# Historic Documents
# of 2018

# Historic Documents
# of 2018

Heather Kerrigan, Editor

⑤SAGE reference |  CQPRESS

FOR INFORMATION:

CQ Press

An Imprint of SAGE Publications, Inc.

2455 Teller Road

Thousand Oaks, California 91320

E-mail: order@sagepub.com

SAGE Publications Ltd.

1 Oliver's Yard

55 City Road

London EC1Y 1SP

United Kingdom

SAGE Publications India Pvt. Ltd.

B 1/I 1 Mohan Cooperative Industrial Area

Mathura Road, New Delhi 110 044

India

SAGE Publications Asia-Pacific Pte. Ltd.

18 Cross Street #10-10/11/12

China Square Central

Singapore 048423

SAGE Editor:   Laura Notton

Editor:   Heather Kerrigan

Managing Editor:   Linda Grimm

Contributors:   Brian P. Beary

      Melissa Feinberg

      Linda Grimm

      Daniel Horner

      Robert William Howard

      Megan Howes

      Heather Kerrigan

Production Editor:   Tracy Buyan

Copy Editor:   Kim Husband

Typesetter:   C&M Digitals (P) Ltd.

Proofreader:   Talia Greenberg

Indexer:   Joan Shapiro

Cover Designer:   Candice Harman

Marketing Manager:   Jennifer Jelinski

Printed in the United States of America

ISBN 978-1-5443-5253-4
ISSN 0892-080X

This book is printed on acid-free paper.

19 20 21 22 23 10 9 8 7 6 5 4 3 2 1

# Contents

## JANUARY

# FEBRUARY

# MARCH

# APRIL

immigration; a memorandum from Attorney General Jeff Sessions on April 6, 2018, calling for zero tolerance in prosecuting illegal border crossers; June 18, 2018, remarks by Department of Homeland Security Secretary Kirstjen M. Nielsen, providing information on the administration's policy on illegal immigration; and a June 20, 2018, executive order ending family separation at the U.S.–Mexico border.

## MAY

# JUNE

# JULY

# AUGUST

# SEPTEMBER

# OCTOBER

# NOVEMBER

# DECEMBER

# Thematic Table of Contents

# GOVERNMENT AND POLITICS

# HEALTH AND SOCIAL SERVICES

# INTERNATIONAL AFFAIRS

## *AFRICA*

# INTERNATIONAL AFFAIRS

## *ASIA*

# INTERNATIONAL AFFAIRS

## *AUSTRALIA*

# INTERNATIONAL AFFAIRS

## *CANADA*

# INTERNATIONAL AFFAIRS

## *EUROPE*

# INTERNATIONAL AFFAIRS

## *LATIN AMERICA AND THE CARIBBEAN*

# INTERNATIONAL AFFAIRS

## *MIDDLE EAST*

# INTERNATIONAL AFFAIRS

## RUSSIA AND THE FORMER SOVIET REPUBLIC

# INTERNATIONAL AFFAIRS

## GLOBAL ISSUES

# NATIONAL SECURITY AND TERRORISM

# RELIGION

# RIGHTS, RESPONSIBILITIES, AND JUSTICE

# List of Document Sources

## CONGRESS

## EXECUTIVE DEPARTMENTS, AGENCIES, FEDERAL OFFICES, AND COMMISSIONS

# INTERNATIONAL GOVERNMENTAL ORGANIZATIONS

# INTERNATIONAL NONGOVERNMENTAL ORGANIZATIONS

# JUDICIARY

# NONGOVERNMENTAL ORGANIZATIONS

# NON-U.S. GOVERNMENTS

# U.S. STATE AND LOCAL GOVERNMENTS

# WHITE HOUSE AND THE PRESIDENT

# Preface

The second year of Donald Trump's presidency, controversial federal policies on immigration and trade, concerns about Facebook and consumer data usage ethics, the continuation of Brexit negotiations, the release of major climate change studies, the installment of a second Trump-appointed justice to the U.S. Supreme Court, and Supreme Court decisions on union dues and the Trump travel ban are just a few of the topics of national and international significance chosen for discussion in *Historic Documents of 2018*. This edition marks the forty-sixth volume of a CQ Press project that began with *Historic Documents of 1972*. This series allows students, librarians, journalists, scholars, and others to research and understand the most important domestic and foreign issues and events of the year through primary source documents. To aid research, many of the lengthy documents written for specialized audiences have been excerpted to highlight the most important sections. The official statements, news conferences, speeches, special studies, and court decisions presented here should be of lasting public and academic interest.

*Historic Documents of 2018* opens with an "Overview of 2018," a sweeping narrative of the key events and issues of the year that provides context for the documents that follow. The balance of the book is organized chronologically, with each article comprising an introduction entitled "Document in Context" and one or more related documents on a specific event, issue, or topic. Often an event is not limited to a particular day. Consequently, readers will find that some events include multiple documents that may span several months. Their placement in the book corresponds to the date of the first document included for that event. The event introductions provide context and an account of further developments during the year. A thematic table of contents (page xvii) and a list of documents organized by source (page xxiii) follow the standard table of contents and assist readers in locating events and documents.

As events, issues, and consequences become more complex and far-reaching, these introductions and documents yield important information and deepen understanding about the world's increasing interconnectedness. As memories of current events fade, these selections will continue to further understanding of the events and issues that have shaped the lives of people around the world.

# How to Use This Book

Each of the entries in this edition consists of two parts: a comprehensive introduction followed by one or more primary source documents. The articles are arranged in chronological order by month. Articles with multiple documents are placed according to the date of the first document. There are several ways to find events and documents of interest:

**By date:** If the approximate date of an event or document is known, browse through the titles for that month in the table of contents. Alternatively, browse the tables of contents that appear at the beginning of each month's articles.

**By theme:** To find a particular topic or subject area, browse the thematic table of contents.

**By document type or source:** To find a particular type of document or document source, such as the White House or Congress, review the list of document sources.

**By index:** The index allows researchers to locate references to specific events or documents as well as entries on the same or related subjects.

An online edition of this volume, as well as an archive going back to 1972, is available and offers advance search and browse functionality.

Each article begins with an introduction. This feature provides historical and intellectual contexts for the documents that follow. Documents are reproduced with the original spelling, capitalization, and punctuation of the original or official copy. Ellipsis points indicate textual omissions (unless they were present in the documents themselves, indicating pauses in speech), and brackets are used for editorial insertions within documents for text clarification. The excerpting of Supreme Court opinions has been done somewhat differently from other documents. In-text references and citations to laws and other cases have been removed when not part of a sentence to improve the readability of opinions. In those documents, readers will find ellipses used only when sections of narrative text have been removed.

Full citations appear at the end of each document. If a document is not available on the Internet, this too is noted. For further reading on a particular topic, consult the "Other *Historic Documents* of Interest" section at the end of each article. These sections provide cross-references for related articles in this edition of *Historic Documents* as well as in previous editions. References to articles from past volumes include the year and page number for easy retrieval.

# Overview of 2018

In the United States, 2018 was characterized by partisan wrangling as Democrats tried to position themselves well before the November midterm elections and the administration of President Donald Trump sought to enact a number of its priorities. During his second year in office, President Trump focused primarily on curbing illegal immigration and addressing trade issues that he felt unfairly targeted the United States and its workers. The president continued to call for construction of a wall along the border between the United States and Mexico but failed to gain enough traction in Congress for passage of funding needed to begin construction. The result was the longest federal government shutdown in history, stretching for thirty-five days from late December into January. The administration enacted various immigration policies, including one, known as "zero tolerance," that resulted in the separation of migrant children from adults at the U.S.–Mexico border and another that sought to prohibit those crossing the border illegally from applying for asylum. Both policies were challenged in federal court.

Addressing another of the president's campaign promises, the White House continued work on renegotiating the North American Free Trade Agreement (NAFTA) and addressing a trade imbalance between the United States and a number of countries, most notably China. By the close of the year, the president had secured a revised trade deal with Mexico and Canada. But his tariffs, intended to boost U.S. manufacturing, resulted in a trade war with China that hampered global economic growth.

Progress on the president's agenda was often clouded by the ongoing investigation into possible ties between the Trump campaign and the Russian government. In 2018, Trump's former campaign manager was found guilty on eight counts, his personal lawyer pleaded guilty to illegal campaign contributions and lying to Congress, and twenty-five Russians and three Russian companies were indicted for hacking and spreading misinformation related to the 2016 presidential election. In the midterm election, Democrats were able to harness some of the discontent with the Trump administration to take control of the House but lost two seats in the Senate and failed to gain much traction in state legislatures and governorships.

Internationally, the year was dominated by ongoing negotiations surrounding the United Kingdom's withdrawal from the European Union and talks between North and South Korea intended to denuclearize and bring peace to the Korean peninsula. In Britain, Prime Minister Theresa May held a tenuous grip on power as she labored to reach a Brexit agreement with the European Union that was palatable enough to win approval in parliament and put the country on track to leave the multinational body by March 2019. Each of her attempts met significant resistance, and by the start of 2019, there was little indication of how and on what terms the UK would leave the EU.

In Asia, hints of progress were seen in the relationship between North and South Korea. The leaders of the two nations came together on multiple occasions and reached an agreement aimed at complete denuclearization and addressing humanitarian issues that were a result of the division of the peninsula. Although broad, the agreement laid the groundwork for ongoing negotiations and is widely considered one of the biggest break-throughs toward peace between the two countries in decades.

There were also a number of notable elections around the globe in 2018, including in Brazil, Sweden, Armenia, and Zimbabwe. Zimbabwe held its first presidential election that did not include longtime ruler Robert Mugabe. The vote was largely peaceful, but a delay in results prompted protests over concern that the electoral body was attempting to fix the outcome on behalf of the interim president, Emmerson Mnangagwa. In Sweden, the general election resulted in a deadlocked parliament, the prime minister's ouster, and four months of negotiations to form a new government that saw the recently removed prime minister returned to power. A similarly complex election took place in Armenia, where the ruling Republican Party was dealt a major defeat, thus signaling a significant power shift in the country. And in Brazil, voter discontent with the sitting government led to the election of Jair Bolsonaro, a far-right candidate known for disparaging rhetoric aimed at women and homosexuals. Bolsonaro promised to use his platform to fight crime and corruption, but many Brazilians were concerned about how the new president would govern, given his distaste for certain segments of society.

## DOMESTIC ISSUES

### Immigration Policy

When he campaigned for president, Trump frequently promised his supporters that he would address illegal immigration, specifically at the U.S.–Mexico border. This included building a wall along the southern perimeter. Throughout 2017 and 2018, President Trump asked Congress for billions of dollars to fund a wall along nearly 1,400 miles of border that did not currently have a barrier in place. Democrats and Republicans could not reach a consensus on providing the money, and as a result, the government shut down twice in 2018—once in January for three days and again from December into January for thirty-five days. No border wall funding was included in the temporary stop-gap measure to end the thirty-five day shutdown, and the final omnibus included only a small fraction of what the president requested. As a result, President Trump declared a national emergency to gain access to additional construction funds.

While Trump continued to push for a wall, the administration enacted policies to address illegal immigration. In April, President Trump signed two memoranda, one that directed the secretary of defense and Department of Homeland Security to secure the southern border and provided permission to utilize the National Guard if needed. The second addressed the existing "catch and release" immigration policy that allows certain migrants to be released into the United States while awaiting immigration hearings. The memorandum did not end catch and release but instead instructed federal agencies to report to the president on the resources and measures necessary to end the practice.

Also in April, Attorney General Jeff Sessions announced that the Department of Justice was implementing a zero-tolerance policy for those attempting to enter the country illegally. As part of that policy, in May, Sessions said that the United States would refer all illegal border crossers for prosecution. This included any migrant who failed to enter the United States at an official port of entry, even those seeking asylum. He admitted that, based on the administration's interpretation of the 1997 Flores Settlement Agreement, minors may be separated from their parents and placed in different detention facilities. Media outlets were quickly flooded with pictures of dark facilities where children, including infants, were being held, sometimes in what appeared to be cages. The Department of Homeland Security (DHS) and the Trump administration held that they did not have a policy of separating families but were required to enforce existing immigration laws that necessitated such separation. On June 20, President Trump signed an executive order ending family separation at the border, and a federal judge subsequently ordered all separated children to be reunited with their parents.

In November, facing a caravan of migrants from Central America that numbered somewhere between 3,500 and more than 8,000, the president issued a proclamation to deny asylum to any migrant attempting to enter the United States illegally, thus forcing those seeking asylum to enter through a designated port of entry. Civil rights groups quickly filed suit, and a federal judge in California blocked the proclamation from going into effect. The administration sought relief from the Ninth Circuit and also asked the Supreme Court for a stay of the initial ruling in order to allow the asylum ban to go into effect while the administration's case was being tried before the Ninth Circuit; the Supreme Court denied that request. Shortly before the close of 2018, DHS announced that it would return all migrants seeking asylum to Mexico while they awaited a court hearing, instead of allowing them to wait in the United States. DHS said the policy would likely reduce the number of asylum seekers and alleviate the burden on immigration courts. Immigration groups promised to challenge the decision in court.

## Ongoing Investigation into Trump Campaign

In May 2017, the Department of Justice appointed former Federal Bureau of Investigation (FBI) director Robert Mueller as special counsel to investigate any coordination between the Trump campaign and the Russian government related to the 2016 presidential election. The president frequently referred to the investigation as a "witch hunt" and alleged that there was significant Democratic bias among those conducting the probe. By the close of 2018, Mueller's team had indicted or gained guilty pleas from at least thirty-two individuals and three companies, including Trump campaign chair Paul Manafort and the president's personal lawyer Michael Cohen.

Manafort, along with his business associate Rick Gates, was the first charged in the Mueller investigation. Charges against Manafort and Gates included money laundering, false statements to the Justice Department, failure to register as a foreign agent under the Foreign Agent Registration Act, failure to file reports regarding foreign bank and financial accounts, and acts of conspiracy against the United States. Many of the charges stemmed from Manafort's work lobbying on behalf of a pro-Russian political party in Ukraine. Gates agreed to a plea bargain in February 2018, but Manafort went to trial. In July, of the eighteen criminal counts against him, Manafort was found guilty on eight, and the jury deadlocked on the remaining ten charges. Manafort faced a second trial in September but reached a deal with the government that required him to cooperate with investigators. In November, the Mueller team noted in court documents that Manafort violated that agreement by lying to the special counsel's office and the FBI.

Cohen was drawn into the Mueller probe in April 2018 when the FBI raided his office and hotel room. In August, he surrendered to the FBI and was charged in federal court with tax evasion, making false statements to a bank, unlawful corporate contributions, and an excessive campaign contribution. The latter two charges were tied to alleged hush money payments made to an adult film star and a *Playboy* model to stop the pair from discussing their relationships with Trump that might discredit his campaign. In November, Cohen was subject to an additional charge for lying to Congress. Cohen accepted plea agreements on all nine charges and was sentenced to more three years in prison.

The Mueller team also investigated Russian intelligence operatives, and in February, the Department of Justice indicted twenty-five Russians and three companies for hacking and spreading misinformation during the 2016 campaign. According to the indictments, the Russians specifically acted to discredit Democratic presidential nominee Hillary Clinton while bolstering Trump. However, there was no indication that their efforts impacted election results or that any Trump campaign officials were involved. The indictment was issued just days before President Trump was set to meet with Russian President Vladimir Putin. The president promised to confront the Russian leader about the allegations.

## Midterm Elections

Political jockeying in Congress over the president's priorities came to a head on November 6, when voters across the country went to the polls to choose their members of Congress, governors, and thousands of state and local leaders. Democrats had significant momentum headed into the vote, given high dissatisfaction with the current administration, an anti-incumbent sentiment, and enthusiasm for a record number of women running for office. In the House, where all 435 seats were up for reelection, Democrats won 235 seats to the Republicans' 199. In the Senate, where Democrats were defending 26 of the 35 seats up for reelection, the path to victory was less clear, and Republicans were able to expand their majority to 53 seats.

The races garnered extensive media attention for their historic firsts. In one of the most talked-about races, twenty-nine-year-old political newcomer Alexandria Ocasio-Cortez defeated ten-term incumbent and Democratic Caucus Chair Joe Crowley in the primary in New York's 14th Congressional District and went on to win the general election, becoming the youngest woman ever elected to Congress. The incoming Congress would include a record 131 women, the average age of the House and Senate decreased by a decade to forty-seven, and a growing number of people of color were elected. The 116th Congress would also include the first two Native American women and the first two Muslim women to serve.

In the states, voters signaled that they were becoming increasingly entrenched in their partisan views. Both Democrats and Republicans did well with their bases and where they already held a majority. Democrats gained seven governorships and six legislative chambers, but Republicans continued to hold a majority of the governorships and nearly two-thirds of all state legislative chambers. A number of races resulted in lawsuits and recounts related to voter disenfranchisement. This included the Georgia governor's race, where 3,000 voters were incorrectly flagged as noncitizens and tens of thousands of voter registrations were improperly put on hold. Both instances disproportionately impacted African Americans.

## Foreign Relations in the Trump Administration

The Trump administration made headway on its foreign policy agenda in 2018. Among the most closely watched activities was a historic meeting between President Trump and

North Korean leader Kim Jong Un. The face-to-face summit in Singapore in June marked the first instance of a sitting U.S. president meeting with a North Korean leader. The talks resulted in a joint statement declaring the intent of the two nations to work toward improving their relationship. While Trump hailed the summit as a major victory, he faced criticism at home and abroad for not reaching more concrete steps with the North Korean leader on denuclearization.

On Iran, another nuclear-armed nation, the president followed through on a campaign promise and announced that he was removing the United States as party to the Joint Comprehensive Plan of Action (JCPOA), a 2015 multilateral deal in which Iran agreed to restrictions on its nuclear program in return for a lifting of sanctions. The president had frequently criticized the deal for not doing enough to outright prohibit Iran from developing nuclear weapons. The move to leave the JCPOA and reimpose U.S. sanctions on Iran drew quick criticism from the other nations included in the deal, all of which maintained their commitment to continuing work with Iran toward denuclearization.

Elsewhere in the Middle East, the Trump administration better defined its intent with regards to U.S. troops deployed in Syria in the ongoing fight against the Islamic State of Iraq and the Levant (ISIL). In January, Secretary of State Rex Tillerson announced that the United States would maintain a troop presence in Syria to ensure that neither Iran nor the Syrian government of President Bashar al-Assad could retake portions of the country that had been liberated. Tillerson cautioned that the deployment was not indefinite but that troops would remain so long as the conditions necessary to maintain stability were warranted. In December, Trump shocked his advisers, U.S. lawmakers, and coalition partners by announcing his intent to withdraw American troops from Syria, explaining that ISIL had been defeated and U.S. troop involvement was no longer necessary in the region. The announcement led to the resignations of Defense Secretary Jim Mattis and Brett McGurk, special presidential envoy to the coalition fighting ISIL. Despite urgings from presidential advisers, who publicly expressed concern that leaving could further destabilize the region and allow ISIL to regain its foothold, the U.S. began withdrawing military equipment in January 2019.

President Trump also spent much of the year focused on what he believed to be unfair trade practices. The president imposed an escalating number of import tariffs on a variety of goods, most notably steel and aluminum. The intent was to discourage Americans from buying cheaper imported goods and shift their purchases to American-made products to benefit domestic manufacturers while also addressing trade imbalance. Impacted nations quickly imposed retaliatory tariffs. The tariffs threatened to derail the year-long renegotiation of NAFTA, but on November 30, the United States–Mexico–Canada Agreement (USMCA) was signed by Trump and his Mexican and Canadian counterparts. To go into effect, the USMCA, which would, among other things, expand access for Mexican and Canadian producers to American markets and incentivize the purchase of vehicles produced by workers making a living wage, required the ratification by each nation's legislature before it could go into effect.

## Supreme Court Decisions

The U.S. Supreme Court issued rulings in several noteworthy cases during its 2017–2018 term, including the closely watched *Trump v. Hawaii,* which centered on the third iteration of the Trump administration's travel ban. The ban in question had been introduced in September 2017 and proclaimed an indefinite ban on travel to the United States by citizens of Iran, Libya, Somalia, Syria, and Yemen, in addition to imposing new restrictions on travel from North Korea and Chad and for some Venezuelan officials. The State of Hawaii claimed that President Trump's comments about the proclamation, which included referring to it as a "Muslim Ban" (many of the countries named in the proclamation are predominantly Muslim), undermined its legitimacy and proved the policy was motivated by religious animosity rather than a real national security concern. The Court rejected Hawaii's challenge on June 26, ruling the president both had the authority to issue such a proclamation and had provided findings to support the new restrictions that did not mention religion.

Earlier in the month, the Court ruled in *Masterpiece Cakeshop v. Colorado Civil Rights Commission* in favor of a baker who refused to make a wedding cake for a gay couple because he said it violated his religious beliefs. While seemingly at odds with the Court's landmark decision in *Obergefell v. Hodges,* which found that same-sex couples have the same constitutionally protected right to marry as opposite-sex couples, the ruling was narrowly written to the case's specific circumstances. The Court found that the baker's case had been tainted by the Colorado Civil Rights Commission's open and public hostility to religion, as well as its inconsistent treatment of similar cases in which bakers had refused to make cakes depicting words or images opposed to same-sex marriage.

The Court also addressed three separate cases involving partisan gerrymandering but opted to send each back to lower judicial bodies for further consideration. The first such case, *Common Cause v. Rucho,* brought North Carolina's federal congressional district map back into the spotlight. On January 9, a panel of judges threw out the state's district map, citing evidence of partisan gerrymandering by the Republicans who drew the map. However, the Court issued a stay of the decision on January 18 and sent the case back to the state for reconsideration. Six months later, the Court ruled in *Gill v. Whitford* that the parties involved in the case lacked standing to bring the suit. That case centered around a complaint filed by Wisconsin voters who alleged the state's district map unconstitutionally favored Republicans. The Court argued the voters had not provided sufficient proof of individual harm and sent the case back to the state. That same day, the Court published an unsigned opinion in *Benisek v. Lamone,* a case out of Maryland in which Republican voters claimed a district had been redrawn to favor Democrats. A federal court had granted a stay pending the Court's ruling in *Gill v. Whitford,* but the case was appealed before it went to trial. The Court's unsigned opinion sent the case back to Maryland, stating there was no reason to intervene before the case was heard in a lower court.

Perhaps the most impactful ruling issued by the Court during the term was its decision in *Janus v. American Federation of State, County, and Municipal Employees.* Released on June 27, the ruling overturned a forty-year precedent under which public-sector unions had been allowed to charge so-called "fair share" fees to nonunion workers as long as those fees were not used for political activity. The purpose of such fees is to ensure that nonunion employees do not receive the same collective bargaining benefits as union workers, who pay higher membership fees. The Court held that public-sector unions can no longer charge these fees without nonunion employees' specific consent, arguing that the fees violate nonmembers' rights to free speech by forcing them to subsidize an organization and its speech. As a result of the ruling, more than twenty states would need to revise their laws, and thousands of collective bargaining agreements involving millions of public employees must be renegotiated.

The same day as the *Janus* decision, Justice Anthony M. Kennedy announced his intent to retire from the Court by the end of July. Kennedy served on the Court for nearly thirty years and, while most frequently voting with the Court's conservative justices, was often the key vote in major liberal decisions. On July 9, President Trump nominated Brett M. Kavanaugh, a judge on the U.S. Court of Appeals for the District of Columbia, to fill Kennedy's seat. Shortly after confirmation hearings were held in the Senate in early September, news broke that Sen. Dianne Feinstein, D-Calif., had received a letter from a woman accusing Kavanaugh of sexual assault while they were in high school. Dr. Christine Blasey Ford went public with her allegations on September 16 and was followed by another accuser from Kavanaugh's college days. The allegations led to dramatic historic testimony before the Senate Judiciary Committee on September 27, during which Dr. Ford recounted her experience and Kavanaugh denied all allegations. An FBI investigation was conducted at the request of Sen. Jeff Flake, R-Ariz., but was limited in scope and did not produce new information, nor were witnesses able to provide concrete evidence either supporting Ford or exonerating Kavanaugh. The Senate ultimately went on to confirm Kavanaugh by a two-vote margin.

## Foreign Affairs

### Brexit Negotiations Progress

After a halting start to talks in 2017, European Union and United Kingdom negotiators began to make progress in setting the terms of the UK's withdrawal from the EU, commonly referred to as Brexit. Negotiators resolved several key issues early in 2018, such as establishing a transition period for the UK to exit the EU's single market, determining the lump sum the UK would pay to the EU for continued access to the single market during the transition period, and agreeing on the rights of expatriate citizens to continue living and working in their adoptive countries.

Despite this progress, the status of the UK's post-Brexit border with the EU in Northern Ireland remained a sticking point in negotiations for much of the rest of the year. Prime Minister Theresa May's government chose not to remain in the EU's single market or customs union and had ruled out the possibility of making a separate arrangement between Northern Ireland and the EU, meaning that border controls would likely be required. However, this would be a violation of the 1998 Good Friday Agreement that ended decades of violence in Northern Ireland and requires the UK to guarantee the free flow of goods and people in Ireland.

In October, negotiators developed a proposed solution known as the "backstop." The arrangement called for the EU and UK to work on a free-trade agreement during the Brexit transition period that would preserve the free movement of people and goods in Ireland. If an agreement was not reached by the end of the transition period, the entire UK would temporarily remain in the EU customs union until a solution could be found. The backstop soon became an issue for parliament's Brexit supporters, who argued that without a prescribed timeframe, the UK's temporary continuation in the customs union could be extended indefinitely.

With support in parliament waning, May postponed a planned December vote on the agreement until January 2019 in hopes of securing clearer backstop commitments from the EU. However, the EU declined to make a binding commitment, leading to an overwhelming rejection of the Brexit agreement by members of parliament. May's government survived a subsequent no-confidence vote, but significant concern and uncertainty remained about the UK's path forward.

## North and South Korean Leaders Pursue Peace

On April 27, South Korean President Moon Jae-in and North Korean leader Kim Jong Un came together for a historic meeting in the demilitarized zone (DMZ) separating the two countries, signaling the potential for a major change in their hostile relationship. The meeting was preceded by a shift in Kim's rhetoric toward South Korea that, while still highly critical of the Moon administration, called for the peninsula's independent reunification. Moon had also been more open to working with North Korea than his predecessors, as evidenced by his assistance in coordinating a summit between Kim and President Trump in June 2018. In another diplomatic breakthrough, athletes from the two Koreas competed alongside each other under a unified flag at the 2018 Olympic Games, hosted in February in the South Korean city of PyeongChang. It was at the Games that Kim's sister, Kim Yo-jong, met with Moon and extended an invitation to a summit in Pyongyang, North Korea's capital. Additionally, North Korea announced a halt to its nuclear weapons tests, which largely remained in effect through the end of the year.

Moon and Kim's April meeting resulted in the Panmunjom Declaration on Peace, Prosperity, and Reunification of the Korean Peninsula. The declaration was primarily a broad-strokes agreement, with commitments including a resolution of humanitarian issues resulting from the peninsula's division, the complete denuclearization of both nations, and an end to propaganda campaigns. The two governments agreed to pursue a peace treaty that would replace the 1953 armistice that ended the Korean War. While broad in its terms, the declaration provided a foundation for subsequent meetings between Moon and Kim in May and September and the development of more concrete agreements, such as the dismantling of specific North Korean nuclear and missile facilities.

## Elections Bring New Leadership across the Globe

Several significant elections and changes in power occurred around the world in 2018. In July, Zimbabwe held its first presidential election in which former leader Robert Mugabe was not a candidate. Mugabe presided over a dictatorial government for nearly forty years before resigning in November 2017 amid a bloodless takeover led by a segment of the Zimbabwe military. Mugabe was replaced by his former prime minister, Emmerson Mnangagwa, who served as interim president until the 2018 election. While the poll was conducted peacefully, a delay in announcing the presidential results prompted allegations of vote rigging and protests in the capital, where demonstrators clashed with the military. Mnangagwa was declared the winner on August 3, an outcome that was challenged by opponents in the Constitutional Court. However, the court ruled unanimously that allegations of election fraud were unsubstantiated and affirmed the results.

Sweden's September 2018 general election left the country's two traditional political blocs deadlocked in parliament and led to Prime Minster Stefan Löfven's ouster after his government lost a no-confidence vote. Efforts to form a new government were complicated by the electoral success of the Sweden Democrats, a far-right, anti-immigrant party that won the third largest portion of seats in parliament following a campaign focused on issues of immigration, migrant integration, and welfare program sustainability. Most political parties were staunchly opposed to working with the Sweden Democrats, but center-right and center-left parties were also reluctant to forge cross-bloc alliances. For three and a half months, Speaker Andreas Norlén charged various party leaders with forming a new government, but each effort failed, leading to speculation that snap elections would be necessary. Then in January 2019, an agreement between the Centre, Green, Liberal, and Social Democratic parties was announced that returned Löfven to the prime minister's office and shepherded in a new government led by the Social Democratic and Green parties.

A different but similarly complex electoral scenario played out in Armenia, where a peaceful public revolution prompted a major power shift from the country's long-dominant Republican Party. Protests began in response to the National Assembly's appointment of outgoing president Serzh Sargsyan as prime minister, which many Armenians viewed as an attempt to cling to power, and were led by Nikol Pashinyan, a member of parliament and vocal critic of the government. Sargsyan resigned in April 2018, opening the door for the National Assembly to elect Pashinyan as the next prime minister in May. Pashinyan pledged to organize a new parliamentary election, saying the National Assembly no longer reflected the will of the voters. After facing some initial resistance from the Republican Party, Pashinyan resigned from office on October 16 to force a snap election. The National Assembly was dissolved the following month and the election held on December 9. The political bloc to which Pashinyan belonged won approximately 70 percent of the votes, securing roughly two-thirds of the seats in parliament and bringing Pashinyan back as prime minister, while the Republican Party suffered a major defeat.

Voters' disillusionment with liberal leaders following a string of corruption scandals and economic stagnation was a major factor in Brazil's general election in October 2018. Initially a minor candidate, far-right politician and longtime legislator Jair Bolsonaro effectively capitalized on voters' discontent, attracting significant support by promising to crack down on crime and corruption despite his history of controversial remarks disparaging women, homosexuals, and other groups. Bolsonaro's campaign was further bolstered by election officials' rejection of Luiz Inácio Lula da Silva's candidacy. At the time, the highly popular former president was serving a prison sentence for corruption and money-laundering convictions. The court's decision forced the leading Workers' Party to put forward a lesser-known candidate, Fernando Haddad, who struggled to leverage da Silva's legacy and name recognition while distancing himself from party scandals. Following a bitter campaign marked by violence—including an incident in which Bolsonaro was stabbed—and widespread misinformation, Bolsonaro and Haddad were the two top vote winners in the first-round poll held on October 7. Since neither candidate received 50 percent of the vote, a runoff was held on October 28. Bolsonaro emerged as the victor, receiving nearly 10 percent more votes than Haddad. While Bolsonaro's supporters celebrated his win, many Brazilians remain concerned about the policies the new president may pursue, given his previous statements.

—Heather Kerrigan and Linda Grimm

# January

# Federal Officials on Presidential War Powers, U.S. Troop Policy to Combat ISIL

DECEMBER 19, 2017, AND JANUARY 29
AND FEBRUARY 12, 2018

U.S. airstrikes conducted in Syria in 2017 raised fresh questions about the president's power to wage war, as did the announcement in January 2018 that the United States would maintain a military presence in Syria beyond the fight with the Islamic State in Iraq and the Levant (ISIL). Sen. Tim Kaine, D-Va., led a push to pressure President Donald Trump's administration to provide a legal justification for the airstrikes and more detailed information about its long-term plan for Syria. Officials including Secretary of State Rex Tillerson argued that the congressionally approved 2001 and 2002 Authorization for the Use of Military Force (AUMF) covered ongoing operations in Syria and against ISIL, but some lawmakers countered that a new authorization with a broader scope was needed to reflect current threats.

## PRESIDENTIAL WAR POWERS

The U.S. Constitution grants Congress the power to declare war; however, the president has the authority to deploy the military without congressional approval if the United States is attacked or if there is a threat of imminent attack. The War Powers Resolution of 1973 requires the president to notify Congress within forty-eight hours of military action and forbids U.S. troops from being deployed for more than sixty days without a formal declaration of war or a congressional AUMF.

In 2001, shortly after the September 11 terrorist attacks, Congress passed an AUMF allowing President George W. Bush "to use all necessary and appropriate force against those nations, organizations, or persons he determines planned, authorized, committed or aided the terrorist attacks that occurred on September 11, 2001, or harbored such organizations or persons, in order to prevent any future acts of international terrorism against the United States by such nations, organizations or persons." A second AUMF was passed in October 2002, this time giving the president power "to use the Armed Forces of the United States as he determines to be necessary and appropriate in order to (1) defend the national security of the United States against the continuing threat posed by Iraq; and (2) enforce all relevant United Nations Security Council resolutions regarding Iraq." These AUMFs provided Bush with the legal authority he needed to go to war in Iraq and Afghanistan.

Both AUMFs remained in place during President Barack Obama's administration and were used to carry out various military operations against terrorist groups in and outside of Iraq and Afghanistan, including ISIL. Obama faced criticism from lawmakers and others who argued the 2001 and 2002 AUMFs did not provide the broad scope required to enable the president to conduct such activities, particularly since some organizations—such as ISIL—did not exist in 2001. Some lawmakers called for a new AUMF that could support the United States' ongoing counterterror operations abroad, and Obama submitted draft AUMF legislation to Congress in 2015. However, lawmakers disagreed on whether the AUMF should be written broadly or limited by timeframe, geographic regions, or terrorist groups; as a result, a new AUMF was not approved.

## TRUMP CHALLENGED OVER AIRSTRIKES IN SYRIA

In April 2017, Trump directed U.S. airstrikes against Syrian military facilities in response to Syria's use of chemical weapons against its own citizens. The administration did not give a legal explanation for its determination that the president had the authority to carry out such airstrikes—which notably targeted another sovereign government, not a terrorist organization—despite calls from Congress that it provide this information. Kaine was the most vocal among these lawmakers, raising concerns that the president had overstepped his authority and Congress was abdicating its responsibilities to declare war. Kaine has persistently pushed for an updated AUMF that reflects current threats, including ISIL. Earlier in the year, Kaine had co-sponsored with Sen. Jeff Flake, R-Ariz., a bill to repeal the 2001 and 2002 AUMFs and replace them with a new measure, but the bill did not make it out of committee.

In October, the Senate Foreign Relations Committee summoned Secretary of State Tillerson and Secretary of Defense James Mattis to a hearing to provide the administration's perspective on authorizations of military force. Both Tillerson and Mattis stated their belief that the 2001 and 2002 AUMF gave the administration legal authority to continue fighting terrorist organizations, including ISIL, and that a new AUMF was unnecessary. They also cautioned that if Congress decided to pursue a new AUMF, it should not include time or geographic limits because that could hinder counterterrorism efforts. "The collapse of ISIS's so-called caliphate in Iraq and Syria means it will attempt to burrow into new countries and find safe havens," said Tillerson. "Our legal authorities for heading off a transnational threat like ISIS cannot be constrained by geographic boundaries. Otherwise, ISIS may reestablish itself and gain strength in vulnerable spaces."

The following month, it was revealed through a Freedom of Information Act (FOIA) request by Protect Democracy that a "secret" memo explaining the Trump administration's interpretation of the president's authority to wage war had been prepared by the U.S. Justice Department. Although the document was not classified, the Justice Department refused to release it. Kaine requested a copy of the memo in a letter to Tillerson on February 8, 2018, stating, "The fact that there is a lengthy memo with a more detailed legal justification that has not been shared with Congress, or the American public, is unacceptable." Kaine also expressed concerns that "this legal justification may now become precedent for additional executive unilateral military action." However, by the end of 2018, the document still has not been shared with Congress.

The administration took a different approach following a second round of U.S. airstrikes against Syrian military facilities in April 2018 (again in response to the government's use of chemical weapons). On May 31, the Justice Department Office of Legal

Counsel issued an opinion that Trump had the authority to legally and unilaterally direct the airstrikes because he had determined that doing so would be in the national interest and would have little risk of escalation. "Given the absence of ground troops, the limited mission and time frame and the efforts to avoid escalation, the anticipated nature, scope and duration of these airstrikes did not rise to the level of a 'war' for constitutional purposes," wrote Steven Engel, the assistant attorney general for the Office of Legal Counsel. The document stated that Engel provided the same guidance to the White House counsel prior to the airstrikes. Kaine dismissed the memo as "ludicrous," declaring it was further proof that "Congress must finally take back its authority when it comes to war."

## ADMINISTRATION ANNOUNCES PLAN FOR LONG-TERM MILITARY PRESENCE IN SYRIA

Separate from the airstrike issue, Kaine raised concerns about statements by administration officials suggesting "a military presence in Syria could be open-ended to pursue objectives unrelated to the counter-ISIS mission." Kaine wrote to Mattis and Tillerson on December 19, 2017, requesting information about the goals of the administration's "counter-ISIS campaign," plans for continued military presence in Iraq and Syria, and an updated count of troops deployed in Syria, among other things. "I am concerned that the United States will soon find itself lacking domestic or international legal standing for operations in Syria based on official statements that our presence, intended for a narrowly scoped campaign to fight ISIS, might now be used to pressure the Syrian government, target Iran and its proxies, and engage other entities not covered under the 2001 AUMF," Kaine wrote.

Roughly one month later, on January 17, Tillerson announced the administration's intention to keep U.S. troops in Syria to ensure neither Iran nor Syrian President Bashar al-Assad took control over parts of the country that had been liberated from ISIL with the United States' help and were now held by rebel groups. Tillerson said the administration did not want to repeat Obama's mistakes, pointing to how "a premature departure from Iraq allowed al Qaeda in Iraq to survive and eventually morph into ISIS." Keeping troops in Syria would help to stabilize the country, Tillerson argued. "ISIS has one foot in the grave, and by maintaining an American military presence in Syria until the full and complete defeat of ISIS is achieved, it will soon have two," he said. The United States' military mission would remain "conditions-based," he said, not an indefinite commitment. (As of December 2017, the United States had approximately 2,000 soldiers in Syria, primarily from engineering units helping to build defenses and Special Operations units fighting and training with local militia.)

Soon after Tillerson's remarks, both the U.S. Defense and State Departments responded to Kaine with letters dated January 29 and February 12, respectively. Both letters indicated the Trump administration's belief that it did not need any new legal authority from Congress to keep troops in Syria and Iraq, including in areas from which ISIL had been driven. "The 2001 AUMF also provides authority to use force to defend U.S., Coalition, and partner forces engaged in the campaign to defeat ISIS to the extent such use of force is a necessary and appropriate measure in support of counter-ISIS operations," wrote Mary Waters, the assistant secretary of state for legislative affairs. "The strikes taken by the United States in May and June 2017 against the Syrian

Government and pro-Syrian Government forces were limited and lawful measures taken under that authority to counter immediate threats to U.S. or partner forces engaged in that campaign."

The letters also argued that the ongoing potential threat from ISIL justified the continued military presence. "Although U.S. and Coalition-backed forces have liberated the vast majority of the territory ISIS once held in Iraq and Syria, more tough fighting remains ahead to defeat ISIS's physical 'caliphate' and achieve the group's permanent defeat," wrote David Trachtenberg, the deputy undersecretary of defense for policy. "ISIS is transitioning to an insurgency in Iraq and Syria, while continuing to support the global terrorist operations of its branches, networks, and individual supporters worldwide." Waters noted that "the threat posed by ISIS and al-Qa'ida is not solely dependent upon the physical control of territory by these groups," adding that "ensuring that ISIS cannot regenerate its forces or reclaim lost ground is essential to the protection of our homeland."

Kaine claimed the administration was stretching to apply existing AUMFs to current military action in Syria and accused Trump of "acting like a king by unilaterally starting a war." He called for a new authorization that would support a longer-term mission, including the authority "to strike pro-Assad forces in areas devoid of ISIS to protect our Syrian partners who seek Assad's overthrow." Not all of Kaine's congressional colleagues were in agreement, however. "He has the authority under the existing AUMF," said House Speaker Paul Ryan, R-Wis., dismissing the need for a new authorization. "What I would hate to do . . . is have an AUMF that ties the hands of our military behind their backs," he added.

On April 16, Sen. Bob Corker, R-Tenn., introduced legislation, co-sponsored by Kaine, providing a new AUMF that did not have an expiration date or limit the expansion of military operations to additional countries or against new terrorist groups. The bill did include provisions establishing a process for lawmakers to review and vote to repeal or modify the AUMF every four years. It also required the president to notify Congress, within forty-eight hours, of military operations in countries where the United States is not already fighting or that target new groups; Congress would then have the opportunity to review and fast-track legislation to block further military action. Republicans and Democrats were sharply divided over the bill's provisions, particularly its lack of a time limit, which some lawmakers said made the bill a "non-starter." The bill did not progress beyond committee before the end of the year.

Kaine continued his efforts to exert pressure on the administration by delaying the confirmation of David Schenker as the next assistant secretary of state for Near Eastern affairs. Schenker was still awaiting confirmation at the start of 2019.

—Linda Grimm

*Following is a letter from Sen. Tim Kaine, D-Va., to Secretary of State Rex Tillerson and Secretary of Defense Jim Mattis, dated December 19, 2017, requesting information about the administration's counter-ISIS campaign in Iraq and Syria; as well as letters from Deputy Under Secretary of Defense for Policy David J. Trachtenberg and Assistant Secretary of State for Legislative Affairs Mary K. Waters, dated January 29, 2018, and February 12, 2018, respectively, to Sen. Tim Kaine, D-Va., in response to his inquiry.*

# Sen. Kaine Requests Information on U.S. Counter-ISIS Campaign

**December 19, 2017**

Dear Secretaries Tillerson and Mattis:

I write to seek clarification and additional information on the counter-ISIS campaign in Iraq and Syria following the submission of the December War Powers notification, statements from a recent Pentagon press briefing and troubling news reports on the changing U.S. mission in Syria. I am concerned that the United States will soon find itself lacking domestic or international legal standing for operations in Syria based on official statements that our presence, intended for a narrowly-scoped campaign to fight ISIS, might now be used to pressure the Syrian government, target Iran and its proxies, and engage other entities not covered under the 2001 AUMF.

The December War Powers Act notification to Congress does not specify the number of U.S. troops in Iraq or Syria, but at a recent Pentagon press conference, a DOD spokesman stated that there are approximately 2,000 troops in Syria, a 397% increase from the 503 troops cited six months earlier in the June notification. He further stated that, "We will be in Syria as long as it takes to make sure that ISIS is not afforded the ability to re-establish safe havens and conduct attacks."

Following this press briefing, Russia's military announced on December 7 that it had accomplished its mission of defeating ISIS in Syria and that there were no remaining settlements there under ISIS control. On December 9, Iraqi Prime Minister Abadi declared victory over ISIS in Iraq and the end of more than three years of battles to regain control over areas that had been under ISIS's dominion. Abadi stated, "Our forces fully control the Iraqi Syrian border, and thus we can announce the end of the war against Daesh." That same day, the State Department agreed with Prime Minister Abadi noting, "The Iraqi announcement signals the last remnants of ISIS's self-proclaimed 'caliphate' in Iraq have been erased and the people living in those areas have been freed from ISIS's brutal control."

However, while welcoming Abadi's announcement, additional Administration statements have suggested that a military presence in Syria could be open-ended to pursue objectives unrelated to the counter-ISIS mission. The original mission relied upon an expansive legal interpretation of the 2001 and 2002 AUMFs detailed in the December 2016 White House report: "Legal and Policy Frameworks Guiding The United States' Use Of Military Force And Related National Security Operations."

Additionally, on December 13, the *Wall Street Journal* published an article quoting an unnamed U.S. official who said, "Our leadership has set as an objective not to allow Iran and its proxies to be able to establish a presence in Syria that they can use to threaten our allies or us in the region." The article also states that the Administration is considering whether to make "confronting Iran an explicit new goal for the more than 2,000 American forces currently in Syria." If these reports accurately reflect your intentions, the actions you are likely considering far exceed the counter-ISIS mandate and lack domestic or international legal authority to support the continued presence of U.S. forces absent host nation approval or evidence of an enemy that poses an imminent threat to the United States.

As such, I request answers to the following questions:

- Is the Administration contemplating a policy that makes "confronting Iran an explicit new goal for the more than 2,000 American forces currently in Syria?"
- Has the Administration previously targeted, or is planning to target Shia militias operating in Iraq that are aligned with the Iraqi government? If so, under what legal authority?
- Does the Administration have any plans to target Shia militias or Iranian proxies in Syria? If so, under what legal authority?
- Does the Administration intend to retain a military presence in Iraq or Syria to combat Iran? If so, under what legal authority?
- Do you agree that ISIS is defeated in Iraq? Syria?
- How does the Administration define the "defeat" of ISIS? Please describe the conditions being evaluated for a "conditions-based" withdrawal of U.S. forces from Syria.
- Please clarify what reporting changes you made, if any, that could have resulted in the stark difference in U.S. troop numbers in Syria between this month and last.
- Do you believe the 2002 AUMF authorizing the war in Iraq is still necessary? What operations in the past 5 years solely relied on the 2002 AUMF for legal justification?
- Secretary Mattis, you announced that the U.S. military would remain in Syria to fight ISIS and to propel Bashar al-Assad into participating in political negotiations in Syria. What would be the legal basis for using military force to compel Bashar al-Assad into participating in political negotiations?
- The December 2017 War Powers notification to Congress states "the Defeat-ISIS campaign in Syria have [sic] undertaken a limited number of strikes against Syrian government and pro-Syrian government forces." Have you deemed that Syrian government and pro-Syrian government forces are Associated Forces of ISIS pursuant to the 2001 AUMF?

Sincerely,
Tim Kaine

Source: Office of U.S. Senator Tim Kaine. "Kaine-Trump ISIS War Power Letters." December 19, 2017. https://www.documentcloud.org/documents/43885-Kaine-Trump-ISIS-war-power-letters.html.

# Defense Department Responds to Sen. Kaine on AUMF

**January 29, 2018**

Dear Senator Kaine:

This letter responds to your December 19, 2017, letter to Secretary Mattis requesting a more detailed explanation of the Department of Defense's (DoD) missions in Syria and Iraq, as well as the conditions for the defeat of ISIS.

The 2001 Authorization for Use of Military Force (AUMF) authorizes the United States to use force against al-Qa'ida, the Taliban, and associated forces and against ISIS. DoD remains particularly focused on targeting ISIS and al-Qa'ida in Iraq and Syria. U.S. and partner forces in both countries continue to fight ISIS and al-Qa'ida and disrupt terrorist attack plotting. The Department of Defense is not targeting other militias or organizations, including Shia militia groups or Iranian proxies.

In support of the President's Iran Strategy, DoD is reviewing the breadth of our security cooperation activities, force posture, and plans. The Department of Defense is identifying new areas where we will work with allies and partners to pressure the Iranian regime, neutralize its destabilizing influences, and constrain its aggressive power projection, particularly its support for terrorist groups and militants. DoD supports State Department-led efforts to collaborate with allies and partners and, through sanctions and multilateral organizations like the United Nations, to pressure Iran to halt its destabilizing activities.

Although U.S. and Coalition-backed forces have liberated the vast majority of the territory ISIS once held in Iraq and Syria, more tough fighting remains ahead to defeat ISIS's physical "caliphate" and achieve the group's permanent defeat. ISIS is transitioning to an insurgency in Iraq and Syria, while continuing to support the global terrorist operations of its branches, networks, and individual supporters worldwide. Just as when we previously removed U.S. forces prematurely, the group will look to exploit any abatement in pressure to regenerate capabilities and reestablish local control of territory. As ISIS evolves, so too, is the campaign to defeat ISIS transitioning to a new phase in Iraq and Syria. DoD is optimizing and adapting our military presence to maintain counterterrorism pressure on the enemy, while facilitating stabilization and political reconciliation efforts needed to ensure the enduring defeat of ISIS. We, along with the Coalition and our partners, remain committed to ISIS's permanent defeat. ISIS will be defeated when local security forces are capable of effectively responding to and containing the group, and when ISIS is unable to function as a global organization.

With the approval of the Government of Iraq, DoD and other foreign partners are working with the Iraqi Security Forces to improve their capabilities and secure areas liberated from ISIS. In Syria, operating under current authorities, the U.S. military will continue to support local partner forces in Syria to complete the military defeat of ISIS and prevent its resurgence. The United States continues to support the Geneva-based political process pursuant to United Nations Security Council Resolution 2254. I would refer you to the State Department for more information regarding stabilization efforts and the political process.

As part of our effort to accelerate the campaign against ISIS, DoD revised how it publicly reports force levels in Iraq and Syria. As a result, DoD now publicly reports that it has approximately 2,000 forces in Syria. These numbers do not reflect an increase in the number of personnel on the ground; rather, they represent a change in how these numbers are publicly reported. Under previous reporting practices, certain forces in Syria on a temporary duty status were not publicly reported, but they are now included in the 2,000 force total. For operational security reasons, U.S. forces conducting sensitive missions are not included in the publicly reported numbers. As you know, DoD provides these classified details to its congressional oversight committees in closed sessions. We anticipate these numbers will decrease as the nature of our operations change in Iraq and Syria, but we do not have a timeline-based approach to our presence in either Iraq or Syria.

In addition to providing authority to conduct offensive counterterrorism operations against al-Qa'ida and ISIS in Iraq and Syria, the 2001 AUMF also provides authority to use force to defend U.S., Coalition, and partner forces engaged in the campaign to defeat ISIS to the extent such force is a necessary and appropriate measure in support of the D-ISIS campaign. The small number of strikes taken by U.S. forces since May 2017 against the Syrian Government and pro-Syrian Government forces, referenced in the June and December 2017 periodic reports to Congress consistent with the War Powers Resolution, were limited and lawful measures taken under this authority to counter immediate threats to U.S. or partner forces engaged in the D-ISIS campaign. There has been no assessment that either the Syrian Government or pro-Syrian Government forces are "associated forces" of ISIS under the 2001 AUMF.

The April 6, 2017, U.S. missile strike on Shayrat airfield in Syria was not based on the authority of either the 2001 or 2002 AUMFs. Rather, as was notified to the Congress on April 8, the President authorized that strike pursuant to his power under Article II of the Constitution as Commander in Chief and Chief Executive to use this sort of military force overseas to defend important U.S. national interests. The U.S. military action was directed against Syrian military targets directly connected to the April 4 chemical weapons attack in Idlib and was justified, legitimate, and proportionate as a measure to deter and prevent Syria's illegal and provocative use of chemical weapons.

Finally, the 2002 Authorization for Use of Military Force Against Iraq Resolution (2002 AUMF) continues to provide authority for military operations against ISIS in Iraq. It also provides authority to respond to threats to U.S. national security emanating from Iraq that may re-emerge and that may not be covered by the 2001 AUMF. The 2002 AUMF thus remains necessary to support the use of military force to assist the Government of Iraq both in the fight against ISIS, and in stabilizing Iraq following the destruction of ISIS's so-called caliphate.

Sincerely,
David J. Trachtenberg
Deputy Under Secretary of Defense (Policy)

SOURCE: Office of the Under Secretary of Defense. "Kaine-Trump ISIS War Power Letters." January 29, 2018. https://www.documentcloud.org/documents/4383185-Kaine-Trump-ISIS-war-power-letters.html.

# State Department Responds to Sen. Kaine on AUMF Use against ISIS

**February 12, 2018**

Dear Senator Kaine:

Thank you for your letter of December 19, 2017 about the U.S. military counter ISIS campaign in Iraq and Syria. This response has been coordinated with the Department of Defense (DoD), which I understand has written to you on January 29, 2018.

Our purpose and reasons for being in Iraq and Syria are unchanged: defeating ISIS and degrading al-Qa'ida. The Iraqi Security Forces, including the Kurdish Peshmerga, and local partner forces in Syria, with the support of the 74-member Global Coalition to Defeat ISIS, have made great progress in destroying ISIS's so-called "caliphate." With Coalition support, our partners on the ground have liberated nearly all of the territory and millions of civilians once under ISIS's despotic control. However, the threat posed by ISIS and al-Qa'ida is not solely dependent upon the physical control of territory by these groups. Ensuring that ISIS cannot regenerate its forces or reclaim lost ground is essential to the protection of our homeland. Realizing that military operations are necessary, but insufficient by themselves, to achieve ISIS's enduring defeat, the U.S.-led Global Coalition to Defeat ISIS is committed to helping stabilize liberated communities through activities including restoring basic essential services, de-mining, and facilitating our partners' transition to sustainable, self-sufficient security forces and credible, inclusive governance. Through this approach, we are laying the groundwork to prevent ISIS's reemergence and setting the conditions that are ultimately conducive to allowing displaced Syrians and refugees to safely and voluntarily return to their homes.

The United States also continues to believe that the Syrian civil conflict must be resolved through a political solution, and a political solution can only be reached through the full implementation of United Nations Security Council Resolution 2254.

The domestic and international legal bases for use of military force by the United States in Iraq and Syria are unchanged, and outlined below.

As a matter of domestic law, legal authority for the use of military force against ISIS and al Qa'ida includes the Authorizations for Use of Military Force (AUMF) of 2001 and 2002. The 2001 AUMF also provides authority to use force to defend U.S., Coalition, and partner forces engaged in the campaign to defeat ISIS to the extent such use of force is a necessary and appropriate measure in support of counter-ISIS operations. The strikes taken by the United States in May and June 2017 against the Syrian Government and pro-Syrian-Government forces were limited and lawful measures taken under that authority to counter immediate threats to U.S. or partner forces engaged in that campaign. The United States does not seek to fight the Government of Syria or Iran or Iranian-supported groups in Iraq or Syria. However, the United States will not hesitate to use necessary and proportionate force to defend U.S., Coalition, or partner forces engaged in operations to defeat ISIS and degrade al-Qa'ida. There has been no assessment that either the Syrian Government or pro-Syrian-Government forces are "associated forces" of ISIS under the 2001 AUMF.

The 2002 AUMF provides authority "to defend the national security of the United States against the continuing threat posed by Iraq." The 2002 AUMF is an important source of authority for the use of military force to assist the Government of Iraq in military operations against ISIS and in continuing counterterrorism operations to address threats to U.S. national security emanating from Iraq following the destruction of ISIS's so-called physical "caliphate."

As a matter of international law, the United States is using force in Iraq with the consent of the Iraqi government. In Syria, the United States is using force against ISIS and al-Qa'ida, and is providing support to Syrian partner forces fighting ISIS such as the Syrian Democratic Forces, in the collective self-defense of Iraq (and other States) and in U.S. national self-defense. Consistent with the inherent right of self-defense, the United States initiated necessary and proportionate actions in Syria against ISIS and al-Qa'ida in 2014, and those actions continue to the present day. Such necessary and proportionate measures include the use of force to defend U.S., Coalition, and U.S.-supported partner forces from any threats from the Syrian Government and pro-Syrian Government forces.

We hope this information is useful. Please do not hesitate to contact us if we can be of further assistance.

Sincerely,
Mary K. Waters
Assistant Secretary
Legislative Affairs

SOURCE: Office of the Under Secretary of State. "Kaine-Trump ISIS War Power Letters." February 12, 2018. https://www.documentcloud.org/documents/4383185-Kaine-Trump-ISIS-war-power-letters.html.

## OTHER HISTORIC DOCUMENTS OF INTEREST

### FROM THIS VOLUME

- Chemical Attack in Syria Sparks International Action, p. 238

### FROM PREVIOUS *HISTORIC DOCUMENTS*

- President Trump, United Nations Respond to Chemical Attack in Syria, *2017*, p. 224
- Congressional Authorization Sought for Military Action against ISIL, *2015*, p. 53
- Al Qaeda Operative Captured in Tripoli, *2013*, p. 497

# Federal Court and Supreme Court Issue Rulings on Gerrymandering

JANUARY 9 AND JUNE 18, 2018

The gerrymandering of political districts has emerged as one of the more challenging issues the federal courts have struggled with in the past decades. The Supreme Court reiterated in 2017 that gerrymandering along racial lines is a clear constitutional violation, but it has never struck down a redistricting map on the grounds of purely partisan gerrymandering. On January 9, 2018, unwilling to wait for guidance from the Supreme Court, a panel of federal judges in North Carolina became the first court ever to throw out a state map of federal congressional districts for purely partisan gerrymandering. In a lengthy opinion, the court explained that there was extensive evidence that Republicans had acted to subvert the interests of non-Republicans in drawing the congressional map. The court ordered the state to draw new boundaries, but the short timeframe for doing so ahead of upcoming candidate filing deadlines resulted, on January 18, in the Supreme Court issuing a stay of the district court's decision pending appeal. The Supreme Court was also asked to weigh in on gerrymandering cases in Maryland and Wisconsin. On June 18, the Supreme Court handed down its rulings but sidestepped the substantive constitutional question and instead ruled that the specific parties to the cases lacked standing even to raise the issue. The cases were sent back to the states to give the parties another chance to show that they suffered the kind of individualized harm necessary to challenge partisan gerrymandering.

## Partisan Gerrymanders Challenged in Three States

As required by the Constitution, every ten years the federal government takes a census of everyone in the country. States use this data to design congressional districts of roughly equal numbers of people. The effort to redraw the congressional maps is led by the party in power, which may or may not take into account opinions of the minority party and public. This partisan methodology sometimes results in a court challenge by those alleging that the map has either been drawn in a way that discriminates based on race or based upon party. Because resolving disputes about the constitutionality of a state's district maps is often extremely time sensitive, these challenges are heard first by a three-judge panel and, if appealed, are sent directly to the Supreme Court, which must review the case on an expedited schedule. Since the last round of redistricting in 2010, challengers in three states—Maryland, North Carolina, and Wisconsin—brought federal cases seeking to strike down voting district maps, arguing that they are unconstitutional partisan gerrymanders, a term defined by the courts as "the drawing of legislative district lines to subordinate adherents of one political party and entrench a rival party in power."

North Carolina is a battleground state, almost evenly split between Democrats and Republicans, with highly contested statewide elections. In 2010, Republicans gained control of all branches of the state government and, thus, had exclusive control over the redistricting process. The resulting 2011 plan was used in two congressional elections. In 2012, Republican candidates received 49 percent of the statewide vote but won nine out of thirteen congressional seats. In 2014, Republican candidates received 54 percent of the vote, but won ten out of thirteen seats. On February 5, 2016, in a decision that was later upheld by the Supreme Court, a three-judge panel of federal judges struck down this plan as an unconstitutional racial gerrymander. Republicans, who still controlled both chambers of the North Carolina General Assembly, drew a remedial districting plan without any input from Democrats or the public. Common Cause, the League of Women Voters of North Carolina, and multiple individual voters filed suit challenging the remedial 2016 plan, this time as an unconstitutional partisan gerrymander.

Wisconsin is also very evenly split between political parties. In fact, following the census in 1980, 1990, and 2000, federal courts were called in to draw the state's legislative districts when the legislature and the governor, who represented different political parties, were unable to agree to new districting plans. However, in 2010, the Republican Party took control of the legislature and governor's mansion and developed new legislative maps in a secret process. In the 2012 elections, the first with the newly drawn map, Democratic candidates won a majority of the votes counted; but because of how the district lines were drawn, Republicans won a 60–32 seat advantage in the State Assembly.

In 2015, voters filed a complaint in federal court in Wisconsin challenging the voter map as a partisan gerrymander that unconstitutionally favors Republican voters and candidates by "cracking" and "packing" Democratic voters in Wisconsin. According to their complaint: "Cracking means dividing a party's supporters among multiple districts so that they fall short of a majority in each one. Packing means concentrating one party's backers in a few districts that they win by overwhelming margins." At the end of a trial, the three-judge panel found that the Wisconsin map was designed "to secure Republican control of the Assembly under any likely future electoral scenario for the remainder of the decade" and concluded that it violated the First and Fourteenth Amendments. The case, *Gill v. Whitford*, was appealed to the Supreme Court.

Maryland primarily elects Democratic candidates, and in 2011, its legislators redrew the district maps with what former governor Martin O'Malley, a Democrat, admitted was partisan intent, to increase the Democratic advantage from 6–2 to 7–1. To do this, they switched out one set of voters from the district held by Rep. Roscoe G. Bartlett, a Republican, and switched back in the same number of different voters. Before the change, Rep. Bartlett won his district by a 28-percentage-point margin, but, after the redraw, he lost to a Democrat by 21 percentage points. Several Republican voters brought suit, alleging that the map was gerrymandered in 2011 for the purpose of retaliating against them for their political views. Before a trial on the merits, the federal court granted a stay pending a Supreme Court ruling in *Gill v. Whitford*.

## NORTH CAROLINA COURT THROWS OUT MAP OF CONGRESSIONAL DISTRICTS

On January 9, 2018, a panel of three judges ruled in *Common Cause v. Rucho*, striking down North Carolina's congressional map, ordering the state to present a remedial plan by

January 24, and making clear that if the court did not find the redrawn map satisfactory, it would impose its own.

In a strongly worded 191-page opinion, the panel concluded that the map violated the Equal Protection Clause, which prohibits a state from "deny[ing] to any person within its jurisdiction the equal protection of the laws." Direct testimony from Republican leaders freely acknowledging that they enacted the plan with the intent of discriminating against voters who favored non-Republican candidates bolstered the court's finding. One such leader proclaimed that he drew the map to advantage Republicans because "electing Republicans is better than electing Democrats." Judge James Wynn dryly replied that this "is not a choice the Constitution" gave him to make. The consultant hired to create the map also testified that he was instructed to "minimize the number of districts in which Democrats would have an opportunity to elect a Democratic candidate." Further, the court reviewed five different types of statistical analyses performed by three different experts all reaching the same conclusion: the North Carolina plan led to and likely will continue to lead to discriminatory effects through multiple election cycles.

The court also found that North Carolina's General Assembly drew district lines to discriminate against voters based on their past political associations and expressions of political beliefs in violation of the First Amendment's prohibition against the government favoring or disfavoring particular viewpoints. Finally, the court found that the invidious partisanship reflected in the district map runs contrary to Article 1, Section 2 of the Constitution, the section that gives states the power to draw up congressional districts but vests the power to choose representatives in "the People." According to the court, the North Carolina partisan gerrymander violates this core constitutional principle "that the voters should choose their representatives, not the other way around."

Although the court found the map to be an unconstitutional partisan gerrymander and blocked North Carolina from using it in future elections, the Supreme Court issued an order staying the decision just a few days later. The Supreme Court had already heard oral arguments in *Gill v. Whitford*, a partisan gerrymander case out of Wisconsin, and the decision in that case would be one of the most anticipated of the year.

## Supreme Court Sidesteps the Central Question on Partisan Gerrymandering

On June 18, 2018, the Supreme Court chose not to rule on the merits of a partisan gerrymander challenge to a redistricting plan written by the Republican legislature in Wisconsin. Instead, Chief Justice John Roberts, writing for a unanimous Court in *Gill v. Whitford*, found that the parties bringing the challenge did not have "standing" to bring the lawsuit. That is, they did not have the necessary personal stake in the outcome of the controversy to invoke the Court's jurisdiction under Article III of the Constitution. As the opinion explains, to have standing, a plaintiff must have suffered "an injury in fact" that is "fairly traceable" to the challenged conduct and will be redressed by a favorable Court decision. If this standard is not met, the courts cannot intervene.

The parties bringing the lawsuit had tried to propose a workable standard for determining whether partisan gerrymandering has reached a level that is unconstitutional.

Their proposal turned on the concept of "the efficiency gap," which relied on the percentage of votes "wasted," based on average measures. They claimed a constitutional right "not to be placed in legislative districts deliberately designed to 'waste' their votes in elections where their chosen candidates will win in landslides (packing) or are destined to lose by closer margins (cracking)." The problem for the Court was that none of the voters bringing the case sought to prove that he or she lives in a gerrymandered district. The plaintiffs instead presented arguments that their legal injury was not just the injury suffered as individual voters, but, rather, encompassed the statewide harm to their interest in "collective representation in the legislature." The Court rejected this notion of collective harm and held that the plaintiffs failed to present meaningful evidence that they had suffered individualized harm. "They instead, rested their case at trial," the chief justice wrote, "on their theory of statewide injury to Wisconsin Democrats." Because the Court cannot resolve a case about group partisan preferences, its prescribed role is "to vindicate the individual rights of the people appearing before it."

Rather than dismissing the case, the Court opted to give the parties the opportunity to prove "concrete and particularized injuries" and sent the case back to Wisconsin. At the same time, it published a short *per curium* (unsigned) opinion, in *Benisek v. Lamone*, the case challenging Democratic redistricting in Maryland from 2011. The Maryland case had been appealed before a trial had been held, and the Supreme Court sent it back to Maryland, saying that the parties had waited too long to seek an injunction and that there is no reason to intervene now before a trial has taken place. The Supreme Court also sent *Common Cause v. Rucho* back to the North Carolina court for reconsideration in light of the guidance provided in *Gill v. Whitford*.

## North Carolina Court Issues New Ruling

On August 27, 2018, the North Carolina federal court issued a new opinion in the case of *Common Cause v. Rucho,* the case that had been returned by the Supreme Court without a ruling. It held that the parties to this case did in fact have standing and, again, ruled for the challengers on all claims, holding that the partisan gerrymander of the state's congressional districts was unconstitutional. In a move designed to ensure that the case would reach the Supreme Court during its next term, the federal court agreed to put its own ruling on hold pending appeal on two conditions: first, that the state must have its appeal in on an expedited basis, and second, that it cannot ask for any extensions. If the legislature violates these terms, the trial court will proceed with drawing its own new map of voting districts.

—Melissa Feinberg

*Following are excerpts from the United States District Court for the Middle District of North Carolina decision in* Common Cause v. Rucho, *decided on January 9, 2018, in which the court threw out the state's congressional district map for partisan gerrymandering; and two Supreme Court decisions,* Gill v. Whitford *and* Benisek v. Lamone, *both from June 18, 2018, on gerrymandering cases brought against the congressional maps in Wisconsin and Maryland, in which the Court failed to rule on the central issue of partisan gerrymandering.*

# Federal Court Rules against North Carolina Congressional District Maps

---

**January 9, 2018**

*[Footnotes have been omitted.]*

## IN THE UNITED STATES DISTRICT COURT
## FOR THE MIDDLE DISTRICT OF NORTH CAROLINA

COMMON CAUSE, et al.,

Plaintiffs,

v.

ROBERT A. RUCHO, in his official capacity as Chairman of the North Carolina Senate Redistricting Committee for the 2016 Extra Session and Co-Chairman of the Joint Select Committee on Congressional Redistricting, et al.,

Defendants.

No. 1:16-CV-1026

LEAGUE OF WOMEN VOTERS OF NORTH CAROLINA, et al.,

Plaintiffs,

v.

ROBERT A. RUCHO, in his official capacity as Chairman of the North Carolina Senate Redistricting Committee for the 2016 Extra Session and Co-Chairman of the Joint Select Committee on Congressional Redistricting, et al.,

Defendants.

No. 1:16-CV-1164

Before WYNN, Circuit Judge, and OSTEEN, JR., District Judge, and BRITT, Senior District Judge.

\* \* \* \* \*

Circuit Judge Wynn wrote the majority opinion in which Senior District Judge Britt concurred. District Judge Osteen, Jr., wrote a separate opinion concurring in part and dissenting in part.

## MEMORANDUM OPINION

WYNN, Circuit Judge:

In these consolidated cases, two groups of Plaintiffs allege that North Carolina's 2016 Congressional Redistricting Plan (the "2016 Plan") constitutes a partisan gerrymander in violation of the First Amendment, the Equal Protection Clause of the Fourteenth Amendment, and Article I, Sections 2 and 4 of the Constitution. Legislative Defendants do not dispute that the General Assembly intended for the 2016 Plan to favor supporters of Republican candidates and disfavor supporters of non-Republican candidates. Nor could they. The Republican-controlled North Carolina General Assembly expressly directed the legislators and consultant responsible for drawing the 2016 Plan to rely on "political data"—past election results specifying whether, and to what extent, particular voting districts had favored Republican or Democratic candidates, and therefore were likely to do so in the future—to draw a districting plan that would ensure Republican candidates would prevail in the vast majority of the state's congressional districts.

Legislative Defendants also do not argue—and have never argued—that the 2016 Plan's intentional disfavoring of supporters of non-Republican candidates advances *any* democratic, constitutional, or public interest. Nor could they. Neither the Supreme Court nor any lower court has recognized any such interest furthered by partisan gerrymandering— "the drawing of legislative district lines to subordinate adherents of one political party and entrench a rival party in power." *Ariz. State Legislature v. Ariz. Indep. Redistricting Comm'n*, 135 S. Ct. 2652, 2658 (2015). And, as further detailed below, partisan gerrymandering runs contrary to numerous fundamental democratic principles and individual rights enshrined in the Constitution.

Rather than seeking to advance any democratic or constitutional interest, the state legislator responsible for drawing the 2016 Plan said he drew the map to advantage Republican candidates because he "think[s] electing Republicans is better than electing Democrats." Ex. 1016, at 34:21–23. But that is not a choice the Constitution allows legislative mapdrawers to make. Rather, "the core principle of [our] republican government [is] that the voters should choose their representatives, not the other way around." *Ariz. State Leg.*, 135 S. Ct. at 2677 (internal quotation marks omitted).

Accordingly, and as further explained below, we conclude that Plaintiffs prevail on all of their constitutional claims.

## I.

*[Sections A and B, and a majority of section C, detailing the background and allegations in the case, have been omitted.]*

. . . For the reasons that follow, we reject Legislative Defendants' standing and justiciability arguments. We further conclude that the 2016 Plan violates the Equal Protection Clause because the General Assembly enacted the plan with the intent of discriminating against voters who favored non-Republican candidates, the plan has had and likely will continue to have that effect, and no legitimate state interest justifies the 2016 Plan's discriminatory partisan effect. We also conclude that the 2016 Plan violates the First Amendment by unjustifiably discriminating against voters based on their previous political expression and affiliation. Finally, we hold that the 2016 Plan violates Article I by exceeding the scope of the General Assembly's delegated authority to enact congressional election regulations and interfering with the right of "the People" to choose their Representatives.

## II.

Before addressing the merits of Plaintiffs' claims, we first address Legislative Defendants' threshold standing and justiciability arguments. . . .

*[Information on previous court precedent and its bearing on claims in the case have been omitted.]*

In conclusion, we find that both the individual and organizational Plaintiffs have suffered injuries-in-fact attributable to the 2016 Plan, and, based on those injuries, Plaintiffs have standing to challenge the 2016 Plan as a whole. Even absent statewide standing, because Plaintiffs reside in each of the state's thirteen districts and have all suffered injuries-in-fact, Plaintiffs, as a group, have standing to lodge district-by-district challenges to the entire 2016 Plan.

*[Section B, detailing the defendants' arguments and relevant precedent, has been omitted.]*

## III.

Having disposed of Legislative Defendants' standing and justiciability arguments, we now turn to Plaintiffs' claims under the Equal Protection Clause of the Fourteenth Amendment. The Equal Protection Clause prohibits a State from "deny[ing] to any person within its jurisdiction the equal protection of the laws." U.S. Const. amend XIV. Partisan gerrymandering potentially runs afoul of the Equal Protection Clause because, by seeking to diminish the electoral power of supporters of a disfavored party, a partisan gerrymander treats individuals who support candidates of one political party less favorably than individuals who support candidates of another party. *Cf. Lehr v. Robertson*, 463 U.S. 248, 265 (1983) ("The concept of equal justice under law requires the State to govern impartially."). . .

As this Court explained in denying Defendants' motions to dismiss, the Supreme Court's splintered partisan gerrymandering decisions establish that in order to prove a prima facie partisan gerrymandering claim under the Equal Protection Clause, "a plaintiff must show both [1] discriminatory intent and [2] discriminatory effects." *Common Cause*, 240 F. Supp. 3d at 387 (citing *Bandemer*, 478 U.S. at 127 (plurality op.); *id.* at 161 (Powell, J., concurring and dissenting)). . . .

## A.

. . . To establish a discriminatory purpose or intent, a plaintiff need not show that the discriminatory purpose is "express or appear[s] on the face of the statute." *Washington*, 426 U.S. at 241. Rather, "an invidious discriminatory purpose may often be inferred from the totality of the relevant facts." *Id.* at 242. In determining whether an "invidious discriminatory purpose was a motivating factor" behind the challenged action, evidence that the impact of the challenged action falls "more heavily" on one group than another "may provide an important starting point." *Vill. of Arlington Heights v. Metro. Hous. Dev. Corp.*, 429 U.S. 252, 266 (1977). . . .

## 2.

We agree with Plaintiffs that a wealth of evidence proves the General Assembly's intent to "subordinate" the interests of non-Republican voters and "entrench" Republican domination of the state's congressional delegation. In particular, we find that the following evidence proves the General Assembly's discriminatory intent: (a) the facts and circumstances surrounding the drawing and enactment of the 2016 Plan; (b) empirical analyses of the 2016 Plan; and (c) the discriminatory partisan intent motivating the 2011 Plan, which the General Assembly expressly sought to carry forward when it drew the 2016 Plan.

### a.

Several aspects of the 2016 redistricting process establish that the General Assembly sought to advance the interests of the Republican Party at the expense of the interests of non-Republican voters. *First*, Republicans had exclusive control over the drawing and enactment of the 2016 Plan. The Committee's Republican leadership and majority denied Democratic legislators access to the principal mapdrawer, Dr. Hofeller. And with the exception of one small change to prevent the pairing of Democratic incumbents, Dr. Hofeller finished drawing the 2016 Plan *before* Democrats had an opportunity to participate in the legislative process. Additionally, all of the key votes—including the Committee votes adopting the Political Data and Partisan Advantage criteria and approving the 2016 Plan, and the House and Senate votes adopting the 2016 Plan—were decided on a party-line basis. As the *Bandemer* plurality recognized, when a single party exclusively controls the redistricting process, "it should not be very difficult to prove that the likely political consequences of the reapportionment were intended." *Bandemer*, 478 U.S. at 129 (plurality op.); *Pope*, 809 F. Supp. at 396.

*Second*, the legislative process "[d]epart[ed] from the normal procedural sequence." *Arlington Heights*, 429 U.S. at 267. Representative Lewis and Senator Rucho instructed Dr. Hofeller regarding the criteria he should follow in drawing the 2016 Plan *before* they had been appointed co-chairs of the Committee and *before* the Committee debated and adopted those criteria. Lewis Dep. 77:7–20. Indeed, Dr. Hofeller completed drawing the 2016 Plan *before* the Committee met and adopted the governing criteria. *Id.* And notwithstanding that the Committee held public hearings and received public input, Dr. Hofeller never received, much less considered, *any* of that input in drawing the 2016 Plan.

*Third*, the plain language of the "Partisan *Advantage*" criterion reflects an express legislative intent to discriminate—to favor voters who support Republican candidates and subordinate the interests of voters who support non-Republican candidates. Moreover, the Partisan Advantage criterion reflects an express intent to entrench the Republican supermajority in North Carolina's congressional delegation by seeking to "maintain" the partisan make-up of the delegation achieved under the unconstitutional 2011 Plan.

. . . Representative Lewis explained that "to the extent [we] are going to use political data in drawing this map, it is to gain partisan advantage ("We did seek a partisan advantage in drawing the map." (Statement of Rep. Lewis)). . . And Representative Lewis "acknowledge[d] freely that this would be a political gerrymander,"—a sentiment with which Senator Rucho "s[aw] nothing wrong". . . .

## b.

We also find that empirical evidence reveals that the 2016 Plan "bears more heavily on [supporters of candidates of one party] than another." *Washington*, 426 U.S. at 242. In particular, two empirical analyses introduced by Plaintiffs demonstrate that the pro-Republican partisan advantage achieved by the 2016 Plan cannot be explained by the General Assembly's legitimate redistricting objectives, including legitimate redistricting objectives that take into account partisan considerations.

Dr. Jonathan Mattingly, a mathematics and statistics professor at Duke University and an expert in applied computational mathematics, drew an ensemble of 24,518 simulated districting plans from a probability distribution of *all* possible North Carolina congressional redistricting plans. To create the ensemble, Dr. Mattingly programmed a computer first to draw a random sample of more than 150,000 simulated plans using a Markov chain Monte Carlo algorithm—a widely employed statistical method used in a variety of settings—that randomly perturbed the lines of an initial districting plan to generate successive new plans. The computer algorithm then eliminated from the 150,000 plan sample all "unreasonable" districting plans—plans with noncontiguous districts, plans with population deviations exceeding 0.1 percent, plans that were not reasonably compact under common statistical measures of compactness, plans that did not minimize the number of county and VTD splits, and plans that did not comply with the Voting Rights Act—yielding the 24,518-plan ensemble. . . .

*[Additional information on Dr. Mattingly's analysis has been omitted.]*

We find that Dr. Mattingly's analyses, which he confirmed through extensive sensitivity testing, provide strong evidence that the General Assembly intended to subordinate the interests of non-Republican voters and entrench the Republican Party in power. In particular, given that 99 percent of Dr. Mattingly's 24,518 simulated plans—which conformed to traditional redistricting criteria and the non-partisan criteria adopted by the Committee—would have led to the election of at least one additional Democratic candidate, we agree with Dr. Mattingly's conclusion that the 2016 Plan's pro-Republican bias is not attributable to a legitimate redistricting objective, but instead reflects an intentional effort to subordinate the interests of non-Republican voters. Dr. Mattingly's analysis that the packing and cracking of non-Republican voters had to have been the product of an intentional legislative effort reinforces that conclusion. And Dr. Mattingly's finding that the 2016 Plan produced "safe Republican majorities in the first eight most Republican districts," shows that the General Assembly intended for the partisan advantage to persist. That the 2016 Plan's intentional pro-Republican bias exists when Dr. Mattingly used the actual votes from *both* 2012 (a relatively good year for Democrats) and 2016 (a relatively good year for Republicans) also speaks to the imperviousness of the 2016 Plan's partisan advantage to changes in candidates and the political environment.

Dr. Jowei Chen, a political science professor at the University of Michigan and expert in political geography and redistricting, also evaluated the 2016 Plan's partisan performance relative to simulated districting plans. . . .

*[Additional findings from Dr. Chen's analyses have been omitted.]*

Like Dr. Mattingly's analyses, we find that Dr. Chen's analyses provide compelling evidence that the General Assembly intended to subordinate the interests of non-Republican voters in drawing the 2016 Plan. In particular, we find it significant that *none* of the 3,000 simulated districts plans generated by Dr. Chen's computer algorithm, which conformed to all of the traditional nonpartisan districting criteria adopted by the Committee, produced a congressional delegation containing 10 Republican and 3 Democrats—the result the General Assembly intended the 2016 Plan to create, and the result the 2016 Plan in fact created. That the 2016 Plan continued to be an "extreme statistical outlier" in terms of its pro-Republican tilt under three separate specifications of criteria for drawing the simulated plans reinforces our confidence that Dr. Chen's conclusions reflect stable and valid results.

*[Court analysis of the work of Dr. Chen and Dr. Mattingly in relation to the case has been omitted.]*

### 3.

. . . Finally, the facts and circumstances surrounding the drawing and enactment of the 2011 Plan—the partisan effects of which the Committee expressly sought to carry forward in the 2016 Plan—further establish that the General Assembly drew the 2016 Plan to maximize partisan advantage. In particular, Representative Lewis and Senator Rucho's "primar[y] goal" in drawing the 2011 Plan was "to create *as many districts as possible* in which GOP candidates would be able to successfully compete for office." Hofeller Dep. 123:1–7 (emphasis added). And, in accordance with that goal, Dr. Hofeller testified that he drew the plan "to *minimize* the number of districts in which Democrats would have an opportunity to elect a Democratic candidate." *Id.* at 127:19–22 (emphasis added). . . .

\* \* \* \* \*

In sum, we find that Plaintiffs presented more-than-adequate evidence to satisfy their burden to demonstrate that the General Assembly was motivated by invidious partisan intent in drawing the 2016 Plan. Although we do not believe the law requires a finding of predominance, we nonetheless find that Plaintiffs' evidence—particularly the facts and circumstances surrounding the drawing and enactment of the 2016 Plan and Dr. Mattingly's and Dr. Chen's analyses—establish that the pursuit of partisan advantage predominated over the General Assembly's non-partisan redistricting objectives. And given that Dr. Chen found that the General Assembly's desire to protect incumbents and express refusal to try to avoid dividing political subdivisions failed to explain the 2016 Plan's partisan bias, we find that Plaintiffs' evidence distinguishes between permissible redistricting objectives that rely on political data or consider partisanship, and what instead here occurred: invidious partisan discrimination.

### B.

Having concluded that the General Assembly intended to discriminate against voters who supported or were likely to support non-Republican candidates, we now must determine whether the 2016 Plan achieved its discriminatory objective.

*[Past court rulings and additional information related to partisan discrimination in drawing congressional boundaries have been omitted.]*

## 2.

We find that Plaintiffs satisfied their burden under the discriminatory effects prong by proving the 2016 Plan dilutes the votes of non-Republican voters and entrenches Republican control of the state's congressional delegation. In reaching this conclusion we rely on the following categories of evidence: (a) the results of North Carolina's 2016 congressional election conducted using the 2016 Plan; (b) expert analyses of those results revealing that the 2016 Plan exhibits "extreme" partisan asymmetry; (c) Dr. Mattingly's and Dr. Chen's simulation analyses; and (d) the results of North Carolina's 2012 and 2014 elections using the 2011 Plan—the partisan effects of which the General Assembly expressly sought to carry forward when it drew the 2016 Plan—and empirical analyses of those results.

## a.

We begin with the results of North Carolina's 2016 congressional election conducted under the 2016 Plan. The General Assembly achieved its goal: North Carolina voters elected a congressional delegation of 10 Republicans and 3 Democrats. That the 2016 Plan resulted in the outcome Representative Lewis, Senator Rucho, Dr. Hofeller, and the General Assembly intended proves both that the precinct-level election data used by the mapdrawers served as a reliable predictor of the 2016 Plan's partisan performance and that the mapdrawers effectively used that data to draw a districting plan that perfectly achieved the General Assembly's partisan objectives.

Following the 2016 election, Republicans hold 76.9 percent of the seats in the state's thirteen-seat congressional delegation, whereas North Carolina voters cast 53.22 percent of their votes for Republican congressional candidates. Notably, the *Whitford* court found that less significant disparities between the favored party's seatshare and vote-share (60.7% v. 48.6% and 63.6% v. 52%) provided evidence of a challenged districting plan's discriminatory effects. 218 F. Supp. 3d at 901. As the court explained, "[i]f it is true that a redistricting 'plan that more closely reflects the distribution of state party power seems a less likely vehicle for partisan discrimination,' . . . then a plan that deviates this strongly from the distribution of statewide power suggests the opposite." *Id.* at 902 (quoting *LULAC,* 548 U.S. at 419 (opinion of Kennedy, J.)).

The results of the 2016 election also reveal that the 2016 Plan "packed" and "cracked" voters who supported Republican candidates. In particular, in the three districts in which Democratic candidates prevailed, the Democratic candidates received an average of 67.95 percent of the vote, whereas Republican candidates received an average of 31.24 percent of the vote. By contrast, in the ten districts in which Republican candidates prevailed, the Republican candidates received an average of 60.27 percent of the vote, and Democratic candidates received an average of 39.73 percent of the vote. Democratic candidates, therefore, consistently won by larger margins than Republican candidates. Additionally, the Democratic candidate's margin in the *least* Democratic district in which a Democratic candidate prevailed (34.04%) was nearly *triple* that of the Republican candidate's margin in the *least* Republican district in which a Republican candidate prevailed (12.20%), reflecting the "S-shaped curve" that Dr. Mattingly described as "the signature of [partisan] gerrymandering."

And the results of the 2016 congressional election establish that the 2016 Plan's discriminatory effects likely will persist through multiple election cycles. To begin, the Republican candidate's vote share (56.10%) and margin of victory (12.20%) in the *least* Republican district electing a Republican candidate, District 13, exceed the thresholds at which political science experts, including Legislative Defendants' expert Dr. Hood, consider a seat to be "safe"—*i.e.*, highly unlikely to change parties in subsequent elections. . . .

*[Background on research conducted by Dr. Simon Jackman into how districting plans can change electoral conditions has been omitted.]*

\* \* \* \* \*

We find Dr. Jackman's partisan asymmetry analyses provide strong evidence that the 2016 Plan subordinates the interests of supporters of non-Republican candidates and serves to entrench the Republican Party's control of the state's congressional delegation. In particular, we find it significant that three different measures of partisan asymmetry all point to the same result—that the 2016 Plan poses a significant impediment to supporters of non-Republican candidates translating their votes into seats, and that the magnitude of that impediment is an extreme outlier relative to other congressional districting plans. We also find it significant that Dr. Jackman's analyses demonstrate the durability of the 2016 Plan's pro-Republican bias, both by comparing the 2016 Plan to other plans that were used in multiple elections and by demonstrating that 2016 Plan is likely to retain its pro-Republican bias "under any *likely* electoral scenario." *Whitford*, 218 F. Supp. 3d at 899, 903. Given that durability, we find that the 2016 Plan has the effect of entrenching Republican candidates in power, even in the face of significant shifts in voter support in favor of non-Republican candidates, and thereby likely making Republican elected representatives less responsive to the interests of non-Republican members of their constituency. . . .

*[Court review of the analyses by Drs. Chen, Mattingly, and Jackman has been omitted.]*

\* \* \* \* \*

When viewed in totality, we find Plaintiffs' evidence more than sufficient to prove that the 2016 Plan has discriminated, and will continue to discriminate, against voters who support non-Republican candidates. In reaching this conclusion, we find it significant that Plaintiffs' evidence proves the 2016 Plan's discriminatory effects in a variety of different ways. Plaintiffs' direct evidence based on the actual results of an election conducted under the 2016 Plan confirmed that the discriminatory effects intended by the 2016 Plan's architects and predicted by Dr. Mattingly's analyses—the election of 10 Republicans by margins that suggest they will retain their seats throughout the life of the plan—in fact occurred. That five different types of statistical analyses performed by three different experts all reached the same conclusion gives us further confidence that 2016 Plan produces discernible discriminatory effects. And although some of those analyses considered "unfair results that would occur in a hypothetical state of affairs," *LULAC*, 548 U.S. at 420 (opinion of Kennedy, J.), others like the efficiency gap and the mean-median difference did not. Given that all of this evidence "point[s] in the same direction"—and Legislative Defendants failed to provide any evidence to the contrary—Plaintiffs have provided "strong proof" of the 2016 Plan's discriminatory effects. *Sylvester*, 453 F.3d at 903.

*[A review of the district map and whether it is justified by a state interest or other explanation has been omitted.]*

* * * * *

In sum, we find that the General Assembly drew and enacted the 2016 Plan with intent to subordinate the interests of non-Republican voters and entrench Republican control of North Carolina's congressional delegation. We further find that a variety of evidence demonstrates that the 2016 Plan achieved the General Assembly's discriminatory partisan objective. And we find that neither North Carolina's political geography nor the General Assembly's interest in protecting incumbents explains the 2016 Plan's discriminatory effects. Accordingly, we conclude that the 2016 Plan constitutes an unconstitutional partisan gerrymander in violation of the Equal Protection Clause of the Fourteenth Amendment.

## IV.

Next, we consider Plaintiffs' claims under the First Amendment. The First Amendment, through the Due Process Clause of the Fourteenth Amendment, prohibits states from making any law "abridging the freedom of speech." U.S. Const. amend. I. Partisan gerrymandering—again, "the drawing of legislative district lines to subordinate adherents of one political party and entrench a rival party in power," *Ariz. State Leg.*, 135 S. Ct. at 2658—implicates First Amendment rights because "political belief and association constitute the core of those activities protected by the First Amendment," *Elrod v. Burns*, 427 U.S. 347, 356 (1976). The First Amendment "has its fullest and most urgent application to speech uttered during a campaign for political office." *Citizens United v. Fed. Election Comm'n*, 558 U.S. 310, 339–40 (2010) (internal quotation marks omitted). To that end, the First Amendment protects "the right of individuals to associate for the advancement of political beliefs, and the right of qualified voters, *regardless of their political persuasion*, to cast their votes effectively." *Williams*, 393 U.S. at 30–31 (emphasis added).

*[The court's application of the First Amendment to drawing congressional boundaries has been omitted.]*

The 2016 Plan, in particular, implicates all four of these lines of precedent. The 2016 Plan discriminates against a particular viewpoint: voters who oppose the Republican platform and Republican candidates. The 2016 Plan also discriminates against a particular group of speakers: non-Republican candidates and voters who support non-Republican candidates. The General Assembly's use of Political Data—individuals' votes in previous elections—to draw district lines to dilute the votes of individuals likely to support non-Republican candidates imposes burdens on such individuals based on their past political speech and association. And the 2016 Plan's partisan favoritism excludes it from the class of "reasonable, politically neutral" electoral regulations that pass First Amendment muster. Burdick, 504 U.S. at 438. . . .

## B.

. . . Drawing on that precedent, we derive a three-prong test requiring Plaintiffs to prove: (1) that the challenged districting plan was intended to favor or disfavor individuals or entities that support a particular candidate or political party, (2) that the districting plan burdened the political speech or associational rights of such individuals or entities, and (3) that a causal relationship existed between the governmental actor's discriminatory motivation and the First Amendment burdens imposed by the districting plan. . . .

Under that standard, the record reveals that the 2016 Plan has had a chilling effect on reasonable North Carolinians' First Amendment activities. Multiple Plaintiffs testified that in "the most recent election, a lot of people did not come out to vote"— despite concerted get-out-the-vote efforts—"[b]ecause they felt their vote didn't count." Evans Dep. 16:4–9; *accord, e.g.,* Peck Dep. 27:20–24 ("I can't tell you how many people told me this election, Republicans as well as Democrats, 'This system is rigged. My vote doesn't count.' It was really hard to try to galvanize people to participate."). Likewise, in the 2016 election under the 2016 Plan, many organizations' "biggest struggle was to get people to vote." Peck Dep. 40:5–6. Voters and advocacy organizations elected not to participate in congressional races because they believed they could not "have a democratic—small "D"—democratic impact. It doesn't really matter for those races because of the gerrymandering because they're not competitive.". . .

\* \* \* \* \*

In sum, we find (1) that the 2016 Plan was intended to disfavor supporters of non-Republican candidates based on those supporters' past expressions of political beliefs, (2) that the 2016 Plan burdened such supporters' political speech and associational rights, and (3) that a causal relationship existed between the General Assembly's discriminatory motivation and the First Amendment burdens imposed by the 2016 Plan. Accordingly, we conclude that the 2016 Plan violates the First Amendment.

## V.

Finally, we turn to Common Clause Plaintiffs' claims under Article I of the Constitution. Common Cause Plaintiffs assert the 2016 Plan runs afoul of two provisions in Article I: Article I, section 2, which provides that the "House of Representatives shall be composed of Members chosen . . . by the People," and the Elections Clause, which provides that "the Times, Places and Manner of holding Elections for . . . Representatives, shall be prescribed in each State by the Legislature thereof; but the Congress may at any time by Law make or alter such Regulations," U.S. Const. art. I, § 4, cl. 1. . . .

The States' broad, delegated power under the Election Clause, however, is not without limit. In particular, "in exercising their powers of supervision over elections and in setting qualifications for voters, the States may not infringe upon basic constitutional protections." *Kusper*, 414 U.S. at 56–57; *see also Tashjian*, 479 U.S. at 217 ("The power to regulate the time, place, and manner of elections does not justify, without more, the abridgement of fundamental rights."). Likewise, the Elections Clause does not serve "as a source of power [for States] to dictate electoral outcomes, to favor or disfavor a class of candidates, or to evade important constitutional restraints." *Thornton*, 514 U.S. at 833–34. Put differently, the States' authority under the elections clause extends *only* to "*neutral* provisions as to the time, place, and manner of elections." *Gralike*, 531 U.S. at 527 (emphasis added).

## B.

Under this precedent, we conclude that the 2016 Plan exceeds the General Assembly's delegated authority under the Elections Clause for three reasons: (1) the Elections Clause did not empower State legislatures to disfavor the interests of supporters of a particular candidate or party in drawing congressional districts; (2) the 2016 Plan's pro-Republican bias violates other constitutional provisions, including the First Amendment, the Equal Protection Clause, and Article I, section 2; and (3) the 2016 Plan represents an impermissible effort to "dictate electoral outcomes" and "disfavor a class of candidates." *Thornton*, 514 U.S. at 833–34.

*[Additional discussion of the Elections Clause and its relevance in the case has been omitted.]*

## VI.

Having concluded that the 2016 Plan violates the Equal Protection Clause, the First Amendment, and Article I of the Constitution, we now must determine the appropriate remedy. Absent unusual circumstances, "such as where an impending election is imminent and a State's election machinery is already in progress," courts should take "appropriate action to insure that no further elections are conducted under the invalid plan." *Reynolds*, 377 U.S. at 585. As the 2018 general election remains many months away and the 2018 election cycle has not yet formally begun, we find no such circumstances exist. Accordingly, we enjoin Defendants from conducting any further elections using the 2016 Plan.

*[Additional direction for drawing a remedial map or alternative plan has been omitted.]*

SO ORDERED

*[The opinion of Judge Osteen Jr., concurring in part and dissenting in part, has been omitted.]*

SOURCE: United States District Court for the Middle District of North Carolina. *Common Cause v. Rucho*. No. 1:16-CV-1026. January 9, 2018. https://www.gpo.gov/fdsys/pkg/USCOURTS-ncmd-1_16-cv-01164/pdf/USCOURTS-ncmd-1_16-cv-01164-3.pdf.

# *Supreme Court Sends Wisconsin Gerrymandering Case Back to Lower Court*

---

**June 18, 2018**

*[Footnotes have been omitted.]*

## SUPREME COURT OF THE UNITED STATES

No. 16–1161

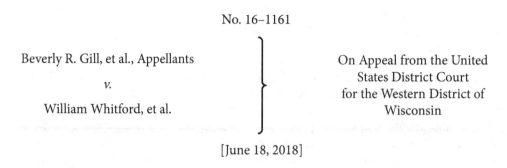

Beverly R. Gill, et al., Appellants

*v.*

William Whitford, et al.

On Appeal from the United
States District Court
for the Western District of
Wisconsin

[June 18, 2018]

CHIEF JUSTICE ROBERTS delivered the opinion of the Court.

The State of Wisconsin, like most other States, entrusts to its legislature the periodic task of redrawing the boundaries of the State's legislative districts. A group of Wisconsin Democratic voters filed a complaint in the District Court, alleging that the legislature carried out this task with an eye to diminishing the ability of Wisconsin Democrats to convert Democratic votes into Democratic seats in the legislature. The plaintiffs asserted that, in so doing, the legislature had infringed their rights under the First and Fourteenth Amendments.

But a plaintiff seeking relief in federal court must first demonstrate that he has standing to do so, including that he has "a personal stake in the outcome," *Baker* v. *Carr*, 369 U. S. 186, 204 (1962), distinct from a "generally available grievance about government," *Lance* v. *Coffman*, 549 U. S. 437, 439 (2007) (*per curiam*). That threshold requirement "ensures that we act *as judges*, and do not engage in policymaking properly left to elected representatives." *Hollingsworth* v. *Perry*, 570 U. S. 693, 700 (2013). Certain of the plaintiffs before us alleged that they had such a personal stake in this case, but never followed up with the requisite proof. The District Court and this Court therefore lack the power to resolve their claims. We vacate the judgment and remand the case for further proceedings, in the course of which those plaintiffs may attempt to demonstrate standing in accord with the analysis in this opinion.

*[Section I, detailing the background and facts in the case, has been omitted.]*

## II

*[Section A, in which the Court remarks on earlier related cases, has been omitted.]*

### B

At argument on appeal in this case, counsel for the plaintiffs argued that this Court *can* address the problem of partisan gerrymandering because it *must*: The Court should exercise its power here because it is the "only institution in the United States" capable of "solv[ing] this problem." Tr. of Oral Arg. 62. Such invitations must be answered with care. "Failure of political will does not justify unconstitutional remedies." *Clinton* v. *City of New York*, 524 U. S. 417, 449 (1998) (KENNEDY, J., concurring). Our power as judges to "say what the law is," *Marbury* v. *Madison*, 1 Cranch 137, 177 (1803), rests not on the default of politically accountable officers, but is instead grounded in and limited by the necessity of resolving, according to legal principles, a plaintiff's particular claim of legal right.

Our considerable efforts in *Gaffney, Bandemer, Vieth,* and *LULAC* leave unresolved whether such claims may be brought in cases involving allegations of partisan gerrymandering. In particular, two threshold questions remain: what is necessary to show standing in a case of this sort, and whether those claims are justiciable. Here we do not decide the latter question because the plaintiffs in this case have not shown standing under the theory upon which they based their claims for relief.

To ensure that the Federal Judiciary respects "the proper—and properly limited—role of the courts in a democratic society," *Allen* v. *Wright,* 468 U. S. 737, 750 (1984), a plaintiff may not invoke federal-court jurisdiction unless he can show "a personal stake in the outcome of the controversy." *Baker,* 369 U. S., at 204. A federal court is not "a forum for generalized grievances," and the requirement of such a personal stake "ensures that courts exercise power that is judicial in nature." *Lance,* 549 U. S., at 439, 441. We enforce that requirement by insisting that a plaintiff satisfy the familiar three-part test for Article III standing: that he "(1) suffered an injury in fact, (2) that is fairly traceable to the challenged conduct of the defendant, and (3) that is likely to be redressed by a favorable judicial decision." *Spokeo, Inc.* v. *Robins,* 578 U. S. ___, ___ (2016) (slip op., at 6). Foremost among these requirements is injury in fact— a plaintiff's pleading and proof that he has suffered the "invasion of a legally protected interest" that is "concrete and particularized," *i.e.,* which "affect[s] the plaintiff in a personal and individual way." *Lujan* v. *Defenders of Wildlife,* 504 U. S. 555, 560, and n. 1 (1992).

We have long recognized that a person's right to vote is "individual and personal in nature." *Reynolds* v. *Sims,* 377 U. S. 533, 561 (1964). Thus, "voters who allege facts showing disadvantage to themselves as individuals have standing to sue" to remedy that disadvantage. *Baker,* 369 U. S., at 206. The plaintiffs in this case alleged that they suffered such injury from partisan gerrymandering, which works through "packing" and "cracking" voters of one party to disadvantage those voters. That is, the plaintiffs claim a constitutional right not to be placed in legislative districts deliberately designed to "waste" their votes in elections where their chosen candidates will win in landslides (packing) or are destined to lose by closer margins (cracking).

To the extent the plaintiffs' alleged harm is the dilution of their votes, that injury is district specific. An individual voter in Wisconsin is placed in a single district. He votes for a single representative. The boundaries of the district, and the composition of its voters, determine whether and to what extent a particular voter is packed or cracked. This "disadvantage to [the voter] as [an] individual[]," *Baker,* 369 U. S., at 206, therefore results from the boundaries of the particular district in which he resides. And a plaintiff's remedy must be "limited to the inadequacy that produced [his] injury in fact." *Lewis* v. *Casey,* 518 U. S. 343, 357 (1996). In this case the remedy that is proper and sufficient lies in the revision of the boundaries of the individual's own district.

For similar reasons, we have held that a plaintiff who alleges that he is the object of a racial gerrymander—a drawing of district lines on the basis of race—has standing to assert only that his own district has been so gerrymandered. See *United States* v. *Hays,* 515 U. S. 737, 744–745 (1995). A plaintiff who complains of gerrymandering, but who does not live in a gerrymandered district, "assert[s] only a generalized grievance against governmental conduct of which he or she does not approve." *Id.,* at 745. Plaintiffs who complain of racial gerrymandering in their State cannot sue to invalidate the whole State's legislative districting map; such complaints must proceed "district-by-district." *Alabama Legislative Black Caucus* v. *Alabama,* 575 U. S. ___, ___ (2015) (slip op., at 6).

The plaintiffs argue that their claim of statewide injury is analogous to the claims presented in *Baker* and *Reynolds*, which they assert were "statewide in nature" because they rested on allegations that "districts *throughout a state* [had] been malapportioned." Brief for Appellees 29. But, as we have already noted, the holdings in *Baker* and *Reynolds* were expressly premised on the understanding that the injuries giving rise to those claims were "individual and personal in nature," *Reynolds*, 377 U. S., at 561, because the claims were brought by voters who alleged "facts showing disadvantage to themselves as individuals," *Baker*, 369 U. S., at 206.

The plaintiffs' mistaken insistence that the claims in *Baker* and *Reynolds* were "statewide in nature" rests on a failure to distinguish injury from remedy. In those malapportionment cases, the only way to vindicate an individual plaintiff's right to an equally weighted vote was through a wholesale "restructuring of the geographical distribution of seats in a state legislature." *Reynolds*, 377 U. S., at 561; see, *e.g., Moss v. Burkhart*, 220 F. Supp. 149, 156–160 (WD Okla. 1963) (directing the county-by-county reapportionment of the Oklahoma Legislature), aff'd *sub nom. Williams* v. *Moss*, 378 U. S. 558 (1964) (*per curiam*).

Here, the plaintiffs' partisan gerrymandering claims turn on allegations that their votes have been diluted. That harm arises from the particular composition of the voter's own district, which causes his vote—having been packed or cracked—to carry less weight than it would carry in another, hypothetical district. Remedying the individual voter's harm, therefore, does not necessarily require restructuring all of the State's legislative districts. It requires revising only such districts as are necessary to reshape the voter's district—so that the voter may be unpacked or uncracked, as the case may be. Cf. *Alabama Legislative Black Caucus*, 575 U. S., at ___ (slip op., at 7). This fits the rule that a "remedy must of course be limited to the inadequacy that produced the injury in fact that the plaintiff has established." *Lewis*, 518 U. S., at 357.

The plaintiffs argue that their legal injury is not limited to the injury that they have suffered as individual voters, but extends also to the statewide harm to their interest "in their collective representation in the legislature," and in influencing the legislature's overall "composition and policymaking." Brief for Appellees 31. But our cases to date have not found that this presents an individual and personal injury of the kind required for Article III standing. On the facts of this case, the plaintiffs may not rely on "the kind of undifferentiated, generalized grievance about the conduct of government that we have refused to countenance in the past." *Lance*, 549 U. S., at 442. A citizen's interest in the overall composition of the legislature is embodied in his right to vote for his representative. And the citizen's abstract interest in policies adopted by the legislature on the facts here is a nonjusticiable "general interest common to all members of the public." *Ex parte Lévitt*, 302 U. S. 633, 634 (1937) (*per curiam*).

We leave for another day consideration of other possible theories of harm not presented here and whether those theories might present justiciable claims giving rise to statewide remedies. JUSTICE KAGAN'S concurring opinion endeavors to address "other kinds of constitutional harm," see *post*, at 8, perhaps involving different kinds of plaintiffs, see *post*, at 9, and differently alleged burdens, see *ibid*. But the opinion of the Court rests on the understanding that we lack jurisdiction to decide this case, much less to draw speculative and advisory conclusions regarding others. See *Public Workers* v. *Mitchell*, 330 U. S. 75, 90 (1947) (noting that courts must "respect the limits of [their] unique authority" and engage in "[j]udicial exposition . . . only when necessary to decide definite issues between litigants"). The reasoning of this Court with respect to the disposition of this case is set forth in this opinion and none other. And the sum of the standing principles articulated here, as applied to this case, is that the harm asserted by the plaintiffs is best understood as arising from a burden on those plaintiffs' own votes. In this gerrymandering context that burden arises through a voter's placement in a "cracked" or "packed" district.

## C

Four of the plaintiffs in this case—Mary Lynne Donohue, Wendy Sue Johnson, Janet Mitchell, and Jerome Wallace—pleaded a particularized burden along such lines. They alleged that Act 43 had "dilut[ed] the influence" of their votes as a result of packing or cracking in their legislative districts. See 1 App. 34–36, Complaint ¶¶20, 23, 24, 26. The facts necessary to establish standing, however, must not only be alleged at the pleading stage, but also proved at trial. See *Defenders of Wildlife*, 504 U. S., at 561. As the proceedings in the District Court progressed to trial, the plaintiffs failed to meaningfully pursue their allegations of individual harm. The plaintiffs did not seek to show such requisite harm since, on this record, it appears that not a single plaintiff sought to prove that he or she lives in a cracked or packed district. They instead rested their case at trial—and their arguments before this Court—on their theory of statewide injury to Wisconsin Democrats, in support of which they offered three kinds of evidence. . . .

Third, the plaintiffs offered evidence concerning the impact that Act 43 had in skewing Wisconsin's statewide political map in favor of Republicans. This evidence, which made up the heart of the plaintiffs' case, was derived from partisan-asymmetry studies similar to those discussed in *LULAC*. The plaintiffs contend that these studies measure deviations from "partisan symmetry," which they describe as the "social scientific tenet that [districting] maps should treat parties symmetrically." Brief for Appellees 37. In the District Court, the plaintiffs' case rested largely on a particular measure of partisan asymmetry—the "efficiency gap" of wasted votes. See *supra*, at 3–4. That measure was first developed in two academic articles published shortly before the initiation of this lawsuit. See Stephanopoulos & McGhee, Partisan Gerrymandering and the Efficiency Gap, 82 U. Chi. L. Rev. 831 (2015); McGhee, Measuring Partisan Bias in Single-Member District Electoral Systems, 39 Leg. Studies Q. 55 (2014).

The plaintiffs asserted in their complaint that the "efficiency gap captures in a single number all of a district plan's cracking and packing." 1 App. 28–29, Complaint ¶5 (emphasis deleted). That number is calculated by subtracting the statewide sum of one party's wasted votes from the statewide sum of the other party's wasted votes and dividing the result by the statewide sum of all votes cast, where "wasted votes" are defined as all votes cast for a losing candidate and all votes cast for a winning candidate beyond the 50% plus one that ensures victory. See Brief for Eric McGhee as *Amicus Curiae* 6, and n. 3. The larger the number produced by that calculation, the greater the asymmetry between the parties in their efficiency in converting votes into legislative seats. Though they take no firm position on the matter, the plaintiffs have suggested that an efficiency gap in the range of 7% to 10% should trigger constitutional scrutiny. See Brief for Appellees 52–53, and n. 17.

The plaintiffs and their *amici curiae* promise us that the efficiency gap and similar measures of partisan asymmetry will allow the federal courts—armed with just "a pencil and paper or a hand calculator"—to finally solve the problem of partisan gerrymandering that has confounded the Court for decades. Brief for Heather K. Gerken et al. as *Amici Curiae* 27 (citing Wang, Let Math Save Our Democracy, N. Y. Times, Dec. 5, 2015). We need not doubt the plaintiffs' math. The difficulty for standing purposes is that these calculations are an average measure. They do not address the effect that a gerrymander has on the votes of particular citizens. Partisan-asymmetry metrics such as the efficiency gap measure something else entirely: the effect that a gerrymander has on the fortunes of political parties.

Consider the situation of Professor Whitford, who lives in District 76, where, defendants contend, Democrats are "naturally" packed due to their geographic concentration, with that of plaintiff Mary Lynne Donohue, who lives in Assembly District 26 in Sheboygan, where Democrats like her have allegedly been deliberately cracked. By all accounts, Act 43 has not affected Whitford's individual vote for his Assembly representative—even plaintiffs' own demonstration map resulted in a virtually identical district for him. Donohue, on the other hand, alleges that Act 43 burdened her individual vote. Yet neither the efficiency gap nor the other measures of partisan asymmetry offered by the plaintiffs are capable of telling the difference between what Act 43 did to Whitford and what it did to Donohue. The single statewide measure of partisan advantage delivered by the efficiency gap treats Whitford and Donohue as indistinguishable, even though their individual situations are quite different.

That shortcoming confirms the fundamental problem with the plaintiffs' case as presented on this record. It is a case about group political interests, not individual legal rights. But this Court is not responsible for vindicating generalized partisan preferences. The Court's constitutionally prescribed role is to vindicate the individual rights of the people appearing before it.

## III

In cases where a plaintiff fails to demonstrate Article III standing, we usually direct the dismissal of the plaintiff's claims. See, *e.g., DaimlerChrysler Corp.* v. *Cuno*, 547 U. S. 332, 354 (2006). This is not the usual case. It concerns an unsettled kind of claim this Court has not agreed upon, the contours and justiciability of which are unresolved. Under the circumstances, and in light of the plaintiffs' allegations that Donohue, Johnson, Mitchell, and Wallace live in districts where Democrats like them have been packed or cracked, we decline to direct dismissal.

We therefore remand the case to the District Court so that the plaintiffs may have an opportunity to prove concrete and particularized injuries using evidence—unlike the bulk of the evidence presented thus far—that would tend to demonstrate a burden on their individual votes. Cf. *Alabama Legislative Black Caucus*, 575 U. S., at ___ (slip op., at 8) (remanding for further consideration of the plaintiffs' gerrymandering claims on a district-by-district basis). We express no view on the merits of the plaintiffs' case. We caution, however, that "standing is not dispensed in gross": A plaintiff's remedy must be tailored to redress the plaintiff's particular injury. *Cuno*, 547 U. S., at 353.

The judgment of the District Court is vacated, and the case is remanded for further proceedings consistent with this opinion.

*[The concurring opinion of Justice Kagan, joined by Justices Ginsburg, Breyer, and Sotomayor, has been omitted, as has the concurring opinion of Justice Thomas, who was joined by Justice Gorsuch concurring in part and concurring in the judgment.]*

*It is so ordered.*

Source: Supreme Court of the United States. *Gill v. Whitford*. 585 U.S. ___ (2018). https://www.supremecourt.gov/opinions/17pdf/16-1161_dc8f.pdf.

# *Supreme Court Fails to Weigh In on Maryland Gerrymandering*

June 18, 2018

## SUPREME COURT OF THE UNITED STATES

No. 17-333

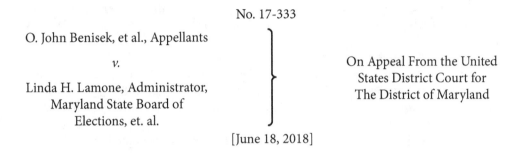

O. John Benisek, et al., Appellants

*v.*

Linda H. Lamone, Administrator, Maryland State Board of Elections, et. al.

On Appeal From the United States District Court for The District of Maryland

[June 18, 2018]

PER CURIAM.

This appeal arises from the denial of a motion for a preliminary injunction in the District Court. Appellants are several Republican voters, plaintiffs below, who allege that Maryland's Sixth Congressional District was gerrymandered in 2011 for the purpose of retaliating against them for their political views.

In May 2017, six years after the Maryland General Assembly redrew the Sixth District, plaintiffs moved the District Court to enjoin Maryland's election officials from holding congressional elections under the 2011 map. They asserted that "extend[ing] this constitutional offense"— *i.e.,* the alleged gerrymander—"into the 2018 election would be a manifest and irreparable injury." Record in No. 1:13–cv–3233, Doc. 177–1, p. 3. In order to allow time for the creation of a new districting map, plaintiffs urged the District Court to enter a preliminary injunction by August 18, 2017. *Id.,* at 32.

On August 24, 2017, the District Court denied plaintiffs' motion and stayed further proceedings pending this Court's disposition of partisan gerrymandering claims in *Gill* v. *Whitford,* No. 16–1161. 266 F. Supp. 3d 799. The District Court found that plaintiffs had failed to show a likelihood of success on the merits sufficient to warrant a preliminary injunction. *Id.,* at 808–814. The District Court also held that it was "in no position to award [p]laintiffs the remedy they . . . requested on the timetable they . . . demanded." *Id.,* at 815. The court explained that, notwithstanding its "diligence in ruling on the pending preliminary injunction motion (which has been a priority for each member of this panel)," plaintiffs' proposed August deadline for injunctive relief had "already come and gone." *Ibid.*

In addition, the District Court emphasized that it was concerned about "measuring the legality and constitutionality of any redistricting plan in Maryland . . . according to the proper legal standard." *Id.,* at 816. In the District Court's view, it would be "better equipped to make that legal determination and to chart a wise course for further proceedings" after this Court issued a decision in *Gill. Ibid.* Plaintiffs ask this Court to vacate the District Court's order and remand for further consideration of whether a preliminary injunction is appropriate.

We now note our jurisdiction and review the District Court's decision for an abuse of discretion, keeping in mind that a preliminary injunction is "an extraordinary remedy never awarded as of right." *Winter v. Natural Resources Defense Council, Inc.*, 555 U. S. 7, 24 (2008). As a matter of equitable discretion, a preliminary injunction does not follow as a matter of course from a plaintiff's showing of a likelihood of success on the merits. *See id.*, at 32. Rather, a court must also consider whether the movant has shown "that he is likely to suffer irreparable harm in the absence of preliminary relief, that the balance of equities tips in his favor, and that an injunction is in the public interest." *Id.*, at 20.

Plaintiffs made no such showing below. Even if we assume—contrary to the findings of the District Court—that plaintiffs were likely to succeed on the merits of their claims, the balance of equities and the public interest tilted against their request for a preliminary injunction.

First, a party requesting a preliminary injunction must generally show reasonable diligence. Cf. *Holmberg v. Armbrecht*, 327 U. S. 392, 396 (1946). That is as true in election law cases as elsewhere. See *Lucas v. Townsend*, 486 U. S. 1301, 1305 (1988) (KENNEDY, J., in chambers); *Fishman v. Schaffer*, 429 U. S. 1325, 1330 (1976) (Marshall, J., in chambers). In this case, appellants did not move for a preliminary injunction in the District Court until six years, and three general elections, after the 2011 map was adopted, and over three years after the plaintiffs' first complaint was filed.

Plaintiffs argue that they have nevertheless pursued their claims diligently, and they attribute their delay in seeking a preliminary injunction to the "convoluted procedural history of the case" and the "dogged refusal to cooperate in discovery" by state officials. Reply Brief 22. Yet the record suggests that the delay largely arose from a circumstance within plaintiffs' control: namely, their failure to plead the claims giving rise to their request for preliminary injunctive relief until 2016. Although one of the seven plaintiffs before us filed a complaint in 2013 alleging that Maryland's congressional map was an unconstitutional gerrymander, that initial complaint did not present the retaliation theory asserted here. See Amended Complaint, Doc. 11, p. 3 (Dec. 2, 2013) (explaining that the gerrymandering claim did not turn upon "the reason or intent of the legislature" in adopting the map).

It was not until 2016 that the remaining plaintiffs joined the case and filed an amended complaint alleging that Maryland officials intentionally retaliated against them because of their political views. See 3 App. 640–643. Plaintiffs' newly presented claims—unlike the gerrymandering claim presented in the 2013 complaint—required discovery into the motives of the officials who produced the 2011 congressional map. See, *e.g.*, Memorandum of Law in Support of Plaintiffs' Motion to Compel, Doc. 111– 1, p. 3 (Jan. 4, 2017) (describing plaintiffs' demand that various state officials "testify . . . and answer questions concerning legislative intent"). It is true that the assertion of legislative privilege by those officials delayed the completion of that discovery. See Joint Motion To Extend Deadlines for Completion of Fact Discovery and Expert Witness Disclosures, Doc. 161, pp. 1–2 (Mar. 3, 2017); Joint Motion To Extend Deadlines for Completion of Fact Discovery and Expert Witness Disclosures, Doc. 170, pp. 1–2 (Mar. 27, 2017). But that does not change the fact that plaintiffs could have sought a preliminary injunction much earlier. See *Fishman, supra*, at 1330. In considering the balance of equities among the parties, we think that plaintiffs' unnecessary, years-long delay in asking for preliminary injunctive relief weighed against their request.

Second, a due regard for the public interest in orderly elections supported the District Court's discretionary decision to deny a preliminary injunction and to stay the proceedings.

See *Purcell* v. *Gonzalez*, 549 U. S. 1, 4–5 (2006) (*per curiam*). Plaintiffs themselves represented to the District Court that any injunctive relief would have to be granted by August 18, 2017, to ensure the timely completion of a new districting scheme in advance of the 2018 election season. Despite the District Court's undisputedly diligent efforts, however, that date had "already come and gone" by the time the court ruled on plaintiffs' motion. 266 F. Supp. 3d, at 815. (Such deadline has also, of course, long since passed for purposes of entering a preliminary injunction on remand from this Court.)

On top of this time constraint was the legal uncertainty surrounding any potential remedy for the plaintiffs' asserted injury. At the time the District Court made its decision, the appeal in *Gill* was pending before this Court. The District Court recognized that our decision in *Gill* had the potential to "shed light on critical questions in this case" and to set forth a "framework" by which plaintiffs' claims could be decided and, potentially, remedied. 266 F. Supp. 3d, at 815–816. In the District Court's view, "charging ahead" and adjudicating the plaintiffs' claims in that fluctuating legal environment, when firmer guidance from this Court might have been forthcoming, would have been a mistake. *Id.*, at 816. Such a determination was within the sound discretion of the District Court. Given the District Court's decision to wait for this Court's ruling in *Gill* before further adjudicating plaintiffs' claims, the court reasonably could have concluded that a preliminary injunction would have been against the public interest, as an injunction might have worked a needlessly "chaotic and disruptive effect upon the electoral process," *Fishman, supra,* at 1330, and because the "purpose of a preliminary injunction is merely to preserve the relative positions of the parties until a trial on the merits can be held," *University of Tex.* v. *Camenisch*, 451 U. S. 390, 395 (1981). In these particular circumstances, we conclude that the District Court's decision denying a preliminary injunction cannot be regarded as an abuse of discretion.

The order of the District Court is

*Affirmed.*

SOURCE: Supreme Court of the United States. *Benisek v. Lamone.* 585 U.S. ___ (2018). https://www .supremecourt.gov/opinions/17pdf/17-333_b97c.pdf.

## OTHER HISTORIC DOCUMENTS OF INTEREST

### FROM PREVIOUS *HISTORIC DOCUMENTS*

▪ Supreme Court Rules on Gerrymandering, *2017*, p. 293

# Cape Town and South African Officials Address Day Zero

JANUARY 24, FEBRUARY 4, AND MARCH 8, 2018

In early 2018, the South African government announced a dire prediction: Cape Town and its more than four million residents would soon experience what it called "Day Zero," when taps for businesses and homes would be shut off and water rations imposed. Political, social, racial, and class tensions flared. Some, including local government leaders, predicted the biggest threat to order since World War II. The premier of the Western Cape Province, which includes Cape Town, wondered how they would "prevent anarchy." The city and national government took drastic actions, imposing strict conservation efforts, rebuilding leaking infrastructure, and assessing new sources of water. In the end, conservation efforts averted the crisis but only temporarily—and at a cost. While a new Day Zero in 2019 looms, the crisis raised a larger question about what a hotter, drier future with more unpredictable weather and shifting climate patterns means not just for Cape Town but for cities across the world.

## A Decade in the Making

Situated on the southern coast of South Africa, Cape Town is a city known for its pristine beaches, warm weather, and natural landmarks. The southernmost point of the African continent, Cape Point, sits nearby, and a diversified local economy built on the nearby harbor supports more than four million people, making it the most populous city in the Western Cape province. The iconic Table Mountain has been the backdrop for many Hollywood blockbusters. However, in the early half of 2018, a different story—one sounding more like a dystopian movie than something that would happen to a populous, modern, cosmopolitan city—emerged.

Situated in an arid region and dependent on heavy rainfall during the wet season to replenish water supplies, Cape Town has long been acutely attuned to changes in climate. In 1904, the area experienced the worst recorded drought in its history, followed by periodic droughts throughout much of the next century. After the turn of the century, however, droughts became more frequent and severe as the climate became hotter and more arid. Low winter rainfall from 2000 to 2004 resulted in new water restrictions. While rainfall rebounded, the threat of El Niño–related droughts, in which average rainfall dropped precipitously, loomed over the region.

Those concerns took on new importance in the summer of 2015, when Cape Town began to experience its worst drought in more than a century. Water levels in the city's dams declined 20 percent from 2014 to 2015. While rain fell in other portions of the country in 2016, the drought remained in the Western Cape. It worsened the next year; overall rainfall in 2017 was the lowest since 1933, the year when official record keeping began. In October 2017, the city had an estimated five months of storage available before water levels would be depleted. At the end of that period, which local leaders dubbed "Day Zero," Cape Town would experience a cataclysmic event with taps shut off, water rationed, and possible social unrest.

## A "Green City" Recognized for Its Conservation Efforts

Cape Town has long been celebrated for its conservation efforts. In years before the drought began, the city stabilized water demand and seemed to be on sure footing. City leaders focused on careful management of existing supplies, improving recycling programs and infrastructure, introducing a "stepped" water tariff to encourage savings, and educating consumers.

The results were stark. In 2014, city officials cut water consumption growth and water waste, resulting in nearly 30 percent total water savings. The city and surrounding areas turned to recycled water to irrigate public parks and green areas. An aggressive consumer education campaign helped curb individual use while city officials repaired leaking water infrastructure for more than 4,000 households and replaced hundreds of kilometers of water pipes to reduce bursts and leaks.

The rest of the world noticed. C40, a collection of cities focused on climate change worldwide, awarded Cape Town in 2015 its "adaptation implementation" prize for the city's water management. The group commended the city for its "comprehensive programme of water conservation and water demand management (WCWDM) aimed at minimising water waste and promoting efficient use of water." Meanwhile, city officials boasted about being a top "green city," a designation awarded several years earlier by a leading social responsibility think tank. "In a world of increasing population pressures and depleting natural resources some cities, such as Cape Town, are proactively adjusting their practices today as well as implementing sustainable long-term practices," a think tank official remarked in announcing the award.

City leaders had proven to be responsible stewards of water resources, and as a result, officials from across the world looked to the city for guidance on conservation efforts. On the surface, Cape Town seemed not only well situated for the future but a leader on water conservation in an increasingly dry world. But just three years later, officials would grapple with becoming the first major city in the world to face a catastrophic water shortage.

## Tensions Rise as Water Levels Drop

The threat of Day Zero intensified in the winter of 2017. A severe drought dropped water supplies to dangerous levels; in just three years, water storage levels fell from 72 percent to 21 percent. City and national leaders grappled with the best approach to extend the dwindling water supply. Officials' main hope was to delay the date when taps would be shut off through an aggressive conservation program, giving dams more time in the wet season to replenish with falling rains.

As water levels dropped, tensions increased, and the political situation did little to ease the situation. Since 2006, Cape Town served as the seat of power of the Democratic Alliance (DA), the opposition political party locked in a power struggle with the African National Congress (ANC), South Africa's main political party that has dominated South Africa since the end of apartheid. City officials laid blame with the national party, while ANC officials blamed the DA for mismanaging the city. Some national leaders even feared that Day Zero would create social unrest across the province and even the country. "When

Day Zero arrives, how do we make water accessible and prevent anarchy?" Helen Zille, the premier of Western Cape Province, wrote.

Even government agencies became embroiled in the political back-and-forth. Nomvula Mokonyane, minister of the South Africa Department of Water and Sanitation, accused the premier and leader of the Democratic Alliance of creating "scapegoats" to shift blame. "What the Premier and Mmusi Maimane are trying to do is to shield the province and their organization from accountability on the water crisis by shifting blame on the issue to National Government without acknowledgment of the interventions implemented thus far in support of the province by the National government working through the National Disaster Management Centre."

City officials fired back, laying blame with the ANC. Much of the responsibility for building water infrastructure lies with the national government, as does regulating the water supply to Cape Town, surrounding townships, and other municipalities. The national government also has control over the province's agricultural sector, including the large wine industry east of Cape Town. The agricultural sector and wine producers account for a sizeable portion of the region's water use; experts say that the national government's failure to limit water supplies to farmers in the first two years of the drought intensified the problem.

The crisis also enflamed social and racial tensions. South Africa is one of the world's most unequal countries. In Cape Town and surrounding townships, the differences are stark. People living in tin-roof shacks in outlying townships share communal taps and carry water in buckets. In former colonial neighborhoods in the shadow of Table Mountain, millionaires live in mansions with glistening pools and private water tanks. Day Zero put a harsh magnifying glass on this social inequity, pushing many to wonder what happens to the less fortunate when the social contract breaks down.

## Aggressive Efforts from City and National Officials Push Back Day Zero

While political tensions simmered beneath the surface, national and local leaders vowed to reverse Day Zero. City officials launched an aggressive consumer education effort called #DefeatDayZero, while national leaders hurried infrastructure improvements. Residents were pushed to curb their usage to eighty-seven liters of water per day that January; a month later, that limit dropped to fifty liters, enforced by harsh fines for any excess. National officials imposed similarly strict conservation measures on business and curtailed groundwater usage for domestic and industrial use by 45 percent and for agricultural use by 60 percent. Officials also cut back on water usage for irrigation systems and installed electronic water recording, monitoring, and measurement devices.

The policies worked, to an extent. In early February, officials announced that Day Zero was pushed back from March to mid-April because of declining agriculture use. Officials stressed, however, that individuals needed to further cut their usage. Cape Town's executive deputy mayor, Alderman Ian Neilson, expressed new hope for the city. "This is a welcome decline in water usage and gives Cape Town and some of the other municipalities hope," Neilson said. But a cloud of uncertainty remained. "We cannot accurately predict the volume of rainfall still to come, or when it will come," Neilson said in the very next sentence.

National leaders also conveyed a new sense of hope and a communal effort to defeat Day Zero. In a report to the National Assembly on the city and national government's response to the crisis, Deputy Minister of Water and Sanitation Pamela Tshwete outlined how other areas of the country have fared—and survived—harsh droughts. Tshwete expressed confidence that just as those areas had recovered, so will Cape Town. "The deeper we dig into the apparent water crisis in Western Cape and Cape Town in particular, the more unjustifiable Day Zero becomes, the further the date shifts." Her speech concluded by calling on the country to pursue "an unconventional approach" to water access. Priorities included developing more groundwater sources, enhancing water reuse, desalinating brackish and sea water, and harvesting upscale rainwater. Without this unconventional approach, climate change will continue to impact the country. "This work will continue," Tshwete said, "because we have the interests of all South Africans, notwithstanding where they live or work."

## AN UNCERTAIN FUTURE FOR CAPE TOWN AND CITIES ACROSS THE WORLD

The Day Zero water crisis still looms over Cape Town. City officials have pegged a new date in 2019 when water levels will drop to dangerous levels. Far from being a single crisis, Day Zero may be the new normal for Cape Town, just as water insecurity will soon threaten other cities worldwide. A changing climate has led to more severe extreme weather, such as harsher droughts and less rainfall, and is creating new problems for towns, cities, and countries in arid regions around the world. Cape Town was the first major city to face a cataclysmic water crisis, but the world may just be feeling the first effects of a hotter, drier globe.

—Robert Howard

*Following is a January 24, 2018, statement from the South African minister of water and sanitation on the Day Zero water crisis; a February 4, 2018, statement by the Cape Town executive deputy mayor postponing Day Zero; and the text of a March 8, 2018, speech delivered by the deputy minister of water and sanitation on the efforts being made by the central government to aid Cape Town.*

# *South African Minister of Water and Sanitation on Government's Response to Water Crisis*

**January 24, 2018**

The Minister of Water and Sanitations, Nomvula Mokonyane, has noted several political utterances by the Premier of the Western Cape, Ms. Helen Zille, and the leader of the Democratic Alliance (DA), Mmusi Maimane, with regards to the water crisis in the Western Cape and in particular, Cape Town.

What the Premier and leader of the Democratic Alliance have sought to do is to absolve themselves of their responsibilities in the management of the water crisis through an attempt to mischievously create scapegoats and shift the blame on the seriousness of the water crisis to national government and the Minister in particular.

The Minister of Water and Sanitation together with the City of Cape Town and the provincial ministry of Local Government, Environment and Development Planning in the Western Cape have held several meetings in an effort to manage and mitigate the effects of the drought on water availability for the province.

These engagements gave birth to the Restrictions Management Committee and the Joint Operations Centre that have been overseeing the drought management functions and interventions in the province with the joint participation of local, provincial and national government.

Through these efforts a Water Indaba, bringing together the whole of government, the private and agricultural sectors along with academics and experts, was convened to look into the various possible solutions and actions necessary to avert a water black-out. Several of the proposals emanating from these engagements have since been pursued including desalination options, the recycling of water, further increases in restrictions, clearing of canals, dredging of dams and expediting the implementation of the Berg River-Voelvlei augmentation scheme.

Currently, the rate of abstraction from the Western Cape Water Supply System has increased despite restrictions gazetted by the department of water and sanitation which placed a 45% water use restriction for domestic users and 60% for agriculture. The Cape Town Water Supply System (Six Dams supplying Cape Town) alone, decreased by a highly concerning 1.43% in the last week leaving the dam levels at 26.94%.

We continue to see falling reservoir capacities and the combined capacity of the 43 dams in the Province which we monitor on a weekly basis decreased by 1.37% in the last week to 25.21%.

The City of Cape Town, now on Level 6 restrictions, are still not achieving their target of 500 megalitres per day and are over by approximately 86 megalitres per day.

Urgency is required in assisting the City of Cape Town to avert #DayZero through increases [in] public awareness and enforcement of compliance with water use restrictions in order to stretch the available water resources and minimize the possibility of a #DayZero.

"The Western Cape drought and current water crisis in Cape Town requires a massive public involvement process where citizens adhere to and assist in identifying those who still continue to use water irresponsibly. No amount of politicking and scapegoats will do away with the imminent water blackout we face in the Western Cape if we fail to act responsibly."

"What the Premier and Mmusi Maimane are trying to do is to shield the province and their organization from accountability on the water crisis by shifting blame on the issue to National Government without acknowledgment of the interventions implemented thus far in support of the province by the National government working through the National Disaster Management Centre."

"As a department we have successfully intervened and saved several provinces who were devastated by the drought over the last three years and will continue to do so in the Western Cape as well. Our mandate for water provision and support knows no politics and we will not be drawn into petty political squabbles whilst the people and economy of the Western Cape are on the verge of a possible water supply blackout."

"Defeating Day Zero has been and continues to be our main priority and the work that has been done over the last year will continue with increased urgency to ensure we guarantee access to water for citizens," said Minister Mokonyane.

On 12 January 2018 the department published additional interventions in the Government Gazette with regard to limiting the use of water in the Breede-Gouritz and Berg-Olifants Water Management Areas. This notice includes inter-alia the following:

- Curtailing groundwater abstractions for domestic and industrial use by 45% and for agricultural use by 60%. This brings the restrictions on groundwater use in line with the restrictions applied to surface water use.

- Curtailment of water for irrigation use from the system dams once the users have depleted their seasonal bulk volumes (for some users this could be as early the end of January 2018).

- The installation of electronic water recording and monitoring/measurement devices.

Additional officials have also been deployed from the department to the province to strengthen our compliance and enforcement capabilities in the province to ensure that water users comply with restrictions and that we deal effectively with any transgressions.

Minister Mokonyane will over the next few days hold several follow-up meetings with the various stakeholders to assess progress on the implementation of current interventions and an assessment of new interventions necessary to avert #DayZero.

SOURCE: Republic of South Africa Department of Water and Sanitation. "Minister Mokonyane on Western Cape Water Crisis and Day Zero." January 24, 2018. http://www.dwa.gov.za/Communications/ PressReleases/2018/MS%20-%20Minister%20Mokonyane%20on%20Western%20Cape%20Water%20 Crisis%20and%20Day%20Zero.pdf.

DOCUMENT    *Cape Town Postpones Day Zero*

**February 4, 2018**

### STATEMENT BY THE CITY'S EXECUTIVE DEPUTY MAYOR, ALDERMAN IAN NEILSON

Day Zero, the day we may have to start queueing for water, is expected to move out to mid-May 2018 due to a decline in agricultural usage. But Capetonians must continue reducing consumption if we are to avoid Day Zero. There has not been any significant decline in urban usage. All Capetonians must therefore continue to use no more than 50 litres per person per day to help stretch our dwindling supplies.

Many of the agricultural users in the Western Cape Supply System, where the City also draws its water from, have used up the water allocated to them as per agreement with the National Department of Water and Sanitation.

Agricultural usage is therefore likely to drop significantly over the next weeks. Currently, the agriculture sector is drawing about 30% of the water in the supply scheme. This should fall to approximately 15% in March and 10% in April. It must be noted that the City does not have any control over agricultural releases, so this is the best estimate we can make with the information at hand.

This is a welcome decline in water usage and gives Cape Town and some of the other municipalities hope but importantly, we need to get our consumption down to 450 million litres per day to prevent the remaining water supplies running out before the arrival of winter rains. We cannot accurately predict the volume of rainfall still to come, or when it will come.

Last year, we had abnormally low winter rainfall, and we cannot assume that this year will be any different. Even if we have been given a slight reprieve at this stage, we are likely to be facing a late and dry winter.

All preparations for the possibility of reaching Day Zero continue in earnest. The City also continues with the roll-out of aggressive pressure management initiatives in an effort to stretch our supplies.

With the hot weather predicted over the week ahead and expected high evaporation rates, coupled with an expected increase in water use by our residents as a result of the weather, we dare not rest on our laurels now. It will be to the detriment of our efforts as Team Cape Town.

In calculating Day Zero, we have consistently taken a conservative approach (based on what we have experienced before, especially in relation to agricultural usage) to water management and demand.

**We've taken into account:**

- Evaporation: The model assumes maximum calculated evaporation rates, based on historic calculations adjusted for increases in temperature and wind.

- Agricultural releases: The City extrapolated the National Department of Water and Sanitation's (NDWS) unverified release data as read from the NDWS hydrology website. In the previous season, agriculture exceeded its unrestricted allocation by a small percentage. The City thus had no historical evidence base to assume that agriculture would remain within their allocation. However, the national department has now shut off supply to two irrigation boards that utilised their full allocation by the end of January 2018. The City therefore feels more confident that agriculture will stay within their allocation this year, as opposed to the previous year. Had agricultural releases not slowed down, the threat of Day Zero would have moved closer.

- Urban usage: While the City has worked tirelessly on fixing bursts and leaks, installing water management devices and implementing advanced pressure management to drive down consumption and minimise leaks and bursts, urban demand is very much reliant on the behaviour of water users. For this reason, the model assumes that consumption will remain at the previous weeks' average usage levels.

### Tariff increases

As of 1 February 2018, level 6B water restrictions and tariffs have come into effect to help finance water services and to reduce usage.

To cover the costs of water and sanitation provision, and to assist in driving down demand further, the water and sanitation tariffs have been increased. The tariffs remain based on usage. The more you use, the more you pay. High users will be hit especially hard. The City does not make a profit on income from the sale of water.

This is part of the City's efforts to avoid Day Zero and to create financial stability for the provision of water services. Although we have brought usage down from 1.1 billion litres per day to just under 600 million litres per day, we need to get to 450 million litres of collective usage per day.

**Latest water dashboard (http://coct.co/water-dashboard/)**

- Day Zero: 11 May 2018 (was 16 April 2018)

- Dam Levels: 25.5% (decline of 0.8%)

- Total consumption: 547 million litres per day (97 million litres above the target of 450 million litres per day)

- % of Capetonians saving: *note, due to the implementation of 50 litre targets, this calculation is under review

SOURCE: City of Cape Town. "Day Zero Projection Moves Out due to Declining Agricultural Usage." February 4, 2018. http://www.capetown.gov.za/Media-and-news/Day%20Zero%20projection%20moves%20out%20due%20to%20declining%20agricultural%20usage.

# Deputy Minister of Water and Sanitation on Efforts and Fallacies in Day Zero Situation

**March 8, 2018**

Speaker of the National Assembly
Ministers and Deputy Ministers
Honourable Members of the National Assembly
Honoured Guests

We are gathered here today about a very crucial issue that is of concern to all of us. We all know that South Africa is a water scarce country and one of 40 driest countries in the world. It is also important to know that married to the dryness, the country as a whole has not recovered from the 2014 drought.

During this truly difficult time of drought, it is good and common practice to stretch available water resources through the practical application of restrictions to ensure that water supply systems do not fail. This is the principle from which we operate as the Department of Water and Sanitation.

This requires that all; and I do stress: ALL of us play our part and comply with the restrictions which are applied from time to time. What is true is that the provinces of KwaZulu-Natal, Limpopo, Free State, North West and the Northern Cape bore the burden of the drought at its greatest height. The devastation that led to huge losses of livestock and crops over a period must always remain in our thoughts.

What we saw in the early parts of the drought is that the reaction to the drought in KwaZulu-Natal, Free State, Limpopo and North West was more serious than what is experienced in the Western Cape and Particularly Cape Town.

The marked appreciation of the situation saw a much quicker response to the warnings and adherence to restrictions imposed at the time. The most affected municipalities in the affected provinces understood and appreciated the need for joint efforts towards enabling positive responses to the drought.

A perfect example to remember is that of a two-day programme that included Department of Water and Sanitation principals meeting with the Premier of KwaZulu-Natal, MEC's in the Disaster Management Committee, District Mayors of the affected Municipalities and Executive Mayor of the City of eThekwini. This was followed by a situational assessment site visit to the UGu and UMvoti Dams then, showing absolute political will.

This visit followed numerous meetings held by the Department of Water and Sanitation and the KwaZulu-Natal provincial government on fast-tracking relief efforts and unlocking interventions meant to bring short, medium and long-term solutions to the water shortages experienced at the time.

We cannot ignore the important decision to put up the Richards Bay Desalination Plant, utilising the expertise of Umgeni Water to research and find the best technology, facilitate and procure the technology in the shortest possible time without flouting the rules.

Engagements with the Strategic Water Partnership Network (SWPN) and members of the public on behavioural changes were necessary to ensure water supply and savings through behavioural change.

The then dire drought situation in the Free State prompted the FS Provincial Government to call on all people of the province to be actively involved in efforts to save water and fight against the devastating effects of global warming and climate change. There was a threat to the livelihood of the people of the Free State.

The province immediately implemented short, medium and long term measures to address and mitigate the potential impact of the drought then; with measures including but not limited to:

- implementing drought operating rules at all dams;

- diversifying the water mix to include ground water utilisation, rainwater harvesting, re-use of return flows and packaged desalination plants;

- reducing operational risks through proper infrastructure operation and maintenance with associated skills development;

- and acquiring and deploying water tanks to affected communities.

The Free State government at the time also warned all its citizens that the water restrictions that were being implemented needed to be adhered to for the situation not to worsen.

We do remember also that in 2016 with the Integrated Vaal River System which was very low, political leadership was shown by the province of Gauteng to encourage all sorts of water saving efforts. The most critical, was the reduction of supplies by Rand Water to municipalities to force water savings, with direction from Department of Water and Sanitation and the Gauteng Provincial Government through the COGTA MEC.

**There is this untrue narrative about the City of Cape Town not receiving assistance from National Government. This is inaccurate.**

The Department of Water and Sanitation, through its Western Cape office, serves not just the City of Cape Town but the whole province. The drought is not just localized but provincial; exactly the same as what happened in other provinces.

Attention has also been given to the province through the work of the Inter-Ministerial Task Team on Drought. The Department of Water and Sanitation has also availed one of its top managers to be part of the City of Cape Town's advisory committee that keeps the City up to date on all matters of the drought on a weekly basis.

It is important to highlight that COGTA through a letter dated 22 August 2017 allocated the following amounts for drought relief in the Western Cape:

- R20.8 million to the City of Cape Town;

- R10.9 million to the Bitou Local Municipality;

- R3.1 million to the Theewaterskloof Local Municipality;

- And on the 25 September 2017 a further R40 million was allocated to the Department of Agriculture for animal feed

The total sum allocated to the Western Cape therefore totalled R74.8 million. It is very important that we get to know how much of this has been utilised and on what? We also need to understand how these allocations impacted on the poor and vulnerable people in Khayelitsha, ImizamoYethu and other places where service delivery is needed.

What we have observed was that at the beginning of this unfortunate situation, the response of consumers in the Western Cape was quite concerning. After the 12 December 2017 restrictions and interventions were announced, with additional interventions published in the Government Gazette on Friday 12 January 2018 with regard to limiting the use of water in the Breede-Gouritz and Berg-Olifants Water Management Areas.

This notice included the following among other things:

- Limiting groundwater abstractions for domestic and industrial use by 45% and for agricultural use by 60%. Bringing the restrictions on groundwater use in line with the restrictions applied to surface water use.

- It was necessary to also limit water for irrigation use from the system dams once the users have depleted their seasonal bulk volumes.

Whilst the City of Cape Town is threatening its people with Day Zero and receiving the lion's share of attention due to its centrality with regards [to] the economy of the Western Cape, we must remember that the current drought has been real in all of South Africa and the SADC Regions for the last four years at least.

To support of the situation in the Western Cape and Cape Town in particular:

- The Department of Water and Sanitation Signed a Memorandum of Agreement (MoA) with the City of Cape Town

- Borehole positions were established within Department of Water and Sanitation premises in the Theewaterskloof Dam basin

- The Department assigned additional staff to compliment the maintenance team

- Encourage implementation of best efforts to manage the Cape Town Systems Dams through the application of restrictions which were recently increased (domestic and industrial use increased from 40% to 45% and agricultural use increased from 50% to 60%)

- Following meetings with the Mayor of the City of Cape Town, a directive was issued to Umgeni Water (11/12/2017) to procure a 10 Million Litres per Day plant as an emergency intervention for City of Cape Town. The procurement process has been concluded. Despite the City of Cape Town wanting the project to be delayed in order to find an alternate site for the plant, we continue with preparation for implementation.

**The deeper we dig into the apparent water crisis in Western Cape and Cape Town in particular, the more unjustifiable Day Zero becomes. The further the date shifts. I'm made to believe leader of the opposition has now announced that Day Zero is no longer in 2018**

- On 18 May 2017 approval was granted to TCTA to build the Berg Rivier Voelvlei Dam Augmentation Scheme (BRVAS)

- In addition to all this, the Department of Water and Sanitation has emergency systems in place should the dam levels reach 13% or lower.

- The joint Compliance Monitoring and Enforcement efforts conducted by the Department of Water and Sanitation and the municipalities has also influenced the reduction in water use (particularly the unauthorised use)

- Department of Water and Sanitation is also fast-tracking the approval of water use licences and has recently granted licences to City of Cape Town for the groundwater programme involving:
  o Steenbras: three phases up to 57 million Cubic Metres per annum,
  o Cape Flats: three phases up to 75 million Cubic Metres per annum,
  o Oranjezicht Springs: up to 1.78 million Cubic Metres per annum.

This work will continue because we have the interests of all South Africans, notwithstanding where they live or work.

**Singu rhulumente okhathalayo, ngoba kaloku amanzi ayimpilo!**
**Yaye xa amanzi engekho ngomama abasokolayo.**

As I conclude, let's separate politics from water. We need to remember that a great deal of consideration needs to be attached to the following:

South Africa's main source remains surface water. The reality therefore is that South Africa needs to go for an unconventional approach towards water access. More groundwater development needs to be undertaken, water reuse must be enhanced, brackish and sea-water desalinated, and most definitely upscale rainwater harvesting.

We need to be more efficient in water use; including reducing the non-revenue water by attending to water losses and leaks from the system. Pollution remains a worry considering the limited water resources that we have.

One of the most important adaptation strategies that need to be prioritized and strengthened is the water conservation and demand management. Without this, climate change will continue to negatively impact on us.

**Enkosi!**

Source: Republic of South Africa Department of Water and Sanitation. "Speech by Deputy Minister of Water and Sanitation, Pamela Tshwete, during the Debate at the National Assembly: The Water Crisis in the Western Cape, the City of Cape Town in Particular, and in Other Provinces, and the Impact It Has on the Country as a Result of Drought, Global Warming and Other Contributing Factors." March 8, 2018. http://www.dwa.gov.za/Communications/MinisterSpeeches/2018/Speech%20-%20 The%20Water%20Crisis%20in%20the%20Western%20Cape%20The%20City%20of%20Cape%20 Town%20in%20Particular%20and%20in%20other%20Provinces%20and%20the%20Impact%20it%20 has%20on%20the%20Country%20as%20a%20Result%20of%20Drought.pdf.

## OTHER HISTORIC DOCUMENTS OF INTEREST

### FROM THIS VOLUME

### FROM PREVIOUS *HISTORIC DOCUMENTS*

# State of the Union Address and Democratic Response

JANUARY 30, 2018

On January 30, 2018, President Donald Trump delivered the first State of the Union address of his presidency. The White House promised that the president would seek to strike a bipartisan tone, looking to bring together a nation deeply divided since the 2016 election. At the time of his speech, the Trump administration was facing record-low approval ratings and was subject to a federal investigation into alleged interactions between his campaign and the Russian government. But the administration was also celebrating its recent legislative victory, a tax cut bill that the president said would provide significant relief to middle-class Americans. The eighty-minute address was similar in format to the speeches delivered by past presidents, touting the successes of his first year in office and laying out his priorities for the coming year, utilizing invitees and their personal stories to highlight the importance of his plans. Included in what the president called a "new American moment" were large funding increases for the U.S. military and the nation's infrastructure, an overhauled immigration plan, and a shift in American policy abroad.

## TRUMP'S FIRST SPEECH HIGHLIGHTS ECONOMIC GAINS

In his letter inviting the president to deliver an address before a joint session of Congress, Speaker Paul Ryan, R-Wis., said the country was "in the midst of a historic effort to provide relief to hardworking taxpayers" and "grow our economy," adding that "the new year will bring an opportunity to take account of the progress we have made but also lay out the work that still remains to be done on behalf of the American people." It was these themes that Trump seized upon as he stood before the body on January 30.

One month earlier, Congress had passed the largest overhaul to the U.S. tax code in decades. Republicans said the move would provide significant relief for middle-class families, something heavily debated by economists. In its first year, 2019, a majority of taxpayers would see their taxes reduced by an average of $100, but by 2027, more than half of taxpayers would be paying more than they did in 2017. This is because certain provisions of the tax law will sunset in 2026 if not renewed by Congress, but Republicans promised to do so. Democrats continued to argue that the greatest benefits in the bill went to the wealthiest Americans. According to a study by the Tax Policy Center, "higher income households receive larger average tax cuts as a percentage of after-tax income, with the largest cuts as a share of income going to taxpayers in the 95th and 99th percentiles of the income distribution."

The president was keen to tout the law's benefits during his address. "Our massive tax cuts provide tremendous relief for the middle class and small business. To lower tax rates for hard-working Americans, we nearly doubled the standard deduction for everyone," the president said in his address. Trump also highlighted a change the tax law made to the

Patient Protection and Affordable Care Act (ACA), President Barack Obama's landmark piece of legislation and a target of Republican criticism since it was signed into law in 2010. The 2017 tax overhaul eliminated a key piece of the ACA, the individual mandate, which requires all Americans to have a health insurance plan or pay an annual penalty. The tax law zeroes out the penalty starting in 2019. "We eliminated an especially cruel tax that fell mostly on Americans making less than $50,000 a year, forcing them to pay tremendous penalties simply because they couldn't afford Government-ordered health plans. We repealed the core of the disastrous Obamacare. The individual mandate is now gone, thank heavens," Trump said.

Trump said that the tax plan passed by Congress and his overall economic agenda would help encourage job growth and bring more businesses back to the United States. Since he took office, unemployment had continued to decline, ending 2017 at 4.1 percent, and job creation remained healthy, although somewhat slower than it was at the end of the Obama presidency. "Since the election, we have created 2.4 million new jobs, including 200,000 new jobs in manufacturing alone. Tremendous numbers. After years and years of wage stagnation, we are finally seeing rising wages. Unemployment claims have hit a 45-year low," Trump said. He added that "very soon, auto plants and other plants will be opening up all over our country. This is all news Americans are totally unaccustomed to hearing. For many years, companies and jobs were only leaving us. But now they are roaring back." In 2017 and 2018, some companies announced plans to move offshore operations back to the United States, including Apple, General Motors, Ford, and Intel. However, Trump's ongoing trade war and the subsequent retaliatory tariffs imposed by China and the European Union forced other manufacturers, like Harley Davidson, to move a portion of their manufacturing overseas.

## IMMIGRATION TAKES CENTER STAGE

Trump's address to Congress took place just a week after a three-day government shutdown that was caused in part by partisan squabbling over a Trump priority, funding for a wall along the U.S.–Mexico border. In his State of the Union address, the president renewed his call for $25 billion to build a border wall, in exchange for an immigration policy that would provide a path to citizenship for 1.8 million undocumented immigrants. This, the president said, would be a significant increase from the estimated 690,000 currently covered by the Deferred Action for Childhood Arrivals (DACA) program. In addition, Trump's immigration policy would end chain migration that gives preference to family members of those already living in the United States and would also end the visa lottery system that benefits 50,000 each year. Trump wanted to replace the visa lottery with a merit-based system, one that "admits people who are skilled, who want to work, who will contribute to our society, and who will love and respect our country." According to the Congressional Research Service, those admitted under the visa lottery are most likely to be in professional and managerial roles and already must meet certain criteria for entry, including education and work experience.

"It is time to reform these outdated immigration rules and finally bring our immigration system into the 21st century," the president said. Trump argued that his policies would help "struggling communities, especially immigrant communities" by focusing "on the best interests of American workers and American families." He went on to describe how the current immigration system has hurt Americans through an increase in drugs, gang violence, and fewer jobs for American workers. These were key talking points highlighted by the president during his campaign; however, most are heavily disputed. The National

Academies of Sciences, Engineering, and Medicine released a report in 2016 indicating that immigrants have "little to no negative effects on overall wages and employment of native-born workers in the longer term," although they do have some short-term impact on the career prospects of Americans without a college education. Trump relied on families in the audience who were victims of violence perpetrated by illegal immigrants to punctuate his call for an overhaul of current immigration law.

Trump's immigration proposal, which he touted as a "fair compromise . . . where nobody gets everything they want, but where our country gets the critical reforms it needs and must have," was widely panned by Democrats and some Republicans who found it anti–legal immigration and who doubted its ability to win enough support in both houses of Congress for passage. Sen. Richard Blumenthal, D-Conn., called the proposal "a red-meat appeal to the anti-immigrant base of his party, not the unifying, coming-together appeal that we all know is necessary." But Sen. John Cornyn, R-Tex., said Democrats needed to come to the table. "If Democrats don't figure out a way to negotiate, then the DACA program will end and that's not an outcome I think anybody would like," he said, adding that "they will be responsible for it. I think they need a little reality check."

## President Calls for Significant Infrastructure Investment

Since his inauguration, Trump had promised to submit a proposal to Congress for making a significant investment in the nation's infrastructure. This is a topic that typically has broad bipartisan support, and one that should have been a relatively easy win for the president. Initial reports from the White House indicated that the president would call for $1.7 trillion in infrastructure spending, but that only $200 billion would come from federal coffers. The rest would be made up by state and local governments and private investors, something that concerned many in Congress given the lagging financial capacity of the nation's municipal governments. However, by the time of his State of the Union address, the president had not yet sent his official proposal to Congress.

During his address, the president spoke with concern about how long it currently takes America to fix or build a new road. "America is a nation of builders. We built the Empire State Building in just 1 year. Isn't it a disgrace that it can now take 10 years just to get a minor permit approved for the building of a simple road?" To address this concern, the president asked Congress "to produce a bill that generates at least $1.5 trillion for the new infrastructure investment that our country so desperately needs." He said such an investment would not only result in new roads, bridges, and highways but that it would be done "with American heart and American hands and American grit."

Republicans and Democrats alike expressed audible shock at the president's request for $1.5 billion in infrastructure funding. "The question is, how are you gonna pay for it," asked Sen. Cornyn, adding, "Leveraging private dollars is a good start but we got a lot of work to do." Sen. James Lankford, R-Okla., said the announcement "kind of sucked the oxygen out of the room for a moment, as no one expected a number that big," adding, "The obvious thing is, where are we with debt and deficit and how are we going to be able to pull it together?"

## Trump Calls for Increased Military Spending

The president had spoken frequently since his election about the importance of supporting America's men and women in uniform, specifically through significantly increased defense spending. During his address, Trump asked Congress to end the defense sequester, the result of the 2011 Budget Control Act that requires across-the-board spending cuts. Trump said it was necessary to end the program and fully fund the military because "around the world we face rogue regimes, terrorist groups, and rivals like China and Russia that challenge our interests, our economy, and our values ... unmatched power is the surest means to our true and great defense." The president asked that some of this spending be directed toward rebuilding the nation's nuclear arsenal and continuing to support efforts against the Islamic State of Iraq and the Levant.

Trump also used his speech to again call for cuts to U.S. foreign aid. In the past he had asked Congress to cut back foreign aid spending by as much as 30 percent, but that drew criticism from both parties in Congress and his secretary of defense; federal officials have long viewed foreign aid as an investment in national security. The cuts Trump proposed in his State of the Union were targeted against nations that fail to support the United States. Trump said that Congress should "pass legislation to help ensure American foreign-assistance dollars always serve American interests and only go to friends of America, not enemies." This was in direct response to a vote in the United Nations General Assembly in which dozens of countries voted against the U.S. decision to recognize Jerusalem as the capital of Israel.

The president also renewed calls to crack down on two nuclear-armed nations: Iran and North Korea. On the former, the president said he would ask Congress to fix the Joint Comprehensive Plan of Action (JCPOA), a multilateral agreement signed during the Obama administration that requires Iran to roll back its nuclear program in return for lifting some economic sanctions. And on North Korea, Trump said his administration is "waging a campaign of maximum pressure to prevent" North Korea's pursuit of nuclear weapons. "Past experience has taught us that complacency and concessions only invite aggression and provocation. I will not repeat the mistakes of past administrations that got us into this very dangerous position," the president declared. Trump punctuated his remarks on North Korea by sharing the stories of those he had invited to the address, including the parents of Otto Warmbier, the American college student who was detained in North Korea and died shortly after returning to the United States, and Ji Seong-ho, a North Korean dissident.

## REP. KENNEDY DELIVERS DEMOCRATIC RESPONSE

Rep. Joe Kennedy, D-Mass., a three-term, thirty-seven-year-old member of Congress, was chosen by Democrats to deliver the official response to the president's address. Kennedy is the grandson of Sen. Robert Kennedy, who was assassinated in 1968 while campaigning for president. Kennedy's speech promised that Democrats had a "better deal" for Americans than the Trump administration, built on the idea that "the strongest, richest, greatest nation in the world shouldn't leave any one behind." Kennedy opened his speech by addressing the division that many in the country had felt since the 2016 election, remarking "this is not right. This is not who we are." Without calling out the president by name, Kennedy said the past year of chaos had been built by an administration working to sew division and pit Americans against one another.

Kennedy hailed the Me Too, Black Lives Matter, and women's movements and praised immigrants who have come to or are seeking a path to the United States. "You are a part of our story. We will fight for you. We will not walk away," Kennedy said. Kennedy asserted that Democrats would continue to work for all Americans and that "our country will be judged by the promises we keep." He added, "Bullies may land a punch. They might leave a mark. But they have never, not once, in the history of our United States, managed to match the strength and spirit of a people united in defense of their future."

Sen. Bernie Sanders, I-Vt.; Rep. Maxine Waters, D-Calif., who did not attend the State of the Union address in protest; and Rep. Donna Edwards, D-Md., delivered their own responses to the State of the Union address that were carried online and through social media platforms.

—Heather Kerrigan

*Following is the full text of President Donald Trump's January 30, 2018, State of the Union address; and the Democratic response, also on January 30, 2018, delivered by Rep. Joe Kennedy, D-Mass.*

# President Trump Delivers the 2018 State of the Union Address

**January 30, 2018**

*The President.* Mr. Speaker, Mr. Vice President, Members of Congress, the First Lady of the United States, and my fellow Americans: Less than 1 year has passed since I first stood at this podium, in this majestic Chamber, to speak on behalf of the American people and to address their concerns, their hopes, and their dreams. That night, our new administration had already taken very swift action. A new tide of optimism was already sweeping across our land. Each day since, we have gone forward with a clear vision and a righteous mission: to make America great again for all Americans.

Over the last year, we have made incredible progress and achieved extraordinary success. We have faced challenges we expected and others we could never have imagined. We have shared in the heights of victory and the pains of hardship. We have endured floods and fires and storms. But through it all, we have seen the beauty of America's soul and the steel in America's spine.

Each test has forged new American heroes to remind us who we are and show us what we can be. We saw the volunteers of the Cajun Navy racing to the rescue with their fishing boats to save people in the aftermath of a totally devastating hurricane. We saw strangers shielding strangers from a hail of gunfire on the Las Vegas strip.

We heard tales of Americans like Coast Guard Petty Officer Ashlee Leppert, who is here tonight in the gallery with Melania. Ashlee was aboard one of the first helicopters on the scene in Houston during the Hurricane Harvey. Through 18 hours of wind and rain, Ashlee braved live power lines and deep water to help save more than 40 lives. Ashlee, we all thank you. Thank you very much.

We heard about Americans like firefighter David Dahlberg. He's here with us also. David faced down walls of flame to rescue almost 60 children trapped at a California summer camp threatened by those devastating wildfires. To everyone still recovering in Texas, Florida, Louisiana, Puerto Rico, and the Virgin Islands—everywhere—we are with you, we love you, and we always will pull through together, always. Thank you to David and the brave people of California. Thank you very much, David. Great job.

Some trials over the past year touched this Chamber very personally. With us tonight is one of the toughest people ever to serve in this House, a guy who took a bullet, almost died, and was back to work 3½ months later: the legend from Louisiana—[*laughter*]—Congressman Steve Scalise. [*Applause*] I think they like you, Steve. [*Laughter*] We are incredibly grateful for the heroic efforts of the Capitol Police officers, the Alexandria Police, and the doctors, nurses, and paramedics who saved his life and the lives of many others; some in this room. In the aftermath—[*applause*]—yes. Yes.

In the aftermath of that terrible shooting, we came together, not as Republicans or Democrats, but as representatives of the people. But it is not enough to come together only in times of tragedy. Tonight I call upon all of us to set aside our differences, to seek out common ground, and to summon the unity we need to deliver for the people. This is really the key. These are the people we were elected to serve. [*Applause*] Thank you. Over the last year, the world has seen what we always knew: that no people on Earth are so fearless or daring or determined as Americans. If there is a mountain, we climb it. If there is a frontier, we cross it. If there's a challenge, we tame it. If there's an opportunity, we seize it. So let's begin tonight by recognizing that the state of our Union is strong because our people are strong. And together, we are building a safe, strong, and proud America.

Since the election, we have created 2.4 million new jobs, including 200,000 new jobs in manufacturing alone. Tremendous numbers. After years and years of wage stagnation, we are finally seeing rising wages. Unemployment claims have hit a 45-year low. And something I'm very proud of: African American unemployment stands at the lowest rate ever recorded. And Hispanic American unemployment has also reached the lowest levels in history.

Small-business confidence is at an all-time high. The stock market has smashed one record after another, gaining $8 trillion and more in value in just this short period of time. The great news for Americans: 401(k), retirement, pension, and college savings accounts have gone through the roof.

And just as I promised the American people from this podium 11 months ago, we enacted the biggest tax cuts and reforms in American history. Our massive tax cuts provide tremendous relief for the middle class and small business. To lower tax rates for hard-working Americans, we nearly doubled the standard deduction for everyone. Now, the first $24,000 earned by a married couple is completely tax free. We also doubled the child tax credit. A typical family of four making $75,000 will see their tax bill reduced by $2,000, slashing their tax bill in half. In April, this will be the last time you will ever file under the old and very broken system, and millions of Americans will have more take-home pay starting next month—a lot more.

We eliminated an especially cruel tax that fell mostly on Americans making less than $50,000 a year, forcing them to pay tremendous penalties simply because they couldn't afford Government-ordered health plans. We repealed the core of the disastrous Obamacare. The individual mandate is now gone, thank heavens. [*Applause*] Great job.

We slashed the business tax rate from 35 percent all the way down to 21 percent, so American companies can compete and win against anyone else anywhere in the world. These changes alone are estimated to increase average family income by more than $4,000, a lot of money. Small businesses have also received a massive tax cut and can now deduct 20 percent of their business income.

Here tonight are Steve Staub and Sandy Keplinger of Staub Manufacturing, a small, beautiful business in Ohio. They've just finished the best year in their 20-year history. Because of tax reform, they are handing out raises, hiring an additional 14 people, and expanding into the building next door. It's a good feeling.

One of Staub's employees, Corey Adams, is also with us tonight. Corey is an all-American worker. He supported himself through high school, lost his job during the 2008 recession, and was later hired by Staub, where he trained to become a welder. Like many hard-working Americans, Corey plans to invest his tax cut raise into his new home and his two daughters' education. Corey, please stand. And he's a great welder. [*Laughter*] I was told that by the man that owns that company that's doing so well. So congratulations, Corey.

Since we passed tax cuts, roughly 3 million workers have already gotten tax cut bonuses, many of them thousands and thousands of dollars per worker. And it's getting more every month, every week. Apple has just announced it plans to invest a total of $350 billion in America and hire another 20,000 workers. And just a little while ago, ExxonMobil announced a $50 billion investment in the United States—just a little while ago.

This, in fact, is our new American moment. There has never been a better time to start living the American Dream. So to every citizen watching at home tonight, no matter where you've been or where you've come from, this is your time. If you work hard, if you believe in yourself, if you believe in America, then you can dream anything, you can be anything, and together, we can achieve absolutely anything.

Tonight I want to talk about what kind of future we are going to have and what kind of a nation we are going to be. All of us, together, as one team, one people, and one American family can do anything. We all share the same home, the same heart, the same destiny, and the same great American flag. Together, we are rediscovering the American way. In America, we know that faith and family, not government and bureaucracy, are the center of American life. The motto is, "In God We Trust." And we celebrate our police, our military, and our amazing veterans as heroes who deserve our total and unwavering support.

Here tonight is Preston Sharp, a 12-year-old boy from Redding, California, who noticed that veterans' graves were not marked with flags on Veterans Day. He decided all by himself to change that and started a movement that has now placed 40,000 flags at the graves of our great heroes. Preston, a job well done. Young patriots, like Preston, teach all of us about our civic duty as Americans. And I met Preston a little while ago, and he is something very special, that I can tell you. Great future. Thank you very much for all you've done, Preston. Thank you very much.

Preston's reverence for those who have served our Nation reminds us of why we salute our flag, why we put our hands on our hearts for the Pledge of Allegiance, and why we proudly stand for the national anthem. Americans love their country, and they deserve a Government that shows them the same love and loyalty in return. For the last year, we have sought to restore the bonds of trust between our citizens and their Government. Working with the Senate, we are appointing judges who will interpret the Constitution as written, including a great new Supreme Court Justice and more circuit court judges than any new administration in the history of our country. We are totally defending our Second Amendment and have taken historic actions to protect religious liberty.

And we are serving our brave veterans, including giving our veterans choice in their health care decisions. Last year, Congress also passed, and I signed, the landmark VA Accountability Act. Since its passage, my administration has already removed more than 1,500 VA employees who failed to give our veterans the care they deserve. And we are hiring talented people who love our vets as much as we do. And I will not stop until our veterans are properly taken care of, which has been my promise to them from the very beginning of this great journey.

All Americans deserve accountability and respect, and that's what we are giving to our wonderful heroes, our veterans. Thank you. So tonight I call on Congress to empower every Cabinet Secretary with the authority to reward good workers and to remove Federal employees who undermine the public trust or fail the American people.

In our drive to make Washington accountable, we have eliminated more regulations in our first year than any administration in the history of our country. We have ended the war on American energy, and we have ended the war on beautiful, clean coal. We are now, very proudly, an exporter of energy to the world. In Detroit, I halted Government mandates that crippled America's great, beautiful autoworkers so that we can get Motor City revving its engines again. And that's what's happening. Many car companies are now building and expanding plants in the United States, something we haven't seen for decades. Chrysler is moving a major plant from Mexico to Michigan. Toyota and Mazda are opening up a plant in Alabama, a big one. And we haven't seen this in a long time. It's all coming back.

Very soon, auto plants and other plants will be opening up all over our country. This is all news Americans are totally unaccustomed to hearing. For many years, companies and jobs were only leaving us. But now they are roaring back. They're coming back. They want to be where the action is. They want to be in the United States of America. That's where they want to be.

Exciting progress is happening every single day. To speed access to breakthrough cures and affordable generic drugs, last year, the FDA approved more new and generic drugs and medical devices than ever before in our country's history. We also believe that patients with terminal conditions and terminal illness should have access to experimental treatment immediately that could potentially save their lives. People who are terminally ill should not have to go from country to country to seek a cure. I want to give them a chance right here at home. It's time for Congress to give these wonderful, incredible Americans the right to try. [*Applause*] Right?

One of my greatest priorities is to reduce the price of prescription drugs. In many other countries, these drugs cost far less than what we pay in the United States. And it's very, very unfair. That is why I have directed my administration to make fixing the injustice of high drug prices one of my top priorities for the year. And prices will come down substantially. Watch.

America has also finally turned the page on decades of unfair trade deals that sacrificed our prosperity and shipped away our companies, our jobs, and our wealth. Our Nation has lost its wealth, but we're getting it back so fast. The era of economic surrender is totally over. From now on, we expect trading relationships to be fair and, very importantly, reciprocal.

We will work to fix bad trade deals and negotiate new ones. And they'll be good ones, but they'll be fair. And we will protect American workers and American intellectual property through strong enforcement of our trade rules.

As we rebuild our industries, it is also time to rebuild our crumbling infrastructure. America is a nation of builders. We built the Empire State Building in just 1 year. Isn't it a disgrace that it can now take 10 years just to get a minor permit approved for the building of a simple road? I am asking both parties to come together to give us safe, fast, reliable, and modern infrastructure that our economy needs and our people deserve.

Tonight I'm calling on Congress to produce a bill that generates at least $1.5 trillion for the new infrastructure investment that our country so desperately needs. Every Federal dollar should be leveraged by partnering with State and local governments and, where appropriate, tapping into private sector investment to permanently fix the infrastructure deficit. And we can do it.

Any bill must also streamline the permitting and approval process, getting it down to no more than 2 years and perhaps even 1. Together, we can reclaim our great building heritage. We will build gleaming new roads, bridges, highways, railways, and waterways all across our land. And we will do it with American heart and American hands and American grit. We want every American to know the dignity of a hard day's work. We want every child to be safe in their home at night. And we want every citizen to be proud of this land that we all love so much. We can lift our citizens from welfare to work, from dependence to independence, and from poverty to prosperity.

As tax cuts create new jobs, let's invest in workforce development, and let's invest in job training, which we need so badly. Let's open great vocational schools so our future workers can learn a craft and realize their full potential. And let's support working families by supporting paid family leave.

As America regains its strength, opportunity must be extended to all citizens. That is why this year, we will embark on reforming our prisons to help former inmates, who have served their time, get a second chance at life.

Struggling communities, especially immigrant communities, will also be helped by immigration policies that focus on the best interests of American workers and American families. For decades, open borders have allowed drugs and gangs to pour into our most vulnerable communities. They've allowed millions of low-wage workers to compete for jobs and wages against the poorest Americans. Most tragically, they have caused the loss of many innocent lives.

Here tonight are two fathers and two mothers: Evelyn Rodriguez, Freddy Cuevas, Elizabeth Alvarado, and Robert Mickens. Their two teenage daughters—Kayla Cuevas and Nisa Mickens—were close friends on Long Island. But in September 2016, on the eve of Nisa's 16th birthday—such a happy time it should have been—neither of them came home. These two precious girls were brutally murdered while walking together in their hometown.

Six members of the savage MS–13 gang have been charged with Kayla and Nisa's murders. Many of these gang members took advantage of glaring loopholes in our laws to enter the country as illegal, unaccompanied alien minors, and wound up in Kayla and Nisa's high school. Evelyn, Elizabeth, Freddy, and Robert: Tonight everyone in this chamber is praying for you. Everyone in America is grieving for you. Please stand. Thank you very much. I want you to know that 320 million hearts are right now breaking for you. We love you. Thank you.

While we cannot imagine the depths of that kind of sorrow, we can make sure that other families never have to endure this kind of pain. Tonight I am calling on Congress to finally close the deadly loopholes that have allowed MS–13 and other criminal gangs to break into our country. We have proposed new legislation that will fix our immigration laws and support our ICE and Border Patrol agents—these are great people; these are great, great people—that work so hard in the midst of such danger so that this can never happen again.

The United States is a compassionate nation. We are proud that we do more than any other country anywhere in the world to help the needy, the struggling, and the under-privileged all over the world. But as President of the United States, my highest loyalty, my greatest compassion, my constant concern is for America's children, America's struggling workers, and America's forgotten communities. I want our youth to grow up to achieve great things. I want our poor to have their chance to rise.

So tonight I am extending an open hand to work with members of both parties, Democrats and Republicans, to protect our citizens of every background, color, religion, and creed. My duty, and the sacred duty of every elected official in this Chamber, is to defend Americans, to protect their safety, their families, their communities, and their right to the American Dream. Because Americans are dreamers too. Here tonight is one leader in the effort to defend our country, Homeland Security Investigations Special Agent Celestino Martinez. He goes by "D.J." and "C.J." He said, "Call me either one." [*Laughter*] So we'll call you "C.J." [*Laughter*] Served 15 years in the Air Force before becoming an ICE agent and spending the last 15 years fighting gang violence and getting dangerous criminals off of our streets. Tough job.

At one point, MS–13 leaders ordered C.J.'s murder. And they wanted it to happen quickly. But he did not cave to threats or to fear. Last May, he commanded an operation to track down gang members on Long Island. His team has arrested nearly 400, including more than 220 MS–13 gang members. And I have to tell you, what the Border Patrol and ICE have done, we have sent thousands and thousands and thousands of MS–13 horrible people out of this country or into our prisons. So I just want to congratulate you, C.J. You're a brave guy. Thank you very much.

And I asked C.J., "What's the secret?" He said, "We're just tougher than they are." And I like that answer. [*Laughter*] Now, let's get Congress to send you—and all of the people in this great Chamber have to do it; we have no choice. C.J., we're going to send you reinforcements, and we're going to send them to you quickly. It's what you need.

Over the next few weeks, the House and Senate will be voting on an immigration reform package. In recent months, my administration has met extensively with both Democrats and Republicans to craft a bipartisan approach to immigration reform. Based on these discussions, we presented Congress with a detailed proposal that should be supported by both parties as a fair compromise, one where nobody gets everything they want, but where our country gets the critical reforms it needs and must have.

Here are the four pillars of our plan: The first pillar of our framework generously offers a path to citizenship for 1.8 million illegal immigrants who were brought here by their parents at a young age. That covers almost three times more people than the previous administration covered. Under our plan, those who meet education and work requirements and show good moral character will be able to become full citizens of the United States over a 12-year period.

The second pillar fully secures the border. That means building a great wall on the southern border, and it means hiring more heroes, like C.J., to keep our communities safe. Crucially, our plan closes the terrible loopholes exploited by criminals and terrorists to enter our country, and it finally ends the horrible and dangerous practice of catch-and-release.

The third pillar ends the visa lottery, a program that randomly hands out green cards without any regard for skill, merit, or the safety of American people. It's time to begin moving toward a merit-based immigration system, one that admits people who are skilled, who want to work, who will contribute to our society, and who will love and respect our country.

The fourth and final pillar protects the nuclear family by ending chain migration. Under the current broken system, a single immigrant can bring in virtually unlimited numbers of distant relatives. Under our plan, we focus on the immediate family by limiting sponsorships to spouses and minor children. This vital reform is necessary, not just for our economy, but for our security and for the future of America.

In recent weeks, two terrorist attacks in New York were made possible by the visa lottery and chain migration. In the age of terrorism, these programs present risks we can just no longer afford. It's time to reform these outdated immigration rules and finally bring our immigration system into the 21st century. These four pillars represent a down-the-middle compromise and one that will create a safe, modern, and lawful immigration system. For over 30 years, Washington has tried and failed to solve this problem. This Congress can be the one that finally makes it happen. Most importantly, these four pillars will produce legislation that fulfills my ironclad pledge to sign a bill that puts America first. So let's come together, set politics aside, and finally get the job done.

These reforms will also support our response to the terrible crisis of opioid and drug addiction. Never before has it been like it is now. It is terrible. We have to do something about it. In 2016, we lost 64,000 Americans to drug overdoses: 174 deaths per day, 7 per hour. We must get much tougher on drug dealers and pushers if we are going to succeed in stopping this scourge.

My administration is committed to fighting the drug epidemic and helping get treatment for those in need, for those who have been so terribly hurt. The struggle will be long, and it will be difficult, but as Americans always do, in the end, we will succeed. We will prevail.

As we have seen tonight, the most difficult challenges bring out the best in America. We see a vivid expression of this truth in the story of the Holets family of New Mexico. Ryan Holets is 27 years old, an officer with the Albuquerque Police Department. He's here tonight with his wife Rebecca. Thank you, Ryan.

Last year, Ryan was on duty when he saw a pregnant, homeless woman preparing to inject heroin. When Ryan told her she was going to harm her unborn child, she began to weep. She told him she didn't know where to turn, but badly wanted a safe home for her baby.

In that moment, Ryan said he felt God speak to him: "You will do it, because you can." He heard those words. He took out a picture of his wife and their four kids. Then, he went home to tell his wife Rebecca. In an instant, she agreed to adopt. The Holets named their new daughter Hope. Ryan and Rebecca, you embody the goodness of our Nation. Thank you. Thank you, Ryan and Rebecca.

As we rebuild America's strength and confidence at home, we are also restoring our strength and standing abroad. Around the world, we face rogue regimes, terrorist groups, and rivals like China and Russia that challenge our interests, our economy, and our values. In confronting these horrible dangers, we know that weakness is the surest path to conflict and unmatched power is the surest means to our true and great defense.

For this reason, I am asking Congress to end the dangerous defense sequester and fully fund our great military. As part of our defense, we must modernize and rebuild our nuclear arsenal, hopefully, never having to use it, but making it so strong and so powerful that it will deter any acts of aggression by any other nation or anyone else. Perhaps someday in the future, there will be a magical moment when the countries of the world will get together to eliminate their nuclear weapons. Unfortunately, we are not there yet, sadly.

Last year, I also pledged that we would work with our allies to extinguish ISIS from the face of the Earth. One year later, I am proud to report that the coalition to defeat ISIS has liberated very close to 100 percent of the territory just recently held by these killers in Iraq and in Syria and in other locations as well. But there is much more work to be done. We will continue our fight until ISIS is defeated.

Army Staff Sergeant Justin Peck is here tonight. Near Raqqa, last November, Justin and his comrade, Chief Petty Officer Kenton Stacy, were on a mission to clear buildings that ISIS had rigged with explosive so that civilians could return to that city, hopefully, soon and, hopefully, safely.

Clearing the second floor of a vital hospital, Kenton Stacy was severely wounded by an explosion. Immediately, Justin bounded into the booby-trapped and unbelievably dangerous and unsafe building, and found Kenton, but in very, very bad shape. He applied pressure to the wound and inserted a tube to reopen an airway. He then performed CPR for 20 straight minutes during the ground transport and maintained artificial respiration through 2½ hours and through emergency surgery.

Kenton Stacy would have died if it were not for Justin's selfless love for his fellow warrior. Tonight Kenton is recovering in Texas, Raqqa is liberated, and Justin is wearing his new Bronze Star, with a "V" for valor. Staff Sergeant Peck, all of America salutes you.

Terrorists who do things like place bombs in civilian hospitals are evil. When possible, we have no choice but to annihilate them. When necessary, we must be able to detain and question them. But we must be clear: Terrorists are not merely criminals, they are unlawful enemy combatants. And when captured overseas, they should be treated like the terrorists they are.

In the past, we have foolishly released hundreds and hundreds of dangerous terrorists, only to meet them again on the battlefield, including the ISIS leader, al-Baghdadi, who we captured, who we had, who we released. So today I'm keeping another promise. I just signed, prior to walking in, an order directing Secretary Mattis—who is doing a great job, thank you—to reexamine our military detention policy and to keep open the detention facilities in Guantanamo Bay. I am asking Congress to ensure that, in the fight against ISIS and Al Qaida, we continue to have all necessary power to detain terrorists, wherever we chase them down, wherever we find them. And in many cases, for them, it will now be Guantanamo Bay.

At the same time, as of a few months ago, our warriors in Afghanistan have new rules of engagement. Along with their heroic Afghan partners, our military is no longer undermined by artificial timelines, and we no longer tell our enemies our plans.

Last month, I also took an action endorsed unanimously by the U.S. Senate just months before. I recognized Jerusalem as the capital of Israel. Shortly afterwards, dozens of countries voted in the United Nations General Assembly against America's sovereign right to make this decision. In 2016, American taxpayers generously sent those same countries more than $20 billion in aid. That is why tonight I am asking Congress to pass legislation to help ensure American foreign-assistance dollars always serve American interests and only go to friends of America, not enemies of America.

As we strengthen friendships all around the world, we are also restoring clarity about our adversaries. When the people of Iran rose up against the crimes of their corrupt dictatorship, I did not stay silent. America stands with the people of Iran in their courageous struggle for freedom. I am asking Congress to address the fundamental flaws in the terrible Iran nuclear deal. My administration has also imposed tough sanctions on the communist and socialist dictatorships in Cuba and Venezuela.

But no regime has oppressed its own citizens more totally or brutally than the cruel dictatorship in North Korea. North Korea's reckless pursuit of nuclear missiles could very soon threaten our homeland. We are waging a campaign of maximum pressure to prevent that from ever happening. Past experience has taught us that complacency and concessions only invite aggression and provocation. I will not repeat the mistakes of past administrations that got us into this very dangerous position. We need only look at the depraved character of the North Korean regime to understand the nature of the nuclear threat it could pose to America and to our allies.

Otto Warmbier was a hard-working student at the University of Virginia, and a great student he was. On his way to study abroad in Asia, Otto joined a tour to North Korea. At its conclusion, this wonderful young man was arrested and charged with crimes against the state. After a shameful trial, the dictatorship sentenced Otto to 15 years of hard labor, before returning him to America last June, horribly injured and on the verge of death. He passed away just days after his return.

Otto's wonderful parents, Fred and Cindy Warmbier, are here with us tonight, along with Otto's brother and sister, Austin and Greta. Please. Incredible people. You are powerful witnesses to a menace that threatens our world, and your strength truly inspires us all. Thank you very much. Thank you. Tonight we pledge to honor Otto's memory with total American resolve. Thank you.

Finally—[*applause*]—thank you. We are joined by one more witness to the ominous nature of this regime. His name is Mr. Ji Sung-ho. In 1996, Sung-ho was a starving boy in North Korea. One day, he tried to steal coal from a railroad car to barter for a few scraps of food, which were very hard to get. In the process, he passed out on the train tracks, exhausted from hunger. He woke up as a train ran over his limbs. He then endured multiple amputations without anything to dull the pain or the hurt. His brother and sister gave what little food they had to help him recover and ate dirt themselves, permanently stunting their own growth.

Later, he was tortured by North Korean authorities after returning from a brief visit to China. His tormentors wanted to know if he'd met any Christians. He had, and he resolved, after that, to be free. Sung-ho traveled thousands of miles on crutches all across China and Southeast Asia to freedom. Most of his family followed. His father was caught trying to escape and was tortured to death.

Today, he lives in Seoul, where he rescues other defectors and broadcasts into North Korea what the regime fears most: the truth. Today, he has a new leg. But, Sung-ho, I understand you still keep those old crutches as a reminder of how far you've come. Your great sacrifice is an inspiration to us all. Please. Thank you. Sung-ho's story is a testament to the yearning of every human soul to live in freedom.

It was that same yearning for freedom that nearly 250 years ago gave birth to a special place called America. It was a small cluster of colonies caught between a great ocean and a vast wilderness. It was home to an incredible people with a revolutionary idea: that they could rule themselves; that they could chart their own destiny; and that, together, they could light up the entire world.

That is what our country has always been about. That is what Americans have always stood for, always strived for, and always done. Atop the dome of this Capitol stands the statue of Freedom. She stands tall and dignified among the monuments to our ancestors who fought and lived and died to protect her: monuments to Washington and Jefferson and Lincoln and King. Memorials to the heroes of Yorktown and Saratoga; to young Americans who shed their blood on the shores of Normandy and the fields beyond; and others, who went down in the waters of the Pacific and the skies all over Asia. And Freedom stands tall over one more monument: this one. This Capitol—this living monument—this is the monument to the American people.

*Audience members.* U.S.A.! U.S.A.! U.S.A.!

*The President.* We're a people whose heroes live not only in the past, but all around us, defending hope, pride, and defending the American way.

They work in every trade. They sacrifice to raise a family. They care for our children at home. They defend our flag abroad. And they are strong moms and brave kids. They are firefighters and police officers and border agents, medics and marines. But above all else, they are Americans. And this Capitol, this city, this Nation, belongs entirely to them. Our task is to respect them, to listen to them, to serve them, to protect them, and to always be worthy of them.

Americans fill the world with art and music. They push the bounds of science and discovery. And they forever remind us of what we should never, ever forget: The people dreamed this country, the people built this country, and it's the people who are making America great again.

As long as we are proud of who we are and what we are fighting for, there is nothing we cannot achieve. As long as we have confidence in our values, faith in our citizens, and trust in our God, we will never fail. Our families will thrive. Our people will prosper. And our Nation will forever be safe and strong and proud and mighty and free.

Thank you. And God bless America. Goodnight.

SOURCE: Executive Office of the President. "Address before a Joint Session of the Congress on the State of the Union." January 30, 2018. *Compilation of Presidential Documents* 2018, no. 00064 (January 30, 2018). https://www.gpo.gov/fdsys/pkg/DCPD-201800064/pdf/DCPD-201800064.pdf.

DOCUMENT

# *Rep. Kennedy Delivers Democratic Response to the State of the Union Address*

**January 30, 2018**

As Prepared for Delivery

Washington, D.C.—Congressman Joe Kennedy III of Massachusetts today delivered the Democratic response to President Donald Trump's State of the Union. Below is a full transcript of his remarks:

Good evening ladies and gentlemen. It is a privilege to join you tonight.

We are here in Fall River, Massachusetts—a proud American city, built by immigrants.

From textiles to robots, this is a place that knows how to make great things.

The students with us this evening in the autoshop at Diman Regional Technical School carry on that rich legacy.

Like many American hometowns, Fall River has faced its share of storms. But people here are tough. They fight for each other. They pull for their city.

It is a fitting place to gather as our nation reflects on the state of our union.

This is a difficult task. Many have spent the past year anxious, angry, afraid. We all feel the fault lines of a fractured country. We hear the voices of Americans who feel forgotten and forsaken.

We see an economy that makes stocks soar, investor portfolios bulge and corporate profits climb but fails to give workers their fair share of the reward.

A government that struggles to keep itself open.

Russia knee-deep in our democracy.

An all-out war on environmental protection.

A Justice Department rolling back civil rights by the day.

Hatred and supremacy proudly marching in our streets.

Bullets tearing through our classrooms, concerts, and congregations. Targeting our safest, sacred places.

And that nagging, sinking feeling, no matter your political beliefs: this is not right. This is not who we are.

It would be easy to dismiss the past year as chaos. Partisanship. Politics.

But it's far bigger than that. This administration isn't just targeting the laws that protect us—they are targeting the very idea that we are all worthy of protection.

For them, dignity isn't something you're born with but something you measure.

By your net worth, your celebrity, your headlines, your crowd size.

Not to mention, the gender of your spouse. The country of your birth. The color of your skin. The God of your prayers.

Their record is a rebuke of our highest American ideal: the belief that we are all worthy, we are all equal and we all count. In the eyes of our law and our leaders, our God and our government.

That is the American promise.

But today that promise is being broken. By an Administration that callously appraises our worthiness and decides who makes the cut and who can be bargained away.

They are turning American life into a zero-sum game.

Where, in order for one to win, another must lose.

Where we can guarantee America's safety if we slash our safety net.

We can extend healthcare to Mississippi if we gut it in Massachusetts.

We can cut taxes for corporations today if we raise them for families tomorrow.

We can take care of sick kids if we sacrifice Dreamers.

We are bombarded with one false choice after another:

Coal miners or single moms. Rural communities or inner cities. The coast or the heartland.

As if the mechanic in Pittsburgh and the teacher in Tulsa and the daycare worker in Birmingham are somehow bitter rivals, rather than mutual casualties of a system forcefully rigged for those at the top.

As if the parent who lies awake terrified that their transgender son will be beaten and bullied at school is any more or less legitimate than the parent whose heart is shattered by a daughter in the grips of opioid addiction.

So here is the answer Democrats offer tonight: we choose both. We fight for both. Because the strongest, richest, greatest nation in the world shouldn't leave any one behind.

We choose a better deal for all who call this country home.

We choose the living wage, paid leave and affordable child care your family needs to survive.

We choose pensions that are solvent, trade pacts that are fair, roads and bridges that won't rust away, and good education you can afford.

We choose a health care system that offers mercy, whether you suffer from cancer or depression or addiction.

We choose an economy strong enough to boast record stock prices AND brave enough to admit that top CEOs making 300 times the average worker is not right.

We choose Fall River.

We choose the thousands of American communities whose roads aren't paved with power or privilege, but with honest effort, good faith, and the resolve to build something better for their kids.

That is our story. It began the day our Founding Fathers and Mothers set sail for a New World, fleeing oppression and intolerance.

It continued with every word of our Independence—the audacity to declare that all men are created equal. An imperfect promise for a nation struggling to become a more perfect union.

It grew with every suffragette's step, every Freedom Riders voice, every weary soul we welcomed to our shores.

And to all the Dreamers watching tonight, let me be clear: *Ustedes son parte de nuestra historia. Vamos a luchar por ustedes y no nos vamos alejar.*

You are a part of our story. We will fight for you. We will not walk away.

America, we carry that story on our shoulders.

You swarmed Washington last year to ensure no parent has to worry if they can afford to save their child's life.

You proudly marched together last weekend—thousands deep—in the streets of Las Vegas and Philadelphia and Nashville.

You sat high atop your mom's shoulders and held a sign that read: "Build a wall and my generation will tear it down."

You bravely say, me too. You steadfastly say, black lives matter.

You wade through flood waters, battle hurricanes, and brave wildfires and mudslides to save a stranger.

You fight your own, quiet battles every single day.

You drag your weary bodies to that extra shift so your families won't feel the sting of scarcity.

You leave loved ones at home to defend our country overseas, or patrol our neighborhoods overnight.

You serve. You rescue. You help. You heal.

That—more than any law or leader, any debate or disagreement—that is what drives us toward progress.

Bullies may land a punch. They might leave a mark. But they have never, not once, in the history of our United States, managed to match the strength and spirit of a people united in defense of their future.

Politicians can be cheered for the promises they make. Our country will be judged by the promises we keep.

That is the measure of our character. That's who we are.

Out of many. One.

Ladies and gentlemen, have faith: The state of our union is hopeful, resilient, enduring.

Thank you, God Bless you and your families, and God Bless the United States of America.

SOURCE: Office of Rep. Nancy Pelosi. "Congressman Joe Kennedy's Democratic Response to President Trump's State of the Union." As prepared for delivery. January 30, 2018.

## OTHER HISTORIC DOCUMENTS OF INTEREST

### FROM THIS VOLUME

- ■ U.S. and Chinese Officials Respond to Trade Dispute, p. 163
- ■ Trump Administration Remarks on U.S. Immigration Policy, p. 221

# February

# Republicans and DOJ Release Information on Potential Political Bias at the FBI

**FEBRUARY 2, MARCH 16, APRIL 13, AND AUGUST 13, 2018**

Throughout 2017 and 2018, President Donald Trump and Republicans attacked the Federal Bureau of Investigation (FBI) and Department of Justice (DOJ) over potential political bias against the president at its highest levels. In 2017, Trump fired FBI director James Comey, shortly before former FBI director Robert Mueller was appointed to lead the investigation into possible coordination between Trump's campaign and Russian officials. In 2018, the Trump administration fired another high-level FBI official, Deputy Director Andrew McCabe, for lying under oath and an unauthorized release of information to the media. The FBI also let go of Agent Peter Strzok, a member of its counterintelligence team, for bias against the Trump administration and other misconduct. The president linked all of these firings to the Mueller investigation as further proof that his campaign had not colluded with the Russians.

## WHITE HOUSE AGREES TO RELEASE OF NUNES MEMO

For weeks, Republican members of the House Select Committee on Intelligence had been hinting to the media that they had indisputable proof that leaders at the FBI and DOJ were utilizing politically biased information to target the Trump administration. The FBI, DOJ, and other intelligence community agencies had urged the president to keep the memo secret, arguing that it could harm national security. The FBI stated it had "grave concerns about material omissions of fact that fundamentally impact the memo's accuracy." However, the president chose to move forward, reportedly telling close aides that he felt the memo cleared him and his campaign of any wrongdoing in the 2016 election. The four-page document, put together by Republican staff on the House Select Intelligence Committee under the direction of chair Rep. Devin Nunes, R-Calif., was okayed for release on February 2, 2018.

The memo detailed possible bias in the information used in October 2016 to obtain a Foreign Intelligence Surveillance Act (FISA) warrant to conduct electronic surveillance of Carter Page, a former Trump foreign policy campaign adviser. Specifically, the memo indicated that the FISA application used by the FBI and DOJ relied heavily on information in a dossier compiled by former British intelligence officer Christopher Steele on alleged links between the Trump campaign and Russian government officials. The dossier was commissioned by Fusion GPS, a political research firm that was hired by the Democratic National Committee (DNC) and the campaign of Hillary Clinton, and the accuracy of its contents has frequently been called into question.

According to the memo, the FBI failed to include in its application to the Foreign Intelligence Surveillance Court (FISC) any indication that the DNC and Clinton campaign had paid for the dossier. This dossier, the memo states, "formed an essential part of the Carter Page FISA application." The memo goes on to note that McCabe testified in December 2017 before a congressional panel "that no surveillance warrant would have been sought from the FISC without the Steele dossier information." Both the information included in the application and the content of McCabe's testimony were highly debated, because the application had not been released at the time the Nunes memo was made public, and McCabe gave a closed-door testimony for which there is no public transcript. According to the Nunes memo, the findings "represent a troubling breakdown of legal processes established to protect the American people from abuses related to the FISA process."

The memo does not include any indication of other information the FBI and DOJ may have used in their application to the FISC. That was a key point of contention among Democrats on the committee, who wrote their own memo, drafted by ranking member Rep. Adam Schiff, D-Calif. On the same day, the committee voted along party lines to release the Nunes memo and ask the president to make it public, then also voted along party lines to block the release of the competing Democratic memo. The Democrats revised their memo, with significant redactions, and the White House permitted its release on February 24. According to the Democrats' memo, "FBI and DOJ officials did not 'abuse' the Foreign Intelligence Surveillance Act (FISA) process, omit material information, or subvert this vital tool to spy on the Trump campaign," and the "DOJ met the rigor, transparency, and evidentiary basis needed to meet FISA's probable cause requirement." The memo developed by Democrats states that the FBI and DOJ relied on multiple sources of evidence for the basis of their application, not just the dossier. The document also notes that Page was the subject of a 2013 surveillance effort by the DOJ and FBI after the intelligence community learned that the Russians were trying to utilize Page as a source. President Trump called the Democratic response "a total political and legal BUST. Just confirms all of the terrible things that were done. SO ILLEGAL," he tweeted.

On July 21, 2018, the Justice Department released a heavily redacted version of the original Page FISA application and three subsequent renewal applications. These versions contradicted the Republican Nunes memo, noting various sources of information as the basis of the application. The application also included a lengthy footnote on potential political bias in relation to the Steele dossier, stating that the research was "likely looking for information to discredit" the Trump campaign. As is standard among law enforcement officials, the application did not reference by name Trump, Clinton, or the DNC. Despite the contents of the application, President Trump responded to its release on Twitter, writing, "Looking more & more like the Trump Campaign for President was illegally being spied upon (surveillance) for the political gain of Crooked Hillary Clinton and the DNC."

## FBI DEPUTY DIRECTOR MCCABE FIRED

On March 16, less than two days before he was set to retire, Attorney General Jeff Sessions fired FBI Deputy Director Andrew McCabe, a twenty-year veteran of the agency. Sessions cited the reason for the firing as lack of candor with FBI officials and DOJ investigators. McCabe called the firing an "attack on my credibility" that was "one part of a larger effort not just to slander me personally, but to taint the FBI, law enforcement, and intelligence professionals more generally."

It was not until April that the Department of Justice Office of the Inspector General (OIG) released a report detailing the findings of an investigation that led to McCabe's firing. The OIG report cited four examples of lack of candor or providing false information, both under oath and not under oath, as well as an unauthorized disclosure of FBI information to the media. All of the findings revolve around a 2016 phone call between an assistant to McCabe and the *Wall Street Journal*. At the time, the newspaper was working on a story alleging that the FBI was intentionally slowing on an investigation into the Clinton Foundation, potentially because McCabe's wife had received a campaign contribution from a political action committee associated with Clinton supporter and Virginia governor Terry McAuliffe when she was running for Virginia senate in 2015. The OIG report alleges that to protect his own reputation, McCabe authorized his assistants to provide information to the *Wall Street Journal* about a phone conversation he had with the principal associate deputy attorney general (PADAG) on the investigation.

The first instance of lack of candor, according to the OIG's report, occurred on October 31, 2016, in a conversation between then–FBI director James Comey and McCabe regarding anonymous quotes that appeared in the *Wall Street Journal* article one day earlier. The report states that McCabe and Comey had "starkly conflicting" recollections of the conversation, with Comey claiming that McCabe did not tell him about the authorization of the release of information. Although the OIG acknowledges that only McCabe and Comey had knowledge of their conversation, there is circumstantial evidence supporting Comey's recollection over that of McCabe, who said that he had informed Comey of the release of information.

The second instance of lack of candor occurred during an interview with the FBI inspection division on May 9, 2017. During the interview, the OIG report states McCabe "falsely told the agents that he had not authorized the disclosure to the WSJ and did not know who did." However, during a later interview with the OIG, McCabe would state that "he did not believe that he denied authorizing the disclosure of the PADAG call during the interview" but "could not provide any alternative account about what he actually said."

The third and fourth instances of lack of candor occurred during interviews with the OIG on July 28, 2017, and November 29, 2017. During the first interview, McCabe again claimed that he was not aware of where his aide was on the day she made the disclosure to the *Wall Street Journal* and said that he did not believe she was authorized to speak to the media. During the November 29 follow-up conversation, McCabe said he "misspoke" about the situation because he was caught off guard by the questions. The OIG found both statements implausible and had FBI records showing that McCabe was in frequent communication with his aide on the day of the disclosure and that the two had discussed the conversation with the *Wall Street Journal*. During the November 29 interview, McCabe also said that he told Comey about his decision to authorize the disclosure of the PADAG phone call.

According to the OIG, McCabe was authorized to release information about the Clinton Foundation investigation, so long as the disclosure was in the public's interest. However, the OIG found that the release was done "in a manner designed to advance his personal interests" and did not meet the public-interest exemption. In a point-by-point rebuttal, McCabe's lawyer, Michael Bromwich, stated that McCabe released the information to protect the FBI's reputation and that doing so was in the public's interest. He called McCabe's firing "completely unjustified" and "nothing short of extraordinary." McCabe's lawyer insinuates that there was pressure from the president on the OIG to produce results to his liking, resulting in an OIG report that was incomplete and misleading.

On Twitter, President Trump highlighted the release of the report. "DOJ just issued the McCabe report—which is a total disaster. He LIED! LIED! LIED! McCabe was totally controlled by Comey—McCabe is Comey!! No collusion, all made up by this den of thieves and lowlifes!" Inspector General Michael Horowitz called on the U.S. attorney to undertake a criminal investigation into McCabe, but McCabe's lawyer indicated a belief that "unless there is inappropriate pressure from high levels of the administration, the U.S. attorney's office will conclude that it should decline to prosecute." In June, McCabe filed a lawsuit against the FBI, DOJ, and OIG, alleging that he was not provided proper documentation on his firing and was not given the requested FBI guidelines on disciplinary action. Media outlets reported in September that a grand jury was impaneled to consider the referral by the inspector general, but neither that nor McCabe's lawsuit had moved forward by the end of 2018.

## FBI Agent Strzok Fired

Peter Strzok, a twenty-year veteran of the FBI and a high-ranking member of the agency's counterintelligence unit, first gained national attention in 2017 when text messages between him and FBI attorney Lisa Page became public. In the texts, the two expressed their significant displeasure over then-candidate Trump and, to a lesser extent, Hillary Clinton. Strzok had worked on both the investigation into Clinton's use of a private e-mail server during her time as secretary of state, as well as Robert Mueller's investigation into potential collusion between the Trump campaign and Russian officials. Strzok left the Mueller investigation after the text messages were uncovered; however, Republicans frequently utilized Strzok's e-mails to characterize the Mueller investigation as politically biased.

The text messages between Strzok and Page were uncovered during an investigation by the DOJ OIG into how the FBI and Justice Department handled the Clinton e-mail-server probe. In one particular exchange, Page texted to Strzok that Trump is "not ever going to become president, right? Right?!" to which Strzok responded, "No. No he won't. We'll stop it." Although the OIG report noted that it found no evidence that Strzok had allowed his opinions to influence his work, that text was "not only indicative of a biased state of mind but, even more seriously, implies a willingness to take official action to impact the presidential candidate's electoral prospects." The OIG also faulted Strzok for waiting a month after receiving information that there were additional e-mails related to the Clinton server investigation to analyze their contents. "Under these circumstances, we did not have confidence that Strzok's decision to prioritize the Russia investigation over following up on the Midyear-related investigative lead . . . was free from bias." Strzok was called before Congress in July 2018 to testify about the texts and denied that he had allowed his personal opinions to interfere with his work. During his testimony, Strzok called it "just another victory notch in Putin's belt and another milestone in our enemies' campaign to tear America apart."

The findings of the OIG report resulted in Strzok's referral to the FBI's Office of Professional Responsibility, which recommended he receive a demotion and a sixty-day suspension both for the text messages and for sending to his personal e-mail account a search warrant containing information that was under seal. The deputy director, however, opted to fire Strzok on August 13. Strzok's lawyer, Aitan Goelman, argued that the firing was politically motivated. "The decision to fire Special Agent Strzok is not only a departure from typical Bureau practice, but also contradicts Director Wray's testimony to Congress and his assurances that the FBI intended to follow its regular process in this and all personnel matters," Strzok's lawyer said. "The decision should be deeply troubling to all

Americans. A lengthy investigation and multiple rounds of congressional testimony failed to produce a shred of evidence that Special Agent Strzok's personal views ever affected his work," Goelman added. Strzok said he was "deeply saddened" by his firing, and that it was "an honor to serve my country and work with the fine men and women of the FBI."

On Twitter, President Trump celebrated Strzok's firing, and attempted to link it to the Mueller investigation: "Agent Peter Strzok was just fired from the FBI—finally. The list of bad players in the FBI & DOJ gets longer & longer. Based on the fact that Strzok was in charge of the Witch Hunt, will it be dropped? It is a total Hoax. No Collusion, No Obstruction—I just fight back!" The president also asked, "Will the FBI ever recover it's [sic] once stellar reputation, so badly damaged by Comey, McCabe, Peter S and his lover, the lovely Lisa Page, and other top officials now dismissed or fired?" Notably, Strzok was the third high-level FBI official fired since the start of President Trump's term.

—Heather Kerrigan

*Following is a letter from White House Counsel Don McGahn on February 2, 2018, agreeing to the release of a memo from the House Select Committee on Intelligence detailing bias at the FBI, and the associated memo; a March 16, 2018, tweet by President Donald Trump upon the firing of FBI deputy director Andrew McCabe; excerpts from a February report, released to the public by the Department of Justice on April 13, 2018, from an investigation into McCabe's conduct at the FBI; and an August 13, 2018, tweet from President Trump on Peter Strzok's firing.*

# *Nunes Memo on DOJ and FBI Bias Released*

**February 2, 2018**

*[All footnotes have been omitted.]*

The Honorable Devin Nunes
Chairman, House Permanent Select Committee on Intelligence
United States Capitol
Washington, DC 20515

Dear Mr. Chairman:

On January 29, 2018, the House Permanent Select Committee on Intelligence (herein after "the Committee") voted to disclose publicly a memorandum containing classified information provided to the Committee in connection with its oversight activities (the "Memorandum," which is attached to this letter). As provided by clause 11(g) of Rule X of the House of Representatives, the Committee has forwarded this Memorandum to the President based on its determination that the release of the Memorandum would serve the public interest.

The Constitution vests the President with the authority to protect national security secrets from disclosure. As the Supreme Court has recognized, it is the President's responsibility to classify, declassify, and control access to information bearing on our intelligence sources and methods of national defense. *See, e.g., Dep't of Navy v. Egan*, 484 U.S. 518, 527 (1988). In order to facilitate appropriate congressional oversight, the Executive Branch may entrust classified information to the appropriate committees of Congress, as it has done in connection with the Committee's oversight activities here. The Executive Branch does so on the assumption that the Committee will responsibly protect such classified information, consistent with the laws of the United States.

The Committee has now determined that the release of the Memorandum would be appropriate. The Executive Branch, across Administrations of both parties, has worked to accommodate congressional requests to declassify specific materials in the public interest. However, public release of classified information by unilateral action of the Legislative Branch is extremely rare and raises significant separation of powers concerns. Accordingly, the Committee's request to release the Memorandum is interpreted as a request for declassification pursuant to the President's authority.

The President understands that the protection of our national security represents his highest obligation. Accordingly, he has directed lawyers and national security staff to assess the declassification request, consistent with established standards governing the handling of classified information, including those under Section 3.1(d) of Executive Order 13526. Those standards permit declassification when the public interest in disclosure outweighs any need to protect the information. The White House review process also included input from the Office of the Director of National Intelligence and the Department of Justice. Consistent with this review and these standards, the President has determined that declassification of the Memorandum is appropriate.

Based on this assessment and in light of the significant public interest in the memorandum, the President has authorized the declassification of the Memorandum. To be clear, the Memorandum reflects the judgements of its congressional authors. The President understands that oversight concerning matters related to the Memorandum may be continuing. Though the circumstances leading to the declassification through this process are extraordinary, the Executive Branch stands ready to work with Congress to accommodate oversight requests consistent with applicable standards and processes, including the need to protect intelligence sources and methods.

Sincerely,
Donald F. McGahn II
Counsel to the President

Cc: The Honorable Paul Ryan
Speaker of the House

The Honorable Adam Schiff
Ranking Member, House Permanent Select Committee on Intelligence

January 18, 2018
Declassified by order of the President, February 2, 2018

To:        HPSCI Majority Members
From:      HPSCI Majority Staff
Subject:   Foreign Intelligence Surveillance Act Abuses at the Department of Justice and
           the Federal Bureau of Investigation

## Purpose

This memorandum provides Members an update on significant facts relating to the Committee's ongoing investigation into the Department of Justice (DOJ) and Federal Bureau of Investigation (FBI) and their use of the Foreign Intelligence Surveillance Act (FISA) during the 2016 presidential election cycle. Our findings, which are detailed below, 1) raise concerns with the legitimacy and legality of certain DOJ and FBI interactions with the Foreign Intelligence Surveillance Court (FISC), and 2) represent a troubling breakdown of legal processes established to protect the American people from abuses related to the FISA process.

## Investigation Update

On October 21, 2016, DOJ and FBI sought and received a FISA probable cause order (not under Title VII) authorizing electronic surveillance on Carter Page from the FISC. Page is a U.S. citizen who served as a volunteer advisor to the Trump presidential campaign. Consistent with requirements under FISA, the application had to be first certified by the Director or Deputy Director of the FBI. It then required the approval of the Attorney General, Deputy Attorney General (DAG), or the Senate-confirmed Assistant Attorney General for the National Security Division.

The FBI and DOJ obtained one initial FISA warrant targeting Carter Page and three FISA renewals from the FISC. As required by statute (50 U.S.C. §1805(d)(1)), a FISA order on an American citizen must be renewed by the FISC every 90 days and each renewal requires a separate finding of probable cause. Then-Director James Comey signed three FISA applications in question on behalf of the FBI, and Deputy Director Andrew McCabe signed one. Then-DAG Sally Yates, then-Acting DAG Dana Boente, and DAG Rod Rosenstein each signed one or more FISA applications on behalf of DOJ.

Due to the sensitive nature of foreign intelligence activity, FISA submissions (including renewals) before the FISC are classified. As such, the public's confidence in the integrity of the FISA process depends on the court's ability to hold the government to the highest standard—particularly as it relates to surveillance of American citizens. However, the FISC's rigor in protecting the rights of Americans, which is reinforced by 90-day renewals of surveillance orders, is necessarily dependent on the government's production to the court of all material and relevant facts. This should include information potentially favorable to the target of the FISA application that is known by the government. In the case of Carter Page, the government had at least four independent opportunities before the FISC to accurately provide an accounting of the relevant facts. However, our findings indicate that, as described below, material and relevant information was omitted.

1) The "dossier" compiled by Christopher Steele (Steele dossier) on behalf of the Democratic National Committee (DNC) and the Hillary Clinton campaign formed an essential part of the Carter Page FISA application. Steele was a long-time FBI source who was paid over $160,000 by the DNC and Clinton campaign, via the law firm Perkins Coie and research firm Fusion GPS, to obtain derogatory information on Donald Trump's ties to Russia.

   a) Neither the initial application in October 2016, nor any of the renewals, disclose or reference the role of the DNC, Clinton campaign, or any party/campaign in funding Steele's efforts, even though the political origins of the Steele dossier were then known to senior DOJ and FBI officials.

b)   The initial FISA application notes Steele was working for a named U.S. person, but does not name Fusion GPS and principal Glenn Simpson, who was paid by a U.S. law firm (Perkins Cole) representing the DNC (even though it was known by DOJ at the time that political actors were involved with the Steele dossier). The application does not mention Steele was ultimately working on behalf of—and paid for by—the DNC and Clinton campaign, or that the FBI had separately authorized payment to Steele for the same information.

2)   The Carter Page FISA application also cited extensively a September 23, 2016, *Yahoo News* article by Michael Isikoff, which focuses on Page's July 2016 trip to Moscow. <u>This article does not corroborate the Steele dossier because it is derived from information leaked by Steele himself to *Yahoo News*</u>. The Page FISA application incorrectly assesses that Steele did not directly provide information to *Yahoo News*. Steele has admitted in British court filings that he met with *Yahoo News*—and several other outlets—in September 2016 at the direction of Fusion GPS. Perkins Coie was aware of Steele's initial media contacts because they hosted at least one meeting in Washington D.C. in 2016 with Steele and Fusion GPS where this matter was discussed.

   a)   Steele was suspended and then terminated as an FBI source for what the FBI defines as the most serious of violations—an unauthorized disclosure to the media of his relationship with the FBI in an October 30, 2016, *Mother Jones* article by David Corn. Steele should have been terminated for his previous undisclosed contacts with Yahoo and other outlets **in September**—before the Page application was submitted to the FISC in October—but Steele improperly concealed from and lied to the FBI about those contacts.

   b)   Steele's numerous encounters with the media violated the cardinal rule of source handling—maintaining confidentiality—and demonstrated that Steele had become a less reliable source for the FBI.

3)   Before and after Steele was terminated as a source, he maintained contact with DOJ via then-Associate Deputy Attorney General Bruce Ohr, a senior DOJ official who worked closely with Deputy Attorneys General Yates and later Rosenstein. Shortly after the election, the FBI began interviewing Ohr, documenting his communications with Steele. For example, in September 2016, Steele admitted to Ohr his feelings against then-candidate Trump when Steele said he "**was desperate that Donald Trump not get elected and was passionate about him not being president.**" This clear evidence of Steele's bias was recorded by Ohr at the time and subsequently in official FBI files—but not reflected in any of the Page FISA applications.

   a)   During this same time period, Ohr's wife was employed by Fusion GPS to assist in the cultivation of opposition research on Trump. Ohr later provided the FBI with all of his wife's opposition research, paid for by the DNC and Clinton campaign via Fusion GPS. The Ohrs' relationship with Steele and Fusion GPS was inexplicably concealed from the FISC.

4)   According to the head of the FBI's counterintelligence division, Assistant Director Bill Priestap, corroboration of the Steele dossier was in its "infancy" at the time of the initial Page FISA application. After Steele was terminated, a source validation report conducted by an independent unit within FBI assessed Steele's reporting as only minimally corroborated. Yet, in early January 2017, Director Comey briefed President-elect Trump on a summary of the Steele dossier, even though

it was—according to his June 2017 testimony—"salacious and unverified." While the FISA application relied on Steele's past record of credible reporting on other unrelated matters, it ignored or concealed his anti-Trump financial and ideological motivations. Furthermore, Deputy Director McCabe testified before the Committee in December 2017 that no surveillance warrant would have been sought from the FISC without the Steele dossier information.

5) The Page FISA application also mentions information regarding fellow Trump campaign advisor George Papadopoulos, but there is no evidence of any cooperation or conspiracy between Page and Papadopoulos. The Papadopoulos information triggered the opening of an FBI counterintelligence investigation in late July 2016 by FBI agent Pete Strzok. Strzok was reassigned by the Special Counsel's Office to FBI Human Resources for improper text messages with his mistress, FBI Attorney Lisa Page (no known relation to Carter Page), where they both demonstrated a clear bias against Trump and in favor of Clinton, whom Strzok had also investigated. The Strzok/Lisa Page texts also reflect extensive discussions about the investigation, orchestrating leaks to the media, and include a meeting with Deputy Director McCabe to discuss an "insurance" policy against President Trump's election.

SOURCE: House of Representatives Select Committee on Intelligence. "Foreign Intelligence Surveillance Act Abuses at the Department of Justice and the Federal Bureau of Investigation." February 2, 2018. https://intelligence.house.gov/uploadedfiles/memo_and_white_house_letter.pdf.

DOCUMENT

## *President Trump on McCabe Firing*

**March 16, 2018**

Andrew McCabe FIRED, a great day for the hard working men and women of the FBI—A great day for Democracy. Sanctimonious James Comey was his boss and made McCabe look like a choirboy. He knew all about the lies and corruption going on at the highest levels of the FBI!

SOURCE: Donald Trump (@realDonaldTrump). Twitter post. March 16, 2018. https://twitter.com/realDonaldTrump/status/974859881827258369.

DOCUMENT

## *DOJ Releases Report on Investigation into McCabe Allegations*

**April 13, 2018**

*[The Table of Contents has been omitted.]*

*[Footnotes have been omitted.]*

## I. Introduction and Summary of Findings

This misconduct report addresses the accuracy of statements made by then-Federal Bureau of Investigation (FBI) Deputy Director Andrew McCabe to the FBI's Inspection Division (INSD) and the Department of Justice (Department or DOJ) Office of the Inspector General (OIG) concerning the disclosure of certain law enforcement sensitive information to reporter Devlin Barrett that was published online in the Wall Street Journal (WSJ) on October 30, 2016, in an article entitled "FBI in Internal Feud Over Hillary Clinton Probe." A print version of the article was published in the WSJ on Monday, October 31, 2016, in an article entitled "FBI, Justice Feud in Clinton Probe."

This investigation was initially opened by INSD to determine whether the information published by the WSJ in the October 30 article was an unauthorized leak and, if so, who was the source of the leak. On August 31, 2017, the OIG opened an investigation of McCabe following INSD's referral of its matter to the OIG after INSD became concerned that McCabe may have lacked candor when questioned by INSD agents about his role in the disclosure to the WSJ. Shortly before that INSD referral, as part of its ongoing Review of Allegations Regarding Various Actions by the Department and the FBI in Advance of the 2016 Election, the OIG identified FBI text messages by McCabe's then-Special Counsel ("Special Counsel") that reflected that she and the then-Assistant Director for Public Affairs ("AD/OPA") had been in contact with Barrett on October 27 and 28, 2016, and the OIG began to review the involvement of McCabe, Special Counsel, and AD/OPA in the disclosure of information to the WSJ in connection with the October 30 article.

In addition to addressing whether McCabe lacked candor, the OIG's misconduct investigation addressed whether any FBI or Department of Justice policies were violated in disclosing non-public FBI information to the WSJ.

The OIG's misconduct investigation included reviewing all of the INSD investigative materials as well as numerous additional documents, e-mails, text messages, and OIG interview transcripts. The OIG interviewed numerous witnesses, including McCabe, Special Counsel, former FBI Director James Comey, and others.

As detailed below, we found that in late October 2016, McCabe authorized Special Counsel and AD/OPA to discuss with Barrett issues related to the FBI's Clinton Foundation investigation (CF Investigation). In particular, McCabe authorized Special Counsel and AD/OPA to disclose to Barrett the contents of a telephone call that had occurred on August 12, 2016, between McCabe and the then-Principal Associate Deputy Attorney General ("PADAG"). Among the purposes of the disclosure was to rebut a narrative that had been developing following a story in the WSJ on October 23, 2016, that questioned McCabe's impartiality in overseeing FBI investigations involving former Secretary of State Hillary Clinton, and claimed that McCabe had ordered the termination of the CF Investigation due to Department of Justice pressure. The disclosure to the WSJ effectively confirmed the existence of the CF Investigation, which then-FBI Director Comey had previously refused to do. The account of the August 12 McCabe-PADAG call, and other information regarding the handling of the CF Investigation, was included in the October 30 WSJ article.

We found that, in a conversation with then-Director Comey shortly after the WSJ article was published, McCabe lacked candor when he told Comey, or made statements that led Comey to believe, that McCabe had not authorized the disclosure and did not know who did. This conduct violated FBI Offense Code 2.5 (Lack of Candor—No Oath).

We also found that on May 9, 2017, when questioned under oath by FBI agents from INSD, McCabe lacked candor when he told the agents that he had not authorized the disclosure to the WSJ and did not know who did. This conduct violated FBI Offense Code 2.6 (Lack of Candor—Under Oath).

We further found that on July 28, 2017, when questioned under oath by the OIG in a recorded interview, McCabe lacked candor when he stated: (a) that he was not aware of Special Counsel having been authorized to speak to reporters around October 30 and (b) that, because he was not in Washington, D.C., on October 27 and 28, 2016, he was unable to say where Special Counsel was or what she was doing at that time. This conduct violated FBI Offense Code 2.6 (Lack of Candor—Under Oath).

We additionally found that on November 29, 2017, when questioned under oath by the OIG in a recorded interview during which he contradicted his prior statements by acknowledging that he had authorized the disclosure to the WSJ, McCabe lacked candor when he: (a) stated that he told Comey on October 31, 2016, that he had authorized the disclosure to the WSJ; (b) denied telling INSD agents on May 9 that he had not authorized the disclosure to the WSJ about the PADAG call; and (c) asserted that INSD's questioning of him on May 9 about the October 30 WSJ article occurred at the end of an unrelated meeting when one of the INSD agents pulled him aside and asked him one or two questions about the article. This conduct violated FBI Offense Code 2.6 (Lack of Candor—Under Oath).

Lastly, we determined that as Deputy Director, McCabe was authorized to disclose the existence of the CF Investigation publicly if such a disclosure fell within the "public interest" exception in applicable FBI and DOJ policies generally prohibiting such a disclosure of an ongoing investigation. However, we concluded that McCabe's decision to confirm the existence of the CF Investigation through an anonymously sourced quote, recounting the content of a phone call with a senior Department official in a manner designed to advance his personal interests at the expense of Department leadership, was clearly not within the public interest exception. We therefore concluded that McCabe's disclosure of the existence of an ongoing investigation in this manner violated the FBI's and the Department's media policy and constituted misconduct.

The OIG is issuing this report to the FBI for such action as it deems appropriate.

*[Sections II and III, outlining relevant statutes, policies, and practices as well as factual findings related to the allegations, have been omitted.]*

## IV. OIG Analysis

### A. Lack of Candor

We concluded that McCabe lacked candor on four separate occasions in connection with the disclosure to the WSJ. Three of those occasions involved his testimony under oath.

#### 1. Lack of Candor with Then-Director Comey on or around October 31, 2016

We concluded that McCabe lacked candor during his conversation with then-Director Comey on or about October 31, 2016, when they discussed the October 30 WSJ article. As detailed above, Comey and McCabe gave starkly conflicting accounts of this conversation. Comey said that McCabe "definitely" did not tell Comey that he had authorized the disclosure about the PADAG call. To the contrary, Comey told the OIG that, on or about October 31, McCabe led him to believe "in form or fashion" that McCabe did not authorize the disclosure about the PADAG call to the WSJ. Comey described how McCabe gave

Comey the impression that McCabe had not authorized the disclosure about the PADAG call, was not involved in the disclosure, and did not know how it happened. By contrast, McCabe asserted that he explicitly told Comey during that conversation that he authorized the disclosure and that Comey agreed it was a "good" idea.

While the only direct evidence regarding this McCabe-Comey conversation were the recollections of the two participants, there is considerable circumstantial evidence and we concluded that the overwhelming weight of that evidence supported Comey's version of the conversation. Indeed, none of the circumstantial evidence provided support for McCabe's account of the discussion; rather, we found that much of the available evidence undercut McCabe's claim.

First, Comey had pointedly refused to confirm the existence of the CF Investigation in testimony to Congress just 3 months earlier. Additionally, 1 month before McCabe authorized the disclosure, Comey also refused to confirm or deny two different investigations during an FBI oversight hearing before the House Judiciary Committee. Comey stated during the hearing: "our standard is we do not confirm or deny the existence of investigations." Comey noted that there is a public interest exception, but "our overwhelming rule is we do not comment except in certain exceptional circumstances." Comey told us that when the FBI made disclosures of this type during his tenure, such as occurred in connection with the Clinton E-mail and Russia investigations, it did so only after careful deliberations as to form and wording; he also noted that such a disclosure would not be made through an anonymously sourced quote given to a single reporter. We found it highly improbable that Comey would have been approving of a decision by McCabe to disclose to a reporter, on background, information essentially confirming the existence of an FBI investigation that Comey himself had refused to confirm when testifying before Congress.

Second, on the morning after the article appeared online (and the same day it appeared in print), Comey expressed concerns at his staff meeting about the volume of leaks, as evidenced by Special Counsel's contemporaneous notes of the meeting. We found it highly unlikely that Comey, in a discussion with McCabe that same day, would have been accepting of a disclosure authorized by McCabe that looked exactly like the type of leak that he was condemning to his staff.

Third, the disclosure occurred less than 10 days before the presidential election and just 2 days after the firestorm surrounding Comey's letter to Congress about taking additional steps in the Clinton E-mail Investigation. Disclosure of the PADAG call risked subjecting the FBI to even more criticism about potentially affecting the imminent presidential election, by confirming the existence of a previously unconfirmed criminal investigation involving candidate Clinton. We highly doubt that Comey, who himself expressed concern to us that the WSJ disclosure occurred 2 days after his October 28 letter, would have countenanced such a disclosure by McCabe within days of the election if he had been told about it.

Fourth, publishing the account of the PADAG call risked further "poisoning" the FBI's relationship with DOJ leadership at a time it was already under great strain because of, among other things, Comey's decision to notify Congress on October 28 that the FBI was taking additional steps in the Clinton E-mail Investigation and the Department leadership's concern about leaks emanating from the FBI.

Fifth, on October 27, Comey and FBI-GC expressed concerns to McCabe about whether McCabe should participate further in the Clinton E-mail Investigation because of the appearance created by the campaign contributions to his wife's campaign. The same logic applied to the CF Investigation. On that same date, McCabe authorized Special Counsel to discuss the August 12 PADAG call with the WSJ reporter, thereby confirming the FBI's criminal investigation. McCabe's text message to Special Counsel late on October 27 ("no decision on recusal will be made until I return and weigh in") shows that he knew the issue of recusal was clearly on the table; indeed, McCabe announced his recusal from both Clinton-related matters on November 1. Under these circumstances, McCabe had a strong reason not to tell Comey on October 31 that he had authorized the disclosure to the WSJ about the CF Investigation: it would have been an admission that McCabe had taken action relating to that investigation at exactly the time that McCabe's recusal from Clinton-related matters was under consideration by Comey. Further, we found it extremely unlikely, as McCabe now claims, that he not only told Comey about his decision to authorize the disclosure, but that Comey thought it was a "good" idea for McCabe to have taken that action.

Sixth, no other senior FBI official corroborated McCabe's testimony that, among FBI executive leadership, "people knew that generally" he had authorized the disclosure. Rather, multiple witnesses identified by McCabe told us that because of the information contained in the WSJ report, they did not believe it was an authorized disclosure. They also said that had they heard about such an authorization they would have recalled it because it would have been so unusual. Other than Special Counsel, *no* witness we interviewed told us that they knew that this disclosure had been authorized at the time. We think it likely that at least some FBI executives would have been aware of McCabe's authorization if he had told Comey what he had done.

Finally, Comey's testimony that McCabe did not tell him that McCabe had authorized the disclosure to the WSJ is entirely consistent with McCabe's statement to INSD on May 9 that he had "no idea where [the disclosure] came from" or "who the source was," as well as his claim to the OIG on July 28 that he was not aware that Special Counsel had disclosed the information to the WSJ. Conversely, McCabe's claim that he told Comey is not only inconsistent with his May 9 and July 28 statements to the INSD and OIG, respectively, but there would be no reason for McCabe to not tell INSD and OIG about his actions on those dates if he had already admitted them to Comey. Indeed, McCabe contacted the OIG on August 1 to attempt to correct his July 28 testimony only after he was made aware on July 28 that the OIG had text messages from Special Counsel that would likely enable the OIG to soon learn the truth about who authorized Special Counsel's actions.

Taking all of these factors into account, we concluded that McCabe did not tell Comey on or around October 31 (or at any other time) that he (McCabe) had authorized the disclosure of information about the CF Investigation to the WSJ.

Had McCabe done so, we believe that Comey would have objected to the disclosure. McCabe's disclosure was an attempt to make himself look good by making senior department leadership, specifically the Principal Associate Deputy Attorney General, look bad. While the disclosure may have served McCabe's personal interests in seeking to rebut the WSJ article on October 23 and to avoid another personally damaging WSJ story on October 30, it did so at the expense of undermining public confidence in the Department as a whole. We do not believe that Comey would have been approving of such a disclosure by McCabe if he had been told about it.

For the same reasons, we reject the suggestion that Comey simply forgot or misremembered what McCabe told him. If McCabe had told Comey that he had authorized this significant disclosure, we believe it would have surprised Comey and that Comey would have remembered it when the OIG interviewed him approximately 1 year later. Similarly, we believe the other FBI executives would have remembered it too had they been told about it.

Comey did not testify that McCabe affirmatively and explicitly denied having authorized the disclosure, but rather that McCabe "in form or fashion" led him to believe that McCabe did not know how the WSJ got the account of the PADAG call, and "definitely didn't tell [Comey] he authorized it." The FBI Offense code 2.5 (Lack of Candor—No Oath) does not require an explicit false statement to establish lack of candor. It applies to "the failure to be fully forthright, or the concealment or omission of a material fact/ information." We concluded that McCabe lacked candor in concealing from Comey his role in authorizing the disclosure to the WSJ.

### 2.   Lack of Candor in Interview under Oath with INSD Agents on May 9, 2017

We concluded that McCabe lacked candor during an INSD interview under oath on May 9, 2017, when he falsely told the agents that he had not authorized the disclosure to the WSJ and did not know who did.

Two INSD investigators [redacted] testified to the OIG that they clearly recalled McCabe telling them under oath on May 9 that he did not know who authorized the disclosure of the PADAG call to the WSJ. The agents said that they provided McCabe with a copy of the article and had him initial it, gave him an opportunity to read it, and then discussed it with him. According to the agents, McCabe told them he recalled the article, yet claimed he had "no idea where [the account of the PADAG call] came from" or "who the source was" for it. Moreover, McCabe told the agents that he had previously told others about the August 12 call with PADAG, leaving INSD SSA1 with the impression that INSD would "not [] get anywhere by asking" McCabe how many people could have known about what appeared to be a private conversation between him and PADAG. The agents' recollections are corroborated by contemporaneous notes of the May 9 interview taken by one of the agents and by the draft SSS that INSD prepared for McCabe's signature within a few days of the interview (which McCabe never signed, despite INSD's repeated efforts to get him to do so). Moreover, McCabe's denial to the INSD agents was consistent with his responses to the OIG during his audio-recorded July 28 interview. We found that these FBI employees—who had nothing to gain and everything to lose if they did anything but tell the truth regarding the interview of the then-FBI Deputy Director—accurately and truthfully recounted the details of what occurred during McCabe's May 9 interview.

By contrast, McCabe's account of this May 9 interview, which he provided to the OIG during his November 29 interview, was wholly unpersuasive. McCabe claimed that the INSD agents "must have" gotten it wrong when they wrote that he told them on May 9 that he did not authorize the conversation and that he did not know who the source was. Although McCabe said he did not believe that he denied authorizing the disclosure of the PADAG call during the interview, he could not provide any alternative account about what he actually said. Rather, McCabe stated that he could not remember what he told the INSD investigators. McCabe did not question the competence or good faith of the INSD interviewers, and also admitted that he could not explain why the investigators got the impression that McCabe had told them the WSJ article was an unauthorized leak.

However, in an apparent effort to provide an excuse for his untruthful responses to INSD, McCabe sought to portray the discussion about the October 30 article as essentially an afterthought by the agents. We found his description of the circumstances surrounding the interview to be demonstrably false. First, INSD-Section Chief flatly contradicted

McCabe's claim that, at the end of an unrelated meeting, as the agents were walking out of his office, one of them (INSD-Section Chief) pulled McCabe aside and asked him a question or two about the October 30 article. Second, INSD-SSA1's two and half pages of notes of the meeting reflected that a significant portion of the interview related specifically to the account of the PADAG call that appeared in the October 30 article. Third, the agent that took the notes (INSD-SSA1) was not the agent (INSD-Section Chief) that McCabe claimed pulled him aside. Indeed, McCabe said that INSD-SSA1 and INSD-SSA2 (who did not attend the May 9 interview) were in the hallway outside of his office when he contends that INSD-Section Chief asked him about the disclosure of the PADAG call in the October 30 article, circumstances that INSD-Section Chief denied. Fourth, McCabe acknowledged that his initials were on a copy of the October 30 article that the agents gave him to review, as reflected in INSD-SSA1's notes.

We also considered whether McCabe simply forgot that he had authorized the WSJ disclosure at the time of his May 9 INSD interview, and therefore made an honest mistake in telling INSD he did not know who did it. In three interviews under oath, including one with outside counsel, McCabe has never made this claim of a failed memory, and in any event we did not find this to be a persuasive explanation for his inaccurate statement given McCabe's other admissions.

First, McCabe acknowledged that the PADAG call was a very memorable event in McCabe's career. It involved a dramatic confrontation between McCabe and the Principal Associate Deputy Attorney General, one of the highest ranking officials in the Department. McCabe told the OIG that, despite his long career in the FBI, he had never had a conversation "like this one" with a high level Department of Justice official before or since August 12, 2016.

Second, McCabe told us this was the one and only time in his career that he authorized a disclosure to the media of an internal discussion with such a high level Department official.

Third, McCabe was deeply involved in the disclosure by Special Counsel to Barrett; this was not a fleeting event but rather one that McCabe was involved in for the entire week. McCabe learned by October 25 about Barrett's intention to write about the CF Investigation. By October 27, McCabe had authorized Special Counsel and AD/OPA to discuss the investigation with Barrett. McCabe then closely followed the progress of their discussions, including having a 51 minute call with Special Counsel on October 27 between Special Counsel's first and second calls that day with Barrett. McCabe also had conversations with Special Counsel on October 28 close in time to her call with Barrett that day. Then, on October 30, the day the article appeared, McCabe called both NY-ADIC and W-ADIC to admonish them for the leaks that appeared in the article. The next day, October 31, McCabe had a conversation with Comey about the article. Finally, on November 4, the day after another WSJ article concerning the CF Investigation, which again included information about the McCabe-PADAG call, McCabe again admonished NY-ADIC for leaks in that article.

Fourth, McCabe viewed the allegations that the WSJ reporter had told Special Counsel and AD/OPA that he would be writing about in the October 30 article as "incredibly damaging" to the credibility of the FBI, as well as an attack on his own integrity. The October 30 WSJ article challenged McCabe's leadership of the FBI directly and personally, specifically his oversight of the CF Investigation. We do not believe McCabe would have forgotten his own actions taken in connection with the publication of an article that was as memorable and personal as this one.

Fifth, McCabe acknowledged that INSD showed him the October 30 WSJ article at the outset of the discussion and gave him an opportunity to read it, and that he initialed the article and told the agents that he remembered it.

In light of the above circumstances, it seems highly implausible that McCabe forgot in May what he recalled in detail during his November OIG testimony: that he made an active choice to authorize Special Counsel and AD/OPA to disclose the PADAG call as the "best evidence" to rebut the assertion that McCabe and the FBI ordered the termination of a criminal investigation due to Department of Justice pressure. We therefore concluded that when McCabe told INSD in May that he did not know who authorized the disclosure to the WSJ, it was not due to a lack of memory. In our view, the evidence is substantial that it was done knowingly and intentionally.

For these reasons, we concluded that McCabe violated FBI Offense Code 2.6 (Lack of Candor—Under Oath) when he falsely told INSD agents on May 9, 2017, that he did not know who authorized the disclosure of the PADAG call to the WSJ.

### 3.   Lack of Candor in Interview under Oath with OIG Investigators on July 28, 2017

We concluded that McCabe lacked candor during his OIG audio-recorded interview under oath on July 28, 2017, when he falsely stated that: (a) he was not aware of Special Counsel being authorized to speak to reporters around October 30 and (b) he did not know, because he was out of town, "where [Special Counsel] was or what she was doing" during the relevant time period.

First, with regard to McCabe's claim that he was not aware of Special Counsel being authorized to speak to reporters around October 30, that claim was essentially the same false denial that McCabe made to the two INSD agents on May 9, except this time the false denial was made in an audio-recorded interview. Thus, McCabe cannot deny that he made the statement, as he has attempted to do with regard to his May 9 response to INSD agents. Instead, McCabe asserted in his November 29 OIG interview that he "misspoke" during the July 28 interview because he was surprised by the topic being raised during that interview and had not thought about the October 30 article in "quite a long time." However, McCabe was shown the article and asked questions about it less than 3 months earlier in the May 9 INSD interview. Moreover, in neither the OIG July interview nor the May 9 INSD interview did McCabe indicate that he lacked recollection or needed more time to think about the matter. As Deputy Director, McCabe well knew the significance of OIG and INSD investigations, and of the importance of being truthful when questioned under oath by agents from those Offices. Moreover, McCabe was a trained law enforcement officer with roughly 20 years of law enforcement experience. On this record, we do not credit his claim that his unequivocal denials under oath, on two occasions within 3 months of one another, were the result of being surprised by the questions.

Second, with regard to McCabe's claim that he did not know where Special Counsel was or what she was doing during the relevant time period, FBI records show that McCabe was in frequent telephone and text communication with Special Counsel during that time period and had several communications with her regarding her calls with Barrett, including a 51 minute call after her first call with Barrett and a 23 minute call after her final call with Barrett. McCabe's own text messages reflect that McCabe was keenly interested to learn about the results of Special Counsel's calls with Barrett. We therefore found that

McCabe's claimed ignorance regarding Special Counsel's activities on those days was demonstrably false.

For these reasons, we concluded that McCabe violated FBI Offense Code 2.6 (Lack of Candor—Under Oath) when he falsely told the OIG on July 28, 2017, that: (a) he was not aware of Special Counsel being authorized to talk to reporters and (b) he did not know what Special Counsel was doing at the relevant time because he was out of town. In reaching this conclusion, we took note of the fact that McCabe called the OIG 4 days later, on August 1, and indicated that he had been thinking about the questions he had been asked and believed that he may have authorized Special Counsel to work with AD/OPA and Barrett on the follow-up WSJ article. McCabe's call to the OIG on August 1 to attempt to correct his prior false testimony to the OIG was the appropriate course for him to take, and was a potentially mitigating factor in this misconduct. However, as detailed in the next section, we found that when McCabe was given the opportunity during his November 29 OIG interview to address and acknowledge his prior false statements to the INSD and the OIG, McCabe made additional false statements. Under these circumstances, we concluded that McCabe's August 1 call to the OIG does not alter our factual determination that his sworn testimony on July 28 lacked candor.

4. **Lack of Candor in Interview under Oath with OIG Investigators on November 29, 2017**

We concluded that McCabe lacked candor during an OIG interview under oath on November 29, 2017, when he falsely told the OIG in a recorded interview that: (a) he told Comey on October 31, 2016, that he (McCabe) had authorized the disclosure to the WSJ and that Comey agreed it was a "good" idea; (b) he did not deny to the INSD agents on May 9 that he had authorized the disclosure to the WSJ; and (c) the May 9 INSD interview occurred at the end of an unrelated meeting when one of the INSD agents pulled him aside and asked him one or two questions about the October 30 article.

First, with regard to his claim of having told Comey that he had authorized the disclosure, Comey stated precisely the opposite in his OIG interview, and the chronology and circumstances then existing (as described above) make it extraordinarily unlikely that McCabe did so and that Comey would simply have agreed after the fact with McCabe's disclosure and thought it was a good idea. As detailed above, the overwhelming weight of evidence supported Comey's version of the conversation and not McCabe's.

Second, with regard to McCabe's claim that he did not deny authorizing the disclosure to the WSJ during the May 9 INSD interview, as noted previously the testimony of the INSD agents, the contemporaneous notes of the interview, the draft Signed Sworn Statement prepared 3 days later, and the similar false statements made by McCabe to the OIG on July 28 wholly undercut the contention by McCabe to the OIG on November 29.

Third, as explained above in Section A.2., we found that McCabe's description of the May 9 INSD interview about the October 30 WSJ article as essentially an afterthought, involving only a question or two from one of the INSD agents as the meeting was ending, was demonstrably false.

As such, we concluded that McCabe's testimony to the OIG lacked candor and violated FBI Offense Code 2.6 (Lack of Candor—Under Oath) when he falsely testified on November 29, 2017, that: (a) he told Comey on October 31, 2016, that he (McCabe) had authorized the disclosure to the WSJ and that Comey agreed it was a "good" idea; (b) he did not deny to the INSD agents on May 9 that he had authorized the disclosure to the WSJ; and (c) the May 9 INSD interview occurred at the end of an unrelated meeting when one of the INSD agents pulled him aside and asked him one or two questions about the October 30 article.

## B. Media Policies

As the FBI's Deputy Director, McCabe was authorized to disclose the existence of the CF Investigation if the "public interest" exception found in Section 3.4 of the FBI's then-existing Policy on Media Relations applied. Similarly, the Department's U.S. Attorneys' Manual included a public interest exception to the general prohibition on disclosing information about an ongoing criminal investigation. However, we concluded that McCabe's decision to confirm the existence of the CF Investigation through an anonymously sourced quote, recounting the content of a phone call with a senior Department official in a manner designed to advance his personal interests, was clearly not within the public interest exception. We therefore concluded that McCabe's disclosure of the existence of an ongoing investigation in this manner violated the FBI's and the Department's media policy and constituted misconduct.

As an initial matter, we found entirely unpersuasive McCabe's claim to us that he did not view the disclosure to the WSJ about the PADAG call as disclosing the existence of the CF Investigation, and that therefore the FBI's prohibitions on commenting about a case did not apply. He asserted that was not the purpose of the disclosure and "there really wasn't any discussion of the case, of the merits of the case, the targets and subjects of the case, so I did not see it as a disclosure about the Clinton Foundation case." We found this explanation lacking in credibility. The sole purpose for authorizing Special Counsel's and AD/OPA's disclosure about the August 12 PADAG conversation was to make the point that McCabe had stood up to the Department so that the FBI could continue to pursue its "validly predicated" CF Investigation. The only possible conclusion that anyone could take from such a disclosure was confirmation that the FBI was conducting a CF Investigation, a fact Comey had pointedly refused to confirm in public testimony several months earlier. McCabe himself acknowledged in his OIG testimony that his authorization of the disclosure of the PADAG call "clearly creates" the effect of confirming the existence of the CF Investigation. We therefore concluded that FBI and Department policies were plainly applicable to the disclosure.

In our view, McCabe's best argument that his decision to disclose the August 12 conversation was at least arguably consistent with the public interest exception in the FBI and Department policies is that it was in the public interest for the FBI to rebut the allegation, from unnamed sources, that FBI leadership had shut down or suppressed the CF Investigation because of improper pressure from the Department. This allegation was described by the WSJ reporter to Special Counsel and AD/OPA in the October 27 call and was ultimately reported in the October 30 WSJ article and in other press accounts. However, the manner in which McCabe addressed the anonymous allegations about the FBI's and the Department's handling of the CF Investigation reflected that McCabe was motivated to defend his integrity and objectivity in relation to the CF Investigation, which had been called into question, and not to advance any public interest.

Had McCabe's primary concern actually been to reassure the public that the FBI was pursuing the CF Investigation despite the anonymous claims in the article, the way that the FBI and the Department would usually accomplish that goal is through a public statement reassuring the public that the FBI is investigating the matter. Of course, that would have required McCabe to alert Comey to the reporter's inquiry and to defer to Comey's and the Department's judgment as to whether the "public interest" exception applied and, even if it did, whether any such statement would be appropriate within days of the election. McCabe did not follow that course. Instead, McCabe, without consulting Comey, authorized disclosure of the PADAG call on background to one news organization that was directed primarily at enhancing McCabe's reputation at the expense of PADAG. Rather than reassuring the public, the disclosure led to further questions about leaks emanating from the FBI within days of an election, was part of a WSJ story that was predictably headlined, "FBI, Justice Feud in Clinton Probe," and resulted in another WSJ article on November 3.

In his testimony to the OIG, Comey disputed the notion that this disclosure was "in the best interest of the FBI." Comey acknowledged that one could argue that the disclosure shows that FBI leadership "is battling the pencil-pushing bureaucrats across the street [at Main Justice]" and "trying to do the right thing by way of the investigators in New York and Andy [McCabe] is their champion," but Comey said he "wouldn't have bought this argument" because it is outweighed by the fact that the disclosure would confirm the existence of a criminal investigation and harm FBI-DOJ relations. Likewise, FBI-GC told us that the problem with the disclosure was that "to put it bluntly, it throws DOJ under the bus," while accomplishing very little in terms of countering the narrative that the FBI was politically motivated. In FBI-GC's view, disclosure of this single conversation amounted to "a lower level effort to influence the narrative when the narrative is at a much higher level and going at a trajectory that it was not possible to change through something like this."

The FBI senior executives we interviewed suspected that this disclosure was an unauthorized leak because it disclosed a high-level conversation that appeared to serve McCabe at the expense of making DOJ look bad. As McCabe's own Chief of Staff stated:

> I just can't imagine that the Deputy would have authorized the leak. It just doesn't seem to serve, I mean, I guess it serves, it serves the purpose of the Deputy by saying, hey look, do you want us to shut this thing down? I guess it serves Andy in that way, but it really, it really highlights a dysfunction between the FBI and the, and DOJ. And to that end, it doesn't really serve the greater good.

We also found that McCabe's actions contemporaneous with the disclosure in October 2016, as well as those following it, reflected an understanding by McCabe that his authorization of the disclosure was not consistent with FBI policy. For example, on October 30 and November 4, following publication of the WSJ articles referencing his authorized disclosure about the PADAG conversation, McCabe called the NY-ADIC to complain about the CF Investigation leaks contained in those stories, without mentioning that he had authorized an anonymous disclosure rebutting the leaks and confirming the CF Investigation. Then, when questioned about the disclosure by INSD agents in May 2017, McCabe issued false denials regarding his involvement in it. Further, after it became apparent that the OIG knew about his role in the disclosure, McCabe sought to legitimize his actions by falsely claiming that he had told Comey that he authorized the disclosure and that Comey was fine with his decision.

We are mindful that McCabe was responding to anonymous, unauthorized leaks about the CF Investigation that may have originated from current or former FBI agents. However, ongoing, non-public FBI investigations are sometimes the subject of media reports, yet the FBI's official response to such reports is typically to refuse to confirm or deny the existence of the investigation, as then-Director Comey did in his July Congressional testimony. Moreover, the FBI never officially confirms the existence of an ongoing criminal investigation through an anonymously quoted source. We concluded that McCabe's decision to confirm the existence of the CF Investigation through an anonymously sourced quote in the WSJ, recounting the content of a telephone conversation between him and a Department official, served only to advance McCabe's personal interests and not the public interest, as required by FBI policy. We therefore found that his actions violated applicable FBI and Department policies and constituted misconduct.

## C. Conclusion

As detailed in this report, the OIG found that then-Deputy Director Andrew McCabe lacked candor, including under oath, on multiple occasions in connection with describing his role in connection with a disclosure to the WSJ, and that this conduct violated FBI Offense Codes 2.5 and 2.6. The OIG also concluded that McCabe's disclosure of the existence of an ongoing investigation in the manner described in this report violated the FBI's and the Department's media policy and constituted misconduct.

The OIG is issuing this report to the FBI for such action that it deems to be appropriate.

SOURCE: Department of Justice. Office of the Inspector General. "A Report of Investigation of Certain Allegations relating to Former FBI Deputy Director Andrew McCabe." April 13, 2018. https://oig.justice .gov/reports/2018/o20180413.pdf.

DOCUMENT   *President Trump on Strzok Firing*

**August 13, 2018**

Agent Peter Strzok was just fired from the FBI—finally. The list of bad players in the FBI & DOJ gets longer & longer. Based on the fact that Strzok was in charge of the Witch Hunt, will it be dropped? It is a total Hoax. No Collusion, No Obstruction—I just fight back!

SOURCE: Donald Trump (@realDonaldTrump). Twitter post. August 13, 2018. https://twitter.com/real donaldtrump/status/1029036065158557701?lang=en.

## OTHER HISTORIC DOCUMENTS OF INTEREST

### FROM PREVIOUS *HISTORIC DOCUMENTS*

# International Olympic Committee President on the Winter Olympic Games

FEBRUARY 5 AND 25, 2018

After years of escalating aggression, the 2018 Olympic Games brought a diplomatic break-through to the Korean peninsula. In January, International Olympic Committee (IOC) President Thomas Bach announced that North Korean athletes would participate in the PyeongChang 2018 Winter Games alongside South Korea as part of a unified team. With this cautiously regarded a first step on a long road to peace, South Korea's President Moon Jae-in led an effort to overcome long-standing mistrust and animosity by leveraging the Olympic Games to ease tensions. Moon referred to the Games as a "Peace Olympics" with the hope of improving relations and moving the two Koreas and their allies toward diplomacy. Ultimately, the Games were hailed as a success and would become the cornerstone of ongoing 2018 peace talks between the two Koreas.

## Sport as a Diplomatic Tool

A cease-fire suspended the Korean War in 1953, leaving the two sides still technically at war. In September 2017, as Pyongyang conducted its sixth and most powerful inter-continental ballistic missile test, and as U.S. President Donald Trump tweeted threats of military action in no abstract terms, the Korean peninsula edged toward conflict. The monolithic, unpredictable Kim dynasty has ruled the isolated and impoverished state for three generations, denying its citizens the most basic civil liberties. The regime is subject to multiple rounds of sanctions imposed by the United States and the United Nations Security Council targeting arms proliferation, missile testing, and human rights abuses.

In the years leading up to the 2018 Games, the IOC monitored the political circum-stances of holding the event just fifty miles from the heavily armed demilitarized zone, and Trump administration officials had raised doubts over American participation, citing security concerns. Among the ice rinks and bobsled tracks, underground evacuation cen-ters were constructed, underscoring how volatile and fraught the relationship had very recently been.

Despite heightened diplomatic and security concerns, sporting events have also proven to be useful diplomatic tools on the Korean peninsula, used to compliment more official diplomatic activities. The Reagan administration used the 1988 Summer Games in Seoul to launch official talks with North Korea to maneuver away from confrontation. A decade later, through South Korea's Sunshine Policy (a foreign policy strategy toward the North, focusing on rapprochement), North and South Korea marched together at various international sporting events under the Korean Unification Flag. In 2014, North and South Korea utilized the Asian Games as an opportunity to allow some family reunifications across the demilitarized zone and forestall greater conflict. At the time, those occasions were lauded as historic breakthroughs, until Pyongyang and Seoul reverted to their familiar postures of mistrust.

North Korea has also used global sporting events held in South Korea as an opportunity to attack its neighbor. In 1987, North Koreans blew up an airliner bound for South Korea shortly before it was due to host the 1988 Olympic Games in Seoul. And during the 2002 FIFA World Cup, co-hosted by South Korea and Japan, North Korea attacked a South Korean navy ship, killing six.

## NORTH KOREA TAKES STEPS TOWARD OLYMPIC PEACE

After months of defying international condemnation, reclusive North Korean dictator Kim Jong Un surprised the global community when, in his New Year's Day address, he expressed hope for a successful Olympic event and offered to send a delegation to participate. Less than three weeks later, the Olympic Korean Peninsula Declaration was announced, outlining the terms of North Korea's participation as negotiated by representatives from both countries, the PyeongChang Organizing Committee and IOC.

Moon welcomed Kim's overture but insisted that discussions must proceed alongside talks addressing his nuclear program. South Korea conducts annual joint military exercises with the United States, which Kim perceives as rehearsal for invasion and has often cited as an obstacle to dialogue. In a gesture of goodwill, these drills were delayed until the Paralympic Games concluded in March, and during this time, North Korea agreed to refrain from conducting further missile tests. A cross-border military phone line was also reestablished, and North Korea's participation in the Games set in motion the first bilateral talks since 2015. Despite the logistical challenges posed by the eleventh-hour accord, arrangements were quickly made for media, government officials, art performers, and spectators to attend, and steps were taken with the United Nations Security Council for Seoul to lift travel sanctions against North Korean officials.

Kim Yong-nam, an elderly political veteran, president of North Korea's Supreme People's Assembly, and the highest-ranking official to visit the country since 2014, led the North Korean delegation. A total of twenty-two North Korean athletes competed across disciplines including figure skating, speed skating, cross-country and alpine skiing, and a joint North–South Korean women's ice hockey team. During the opening ceremony, a unified Korean delegation entered the Olympic stadium behind the Korean Unification Flag. A traditional folk song reflecting shared cultural heritage was played instead of either national anthem. Evoking a narrative of reconciliation and the Olympic truce, their exceptional rapprochement shifted the global focus from impending conflict to the emerging possibility of meaningful dialogue.

## KIM EMBARKS ON A CHARM OFFENSIVE

Kim again surprised the international community by dispatching his sister, Kim Yo-jong, to soften his image. According to the *New York Times*, Kim Yo-jong is believed to be a deputy director of the Department of Propaganda and Agitation. She is the first member of the North Korean ruling family to cross the border since 1953 and, upon her global debut, was called by South Korean media "North Korea's Ivanka," likening her influence and stature to President Trump's daughter. In an unprecedented and unexpected display of unity, Moon shook hands with Kim Yong-nam and Kim Yo-jong, who invited South Korea to an official summit in Pyongyang following the Games.

The American delegation, led by Vice President Mike Pence, aimed to lessen the propaganda opportunity for North Korea while reminding the public and other foreign leaders of the administration's position. To that end, Pence skipped a dinner hosted by Moon where he was to be seated across from North Korea's head of state. He briefly exchanged greetings with Moon and close ally Japanese Prime Minister Shinzo Abe before leaving but avoided Kim Yong-nam and Kim Yo-jong. Speaking to reporters in Japan before the event, Pence warned that Kim would try to co-opt the media attention and narrative, using imagery of the Games while hiding "behind the Olympic banner the reality that they enslave their people and threaten the wider region." By avoiding a handshake, Pence and the Trump administration believed they could avert publicity that would have played to North Korea's benefit. Pence, who was with leaders of the North and South Korean delegations during the opening ceremony, remained seated while those around him stood for the joint Korean team.

## SKEPTICISM AMONG INTERNATIONAL COMMUNITY SURROUNDS NORTH KOREA'S PARTICIPATION

The response of the South Korean people to the North's inclusion in the Games was frosty. Many felt that Moon used the Olympics for diplomatic expediency, and conservatives who would prefer a tougher stance on the North called the Games the "Pyongyang Olympics," referencing North Korea's capital city. Moon's popularity also fell among young voters, who tend to be globally minded and economically well off. While the North is subject to heavy sanctions, the democratic South has grown into the world's eleventh-largest economy following a concerted postwar recovery effort. Many young South Koreans are opposed to reunification, since they do not readily identify with their northern counterparts and are not willing to undertake the economic sacrifice. As the son of North Korean refugees, Moon favors engagement and strongly encouraged North Korea's participation in the Games but appeared to understand that he is likely to be the last president with personal ties across the thirty-eighth parallel and warned that if North Korea's participation in the Winter Olympics does not lead to more talks, "it will not be easy to find another occasion for a dialogue."

Kim's overtures were largely viewed as an appeal to Moon's value of diplomacy, and the pursuit of concessions on sanctions in exchange for increased communication. Moon's temperate tone was increasingly at odds with the Trump administration's confrontational approach to foreign policy, and Kim, constrained by the need to appear powerful to foreign leaders, played on tensions between the two allies. Over the course of the Games, the United States pivoted from expressing openness to diplomacy to repeating threats of military force. The PyeongChang Games created space for unofficial, nonstructured interaction, and Kim recognized the opportunity to adjust his image abroad, broach negotiations while not giving in to international pressure, and push a narrative of strength at home.

Much of the international community remained skeptical about Kim's intentions to move toward denuclearization. Implied in his rhetoric was a willingness to engage with others, including the United States, conditional on their acceptance of North Korea as a nuclear state. But the United States maintained that it would not enter any serious negotiations or ease sanctions without a commitment to disarmament. In a meeting with Senior White House Adviser Ivanka Trump, who attended the closing ceremony, Moon emphasized the need to improve ties "in parallel" with efforts to denuclearize the North and pushed for United States–North Korea talks. But the Trump administration announced further sanctions against North Korea and expressed frustration that Moon was "working at cross-purposes" with its efforts to further isolate and pressure North Korea to give up its nuclear program.

Moon, however, remained committed to the peace process started at the Games. In September, Moon addressed the 73rd Session of the United Nations General Assembly, noting, "The Olympic truce resolution adopted at the UN General Assembly in November 2017 came to precious fruition. . . . The Republic of Korea will spare no effort to guide North Korea towards that path." While it may not have caused goodwill so much as it reflected political objectives, North Korea's intentions to participate in the next two Olympic Games in Japan and China and its interest in a joint 2032 host bid suggest potential for lasting developments.

### PyeongChang Olympics Hailed as a Success

The Winter Olympics in PyeongChang, held from February 9 to February 25, included nearly 3,000 athletes from ninety-two countries who participated in 102 events. Four new events were included, including big-air snowboarding, mass-start speed skating, mixed team alpine skiing, and mixed doubles curling. The Winter Games also featured participants from six new countries: Ecuador, Eritrea, Kosovo, Malaysia, Nigeria, and Singapore, nations that typically only field Summer Olympic teams.

Bach called the Games a "new beginning on the Korean Peninsula" that "brought real hope for a brighter future for everyone." He also celebrated the ability of technology to allow greater viewership of the Games than ever before, and the record number of nations participating. "Therefore," Bach said, "the Olympic Winter Games PyeongChang 2018 are the Games of New Horizons. We are embracing these new horizons. We offer our hand to everybody to join forces in this faith in the future."

—Megan Howes

*Following are the text of the remarks made by International Olympic Committee President Thomas Bach upon the opening of the 132nd Olympic Games in PyeongChang on February 5, 2018; and the text of remarks by Bach on February 25, 2018, reflecting on the event at the closing ceremony.*

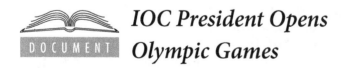

## IOC President Opens
## Olympic Games

**February 5, 2018**

*[The opening of Bach's remarks, delivered in French, has been omitted.]*

The Olympic Winter Games PyeongChang 2018 have allowed another new beginning on the Korean Peninsula. They have opened the door for a peaceful dialogue between the Republic of Korea and the Democratic People's Republic of Korea. The Olympic spirit has brought two sides together that for too long were divided by mistrust and animosity. The Olympic spirit has brought real hope for a brighter future for everyone on the Korean Peninsula. The Olympic spirit has brought us all together in mutual respect and understanding.

Your Excellency, President Moon, you deserve our thanks for your faith in this Olympic spirit.

It was a long and difficult journey. With regard to the athletes from the NOC of the DPRK, in 2014, the IOC started a special programme to support them in the qualification process. At the same time we started addressing the special political situation of having the Olympic Winter Games on the Korean peninsula. For this purpose, we began preliminary talks at the highest level of government with different partners to explore the political implications. Since then, we have maintained and reinforced these contacts with all sides, in particular during the most difficult phases of political tensions. As I reported to you at our last session in Lima, we have held many discussions, always promoting a solution by dialogue and diplomacy. In all the conversations we had, the Olympic Winter Games PyeongChang 2018 were never put in doubt. On the contrary, we could always feel support. All the leaders gave us confidence in the Games, which allowed us to proceed with the preparations. Despite the sometimes worrying political circumstances, we were always standing at the side of our Korean hosts, and never talked of a Plan B.

All these efforts finally led to the "Olympic Korean Peninsula Declaration" on January 20th, at the IOC in Lausanne. On this day, the IOC took a number of exceptional decisions. As a result, we will see 22 athletes from the NOC of DPRK participate in these Olympic Winter Games. Together with athletes from the NOC of the Republic of Korea, they will march as one team, behind one flag, at the Opening Ceremony, and form a unified team in ice hockey. Coming myself from, and having competed for, a formerly divided country, I am looking forward to this with great anticipation and great emotion.

Two years ago in Rio de Janeiro, with the first ever Refugee Olympic Team, the IOC sent a message of hope to the world. Now in PyeongChang, by marching together behind one flag, the athletes from the teams of the ROK and DPRK, will send a powerful message of peace to the world.

My thanks go to the leaders of the delegations from the NOCs of the ROK and DPRK, and to the governments of the ROK and DPRK who paved the way.

This initiative gives all parties the chance to reflect on what the future could look like, if we were all guided by this Olympic spirit.

But Korea's journey does not end here. The political tensions will not disappear overnight. Sport cannot create peace, but the Olympic Games can open the way with powerful symbols. It is our fervent wish for the Korean people, and indeed for the whole world, that this dialogue which has only just begun, will continue. It is my hope that all the political parties involved will also be inspired by this Olympic Spirit of respect and understanding, demonstrated by the athletes.

The Olympic Value of excellence is clearly shown in the organisation of these Olympic Winter Games. Here again, President Moon, you played—and play—an instrumental and essential role from the first day of your mandate. You supported and promoted these Games, making them your project. You even spent your first official holiday here in PyeongChang: this was indeed a powerful way of showing your commitment. And I know that in this way, you inspired the Korean people and in particular, the PyeongChang 2018 Organising Committee, under the able leadership of President Lee Hee-beom.

President Lee, we are aware that when you took office, you had many challenges to overcome. You have risen to those challenges in a most dynamic and efficient way. For this reason, I would like to personally thank you very much for your determination and commitment. Through the efforts of our Korean partners and friends we can confidently say today: it is time for PyeongChang. In the meantime, you have got to know me well. So it will not come as a surprise to you when, at the beginning of the Games, I say it is too early for congratulations. But I am extremely confident that I will be able to warmly congratulate the PyeongChang Organising Committee and the Korean people on the occasion of the closing ceremony. Already now I congratulate you on an Olympic record, with 92 National Olympic Committees participating—6 of them for the very first time.

All this would not have been possible without the great work of our Coordination Commission. Therefore I would like to thank very warmly our dear colleague and friend Mrs Gunilla Lindberg and all her colleagues. I would also like to thank the International Winter Sports Federations for their great help and cooperation in delivering these Games, and in particular their chair, Gian-Franco Kasper.

The Olympic Winter Games PyeongChang 2018 give the Olympic Movement the best start to look ahead with confidence and optimism. This year, there will be many occasions, when we will see the reforms of our Olympic Agenda 2020 come to fruition.

One important reform is to strengthen the WADA-led worldwide anti-doping system. Initiated by the IOC, the newly established International Testing Agency will soon be operational. We are proud that with the establishment of the ITA, we have opened a new chapter in the fight against doping.

In addition, for the very first time at Olympic Games, both testing and sanctioning will be independent of the IOC. In today's world, it is more important than ever before to avoid even the perception of a conflict of interest. Making testing and sanctioning independent from sport organisations and national interests is therefore a vital step in that direction. This is why we call on all International Federations and major sports organisers to follow our lead.

On 5 December 2017, the IOC had to sanction the systemic manipulation of the anti-doping system in Russia, as established by the Schmid Commission. This was an unprecedented attack on the integrity of the Olympic Games. This is why the Executive Board reacted with the toughest sanction for an NOC: the suspension from the Olympic Games. There will be no Russian flag and no Russian anthem here in PyeongChang. There will be no officials from the Russian Ministry of Sport. The deputy Prime Minister and the then Deputy Minister of Sport have been excluded from any participation in all future Olympic Games for life.

On the other hand, we had to uphold the principle of individual justice to which every human being is entitled. This is why we created a pathway for clean, individual Russian athletes to compete in PyeongChang, but only under the strictest conditions. They were under the scrutiny of an independent panel, which had to establish that there is no doubt about their integrity.

Furthermore, they underwent 50 per cent more tests than the next highest NOC. As a result, three out of four of those invited athletes did not compete at Sochi.

We applied the same strict procedure after the extremely disappointing CAS decisions upholding a number of appeals. The privilege to be invited requires more than just the absence of a sanction. So we have not invited them.

In this way we want to do justice to all athletes, regardless of their passport. The invited clean Russian athletes can be ambassadors of a new generation. They can be the new role models for a change of culture in Russian sports. They can demonstrate to their fellow athletes that if you're clean you are rewarded, and not punished for the rule violations of others. Now it is up to Russia whether they want to be welcomed back to the Olympic Movement. Our Implementation Group will closely monitor the situation, and make a recommendation to the IOC Executive Board at the end of the Olympic Games.

This important issue goes to the heart of fair play, and we will discuss it fully tomorrow during our Session.

I would like to pay tribute to all those who have worked so hard on these complex issues, IOC Executive Board member Denis Oswald, former President of Switzerland, Samuel Schmid, former minister of sport of France, Valérie Fourneyron, IOC Executive Board member Nicole Hoeverts. Each of them has worked together with dedicated colleagues to ensure the protection of clean athletes, and I would like to express our gratitude to all of them.

Later this year, we will see the transformation of the concept for the Youth Olympic Games—another reform of Olympic Agenda 2020 coming to fruition. At the Youth Olympic Games Buenos Aires 2018, we will experience this new format, making the YOG more youthful, more urban, more inclusive and more female. It will be the first Olympic programme with complete gender equality, the same number of girls and boys taking part in the same number of sport events. In Buenos Aires, the population will not be invited just to watch but to be part of the Games. This will be demonstrated with the Opening Ceremony taking place in the heart of the city, rather than in a stadium, and by many other inclusive sports activities. With this new YOG concept, in Buenos Aires we are taking sport to where the people are, instead of waiting for the people to come to sport. All the elements are in place for the YOG Buenos Aires 2018 to showcase the first Youth Olympic Games of a new era.

Another direct result of our Agenda reforms will be the very first "Olympism in Action" Forum. This will also take place in Buenos Aires, just before the YOG. This Forum will bring together a community of 2,000 stakeholders from the Olympic Movement, business, politics and civil society to discuss the most important topics for the future of sport. Together with our stakeholders, benefiting from the involvement of many young athletes, we will discuss the role of sport in today's society. We will cover a wide range of subjects including education and health, the future of the Olympic Games, anti-doping, good governance, digitalisation and esports.

Speaking of e-sports, we know that we do not have the solution yet. What we can say is that the intensity that competitive "e-Sports" players show in their preparation and training is comparable to that you will find among athletes in traditional sports. This however is not the only point to be taken into consideration. The IOC is a values-based organisation. Therefore it is fundamental that we do not give recognition to an activity which infringes on our Olympic Values. There can be no place for those video games which are about killing, which glorify violence or which promote discrimination. We are looking forward to a pretty lively debate in Buenos Aires! And I guess our Korean friends will play a major role in this; e-sports being popular here.

The creation of the Olympic Channel is the most visible result of our efforts to engage with youth. So far it has been a great success, already reaching more than 1.2 billion video views, with 85 per cent of those engaging with Olympic Channel content on social media below the age of 35. (So our generation!) The channel promises to be even more successful this year. Its new cooperation deal with Snapchat will reach the perfect demographic. New projects will make the channel even more interactive, and it will benefit from the Olympic Winter Games and from the live coverage of the Youth Olympic Games.

Another journey we are on is to the Olympic Winter Games 2026. There, you the IOC members, have reformed substantially the candidature process just recently. Because of this, we are confident that we can better address the special challenges we have concerning the Olympic Winter Games: to name just a few—geographic conditions, climate change and ways of political decision-making, with a lack of confidence in the future in a number of western countries.

At this moment, we are in the non-committal dialogue phase with a number of cities and NOCs from three continents. By concentrating on quality rather than quantity of the candidatures, we can be confident that at the next IOC Session in Buenos Aires, we will be able to formally appoint candidate cities promising excellent Olympic Winter Games 2026. These candidates will benefit from our new approach to the organisation of the Olympic Games, offering the potential of savings of five hundred million dollars for the Olympic Winter Games, and one billion dollars for the Games of the Olympiad.

As you can see, we have a full agenda this year. We can tackle this agenda with great anticipation and with confidence.

In an otherwise extremely fragile world, despite all the challenges we face, we are still an anchor of stability.

Let us all spread this positive message. Let us all promote the unifying power of this, our Olympic spirit.

SOURCE: International Olympic Committee. "Opening Ceremony of the IOC Session." February 5, 2018. https://stillmed.olympic.org/media/Document%20Library/OlympicOrg/News/2018/02/2018-02-05-IOC-Session-Opening-Ceremony-Speech-President-Bach.pdf.

# IOC President Remarks on the Closing of the 2018 Winter Olympic Games

**February 25, 2018**

Congratulations, PyeongChang!

Dear Olympic friends around the world,

Your Excellency, Moon Jae-in, President of the Republic of Korea,

Dear President of POCOG, Lee Heebeom,

Excellencies,

Dear athletes,

Dear members of the Olympic family,

Ladies and gentlemen.

Over the past 17 days, we have experienced Olympic Games rooted in tradition and showing the way to the future.

They have proved true the words of our founder, Pierre de Coubertin, when he said the Olympic Games are a homage to the past and an act of faith in the future.

A true homage to the past was the respect of the Olympic Truce, just as it was three thousand years ago in ancient Olympia.

Dear athletes from the NOCs of the Republic of Korea and the Democratic People's Republic of Korea, with your joint march, you have shared your faith in a peaceful future with all of us.

You have shown how sport brings people together in our fragile world; you have shown how sport builds bridges. The IOC will continue this Olympic dialogue, even after we extinguish the Olympic flame.

In this, we are driven by our faith in the future.

These Olympic Winter Games have introduced new events that appeal to new generations.

Digital technology has enabled more people in more countries to see winter sports in more ways.

We have brought together a record number of National Olympic Committees to participate in Olympic Winter Games.

Therefore I can truly say: the Olympic Winter Games PyeongChang 2018 are the Games of New Horizons.

We are embracing these new horizons. We offer our hand to everybody to join forces in this faith in the future.

Dear athletes, you are the best ambassadors of our optimism. Thank you for sharing it with us. Thank you for your competitive spirit. Thank you for your fair play.

To the organisers of the Olympic Winter Games PyeongChang 2018, I say: thank you from the bottom of my heart. I congratulate you for showing us new horizons.

For your contributions, I thank the International Winter Sports Federations, the participating National Olympic Committees, our sponsors, and the television rights holders.

To the President of the Republic of Korea, Your Excellency Moon Jae-in, I say thank you for your personal commitment and determination to make these Games so successful in every way.

To the volunteers, I say a special thank you for warming our hearts even in the coldest temperatures.

Volunteers, Thank you for your dedication.

To our gracious hosts, the people of Korea, I say: thank you.

Athletes from the five continents of the world and future host countries of the Olympic Games would like to join in this thanks.

*Martin Fourcade, Nao Kodaira, Seun Adigun, Yun Sungbin, Ryom Tae-ok, Lindsey Vonn, Liu Jiayu, Pita Taufatofua*

Welcome . . . Together we would like to express our gratitude, with the typical Korean gesture of a heart, which we have appreciated so much during these Games.

And now it is my obligation to declare the Olympic Winter Games PyeongChang 2018 closed.

In accordance with tradition, I call upon the youth of the world to assemble four years from now in Beijing, People's Republic of China, to celebrate with all of us, the 24th Olympic Winter Games.

SOURCE: International Olympic Committee. "Closing Ceremony of the Olympic Winter Games PyeongChang 2018." February 25, 2018. https://stillmed.olympic.org/media/Document%20Library/ OlympicOrg/News/2018/02/closing-ceremony/President-speech-PyeongChang-2018-Closing- Ceremony.pdf.

# OTHER HISTORIC DOCUMENTS OF INTEREST

**FROM THIS VOLUME**

- North and South Korean Leaders Issue Declaration for Peace, p. 260
- President Trump, Chairman Kim Remark on Historic Summit, p. 347

**FROM PREVIOUS *HISTORIC DOCUMENTS***

- United Nations and United States Issue Sanctions against North Korea, *2017*, p. 169
- United Nations Report on North Korea's Human Rights Abuses, *2014*, p. 49

# Administration Officials Respond to Leadership Changes in Trump White House

FEBRUARY 8, MARCH 13, JULY 5, OCTOBER 3, NOVEMBER 7, AND DECEMBER 15, 2018

Within the first eight months of his presidency, Donald Trump fired or accepted the resignations of fourteen cabinet-level officials and senior White House staff. This significant turnover continued throughout 2018 with the departure of Secretary of State Rex Tillerson, Environmental Protection Agency (EPA) Administrator Scott Pruitt, Veterans Affairs Secretary David Shulkin, Interior Secretary Ryan Zinke, and U.S. Ambassador to the United Nations Nikki Haley. Attorney General Jeff Sessions, White House Chief of Staff John Kelly, and White House Staff Secretary Rob Porter were also among the top officials who left the administration.

## DOMESTIC VIOLENCE ALLEGATIONS PROMPT PORTER'S RESIGNATION

Porter's resignation was among the administration's first personnel changes in 2018. As the staff secretary for Trump, Porter helped manage the flow of information to the president, particularly news clips and briefing books. As he was well liked by Trump and other senior staff, Porter's responsibilities quickly grew beyond the typical staff secretary role to include opportunities such as helping draft the 2018 State of the Union address and attending the World Economic Forum.

Porter's rising star was tarnished in early February after *The Daily Mail* reported allegations by his ex-wives that Porter had verbally and physically abused them. The report revealed Porter's second wife had obtained a protective order against him in 2010 after he violated a private separation agreement and refused to leave her apartment until she called the police. A subsequent report from *The Intercept* included photos of Porter's first wife with a black eye, which she claimed Porter gave her.

Porter decried the allegations as "outrageous," claiming that he took the photos of his first wife and that "the reality behind them is nowhere close to what is being described." He added, "I have been transparent and truthful about these vile claims, but I will not further engage publicly with a coordinated smear campaign." The White House initially defended Porter, saying that "the president and chief of staff have full confidence in his abilities and his performance." Chief of Staff John Kelly described Porter as "a man of true integrity and honor." However, the administration reversed course once the photos were released. "There is no place for domestic violence in our society," Kelly said.

Porter resigned on February 7. Reports quickly circulated that Kelly knew about the 2010 protective order against Porter and that this issue had prevented Porter from obtaining full security clearance. Speaking to reporters on February 8, Deputy Press Secretary Raj Shah said Porter had been "operating on an interim security clearance" and that his "background investigation was ongoing" at the time of his resignation. The White House claimed that, due to the ongoing nature of the investigation, a final report of findings had not been submitted, and thus senior staff were not aware of the allegations. "The background check investigates both the allegations and the denials," Shah said. "The investigation does not stop when allegations come to light." Porter was succeeded by Deputy Staff Secretary Derek Lyons.

## TRUMP FIRES TILLERSON OVER POLICY DISAGREEMENTS

On March 13, Trump announced via Twitter that he had fired Tillerson and would be nominating CIA Director Mike Pompeo to become the next secretary of state. The president reportedly called Tillerson several hours later to give him the news.

Tensions between Trump and Tillerson had been brewing for months, due in part to ongoing policy disagreements. Tillerson supported the nuclear deal with Iran and pushed Trump to certify the agreement in the summer of 2017, though Trump had described it as "the worst deal ever." Tillerson also wanted the United States to remain in the Paris Agreement, but Trump withdrew from the deal. When it came to addressing the nuclear threat posed by North Korea, Tillerson favored dialogue, while Trump warned of military action. This was also an instance in which Trump seemed to publicly undercut his secretary of state: following reports that Tillerson was pursuing talks with North Korea, Trump tweeted that he was "wasting his time trying to negotiate with Little Rocket Man."

Also, in October 2017, NBC News reported that Tillerson called Trump a "moron" during a meeting with cabinet officials, in response to a controversial political speech Trump gave to the Boy Scouts of America in July. Tillerson called an unprecedented press conference to address the issue, though he declined to directly confirm or deny calling the president a moron. While the incident reportedly exacerbated tensions between the two, Trump publicly brushed it off as "fake news," and administration officials said there was no talk of Tillerson's resignation at that point.

Explaining his decision to let Tillerson go, Trump said, "We were not really thinking the same. With Mike Pompeo, we have a similar thought process." Trump said he respected Tillerson's "intellect" and got along well with him, but "Rex will be much happier now." Reports indicated that Trump wanted to have a new secretary of state in place before his meeting with North Korean leader Kim Jong Un, planned for May.

Tillerson declined to thank or even mention Trump in his farewell address to the State Department on March 13, instead thanking agency staff "for the privilege of serving beside you for the last 14 months." Tillerson acknowledged the State Department's close working relationship with the Defense Department and the two agencies' agreement that "U.S. leadership starts with diplomacy." He also highlighted several key State Department accomplishments, including North Korea's agreement to nuclear talks, while acknowledging that "much remains to be done to achieve our mission on behalf of the American people with allies and with partners."

Deputy Secretary of State John Sullivan assumed Tillerson's responsibilities until Pompeo was confirmed by the Senate on April 26. Pompeo faced strong opposition from most Democrats due to his hawkish foreign policy views, and from Sen. Rand Paul, R-Ky., because of his support for the Iraq War and enhanced interrogation techniques. However, Paul declared his support for Pompeo after the administration said the Iraq War was a mistake and the United States should wind down its presence in Afghanistan, and six Democrats facing tough reelection challenges in the midterms joined with Republicans to approve Pompeo's nomination.

## Veterans Affairs Secretary Ousted

David Shulkin, secretary for the U.S. Department of Veterans Affairs (VA), was the next cabinet member to go, but whether he resigned or was fired remains unclear. The White House claims Shulkin resigned, but Shulkin insists he was fired, stating Kelly called to tell him he was being relieved and that he was not asked to submit a letter of resignation. Several news reports also suggested Shulkin was not given a chance to return to his office or deliver a farewell address to VA employees. His departure was officially announced by Trump on March 28. "I appreciate the work of Dr. David Shulkin and the many great things we did together at Veterans Affairs, including the VA Accountability Act that he was helpful in getting passed," Trump said in a statement. "He has been a great supporter of veterans across the country and I am grateful for his service."

Shulkin's early accomplishments at the VA—which included expanding the G.I. Bill to cover veterans of the War on Terror, streamlining the disability benefits appeal process, and pushing for legislation that made it easier for the department to fire employees with poor performance—earned him praise from Trump, but an internal power struggle and an ethics investigation caused trouble for the secretary in 2018. In February, the VA inspector general released a report finding Shulkin spent most of his time sightseeing while on a taxpayer-funded trip to Europe in 2017 and improperly accepted tickets to the Wimbledon tennis championship as a gift. Shulkin repaid the department for the trip but also warned about officials "trying to undermine the department from within," a reference to senior VA staff who wanted to privatize veterans' health care—a move Shulkin generally opposed. "I do believe that there were no ethical violations here, that this was being used in a political context to exploit the situation," Shulkin said. "And I do believe that the issue at hand is the future of VA and whether it's going to be privatized or not."

To replace Shulkin, Trump nominated Adm. Ronny Jackson, the White House physician. Notably, Trump bypassed Deputy Secretary for Veterans Affairs Thomas Bowman to name Robert Wilkie, the under secretary of defense for personnel and readiness, as acting secretary. Bowman has, along with Shulkin, opposed efforts to privatize the VA. Jackson ultimately withdrew his nomination amid allegations that he fostered a hostile work environment and behaved improperly while leading the White House Medical Unit. Jackson said the allegations were "baseless and anonymous attacks on my character and integrity." Trump subsequently nominated Wilkie to the secretary's post. Wilkie's nomination was generally uncontested, and he was confirmed by the Senate in July.

## Plagued by Ethics Scandals, Pruitt Resigns

Controversy had surrounded EPA Administrator Scott Pruitt since his nomination, with Democrats strongly opposed to the selection of a former state attorney general who had earned a reputation for suing the EPA. Pruitt also oversaw an aggressive rollback of President Barack Obama's environmental policies, garnering further criticism from Democrats and conservation groups. The controversy only grew as Pruitt became the subject of an ever-expanding list of federal investigations into alleged legal and ethical violations. These allegations included a potential violation of federal gift rules. In 2017, Pruitt paid only $50 a night to live in a condo co-owned by the wife of an energy lobbyist who sought assistance from the EPA that same year. Pruitt also faced scrutiny for meeting with industry groups including the National Mining Association and encouraging them to push the administration for certain policies. Another inquiry focused on the management and payment of

Pruitt's twenty-four-hour security detail. The team of at least twenty people was more than three times the size of previous administrators' details, and Pruitt's team was paid more than double what their predecessors had been. Additionally, the Government Accountability Office found that Pruitt and the EPA broke federal law with the $43,000 purchase and installation of a soundproof phone booth for the secretary. (The EPA is required to notify Congress before spending more than $5,000 on office equipment.) Republicans began to join Democrats in turning against Pruitt—with some even calling for his resignation—and lawmakers grilled him on various allegations during budget hearings before Congress.

Pruitt submitted his letter of resignation to Trump on July 5, writing that it was "extremely difficult for me to cease serving you in this role first because I count it a blessing to be serving you in any capacity, but also, because of the transformative work that is occurring." Pruitt heaped praise on Trump for his "courage, steadfastness and resolute commitment to get results for the American people" and said he believed Trump was president "because of God's providence." Trump later tweeted that Pruitt had done "an outstanding job" and said Andrew Wheeler, Pruitt's deputy, would serve as acting EPA administrator. Wheeler remains interim administrator at the time of writing. At least five inquiries into Pruitt's conduct are ongoing, according to the EPA inspector general.

## Haley Departs on Friendly Terms

Notable administration departures continued into the fall with the October 9 announcement that Haley would step down as U.S. ambassador to the United Nations at the end of 2018. "It has been an immense honor to serve our country in your Administration," Haley wrote in her letter of resignation. "We stood strong for American values and interests, always placing America first. I am proud of our record." Trump praised Haley, saying that she had done an "incredible job" and could have her pick of jobs if she decided to return to the administration in the future. UN Secretary-General Antonio Guterres thanked Haley for her "excellent cooperation and support," noting the two had "a very productive and strong working relationship."

Haley explained that she was leaving her position because she had accomplished her goals and wanted to return to the private sector. She also declared she did not intend to run for president in 2020, instead pledging to support Trump's reelection. Washington insiders observed that Haley managed to leave the administration with her reputation and relationship with Trump intact, unlike many of her departed colleagues.

On December 7, Trump announced his intention to nominate State Department spokeswoman Heather Nauert to replace Haley. Nauert previously anchored Fox News' *Fox & Friends* program and was praised by Trump as "very talented, very smart, very quick."

## Trump Requests Embattled Attorney General's Resignation

After criticizing his attorney general for more than a year, Trump requested Sessions's resignation on November 7. Sessions complied later that day. "I came to work at the Department of Justice every day determined to do my duty and serve my country," Sessions wrote. "I have done so to the best of my ability to support the fundamental legal processes that are the foundation of justice."

Tensions between Trump and Sessions formed early, after Sessions recused himself from the U.S. Department of Justice's investigation into Russia's alleged meddling in the 2016 election. This paved the way for former Federal Bureau of Investigation (FBI) director Robert Mueller's appointment as special counsel to lead the investigation. Sessions recused himself because he had failed to disclose election-year meetings with Russian Ambassador Sergey Kislyak. Trump repeatedly lashed out at Sessions in tweets, press conferences, and interviews as the Mueller probe progressed, stating in one instance that he would have nominated someone else to be attorney general if he had known Sessions was going to recuse himself. Trump also criticized Sessions for not investigating "crooked Hillary."

The president's consistent criticism of Sessions prompted concerns that Trump was hoping to push the attorney general out of office in order to gain control over the Russia investigation, which he has called a "witch hunt." Democratic leaders including Sen. Chuck Schumer, D-N.Y., and House Minority Leader Nancy Pelosi, D-Calif., said they found the timing of Sessions's resignation amid suspect and characterized it as an effort to derail Mueller's investigation. Democrats also called for Matthew Whitaker, Sessions's chief of staff and Trump's pick for acting attorney general, to recuse himself from the Russia probe. Whitaker had previously called for Deputy Attorney General Rod Rosenstein to "limit the scope" of the investigation.

Trump nominated William Barr to become the next attorney general. Barr previously served as attorney general under former president George H. W. Bush from 1991 to 1993. Senate Democrats challenged Barr's nomination, but he was ultimately confirmed by the Senate on February 14, 2019, by a vote of 54–48.

## CHIEF OF STAFF TO STEP DOWN

After months of rumors that the change was coming, Trump announced on December 8 that White House Chief of Staff John Kelly would be stepping down by the end of the year. A retired four-star Marine Corps general, Kelly was brought on as chief of staff in July 2017—after briefly serving as Trump's first secretary of the Department of Homeland Security—to help bring order to a White House that was widely reported to be chaotic and to guide a staff with relatively little government experience. However, the president reportedly chafed at Kelly's efforts to restrict access to the president and some of his personnel decisions, while Kelly complained about Trump circumventing the chain of command by taking meetings and making decisions without his knowledge. Both men regularly—and sometimes publicly—expressed unhappiness with their relationship, although administration officials confirmed in July that Kelly had agreed to stay on as chief of staff through the 2020 election.

Nick Ayers, Pence's chief of staff, was widely reported to be Trump's top pick to replace Kelly. However, on December 9, Ayers announced via Twitter that he intended to leave the White House at the end of the year. After several days of media speculation about other candidates for the position, Trump announced on December 14 that Office of Management and Budget (OMB) director Mick Mulvaney would become his acting chief of staff. Administration officials did not offer an explanation for Mulvaney's "acting" title, nor did they indicate how long he was expected to serve as chief of staff. OMB deputy director Russ Vought has since assumed temporary responsibility for overseeing the office's day-to-day operations.

## ZINKE PRESSURED TO LEAVE AMID ETHICS INVESTIGATIONS

On December 15, Interior Secretary Ryan Zinke became the fourth Cabinet-level official to leave the administration due to alleged ethics violations. Media reports indicated that administration officials had pressured Zinke to resign for weeks, warning that if he did not step down by the end of the year, he would be fired.

According to Citizens for Responsibility and Ethics in Washington, D.C., Zinke had been the subject of eighteen different ethics investigations since he took office, some of which cleared the secretary of misconduct. The primary investigation centered on Zinke's involvement in a land development deal in his hometown of Whitefish, Montana. Some of the land owned by a foundation associated with Zinke and his wife, who was the group's president, would be developed as part of the deal; the Zinkes also owned property adjacent to the development that stood to increase in value once the project was complete. The deal was backed by the chairman of Halliburton, an oil field services firm directly affected by the Interior Department's policies regarding oil and gas drilling and energy production prospecting on public lands and in federal waters. Zinke reportedly remained involved in discussions about the deal after becoming secretary, prompting the Interior Department's inspector general to open an investigation into possible conflicts of interest. (As secretary, Zinke opened more federal lands and waters for oil and gas exploration.) The investigation was referred to the Justice Department in October, suggesting federal officials may consider criminal charges against Zinke. Other issues under investigation included Zinke's rejection of two proposed tribal casino projects in Connecticut due to pressure from MGM Resorts International lobbyists, his violation of Interior Department policies by allowing his wife to ride in government vehicles, and his alleged censorship of a National Park Service report to remove mentions of humans' role in climate change.

In his resignation letter, Zinke decried "vicious and politically motivated attacks" against him, declaring they had "created an unfortunate distraction" from the department's mission. On Twitter, Zinke said he was "incredibly proud of all the good work [the president and I] accomplished together" but that he could not "justify spending thousands of dollars defending myself and my family against false allegations." Trump thanked Zinke for his service, saying he "has accomplished much during his tenure." Zinke's deputy, David Bernhardt, was named acting secretary.

—Linda Grimm

*Following are excerpts from a press briefing conducted by Deputy Press Secretary Raj Shah on February 8, 2018, during which Shah made a statement and answered questions about Rob Porter's resignation; a tweet from President Donald Trump on March 13, 2018, announcing Secretary of State Rex Tillerson's resignation and replacement; farewell remarks made by Tillerson on March 13, 2018; EPA Administrator Scott Pruitt's resignation letter, dated July 5, 2018; U.S. Ambassador to the UN Nikki Haley's resignation letter, submitted on October 3, 2018; Attorney General Jeff Sessions's resignation letter from November 7, 2018; and a December 15, 2018, tweet from Trump announcing Interior Secretary Ryan Zinke's resignation and Zinke's response.*

# Deputy Press Secretary Raj Shah Answers Questions about Porter Resignation

**February 8, 2018**

MR. SHAH: Good afternoon, everyone. I want to start with a statement, and then we'll take your questions.

Our normal policy, consistent with the policies of past administrations, is to not comment on background checks and security clearances. Given the unusual nature of these circumstances and a number of false reports floating around, we wanted to try to explain as best that we can, within our security limitations, how the background investigation process works, and then talk a little bit about Rob Porter and how his situation fits within that process. . . .

. . . The allegations made against Rob Porter, as we understand them, involve incidents long before he joined the White House. Therefore, they are best evaluated through the background check process.

It's important to remember that Rob Porter has repeatedly denied these allegations, and done so publicly. That doesn't change how serious and disturbing these allegations are. They're upsetting. And the background check investigates both the allegations and the denials. The investigation does not stop when allegations comes [sic] to light. It continues to determine the truth.

We should not short-circuit an investigation just because allegations are made, unless they could compromise national security or interfere with operations at the White House. The truth must be determined.

And that was what was going on with Rob Porter. His background investigation was ongoing. He was operating on an interim security clearance. His clearance was never denied, and he resigned. . . .

During his time at the White House, Rob received no waivers and no special treatment. And this is the tried and true process. It was followed meticulously.

We hope this helps explain how seriously these matters are taken and how the process works to investigate such allegations.

With that, I'll take your questions.

Q Can you tell us, Raj, when the White House first became aware of these allegations?

MR. SHAH: Well, I know there's been some reports about the Chief of Staff. He became fully aware about these allegations yesterday.

I'm not going to get into the specifics regarding who may have known what pieces of information because they were all part of an ongoing background check investigation. . . .

Q Let me ask you if I can: The statement changed from John Kelly yesterday morning to the statement yesterday evening. He said, "based on new allegations." But what changed yesterday, absent a photograph, in terms of new allegations?

MR. SHAH: Well, I think what I just referenced. The reports had additional allegations; they had more information.

Q So you're saying the initial reports where two former wives accused him of violence, both physical and verbal abuse, was not sufficient for him to say that I think he's a man of honor?

MR. SHAH: There were a number of statements from the Press Secretary, from the Chief of Staff, and from others that reflected the Rob Porter that we've come to know working here for over a year, and the Chief of Staff for about the last six months. But the reports are troubling, and I think the statement from Wednesday night reflects the Rob Porter that we had seen in these news reports and some of these credible allegations. . . .

Q . . . You talked about the fact there weren't any concerns, you said, that could compromise national security or interfere with operations here at the White House. But we've spoken to one of Porter's ex-wives who told us that she warned the FBI that he could be susceptible to blackmail because of the allegations against him. Is that—

MR. SHAH: Look, again, I'm not going to get into the specifics of the investigation itself. I think that's a question for the FBI and others. But this is not our process. This is the process the U.S. government uses across agencies and has existed over numerous administrations. . . .

Q Are you saying that the Chief of Staff of this White House had no idea that Rob Porter's two ex-wives had domestic violence allegations against him, when they made those claims to the FBI; that John Kelly did not know that? How is that possible that the Chief of Staff did not know that?

MR. SHAH: Well, again, this is part of an ongoing investigation. We trust the background check process. And the Chief of Staff does not get detailed updates about what may or may not have been alleged. . . .

Q But let me ask you, if I could follow up that—because as you were coming out here yesterday—or Sarah Sanders was coming out here yesterday, you were releasing a statement from Rob Porter, saying that he took those photographs. That appears to be an acknowledgment that this abuse took place, that he helped document it.

How can the White House Chief of Staff, how can the Press Secretary, how can this White House still be standing behind him when Mr. Porter appeared to be acknowledging that he had this past?

MR. SHAH: I think it's fair to say that we all could have done better over the last few hours—or last few days in dealing with this situation. But this was the Rob Porter that I and many others have dealt with, that Sarah dealt with, that other officials, including the Chief of Staff, have dealt with. And the emerging reports were not reflective of the individual who we had come to know. . . .

Q Normally, when you hire people, do you wait for the investigation to come back before hiring them? Is the burden of proof not on the people seeking the job to prove that they are qualified and don't have any skeletons in their closet? Or do they just get to come aboard and you wait and see what happens with the investigation?

MR. SHAH: The process tends to be a little bit different with the White House because there's a lot of officials coming in with the new administration, and a lot of individuals coming in have an interim clearance. . . .

Q The interim security clearance, does that allow Rob Porter to be able to touch—at the time when he was employed—to be able to touch and see classified materials?

MR. SHAH: It would, yes. . . .

Q If I understood your description of the background check process correctly, the fact that the two ex-wives had made statements to the FBI about alleged abuse during that investigation was not a disqualifying factor in his initial hiring. Does the White House regret that? And going forward, do you plan to change the way you consider allegations of domestic abuse?

MR. SHAH: Well, again, understand that the background investigation was not completed. There was no determination made about Rob Porter's security clearance. There was not a thumbs up or thumbs down. There was no denial of his security clearance. He was operating off an interim clearance. That is the clearance that many individuals who have never had a security clearance would get when they first come to the White House.

With respect to allegations made, again, every allegation has to be investigated. Any denial has to be thoroughly and fully investigated. We allow that process to play out. . . .

Q And then the last thing on that is, you said that there are things that this White House could have done better with respect to this. Could you please detail that? What could the White House have done better?

MR. SHAH Well, again, I'm not going to get into a tick-tock and all these detailed specifics. I think a lot of individuals were involved with the White House response to this, myself included. And I think a lot of us could have done better. . . .

SOURCE: The White House. "Press Briefing by Principal Deputy Press Secretary Raj Shah." February 8, 2018. https://www.whitehouse.gov/briefings-statements/press-briefing-principal-deputy-press-secretary-raj-shah-020818.

## *President Trump Announces Tillerson Resignation, Replacement*

**March 13, 2018**

Mike Pompeo, Director of the CIA, will become our new Secretary of State. He will do a fantastic job! Thank you to Rex Tillerson for his service! Gina Haspel will become the new Director of the CIA, and the first woman so chosen. Congratulations to all!

SOURCE: Donald Trump (@realDonaldTrump). Twitter post. March 13, 2018. https://twitter.com/realdonaldtrump/status/973540316656623616?lang=en.

## *Farewell Remarks by Secretary of State Rex Tillerson*

**March 13, 2018**

Good afternoon, all. I received a call today from the President of the United States a little after noontime from Air Force One, and I've also spoken to White House Chief of Staff Kelly to ensure we have clarity as to the days ahead. What is most important is to ensure an orderly and smooth transition during a time that the country continues to face significant policy and national security challenges.

As such, effective at the end of the day, I'm delegating all responsibilities of the office of the Secretary to Deputy Secretary of State Sullivan. My commission as Secretary of State will terminate at midnight, March the 31st. Between now and then, I will address a few administrative matters related to my departure and work towards a smooth and orderly transition for Secretary of State–Designate Mike Pompeo.

I'm encouraging my policy planning team and under secretaries and assistant secretaries—those confirmed as well as those in acting positions—to remain at their post and continue our mission at the State Department in working with the interagency process. I will be meeting members of my front office team and policy planning later today to thank them for their service. They have been extraordinarily dedicated to our mission, which includes promoting values that I view as being very important: the safety and security of our State Department personnel; accountability, which means treating each other with honesty and integrity; and respect for one another, most recently in particular to address challenges of sexual harassment within the department.

I want to speak now to my State Department colleagues and to our interagency colleagues and partners at DOD and the Joint Chiefs of Staff most particularly. To my Foreign Service officers and Civil Service colleagues, we all took the same oath of office. Whether you're career, employee, or political appointee, we are all bound by that common commitment: to support and defend the constitution, to bear true faith and allegiance to the same, and to faithfully discharge the duties of our office.

As a State Department, we're bound together by that oath. We remain steadfast here in Washington and at posts across the world, many of whom are in danger pay situations without their families. The world needs selfless leaders like these, ready to work with long-standing allies, new emerging partners and allies, who now—many are struggling as democracies, and in some cases are dealing with human tragedy, crisis of natural disasters, literally crawling themselves out of those circumstances. These are experiences that no lecture hall in a [sic] academic environment or at a think tank can teach you. Only by people going to the front lines to serve can they develop this kind of talent.

To the men and women in uniform, I'm told for the first time in most people's memory, the Department of State and Department of Defense have a close working relationship where we all agree that U.S. leadership starts with diplomacy. The men and women in uniform at the Department of Defense, under the leadership of Secretary Mattis and General Dunford, protect us as Americans and our way of life daily, at home and abroad. As an all-volunteer military, they do it for love of country, they do it for you, and they do it for me, and for no other reason. As Americans, we are all eternally grateful to each of them, and we honor their sacrifices.

The rewarding part of having leadership and partnerships in place is that you can actually get some things done. And I want to give recognition to the State Department and our partners for a few of their accomplishments under this administration.

First, working with allies, we exceeded the expectations of almost everyone with the DPRK maximum pressure campaign. With the announcement on my very first trip as Secretary of State to the region that the era of strategic patience was over, and we commenced the steps to dramatically increase not just the scope but the effectiveness of the sanctions. The department undertook a global campaign to bring partners and allies on board in every country around the world, with every embassy and mission raising this to the highest levels. And at every meeting I've had throughout the year, this has been on the agenda to discuss.

The adoption of the South Asia strategy with a conditions-based military plan is the tool to compel the Taliban to reconciliation and peace talks with the Afghan Government.

Finally equipped are military planners with a strategy which they can execute as opposed to a succession of 16 one-year strategies. This clear military commitment attracted the support of allies broadly and equipped our diplomats with a whole new level of certainty around how to prepare for the peace talks and achieve the final objectives.

In other areas, while progress has been made, much work remains. In Syria, we did achieve important ceasefires and stabilizations, which we know has saved thousands of lives. There's more to be done in Syria, particularly with respect to achieving the peace, as well as stabilizing Iraq and seeing a healthy government installed, and more broadly in the entire global campaign to defeat ISIS. Nothing is possible without allies and partners, though.

Much work remains to establish a clear view of the nature of our future relationship with China. How shall we deal with one another over the next 50 years and ensure a period of prosperity for all of our peoples, free of conflict between two very powerful nations?

And much work remains to respond to the troubling behavior and actions on the part of the Russian Government. Russia must assess carefully as to how its actions are in the best interest of the Russian people and of the world more broadly. Continuing on their current trajectory is likely to lead to greater isolation on their part, a situation which is not in anyone's interest.

So to my colleagues in the State Department and in the interagency, much remains to be done to achieve our mission on behalf of the American people with allies and with partners. I close by thanking all for the privilege of serving beside you for the last 14 months. Importantly, to the 300-plus million Americans, thank you for your devotion to a free and open society, to acts of kindness towards one another, to honesty, and the quiet hard work that you do every day to support this government with your tax dollars.

All of us, we know, want to leave this place as a better place for the next generation. I'll now return to private life as a private citizen, as a proud American, proud of the opportunity I've had to serve my country. God bless all of you. God bless the American people. God bless America.

SOURCE: U.S. State Department. "Remarks in Press Briefing Room." March 13, 2018. https://www.state
.gov/secretary/20172018tillerson/remarks/2018/03/279233.htm.

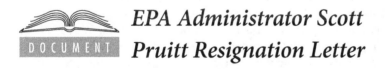

# EPA Administrator Scott Pruitt Resignation Letter

**July 5, 2018**

Mr. President, it has been an honor to serve you in the Cabinet as Administrator of the EPA. Truly, your confidence in me has blessed me personally and enabled me to advance your agenda beyond what anyone anticipated at the beginning of your Administration. Your courage, steadfastness and resolute commitment to get results for the American people, both with regard to improved environmental outcomes as well as historical regulatory reform, is in fact occurring at an unprecedented pace and I thank you for the opportunity to serve you and the American people in helping achieve those ends.

That is why it is hard for me to advise you I am stepping down as Administrator of the EPA effective as of July 6. It is extremely difficult for me to cease serving you in this role first because I count it a blessing to be serving you in any capacity, but also, because of the transformative work that is occurring. However, the unrelenting attacks on me personally, my family, are unprecedented and have taken a sizable toll on all of us.

My desire in service to you has always been to bless you as you make important decisions for the American people. I believe you are serving as President today because of God's providence. I believe that same providence brought me into your service. I pray as I have served you that I have blessed you and enabled you to effectively lead the American people. Thank you again Mr. President for the honor of serving you and I wish you Godspeed in all that you put your hand to.

Your Faithful Friend,
Scott Pruitt

SOURCE: Scott Pruitt. "Scott Pruitt's Resignation Letter." July 5, 2018.

# U.S. Ambassador to the UN Nikki Haley's Resignation Letter

**October 3, 2018**

Dear Mr. President:

It has been an immense honor to serve our country in your Administration. I cannot thank you enough for giving me this opportunity.

You will recall that when you offered me the position of United States Ambassador to the United Nations in November 2016, I accepted the offer based on some conditions. Those conditions included serving in your Cabinet and on the National Security Council and being free to speak my mind on the issues of the day. You made those commitments and you have absolutely kept them all. For that too, I will always be grateful.

We achieved great successes at the UN. We passed the toughest sanctions against any country in a generation, pressuring North Korea toward denuclearization. We passed an arms embargo on South Sudan that will help reduce violence and hopefully bring peace to that troubled country. We stood up for our ally Israel and began to roll back the UN's relentless bias against her. We reformed UN operations and saved over $1.3 billion. We spoke out resolutely against dictatorships in Iran, Syria, Venezuela, Cuba, and yes, Russia. Through it all, we stood strong for American values and interests, always placing America first. I am proud of our record. As a strong supporter of term limits, I have long believed that rotation in office benefits the public. Between the UN Ambassadorship and serving in the South Carolina Governorship and General Assembly, I have been in public office for fourteen straight years. As a businessman, I expect you will appreciate my sense that returning from government to the private sector is not a step down but a step up.

Accordingly, I am resigning my position. To give you time to select a replacement, and to give the Senate time to consider your selection, I am prepared to continue to serve until January 2019. At that point, I will once again become a private citizen. I expect to continue to speak out from time to time on important public policy matters, but I will surely not be a candidate for any office in 2020. As a private citizen, I look forward to supporting your re-election as President, and supporting the policies that will continue to move our great country toward even greater heights.

With best wishes and deep gratitude,
Nikki Haley

SOURCE: Nikki Haley. "Nikki Haley Resignation Letter." October 3, 2018.

## Attorney General Jeff Sessions's Resignation Letter

**November 7, 2018**

Dear Mr. President,

At your request, I am submitting my resignation.

Since the day I was honored to be sworn in as Attorney General of the United States, I came to work at the Department of Justice every day determined to do my duty and serve my country. I have done so to the best of my ability, working to support the fundamental legal processes that are the foundation of justice.

The team we assembled embraced your directive to be a law and order Department of Justice. We prosecuted the largest number of violent offenders and firearm defendants in our country's history. We took on transnational gangs that are bringing violence and death across our borders and protected national security. We did our part to restore immigration enforcement. We targeted the opioid epidemic by prosecuting doctors, pharmacists, and anyone else who contributes to this crisis with new law enforcement tools and determination. And we have seen results. After two years of rising violent crime and homicides prior to this administration, those trends have reversed—thanks to the hard work of our prosecutors and law enforcement around the country. I am particularly grateful to the fabulous men and women in law enforcement all over this country with whom I have served. I have had no greater honor than to serve alongside them. As I have said many times, they have my thanks and I will always have their backs.

Most importantly, in my time as Attorney General we have restored and upheld the rule of law—a glorious tradition that each of us has a responsibility to safeguard. We have operated with integrity and have lawfully and aggressively advanced the policy agenda of this administration.

I have been honored to serve as Attorney General and have worked to implement the law enforcement agenda based on the rule of law that formed a central part of your campaign for the Presidency.

Thank you for the opportunity, Mr. President.

Sincerely,
Jefferson B. Sessions III
Attorney General

SOURCE: Jeff Sessions. "Jeff Sessions Resignation Letter." November 7, 2018.

# *Trump Announces Zinke Resignation*

**December 15, 2018**

Secretary of the Interior @RyanZinke will be leaving the Administration at the end of the year after having served for a period of almost two years. Ryan has accomplished much during his tenure and I want to thank him for his service to our Nation.......

SOURCE: Donald Trump (@realDonaldTrump). Twitter post. December 15, 2018. https://twitter.com/realDonaldTrump/status/1073944491588022272.

# *Zinke Statement on Resignation*

**December 15, 2018**

I love working for the President and am incredibly proud of all the good work we've accomplished together. However, after 30 years of public service, I cannot justify spending thousands of dollars defending myself and my family against false allegations. Full statement attached.

"It is a great honor to serve the American people as their Interior Secretary. I love working for the President and am incredibly proud of all the good work we've accomplished together. However, after 30 years of public service, I cannot justify spending thousands of dollars defending myself and my family against false allegations. It is better for the President and Interior to focus on accomplishments rather than fictitious allegations." Secretary of the Interior Ryan Zinke

SOURCE: Secretary Ryan Zinke (@SecretaryZinke). Twitter post. December 15, 2018. https://twitter.com/SecretaryZinke/status/1074014810830974977.

## OTHER HISTORIC DOCUMENTS OF INTEREST

**FROM PREVIOUS *HISTORIC DOCUMENTS***

# State and Federal Officials Respond to Parkland Shooting

FEBRUARY 15 AND 23, 2018

The United States experienced another gun-related tragedy in February 2018 when Nikolas Cruz, a former student at Marjory Stoneman Douglas High School in Parkland, Florida, opened fire on the school's campus, killing seventeen people and injuring another fourteen. The shooting revived debate over legislative proposals to increase restrictions on gun purchases and ownership—a debate that last stagnated in 2017 following mass shootings in Las Vegas and Texas—and prompted an examination of state and school officials' handling of students with mental, emotional, and behavioral concerns. While the Parkland shooting bore many similarities to previous school shootings, it was unique in that it sparked a new movement of student activism, as survivors demanded gun reform, threatened to vote out the lawmakers who refused to make changes, and called on their representatives to reject contributions from the influential National Rifle Association (NRA). It also spurred a wave of legislative action in the states, with lawmakers passing fifty new gun laws—including in fourteen states with Republican governors.

## TRAGEDY IN FLORIDA

A shooter entered Marjory Stoneman Douglas High School around 2:30 p.m. on February 14 and began firing at students in the hallways and classrooms of the school's freshman building. Using a semiautomatic AR-15 rifle, the shooter killed seventeen people and wounded another fourteen in roughly six minutes. The victims included fourteen students—ranging in age from fourteen to eighteen—as well as a geography teacher, an assistant football coach, and the school's athletic director. Aaron Feis, the assistant football coach, was killed after putting himself between the shooter and students. Scott Beigel, the geography teacher, was killed as he ushered students into his classroom to hide. Beigel and Feis were among the teachers and school staff heralded as heroes for their efforts to protect students during the incident.

President Donald Trump offered his condolences via televised address. "To every parent, teacher, and child who is hurting so badly, we are here for you—whatever you need, whatever we can do—to ease your pain," he said. "No child, no teacher, should ever be in danger in an American school. No parent should ever have to fear for their sons and daughters when they kiss them goodbye in the morning."

The shooter was later identified as nineteen-year-old Nikolas Cruz, a former Stoneman Douglas student. Cruz was arrested while walking down a street in a residential neighborhood about an hour after the shooting occurred. According to police reports, Cruz had discarded his gun and ammunition somewhere in the school and blended in with fleeing students to escape. Cruz confessed to the killings and was ultimately indicted on thirty-four counts: seventeen of premeditated murder in the first degree and seventeen of attempted murder in the first degree. The state prosecutor assigned to the case announced he would seek the death penalty.

## A Student with a Troubled Past

With Cruz's identity revealed, a picture of a young man with a history of emotional and behavioral issues began to take shape. Reports from those who knew Cruz suggested he had always been a troublemaker, though he did not have a criminal record. Neighbors said that Cruz's mother had called the cops several times for help keeping her son under control, including once to break up a fight between Cruz and his brother. This was confirmed by a list of calls released by the Broward County Sheriff's Office showing they had received eighteen calls from Cruz's mother regarding her son. In another incident in early 2016, police were called after a neighbor's child saw an Instagram post from Cruz that seemed to suggest he "planned to shoot up the school." The deputies found that Cruz only owned knives and a BB gun at that point but provided information on the incident to a school resource officer at Stoneman Douglas. Additionally, Cruz was referred to the Florida Department of Children and Families in 2016 after he began cutting himself and posting pictures of it on Snapchat. After looking into the matter, the department concluded that Cruz was "not a risk to harm himself or others" even though he had been diagnosed with a variety of conditions, including depression.

Cruz also got into trouble at school. Teachers and students at Stoneman Douglas reported that Cruz kicked doors, cursed at teachers, fought with classmates, and once brought a backpack with bullets in it to school. When he was younger, Cruz was referred to the Broward County school district's PROMISE Program, an alternative school, after vandalizing a bathroom at Westglades Middle School. Students who commit any of a specific set of misdemeanors at their school can attend PROMISE and receive counseling and other support instead of facing charges through the criminal justice system. Cruz was recommended for a three-day assignment, but a spokesperson for the school district was not able to confirm he had completed the assignment. Cruz was transferred to the district's Cross Creek School for kids with emotional and behavioral disabilities in 2014, where his behavior and academic performance appeared to improve. He was allowed to enroll at Stoneman Douglas in 2016 but was expelled for "disciplinary reasons" in 2017. Cruz was then transferred to another alternative school, the Off Campus Learning Center, but he only attended for five months.

The school district's handling of Cruz became a major focus after the shooting, with the victims' families and other parents claiming administrators' negligence had contributed to the tragedy. The school district later commissioned an investigation of itself, which generally found that officials handled Cruz's situation appropriately, with two exceptions. The details of these exceptions were not included in the heavily redacted version of the report that was released publicly; however, the *Sun-Sentinel* was able to extract the redacted text. The paper reported that Cruz had been encouraged to transfer back to Cross Creek when he was a junior, but administrators failed to present his options appropriately: Cruz was told he could either transfer to Cross Creek, stay at Stoneman Douglas without the special education assistance he had been receiving, or sue the school district, but he should have had the option to stay at Stoneman Douglas and continue with special education services. Cruz chose to remain at Stoneman Douglas without assistance. The *Sun-Sentinel*'s report also revealed that Cruz tried to reenroll at Cross Creek two months after being expelled from Stoneman Douglas. The district told Cruz that they needed to reevaluate his eligibility and that he would have to reenroll at Stoneman Douglas before they could do so, but it was too late in the school year to process the reenrollment.

The FBI also drew criticism for its failure to investigate a tip received about Cruz the month before the shooting. According to an FBI statement, a caller to the bureau's public tip line "provided information about Cruz's gun ownership, desire to kill people, erratic behavior, and disturbing social media posts, as well as the potential of him conducting a school shooting." Per FBI protocol, this information should have been assessed as a potential "threat to life" and forwarded to the Miami field office for investigation; however, the FBI stated these protocols were not followed and no investigation was conducted. "Every red flag was there and nobody did anything," said Howard Finkelstein, chief public defender for Broward County.

## STUDENTS CALL FOR GUN REFORM

As has been the case after nearly every mass shooting in recent U.S. history, the nation's gun laws quickly became a focus of conversation, though law enforcement officials reported that Cruz's gun was legally purchased at a tactical supply store one year before the incident. What made the Parkland shooting unique, however, was that most calls for tighter gun restrictions came from students. "The fact that a student is not surprised that there was another mass shooting—but this time it was at his school—says so much about the current state that our country is in, and how much has to be done," said David Hogg, a seventeen-year-old Stoneman Douglas student. "We need to do something . . . Congress needs to get over their political bias with each other and work toward saving children's lives."

On February 21, thousands of students rallied at the Old Capitol in Tallahassee to demand gun reform. Students also met with lawmakers and state officials from both parties to discuss gun control legislation. "We've had enough of thoughts and prayers," said Delaney Tarr. "If you supported us you would have made a change long ago and you would be making change now."

Led by Parkland survivors, a new national student movement soon emerged and quickly gained momentum. The first major coordinated action of this student-led movement took place on March 14, when thousands of students in cities and towns across the country walked out of their classrooms. Beginning at 10:00 a.m., the walkouts generally lasted about seventeen minutes (one minute for each Parkland victim). School administrators in some localities were publicly supportive, while others warned participants would be disciplined. Some schools opted to conduct assemblies about student safety or hold a moment of silence instead. A second national school walkout took place on April 20, the nineteenth anniversary of the Columbine High School shooting. Organizers estimated that students from more than 2,500 schools participated.

Parkland students also spearheaded planning for the March for Our Lives. An estimated 180,000 people attended the main event in Washington, D.C., on March 24, with smaller marches planned in every state. Marches were also held across the globe in cities such as London, Copenhagen, Tokyo, Madrid, Rome, and Paris. Organizers said their goal was to "demand that a comprehensive and effective bill be immediately brought before Congress to address these gun issues." The students also made a major push to register and encourage other young people to vote.

Several Parkland students spoke at the event in Washington, D.C., including sophomore Cameron Kasky, who declared, "To the leaders, skeptics and cynics who told us to sit down and stay silent: Wait your turn. Welcome to the revolution." Emma Gonzalez spoke for less than two minutes, taking most of that time to recite the names of the Parkland shooting victims, before standing in silence. When a timer went off after six minutes and twenty seconds, Gonzalez noted that was how long it took Cruz to kill those named. "Fight for your lives," she said, "before it's someone else's job."

Although the Parkland incident and other school shootings were a major focus of the march, speakers also sought to call attention to other gun violence affecting youth, including those living in cities like Chicago. "We recognize that Parkland received more attention because of its affluence, but we share this stage today and forever with those communities who have always stared down the barrel of a gun," said Stoneman Douglas student Jaclyn Corin. "We deserve the right to have a life without fear of being gunned down," said Trevon Bosley, a nineteen-year-old Chicago resident whose older brother Terrell died of a gunshot wound.

In a statement, the White House applauded "the many courageous young Americans exercising their First Amendment rights today." Deputy Press Secretary Raj Shah had previously said the president "shares the students' concerns about school safety" and cited his support for mental health and background check improvements. The NRA did not provide an official response to the march, but a Facebook post claimed the protests were a result of "gun-hating billionaires and Hollywood elites" manipulating young people "as part of their plan to DESTROY the Second Amendment and strip us of our right to defend ourselves and our loved ones." Gun-control opponents held smaller rallies the same day in Boston and Salt Lake City.

## Congress Takes Limited Action

Federal lawmakers quickly assumed their usual stances in the wake of similar tragedies, with most Democrats calling for greater restrictions on guns while Republicans warned about trampling Second Amendment rights and often tried to refocus the conversation on mental health. House Speaker Paul Ryan, R-Wis., called for unity, stating that policymakers should not make "knee-jerk" decisions before all the facts were available and should "think less about taking sides and fighting each other politically." Trump largely remained focused on enhancing school safety, expressing support for arming teachers and allowing concealed carry in schools, and mental health issues, emphasizing during his televised address that he would work with state and local leaders to "tackle the difficult issue of mental health." He also posted on Twitter that there were "so many signs that the Florida shooter was mentally disturbed."

Despite the usual partisan divisions, reports suggested that lawmakers might take action on several gun-related proposals, including a ban on bump stocks (a device that allows semiautomatic weapons to fire like fully automatic weapons), raising the age limit for rifle purchases from eighteen to twenty-one, expanding background checks to online sales and purchases at gun shows, and improving the national background check system by better enforcing reporting requirements. This last proposal, known as the Fix NICS Act, was widely considered to have the best chance of passage in Congress. The bill was introduced by Sen. John Cornyn, R-Tex., following a mass shooting at a church in Sutherland Springs, Texas. The Air Force admitted after the incident that it had not submitted criminal records to the National Instant Check System (NICS) that would have prevented the shooter from obtaining a gun. The Fix NICS Act sets out a series of incentives and punishments to encourage states, federal agencies, and the military to report more data to the NICS.

On March 14, the House passed the STOP School Violence Act to provide more funding for school security. Measures included increased funding for development of anonymous reporting systems, additional training for school officials and local law enforcement to respond to mental health crises, and funding for protective measures such as metal detectors. The bill did not include a call to arm teachers, which had been sought by the White House. While the bill passed with bipartisan support, Democrats expressed frustration that it did not include gun-control measures. "This is a pretense that we are doing something while assuring the NRA that we aren't doing anything," said Rep. Steny Hoyer, D-Md.

One week later, Congress approved a $1.3 trillion spending bill that included two gun-related measures. One was the Fix NICS Act, which had been folded into the omnibus spending package. In addition, a report accompanying the bill clarified the intent of the 1996 Dickey Amendment. Democrats have long sought the amendment's repeal because it has often been cited as broadly prohibiting research studies of gun-related issues. "While appropriations language prohibits the CDC and other agencies from using appropriated funding to advocate or promote gun control, the Secretary of Health and Human Services has stated the CDC has the authority to conduct research on the causes of gun violence," the report stated. Trump signed the bill on March 23.

A separate proposal put forward by Sens. Marco Rubio, R-Fla., Ben Nelson, D-Fla., and Jack Reed, D-R.I., on March 22 sought to provide grants to encourage states to pass extreme risk-protection-order laws. Also known as "red flag" laws, such measures generally allow law enforcement officials to temporarily prohibit someone from purchasing or possessing firearms if they are deemed a significant risk of injury to themselves or others. "What we're really focused on here more than anything else is identifying the people that are going to commit a violent act irrespective of where they're going to commit it and stopping them before they do it," said Rubio. The bill did not advance by the end of the year.

Absent further congressional action on the matter, Trump declared his intention to ban bump stocks via executive order, though he later delegated the task to the U.S. Department of Justice. On March 23, Attorney General Jeff Sessions announced the department was proposing a rulemaking to define the term *machinegun*, as used in the National Firearms Act and Gun Control Act, to include "all bump-stock-type devices that harness recoil energy to facilitate the continuous operation of a semiautomatic long gun after a single pull of the trigger." The proposal was accepted, and the rule is set to go into effect on March 26, 2019.

## Gun Control in the States

While Congress made limited progress on gun reform, state lawmakers moved quickly to pass fifty new gun-control bills in 2018. "Legislators are starting to realize that mass shootings can happen in their state anytime, and they don't want to be in a position that this kind of thing can happen in their state at all," said Allison Anderman, the managing attorney at the Giffords Law Center.

Florida was the first state to take action, with Gov. Rick Scott pledging to "do everything I can to make sure this never happens again." In addition to ordering the state's Department of Law Enforcement to investigate local authorities' response to the shooting, Scott released a "major action plan" consisting of new programs, regulations, and funding to help make schools and communities safer. Many of Scott's proposals were approved by the Florida legislature and signed into law on March 9. These included raising the age limit for gun purchases to twenty-one, creating a three-day waiting period for gun purchases, increasing funding for schools to provide mental health care to students and implement stronger security measures, implementing a "red flag" law, and prohibiting gun sales to people committed to mental institutions or deemed mentally incompetent by a judge. "I want to make it virtually impossible for anyone who is a danger to themselves or others to use a gun," said Scott. "It's obvious we can't trust the federal process which is why we have to make these changes here in Florida." The new gun limits were particularly noteworthy for Florida, which has steadily sought to expand gun rights since the mid-1990s and is known for its Stand Your Ground laws. (Stand Your Ground laws allow a person to use force—even deadly force—to defend themselves against a threat.) The NRA responded by filing a lawsuit in federal district court arguing the age limit is a "blanket ban" that violates both the Second and Fourteenth Amendments.

In California, Gov. Jerry Brown signed a package of laws raising the minimum gun-buying age to twenty-one, requiring gun-safety training for those applying for concealed carry permits, banning people convicted of serious domestic violence charges and people who have been hospitalized for mental health problems more than once a year from owning guns, and strengthening reporting requirements for lost or stolen guns. New Jersey Gov. Phil Murphy approved a new "red flag" law as well as measures prohibiting the possession and manufacture of armor-piercing ammunition, reducing the maximum allowed magazine capacity from fifteen to ten rounds, and requiring mental health practitioners to alert law enforcement if a patient has threatened serious physical violence against themselves or others. Similar measures were passed in gun-friendly Vermont, which also banned guns in K–12 schools and expanded background checks to private sales. Connecticut, Hawaii, New York, Oregon, Rhode Island, and Washington were among the other states that passed new or tightened existing gun regulations in the wake of the Parkland shooting. At least two states—Idaho and Wyoming—loosened gun regulations, opting to expand their Stand Your Ground laws.

—Linda Grimm

*Following are remarks by President Donald Trump from February 15, 2018, responding to the Parkland shooting; and remarks by Florida Gov. Rick Scott on February 23, 2018, announcing his school safety action plan.*

DOCUMENT

# President Trump's Remarks on the Parkland Shooting

**February 15, 2018**

My fellow Americans, today I speak to a nation in grief. Yesterday, a school filled with innocent children and caring teachers became the scene of terrible violence, hatred, and evil.

Around 2:30 yesterday afternoon, police responded to reports of gunfire at Marjory Stoneman Douglas High School in Parkland, Florida, a great and safe community. There, a shooter, who is now in custody, opened fire on defenseless students and teachers. He murdered 17 people and badly wounded at least 14 others.

Our entire Nation, with one heavy heart, is praying for the victims and their families. To every parent, teacher, and child who is hurting so badly, we are here for you—whatever you need, whatever we can do—to ease your pain. We are all joined together as one American family, and your suffering is our burden also.

No child, no teacher, should ever be in danger in an American school. No parent should ever have to fear for their sons and daughters when they kiss them goodbye in the morning. Each person who was stolen from us yesterday had a full life ahead of them, a life filled with wondrous beauty and unlimited potential and promise. Each one had dreams to pursue, love to give, and talents to share with the world. And each one had a family to whom they meant everything in the world.

Today we mourn for all of those who lost their lives. We comfort the grieving and the wounded. And we hurt for the entire community of Parkland, Florida, that is now in shock, in pain, and searching for answers.

To law enforcement, first responders, and teachers who responded so bravely in the face of danger: We thank you for your courage. Soon after the shooting, I spoke with Governor Scott to convey our deepest sympathies to the people of Florida and our determination to assist in any way that we can. I also spoke with Florida Attorney General Pam Bondi and Broward County Sheriff Scott Israel. I'm making plans to visit Parkland to meet with families and local officials and to continue coordinating the Federal response.

In these moments of heartache and darkness, we hold on to God's word in scripture: "I have heard your prayer and seen your tears. I will heal you." We trust in that promise, and we hold fast to our fellow Americans in their time of sorrow.

I want to speak now directly to America's children, especially those who feel lost, alone, confused, or even scared: I want you to know that you are never alone and you never will be.

You have people who care about you, who love you, and who will do anything at all to protect you. If you need help, turn to a teacher, a family member, a local police officer, or a faith leader. Answer hate with love; answer cruelty with kindness.

We must also work together to create a culture in our country that embraces the dignity of life, that creates deep and meaningful human connections, and that turns classmates and colleagues into friends and neighbors.

Our administration is working closely with local authorities to investigate the shooting and learn everything we can. We are committed to working with State and local leaders to help secure our schools and tackle the difficult issue of mental health.

Later this month, I will be meeting with the Nation's Governors and attorney generals, where making our schools and our children safer will be our top priority. It is not enough to simply take actions that make us feel like we are making a difference. We must actually make that difference.

In times of tragedy, the bonds that sustain us are those of family, faith, community, and country. These bonds are stronger than the forces of hatred and evil, and these bonds grow even stronger in the hours of our greatest need.

And so always, but especially today, let us hold our loved ones close, let us pray for healing and for peace, and let us come together as one Nation to wipe away the tears and strive for a much better tomorrow.

Thank you, and God bless you all. Thank you very much.

SOURCE: Executive Office of the President. "Remarks on the Shooting in Parkland, Florida." February 15, 2018. *Compilation of Presidential Documents* 2018, no. 00096 (February 15, 2018). https://www.gpo.gov/fdsys/pkg/DCPD-201800096/pdf/DCPD-201800096.pdf.

# Florida Gov. Rick Scott Remarks on School Safety Action Plan

**February 23, 2018**

Alyssa Alhadeff, Scott Beigel, Martin Duque Anguiano, Nicholas Dworet, Aaron Feis, Jamie Guttenberg, Chris Hixon, Luke Hoyer, Cara Loughran, Gina Montalto, Joaquin Oliver, Alaina Petty, Meadow Pollack, Helena Ramsay, Alexander Schachter, Carmen Schentrup, Peter Wang.

Unfortunately, none of the plans I'm announcing today will bring any of them back, but it's important to remember them. The seventeen lives that were cut short and all the hopes and dreams that were ruined have changed our state forever. Florida will never be the same.

Today, I am announcing a major action plan. I will be working with the legislature aggressively over the next two weeks to get it done.

This week we asked law enforcement leaders, education leaders, and health leaders from all over the state to drop what they were doing, clear their schedules, and immediately get up to Tallahassee for urgent conversations about what we can—and must do—to make our schools and communities safer. We must take care of our kids.

I can tell you that everyone said yes, and they came, and they got to work.

I have also spent a lot of time in Parkland meeting with families and students. I've been there nearly every day since the shooting. I have listened to their ideas to make sure this never happens again.

I also met with students who courageously came to Tallahassee to have their voices heard. What we saw in this building on Wednesday is what our democracy is about and why we live in the greatest nation on earth.

My message to them has been very simple—you are not alone. Change is coming . . . and it will come fast.

This is a time when I believe we must all come together, and even cross party lines. Of course, we won't all agree on every issue, but I do believe this is a moment when our state can come together around a common sense set of actions.

I also want to encourage people to listen to each other and keep listening to each other. I've done a lot more listening than talking this week. Sometimes leading involves more listening than talking.

I've listened to things that I agree with, and to things I don't agree with. It's important to consider all viewpoints.

I've broken my action plan down into three sections. Gun laws, school safety, and mental health. We must get this done in the next two weeks.

First, on guns:

I want to make it virtually impossible for anyone who has mental issues to use a gun. I want to make it virtually impossible for anyone who is a danger to themselves or others to use a gun.

I want to create a new program in Florida—I call it the Violent Threat Restraining Order. This concept is very simple, and very common sense in my view.

This will allow a court to prohibit a violent or mentally ill person from purchasing or possessing a firearm or any other weapon when either a family member, community welfare expert or law enforcement officer files a sworn request, and presents evidence to the court of a threat of violence involving firearms or other weapons. There would be speedy due process for the accused and any fraudulent or false statements would face criminal penalties.

Let's take a moment to look at the case of this killer. This person was not stopped from legally purchasing a weapon, was not arrested, was not detained, and was never forced to turn in his weapons.

Let's review the warning signs here . . . he had 39 visits from police, his mother called him in, DCF investigated, he was kicked out of school, he was known to students as a danger to shoot people, and he was reported to the FBI last month as a possible school shooter.

And yet, he was never put on the list to be denied the ability to buy a gun, and his guns were never removed from him.

We will also strengthen gun purchase and possession restrictions for mentally ill individuals under the Baker Act. If a court involuntarily commits someone because they are a risk to themselves or others, they would be required to surrender all firearms and not regain their right to purchase or possess a firearm until a court hearing. We are also proposing a minimum 60-day period before individuals can ask a court to restore access to firearms.

Also, we will require all individuals purchasing firearms to be 21 or older. Let me repeat—we will require all individuals purchasing firearms to be 21 or older.

There will be exceptions for active duty and reserve military and spouses, National Guard members, and law enforcement.

Next, we will prohibit a person from possessing or purchasing a firearm if they are subject to an injunction for protection against stalking, cyberstalking, dating violence, repeat violence, sexual violence, or domestic violence.

We will establish enhanced criminal penalties for threats to schools, like social media threats of shootings or bombings. We will also enhance penalties if any person possesses or purchases a gun after they have been deemed by state law to not have access to a gun.

And, we will completely ban the purchase or sale of bump stocks.

The second part of my action plan provides $450 million to keep students safe.

Today, I am calling for a mandatory law enforcement officer in every public school. These law enforcement officers must either be sworn sheriff's deputies or police officers and be present during all hours students are on campus.

The size of the campus should be a factor in determining staffing levels by the county sheriff's office, and I am proposing at least one law enforcement officer for every 1,000 students. This must be implemented by the start of the 2018 school year.

We will also provide sheriff's departments the authority to train additional school personnel or reserve law enforcement officers to protect students if requested by the local school board.

And, we will require mandatory active shooter training as outlined by the Department of Homeland Security. All training and code red drills must be completed during the first week of each semester in all public schools. Both faculty and students must participate in active shooter drills and local sheriff's offices must approve and be involved in training.

We are also increasing funding in the Safe Schools Allocation to address specific school safety needs within each school district. This includes school hardening measures like metal detectors, bullet-proof glass, steel doors, and upgraded locks. The Florida Department of Education, with FDLE, will also provide minimum school safety and security standards by July 1st to all school districts.

All school safety plans must be submitted to their county sheriff's office by July 1st each year for approval. Once all plans and requests for school hardening have been approved by the county sheriff's office, in consultation with local police, plans will be forwarded to the Department of Education by the school district to receive any state funds.

School districts must also take all capital outlay funds received from taxpayers and use it for school hardening before it can be spent on any other capital outlay. All safe school allocations must be spent in accordance with the sheriff approved plans.

We will also require each school district that receives a Safe Schools Allocation to enter into an agreement with the local sheriff's office, the Department of Juvenile Justice, the Department of Children and Families, the Department of Law Enforcement and any community behavioral health provider for the purpose of sharing information. That will allow us to better coordinate services in order to provide prevention or intervention strategies.

We will also establish a new, anonymous K–12 "See Something, Say Something" statewide, dedicated hotline, website and mobile app.

Next, we will establish funding to require access to dedicated mental health counselors to provide direct counseling services to students at every school. These counselors cannot serve dual roles, like teaching or academic advising. Every student must have the opportunity to meet one-on-one with a mental health professional, and receive ongoing counseling as needed.

Each school will be required to have a threat assessment team including a teacher, a local law enforcement officer, a human resource officer, a DCF employee, a DJJ employee, and the principal to meet monthly to review any potential threats to students and staff at the school.

Finally, we will require crisis intervention training for all school personnel. This training must be completed before the start of the 2018 school year.

The final part of my action plan includes $50 million in additional funding for mental health initiatives.

We must expand mental health service teams statewide to serve youth and young adults with early or serious mental illness by providing counseling, crisis management and other critical mental health services.

We are also requiring every sheriffs' office to have a DCF case manager embedded in their department to solely work as a crisis welfare worker for repeat cases in the community. This will require 67 additional employees to be hired at DCF by July 15th.

Finally, we will provide law enforcement and mental health coordination matching grants to allow sheriffs to establish special law enforcement teams to coordinate with DCF case managers.

Before I take your questions, I want to close with this.

The goal of this plan of action is to make massive changes in protecting our schools, provide significantly more resources for mental health, and do everything we can to keep guns out of the hands of those dealing with mental problems or threating harm to themselves or others.

I know there are some who are advocating a mass takeaway of 2nd amendment rights for all Americans. That is not the answer.

Keeping guns away from dangerous people and people with mental issues is what we need to do.

I do know that some are going to accuse me of unfairly stigmatizing those who struggle with mental illness. I reject that. I am not asking them to wear a scarlet letter, nor am I unsympathetic to their plight. I have a family member who has dealt with these issues. It is hard on them and it is hard on the family.

But, what I am saying is no one with mental issues should have access to guns.

It's common sense, and it is in their own best interest, not to mention the interests of our communities.

And much of what I'm proposing involves giving law enforcement the ability to stop people from harming themselves and others, while giving them the tools to keep our schools safe.

We know for certain that we cannot simply rely on the current federal background check system.

This killer should not have been able to purchase or even possess a weapon.

And we know that the federal government can't even be counted on to investigate or act on serious and credible threats as we saw with the FBI's complete failure.

It's obvious we can't trust the federal process[,] which is why we have to make these changes here in Florida.

I'm an NRA member, a supporter of the 2nd amendment, and the 1st amendment, and the entire bill of rights for that matter. I'm also a father, and a grandfather, and a Governor.

We all have a difficult task in front of us . . . balancing our individual rights with our obvious need for public safety.

But of course, some will say it's too much, and some will say it is not enough. I respect everyone's opinion, and I don't ridicule those who disagree with me. An open dialogue is crucial.

But, I will not accept the old, tired political notion that we don't have enough time to get anything done. Government does not have to be slow or lethargic. And when it comes to protecting our schools and our kids, we need to be swift and decisive.

I also understand that I am proposing half a billion dollars for school safety and mental health initiatives.

But let me be clear—there is nothing more important than the safety of our children. Our kids deserve nothing less. Fortunately, our economy is booming, and we have the resources to protect our schools and our students.

And, if providing this funding means we won't be able to cut taxes this year—so be it.

And, if we have to give up some of the projects we all hold near and dear—so be it.

We are all elected to come to Tallahassee to represent the best interests of Floridians. And, today, there is nothing more important than to do all we can to make sure a horrific and evil act like the Parkland shooting never happens again.

SOURCE: Office of the Governor of Florida. "Gov. Scott Announces Major Action Plan to Keep Florida Students Safe following Tragic Parkland Shooting." February 23, 2018. https://www.flgov .com/2018/02/23/gov-scott-announces-major-action-plan-to-keep-florida-students-safe-following-tragic-parkland-shooting [cached].

## OTHER HISTORIC DOCUMENTS OF INTEREST

### FROM PREVIOUS *HISTORIC DOCUMENTS*

# Department of Justice Issues Indictments against Russians; Trump and Putin Meet for Summit

FEBRUARY 16, AND JULY 13 AND 16, 2018

In 2018, the investigation led by Special Counsel former FBI director Robert Mueller into possible coordination between the 2016 presidential campaign of Donald Trump and Russian officials resulted in two separate court filings indicting twenty-five Russians for both hacking and the spread of misinformation. The indictments stated that the Russians had acted to discredit the campaign of Hillary Clinton while bolstering that of Trump; however, there was no indication that their efforts impacted election results or that Trump campaign officials were involved. The second of the grand jury indictments came just days ahead of a scheduled summit between President Trump and Russian President Vladimir Putin. Despite being encouraged otherwise, Trump pressed forward with the summit and drew fire for seeming to disagree with American intelligence agencies and their assessment that Russia had attempted to influence the 2016 presidential election. President Trump spoke at length during a news conference about his faith in Putin's strong denial of any attempted interference, comments he would soon walk back.

## Thirteen Indicted for Russian Disinformation Campaign

Mueller's work began in May 2017, when he was appointed by the Department of Justice as special counsel to lead an investigation into "any links and/or coordination between the Russian government and individuals associated with the campaign of President Donald Trump." He was also granted authority "to prosecute federal crimes arising from the investigation of these matters." President Trump frequently sought to undermine Mueller's investigation, which he referred to as a politically motivated "witch hunt." By the end of 2018, Mueller's team had either indicted or garnered guilty pleas from at least thirty-three individuals and three companies. Included in that group were Trump campaign officials, including foreign policy adviser George Papadopoulos, chair Paul Manafort, aide Rick Gates, and aide and U.S. National Security Adviser Michael Flynn.

The indictments also took aim at Russian intelligence operatives. In early 2017, U.S. intelligence agencies announced their conclusion that Russia had in fact attempted to influence the 2016 U.S. presidential election. According to their report, the Russians did this through a number of means, including hacking e-mail servers belonging to the Democratic National Committee (DNC), Democratic Congressional Campaign Committee (DCCC), and Clinton campaign chair John Podesta to gather and leak information and through spreading misinformation and propaganda, primarily via social media platforms. The latter was the subject of an indictment in February 2018 against thirteen Russians and three companies.

The indictment, filed in the District Court for the District of Columbia on February 16, 2018, alleges that the Russians and the three companies—Internet Research Agency, Concord Management and Consulting LLC, and Concord Catering—under the direction of Kremlin-connected oligarch Yevgeny Prigozhin, created hundreds of fake Twitter and Facebook accounts and even coordinated in-person pro-Trump events, posing as Americans with the intent of spreading information to discredit Clinton's campaign. According to Deputy Attorney General Rod Rosenstein, who announced the charges, "The defendants allegedly conducted what they called information warfare against the United States, with the stated goal of spreading distrust towards the candidates and the political system in general." The effort employed hundreds of Russian citizens, utilized shell companies to hide its funding and activities, and frequently conducted research by contacting actual U.S. political activists and even visiting the United States. Those named in the indictment were charged with conspiracy to defraud the United States, conspiracy to commit wire and bank fraud, and aggravated identify theft.

The campaign to spread misinformation began as early as 2014, according to the indictment, when at least three Russians traveled to ten states including Michigan, Texas, and New York on an intelligence-gathering mission. Prior to the trip, they "planned travel itineraries, purchased equipment (such as cameras, SIM cards, and drop phones), and discussed security measures (including 'evacuation scenarios')," the indictment stated. The travel is considered an attempt to conspire to obstruct U.S. government agencies "by making expenditures in connection with the 2016 U.S. presidential election without proper regulatory disclosure; failing to register as foreign agents carrying out political activities within the United States; and obtaining visas through false and fraudulent statements." The 2014 time frame is a year earlier than previously reported by former Federal Bureau of Investigation (FBI) director James Comey, who told Congress that the Russian campaign to influence the election began in 2015.

The indictment provides additional facts supporting the 2017 intelligence agency claims that the Russians were attempting to help the Trump campaign. In one memo to staff at the Internet Research Agency quoted in the indictment, they are told to "use any opportunity to criticize Hillary and the rest (except Sanders and Trump—we support them)," and were later chastised for a "low number of posts dedicated to criticizing Hillary Clinton" and were reminded it was "imperative to intensify criticizing Hillary Clinton." Facebook, Twitter, and Google reported in 2017 that they were aware that so-called Russian trolls were using their platforms and were also purchasing advertisements and that they had begun cooperating with the Mueller investigation and working to strengthen their own safeguards to prevent the same situation in the future. Around the same time, the Russians became aware that they had been caught, according to the indictment, with one writing to the others, "We have a slight crisis here at work: the FBI busted our activity (not a joke)."

The indictment details communication between three Trump campaign officials and the Russian defendants. The three were working for the Trump campaign in Florida and communicated with the fake Russian personas. The indictment does not indicate whether the campaign staff ever responded to Russian requests for on-the-ground assistance at planned rallies or what information they may have provided. Despite the use of Americans in their operation, there are no U.S. citizens named in the indictment. "There is no allegation in this indictment that any American was a knowing participant in this illegal activity," Rosenstein said at the press briefing announcing the charges. The February indictment does not show any direct ties with the Trump campaign and also did not indicate whether the highest levels of the Russian government, or Putin himself, had any knowledge of or provided direction for the disinformation campaign.

On Twitter, President Trump called the indictment a vindication for his campaign. "Russia started their anti-US campaign in 2014, long before I announced that I would run for President. The results of the election were not impacted. The Trump campaign did nothing wrong—no collusion!" The White House also released an official statement echoing the president's tweet and adding, "It's time we stop the outlandish partisan attacks, wild and false allegations, and far-fetched theories, which only serve to further the agendas of bad actors, like Russia, and do nothing to protect the principles of our institutions. We must unite as Americans to protect the integrity of our democracy and our elections."

It is unlikely that those named in the indictment will ever appear in court because Russia does not have an extradition treaty with the United States. Russian Foreign Ministry spokesperson Maria Zakharova wrote on Facebook, "13 against billion-dollar budgets of special services? Against intelligence and counterintelligence, against the latest developments and technologies? . . . Absurd? Yes," adding, "This is modern American political reality."

## Twelve Russians Accused of Hacking

Another grand jury indictment was handed down on July 13, 2018, this time against twelve Russian officers, all members of the GRU, the military's intelligence directorate, who allegedly hacked into the e-mail servers of the DNC, Clinton campaign, and DCCC in 2016, as well as a state election board website and company that supplies software used to verify voter registration information. Those named in the indictment were charged with crimes including conspiracy to launder money, conspiracy to commit computer crimes, and identity theft. As with the February indictment, there was no direct link drawn between Trump campaign officials and the named defendants and no indication that the efforts by the accused had any impact on the election outcome.

According to the indictment, the Russians first tried to gain access to Clinton's e-mail servers on July 27, 2016, the same day Trump said on the campaign trail, "Russia, if you're listening, I hope you're able to find the 30,000 e-mails that are missing," referencing the DOJ and FBI investigation into Clinton's use of a private e-mail server during her time as secretary of state. The hackers would go on to attempt to gain access to the computers of more than 300 Clinton-affiliated individuals. When successful, they installed code into the computers allowing them to steal files and leak any worthwhile information. The contents of the stolen information were primarily shared on DCLeaks, an account set up by the Russian intelligence operatives, and through a persona known as Guccifer 2.0. According to the indictment, the information was also shared by "Organization #1," assumed by members of the media to be WikiLeaks. According to the indictment, Organization #1 had contacted Guccifer 2.0 to request "anything Hillary related." Among the most critical leaked content were e-mails indicating that the DNC had attempted to sabotage the campaign of Sen. Bernie Sanders, I-Vt. Once the DNC became aware of the hack, it took steps to lock down its servers, and Guccifer 2.0 claimed to be a Romanian. According to the indictment, this was done to cover their tracks and "undermine the allegations of Russian responsibility."

To pay for their activities, including the purchase of servers and other computer infrastructure, the Russians named in the indictment relied on the cryptocurrency bitcoin and at one point even mined the currency themselves. The indictment says the online currency "allowed the conspirators to avoid direct relations with traditional financial institutions, allowing them to evade greater scrutiny of their identities and sources of funds."

Although no American is named in the indictment, it does indicate that the hackers were communicating with "a person who was in regular contact with senior members of the presidential campaign." There is no indication in the indictment or in Rosenstein's comments announcing the charges that this individual knew that the Russians were on the other end of the conversation. In one communication noted in the indictment, Guccifer 2.0 writes to the individual, "what do u think of the info on the turnout model for the democrats entire presidential campaign [sic]," in reference to a stolen document from the DCCC. The individual replies, "Pretty standard."

White House Deputy Press Secretary Lindsay Walters said the July indictment made clear there was no "knowing involvement by anyone on the campaign and no allegations that the alleged hacking affected the election result." Instead of his more traditional tweets about a lack of collusion between his campaign and the Russians, Trump used the indictment as an opportunity to question the actions of his predecessor's administration. "The stories you heard about the 12 Russians yesterday took place during the Obama Administration, not the Trump Administration. Why didn't they do something about it, especially when it was reported that President Obama was informed by the FBI in September, before the Election," he said. In a second tweet, the president added, "Why didn't Obama do something about it? Because he thought Crooked Hillary Clinton would win, that's why." Obama had taken some action in 2016 after learning about the suspected interference, including imposing sanctions and expelling Russian diplomats.

The July indictment came just days before President Trump was scheduled to meet with President Putin in Helsinki, Finland, following a North Atlantic Treaty Organization (NATO) summit. The indictment raised questions about whether the president would move forward with the meeting, and he was even encouraged to withdraw by members of his own party. "If President Trump is not prepared to hold Putin accountable, the summit in Helsinki should not move forward," said Sen. John McCain, R-Ariz. Trump, however, chose to move forward but promised to press Putin on the issue. "I don't think you'll have any 'Gee, I did it, you got me,'" Trump said, but added that he would "absolutely firmly ask the question" about whether Russia had meddled in the 2016 election. After the indictment was released, the Kremlin again denied its involvement and said the findings were intended to "spoil the atmosphere before the Russian–American summit." The statement from Russia went on to call the indictment "regrettable" and a "duplication of false information . . . worked up for obvious political reasons."

## Trump and Putin Meet for Summit

The night before the July 16 scheduled meeting between Trump and Putin in Helsinki, the president tweeted about the United States' relationship with Russia, blaming tension between the two countries on the United States itself and on previous administrations. "Our relationship with Russia has NEVER been worse thanks to many years of U.S. foolishness and stupidity and now, the Rigged Witch Hunt!" The tweet was shared by the Russian Foreign Ministry's Twitter account, with the comment, "We agree."

Trump and Putin met privately—with only their interpreters present—for nearly two hours before emerging for a joint press conference. At the start of their remarks, each president commented on the importance of improving the U.S.-Russia relationship. Putin said the conversation reflected the desire "to redress this negative situation in the bilateral relationship, outline the first steps for improving this relationship to restore the acceptable level of trust, and going back to the previous level of interaction on all mutual interests issues." Trump echoed Putin's comments, adding, "our relationship has never been worse than it is now. However, that changed as of about 4 hours ago. . . . Constructive dialogue between the United States and Russia affords the opportunity to open new pathways toward peace and stability in our world. I would rather take a political risk in pursuit of peace than to risk peace in pursuit of politics."

The forty-minute press conference was expected to focus on what the two had discussed and where they may have reached common ground on international affairs, especially on Syria (Russia supports the Assad regime, while the United States has backed the rebels); Ukraine, where pro-Russian separatists are still fighting the government for control of territory; and global efforts against terrorist groups. Putin did speak briefly on Ukraine, acknowledging that Trump and the United States view Russian incursion in the region illegal and that Russia has a different opinion. And the pair also touched on Syria, nuclear-armed states including North Korea, the Islamic State of Iraq and the Levant (ISIL), and military cooperation. However, the press conference focused primarily on Russian meddling in the 2016 U.S. presidential election, and Trump frequently turned that into a conversation about Democratic attempts to undermine his campaign and presidency.

When asked, Putin denied that Russia had any involvement in the U.S. presidential election. He said, "As to who is to be believed and to who is not to be believed, you can trust no one. . . . Where did you get this idea that President Trump trusts me or I trust him? He defends the interests of the United States of America, and I do defend the interests of the Russian Federation. We do have interests that are common. We are looking for points of contact." Putin added that Trump had "mentioned the issue of the so-called interference of Russia when [sic] the American elections, and I had to reiterate things I said several times . . . that the Russian state has never interfered and is not going to interfere into internal American affairs, including the election process."

Trump shared that he had asked Putin during their meeting about the issue, and that Putin gave an "extremely strong and powerful" denial of involvement. "They think it's Russia," Trump said, adding, "I have President Putin; he just said it's not Russia. . . . I don't see any reason why it would be." Trump also said that Putin had offered to have Russian intelligence agencies assist with the Mueller investigation, which Trump called "an incredible offer." The president also repeated his claim that there was "no collusion" between his campaign and the Russian government, while Putin noted that his preference was for Trump to defeat Clinton because Trump had talked on the campaign trail about normalizing relations with Russia.

Some in Trump's cabinet, as well as congressional leaders on both sides of the aisle, expressed dismay at Trump's seeming rejection of the findings of the U.S. intelligence community in favor of Putin's words. Dan Coats, director of national intelligence, said the work done was "clear in our assessments of Russian meddling in the 2016 election and their ongoing, pervasive efforts to undermine our democracy," adding, "We will continue to provide unvarnished and objective intelligence in support of our national security." Republicans were quick to share their concern as well. Sen. Jeff Flake, R-Ariz., who has frequently sparred with the president, called the press conference "shameful," and Sen. Ben Sasse, R-Neb., said Trump's comments were "bizarre and flat-out wrong." He went on to say that, while the United States should want a good relationship with Russia, "Vladimir Putin and his thugs are responsible for Soviet-style aggression. When the president plays these moral equivalence games, he gives Putin a propaganda win he desperately needs." Speaker of the House Paul Ryan, R-Wis., said there was "no question that Russia interfered in our election and continues attempts to undermine democracy here and around the world. That is not just the finding of the American intelligence community but also the House Committee on Intelligence. The president must appreciate that Russia is not our ally." In response to the blowback, the president said on Twitter that he respected the intelligence election community but that America could never put its relationship with Russia on a positive footing if they continued to focus on the past.

On July 17, President Trump walked back his remarks made during the summit with Putin, stating that he accepted the findings of the U.S. intelligence community in their investigation into Russian meddling in the 2016 election and that he had "full faith and support for America's great intelligence agencies." But he also said that the meddling "could be other people also, there are a lot of people out there." Trump admitted that he misspoke during his press conference with the Russian leader when he said he could see no reason why it "would" be Russia that interfered, noting that he meant to say "wouldn't."

In addition to his comments on Russian meddling in the 2016 election, Trump was also criticized for failing to produce any meaningful outcome from his summit. The administration characterized the summit itself as a positive outcome and said that follow-up meetings between the two leaders to establish areas of partnership would be forthcoming. In November, confusion arose over a potential second meeting between Trump and Putin in Paris before the annual Armistice Day celebration. Trump stated that he would likely delay their meeting until the Group of 20 meeting in Argentina, scheduled for November 30 to December 1. A Kremlin spokesperson, however, said that the pair would meet briefly in Paris. Trump and Putin never ended up meeting in Argentina, either.

—Heather Kerrigan

*Following are excerpts from the indictment in the case of* United States v. Internet Research Agency, *released on February 16, 2018, against thirteen Russians and three companies who are alleged to have conducted a propaganda and misinformation campaign with the aim of influencing the 2016 U.S. presidential election; excerpts from the July 13, 2018, indictment against twelve Russians for hacking offenses during the 2016 election; and the text of a July 16, 2018, press conference held by U.S. President Donald Trump and Russian President Vladimir Putin following a summit between the two leaders.*

# *DOJ Files Indictments against Thirteen Russians for Interference in U.S. Election*

**February 16, 2018**

IN THE UNITED STATES DISTRICT COURT
FOR THE DISTRICT OF COLUMBIA

UNITED STATES OF AMERICA

v.

INTERNET RESEARCH AGENCY LLC A/K/A MEDIASINTEZ LLC A/K/A GLAVSET LLC A/K/A MIXINFO LLC A/K/A AZIMUT LLC A/K/A NOVINFO LLC, CONCORD MANAGEMENT AND CONSULTING LLC, CONCORD CATERING, YEVGENIY VIKTOROVICH PRIGOZHIN, MIKHAIL IVANOVICH BYSTROV, MIKHAIL LEONIDOVICH BURCHIK A/K/A MIKHAIL ABRAMOV, ALEKSANDRA YURYEVNA KRYLOVA, ANNA VLADISLAVOVNA BOGACHEV A, SERGEY PAVLOVICH POLOZOV, MARIA ANATOLYEVNA BOVDA A/K/A MARIA ANATOLYEVNA BELYAEVA, ROBERT SERGEYEVICH BOVDA, DZHEYKHUN NASIMI OGLY ASLANOV A/K/A JAYHOON ASLANOV A/K/A JAY ASLANOV, VADIM VLADIMIROVICH PODKOPAEV, GLEB IGOREVICH VASILCHENKO, IRINA VIKTOROVNA KAVERZINA, and VLADIMIR VENKOV.

Defendants.

CRIMINAL NO.
(18 U.S.C. §§ 2, 371, 1349, 1028A)

## INDICTMENT

The Grand Jury for the District of Columbia charges:

### Introduction

1. The United States of America, through its departments and agencies, regulates the activities of foreign individuals and entities in and affecting the United States in order to prevent, disclose, and counteract improper foreign influence on U.S. elections and on the U.S. political system. U.S. law bans foreign nationals from making certain expenditures or financial disbursements for the purpose of influencing federal elections. U.S. law also bars agents of any foreign entity from engaging in political activities within the United States without first registering with the Attorney General. And U.S. law requires certain foreign nationals seeking entry to the United States to obtain a visa by providing truthful and accurate information to the government. Various federal agencies, including the Federal Election Commission, the U.S. Department of Justice, and the U.S. Department of State, are charged with enforcing these laws.

2. Defendant INTERNET RESEARCH AGENCY LLC ("ORGANIZATION") is a Russian organization engaged in operations to interfere with elections and political processes. Defendants MIKHAIL IVANOVICH BYSTROV, MIKHAIL LEONIDOVICH BURCHIK, ALEKSANDRA YURYEVNA KRYLOVA, ANNA VLADISLAVOVNA BOGACHEVA, SERGEY PAVLOVICH POLOZOV, MARIA ANATOLYEVNA BOVDA, ROBERT SERGEYEVICH BOVDA, DZHEYKHUN NASIMI OGLY ASLANOV, VADIM VLADIMIROVICH PODKOPAEV, GLEB IGOREVICH VASILCHENKO, IRINA VIKTOROVNA KAVERZINA, and VLADIMIR VENKOV worked in various capacities to carry out Defendant ORGANIZATION's interference operations targeting the United States. From in or around 2014 to the present, Defendants knowingly and intentionally conspired with each other (and with persons known and unknown to the Grand Jury) to defraud the United States by impairing, obstructing, and defeating the lawful functions

of the government through fraud and deceit for the purpose of interfering with the U.S. political and electoral processes, including the presidential election of 2016.

3. Beginning as early as 2014, Defendant ORGANIZATION began operations to interfere with the U.S. political system, including the 2016 U.S. presidential election. Defendant ORGANIZATION received funding for its operations from Defendant YEVGENIY VIKTOROVICH PRIGOZHIN and companies he controlled, including Defendants CONCORD MANAGEMENT AND CONSULTING LLC and CONCORD CATERING (collectively "CONCORD"). Defendants CONCORD and PRIGOZHIN spent significant funds to further the ORGANIZATION's operations and to pay the remaining Defendants, along with other uncharged ORGANIZATION employees, salaries and bonuses for their work at the ORGANIZATION.

4. Defendants, posing as U.S. persons and creating false U.S. personas, operated social media pages and groups designed to attract U.S. audiences. These groups and pages, which addressed divisive U.S. political and social issues, falsely claimed to be controlled by U.S. activists when, in fact, they were controlled by Defendants. Defendants also used the stolen identities of real U.S. persons to post on ORGANIZATION-controlled social media accounts. Over time, these social media accounts became Defendants' means to reach significant numbers of Americans for purposes of interfering with the U.S. political system, including the presidential election of 2016.

5. Certain Defendants traveled to the United States under false pretenses for the purpose of collecting intelligence to inform Defendants' operations. Defendants also procured and used computer infrastructure, based partly in the United States, to hide the Russian origin of their activities and to avoid detection by U.S. regulators and law enforcement.

6. Defendant ORGANIZATION had a strategic goal to sow discord in the U.S. political system, including the 2016 U.S. presidential election. Defendants posted derogatory information about a number of candidates, and by early to mid-2016, Defendants' operations included supporting the presidential campaign of then-candidate Donald J. Trump ("Trump Campaign") and disparaging Hillary Clinton. Defendants made various expenditures to carry out those activities, including buying political advertisements on social media in the names of U.S. persons and entities. Defendants also staged political rallies inside the United States, and while posing as U.S. grassroots entities and U.S. persons, and without revealing their Russian identities and ORGANIZATION affiliation, solicited and compensated real U.S. persons to promote or disparage candidates. Some Defendants, posing as U.S. persons and without revealing their Russian association, communicated with unwitting individuals associated with the Trump Campaign and with other political activists to seek to coordinate political activities.

7. In order to carry out their activities to interfere in U.S. political and electoral processes without detection of their Russian affiliation, Defendants conspired to obstruct the lawful functions of the United States government through fraud and deceit, including by making expenditures in connection with the 2016 U.S. presidential election without proper regulatory disclosure; failing to register as foreign agents carrying out political activities within the United States; and obtaining visas through false and fraudulent statements.

*[The remaining sections of the indictment, outlining the specific counts against those named in the filing, have been omitted.]*

Source: Department of Justice. *United States v. Internet Research Agency.* Criminal no. 18 U.S.C. §§ 2, 371, 1349, 1028A. Filed February 16, 2018. https://www.justice.gov/file/1035477/download.

# Grand Jury Indicts Twelve Russians for Hacking Offenses in U.S. Election

DOCUMENT

**July 13, 2018**

### IN THE UNITED STATES DISTRICT COURT
### FOR THE DISTRICT OF COLUMBIA

UNITED STATES OF AMERICA

v.

VIKTOR BORISOVICH NETYKSHO, BORIS ALEKSEYEVICH ANTONOV, DMITRIY SERGEYEVICH BADIN, IVAN SERGEYEVICH YERMAKOV, ALEKSEY VIKTOROVICH

LUKASHEV, SERGEY ALEKSANDROVICH MORGACHEV, NIKOLAY YURYEVICH KOZACHEK, PAVEL VYACHESLAVOVICH YERSHOV, ARTEM ANDREYEVICH MALYSHEV, ALEKSANDR VLADIMIROVICH OSADCHUK, ALEKSEY ALEKSANDRO VICH POTEMKIN, and ANATOLIY SERGEYEVICH KOVALEV,

Defendants.

CRIMINAL NO.

(18 U.S.C. §§ 2, 371, 1030, 1028A, 1956, and 3551 et seq.)

## INDICTMENT

The Grand Jury for the District of Columbia charges:

## COUNT ONE

### (Conspiracy to Commit an Offense Against the United States)

1. In or around 2016, the Russian Federation ("Russia") operated a military intelligence agency called the Main Intelligence Directorate of the General Staff ("GRU"). The GRU had multiple units, including Units 26165 and 74455, engaged in cyber operations that involved the staged releases of documents stolen through computer intrusions. These units conducted large-scale cyber operations to interfere with the 2016 U.S. presidential election.

2. Defendants VIKTOR BORISOVICH NETYKSHO, BORIS ALEKSEYEVICH ANTONOV, DMITRIY SERGEYEVICH BADIN, IVAN SERGEYEVICH YERMAKOV, ALEKSEY VIKTOROVICH LUKASHEV, SERGEY ALEKSANDROVICH MORGACHEV, NIKOLAY YURYEVICH KOZACHEK, PAVEL VYACHESLAVOVICH YERSHOV, ARTEM ANDREYEVICH MALYSHEV, ALEKSANDR VLADIMIROVICH OSADCHUK, and ALEKSEY ALEKSANDROVICH POTEMKIN were GRU officers who knowingly and intentionally conspired with each other, and with persons known and unknown to the Grand Jury (collectively the "Conspirators"), to gain unauthorized access (to "hack") into the computers of U.S. persons and entities involved in the 2016 U.S. presidential election, steal documents from those computers, and stage releases of the stolen documents to interfere with the 2016 U.S. presidential election.

3. Starting in at least March 2016, the Conspirators used a variety of means to hack the email accounts of volunteers and employees of the U.S. presidential campaign of Hillary Clinton (the "Clinton Campaign"), including the email account of the Clinton Campaign's chairman.

4. By in or around April 2016, the Conspirators also hacked into the computer networks of the Democratic Congressional Campaign Committee ("DCCC") and the Democratic National Committee ("DNC"). The Conspirators covertly monitored the computers of dozens of DCCC and DNC employees, implanted hundreds of files containing malicious computer code ("malware"), and stole emails and other documents from the DCCC and DNC.

5. By in or around April 2016, the Conspirators began to plan the release of materials stolen from the Clinton Campaign, DCCC, and DNC.

6. Beginning in or around June 2016, the Conspirators staged and released tens of thousands of the stolen emails and documents. They did so using fictitious online personas, including "DCLeaks" and "Guccifer 2.0."

7. The Conspirators also used the Guccifer 2.0 persona to release additional stolen documents through a website maintained by an organization ("Organization 1"), that had previously posted documents stolen from U.S. persons, entities, and the U.S. government. The Conspirators continued their U.S. election-interference operations through in or around November 2016.

8. To hide their connections to Russia and the Russian government, the Conspirators used false identities and made false statements about their identities. To further avoid detection, the Conspirators used a network of computers located across the world, including in the United States, and paid for this infrastructure using cryptocurrency. . . .

*[Information on each of the defendants charged under this count has been omitted.]*

### Object of the Conspiracy

20. The object of the conspiracy was to hack into the computers of U.S. persons and entities involved in the 2016 U.S. presidential election, steal documents from those computers, and stage releases of the stolen documents to interfere with the 2016 U.S. presidential election.

*[A section on the manner and means under which the conspiracy was undertaken has been omitted.]*

## Statutory Allegations

... 51. From at least in or around March 2016 through November 2016, in the District of Columbia and elsewhere, Defendants NETYKSHO, ANTONOV, BADIN, YERMAKOV, LUKASHEV, MORGACHEV, KOZACHEK, YERSHOV, MALYSHEV, OSADCHUK, and POTEMKIN, together with others known and unknown to the Grand Jury, knowingly and intentionally conspired to commit offenses against the United States, namely:

a. To knowingly access a computer without authorization and exceed authorized access to a computer, and to obtain thereby information from a protected computer, where the value of the information obtained exceeded $5,000, in violation of Title 18, United States Code, Sections 1030(a)(2)(C) and 1030(c)(2)(B); and

b. To knowingly cause the transmission of a program, information, code, and command, and as a result of such conduct, to intentionally cause damage without authorization to a protected computer, and where the offense did cause and, if completed, would have caused, loss aggregating $5,000 in value to at least one person during a one-year period from a related course of conduct affecting a protected computer, and damage affecting at least ten protected computers during a one-year period, in violation of Title 18, United States Code, Sections 1030(a)(5)(A) and 1030(c)(4)(B).

52. In furtherance of the Conspiracy and to effect its illegal objects, the Conspirators committed the overt acts set forth in paragraphs 1 through 19, 21 through 49, 55, and 57 through 64, which are re-alleged and incorporated by reference as if fully set forth herein.

53. In furtherance of the Conspiracy, and as set forth in paragraphs 1 through 19, 21 through 49, 55, and 57 through 64, the Conspirators knowingly falsely registered a domain name and knowingly used that domain name in the course of committing an offense, namely, the Conspirators registered domains, including dcleaks.com and actblues.com, with false names and addresses, and used those domains in the course of committing the felony offense charged in Count One. ...

## COUNTS TWO THROUGH NINE

### (Aggravated Identity Theft)

... 55. On or about the dates specified below, in the District of Columbia and elsewhere, Defendants VIKTOR BORISOVICH NETYKSHO, BORIS ALEKSEYEVICH ANTONOV, DMITRIY SERGEYEVICH BADIN, IVAN SERGEYEVICH YERMAKOV, ALEKSEY VIKTOROVICH LUKASHEV, SERGEY ALEKSANDROVICH MORGACHEV, NIKOLAY YURYEVICH KOZACHEK, PAVEL VYACHESLAVOVICH YERSHOV, ARTEM ANDREYEVICH MALYSHEV, ALEKSANDR VLADIMIROVICH OSADCHUK, and ALEKSEY ALEKSANDROVICH POTEMKIN did knowingly transfer, possess, and use, without lawful authority, a means of identification of another person during and in relation to a felony violation enumerated in Title 18, United States Code, Section 1028A(c), namely, computer fraud in violation of Title 18, United States

Code, Sections 1030(a)(2)(C) and 1030(c)(2)(B), knowing that the means of identification belonged to another real person:

*[A table of the counts and dates of each instance of identity theft has been omitted.]*

## COUNT TEN

### (Conspiracy to Launder Money)

...57. To facilitate the purchase of infrastructure used in their hacking activity—including hacking into the computers of U.S. persons and entities involved in the 2016 U.S. presidential election and releasing the stolen documents—the Defendants conspired to launder the equivalent of more than $95,000 through a web of transactions structured to capitalize on the perceived anonymity of cryptocurrencies such as bitcoin.

58. Although the Conspirators caused transactions to be conducted in a variety of currencies, including U.S. dollars, they principally used bitcoin when purchasing servers, registering domains, and otherwise making payments in furtherance of hacking activity. Many of these payments were processed by companies located in the United States that provided payment processing services to hosting companies, domain registrars, and other vendors both international and domestic. The use of bitcoin allowed the Conspirators to avoid direct relationships with traditional financial institutions, allowing them to evade greater scrutiny of their identities and sources of funds.

59. All bitcoin transactions are added to a public ledger called the Blockchain, but the Blockchain identifies the parties to each transaction only by alpha-numeric identifiers known as bitcoin addresses. To further avoid creating a centralized paper trail of all of their purchases, the Conspirators purchased infrastructure using hundreds of different email accounts, in some cases using a new account for each purchase. The Conspirators used fictitious names and addresses in order to obscure their identities and their links to Russia and the Russian government. For example, the dcleaks.com domain was registered and paid for using the fictitious name "Carrie Feehan" and an address in New York. In some cases, as part of the payment process, the Conspirators provided vendors with non-sensical addresses such as "usa Denver AZ," "gfhgh ghfhgfh fdgfdg WA," and "1 2 dwd District of Columbia."

60. The Conspirators used several dedicated email accounts to track basic bitcoin transaction information and to facilitate bitcoin payments to vendors. One of these dedicated accounts, registered with the username "gfadel47," received hundreds of bitcoin payment requests from approximately 100 different email accounts. For example, on or about February 1, 2016, the gfadel47 account received the instruction to "[p]lease send exactly 0.026043 bitcoin to" a certain thirty-four character bitcoin address. Shortly thereafter, a transaction matching those exact instructions was added to the Blockchain.

61. On occasion, the Conspirators facilitated bitcoin payments using the same computers that they used to conduct their hacking activity, including to create and send test spearphishing emails. Additionally, one of these dedicated accounts was used by the Conspirators in or around 2015 to renew the registration of a

domain (linuxkrnl.net) encoded in certain X-Agent malware installed on the DNC network.

62. The Conspirators funded the purchase of computer infrastructure for their hacking activity in part by "mining" bitcoin. Individuals and entities can mine bitcoin by allowing their computing power to be used to verify and record payments on the bitcoin public ledger, a service for which they are rewarded with freshly-minted bitcoin. The pool of bitcoin generated from the GRU's mining activity was used, for example, to pay a Romanian company to register the domain dcleaks .com through a payment processing company located in the United States.

63. In addition to mining bitcoin, the Conspirators acquired bitcoin through a variety of means designed to obscure the origin of the funds. This included purchasing bitcoin through peer-to-peer exchanges, moving funds through other digital currencies, and using pre-paid cards. They also enlisted the assistance of one or more third-party exchangers who facilitated layered transactions through digital currency exchange platforms providing heightened anonymity.

64. The Conspirators used the same funding structure—and in some cases, the very same pool of funds—to purchase key accounts, servers, and domains used in their election-related hacking activity. . . .

## COUNT ELEVEN

### (Conspiracy to Commit an Offense Against the United States)

66. Paragraphs 1 through 8 of this Indictment are re-alleged and incorporated by reference as if fully set forth herein.

### Defendants

67. Paragraph 18 of this Indictment relating to ALEKSANDR VLADIMIROVICH OSADCHUK is re-alleged and incorporated by reference as if fully set forth herein.

68. Defendant ANATOLIY SERGEYEVICH KOVALEV (Ковалев Анатолий Сергеевич) was an officer in the Russian military assigned to Unit 74455 who worked in the GRU's 22 Kirova Street building (the Tower).

69. Defendants OSADCHUK and KOVALEV were GRU officers who knowingly and intentionally conspired with each other and with persons, known and unknown to the Grand Jury, to hack into the computers of U.S. persons and entities responsible for the administration of 2016 U.S. elections, such as state boards of elections, secretaries of state, and U.S. companies that supplied software and other technology related to the administration of U.S. elections.

Object of the Conspiracy

70. The object of the conspiracy was to hack into protected computers of persons and entities charged with the administration of the 2016 U.S. elections in order to access those computers and steal voter data and other information stored on those computers.

*[The details of the manner under which activities listed under Count Eleven were carried out, as well as the forfeiture required of the defendants if found guilty, have been omitted.]*

Source: Department of Justice. *United States v. Viktor Borisovich Netyksho.* Criminal no. 18 U.S.C. §§ 2, 371, 1030, 1028A, 1956, and 3551 et seq. Filed July 13, 2018. https://www.justice.gov/file/1080281/download.

# Trump and Putin Remark on Election Interference during Summit

**July 16, 2018**

*President Putin.* Thank you so much. Shall we start working, I guess? Distinguished Mr. President, ladies and gentlemen: Negotiations with the President of the United States, Donald Trump, took place in a frank and businesslike atmosphere. I think we can call it a success and a very fruitful round of negotiations.

We carefully analyzed the current status—the present and the future of the Russia-United States relationship; key issues of the global agenda. It's quite clear to everyone that the bilateral relationship are [*sic*] going through a complicated stage, and yet those impediments—the current tension, the tense atmosphere—essentially have no solid reason behind it.

The cold war is a thing of past. The era of acute ideological confrontation of the two countries is a thing of the remote past, is a vestige of the past. The situation in the world changed dramatically.

Today, both Russia and the United States face a whole new set of challenges. Those include a dangerous maladjustment of mechanisms for maintaining international security and stability, regional crises, the creeping threats of terrorism and transnational crime. It's the snowballing problems in the economy, environmental risks, and other sets of challenges. We can only cope with these challenges if we join the ranks and work together. Hopefully, we will reach this understanding with our American partners.

Today's negotiations reflected our joint wish—our joint wish with President Trump to redress this negative situation in the bilateral relationship, outline the first steps for improving this relationship to restore the acceptable level of trust, and going back to the previous level of interaction on all mutual interests issues.

As major nuclear powers, we bear special responsibility for maintaining international security. And it made it vital—and we mentioned this during the negotiations—it's crucial that we fine-tune the dialogue on strategic stability and global security and nonproliferation of weapons of mass destruction. We submitted our American colleagues a note with a number of specific suggestions.

We believe it necessary to work together further on to interact on the disarmament agenda, military, and technical cooperation. This includes the extension of the Strategic Offensive Arms Limitation Treaty. It's a dangerous situation with the global American antimissile defense system; it's the implementation issues with the INF treaty; and of course, the agenda of nonplacement of weapons in space.

We favor the continued cooperation in counterterrorism and maintaining cybersecurity. And I'd like to point out specifically that our special services are cooperating quite successfully together. The most recent example is their operational cooperation within the recently concluded World Football Cup.

In general, the contacts among the special services should be put to a systemwide basis—should be brought to a systemic framework. I recall—I reminded President Trump about the suggestion to reestablish the working group on antiterrorism. We also mentioned a plethora of regional crises. It's not always that our postures dovetail exactly. And yet, the overlapping and mutual interests abound. We have to look for points of contact and interact closer in a variety of international fora.

Clearly, we mentioned the regional crisis; for instance, Syria. As far as Syria is concerned, the task of establishing peace and reconciliation in this country could be the first showcase example of this successful joint work. Russia and the United States apparently can act proactively and take—assume the leadership in this issue, and organize the interaction to overcome humanitarian crisis, and help Syrian refugees to go back to their homes.

In order to accomplish this level of successful cooperation in Syria, we have all the required components. Let me remind you that both Russian and American military have acquired a useful experience of coordination of their action, established the operational channels of communication which permitted to avoid dangerous incidents and unintentional collisions in the air and in the ground.

Also, crushing terrorists in the southwest of Syria—the south of Syria—should be brought to the full compliance with the treaty of 1974 about the separation of forces—about separation of forces of Israel and Syria. This will bring peace to Golan Heights and bring a more peaceful relationship between Syria and Israel, and also to provide security of the State of Israel.

Mr. President paid special attention to the issue during today's negotiations, and I would like to confirm that Russia is interested in this development, and [thus] will act accordingly. Thus far, we will make a step toward creating a lasting peace in compliance with the respective resolutions of Security Council, for instance, the Resolution 338.

We—it is—we're glad that the Korean Peninsula issue is starting to resolve. To a great extent, it was possible thanks to the personal engagement of President Trump, who opted for dialogue instead of confrontation.

You know, we also mentioned our concern about the withdrawal of the United States from the JCPOA. Well, the U.S.—our U.S. counterparts are aware of our posture. Let me remind you that thanks to the Iranian nuclear deal, Iran became the most controlled country in the world; it submitted to the control of IAEA. It effectively ensures the exclusively peaceful nature of the Iranian nuclear program and strengthens the nonproliferation regime.

While we discussed the internal Ukrainian crisis, we paid special attention to the bona fide implementation of Minsk Agreements by Kiev. At the same time, the United States could be more decisive in nudging the Ukrainian leadership and encourage it to work actively on this. We paid more attention to economic ties and economic cooperation. It's clear that both countries—the businesses of both countries are interested in this.

American delegation was one of the largest delegations in the St. Petersburg Economic Forum. It featured over 500 representatives from American businesses. We agreed—me and President Trump—we agreed to create the high-level working group that would bring together captains of Russian and American business. After all, entrepreneurs and businessmen know better how to articulate this successful business cooperation. We'll let them think and make their proposals and their suggestions in this regard.

Once again, President Trump mentioned the issue of the so-called interference of Russia when the American elections [*sic*], and I had to reiterate things I said several times, including during our personal contacts, that the Russian state has never interfered and is not going to interfere into internal American affairs, including the election process.

Any specific material, if such things arise, we are ready to analyze together. For instance, we can analyze them through the joint working group on cybersecurity, the establishment of which we discussed during our previous contacts.

And clearly, it's past time we restore our cooperation in the cultural area, in the humanitarian area. As far as—I think you know that recently we hosted the American Congressmen delegation, and now it's perceived and portrayed almost as a historic event, although it should have been just a current affairs—just business as usual. And in this regard, we mentioned this proposal to the President.

But we have to think about the practicalities of our cooperation, but also about the rationale, the underlying logic of it. And we have to engage experts on bilateral relationship who know history and the background of our relationship. The idea is to create an expert council that would include political scientists, prominent diplomats, and former military experts from both countries who would look for points of contact between the two countries, that would look for ways on putting the relationship on the trajectory of growth.

In general, we are glad with the outcome of our first full-scale meeting, because previously we only had a chance to talk briefly on international fora. We had a good conversation with President Trump, and I hope that we start to understand each other better. And I'm grateful to Donald for it.

Clearly, there are some challenges left when we were not able to clear all the backlog. But I think that we made a first important step in this direction.

And in conclusion, I want to point out that this atmosphere of cooperation is something that we are especially grateful for to our Finnish hosts. We're grateful for Finnish people and Finnish leadership for what they've done. I know that we've caused some inconvenience to Finland, and we apologize for it.

Thank you for your attention.

*President Trump.* Thank you. Thank you very much.

Thank you. I have just concluded a meeting with President Putin on a wide range of critical issues for both of our countries. We had direct, open, deeply productive dialogue. It went very well.

Before I begin, I want to thank President Niinistö of Finland for graciously hosting today's summit. President Putin and I were saying how lovely it was and what a great job they did.

I also want to congratulate Russia and President Putin for having done such an excellent job in hosting the World Cup. It was really one of the best ever, and your team also did very well. It was a great job.

I'm here today to continue the proud tradition of bold American diplomacy. From the earliest days of our Republic, American leaders have understood that diplomacy and engagement is preferable to conflict and hostility. A productive dialogue is not only good for the United States and good for Russia, but it is good for the world.

The disagreements between our two countries are well known, and President Putin and I discussed them at length today. But if we're going to solve many of the problems facing our world, then we are going to have to find ways to cooperate in pursuit of shared interests. Too often, in both recent past and long ago, we have seen the consequences when diplomacy is left on the table. We have also seen the benefits of cooperation. In the last century, our nations fought alongside one another in the Second World War. Even during the tensions of the cold war, when the world looked much different than it does today, the United States and Russia were able to maintain a strong dialogue.

But our relationship has never been worse than it is now. However, that changed as of about 4 hours ago. I really believe that. Nothing would be easier politically than to refuse to meet, to refuse to engage. But that would not accomplish anything. As President, I cannot make decisions on foreign policy in a futile effort to appease partisan critics or the media or Democrats who want to do nothing but resist and obstruct.

Constructive dialogue between the United States and Russia affords the opportunity to open new pathways toward peace and stability in our world. I would rather take a political risk in pursuit of peace than to risk peace in pursuit of politics. As President, I will always put what is best for America and what is best for the American people.

During today's meeting, I addressed directly with President Putin the issue of Russian interference in our elections. I felt this was a message best delivered in person. We spent a great deal of time talking about it, and President Putin may very well want to address it, and very strongly—because he feels very strongly about it, and he has an interesting idea.

We also discussed one of the most critical challenges facing humanity: nuclear proliferation. I provided an update on my meeting last month with Chairman Kim on the denuclearization of North Korea. And after today, I am very sure that President Putin and Russia want very much to end that problem. They're going to work with us, and I appreciate that commitment.

The President and I also discussed the scourge of radical Islamic terrorism. Both Russia and the United States have suffered horrific terrorist attacks, and we have agreed to maintain open communication between our security agencies to protect our citizens from this global menace.

Last year, we told Russia about a planned attack in St. Petersburg, and they were able to stop it cold. They found them. They stopped them. There was no doubt about it. I appreciated President Putin's phone call afterwards to thank me.

I also emphasized the importance of placing pressure on Iran to halt its nuclear ambitions and to stop its campaign of violence throughout the area, throughout the Middle East.

As we discussed at length, the crisis in Syria is a complex one. Cooperation between our two countries has the potential to save hundreds of thousands of lives. I also made clear that the United States will not allow Iran to benefit from our successful campaign against ISIS. We have just about eradicated ISIS in the area.

We also agreed that representatives from our national security councils will meet to follow up on all of the issues we addressed today and to continue the progress we have started right here in Helsinki.

Today's meeting is only the beginning of a longer process. But we have taken the first steps toward a brighter future and one with a strong dialogue and a lot of thought. Our expectations are grounded in realism, but our hopes are grounded in America's desire for friendship, cooperation, and peace. And I think I can speak on behalf of Russia when I say that also. President Putin, I want to thank you again for joining me for these important discussions and for advancing open dialogue between Russia and the United States. Our meeting carries on a long tradition of diplomacy between Russia, the United States, for the greater good of all.

And this was a very constructive day. This was a very constructive few hours that we spent together. It's in the interest of both of our countries to continue our conversation, and we have agreed to do so.

I'm sure we'll be meeting again in the future often, and hopefully, we will solve every one of the problems that we discussed today.

So, again, President Putin, thank you very much.

*[At this point, President Trump and President Putin shook hands, and President Putin spoke briefly in English as follows.]*

*President Putin.* Thank you, sir. . . .

*[A question about natural gas production has been omitted.]*

*White House Press Secretary Sarah Huckabee Sanders.* The first question for a U.S. journalist goes to Jeff Mason, from Reuters.

## Russia–U.S. Relations/Investigation into Russia's Interference in 2016 Presidential Election

Q. Thank you. Mr. President, you tweeted this morning that it's U.S. foolishness, stupidity, and the Mueller probe that is responsible for the decline in U.S. relations with Russia. Do you hold Russia at all accountable for anything in particular? And if so, what would you consider them—that they are responsible for?

*President Trump.* Yes, I do. I hold both countries responsible. I think that the United States has been foolish. I think we've all been foolish. We should have had this dialogue a long time ago—a long time, frankly, before I got to office. And I think we're all to blame. I think that the United States now has stepped forward, along with Russia. And we're getting together. And we have a chance to do some great things, whether it's nuclear proliferation, in terms of stopping—because we have to do it. Ultimately, that's probably the most important thing that we can be working on.

But I do feel that we have both made some mistakes. I think that the probe is a disaster for our country. I think it's kept us apart. It's kept us separated. There was no collusion at all. Everybody knows it. People are being brought out to the fore.

So far, that I know, virtually none of it related to the campaign. And they're going to have to try really hard to find somebody that did relate to the campaign. That was a clean campaign. I beat Hillary Clinton easily. And frankly, we beat her—and I'm not even saying from the standpoint—we won that race. And it's a shame that there can even be a little bit of a cloud over it.

People know that. People understand it. But the main thing, and we discussed this also, is zero collusion. And it has had a negative impact upon the relationship of the two largest nuclear powers in the world. We have 90 percent of nuclear power between the two countries. It's ridiculous. It's ridiculous what's going on with the probe.

### Investigation into Russia's Interference in 2016 Presidential Election

*Q.* For President Putin, if I could follow up as well. Why should Americans and why should President Trump believe your statement that Russia did not intervene in the 2016 election, given the evidence that U.S. intelligence agencies have provided? And will you consider extraditing the 12 Russian officials that were indicted last week by a U.S. grand jury?

*President Trump.* Well, I'm going to let the President answer the second part of that question. But, as you know, the whole concept of that came up perhaps a little bit before, but it came out as a reason why the Democrats lost an election, which, frankly, they should have been able to win, because the electoral college is much more advantageous for Democrats, as you know, than it is to Republicans.

We won the electoral college by a lot—306 to 223, I believe. And that was a well-fought—that was a well-fought battle. We did a great job.

And, frankly, I'm going to let the President speak to the second part of your question. But just to say it one time again, and I say it all the time: There was no collusion. I didn't know the President. There was nobody to collude with. There was no collusion with the campaign. And every time you hear all of these—you know, 12 and 14—it's stuff that has nothing to do—and frankly, they admit, these are not people involved in the campaign.

But to the average reader out there, they're saying, "Well, maybe that does." It doesn't. And even the people involved, some perhaps told mis-stories or, though in one case, the FBI said there was no lie. There was no lie. Somebody else said there was.

We ran a brilliant campaign, and that's why I'm President. Thank you.

*President Putin.* As to who is to be believed and to who is not to be believed, you can trust no one, if you take this. Where did you get this idea that President Trump trusts me or I trust him? He defends the interests of the United States of America, and I do defend the interests of the Russian Federation.

We do have interests that are common. We are looking for points of contact. There are issues where our postures diverge, and we are looking for ways to reconcile our differences; how to make our effort more meaningful.

We should not proceed from the immediate political interests that guide certain political powers in our countries. We should be guided by facts. Could you name a single fact that would definitively prove the collusion? This is utter nonsense, just like the President recently mentioned.

Yes, the public at large in the United States had a certain perceived opinion of the candidates during the campaign, but there's nothing particularly extraordinary about it. That's the usual thing.

President Trump, when he was a candidate, he mentioned the need to restore the Russia-U.S. relationship, and it's clear that a certain part of American society felt sympathetic about it, and different people could express their sympathy in different ways. But isn't that natural? Isn't it natural to be sympathetic towards a person who is willing to restore the relationship with our country, who wants to work with us?

We heard the accusations about the Concord country. Well, as far as I know, this company hired American lawyers. And the accusations doesn't—doesn't have a fighting chance in the American courts. So there's no evidence when it comes to the actual facts. So we have to be guided by facts and not by rumors.

Now, let's get back to the issue of these 12 alleged intelligence officers of Russia. I don't know the full extent of the situation, but the President Trump mentioned this issue, and I will look into it.

So far, I can say the following, the things that—off the top of my head: We have an acting—an existing agreement between the United States of America and the Russian Federation, an existing treaty that dates back to 1999, the Mutual Assistance on Criminal Cases. This treaty is in full effect. It works quite efficiently.

On average, we initiate about a hundred, hundred and fifty criminal cases upon request from foreign states. For instance, the last year, there was one extradition case, upon the request, sent by the United States. So this treaty has specific legal procedures.

We can offer that the appropriate commission headed by Special Attorney Mueller—he can use this treaty as a solid foundation, and send a formal, an official request to us so that we would interrogate—we would hold the questioning of these individuals who he believes are privy to some crimes. And our law enforcement are perfectly able to do this questioning and send the appropriate materials to the United States.

Moreover, we can meet you halfway; we can make another step. We can actually permit official representatives of the United States, including the members of this very commission headed by Mr. Mueller—we can let them into the country and they will be present at this questioning.

But in this case, there is another condition. This kind of effort should be a mutual one. Then we would expect that the Americans would reciprocate, and they would question officials, including the officers of law enforcement and intelligence services of the United States whom we believe are—who have something to do with illegal actions on the territory of Russia, and we have to request the presence of our law enforcement.

For instance, we can bring up the—Mr. Browder in this particular case. Business associates of Mr. Browder have earned over $1½ billion in Russia. They never paid any taxes, neither in Russia nor in the United States, and yet the money escaped the country. They were transferred to the United States. They sent a huge amount of money—400 million—as a contribution to the campaign of Hillary Clinton. Well, that's their personal case. It might have been legal, the contribution itself, but the way the money was earned was illegal.

So we have a solid reason to believe that some intelligence officers accompanied and guided these transactions. So we have an interest of questioning them. We can—that could be a first step, and we can also extend it. Options abound, and they all can be found in an appropriate legal framework.

Q. President Putin, did you want President Trump to win the election? And did you direct any of your officials to help him do that?

*President Putin.* Yes, I did. Yes, I did. Because he talked about bringing the U.S.–Russia relationship back to normal. . . .

*[Questions about the Islamic State, military coordination between the two countries, and the World Cup have been omitted.]*

*Press Secretary Sanders.* The final question from the United States will go to Jonathan Lemire, from the AP.

## Russia's Interference in 2016 Presidential Election

Q. Thank you. A question for each President. President Trump—

*President Trump.* Yes.

Q. —you first. Just now, President Putin denied having anything to do with the election interference in 2016. Every U.S. intelligence agency has concluded that Russia did. What—who—my first question for you, sir, is, who do you believe?

My second question is, would you now, with t0he whole world watching, tell President Putin—would you denounce what happened in 2016? And would you warn him to never do it again?

*President Trump.* So let me just say that we have two thoughts. You have groups that are wondering why the FBI never took the server. Why haven't they taken the server? Why was the FBI told to leave the office of the Democratic National Committee? I've been wondering that. I've been asking that for months and months, and I've been tweeting it out and calling it out on social media. Where is the server? I want to know: Where is the server? And what is the server saying?

With that being said, all I can do is ask the question. My people came to me—Dan Coats came to me and some others—they said they think it's Russia. I have President Putin; he just said it's not Russia.

I will say this: I don't see any reason why it would be, but I really do want to see the server. But I have—I have confidence in both parties. I really believe that this will probably go on for a while, but I don't think it can go on without finding out what happened to the server. What happened to the servers of the Pakistani gentleman that worked on the DNC? Where are those servers? They're missing. Where are they? What happened to Hillary Clinton's e-mails? Thirty-three thousand e-mails gone—just gone. I think, in Russia, they wouldn't be gone so easily. I think it's a disgrace that we can't get Hillary Clinton's 33,000 e-mails.

So I have great confidence in my intelligence people, but I will tell you that President Putin was extremely strong and powerful in his denial today. And what he did is an incredible offer; he offered to have the people working on the case come and work with their investigators with respect to the 12 people. I think that's an incredible offer.

Okay? Thank you. Yes, please.

*President Putin.* I'd like to add something to this. After all, I was an intelligence officer myself, and I do know how dossiers are made up. Just a quick—just a second. That's the first thing.

Now, the second thing: I believe that Russia is a democratic state, and I hope you're not denying this right to your own country. You're not denying that United States is a democracy. Do you believe the United States is a democracy? And if so, if it is a democratic state, then the final conclusion in this kind of dispute can only be delivered by a trial by the court, not by the executive—by the law enforcement.

For instance, the Concord company that was brought up is being accused—it's been accused of interference. But this company does not constitute the Russian state. It does not represent the Russian state. And I brought several examples before.

Well, you have a lot of individuals in the United States—take George Soros, for instance—with multibillion capitals, but it doesn't make him—his position, his posture— the posture of the United States? No, it does not. Well, it's the same case. There is the issue of trying a case in the court, and the final say is for the court to deliver. We are now talking about the private—the individuals, and not about particular states. And as far as the most recent allegation is concerned about the Russian intelligence officers, we do have an inter-governmental treaty. Please, do send us the request. We will analyze it properly, and we'll send a formal response.

And as I said, we can extend this cooperation, but we should do it on a reciprocal basis, because we would await our Russian counterparts to provide us access to the persons of interest for us who we believe can have something to do with intelligence services.

Let's discuss the specific issues, and not use the Russia and the U.S. relationship as a loose change—the loose change for this internal political struggle.

*Investigation into Russia's Interference in 2016 Presidential Election*

Q. My question for President—for President Putin. Thank you. Two questions for you, sir. Can you tell me what President Trump may have indicated to you about officially recognizing Crimea as part of Russia?

And then secondly, sir, do you—does the Russian Government have any compromising material on President Trump or his family?

*President Putin.* [*Laughter*] President Trump and—well, the posture of President Trump on Crimea is well known, and he stands firmly by it. He continued to maintain that it was illegal to annex it. We—our viewpoint is different. We held a referendum in strict compliance with the U.N. Charter and the international legislation. For us, this issue— we—[*inaudible*]—to this issue.

And now to the compromising material. Yes, I did heard these rumors that we alleg-edly collected compromising material on Mr. Trump when he was visiting Moscow. Now, distinguished colleague, let me tell you this: When President Trump visit Moscow back then, I didn't even know that he was in Moscow. I treat President Trump with utmost respect. But back then, when he was a private individual, a businessman, nobody informed me that he was in Moscow.

Well, let's take St. Petersburg Economic Forum, for instance. There were over 500 American businessmen—the high-ranking, the high-level ones. I don't even remember the last names of each and every one of them. Well, do you remember—do you think that we try to collect compromising material on each and every single one of them? Well, it's difficult to imagine an utter nonsense of a bigger scale than this.

Well, please, just disregard these issues and don't think about this anymore again.

*President Trump.* And I have to say, if they had it, it would have been out long ago. And if anybody watched Peter Strzok testify over the last couple of days—and I was in

Brussels watching it—it was a disgrace to the FBI, it was a disgrace to our country, and, you would say, that was a total witch hunt.

Thank you very much, everybody. Thank you. Thank you.

SOURCE: Executive Office of the President. "The President's News Conference with President Vladimir Vladimirovich Putin of Russia in Helsinki, Finland." July 16, 2018. *Compilation of Presidential Documents* 2018, no. 00488 (July 16, 2018). https://www.gpo.gov/fdsys/pkg/DCPD-201800488/pdf/DCPD-201800488.pdf.

## OTHER HISTORIC DOCUMENTS OF INTEREST

### FROM THIS VOLUME

### FROM PREVIOUS *HISTORIC DOCUMENTS*

# Ethiopian Prime Minister Resigns

FEBRUARY 17 AND 23, 2018

Beset by political and ethnic unrest and fractures in its ruling coalition, the Ethiopian government began implementing reforms early in 2018 to stop the spread of antigovernment protests. In February, Prime Minister Hailemariam Desalegn announced his resignation, stating that it was necessary to allow further reforms to take place. Desalegn's successor, Abiy Ahmed, moved quickly to accelerate the pace of reform upon taking office, including freeing opposition leaders from jail, lifting restrictions on assembly and expression, and reshuffling cabinet-level positions.

## PROTESTORS DEMAND CHANGE

Since 2015, Ethiopia has been racked by antigovernment protests, many of which have occurred in the Oromia and Amhara regions—the largest of the country's nine ethnically based states. The protests reportedly began over land rights issues such as the now-abandoned plan to expand the capital, Addis Ababa, into the surrounding Oromia region, which involved the seizure of farmland for development purposes. Long-simmering ethnic tensions between the Amhara and the Tigrayan over the government's division of the Wolkayt district also led to protests during this time. (The Amhara claim to be the majority in the Wolkayt district and believe its partial incorporation into the Tigray region was illegal.)

However, the protests soon expanded to encompass calls for broad political and economic reforms and spread to more regions of the country. Ethiopia is a democracy and has held general elections every five years since 1995, but the Ethiopian People's Revolutionary Democratic Front (EPRDF) has run the government for more than twenty-five years and has had complete control of parliament since the last election in 2015. Although the Oromo People's Democratic Organization and the Amhara National Democratic Movement are among the four ethnic parties comprising the EPRDF, the Oromo and Amhara people claim they have been marginalized economically, politically, and culturally by the minority Tigrayans. The Oromo and Amhara are roughly 35 percent and 27 percent, respectively, of Ethiopia's population, while the Tigrayans make up approximately 6 percent of the population. However, the Tigray People's Liberation Front (TPLF)—also part of the EPRDF—has largely dominated the military and intelligence services, and the TPLF's Meles Zenawi served as Ethiopia's prime minister for seventeen years. Desalegn, who succeeded Zenawi in 2012, chaired the fourth coalition member, the Southern Ethiopian People's Democratic Movement, which represents minority tribes in the country's south.

Human rights organizations estimate that hundreds of Ethiopians were killed and tens of thousands arrested in the government's crackdown on protestors and efforts to repress opposition, which, in addition to the use of violence by security forces to disperse demonstrations, involved tight restrictions on Internet and social media use. The government was also accused of using trumped-up charges under Ethiopia's antiterrorism laws to justify mass arrests of opposition members, and some opposition groups, such as Ginbot 7, were deemed terrorist organizations. The government's harsh response in turn prompted further protests, including an August 2016 demonstration involving hundreds of thousands of protestors marching in more than 200 towns and cities.

Then in October 2016, an antigovernment protest took place at the annual Irreechaa festival in the Oromia region. Police fired tear gas and rubber bullets into the crowd, prompting a stampede that killed more than fifty people. Fresh demonstrations against the government's response broke out and ultimately led officials to declare a ten-month state of emergency. Under the state of emergency, the government banned protests, involvement in political campaigns "likely to cause disturbances," political gestures (such as crossing one's arms over one's head to represent protestors being arrested), and the communication of political messages to the public without the government's permission. The government also blocked two foreign-based broadcast channels, ESAT and OMN, that it claimed belonged to terrorist organizations and restricted social media use, saying it could not be used to contact "outside forces" such as "terrorist organizations and anti-peace groups designated as terrorist."

Protests dropped off somewhat but continued throughout 2017 despite the state of emergency, leading the government to consider other measures to quiet the discord. In January 2018, the government released hundreds of opposition supporters from jail and announced it would close the notorious Maekelawi detention center, which Amnesty International has described as a "torture chamber, used by the Ethiopian authorities to brutally interrogate anybody who dares to dissent including peaceful protestors, journalists and opposition figures." Desalegn said he wanted to "widen the democratic space for all" and "foster national reconciliation" with these actions.

## Desalegn Resigns, State of Emergency Declared

Facing unending protests and infighting within the EPRDF, Desalegn submitted a letter of resignation to parliament on February 15, 2018. Desalegn said he would step down as prime minister and as chair of the EPRDF, though he would remain in office until his resignation was accepted and his replacement was chosen. Desalegn wrote that "unrest and a political crisis have led to the loss of lives and displacement of many" and that his resignation was "vital in the bid to carry out reforms that would lead to sustainable peace and democracy."

The EPRDF quickly declared a new state of emergency, with the state-run Ethiopian Broadcasting Corporation reporting the coalition had concluded "imposing emergency rule would be vital to safeguarding the constitutional order of our country." Parliament ratified the six-month state of emergency on March 2. Notably, eighty-eight deputies voted against the measure, an unprecedented show of dissent given the EPRDF's total control of parliament. The new state of emergency prohibited most public gatherings and increased the security forces' power to respond to the ongoing unrest. Officials at the U.S. Embassy in Ethiopia issued a statement saying they "strongly disagree" with the government's imposition of "restrictions on fundamental rights" under the state of emergency, acknowledging the government's concerns about violence but declaring that "the answer is greater freedom, not less." Similarly, UN Secretary-General Antonió Guterres emphasized "the importance of avoiding actions that would infringe on the human rights and fundamental freedoms of citizens." Guterres also welcomed the steps taken by Ethiopia to implement government reforms and pledged the UN's continued support for reforms that "enhance governance, stability and development."

## New Prime Minister Accelerates Reform

The EPRDF selected Abiy Ahmed of the Oromo People's Democratic Organization as Desalegn's successor. Taking office on April 2, Ahmed became Ethiopia's first Oromo prime minister and moved quickly to initiate a series of reforms. Hundreds of additional political prisoners were freed in May, including Ginbot 7 leader Andargachew Tsege. The group later announced the suspension of its armed resistance against the government, saying Ahmed gave it hope that "genuine democracy" was "a real possibility." Ahmed invited opposition leaders to return from exile and welcomed UN High Commissioner for Human Rights Zeid Raad al-Hussein back to Ethiopia. He also ended the state of emergency in June, two months early.

One of Ahmed's most significant early accomplishments was ending Ethiopia's violent twenty-year dispute with neighboring country Eritrea. On June 5, Ahmed agreed to accept the terms of a peace agreement reached in 2000, following a nasty two-year war, which included granting disputed border territory to Eritrea. He and Eritrean President Isaias Afwerki appeared together in public on July 9 to officially declare the end of hostilities. The two countries subsequently reopened their respective embassies and their land border, restored flights, and allowed direct phone calls between their citizens.

Also in July, the government announced the firing of five senior prison officials for alleged human rights abuses. Ahmed had previously described the use of torture by security services as "the terrorist act" of the government. Other reforms under Ahmed included the unblocking of websites and broadcast channels and a promise that Ethiopia will hold free and competitive elections in 2020. Ahmed has also embarked on a listening tour, holding town hall–style meetings with citizens across the country. "Inclusiveness and coexistence is critical in Ethiopia because of differences in terms of tribalism, and religion and the virtually feudal system of land ownership which prevailed in the past," said Ahmed. "Democracy is an existential issue for Ethiopia. There is no option but multi-partyism."

While the antigovernment protests stopped after Ahmed took office, a fresh wave of ethnic violence broke out over the summer: Muslims and Christians fought each other in Oromia; violence erupted between the Gedeo and Guji Oromo people during a land dispute; and mobs attacked minorities including the Somalis and Tigrayans. In mid-September, violent clashes were reported in the villages on the outskirts of Addis Ababa. According to the Oromia Police Commission, twenty-three people were killed, and hundreds of suspects were arrested. Young Oromo men connected with the Oromo Liberation Front—an opposition group recently returned from exile—were blamed for leading the attacks against the smaller Dorze, Famo, and Wolaita ethnic groups. Protests against the Oromo group were held in Addis Ababa in response to the attacks. Observers speculated that these conflicts were linked to the government's reforms and its relaxation of long-held control.

## Changes in Leadership Bring Greater Diversity

Ahmed's reforms continued into the fall of 2018 with a cabinet reshuffle in October. The total number of cabinet posts was reduced from twenty-eight to twenty, and women were named to half of these positions. Women were appointed to lead the ministries of trade, transport and labor, culture, science, and revenue, and—for the first time—were also tapped to fill top security roles. Aisha Mohammed was named as defense minister and Muferiat Kamil was named the minister of peace, with oversight of the federal police, intelligence agencies, and information security agency.

Then, on October 25, the Ethiopian parliament approved Sahle-Work Zewde as the country's first female president. Zewde had previously served as the special representative to the African Union for the UN secretary-general and had also led the UN's Nairobi office. The presidency is a ceremonial position in Ethiopia, but officials acknowledged the significance of Zewde's selection. "In a patriarchal society such as ours, the appointment of a female head of state not only sets the standard for the future but also normalizes women as decision makers in public life," said Fitsum Arega, Ahmed's chief of staff.

—Linda Grimm

*Following is a statement from the U.S. Embassy in Ethiopia from February 17, 2018, responding to the government's declaration of a state of emergency; and a statement from UN Secretary-General Antonió Guterres issued on February 23, 2018, in response to Prime Minister Hailemariam Desalegn's resignation.*

# U.S. Embassy on the Ethiopian Government's State of Emergency

**February 17, 2018**

We strongly disagree with the Ethiopian government's decision to impose a state of emergency that includes restrictions on fundamental rights such as assembly and expression.

We recognize and share concerns expressed by the government about incidents of violence and loss of life, but firmly believe that the answer is greater freedom, not less.

The challenges facing Ethiopia, whether to democratic reform, economic growth, or lasting stability, are best addressed through inclusive discourse and political processes, rather than through the imposition of restrictions.

The declaration of a state of emergency undermines recent positive steps toward creating a more inclusive political space, including the release of thousands of prisoners. Restrictions on the ability of the Ethiopian people to express themselves peacefully sends a message that they are not being heard.

We strongly urge the government to rethink this approach and identify other means to protect lives and property while preserving, and indeed expanding, the space for meaningful dialogue and political participation that can pave the way to a lasting democracy.

SOURCE: U.S. Embassy in Ethiopia. "U.S. Embassy Statement on the Ethiopian Government's Declared State of Emergency." February 17, 2018. https://et.usembassy.gov/u-s-embassy-statement-ethiopian-governments-declared-state-emergency.

# United Nations Welcomes Ethiopia's Intention to Continue Governance Reforms

**February 23, 2018**

The following statement was issued today by the Spokesman for UN Secretary-General António Guterres:

> The United Nations takes note of the recent decision by the Prime Minister of Ethiopia, Hailemariam Desalegn, to resign, to "allow further political reforms to take place in the country aimed at widening democratic space". The Government of Ethiopia has expressed the intention to continue with implementation of governance reforms and increase participation in the political process.
>
> The United Nations welcomes the steps so far undertaken in that direction, including the release of detainees. The United Nations considers Ethiopia a valued partner in peace and security, development, humanitarian and human rights issues in the Horn of Africa and the African continent, and will continue to support the Government and people of Ethiopia in implementing reforms that would enhance governance, stability and development.
>
> The United Nations also takes note of the recent declaration of a state of emergency and stresses the importance of avoiding actions that would infringe on the human rights and fundamental freedoms of citizens, the peace, security and stability of the country, or impact on the delivery of humanitarian assistance.

SOURCE: United Nations. "United Nations Welcomes Government of Ethiopia's Intention to Continue Governance Reforms following Resignation Announcement by Prime Minister." February 23, 2018. https://www.un.org/press/en/2018/sgsm18908.doc.htm.

# Governors Respond to Teacher Strikes in West Virginia, Oklahoma, and Arizona

FEBRUARY 21, MARCH 6, APRIL 12, AND MAY 3, 2018

In February 2016, West Virginia teachers walked out of their classrooms, shuttering schools and creating a ripple effect across the United States as a growing number of educators came together to protest low wages, slashed school budgets, high health-care costs, and changes to pension programs. In addition to West Virginia, statewide strikes took place in Arizona and Oklahoma, while smaller, district-based walkouts took place in Colorado, Kentucky, and North Carolina. Results were mixed. In states such as Oklahoma, teachers returned to their classrooms without new concessions (they had already received a $6,000 pay increase before walking out), but in Arizona, the governor signed into law a requirement that would progressively raise teacher pay by 20 percent by 2020.

## WEST VIRGINIA EDUCATORS START A TREND

On February 22, 2018, three unions representing West Virginia teachers—the American Federation of Teachers–West Virginia, West Virginia Education Association, and West Virginia School Service Personnel—called on educators to walk out of their classrooms in protest over low wages. At the time, teachers in the state earned an average of $45,555, according to the National Education Association, one of the lowest teacher salaries in the nation. The strike began one day after Gov. Jim Justice signed a 2 percent pay increase into law that would take effect in 2019 and that would be followed by a 1 percent increase in both 2020 and 2021. The teachers argued that the increase did not go far enough, especially in light of benefit cuts and increases in the cost of their health insurance.

The move quickly drew national attention, not only because it put nearly 277,000 kids out of school but also because strikes in the public education sector had become increasingly rare since their heyday of the 1970s. Part of the decline is driven by the growing number of states adopting right-to-work legislation, which has decreased union membership and their influence among educators.

Republicans, who control all statewide offices and the legislature, pushed back. "This illegal work stoppage affects hundreds of thousands of students and families across our state," said the state's attorney general, Patrick Morrisey, who added that his office was prepared to take legal action if necessary to force teachers back into the classroom. In the legislature, state house Finance Chair Eric Nelson said that while "we'd all like to do a lot more," the state budget simply did not have enough left over for additional raises for teachers.

The unions leading the strike advocated for a 5 percent raise for teachers and refused to ask their members to return to the classroom until it was signed into law. In response, the state house passed a bill—one supported by the governor—that would provide the requested 5 percent raise. The senate, however, considered legislation to provide a 4 percent hike, which the house rejected. Gov. Justice encouraged the legislators to find a middle ground, tweeting, "Mistakes and differences aside, we've got to get our kids back to school. While everyone is focused on the mistakes, my focus is solely on getting our children back to school. It's time to quit playing politics and get our kids back in school." As teachers and their supporters flooded the state capitol building, the conference committee met and agreed on the house version, with a caveat from Republican senators that the raises could not be covered by an anticipated increase in revenue in the coming fiscal year but would rather need to be funded by deep cuts to other budgetary items like entitlement programs. The bill passed both houses unanimously.

On March 6, the West Virginia legislature sent the bill to the governor for his signature, and educators returned to their classrooms one day later. Additionally, Gov. Justice convened a task force to review a lingering concern of teachers—the high cost of their health insurance. At the same time, he temporarily froze insurance rates at the fiscal year 2018 level, pending the task force's recommendations.

## Oklahoma Teachers See Small Gains, Some Defeat

In late March, the Oklahoma legislature passed a bill giving teachers an average raise of around $6,000 each, far lower than the $10,000 requested by the union representing the state's teachers, the Oklahoma Education Association (OEA). The OEA soon began floating the idea of a strike, calling not only for increased pay for teachers and support staff but for an overall increase in funding for education. In the past decade, the state had suffered millions of dollars in cuts to education, which not only led schools to cut programming including arts and music but left some districts with four-day weeks.

On April 2, the first day of the walkout, many teachers and supporters rallied at the state capitol to encourage the governor and legislature to take additional action to increase school funding. A few days after the strike began, the OEA put together a list of demands for lawmakers to end the walkout, including restoring cuts to education. The OEA suggested that if two specific tax bills were eliminated—including a capital gains tax exemption and a hotel/motel tax—they could increase state revenue. That revenue could, in theory, be directed back to schools and take teachers off the picket lines. The state senate passed a $40 million increase in funding for education, but it was not enough to placate the OEA.

The strike lasted nine days before the teachers' unions asked their members to return to the classrooms. The teachers were unable to garner any new concessions outside of the already agreed-upon $6,000 pay increase that would be funded by a major tax hike. "We're angry that the legislature—the senate in particular—wasn't willing to talk about funding any more for education," OEA President Alicia Priest said. But, she added, "We recognize that our formal efforts to lobby elected leaders have achieved all that we will be able to accomplish this legislative session."

## Arizona Teachers Receive a Substantial Pay Raise

As an increasing number of teachers were walking out of classrooms across the country, Arizona Gov. Doug Ducey attempted to stave off a strike in his own state, promising teachers that he would raise their pay by 20 percent by 2020. The teachers' union rejected the offer, noting that the raises called for in the governor's plan would not be across the board and did not include support staff, nor was any additional money allocated to classrooms. In the weeks that followed, teachers began holding "walk-ins" to speak with parents and concerned community members about the state of education in Arizona and the importance of taking a stand.

On April 19, an overwhelming majority of teachers voted in favor of the first-ever statewide walkout in Arizona history, to begin on April 26. The decision closed 110 school districts and left 850,000 students out of the classroom. Because Arizona is a right-to-work state where individuals are not required to join a union, and the school districts do not collectively bargain with teachers' unions, the move was risky. In fact, teachers received a notice from the Arizona Education Association that the strike was illegal under a 1971 attorney general's opinion and that participating could result in the loss of teaching credentials.

The Arizona Education Association (AEA) and Arizona Educators United, the union and grassroots movement, respectively, backing the teachers called on the legislature to develop a long-term solution to Arizona's education funding if they wanted to get teachers back on the job. The teachers' union repeatedly called for meetings with the governor and for the legislature to restore $1 billion in cuts to education, increase teacher pay by 20 percent, and raise support staff wages in its budget bill before the end of their annual session. They also asked the state to maintain a sales tax that was set to expire and that makes up hundreds of millions of dollars in annual education funding.

On May 1, the AEA announced that if the legislature passed a budget by May 3, teachers would return to their classrooms. The union vowed, however, to maintain pressure on the governor and legislature for additional funding for schools in future budgets. On May 4, teachers went back to work after the governor signed a budgetary measure acquiescing to some of their demands but not all. Teachers would receive a 20 percent pay increase by 2020, with 9 percent of that coming in late 2018, and an additional $371 million was added to education funding over the next five years. The legislation signed by the governor did not include additional money for support staff or meet the $1 billion funding goal set by the AEA.

## STATE CAPITOL RALLIES AND DISTRICT WALKOUTS

Teachers in some Colorado, Kentucky, and North Carolina districts also staged rallies and walkouts. In Colorado, Pueblo County teachers went on strike, while educators from across the state rallied at the capitol, calling for pay increases for teachers and the restoration of the education budget to its prerecession level. In late April, the governor signed legislation adding $150 million per year back into the education budget, and Pueblo County was successful in winning a 2 percent pay raise. Following the protests, one state Republican lawmaker, Sen. Bob Gardner, introduced a bill that would prevent Colorado teachers from going on strike. Under the bill, any teacher participating in a strike could be fired by the school district immediately, face fines of up to $500 per day, and spend six months in jail. The bill's sponsor killed his own proposal, citing an overwhelming volume of other work before the legislature.

Similarly, in North Carolina, thousands of teachers walked out of their classrooms on May 16 to rally at the capitol for higher wages, better working conditions, and more education funding. Chanting, "Remember, remember, we vote in November," teachers, students, and parents were supported by Democratic Gov. Roy Cooper, who called on the legislature to pass his proposed budget that asked for an average 8 percent pay raise for teachers.

The Republican-controlled legislature's budget proposal at the time would have boosted pay by only around 5 percent. In June, the legislature passed its biennial budget that included an average 6.5 percent pay increase for teachers. Gov. Cooper vetoed the bill, but the legislature overrode the veto.

In Kentucky, teachers battled with the legislature and governor over changes to the pension plan structure that put them into a cash-balance plan rather than a traditional pension and would limit the amount of sick days new hires could put toward their retirement. They also called on the legislature to overturn the governor's veto on legislation that would increase funding for education. More than thirty school districts closed as thousands of teachers rallied at the state capitol, something the governor spoke fiercely against. "I guarantee you somewhere today a child was physically harmed or ingested poison because they were home alone because a single parent didn't have any money to take care of them. I'm offended by the idea that people so cavalierly and so flippantly disregarded what's truly best for children," the governor said. Ultimately, the legislature overrode the governor's veto and put in place a two-year budget that would raise public education spending by record levels through increases in the cigarette tax and sales tax for certain services.

Nearly all of the states where protests took place are right-to-work states, where unions cannot require employees to become members or pay dues as part of their employment at a specific job. However, U.S. labor law still requires that unions represent all employees in any workplace they represent. Unions argue that right-to-work laws decimate their dues and impact their ability to collectively bargain effectively for the membership. Conservatives and business leaders who support such legislation see it as an individual liberty issue. The states with teacher walkouts had another thing in common: they were among the locations with the lowest salaries for teachers and the greatest post-recession cuts to education budgets. Because of this, in many states, the walkouts were not focused solely on teacher pay but also on replacing the funding for classrooms.

—Heather Kerrigan

*Following are two press releases from West Virginia Gov. Jim Justice on February 21, 2018, upon signing legislation to increase teacher pay, and on March 6 announcing the end of the teacher strike; an April 12, 2018, statement by Oklahoma Gov. Mary Fallin on ending a nine-day teacher walkout; and a press release from Arizona Gov. Doug Ducey on May 3, 2018, announcing a 20 percent progressive increase in teacher pay.*

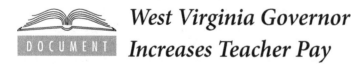

# *West Virginia Governor Increases Teacher Pay*

**February 21, 2018**

Gov. Jim Justice has signed legislation today that will provide teachers, school service personnel and state police with a 2 percent pay increase starting in July and has taken the steps in the budget to include a 2 percent pay raise for all other state employees effective July 1 as well.

Teachers are also scheduled to get an additional 1 percent hike in each of the following two years, FY 2020 and 2021, while school service personnel and state police will get an additional 1 percent in FY 2020.

Gov. Justice said that members of the West Virginia Legislature "did the responsible thing to help our teachers and state employees" by passing the pay raise package on Tuesday.

"We need to keep our kids and teachers in the classroom," Gov. Justice said. "We certainly recognize our teachers are underpaid and this is a step in the right direction to addressing their pay issue. The PEIA board has also voted to approve changes I recommended—I've asked and the PEIA board has voted to eliminate the mandated participation in the Go365 program, the use of combined household income to determine rates, and to freeze the plan for 16 months while we examine it and enact a long-term solution to the PEIA problems.

"Now we need to turn our focus back to continuing public education reforms and making our state educational system the best in the country."

SOURCE: Office of the Governor of West Virginia. "Gov. Justice Signs Pay Raise Bill." February 21, 2018. https://governor.wv.gov/News/press-releases/2018/Pages/Gov.-Justice-signs-pay-raise-bill.aspx.

## Gov. Justice Announces End of Teacher Strike

**March 6, 2018**

Governor Justice stood rock solid on the 5 percent Teacher pay raise and delivered. Not only this, but he and his staff made additional cuts which gave all State employees 5 percent as well. All the focus should have always been on fairness and getting the kids back in school.

Because of the Governor's leadership our state is now growing at a 4.7 percent growth rate and can afford helping our people.

SOURCE: Office of the Governor of West Virginia. "Governor Justice Announces That Our Kids Are Going Back to the Classroom." March 6, 2018. https://governor.wv.gov/News/press-releases/2018/Pages/Governor-Justice-Announces-That-Our-Kids-Are-Going-Back-to-the-Classroom.aspx.

## Oklahoma Governor on End of Teacher Walkout

**April 12, 2018**

Governor Mary Fallin this evening issued the following statement on the announced end of the nine-day public school teacher walkout:

"Oklahomans and our elected officials have proven they are committed to school children, teachers and educators. We appreciate our professional teachers. I'm glad teachers who participated in the union strike will return to teaching their students. They've been out for two weeks, and it's time for them to get back to school. Student learning at schools affected by the strike has been halted for nearly two weeks at a critical time in the academic year when federal and state testing requirements need to be completed.

"Three weeks ago, before the walkout, I gave final approval to an historic raise for teachers, which allows for a $6,100, or 16 percent, pay raise on average. Now, Oklahoma's teacher pay moves up from the lowest, in average teacher pay, to second in the seven-state region and up to 29th from 49th nationally. Oklahoma's teacher-pay ranking improves to 12th in the nation when adjusted for cost of living. And last week I signed a bill—approved by legislators before the walk-out—which allocates $2.9 billion for common education for the upcoming 2019 fiscal year, which is the largest amount ever appropriated in Oklahoma for K–12 public education and a 19.7 percent increase over this fiscal year's appropriation for public schools.

"I am very proud that Republican lawmakers have led the way on increasing educational expenditures for Oklahoma's students this session. In addition, they have protected Oklahomans, especially small businesses and farmers, from an irresponsible capital gains tax. The Legislature still has important work to do for the people of Oklahoma before they adjourn, including criminal justice reform and meeting the financial needs of other core services such as public safety, health and human services. I appreciate their ongoing efforts to address all of the priorities in the state.

"I want to thank the more than 100 Oklahoma Highway Patrol troopers who worked long hours at the state Capitol to keep teachers, visitors and state employees safe. The state employees who work at the Capitol deserve our state's gratitude for their service, too."

SOURCE: Office of the Governor of Oklahoma. "Gov. Fallin Statement on End of Nine-Day Public School Teacher Walkout." April 12, 2018. https://www.ok.gov/triton/modules/newsroom/newsroom_article .php?id=223&article_id=42123.

# *Arizona Governor Raises Teacher Pay by 20 Percent*

**May 3, 2018**

Raises are on the way to Arizona teachers.

Governor Doug Ducey has signed the full #20x2020 plan into law, providing a 20 percent boost in teacher pay over the next three years—including 10 percent in school year

2018—and a significant increase in flexible dollars to Arizona schools for support staff, new textbooks, upgraded technology and infrastructure.

This package—proposed by Governor Ducey on April 12 and passed today on a bipartisan basis—represents an increase of more than $1 billion in education spending when fully implemented, including a more than $520 million increase in K–12 education spending this year alone.

"Arizona teachers have earned a raise, and this plan delivers," said Governor Doug Ducey. "The impact our teachers have on the lives of Arizona kids cannot be overstated. They work incredibly hard to make a difference for their students. This plan not only provides our teachers with a 20 percent increase in pay by school year 2020, it also provides millions in flexible dollars to improve our public education system. I've had the honor of hearing directly from Arizona teachers, over these last several weeks in particular. It's their input that has shaped and improved this plan. We will never check the box on public education, but this is one big, positive step in the right direction for our teachers and their students."

Investments in Arizona's classrooms include $371 million to fully restore recession-era cuts to Additional Assistance over the next five years, starting with $100 million this fiscal year. These flexible and permanent dollars will be available for updating curriculum, modernizing classroom technology and increasing support staff salaries.

The budget also includes other important K-12 education investments, including $1.8 million to fund career and technical education, $10 million for behavioral health specialists, $53 million for building renewal to improve school infrastructure—the highest funding level since 2007—and $86 million over two years for construction of five new schools.

This budget was very much influenced and shaped by Arizona school leaders.

On April 10, Governor Ducey met with a group of superintendents representing students from across the state specifically to talk about the impact a strike would have on their schools and communities. During that meeting, they described the challenges of recruiting and retaining staff, and at the same time, managing all of the remaining needs in their schools.

The next day, on April 11, the Finance Advisory Committee, consisting of independent economists, recognized that revenues through March were $262 million above forecast and included significant increases in ongoing revenues available to the state over the next several years. This report confirmed news released on April 9 from the nonpartisan Congressional Budget Office announcing a 75 percent upward revision to growth forecasts for the national economy over the next two years. With that improved outlook, Arizona could realize over $1.5 billion in additional revenues over the next five years.

The budget does not compromise other essential state services to accommodate our teacher pay package. In fact, it increases the state's commitments to developmental disabilities, skilled nursing facilities, Medicaid, critical access hospitals, the arts, food banks and higher education.

*[A breakdown of other budgetary measures signed by the governor has been omitted.]*

SOURCE: Office of the Governor of Arizona. "Governor Ducey Signs 20 Percent Increase in Teacher Pay." May 3, 2018. https://azgovernor.gov/governor/news/2018/05/governor-ducey-signs-20-percent-increase-teacher-pay-0.

# March

# U.S. and Chinese Officials
# Respond to Trade Dispute

MARCH 2, 8, 22, AND 24, APRIL 3, AND JUNE 16, 2018

Throughout 2018, the United States imposed import tariffs on a variety of goods, including washing machines, solar cells, aluminum, and steel. The intent of the administration of President Donald Trump was to raise prices on imported goods to discourage Americans from buying them, and instead shift their purchases to American-made goods for the benefit of domestic manufacturers. The president also sought to use the tariffs to address the trade imbalance between the United States and many other countries, most specifically China. Many economists argued that these so-called trade wars would ultimately have a negative impact on Americans, who may face higher prices due to both retaliatory tariffs and increased raw material prices that are passed on to consumers in the finished product. By mid-year, the United States narrowed the scope of its rising tariffs and targeted China, a nation it has long accused of economic policies that violate international trade agreements and hurt consumers and manufacturers around the globe. In response, China levied tariffs on goods imported from the United States, and the two countries soon found themselves at an impasse. By the end of 2018, the United States had placed tariffs on $250 billion worth of Chinese goods, while China imposed tariffs on $110 billion worth of U.S. products.

## SOLAR PANELS, WASHING MACHINES
## FIRST TARGETS OF INCREASED TARIFFS

President Trump campaigned on the platform of putting "America first," which extended to addressing what he saw as imbalances in the global market for American goods. In particular, then-candidate Trump took issue with the United States' trade deficit with China, estimated at approximately $375 billion in 2017, and blamed former presidents for "allowing this out-of-control trade deficit to take place and to grow." At a campaign rally in 2016, Trump told the audience that the United States "can't continue to allow China to rape our country and that's what they're doing. It's the greatest theft in the history of the world." He also took aim at China's economic policies, saying "the single biggest weapon used against us and to destroy our companies is devaluation of currencies, and the greatest ever at that is China." The United States has in the past urged China to stop manipulating its currency, and Congress has unsuccessfully attempted to give the Treasury expanded authority to take action against nations that devalue their currency.

Under Section 201 of the U.S. Trade Act of 1974, the president has the ability to temporarily raise import duties on products deemed to threaten or injure domestic producers of the same goods. In late 2017, President Trump called on the Commerce Department and the U.S. International Trade Commission (ITC) to look into whether there are certain imported products that harm American manufacturers more than others. The ITC responded that an increase in washing machine and solar cell and module imports posed that serious threat. The Office of the U.S. Trade Representative (USTR) proposed, and the president accepted, a sliding scale of tariffs on these items. The first 1.2 million imported finished washing machine units would be subject to a 20 percent tariff in year one, and any additional machines beyond the first 1.2 million would face a 50 percent tariff. These rates would fall slightly in years two and three. Solar modules and cells were subject to a 30 percent tariff in year one, which would decrease by 5 percentage points each year through year four. The first 2.5 gigawatts of imported unassembled solar cells would be exempt from the tariff. Robert Lighthizer, U.S. trade representative, said the action "makes clear that the Trump Administration will always defend American workers, farmers, ranchers, and businesses."

The response from solar cell and washing machine producers was mixed. Solar energy groups around the globe were vehemently against the tariffs, arguing that they had the potential to slow the shift to clean energy and were likely to result in the loss of thousands of jobs in the industry. "These policies have been tried in many parts of the world and in not one case have the measures led to more jobs, more manufacturing, and more value," said James Watson, CEO of SolarPower Europe. Abigail Ross Hopper, president of the U.S. Solar Energy Industries Association, agreed. "It's just basic economics—if you raise the price of a product it's going to decrease demand for that product." On the washing machine side, Whirlpool, which manufacturers its machines in the United States, supported the decision. Chair Jeff Fettig said the tariffs help American companies "compete on a level playing field with their foreign counterparts." However, foreign manufacturers such as Samsung and LG, South Korean companies with operations in the United States that had recently begun production on new U.S. factories, said the tariff would have the largest negative impact on consumers who would find themselves facing higher costs and that foreign companies might be less likely to build factories and hire American workers in the future. In fact, the ITC had recommended that the Trump administration exempt LG's washing machines from the tariffs after earlier anti-dumping duties were removed; LG was not exempted in the final tariff.

Large U.S. trading partners, including the European Union, Canada, Mexico, China, and South Korea, bore the brunt of the tariffs, and all responded in kind, increasing their own import tariffs on some U.S. goods. Mexico's Economy Department promised to "use all available legal resources . . . to apply protections on Mexican washing machines and solar panels," and some Canadian solar companies went on to sue the Trump administration, arguing these tariffs were a violation of the North American Free Trade Agreement (NAFTA). South Korea called the tariffs a clear violation of World Trade Organization (WTO) rules and filed a formal complaint with the international body. China urged "restraint in using trade restrictions" but said that if the United States continued to add tariffs, it would "resolutely defend its legitimate interests."

## ALUMINUM, STEEL INCLUDED IN SECOND ROUND OF TARIFFS

On March 8, on recommendation from the Commerce Department, Trump announced a tariff on all steel and aluminum imports, at 25 percent and 10 percent, respectively. "Our industries have been targeted for years and years—decades, in fact—by unfair foreign trade practices leading to the shuttered plants and mills, the laying off of millions of workers, and the decimation of entire communities. And that's going to stop," President

Trump said. "Today I'm defending America's national security by placing tariffs on foreign imports of steel and aluminum." He added, "we're urging all companies to buy American." During the signing ceremony, the president pointed to successes that were already being seen around the country in anticipation of the tariffs, including the reopening of a U.S. Steel plant in Illinois and a forthcoming investment of $100 million to upgrade and restart the Century Aluminum plant in Kentucky.

U.S. trade partners again responded with retaliatory tariffs, with the European Union placing tariffs on more than $3 billion worth of items such as motorcycles and whiskey. Mexico increased duties on whiskey, cheese, pork, and other products, and Canada announced that more than $12 billion worth of products would be taxed. Although the U.S. tariff applied to any nation from which these materials were imported, the greatest impact was felt in China, the world's largest producer of steel and aluminum. In response, China announced that it would raise tariffs on $3 billion in U.S. imports—including recycled aluminum, some foods, and some steel products including consumer vehicles—to 15 percent or 25 percent. China accused the United States of provoking the "largest trade war in economic history" and raised a concern through the WTO.

China is the United States' largest merchandise trading partner, third-largest export market, and largest source of imports. A close trading relationship between the two countries benefits the United States in a number of ways. For example, Chinese-made products are often cheaper and therefore easier on the American consumer's wallet. Those companies that either rely on Chinese labor as a final point of production or acquire Chinese parts for assembly in the United States can often lower costs to consumers. However, the United States has been critical of the Chinese economy, frequently accusing it of devaluing its currency and poorly enforcing intellectual property rights. U.S. leaders have often raised concern that the subpar policies the Chinese government imposes on its economy hurt American businesses and jobs.

In mid-May, amid growing threats of new tariffs from both the United States and China, the two nations released a joint statement announcing that they had agreed upon a trade framework and that they would stop escalating trade tensions while negotiations were underway. In the framework, China agreed to "significantly increase" its purchase of U.S. goods and services and cut passenger vehicle import duties from 25 percent to 15 percent. "Getting China to open its market to more U.S. exports is significant, but the far more important issues revolve around forced technology transfers, cyber theft and the protection of our innovation," Lighthizer said. By late May, negotiations had broken down, and the two sides again began threatening to impose new tariffs. "We feel sorry that the U.S. has ignored the consensus already reached and capriciously initiate the trade war. It has impaired the interest of both sides, and destroyed the world trade order," the Chinese Ministry of Commerce said in a June statement.

In September, the United States followed through on its threats and issued tariffs on another $200 billion in Chinese goods, declaring that tariffs would begin at 10 percent but would increase to 25 percent at the start of 2019 if the two nations could not finalize their trade agreement. China retaliated with tariffs on an additional $60 billion in U.S. goods and called off negotiations, at least until after the U.S. midterm elections in November. "The door for trade talks is always open, but negotiations must be held in an environment of mutual respect," the Chinese government announced, adding that negotiations "cannot be carried out under the threat of tariffs." Lindsay Walters, deputy White House press secretary, responded, "We remain open to continuing discussions with China, but China must meaningfully engage on the unfair trading practices."

## ADDITIONAL PRODUCTS SUBJECT TO TARIFF OVER INTELLECTUAL PROPERTY RIGHTS VIOLATIONS

On March 22, President Trump called on the U.S. Trade Representative to research and determine which products should be subject to additional tariffs to address Chinese activities that "are unreasonable or discriminatory and that burden or restrict U.S. commerce." This announcement was meant to specifically target China for alleged intellectual property rights (IPR) violations. Trump's concern was in part driven by the Made in China 2025 initiative, first outlined in 2015, that aims to increase Chinese industrial production to allow the country to become a bigger player on the world stage. Trump and many other U.S. leaders see this as a threat to U.S. economic dominance. The concern isn't just their growing manufacturing output but more specifically their growth in the technology sector and the share of goods that the nation is exporting that are considered medium or high tech.

In May, the White House announced new tariffs on $50 billion worth of goods from China that contain "industrially significant technologies." According to the U.S. Trade Representative, "Today's action comes after an exhaustive Section 301 investigation in which USTR found that China's acts, policies and practices related to technology transfer, intellectual property, and innovation are unreasonable and discriminatory, and burden U.S. commerce." Lighthizer said the tariffs were an important step toward protecting American companies from what he called "the unprecedented threat posed by China's theft of our intellectual property, the forced transfer of American technology, and its cyberattacks on our computer networks," adding, "China's government is aggressively working to undermine America's high-tech industries and our economic leadership through unfair trade practices and industrial policies like 'Made in China 2025.'"

On June 15, the Office of the U.S. Trade Representative said it had developed a two-stage plan to implement the $50 billion in tariffs related to intellectual property theft. Through a 25 percent tax, the first stage would increase tariffs on $34 billion worth of Chinese products, and the second stage would raise tariffs on $16 billion in Chinese goods. China quickly retaliated with its own two-stage tariff increase, and the Trump administration threatened to continue raising tariffs until China agreed to deescalate the situation.

## DOMESTIC AND GLOBAL RESPONSE TO THE TRADE WAR

The president frequently asserted that trade wars are good for the American economy and consumer. "When a country (USA) is losing many billions of dollars on trade with virtually every country it does business with, trade wars are good, and easy to win. Example, when we are down $100 billion with a certain country and they get cute, don't trade anymore—we win big. It's easy!" the president tweeted on March 2. The president has explained that by taxing imports, the United States can reduce its trade deficit with other nations and American manufacturers come out on top. Economists argue that in reality, while tariffs could boost the price of U.S. steel and aluminum, the manufacturers that require these materials will face higher costs that are likely to be passed on to consumers through the end product. They also note that trade deficits, especially for nations that have moved from a manufacturing to a service-based economy, are not necessarily negative. Economist Mark Zandi, pointing to the rise in the cost of washing machines in the spring, wrote, "Higher tariffs act much like a tax increase, weakening the purchasing power of households; if households need to spend more on imported goods, they have less income to spend on other things."

The president faced resistance to enhanced tariffs from within his own cabinet and the Republican Party. "I disagree with this action and fear its unintended consequences," Speaker of the House Paul Ryan, R-Wis., said, arguing that such tactics should only be utilized to target those who violate trade law. "Our economy and our national security are strengthened by fostering free trade with our allies and promoting the rule of law," Ryan said. Senate Majority Leader Mitch McConnell, R-Ky., agreed with Ryan. According to McConnell, "We've been arguing aggressively that this is the wrong path for us," but, he added, "The president does have the right to do what he's doing." Congressional Republicans made a few attempts at reining in the president's tariffs but failed to gain enough traction to bring legislation to the floor.

The tariffs did not impact just the United States and its largest trading partners. The *Economist* reported that smaller nations might feel a significant impact because 30 percent of the value of products imported by the United States from China originate in a third country. According to the International Monetary Fund, the escalation between the United States and China had the potential to reduce global economic growth by 0.5 percent by 2020. Similarly, Fitch Ratings downgraded by 0.1 percentage point its global growth forecast for 2019 to 3.1 percent.

—Heather Kerrigan

*Following are a March 2, 2018, tweet from President Donald Trump on trade wars; a March 8, 2018, statement from President Trump announcing new import tariffs on steel and aluminum, along with two associated presidential proclamations; March 22, 2018, remarks by President Trump on Chinese intellectual property violations and an associated presidential memo calling on federal departments to investigate intellectual property theft; March 24 and April 3, 2018, statements from the Chinese government announcing new tariffs on imports from the United States; and a June 16, 2018, statement from the Chinese government regarding ongoing trade negotiations with the United States.*

# President Trump on the Value of Trade Wars

**March 2, 2018**

When a country (USA) is losing many billions of dollars on trade with virtually every country it does business with, trade wars are good, and easy to win. Example, when we are down $100 billion with a certain country and they get cute, don't trade anymore—we win big. It's easy!

SOURCE: Donald Trump (@realDonaldTrump). Twitter post. March 2, 2018. https://twitter.com/realdonald trump/status/969525362580484098?lang=en.

# President Trump Adjusts Tariffs on Aluminum and Steel Imports

**March 8, 2018**

*The President.* Well, thank you very much, everybody. I'm honored to be here with our incredible steel and aluminum workers, and you are truly the backbone of America. You know that. Very special people. I've known you and people that are very closely related to you for a long time. You know that. I think it's probably the reason I'm here. So I want to thank you.

I also want to thank Secretary Mnuchin, Ambassador Lighthizer, Secretary Ross, Peter Navarro, Mike Pence, our great Vice President. They've worked so hard on getting this going and getting it done. And people are starting to realize how important it is. We have to protect and build our steel and aluminum industries, while at the same time showing great flexibility and cooperation toward those that are really friends of ours, both on a trade basis and a military basis.

A strong steel and aluminum industry are vital to our national security. Absolutely vital. Steel is steel. You don't have steel, you don't have a country. Our industries have been targeted for years and years—decades, in fact—by unfair foreign trade practices leading to the shuttered plants and mills, the laying off of millions of workers, and the decimation of entire communities. And that's going to stop, right? It's going to stop.

This is not merely an economic disaster, but it's a security disaster. We want to build our ships, we want to build our planes, we want to build our military equipment with steel, with aluminum from our country. And now we're finally taking action to correct this long-overdue problem. It's a travesty.

Today I'm defending America's national security by placing tariffs on foreign imports of steel and aluminum. We will have a 25-percent tariff on foreign steel and a 10-percent tariff on foreign aluminum when the product comes across our borders. It's a process called dumping. And they dumped more than at any time, on any nation, anywhere in the world. And it drove our plants out of business. It drove our factories out of business. And we want a lot of steel coming into our country, but we want it to be fair, and we want our workers to be protected. And we want, frankly, our companies to be protected.

By contrast, we will not place any new tax on product made in the U.S.A. So there's no tax if a product is made in the U.S.A. You don't want to pay tax? Bring your plant to the U.S.A.; there's no tax. Which we will benefit from the massive tax cuts that we have in place. We have passed the largest tax cut plan in the country's history, and that has caused really tremendous success between that and regulation cutting. And I think maybe regulation cutting every bit as much. And we have a long way to go on regulations, but we've already cut more than any President in history.

So we're urging all companies to buy American. That's what we want, buy American. The action that I'm taking today follows a 9-month investigation by the Department of Commerce, Secretary Ross, documenting a growing crisis in our steel and aluminum production that threatens the security of our Nation and also is bad for us economically and with jobs.

The American steel and aluminum industry has been ravaged by aggressive, foreign trade practices. It's really an assault on our country. It's been an assault. They know better than anybody. Other countries have added production capacity that far exceeds demand and flooded the world market with cheap metal that is subsidized by foreign governments, creating jobs for their country and taking away jobs from our country. I've been talking about this for a long time, a lot longer than my political career. I've been talking about this for many years.

For example, it takes China about 1 month to produce as much steel as they produce in the United States in an entire year, because we've closed down so much capacity. Plants closed all over the United States, and some plants—I see massive plants from 40 years ago, and they're working now in a little corner of the building. Well, we're going to get those buildings open again and producing again. And that's going to be a great thing for our country. And this is only the first stop.

Aluminum imports now account for more than 90 percent of the primary American demand. Over the last two decades, nearly two-thirds of American raw steel companies have gone out of business. More than one-third of the steel jobs have disappeared. Six primary aluminum smelters—which is a big deal—have permanently shut down since just 2012. The actions we're taking today are not a matter of choice, they're a matter of necessity for our security.

We're already seeing the national security benefits of this order. Yesterday, in anticipation that we'd be here today, U.S. Steel announced it's reopening a mill in Illinois, a big one, and recalling 500 workers immediately. That's going on all over the country. And by the way, it went on with solar panels, which we did 3 months ago, and washing machines, where they were dumping washing machines all over our country. And now they're expanding plants to make washing machines. We put the tax on it; a lot of you were here.

A skilled, trained workforce in steel is a crucial element of America's national security and must be protected. After the signing of this proclamation, Century Aluminum in Kentucky—Century is a great company—will be investing over $100 million to restart and upgrade their idled military-grade, high-quality aluminum production, which is also critically important to our national security. That's 150,000 additional tons of aluminum. And think of it: This is a closed plant, and now they're doing 150,000 tons production, and an additional 300 workers, and ultimately many more hired in the great State of Kentucky—a package of, sometimes, $90,000 per worker.

Our greatest Presidents all understood, from Washington to Lincoln, to Jackson, to Teddy Roosevelt, that America must have a strong, vibrant, and independent manufacturing base. Has to have it. President McKinley, who felt very, very strongly about this—the country was very, very successful. We actually operated out of cash flow, if you can believe it. "The protective tariff policy of the Republicans," he said, ". . . has made the lives of the masses of our countrymen sweeter and brighter" and brighter and brighter. It is the best for our citizenship and our civilization, and it opens up a higher and better destiny for our people.

Many politicians lamented the decline of our once-proud industries, and many countries denounced global excess capacity, but no one took action. All of our politicians, they saw what was happening to our country. I've seen it. For 25 years, I've been talking about it. Talked about Japan, talked about China. But the politicians never did anything about it. But now they are.

Our factories were left to rot and to rust all over the place. Thriving communities turned into ghost towns. You guys know that, right? Not any longer. The workers who poured their souls into building this great Nation were betrayed, but that betrayal is now over. I'm delivering on a promise I made during the campaign, and I've been making it for a good part of my life. If I ever did this—I never really thought I would—I said, "Let's run for President," and look what happened. And part of the reason it happened is you and my message having to do with you and other messages also: security, military, the wall, the border. A lot of good messages. But this was one of the most important.

My most important job is to keep American people safe. And as you know, we just had approved a $700 billion military budget—the largest ever—$716 billion next year. That means not only safety, but it means jobs. It also means the use of steel from our country.

But if the same goals can be accomplished by other means, America will remain open to modifying or removing the tariffs for individual nations, as long as we can agree on a way to ensure that their products no longer threaten our security. So I've put Ambassador Lighthizer—great gentleman—in charge of negotiating with countries that seek an alternative to the steel and aluminum tariffs.

The fact is, we've been treated—really, I mean, we've been treated so badly over the years by other countries. I think, really, we've been treated very badly by our politicians, by our Presidents, by people that represented us that didn't, frankly, know what they were doing.

And we lose $800 billion a year on trade. Every year, $800 billion. It's been going on for a long time: $300 billion, $400 billion, $500 billion. It got up to $600 billion, and it keeps going. But it's going to start changing; it has to change.

We're negotiating now with China. We're in the midst of a big negotiation. I don't know that anything is going to come of it. They have been very helpful. President Xi, I have great respect for, a lot of respect. But I don't know that anything is going to come of that.

But we're going to cut down the deficits one way or the other. We have a deficit with China of at least $500 billion. And when you add intellectual property, it's much higher than that. That's a year.

At the same time, due to the unique nature of our relationship with Canada and Mexico, we're negotiating, right now, NAFTA. And we're going to hold off the tariff on those two countries to see whether or not we're able to make the deal on NAFTA. National security—very important aspect of that deal. And if we're making the deal on NAFTA, this will figure into the deal, and we won't have the tariffs on Canada or Mexico.

If we don't make the deal on NAFTA, and if we terminate NAFTA because they're unable to make a deal that's fair for our workers and fair for our farmers—we love our farmers—and fair for our manufacturers, then we're going to terminate NAFTA, and we'll start all over again, or we'll just do it a different way. But we'll terminate NAFTA, and that will be it.

But I have a feeling we're going to make a deal on NAFTA. I've been saying it for a long time: We either make a deal, or we terminate. And if we do, there won't be any tariffs on Canada, and there won't be any tariffs on Mexico.

One other thing: Some of the countries that we're dealing with are great partners, great military allies, and we're going to be looking at that very strongly. The tariffs don't go effective for at least another 15 days. And we're going to see who's treating us fairly, who's not treating us fairly. Part of that is going to be military: who's paying the bills, who's not paying the bills. We subsidize many rich countries with our military. They pay not a 100 cents on the dollar, in some cases, not 50 cents on the dollar, and they're massive wealthy countries. So we have to stop that. And that will enter into the equation also. Very interesting, I saw a tweet—it just came in from Elon Musk, who's using our wonderful space facilities and did a great job 3 weeks ago—he said, "For example, an American car going to China pays 25-percent import duty, but a Chinese car coming to the United States only pays 2.5 percent, a tenfold difference." So an American car going to China—think of that—pays 25-percent import duty. So we send our car over there, pay 25 percent. They send their car over here, 2.5 percent. Ten point—that's from Elon, but everybody knows it. They've known it for years. They never did anything about it. It's got to change.

We're going to be doing a reciprocal tax program at some point so that if China is going to charge us 25 percent, or if India is going to charge us 75 percent, and we charge them nothing—if they're at 50 or they're at 75 or they're at 25—we're going to be at those same numbers. It's called reciprocal. It's a mirror tax. So they charge us 50; we charge them 50. Right now they'll charge us 50; we charge them nothing. Doesn't work.

So that's called a reciprocal tax or mirror tax. And we're going to be doing a lot of that. It's—we've really—the first year, we've really set the stage. A lot of it had to do with—structurally, we had to go through certain procedures in order to get to this point. But now we're at this point.

American companies have not been treated fairly. And some American companies, frankly, have taken advantage of it and gone to other countries and developed in Mexico massive automobile plants, taking our jobs away and taking our companies down to Mexico to make the cars. And then, they send them right across the border without tax, without anything. So we lose the jobs. They make the cars. They get all the benefits. Then, they sell the cars back into the United States.

So we're changing things, and we're going to have a lot of great relationships. I think companies are going to be very happy in the end. I think that countries are going to be very happy. We're going to show great flexibility. And again, many of the countries that treat us the worst on trade and on military are our allies, as they like to call them.

So we just want fairness. We just want fairness. We want everything to be reciprocal. And I think, in the end, we're going to have a lot of great jobs, we're going to have a lot of great companies, all coming back into our country. You see it—the other day, Chrysler announced they're leaving Mexico, and they're coming back into Michigan with a big plant. You haven't seen that in a long time, folks. You haven't seen that in a long time.

So because I sort of grew up with this group of people—I know a lot about the steel industry and I know lot about the aluminum industry; we've got to bring them back—I thought maybe a few of you might like to say a couple of words. And there's only about 25 million people watching, so don't worry about it. You want to say something? Come on up.

*[An exchange with attendees at the signing has been omitted.]*

Source: Executive Office of the President. "Remarks on Signing Proclamations on Adjusting Imports of Aluminum and Steel into the United States and an Exchange with Reporters." March 8, 2018. *Compilation of Presidential Documents* 2018, no. 00146 (March 8, 2018). https://www.gpo.gov/fdsys/pkg/DCPD-201800146/pdf/DCPD-201800146.pdf.

# *Presidential Proclamation on Aluminum Imports*

**March 8, 2018**

*By the President of the United States of America*

*A Proclamation*

1. On January 19, 2018, the Secretary of Commerce (Secretary) transmitted to me a report on his investigation into the effect of imports of aluminum on the national security

of the United States under section 232 of the Trade Expansion Act of 1962, as amended (19 U.S.C. 1862).

2. The Secretary found and advised me of his opinion that aluminum is being imported into the United States in such quantities and under such circumstances as to threaten to impair the national security of the United States. The Secretary found that the present quantities of aluminum imports and the circumstances of global excess capacity for producing aluminum are "weakening our internal economy," leaving the United States "almost totally reliant on foreign producers of primary aluminum" and "at risk of becoming completely reliant on foreign producers of high-purity aluminum that is essential for key military and commercial systems." Because of these risks, and the risk that the domestic aluminum industry would become "unable to satisfy existing national security needs or respond to a national security emergency that requires a large increase in domestic production," and taking into account the close relation of the economic welfare of the Nation to our national security, see 19 U.S.C. 1862(d), the Secretary concluded that the present quantities and circumstances of aluminum imports threaten to impair the national security as defined in section 232 of the Trade Expansion Act of 1962, as amended.

3. In light of this conclusion, the Secretary recommended actions to adjust the imports of aluminum so that such imports will not threaten to impair the national security. Among those recommendations was a global tariff of 7.7 percent on imports of aluminum articles in order to reduce imports to a level that the Secretary assessed would enable domestic aluminum producers to use approximately 80 percent of existing domestic production capacity and thereby achieve long-term economic viability through increased production. The Secretary has also recommended that I authorize him, in response to specific requests from affected domestic parties, to exclude from any adopted import restrictions those aluminum articles for which the Secretary determines there is a lack of sufficient U.S. production capacity of comparable products, or to exclude aluminum articles from such restrictions for specific national security-based considerations.

4. I concur in the Secretary's finding that aluminum articles are being imported into the United States in such quantities and under such circumstances as to threaten to impair the national security of the United States, and I have considered his recommendations.

5. Section 232 of the Trade Expansion Act of 1962, as amended, authorizes the President to adjust the imports of an article and its derivatives that are being imported into the United States in such quantities or under such circumstances as to threaten to impair the national security.

6. Section 604 of the Trade Act of 1974, as amended (19 U.S.C. 2483), authorizes the President to embody in the Harmonized Tariff Schedule of the United States (HTSUS) the substance of acts affecting import treatment, and actions thereunder, including the removal, modification, continuance, or imposition of any rate of duty or other import restriction.

7. In the exercise of these authorities, I have decided to adjust the imports of aluminum articles by imposing a 10 percent ad valorem tariff on aluminum articles, as defined below, imported from all countries except Canada and Mexico. In my judgment, this tariff is necessary and appropriate in light of the many factors I have considered, including the

Secretary's report, updated import and production numbers for 2017, the failure of countries to agree on measures to reduce global excess capacity, the continued high level of imports since the beginning of the year, and special circumstances that exist with respect to Canada and Mexico. This relief will help our domestic aluminum industry to revive idled facilities, open closed smelters and mills, preserve necessary skills by hiring new aluminum workers, and maintain or increase production, which will reduce our Nation's need to rely on foreign producers for aluminum and ensure that domestic producers can continue to supply all the aluminum necessary for critical industries and national defense. Under current circumstances, this tariff is necessary and appropriate to address the threat that imports of aluminum articles pose to the national security.

8. In adopting this tariff, I recognize that our Nation has important security relationships with some countries whose exports of aluminum to the United States weaken our internal economy and thereby threaten to impair the national security. I also recognize our shared concern about global excess capacity, a circumstance that is contributing to the threatened impairment of the national security. Any country with which we have a security relationship is welcome to discuss with the United States alternative ways to address the threatened impairment of the national security caused by imports from that country. Should the United States and any such country arrive at a satisfactory alternative means to address the threat to the national security such that I determine that imports from that country no longer threaten to impair the national security, I may remove or modify the restriction on aluminum articles imports from that country and, if necessary, make any corresponding adjustments to the tariff as it applies to other countries as our national security interests require.

9. I conclude that Canada and Mexico present a special case. Given our shared commitment to supporting each other in addressing national security concerns, our shared commitment to addressing global excess capacity for producing aluminum, the physical proximity of our respective industrial bases, the robust economic integration between our countries, the export of aluminum produced in the United States to Canada and Mexico, and the close relation of the economic welfare of the United States to our national security, see 19 U.S.C. 1862(d), I have determined that the necessary and appropriate means to address the threat to the national security posed by imports of aluminum articles from Canada and Mexico is to continue ongoing discussions with these countries and to exempt aluminum articles imports from these countries from the tariff, at least at this time. I expect that Canada and Mexico will take action to prevent transshipment of aluminum articles through Canada and Mexico to the United States.

10. In the meantime, the tariff imposed by this proclamation is an important first step in ensuring the economic viability of our domestic aluminum industry. Without this tariff and satisfactory outcomes in ongoing negotiations with Canada and Mexico, the industry will continue to decline, leaving the United States at risk of becoming reliant on foreign producers of aluminum to meet our national security needs—a situation that is fundamentally inconsistent with the safety and security of the American people. It is my judgment that the tariff imposed by this proclamation is necessary and appropriate to adjust imports of aluminum articles so that such imports will not threaten to impair the national security as defined in section 232 of the Trade Expansion Act of 1962, as amended.

*Now, Therefore, I, Donald J. Trump*, President of the United States of America, by the authority vested in me by the Constitution and the laws of the United States of America, including section 301 of title 3, United States Code, section 604 of the Trade Act of 1974, as amended, and section 232 of the Trade Expansion Act of 1962, as amended, do hereby proclaim as follows:

(1) For the purposes of this proclamation, "aluminum articles" are defined in the Harmonized Tariff Schedule (HTS) as: (a) unwrought aluminum (HTS 7601); (b) aluminum bars, rods, and profiles (HTS 7604); (c) aluminum wire (HTS 7605); (d) aluminum plate, sheet, strip, and foil (flat rolled products) (HTS 7606 and 7607); (e) aluminum tubes and pipes and tube and pipe fitting (HTS 7608 and 7609); and (f) aluminum castings and forgings (HTS 7616.99.51.60 and 7616.99.51.70), including any subsequent revisions to these HTS classifications.

(2) In order to establish increases in the duty rate on imports of aluminum articles, subchapter III of chapter 99 of the HTSUS is modified as provided in the Annex to this proclamation. Except as otherwise provided in this proclamation, or in notices published pursuant to clause 3 of this proclamation, all imports of aluminum articles specified in the Annex shall be subject to an additional 10 percent ad valorem rate of duty with respect to goods entered, or withdrawn from warehouse for consumption, on or after 12:01 a.m. eastern daylight time on March 23, 2018. This rate of duty, which is in addition to any other duties, fees, exactions, and charges applicable to such imported aluminum articles, shall apply to imports of aluminum articles from all countries except Canada and Mexico.

(3) The Secretary, in consultation with the Secretary of State, the Secretary of the Treasury, the Secretary of Defense, the United States Trade Representative (USTR), the Assistant to the President for National Security Affairs, the Assistant to the President for Economic Policy, and such other senior Executive Branch officials as the Secretary deems appropriate, is hereby authorized to provide relief from the additional duties set forth in clause 2 of this proclamation for any aluminum article determined not to be produced in the United States in a sufficient and reasonably available amount or of a satisfactory quality and is also authorized to provide such relief based upon specific national security considerations. Such relief shall be provided for an aluminum article only after a request for exclusion is made by a directly affected party located in the United States. If the Secretary determines that a particular aluminum article should be excluded, the Secretary shall, upon publishing a notice of such determination in the Federal Register, notify Customs and Border Protection (CBP) of the Department of Homeland Security concerning such article so that it will be excluded from the duties described in clause 2 of this proclamation. The Secretary shall consult with CBP to determine whether the HTSUS provisions created by the Annex to this proclamation should be modified in order to ensure the proper administration of such exclusion, and, if so, shall make such modification to the HTSUS through a notice in the *Federal Register*.

(4) Within 10 days after the date of this proclamation, the Secretary shall issue procedures for the requests for exclusion described in clause 3 of this proclamation. The issuance of such procedures is exempt from Executive Order 13771 of January 30, 2017 (Reducing Regulation and Controlling Regulatory Costs).

(5) (a) The modifications to the HTSUS made by the Annex to this proclamation shall be effective with respect to goods entered, or withdrawn from warehouse for

consumption, on or after 12:01 a.m. eastern daylight time on March 23, 2018, and shall continue in effect, unless such actions are expressly reduced, modified, or terminated.

(b) The Secretary shall continue to monitor imports of aluminum articles and shall, from time to time, in consultation with the Secretary of State, the Secretary of the Treasury, the Secretary of Defense, the USTR, the Assistant to the President for National Security Affairs, the Assistant to the President for Economic Policy, the Director of the Office of Management and Budget, and such other senior Executive Branch officials as the Secretary deems appropriate, review the status of such imports with respect to the national security. The Secretary shall inform the President of any circumstances that in the Secretary's opinion might indicate the need for further action by the President under section 232 of the Trade Expansion Act of 1962, as amended. The Secretary shall also inform the President of any circumstance that in the Secretary's opinion might indicate that the increase in duty rate provided for in this proclamation is no longer necessary.

(6) Any provision of previous proclamations and Executive Orders that is inconsistent with the actions taken in this proclamation is superseded to the extent of such inconsistency.

*In Witness Whereof,* I have hereunto set my hand this eighth day of March, in the year of our Lord two thousand eighteen, and of the Independence of the United States of America the two hundred and forty-second.

DONALD J. TRUMP

SOURCE: Executive Office of the President. "Proclamation 9704—Adjusting Imports of Aluminum into the United States." March 8, 2018. *Compilation of Presidential Documents* 2018, no. 00147 (March 8, 2018). https://www.gpo.gov/fdsys/pkg/DCPD-201800147/pdf/DCPD-201800147.pdf.

# *Presidential Proclamation on Steel Imports*

**March 8, 2018**

*By the President of the United States of America*

*A Proclamation*

1. On January 11, 2018, the Secretary of Commerce (Secretary) transmitted to me a report on his investigation into the effect of imports of steel mill articles (steel articles) on the national security of the United States under section 232 of the Trade Expansion Act of 1962, as amended (19 U.S.C. 1862).

2. The Secretary found and advised me of his opinion that steel articles are being imported into the United States in such quantities and under such circumstances as to threaten to impair the national security of the United States. The Secretary found that the present quantities of steel articles imports and the circumstances of global excess capacity for producing steel are "weakening our internal economy," resulting in the persistent threat

of further closures of domestic steel production facilities and the "shrinking [of our] ability to meet national security production requirements in a national emergency." Because of these risks and the risk that the United States may be unable to "meet [steel] demands for national defense and critical industries in a national emergency," and taking into account the close relation of the economic welfare of the Nation to our national security, *see* 19 U.S.C. 1862(d), the Secretary concluded that the present quantities and circumstances of steel articles imports threaten to impair the national security as defined in section 232 of the Trade Expansion Act of 1962, as amended.

3. In reaching this conclusion, the Secretary considered the previous U.S. Government measures and actions on steel articles imports and excess capacity, including actions taken under Presidents Reagan, George H.W. Bush, Clinton, and George W. Bush. The Secretary also considered the Department of Commerce's narrower investigation of iron ore and semi-finished steel imports in 2001, and found the recommendations in that report to be outdated given the dramatic changes in the steel industry since 2001, including the increased level of global excess capacity, the increased level of imports, the reduction in basic oxygen furnace facilities, the number of idled facilities despite increased demand for steel in critical industries, and the potential impact of further plant closures on capacity needed in a national emergency.

4. In light of this conclusion, the Secretary recommended actions to adjust the imports of steel articles so that such imports will not threaten to impair the national security. Among those recommendations was a global tariff of 24 percent on imports of steel articles in order to reduce imports to a level that the Secretary assessed would enable domestic steel producers to use approximately 80 percent of existing domestic production capacity and thereby achieve long-term economic viability through increased production. The Secretary has also recommended that I authorize him, in response to specific requests from affected domestic parties, to exclude from any adopted import restrictions those steel articles for which the Secretary determines there is a lack of sufficient U.S. production capacity of comparable products, or to exclude steel articles from such restrictions for specific national security based considerations.

5. I concur in the Secretary's finding that steel articles are being imported into the United States in such quantities and under such circumstances as to threaten to impair the national security of the United States, and I have considered his recommendations.

6. Section 232 of the Trade Expansion Act of 1962, as amended, authorizes the President to adjust the imports of an article and its derivatives that are being imported into the United States in such quantities or under such circumstances as to threaten to impair the national security.

7. Section 604 of the Trade Act of 1974, as amended (19 U.S.C. 2483), authorizes the President to embody in the Harmonized Tariff Schedule of the United States (HTSUS) the substance of acts affecting import treatment, and actions thereunder, including the removal, modification, continuance, or imposition of any rate of duty or other import restriction.

8. In the exercise of these authorities, I have decided to adjust the imports of steel articles by imposing a 25 percent ad valorem tariff on steel articles, as defined below, imported from all countries except Canada and Mexico. In my judgment, this tariff is

necessary and appropriate in light of the many factors I have considered, including the Secretary's report, updated import and production numbers for 2017, the failure of countries to agree on measures to reduce global excess capacity, the continued high level of imports since the beginning of the year, and special circumstances that exist with respect to Canada and Mexico. This relief will help our domestic steel industry to revive idled facilities, open closed mills, preserve necessary skills by hiring new steel workers, and maintain or increase production, which will reduce our Nation's need to rely on foreign producers for steel and ensure that domestic producers can continue to supply all the steel necessary for critical industries and national defense. Under current circumstances, this tariff is necessary and appropriate to address the threat that imports of steel articles pose to the national security.

9. In adopting this tariff, I recognize that our Nation has important security relationships with some countries whose exports of steel articles to the United States weaken our internal economy and thereby threaten to impair the national security. I also recognize our shared concern about global excess capacity, a circumstance that is contributing to the threatened impairment of the national security. Any country with which we have a security relationship is welcome to discuss with the United States alternative ways to address the threatened impairment of the national security caused by imports from that country. Should the United States and any such country arrive at a satisfactory alternative means to address the threat to the national security such that I determine that imports from that country no longer threaten to impair the national security, I may remove or modify the restriction on steel articles imports from that country and, if necessary, make any corresponding adjustments to the tariff as it applies to other countries as our national security interests require.

10. I conclude that Canada and Mexico present a special case. Given our shared commitment to supporting each other in addressing national security concerns, our shared commitment to addressing global excess capacity for producing steel, the physical proximity of our respective industrial bases, the robust economic integration between our countries, the export of steel articles produced in the United States to Canada and Mexico, and the close relation of the economic welfare of the United States to our national security, see 19 U.S.C. 1862(d), I have determined that the necessary and appropriate means to address the threat to the national security posed by imports of steel articles from Canada and Mexico is to continue ongoing discussions with these countries and to exempt steel articles imports from these countries from the tariff, at least at this time. I expect that Canada and Mexico will take action to prevent transshipment of steel articles through Canada and Mexico to the United States.

11. In the meantime, the tariff imposed by this proclamation is an important first step in ensuring the economic viability of our domestic steel industry. Without this tariff and satisfactory outcomes in ongoing negotiations with Canada and Mexico, the industry will continue to decline, leaving the United States at risk of becoming reliant on foreign producers of steel to meet our national security needs—a situation that is fundamentally inconsistent with the safety and security of the American people. It is my judgment that the tariff imposed by this proclamation is necessary and appropriate to adjust imports of steel articles so that such imports will not threaten to impair the national security as defined in section 232 of the Trade Expansion Act of 1962, as amended.

*Now, Therefore, I, Donald J. Trump*, President of the United States of America, by the authority vested in me by the Constitution and the laws of the United States of America, including section 301 of title 3, United States Code, section 604 of the Trade Act of 1974, as amended, and section 232 of the Trade Expansion Act of 1962, as amended, do hereby proclaim as follows:

(1) For the purposes of this proclamation, "steel articles" are defined at the Harmonized Tariff Schedule (HTS) 6-digit level as: 7206.10 through 7216.50, 7216.99 through 7301.10, 7302.10, 7302.40 through 7302.90, and 7304.10 through 7306.90, including any subsequent revisions to these HTS classifications.

(2) In order to establish increases in the duty rate on imports of steel articles, subchapter III of chapter 99 of the HTSUS is modified as provided in the Annex to this proclamation. Except as otherwise provided in this proclamation, or in notices published pursuant to clause 3 of this proclamation, all steel articles imports specified in the Annex shall be subject to an additional 25 percent ad valorem rate of duty with respect to goods entered, or withdrawn from warehouse for consumption, on or after 12:01 a.m. eastern daylight time on March 23, 2018. This rate of duty, which is in addition to any other duties, fees, exactions, and charges applicable to such imported steel articles, shall apply to imports of steel articles from all countries except Canada and Mexico.

(3) The Secretary, in consultation with the Secretary of State, the Secretary of the Treasury, the Secretary of Defense, the United States Trade Representative (USTR), the Assistant to the President for National Security Affairs, the Assistant to the President for Economic Policy, and such other senior Executive Branch officials as the Secretary deems appropriate, is hereby authorized to provide relief from the additional duties set forth in clause 2 of this proclamation for any steel article determined not to be produced in the United States in a sufficient and reasonably available amount or of a satisfactory quality and is also authorized to provide such relief based upon specific national security considerations. Such relief shall be provided for a steel article only after a request for exclusion is made by a directly affected party located in the United States. If the Secretary determines that a particular steel article should be excluded, the Secretary shall, upon publishing a notice of such determination in the *Federal Register*, notify Customs and Border Protection (CBP) of the Department of Homeland Security concerning such article so that it will be excluded from the duties described in clause 2 of this proclamation. The Secretary shall consult with CBP to determine whether the HTSUS provisions created by the Annex to this proclamation should be modified in order to ensure the proper administration of such exclusion, and, if so, shall make such modification to the HTSUS through a notice in the *Federal Register*.

(4) Within 10 days after the date of this proclamation, the Secretary shall issue procedures for the requests for exclusion described in clause 3 of this proclamation. The issuance of such procedures is exempt from Executive Order 13771 of January 30, 2017 (Reducing Regulation and Controlling Regulatory Costs).

(5) (a) The modifications to the HTSUS made by the Annex to this proclamation shall be effective with respect to goods entered, or withdrawn from warehouse for consumption, on or after 12:01 a.m. eastern daylight time on March 23, 2018, and shall continue in effect, unless such actions are expressly reduced, modified, or terminated.

(b) The Secretary shall continue to monitor imports of steel articles and shall, from time to time, in consultation with the Secretary of State, the Secretary of the Treasury, the Secretary of Defense, the USTR, the Assistant to the President for National Security Affairs, the Assistant to the President for Economic Policy, the Director of the Office of Management and Budget, and such other senior Executive Branch officials as the Secretary deems appropriate, review the status of such imports with respect to the national security. The Secretary shall inform the President of any circumstances that in the Secretary's opinion might indicate the need for further action by the President under section 232 of the Trade Expansion Act of 1962, as amended. The Secretary shall also inform the President of any circumstance that in the Secretary's opinion might indicate that the increase in duty rate provided for in this proclamation is no longer necessary.

(6) Any provision of previous proclamations and Executive Orders that is inconsistent with the actions taken in this proclamation is superseded to the extent of such inconsistency.

*In Witness Whereof*, I have hereunto set my hand this eighth day of March, in the year of our Lord two thousand eighteen, and of the Independence of the United States of America the two hundred and forty-second.

DONALD J. TRUMP

SOURCE: Executive Office of the President. "Proclamation 9705—Adjusting Imports of Steel into the United States." March 8, 2018. *Compilation of Presidential Documents* 2018, no. 00148 (March 8, 2018). https://www.gpo.gov/fdsys/pkg/DCPD-201800148/pdf/DCPD-201800148.pdf.

## President Trump Remarks on Chinese Intellectual Property Violations

**March 22, 2018**

*The President.* Well, thank you everybody. This has been long in the making. You've heard many, many speeches by me and talks by me and interviews where I talk about unfair trade practices. We've lost, over a fairly short period of time, 60,000 factories in our country: closed, shuttered, gone. Six million jobs, at least, gone. And now they're starting to come back. You see what's happening with Chrysler, with Foxconn, with so many other companies wanting to come back into the United States.

But we have one particular problem. And I view them as a friend; I have tremendous respect for President Xi. We have a great relationship. They're helping us a lot in North Korea. And that's China.

But we have a trade deficit, depending on the way you calculate, of $504 billion. Now, some people would say it's really $375 billion. Many different ways of looking at it, but any way you look at it, it is the largest deficit of any country in the history of our world. It's out of control.

We have a tremendous intellectual property theft situation going on, which likewise is hundreds of billions of dollars. And that's on a yearly basis. I've spoken to the President. I've spoken to representatives of China. We've been dealing with it very seriously.

As you know, we're renegotiating NAFTA. We'll see how that turns out. Many countries are calling to negotiate better trade deals because they don't want to have to pay the steel and aluminum tariffs that we are negotiating with various countries—Mr. Lighthizer, Mr. Ross.

We are just starting a negotiation with the European Union because they've really shut out our country to a large extent. They have barriers that they can trade with us, but we can't trade with them. They're very strong barriers. They have very high tariffs. We don't. It's just not fair.

NAFTA has been a very bad deal for the United States, but we'll make it better, or we'll have to do something else. The deal we have with South Korea is a very one-sided deal. It's a deal that has to be changed.

So we have a lot of things happening. But in particular, with China, we're going to be doing a section 301 trade action. It could be about $60 billion, but that's really just a fraction of what we're talking about.

I've been speaking with the highest Chinese representatives, including the President, and I've asked them to reduce the trade deficit immediately by $100 billion. It's a lot. So that would be anywhere from 25 percent, depending on the way you figure, to maybe something even more than that. But we have to do that.

The word that I want to use is "reciprocal." When they charge 25 percent for a car to go in, and we charge 2 percent for their car to come into the United States, that's not good. That's how China rebuilt itself. The tremendous money that we've paid since the founding of the World Trade Organization—which has actually been a disaster for us. It's been very unfair to us. The arbitrations are very unfair. The judging has been very unfair. And knowingly, we always have a minority, and it's not fair.

So we're talking to World Trade, we're talking to NAFTA, we're talking to China, we're talking to European Union. And I will say, every single one of them wants to negotiate. And I believe that, in many cases—maybe all cases—we'll end up negotiating a deal.

So we've spoken to China, and we're in the midst of a very large negotiation. We'll see where it takes us. But in the meantime, we are sending a section 301 action. I'll be signing it right here, right now. I'd like to ask Bob Lighthizer to say a few words about the 301 and where we are in that negotiation.

And we're doing things for this country that should have been done for many, many years. We've had this abuse by many other countries and groups of countries that were put together in order to take advantage of the United States, and we don't want that to happen. We're not going to let that happen. It's probably one of the reasons I was elected, maybe one of the main reasons. But we're not going to let that happen.

We have, right now, an $800 billion trade deficit with the world. So think of that. So let's say we have 500 to 375, but let's say we have 500 with China, but we have 800 total with the world. That would mean that China is more than half. So we're going to get it taken care of. And frankly, it's going to make us a much stronger, much richer nation.

The word is "reciprocal." That's the word I want everyone to remember. We want reciprocal—mirror. Some people call it a mirror tariff or a mirror tax. Just use the word reciprocal. If they charge us, we charge them the same thing. That's the way it's got to be. That's not the way it is. For many, many years—for many decades, it has not been that way.

And I will say, the people we're negotiating with—smilingly, they really agree with us. I really believe they cannot believe they've gotten away with this for so long.

I'll talk to Prime Minister Abe of Japan and others—great guy, friend of mine—and there will be a little smile on their face. And the smile is, "I can't believe we've been able to take advantage of the United States for so long." So those days are over.

Ambassador Lighthizer, thank you.

*U.S. Trade Representative Robert E. Lighthizer.* Well, thank you very much, Mr. President. First of all, for those of you who don't know, section 301 is a statute that gives substantial power, authority to the President to correct actions in certain circumstances where there's unfair acts, policies, or practices by our trading partners.

In this case, the area is technology. Technology is probably the most important part of our economy. There's 44 million people who work in high-technology areas. No country has as much technology-intensive industry as the United States. And technology is really the backbone of the future of the American economy.

Given these problems, the President asked USTR to conduct a study. We conducted a thorough study. We had hearings. We reviewed tens of thousands of pages of documents. We talked to many, many businesspeople. We had testimony, as I say. And we concluded that, in fact, China does have a policy of forced technology transfer; of requiring licensing at less than economic value; at—of state capitalism, wherein they go in and buy technology in the United States in noneconomic ways; and then, finally, of cyber theft. The result of this has been that the President has analyzed it—we have a 200-page study which we will put out—and he concluded that we should put in place tariffs on appropriate products—we can explain later how we concluded what products they are; that we would put investment restrictions on China with respect to high technology; and that we'll file a WTO case. Because one of the actions here does involve a WTO violation. This is an extremely important action, very significant and very important for the future of the country, really, across industries. And I would really like to thank you very much, Mr. President, for giving me the opportunity to work on it.

*The President.* Thank you very much, Bob.

Secretary Ross.

*Secretary of Commerce Wilbur L. Ross, Jr.* Intellectual property rights are our future, and it's no accident that in June of this year, the U.S. Patent and Trademark Office will issue its 10 millionth patent—10 million patents. There's no country in the history of the world that remotely approaches that.

So the steel and aluminum actions we've taken deal more or less with the present. This action on intellectual property rights deals with the future. So we're trying to solve both today's problem and problems that otherwise will be forthcoming. That's why these actions are so important and so important in unison with each other. We will end up negotiating these things, rather than fighting over them, in my view.

*The President.* Mike Pence, would you like to say something?

*Vice President Michael R. Pence.* Thank you, Mr. President, and to all our honored guests. Today's action sends a clear message that this President and our entire administration are determined to put American jobs and American workers first.

The action the President will take today under section 301 also makes it clear that the era of economic surrender is over. The United States of America is taking targeted and focused action to protect not only American jobs, but America's technology, which will power and drive an innovation economy for decades to come.

It is just one more step of a promise made and a promise kept by President Trump.

*The President.* So we'll sign right now. I just want to let everybody know, just for a second time, that we are in the midst of very major and very positive negotiations. Positive for the United States and, actually, very positive for other countries also.

*[A brief Q&A with attendees has been omitted.]*

SOURCE: Executive Office of the President. "Remarks on Signing a Memorandum on Actions by the United States related to the Section 301 Investigation of China's Laws, Policies, Practices, or Actions related to Technology Transfer, Intellectual Property, and Innovation and an Exchange with Reporters." March 22, 2018. *Compilation of Presidential Documents* 2018, no. 00179 (March 22, 2018). https://www.gpo.gov/fdsys/pkg/DCPD-201800179/pdf/DCPD-201800179.pdf.

# Memorandum on Chinese Intellectual Property Violations

**March 22, 2018**

*Memorandum for the Secretary of the Treasury, the United States Trade Representative, the Senior Advisor for Policy, the Assistant to the President for Economic Policy, the Assistant to the President for National Security Affairs, and the Assistant to the President for Homeland Security and Counterterrorism*

*Subject:* Actions by the United States Related to the Section 301 Investigation of China's Laws, Policies, Practices, or Actions Related to Technology Transfer, Intellectual Property, and Innovation

On August 14, 2017, I directed the United States Trade Representative (Trade Representative) to determine whether to investigate China's laws, policies, practices, or actions that may be unreasonable or discriminatory and that may be harming American intellectual property rights, innovation, or technology development. On August 18, 2017, the Trade Representative initiated an investigation under section 301 of the Trade Act of 1974, as amended (the "Act") (19 U.S.C. 2411).

During its investigation, the Office of the United States Trade Representative (USTR) consulted with appropriate advisory committees and the interagency section 301 Committee. The Trade Representative also requested consultations with the Government of China, under section 303 of the Act (19 U.S.C. 2413). The USTR held a public hearing on October 10, 2017, and two rounds of public written comment periods. The USTR received approximately 70 written submissions from academics, think tanks, law firms, trade associations, and companies.

The Trade Representative has advised me that the investigation supports the following findings:

First, China uses foreign ownership restrictions, including joint venture requirements, equity limitations, and other investment restrictions, to require or pressure technology transfer from U.S. companies to Chinese entities. China also uses administrative review and licensing procedures to require or pressure technology transfer, which, inter alia, undermines the value of U.S. investments and technology and weakens the global competitiveness of U.S. firms.

Second, China imposes substantial restrictions on, and intervenes in, U.S. firms' investments and activities, including through restrictions on technology licensing terms. These restrictions deprive U.S. technology owners of the ability to bargain and set market-based terms for technology transfer. As a result, U.S. companies seeking to license technologies must do so on terms that unfairly favor Chinese recipients.

Third, China directs and facilitates the systematic investment in, and acquisition of, U.S. companies and assets by Chinese companies to obtain cutting-edge technologies and intellectual property and to generate large-scale technology transfer in industries deemed important by Chinese government industrial plans.

Fourth, China conducts and supports unauthorized intrusions into, and theft from, the computer networks of U.S. companies. These actions provide the Chinese government with unauthorized access to intellectual property, trade secrets, or confidential business information, including technical data, negotiating positions, and sensitive and proprietary internal business communications, and they also support China's strategic development goals, including its science and technology advancement, military modernization, and economic development.

It is hereby directed as follows:

*Section 1. Tariffs.* (a) The Trade Representative should take all appropriate action under section 301 of the Act (19 U.S.C. 2411) to address the acts, policies, and practices of China that are unreasonable or discriminatory and that burden or restrict U.S. commerce. The Trade Representative shall consider whether such action should include increased tariffs on goods from China.

(b) To advance the purposes of subsection (a) of this section, the Trade Representative shall publish a proposed list of products and any intended tariff increases within 15 days of the date of this memorandum. After a period of notice and comment in accordance with section 304(b) of the Act (19 U.S.C. 2414(b)), and after consultation with appropriate agencies and committees, the Trade Representative shall, as appropriate and consistent with law, publish a final list of products and tariff increases, if any, and implement any such tariffs.

*Sec. 2. WTO Dispute Settlement.* (a) The Trade Representative shall, as appropriate and consistent with law, pursue dispute settlement in the World Trade Organization (WTO) to address China's discriminatory licensing practices. Where appropriate and consistent with law, the Trade Representative should pursue this action in cooperation with other WTO members to address China's unfair trade practices.

(b) Within 60 days of the date of this memorandum, the Trade Representative shall report to me his progress under subsection (a) of this section.

*Sec. 3. Investment Restrictions.* (a) The Secretary of the Treasury (Secretary), in consultation with other senior executive branch officials the Secretary deems appropriate, shall propose executive branch action, as appropriate and consistent with law, and using any available statutory authority, to address concerns about investment in the United States directed or facilitated by China in industries or technologies deemed important to the United States.

(b) Within 60 days of the date of this memorandum, the Secretary shall report to me his progress under subsection (a) of this section.

*Sec. 4. Publication.* The Trade Representative is authorized and directed to publish this memorandum in the Federal Register.

DONALD J. TRUMP

SOURCE: Executive Office of the President. "Memorandum on Actions by the United States related to the Section 301 Investigation of China's Laws, Policies, Practices, or Actions related to Technology Transfer, Intellectual Property, and Innovation." March 22, 2018. *Compilation of Presidential Documents* 2018, no. 00180 (March 22, 2018). https://www.gpo.gov/fdsys/pkg/DCPD-201800180/pdf/DCPD-201800180.pdf.

 # Chinese Ministry of Commerce Releases Retaliatory Tariffs

**March 24, 2018**

The Ministry of Commerce issued a list of discontinuation concessions against the U.S. Section 232 measures for imported steel and aluminum products and solicited public comments on March 23, 2018, intending to impose tariffs on certain products imported from the U.S. to balance losses to Chinese interests as a result of tariffs levied by the U.S. government on steel and aluminum imports. The spokesperson of the Ministry of Commerce made a statement on that.

This list tentatively contains 128 tax products across 7 categories. According to the 2017 statistics, it involves U.S. exports to China of some US$3 billion. The first part covers a total of 120 taxes involving US$977 million in U.S. exports to China, including fresh fruits, dried fruits and nut products, wines, modified ethanol, American ginseng, and seamless steel pipes, which is expected to impose a tariff of 15 percent. And the second part covers a total of 8 taxes involving US$1.992 billion of US exports to China, including pork and its products, recycled aluminum and other products, with a proposed tariff of 25 percent.

The fact that the United States imposed tariffs of 25 percent and 10 percent on imported steel and aluminum products on the grounds of "national security" actually constitutes a safeguard measure. According to the relevant provisions of the WTO's Agreement on Safeguard Measures, China has formulated a list of suspension of concessions. If China and the United States fail to reach a trade compensation agreement within the stipulated time, China will exercise the right to suspend concessions for products mentioned in the first part; China will implement the second part list after further evaluating the impact of the U.S. measures on China. China reserves the right to adjust measures based on actual conditions and will implement necessary procedures in accordance with relevant WTO rules.

The United States' practice of import restrictions based on "national security" has severely damaged the multilateral trade system fronted by the WTO and seriously interfered with the normal international trade order, which has been opposed by many WTO members. The Chinese side also negotiated with the United States through multiple levels and channels, and will take legal actions under the WTO framework to jointly maintain the stability and authority of the multilateral trade rules with other WTO members.

As the world's two largest economies, it is the only correct choice for China and the United States to cooperate with each other. It is our hope that both sides can proceed from the overall interests of both China and the United States, with a focus on each other, cooperation, and control disagreements, jointly promoting the healthy and stable development of China–US economic and trade relations. China urges the United States to resolve China's concerns as soon as possible, and resolve differences through dialogue and consultation, thus avoiding harming the overall situation of Sino–U.S. cooperation.

SOURCE: Chinese Ministry of Commerce Website. "The Spokesperson of the Ministry of Commerce Makes Remarks on China's Release of a List of Discontinuation Concessions against the U.S. Steel and Aluminum Imports under Section 232." March 24, 2018. http://english.mofcom.gov.cn/article/news release/policyreleasing/201803/20180302723376.shtml.

# Chinese Government Announces Additional Tariffs on U.S. Products

**April 3, 2018**

The Customs Tariff Commission of the State Council decided to slap additional tariff of 15% or 25% on 128 items of products imported from the US since April 2, 2018. The Spokesman of Ministry of Commerce commented on it.

On March 23, the Ministry of Commerce issued a product list of termination and concessions against the U.S. Section 232 measures for imported steel and aluminum products, and solicited public comments. On March 31, comments period was over, during which, many citizens expressed their supports for the measures and lists through telephones or e-mail, endorsing the government's taking measures to safeguard the interests of the country and its industries. Part of the citizens suggested strengthening the measures. After evaluation, China decided to take above measures against 128 products imported from the US.

China said that the US took 232 measures against imported steel and aluminum products, abused the WTO article of "Security Exception", formed safeguard measures actually, only targeted at a few countries, severely violated the non-discrimination principle which is the footstone of multilateral trading system, and infringed the interests of China. On March 26, according to the Agreement of Safeguards, China raised the requirements for trade compensation consultation to the US through the WTO but the US refused to answer. Considering that there was no possibility to reach consensus between the two countries, on March 29, China reported the product list of termination and concessions to WTO and decided to slap additional tariff on part of products imported from the US, so as to balance China's loss caused by the US 232 measures.

It is China's legitimate right to suspend part of its obligations to the US as a WTO member. China hoped the US would revoke the measures that violated the WTO rules and brought China-US trade to the normal track regarding related products. As the two largest economies in the world, cooperation is the only correct choice for China and the US. The two parties should solve each other's concerns through dialogues and realize common development, so as to avoid bigger harms to the overall situation of China–US cooperation caused by the follow-up actions.

Source: Chinese Ministry of Commerce Website. "Spokesman of Ministry of Commerce Comments on China's Decision to Slap Tariffs on Part of Products Imported from US." April 3, 2018. http://english .mofcom.gov.cn/article/newsrelease/policyreleasing/201804/20180402733539.shtml.

# Chinese Government on Trade Negotiations

DOCUMENT

June 16, 2018

The US and China have conducted several rounds of negotiations, aiming to resolve the differences and realize mutually beneficial results. But we feel sorry that the US has ignored the consensus already reached and capriciously initiate the trade war. It has impaired the interest of both sides, and destroyed the world trade order. China was resolutely against it.

China doesn't want a trade war, but we have to strike back to defend the interest of our country and its people and resolutely safeguard the economic globalization and multilateral trading system while facing the US harming others without benefiting itself. We will impose tariffs with the same size and force and all the trade and economic achievements reached by the two sides will be invalid at the same time.

Nowadays, the trade war is not in line with global interest. We call on all countries to jointly take actions to stop outdated and backward behavior and jointly defend common interest of the mankind.

Source: Chinese Ministry of Commerce Website. "MOFCOM Spokesman Comments on the US Trade Measures against China." June 16, 2018. http://english.mofcom.gov.cn/article/newsrelease/policyreleasing/ 201806/20180602757671.shtml.

## OTHER HISTORIC DOCUMENTS OF INTEREST

### FROM THIS VOLUME

FROM PREVIOUS *HISTORIC DOCUMENTS*

- Senate Passes Currency Misalignment Act, *2011*, p. 527
- Bureau of Labor Statistics on the U.S. Employment Situation, *2003*, p. 441

# China Adopts Amendment Eliminating Term Limits

MARCH 11 AND 12, 2018

On February 25, 2018, the Central Committee of the Communist Party of China announced several proposed amendments to the Chinese Constitution, including one eliminating presidential term limits. The amendment's approval—virtually guaranteed by the National People's Congress (NPC)—provides an opportunity for President Xi Jinping to remain in office after his second term ends in 2023. The Communist Party claimed the amendment would help ensure political stability, but others raised concerns about a perceived power grab by Xi and the potential for an indefinite presidency.

## CHINA'S "THREE-IN-ONE" SYSTEM

Chinese presidents have been limited to serving two consecutive five-year terms since 1982, when China's fourth and current Constitution was adopted. The president also typically serves as the general secretary of the Central Committee and the chair of the Central Military Commission. This "three-in-one" system, as it is known, has been the norm since 1993, when Deng Xiaoping was president. Two of Deng's potential successors were forced to resign following the Chinese student protests of the late 1980s, leading Deng to choose Jiang Zemin as the next president. Deng also appointed Jiang to the general secretary and chair positions to help clearly establish his authority and provide for a smooth transition of power. There are no limits on the length of time someone can serve as the Communist Party's leader or leader of the military.

Communist Party leaders and state-run media frequently cited the lack of limits on the general secretary and chair positions as part of the reason for the term-limit amendment. Doing away with presidential term limits, they said, would help align the three positions and provide political stability. *People Daily*, a Communist Party newspaper, stated the amendment was "an important measure for perfecting the system of the party and the state" and that it did "not mean changing the retirement system for party and national leaders" or "a life-long term system for leading officials."

China observers characterized the term-limit amendment as a further effort by Xi to consolidate and retain his control over the Communist Party and thus China's government for the long term. Xi declined to identify a potential successor in 2017 during the Communist Party's National Congress, as has been the custom for Chinese presidents nearing the start of their second term, fueling speculation that he would try to seek a third term.

## GOVERNMENT CENSORS PUBLIC DISSENT

In the hours following the amendment's public announcement, Chinese citizens took to social media to express their support for or opposition to Xi and the elimination of term limits. Xi was unfavorably compared to former leader Mao Zedong, who also sought to centralize power, demanded absolute loyalty to the Communist Party, and leveraged propaganda to build a base of support and remain in power. Some social media users also complained that China was becoming like its neighbor, North Korea. Others used *Winnie the Pooh* memes to express their opposition. (Some believe Xi resembles Winnie the Pooh; as such, the Disney character is sometimes used to represent Xi.)

Government censors soon began to remove such content and blocked the use of terms including *lifelong, disagree,* and *my emperor.* The English letter *N* was also blocked for some time because it can be used to represent infinity. An open letter to NPC delegates from a former editor of *China Youth Daily,* the official newspaper of the Communist Youth League of China, was also taken down after circulating on social media. The letter called for delegates to vote against the term-limit amendment, arguing that it risked "once again planting seeds of chaos in China and causing untold damage."

## NATIONAL PEOPLE'S CONGRESS VOTES

The term-limit amendment was submitted to the first session of the 13th NPC on March 5. It was considered by the NPC delegates as part of a package of amendments, which also included a measure adding Xi Jinping Thought on Socialism with Chinese Characteristics for a New Era to the Constitution. Xi Jinping Thought is a political doctrine comprised of fourteen principles—including the supremacy of the Communist Party, the importance of governing according to the rule of law, and the need to take a people-centric approach to governance—guiding policy development. It was added to the Communist Party's constitution in 2017, alongside Marxism-Leninism, Mao Zedong Thought, and other foundational theories, as one of the "guides to action of the Party" in the Constitution.

Another amendment allowed for the creation of a National Supervision Commission (NSC) to investigate Communist Party members and civil servants for corruption. Designed to function independently of China's judiciary and other state agencies, the NSC will extend and broaden the anticorruption campaign launched by the government in 2012. That campaign is overseen by the Communist Party Central Commission for Discipline Inspection (CCDI) and has focused solely on party members. To date, more than 1.5 million officials, including thirty-five members of the Central Committee and nine members of CCDI, have been disciplined because of anticorruption investigation findings.

Since the NPC is widely regarded as a "rubber stamp," having never rejected a proposal or amendment from Communist Party leadership, there was no doubt the amendments would be approved. On March 11, the NPC voted overwhelmingly in favor of the measures, with only two delegates voting against the amendments and three delegates abstaining. "Doesn't the emperor of Japan rule for life? Doesn't the Queen of England rule for life?" asked delegate Chen Jinshi. "So why can't our president rule for life?" Chen added, "As long as his health is good, what's there to be worried about?" Shen Chunyao, chair of the Commission for Legislative Affairs of the National People's Congress Standing Committee, told reporters the amendment was "a key measure to improve the state leadership system," adding, "The 'three in one' leadership is not only necessary, but proves to be the most suitable system for a big party and country like ours."

Reactions from Western leaders were largely muted, with observers speculating they feared criticisms might be met with economic reprisals. U.S. President Donald Trump appeared to support the change, telling a group of donors that it was "great" and that "maybe we'll want to give that a shot someday." However, Press Secretary Sarah Huckabee Sanders told reporters the president supported term limits in the United States and that it was up to China to decide "what's best for their country."

Xi's second term began in March 2018. He may not be formally granted a third term until the 20th National Congress of the Communist Party of China convenes in 2022.

—Linda Grimm

*Following are two documents from the National People's Congress of the People's Republic of China from March 11 and March 12, 2018, announcing the National People's Congress's adoption of constitutional amendments and reporting comments made by Shen Chunyao, Chair of the Commission for Legislative Affairs of the National People's Congress Standing Committee, during a press conference following the vote.*

# China's National Legislature Adopts Constitutional Amendment

**March 11, 2018**

China's National People's Congress (NPC), the national legislature, adopted an amendment to the country's Constitution on Sunday.

Lawmakers at the ongoing NPC annual session agreed that the constitutional revision, which accords with the aspiration of the Communist Party of China (CPC) and the people and has won approval from both inside and outside the Party, is of historic significance for ensuring prosperity and lasting security of both the Party and the country.

The draft amendment was submitted to the first session of 13th NPC for deliberation on Monday.

Revising part of the Constitution is a major decision made by the CPC Central Committee from the overall and strategic height of upholding and developing socialism with Chinese characteristics in the new era, said Xi Jinping, general secretary of the CPC Central Committee, when joining NPC deputies in a panel discussion on Wednesday.

This was the first amendment to the country's fundamental law in 14 years.

The People's Republic of China enacted its first Constitution in 1954. The current Constitution was adopted in 1982 and amended in 1988, 1993, 1999 and 2004.

While the reform and opening-up drive, which began 40 years ago, has made amazing progress, it brought major changes to the country's Constitution.

From 1988 to 1999, amendments included reform of land-use rights, a legal status for the private economy, the theory of building socialism with Chinese characteristics, replacing the phrase "planned economy" with "socialist market economy," and incorporation of Deng Xiaoping Theory.

The most recent amendment in 2004 protected private property and human rights and gave the Theory of Three Represents constitutional authority.

China's Constitution has been developed along with the people's practices of building socialism with Chinese characteristics under the CPC leadership, according to Li Shuzhong, vice president of the China University of Political Science and Law.

"The amendment makes the Constitution in keeping with the times by incorporating new achievements, experiences and requirements of the Party and the country's development as socialism with Chinese characteristics has entered a new era," Li said.

A constitutional change is either proposed by the NPC Standing Committee or by more than one-fifth of all NPC deputies, and then requires the approval of two-thirds or more of NPC deputies during the annual session.

SOURCE: National People's Congress of the People's Republic of China. "China's National Legislature Adopts Constitutional Amendment." March 11, 2018. http://www.npc.gov.cn/englishnpc/Special_13_1/2018-03/11/content_2046558.htm.

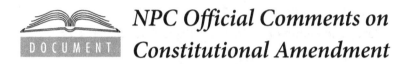

## NPC Official Comments on Constitutional Amendment

**March 12, 2018**

The constitutional amendment adopted by China's national legislature Sunday, including a revision regarding the President's term of office, is good for China's enduring peace and stability, an official said.

Shen Chunyao, chairman of the Commission for Legislative Affairs of the National People's Congress Standing Committee, said the revision is good for upholding the authority and centralized, unified leadership of the Communist Party of China (CPC) Central Committee with Comrade Xi Jinping at the core.

"It is a key measure to improve the state leadership system," Shen told reporters at a press conference held right after the amendment was adopted.

He said the experience of the past 20 plus years showed that the "three in one" leadership system was a successful, effective and pivotal one for China. The "three" refers to general secretary of the CPC Central Committee, the chairman of the Central Military Commission and the state president—the top positions of the ruling party, the armed forces and the state.

Shen said there has been a growing and across-the-board call for the provision of the president's term in the Constitution to be compatible with that of the other two top positions.

"The 'three in one' leadership is not only necessary, but proves to be the most suitable system for a big party and country like ours," he said.

"It is a successful experience we draw from the Party's long-term governance," he said, adding that this revision is "very important" and its meanings need to be learnt well and correctly.

Shen said the revision has a wide and solid political, legal and social base. Lawmakers applauded twice when it was introduced at the NPC annual session on March 5 for deliberation.

In response to a reporter's question, he said the hypothesis of a repetition of political turmoil linked to leadership reshuffle is unfounded because the CPC has managed to solve a number of key challenges in its over 90 years' history, including how to ensure the orderly transition of the party and state leaders at all levels.

The path of socialist political advancement with Chinese characteristics the CPC has explored will lead China to an even brighter future, Shen said.

SOURCE: National People's Congress of the People's Republic of China. "Constitutional Amendment Good for China's Enduring Peace, Stability." March 12, 2018. http://www.npc.gov.cn/englishnpc/news/Legislation/2018-03/12/content_2046857.htm.

## OTHER HISTORIC DOCUMENTS OF INTEREST

### FROM PREVIOUS *HISTORIC DOCUMENTS*

# British and Russian Officials
# Respond to Nerve Agent Attack

MARCH 12, 13, 14, AND 22, SEPTEMBER 5,
AND OCTOBER 3, 2018

On March 4, 2018, Sergei Skripal and his daughter Yulia, two Russian nationals, were spotted by passers-by in a semicomatose state on a public bench in the city of Salisbury, England. Later tests revealed that they had been exposed to the deadly nerve agent Novichok, a chemical substance developed by the Soviet Union in the 1970s. Following an investigation, the United Kingdom government made a determination that the Russian state was responsible for the poisoning. European and North Atlantic Treaty Organization (NATO) allies showed solidarity with the United Kingdom by collectively expelling 145 Russian diplomats. The expulsions triggered equivalent, retaliatory expulsions of Western diplomats by Russia. The Skripals slowly recovered from the poisoning, but three months later, a woman in Salisbury was killed after seemingly accidental exposure to the nerve agent. By September, the United Kingdom identified two Russian nationals that it said had carried out the poisoning. Russian authorities, including President Vladimir Putin, firmly denied involvement and demanded that the United Kingdom provide it with material evidence, including samples of the Novichok, but the United Kingdom declined to do so.

## RUSSIAN NATIONALS POISONED WITH
## NERVE AGENT IN THE UNITED KINGDOM

Earlier in his life, Sergei Skripal worked as a spy for the Russian government before switching sides and beginning to turn over secrets to UK intelligence agents. Although he was found guilty of treason by Russia and sentenced to imprisonment, he was later released as part of a spy prisoner swap agreement. Skripal was living in Salisbury, a small city in England, when the nerve agent attack occurred. His daughter Yulia, a Russian resident, had flown to the UK from Moscow the day before the poisoning to visit her father. Around lunchtime, they drove from Skripal's home to Salisbury city center. They visited The Mill pub and dined at Zizzi's restaurant. Later that afternoon, they were found slipping in and out of consciousness on a public bench. The pair was rushed to the hospital, where they remained for weeks in a grave condition. The Skripals would eventually recover from the attack and are believed to have gone into hiding.

Meanwhile, UK authorities launched a major investigation into the incident, with hundreds of police officers involved and parts of Salisbury cordoned off and tested to ensure that no one else would be exposed to the poisoning agent. (A police officer who had searched the Skripal residence fell seriously ill after exposure to the agent but survived.) Laboratory analyses concluded that the Skripals had come into contact with Novichok, a potentially lethal nerve agent that the Soviet Union had developed in the 1970s, stocks of which were held by Russia after the collapse of the Soviet Union in 1991.

The idea that such an attack would be perpetrated by the Russian authorities so brazenly on UK soil sent shockwaves through diplomatic circles and provoked a swift and resolute response from the UK government.

## ACCUSATIONS, DENIALS, AND EXPULSIONS

Addressing the UK parliament on March 12, Prime Minister Theresa May called the poisoning a "reckless and despicable act" and asserted that it was "highly likely" the Russian state was responsible. "Russia has previously produced this agent and would still be capable of doing so," May said. The poisoning occurred in a "backdrop of a well-established pattern of Russian state aggression," she added. Such acts of aggression included, she said, Russia's annexation of Crimea, which it took from Ukraine in 2014; Moscow's material support for pro-Russian separatist militias in eastern Ukraine; various cyber-espionage instances and disruption operations; and meddling in the elections of several countries. The Russian parliament in 2006 had even approved the extrajudicial killing of terrorists and dissidents outside of Russia, she noted. The poisoning was "not just a crime against the Skripals, but an indiscriminate and reckless act against the United Kingdom, putting the lives of innocent civilians at risk," May said. The UK's approach in dealing with Russia henceforth would be "engage but beware," she said.

The Russian response to the accusations was presented to the Organisation for the Prohibition of Chemical Weapons (OPCW), an international entity based in The Hague with 193 member countries whose mission is to permanently and verifiably eliminate chemical weapons. Russia's ambassador to the OPCW, Alexander Shulgin, on March 13 denounced as "unacceptable" the United Kingdom's "unfounded accusations of Russia's alleged involvement." Shulgin added, caustically, "Our British colleagues should save their propaganda fervour and slogans for their unenlightened domestic audience." As for next steps, the Russian ambassador to the OPCW called on London to "officially formalise your request to begin consultations with us" before adding, "We will require material evidence of the alleged Russian trace in this high-profile case."

On March 14, Prime Minister May returned to Parliament to outline her government's policy response to the poisoning. She said that Russia's "response has demonstrated complete disdain for the gravity of these events." She unveiled retaliatory measures, including expulsion of twenty-three Russian diplomats with a week's notice; new legislation to detain at the UK border those suspected of hostile state activity; financial sanctions; and new powers to monitor and track suspected state agents. May suspended high-level bilateral UK–Russia contacts, including revoking an invitation to Russian foreign minister Sergey Lavrov and declining to send a UK government minister or royal family member to attend the football World Cup that Russia was hosting that summer. "Many of us looked at a post–Soviet Russia with hope. We wanted a better relationship, and it is tragic that President Putin has chosen to act in this way," May concluded.

The United Kingdom received strong support from its European and NATO allies following the attack. A meeting of the European Council on March 22 and 23 resulted in a joint statement endorsing the "United Kingdom government's assessment that it is highly likely that the Russian Federation is responsible and that there is no plausible alternative explanation" for the poisoning. On top of the twenty-three Russian diplomats the United Kingdom expelled, the following eighteen EU countries announced expulsions: Belgium (one), Croatia (one), Czech Republic (three), Denmark (two), Estonia (one), Finland (one), France (four), Germany (four), Hungary (one), Ireland (one), Italy (two),

Latvia (one), Lithuania (three), the Netherlands (two), Poland (four), Romania (one), Spain (two), and Sweden (one). The remaining nine EU countries declined to expel Russian diplomats. Some, like Luxembourg, did so because of the small size of their diplomatic missions, which mean that expulsions could result in bilateral relations with Russia being entirely terminated. For others, such as Bulgaria and Greece, their strong business and/or political ties to Russia were more likely the determining factors in their decisions not to expel diplomats.

Some non-EU member states in Europe joined their EU counterparts in ordering Russian diplomats out, including Albania, Macedonia, Moldova, Montenegro, Norway, and Ukraine. Beyond Europe, Australia and Canada announced their own expulsions. The country that expelled more Russian diplomats than any other—including the UK itself—was the United States, which ordered sixty to leave, forty-eight from Washington, D.C., and twelve from New York, and shut down a Russian consulate in Seattle. Commentators noted how the firm U.S. response, spearheaded by the State Department, was somewhat at odds with the friendly overtures to Russia that President Donald Trump had been making since entering the White House in January 2017.

Throughout the year, the Trump administration continued to send mixed signals on Russia. On the one hand, President Trump called Putin to congratulate him on his overwhelming reelection as Russian president on March 18—just days after the Skripal poisoning—and Trump did not raise the poisoning episode in their conversation. Following a summit between Trump and Putin in Helsinki on July 16, Trump was roundly criticized by Democrats and many fellow Republicans for being too friendly with Putin and for too readily accepting Putin's denials that Russia had meddled in the 2016 U.S. presidential election. On the other hand, the State Department conducted its own inquiry into the Skripal poisoning and concluded that the UK government had correctly determined that the Russian state was responsible. This determination prompted additional U.S. sanctions, rolled out in August, which included limits on exporting certain products to Russia.

## SECOND NERVE AGENT ATTACK RESULTS IN DEATH, SUSPECTS IDENTIFIED

The Salisbury operation led to an unintended fatality four months later. On June 30, Dawn Sturgess, a woman living in a homeless hostel in Salisbury, became ill after she sprayed what she thought was perfume on her wrist. The bottle she had handled had in fact contained Novichok. Sturgess's boyfriend, Charlie Rowley, gave her the bottle as a present, having found it discarded in Salisbury, most likely—UK authorities contended—by the individuals who brought it to Salisbury to poison Skripal. Rowley became ill from the exposure but recovered; Sturgess, however, died on July 8.

The UK investigation culminated in an announcement on September 5 of criminal charges against two Russian nationals who had been seen on multiple security cameras in the Salisbury area. Investigators concluded that the two had flown to London using aliases, taken a train to Salisbury on two successive days—once for reconnaissance and once to carry out the poisoning—and that they had sprayed Novichok on the door of the Skripal residence. The passports they used to enter the United Kingdom gave their names as Alexander Petrov and Ruslan Boshirov. The UK authorities concluded that these aliases were given to them by Russian military intelligence, for whom they worked.

Days after being identified, the two men came forward to give a version of events in an interview aired on Russian state television. They claimed to be businessmen on a tourist trip to Salisbury to visit its renowned cathedral. They came to the city on two successive days, they claimed, because adverse weather conditions deterred them from completing their itinerary the first day. Their story was received with widespread disbelief and even derision. Meanwhile, with their faces now known, investigative reporters started digging into their backgrounds. One media outlet, Bellingcat, reported that the men were Russian intelligence operatives whose real names were Anatoly Chepiga and Alexander Mishkin.

Russian authorities continued to deny involvement. Speaking at an energy forum in Russia in October, President Putin denied ordering the attack and mocked the UK investigation. However, Putin also condemned Sergei Skripal as a traitor to his motherland, calling him a "scumbag," and said, "traitors will kick the bucket." In a further twist to the story, the authorities in the Netherlands announced in October that they had discovered four Russians trying to hack into the information system of The Hague–based OPCW, which was investigating the poisoning.

—Brian Beary

*Following are two speeches delivered by Prime Minister Theresa May, on March 12 and March 14, 2018, regarding the poisoning of two Russian nationals with a nerve agent in the United Kingdom; a March 13, 2018, reaction to the poisoning from Russian officials delivered before the Organisation for the Prohibition of Chemical Weapons; a March 22, 2018, conclusion from the European Council regarding the Salisbury attack; Prime Minister May's announcement on September 5, 2018, that charges had been brought against two Russians for the nerve agent attacks; and an October 3, 2018, statement by Russian President Vladimir Putin on the UK's investigation into the nerve attacks.*

DOCUMENT

# Prime Minister May on the Salisbury Poisoning Incident

**March 12, 2018**

With permission, Mr Speaker, I would like to update the House on the incident in Salisbury and the steps we are taking to investigate what happened and to respond to this reckless and despicable act.

Last week, my right hon. Friends the Foreign and Home Secretaries set out the details of events as they unfolded on Sunday 4 March. I am sure that the whole House will want to pay tribute again to the bravery and professionalism of our emergency services and armed forces in responding to this incident, as well as the doctors and nurses who are now treating those affected. In particular, our thoughts are with Detective Sergeant Nick Bailey, who remains in a serious but stable condition. In responding to this incident, he exemplified the duty and courage that define our emergency services and in which our whole nation takes the greatest pride.

I want to pay tribute to the fortitude and calmness with which people in Salisbury have responded to these events and to thank all those who have come forward to assist the police with their investigation. The incident has, of course, caused considerable concern across the community. Following the discovery of traces of nerve agent in a Zizzi restaurant and the Mill pub, the chief medical officer issued further precautionary advice, but, as Public Health England has made clear, the risk to public health is low.

I share the impatience of the House and the country at large to bring those responsible to justice and to take the full range of appropriate responses against those who would act against our country in this way. But as a nation that believes in justice and the rule of law, it is essential that we proceed in the right way, led not by speculation but by the evidence. That is why we have given the police the space and time to carry out their investigation properly. Hundreds of officers have been working around the clock, together with experts from our armed forces, to sift and assess all the available evidence, to identify crime scenes and decontamination sites and to follow every possible lead to find those responsible. That investigation continues and we must allow the police to continue with their work.

This morning, I chaired a meeting of the National Security Council in which we considered the information available so far. As is normal, the council was updated on the assessment and intelligence picture, as well as on the state of the investigation. It is now clear that Mr Skripal and his daughter were poisoned with a military-grade nerve agent of a type developed by Russia. It is part of a group of nerve agents known as Novichok.

Based on the positive identification of this chemical agent by world-leading experts at the Defence Science and Technology Laboratory at Porton Down, our knowledge that Russia has previously produced this agent and would still be capable of doing so, Russia's record of conducting state-sponsored assassinations and our assessment that Russia views some defectors as legitimate targets for assassinations, the Government have concluded that it is highly likely that Russia was responsible for the act against Sergei and Yulia Skripal. There are, therefore, only two plausible explanations for what happened in Salisbury on 4 March: either this was a direct act by the Russian state against our country; or the Russian Government lost control of their potentially catastrophically damaging nerve agent and allowed it to get into the hands of others.

This afternoon, my right hon. Friend the Foreign Secretary has summoned the Russian ambassador to the Foreign and Commonwealth Office and asked him to explain which of the two possibilities it is and to account for how this Russian-produced nerve agent could have been deployed in Salisbury against Mr Skripal and his daughter. My right hon. Friend has stated to the ambassador that the Russian Federation must immediately provide full and complete disclosure of the Novichok programme to the Organisation for the Prohibition of Chemical Weapons, and he has requested the Russian Government's response by the end of tomorrow.

This action has happened against a backdrop of a well-established pattern of Russian state aggression. Russia's illegal annexation of Crimea was the first time since the second world war that one sovereign nation has forcibly taken territory from another in Europe. Russia has fomented conflict in the Donbass, repeatedly violated the national airspace of several European countries and mounted a sustained campaign of cyber-espionage and disruption, which has included meddling in elections and hacking the Danish Ministry of Defence and the Bundestag, among many others.

During his recent state of the union address, President Putin showed video graphics of missile launches, flight trajectories and explosions, including the modelling of attacks on the United States with a series of warheads impacting in Florida. The extra-judicial killing of terrorists and dissidents outside Russia was given legal sanction by the Russian Parliament in 2006, and, of course, Russia used radiological substances in its barbaric assault on Mr Litvinenko. We saw promises to assist the investigation then, but they resulted in denial and obfuscation and the stifling of due process and the rule of law.

Following Mr Litvinenko's death, we expelled Russian diplomats, suspended security co-operation, broke off bilateral plans on visas, froze the assets of the suspects and put them on international extradition lists, and those measures remain in place. Furthermore, our commitment to collective defence and security through NATO remains as strong as ever in the face of Russian behaviour. Indeed, our armed forces have a leading role in NATO's enhanced forward presence, with British troops leading a multinational battle-group in Estonia. We have led the way in securing tough sanctions against the Russian economy, and we have at all stages worked closely with our allies and will continue to do so. We must now stand ready to take much more extensive measures.

On Wednesday, we will consider in detail the response from the Russian state. Should there be no credible response, we will conclude that this action amounts to an unlawful use of force by the Russian state against the United Kingdom, and I will come back to this House to set out the full range of measures that we will take in response.

This attempted murder using a weapons-grade nerve agent in a British town was not just a crime against the Skripals, but an indiscriminate and reckless act against the United Kingdom, putting the lives of innocent civilians at risk. We will not tolerate such a brazen attempt to murder innocent civilians on our soil. I commend this statement to the House.

*[Additional comments by other members of Parliament and the prime minister have been omitted.]*

SOURCE: United Kingdom Parliament House of Commons Hansard. "Salisbury Incident." March 12, 2018. Volume 637. https://hansard.parliament.uk/Commons/2018-03-12/debates/722E1DF5-68E2-41A0-8F3C-23B6480B93BF/SalisburyIncident.

# *Russian Official Responds to Toxic Agent Attack in Salisbury*

**March 13, 2018**

Mr Chairperson,

In connection with the vicious attacks launched by British officials in London, as well as the statement by the head of the British delegation to the OPCW with regard to Russia concerning the suspicious story of two persons poisoned with a toxic agent in Salisbury, we would like to state the following.

The British authorities' unfounded accusations of Russia's alleged involvement in using poisonous agents on their territory are absolutely unacceptable. Our British colleagues should recall that Russia and the United Kingdom are members of the OPCW which is one of the most successful and effective disarmament and non-proliferation mechanisms. We call upon them to abandon the language of ultimatums and threats and return to the legal framework of the chemical convention, which makes it possible to resolve this kind of situation.

If London does have serious reasons to suspect Russia of violating the CWC—and the statement read by distinguished Ambassador Peter Wilson indicates directly that this is so—we suggest that Britain immediately avail itself of the procedures provided for by paragraph 2 of Article 9 of the CWC. They make it possible, on a bilateral basis, to officially contact us for clarifications regarding any issues that raise doubts or concerns.

We would also like to emphasise that such clarifications under the Convention are provided to the requesting member state as soon as possible, but in any case no later than 10 days following receipt of the request. As such, the ultimatum's demand that information be provided immediately, by the end of today, is absolutely unacceptable.

Our British colleagues should save their propaganda fervour and slogans for their unenlightened domestic audience, where perhaps they will have some effect. Here, within the walls of a specialised international organisation, such as the OPCW, one must use facts and nothing but the facts. Stop fomenting hysteria, go ahead and officially formalise your request to begin consultations with us in order to clarify the situation. A fair warning, we will require material evidence of the alleged Russian trace in this high-profile case. Britain's allegations that they have everything, and their world-famous scientists have irrefutable data, but they will not give us anything, will not be taken into account. For us, this will mean that London has nothing substantial to show, and all its loud accusations are nothing but fiction and another instance of the dirty information war being waged on Russia. Sooner or later, they will have to be held accountable for their lies.

In addition, in this particular case, it would be legitimate for the British side to seek assistance from the OPCW Technical Secretariat in conducting an independent laboratory analysis of the available samples that allegedly show traces of nerve agents in Salisbury.

Thank you, Mr Chairperson.

We ask you to circulate this statement as an official document of the 87th session of the OPCW's Executive Council and post it on the Organisation's external server.

SOURCE: Organisation for the Prohibition of Chemical Weapons. "Statement by H.E. Ambassador A.V. Shulgin Permanent Representative of the Russian Federation to the OPCW at the Eighty-Seventh Session of the Executive Council (on the Chemical Incident in Salisbury)." March 13, 2018. https://www.opcw .org/sites/default/files/documents/EC/87/en/ec87nat09_e_.pdf.

# *Prime Minister May Provides Parliament Additional Details on Salisbury Nerve Agent Attack*

**March 14, 2018**

With permission, Mr Speaker, I would like to make a statement on the response of the Russian Government to the incident in Salisbury.

First, on behalf of the whole House, let me pay tribute once again to the bravery and professionalism of all the emergency services, doctors, nurses and investigation teams who have led the response to this appalling incident, and also to the fortitude of the people of Salisbury. I reassure them that, as Public Health England has made clear, the ongoing risk to public health is low, and the Government will continue to do everything possible to support this historic city to recover fully.

On Monday I set out that Mr Skripal and his daughter were poisoned with Novichok—a military-grade nerve agent developed by Russia. Based on this capability, combined with Russia's record of conducting state-sponsored assassinations—including against former intelligence officers whom it regards as legitimate targets—the UK Government concluded it was highly likely that Russia was responsible for this reckless and despicable act. There are only two plausible explanations: either this was a direct act by the Russian state against our country; or, conceivably, the Russian Government could have lost control of a military-grade nerve agent and allowed it to get into the hands of others.

It was right to offer Russia the opportunity to provide an explanation, but its response has demonstrated complete disdain for the gravity of these events. The Russian Government have provided no credible explanation that could suggest that they lost control of their nerve agent, no explanation as to how this agent came to be used in the United Kingdom, and no explanation as to why Russia has an undeclared chemical weapons programme in contravention of international law. Instead it has treated the use of a military-grade nerve agent in Europe with sarcasm, contempt and defiance.

There is no alternative conclusion other than that the Russian state was culpable for the attempted murder of Mr Skripal and his daughter, and for threatening the lives of other British citizens in Salisbury, including Detective Sergeant Nick Bailey. This represents an unlawful use of force by the Russian state against the United Kingdom. As I set out on Monday, it has taken place against the backdrop of a well-established pattern of Russian state aggression across Europe and beyond. It must therefore be met with a full and robust response beyond the actions we have already taken since the murder of Mr Litvinenko and to counter this pattern of Russian aggression elsewhere.

As the discussion in this House on Monday made clear, it is essential that we now come together with our allies to defend our security, to stand up for our values and to send a clear message to those who would seek to undermine them. This morning I chaired a further meeting of the National Security Council, where we agreed immediate actions to dismantle the Russian espionage network in the UK, urgent work to develop new powers to tackle all forms of hostile state activity and to ensure that those seeking to carry out such activity cannot enter the UK, and additional steps to suspend all planned high-level contacts between the United Kingdom and the Russian Federation.

Let me start with the immediate actions. The House will recall that, following the murder of Mr Litvinenko, the UK expelled four diplomats. Under the Vienna convention, the United Kingdom will now expel 23 Russian diplomats who have been identified as undeclared intelligence officers. They have just one week to leave. This will be the single biggest expulsion for over 30 years and it reflects the fact that this is not the first time that the Russian state has acted against our country. Through these expulsions, we will fundamentally degrade Russian intelligence capability in the UK for years to come, and if Russia seeks to rebuild it, we will prevent it from doing so.

We will also urgently develop proposals for new legislative powers to harden our defences against all forms of hostile state activity. This will include the addition of a targeted power to detain those suspected of hostile state activity at the UK border. This power is currently only permitted in relation to those suspected of terrorism. And I have asked the Home Secretary to consider whether there is a need for new counter-espionage powers to clamp down on the full spectrum of hostile activities of foreign agents in our country.

As I set out on Monday, we will also table a Government amendment to the Sanctions and Anti-Money Laundering Bill to strengthen our powers to impose sanctions in response to the violation of human rights. In doing so, we will play our part in an international effort to punish those responsible for the sorts of abuses suffered by Sergei Magnitsky. I hope, as with all the measures I am setting out today, that this will command cross-party support.

We will also make full use of existing powers to enhance our efforts to monitor and track the intentions of those travelling to the UK who could be engaged in activity that threatens the security of the UK and of our allies. So we will increase checks on private flights, customs and freight. We will freeze Russian state assets wherever we have the evidence that they may be used to threaten the life or property of UK nationals or residents. Led by the National Crime Agency, we will continue to bring all the capabilities of UK law enforcement to bear against serious criminals and corrupt elites. There is no place for these people, or their money, in our country.

Let me be clear. While our response must be robust, it must also remain true to our values as a liberal democracy that believes in the rule of law. Many Russians have made this country their home, abide by our laws, and make an important contribution to our country which we must continue to welcome. But to those who seek to do us harm, my message is simple: you are not welcome here.

Let me turn to our bilateral relationship. As I said on Monday, we have had a very simple approach to Russia: engage but beware. I continue to believe that it is not in our national interest to break off all dialogue between the United Kingdom and the Russian Federation. But in the aftermath of this appalling act against our country, this relationship cannot be the same. So we will suspend all planned high-level bilateral contacts between the United Kingdom and the Russian Federation. This includes revoking the invitation to Foreign Minister Lavrov to pay a reciprocal visit to the UK and confirming that there will be no attendance by Ministers, or indeed members of the royal family, at this summer's World [C]up in Russia.

Finally, we will deploy a range of tools from across the full breadth of our national security apparatus in order to counter the threats of hostile state activity. While I have set out some of these measures today, Members on all sides will understand that there are some that cannot be shared publicly for reasons of national security. And of course there are other measures we stand ready to deploy at any time should we face further Russian provocation.

None of the actions we take is intended to damage legitimate activity or prevent contacts between our populations. We have no disagreement with the people of Russia, who have been responsible for so many great achievements throughout their history. Many of us looked at a post-Soviet Russia with hope. We wanted a better relationship, and it is tragic that President Putin has chosen to act in this way. But we will not tolerate the threat to the life of British people and others on British soil from the Russian Government. Nor will we tolerate such a flagrant breach of Russia's international obligations.

As I set out on Monday, the United Kingdom does not stand alone in confronting Russian aggression. In the last 24 hours I have spoken to President Trump, Chancellor Merkel and President Macron. We have agreed to co-operate closely in responding to this barbaric act and to co-ordinate our efforts to stand up for the rules-based international order which Russia seeks to undermine. I will also speak to other allies and partners in the coming days. I welcome the strong expressions of support from NATO and from partners across the European Union and beyond. Later today in New York, the UN Security Council will hold open consultations where we will be pushing for a robust international response. We have also notified the Organisation for the Prohibition of Chemical Weapons about Russia's use of this nerve agent, and we are working with the police to enable the OPCW to independently verify our analysis.

This was not just an act of attempted murder in Salisbury, nor just an act against the UK. It is an affront to the prohibition on the use of chemical weapons, and it is an affront to the rules-based system on which we and our international partners depend. We will work with our allies and partners to confront such actions wherever they threaten our security, at home and abroad. I commend this statement to the House.

*[Additional comments by other members of Parliament and the prime minister have been omitted.]*

SOURCE: United Kingdom Parliament House of Commons Hansard. "Salisbury Incident: Further Update." March 14, 2018. Volume 637. https://hansard.parliament.uk/Commons/2018-03-14/debates/071C37BB-DF8F-4836-88CA-66AB74369BC1/SalisburyIncidentFurtherUpdate.

# European Council Concurs with UK Findings on Nerve Agent Attack

**March 22, 2018**

9. The European Council condemns in the strongest possible terms the recent attack in Salisbury, expresses its deepest sympathies to all whose lives have been threatened and lends its support to the ongoing investigation. It agrees with the United Kingdom government's assessment that it is highly likely that the Russian Federation is responsible and that there is no plausible alternative explanation. We stand in unqualified solidarity with the United Kingdom in the face of this grave challenge to our shared security.

10. The use of chemical weapons, including the use of any toxic chemicals as weapons under any circumstances, is completely unacceptable, must be systematically and rigorously condemned and constitutes a security threat to us all. Member States will coordinate on the consequences to be drawn in the light of the answers provided by the Russian authorities. The European Union will remain closely focused on this issue and its implications.

11. Against this background, the European Union must strengthen its resilience to Chemical, Biological, Radiological and Nuclear-related risks, including through closer cooperation between the European Union and its Member States as well as NATO. The European Union and its Member States should also continue to bolster their capabilities to address hybrid threats, including in the areas of cyber, strategic communication and counter-intelligence. The European Council invites the European Commission and the High Representative to take this work forward and report on progress by the June European Council.

SOURCE: Council of the European Union. "European Council Conclusions on the Salisbury Attack, 22 March 2018." March 22, 2018. https://www.consilium.europa.eu/en/press/press-releases/2018/03/22/european-council-conclusions-on-the-salisbury-attack/pdf.

## Prime Minister May Announces Charges in Nerve Agent Attack

**September 5, 2018**

With permission, Mr Speaker, I would like to update the House on the investigation into the attempted murder of Sergey and Yulia Skripal—and the subsequent poisoning of Dawn Sturgess and Charlie Rowley earlier this year.

This was a sickening and despicable act in which a devastatingly toxic nerve agent—known as Novichok—was used to attack our country. It left four people fighting for their lives and one innocent woman dead. And I know the thoughts of the whole House will be with the family of Dawn Sturgess in particular, following their tragic loss.

In March I set out for the House why the government concluded that the Russian State was culpable for the attempted murder of Mr Skripal and his daughter.

I also said that—while we all share a sense of impatience to bring those responsible to justice—as a nation that believes in the rule of law we would give the police the space and time to carry out their investigation properly.

Since then around 250 detectives have trawled through more than 11,000 hours of CCTV and taken more than 1,400 statements.

Working around the clock they have carried out painstaking and methodical work to ascertain exactly which individuals were responsible and the methods they used to carry out this attack.

Mr Speaker, this forensic investigation has now produced sufficient evidence for the independent Director of Public Prosecutions to bring charges against two Russian nationals for:

- the conspiracy to murder Sergei Skripal;

- the attempted murder of Sergei and Yulia Skripal and Detective Sergeant Nick Bailey;

- the use and possession of Novichok; and

- causing grievous bodily harm with intent to Yulia Skripal and Nick Bailey.

This morning, the police have set out how the two Russian nationals travelled under the names of Alexander Petrov and Ruslan Boshirov—names the police believe to be aliases.

They arrived at Gatwick Airport at 3pm on Friday 2nd March, having flown from Moscow on flight SU2588.

They travelled by train to London Victoria, then on to Waterloo before going to the City Stay Hotel in Bow Road East London.

They stayed there on both Friday and Saturday evenings—and traces of Novichok were found in their hotel room.

On Saturday 3rd March they visited Salisbury, arriving at approximately 2.25pm and leaving less than two hours later, at 4.10pm. The police are confident this was for reconnaissance of the Salisbury area.

On Sunday 4th March they made the same journey, travelling by underground from Bow to Waterloo station at approximately 8.05am, before continuing by train to Salisbury.

The police have today released CCTV footage of the two men which clearly places them in the immediate vicinity of the Skripals' house at 11.58am, which the police say was moments before the attack.

They left Salisbury and returned to Waterloo arriving at approximately 4.45pm and boarded the underground at approximately 6.30pm to Heathrow—from where they returned to Moscow on flight SU2585, departing at 10.30pm.

Mr Speaker, this hard evidence has enabled the independent Crown Prosecution Service to conclude they have a sufficient basis on which to bring charges against these two men for the attack in Salisbury.

The same two men are now also the prime suspects in the case of Dawn Sturgess and Charlie Rowley too.

There is no other line of inquiry beyond this.

And the police have today formally linked the attack on the Skripals and the events in Amesbury—such that it now forms one investigation.

There are good reasons for doing so.

Our own analysis, together with yesterday's report from the Organisation for the Prohibition of Chemical Weapons, has confirmed that the exact same chemical nerve agent was used in both cases.

There is no evidence to suggest that Dawn and Charlie may have been deliberately targeted, but rather were victims of the reckless disposal of this agent.

The police have today released further details of the small glass counterfeit perfume bottle and box discovered in Charlie Rowley's house which was found to contain this nerve agent.

And the manner in which the bottle was modified leaves no doubt it was a cover for smuggling the weapon into the country, and for the delivery method for the attack against the Skripals' front door.

Mr Speaker, the police investigation into the poisoning of Dawn and Charlie is ongoing and the police are today appealing for further information. But were these two suspects within our jurisdiction there would be a clear basis in law for their arrest for murder.

Mr Speaker, we repeatedly asked Russia to account for what happened in Salisbury in March, and they have replied with obfuscation and lies.

This has included trying to pass the blame for this attack onto terrorists, onto our international partners, and even onto the future mother-in-law of Yulia Skripal.

They even claimed that I, myself, invented Novichok.

Their attempts to hide the truth by pushing out a deluge of disinformation simply reinforces their culpability.

As we made clear in March, only Russia had the technical means, operational experience and motive to carry out the attack.

Novichok nerve agents were developed by the Soviet Union in the 1980s under a programme codenamed FOLIANT.

Within the past decade Russia has produced and stockpiled small quantities of these agents, long after it signed the Chemical Weapons Convention.

And during the 2000s, Russia commenced a programme to test means of delivering nerve agents including by application to door handles.

We were right to say in March that the Russian State was responsible.

And now we have identified the individuals involved, we can go even further.

Mr Speaker, just as the police investigation has enabled the CPS to bring charges against the two suspects, so the Security and Intelligence Agencies have carried out their own investigations into the organisation behind this attack.

Based on this work, I can today tell the House that, based on a body of intelligence, the Government has concluded that the two individuals named by the police and CPS are officers from the Russian military intelligence service, also known as the GRU.

The GRU is a highly disciplined organisation with a well-established chain of command.

So this was not a rogue operation. It was almost certainly also approved outside the GRU at a senior level of the Russian state.

Mr Speaker, the House will appreciate that I cannot go into details about the work of our security and intelligence agencies. But we will be briefing Opposition leaders and others on Privy Council terms and also giving further detail to the Intelligence and Security Committee.

Let me turn to our response to this appalling attack and the further knowledge we now have about those responsible.

First, with respect to the two individuals, as the Crown Prosecution Service and Police announced earlier today, we have obtained a European Arrest Warrant and will shortly issue an Interpol red notice.

Of course, Russia has repeatedly refused to allow its nationals to stand trial overseas, citing a bar on extradition in its constitution.

So, as we found following the murder of Alexander Litvinenko, any formal extradition request in this case would be futile.

But should either of these individuals ever again travel outside Russia, we will take every possible step to detain them, to extradite them and to bring them to face justice here in the United Kingdom.

Mr Speaker, this chemical weapons attack on our soil was part of a wider pattern of Russian behaviour that persistently seeks to undermine our security and that of our allies around the world.

They have fomented conflict in the Donbas, illegally annexed Crimea, repeatedly violated the national airspace of several European countries and mounted a sustained campaign of cyber espionage and election interference.

They were behind a violent attempted coup in Montenegro. And a Russian-made missile, launched from territory held by Russian-backed separatists, brought down MH17.

We must step up our collective effort to protect ourselves in response to this threat— and that is exactly what we have done since the attack in March, both domestically and collectively with our allies.

We have introduced a new power to detain people at the UK border to determine whether they are engaged in hostile state activity.

We have introduced the Magnitsky amendment to the Sanctions and Money Laundering Act in response to the violation of human rights. And we have radically stepped up our activity against illicit finance entering our country.

We also expelled 23 Russian diplomats who had been identified as undeclared Russian intelligence officers, fundamentally degrading Russian intelligence capability in the UK for years to come.

And in collective solidarity—and in recognition of the shared threat posed to our allies—28 other countries as well as NATO joined us in expelling a total of over 150 Russian intelligence officers: the largest collective expulsion ever.

Since then, the EU agreed a comprehensive package to tackle hybrid threats.

The G7 agreed a Rapid Response Mechanism to share intelligence on hostile state activity.

NATO has substantially strengthened its collective deterrence, including through a new Cyber Operations Centre.

And the US has announced additional sanctions against Russia for the Salisbury attack.

Mr Speaker, our allies acted in good faith—and the painstaking work of our police and intelligence agencies over the last six months further reinforces that they were right to do so.

Together, we will continue to show that those who attempt to undermine the international rules based system cannot act with impunity.

We will continue to press for all of the measures agreed so far to be fully implemented, including the creation of a new EU Chemical Weapons sanctions regime.

But we will not stop there.

We will also push for new EU sanctions regimes against those responsible for cyber-attacks and gross human rights violations—and for new listings under the existing regime against Russia.

And we will work with our partners to empower the OPCW to attribute chemical weapons attacks to other states beyond Syria.

Most significantly, Mr Speaker, what we have learnt from today's announcement is the specific nature of the threat from the Russian GRU.

We know that the GRU has played a key part in malign Russian activity in recent years.

And today we have exposed their role behind the despicable chemical weapons attack on the streets of Salisbury.

The actions of the GRU are a threat to all our allies and to all our citizens.

And on the basis of what we have learnt in the Salisbury investigation—and what we know about this organisation more broadly—we must now step up our collective efforts, specifically against the GRU.

We are increasing our understanding of what the GRU is doing in our countries, shining a light on their activities, exposing their methods and sharing them with our allies, just as we have done with Salisbury.

And, Mr Speaker, while the House will appreciate that I cannot go into details, together with our allies we will deploy the full range of tools from across our National Security apparatus in order to counter the threat posed by the GRU.

I have said before, and I say again now, that the UK has no quarrel with the Russian people.

And we continue to hold out hope that we will one day once again enjoy a strong partnership with the Government of this great nation.

As a fellow Permanent Member of the UN Security Council, we will continue to engage Russia on topics of international peace and security.

But we will also use these channels of communication to make clear there can be no place in any civilised international order for the kind of barbaric activity which we saw in Salisbury in March.

Finally, Mr Speaker let me pay tribute to the fortitude of the people of Salisbury, Amesbury and the surrounding areas, who have faced such disruption to their daily lives over the past six months.

Let me once again thank the outstanding efforts of the emergency services and National Health Service in responding to these incidents.

And let me thank all those involved in the police and intelligence community for their tireless and painstaking work which has led to today's announcement.

Mr Speaker, back in March, Russia sought to sow doubt and uncertainty about the evidence we presented to this House—and some were minded to believe them.

Today's announcement shows that we were right.

We were right to act against the Russian State in the way we did. And we are right now to step up our efforts against the GRU.

We will not tolerate such barbaric acts against our country.

And—together with our allies—this government will continue to do whatever is necessary to keep our people safe.

And I commend this statement to the House.

Source: Government of the United Kingdom. "PM Statement on the Salisbury Investigation: 5 September 2018." September 5, 2018. https://www.gov.uk/government/speeches/pm-statement-on-the-salisbury-investigation-5-september-2018.

# Russian President Putin Responds to UK Investigation into Nerve Agent Attack

**October 3, 2018**

*[Remarks made by President Putin not related to the nerve agent attack have been omitted.]*

*Vladimir Putin:* . . . As regards the Skripals and all that, this latest spy scandal is being artificially inflated. I have seen some media outlets and your colleagues push the idea that Skripal is almost a human rights activist. But he is just a spy, a traitor to the motherland. There is such a term, a 'traitor to the motherland,' and that's what he is.

Imagine you are a citizen of a country, and suddenly somebody comes along who betrays your country. How would you, or anybody present here, a representative of any country, feel about such a person? He is scum, that's all. But a whole information campaign has been deployed around it.

I think it will come to an end, I hope it will, and the sooner the better. We have repeatedly told our colleagues to show us the documents. We will see what can be done and conduct an investigation.

We probably have an agreement with the UK on assistance in criminal cases that outlines the procedure. Well, submit the documents to the Prosecutor General's Office as required. We will see what actually happened there.

The fuss between security services did not start yesterday. As you know, espionage, just like prostitution, is one of the most 'important' jobs in the world. So what? Nobody shut it down and nobody can shut it down yet.

*Ryan Chilcote:* Espionage aside, I think there are two other issues. One is the use of chemical weapons, and let's not forget that in addition to the Skripal family being affected in that attack, there was also a homeless person who was killed when they came in contact with the nerve agent Novichok.

*Vladimir Putin:* Listen, since we are talking about poisoning Skripal, are you saying that we also poisoned a homeless person there? Sometimes I look at what is happening around this case and it amazes me. Some guys came to England and started poisoning homeless people. Such nonsense. What is this all about? Are they working for cleaning services? Nobody wanted to poison. . . . This Skripal is a traitor, as I said. He was caught and punished. He spent a total of five years in prison. We released him. That's it. He left. He continued to cooperate with and consult some security services.

Source: President of Russia. "Russian Energy Week International Forum." October 3, 2018. http://en.kremlin.ru/events/president/transcripts/58701.

## OTHER HISTORIC DOCUMENTS OF INTEREST

### FROM THIS VOLUME

### FROM PREVIOUS *HISTORIC DOCUMENTS*

# Trump Administration and Courts Rule on Tech Mergers

MARCH 12, JUNE 12, AND SEPTEMBER 11, 2018

Three major mergers within the U.S. technology sector drew federal regulators' attention in 2018. In an unusual move, President Donald Trump issued an executive order to block the proposed takeover of Qualcomm by foreign-based Broadcom before a final agreement had been reached, citing national security concerns. In June, a federal district court denied the government's request to prevent AT&T and Time Warner from merging; less than two months later, the U.S. Justice Department appealed the ruling. Finally, the Federal Communications Commission (FCC) began its review of a proposed merger between T-Mobile and Sprint.

## ADMINISTRATION BLOCKS CHIP MAKER MERGER

On March 12, President Trump issued an executive order blocking the proposed merger of Qualcomm Incorporated and Broadcom Limited. San Diego–based Qualcomm is the largest producer of smartphone chips in the world, while Singapore-based Broadcom makes chips for everything from cars to TVs to computers. Broadcom first offered to buy Qualcomm in November 2017 for $105 billion, but Qualcomm's management quickly rejected the offer, saying the price dramatically undervalued the company. The rejection prompted Broadcom to launch a hostile takeover, going directly to shareholders to convince them to accept the deal and acquiring proxies to elect a Broadcom-proposed slate of directors who supported the merger to Qualcomm's board.

In his executive order, Trump argued that Broadcom "might take action that threatens to impair the national security of the United States" and that existing laws did not provide "adequate and appropriate authority for me to protect the national security in this matter." Therefore, he prohibited the merger and any "substantially equivalent merger, acquisition, or takeover, whether effected directly or indirectly."

The language of the executive order reflected concerns previously identified by the Committee on Foreign Investment in the United States (CFIUS) in an interim order issued on March 4. CFIUS is an interagency committee that reviews certain types of transactions that involve foreign investment in the United States to assess their potential impact on national security. The committee determined the merger posed national security risks to the United States and imposed two measures intended to mitigate these risks. Specifically, the order delayed Qualcomm's annual shareholder meeting—at which shareholders were expected to vote on the proposed board nominees—for thirty days and prohibited Qualcomm's board, executives, and agents from accepting the merger or taking any action that could further consideration of the agreement.

CFIUS sent a letter to the two companies' lawyers to explain their concerns, which included that the merger could disadvantage the United States' development of mobile technology, particularly 5G. The fifth generation of wireless technology, 5G is projected to be one hundred times faster and provide better connections than current 4G technology. Those in the technology sector speculate that 5G could play a critical role in establishing the communications systems needed to support emerging technologies such as self-driving cars, virtual reality, and advanced telemedicine, in addition to increasing the amount of information that can be stored in the cloud. Unlike earlier generations of mobile technology, 5G is formed by a global standard that every company and country must agree to, meaning a leader in 5G has more opportunity to shape the technology than before. (With previous generations, such as 3G, companies had separate wireless networks, and mobile devices produced by one company would not work on another's network.) CFIUS noted that no American company was presently a leader in 5G technology but that Qualcomm had invested heavily in 5G research and development. If the merger went through, Broadcom would be buying Qualcomm's 5G research in addition to its smartphone chips. CFIUS expressed concern that Broadcom may hinder Qualcomm's 5G research through cost-cutting measures, which could weaken Qualcomm's position and thus the United States' position in relation to foreign rivals who are trying to develop 5G technology first—specifically, China. "Given well-known U.S. national security concerns about Huawei and other Chinese telecommunications companies, a shift to Chinese dominance in 5G would have substantial negative national security consequences for the United States," the committee wrote.

Industry observers noted the administration's intervention in the merger was unprecedented because a final agreement had not been reached prior to the committee's or Trump's order. CFIUS typically does not become involved until a deal has been finalized and is ready to go through the formal regulatory review process. Further, only five transactions have been blocked by presidential order since CFIUS's creation in 1975, including a 2017 proposal by Chinese government-backed Canyon Bridge Capital Partners to buy Oregon-based Lattice Semiconductor Corp. (also prohibited due to national security concerns).

Broadcom had sought to redomicile in the United States on an expedited timeline to allay regulators' concerns and offered assurances that it would not only continue Qualcomm's 5G research and development efforts, it would "focus R&D spend to those critical technologies that are essential to the U.S." However, these actions proved ineffective. Although Broadcom said it strongly disagreed that its purchase of Qualcomm would pose a security threat, the company officially withdrew its offer on March 14.

## JUSTICE DEPARTMENT APPEALS COURT DECISION ON AT&T–TIME WARNER MERGER

On June 12, United States District Court for the District of Columbia Senior Judge Richard Leon handed AT&T and Time Warner a victory when he ruled the companies' proposed merger could proceed. "I conclude that the Government has failed to meet its burden to establish that the proposed 'transaction is likely to lessen competition substantially,'" Leon wrote in his opinion. "Based on that conclusion, and for all the reasons set forth in greater detail in this Opinion, the Court DENIES the Government's request to enjoin the proposed merger." Leon declined to impose any conditions on the deal's execution; these conditions, such as the requirement that the companies sell off certain assets, are sometimes sought by the government to reduce a merger's anticipated impact on competition.

"We are pleased that, after conducting a full and fair trial on the merits, the Court has categorically rejected the government's lawsuit to block our merger with Time Warner," said David McAtee, AT&T's general counsel. Assistant Attorney General Makan Delrahim, head of the Justice Department's Antitrust Division, said the agency would "closely review the court's opinion and consider next steps in light of our commitment to preserving competition for the benefit of American consumers."

Originally announced in October 2016, AT&T's agreement to buy Time Warner for $108 billion (which included the acquisition of Time Warner debt) was one of the largest transactions in American history. The deal was a classic vertical merger, in which two or more companies operate at different levels of production for the same product: Time Warner provides media content, and AT&T provides distribution. The government has generally approved vertical transactions since it lost a case against this type of merger in the trucking industry in 1979. In the instance of AT&T and Time Warner, the Justice Department wanted the companies to agree to divest of Turner Broadcasting or DirecTV before the merger was approved and finalized. Both companies refused. As a result, the federal government filed a civil antitrust lawsuit in November 2017 to block the merger, claiming it "would greatly harm American consumers" and result in "higher monthly television bills and fewer of the new, emerging innovative options that consumers are beginning to enjoy." AT&T countered the government's filing by pointing to an "intensely competitive and rapidly changing" marketplace in which Americans are increasingly consuming content via direct-to-consumer platforms such as Netflix, Hulu, YouTube, and Amazon Video. Some questioned whether the suit was politically motivated, since Time Warner is the parent company of CNN—a cable news network that is frequently derided by Trump for its political coverage. Justice Department and White House officials denied this, and in February 2018, Leon rejected AT&T's request for the administration's logs of communications about the merger, ruling that the company had not provided sufficient proof of unfair targeting.

With the court's approval, the merger was completed on June 15. On August 6, the Justice Department filed its appeal with the United States Court of Appeals for the District of Columbia Circuit. The government argued in its brief that the lower court made "fundamental errors of economic logic and reasoning" in analyzing the impact of the merger. Specifically, it failed to consider how AT&T would have greater leverage during negotiations with rival distributors because it could threaten to pull Time Warner content from those distributors, potentially causing consumers to switch their provider to AT&T to get that content. This would also allow AT&T to charge its rivals higher fees to carry Time Warner content. "These errors distorted its view of the evidence and rendered its factual findings clearly erroneous, and they are the subject of this appeal," read the filing.

"Appeals aren't 'do-overs,'" AT&T general counsel McAtee said in a statement. "After a long trial, Judge Leon weighed the evidence and rendered a comprehensive 172-page decision that systematically exposed each of the many holes in the Government's case. There is nothing in DOJ's brief today that should disturb that decision."

Oral arguments for the appeal began on December 6.

## T-Mobile–Sprint Merger under FCC Review

Another major technology merger was announced on April 29, this time between wireless providers T-Mobile and Sprint. In a joint release, the companies said their merger would "be a force for positive change in the U.S. wireless, video, and broadband industries" and would "lay the foundation for U.S. companies and innovators to lead in the 5G era." The new company, to be called simply T-Mobile, would have the capacity to create a nation-wide 5G network that would enable U.S. companies and entrepreneurs to lead in 5G technology, they said. "The combined company will have lower costs, greater economies of scale, and the resources to provide U.S. consumers and businesses with lower prices, better quality, unmatched value, and greater competition," they added.

Although the $26 billion merger was widely anticipated (the two companies had considered merging before), consumer groups remained skeptical. "If the national wireless market shrinks from essentially four companies to three, history suggests the negative impact on competition would mean higher prices for many people," said Jonathan Schwantes, senior policy counsel for Consumers Union. The government officially began its review of the proposed merger on June 19, after T-Mobile and Sprint filed their formal application with the FCC. The FCC typically reviews and approves or denies mergers and other business transactions within 180 days of being notified about the deal, but on September 11, the commission announced it was pausing this informal clock. The companies had reportedly submitted new information to the FCC, including a "substantially revised" network engineering model, business model, and economic modeling. "Considering the complexity and potential importance of these newly-provided and expected models, it is appropriate to stop the informal 180-day clock to allow time for their review," FCC officials said in a letter to the two companies. "The Commission will decide whether to extend the deadline for reply comments after receiving the remainder of the Applicants' modeling submissions." At the time of writing, the FCC had not indicated when it would resume its review.

—Linda Grimm

*Following is President Donald Trump's executive order from March 12, 2018, blocking the Qualcomm–Broadcom merger; the summary of Senior Judge Richard Leon's ruling on June 12, 2018, that the AT&T–Time Warner merger could proceed; and an FCC letter, dated September 11, 2018, announcing that the body intends to pause its review of the T-Mobile and Sprint merger pending additional information.*

DOCUMENT

# Executive Order Blocking
# Qualcomm–Broadcom Merger

**March 12, 2018**

By the authority vested in me as President by the Constitution and the laws of the United States of America, including section 721 of the Defense Production Act of 1950, as amended (section 721), 50 U.S.C. 4565, it is hereby ordered as follows:

*Section 1. Findings.* (a) There is credible evidence that leads me to believe that Broadcom Limited, a limited company organized under the laws of Singapore (Broadcom), along with its partners, subsidiaries, or affiliates, including Broadcom Corporation, a California corporation, and Broadcom Cayman L.P., a Cayman Islands limited partnership, and their partners, subsidiaries, or affiliates (together, the Purchaser), through exercising control of Qualcomm Incorporated (Qualcomm), a Delaware corporation, might take action that threatens to impair the national security of the United States; and

(b) Provisions of law, other than section 721 and the International Emergency Economic Powers Act (50 U.S.C. 1701 et seq.), do not, in my judgment, provide adequate and appropriate authority for me to protect the national security in this matter.

*Sec. 2. Actions Ordered and Authorized.* On the basis of the findings set forth in section 1 of this order, considering the factors described in subsection 721(f) of the Defense Production Act of 1950, as appropriate, and pursuant to my authority under applicable law, including section 721, I hereby order that:

(a) The proposed takeover of Qualcomm by the Purchaser is prohibited, and any substantially equivalent merger, acquisition, or takeover, whether effected directly or indirectly, is also prohibited.

(b) All 15 individuals listed as potential candidates on the Form of Blue Proxy Card filed by Broadcom and Broadcom Corporation with the Securities and Exchange Commission on February 20, 2018 (together, the Candidates), are hereby disqualified from standing for election as directors of Qualcomm. Qualcomm is prohibited from accepting the nomination of or votes for any of the Candidates.

(c) The Purchaser shall uphold its proxy commitments to those Qualcomm stockholders who have returned their final proxies to the Purchaser, to the extent consistent with this order.

(d) Qualcomm shall hold its annual stockholder meeting no later than 10 days following the written notice of the meeting provided to stockholders under Delaware General Corporation Law, Title 8, Chapter 1, Subchapter VII, section 222(b), and that notice shall be provided as soon as possible.

(e) The Purchaser and Qualcomm shall immediately and permanently abandon the proposed takeover. Immediately upon completion of all steps necessary to terminate the proposed takeover of Qualcomm, the Purchaser and Qualcomm shall certify in writing to the Committee on Foreign Investment in the United States (CFIUS) that such termination has been effected in accordance with this order and that all steps necessary to fully and permanently abandon the proposed takeover of Qualcomm have been completed.

(f) From the date of this order until the Purchaser and Qualcomm provide a certification of termination of the proposed takeover to CFIUS pursuant to subsection (e) of this section, the Purchaser and Qualcomm shall certify to CFIUS on a weekly basis that they are in compliance with this order and include a description of efforts to fully and permanently abandon the proposed takeover of Qualcomm and a timeline for projected completion of remaining actions.

(g) Any transaction or other device entered into or employed for the purpose of, or with the effect of, avoiding or circumventing this order is prohibited.

(h) If any provision of this order, or the application of any provision to any person or circumstances, is held to be invalid, the remainder of this order and the application of its other provisions to any other persons or circumstances shall not be affected thereby. If any provision of this order, or the application of any provision to any person or circumstances, is held to be invalid because of the lack of certain procedural requirements, the relevant executive branch officials shall implement those procedural requirements.

(i) This order supersedes the Interim Order issued by CFIUS on March 4, 2018.

(j) The Attorney General is authorized to take any steps necessary to enforce this order.

*Sec. 3. Reservation.* I hereby reserve my authority to issue further orders with respect to the Purchaser and Qualcomm as shall in my judgment be necessary to protect the national security of the United States.

*Sec. 4. Publication and Transmittal.* (a) This order shall be published in the *Federal Register*.

(b) I hereby direct the Secretary of the Treasury to transmit a copy of this order to Qualcomm and Broadcom.

DONALD J. TRUMP

SOURCE: Executive Office of the President. "Order—Regarding the Proposed Takeover of Qualcomm Incorporated by Broadcom Limited." *Compilation of Presidential Documents* 2018, no. 00154 (March 12, 2018). March 12, 2018. https://www.gpo.gov/fdsys/pkg/DCPD-201800154/pdf/DCPD-201800154.pdf.

# *United States District Court for the District of Columbia Ruling in U.S. v. AT&T Inc.*

**June 12, 2018**

### UNITED STATES DISTRICT COURT FOR THE DISTRICT OF COLUMBIA

UNITED STATES OF AMERICA,
  Plaintiff,

v.                                        Civil Case No. 17-2511 (RJL)

AT&T Inc., *et. al.*,
  Defendants

If there ever were an antitrust case where the parties had a dramatically different assessment of the current state of the relevant market and a fundamentally different vision of its future development, this is the one. Small wonder it had to go to trial!

On November 20, 2017, the U.S. Department of Justice's Antitrust Division brought this suit, on behalf of the United States of America ("the Government" or "the plaintiff"), to block the merger of AT&T Inc. ("AT&T") and Time Warner Inc. ("Time Warner") as a violation of Section 7 of the Clayton Act, 15 U.S.C. § 18. The Government claims, in essence, that permitting AT&T to acquire Time Warner is likely to substantially lessen competition in the video programming and distribution market nationwide by enabling AT&T to use Time Warner's "must have" television content to either raise its rivals' video programming costs or, by way of a "blackout," drive those same rivals' customers to its subsidiary, DirecTV. Thus, according to the Government, consumers nationwide will be harmed by increased prices for access to Turner networks, notwithstanding the Government's concession that this vertical merger would result in hundreds of millions of dollars in annual cost savings to AT&T's customers and notwithstanding the fact that (unlike in "horizontal" mergers) no competitor will be eliminated by the merger's proposed vertical integration.

Not surprisingly, the defendants, AT&T, Time Warner, and DirecTV, strongly disagree. Their vision couldn't be more different. The video programming and distribution market, they point out, has been, and is, in the middle of a revolution where high-speed internet access has facilitated a "veritable explosion" of new, innovative video content and advertising offerings over the past five years. Trial Tr. ("Tr.") 1397: 1–4 (Montemagno (Charter)). Vertically integrated entities like Netflix, Hulu, and Amazon have achieved remarkable success in creating and providing affordable, on-demand video content directly to viewers over the internet. Meanwhile, web giants Facebook and Google have developed new ways to use data to create effective—and lucrative—digital advertisements tailored to the individual consumer.

As a result of these "tectonic changes" brought on by the proliferation of high-speed internet access, video programmers such as Time Warner and video distributors such as AT&T find themselves facing two stark realities: declining video subscriptions and flatlining television advertising revenues. *Id.* at 3079: 18 (Bewkes (Time Warner)). Indeed, cost-conscious consumers increasingly choose to "cut" or "shave" the cord, abandoning their traditional cable- or satellite- TV packages for cheaper content alternatives available over the internet. At the same time, Facebook's and Google's dominant digital advertising platforms have surpassed television advertising in revenue. Watching vertically integrated, data-informed entities thrive as television subscriptions and advertising revenues declined, AT&T and Time Warner concluded that each had a problem that the other could solve: Time Warner could provide AT&T with the ability to experiment with and develop innovative video content and advertising offerings for AT&T's many video and wireless customers, and AT&T could afford Time Warner access to customer relationships and valuable data about its programming. Together, AT&T and Time Warner concluded that both companies could stop "chasing taillights" and catch up with the competition. 2/16/18 Hr'g Tr. 34:16 [Dkt # 67]. Those were the circumstances that drove AT&T, a distributor of content, and Time Warner, a content creator and programmer, to announce their historic $108 billion merger in October 2016 (the "proposed merger" or "challenged merger"). Those are the circumstances that cause them to claim today that their merger will increase not only innovation, but competition in this marketplace for years to come.

Section 7 of the Clayton Act assigns this Court the "uncertain task" of weighing the parties' competing visions of the future of the relevant market and the challenged merger's place within it. *United States v. Baker Hughes Inc.*, 908 F.2d 981, 991 (D.C. Cir. 1990). Nothing less than a comprehensive inquiry into future competitive conditions in that market is expected. And the Government has the burden of proof to demonstrate that the merger is likely to lessen competition substantially in that uncertain future.

Since announcing the transaction in late October 2016, defendants have delayed closing on the merger agreement for about 18 months as a result of the Government's investigation and suit. The deal is now set to expire if not consummated on or before June 21, 2018—a turn of events that would require AT&T to pay Time Warner a "break-up fee" of $500 million. The parties have engaged in a highly accelerated discovery schedule to prepare themselves to try this case in March and April of this year. The trial itself lasted nearly six weeks. Both sides put on a case-in-chief and the Government put on a rebuttal case as well. At the conclusion of the trial, I advised the parties I would issue a ruling, if not an opinion, no later than June 12, 2018 so that the losing side would have the agreed upon time remaining to pursue its appellate rights *before* the merger or the $500 million break-up fee went into effect.

The following is the Court's Opinion. Initially, I provide context for this suit by reviewing the background of the video programming and distribution industry, the proposed merger, and the procedural history of this case. Thereafter, I discuss the legal standards governing a suit under Section 7 of the Clayton Act, emphasizing in particular the considerations at play in evaluating vertical mergers. With that in place, I next analyze each of the Government's three theories of harm to competition, balancing, as appropriate, the conceded proconsumer benefits of the merger with the consumer harms alleged and the evidence offered to support them. Ultimately, I conclude that the Government has failed to meet its burden to establish that the proposed "transaction is likely to lessen competition substantially." *Baker Hughes*, 908 F.2d at 985.

As such, based on that conclusion, and for all the reasons set forth in greater detail in this Opinion, the Court **DENIES** the Government's request to enjoin the proposed merger.

SOURCE: United States District Court for the District of Columbia. *United State of America, Plaintiff, v. AT&T, Inc., et al., Defendants.* June 12, 2018. http://www.dcd.uscourts.gov/sites/dcd/files/17-2511opinion.pdf.

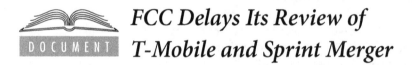

# FCC Delays Its Review of T-Mobile and Sprint Merger

September 11, 2018

*[All footnotes have been omitted.]*

<u>VIA E-MAIL</u>

Kathleen O'Brien Ham
T-Mobile U.S., Inc.
601 Pennsylvania Avenue, N.W.
North Building, Suite 800
Washington, DC 20004
*[kathleen.ham@t-mobile.com]*

Vonya B. McCann
Sprint Corporation
900 7th Street, N.W.
Washington, DC 20001
*[vonya.b.mccann@sprint.com]*

Re: Applications of T-Mobile U.S., Inc., and Sprint Corporation for Consent to Transfer Control of Licenses and Authorizations (WT Docket No. 18-197)

Dear Ms. Ham and Ms. McCann:

Today we are pausing the Commission's informal 180-day transaction shot clock in this proceeding. Additional time is necessary to allow for thorough staff and third-party review of newly-submitted and anticipated modeling relied on by the Applicants.

Each of three separate developments requires more time. First, on September 5, 2018, the Applicants submitted a substantially revised network engineering model. Although the Applicants previously provided a network engineering model as backup for certain network claims, you explained that since that time "the model has been extended," and that the newly-provided model "completes" the prior work. Moreover, the Applicants asserted that this is now the "engineering model on which they rely in support of this transaction."

The newly-provided network engineering model is significantly larger and more complex than the engineering submissions already in the record. It appears to incorporate new logic, methodologies, facts and assumptions, on a subject central to the Applications—the transaction's claimed network benefits. Accordingly, the Commission and third parties will require additional time to review it.

Further, in an August 29, 2018, *ex parte* meeting, T-Mobile executives Mike Sievert and Peter Ewens described T-Mobile's reliance on a business model, titled "Build 9," which apparently provides the financial basis for the projected new network buildout. The Commission did not receive Build 9, and third parties did not have access to it, until September 5. Build 9 therefore requires further review.

Finally, T-Mobile recently disclosed that it intends to submit additional economic modeling in support of the Applications, beyond that strictly responsive to the various economic analyses in the Petitions to Deny. This new economic modeling will also require additional time for review.

We also understand that these models may interact with or support one another in ways still unknown to the Commission and third parties. It will take time to evaluate, understand the relationships between, and prepare responses to these models. Moreover, those evaluations may also require additional information and explanation about the new modeling.

The Commission has a strong interest in ensuring a full and complete record upon which to base its decision in this proceeding. Considering the complexity and potential importance of these newly-provided and expected models, it is appropriate to stop the informal 180-day clock to allow time for their review. The clock will remain stopped until the Applicants have completed the record on which they intend to rely and a reasonable period of time has passed for staff and third-party review. The Commission will decide whether to extend the deadline for reply comments after receiving the remainder of the Applicants' modeling submissions.

Please feel free to reach out to us if you have any questions.

Sincerely,
David B. Lawrence
Director
T-Mobile/Sprint Transaction Task Force

Donald Stockdale
Chief
Wireless Telecommunications Bureau

cc: Nancy J. Victory
Regina M. Keeny

SOURCE: Federal Communications Commission. "Letter Pausing the T-Mobile-Sprint Transaction Clock." September 11, 2018. https://docs.fcc.gov/public/attachments/DOC-354053A1.pdf.

## OTHER HISTORIC DOCUMENTS OF INTEREST

### FROM PREVIOUS *HISTORIC DOCUMENTS*

- U.S. Department of Justice Sues to Block AT&T and Time Warner Merger, *2017*, p. 609

# April

# Trump Administration Remarks on U.S. Immigration Policy

APRIL 4 AND 6, AND JUNE 18 AND 20, 2018

Illegal immigration into the United States, most commonly measured by the number apprehended at a U.S. border, has been on a downward trend during the past decade. By 2017, arrests of illegal border crossers had reached a forty-six-year low. However, following an uptick in illegal border crossings in the southwest at the start of 2018, the Trump administration took action to stem the flow of illegal immigrants into the United States. This included the implementation of controversial policies that resulted in migrant children being separated from their parents at the border and placed in detention facilities. Multiple legal challenges followed, and federal courts issued orders calling on the Trump administration to end the separation policy and reunite children with their parents. By the end of the year, hundreds of migrant children remained under the care of the U.S. government, and the president was still pushing for congressional action on revised immigration policy that included funding for a wall along the U.S.–Mexico border.

## PRESIDENT ISSUES MEMORANDA ON BORDER SECURITY

When he announced his presidential run, Trump promised to "build a great wall on our southern border" and have Mexico pay for it. Often using it as a tactic to rally his base, Trump said a wall along the 2,000-mile U.S.–Mexico border would deter illegal immigration and keep Americans safe. After his election, Trump asked Congress to include billions of dollars for this wall in annual appropriations bills, and the federal government awarded contracts to build prototypes of a wall that could cover the nearly 1,400 miles of border that do not currently have a barrier in place. Democrats and Republicans sparred over border wall funding, and even Republicans were hesitant to give the president the money he requested. In January 2018, funding for the border wall—along with an extension of the Deferred Action for Childhood Arrivals (DACA) immigration policy—resulted in a three-day government shutdown. Trump ultimately signed a short-term budget to reopen the government but promised that his "administration will work toward solving the problem of very unfair illegal immigration." An omnibus spending bill signed by the president in March included $1.6 billion for projects at the border, but none of that money could be used to build the border wall Trump sought. Similarly, a September continuing resolution (CR) to fund the government did not include border wall funding in order to stave off a government shutdown, nor did a short-term December CR. The border wall fight was, however, the primary cause of the longest federal government shutdown in U.S. history that began at midnight on December 22, 2018.

Without a long-term immigration reform plan or funding for a border wall, in April, President Trump issued two memoranda on security along the southern border and deterring illegal immigration. The first memorandum, issued on April 4, came shortly after Trump surprised even Defense Department officials by indicating that he was considering a plan to send National Guard troops to the U.S.–Mexico border. Past presidents have deployed the National Guard to the border for limited missions, primarily to provide surveillance and support to border agents. An 1878 law prohibits the National Guard from acting in a law enforcement role, making arrests, or using force along the border. Ahead of the release of the memo, Trump tweeted, "Our Border Laws are very weak while those of Mexico & Canada are very strong. Congress must change these Obama era, and other, laws NOW! The Democrats stand in our way—they want people to pour into our country unchecked. . . . CRIME! We will be taking strong action today."

In the memorandum, Trump stated, "The situation at the border has now reached a point of crisis. The lawlessness that continues at our southern border is fundamentally incompatible with the safety, security, and sovereignty of the American people. My Administration has no choice but to act." The memo mentioned an influx of illegal drugs, dangerous gang activity, and extensive illegal immigration that was threatening U.S. security. The order directed the secretary of defense to work with the Department of Homeland Security (DHS) to secure the southern border, including utilizing the National Guard to assist.

Two days later, Trump released a memo on the "catch and release" border policy, which refers to the practice of releasing migrants into the United States while they await immigration hearings. Most of the migrants who benefit from catch and release are protected classes, including unaccompanied minors, families traveling together with children, and those seeking asylum for fear of returning to their home countries. According to the president, when catch and release is enforced, "nobody ever comes back" for their court date and people instead remain illegally in the country. Justice Department data indicate, however, that a majority of migrants released into the country ahead of a court date do appear at their hearings.

The president's April 6 memorandum did not end the catch and release policy but instead called on federal agencies to report to the president on actions being taken to end the policy, resources required to do so, and measures being considered to target nations that reject repatriation of their citizens that cross into the United States illegally. The memo also called on the applicable federal agencies to review their policies for determining whether migrants have a "credible fear" of returning to their home countries and includes a list of facilities that could be used to detain illegal immigrants. Attorney General Jeff Sessions announced on the same day a "zero-tolerance policy" for those attempting to enter the United States illegally. "The situation at our Southwest Border is unacceptable. Congress has failed to pass effective legislation that serves the national interest—that closes dangerous loopholes and fully funds a wall along our southern border. As a result, a crisis has erupted . . . that necessitates an escalated effort to prosecute those who choose to illegally cross our border," Sessions said. According to the Department of Justice, the move came "as the Department of Homeland Security reported a 203 percent increase in illegal border crossings from March 2017 to March 2018, and a 37 percent increase from February 2018 to March 2018—the largest month-to-month increase since 2011."

## Migrant Detention Facilities Spark Outcry

Citing eleven million immigrants in the country illegally and a failure of Congress to act to secure the southern border, Sessions announced in May that the Department of Homeland Security would refer all illegal border crossers for prosecution. This included any immigrants, even those seeking asylum, who do not enter the United States at an official port of entry. Sessions said, "This is a great nation—the greatest in the history of the world. It is no surprise that people want to come here. But they must do so properly. They must follow our laws—or not come here at all. . . . And so this Department, under President Trump's leadership, is enforcing the law without exception. We will finally secure this border so that we can give the American people safety and peace of mind. That's what the people deserve." To aid in the increase of Department of Justice cases, Sessions ordered eighteen immigration judges to the border and moved thirty-five prosecutors to the southwestern United States.

Sessions admitted that the policies now being enforced at the border might result in the separation of parents from children. "If you are smuggling a child, then we will prosecute you. And that child may be separated from you, as required by law," Sessions said. Sessions was referring to the Flores Settlement Agreement, a 1997 consent decree that outlined how the Immigration and Naturalization Service (INS), the precursor to the Department of Homeland Security, would handle minor children of migrants. Flores states that children must be placed "in the least restrictive setting appropriate to the minor's age and special needs" and stresses the importance of keeping children close to their parents or other family members. Additionally, Flores notes that if detaining the minor is not necessary to ensure timely appearance before a judge, the minor is to be released to a parent, legal guardian, adult relative, or, as a last resort, a licensed child care program or foster care. Under Flores, minors are limited to twenty days in immigration detention.

Trump called on Democrats to end the law that was in place requiring the separation of children from families. "I hate the children being taken away," Trump said, adding, "The Democrats have to change their law—that's their law." However, no such law exists. The Obama administration previously wrestled with the specifics of Flores and was subject to a lawsuit in 2015 regarding immigrant families that were being held in detention facilities together. In that instance, the court ruled that Flores applies to accompanied as well as unaccompanied children and that they cannot be detained for more than twenty days. And, so long as the parent did not pose a security or a flight risk, the parent should be released with the child. In 2016, the U.S. Court of Appeals for the Ninth Circuit reversed a portion of the 2015 ruling, noting that parents do not have the same right to release as their children, but rather must have a determination made based on the same rules that apply to adults traveling without children. The Trump administration appeared to interpret this to allow for the separation of parents from their children and the holding of those children for no more than twenty days before their release to a related adult or a licensed facility.

What resulted was a period of chaos at the border as children were separated from their parents and placed in detention centers. Media outlets requested, and were eventually granted, access to some of the facilities, where they found children, some as young as infants, being housed in cage-like settings. The Associated Press reported on a "large dark facility" with "a series of cages created by metal fencing. One cage had 20 children inside. Scattered about are bottles of water, bags of chips and large foil sheets intended to serve as blankets." The Texas Civil Rights Project found that parents were not being told of their children's whereabouts and that they were sometimes fooled into letting their children leave with border agents. Homeland Security officials told the *Los Angeles Times* that those "accusations of surreptitious efforts to separate are completely false." According to lawyers advocating on behalf of the parents, there was no formal method in place for tracking the children and their parents. Secretary of Homeland Security Kirstjen Nielsen was called before Congress to answer questions about the Trump administration's policy on family separations at the border and the detention of minors. "We do not have a policy to separate children from their parents. Our policy is, if you break the law, we will prosecute you," she said.

In a separate press briefing on June 18, Secretary Nielsen reiterated the position of the Trump administration, stating, "We have a statutory responsibility that we take seriously to protect alien children from human smuggling, trafficking, and other criminal actions, while enforcing our immigration laws." She went on to note that DHS has a long-running policy of separating children from parents if "we cannot determine a familial or custodial relationship," "the adult is suspected of human trafficking," "the parent is charged with human smuggling," or "the parent is a national security, public or safety risk." She further called on Congress to support the administration's goals of protecting the country from dangerous illegal immigrants by closing loopholes in current law to stop parents from giving children to smugglers, end abuse of the asylum system, and amend the Flores Settlement. "Until these loopholes are closed by Congress, it is not possible—as a matter of law—to detain and remove whole family units who arrive illegally in the United States. Congress and the courts created this problem, and Congress alone can fix it. Until then, we will enforce every law we have on the books to defend the sovereignty and security of the United States," Nielsen said.

## FEDERAL COURTS RULE ON FAMILY REUNIFICATION

On June 20, President Trump signed an executive order to end family separations at the border. The order states that families crossing the border illegally would be detained together until criminal proceedings or asylum claims are complete: "It is . . . the policy of this Administration to maintain family unity, including by detaining alien families together where appropriate and consistent with law and available resources." An exception was included if federal authorities felt that the child would be in danger. The order also directed the Department of Justice to expedite immigration proceedings that involved families. In order to keep the children detained with their parents for the duration of those proceedings—which frequently last more than twenty days—the Trump administration needed a court to alter Flores. Attorney General Sessions made the official request on June 21 to the United States District Court for the Central District of California. That request was rejected by Judge Dolly Gee on July 9. Gee noted that the Trump administration had not used any argument different than those submitted by the Obama administration related to family detention and that she had rejected in 2016. Gee called the request an attempt to make the courts responsible for "over 20 years of congressional inaction and ill-considered executive action that have led to the current stalemate."

On June 26, less than one week after Trump's executive order was released, Democratic attorneys general in seventeen states and Washington, D.C., filed a lawsuit calling on a federal circuit court to block family separations at the border, which it called "cruel and unlawful," and immediately reunite children with their families. The lawsuit alleged that Trump's executive order does nothing to reunite families who have already been separated and is "so vague and equivocal that it is unclear when or if any changes will actually be made." New York Attorney General Barbara Underwood, who joined the suit, said of the family separations, "This is not who we are as a country." California Attorney General Xavier Becerra, also party to the lawsuit, said in a statement, "President Trump's indifference towards the human rights of the children and parents who have been ripped away from one another is chilling." Separate lawsuits were filed on behalf of migrant families calling for parents who were separated to be released and reunited with their children.

The same day the attorneys general filed their case, a federal judge ruled on a separate lawsuit that family separations at the border must end and that families already separated should be reunified. "Plaintiffs have demonstrated a likelihood of success on the merits, irreparable harm, and that the balance of equities and the public interest weigh in their favor, thus warranting issuance of a preliminary injunction," wrote U.S. District Court Judge Dana Sabraw. The Trump administration was directed by Sabraw to reunite all children under age five within fourteen days and those over age five within thirty days. Exceptions were made for parents who declined reunification and opted to allow their children to seek asylum independently and parents who were deemed unfit (such as those viewed as abusive). Under the order, parents could not be deported without their children unless they waived their rights to reunification.

Following the June court order, DHS began working toward reunifying the detained children with their families. Adults with deportation orders were given the option to wait to be reunited with their children or leave the United States and allow their children to pursue their own asylum claims. One week ahead of the court-ordered reunification deadline, only 364 of the more than 2,500 children were with their parents. Once the deadline was reached, that number had grown to around 1,440, according to the Trump administration. The children who had not been reunited, according to the White House, were ineligible for reunification because DHS was unable to confirm parental ties or the parent had a communicable disease or criminal record. Nielsen told the media that her agency was working to reunify children with their parents but would "not cut corners" in order to ensure the children were safe.

## Migrant Caravan Reaches U.S.–Mexico Border

Shortly before the November midterm elections, President Trump announced that he was deploying more than 5,000 active-duty troops to the U.S.–Mexico border, this time to stop a migrant caravan that was making its way from Central America through Mexico. Democrats called the move a political stunt, intended to increase support for Republicans in tough reelection battles, but Trump said the caravan was an "invasion of our country" by "a lot of bad people" and he had no option but to send the troops in defense of the country. "I am bringing out the military for this National Emergency. They will be stopped!" the president tweeted. At the time of the announcement, the caravan was thought to have shrunk, but estimates of its size varied widely from 3,500 individuals to upwards of 8,000, and the group was hundreds of miles away from reaching the southern border of the United States. According to media reports, many in the caravan were women and children who intended to seek asylum in the United States, but the Department of Homeland Security reported that the group included many single men and individuals with criminal histories.

The troops that were deployed to the border acted in a support role for U.S. Border Patrol agents. Duties included building barriers to stop migrants who failed to cross at an official port of entry, providing helicopter transport to border agents, and assisting with planning and surveillance activities. Mexican police attempted to stop many of those who were trying to cross into the United States, and their efforts were only marginally effective. On November 25, some of the migrants attempted to cross from Tijuana, Mexico, into San Diego and were met with tear gas fired by Border Patrol agents after some migrants reportedly threw rocks at the border guards. Media reports featured pictures of parents dragging children away from the assault. President Trump defended the use of tear gas, saying the border agents were "being rushed by some very tough people."

The troops were expected to begin returning home in mid-November, despite the bulk of the caravan not having reached U.S. soil. However, on November 28, Pentagon officials announced that the president would extend their mission into 2019.

—Heather Kerrigan

*Following are two memoranda issued by President Donald Trump on April 4 and 6, 2018, regarding security along the U.S.–Mexico border and illegal immigration; a memorandum from Attorney General Jeff Sessions on April 6, 2018, calling for zero tolerance in prosecuting illegal border crossers; June 18, 2018, remarks by Department of Homeland Security Secretary Kirstjen M. Nielsen, providing information on the administration's policy on illegal immigration; and a June 20, 2018, executive order ending family separation at the U.S.–Mexico border.*

# President Trump Calls for Increased Border Security

**April 4, 2018**

*Memorandum for the Secretary of Defense, the Attorney General, and the Secretary of Homeland Security*

*Subject: Securing the Southern Border of the United States*

1. The security of the United States is imperiled by a drastic surge of illegal activity on the southern border. Large quantities of fentanyl, other opioids, and other dangerous and illicit drugs are flowing across our southern border and into our country at unprecedented levels, destroying the lives of our families and loved ones. Mara Salvatrucha (MS-13) and other deadly transnational gangs are systematically exploiting our unsecured southern border to enter our country and develop operational capacity in American communities throughout the country. The anticipated rapid rise in illegal crossings as we head into the spring and summer months threatens to overwhelm our Nation's law enforcement capacities.

2. The combination of illegal drugs, dangerous gang activity, and extensive illegal immigration not only threatens our safety but also undermines the rule of law. Our American way of life hinges on our ability as a Nation to adequately and effectively enforce our laws and protect our borders. A key and undeniable attribute of a sovereign nation is the ability to control who and what enters its territory.

3. Our professional and dedicated U.S. Customs and Border Protection agents and officers, U.S. Immigration and Customs Enforcement officers, and other Federal, State, and local law enforcement personnel work tirelessly to defend our homeland against these threats. They risk their lives daily to protect the people of this country. Theirs is a record of dedication and sacrifice, meriting the unwavering support of the entire United States Government.

4. The situation at the border has now reached a point of crisis. The lawlessness that continues at our southern border is fundamentally incompatible with the safety, security, and sovereignty of the American people. My Administration has no choice but to act.

5. The Department of Defense currently assists other nations in many respects, including assisting with border security, but the highest sovereign duty of the President is to defend this Nation, which includes the defense of our borders.

6. The President may assign a mission to the Secretary of Defense to support the operations of the Department of Homeland Security in securing our southern border, including by requesting use of the National Guard, and to take other necessary steps to stop the flow of deadly drugs and other contraband, gang members and other criminals, and illegal aliens into the country. The Secretary of Defense may use all available authorities as appropriate, including use of National Guard forces, to fulfill this mission. During the administrations of Presidents George W. Bush and Barack Obama, the National Guard provided support for efforts to secure our southern border. The crisis at our southern border once again calls for the National Guard to help secure our border and protect our homeland.

Therefore, by the authority vested in me as President by the Constitution and the laws of the United States, including section 502 of title 32, United States Code, and section 301 of title 3, United States Code, I hereby direct as follows:

*Section 1.* The Secretary of Defense shall support the Department of Homeland Security in securing the southern border and taking other necessary actions to stop the flow of deadly drugs and other contraband, gang members and other criminals, and illegal aliens into this country. The Secretary of Defense shall request use of National Guard personnel to assist in fulfilling this mission, pursuant to section 502 of title 32, United States Code, and may use such other authorities as appropriate and consistent with applicable law.

*Sec. 2.* The Secretary of Homeland Security shall work with the Secretary of Defense to provide any training or instruction necessary for any military personnel, including National Guard units, to effectively support Department of Homeland Security personnel in securing the border.

*Sec. 3.* The Secretary of Defense and the Secretary of Homeland Security, in coordination with the Attorney General, are directed to determine what other resources and actions are necessary to protect our southern border, including Federal law enforcement and United States military resources. Within 30 days of the date of this memorandum, the Secretary of Defense and the Secretary of Homeland Security, in coordination with the Attorney General, shall submit to the President a report detailing their findings and an action plan, including specific recommendations as to any other executive authorities that should be invoked to defend the border and security of the United States.

*Sec. 4.* Any provision of any previous proclamation, memorandum, or Executive Order that is inconsistent with the actions taken in this memorandum is superseded to the extent of such inconsistency.

*Sec. 5.* (a) Nothing in this memorandum shall be construed to impair or otherwise affect:

(i) the authority granted by law to an executive department or agency, or the head-thereof; or

(ii) the functions of the Director of the Office of Management and Budget relating to budgetary, administrative, or legislative proposals.

(b) This memorandum shall be implemented consistent with applicable law and subject to the availability of appropriations.

(c) This memorandum is not intended to, and does not, create any right or benefit, substantive or procedural, enforceable at law or in equity by any party against the United States, its departments, agencies, or entities, its officers, employees, or agents, or any other person.

DONALD J. TRUMP

Source: Executive Office of the President. "Memorandum on Securing the Southern Border of the United States." April 4, 2018. *Compilation of Presidential Documents* 2018, no. 00218 (April 4, 2018). https://www.gpo.gov/fdsys/pkg/DCPD-201800218/pdf/DCPD-201800218.pdf.

# President Trump Announces End of Catch and Release

**April 6, 2018**

*Memorandum for the Secretary of State, the Secretary of Defense, the Attorney General, the Secretary of Health and Human Services, and the Secretary of Homeland Security*

*Subject: Ending "Catch and Release" at the Border of the United States and Directing Other Enhancements to Immigration Enforcement*

*Section 1. Purpose.* (a) Human smuggling operations, smuggling of drugs and other contraband, and entry of gang members and other criminals at the border of the United States threaten our national security and public safety. The backlog of immigration-related cases in our administrative system is alarmingly large and has hindered the expeditious adjudication of outstanding cases. Border-security and immigration enforcement personnel shortages have become critical.

(b) In Executive Order 13767 of January 25, 2017 (Border Security and Immigration Enforcement Improvements), I directed the Secretary of Homeland Security to issue new policy guidance regarding the appropriate and consistent use of detention authority under the Immigration and Nationality Act (INA), including the termination of the practice known as "catch and release," whereby aliens are released in the United States shortly after their apprehension for violations of our immigration laws. On February 20, 2017, the Secretary issued a memorandum taking steps to end "catch and release" practices. These steps have produced positive results. Still, more must be done to enforce our laws and to protect our country from the dangers of releasing detained aliens into our communities while their immigration claims are pending.

Therefore, by the authority vested in me as President by the Constitution and the laws of the United States of America, I hereby direct as follows:

*Sec. 2. Ending "Catch and Release".* (a) Within 45 days of the date of this memorandum, the Secretary of Homeland Security, in coordination with the Secretary of Defense, the Attorney General, and the Secretary of Health and Human Services, shall submit a report to the President detailing all measures that their respective departments have pursued or are pursuing to expeditiously end "catch and release" practices. At a minimum, such report shall address the following:

(i) All measures taken pursuant to section 5(a) of Executive Order 13767 to allocate all legally available resources to construct, operate, control, or modify—or establish contracts to construct, operate, control, or modify—facilities to detain aliens for violations of immigration law at or near the borders of the United States;

(ii) All measures taken pursuant to section 5(b) of Executive Order 13767 to assign asylum officers to immigration detention facilities for the purpose of accepting asylum referrals and conducting credible fear determinations and reasonable fear determinations;

(iii) All measures taken pursuant to section 6 of Executive Order 13767 to ensure the detention of aliens apprehended for violations of immigration law;

(iv) All measures taken pursuant to section 11(a) of Executive Order 13767 to ensure that the parole and asylum provisions of Federal immigration law are not illegally exploited to prevent the removal of otherwise removable aliens;

(v) All measures taken pursuant to section 11(b) of Executive Order 13767 to ensure that asylum referrals and credible fear determinations pursuant to section 235(b)(1) of the INA (8 U.S.C. 1125(b)(1)) and 8 CFR 208.30, and reasonable fear determinations pursuant to 8 CFR 208.31, are conducted in a manner consistent with those provisions;

(vi) All measures taken pursuant to section 6 of Executive Order 13768 of January 25, 2017 (Enhancing Public Safety in the Interior of the United States), to ensure the assessment and collection of all authorized fines and penalties from aliens unlawfully present in the United States and from those who facilitate their unlawful presence in the United States;

(vii) A detailed list of all existing facilities, including military facilities, that could be used, modified, or repurposed to detain aliens for violations of immigration law at or near the borders of the United States; and

(viii) The number of credible fear and reasonable fear claims received, granted, and denied—broken down by the purported protected ground upon which a credible fear or reasonable fear claim was made—in each year since the beginning of fiscal year 2009.

(b) Within 75 days of the date of this memorandum, the Attorney General and the Secretary of Homeland Security, in consultation with the Secretary of Defense and the Secretary of Health and Human Services, shall submit a report to the President identifying any additional resources or authorities that may be needed to expeditiously end "catch and release" practices.

*Sec. 3. Return of Removable Aliens to Their Home Countries or Countries of Origin.* Within 60 days of the date of this memorandum, the Secretary of State and the Secretary of Homeland Security shall submit a report to the President detailing all measures, including diplomatic measures, that are being pursued against countries that refuse to expeditiously accept the repatriation of their nationals. The report shall include all measures taken pursuant to section 12 of Executive Order 13768 to implement the sanctions authorized by section 243(d) of the INA (8 U.S.C. 1253(d)), or a detailed explanation as to why such sanctions have not yet been imposed.

*Sec. 4. General Provisions.* (a) Nothing in this memorandum shall be construed to impair or otherwise affect:

(i) the authority granted by law to an executive department or agency, or the head thereof; or

(ii) the functions of the Director of the Office of Management and Budget relating to budgetary, administrative, or legislative proposals.

(b) This memorandum shall be implemented consistent with applicable law and subject to the availability of appropriations.

(c) This memorandum is not intended to, and does not, create any right or benefit, substantive or procedural, enforceable at law or in equity by any party against the United States, its departments, agencies, or entities, its officers, employees, or agents, or any other person.

(d) The Secretary of State is hereby authorized and directed to publish this memorandum in the *Federal Register*.

DONALD J. TRUMP

SOURCE: Executive Office of the President. "Memorandum on Ending 'Catch and Release' at the Border of the United States and Directing Order Enhancements to Immigration Enforcement." April 6, 2018. *Compilation of Presidential Documents* 2018, no. 00225 (April 6, 2018). https://www.gpo.gov/fdsys/pkg/DCPD-201800225/pdf/DCPD-201800225.pdf.

# *Attorney General Sessions Enforces Zero Tolerance Policy for Illegal Border Crossers*

DOCUMENT

**April 6, 2018**

MEMORANDUM FOR FEDERAL PROSECUTORS ALONG THE SOUTHWEST BORDER

FROM: THE ATTORNEY GENERAL
SUBJECT: Zero-Tolerance for Offenses Under 8 U.S.C. § 1325(a)

On April 11, 2017, I issued a memorandum to all federal prosecutors entitled "Renewed Commitment to Criminal Immigration Enforcement," in which I directed the prioritization of the prosecution of certain criminal immigration offenses. I further directed each United States Attorney's Office along the Southwest Border to work with the Department of Homeland Security to develop guidelines for prosecuting offenses under 8 U.S.C. § 1325(a).

Those seeking to further an illegal goal constantly alter their tactics to take advantage of weak points. That means we must effectively respond with smart changes also. The recent increase in aliens illegally crossing our Southwest Border requires an updated approach. Past prosecution initiatives in certain districts—such as Operation Streamline— led to a decrease in illegal activities in those districts. We must continue to execute effective policies to meet new challenges.

Accordingly, I direct each United States Attorney's Office along the Southwest Border to the extent practicable, and in consultation with DHS—to adopt immediately a zero-tolerance policy for all offenses referred for prosecution under section 1325(a). This zero-tolerance policy shall supersede any existing policies. If adopting such a policy requires additional resources, each office shall identify and request such additional resources.

You are on the front lines of this battle. I respect you and your team. Your dedication and insight into border reality is invaluable. Keep us informed, and don't hesitate to give us suggestions for improvement. Remember, our goal is not simply more cases. It is to end the illegality in our immigration system.

This guidance is not intended to, does not, and may not be relied upon to create, any right or benefit, substantive or procedural, enforceable at law or in equity by any party against the United States, its departments, agencies, or entities, its officers, employees, or agents, or any other person.

SOURCE: U.S. Department of Justice. "Memorandum for Federal Prosecutors along the Southwest Border." April 6, 2018. https://www.justice.gov/opa/press-release/file/1049751/download.

# DHS Secretary Addresses Administration Policy on Immigration

**June 18, 2018**

WASHINGTON—Today, Secretary of Homeland Security Kirstjen M. Nielsen delivered the below remarks at the White House Press Briefing on the illegal immigration crisis at the southern border:

SECRETARY NIELSEN: Good afternoon. It is my pleasure to be here because I would love to see if I can help explain some of what is going on and give you some of the facts. I know there have been a lot put out there but hopefully we clarify some things today. I just wanted to start by thanking the sheriffs of the United States, I had the privilege of speaking to them this morning at the National Sheriffs' Association Conference. We are so thankful for their partnership here at DHS and all they do to protect our communities so, I thank them. I want to provide you an update on the illegal immigration crisis on our Southern

Border and the efforts the Administration is taking to solve this crisis and to stop the flood of illegal immigrants, drugs, contraband, and crime coming across the border. So let's just start with a few numbers and facts.

So, in the last three months we have seen illegal immigration on our Southern Border exceed 50,000 people each month—multiples over each month last year. Since this time last year, there has been a 325 percent increase in Unaccompanied Alien Children and a 435 percent increase in family units entering the country illegally. Over the last ten years, there has been a 1,700% increase in asylum claims, resulting in an Asylum Backlog today, in our country[,] of 600,000 cases.

Since 2013, the United States has admitted more than half a million illegal immigrant minors and family units from Central America—most of whom today, are at large in the United States.

At the same time, large criminal organizations such as MS-13 have violated our borders and gained a deadly foothold within the United States.

This entire crisis, just to be clear, is not new. It has been occurring and expanding over many decades. Currently, it is the exclusive product of loopholes in our federal immigration laws that prevent illegal immigrant minors and family members from being detained and removed to their home countries. In other words, these loopholes create a functionally open border. Apprehension without detention and removal is not border security.

We have repeatedly called on Congress to close these loopholes. I myself have met with as many members that have been willing to meet with me, I've testified seven times. I will continue to make myself available to ask that they work with us to solve this crisis. Yet, the voices most loudly criticizing the enforcement of our current laws are those whose policies created this crisis—and whose policies perpetuate it.

In particular, we need to reform three major loopholes, let me quickly walk you through them. First, we need to amend the 2008 Trafficking Victims Protection Reauthorization Act or TVPRA, which is much easier to say—this law encourages families to put children in the hands of smugglers to bring them alone on the dangerous trek northward. And make no mistake, we've talked about this before, this trek is dangerous and deadly.

Second, we need to reform our asylum laws to end the systemic abuse of our asylum system and stop fraud. Right now our asylum system fails to assist asylum seekers who legitimately need it. We are a country of compassion, we are a country of heart, we must fix the system so that those who truly need asylum can, in fact, receive it.

Third, we need to amend the Flores Settlement agreement and recent expansions which would allow allow [sic] for family detention during the removal process—and we need Congress [to] fund our ability to hold families together through the immigration process.

Until these loopholes are closed by Congress, it is not possible—as a matter of law—to detain and remove whole family units who arrive illegally in the United States.

Congress and the courts created this problem, and Congress alone can fix it. Until then, we will enforce every law we have on the books to defend the sovereignty and security of the United States. Those who criticize the enforcement of our laws, have offered only one counter-measure: open borders—the quick release of all illegal alien families, and the decision not to enforce our laws. This policy would be disastrous, its prime beneficiaries would be the smuggling organizations themselves, and the prime victims would be the children who would be plunged into the smuggling machines and gang recruitment on the trip north.

There is a lot of misinformation about what DHS is and is not doing as it relates to families at the border, and I want to correct the record.

Here are the facts:

First, this Administration did not create a policy of separating families at the border.

We have a statutory responsibility that we take seriously to protect alien children from human smuggling, trafficking, and other criminal actions, while enforcing our immigration laws.

We have a long existing policy—multiple administrations have followed—that outline when we may take action to protect children.

We will separate those who claim to be parent and child if we cannot determine a familial or custodial relationship exists. For example, if there is no documentation to confirm the claimed relationship between an adult and a child.

We do so if the parent is a national security, public or safety risk, including where there are criminal charges at issue, and it may not be appropriate to maintain the family in detention together.

We also separate a parent and child if the adult is suspected of human trafficking. There have been cases where minors have been used and trafficked by unrelated adults in an effort to avoid detention. I'll stop here to say that in the last five months, we've had a 314 percent increase in adults and children arriving at the border fraudulently claiming to be a family unit. This is, obviously, of concern.

And separation can occur when the parent is charged with human smuggling. Under those circumstances, we would detain the parent in an appropriate, secure detection facility, separate from the child.

What has changed is that we no longer exempt entire classes of people who break the law. Everyone is subject to prosecution.

When DHS refers a case against a parent or legal guardian for criminal prosecution, the parent or legal guardian will be placed into U.S. Marshals Service custody for pre-trial detention pursuant to an order by a federal judge and any accompanying child will be transferred to the Department of Health and Human Services and will be reclassified as an Unaccompanied Alien Child.

That is in accordance with the TVPRA—a law that was passed by Congress—and a following court order—neither are actions the Trump Administration has taken.

And let's be clear—if an American were to commit a crime anywhere in the United States, they would go to jail and be separated from their family. This is not a controversial ideal.

Second, children in DHS and HHS custody are being well taken care of.

The Department of Health and Human Services' Office of Refugee Resettlement provides meals, medical care, and educational services to these children. They are provided temporary shelter, and HHS works hard to find a parent, relative, or foster home to care for these children.

Parents can still communicate with their children through phone calls and video conferencing.

And a parent who is released from custody can be a sponsor and ask HHS to release the child back into their care.

Further, these minors can still apply for asylum and other protections under U.S. immigration law if eligible.

We take allegation of mistreatment seriously and I want to stress this point. We investigate, we hold those accountable when and if it should occur. We have some of the highest detention standards in the country. Claiming these children and their parents are treated inhumanely is not true, and completely disrespects the hardworking men and women at the Office of Refugee Resettlement.

Third, parents who entered illegally are—by definition—criminals.

Illegal entry is a crime as determined by Congress.

By entering our country illegally—often in dangerous circumstances—illegal immigrants have put their children at risk.

Fourth, CBP and ICE officers are properly trained to care for minors in their custody.

DHS and HHS treats all individuals in its custody with dignity and respect, and complies with all laws and policy.

This reinforces and reiterates the need to consider the best interest of the children and mandates adherence to established protocols to protect at-risk populations, to include standards for the transport and treatment of minors in DHS and HHS custody.

Additionally, all U.S. Border Patrol personnel on the southwest border are bilingual. Every last one of them. They are directed to clearly explain the relevant process to apprehended individuals, and provide detainees with written documentation—in both Spanish and English—that lays out the process and appropriate phone numbers to contact.

And finally, DHS is not separating families legitimately seeking asylum at ports of entry.

If an adult enters at a port of entry and claims asylum, they will not face prosecution for illegal entry. They have not committed a crime by coming to the port of entry.

As I mentioned, DHS does have a responsibility to protect minors and in that case as well, we will only separate the family if we cannot determine there is a familial relationship; if the child may be at risk with the parent or legal guardian; or if the parent or legal guardian is referred for prosecution.

We have a duty to protect the American people, and it's one that I take very seriously.

Here is the bottom line: DHS is no longer ignoring the law. We are enforcing the laws as they exist on the books. As long as illegal entry remains a criminal offense, DHS will not look the other way. DHS will faithfully execute the laws enacted by Congress as we are sworn to do.

As I said earlier today, surely it is the beginning of the unraveling of democracy when the body who makes the laws—instead of changing them—tells the enforcement body not to enforce the law.

I ask Congress to act this week so that we can secure our borders and uphold our humanitarian ideas. These two missions should not be pitted against each other. If we close the loopholes we can accomplish both.

Before I take questions, I just want to ask that in your reporting, please consider the men and women of DHS who are dedicated law enforcement officers who often put their lives at risk. Let's remember their sacrifice and commitment to this country. And with that I'll take some questions.

SOURCE: U.S. Department of Homeland Security. "DHS Secretary Nielsen's Remarks on the Illegal Immigration Crisis." June 18, 2018. https://www.dhs.gov/news/2018/06/18/dhs-secretary-nielsens-remarks-illegal-immigration-crisis.

 *President Trump Issues Executive Order Stopping Border Separations*

DOCUMENT

June 20, 2018

By the authority vested in me as President by the Constitution and the laws of the United States of America, including the Immigration and Nationality Act (INA), 8 U.S.C. 1101 et seq., it is hereby ordered as follows:

*Section 1. Policy.* It is the policy of this Administration to rigorously enforce our immigration laws. Under our laws, the only legal way for an alien to enter this country is at a designated port of entry at an appropriate time. When an alien enters or attempts to enter the country anywhere else, that alien has committed at least the crime of improper entry and is subject to a fine or imprisonment under section 1325(a) of title 8, United States Code. This Administration will initiate proceedings to enforce this and other criminal provisions of the INA until and unless Congress directs otherwise. It is also the policy of this Administration to maintain family unity, including by detaining alien families together where appropriate and consistent with law and available resources. It is unfortunate that Congress's failure to act and court orders have put the Administration in the position of separating alien families to effectively enforce the law.

*Sec. 2. Definitions.* For purposes of this order, the following definitions apply:

(a) "Alien family" means

(i) any person not a citizen or national of the United States who has not been admitted into, or is not authorized to enter or remain in, the United States, who entered this country with an alien child or alien children at or between designated ports of entry and who was detained; and

(ii) that person's alien child or alien children.

(b) "Alien child" means any person not a citizen or national of the United States who

(i) has not been admitted into, or is not authorized to enter or remain in, the United States;

(ii) is under the age of 18; and

(iii) has a legal parent-child relationship to an alien who entered the United States with the alien child at or between designated ports of entry and who was detained.

*Sec. 3. Temporary Detention Policy for Families Entering [T]his Country Illegally.* (a) The Secretary of Homeland Security (Secretary), shall, to the extent permitted by law and subject to the availability of appropriations, maintain custody of alien families during the pendency of any criminal improper entry or immigration proceedings involving their members.

(b) The Secretary shall not, however, detain an alien family together when there is a concern that detention of an alien child with the child's alien parent would pose a risk to the child's welfare.

(c) The Secretary of Defense shall take all legally available measures to provide to the Secretary, upon request, any existing facilities available for the housing and care of alien families, and shall construct such facilities if necessary and consistent with law. The Secretary, to the extent permitted by law, shall be responsible for reimbursement for the use of these facilities.

(d) Heads of executive departments and agencies shall, to the extent consistent with law, make available to the Secretary, for the housing and care of alien families pending court proceedings for improper entry, any facilities that are appropriate for such purposes. The Secretary, to the extent permitted by law, shall be responsible for reimbursement for the use of these facilities.

(e) The Attorney General shall promptly file a request with the U.S. District Court for the Central District of California to modify the Settlement Agreement in *Flores v. Sessions*, CV 85–4544 ("*Flores* settlement"), in a manner that would permit the Secretary, under present resource constraints, to detain alien families together throughout the pendency of criminal proceedings for improper entry or any removal or other immigration proceedings.

*Sec. 4. Prioritization of Immigration Proceedings Involving Alien Families.* The Attorney General shall, to the extent practicable, prioritize the adjudication of cases involving detained families.

*Sec. 5. General Provisions.* (a) Nothing in this order shall be construed to impair or otherwise affect:

> (i) the authority granted by law to an executive department or agency, or the head thereof; or

> (ii) the functions of the Director of the Office of Management and Budget relating to budgetary, administrative, or legislative proposals.

(b)  This order shall be implemented in a manner consistent with applicable law and subject to the availability of appropriations.

(c)  This order is not intended to, and does not, create any right or benefit, substantive or procedural, enforceable at law or in equity by any party against the United States, its departments, agencies, or entities, its officers, employees, or agents, or any other person.

DONALD J. TRUMP

SOURCE: Executive Office of the President. "Executive Order 13841—Affording Congress an Opportunity to Address Family Separation." June 20, 2018. *Compilation of Presidential Documents* 2018, no. 00439 (June 20, 2018). https://www.gpo.gov/fdsys/pkg/DCPD-201800439/pdf/DCPD-201800439.pdf.

## OTHER HISTORIC DOCUMENTS OF INTEREST

### FROM THIS VOLUME

### FROM PREVIOUS *HISTORIC DOCUMENTS*

# Chemical Attack in Syria
# Sparks International Action

APRIL 10 AND 13, 2018

On April 7, 2018, the Syrian government launched a chemical weapons strike against the city of Douma in an attempt to clear the rebels and return the region to government control. The government of President Bashar al-Assad denied that the attack had occurred, alleging that it was staged by Western governments. In response, the United States led a coalition with France and the United Kingdom to carry out a limited airstrike against Assad's chemical weapons facilities. The strikes were deemed successful, but they had little lasting impact on ending the long-running Syrian civil war.

## SUSPECTED CHEMICAL WEAPONS STRIKE HITS STRATEGIC REBEL STRONGHOLD

In 2011, as the Arab Spring swept across the Middle East and Northern Africa, Syrians took to the streets in protest of the unlawful acts committed by President Assad and his security forces. Seven years later, the nation remained locked in a civil war between the Assad regime and rebel groups trying to bring down the government. Since that time, the Syrian government has launched dozens of chemical weapons attacks, most of which included either chlorine gas or the nerve agent sarin. The deadliest attack was carried out in August 2013, when more than 1,000 were killed in Eastern Ghouta, the region just outside of Damascus. The United States opted not to respond militarily but instead reached an agreement with Russia, which backs the Assad regime, to dismantle Syria's chemical weapons capabilities. That agreement did not ban Assad's government from maintaining chlorine stocks; however, the Chemical Weapons Convention, which Syria became party to in 2013 as part of the agreement between the United States and Russia, expressly prohibits the use of any chemical weapon, including chlorine.

On April 7, 2018, the Syrian government launched another chemical attack in Douma, the largest city in Eastern Ghouta, which had been under rebel control since late 2012. In the weeks preceding the attack, the Syrian army had launched an operation to retake Eastern Ghouta, one of the last strategic rebel strongholds in Syria. Tens of thousands of Syrians left the area in evacuation deals secured between the government and rebels. The Syrian army was able to clear most of the territory, with the exception of Douma. Russia led negotiations between the Jaish al-Islam rebels operating in the region and the Syrian government, which resulted in a temporary cease-fire, but ultimately no agreement for the rebels to leave Douma, resulting in a ramp-up of Syrian army airstrikes. According to the Violations Documentation Center, a Syrian group that tracks human rights violations, two of the bombs contained chemical substances. The Syrian Civil Defense, also known as the White Helmets, reported smelling chlorine in the air, and patients quickly began filling medical centers with symptoms indicating exposure to a chemical agent. Dozens were killed and hundreds were injured in the chemical attack. One day later, the estimated 8,000 rebels in Douma agreed to leave the area and surrender it to the Syrian army.

The United States, United Kingdom, and France attributed the attack to the Syrian army, while Syria and Russia denied that the attack had even occurred. Assad claimed that "after we liberated that area, our information confirmed the attack did not take place." Russian Foreign Minister Sergey Lavrov said that there was "irrefutable evidence" that the attack was staged by the White Helmets with backing from the United Kingdom. On Twitter, President Donald Trump said many were killed in a "mindless CHEMICAL attack in Syria," adding, "President Putin, Russia and Iran are responsible for backing Animal Assad." The Organisation for the Prohibition of Chemical Weapons (OPCW) attempted to gain access to Douma to investigate the site of the suspected attack but was prevented from doing so by the Syrian army. The OPCW did not reach the site until April 21. It released a report on July 6 noting that the samples it took indicated chlorinated organic chemicals but no nerve agents.

## United Nations Fails to Respond, Coalition Launches Retaliatory Airstrike

Members of the United Nations Security Council called an emergency meeting on April 10 and were urged by the Syrian envoy to act to prevent further escalation of the conflict in Syria. The United States put forward a resolution to investigate the chemical weapons attacks in Syria and determine the responsible party; Russia, a permanent member of the Security Council, vetoed the move. This marked the twelfth time Russia acted to veto attempted action on Syria since its civil war began. "History will record that, on this day, Russia chose protecting a monster over the lives of the Syrian people," said U.S. Ambassador Nikki Haley. Russia issued its own resolution, also calling for an investigation, but asked that no blame be assigned. Seven nations, including the United States, United Kingdom, and France, voted against the resolution. The United Nations Commission of Enquiry would issue its own report into the attack in September, noting that "a vast body of evidence collected . . . suggests that . . . a gas cylinder containing a chlorine payload delivered by helicopter struck a multi-story residential apartment building." The UN Commission concluded that this resulted in the death of at least forty-nine people.

On the evening of April 13, President Trump addressed the nation and announced that he had authorized airstrikes against targets in Syria. The United States was joined by the United Kingdom and France. This marked the second time Trump had acted to strike Syria over its use of chemical weapons. His first retaliatory strike took place in April 2017 when fifty-nine cruise missiles were fired at a Syrian airbase with little effect. In his address, Trump called out Assad's primary supporters, Iran and Russia, asking, "What kind of a nation wants to be associated with the mass murder of innocent men, women, and children?" He added, "No nation can succeed in the long run by promoting rogue states, brutal tyrants, and murderous dictators." UK Prime Minister Theresa May, who did not provide forces for the 2017 strike, said that the United Kingdom had no choice but to act in response to the 2018 attack. "This persistent pattern of behavior must be stopped— not just to protect innocent people in Syria from the horrific deaths and casualties caused by chemical weapons, but also because we cannot allow the erosion of the international norm that prevents the use of these weapons."

The April 2018 attack was a limited strike, reflecting President Trump's desire to avoid becoming entangled in the region. Since taking office, the president had focused primarily on targeting the Islamic State of Iraq and the Levant (ISIL) instead of backing the rebels in their fight against Assad. Trump called the area "a troubled place" during his televised address, saying that while the United States would remain a partner, "the fate of the region lies in the hands of its own people." The strike was carried out with missiles fired from aircrafts, ships, and submarines. According to the coalition, a chemical weapons storage facility, chemical weapons bunker, and chemical weapons research center were destroyed. In total, 105 missiles were launched; the United States claimed that none were intercepted, but Russia said that Syria shot down seventy-one. The Pentagon said that the strikes successfully eliminated the "heart" of the Syrian government's chemical weapons program but admitted that Assad could likely continue targeting civilians with chemical weapons.

—Heather Kerrigan

*Following is an April 10, 2018, United Nations news report announcing the body's failure to adopt a resolution in response to the Syrian chemical weapons attack; and the text of a statement from President Donald Trump on April 13, 2018, about U.S. airstrikes in Syria in response to the use of chemical weapons by the Assad regime.*

# UN Security Fails to Adopt Resolution in Response to Chemical Weapons Attack

**April 10, 2018**

Days after an alleged chemical weapons attack in the Damascus suburb of Douma, the United Nations Security Council failed to adopt two competing resolutions that would have established a mechanism to investigate use of such weapons in Syria, as well as another concerning a fact-finding mission in the war-torn country.

Had one of the two mechanisms proposed in the drafts been approved, it could have filled the vacuum left by the Organisation for Prevention of Chemical Weapons (OPCW)-UN Joint Investigative Mechanism (JIM) when its mandate expired last November.

The first draft considered today—penned by the United States—which would have established a new investigative mechanism for one year, as well as identify those responsible for the use of chemical weapons, was rejected owing to a negative vote from Russia.

The draft received 12 votes in favour, two against (Bolivia and Russia) and one abstention (China).

A negative vote—or veto—from one of the Council's five permanent members—China, France, Russia, United Kingdom and the United States—blocks passage of a resolution.

Today's meeting marked the twelfth time Russia has used its veto to block Council action on Syria.

Similarly, a competing draft—penned by Russia—which would have established the mechanism for one year as well but would have given the Security Council the responsibility to assign accountability for the use of chemical weapons in Syria, was also not adopted.

This draft received six Council members' votes in favour (Bolivia, China, Ethiopia, Equatorial Guinea, Kazakhstan and Russia), seven against (France, the Netherlands, Peru, Poland, Sweden, United Kingdom and United States) and two abstentions (Cote d'Ivoire and Kuwait).

The Council rejected a third text—also proposed by Russia—which concerned the work of the OPCW Fact-Finding Mission (FFM).

The draft received five votes in favour (Bolivia, China, Ethiopia, Kazakhstan and Russia), four against (France, Poland, the United Kingdom and the United States), and six abstentions (Cote d'Ivoire, Equatorial Guinea, Kuwait, the Netherlands, Peru, and Sweden).

Ahead of the Security Council meetings today, UN Secretary-General António Guterres had repeated his call on 15-member body to "find unity" on the issue of use of chemical weapons in Syria and ensure accountability.

"The norms against chemical weapons must be upheld. I appeal to the Security Council to fulfil its responsibility and find unity on this issue," he said.

"I also encourage the Council to redouble its efforts to agree on a dedicated mechanism for accountability."

SOURCE: United Nations. "Security Council Fails to Adopt Three Resolutions on Chemical Weapons Use in Syria." April 10, 2018. https://news.un.org/en/story/2018/04/1006991.

# *President Trump Addresses Syria Airstrike and Chemical Weapons Attack*

**April 13, 2018**

My fellow Americans, a short time ago, I ordered the United States Armed Forces to launch precision strikes on targets associated with the chemical weapons capabilities of Syrian dictator Bashar al-Asad. A combined operation with the armed forces of France and the United Kingdom is now underway. We thank them both.

Tonight I want to speak with you about why we have taken this action. One year ago, Asad launched a savage chemical weapons attack against his own innocent people. The United States responded with 58 missile strikes that destroyed 20 percent of the Syrian Air Force.

Last Saturday, the Asad regime again deployed chemical weapons to slaughter innocent civilians, this time, in the town of Douma, near the Syrian capital of Damascus. This massacre was a significant escalation in a pattern of chemical weapons use by that very terrible regime. The evil and the despicable attack left mothers and fathers, infants and children, thrashing in pain and gasping for air. These are not the actions of a man; they are crimes of a monster instead.

Following the horrors of World War I a century ago, civilized nations joined together to ban chemical warfare. Chemical weapons are uniquely dangerous not only because they inflict gruesome suffering, but because even small amounts can unleash widespread devastation.

The purpose of our actions tonight is to establish a strong deterrent against the production, spread, and use of chemical weapons. Establishing this deterrent is a vital national security interest of the United States. The combined American, British, and French response to these atrocities will integrate all instruments of our national power: military, economic, and diplomatic. We are prepared to sustain this response until the Syrian regime stops its use of prohibited chemical agents.

I also have a message tonight for the two governments most responsible for supporting, equipping, and financing the criminal Asad regime. To Iran and to Russia, I ask: What kind of a nation wants to be associated with the mass murder of innocent men, women, and children? The nations of the world can be judged by the friends they keep. No nation can succeed in the long run by promoting rogue states, brutal tyrants, and murderous dictators.

In 2013, President Putin and his Government promised the world that they would guarantee the elimination of Syria's chemical weapons. Asad's recent attack—and today's response—are the direct result of Russia's failure to keep that promise. Russia must decide if it will continue down this dark path or if it will join with civilized nations as a force for stability and peace. Hopefully, someday we'll get along with Russia and maybe even Iran, but maybe not.

I will say this: The United States has a lot to offer, with the greatest and most powerful economy in the history of the world. In Syria, the United States—with but a small force being used to eliminate what is left of ISIS—is doing what is necessary to protect the American people. Over the last year, nearly 100 percent of the territory once controlled by the so-called ISIS caliphate in Syria and Iraq has been liberated and eliminated.

The United States has also rebuilt our friendships across the Middle East. We have asked our partners to take greater responsibility for securing their home region, including contributing large amounts of money for the resources, equipment, and all of the anti-ISIS effort. Increased engagement from our friends, including Saudi Arabia, the United Arab Emirates, Qatar, Egypt, and others can ensure that Iran does not profit from the eradication of ISIS.

America does not seek an indefinite presence in Syria under no circumstances. As other nations step up their contributions, we look forward to the day when we can bring our warriors home. And great warriors they are.

Looking around our very troubled world, Americans have no illusions. We cannot purge the world of evil or act everywhere there is tyranny. No amount of American blood or treasure can produce lasting peace and security in the Middle East. It's a troubled place. We will try to make it better, but it is a troubled place. The United States will be a partner and a friend, but the fate of the region lies in the hands of its own people.

In the last century, we looked straight into the darkest places of the human soul. We saw the anguish that can be unleashed and the evil that can take hold. By the end of the World War I, more than 1 million people had been killed or injured by chemical weapons. We never want to see that ghastly specter return.

So today the nations of Britain, France, and the United States of America have marshaled their righteous power against barbarism and brutality. Tonight I ask all Americans to say a prayer for our noble warriors and our allies as they carry out their missions.

We pray that God will bring comfort to those suffering in Syria. We pray that God will guide the whole region toward a future of dignity and of peace. And we pray that God will continue to watch over and bless the United States of America.

Thank you, and goodnight. Thank you.

SOURCE: Executive Office of the President. "Remarks on United States Military Operations in Syria." April 13, 2018. *Compilation of Presidential Documents* 2018, no. 00242 (April 13, 2018). https://www.gpo .gov/fdsys/pkg/DCPD-201800242/pdf/DCPD-201800242.pdf.

## OTHER HISTORIC DOCUMENTS OF INTEREST

### FROM PREVIOUS *HISTORIC DOCUMENTS*

# Facebook CEO Testifies before Congress on Use of Consumer Data

APRIL 11 AND JUNE 29, 2018

In March 2018, an investigation by the *New York Times* revealed that political data firm Cambridge Analytica had accessed tens of millions of users' private information on Facebook. A month later, on April 11, 2018, Facebook CEO Mark Zuckerberg arrived on Capitol Hill for his first-ever appearance before Congress to address lawmakers' concerns about the data breach. At the heart of the testimony was how technology giants, Facebook included, collect, store, and share consumers' personal data. Lawmakers from both sides of the aisle pressed Zuckerberg to explain not only the data breach but also other controversies, such as alleged censorship of conservative voices and Russia's use of the platform to influence U.S. elections. Zuckerberg took full and personal responsibility for the breach and vowed to review every third-party application and enact more stringent privacy policies. Despite probing questions from the Senate and a more hostile treatment in the House, Zuckerberg and Facebook emerged from ten hours of questioning largely unscathed. Lawmakers did not provide specific legislative solutions that could prevent similar incidents, but it is widely anticipated that Congress will move to strengthen oversight of Facebook and similar Internet companies in the future.

## Donald Trump, a Little-Known Data Firm, and an Unprecedented Privacy Breach

On April 11, 2018, Zuckerberg arrived in Washington, D.C., for his first appearance before Congress. Lawmakers from both sides of the aisle requested the Facebook CEO provide testimony explaining the company's use of consumer data and the steps it was taking to protect users' private information. At the heart of the inquiry, however, was Facebook's relationship with a single data firm.

Two years before Zuckerberg's testimony on Capitol Hill, as the 2016 presidential election ramped up, the Trump campaign contracted a relatively unknown data firm to boost its paid digital advertising. The firm, Cambridge Analytica, was hired to collect data and identify individual voters' personalities, psychologically profiling individual voters to better direct the campaign's paid advertisements and messaging. As revealed by a whistleblower more than a year after the election, the firm, together with a Russian American psychology professor, went further than mere digital targeting.

Starting in 2014, Cambridge University's Psychometrics Centre professor Aleksandr Kogan developed an application on Facebook that scraped private information from individual users' profiles and those of their friends. The practice was done without Facebook's knowledge but was permitted at the time under Facebook's terms of service. (The practice has since been banned.) Kogan then shared that data with Cambridge Analytica. Only around 270,000 users downloaded the application, but the final reach was magnitudes more: In total, Cambridge Analytica had gained access to the private information, including the users' location, of more than 87 million Facebook users. It was one of the largest data breaches in the social network's history.

## FACEBOOK AND POLICY MAKERS RESPOND

Facebook responded to the data breach quickly. The company issued a statement claiming that when it learned data had been shared with Cambridge Analytica against the company's terms of service, it removed the application from the site. Since then, the company said, it had demanded and received certification that the data had been destroyed. A few days later, Facebook announced that it had hired a digital forensics firm "to determine the accuracy of the claims that the Facebook data in question still exists."

Federal regulators and U.S. and British lawmakers were not satisfied. The Federal Trade Commission launched an investigation into whether Facebook violated a 2011 consent agreement to keep users' data private. Senators from both parties, led by Sens. Amy Klobuchar, D-Minn., and John Kennedy, R-La., called for congressional hearings. Republicans on the Senate Commerce Committee, led by Chair John Thune, R-S.D., wrote a letter to Zuckerberg demanding answers. In the United Kingdom, a British parliament committee sent a similar letter requesting Zuckerberg appear before the panel, noting that Facebook's lack of disclosure potentially violated privacy laws in Britain. Politicians in the states took note as well. Massachusetts Attorney General Maura Healey launched an investigation, saying, "Massachusetts residents deserve answers immediately from Facebook and Cambridge Analytica."

Facebook acquiesced to lawmakers' requests, with Zuckerberg agreeing in March to appear before Congress.

## DAY ONE: ZUCKERBERG APPEARS BEFORE THE SENATE

A little less than a month after the data breach was revealed, Zuckerberg appeared before both chambers of Congress. Lawmakers pressed Zuckerberg on what he personally knew about Cambridge Analytica's data collection efforts and what steps he and Facebook were taking to prevent future data breaches. Senators also questioned whether this issue was larger than just Cambridge Analytica, asking if other firms and services were using similar data collection tactics, for example.

Zuckerberg first appeared before a joint session of the Senate Commerce and Judiciary Committees. In his opening remarks, Zuckerberg struck a humble tone and took personal responsibility for the data breach. "We didn't take a broad enough view of our responsibility, and that was a big mistake. It was my mistake, and I'm sorry," he said. "I started Facebook, I run it, and I'm responsible for what happens here."

Despite this admission, Facebook held onto its "social mission," he said. "My top priority has always been our social mission of connecting people, building community, and bringing the world closer together," Zuckerberg reassured the senators. He continued, "I believe deeply in what we are doing. And I know that, when we address these challenges we'll look back and view helping people connect and giving more people a voice as a positive force in the world."

At the center of the committees' concerns was whether a massive technology giant could appropriately regulate itself. Thune said Congress would no longer defer to technology companies, a sentiment Sen. Bill Nelson, D-Fla., echoed. "If you and other social media companies do not get your act in order, none of us are going to have any privacy anymore," said Nelson.

Nelson also asked Zuckerberg why Facebook did not notify users whose data were compromised when the company first discovered the breach. Zuckerberg explained that they had mistakenly trusted Cambridge Analytica. "When we heard back from Cambridge Analytica that they had told us that they weren't using the data and deleted it, we considered it a closed case," Zuckerberg said. "In retrospect, that was clearly a mistake. We shouldn't have taken their word for it."

Zuckerberg vowed to root out bad actors from the platform. Facebook, its CEO said, would be "investigating many apps, tens of thousands of apps, and if we find any suspicious activity, we're going to conduct a full audit of those apps to understand how they're using their data and if they're doing anything improper." He added, "If we find that they're doing anything improper, we'll ban them from Facebook and we will tell everyone affected."

Other senators used the opportunity to raise more partisan concerns. Sen. Ted Cruz, R-Tex., peppered Zuckerberg on whether the platform was unfairly censoring conservative voices. Democratic senators, including Klobuchar, pressed him on Russian use of the platform to interfere with the 2016 election. The questioning lasted for about five hours, during which lawmakers continued to admonish Zuckerberg, and the CEO repeatedly acknowledged his guilt.

## DAY TWO: ZUCKERBERG APPEARS BEFORE THE HOUSE

The following day, Zuckerberg appeared before the House Energy and Commerce Committee, where he found a less receptive audience. Representatives took a sharper tone than their Senate counterparts, pushing Zuckerberg to commit to "yes or no" answers.

Committee Chair Greg Walden, R-Ore., opened the hearing by outlining its two main objectives: to investigate the Cambridge Analytica data breach and to "widen our lens to larger questions about the fundamental relationship between tech companies and their users." Walden applauded Facebook's unique place in modern society as an American success story. However, he explained, "While Facebook has certainly grown, I worry it has not matured. I think it is time to ask whether Facebook may have moved too fast and broken too many things."

Walden also questioned Facebook's core identity. "What exactly is Facebook—a social platform, a data company, an advertising company, a media company, a common carrier in the information age, all of the above, or something else?" He noted that the answer to that question had important implications for how Facebook collects and shares users' personal data and that "if a company fails to keep its promises about how personal data are being used, that breach of trust must have consequences."

Zuckerberg made an opening statement similar to the one he provided to the Senate the day before, once again offering his apologies for the incident. The reception, however, was starkly different. Representatives were sharper in their critiques and less open to the idea that Zuckerberg did not know what was happening at his company, including the data breach. Rep. Mike Doyle, D-Penn., mocked Zuckerberg after the CEO stated he learned about the data breach from news reports. "Do you routinely learn about these violations through the press?" Doyle asked.

Other members were more pointed. Rep. Bobby Rush, D-Ill., accused Facebook of "the wholesale invasion and manipulation of users' right to privacy," likening the company's tactics to those of former Federal Bureau of Investigation director J. Edgar Hoover. Rep. Diana DeGette, D-Colo., questioned why there have been no financial penalties for prior privacy breaches. "We continue to have these abuses and these data breaches, but at the same time, it doesn't seem like future activities are prevented," she said. "I think one of the things that we need to look at in the future . . . is putting really robust penalties in place in case of improper actions."

The questions extended far beyond concerns about security, privacy, and data sharing. Rep. George Kenneth Butterfield, D-N.C., asked about diversity at Facebook headquarters, while Rep. David McKinley, R-W.V., questioned whether the company is tacitly allowing illegal drug sales on its platform.

## FUTURE REGULATION IS EXPECTED BUT UNCERTAIN

After two days of answering more than 600 questions from nearly 100 lawmakers in the House and Senate, Zuckerberg and Facebook emerged bruised but intact. Zuckerberg managed to evade the most probing and potentially damaging questions by promising "my team will get back to you"—a phrase he used more than twenty times.

On June 29, 2018, Facebook kept that promise. In a 752-page document, the company responded to nearly 2,000 outstanding questions from lawmakers, addressing issues ranging from the platform's privacy policy to why individual Facebook advertisements were taken down to the mechanics behind the platform's Trending Topics section.

Lawmakers, meanwhile, continue to grapple with how best to regulate massive Internet companies such as Facebook. Many privacy experts agree with calls for increased regulation on the use of personal data, pointing to a changing society in which users are now conscious enough of how their data are collected and used to allow lawmakers to make meaningful regulatory changes. Some in Congress have suggested they may look to Europe for guidance on data privacy. European regulators have led the charge in cracking down on Facebook, forcing it to stop using facial recognition technology and curtailing some of its Internet-use tracking practices. While exact specifications for future regulations of Internet companies including Facebook remain uncertain, data experts, lawmakers, and even Zuckerberg agree that increased oversight is inevitable.

—Robert Howard

*Following is a statement from House Energy and Commerce Committee Chair Greg Walden, R-Ore., delivered at a hearing on April 11, 2018, about Facebook's use of consumer data; and excerpts from Facebook's June 29, 2018, response to additional questions submitted by members of Congress.*

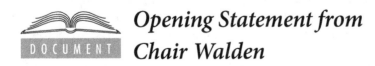 *Opening Statement from Chair Walden*

DOCUMENT

---

**April 11, 2018**

Good morning and welcome, Mr. Zuckerberg, to the Energy and Commerce Committee.

We've called you here today for two reasons: One is to examine alarming reports regarding breaches of trust between your company—one of the biggest and most powerful in the world—and its users. And the second reason is to widen our lens to larger questions about the fundamental relationship between tech companies and their users.

The incident involving Cambridge Analytica and the compromised personal information of approximately 87 million users, mostly Americans, is deeply disturbing to this committee.

The American people are concerned about how Facebook protects and profits from its users' data. In short, does Facebook keep its end of the agreement with its users? How should we, as policy makers, evaluate and respond to these events?

Does Congress need to clarify whether or not consumers own or have any real power over their online data? Have edge providers grown to the point that they need federal supervision?

You and your co-founders started a company in your dorm room that has grown to be one of the biggest and most successful businesses in the world. Through innovation and a quintessentially American entrepreneurial spirit, Facebook and the tech companies that have flourished in Silicon Valley join a legacy of great American companies who built our nation, drove our economy forward, and created jobs and opportunity. And you did it all without having to ask permission from the federal government, and with very little regulatory involvement. The company you created disrupted entire industries and has become an integral part of our lives.

Your success story is an American success story, embodying our shared values of freedom of speech, freedom of association, and freedom of enterprise. Facebook also provides jobs for thousands of Americans, including in my own congressional district at the data center in Prineville, Oregon. Many of our constituents feel a genuine sense of pride and gratitude for what you have created, and you are rightly considered one of this era's greatest entrepreneurs.

This unparalleled achievement is why we look to you with a special sense of obligation and hope for deep introspection.

While Facebook has certainly grown, I worry it has not matured. I think it is time to ask whether Facebook may have moved too fast and broken too many things.

There are critical, unanswered questions surrounding Facebook's business model and the entire digital ecosystem regarding online privacy and consumer protection.

What exactly is Facebook—a social platform, a data company, an advertising company, a media company, a common carrier in the information age, all of the above, or something else?

Users trust Facebook with a great deal of information—their name, hometown, email, phone number, photos, private messages, and much, much more. But in many instances, users aren't actively providing Facebook with data. Facebook collects this information while users simply browse other websites, shop online, or use a third-party app.

People are willing to share quite a bit about their lives online based on the belief that they can easily navigate and control privacy settings and trust that their personal information is in good hands.

If a company fails to keep its promises about how personal data are being used, that breach of trust must have consequences.

Today, we hope to shed light on Facebook's policies and practices surrounding third party access to and use of user data. We also hope you can help clear up the considerable confusion that exists about how people's Facebook data are used outside the platform.

We hope you can help Congress, but more importantly the American people, better understand how Facebook user information has been accessed by third parties, from Cambridge Analytica and CubeYou, to the Obama for America presidential campaign.

And we ask that you share any suggestions you have for ways policymakers can help reassure our constituents that data they believe was only shared with friends or certain groups, remains private to those circles.

As policymakers we want to be sure that consumers are adequately informed about how their online activities and information are used. These issues apply not just to Facebook, but equally to the other Internet-based companies that collect information about users on-line.

Mr. Zuckerberg, your expertise in this field is without rival. Thank you for joining us today to help us learn more about these vital matters.

SOURCE: U.S. House of Representatives Committee Repository. "Opening Statement of Chairman Greg Walden Energy and Commerce Committee, 'Facebook: Transparency and Use of Consumer Data.'" April 11, 2018. https://docs.house.gov/meetings/IF/IF00/20180411/108090/HHRG-115-IF00-MState-W000791-20180411.pdf.

# Facebook Response to Additional Questions from Congress

**June 29, 2018**

*[The following questions and answers have been excerpted from a 752-page document providing Facebook's responses to questions submitted by lawmakers for the record from the April 11, 2018 House Energy and Commerce Committee hearing.]*

### House Energy and Commerce Questions for the Record

#### The Honorable Greg Walden

**1. Restricting outside parties' access to Facebook data was a major topic of discussion at the Energy and Commerce Committee hearing. What additional data and information, from Facebook users or from other third-party companies about Facebook users, does the company collect?**

    **a. Please provide a complete accounting of every data element collected on Facebook users, non-users, and from third-party companies.**

    **b. Are there data elements collected beyond what is necessary to operate the social network platform? If yes, please identify each data element.**

As explained in our Data Policy, we collect three basic categories of data about people:

(1)  data about things people do and share (and who they connect with) on our services;

(2)  data about the devices people use to access our services; and

(3)  data we receive from partners, including the websites and apps that use our business tools.

As far as the amount of data we collect about people, the answer depends on the person. People who have only recently signed up for Facebook have usually shared only a few things—such as name, contact information, age, and gender. Over time, as people use our products, we receive more data from them, and this data helps us provide more relevant content and services. That data will fall into the categories noted above, but the specific data we receive will, in large part, depend on how the person chooses to use Facebook. For example, some people use Facebook to share photos, so we receive and store photos for those people. Some people enjoy watching videos on Facebook; when they do, we receive information about the video they watched, and we can use that information to help show other videos in their News Feeds. Other people seldom or never watch videos, so we do not receive the same kind of information from them, and their News Feeds are likely to feature fewer videos.

The data we have about people also depends on how they have used our controls. For example, people who share photos can easily delete those photos. The same is true of any other kind of content that people post on our services. Through Facebook's Activity Log tool, people can also control the information about their engagement—i.e., their likes, shares and comments—with other people's posts. The use of these controls of course affects the data we have about people.

When people visit apps or websites that feature our technologies—like the Facebook Like or Comment button—our servers automatically log (i) standard browser or app records of the fact that a particular device or user visited the website or app (this connection to Facebook's servers occurs automatically when a person visits a website or app that contains our technologies, such as a Like button, and is an inherent function of internet design); and (ii) any additional information the publisher of the app or website chooses to share with Facebook about the person's activities on that site (such as the fact that a purchase was made on the site). This is a standard feature of the internet, and most websites and apps share this same information with multiple different third-parties whenever people visit their website or app. For example, the House Energy and Commerce Committee's website shares information with Google Analytics to help improve the site. This means that, when a person visits the Committee's website, it sends browser information about their visit to that third party. More information about how this works is available at https://newsroom.fb.com/news/2018/04/data-off-facebook/.

When the person visiting a website featuring Facebook's tools is not a registered Facebook user, Facebook does not have information identifying that individual, and it does not create profiles for this individual.

We use the browser and app logs that apps and websites send to us—described above—in the following ways for non-Facebook users. First, these logs are critical to protecting the security of Facebook and to detecting or preventing fake account access. For example, if a browser has visited hundreds of sites in the last five minutes, that's a sign the device might be a bot, which would be an important signal of a potentially inauthentic account if that browser then attempted to register for an account. Second, we aggregate those logs to provide summaries and insights to websites and apps about how many people visit or use their product, or use specific features like our Like button—but without providing any information about a specific person. We do not create profiles for non-Facebook users, nor do we use browser and app logs for non-Facebook users to show targeted ads from our advertisers to them or otherwise seek to personalize the content they see. However, we may take the opportunity to show a general ad that is unrelated to the attributes of the person or an ad encouraging the non-user to sign up for Facebook.

We do receive some information from devices and browsers that may be used by non-users. For example:

- We also may receive information about the device of a non-registered user if that user visits a part of Facebook that does not require people to log in—such as a public Facebook Page. The information we log when people visit our websites or apps is the same as described above and is the same information that any provider of an online service would receive.

- In addition, Facebook may receive some basic information about devices where Facebook apps are installed, including before people using those devices have registered for Facebook (such as when a user downloads a Facebook app, but has not yet created an account, or if the app is preloaded on a given device). This device data includes things like device model, operating system, IP address, app version and device identifiers. We use this information to provide the right version of the app, help people who want to create accounts (for example, optimizing the registration flow for the specific device), retrieving bug fixes and measuring and improving app performance. We do not use this information to build profiles about non-registered users.

**2. At the April 11 hearing, it was revealed that Facebook's 2 billion users likely had their public profiles scraped (meaning information about individuals, accessible to third party apps on the Facebook Platform, was easily pulled off the service, typically in large quantities, and made accessible to others outside the platform) by outsiders—third-party developers.**

    a.   **How long have third-parties been able to scrape data from Facebook users and their friends' pages? The testimony indicated the mechanisms used by Cambridge Analytica, Obama for America, and countless other third-party applications were no longer available after 2014. Please detail what information third-party applications can remove from Facebook about users and their friends as of January 2018 and, separately, today, if there is any difference.**

We understand your question to be about updates to our app platform. In 2007, there was industry-wide interest in enriching and expanding users' experiences on various platforms by allowing them to take their data (from a device or service) to third-party developers to receive new experiences. For example, around that time, Apple and Google respectively launched their iOS and Android platforms, which were quickly followed by platform technologies and APIs that allowed developers to develop applications for those two platforms and distribute them to users through a variety of channels. Similarly, in 2007, Facebook launched a set of platform technologies that allowed third parties to build applications that could run on and integrate with the Facebook service and that could be installed by Facebook users who chose to do so. In December 2009, Facebook launched new privacy controls that enabled users to control which of the types of information that they made available to their friends could be accessed by apps used by those friends.

As with all of these platforms, the permissions model that governed the information that third-party applications could access from the Platform evolved. For example, in April 2010, Facebook launched granular data permissions (GDP), which allowed users to examine a list of categories of information that an app sought permission to access before they authorized the app.

In November 2013, when Kogan launched the app, apps generally could be launched on the Platform without affirmative review or approval by Facebook. The app used the Facebook Login service, which allowed users to utilize their Facebook credentials to authenticate themselves to third-party services. Facebook Login and Facebook's Graph API also allowed the app to request permission from its users to bring their Facebook data (their own data and data shared with them by their friends) to the app, to obtain new experiences.

At that time, the Graph API V1 allowed app developers to request consent to access information from the installing user such as name, gender, birthdate, location (i.e., current city or hometown), photos and Page likes—and also (depending on, and in accordance with, each friend's own privacy settings) the same or similar categories of information the user's friends had shared with the installing user. Permitting users to share data made available to them by their friends had the upside of making the experience of app users more personalized and social. For example, a Facebook user might want to use a music app that allowed the user to (1) see what his or her friends were listening to and (2) give the app permission to access the user's friend list and thereby know which of the user's friends were also using the app. Such access to information about an app user's friends required not only the consent of the app user, but also required that the friends whose data would be accessed have their own privacy settings set to permit such access by third-party apps. In other words, Kogan's app could have accessed a user's friends' information only for friends whose privacy settings permitted such sharing.

In April 2014, we announced that we would more tightly restrict our platform APIs to prevent abuse. At that time, we made clear that existing apps would have a year to transition—at which point they would be forced (1) to migrate to the more restricted API and (2) be subject to Facebook's new review and approval protocols. The vast majority of companies were required to make the changes by May 2015; a small number of companies (fewer than 100) were given a one-time extension of less than six months beyond May 2015 to come into compliance. (One company received an extension to January 2016.) In addition, in the context of our ongoing review of third-party apps, we discovered a very small number of companies (fewer than 10) that theoretically could have accessed limited friends' data as a result of API access that they received in the context of a beta test. We are not aware that any of this handful of companies used this access, and we have now revoked any technical capability they may have had to access any friends' data.

New apps that launched after April 30, 2014 were required to use our more restrictive platform APIs, which incorporated several key new elements, including:

- Institution of a review and approval process, called App Review (also called Login Review), for any app seeking to operate on the new platform that would request access to data beyond the user's own public profile, email address, and a list of friends of the user who had installed and authorized the same app;

- Generally preventing new apps on the new platform from accessing friends data without review; and

- Providing users with even more granular controls over their permissions as to what categories of their data an app operating on the new platform could access.

Our investigation is ongoing and as part of it we are taking a close look at applications that had access to friends data under Graph API V1 before we made technical changes to our platform to change this access.

The App Review process introduced in 2014 required developers who create an app that asks for more than certain basic user information to justify the data they are looking to collect and how they are going to use it. Facebook then reviewed whether the developer has a legitimate need for the data in light of how the app functions. Only if approved following such review can the app ask for a user's permission to get their data. Facebook has rejected more than half of the apps submitted for App Review between April 2014 and April 2018, including Kogan's second app. We are changing Login so that the only data that an app can request without app review will include name, profile photo, and email address.

We review apps to ensure that the requested permissions clearly improve the user experience and that the data obtained is tied to an experience within the app. We conduct a variety of manual and automated checks of applications on the platform for Policy compliance, as well as random sampling. When we find evidence of or receive allegations of violations, we investigate and, where appropriate, employ a number of measures, including restricting applications from our platform, preventing developers from building on our platform in the future, and taking legal action where appropriate.

Separately, in April, we found out that a feature that lets users look someone up by their phone number and email may have been misused by browsers looking up people's profiles in large volumes with phone numbers they already had. When we found out about the abuse, we shut this feature down. In the past, we have been aware of scraping as an industry issue, and have dealt with specific bad actors previously.

b.   **While the company represents that users could choose what information—if any—to share with Facebook, what steps could Facebook have taken, between 2007-2014, to better inform its users that their privacy settings could result in their Facebook content being scraped by third-parties when their friends used an app?**

We believe that it's important to communicate with people about the information that we collect and how people can control it. That is why we work hard to provide this information to people in a variety of ways: in our Data Policy, and in Privacy Basics, which provides walkthroughs of the most common privacy questions we receive. Beyond simply disclosing our practices, we also think it's important to give people access to their own information, which we do through our Download Your Information and Access Your

Information tools, Activity Log, and Ad Preferences, all of which are accessible through our Privacy Shortcuts tool. We also provide information about these topics as people are using the Facebook service itself.

We've heard loud and clear that privacy settings and other important tools are too hard to find and that we must do more to keep people informed. So, we're taking additional steps to put people more in control of their privacy. For instance, we redesigned our entire settings menu on mobile devices from top to bottom to make things easier to find. We also created a new Privacy Shortcuts in a menu where users can control their data in just a few taps, with clearer explanations of how our controls work. The experience is now clearer, more visual, and easy-to-find. Furthermore, we also updated our terms of service that include our commitments to everyone using Facebook. We explain the services we offer in language that's easier to read. We also updated our Data Policy to better spell out what data we collect and how we use it in Facebook, Instagram, Messenger, and other products.

People own what they share on Facebook, and they can manage things like who sees their posts and the information they choose to include on their profile.

Any person can see each of the specific interests we maintain about them for advertising by visiting Ads Preferences, which lets people see what interests we use to choose ads for them—and to edit or delete these interests. They can choose not to see ads from a particular advertiser or not to see ads based on their use of third-party websites and apps. They also can choose not to see ads off Facebook that are based on the interests we derive from their activities on Facebook.

Our Download Your Information or "DYI" tool is Facebook's data portability tool and was launched many years ago to let people access and download many types of information that we maintain about them. The data in DYI and in our Ad Preferences tool contain each of the interest categories that are used to show people ads, along with information about the advertisers that are running ads based on their use of an advertiser's website or app. People also can choose not to see ads from those advertisers. We recently announced expansions to Download Your Information, which, among other things, will make it easier for people to see their data, delete it, and easily download and export it. More information is available at https://newsroom.fb.com/news/2018/04/new-privacy-protections/.

We have also introduced Access Your Information, a new tool that builds on the functionality we provide in Download Your Information. This feature provides a new way for people to access and manage their information. Users can go here to delete anything from their timeline or profile that they no longer want on Facebook. They can also see their ad interests, as well as information about ads they've clicked on and advertisers who have provided us with information about them that influence the ads they see. From here, they can go to their ad settings to manage how this data is used to show them ads.

And we recently announced plans to build Clear History. This feature will enable users to see the websites and apps that send us information when they use them, clear this information from their accounts, and turn off our ability to store it associated with their accounts going forward. Apps and websites that use features such as the Like button or Facebook

Analytics send us information to make their content and ads better. We also use this information to make users' experiences on Facebook better. If a user clears their history or uses the new setting, we'll remove identifying information so a history of the websites and apps they've used won't be associated with their account. We'll still provide apps and websites with aggregated analytics—for example, we can build reports when we're sent this information so we can tell developers if their apps are more popular with men or women in a certain age group. We can do this without storing the information in a way that's associated with a user's account, and as always, we don't tell advertisers who a user is.

**c.   Did Facebook have a duty to inform users about scraping by third-parties?**

Facebook allows people to view, manage, and remove the apps that they have logged into with Facebook through the App Dashboard. We recently prompted everyone to review their App Dashboard as a part of a Privacy Checkup, and we also provided an educational notice on Facebook to encourage people to review their settings. More information about how users can manage their app settings is available at https://www.facebook.com/help/218345114850283? helpref=about_content.

The categories of information that an app can access is clearly disclosed before the user consents to use an app on the Facebook platform. Users can view and edit the categories of information that apps they have used have access to through the App Dashboard.

In addition, Facebook notifies users in accordance with its obligations under applicable law and has also notified people in cases where there was no legal obligation to do so but we nevertheless determined it was the right thing to do under the circumstances. . . .

**f.   Which company executive(s) at Facebook were responsible for the decision not to notify users affected in 2015?**

When Facebook learned about Kogan's breach of Facebook's data use policies in December 2015, we took immediate action. The company retained an outside firm to assist in investigating Kogan's actions, to demand that Kogan and each party he had shared data with delete the data and any derivatives of the data, and to obtain certifications that they had done so. Because Kogan's app could no longer collect most categories of data due to changes in Facebook's platform, our highest priority at that time was ensuring deletion of the data that Kogan may have accessed before these changes took place. With the benefit of hindsight, we wish we had notified people whose information may have been impacted. Facebook has since notified all people potentially impacted with a detailed notice at the top of their News Feed.

**g.   Is data scraping ever consistent with Facebook's own policies and, if so, please identify the specific policies?**

Facebook's policies regarding third-party usage of its platform technologies have prohibited—and continue to prohibit—third-party app developers from selling or licensing user data accessed from Facebook and from sharing any user data accessed from Facebook with any ad network, data broker or other advertising or monetization-related service. . . .

## The Honorable Robert Latta

**1. What policies, mechanisms or procedures were in place prior to November 2016 to verify whether Russian or Chinese authorities used data acquisition and sharing methods as other third parties, including Obama for America and Dr. Kogan, to scrape the entire Facebook Platform for their own gain? Please describe the policies, mechanisms, or procedures that were put in place since 2016, as well as when they were implemented, to protect against nation-states from using similar techniques and methods.**

In the run-up to the 2016 elections, we were focused on the kinds of cybersecurity attacks typically used by nation states, for example phishing and malware attacks. And we were too slow to spot this type of information operations interference. Since then, we've made important changes to prevent bad actors from using misinformation to undermine the democratic process.

Protecting a global community of more than 2 billion involves a wide range of teams and functions, and our expectation is that those teams will grow across the board. For example, we have dedicated information security and related engineering teams.

Protecting the security of information on Facebook is at the core of how we operate. Security is built into every Facebook product, and we have dedicated teams focused on each aspect of data security. From encryption protocols for data privacy to machine learning for threat detection, Facebook's network is protected by a combination of advanced automated systems and teams with expertise across a wide range of security fields. Our security protections are regularly evaluated and tested by our own internal security experts and independent third parties. For the past seven years, we have also run an open bug bounty program that encourages researchers from around the world to find and responsibly submit security issues to us so that we can fix them quickly and better protect the people who use our service.

We anticipate continuing to grow these teams by hiring a range of experts, including people with specific types of threat intelligence expertise.

This will never be a solved problem because we're up against determined, creative and well-funded adversaries. But we are making steady progress. Here is a list of the 10 most important changes we have made:

- **Ads transparency.** Advertising should be transparent: users should be able to see all the ads an advertiser is currently running on Facebook, Instagram and Messenger. And for ads with political content, we've created an archive that will hold ads with political content for seven years—including information about ad impressions and spend, as well as demographic data such as age, gender, and location. People in Canada and Ireland can already see all the ads that a Page is running on Facebook—and we just launched View Active Ads globally.

- **Verification and labeling.** Every advertiser will now need to confirm their ID and location before being able to run any ads with political content in the US. All ads with political content will also clearly state who paid for them.

- **Updating targeting.** We want ads on Facebook to be safe and civil. We thoroughly review the targeting criteria advertisers can use to ensure they are consistent with our principles. As a result, we removed nearly one-third of the targeting segments used by the IRA. We continue to allow some criteria that people may find controversial. But we do see businesses marketing things like historical books, documentaries or television shows using them in legitimate ways.

- **Better technology.** Over the past year, we've gotten increasingly better at finding and disabling fake accounts. We now block millions of fake accounts each day as people try to create them—and before they've done any harm. This is thanks to improvements in machine learning and artificial intelligence, which can proactively identify suspicious behavior at a scale that was not possible before— without needing to look at the content itself.

- **Action to tackle fake news.** We are working hard to stop the spread of false news. We work with third-party fact-checking organizations to limit the spread of articles rated false. To reduce the spread of false news, we remove fake accounts and disrupt economic incentives for traffickers of misinformation. We also use various signals, including feedback from our community, to identify potential false news. In countries where we have partnerships with independent third-party fact-checkers, stories rated as false by those fact-checkers are shown lower in News Feed. If Pages or domains repeatedly create or share misinformation, we significantly reduce their distribution and remove their advertising rights. We also want to empower people to decide for themselves what to read, trust, and share. We promote news literacy and work to inform people with more context. For example, if third-party fact-checkers write articles about a news story, we show them immediately below the story in the Related Articles unit. We also notify people and Page Admins if they try to share a story, or have shared one in the past, that's been determined to be false. In addition to our own efforts, we're learning from academics, scaling our partnerships with third- party fact-checkers and talking to other organizations about how we can work together.

- **Significant investments in security.** We're doubling the number of people working on safety and security from 10,000 last year to over 20,000 this year. We expect these investments to impact our profitability. But the safety of people using Facebook needs to come before profit.

- **Industry collaboration.** Recently, we joined 34 global tech and security companies in signing a TechAccord pact to help improve security for everyone.

- **Information sharing and reporting channels.** In the 2017 German elections, we worked closely with the authorities there, including the Federal Office for Information Security (BSI). This gave them a dedicated reporting channel for security issues related to the federal elections.

- **Tracking 40+ elections.** In recent months, we've started to deploy new tools and teams to proactively identify threats in the run-up to specific elections. We first tested this effort during the Alabama Senate election, and plan to continue these efforts for elections around the globe, including the US midterms. Last year we used public service announcements to help inform people about fake news in 21 separate countries, including in advance of French, Kenyan and German elections.

- **Action against the Russia-based IRA.** In April, we removed 70 Facebook and 65 Instagram accounts—as well as 138 Facebook Pages—controlled by the IRA primarily targeted either at people living in Russia or Russian-speakers around the world including from neighboring countries like Azerbaijan, Uzbekistan, and Ukraine. The IRA has repeatedly used complex networks of inauthentic accounts to deceive and manipulate people in the US, Europe, and Russia—and we don't want them on Facebook anywhere in the world. . . .

**5. Apparently, Facebook's algorithm change may have resulted in intentional or unintentional censoring of certain types of information and news. As indication of such, some conservative pages, like Diamond and Silk, have been deemed "unsafe to the community." Previously, certain Facebook features allowed users and advertisers to manipulate how information and news was posted.**

a.   **All of these instances lead many to believe that Facebook tailors its products and services based on political agenda? Is this true?**

Being a platform for all ideas is a foundational principle of Facebook. We are committed to ensuring there is no bias in the work we do.

Suppressing content on the basis of political viewpoint or preventing people from seeing what matters most to them is directly contrary to Facebook's mission and our business objectives.

For example, when allegations of political bias surfaced in relation to Facebook's Trending Topics feature, we immediately launched an investigation to determine if anyone violated the integrity of the feature or acted in ways that are inconsistent with Facebook's policies and mission. We spoke with current reviewers and their supervisors, as well as a cross-section of former reviewers; spoke with our contractor; reviewed our guidelines, training, and practices; examined the effectiveness of operational oversight designed to identify and correct mistakes and abuse; and analyzed data on the implementation of our guidelines by reviewers.

Ultimately, our investigation revealed no evidence of systematic political bias in the selection or prominence of stories included in the Trending Topics feature. In fact, our analysis indicated that the rates of approval of conservative and liberal topics are virtually identical in Trending Topics. Moreover, we were unable to substantiate any of the specific allegations of politically-motivated suppression of subjects or sources, as reported in the media. To the contrary, we confirmed that most of those subjects were in fact included as trending topics on multiple occasions, on dates and at intervals that would be expected given the volume of discussion around those topics on those dates.

Nonetheless, as part of our commitment to continually improve our products and to minimize risks where human judgment is involved, we are making a number of changes:

- We have engaged an outside advisor, former Senator Jon Kyl, to advise the company on potential bias against conservative voices. We believe this external feedback will help us improve over time and ensure we can most effectively serve our diverse community and build trust in Facebook as a platform for all ideas.

- We continue to expand our list of outside partner organizations to ensure we receive feedback on our content policies from a diverse set of viewpoints.

- We have made our detailed reviewer guidelines public to help people understand how and why we make decisions about the content that is and is not allowed on Facebook.

- We have launched an appeals process to enable people to contest content decisions with which they disagree.

- We are instituting additional controls and oversight around the review team, including robust escalation procedures and updated reviewer training materials.

These improvements and safeguards are designed to ensure that Facebook remains a platform for all ideas and enables the broadest spectrum of free expression possible.

As to Diamond and Silk, we mishandled communication with Diamond and Silk for months. Their frustration was understandable, and we apologized to them. The message they received on April 5, 2018 that characterized their Page as "dangerous" was incorrect and not reflective of the way we seek to communicate with our community and the people who run Pages on our platform. . . .

SOURCE: U.S. House of Representatives Committee Repository. "Facebook: Transparency and Use of Consumer Data." June 29, 2018. https://docs.house.gov/meetings/if/if00/20180411/108090/hhrg-115-if00-wstate-zuckerbergm-20180411.pdf.

## OTHER HISTORIC DOCUMENTS OF INTEREST

### FROM THIS VOLUME

### FROM PREVIOUS *HISTORIC DOCUMENTS*

# North and South Korean Leaders Issue Declaration for Peace

APRIL 27 AND SEPTEMBER 19, 2018

The border area between North and South Korea, sometimes described as the last remaining border of the Cold War, was the scene for the beginnings of a potentially historic change in the relationship between the two countries. On April 27, South Korean President Moon Jae-in and North Korean leader Kim Jong Un met in the Peace House in the southern portion of the village of Panmunjom in the Demilitarized Zone (DMZ) separating the two countries. There, they issued the Panmunjom Declaration on Peace, Prosperity, and Reunification of the Korean peninsula, in which they pledged to "reconnect the blood relations of the nation and bring forward the future of co-prosperity and independent reunification led by Koreans." Moon and Kim also "confirmed the common goal of realizing, through complete denuclearization, a nuclear-free Korean peninsula." They followed their April face-to-face meeting with two more, in May at Panmunjom and in September in the North Korean capital of Pyongyang. At the latter, they agreed to a longer, more concrete set of commitments.

## LEAD-UP TO THE PANMUNJOM SUMMIT

One of the first signals of possible change on the Korean peninsula came in Kim's New Year's Day address. Much of the address consisted of typical North Korean rhetoric and contained multiple references to "the United States and its vassal forces" and criticized the Moon administration by saying that "nothing has been changed in the relations between the north and the south" after Moon replaced the "fascist" regime of Park Geun-hye. But then Kim pivoted by asserting that the North and the South should "take decisive measures for achieving a breakthrough for independent reunification without being obsessed by bygone days." There have been periods of eased tension between the Koreas before, and experts frequently warn against overreading the New Year's addresses of North Korean leaders, but Kim's calls for cooperation seemed to signal a shift, at least in rhetoric. Kim also mentioned the Winter Olympics that South Korea was to host in February in PyeongChang, wishing the Games success and offering to send a North Korean delegation. He also indicated that North Korea was finished with nuclear testing, noting, "The nuclear weapons research sector and the rocket industry should mass-produce nuclear warheads and ballistic missiles, the power and reliability of which have already been proved to the full."

Kim had a willing partner in Moon, the descendent of North Korean refugees, who came into office advocating a North Korea policy that was less hardline than that of his predecessor. In addition to leading South Korea into talks with the North, Moon helped bring together North Korea and the United States for their own summit in Singapore in June and forged a partnership for the two Koreas to appear under a unified flag at the Winter Olympics. While in South Korea to attend the opening ceremony, Kim Jong Un's sister, Kim Yo-jong, met with Moon and invited him to come to North Korea for a summit with her brother.

## INITIAL MEETING PROVIDES SYMBOLISM AND SUBSTANCE

At the April 27 meeting, the North and South Korean leaders took advantage of the location to put on an event rich in symbolism. When Kim stepped over the barrier between the two countries, he became the first ruling member of the Kim dynasty to do so, and Moon reciprocated, stepping into the northern side of the DMZ.

These symbolic gestures were buttressed by substantive discussions that resulted in the Panmunjom Declaration on Peace, Prosperity, and Reunification of the Korean Peninsula. This sweeping document addresses the nations' issues mostly in broad strokes but in doing so sets the stage for the more specific and concrete commitments that the two countries made less than five months later in Pyongyang.

The two sides "affirmed the principle of national independence which specifies that the destiny of our nation is determined on their own accord." They "agreed to endeavor to swiftly resolve the humanitarian issues that resulted from the division of the nation," in particular the separation of families, "with the upcoming August 15 as an occasion." August 15 is National Liberation Day, marking the liberation of the Korean peninsula from Japanese occupation at the end of World War II. It is the only Korean holiday celebrated on both sides of the DMZ. The promised reunion took place in late August at Mount Kumsang, a resort on North Korea's southeastern coast. Of the 57,000 families that applied, 89 were chosen, according to a CNN report. It was the first such reunion since 2015.

Other sections of the declaration deal with war and peace: "Alleviating the military tension and eliminating the danger of war is a very important issue related to the destiny of the nation and a very crucial issue for ensuring peaceful and stable life of the Koreans." The declaration continued, "The two sides agreed to completely cease all hostile acts against each other in every domain including land, sea and air that are the root cause of military tension and conflicts." As a starting point, Kim and Moon agreed to stop scattering propaganda leaflets and broadcasting propaganda and music through loudspeakers along the Military Demarcation Line—the DMZ's dividing line between North and South. The larger goal, they said, is "to transform the DMZ into a peace zone in a genuine sense."

One of the major issues for the two governments was to bring "an end to the current unnatural state of armistice" and establish "a firm peace regime on the Korean peninsula." In 1953, an armistice ended the hostilities of the Korean War, but no peace treaty was ever signed. In the Panmunjom Declaration, the two countries declared an end to the war and announced their intent to hold trilateral meetings between North and South Korea and the United States—potentially also with China—to replace the 1953 armistice with a new peace agreement. Besides the Koreas, the United States and China were the main participants in the Korean War. U.S. involvement came through the United Nations Command, and although the United States was the dominant member of the command, it also included troops from South Korea and fifteen other "sending states."

Kim and Moon also "confirmed the common goal of realizing, through complete denuclearization, a nuclear-free Korean peninsula." In 1992, North and South Korea issued the Joint Declaration of the Denuclearization of the Korean Peninsula, in which the two sides agreed not to "test, manufacture, produce, receive, possess, store, deploy, or use nuclear weapons." They also agreed not to have facilities to enrich uranium or reprocess spent fuel to separate plutonium, the two paths for making weapon-usable nuclear material. Since then, North Korea—which joined the Nuclear Non-Proliferation Treaty in 1985 and announced its withdrawal in 2003—violated a number of agreements imposing restrictions on its nuclear program. It conducted numerous nuclear weapon tests, with the most recent taking place in September 2017.

Since the start of 2018, North Korea took a number of steps apparently aimed at demonstrating that it was serious about restricting or ending its nuclear weapon program—or at least that it would be open to doing so if the United States would make corresponding goodwill gestures. Shortly before the April summit, North Korea announced that it had halted testing of nuclear weapons and long-range missiles, a pledge that it kept through the end of 2018 (although it did test an unspecified "ultramodern tactical weapon"). North Korea also said it would not transfer nuclear weapons or related technology to other countries or groups and would close the site that it had used for its nuclear tests. On May 24, a group of invited journalists watched a North Korean team set off explosions in tunnels at the Punggye-ri nuclear test site. North Korea asserted that the explosions rendered the site unusable for further tests, but Kim did not bring in international inspectors or independent experts to verify that claim. On October 7, after Kim and U.S. Secretary of State Mike Pompeo met in Pyongyang, State Department spokesperson Heather Nauert issued a statement saying that Kim had "invited inspectors to visit the Punggye-ri nuclear test site to confirm that it has been irreversibly dismantled." In comments to reporters the next day, Pompeo said the visit would take place "as soon as we get it logistically worked out." As of the close of 2018, this visit had not taken place.

The September 19 joint declaration from the Kim–Moon summit in Pyongyang said that North Korea would "permanently dismantle the Dongchang-ri missile engine test site and launch platform under the observation of experts from relevant countries" and "expressed its willingness to continue to take additional measures, such as the permanent dismantlement of the nuclear facilities in Yongbyon, as the United States takes corresponding measures in accordance with the spirit" of the joint statement from the June 12 Kim–Trump summit in Singapore.

## SUBSEQUENT SUMMITS BUILD ON APRIL MEETING

Kim and Moon met for a second summit on May 26, this time in the northern portion of Panmunjom. The meeting was not publicized in advance and was specifically focused on Kim's meeting with President Trump the following month.

The next summit was held in Pyongyang from September 18 to 20. In addition to the statements on dismantling North Korean nuclear and missile facilities, the commitments covered areas such as rail and road connections along the peninsula's east and west coasts, the establishment of a joint special economic zone and a joint special tourism zone, and cooperation in public health and medical care. The most detailed pledges, however, were spelled out in a separate document listing commitments "in the military domain." For example, the two sides agreed to remove all mines from the Joint Security Area in the DMZ, a task they completed in October.

## SANCTIONS POSE OBSTACLE

Cooperation between North and South Korea advanced steadily throughout 2018 but at times appeared halting due to some dependency on the U.S.–North Korea talks and the willingness of the United States to make goodwill gestures toward North Korea. In late 2018, the latter appeared to have stalled after the breakthrough of the June summit, although there continued to be talk of a second Kim–Trump summit in early 2019. While the two relationships with Pyongyang can proceed independently, the United States and South Korea historically have tried to align their policies with regard to North Korea, especially as it relates to sanctions.

North Korea is subject to sanctions under a series of UN Security Council resolutions, starting with one in October 2006 in response to North Korea's first nuclear test and running through two resolutions in late 2017—in September following North Korea's sixth nuclear test and in December in response to North Korea's test launch of an intercontinental ballistic missile.

The sanctions cover a wide variety of imports, exports, financial transactions, and joint business ventures, and some of the contemplated North–South cooperative projects, such as the rail and road links, would require a waiver of the sanctions. But the United States, which has been the driving force behind the sanctions—and, as a permanent member of the Security Council, could block any effort to lift them—said North Korea must complete its denuclearization before UN and U.S. sanctions are lifted. North Korea argued that its recent moves with regard to its nuclear weapon and missile programs warrant sanctions relief, but the United States has dismissed that idea.

North Korea garnered some support from key countries. In October, after a trilateral meeting in Moscow, China, North Korea, and Russia issued a joint statement noting "the significant, practical steps for denuclearization" that North Korea had taken and announced "their consensus on the need for the [Security Council] to activate the process of adjusting sanctions upon [North Korea] in time." South Korea also suggested that some sanctions relief could come before denuclearization was complete. Moon said that "if North Korea's denuclearization is judged to enter an irreversible phase, its denuclearization should be further facilitated by easing UN sanctions." He also has argued that the international community must "respond positively" to North Korea's moves. "We must assure Chairman Kim that he has made the right decision in committing to denuclearization. We must encourage North Korea to stay on the path that leads to permanent and solid peace," Moon said. South Korea and the United States agreed to establish a working group to improve cooperation on a range of issues relating to North Korea issues, including sanctions.

—Daniel Horner

*Following is the joint declaration issued by North and South Korea on April 27, 2018, affirming their intent to improve the relationship between their two nations and seek peace on the Korean peninsula; and a second declaration, issued on September 19, 2018, expanding upon the April declaration and adding concrete steps toward normalization of the relationship.*

# North and South Korea
# Issue Joint Declaration

**April 27, 2018**

Panmunjom Declaration on Peace, Prosperity, and Reunification of the Korean Peninsula

Kim Jong Un, Chairman of the State Affairs Commission of the Democratic People's Republic of Korea and Moon Jae-in, President of the Republic of Korea, reflecting the unanimous aspiration of all the Koreans for peace, prosperity and reunification, held the Inter-Korean Summit Meeting at the "Peace House" at Panmunjom on 27 April, 2018 at the significant period of historic turn being made on the Korean peninsula.

The two leaders solemnly declared before the 80 million Koreans and the whole world that there will be no more war and a new era of peace has begun on the Korean peninsula.

They, sharing the firm commitment to bring a swift end to the Cold War relic of long-standing division and confrontation, to boldly open up a new era of national reconciliation, peace and prosperity, and to improve and cultivate inter-Korean relations in a more active manner, declared at this historic site of Panmunjom as follows:

1. The two sides will reconnect the blood relations of the nation and bring forward the future of co-prosperity and independent reunification led by Koreans by achieving comprehensive and epochal improvement and development in inter-Korean relations.

Improving and developing inter-Korean relations is the prevalent desire of the whole nation and the urgent calling of the times that cannot be held back any further.

① The two sides affirmed the principle of national independence which specifies that the destiny of our nation is determined on their own accord and agreed to open up a watershed moment for the improvement and development of inter-Korean relations by fully implementing all existing inter-Korean declarations and agreements adopted thus far.

② The two sides agreed to hold dialogue and negotiations in various fields including the high-level talks at an early date and take active measures for the implementation of the agreements reached at the Summit.

③ The two sides agreed to establish a joint liaison office with resident representatives of both sides in Kaesong area in order to ensure close consultation between the authorities and to satisfactorily facilitate civil exchanges and cooperation.

④ The two sides agreed to invigorate multi-faceted cooperation, exchanges, visits and contacts of people from all levels of society in order to give further momentum to the atmosphere of national reconciliation and unity.

Between the north and the south, the two sides will boost the atmosphere of reconciliation and cooperation by actively staging various joint events on the dates that hold special meaning for both South and North Korea, such as June 15, in which people from all levels of society including the authorities, parliaments, political parties, local governments and civil organizations, will be involved. On the international front, the two sides agreed to demonstrate the nation's wisdom, talents and unity by jointly participating in international sports events such as the 2018 Asian Games.

⑤ The two sides agreed to endeavor to swiftly resolve the humanitarian issues that resulted from the division of the nation, and to convene the Inter-Korean Red Cross Meeting to discuss and solve various issues including the reunion of separated families and relatives.

For the present, the two sides agreed to hold the reunion of separated families and relatives with the upcoming August 15 as an occasion.

⑥ The two sides agreed to actively promote the projects agreed in the October 4 declaration in order to achieve the balanced development and co-prosperity of the nation's economy, and to take practical measures to relink and modernize railways and roads on the eastern and western coasts on a priority basis for their active use.

2. The two sides will make joint efforts to defuse the acute military tensions and to substantially remove the danger of a war on the Korean peninsula.

Alleviating the military tension and eliminating the danger of war is a very important issue related to the destiny of the nation and a very crucial issue for ensuring peaceful and stable life of the Koreans.

① The two sides agreed to completely cease all hostile acts against each other in every domain including land, sea and air that are the root cause of military tension and conflicts.

For the present, they agreed to stop all the hostile acts including the loud-speaker broadcasting and scattering of leaflets in the areas along the Military Demarcation Line (MDL) from May 1, to dismantle their means, and further to transform the DMZ into a peace zone in a genuine sense.

② The two sides agreed to devise a practical scheme to turn the area of the Northern Limit Line in the West Sea into a maritime peace zone to prevent accidental military clashes and ensure safe fishing activities there.

③ The two sides agreed to, along with the reinvigoration of mutual cooperation, exchanges, visits and contacts, take various military measures to ensure such endeavors.

The two sides agreed to hold frequent meetings between military authorities including the defense ministers' meeting in order to discuss and settle the military issues that may arise between the two sides without delay, and to convene military talks first at the rank of general within May to begin with.

3. The two sides will actively cooperate to build a permanent and stable peace regime on the Korean peninsula.

Bringing an end to the current unnatural state of armistice and establishing a firm peace regime on the Korean peninsula is a historic mission that must not be delayed any further.

① The two sides reaffirmed the non-aggression agreement that precludes the use of force in any form against each other and agreed to strictly abide by it.

② The two sides agreed to carry out disarmament in a phased manner, as military tension is alleviated and substantial progress is made in military confidence-building.

③ The two sides agreed to declare the end of war this year that marks the 65th anniversary of the Armistice Agreement and actively promote the holding of trilateral meetings involving the two sides and the United [S]tates, or quadrilateral meetings involving the two sides, the United States and China with a view to replacing the Armistice Agreement with a peace agreement and establishing a permanent and solid peace regime.

④ The two sides confirmed the common goal of realizing, through complete denuclearization, a nuclear-free Korean peninsula.

The two sides shared the view that the measures being initiated by the north side are very meaningful and crucial for the denuclearization of the Korean peninsula, and agreed to fulfill their respective responsibility and role.

The two sides agreed to make active efforts to seek the support and cooperation of the international community for the denuclearization of the Korean peninsula.

The two leaders agreed to frequently have an in-depth discussion on the important matters for the nation through regular meetings and hotlines, deepen confidence and jointly endeavor to further expand the favorable trend toward the sustained development of the north-south ties and peace, prosperity and reunification of the Korean peninsula.

In this context, President Moon Jae-in agreed to visit Pyongyang this fall.

27 April 2018
Done in Panmunjom

(Signed) Kim Jong Un                          (Signed) Moon Jae-in
Chairman                                      President
State Affairs Commission                      Republic of Korea
Democratic People's Republic of Korea

SOURCE: President of the Republic of Korea. "Panmunjom Declaration on Peace, Prosperity and Reunification of the Korean Peninsula." April 27, 2018. http://english1.president.go.kr/BriefingSpeeches/Speeches/32.

# North, South Korea Begin
# Outlining Steps toward Peace

DOCUMENT

**September 19, 2018**

Moon Jae-in, President of the Republic of Korea and Kim Jong-un, Chairman of the State Affairs Commission of the Democratic People's Republic of Korea held the Inter-Korean Summit Meeting in Pyongyang on September 18-20, 2018.

The two leaders assessed the excellent progress made since the adoption of the historic Panmunjom Declaration, such as the close dialogue and communication between the authorities of the two sides, civilian exchanges and cooperation in many areas, and epochal measures to defuse military tension.

The two leaders reaffirmed the principle of independence and self-determination of the Korean nation, and agreed to consistently and continuously develop inter-Korean relations for national reconciliation and cooperation, and firm peace and co-prosperity, and to make efforts to realize through policy measures the aspiration and hope of all Koreans that the current developments in inter-Korean relations will lead to reunification.

The two leaders held frank and in-depth discussions on various issues and practical steps to advance inter-Korean relations to a new and higher dimension by thoroughly implementing the Panmunjom Declaration, shared the view that the Pyongyang Summit will be an important historic milestone, and declared as follows.

1. The two sides agreed to expand the cessation of military hostility in regions of confrontation such as the DMZ into the substantial removal of the danger of war across the entire Korean Peninsula and a fundamental resolution of the hostile relations.

① The two sides agreed to adopt the "Agreement on the Implementation of the Historic Panmunjom Declaration in the Military Domain" as an annex to the Pyongyang Declaration, and to thoroughly abide by and faithfully implement it, and to actively take practical measures to transform the Korean Peninsula into a land of permanent peace.

② The two sides agreed to engage in constant communication and close consultations to review the implementation of the Agreement and prevent accidental military clashes by promptly activating the Inter-Korean Joint Military Committee.

2. The two sides agreed to pursue substantial measures to further advance exchanges and cooperation based on the spirit of mutual benefit and shared prosperity, and to develop the nation's economy in a balanced manner.

① The two sides agreed to hold a ground-breaking ceremony within this year for the east-coast and west-coast rail and road connections.

② The two sides agreed, as conditions ripe, to first normalize the Gaeseong industrial complex and the Mt. Geumgang Tourism Project, and to discuss the issue of forming a west coast joint special economic zone and an east coast joint special tourism zone.

③ The two sides agreed to actively promote south-north environment cooperation so as to protect and restore the natural ecology, and as a first step to endeavor to achieve substantial results in the currently on-going forestry cooperation.

④ The two sides agreed to strengthen cooperation in the areas of prevention of epidemics, public health and medical care, including emergency measures to prevent the entry and spread of contagious diseases.

3. The two sides agreed to strengthen humanitarian cooperation to fundamentally resolve the issue of separated families.

① The two sides agreed to open a permanent facility for family reunion meetings in the Mt. Geumgang area at an early date, and to promptly restore the facility toward this end.

② The two sides agreed to resolve the issue of video meetings and exchange of video messages among the separated families as a matter of priority through the inter-Korean Red Cross talks.

4. The two sides agreed to actively promote exchanges and cooperation in various fields so as to enhance the atmosphere of reconciliation and unity and to demonstrate the spirit of the Korean nation both internally and externally.

① The two sides agreed to further promote cultural and artistic exchanges, and to first conduct a performance of the Pyongyang Art Troupe in Seoul in October this year.

② The two sides agreed to actively participate together in the 2020 Summer Olympic Games and other international games, and to cooperate in bidding for the joint hosting of the 2032 Summer Olympic Games.

③ The two sides agreed to hold meaningful events to celebrate the 11th anniversary of the October 4 Declaration, to jointly commemorate the 100th anniversary of the March First Independence Movement Day, and to hold working-level consultations toward this end.

5. The two sides shared the view that the Korean Peninsula must be turned into a land of peace free from nuclear weapons and nuclear threats, and that substantial progress toward this end must be made in a prompt manner.

① First, the North will permanently dismantle the Dongchang-ri missile engine test site and launch platform under the observation of experts from relevant countries.

② The North expressed its willingness to continue to take additional measures, such as the permanent dismantlement of the nuclear facilities in Yongbyon, as the United States takes corresponding measures in accordance with the spirit of the June 12 US-DPRK Joint Statement.

③ The two sides agreed to cooperate closely in the process of pursuing complete denuclearization of the Korean Peninsula.

6. Chairman Kim Jong-un agreed to visit Seoul at an early date at the invitation of President Moon Jae-in.

September 19, 2018

Moon Jae-in
President
Republic of Korea

Kim Jong Un
Chairman
State Affairs Commission
Democratic People's Republic of Korea

SOURCE: President of the Republic of Korea. "Pyongyang Joint Declaration of September 2018." September 19, 2018. http://english1.president.go.kr/BriefingSpeeches/Briefings/322.

## OTHER HISTORIC DOCUMENTS OF INTEREST

### FROM THIS VOLUME

**FROM PREVIOUS *HISTORIC DOCUMENTS***

# United Nations Climate Change Releases First Annual Report

APRIL 30, 2018

For twenty-five years, United Nations Climate Change has facilitated intergovernmental climate change negotiations, in addition to providing expertise and other resources to support partnerships and programs aimed at mitigating and adapting to the effects of climate change around the world. In April 2018, the secretariat released its first-ever annual report detailing its multifaceted work to build momentum and capacity for the global response to climate change, including steps taken toward implementation of the historic 2015 Paris Agreement.

## EVOLUTION OF ENVIRONMENTAL DIPLOMACY

Since 1992, the United Nations Framework Convention on Climate Change (UNFCCC) has provided a foundation for formal consideration of climate change actions at the international level. A 1997 extension of the framework, the Kyoto Protocol, attempted with limited success to set legally binding emission reduction targets for industrialized nations while allowing developing countries like China to increase their emissions. Based on the principle of "common but differentiated responsibility," the agreement acknowledged that developed states have both greater liability for emissions and greater economic and technological resources to lead on solutions. The United States never ratified the treaty, and other industrialized nations withdrew support.

At the fifteenth Conference of the Parties (COP15) in 2009, the annual meeting of parties to the UNFCCC during which the convention's implementation is reviewed, participating countries—including developing and developed states—agreed to a common goal of keeping the increase in global temperatures below 2°C. Beyond this point, the international scientific community projects that the environmental impacts of climate change will be drastic and irreversible, compounding stress on economic and political systems at unprecedented scales. Six years later, the landmark Paris Agreement was announced during COP21. Under the nonbinding agreement, participating countries committed to achieving the 2°C goal and agreed to aim for the smaller, more ambitious increase of 1.5°C. Each country submitted its own Nationally Determined Commitment (NDC) to guide its emissions-reduction and climate change–mitigation efforts. Due to the significant gap between the submitted NDCs and what was necessary to achieve the parties' stated goal, the agreement required countries to review their commitments every five years, starting in 2020, with the goal of increasing their pledges to cut emissions. Beyond setting ambitious goals for mitigation, the agreement sought to foster climate-resilient development and broaches the technical and financial dimensions of adapting to inevitable impacts of climate change.

## COP23 Outcomes

Several of the most notable achievements highlighted by UN Climate Change's annual report came out of COP23, convened in Germany in November 2017. A focus of the event and of UN Climate Change efforts throughout the year was encouraging parties to increase their commitments under the Paris Agreement. "Paris was a beginning, not an end," wrote UN Secretary-General António Guterres in the report's forward. "The world is currently not on track to achieve the Paris targets. We need urgent climate action and greatly increased ambition—in emissions reductions and in promoting adaptation to current and future impacts of climate change." To further underscore this point, the report cited findings from a recent UN Climate Change analysis of 189 countries' NDCs, which concluded that while implementation of the Paris Agreement would lead to lower emissions than previously expected in 2025 and 2030, they would still not be enough to limit global temperature rise to 2°C.

To help push countries toward more ambitious NDCs, COP23 delegates launched the Talanoa Dialogue. Described as a "year-long process of engagement," the Dialogue is intended to serve as an initial stocktaking, or assessment of progress toward meeting the Paris Agreement goals, before the first full, global stock take formally occurs in 2023. All climate stakeholders—ranging from state and local governments to nongovernmental organizations, corporations, and individuals—were invited to submit assessments of where the parties to the Paris Agreement stand, where they want to go, and what more can be done to achieve their stated goals, with an emphasis on pre-2020 action.

Other achievements from COP23 highlighted by the annual report included the development of the first-ever Gender Action Plan, which seeks to increase the representation of women in all levels of climate change negotiation and empower them to develop and implement climate solutions. COP23 delegates also agreed to the Koronivia joint work on agriculture, a landmark agreement that acknowledges agriculture's significant role in both causing and combatting climate change and provides a framework for addressing food security issues, reducing greenhouse gas emissions produced by the agriculture sector, and building resilience to the effects of climate change. An innovative knowledge-sharing platform for indigenous and local communities was also established to broaden the reach of insights and best practices related to mitigation and adaptation.

The report further stated that COP23 delegates made important progress toward "clear and comprehensive implementation guidelines for the Paris Agreement," which is also known as the "work programme" and considered crucial to "transforming the Agreement into action." COP24 delegates adopted the guidelines in December 2018.

## Support from UN Climate Change

Robust measurement, reporting, and verification mechanisms form a key element of UN Climate Change's work to monitor climate action and evaluate the related needs of developing countries. The annual report highlighted a variety of tools and programs that the secretariat made available to developing countries in 2017, including trainings and certifications for new and existing experts charged with reviewing and analyzing greenhouse gas emission inventories, biennial climate action reports, and compliance with the Kyoto Protocol. Similarly, UN Climate Change led five regional training sessions and two expos in locations across Asia and Africa to help experts from least developed countries develop national climate change adaptation plans and align them with the UN's

Sustainable Development Goals (SDGs). SDGs call for bold and transformative steps by all countries to more closely align economic growth with social inclusion and protection of natural resources. The report also highlighted initiatives to support developing countries in their adaptation to climate change. At COP23, the Executive Committee of the Warsaw International Mechanism for Loss and Damage Associated with Climate Change Impacts launched the Fiji Clearing House for Risk Transfer. The clearing house will help countries prepare and implement comprehensive risk-management strategies for limiting losses and damage incurred by climate change.

UN Climate Change's work also involves facilitating the investment of financial and technological resources to support emissions reduction and adaptation. According to the report, the secretariat's Adaptation Fund broke its single-year fund-raising record in 2017, drawing $95.5 million from contributors including Germany, Sweden, Italy, and Ireland. Approximately $100 million in funding for adaptation and resilience activities was approved by the fund's board in 2017. Providing an update on the Kyoto Protocol's clean development mechanism, which rewards certified emissions reductions in developing countries with credits that can be sold to finance sustainable development, the report stated that 124 million certified emission reductions had been issued in fifty-one countries in 2017.

Additionally, the Green Climate Fund's (GCF) portfolio reportedly grew to seventy-six projects and programs designed to help least developed populations to limit emissions and adapt to impacts, with $3.7 billion in funding provided by October 2017. The annual report noted that in addition to its existing portfolio, the GCF shortlisted thirty proposals in 2017 that had the potential to leverage $3 in private capital for every $1 of public funds invested. The GCF is a central feature of the UNFCCC, established in 2010 as part of the convention's financing mechanism, and is designed to catalyze a flow of private finance through public investment. Executive Director Howard Bamsey has described the GCF as "the dedicated climate fund serving the Paris Agreement."

In terms of securing new financing for planned and ongoing climate action, the secretariat reported that nearly $1 billion in support was pledged during COP23. The European Investment Bank, for example, announced $75 million in funding for an investment program aimed at improving the resilience of water distribution and wastewater treatment in Fiji. Another pledge, of roughly $150 million, was made by Germany, the United Kingdom, and several partners to expand programs fighting climate change and deforestation in the Amazon rainforest. The secretariat also announced a pilot of a new Needs-Based Climate Finance project in more than ten developing countries that will help assess the countries' financial, capacity-building, and technological needs and mobilize support to meet those needs. The Green Investment Catalyst roundtable was launched by UN Climate Change in 2017 as well, with the goal of attracting private-sector investments that will help Paris Agreement signatories implement their NDCs. Early outcomes from this roundtable included an agreement between the Infrastructure Development Bank of Zimbabwe and the Development Bank of South Africa to establish a climate finance facility and green finance framework for Zimbabwe.

## New Partnerships

Partnerships with public and private entities and nongovernmental organizations are central to UN Climate Change's ability to implement the Paris Agreement, the Kyoto Protocol, and the UNFCCC. In 2017, the secretariat piloted a new initiative to help build innovative partnerships with the private sector, media, and nongovernmental organizations around COP23. Of the 112 potential partners who responded to the secretariat's call through this initiative, UN Climate Change signed agreements with 24 of them, including DHL, which provided pro bono climate-neutral logistics services, and BNP Paribas, which produced a series of articles and social media posts highlighting developments in sustainable finance.

The Climate Action Leadership Network also launched in 2017. Established by the Marrakech Partnership for Global Climate Action—a group of parties and nonparty stakeholders working to support achievement of NDCs—the network consists of high-level private- and public-sector decision makers who serve as "champions," advocating for early climate action and sustainable development across the globe.

Other partnership highlights from the year included increased participation in Climate Neutral Now, a program offered in collaboration with UN Environment through which companies, organizations, and individuals are invited to voluntarily reduce their emissions and purchase "credits" to offset emissions that cannot be avoided; credit sales provide financial support for climate-friendly development projects approved by the UNFCCC. Seventy new companies and organizations registered to participate in this program in 2017.

The secretariat noted in its report that "action and support will be critical on all fronts of the global response to climate change" and that nonparty stakeholders "comprise a vast collective with great significance in the response to climate change. The action and investment decisions of these stakeholders will, alongside government policies and measures, determine the future trajectory of global emissions."

—Megan Howes

*Following are excerpts from the first annual report by the United Nations Climate Change secretariat released on April 30, 2018, detailing the work done in 2017 by the secretariat to lead and manage the global response to the mounting climate crisis.*

# UN Issues First Annual Climate Change Report

**April 30, 2018**

*[The table of contents and all sidebars and graphics have been omitted.]*

## Foreword

by António Guterres, United Nations Secretary-General

Climate change is the defining challenge of our time, yet it is still accelerating faster than our efforts to address it. Atmospheric levels of carbon dioxide are higher than they have been for 800,000 years, and they are increasing. So, too, are the catastrophic effects of our warming planet—extreme storms, droughts, fires, floods, melting ice and rising sea levels.

In 2015, the world's nations recognized the urgency and magnitude of the challenge when they adopted the historic Paris Agreement on climate change with a goal of limiting global average temperature rise to well below 2 °C while aiming for a safe 1.5 °C target. The unity forged in Paris was laudable—and overdue. But, for all its significance, Paris was a beginning, not an end. The world is currently not on track to achieve the Paris targets. We need urgent climate action and greatly increased ambition—in emissions reductions and in promoting adaptation to current and future impacts of climate change.

Success demands broad-based concerted action from all levels of society, public and private, action coalitions across all sectors and the engagement of all key actors. There is no time, nor reason, to delay. The dogma that pollution and high emissions are the unavoidable cost of progress is dead. Investing in climate action makes sense for the global environment, improved public health, new markets, new jobs and new opportunities for sustainable prosperity. Failing to act will simply consign all of humanity to ever-worsening climate calamity.

That is why I urge Parties to vigorously implement the Paris Agreement and to increase their ambition commensurate with the demands of science. The United Nations—led by UN Climate Change—will provide support every step of the way. There is no alternative to decisive, immediate climate action if we are to safeguard the future of this and future generations.

## Highlights of 2017

by Patricia Espinosa, UN Climate Change Executive Secretary

Our planet is warming. An astonishing 17 of the 18 warmest years on record have occurred in the twenty-first century. The past three years were the hottest since records began.

With this warming comes climate change, causing extreme storms, droughts and floods. We witnessed these climate disasters many times in 2017 and were shocked. Yet, these are only the most dramatic and visible impacts. Other upheavals range from reduced crop productivity to forced migration. Climate change is the single biggest threat to life, security and prosperity on Earth.

Faced with the challenges of climate change, the United Nations, governments at all levels, civil society, the private sector and individuals are acting to limit global temperature rise to agreed levels and to help vulnerable communities adapt to the effects of climate change we cannot avoid.

UN Climate Change's mandate is to lead and support the global community in this international response, with the Paris Agreement and the Convention being the long-term vehicles for united global climate action.

For UN Climate Change, much of 2017 was about the hard work of ironing out the details of the new climate regime. This is a laborious process. Without it, however, the Paris Agreement will have no impact.

COP 23, presided over by Fiji, demonstrated that there is an unstoppable climate movement supported by all sectors of society across the globe. Almost 30,000 people took part: Heads of State, ministers, delegates from Parties, private sector and civil society leaders, representatives of international organizations, youth groups and indigenous peoples, and many more. During the conference, financial commitments amounting to almost USD 1 billion to tackle climate change were made.

Building on the negotiations over the years, we saw key decisions made by governments, many of which broke new ground. The Talanoa Dialogue, which will inform and inspire Parties as they review their commitments and revise them upwards. The first-ever Gender Action Plan, which will increase the participation of women in climate change responses. The first-ever agreement on agriculture and climate, which will address both vulnerabilities and emissions in this key sector. The first-ever platform for indigenous peoples and local communities, who can now share their valuable perspectives on climate change.

These decisions to bring in new voices, partners and action areas are vital if we are to succeed in meeting the challenges of climate change. This is why UN Climate Change in 2017 focused increasingly on cooperation and coherent action on climate, sustainable development and disaster risk reduction, both within the United Nations system and with external partners.

We also saw advances in climate finance. The Adaptation Fund broke its single-year resource mobilization record, raising USD 95 .5 million.

UN Climate Change continued to deliver on its core tasks: supporting negotiations, including laying the groundwork for the Paris Agreement work programme, monitoring and analysing commitments to build transparency and trust, increase the capacity of developing countries to adapt to climate change and providing science to help Parties shape their actions on climate change.

There is much to do in 2018. We need to support Parties to increase pre-2020 action. Those Parties that have not yet done so should ratify the Doha Amendment to the Kyoto Protocol. Parties should use the Talanoa Dialogue as an opportunity to engage with one another and increase ambition under the Paris Agreement. In 2018, it is critical that the outcomes of the Paris Agreement work programme are adopted at COP 24 in Katowice to ensure we are ready for the implementation of the Agreement.

At the same time, we must further align planning and action on climate change with the United Nations Sustainable Development Goals and the Sendai Framework for Disaster Risk Reduction 2015–2030, taking advantage of complementary action that supports all three global agendas.

In this regard, the work of the clean development mechanism deserves a mention. Work under the mechanism, highlighted in this report, shows that actions to mitigate climate change bring many co-benefits in human health, green jobs, poverty reduction and other aspects of development. As we look towards establishing a new sustainable development mechanism under Article 6 of the Paris Agreement, we should bear these successes in mind.

We all know the magnitude of the task ahead, and what we must do. This annual report—another first—shows how UN Climate Change is doing everything it can to support, encourage and build on the global response to climate change.

The motto of COP 23 was "Further, faster, together". Throughout 2018 and beyond, let us continue to be inspired by this message and do all in our power, together, to accelerate action. Only by doing so can we succeed in protecting our planet from climate change and securing a low-carbon, sustainable future.

*[Two sections on UN climate change initiatives and achievements have been omitted.]*

## Outlook for 2018 and beyond

The Paris Agreement is an historic achievement that builds on more than two decades of progress in negotiations on climate change. It shows the firm commitment of countries to work together to limit global temperature rise, foster climate resilience, and align global financial flows towards low-emission, climate-resilient development.

After a three-year effort since adoption of the Paris Agreement, Parties are expected, at COP 24 in December 2018, to adopt the outcomes of the Paris Agreement work programme, detailing the modalities, procedures and guidelines needed to give full effect to the Agreement. Subnational authorities and other non-Party stakeholders are meanwhile taking decisive action, transforming the global economy, and national governments are putting in place policies and measures to deliver on their nationally determined contributions under the Paris Agreement.

Parties are also committed to increasing the level of ambition described in their nationally determined contributions. This is crucial if we are to reach the Paris goal of limiting temperature rise to well below 2°C and as close as possible to the safer 1.5°C target.

The nationally determined contributions will be informed and inspired throughout 2018 by the Talanoa Dialogue, a global conversation that is inclusive, participatory and transparent. Following the spirit of the Pacific island tradition of talanoa, the Dialogue is aimed at building empathy and trust and promoting cooperation, and through this, enhancing ambition.

The Talanoa Dialogue will be in turn informed by a special report by the Intergovernmental Panel on Climate Change, requested by COP 21, on the impacts of global warming of 1.5°C above preindustrial levels, and will be structured around three questions: Where are we? Where do we want to go? How do we get there? This crucial global conversation will set the direction of the global response to climate change until the first global stocktake under the Paris Agreement in 2023.

Three years to the end of 2020, a milestone year for the Paris Agreement, action and support will be critical on all fronts of the global response to climate change. Non-Party stakeholders, meaning almost all entities and individuals that do not negotiate directly in the Convention process, comprise a vast collective with great significance in the response to climate change. The action and investment decisions of these stakeholders will, alongside government policies and measures, determine the future trajectory of global emissions.

Parties recognized the crucial role of non-Party stakeholders in Paris. They built this recognition firmly into the Paris Agreement. In 2016, the Marrakech Partnership for Global Climate Action was launched to scale up pre-2020 effort and investment by nations and all climate stakeholders.

The high-level champions of the Marrakech Partnership will in 2018 rally non-Party stakeholders, encouraging still greater efforts and soliciting views in a systematic way through the Talanoa Dialogue and at events in 2018 such as the Global Climate Action Summit and regional climate weeks.

Parties will take stock of progress on pre-2020 implementation and ambition at COP 24 in December. They will do so on the basis of a synthesis of information they provide on progress they have made. They will also consider mitigation efforts by governments, the provision of support to developing countries, and progress made by the Marrakech Partnership. The Standing Committee on Finance will present its biennial assessment and overview of climate finance flows before the COP, which will also inform Parties as they take stock of progress.

In 2018, countries can also bring into effect the second commitment period of the Kyoto Protocol. In 2017, 33 Parties accepted the Doha Amendment to the Kyoto Protocol, which establishes its second commitment period (2013–2020), 33 short of the required 144 Parties needed for its entry into force. That important milestone is within reach.

The Kyoto Protocol was the first breakthrough in global action on climate change. It can transfer a practical legacy to the Paris Agreement, as well as a legacy of cooperation and trust.

Policymakers at all levels, state and non-state actors, should systematically pursue coherence, collaboration and coordination in national and international climate and development policy. Such concerted effort across sectors, frameworks and levels of governance could multiply benefits to produce fundamental and transformative change.

To this end, policies need to be set in place now, technologies developed, matured, commercialized and deployed at scale, and practices and behaviors of economic actors need to move ever faster towards low-emission and sustainable business and investment.

The UN Climate Change secretariat, working with Parties and non-Party stakeholders can help facilitate all of this. Indeed, Parties' expectations of the secretariat have grown and evolved year by year. The UN Climate Change secretariat, and each of its staff members, remains fully committed to adding value to the global response to climate change.

Building on decades of success under the Convention and driven by necessity, the UN Climate Change secretariat will, with sufficient levels of support, enhance its ability to deliver on behalf of Parties, and now non-Party stakeholders, as countries and the UN system strive for broad-based, global action sufficient to safeguard present and future generations from the worst effects of climate change.

*[A section providing background on the UN Climate Change secretariat, and one on the secretariat's finances, have been omitted.]*

SOURCE: United Nations Framework Convention on Climate Change. "UN Climate Change Annual Report 2017." April 30, 2018. https://unfccc.int/sites/default/files/resource/UNClimateChange_annual report2017_final.pdf.

## OTHER HISTORIC DOCUMENTS OF INTEREST

### FROM THIS VOLUME

- IPCC and U.S. Reports Warn of Climate Change Impacts, p. 576

### FROM PREVIOUS *HISTORIC DOCUMENTS*

- United States Withdraws from the Paris Climate Accord, *2016*, p. 323
- U.S. and Chinese Presidents Remark on Ratification of Paris Climate Agreement, *2016*, p. 407
- United Nations Climate Change Conference Reaches Historic Agreement, *2015*, p. 656

# May

# NASA Announces Launch of New Mission to Mars; European Scientists Find Martian Lake

MAY 5 AND JULY 25, 2018

In May 2018, the National Aeronautics and Space Administration (NASA) launched its latest mission to Mars, sending the InSight spacecraft on a nearly seven-month journey to the red planet to explore below its surface. While the spacecraft was en route to Mars, the European Space Agency (ESA) announced the discovery of a liquid body of water under the planet's south pole. NASA and ESA also signed a statement of intent to collaborate on future missions to Mars, with the goal of bringing Martian samples back to Earth for further study.

## InSight Goes to the Red Planet

NASA's Mars Interior Exploration using Seismic Investigations, Geodesy and Heat Transport mission—dubbed InSight for short—launched from Vandenberg Air Force Base in California on May 5, 2018. Managed by the Jet Propulsion Laboratory, the InSight mission is part of NASA's Discovery Program, through which the agency is collaborating with universities and private companies to launch a series of smaller, lower-cost missions to explore the planets, their moons, and small bodies such as comets and asteroids. InSight is unique among NASA's Mars missions in that its lander was designed to study the planet's subsurface components, including its crust, mantle, and core, as well as its tectonic activity. (Past and ongoing missions have largely focused on exploring Mars's canyons, volcanos, rocks, and soil.) Specifically, the InSight lander will be used to study "marsquakes" and how they travel through the planet to help determine how Mars's interior materials are layered. Scientists will also use InSight's communication system to precisely measure Mars's rotation and how it "wobbles" in response to the gravitational pull of its moons and the sun. The flow of heat from the planet's interior will also be a focus of study and, when combined with information about Mars's rotation, will provide insights into how Mars lost its once-strong magnetic field.

Since there has been less geologic activity and internal disruption on Mars than on Earth, the planet's interior can provide more information about its formation and evolution, thereby helping scientists better understand the origins of other rocky planets in our solar system. "InSight will not only teach us about Mars, it will enhance our understanding of formation of other rocky worlds like Earth and the Moon, and thousands of planets around other stars," said Thomas Zurbuchen, associate administrator for NASA's Science Mission Directorate, upon InSight's launch. Scientists also hope to learn more about how a planet's makeup and evolution make it more or less likely to support life. For example, the convergence and separation of Earth's tectonic plates push older crust into the planet's interior and reveal new crust. This effective recycling of crust in turn churns up materials such as water and carbon dioxide that are vital to life. Mars does not have tectonic plates and thus far has not been found to support life, leading scientists to hypothesize that plate tectonics could be a key element in determining whether life exists on a planet. "Earth and Mars were molded out of very similar stuff," said Bruce Banerdt, InSight's principal investigator at NASA's Jet Propulsion Laboratory. "Why did the finished planets turn out so differently? Our measurements will help us turn back the clock and understand what produced a verdant Earth but a desolate Mars."

The InSight spacecraft took nearly seven months to travel the 300-million-mile distance to Mars. During that time, the mission team tested the InSight lander's science instruments: the Heat Flow and Physical Properties Package, and the Seismic Experiment for Interior Structure. These instruments were contributed by the German Aerospace Center and France's Centre National d'Études Spatiales, respectively. The spacecraft was followed on its journey by two experimental CubeSats, known as MarCO. NASA has been working with academic, nonprofit, and developer partners to use the small, briefcase-sized satellites to conduct near-Earth research and test new technologies. Since they are relatively inexpensive to build and launch, CubeSats are expected to provide greater and more cost-effective opportunities to explore other areas of space. The InSight mission marked the first time CubeSats were sent to deep space; they conducted in-flight communications and navigation experiments on the journey to Mars, then were positioned to receive transmissions from the spacecraft during its descent and landing.

InSight landed on Mars on November 26, 2018, at a site named Elysium Planitia. In NASA parlance, the descent to Mars is known as "seven minutes of terror," because a spacecraft goes from traveling about 12,300 miles per hour to five miles per hour in less than seven minutes, relying heavily on a parachute and thrusters to slow down in Mars's thin atmosphere. The mostly pre-programmed landing went smoothly, with InSight successfully deploying its two solar arrays in its first few hours on the planet's surface. "Today, we successfully landed on Mars for the eighth time in human history," said NASA Administrator Jim Bridenstine. "This accomplishment represents the ingenuity of America and our international partners, and it serves as a testament to the dedication and perseverance of our team. The best of NASA is yet to come, and it is coming soon."

Mission scientists said the lander would begin collecting data within a week. However, the team's initial focus will be on deploying the craft's instruments over a period of five to six weeks. InSight is scheduled to remain in operation until November 24, 2020. It joins two other vehicles—NASA's Curiosity and Opportunity—on the planet's surface.

## Liquid Water Found at Mars's South Pole

On July 25, the journal *Science* published a paper by Italian researchers working on ESA's Mars Express mission concluding that a subsurface lake exists at Mars's south pole. The Mars Express spacecraft has been orbiting and studying the planet since December 2003. The team used data collected by the spacecraft's MARSIS instrument—short for Mars Advanced Radar for Subsurface and Ionosphere Sounding instrument—between May 2012 and December 2015 to develop their findings. MARSIS sends radar pulses toward Mars's surface and measures how long it takes for the signals to be reflected to the spacecraft, as well as the strength of the reflections. Different surface and subsurface materials reflect the radar pulses at different speeds and strengths, helping scientists map the planet's topography. The same technique has been used on Earth to find subsurface lakes in the Antarctic and Greenland.

During the period of study, MARSIS received a particularly bright radar reflection from an area roughly 1.5 kilometers below Mars's south pole. These signals, the scientists said, were consistent with the higher radar reflectivity of liquid water. The composition of the polar layers and the projected subsurface temperature further supported this conclusion, they found. The team estimated that the body of water had a diameter of about 20 kilometers; they were not able to measure its depth but stated that it must be at least a few feet deep or MARSIS would not have detected it.

The Mars Express mission previously found water ice at Mars's north and south poles and buried in layers at various locations under the planet's surface. Other missions have also found fossil waterways, minerals that can only be formed when water is present, and possibly the site of an ancient ocean. Liquid water findings have been minimal: droplets collected on NASA's Phoenix Lander in 2008, and some type of water appears to flow down Mars's steeper slopes in the summer, when temperatures rise.

The amount of water that once existed on Mars has major implications for whether the planet ever supported life. The Italian scientists' discovery prompted questions about whether some form of microbial life might exist in the underground lake. Microbial life has been found on Earth in subsurface water that is salty and sediment rich, which researchers believe the Martian water to be. The research team's next project will be to look for other, similar bodies of water on Mars, the presence of which could mean that early Mars was wetter than initially thought and had a water cycle like Earth's. If no other bodies of water are found, the polar lake will likely be considered an anomaly.

## NASA, ESA Signal Intent to Collaborate

While they were pursuing their respective Mars missions, NASA and ESA came together in April 2018 to sign a statement of intent to collaborate on a Mars sample return plan. Through this plan, the two agencies will coordinate a series of missions to bring Martian samples back to Earth for research and analysis that cannot feasibly be conducted on the red planet. According to ESA, bringing samples back from Mars will require at least three missions. The first mission will require a rover—possibly NASA's upcoming 2020 Mars Rover—to collect small surface samples in canisters. A second mission would send a rover to collect the samples gathered by the first rover and bring them to a Mars Ascent Vehicle, which would launch the samples into Mars orbit. The third mission would send a spacecraft to Mars to rendezvous with the orbiting samples, collect them, and transport them back to Earth.

"This signing is historic, as it signals the desire, the readiness, and the willingness to work together to execute this inspiring mission," said Jim Watzin, NASA Mars Exploration Program director. Each agency is expected to submit the proposed Mars sample return plan to their respective authorizing entities (the U.S. Congress and ESA's Ministerial Council) by the end of 2019.

—Linda Grimm

*Following is a press release issued by the National Aeronautics and Space Administration on May 5, 2018, announcing the InSight spacecraft's launch; and an announcement from the European Space Agency on July 25, 2018, about researchers' discovery of a subsurface body of water on Mars.*

## NASA Launches InSight Mission to Study Mars

**May 5, 2018**

NASA's Mars Interior Exploration using Seismic Investigations, Geodesy and Heat Transport (InSight) mission is on a 300-million-mile (483-million-kilometer) trip to Mars to study for the first time what lies deep beneath the surface of the Red Planet. InSight launched at 4:05 a.m. PDT (7:05 a.m. EDT) Saturday from Vandenberg Air Force Base, California.

"The United States continues to lead the way to Mars with this next exciting mission to study the Red Planet's core and geological processes," said NASA Administrator Jim Bridenstine. "I want to congratulate all the teams from NASA and our international partners who made this accomplishment possible. As we continue to gain momentum in our work to send astronauts back to the Moon and on to Mars, missions like InSight are going to prove invaluable."

First reports indicate the United Launch Alliance (ULA) Atlas V rocket that carried InSight into space was seen as far south as Carlsbad, California, and as far east as Oracle, Arizona. One person recorded video of the launch from a private aircraft flying along the California coast.

Riding the Centaur second stage of the rocket, the spacecraft reached orbit 13 minutes and 16 seconds after launch. Sixty-one minutes later, the Centaur ignited a second time, sending InSight on a trajectory toward the Red Planet. InSight separated from the Centaur about 9 minutes later—93 minutes after launch—and contacted ground controllers via NASA's Deep Space Network at 5:41 a.m. PDT (8:41 a.m. EDT).

"The Kennedy Space Center and ULA teams gave us a great ride today and started InSight on our six-and-a-half-month journey to Mars," said Tom Hoffman, InSight project manager at NASA's Jet Propulsion Laboratory in Pasadena, California. "We've received positive indication the InSight spacecraft is in good health and we are all excited to be going to Mars once again to do groundbreaking science."

With its successful launch, NASA's InSight team now is focusing on the six-month voyage. During the cruise phase of the mission, engineers will check out the spacecraft's subsystems and science instruments, making sure its solar arrays and antenna are oriented properly, tracking its trajectory and performing maneuvers to keep it on course.

InSight is scheduled to land on the Red Planet around 3 p.m. EST (noon PST) Nov. 26, where it will conduct science operations until Nov. 24, 2020, which equates to one year and 40 days on Mars, or nearly two Earth years.

"Scientists have been dreaming about doing seismology on Mars for years. In my case, I had that dream 40 years ago as a graduate student, and now that shared dream has been lofted through the clouds and into reality," said Bruce Banerdt, InSight principal investigator at JPL.

The InSight lander will probe and collect data on marsquakes, heat flow from the planet's interior and the way the planet wobbles, to help scientists understand what makes Mars tick and the processes that shaped the four rocky planets of our inner solar system.

"InSight will not only teach us about Mars, it will enhance our understanding of formation of other rocky worlds like Earth and the Moon, and thousands of planets around other stars," said Thomas Zurbuchen, associate administrator for NASA's Science Mission Directorate at the agency headquarters in Washington. "InSight connects science and technology with a diverse team of JPL-led international and commercial partners."

Previous missions to Mars investigated the surface history of the Red Planet by examining features like canyons, volcanoes, rocks and soil, but no one has attempted to investigate the planet's earliest evolution, which can only be found by looking far below the surface.

"InSight will help us unlock the mysteries of Mars in a new way, by not just studying the surface of the planet, but by looking deep inside to help us learn about the earliest building blocks of the planet," said JPL Director Michael Watkins.

JPL manages InSight for NASA's Science Mission Directorate. InSight is part of NASA's Discovery Program, managed by the agency's Marshall Space Flight Center in Huntsville, Alabama. The InSight spacecraft, including cruise stage and lander, was built and tested by Lockheed Martin Space in Denver. NASA's Launch Services Program at the agency's Kennedy Space Center in Florida is responsible for launch service acquisition, integration, analysis, and launch management. United Launch Alliance of Centennial, Colorado, is NASA's launch service provider.

A number of European partners, including France's Centre National d'Études Spatiales (CNES) and the German Aerospace Center (DLR), are supporting the InSight mission. CNES provided the Seismic Experiment for Interior Structure (SEIS) instrument, with significant contributions from the Max Planck Institute for Solar System Research (MPS) in Göttingen, Germany. DLR provided the Heat Flow and Physical Properties Package (HP3) instrument.

For more information about InSight, and to follow along on its flight to Mars, visit: https://www.nasa.gov/insight.

SOURCE: NASA Jet Propulsion Laboratory. "NASA, ULA Launch Mission to Study How Mars Was Made." May 5, 2018. https://www.jpl.nasa.gov/news/news.php?feature=7114.

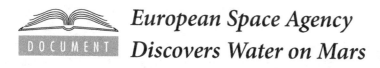

# European Space Agency Discovers Water on Mars

**July 25, 2018**

Radar data collected by ESA's Mars Express point to a pond of liquid water buried under layers of ice and dust in the south polar region of Mars.

Evidence for the Red Planet's watery past is prevalent across its surface in the form of vast dried-out river valley networks and gigantic outflow channels clearly imaged by orbiting spacecraft. Orbiters, together with landers and rovers exploring the martian surface, also discovered minerals that can only form in the presence of liquid water.

But the climate has changed significantly over the course of the planet's 4.6 billion year history and liquid water cannot exist on the surface today, so scientists are looking underground. Early results from the 15-year-old Mars Express spacecraft already found that water-ice exists at the planet's poles and is also buried in layers interspersed with dust.

The presence of liquid water at the base of the polar ice caps has long been suspected; after all, from studies on Earth, it is well known that the melting point of water decreases under the pressure of an overlying glacier. Moreover, the presence of salts on Mars could further reduce the melting point of water and keep the water liquid even at below-freezing temperatures.

But until now evidence from the Mars Advanced Radar for Subsurface and Ionosphere Sounding instrument, MARSIS, the first radar sounder ever to orbit another planet, remained inconclusive.

It has taken the persistence of scientists working with this subsurface-probing instrument to develop new techniques in order to collect as much high-resolution data as possible to confirm their exciting conclusion.

Ground-penetrating radar uses the method of sending radar pulses towards the surface and timing how long it takes for them to be reflected back to the spacecraft, and with what strength. The properties of the material that lies between influences the returned signal, which can be used to map the subsurface topography.

The radar investigation shows that south polar region of Mars is made of many layers of ice and dust down to a depth of about 1.5 km in the 200 km-wide area analysed in this study. A particularly bright radar reflection underneath the layered deposits is identified within a 20 km-wide zone.

Analysing the properties of the reflected radar signals and considering the composition of the layered deposits and expected temperature profile below the surface, the scientists interpret the bright feature as an interface between the ice and a stable body of liquid water, which could be laden with salty, saturated sediments. For MARSIS to be able to detect such a patch of water, it would need to be at least several tens of centimetres thick.

"This subsurface anomaly on Mars has radar properties matching water or water-rich sediments," says Roberto Orosei, principal investigator of the MARSIS experiment and lead author of the paper published in the journal *Science* today.

"This is just one small study area; it is an exciting prospect to think there could be more of these underground pockets of water elsewhere, yet to be discovered."

"We'd seen hints of interesting subsurface features for years but we couldn't reproduce the result from orbit to orbit, because the sampling rates and resolution of our data was previously too low," adds Andrea Cicchetti, MARSIS operations manager and a co-author on the new paper.

"We had to come up with a new operating mode to bypass some onboard processing and trigger a higher sampling rate and thus improve the resolution of the footprint of our dataset: now we see things that simply were not possible before."

The finding is somewhat reminiscent of Lake Vostok, discovered some 4 km below the ice in Antarctica on Earth. Some forms of microbial life are known to thrive in Earth's subglacial environments, but could underground pockets of salty, sediment-rich liquid water on Mars also provide a suitable habitat, either now or in the past? Whether life has ever existed on Mars remains an open question, and is one that Mars missions, including the current European-Russian ExoMars orbiter and future rover, will continue to explore.

"The long duration of Mars Express, and the exhausting effort made by the radar team to overcome many analytical challenges, enabled this much-awaited result, demonstrating that the mission and its payload still have a great science potential," says Dmitri Titov, ESA's Mars Express project scientist.

"This thrilling discovery is a highlight for planetary science and will contribute to our understanding of the evolution of Mars, the history of water on our neighbour planet and its habitability."

Mars Express launched 2 June 2003 and celebrates 15 years in orbit on 25 December this year.

SOURCE: European Space Agency. "Mars Express Detects Liquid Water Hidden under Planet's South Pole." July 25, 2018. https://www.esa.int/Our_Activities/Space_Science/Mars_Express/Mars_Express_detects_liquid_water_hidden_under_planet_s_south_pole.

## OTHER HISTORIC DOCUMENTS OF INTEREST

### FROM PREVIOUS *HISTORIC DOCUMENTS*

- NASA, SpaceX Announce Milestones in Space Exploration; Congress Sets Timeline for Mission to Mars, *2017*, p. 128
- NASA Announces Milestones in Human Spaceflight and Space Exploration, *2016*, p. 150
- NASA Announces Successful Orbiting of Dwarf Planet, *2015*, p. 120
- New Horizons Spacecraft Reaches Pluto, *2015*, p. 384
- NASA's *Voyager 1* Reaches Interstellar Space, *2013*, p. 423

# President Trump and European Leaders on Decision to Remove the U.S. from the Iran Nuclear Deal

MAY 8, 2018

As a presidential candidate, Donald Trump repeatedly denounced the Joint Comprehensive Plan of Action (JCPOA), a multilateral nuclear deal with Iran. Under that 2015 agreement, Iran accepted a variety of restrictions on its nuclear program in return for the lifting of national and international sanctions. Critics of the deal, including Trump, argued that it did not put an effective, permanent brake on Iran's capacity to develop nuclear weapons. After taking office in January 2017, Trump continued to criticize the deal but did not immediately pull the United States out of it. While signaling that he was moving toward withdrawal, he did not take the steps that would cut off the agreement's economic benefits to Iran. That changed in May 2018, when Trump announced that he was removing the United States from the deal and putting back in place the U.S. sanctions that had been lifted.

## JCPOA Takes Shape, Faces Criticism

On July 14, 2015, Iran and a group of six other countries—China, France, Germany, Russia, the United Kingdom, and the United States—agreed to a document known as the JCPOA. In return for the lifting of nuclear-related sanctions imposed by the European Union, the United Nations, and the United States, Iran agreed to limit certain aspects of its nuclear program and allow more intrusive monitoring. For example, one key provision of the JCPOA is that the level of uranium enrichment cannot exceed 3.67 percent uranium-235 for fifteen years. (Uranium-235 is the uranium isotope used in both nuclear power reactors and nuclear weapons. Uranium at an enrichment level of 3.67 percent is usable in reactors but not weapons. Enrichment is the process for increasing the concentration of uranium-235.) The agreement also sets a ceiling of 300 kilograms for Iran's stockpile of enriched uranium and restricts the number and type of centrifuges—machines used in the preferred process for uranium enrichment—it can build and operate.

Under a U.S. law passed in the run-up to the July 2015 signing of the JCPOA, the president is required to make certain periodic certifications to Congress related to Iran's compliance with the accord and the value of the deal to U.S. national security. Trump made that certification every ninety days until October 2017. The October decision to "decertify" did not pull the United States out of the deal, but it signaled Trump's decreasing willingness to tolerate it. In October 13, 2017, remarks, Trump announced, "I am directing my administration to work closely with Congress and our allies to address the deal's many serious flaws so that the Iranian regime can never threaten the world with nuclear weapons." He warned that "in the event we are not able to reach a solution working with Congress and our allies, then the agreement will be terminated."

The congressionally required certification encompasses more than Iranian compliance with the terms of the JCPOA. Trump's decision to withhold certification was based on his assessment of U.S. national security interests, not Iranian compliance with the deal. The International Atomic Energy Agency (IAEA), the Vienna-based organization charged with monitoring Iran's performance under the JCPOA, issues quarterly reports on its inspections and has not found any substantial violations of the agreement. Similarly, the 2018 edition of the State Department's annual report on compliance with arms-control and nonproliferation agreements said, "At the end of December 2017, Iran continued to fulfill its nuclear-related commitments under the Joint Comprehensive Plan of Action."

Although the decertification announcement did not withdraw the United States from the JCPOA, it did start a sixty-day clock under which Congress could end U.S. participation in the deal and reimpose sanctions on an expedited basis. Congress did not act within the allotted time. In January 2018, Trump again declined to make the certification and issued a warning similar to that from October, saying it was "a last chance" to avoid U.S. withdrawal from the deal.

## Trump Announces JCPOA Withdrawal

On May 8, President Trump announced the United States was pulling out of the Iran deal. In a national security presidential memorandum, he said the "understanding to fix the JCPOA" that he had demanded "has not materialized." In the memorandum and in accompanying remarks made during the signing ceremony, Trump cited not only the shortcomings he said were in the agreement itself but also Iran's program to develop ballistic missiles and its support for "destabilizing activities" in the Middle East. In his remarks, Trump declared, "Since the agreement, Iran's bloody ambitions have grown only more brazen." He noted, "I do not believe that continuing to provide JCPOA-related sanctions relief to Iran is in the national interest of the United States, and I will not affirm what I know to be false." Trump said in the memorandum that he was "open to consultations with allies and partners on future international agreements to counter the full range of Iran's threats," but the administration had made clear that the bar for any such agreement is very high.

A detailed description of the Trump administration's approach to Iran came in remarks that Secretary of State Mike Pompeo delivered at the Heritage Foundation on May 21. Pompeo listed a dozen elements that the administration was demanding as part of a new agreement. On the nuclear side, one requirement was that Iran "stop enrichment" of uranium—a constraint considerably tighter than the one in the JCPOA. Beyond the nuclear program, Pompeo said that "Iran must end its proliferation of ballistic missiles and halt further launching or development of nuclear-capable missile systems," "withdraw all forces under Iranian command throughout the entirety of Syria," and "end its threatening behavior against its neighbors—many of whom are U.S. allies." Pompeo acknowledged that the "list is pretty long," but argued, "The length of the list is simply a scope of the malign behavior of Iran. We didn't create the list, they did." Many analysts, however, said Pompeo's required elements for a deal were unrealistic.

## U.S. Decision Assailed

The other parties to the JCPOA sharply criticized the U.S. decision to withdraw. In a joint press release on May 8, the day the decision was announced, the leaders of the three European countries party to the agreement—French President Emmanuel Macron, UK Prime Minister Theresa May, and German Chancellor Angela Merkel—emphasized their "continuing commitment to the JCPoA" and directly addressed some of the Trump administration's key arguments for leaving.

The three leaders said the deal "remains important for our shared security" and noted that the IAEA has found that Iran is complying with its obligations under the JCPOA and the Nuclear Non-Proliferation Treaty. "The world is a safer place as a result," they said. They also acknowledged and responded to the Trump administration's argument that there had to be an agreement restraining Iran in areas beyond its nuclear program: "Because our commitment to the security of our allies and partners in the region is unwavering, we must also address in a meaningful way shared concerns about Iran's ballistic missile programme and its destabilising regional activities, especially in Syria, Iraq and Yemen. We have already started constructive and mutually beneficial discussions on these issues."

The statement noted that the UN Security Council had endorsed the JCPOA in resolution 2231, adopted on July 20, 2015. That resolution "remains the binding international legal framework for the resolution of the dispute about the Iranian nuclear programme. We urge all sides to remain committed to its full implementation and to act in a spirit of responsibility," the leaders said, suggesting that they considered the United States to be violating an international legal obligation by withdrawing from the JCPOA. In their statement, the three European leaders urged "the US to ensure that the structures of the JCPoA can remain intact, and to avoid taking action which obstructs its full implementation by all other parties to the deal." At the same time, the leaders encouraged "Iran to show restraint in response to the decision by the US; Iran must continue to meet its own obligations under the deal, cooperating fully and in a timely manner with IAEA inspection requirements."

In a statement from its foreign ministry, Russia declared that the JCPOA "does not belong to the United States alone but is a domain of the entire international community." Moscow said it "is open to further cooperation with the other JCPOA participants and will continue to actively develop bilateral collaboration and political dialogue with the Islamic Republic of Iran."

For its part, Iran took a two-pronged approach to the withdrawal. Iran's semiofficial Fars News Agency described the country's president, Hassan Rouhani, as saying that Iran would remain in the deal because it serves the country's national interests. But he also signaled a willingness to resume the nuclear activities suspended under the JCPOA if the other remaining parties to the deal did not provide the economic benefits that Iran was promised in return for the restrictions on its nuclear program.

## EU Parries on Sanctions

The JCPOA had lifted sanctions that the United States, the European Union, and the United Nations had imposed on Iran over its nuclear program. Trump's May 8 action reinstated only the U.S. measures, but they have a large impact on countries in the European Union and elsewhere because they include so-called secondary sanctions. Such sanctions penalize businesses and banks in third countries that trade with the country that is the object of the sanctions. In this case, that meant a foreign entity that trades with Iran is subject to U.S. penalties, potentially including a ban on trade with the United States or a cutoff from the U.S. financial system.

The European Union responded by updating a "blocking statute" that had originally been proposed in 1996 to counter the U.S. embargo on Cuba and sanctions on Iran and Libya. As the European body described it, the revised statute "allows EU operators to recover damages arising from US extraterritorial sanctions from the persons causing them and nullifies the effect in the EU of any foreign court rulings based on them. It also forbids EU persons from complying with those sanctions, unless exceptionally authorized to do so by the [European] Commission in case non-compliance seriously damages their interests or the interests of the Union."

The EU also began working to set up a so-called special-purpose vehicle (SPV), a legal mechanism that would allow European companies to trade with Iran without making monetary transfers in dollars. In effect, it would operate as a barter system, but with a credit account. It was anticipated that the SPV would be formally established in January 2019.

For many multinational companies that do business in the United States, the EU actions were not enough to offset the risk of U.S. sanctions penalties. Dozens of companies have pulled back from ongoing or planned projects with Iran. In a June 12 speech to the European parliament, EU foreign policy chief Federica Mogherini said the EU actions had "a strong focus" on small and medium-sized enterprises, which are "less engaged" with the U.S. market. The EU blocking statute went into effect on August 6, to coincide with the return of a number of key U.S. sanctions, following a ninety-day "wind-down" period after the May 8 announcement.

Other major sanctions, including those on imports of Iranian oil, came into effect November 5 after a 180-day wind-down. Rouhani vowed that Iran would "proudly break the sanctions." The relevant U.S. sanctions law allows the president to grant exceptions from the oil ban to recipients of Iranian oil if they are making a "significant reduction" in their purchases. On November 5, the Trump administration granted this exception to eight countries—China, Greece, India, Italy, Japan, South Korea, Taiwan, and Turkey. To continue receiving the exemption, the countries have to be certified every 180 days as continuing to make reductions. China, in addition to being a signatory of the JCPOA, is Iran's largest oil customer.

—Daniel Horner

*Following is a memorandum and accompanying statement issued by President Donald Trump on May 8, 2018, ending the United States' participation in the Joint Comprehensive Plan of Action on Iran; and a May 8, 2018, statement from the leaders of France, Germany, and the United Kingdom on the U.S. withdrawal decision.*

# *President Trump Speaks on Decisions on Iran*

**May 8, 2018**

*The President.* My fellow Americans: Today I want to update the world on our efforts to prevent Iran from acquiring a nuclear weapon.

The Iranian regime is the leading state sponsor of terror. It exports dangerous missiles, fuels conflicts across the Middle East, and supports terrorist proxies and militias such as Hizballah, Hamas, the Taliban, and Al Qaida. Over the years, Iran and its proxies have bombed American Embassies and military installations, murdered hundreds of American servicemembers, and kidnapped, imprisoned, and tortured American citizens.

The Iranian regime has funded its long reign of chaos and terror by plundering the wealth of its own people. No action taken by the regime has been more dangerous than its pursuit of nuclear weapons and the means of delivering them. In 2015, the previous administration joined with other nations in a deal regarding Iran's nuclear program. This agreement was known as the Joint Comprehensive Plan of Action, or JCPOA.

In theory, the so-called Iran deal was supposed to protect the United States and our allies from the lunacy of an Iranian nuclear bomb, a weapon that will only endanger the survival of the Iranian regime. In fact, the deal allowed Iran to continue enriching uranium and, over time, reach the brink of a nuclear breakout. The deal lifted crippling economic sanctions on Iran in exchange for very weak limits on the regime's nuclear activity and no limits at all on its other malign behavior, including its sinister activities in Syria, Yemen, and other places all around the world.

In other words, at the point when the United States had maximum leverage, this disastrous deal gave this regime—and it's a regime of great terror—many billions of dollars, some of it in actual cash, a great embarrassment to me as a citizen and to all citizens of the United States. A constructive deal could easily have been struck at the time, but it wasn't. At the heart of the Iran deal was a giant fiction that a murderous regime desired only a peaceful nuclear energy program.

Today, we have definitive proof that this Iranian promise was a lie. Last week, Israel published intelligence documents long concealed by Iran, conclusively showing the Iranians' regime and its history of pursuing nuclear weapons. The fact is this was a horrible, one-sided deal that should have never, ever been made. It didn't bring calm, it didn't bring peace, and it never will.

In the years since the deal was reached, Iran's military budget has grown by almost 40 percent, while its economy is doing very badly. After the sanctions were lifted, the dictatorship used its new funds to build nuclear-capable missiles, support terrorism, and cause havoc throughout the Middle East and beyond. The agreement was so poorly negotiated that even if Iran fully complies, the regime can still be on the verge of a nuclear breakout in just a short period of time. The deal's sunset provisions are totally unacceptable.

If I allowed this deal to stand, there would soon be a nuclear arms race in the Middle East. Everyone would want their weapons ready by the time Iran had theirs. Making matters worse, the deal's inspection provisions lack adequate mechanisms to prevent, detect, and punish cheating and don't even have the unqualified right to inspect many important locations, including military facilities. Not only does the deal fail to halt Iran's nuclear ambitions, but it also fails to address the regime's development of ballistic missiles that could deliver nuclear warheads.

Finally, the deal does nothing to constrain Iran's destabilizing activities, including its support for terrorism. Since the agreement, Iran's bloody ambitions have grown only more brazen. In light of these glaring flaws, I announced last October that the Iran deal must either be renegotiated or terminated. Three months later, on January 12, I repeated these conditions. I made clear that if the deal could not be fixed, the United States would no longer be a party to the agreement.

Over the past few months, we have engaged extensively with our allies and partners around the world, including France, Germany, and the United Kingdom. We have also consulted with our friends from across the Middle East. We are unified in our understanding of the threat and in our conviction that Iran must never acquire a nuclear weapon.

After these consultations, it is clear to me that we cannot prevent an Iranian nuclear bomb under the decaying and rotten structure of the current agreement. The Iran deal is defective at its core. If we do nothing, we know exactly what will happen. In just a short period of time, the world's leading state sponsor of terror will be on the cusp of acquiring the world's most dangerous weapons.

Therefore, I am announcing today that the United States will withdraw from the Iran nuclear deal. In a few moments, I will sign a Presidential memorandum to begin reinstating U.S. nuclear sanctions on the Iranian regime. We will be instituting the highest level of economic sanction. Any nation that helps Iran in its quest for nuclear weapons could also be strongly sanctioned by the United States.

America will not be held hostage to nuclear blackmail. We will not allow American cities to be threatened with destruction. And we will not allow a regime that chants "Death to America" to gain access to the most deadly weapons on Earth.

Today's action sends a critical message: The United States no longer makes empty threats. When I make promises, I keep them. In fact, at this very moment, Secretary Pompeo is on his way to North Korea in preparation for my upcoming meeting with Kim Jong Un. Plans are being made. Relationships are building. Hopefully, a deal will happen and, with the help of China, South Korea, and Japan, a future of great prosperity and security can be achieved for everyone.

As we exit the Iran deal, we will be working with our allies to find a real, comprehensive, and lasting solution to the Iranian nuclear threat. This will include efforts to eliminate the threat of Iran's ballistic missile program, to stop its terrorist activities worldwide, and to block its menacing activity across the Middle East. In the meantime, powerful sanctions will go into full effect. If the regime continues its nuclear aspirations, it will have bigger problems than it has ever had before.

Finally, I want to deliver a message to the long-suffering people of Iran: The people of America stand with you. It has now been almost 40 years since this dictatorship seized power and took a proud nation hostage. Most of Iran's 80 million citizens have sadly never known an Iran that prospered in peace with its neighbors and commanded the admiration of the world.

But the future of Iran belongs to its people. They are the rightful heirs to a rich culture and an ancient land. And they deserve a nation that does justice to their dreams, honor to their history, and glory to God.

Iran's leaders will naturally say that they refuse to negotiate a new deal; they refuse. And that's fine. I'd probably say the same thing if I was in their position. But the fact is, they are going to want to make a new and lasting deal, one that benefits all of Iran and the Iranian people. When they do, I am ready, willing, and able.

Great things can happen for Iran, and great things can happen for the peace and stability that we all want in the Middle East. There has been enough suffering, death, and destruction. Let it end now.

Thank you. God bless you. Thank you.

*[A brief Q&A with reports on matters related to Iran and North Korea has been omitted.]*

SOURCE: Executive Office of the President. "Remarks on the Joint Comprehensive Plan of Action to Prevent Iran from Obtaining a Nuclear Weapon and an Exchange with Reporters." May 8, 2018. *Compilation of Presidential Documents* 2018, no. 00310 (May 8, 2018). https://www.gpo.gov/fdsys/pkg/DCPD-201800310/pdf/DCPD-201800310.pdf.

# President Trump Issues Memo
# Pulling U.S. out of JCPOA

**May 8, 2018**

National Security Presidential Memorandum/NSPM–11

*Memorandum for the Secretary of State, the Secretary of the Treasury, the Secretary of Defense, the Attorney General, the Secretary of Energy, the Secretary of Homeland Security, the Assistant to the President and Chief of Staff, the United States Trade Representative, the United States Permanent Representative to the United Nations, the Director of National Intelligence, the Director of the Central Intelligence Agency, the Assistant to the President for National Security Affairs, the Counsel to the President, the Assistant to the President for Economic Policy, the Chairman of the Joint Chiefs of Staff, and the Director of the Federal Bureau of Investigation*

*Subject*: Ceasing United States Participation in the Joint Comprehensive Plan of Action and Taking Additional Action to Counter Iran's Malign Influence and Deny Iran All Paths to a Nuclear Weapon

As President, my highest priority is to ensure the safety and security of the United States and the American people. Since its inception in 1979 as a revolutionary theocracy, the Islamic Republic of Iran has declared its hostility to the United States and its allies and partners. Iran remains the world's leading state sponsor of terrorism, and provides assistance to Hezbollah, Hamas, the Taliban, al-Qa'ida, and other terrorist networks. Iran also continues to fuel sectarian violence in Iraq, and support vicious civil wars in Yemen and Syria. It commits grievous human rights abuses, and arbitrarily detains foreigners, including United States citizens, on spurious charges without due process of law.

There is no doubt that Iran previously attempted to bolster its revolutionary aims through the pursuit of nuclear weapons and that Iran's uranium enrichment program continues to give it the capability to reconstitute its weapons-grade uranium program if it so chooses. As President, I have approved an integrated strategy for Iran that includes the strategic objective of denying Iran all paths to a nuclear weapon.

The preceding administration attempted to meet the threat of Iran's pursuit of nuclear capabilities through United States participation in the Joint Comprehensive Plan of Action (JCPOA) on Iran's nuclear program. The JCPOA lifted nuclear-related sanctions on Iran and provided it with other significant benefits in exchange for its temporary commitments to constrain its uranium enrichment program and to not conduct work related to nuclear fuel reprocessing, the two critical pathways to acquiring weapons-grade nuclear material. Some believed the JCPOA would moderate Iran's behavior. Since the JCPOA's inception, however, Iran has only escalated its destabilizing activities in the surrounding region. Iranian or Iran-backed forces have gone on the march in Syria, Iraq, and Yemen, and continue to control parts of Lebanon and Gaza. Meanwhile, Iran has publicly declared it would deny the International Atomic Energy Agency (IAEA) access to military sites in direct conflict with the Additional Protocol to its Comprehensive Safeguards Agreement with the IAEA. In 2016, Iran also twice violated the JCPOA's heavy water stockpile limits. This behavior is unacceptable, especially for a regime known to have pursued nuclear weapons in violation of its obligations under the Treaty on the Non-Proliferation of Nuclear Weapons.

Iran's behavior threatens the national interest of the United States. On October 13, 2017, consistent with certification procedures stipulated in the Iran Nuclear Agreement Review Act, I determined that I was unable to certify that the suspension of sanctions related to Iran pursuant to the JCPOA was appropriate and proportionate to the specific and verifiable measures taken by Iran with respect to terminating its illicit nuclear program. On January 12, 2018, I outlined two possible paths forward—the JCPOA's disastrous flaws would be fixed by May 12, 2018, or, failing that, the United States would cease participation in the agreement. I made clear that this was a last chance, and that absent an understanding to fix the JCPOA, the United States would not continue to implement it.

That understanding has not materialized, and I am today making good on my pledge to end the participation of the United States in the JCPOA. I do not believe that continuing to provide JCPOA-related sanctions relief to Iran is in the national interest of the United States, and I will not affirm what I know to be false. Further, I have determined that it is in the national interest of the United States to re-impose sanctions lifted or waived in connection with the JCPOA as expeditiously as possible.

*Section 1. Policy.* It is the policy of the United States that Iran be denied a nuclear weapon and intercontinental ballistic missiles; that Iran's network and campaign of regional aggression be neutralized; to disrupt, degrade, or deny the Islamic Revolutionary Guards Corps and its surrogates access to the resources that sustain their destabilizing activities; and to counter Iran's aggressive development of missiles and other asymmetric and conventional weapons capabilities. The United States will continue to pursue these aims and the objectives contained in the Iran strategy that I announced on October 13, 2017, adjusting the ways and means to achieve them as required.

*Sec. 2. Ending United States Participation in the JCPOA.* The Secretary of State shall, in consultation with the Secretary of the Treasury and the Secretary of Energy, take all appropriate steps to cease the participation of the United States in the JCPOA.

*Sec. 3. Restoring United States Sanctions.* The Secretary of State and the Secretary of the Treasury shall immediately begin taking steps to re-impose all United States sanctions lifted or waived in connection with the JCPOA, including those under the National Defense Authorization Act for Fiscal Year 2012, the Iran Sanctions Act of 1996, the Iran Threat Reduction and Syria Human Rights Act of 2012, and the Iran Freedom and Counter-proliferation Act of 2012. These steps shall be accomplished as expeditiously as possible, and in no case later than 180 days from the date of this memorandum. The Secretary of State and the Secretary of the Treasury shall coordinate, as appropriate, on steps needed to achieve this aim. They shall, for example, coordinate with respect to preparing any recommended executive actions, including appropriate documents to re-impose sanctions lifted by Executive Order 13716 of January 16, 2016; preparing to re-list persons removed, in connection with the JCPOA, from any relevant sanctions lists, as appropriate; revising relevant sanctions regulations; issuing limited waivers during the wind-down period, as appropriate; and preparing guidance necessary to educate United States and non-United States business communities on the scope of prohibited and sanctionable activity and the need to unwind any such dealings with Iranian persons. Those steps should be accomplished in a manner that, to the extent reasonably practicable, shifts the financial burden of unwinding any transaction or course of dealing primarily onto Iran or the Iranian counterparty.

*Sec. 4. Preparing for Regional Contingencies.* The Secretary of Defense and heads of any other relevant agencies shall prepare to meet, swiftly and decisively, all possible modes of

Iranian aggression against the United States, our allies, and our partners. The Department of Defense shall ensure that the United States develops and retains the means to stop Iran from developing or acquiring a nuclear weapon and related delivery systems.

*Sec. 5. Monitoring Iran's Nuclear Conduct and Consultation with Allies and Partners.* Agencies shall take appropriate steps to enable the United States to continue to monitor Iran's nuclear conduct. I am open to consultations with allies and partners on future international agreements to counter the full range of Iran's threats, including the nuclear weapon and intercontinental ballistic missile threats, and the heads of agencies shall advise me, as appropriate, regarding opportunities for such consultations.

*Sec. 6. General Provisions.* (a) Nothing in this memorandum shall be construed to impair or otherwise affect:

(i) the authority granted by law to an executive department or agency, or the head thereof; or

(ii) the functions of the Director of the Office of Management and Budget relating to budgetary, administrative, or legislative proposals.

(b) This memorandum shall be implemented consistent with applicable law and subject to the availability of appropriations.

(c) This memorandum is not intended to, and does not, create any right or benefit, substantive or procedural, enforceable at law or in equity by any party against the United States, its departments, agencies, or entities, its officers, employees, or agents, or any other person.

DONALD J. TRUMP

SOURCE: Executive Office of the President. "National Security Presidential Memorandum on Ceasing United States Participation in the Joint Comprehensive Plan of Action and Taking Additional Action to Counter Iran's Malign Influence and Deny Iran All Paths to a Nuclear Weapon." May 8, 2018. *Compilation of Presidential Documents* 2018, no. 00311 (May 8, 2018). https://www.gpo.gov/fdsys/pkg/DCPD-201800311/pdf/DCPD-201800311.pdf.

# *European Leaders Respond to U.S. Withdrawal Decision*

**May 8, 2018**

It is with regret and concern that we, the Leaders of France, Germany and the United Kingdom take note of President Trump's decision to withdraw the United States of America from the Joint Comprehensive Plan of Action.

Together, we emphasise our continuing commitment to the JCPoA. This agreement remains important for our shared security. We recall that the JCPoA was unanimously endorsed by the UN Security Council in resolution 2231. This resolution remains the binding international legal framework for the resolution of the dispute about the Iranian nuclear programme. We urge all sides to remain committed to its full implementation and to act in a spirit of responsibility.

According to the IAEA, Iran continues to abide by the restrictions set out by the JCPoA, in line with its obligations under the Treaty on the Non-Proliferation of Nuclear Weapons. The world is a safer place as a result. Therefore we, the E3, will remain parties to the JCPoA. Our governments remain committed to ensuring the agreement is upheld, and will work with all the remaining parties to the deal to ensure this remains the case including through ensuring the continuing economic benefits to the Iranian people that are linked to the agreement.

We urge the US to ensure that the structures of the JCPoA can remain intact, and to avoid taking action which obstructs its full implementation by all other parties to the deal. After engaging with the US Administration in a thorough manner over the past months, we call on the US to do everything possible to preserve the gains for nuclear non-proliferation brought about by the JCPoA, by allowing for a continued enforcement of its main elements.

We encourage Iran to show restraint in response to the decision by the US; Iran must continue to meet its own obligations under the deal, cooperating fully and in a timely manner with IAEA inspection requirements. The IAEA must be able to continue to carry out its long-term verification and monitoring programme without restriction or hindrance. In turn, Iran should continue to receive the sanctions relief it is entitled to whilst it remains in compliance with the terms of the deal.

There must be no doubt: Iran's nuclear program must always remain peaceful and civilian. While taking the JCPOA as a base, we also agree that other major issues of concern need to be addressed. A long-term framework for Iran's nuclear programme after some of the provisions of the JCPOA expire, after 2025, will have to be defined. Because our commitment to the security of our allies and partners in the region is unwavering, we must also address in a meaningful way shared concerns about Iran's ballistic missile programme and its destabilising regional activities, especially in Syria, Iraq and Yemen. We have already started constructive and mutually beneficial discussions on these issues, and the E3 is committed to continuing them with key partners and concerned states across the region.

We and our Foreign Ministers will reach out to all parties to the JCPoA to seek a positive way forward.

SOURCE: Office of the Prime Minister of the United Kingdom. "Joint Statement from Prime Minister May, Chancellor Merkel and President Macron following President Trump's Statement on Iran." May 8, 2018. https://www.gov.uk/government/news/joint-statement-from-prime-minister-may-chancellor-merkel-and-president-macron-following-president-trumps-statement-on-iran.

## OTHER HISTORIC DOCUMENTS OF INTEREST

### FROM PREVIOUS *HISTORIC DOCUMENTS*

# U.S., Israeli Officials Remark on Embassy Move to Jerusalem; UN Responds to Gaza Violence

MAY 14 AND 18, AND JUNE 13, 2018

The United States' recognition of Jerusalem as Israel's capital and relocation of its embassy to the city remained highly controversial in 2018. While celebrated by U.S. and Israeli officials, the embassy's official opening on May 14 fueled protests by tens of thousands of Palestinians in the Gaza Strip. The Israeli military's use of force to disperse the mostly unarmed protestors drew sharp condemnations from the international community, including the United Nations (UN) General Assembly and Human Rights Council, the latter of which called for an investigation into Israel's potential violation of international law.

## U.S. Embassy Opens in Jerusalem

In December 2017, President Donald Trump broke with nearly sixty years of U.S. foreign policy precedent when he formally recognized Jerusalem as Israel's capital and announced the U.S. embassy would relocate from Tel Aviv to Jerusalem. Israel and Palestine have both laid claim to Jerusalem, which is home to some of the holiest Islamic and Jewish religious sites and is currently divided between the majority-Palestinian East and the Israel-controlled West. The international community has generally maintained that Jerusalem is occupied territory, despite Israel declaring the city its capital in 1980, and that its final status should be decided through peace negotiations between the Israelis and Palestinians. The UN Security Council has actively discouraged members from recognizing the city as Israel's capital, prompting countries that once maintained embassies in Jerusalem to move them to Tel Aviv.

The United States successfully deflected an effort by the UN Security Council to pass a resolution that would have rescinded Trump's proclamation and pushed forward with plans to move the embassy. On May 14, 2018—the day of Israel's seventieth anniversary—the former U.S. consulate in Israel officially became the U.S. embassy. President Trump did not attend the opening ceremony in person but recorded a video message in which he said the move had been "a long time coming" and that it was "plain reality" that Jerusalem was Israel's capital. He also reaffirmed the United States' commitment "to facilitating a lasting peace agreement." The president's son-in-law, Jared Kushner, who was charged with managing U.S. efforts to negotiate an Israeli–Palestinian peace deal, said the United States believes "it is possible for both sides to gain more than they give—so that all people can live in peace—safe from danger, free from fear and able to pursue their dreams." Kushner was joined at the ceremony by his wife, Ivanka Trump; U.S. Treasury Secretary Steve Mnuchin; and U.S. Ambassador to Israel David Friedman. Israeli Prime Minister Benjamin Netanyahu also spoke at the ceremony, declaring it a "glorious day" and saying that Israel had "no better friends in the world" than the United States. "We are in Jerusalem and we are here to stay," he said. That evening, during a celebration marking Israel's anniversary, Vice President Mike Pence echoed sentiments shared by the president and Kushner, declaring, "By finally recognizing Jerusalem as Israel's capital, the United States has chosen fact over fiction. And fact is the only true foundation for a just and lasting peace."

Palestinian leaders offered a very different perspective of the embassy's opening. Palestinian President Mahmoud Abbas described the embassy as "an illegal outpost," a term typically used to refer to contested Israeli settlements in the West Bank. Riyad Mansour, ambassador and permanent observer of the state of Palestine to the UN, said there was now "no chance" Palestinians would participate in U.S. efforts to procure peace.

## VIOLENCE ERUPTS ALONG GAZA BORDER

Palestinians were outraged by the change in U.S. policy and resulting embassy relocation. Immediately following Trump's 2017 announcement, Hamas and other Palestinian groups called for three days of "popular anger" across Palestinian territories and in front of U.S. embassies and consulates around the world to protest the decision. Protests broke out in the West Bank and Gaza Strip, with demonstrators burning U.S. and Israeli flags along with pictures of Trump and Netanyahu. More than 100 people were injured when Israeli security forces attempted to disperse the crowds using tear gas and stun grenades.

On March 30, 2018, Palestinians began a six-week series of demonstrations, dubbed "the Great March of Return" by organizers, to protest the embassy's relocation and Israel's economic blockade of the Gaza Strip and demand that Palestinian refugees be allowed to return to the land in Israel from which they had been displaced. The protests were mostly peaceful, though some Palestinians reportedly threw gasoline bombs or rolled burning tires at Israeli soldiers. On the day of the embassy opening in Jerusalem, Palestinians once again gathered at the Gaza border fence to protest. Israeli military officials estimated that at least 40,000 protestors demonstrated at thirteen different locations along the fence. The military claimed that some protestors detonated explosives and flew burning kites over the fence to start fires, but most reports from the border indicated that protestors were largely unarmed except for those who threw stones at Israeli soldiers. Israeli security forces used drones to drop pamphlets urging protestors to move back from the fence; drones also dropped tear gas to try and disperse protestors. Various reports indicated that some protestors tried to break through the fence, prompting Israeli soldiers to open fire on the crowds.

Protests also took place in the West Bank but were much more subdued. Palestinians demonstrated in cities including Hebron and Nablus, and a group of protestors marched from Ramallah toward the Qalandiya checkpoint into Jerusalem. Some in this group threw rocks and Molotov cocktails at Israeli soldiers, who responded by firing tear gas and rubber bullets into the crowd.

According to the Palestinian Health Ministry in Gaza, fifty-eight Palestinians were killed and more than 2,700 were injured in the clashes with Israeli forces. The dead included some children, and roughly 1,300 of the wounded had been injured by gunfire, the ministry said. No Israeli soldiers were injured. The number of casualties made it the bloodiest single day since Israel invaded Gaza in 2014. Abbas said the killings were a "massacre" and called on the international community to intervene immediately to help the Palestinian people. Lt. Col. Jonathan Conricus, a spokesman for the Israel Defense Forces, defended the military's actions against an "unprecedented level of violence" in Gaza, blaming Hamas for Palestinian casualties. "Hamas is killing Gaza," he said. "We, on the other hand, are defending our homes." Conricus added, "Whatever comes close to the fence are rioters, with one purpose, of crossing the fence—nothing else." Raj Shah, the White House's deputy press secretary, declared that "the responsibility for these tragic deaths rests squarely with Hamas," adding, "Hamas is intentionally and cynically provoking this response and as the secretary of state said, Israel has a right to defend itself." Senior Hamas official Khalil al-Hayya said the protests would continue "until the occupation leaves forever."

## THE UN RESPONDS

The international community was mostly critical of Israel's handling of the protests in Gaza. Saudi Arabia strongly condemned Israel's use of force against Palestinian civilians, while Queen Rania of Jordan said it was "a dark and sad day in history, marked with more Palestinian sacrifices." Alistair Burt, the United Kingdom's Minister of State for the Middle East, said that his government would "not waiver from our support for Israel's right to defend its borders. But the large volume of live fire is extremely concerning," adding that Israel needed to "show greater restraint." South Africa recalled its envoy from Tel Aviv, and Turkey pulled its ambassadors from its embassies in Washington, D.C., and Tel Aviv. B'Tselem, an Israeli human rights group, was also among the government's critics. "The fact that live gunfire is once again the sole measure that the Israeli military is using in the field evinces appalling indifference towards human life on the part of senior Israeli government and military officials," the group said in a statement.

UN officials expressed their concern over the clashes as well. A spokesperson for UN Secretary-General António Guterres said he was "profoundly alarmed by the sharp escalation of violence in the occupied Palestinian territory and the high number of Palestinians killed and injured in the Gaza protests." He added that Israeli security forces "must exercise maximum restraint in the use of live fire" and "Hamas and the leaders of the demonstrations have a responsibility to prevent all violent actions and provocations."

On May 18, the UN Human Rights Council approved a resolution condemning "the disproportionate and indiscriminate use of force by the Israeli occupying forces against Palestinian civilians." The group called for the formation of an independent, international commission, to be appointed by the council's president, to investigate "all alleged violations and abuses of international humanitarian law and international human rights law in the Occupied Palestinian Territory." The council said the investigation should, among other things, determine whether any violations of international law amounted to war crimes, and the commission should recommend "accountability measures" including "criminal and command responsibility" for identified violations. The council further demanded that Israel "immediately and fully end its illegal closure of the occupied Gaza Strip," including by resuming the flow of humanitarian aid and commercial goods, and called for the government to cooperate with the commission's investigation.

About a month later, on June 13, the UN General Assembly held an emergency meeting at which it adopted a resolution "deploring the use of excessive, disproportionate and indiscriminate force by Israeli forces against Palestinian civilians." The resolution was approved by a vote of 120–8, with forty-five members abstaining. It demanded that Israel fully comply with its legal obligations under the Fourth Geneva Convention on the protection of civilians in wartime and called for immediate action to implement a "durable and fully respected ceasefire." The resolution also asked Guterres to come up with proposals for ways to ensure Palestinians' safety. Before voting to approve the resolution, assembly members rejected a U.S.-proposed amendment that would have condemned Hamas for inciting violence and called for the organization to cease all violent activity.

Mansour applauded the resolution, stating that Palestine "cannot remain silent in the face of the most violent crimes and human rights violations being systematically perpetrated against our people." Israeli representative Danny Ben Yosef Danon spoke in opposition to the resolution, claiming that the assembly was "colluding with a terrorist organization and empowering Hamas" with its passage.

## U.S. Aid to Palestine Cut

On August 24, the U.S. State Department announced that unspent FY 2017 funds that had been earmarked for aid to Palestine would be redirected to "high-priority projects elsewhere." The move effectively cut more than $200 million in Palestinian aid, including money that had been set aside to address the humanitarian crisis in the Gaza Strip.

The administration froze Palestinian aid earlier in the year after the Palestinian National Authority objected to the United States' recognition of Jerusalem as Israel's capital. Trump had also publicly questioned on Twitter why Palestinians continued to receive "HUNDREDS OF MILLIONS OF DOLLARS a year" in aid without showing any "appreciation or respect." State Department officials noted that Hamas's control of the Gaza Strip was another factor in the administration's decision and said they would review whether continuing to provide aid to Palestinians was beneficial to U.S. taxpayers and the country's national interests. In addition, officials had announced in January that the United States would withhold roughly half of the $125 million that had been budgeted for the United Nations Relief Works Agency (UNRWA), claiming that the organization was perpetuating the Palestinian refugee crisis. UNRWA provides food, education, and health care to Palestinian refugees.

Aid groups said the cuts would force them to lay off staff and discontinue programs that provided assistance such as food vouchers and health care subsidies to poor Palestinians. Critics of the move accused the United States of leveraging critical humanitarian aid to force Palestinians to participate in peace talks and accept a U.S.-brokered peace deal. "The U.S. administration is demonstrating the use of cheap blackmail as a political tool," said Hanan Ashrawi, a Palestinian lawmaker and activist. "The Palestinian people and leadership will not be intimidated and will not succumb to coercion." J Street, a liberal pro-Israel group, said the aid cut was a "moral outrage and a major strategic blunder."

Several days later, the Trump administration announced it was cutting all funding for UNRWA. "The United States will no longer commit further funding to this irredeemably flawed operation," explained the State Department in a statement, adding that the United States was not willing to "shoulder the very disproportionate burden" for UNRWA, which is funded entirely by voluntary donations from UN member states. Then in September, administration officials barred the Conflict Management and Mitigation Program from using its remaining $10 million in funds to support efforts benefiting Palestinians. The program has provided millions of dollars in grants to initiatives that build relationships between Israelis and Palestinians, particularly youth exchange programs. This decision cut off the last remaining source of U.S. aid to Palestinians.

—Linda Grimm

*Following are remarks by Israeli Prime Minister Benjamin Netanyahu on May 14, 2018, at the U.S. embassy opening in Jerusalem; remarks by U.S. Vice President Mike Pence on May 14, 2018, at a celebration of Israel's seventieth anniversary; a*

*UN Human Rights Council resolution approved on May 18, 2018, creating a commission to investigate potential violations of international law by Israel; and a press release issued by the UN on June 13, 2018, announcing the General Assembly's passage of a resolution condemning Israel's use of force and calling for protections for Palestinians.*

## *Prime Minister Netanyahu's Remarks on the U.S. Embassy Opening in Jerusalem*

**May 14, 2018**

We have no better friends in the world. You stand for Israel and you stand for Jerusalem. Thank you.

Your presence here today is a testament to the importance of this occasion, not only for the Trump administration, but in a very personal way for you. For you, each of you, for the pursuit of peace, and for President Trump himself. Thank you.

Dear friends,

What a glorious day. Remember this moment. This is history. President Trump, by recognizing history, you have made history.

All of us are deeply moved. All of us are deeply grateful.

For me, being here brings back wonderful memories from my childhood. *[Hebrew]* So, I know some of you didn't follow every word I said in Hebrew, and I'll tell you that I spent the first three years of my life in this neighborhood, in Ein Gedi Street in Talpiot, which is not very far away. There were a few charming houses here, many open fields. I remember ambling in these fields with my brother, Yoni. He was six; I was three. He held my hand very tight. We'd walk to this wondrous house of Professor Joseph Klausner, the renowned Jewish historian who was my father's teacher. I used to peer through the slats of the wooden synagogue where he and the great Israeli writer, Shai Agnon, used to pray on Shabbat. And David, I would approach this place right here, but only so far, because my mother told me, 'You can't go any further.' This was near the border. It was exposed to sniper fire. That was then. This is now, today.

Today, the embassy of the most powerful nation on earth, our greatest ally, the United States of America, today its embassy opened here.

So for me this spot brings back personal memories, but for our people, it evokes profound collective memories of the greatest moments we have known on this City on a Hill.

In Jerusalem, Abraham passed the greatest test of faith and the right to be the father of our nation.

In Jerusalem, King David established our capital three thousand years ago.

In Jerusalem, King Solomon built our Temple, which stood for many centuries.

In Jerusalem, Jewish exiles from Babylon rebuilt the Temple, which stood for many more centuries.

In Jerusalem, the Maccabees rededicated that Temple and restored Jewish sovereignty in this land.

And it was here in Jerusalem some two thousand years later that the soldiers of Israel spoke three immortal words, 'Har ha'bayit be'yadeinu,' 'The Temple Mount is in our hands,' words that lifted the spirit of the entire nation.

We are in Jerusalem and we are here to stay.

We are here in Jerusalem, protected by the brave soldiers of the army of Israel, led by our Chief of Staff Gadi Eisenkot, and our brave soldiers, our brave soldiers are protecting the borders of Israel as we speak today. We salute them all, and the members of our security forces, the Shin Bet and the Mossad, whose head is with us today. We salute you all, all of you.

Over a century ago, the Balfour Declaration recognized the right of the Jewish people to a national home in this land. And exactly 70 years ago today, President Truman became the first world leader to recognize the newborn Jewish state. Last December, President Trump became the first world leader to recognize Jerusalem as our capital. And today, the United States of America is opening its embassy right here in Jerusalem.

Thank you. Thank you, President Trump, for having the courage to keep your promises. Thank you, President Trump, and thank you all, for making the alliance between America and Israel stronger than ever. And thank you, a special thank you, to you, Ambassador Friedman. Thank you, David, for everything you do to bring our countries and our peoples closer together. Today, you have a special privilege. You are privileged to become the first American ambassador to serve your country in Jerusalem, and this is a distinct honor that will be yours forever. Nobody can be first again.

My friends, this is a great day for Israel. It's a great day for America. It's a great day for our fantastic partnership. But I believe it's also a great day for peace.

I want to thank Jared, Jason and David for your tireless efforts to advance peace, and for your tireless efforts to advance the truth. The truth and peace are interconnected. A peace that is built on lies will crash on the rocks of Middle Eastern reality. You can only build peace on truth, and the truth is that Jerusalem has been and will always be the capital of the Jewish people, the capital of the Jewish state. Truth, peace and justice—as our Supreme Court Justice here. Hanan Melcer, can attest—truth, peace and justice, this is what we have and this is what we believe in.

The prophet, Zechariah, declared over 2,500 years ago, "So said the Lord, 'I will return to Zion and I will dwell in the midst of Jerusalem. And Jerusalem shall be called the City of Truth.'"

May the opening of this embassy in this city spread the truth far and wide, and may the truth advance a lasting peace between Israel and all our neighbors.

G-d bless the United States of America and G-d bless Jerusalem, the eternal, undivided capital of Israel.

Baruch atah A-donai Elokeinu melekh ha'olam shehecheyanu vekiymanu vehigi'anu lazman hazeh [*Blessed are You, Lord our G-d, King of the Universe, who has granted us life, sustained us and enabled us to reach this occasion.*]

Source: Israel Ministry of Foreign Affairs. "PM Netanyahu's Remarks at the Opening of the US Embassy in Jerusalem." May 14, 2018. http://mfa.gov.il/MFA/PressRoom/2018/Pages/PM-Netanyahu-s-remarks-at-the-opening-of-the-US-embassy-in-Jerusalem-14-May-2018.aspx.

# *Vice President Pence Speaks at Israel's Seventieth Independence Day Celebration*

**May 14, 2018**

Thank you, Mr. Ambassador, members of the Cabinet, members of Congress, all of tonight's honorees, and to all of you who've come from near and far. It is deeply humbling for me to stand here tonight with all of you on this extraordinary day as we celebrate 70 years of Israel's independence.

And I bring greetings and congratulations from a leader who has done more to bring our two countries closer together in a year than any President in the past 70 years. I bring greetings from the 45th President of the United States of America, President Donald Trump. . . .

We gather here to celebrate nothing less than a miracle of history: the day when the Jewish people ended the longest exile of any people, anywhere, and reclaimed a Jewish future and rebuilt the Jewish State.

As we look at Israel today, it is extraordinary to behold all the progress she's made and the example she sets. The truth is, today, the modern State of Israel is not just 70 years old; Israel is 70 years strong. And the world marvels at her strength.

The United States of America was proud to be the first nation in the world to recognize the State of Israel seven decades ago.

And just as President Truman made history then, President Trump made history now. And thanks to the President's leadership, almost exactly 70 years to the minute from the rebirth of the Jewish State, the American Embassy officially opened in Jerusalem, the capital of the State of Israel, today.

It was just over five months ago, on December 6, our President officially recognized Jerusalem as Israel's capital. And it was my honor to stand with him on the day that he made that announcement to the world. Today, that recognition became concrete reality.

From King David's time to our own, President Trump has now etched his name into the ineffaceable story of Jerusalem. And as the President said just this morning, today is nothing less than a great day for Israel.

And our administration was proud to send a remarkable delegation to mark this milestone—a delegation of 250 leaders in Congress; leaders from our administration; the President's daughter, Ivanka Trump; and his son-in-law, Jared Kushner.

And to Jared, who's on his way home as we speak after an unforgettable day, let me just say: Jared, your moving remarks this morning will stand forever as a testament, not just to our country and the Jewish people, but to you and your family.

And as Jared said this morning, so I say now, what the world saw in high relief today is, when President Donald Trump makes a promise, he keeps it.

By finally recognizing Jerusalem as Israel's capital, the United States has chosen fact over fiction. And fact is the only true foundation for a just and lasting peace. And as President Trump made clear this morning, "Our greatest hope is for peace."

And as Jared also said, the United States of America "is prepared to support a peace agreement in every way we can." We believe that peace "is possible for both sides to gain more than they give, so that all people can live in peace, safe from danger, free from fear, and able to pursue their dreams."

Jerusalem is a city whose very name means peace. And as for me and my family, and for millions around the globe, we pray for the peace of Jerusalem, that "those who love her be secure," that "there be peace within [her] walls, and security within [her] citadels." And we will keep praying that until peace finally comes to Jerusalem.

And while any peace will undoubtedly require compromise, you can know with confidence: Under President Donald Trump, the United States of America will never compromise the safety and security of the State of Israel. . . .

For 70 years, we've marveled at all the Jewish State and the Jewish people have endured and accomplished. How unlikely was Israel's birth. How more unlikely has been her survival. And how confounding, against the odds, both past and present, has been her thriving. In 70 short years, Israel has become one of the freest, strongest, and most prosperous nations on Earth.

Its booming, hi-tech, start-up nation has turned Israel into a global economic powerhouse that has benefitted the whole world with untold innovations in agriculture, medicine, information, nanotechnology, and so many other areas of human endeavor.

The citizens of Israel have awed the world with the strength of their will, the nobility of their character, and the steadfastness of their faith.

They have, in a very real sense, over the past 70 years, turned the desert into a garden, sickness into health, scarcity into plenty, and despair into hope.

And what has been true for the past 70 years I know will be true for the next. One unalterable truth stands in evidence at this gathering and all across the world: As it has been in the past, so it shall be in the future: America stands with Israel.

We stand with Israel because her cause is our cause, her values are our values, and her fight is our fight. We stand with Israel because we believe in right over wrong, and good over evil, and liberty over tyranny. We stand with Israel because that's what Americans have always done. For in the story of Israel, we see the power of faith, and the promise of hope. . . .

So thank you for giving me the honor of sharing this evening with you, and accepting this well-deserved recognition from the State of Israel for President Donald Trump. And on behalf of the President and all the American people, on this big day for Israel, we say, Mazel Tov.

It's a day of celebration, so I'll let you get back to it. And I'll leave here today absolutely confident with the unwavering support of all of you, the American people, and all who cherish the U.S.-Israel relationship, with the leadership of President Donald Trump in the White House, and with God's help, I know Israel will go from strength to strength. Her first 70 years will just be a glimpse of what's to come, and the United States and Israel will meet our glorious future together.

God bless you. God bless Israel. And God Bless the United States of America.

SOURCE: The White House. "Remarks by Vice President Pence at Israel's 70th Independence Day Celebration." May 14, 2018. https://www.whitehouse.gov/briefings-statements/remarks-vice-president-pence-israels-70th-independence-day-celebration.

# UN Human Rights Council
# Resolution on Violence in Gaza

**May 18, 2018**

*The Human Rights Council,*

*Guided* by the purposes and principles of the Charter of the United Nations and the Universal Declaration of Human Rights,

*Recalling* General Assembly resolution 60/251 of 15 March 2006, Human Rights Council resolutions 5/1 and 5/2 of 18 June 2007, and all other relevant United Nations resolutions,

*Affirming* the applicability of international human rights law and international humanitarian law, in particular the Geneva Convention relative to the Protection of Civilian Persons in Time of War, of 12 August 1949, to the Occupied Palestinian Territory, including East Jerusalem,

*Reaffirming* that all High Contracting Parties to the Fourth Geneva Convention are under the obligation to respect and ensure respect for the obligations arising from the said Convention in relation to the Occupied Palestinian Territory, including East Jerusalem, and reaffirming also their obligations under articles 146, 147 and 148 with regard to penal sanctions, grave breaches and the responsibilities of the High Contracting Parties,

*Convinced* that the lack of accountability for violations of international law reinforces a culture of impunity, leading to a recurrence of violations and seriously endangering international peace,

*Noting* the systematic failure by Israel to carry out genuine investigations in an impartial, independent, prompt and effective way, as required by international law, into the violence and offences against Palestinians by the occupying forces, and to establish judicial accountability for its actions in the Occupied Palestinian Territory, including East Jerusalem,

*Emphasizing* the obligations of Israel as the occupying Power to ensure the safety, well-being and protection of the Palestinian civilian population under its occupation in the Occupied Palestinian Territory, including East Jerusalem,

*Emphasizing also* that the intentional targeting of civilians and other protected persons in situations of armed conflict, including foreign occupation, constitutes a grave breach of international humanitarian law and international human rights law, and poses a threat to international peace and security,

*Recognizing* the importance of the right to life and the right to freedom of peaceful assembly and association to the full enjoyment of all human rights,

1.  *Condemns* the disproportionate and indiscriminate use of force by the Israeli occupying forces against Palestinian civilians, including in the context of peaceful protests, particularly in the Gaza Strip, in violation of international humanitarian law, international human rights law and relevant United Nations

resolutions, and expresses its grief at the extensive loss of life, including of children, women, health workers and journalists, and at the high number of injuries;

2.  *Calls for* an immediate cessation of all attacks, incitement and violence against civilians throughout the Occupied Palestinian Territory, including East Jerusalem;

3.  *Calls upon* all parties to ensure that future demonstrations remain peaceful and to abstain from actions that could endanger the lives of civilians;

4.  *Demands* that Israel, the occupying Power, immediately and fully end its illegal closure of the occupied Gaza Strip, which amounts to collective punishment of the Palestinian civilian population, including through the immediate, sustained and unconditional opening of crossings to the flow of humanitarian aid, commercial goods and persons, especially those in need of urgent medical attention, to and from the Gaza Strip, in compliance with its obligations under international humanitarian law;

5.  *Decides* to urgently dispatch an independent, international commission of inquiry, to be appointed by the President of the Human Rights Council, to investigate all alleged violations and abuses of international humanitarian law and international human rights law in the Occupied Palestinian Territory, including East Jerusalem, particularly in the occupied Gaza Strip, in the context of the military assaults on the large-scale civilian protests that began on 30 March 2018, whether before, during or after; to establish the facts and circumstances, with assistance from relevant experts and special procedure mandate holders, of the alleged violations and abuses, including those that may amount to war crimes; to identify those responsible; to make recommendations, in particular on accountability measures, all with a view to avoiding and ending impunity and ensuring legal accountability, including individual criminal and command responsibility, for such violations and abuses, and on protecting civilians against any further assaults; and to present an oral update thereon to the Council at its thirty-ninth session and a final, written report at its fortieth session;

6.  *Calls upon* Israel, the occupying Power, and all relevant parties to cooperate fully with the commission of inquiry and to facilitate its access, requests the cooperation, as appropriate, of other relevant United Nations bodies with the commission of inquiry to carry out its mission, and requests the assistance of the Secretary-General and the United Nations High Commissioner for Human Rights in this regard, including in the provision of all administrative, technical and logistical assistance required to enable the commission of inquiry and special procedure mandate holders to fulfil their mandates promptly and efficiently;

7.  *Decides* to remain seized of the matter.

SOURCE: United Nations. Office of the High Commissioner for Human Rights. "Violations of International Law in the Context of Large-Scale Civilian Protests in the Occupied Palestinian Territory, Including East Jerusalem." May 22, 2018. https://documents-dds-ny.un.org/doc/UNDOC/GEN/G18/137/36/PDF/G1813736.pdf?OpenElement.

# UN General Assembly Adopts
# Resolution on Protecting Palestinians

**June 13, 2018**

In an emergency meeting, the General Assembly today adopted a resolution deploring the use of excessive, disproportionate and indiscriminate force by Israeli forces against Palestinian civilians in the Occupied Palestinian Territory, including East Jerusalem, and particularly the Gaza Strip.

By the text titled "Protection of the Palestinian civilian population"—adopted by a vote of 120 in favour to 8 against with 45 abstentions—the Assembly demanded that Israel refrain from such actions and fully abide by its legal obligations under the Fourth Geneva Convention relating to the Protection of Civilian Persons in Time of War, of 12 August 1949.

It also deplored the firing of rockets from the Gaza Strip into Israeli civilian areas—and any actions that could endanger civilian lives—and called for urgent steps to ensure an immediate, durable and fully respected ceasefire, as well as for the exercise of maximum restraint by all parties. It requested the Secretary-General to submit a report in no later than 60 days, outlining proposals on ways and means for ensuring the safety of Palestinian civilians, including on an international protection mechanism.

The resolution was adopted following the Assembly's rejection of a United States-sponsored amendment—by a vote of 78 against to 59 in favour, with 26 abstentions—which would have condemned Hamas for repeatedly firing rockets into Israel and inciting violence along the boundary fence. It would have demanded that Hamas cease all violent activity and expressed grave concern over the destruction of the Kerem Shalom crossing by actors in Gaza.

Introducing the proposed amendment, the United States delegate said the resolution, presented by Algeria's delegate, had failed to even mention Hamas, sacrificing honesty in favour of a narrow political agenda that exclusively blamed Israel in what had become a favourite political sport. The modest amendment rightly condemned rocket fire by Hamas, as well as its diversion of resources from civilians to military resources. "It is the least that any self-respecting international organization or nation can do for the cause of peace," she said.

Algeria's representative, introducing the resolution, said Israel had not only set aside its responsibilities under international law, it had purposely violated those obligations. "They have, in a premeditated way, harmed Palestinians, denying them their basic rights," he stressed. "Vote for rights, peace and stability in all of the Middle East," he said.

Bangladesh's delegate, speaking on behalf of the Organization of Islamic Cooperation, said the Security Council's failure to take action, due to a veto cast by a permanent member, had encouraged the occupying Power to continue its aggressions. Without fear of accountability, Israeli forces had continued their brutality.

"By supporting this resolution, you are colluding with a terrorist organization and empowering Hamas," said Israel's representative, stressing that his country had the right to defend itself and asking Member States how they would react if 40,000 rioters attempted to flood their borders. It was Hamas that decided when to attack, when to retreat and when to send its own people straight into harm's way and even to their death. Israel had taken many steps to improve the humanitarian situation in Gaza, while Hamas had spent countless resources on terrorism. To those supporting today's resolution, "you are the ammunition in Hamas' gun; you are the warheads on Hamas' missiles", he said.

The Permanent Observer of the State of Palestine said Member States must do everything possible to uphold the collective obligation to protect civilians in all circumstances, including Palestinian civilians. "We cannot remain silent in the face of the most violent crimes and human rights violations being systematically perpetrated against our people," he stressed. The text was balanced. It had been forged after extensive negotiations during the preceding Security Council process, as well as follow-up consultations and good-faith outreach. He rejected the "bad-faith" attempt to insert an amendment that would radically shift the focus away from the core objective of protecting civilians. . . .

### Action

SABRI BOUKADOUM (Algeria), introducing the draft resolution on the Protection of the Palestinian civilian population (document A/ES-10/L.23), said the situation represented a major threat to international peace and security. "I will not quote the terrifying numbers of the dead and wounded," he emphasized, adding that Israel's aggressions had not spared children, women, the elderly, nurses or humanitarian workers. Razan al-Najjar, a 21-year-old Palestinian nurse, was shot dead at the Gaza Border where she had worked to save the wounded. Israel had not only set aside its responsibilities under international law, it had purposely violated those obligations. "They have, in a premeditated way, harmed Palestinians, denying them their basic rights," he stressed.

The draft resolution was merely reminding the international community of its responsibility to provide civilians protection in times of conflict, he continued. It stressed the need to ensure the well-being and safety of civilians, and called for holding all violators accountable. The draft also called for utmost restraint and calm by all parties, as well as for immediate steps to stabilize the situation on the ground and end the siege imposed on the Gaza Strip by Israel. Given the Security Council's inability to uphold its responsibility, the international community was called upon to redouble its efforts to end the Arab-Israeli conflict on the premise of setting up a Palestinian State based on relevant resolutions on international legitimacy and the Arab Peace Initiative.

On behalf of the Arab Group, he expressed gratitude to Kuwait for recently tabling a similar resolution in the Security Council. He called on all "peace loving" States to stand firmly on the side of the rule of law and to support the draft. "Vote for rights, peace and stability in all of the Middle East," he said.

NIKKI R. HALEY (United States), introducing her delegation's proposed amendment to that draft resolution (document A/ES-10/L.24), said that today, demonstrations were taking place in Nicaragua, civilians peacefully protesting their Government in Iran had been arrested and the world's worst humanitarian crisis continued to unfold in Yemen. In Myanmar, almost a million civilians had been driven from their homes. But the Assembly was not meeting in an emergency session on any of those situations. "Instead, the General Assembly is devoting its valuable time to the situation in Gaza," she said, asking what made that situation different from conflicts in other desperate places around the world.

The answer, she said, was that for many delegations, attacking Israel had become a "favourite political sport". Such one-sided resolutions as the one presented today, which failed to even mention Hamas, did nothing to advance peace. Moreover, everyone knew its passage would accomplish nothing, and could even make peace less likely by feeding the narrative that Gaza's leaders were not responsible. It would also further stoke tensions in favour of a narrow political agenda, she said, emphasizing that "there are no perfect actors on either side". Israel had withdrawn completely from Gaza in 2005 and Hamas had been the de facto leader since 2007. Eleven years later, the territory was stricken with poverty and had become a haven for terrorist activities. Hamas and its allies had fired over a hundred rockets into Israel in just the last month, used civilians as human shields and refused to unite with the Palestinian Authority to pursue peace.

"We still have the opportunity to salvage something honest from this," she said, stressing that the modest amendment proposed by the United States rightly condemned the firing of rockets by Hamas as well as its diversion of resources from civilians to military resources. "It is the least that any self-respecting international organization or nation can do for the cause of peace," she said, urging all Member States to vote in favour it. Today's vote would reveal which stories were serious about the cause of peace, and which were only bound by their political agendas.

RIYAD H. MANSOUR, Permanent Observer of the State of Palestine, said today's initiative represented a genuine effort to address the recent violence and worsening conditions on the ground. "It is firmly based on the belief that, by upholding shared responsibilities in line with the [United Nations] Charter, international law and relevant United Nations resolutions, we can contribute to the efforts to defuse tensions, de-escalate the situation, deter further violence and protect civilian lives," he said. His delegation's decision to approach the Assembly had been prompted by the Security Council's failure to act on the matter, due to the veto cast on 1 June by one of its permanent members. The resolution submitted to the Council by Kuwait had been supported by the vast majority of its members, he said, adding that, on the heels of that regrettable vote, Palestinians had also marked the fifty-first anniversary of the Israeli occupation. "This illegal, belligerent, military occupation is the primary source and root cause of the recurrent emergency crises we face," he said.

While Palestine would have preferred that the Security Council uphold its duties, he said, the negative outcome had emboldened Israel's impunity and forced his delegation to continue its efforts in the Assembly. "We cannot remain silent in the face of the most violent crimes and human rights violations being systematically perpetrated against our people," he said. It was the international community's duty to address all aspects of the crisis and the grave injustice and alleviate, in any way it could, the suffering of the Palestinian people. The draft resolution before the Assembly today was rooted in international law and United Nations resolutions, both on the question of Palestine and on the protection of civilians, medics, humanitarian personnel and journalists. It was a balanced text achieved after extensive negotiations during the preceding Security Council process, and the follow-up consultations and good-faith outreach seeking the support of all delegations.

"We therefore firmly reject the bad-faith attempt to insert an amendment that would radically unbalance the text and shift the Assembly's focus away from the core objective of protecting civilians and upholding international law," he said, calling on delegations to support the longstanding Palestinian cause, advance peace and support the work of United Nations agencies working to meet the needs of Palestinian civilians on the ground—particularly the United Nations Relief and Works Agency for Palestine Refugees in the Near East (UNRWA). Member States must do everything possible to uphold the collective obligation to protect civilians in all circumstances, including Palestinian civilians, and to avert further destabilization of the situation with a view to salvaging the prospects for peace. . . .

DANNY BEN YOSEF DANON (Israel) said he was here today to stand up for a basic right afforded to every country in the world: the right to defend its citizens. The Assembly had convened two emergency sessions in the last six months, both on Israel. Today's meeting was about Israel's right to defend itself. "It is the international community's attempt to take away that right," he said, adding that the draft resolution protected neither Palestinians nor Israelis. "By supporting this resolution, you are colluding with a terrorist organization and empowering Hamas," he stressed. Turkey and Algeria "were not exactly champions of human rights." The Palestinian rioters wanted to seize Tel Aviv, Haifa, and Jerusalem and replace the Jewish State. "We take them at their word," he said, adding that the so-called "March of Return" was a violent attack on Israel. Hamas was using children's toys as weapons. "How would you react if 40,000 rioters attempted to flood your borders," he asked. If the rioters had breached the wall, the world would have witnessed the death of many Israelis and Palestinians.

It was time to expose the forces behind the situation in Gaza and draw a clear demarcation between right and wrong, he continued, reiterating that those who supported the resolution were directly supporting Hamas. It was Hamas that decided when to attack, when to retreat and when to send its own people straight into harm's way and even to their death. Hamas had been recognized as a terrorist organization by many, including Australia, New Zealand, the European Union, Egypt[,] the United Kingdom and the United States. The Assembly's hypocrisy should come as no surprise, he said, recalling that it had called 10 emergency sessions since the founding of the United Nations. Five had been on Israel. The devastation in Syria, which had claimed half a million lives and displaced 7 million people, had never resulted in an emergency session of the Assembly. "This type of worldwide assault is reserved only for Israel," he said. "It is anti-Semitism."

He said Israel had taken many steps to improve the humanitarian situation in Gaza, while Hamas had spent countless resources on terrorism. Yet, Hamas was not even mentioned once in today's resolution. He asked the ambassadors of Turkey, Algeria, Bangladesh, and Venezuela, authors of the resolution: "Do you support terrorism?" Israel wanted to help the civilians in Gaza but the situation at the border was clear. Israel was a democracy defending itself. Hamas was a terrorist organization attacking Israel. The moral majority at the United Nations must not stand for that. To those supporting today's resolution, "you are the ammunition in Hamas' gun; you are the warheads on Hamas' missiles," he said. . . .

The Assembly then rejected the motion to take no action on the proposed amendment (document A/ES-10/L.24), by a vote of 78 against to 59 in favour, with 26 abstentions.

It then took up the amendment (document A/ES-10/L.24), voting 62 in favour to 58 against, with 42 abstentions.

Mr. LAJČÁK, citing the Assembly's Rules of Procedure, said the Assembly did not adopt L.24 because it lacked the required two-thirds majority.

The representative of the <u>United States</u>, on a point of order, said that under rule 71 of the General Assembly's Rules of Procedure, the required majority was a simple majority of those Member States present and voting. She requested that the amendment be adopted.

The President of the General Assembly said that under rule 84, decisions by the Assembly on amendments to proposals relating to important questions required a two-thirds majority. He had ruled accordingly. However, the United States had appealed against his ruling. Pursuant to rule 71, he said the appeal would be put to a vote. His ruling would stand unless overruled by a majority of Member States present and voting.

The representative of the <u>United States</u> thanked the President for putting the appeal to a vote and requested that all delegations vote in favour of it.

The Assembly then took action on the United States' appeal to the ruling of the General Assembly President on the majority required for the adoption of L.24, rejecting it by a vote of 73 against to 66 in favour, with 26 abstentions.

Finally, the Assembly took up L.23, adopting the resolution by a vote of 120 in favour to 8 against (Australia, Israel, Marshall Islands, Micronesia, Nauru, Solomon Islands, Togo, United States), with 45 abstentions. . . .

SOURCE: United Nations. "General Assembly Adopts Resolution on Protecting Palestinian Civilians following Rejection of United States Amendment to Condemn Hamas Rocket Fire." June 13, 2018. https://www.un.org/press/en/2018/ga12028.doc.htm.

## OTHER HISTORIC DOCUMENTS OF INTEREST

### FROM PREVIOUS *HISTORIC DOCUMENTS*

# International Community Responds to Venezuelan Presidential Election

MAY 21, 2018

At the beginning of 2018, Venezuela's National Constituent Assembly called for a snap presidential election to take place in the spring instead of in December, as had been scheduled. The significant reduction in campaign time and restrictions placed on opposition groups by other official measures were widely viewed as a government-led effort to rig the election in President Nicolás Maduro's favor. Opposition leaders and many within the international community declared the election illegitimate and refused to recognize Maduro's victory.

## EARLY ALLEGATIONS OF ELECTION RIGGING

Venezuela has typically held its presidential elections in the last December of a president's six-year term, since new presidential terms begin in January. However, on January 23, the National Constituent Assembly voted unanimously to move the 2018 presidential election up to April; the National Electoral Council subsequently announced the election would take place on April 22. Opposition members and some within the international community decried the move as a government-orchestrated effort to capitalize on opposition parties' disarray following staggering, unexpected losses in the October 2017 gubernatorial elections and to place them at a further disadvantage by significantly reducing the campaign's length. The National Constituent Assembly is comprised entirely of Maduro supporters (opposition parties boycotted the 2017 election of the first cohort of assembly members in protest of the body's formation), and the National Electoral Council is widely viewed as pro-Maduro, particularly following its suspension of an opposition-led effort to recall the president in 2016.

The National Constituent Assembly had also approved two measures that limited opposition parties' ability to participate in the election. In November 2017, the assembly passed an antihate law banning the use of broadcast or social media to disseminate messages that incite hate. It also prohibited any opposition groups that did not comply with the law from registering with the National Electoral Council. Assembly President Delcy Rodriguez said the law's goal was to stop the purported campaign of hate and violence pushed by right-wing opposition extremists and help promote peace and unity. Then in December, the assembly unanimously adopted a measure prohibiting opposition parties that did not participate in that month's mayoral elections from participating in the presidential election. Leaders from the Justice First, Popular Will, and Democratic Action Parties had boycotted the mayoral election to protest perceived bias in the country's electoral system. This action was bolstered by a January 26, 2018, ruling by Venezuela's Supreme Court that the opposition coalition—the Democratic Unity Roundtable, or MUD—would not be allowed to register for the presidential election. Prior to the Court's ruling, MUD had been planning to conduct primaries to select one candidate to represent all of its member parties. The government's actions left the opposition scrambling to determine if individual parties would still field a candidate and if so, who those candidates would be. (Several popular opposition leaders, including Justice First's Henrique Capriles and Popular Will's Leopoldo López, had previously been barred from participating in the election; others were in jail or in self-imposed exile.)

The National Electoral Council eventually pushed the election date back to May 20 following talks between the Maduro government and some opposition parties. MUD ultimately called for a full boycott of the election—one that would see no candidates entered by MUD and would encourage voters to avoid the polls—declaring that it had been rigged in favor of Maduro. The president would, however, face two challengers: Javier Bertucci, an evangelical minister running as an independent, and Henri Falcón, a former state governor who founded his own right-leaning party, Progressive Advance, after breaking with late-president Hugo Chavez and the Socialist Party in 2010.

## ELECTION DAY

The election took place as scheduled on May 20, with Maduro declared the winner that evening. Fewer than half of registered voters cast a ballot, remarkably low participation for a country that had had roughly 80 percent turnout in its two previous presidential elections. Election officials announced that with 92 percent of voting centers reporting, Maduro had received 5.8 million votes, or about 68 percent of all votes cast. Falcón received 1.8 million votes, while Bertucci received 925,000 votes. "So much they have underestimated the revolutionary people! So much they have underestimated me," Maduro said to a rally of supporters. "And here we are again, victorious!"

Allegations of irregularities at polling places and election fraud swirled, including accusations that the government was leveraging the distribution of food aid to pressure Venezuelans into casting a vote for Maduro. The government has been providing boxes of food to help citizens through the country's ongoing economic crisis, which has resulted in severe shortages of basic goods and caused prices for food and medicine to soar. Various reports indicated that it would cost an entire month's minimum wage to buy two pounds of meat or three bags of rice. The day of the election, the Socialist Party set up so-called Red Spots—named for the party's signature color—next to polling places. Voters would cast their ballot, then go to the Red Spots to give their names to workers tracking who voted for Maduro. Workers denied that their tracking would somehow be linked to future food deliveries, but some Venezuelans expressed concern that they would be cut off from assistance if they did not vote for the president. The government was also accused of buying votes: Venezuelans randomly received surprise text messages telling them they would be getting a cash bonus that, for some poor Venezuelans, was equivalent to several weeks of wages.

Falcón declared the election invalid. "For us, there was no election," he said, explaining that "we have serious, serious questions on our part and in addition to the questioning that we may have about the process, without any doubt it lacks legitimacy and in this sense, we do not recognize this electoral process."

## VOTE CONDEMNED BY MANY IN INTERNATIONAL COMMUNITY

Leaders from some countries—including China, Cuba, Iran, North Korea, Russia, Syria, and Turkey—accepted the vote's outcome and congratulated Maduro on his win. However, many others echoed Falcón's declaration that the election was invalid.

On May 21, members of the Lima Group—including Argentina, Mexico, Brazil, Chile, Colombia, Panama, Paraguay, St. Lucia, Guyana, Peru, Honduras, Guatemala, and Costa Rica—released, with Canada, a statement saying they did "not recognize the legitimacy of the electoral process" because it "did not comply with international standards for a democratic, free, fair and transparent process." The group added that they would decrease "their diplomatic relations with Venezuela" and recall their ambassadors to Caracas, in addition to coordinating a regional response to Venezuelans "who are forced to leave their country." (The International Organization for Migration estimated in April 2018 that more than 1.6 million Venezuelans left the country between 2015 and 2017 to escape the ongoing crisis.) The Organization of American States (OAS) was similarly critical of the election. "There can be no democracy without elections, but yesterday Nicolás Maduro showed that elections can be held without democracy," said OAS Secretary General Luis Almagro. "The elections of yesterday in Venezuela were an exercise without the minimum guarantees for the people. They were held with a generalized lack of public freedoms, with outlawed candidates and parties and with electoral authorities lacking any credibility, subject to the executive power."

In the United States, Trump administration officials had decried the election as unfair and undemocratic for months and said they would not recognize the results before the vote had taken place. Responding to Maduro's victory, Vice President Mike Pence said, "The illegitimate result of this fake process is a further blow to the proud democratic tradition of Venezuela. . . . The United States will not sit idly by as Venezuela crumbles and the misery of their brave people continues." U.S. Secretary of State Mike Pompeo added, "Until the Maduro regime restores a democratic path in Venezuela through free, fair, and transparent elections, the government faces isolation from the international community." Shortly after results were announced, Maduro expelled Todd Robinson, the United States' charge d'affaires in Venezuela, and his deputy head of mission, Brian Naranjo, accusing them of conspiring against the government. The United States has not had an ambassador in Venezuela for eight years; Robinson and Naranjo were leading diplomatic efforts on the ground in an ambassador's absence.

The day following the election, President Donald Trump signed an executive order imposing new sanctions on the Venezuelan government. The measure barred U.S. companies or individuals from buying debts or accounts receivable from the Venezuelan government, including the government-owned oil company Petróleos de Venezuela. Maduro and other officials had reportedly been selling government debt and keeping the cash from such sales for themselves. An earlier round of sanctions, imposed in January, charged four current or former military officials with involvement in political repression and public corruption, froze their assets that were under U.S. jurisdiction, and prohibited Americans from doing business with them. Six other Venezuelan officials—including newly named vice president Delcy Rodriguez; Defense Minister Vladimir Padrino; and Maduro's wife, Cilia Flores—were sanctioned in September, bringing the total number of U.S.-sanctioned Venezuelans to fifty.

Also in September, it was revealed that U.S. officials held a series of secret meetings from fall 2017 to early 2018 with Venezuelan military officers who no longer supported Maduro to discuss a potential coup. According to various media reports, the officers told U.S. officials that they represented several hundred others in the armed forces who wanted to oust Maduro. In a statement explaining the meetings, the White House said it was important to "dialogue with all Venezuelans who demonstrate a desire for democracy" to "bring positive change to a country that has suffered so much under Maduro." The United

States denied the military officers' request for material support, such as the provision of encrypted radios to ensure confidential communications and withdrew from talks after dozens of officers were arrested in a government crackdown. The reports raised questions about whether the meetings would give credibility to Maduro's long-standing claims that the United States is conspiring against him and is waging an economic war with Venezuela that has fueled its current crisis. Venezuelan Foreign Minister Jorge Arreaza responded to the news on Twitter. "We denounce before the world the intervention plans and the support to military conspiracies by the US government against Venezuela," he wrote.

The European Union (EU) announced its own sanctions against eleven Venezuelan officials on June 25. The list included Rodriguez and former vice president Tareck El Aissami. EU officials said the sanctioned individuals were "responsible for human rights violations and for undermining democracy and the rule of law in Venezuela," adding that the election "lacked any credibility as the electoral process did not ensure the necessary guarantees for them to be inclusive and democratic." Those listed were banned from traveling to the EU and had their assets frozen. The EU had imposed similar sanctions on seven officials "involved in the non-respect of democratic principles or the rule of law as well as in the violation of human rights" on January 22 and warned that it would sanction more individuals if Venezuela proceeded with the election. The Venezuelan government said it would not be threatened and condemned "the continued aggression and meddling by the EU."

—Linda Grimm

*Following are statements by the Lima Group, U.S. Vice President Mike Pence, U.S. Secretary of State Mike Pompeo, and Organization of American States Secretary General Luis Almagro, issued on May 21, 2018, in response to Venezuela's presidential election.*

# Statement by Lima Group on Venezuelan Presidential Election

**May 21, 2018**

The governments of Argentina, Brazil, Canada, Chile, Colombia, Costa Rica, Guatemala, Guyana, Honduras, Mexico, Panama, Paraguay, Peru and Saint Lucia, express the following:

1. They do not recognize the legitimacy of the electoral process held in the Bolivarian Republic of Venezuela that concluded on May 20, as it did not comply with international standards for a democratic, free, fair and transparent process.

2. They agree to downgrade the level of their diplomatic relations with Venezuela, and will therefore recall their Ambassadors in Caracas for consultations and summon the Ambassadors of Venezuela to express our protest.

3. They reiterate their concern about the deepening political, economic, social and humanitarian crisis that has deteriorated the standard of living in Venezuela, which is reflected in the massive migration of Venezuelans who arrive in our

countries in difficult conditions, and in the loss of democratic institutions and the rule of law, as well as by the lack of guarantees and political freedoms of their citizens.

4.  They decide to submit a new resolution on the situation in Venezuela at the 48th session of the General Assembly of the Organization of the American States.

5.  In order to address the situation resulting from the worrying increase in the flows of Venezuelans who are forced to leave their country, and due to the impact that this situation is having on the entire region, they decide to adopt the following measures:

    i.  Convene a high-level meeting with authorities responsible for migration and refugee matters to exchange best practices and define the guidelines for a comprehensive response, including issues of migratory accommodations and identity documents. In this regard, they accept the offer of Peru to host said meeting during the first half of June.

    ii. Consider the possibility of making financial contributions to the relevant international organizations to strengthen the institutional capacities of countries in the region, especially neighbouring countries, to address the migratory flows of Venezuelans.

6.  They deplore the serious humanitarian situation in Venezuela and, considering the public health implications for the entire region, decide to adopt the following measures:

    i.  Convene a high-level meeting with health authorities to coordinate actions in the area of public health and strengthen cooperation to address the epidemiological emergency.

    ii. Support the supply of medicines by independent institutions as well as epidemiological surveillance actions in Venezuela and its neighbouring countries, particularly due to the reappearance of diseases such as measles, malaria and diphtheria.

7.  Reiterate paragraph 4 of the Lima Declaration of August 8, 2017, and, with a view to helping preserve the powers of the National Assembly, agree to adopt, where their legislation and internal regulations allow, the following economic and financial measures:

    I.  Request that the competent authorities of each country issue and update nationwide circulars or bulletins that convey to the financial and banking sector the risk they might incur if they carry out operations with the Venezuelan government that do not have the endorsement of the National Assembly, including payment agreements and reciprocal credits for foreign trade operations, including military and security goods.

    II. Coordinate actions so that international and regional financial organizations do not grant loans to the Government of Venezuela, due to the unconstitutional nature of acquiring debt without the endorsement of its National Assembly, except when financing is intended for humanitarian assistance, and taking into account prior to its granting the possible unwanted effects in the economy of vulnerable third countries.

III.   Intensify and expand the exchange of financial intelligence information, through existing mechanisms, on the activities of Venezuelan individuals and companies that could be linked to acts of corruption, money laundering or other illicit behaviours that could result in judicial proceedings that penalize said criminal activities, such as asset freezing and the application of financial restrictions.

IV.   In the framework of the international standards set by the Financial Action Task Force and the existing operational mechanisms, they are encouraged to ensure risk assessment of money laundering and terrorism financing and it is further suggested that countries inform the private sector within their jurisdictions of the threats and risks of money laundering and corruption that have been identified in Venezuela and that affect the region, which will enhance the ability to prevent or detect possible illicit acts.

V.   Furthermore, the Financial Intelligence Units and relevant authorities of each country are urged to issue and update nationwide advisories, circulars, or bulletins to alert financial institutions to corruption in Venezuela's public sector and to the methods that Venezuelan officials and their networks may be using to hide and transfer resources derived from acts of corruption.

8.   The Group will continue to follow the evolution of the situation in Venezuela in order to adopt further appropriate measures, individually or collectively, to promote the reestablishment of the rule of law and the democratic order in that country.

SOURCE: Government of Canada. "Statement by Lima Group on Electoral Process in Venezuela." May 21, 2018. http://international.gc.ca/world-monde/international_relations-relations_internationales/latin_america-amerique_latine/2018-05-21-lima_group-groupe_lima.aspx?lang=eng.

# Statement from Vice President Mike Pence on Venezuela's Elections

**May 21, 2018**

Venezuela's election was a sham—neither free nor fair. The illegitimate result of this fake process is a further blow to the proud democratic tradition of Venezuela. Every day, thousands of Venezuelans flee brutal oppression and grinding poverty—literally voting with their feet. The United States will not sit idly by as Venezuela crumbles and the misery of their brave people continues. America stands against dictatorship and with the people of Venezuela. The Maduro regime must allow humanitarian aid into Venezuela and must allow its people to be heard.

SOURCE: The White House. "Statement from Vice President Mike Pence on Venezuela's Elections." May 21, 2018. https://www.whitehouse.gov/briefings-statements/statement-vice-president-mike-pence-venezuelas-elections.

# U.S. Secretary of State Responds to Election in Venezuela

**May 21, 2018**

The United States condemns the fraudulent election that took place in Venezuela on May 20. This so-called "election" is an attack on constitutional order and an affront to Venezuela's tradition of democracy. Until the Maduro regime restores a democratic path in Venezuela through free, fair, and transparent elections, the government faces isolation from the international community.

Sunday's process was choreographed by a regime too unpopular and afraid of its own people to risk free elections and open competition. It stacked the Venezuelan courts and National Electoral Council with biased members aligned with the regime. It silenced dissenting voices. It banned major opposition parties and leaders from participating. As of May 14, more than 338 political prisoners remained jailed, more than in all other countries in the hemisphere combined. The regime stifled the free press. State sources dominated media coverage, unfairly favoring the incumbent. Most contemptible of all, the regime selectively parceled out food to manipulate the votes of hungry Venezuelans.

The Maduro regime fails to defend the Venezuelan people's right to democracy as reflected in the Inter-American Democratic Charter. The United States stands with democratic nations in support of the Venezuelan people and will take swift economic and diplomatic actions to support the restoration of their democracy.

SOURCE: U.S. Department of State. "An Unfair, Unfree Vote in Venezuela." May 21, 2018. https://www .state.gov/secretary/remarks/2018/05/282303.htm.

# Organization of American States Secretary General on Elections in Venezuela

**May 21, 2018**

The Day after the Farce

Yesterday was an infamous day for democracy in the Americas. Faced with the strength of democracy in the regional consciousness, the dictator Maduro tried—without success—to give a democratic veneer to his totalitarian regime.

And that is impossible. Totalitarianism and democracy cannot coexist. The elections of yesterday in Venezuela were an exercise without the minimum guarantees for the people. They were held with a generalized lack of public freedoms, with outlawed candidates and parties and with electoral authorities lacking any credibility, subject to the executive power. The elections were held with more than 300 political prisoners behind bars and with the State using all the resources at its disposal for the farce.

There can be no democracy without elections, but yesterday Nicolás Maduro showed that elections can be held without democracy.

We do not recognize Nicolás Maduro as the legitimate president of Venezuela. Venezuela needs a transitional government that can generate a legitimate electoral system, which in turn would allow for solutions for the country.

But yesterday was also a day of hope for Venezuela. In spite of all the noise made by the state machinery at the service of Nicolás Maduro, the democrats of Venezuela made their voices heard loud and clear by abstaining massively. So much so that not even the electoral authorities of the regime could deny it. The people who left blood in the streets defending their rights are the increasingly clear and evident majority, and their triumph will come with the return of democracy to Venezuela.

The worst thing that can happen to Venezuela is the prolongation of the dictatorship. The humanitarian crisis resulting from the lack of food and medicines is growing more severe, as shown by the thousands of Venezuelans who leave the country every day.

The institutions lack any legitimacy or credibility. The political system, its authorities and its president, are a fraud. We are going to respond to the lack of democracy in Venezuela. We cannot be indifferent and we will not be. We will continue fighting for stronger sanctions against the regime, we will continue struggling for the end of the Venezuelan dictatorship.

SOURCE: Organization of American States. "Message from OAS Secretary General on Elections in Venezuela." May 21, 2018. http://www.oas.org/en/media_center/press_release.asp?sCodigo=S-019/18.

## OTHER HISTORIC DOCUMENTS OF INTEREST

### FROM PREVIOUS *HISTORIC DOCUMENTS*

# Ireland Votes to Legalize Abortion

MAY 28 AND OCTOBER 4, 2018

In May 2018, Irish citizens voted overwhelmingly to repeal the Eighth Amendment to Ireland's Constitution and legalize abortion services. The amendment's repeal was the most recent in a series of social reforms Ireland has undertaken in the past twenty-five years and reflected the greatly diminished influence of the Catholic Church in what has historically been a strongly pious and conservative country. The first papal visit in nearly forty years followed on the heels of the referendum, with Pope Francis seeking forgiveness for sexual and institutional abuse scandals that have undermined the church's credibility in Ireland and left many disillusioned by the Vatican's weak response.

## THE REFERENDUM TAKES SHAPE

Abortion had been illegal in Ireland since 1861, when passage of the Offense Against the Person Act made "attempts to procure abortion" and administration of abortion services a felony offense, punishable by a life sentence. However, the U.S. Supreme Court's 1973 decision in *Roe v. Wade* generated concerns about a possible push to loosen abortion restrictions on the conservative Catholic island. Catholic groups subsequently led the charge for a referendum, held in 1983, in which voters approved the Eighth Amendment to the Irish Constitution. The amendment gave the unborn equal rights as pregnant women and made abortion illegal even in cases of rape, incest, and severe danger to the mother. As a result, Irish women have been forced to travel to Britain if they want an abortion, or they order abortion pills online. The latter option carries considerable risk: if a woman is caught ordering or taking abortion pills, she could be punished with up to fourteen years of jail time.

The call to repeal the Eighth Amendment was triggered by several high-profile cases of women who sought abortions when their health was threatened. In 1992, a fourteen-year-old Irish girl who was raped and impregnated by a friend of her parents was—after a three-month ordeal—permitted by the Supreme Court to travel abroad to obtain an abortion because the rape and pregnancy had made her suicidal. Then in 2012, a woman named Savita Halappanavar died of complications from a miscarriage. Despite determining at seventeen weeks that Halappanavar would miscarry, doctors denied her and her husband's repeated requests for an abortion because they detected a fetal heartbeat—reportedly saying that Ireland was unfortunately "a Catholic country." An independent investigation subsequently commissioned by Ireland's Health Service Executive concluded that Halappanavar would not have died if it had been legally possible to end her pregnancy. Investigators said the hospital had placed an "over-emphasis on the need not to intervene until the fetal heart had stopped" and recommended that Parliament consider revising abortion law and "any necessary constitutional change." Halappanavar's death outraged Irish citizens, thousands of whom gathered in Dublin to demand changes to the country's laws. The government later introduced and Parliament approved the Protection of Life During Pregnancy Act 2013, which allows abortions when there is "substantial risk to life, including risk of suicide."

The Eighth Amendment continued to be a subject of political debate despite the 2013 law's passage. The United Nations Committee on Economic, Social and Cultural Rights recommended in 2015 that Ireland hold a referendum on the amendment. The following year, Ireland's parliament formed a Citizens Assembly with a mandate to consider and provide recommendations to lawmakers on a select set of issues, including the Eighth Amendment. The assembly voted in 2017 to recommend the government provide unrestricted access to abortions.

On January 30, 2018, Taoiseach Leo Varadkar announced that a referendum asking voters if the Eighth Amendment should be repealed would take place by the end of May 2018 and that Health Minister Simon Harris would draft legislation relaxing abortion restrictions that could be introduced in Parliament based on the vote's outcome. If voters supported repeal, the Eighth Amendment would be replaced with text reading, "Provision may be made by law for the regulation of termination of pregnancies," essentially granting Parliament the ability to legislate on the issue. The government published a document titled "General scheme of a bill to regulate termination of pregnancy" on March 27 and announced the following day that the referendum had been scheduled for May 25.

## "Yes" Campaign Wins Overwhelming Victory

Roughly two million voters participated in the referendum, which was the highest recorded turnout for a ballot on social issues and the third-highest turnout for a referendum since the Constitution was adopted in 1937. Approximately 66 percent of voters supported repeal, handing a major victory to the "Yes" campaign. Exit poll data showed that repeal supporters were well distributed across Ireland's urban and rural areas, age brackets, and economic backgrounds.

"A quiet revolution has taken place, and a great act of democracy," said Varadkar. "No more doctors telling their patients there is nothing that can be done for them in their own country. No more lonely journeys across the Irish Sea. No more stigma. The veil of secrecy is lifted. . . . The burden of shame is gone." He acknowledged that those who voted against repeal may be concerned that "the country has taken the wrong turn" but sought to reassure them that "Ireland is still . . . the same country today as it was before, just a little more tolerant, open and respectful." Orla O'Connor, codirector of the Together for Yes campaign, called the vote "a rejection of an Ireland that treats women as second-class citizens." John McGuirk, communications director for the Save the 8th Campaign, lamented that Ireland no longer recognized an unborn child's right to life. "Shortly, legislation will be introduced that will allow babies to be killed in our country," he said, vowing that repeal opponents would fight any such proposals. Harris indicated that the government would move quickly to act on the public's choice, saying that the cabinet would meet on May 29 to discuss the draft abortion bill and approve turning it into a formal legislative proposal to the parliament.

The vote's outcome was widely viewed as further evidence of the Catholic Church's waning influence in Ireland. The country has implemented a series of social reforms since the early 1990s, including those legalizing divorce, homosexuality, and same-sex marriage, that contradict long-held Catholic beliefs. Continued allegations of child sexual abuse by Catholic priests and recent revelations that the church forced thousands of unwed Irish mothers into servitude at Magdalene Laundries or committed them to mental asylums and made them give up their children for adoption have also undermined the church's credibility. "This is devastating for the Roman Catholic hierarchy," said Gail McElroy, a politics professor at Trinity College in Dublin. "It is the final nail in the coffin for them. They're no longer the pillar of society, and their hopes of re-establishing themselves are gone." The church had largely been absent from the debate surrounding the referendum, even though it strongly opposed the Eighth Amendment's repeal. The Association of Catholic Priests told members not to preach on the matter, and "No" campaign representatives reportedly discouraged the church's involvement, seeking to downplay the religious aspects of abortion in favor of a focus on moral values and human rights.

## PARLIAMENT TAKES UP ABORTION BILL

The Eighth Amendment was officially repealed on September 18, when President Michael Higgins signed the referendum bill into law. The government did not formally introduce its proposed abortion legislation in Parliament until October 4, however, deciding to wait until three court cases challenging the referendum result were resolved. The bill would allow abortions on request up to the twelfth week of pregnancy. Between the twelfth and twenty-fourth weeks, abortions would be allowed if there was a risk to the woman's life or a risk of serious harm to the mother's health. Two doctors would need to be consulted and agree that these conditions are met before the abortion is performed. Abortions would not be allowed after twenty-four weeks except in cases of fatal fetal abnormalities. The bill would require general practitioners, obstetricians, and gynecologists to provide abortions. Doctors will have a legal obligation to discuss a woman's options with her, after which the woman must wait three days before deciding whether to go through with the abortion. The bill gives doctors the ability to conscientiously object to providing an abortion; however, they will be expected to arrange for the woman to be transferred to another practitioner who will conduct the abortion. Anyone who performs an abortion outside of the law faces a potential penalty of fourteen years of jail time.

"On May 25th, the Irish people gave us a very clear message to legislate for the introduction of abortion services in this country," said Harris upon introducing the bill in Parliament. "Today, we begin the job they have given us . . . in so doing we are also making history." Harris described the referendum as "a resounding affirmation of respect and support for women and their right to make choices about their own lives," adding that he was determined that Ireland could "begin a new chapter on women's health."

Harris has expressed hope that the law will pass by the end of the year, enabling women to receive abortions in Ireland as early as January 2019. The strength of support for Eighth Amendment repeal is expected to make it difficult for opponents to block the proposed legislation. Both the Irish parliament and senate must pass the bill before it can be signed into law.

## POPE FRANCIS VISITS IRELAND

The Eighth Amendment referendum took place three months before Pope Francis was scheduled to visit Ireland for the World Meeting of Families, an event held by the Catholic Church every three years to celebrate the role of the family. Roughly 70,000 people were expected to attend the star-studded celebration, at which the pope was scheduled to speak.

The pope arrived in a very different Ireland than the one Pope John Paul II had visited nearly forty years prior. In addition to recent social reforms that challenged church positions on issues including marriage and conception, attendance at church had significantly decreased: About one-third of Irish Catholics were going to weekly mass, compared to roughly 80 percent at the time of the last papal visit. Demonstrators gathered to protest the church's failure to address sexual abuse by priests, as well as the exclusion of LGBTQ families from the global celebration.

Meeting with the pope at Dublin Castle, Varadkar issued a stinging criticism of the Catholic Church. "In place of Christian charity, forgiveness, and compassion, far too often there was judgment, severity, and cruelty, in particular, towards women and children and those on the margins," he said. "People kept in dark corners, behind closed doors, cries for help that went unheard." Varadkar urged the pope to use his "office and influence" to help protect children in Ireland and around the world. The pope acknowledged the "grave scandal" caused by the abuse of children and that the "failure of ecclesiastical authorities—bishops, religious superiors, priests and others—adequately to address these repugnant crimes has rightly given rise to outrage, and remains a source of pain and shame for the Catholic community. I myself share those sentiments." However, the pope declined to identify any proposed solutions to the ongoing scandal, disappointing many Irish.

The pope also met with eight abuse survivors during his trip, stating their conversation had a "profound effect" on him, as well as with Higgins, church leaders, the Council of State, Ireland's members of the European parliament, and political leaders from Northern Ireland. He visited a homeless center in Dublin and St. Mary's Pro-Cathedral, which is the episcopal seat of the Roman Catholic Archbishop of Dublin. Before returning to Vatican City, the pope conducted a public mass in Dublin's Phoenix Park, during which he asked "forgiveness for the abuses in Ireland, abuses of power and conscience, sexual abuses on the part of qualified members of the church," and "forgiveness for some members of the hierarchy who did not take care of these painful situations and kept silent."

—Linda Grimm

*Following is a speech by Taoiseach Leo Varadkar on May 28, 2018, responding to the referendum results; and remarks delivered by Health Minister Simon Harris on October 4, 2018, on the introduction of proposed legislation permitting abortions.*

# Taoiseach Varadkar Speaks
# on the Referendum Results

DOCUMENT

**May 28, 2018**

Today is an historic day for Ireland. A quiet revolution has taken place, and a great act of democracy. A hundred years since women got the right to vote. Today, we as a people have spoken. And we say that we trust women and we respect women and their decisions.

For me it is also the day when we said No More.

No more doctors telling their patients there is nothing that can be done for them in their own country.

No more lonely journeys across the Irish Sea.

No more stigma. The veil of secrecy is lifted.

No more isolation. The burden of shame is gone.

When we went to the polls yesterday, some voted yes with enthusiasm and pride, but many others in sorrowful acceptance, with heavy hearts.

The 'X' marked on the ballot paper represented so much more than an individual vote.

In 1983, 841,000 people voted to insert the eighth amendment into our constitution.

In 2018, almost every county, every constituency, men and women, all social classes, almost all age groups. We are not a divided country. The result is resounding.

This gives us the mandate we need to bring forward legislation and secure its passage by the end of the year.

We voted:

- For the 200,000 Irish women who have travelled to Britain since 1983 to end their pregnancies.

- For the couples who shared their stories of returning home with tiny coffins.

- For the young and the not so young women, who spoke their truth.

- For those whose stories have still not been heard.

I said in recent days that this was a once in a generation vote.

Today I believe we have voted for the next generation.

We have voted to look reality in the eye and we did not blink.

We have voted to provide compassion where there was once a cold shoulder, and to offer medical care where once we turned a blind eye.

At the beginning of this campaign I called for a respectful debate, one that was never angry or personalised. I think that by and large we succeeded.

Our democracy is vibrant and robust and can survive divisive debates and make difficult decisions.

To those who voted NO I know today is not welcome. You may feel that the country has taken the wrong turn, is no longer a country you recognise.

I would like to reassure you that Ireland is still be the same country today as it was before, just a little more tolerant, open and respectful.

I would like to thank all of you who brought us here—the members of the Citizens Assembly, the Oireachtas All-Party Committee, the leaders of all the main political parties, the Independent Alliance and independent Ministers, those involved in the civil society campaign who have been working on this issue for many, many years, especially those who opened their hearts and shared their personal stories.

As leader of Fine Gael, I would also like to acknowledge the role of Senator Catherine Noone, the Minister for Health, Simon Harris, and Minister Josepha Madigan.

Above all, I would like to thank the citizens for coming out and voting in such numbers.

Listening to the arguments on both sides over the past few weeks I was struck by what we had in common, rather than what divided us. Both sides expressed a desire to care for women in a crisis, both sides wanted compassion, both sides wanted to choose life.

We all want to ensure that there are fewer crisis pregnancies and fewer abortions. Thanks to sex education, wider availability of contraceptives and emergency contraception, abortion rates are already falling and teenage pregnancy is at its lowest since the 1960s. We will continue to improve access to sexual health and education to reduce crisis pregnancies and abortions further in the year ahead.

We will also continue to make Ireland a better place to raise a family. We've made a good start with two years of free pre-school, free GP visits for young children, subsidised childcare, paid paternity leave and increases in the Working Family Payment and Home Carers Tax Credit.

In the years ahead we will build on these policies so Ireland will become one of the best places in the world to raise a family. Families of all forms.

Everyone deserves a second chance. This is Ireland's second chance to treat everyone equally and with compassion and respect.

For 35 years we have hidden the reality of crisis pregnancies behind our laws. We have hidden our conscience behind the Constitution.

This majority decision changes all that. . . .

I believe today will be remembered as the day we embraced our responsibilities as citizens and as a country.

The day Ireland stepped out from under the last of our shadows and into the light.

The day we came of age as a country. The day we took our place among the nations of the world.

Today, we have a modern constitution for a modern people.

I want to finish with one of my favourite poets, Maya Angelou.

"History, despite its wrenching pain, cannot be unlived, but if faced with courage, need not be lived again."

The wrenching pain of decades of mistreatment of Irish women cannot be unlived. However, today we have ensured that it does not have to be lived again.

SOURCE: Department of the Taoiseach. "Speech by An Taoiseach, Leo Varadkar following the Declaration on the Referendum on the Eighth Amendment." May 28, 2018. https://www.gov.ie/en/publication/d7a266-speech-by-an-taoiseach-leo-varadkar-following-the-declaration-on-the.

# *Health Minister Harris Remarks on Abortion Legislation*

**October 4, 2018**

I move that the Health (Regulation of Termination of Pregnancy) Bill be read a second time.

As legislators in our national parliament, we hold a privileged position, and never more so than when we are acting on the instruction of the people in a referendum.

On May 25th, the Irish people gave us a very clear message to legislate for the introduction of abortion services in this country.

Today, we begin the job they have given us of making the law that follows the repeal of the Eighth Amendment and, after 35 years in our constitution, in so doing we are also making history.

Of course, history is not made only in this House. This history was made on streets, in homes and in ballot boxes across this country.

By people, including colleagues here, who have campaigned steadfastly for many years. By young people who had never had a say on an issue they cared deeply about and who were galvanised by a movement of equality. By everybody who thought deeply and felt strongly on this subject, in their different ways, and came out on May 25th to make their decision known in the ballot box, resulting in an emphatic majority to repeal the Eighth and for us to legislate.

It was a resounding affirmation of respect and support for women and their right to make choices about their own lives. It was a reaffirmation of the primacy of equality in our modern democracy. And it was a call on us all to do more. On women's health. On women's equality. On continuing to shape an inclusive and more equal society.

As Minister for Health, after all we heard during the campaign, after all I've learnt since I took this role, after everything we know of the dark past, I am determined we can begin a new chapter on women's health. A chapter in which women are valued, their decisions are respected and they are cared for without judgment. This will be a priority for me in the time ahead.

I turn now to the legislation before us.

## Purpose of the Bill

The main purpose of the Health (Regulation of Termination of Pregnancy) Bill is to set out the law governing access to termination of pregnancy in this country.

The legislation permits termination to be carried out in cases where there is a risk to the life, or of serious harm to the health, of the pregnant woman; where there is a condition present which is likely to lead to the death of the foetus either before or within 28 days of birth; and up to 12 weeks of pregnancy as set out in Head 13.

## Overview of the Bill

I will now take you through the Bill to clarify its provisions.

I want to note, from the outset that, while the Bill is now arranged slightly differently, its key provisions are the same as those of the draft General Scheme approved by Government which I published in March ahead of the Referendum, and of the updated Scheme approved by Government and made public in July.

The Bill is now divided into three parts.

## Part 1. Preliminary and General

The first part of the Bill has sections on definitions, regulations, offences under the Bill, repeals and transitional provisions.

Section 1 of the Bill makes standard provisions setting out the short title of the Bill and arrangements for its commencement.

Section 2 deals with definitions. It defines the meanings of some of the terms used for the purposes of the Bill, including foetus, medical practitioner, medical procedure, and termination of pregnancy.

Section 3 deals with Regulations, allowing me as Minister to make regulations to bring the legislation into operation and other such procedural matters. Any such regulations will have to be laid before the Houses of the Oireachtas for approval.

Section 4 allows that approved expenses associated with the administration of the Bill may be paid for from public funds.

Section 5 sets out the substantive offences under the Bill. It provides that it shall be an offence for a person, by any means whatsoever, to intentionally end the life of a foetus otherwise than in accordance with the provisions of the Bill.

These provisions will not apply to a pregnant woman who has ended or attempted to end her own pregnancy.

It is further an offence for a person to aid, abet, counsel, or procure a pregnant woman to intentionally end or attempt to end the life of that pregnant woman's foetus otherwise than in accordance with the provisions of the Bill.

The penalty in the Bill for intentionally ending the life of a foetus otherwise than in accordance with the provisions of the legislation is, on conviction, a fine or imprisonment for up to 14 years, or both.

It should be noted that nothing in the Bill will prevent or restrict access to services lawfully carried out outside the State—this means that, for example, a doctor referring a patient to services abroad, or a person paying for flights or accompanying a woman to another jurisdiction to access the procedure will not be committing an offence under the legislation.

Section 6 of the Bill provides for the offence by a body corporate.

Section 7 repeals certain laws which are in contravention with the principle of the Bill. In particular, it repeals the Information Act and I hope to be in a position to commence this particular part of the legislation when the law is enacted. This will allow doctors here share information with doctors abroad, which will of vital assistance to women. *[sic]*

Section 8 puts arrangements in place to cover situations where a review committee has been convened under the Act of 2013 and is ongoing at the time the present Bill comes into effect. It also obliges the HSE to prepare and submit a final report on reviews to me as Minister, not later than 6 months after the commencement date of the present legislation.

## Part 2. Termination of Pregnancy

Part 2 of the Bill covers the grounds on which terminations of pregnancy may be lawfully provided under the legislation, arrangements for conducting reviews, and provisions on certification and notification of procedures under the legislation.

Section 9 offers definitions on health, appropriate medical practitioner, medical specialty, relevant specialty, obstetrician, review committee, and viability.

Sections 10 to 12 of the Bill set out the grounds on which termination of pregnancy may lawfully be provided, where there is a risk to life, or of serious harm to the health of the pregnant woman; where there is a risk to life or health in emergency; and where there is a condition likely to lead to the death of the foetus.

Section 13 provides that a termination of pregnancy may be carried out by a medical practitioner who, having examined the pregnant woman, is of the reasonable opinion formed in good faith that the pregnancy concerned has not exceeded 12 weeks of pregnancy. A 3-day period must elapse between certification and the procedure being carried out. This requirement is not unusual; several countries in Europe, including Belgium and Germany, have similar provisions.

The certifying doctor must then make arrangements for the procedure to be carried out as soon as possible once the 3-day period has elapsed.

Sections 14 to 19 of the Bill set out the arrangements for reviews of medical opinions, where this is sought by a pregnant woman or person acting on her behalf. The purpose of the review process is to provide a formal mechanism whereby the woman can access to a review of the clinical assessment made by the original doctor or doctors. I should make it clear that the formal review pathway is in addition to—and not in substitution for—the option of a woman seeking a second opinion as with normal medical practice.

Section 14 states that where a medical practitioner has not given an opinion or has not given an opinion which would certify a procedure being carried out under section 10 or 12, he/she must inform the pregnant woman in writing that she or a person acting on her behalf may apply for a review of this decision.

Section 15 provides for the establishment of a review panel by the HSE, which may be drawn upon to form a review committee.

Section 16 deals with the establishment of the review committee. As soon as possible, but no later than 3 days after receiving a written request from a pregnant woman, the HSE will convene a committee drawn from the review panel, to consider the relevant decision in question.

Section 17 specifies that the committee shall complete its review as soon as possible, but no later than 7 days after it is established. Where certification is made, the committee must then arrange for the termination of pregnancy to be carried out as soon as possible. Where the committee is not of the opinion that that [sic] a termination may be carried out, this decision must also be communicated to the pregnant woman and the HSE as soon as possible.

Section 18 sets out the procedures of the review committee.

It aims to empower the review committee to obtain whatever manner of clinical evidence it requires to reach a decision, and to call any relevant medical practitioners to give evidence in person. It provides for the woman herself, or a person authorised to do so on her behalf, to be heard by the review committee.

Section 19 provides that the HSE must submit a report to me, as Minister for Health, not later than 30 June each year on the operation of review committees. Information that will have to be provided in the report includes:

a.   the total number of applications received

b.   the number of reviews carried out

c.   in the case of reviews carried out, the reason why the review was sought and

d.   the outcome of the review.

Any information that might identify a woman who has made an application for a review, a person applying on her behalf, or any medical practitioner involved shall be excluded from the report by the HSE.

This information is required to monitor the implementation of the legislation to ensure that the principles and requirements of the system are being upheld.

Sections 20 and 21 set out requirements under the legislation around certification and notification of procedures carried out under the Bill.

Section 21 also contains a requirement for me, as Minister for Health, to prepare and publish an annual report on the notifications received. This will be done without disclosing the names of the women or the medical practitioners involved.

## Part 3. Miscellaneous

The third and final part of the Bill includes provisions covering consent, conscientious objection and provisions for providing universal access to services for persons ordinarily resident in the state.

Section 22 deals with consent, and states that nothing in the Bill will affect the law relating to consent to medical treatment.

The intention is that the provisions of the Bill will operate within the existing legal provisions regarding consent for medical procedures.

Section 23 of the Bill covers conscientious objection. It states that where he/she has a conscientious objection, a medical practitioner, nurse or midwife shall not be obliged to carry out, or to participate in carrying out, a termination of pregnancy. This is in line with Section 49 of the Medical Council's Guide to Professional Conduct and Ethics for Registered Medical Practitioners (2016) which obliges doctors to enable patients to transfer to another doctor for treatment in cases of conscientious objection.

Section 24 prohibits receiving financial or other benefits-in-kind in cases where referrals are made to services providing terminations of pregnancy. It states that a person shall not receive or agree to receive any special benefit or advantage in consideration of a termination of pregnancy within or outside the State, or for making any arrangements for a termination of pregnancy within or outside the State. A person contravening this section shall be guilty of an offence, and liable on summary conviction to a class A fine.

The aim of section 24 is to protect a woman's interests and to ensure that she receives objective advice and information, uncoloured by any financial or other considerations. It will prevent a counsellor, GP or other service provider from receiving "commission" for referring a woman for a termination of pregnancy either in Ireland or abroad.

It will ensure that the person or body cannot derive any benefit from recommending that a termination be procured—with benefits to include financial incentives as well as any other types of advantages or benefits in kind, e.g. holidays, cars, etc.

Sections 25 to 27 of the Bill provide the legislative basis for providing universal access to termination of pregnancy services for persons who are ordinarily resident in the State.

Section 28 of the Bill amends the Schedule to the Bail Act 1997 to include an offence under the Bill.

## Service Delivery

I would now like to turn to what the service would look like, should the Bill become law.

The Bill allows the service to be provided in the primary care setting. It is my intention that termination of pregnancy services should be provided as part of the continuum of women's health services. This would mean that in the future, women would be able to choose to have this service from their own GP—from a person with whom they are comfortable and familiar.

The international evidence and advice I have received shows that most women can have their care provided safely and effectively in the community setting.

This is particularly the case where the service is carried out in early pregnancy.

The evidence shows that the earlier in a pregnancy that a woman seeks the service, the safer it is to provide it without recourse to hospital treatment and with minimal complications or other risks to her health.

Officials in my Department and the HSE are at an advanced stage in drafting contract proposals to allow for as many members of the general practitioner community as possible to participate in providing this service. I look forward to a high rate of participation among general practitioners, so that women's access to the service at the stage in pregnancy when it is safest can be facilitated.

So, up to 9 weeks gestation it is envisaged, as I have said, that most terminations will take place in the community setting and without recourse to referral to hospital or ultrasound scans.

I do understand that not every woman will present early in pregnancy and during the first 9 weeks.

In situations where women present between 9 and 12 weeks of pregnancy, the international evidence and advice I have received indicates that GPs should refer women to the care of consultant obstetricians in hospital environments.

Terminations after 12 weeks of pregnancy will only take place on the grounds of a risk to the life or health of the pregnant woman; a risk to the life or health of the pregnant woman in an emergency; or where there is a condition likely to lead to the death of the foetus before birth or shortly after birth. These will occur in the hospital setting.

I understand that detailed work is ongoing under the auspices of the relevant medical colleges to develop more detailed clinical guidance to assist practitioners in the clinical decision making involved in dealing with these women. My Department has provided financial assistance to the colleges to enable them to complete this work as a key component of the delivery of an integrated service.

I was pleased yesterday to welcome the appointment of Dr Peter Boylan to assist with the HSE's preparations for the implementation of arrangements for termination of pregnancy and related services. Dr Boylan is a leading figure in obstetrics and gynaecology and we are so pleased to have him assist in this work.

Following similar models in other countries, I have directed the HSE to make arrangements to put in place a medically-staffed national telephone helpline to be available on a 24-7 basis once the expanded termination of pregnancy services are in place.

My Department and the HSE are collaborating on developing a comprehensive plan for communicating with the general public and with stakeholder groups for use in introducing expanded and new services. Messages to the general public will highlight the pathways to accessing services, sources of crisis pregnancy counselling and information where the woman may wish to access them, and medical information on the procedure at different stages of gestation.

The importance of attending services early will be one of the key messages of the communications plan.

I want to reiterate that the Government is also committed to working to reduce crisis pregnancies by improving sexual education and ensuring cost is not a barrier in accessing contraception.

## Conclusion

Ceann Comhairle, it has been a long road to get this to juncture. I think today of the many people who have fought this battle over the past 35 years.

I think of the women who shared their private, intimate experiences with the public in order to seek change. I think of the women, and their families, who have endured hardship as a result of the Eighth Amendment but felt unable to share their stories. I hope the work we begin today and the referendum result sends them a message of solidarity and support they were long without.

So in closing, I would ask that we continue to be constructive and not obstructive and ensure we are respectful of each other and of the views of the people of this country as we start the debate on the Health (Regulation of Termination of Pregnancy) Bill.

I hope that we can all work together constructively on this legislation so that we can put services in place for women who need them as soon as possible.

The voices of women who spoke up so movingly during the referendum campaign earlier this year cannot be unheard. Their stories cannot be untold.

If, as I believe to be the case, the people decided they could no longer countenance women being denied care in their own country then we have to make that change. It's time to end the lonely journeys.

Time to finish lifting the shame and stigma that have cast shadows on so many lives. Time to 'stop punishing tragedy'.

I look forward to a future where any woman facing a crisis pregnancy can be assured that she will be treated with compassion and will be able to access all the care she and her family need in this country, supported by those who love them.

Thank you.

SOURCE: Houses of the Oireachtas. "Dáil Éireann Debate - Thursday, 4 Oct 2018 - Health (Regulation of Termination of Pregnancy) Bill 2018: Second Stage." © Houses of the Oireachtas. October 4, 2018. https://www.oireachtas.ie/en/debates/debate/dail/2018-10-04/37/#spk_198. Printed in accordance with the terms of the Oireachtas (Open Data) PSI License. Disclaimer: The Houses of the Oireachtas is not liable for any loss or liability associated with the re-use of information and does not certify that the information is up-to-date or error free. The publication of legislation on our website does not indicate that any particular provision in a statute was, or is currently, in force. The Houses of the Oireachtas does not authorise any user to have exclusive rights to re-use of its information.

## OTHER HISTORIC DOCUMENTS OF INTEREST

### FROM THIS VOLUME

### FROM PREVIOUS *HISTORIC DOCUMENTS*

# June

# Supreme Court Rules on Religious Freedom in Wedding Cake Decision

JUNE 4, 2018

On June 4, 2018, the Supreme Court, in *Masterpiece Cakeshop v. Colorado Civil Rights Commission*, ruled in favor of a Colorado baker who had refused to make a custom wedding cake for a gay couple because he believed that doing so violated his religious beliefs. Some religious groups hoped the opinion would grant business owners with religious objections to same-sex marriage wide latitude to refuse to provide goods and services for such weddings, while civil rights groups worried that such a ruling could open the door to more antigay discrimination. The 7–2 decision was written by Justice Anthony Kennedy, the author of every major decision involving the rights of gay people in the past twenty years. But, in what would turn out to be one of his last decisions before his retirement, he chose not to take the opportunity for a broad ruling on how to balance these competing constitutional concerns. Instead, he wrote a relatively narrow opinion. Although the case came out in favor of the religious baker, it did so on grounds that were very specific to the unique facts of this case and provided little guidance going forward.

## WEDDING CAKE GOES TO COURT

In 2012, Colorado did not recognize same-sex marriages, and the Supreme Court ruling making such recognition mandatory was still three years away. Charlie Craig and Dave Mullins planned to marry legally in Massachusetts and then return to Colorado for a reception for their friends and family. In preparation for this reception, they went to Masterpiece Cakeshop and spoke with the owner, Jack Phillips, to order a cake. Phillips is an expert baker and devout Christian who has owned and operated his shop for twenty-four years and has said that he seeks to "honor God through his work at Masterpiece Cakeshop." Phillips told the couple that he does not create wedding cakes for same-sex weddings but that he would sell them cookies, brownies, birthday cakes, or anything other than wedding cakes. He explained, "I just don't make cakes for same-sex weddings." He later elaborated his belief that "to create a wedding cake for an event that celebrates something that directly goes against the teachings of the Bible, would have been a personal endorsement and participation in the ceremony and relationship that they were entering into."

Shortly afterward, Craig and Mullins filed a discrimination complaint against Masterpiece Cakeshop and Phillips, alleging that they had been denied "full and equal service" at the bakery because of their sexual orientation. The Colorado Anti-Discrimination Act prohibits discrimination in places of public accommodation for reason of "disability, race, creed, color, sex, sexual orientation, marital status, national origin, or ancestry." A state administrative law judge ruled that declining to create a wedding cake for Craig and Mullins constituted prohibited discrimination on the basis of sexual orientation in violation of Colorado law. Phillips had raised two constitutional arguments in his defense, both of which were rejected by the judge. First, that compelling him to use his artistic talents to create a cake would, in effect, force him to express a message with which he disagreed in violation of his First Amendment free-speech rights and, second, would violate his right to free exercise of religion, also protected by the First Amendment.

The Colorado Civil Rights Commission affirmed the administrative judge's decision in full and ordered Phillips to desist from discriminating against same-sex couples by refusing to sell them wedding cakes. Phillips appealed to the Colorado Court of Appeals, which, again, affirmed the ruling. When the Colorado supreme court declined to hear the case, he appealed it to the U.S. Supreme Court.

## NARROW DECISION FAVORS COLORADO BAKER

Justice Kennedy wrote the opinion in *Masterpiece Cakeshop* ruling in favor of Phillips. The opinion, however, was notable for its narrowness. From the start, the Court avoided one of the main arguments presented by Phillips: that compelling him to bake wedding cakes would violate his free-speech rights. Much of the oral argument questioning had focused on whether baking a cake can be speech. Kennedy touched on this, calling that aspect of the case "difficult, for few persons who have seen a beautiful wedding cake might have thought of its creation as an exercise of protected speech." But then he framed the decision entirely as a question of free exercise of religion. The narrow ruling, joined by seven justices, likely indicated that, to the Court, this case contained too many unique facts to make it an appropriate vehicle for a broader ruling on the intersection of the principles of equal protection for gay couples and religious freedom. First off, the case arose before the Supreme Court cases that had recognized the constitutional right to gay marriage. "Phillips' dilemma was particularly understandable," Justice Kennedy wrote, "given the background of legal principles and administration of the law in Colorado at that time."

Further, the Court found that Phillips's case before the Colorado Civil Rights Commission had been tainted by hostility to religion. The Commission, according to the Court, had evidenced "clear and impermissible hostility toward the sincere religious beliefs" motivating Phillips's objection to providing wedding cakes to same-sex weddings. The Court focused on multiple derisive comments made on the record during formal, public hearings, detailing that some commissioners had, according to the Court, "endorsed the view that religious beliefs cannot legitimately be carried into the public sphere or commercial domain, disparaged Phillips' faith as despicable and characterized it as merely rhetorical, and compared his invocation of his sincerely held religious beliefs to defenses of slavery and the Holocaust." Kennedy wrote that these views were "inappropriate for a Commission charged with the solemn responsibility of fair and neutral enforcement of Colorado's antidiscrimination law." Kennedy also found evidence of hostility to religion in the inconsistent treatment of Phillips's claim and at least three other cases of bakers who had objected to a cake order because of conscience. In the other cases, customers had ordered cakes with images and messages in opposition to same-sex marriage and the bakers had objected. In each of these cases, the Commission found the baker to have acted lawfully in refusing service because of the "offensive nature of the requested message." Relying on its own assessment of "offensiveness" to justify a difference in treatment, Kennedy wrote "sends a signal of official disapproval of Phillips' religious beliefs." Evidence of the Commission's hostility to Phillips's sincere religious objections, the Court concluded, "was inconsistent with the First Amendment's guarantees that our laws be applied in a manner that is neutral toward religion." For that reason, the ruling against Phillips must be "set aside."

Despite the outcome, the case left open the possibility that a future case may result in a different ruling. In fact, the opinion repeatedly asserted the legal and constitutional rights of gay Americans. For example, Kennedy wrote that "[o]ur society has come to the recognition that gay persons and gay couples cannot be treated as social outcasts or as inferior in dignity and worth." And, while at the same time, Kennedy recognized that religious objections to gay marriage are protected views, he nevertheless cited the general rule that such objections do not allow businesses to "deny protected persons equal access to goods and services under a neutral and generally applicable public accommodations law." Notably, one of the cases cited for this principle is *Newman v. Piggie Park Enterprises, Inc.*, in which the Supreme Court rejected the claims of owners of a BBQ that their religion required them to refuse service to black customers. And, further, Kennedy wrote that any exception to the general antidiscrimination rule must be narrowly confined; otherwise "a long list of persons who provide goods and services for marriages and weddings might refuse to do so for gay persons, thus resulting in a community-wide stigma inconsistent with the history and dynamics of civil rights laws that ensure equal access to goods, services, and public accommodations."

Although seven justices signed on to the opinion, it was nonetheless deeply fractured, with three separate concurring opinions and one dissent. Justices Ruth Bader Ginsburg and Sonia Sotomayor were the sole dissenters and would have ruled to uphold the Colorado Civil Rights Commission. According to Justice Ginsburg, the comments of two commissioners, given the many layers of independent decision making as the case progressed, did not justify reversing the Commission. Justice Elena Kagan wrote a concurrence, joined by Justice Stephen Breyer. While agreeing with the outcome of the case, she wrote separately to suggest a line of reasoning that the Commission could have used to account for the disparate results between this case and the cases in which bakers refused to bake cakes with antigay messages. This led Justice Neil Gorsuch, joined by Justice Samuel Alito, to write a concurrence to disagree with Justice Kagan, stating that there is no way to "rescue the Commission from its error." Justice Clarence Thomas wrote a separate concurrence to argue that the case should have been decided on much broader free-speech grounds. Justice Gorsuch joined this concurrence, indicating that he is open to a broader ruling shielding merchants who have religious objections to same-sex marriages.

## Reaction to the Narrow Ruling

Reaction to the narrow decision was muted, as supporters of each side found something in the opinion to like. The American Civil Liberties Union (ACLU) statement declared, "the Supreme Court today reaffirmed the core principle that businesses open to the public must be open to all." On the other side, Jeff Hunt, director of the Centennial Institute at Colorado Christian University, described the decision as "a victory for all Americans regardless of religious affiliation as the Supreme Court reaffirmed the importance of religious freedom and freedom of conscience from government interference." On the day of the decision, gay rights activists held a rally on the steps of the Colorado capitol and were joined by Colorado Gov. John Hickenlooper, a Democrat. Reflecting on the *Masterpiece Cakeshop* decision, Hickenlooper commented, "Maybe it was a little naive to think the rapid change in the rights of the gay and lesbian community came so quickly and the battle was done," adding, "I think there will continue to be more skirmishes."

The conflict between claims of religious liberty and antidiscrimination principles is unlikely to abate, and this opinion gave little guidance on how to balance competing claims. One case likely to reach the Court in the future is *Ingersoll v. Arlene's Flowers*, a case from Washington State in which the owner of a flower shop refused to sell flowers to a gay couple for their wedding. Whether in this case or another case, the next time the Supreme Court is presented with the opportunity to rule broadly on the collision between principles of equal protection for LGBTQ people and those of religious liberty, it will not be the same Court. Justice Kennedy, who, in the past decade, has written a series of historic decisions recognizing an expansion of gay rights, officially retired on June 27, 2018, and was replaced by Justice Brett Kavanaugh in October.

—Melissa Feinberg

*Following are excerpts from the Supreme Court decision in the case of* Masterpiece Cakeshop v. Colorado Civil Rights Commission, *on June 4, 2018, in which the Court ruled in favor of a baker who refused to make a cake for a same-sex couple.*

# Supreme Court Issues
# *Ruling on Religious Hostility*

---

**June 4, 2018**

*[Footnotes have been omitted.]*

## SUPREME COURT OF THE UNITED STATES

No. 16-111

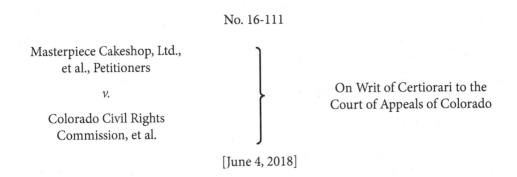

| Masterpiece Cakeshop, Ltd., et al., Petitioners | |
| --- | --- |
| *v.* | On Writ of Certiorari to the Court of Appeals of Colorado |
| Colorado Civil Rights Commission, et al. | |

[June 4, 2018]

JUSTICE KENNEDY delivered the opinion of the Court.

In 2012 a same-sex couple visited Masterpiece Cakeshop, a bakery in Colorado, to make inquiries about ordering a cake for their wedding reception. The shop's owner told the couple that he would not create a cake for their wedding because of his religious opposition to same sex marriages—marriages the State of Colorado itself did not recognize at that time. The couple filed a charge with the Colorado Civil Rights Commission alleging discrimination on the basis of sexual orientation in violation of the Colorado Anti-Discrimination Act.

The Commission determined that the shop's actions violated the Act and ruled in the couple's favor. The Colorado state courts affirmed the ruling and its enforcement order, and this Court now must decide whether the Commission's order violated the Constitution.

The case presents difficult questions as to the proper reconciliation of at least two principles. The first is the authority of a State and its governmental entities to protect the rights and dignity of gay persons who are, or wish to be, married but who face discrimination when they seek goods or services. The second is the right of all persons to exercise fundamental freedoms under the First Amendment, as applied to the States through the Fourteenth Amendment.

The freedoms asserted here are both the freedom of speech and the free exercise of religion. The free speech aspect of this case is difficult, for few persons who have seen a beautiful wedding cake might have thought of its creation as an exercise of protected speech. This is an instructive example, however, of the proposition that the application of constitutional freedoms in new contexts can deepen our understanding of their meaning.

One of the difficulties in this case is that the parties disagree as to the extent of the baker's refusal to provide service. If a baker refused to design a special cake with words or images celebrating the marriage—for instance, a cake showing words with religious meaning—that might be different from a refusal to sell any cake at all. In defining whether a baker's creation can be protected, these details might make a difference.

The same difficulties arise in determining whether a baker has a valid free exercise claim. A baker's refusal to attend the wedding to ensure that the cake is cut the right way, or a refusal to put certain religious words or decorations on the cake, or even a refusal to sell a cake that has been baked for the public generally but includes certain religious words or symbols on it are just three examples of possibilities that seem all but endless.

Whatever the confluence of speech and free exercise principles might be in some cases, the Colorado Civil Rights Commission's consideration of this case was inconsistent with the State's obligation of religious neutrality. The reason and motive for the baker's refusal were based on his sincere religious beliefs and convictions. The Court's precedents make clear that the baker, in his capacity as the owner of a business serving the public, might have his right to the free exercise of religion limited by generally applicable laws. Still, the delicate question of when the free exercise of his religion must yield to an otherwise valid exercise of state power needed to be determined in an adjudication in which religious hostility on the part of the State itself would not be a factor in the balance the State sought to reach. That requirement, however, was not met here. When the Colorado Civil Rights Commission considered this case, it did not do so with the religious neutrality that the Constitution requires.

Given all these considerations, it is proper to hold that whatever the outcome of some future controversy involving facts similar to these, the Commission's actions here violated the Free Exercise Clause; and its order must be set aside.

*[Section I, detailing the factual and legal background of the case, has been omitted.]*

## II

### A

Our society has come to the recognition that gay persons and gay couples cannot be treated as social outcasts or as inferior in dignity and worth. For that reason the laws and the

Constitution can, and in some instances must, protect them in the exercise of their civil rights. The exercise of their freedom on terms equal to others must be given great weight and respect by the courts. At the same time, the religious and philosophical objections to gay marriage are protected views and in some instances protected forms of expression. As this Court observed in *Obergefell* v. *Hodges*, 576 U. S. ___ (2015), "[t]he First Amendment ensures that religious organizations and persons are given proper protection as they seek to teach the principles that are so fulfilling and so central to their lives and faiths." *Id.*, at ___ (slip op., at 27). Nevertheless, while those religious and philosophical objections are protected, it is a general rule that such objections do not allow business owners and other actors in the economy and in society to deny protected persons equal access to goods and services under a neutral and generally applicable public accommodations law. See *Newman* v. *Piggie Park Enterprises, Inc.*, 390 U. S. 400, 402, n. 5 (1968) (*per curiam*); see also *Hurley* v. *Irish-American Gay, Lesbian and Bisexual Group of Boston, Inc.*, 515 U. S. 557, 572 (1995). . . .

When it comes to weddings, it can be assumed that a member of the clergy who objects to gay marriage on moral and religious grounds could not be compelled to perform the ceremony without denial of his or her right to the free exercise of religion. This refusal would be well understood in our constitutional order as an exercise of religion, an exercise that gay persons could recognize and accept without serious diminishment to their own dignity and worth. Yet if that exception were not confined, then a long list of persons who provide goods and services for marriages and weddings might refuse to do so for gay persons, thus resulting in a community-wide stigma inconsistent with the history and dynamics of civil rights laws that ensure equal access to goods, services, and public accommodations.

It is unexceptional that Colorado law can protect gay persons, just as it can protect other classes of individuals, in acquiring whatever products and services they choose on the same terms and conditions as are offered to other members of the public. And there are no doubt innumerable goods and services that no one could argue implicate the First Amendment. Petitioners conceded, moreover, that if a baker refused to sell any goods or any cakes for gay weddings, that would be a different matter and the State would have a strong case under this Court's precedents that this would be a denial of goods and services that went beyond any protected rights of a baker who offers goods and services to the general public and is subject to a neutrally applied and generally applicable public accommodations law. See Tr. of Oral Arg. 4–7, 10.

Phillips claims, however, that a narrower issue is presented. He argues that he had to use his artistic skills to make an expressive statement, a wedding endorsement in his own voice and of his own creation. As Phillips would see the case, this contention has a significant First Amendment speech component and implicates his deep and sincere religious beliefs. In this context the baker likely found it difficult to find a line where the customers' rights to goods and services became a demand for him to exercise the right of his own personal expression for their message, a message he could not express in a way consistent with his religious beliefs. In this context the baker likely found it difficult to find a line where the customers' rights to goods and services became a demand for him to exercise the right of his own personal expression for their message, a message he could not express in a way consistent with his religious beliefs.

*[Discussion about the fact that Colorado did not recognize same-sex marriage at the time of this case has been omitted.]*

There were, to be sue, responses to these arguments that the State could make when it contended for a different result in seeking the enforcement of its generally applicable state regulations of businesses that serve the public. And any decision in favor of the baker would have to be sufficiently constrained lest all purveyors of goods and services who object to gay marriages for moral and religious reasons in effect be allowed to put up signs saying "no goods or services will be sold if they will be used for gay marriages," something that would impose a serious stigma on gay persons. But, nonetheless, Phillips was entitled to the neutral and respectful consideration of his claims in all the circumstances of the case.

## B

The neutral and respectful consideration to which Phillips was entitled was compromised here, however. The Civil Rights Commission's treatment of his case has some elements of a clear and impermissible hostility toward the sincere religious beliefs that motivated his objection.

That hostility surfaced at the Commission's formal, public hearings, as shown by the record. On May 30, 2014, the seven-member Commission convened publicly to consider Phillips' case. At several points during its meeting, commissioners endorsed the view that religious beliefs cannot legitimately be carried into the public sphere or commercial domain, implying that religious beliefs and persons are less than fully welcome in Colorado's business community. . . .

. . . On July 25, 2014, the Commission met again. This meeting, too, was conducted in public and on the record. On this occasion another commissioner made specific reference to the previous meeting's discussion but said far more to disparage Phillips' beliefs. The commissioner stated:

> "I would also like to reiterate what we said in the hearing or the last meeting. Freedom of religion and religion has been used to justify all kinds of discrimination throughout history, whether it be slavery, whether it be the holocaust, whether it be—I mean, we—we can list hundreds of situations where freedom of religion has been used to justify discrimination. And to me it is one of the most despicable pieces of rhetoric that people can use to—to use their religion to hurt others." Tr. 11–12.

To describe a man's faith as "one of the most despicable pieces of rhetoric that people can use" is to disparage his religion in at least two distinct ways: by describing it as despicable, and also by characterizing it as merely rhetorical—something insubstantial and even insincere. The commissioner even went so far as to compare Phillips' invocation of his sincerely held religious beliefs to defenses of slavery and the Holocaust. This sentiment is inappropriate for a Commission charged with the solemn responsibility of fair and neutral enforcement of Colorado's antidiscrimination law—a law that protects against discrimination on the basis of religion as well as sexual orientation. . . .

. . . Another indication of hostility is the difference in treatment between Phillips' case and the cases of other bakers who objected to a requested cake on the basis of conscience and prevailed before the Commission.

As noted above, on at least three other occasions the Civil Rights Division considered the refusal of bakers to create cakes with images that conveyed disapproval of same-sex marriage, along with religious text. Each time, the Division found that the baker acted lawfully in refusing service. It made these determinations because, in the words of the

Division, the requested cake included "wording and images [the baker] deemed derogatory," *Jack* v. *Gateaux, Ltd.*, Charge No. P20140071X, at 4; featured "language and images [the baker] deemed hateful," *Jack* v. *Le Bakery Sensual, Inc.*, Charge No. P20140070X, at 4; or displayed a message the baker "deemed as discriminatory, *Jack* v. *Azucar Bakery*, Charge No. P20140069X, at 4.

The treatment of the conscience-based objections at issue in these three cases contrasts with the Commission's treatment of Phillips' objection. The Commission ruled against Phillips in part on the theory that any message the requested wedding cake would carry would be attributed to the customer, not to the baker. Yet the Division did not address this point in any of the other cases with respect to the cakes depicting anti-gay marriage symbolism. Additionally, the Division found no violation of CADA in the other cases in part because each bakery was willing to sell other products, including those depicting Christian themes, to the prospective customers. But the Commission dismissed Phillips' willingness to sell "birthday cakes, shower cakes, [and] cookies and brownies," App. 152, to gay and lesbian customers as irrelevant. The treatment of the other cases and Phillips' case could reasonably be interpreted as being inconsistent as to the question of whether speech is involved, quite apart from whether the cases should ultimately be distinguished. In short, the Commission's consideration of Phillips' religious objection did not accord with its treatment of these other objections. . . .

A principled rationale for the differences in treatment of these two instances cannot be based on the government's own assessment of offensiveness. Just as "no official, high or petty, can prescribe what shall be orthodox in politics, nationalism, religion, or other matters of opinion." *West Virginia Bd. Of Ed. V. Barnette*, 319 U.S. 624, 642 (1943), it is not as the Court has repeatedly held, the role of the State or its officials to prescribe what shall be offensive. [*citation omitted*] The Colorado court's attempt to account for the difference in treatment elevates one view of what is offensive over another and itself sends a signal of official disapproval of Phillips' religious beliefs. . . .

## C

For the reasons just described, the Commission['s] treatment of Phillips' case violated the State's duty under the First Amendment not to base laws or regulations on hostility to a religion or religious viewpoint. . . .

*[Discussion of the relevant precedents regarding hostility to religious belief has been omitted.]*

. . . In view of these factors the record here demonstrates that the Commission's consideration of Phillips' case was neither tolerant nor respectful of Phillips' religious beliefs. The Commission gave "every appearance," *id.*, at 545, of adjudicating Phillips' religious objection based on a negative normative "evaluation of the particular justification" for his objection and the religious grounds for it. *Id.*, at 537. It hardly requires restating that government has no role in deciding or even suggesting whether the religious ground for Phillips' conscience-based objection is legitimate or illegitimate. On these facts, the Court must draw the inference that Phillips' religious objection was not considered with the neutrality that the Free Exercise Clause requires.

While the issues here are difficult to resolve, it must be concluded that the State's interest could have been weighed against Phillips' sincere religious objections in a way consistent with the requisite religious neutrality that must be strictly observed. The official expressions of hostility to religion in some of the commissioners' comments—comments that were not disavowed at the Commission or by the State at any point in the proceedings that led to affirmance of the order—were inconsistent with what the Free Exercise Clause requires. The Commission's disparate consideration of Phillips' case compared to the cases of the other bakers suggests the same. For these reasons, the order must be set aside.

### III

The Commission's hostility was inconsistent with the First Amendment's guarantee that our laws be applied in a manner that is neutral toward religion. Phillips was entitled to a neutral decisionmaker who would give full and fair consideration to his religious objection as he sought to assert it in all of the circumstances in which this case was presented, considered, and decided. In this case the adjudication concerned a context that may well be different going forward in the respects noted above. However later cases raising these or similar concerns are resolved in the future, for these reasons the rulings of the Commission and of the state court that enforced the Commission's order must be invalidated.

The outcome of cases like this in other circumstances must await further elaboration in the courts, all in the context of recognizing that these disputes must be resolved with tolerance, without undue disrespect to sincere religious beliefs, and without subjecting gay persons to indignities when they seek goods and services in an open market.

The judgment of the Colorado Court of Appeals is reversed.

*It is so ordered.*

*[The concurring opinion of Justice Kagan, joined by Justice Breyer, has been omitted.]*

JUSTICE GORSUCH, with whom JUSTICE ALITO joins, concurring.

*[A review of the facts in the case and the Court's ruling has been omitted.]*

\* \* \*

In *Obergefell*, I warned that the Court's decision would "inevitabl[y] . . . come into conflict" with religious liberty, "as individuals . . . are confronted with demands to participate in and endorse civil marriages between same-sex couples." 576 U. S., at ___ (dissenting opinion) (slip op., at 15). This case proves that the conflict has already emerged. Because the Court's decision vindicates Phillips' right to free exercise, it seems that religious liberty has lived to fight another day. But, in future cases, the freedom of speech could be essential to preventing *Obergefell* from being used to "stamp out every vestige of dissent" and "vilify Americans who are unwilling to assent to the new orthodoxy." *Id.,* at ___ (ALITO, J., dissenting) (slip op., at 6). If that freedom is to maintain its vitality, reasoning like the Colorado Court of Appeals' must be rejected.

JUSTICE GINSBURG, with whom JUSTICE SOTOMAYOR joins, dissenting.

There is much in the Court's opinion with which I agree. "[I]t is a general rule that [religious and philosophical] objections do not allow business owners and other actors in the economy and in society to deny protected persons equal access to goods and services under a neutral and generally applicable public accommodations law." "Colorado law can

protect gay persons, just as it can protect other classes of individuals, in acquiring whatever products and services they choose on the same terms and conditions as are offered to
other members of the public." "[P]urveyors of goods and services who object to gay marriages for moral and religious reasons [may not] put up signs saying 'no goods or services
will be sold if they will be used for gay marriages.'" Gay persons may be spared from
"indignities when they seek goods and services in an open market." I strongly disagree,
however, with the Court's conclusion that Craig and Mullins should lose this case. All of
the above-quoted statements point in the opposite direction.

The Court concludes that "Phillips' religious objection was not considered with the
neutrality that the Free Exercise Clause requires." This conclusion rests on evidence said
to show the Colorado Civil Rights Commission's (Commission) hostility to religion.
Hostility is discernible, the Court maintains, from the asserted "disparate consideration of
Phillips' case compared to the cases of" three other bakers who refused to make cakes
requested by William Jack, an amicus here. The Court also finds hostility in statements
made at two public hearings on Phillips' appeal to the Commission. The different outcomes the Court features do not evidence hostility to religion of the kind we have previously held to signal a free-exercise violation, nor do the comments by one or two members
of one of the four decisionmaking entities considering this case justify reversing the judgment below.

# I

On March 13, 2014—approximately three months after the ALJ ruled in favor of the same-
sex couple, Craig and Mullins, and two months before the Commission heard Phillips'
appeal from that decision—William Jack visited three Colorado bakeries. His visits followed a similar pattern. He requested two cakes

> "made to resemble an open Bible. He also requested that each cake be decorated
> with Biblical verses. [He] requested that one of the cakes include an image of two
> groomsmen, holding hands, with a red 'X' over the image. On one cake, he requested
> [on] one side[,] . . . 'God hates sin. Psalm 45:7' and on the opposite side of the cake
> 'Homosexuality is a detestable sin. Leviticus 18:2.' On the second cake, [the one]
> with the image of the two groomsmen covered by a red 'X' [Jack] requested [these
> words]: 'God loves sinners' and on the other side 'While we were yet sinners Christ
> died for us. Romans 5:8.'"

In contrast to Jack, Craig and Mullins simply requested a wedding cake: They mentioned no message or anything else distinguishing the cake they wanted to buy from any
other wedding cake Phillips would have sold.

One bakery told Jack it would make cakes in the shape of Bibles, but would not deco-
rate them with the requested messages; the owner told Jack her bakery "does not discriminate" and "accept[s] all humans." The second bakery owner told Jack he "had done
open Bibles and books many times and that they look amazing," but declined to make the
specific cakes Jack described because the baker regarded the messages as "hateful."
The third bakery, according to Jack, said it would bake the cakes, but would not include
the requested message.

Jack filed charges against each bakery with the Colorado Civil Rights Division
(Division). The Division found no probable cause to support Jack's claims of unequal

treatment and denial of goods or services based on his Christian religious beliefs. In this regard, the Division observed that the bakeries regularly produced cakes and other baked goods with Christian symbols and had denied other customer requests for designs demeaning people whose dignity the Colorado Anti-discrimination Act (CADA) protects. The Commission summarily affirmed the Division's no-probable-cause finding.

The Court concludes that "the Commission's consideration of Phillips' religious objection did not accord with its treatment of [the other bakers'] objections." But the cases the Court aligns are hardly comparable. The bakers would have refused to make a cake with Jack's requested message for any customer, regardless of his or her religion. And the bakers visited by Jack would have sold him any baked goods they would have sold anyone else. The bakeries' refusal to make Jack cakes of a kind they would not make for any customer scarcely resembles Phillips' refusal to serve Craig and Mullins: Phillips would not sell to Craig and Mullins, for no reason other than their sexual orientation, a cake of the kind he regularly sold to others. When a couple contacts a bakery for a wedding cake, the product they are seeking is a cake celebrating their wedding—not a cake celebrating heterosexual weddings or same-sex weddings—and that is the service Craig and Mullins were denied. Colorado, the Court does not gainsay, prohibits precisely the discrimination Craig and Mullins encountered. See supra, at 1. Jack, on the other hand, suffered no service refusal on the basis of his religion or any other protected characteristic. He was treated as any other customer would have been treated—no better, no worse.

The fact that Phillips might sell other cakes and cookies to gay and lesbian customers was irrelevant to the issue Craig and Mullins' case presented. What matters is that Phillips would not provide a good or service to a same-sex couple that he would provide to a heterosexual couple. In contrast, the other bakeries' sale of other goods to Christian customers was relevant: It shows that there were no goods the bakeries would sell to a non-Christian customer that they would refuse to sell to a Christian customer.

Nor was the Colorado Court of Appeals' "difference in treatment of these two instances . . . based on the government's own assessment of offensiveness." Phillips declined to make a cake he found offensive where the offensiveness of the product was determined solely by the identity of the customer requesting it. The three other bakeries declined to make cakes where their objection to the product was due to the demeaning message the requested product would literally display. As the Court recognizes, a refusal "to design a special cake with words or images . . . might be different from a refusal to sell any cake at all." The Colorado Court of Appeals did not distinguish Phillips and the other three bakeries based simply on its or the Division's finding that messages in the cakes Jack requested were offensive while any message in a cake for Craig and Mullins was not. The Colorado court distinguished the cases on the ground that Craig and Mullins were denied service based on an aspect of their identity that the State chose to grant vigorous protection from discrimination. See App. to Pet. for Cert. 20a, n. 8 ("The Division found that the bakeries did not refuse [Jack's] request because of his creed, but rather because of the offensive nature of the requested message. . . .[T]here was no evidence that the bakeries based their decisions on [Jack's] religion . . . [whereas Phillips] discriminat[ed] on the basis of sexual orientation."). I do not read the Court to suggest that the Colorado Legislature's decision to include certain protected characteristics in CADA is an impermissible government prescription of what is and is not offensive. To repeat, the Court affirms that "Colorado law can protect gay persons, just as it can protect other classes of individuals, in acquiring whatever products and services they choose on the same terms and conditions as are offered to other members of the public."

## II

Statements made at the Commission's public hearings on Phillips' case provide no firmer support for the Court's holding today. Whatever one may think of the statements in historical context, I see no reason why the comments of one or two Commissioners should be taken to overcome Phillips' refusal to sell a wedding cake to Craig and Mullins. The proceedings involved several layers of independent decisionmaking, of which the Commission was but one. First, the Division had to find probable cause that Phillips violated CADA. Second, the ALJ entertained the parties' cross-motions for summary judgment. Third, the Commission heard Phillips' appeal. Fourth, after the Commission's ruling, the Colorado Court of Appeals considered the case de novo. What prejudice infected the determinations of the adjudicators in the case before and after the Commission? The Court does not say. Phillips' case is thus far removed from the only precedent upon which the Court relies, *Church of Lukumi Babalu Aye, Inc. v. Hialeah*, 508 U. S. 520 (1993), where the government action that violated a principle of religious neutrality implicated a sole decisionmaking body, the city council.

* * *

For the reasons stated, sensible application of CADA to a refusal to sell any wedding cake to a gay couple should occasion affirmance of the Colorado Court of Appeals' judgment. I would so rule.

SOURCE: Supreme Court of the United States. *Masterpiece Cakeshop v. Colorado Civil Rights Commission.* 584 U.S. __ (2018). https://www.supremecourt.gov/opinions/17pdf/16-111diff2_e1pf.pdf.

## OTHER HISTORIC DOCUMENTS OF INTEREST

### FROM PREVIOUS *HISTORIC DOCUMENTS*

# President Trump, Chairman Kim Remark on Historic Summit

JUNE 12, 2018

After months of name calling and veiled threats about preemptive military strikes, President Donald Trump and North Korean Chairman Kim Jong Un came face to face for a historic summit in Sentosa, Singapore, on June 12, 2018. The meeting marked the first time a sitting U.S. president and North Korean leader had met. Little is known about what Trump and Kim discussed during their thirty-five-minute, one-on-one conversation, but the extended talks with advisers from both nations resulted in the issuance of a joint statement declaring the intent of the two countries to work toward improving their relationship. The president faced criticism at home both during the lead-up to the meeting and after for giving too much credence to a nuclear-armed leader who has starved his citizens and walking away from the summit without any gains. Trump, however, celebrated the summit as a success and announced his intention to meet again with Kim to further the relationship between the two nations.

## ON-AGAIN, OFF-AGAIN SUMMIT

Throughout most of 2017, North Korea and the United States appeared locked in a war of words that many hoped would not result in actual military activity. Trump referred to Kim as "little rocket man" and at one point promised to bring the "fire and fury" of the United States to North Korea. For his part, Kim continued his nuclear weapons buildup and missile tests and was subject to a growing number of sanctions issued by the United Nations, United States, and other Western governments. By 2018, Kim was taking a slightly more diplomatic tack with neighboring South Korea and was positioning his country as a larger player on the international stage. Kim was the first North Korean leader to enter South Korea since the end of the Korean War, and he began making inroads with South Korean leader Moon Jae-in toward normalized relations and denuclearization. The two nations even competed on a unified team at the Winter Olympics in PyeongChang, South Korea, in February 2018.

Utilizing the Olympics as a diplomatic springboard, the North and South Koreans held several summits, and the South Koreans traveled to the United States in March and delivered an invitation to Trump from North Korea to meet. Multiple high-level talks took place before a summit date in May was agreed to. The Singapore island of Sentosa was chosen as the site of the summit. Each nation would bring a delegation to the meeting, which for the United States would include Secretary of State Mike Pompeo, White House Chief of Staff John Kelly, senior policy adviser Stephen Miller, and National Security Adviser John Bolton. (Pompeo held advance meetings in Pyongyang to prepare for the summit and, as part of those negotiations, secured the release of three Americans being detained in North Korea.)

In mid-May, questions swirled about whether the summit would take place after National Security Adviser Bolton and Vice President Mike Pence suggested that North Korea use Libya's model toward denuclearization, one of abandoning the program first before receiving concessions from other countries. Kim Kye Gwan, first vice minister of foreign affairs for North Korea, called the statement "not an expression of intention to address the issue through dialogue. It is essentially a manifestation of [an] awfully sinister move to impose on our dignified state the destiny of Libya or Iraq which had been collapsed due to yielding the whole of their countries to big powers." On May 24, Trump wrote a letter to Kim declaring that he would no longer participate in the summit, citing a statement from North Korea indicating the reclusive nation could "make the U.S. taste an appalling tragedy it has neither experienced nor even imagined." But that changed a week later after Trump met with Kim's deputy, Kim Yong Chol, at the White House. Trump declared the summit would be pushed back to June and he cautioned, "This will not be just a photo-op" but that North Korea has "to de-nuke. If they don't denuclearize, that will not be acceptable."

The acrimonious relationship between the United States and North Korea finally reached a head when the two leaders shook hands in front of a row of U.S. and North Korean flags on June 12, 2018. During the highly choreographed event, the pair walked together to a private meeting with just their interpreters before a bilateral session and working lunch that included other U.S. and North Korean officials. Trump, who claimed that he did not require much preparation for the meeting because it was based more on "attitude," showed Kim a video on his iPad he had commissioned about the possibilities if the United States and North Korea could form a firm bond. At the conclusion of the summit, the pair signed a joint agreement to work together on issues including the denuclearization of the Korean peninsula in return for security promises from the United States. "Today we had a historic meeting and decided to leave the past behind," Kim said in Korean. "The world will see a major change."

## SUMMIT OUTCOMES

Trump kept many of the details from his meeting with Kim private but felt that the two had established a strong relationship that the United States could leverage. "We both want to do something. We both are going to do something. And we have developed a very special bond," Trump said, adding, "people are going to be very impressed. People are going to be very happy." Despite Trump's declaration of his own success at the summit, international analysts largely agreed that Kim walked away the victor. Trump did not press for concrete steps toward denuclearization during the talks but did agree to halt joint U.S.–South Korea military drills and also questioned the future of U.S. troops in South Korea. "I want to get our soldiers out. I want to bring our soldiers back home," Trump said but added, "That's not part of the equation right now. I hope it will be eventually."

Democrats criticized the president for his handling of Kim. "In his haste to reach an agreement, President Trump elevated North Korea to the level of the United States while preserving the regime's status quo," House Minority Leader Nancy Pelosi, D-Calif., said. Republicans were more optimistic about the meeting but did remain cautious. "We must always be clear that we are dealing with a brutal regime with a long history of deceit," said House Speaker Paul Ryan, R-Wis. "Only time will tell if North Korea is serious this time, and in the meantime we must continue to apply maximum economic pressure," he said. Sen. Tom Cotton, R-Ark., said the meeting was "not something that we should celebrate. It's not a pretty sight. But it's a necessary part of the job to try to protect Americans from a terrible threat."

The summit drew particular criticism for the 400-word joint statement, known as the Singapore Declaration. In it, Trump "committed to provide security guarantees to the DPRK," while Kim "reaffirmed his firm and unwavering commitment to complete denuclearization of the Korean Peninsula." However, the document called only for working "toward complete denuclearization" and an "unwavering commitment to complete denuclearization" rather than establishing firm commitments and next steps toward denuclearizing the Korean peninsula, including concessions from Kim. Christopher Hill, ambassador to South Korea under former president Barack Obama, said Kim had not "given up anything that hasn't been given up before." Ahead of the summit, the United States said it would not accept anything but "complete, verifiable, irreversible denuclearization," and Pompeo told the media the "v" for "verification" matters. The declaration did not contain the word *verification*.

## ONGOING WORK TOWARD DENUCLEARIZATION

Following the Trump–Kim summit, the two nations met infrequently, and many diplomatic talks aimed at developing a roadmap for denuclearization were canceled. By the end of the year, there were few signs that any significant progress had been made toward a denuclearized North Korea. The two nations remained at odds over what must happen before steps could be taken to denuclearize. North Korea was unwavering in its opinion that the relationship between the United States and North Korea must be normalized—including the end of sanctions—before any denuclearization activities could begin, while the United States said destruction or surrender of nuclear weapons must come first. Secretary Pompeo frequently defended the administration's progress, noting, "We continue to have conversations about the right next step that is the right substantive next step."

In early December, Trump announced that he intended to meet again with Kim in early 2019. "We're getting along very well. We have a good relationship," Trump said during the G20 Summit in Argentina while announcing that three sites were currently under consideration for the meeting and that Kim may at some point visit the United States. According to Vice President Pence, the next meeting would be held without a full list of the North Korean nuclear weapons and sites, despite the United States pressing for such information before additional talks could be held. Pence did say, however, that the 2019 meeting would be used to develop a clearer plan for denuclearization. "I think it will be absolutely imperative in this next summit that we come away with a plan for identifying all of the weapons in question, identifying all the development sites, allowing for inspections of the sites and the plan for dismantling nuclear weapons," Pence said.

—Heather Kerrigan

*Following is a joint statement issued by U.S. President Donald Trump and North Korean leader Kim Jong Un on the relationship between the two countries, and a subsequent press conference, both on June 12, 2018.*

# Trump, Kim Release Joint Statement on U.S.–North Korea Relationship

**June 12, 2018**

President Donald J. Trump of the United States of America and Chairman Kim Jong Un of the State Affairs Commission of the Democratic People's Republic of Korea (DPRK) held a first, historic summit in Singapore on June 12, 2018.

President Trump and Chairman Kim Jong Un conducted a comprehensive, in-depth, and sincere exchange of opinions on the issues related to the establishment of new U.S.–DPRK relations and the building of a lasting and robust peace regime on the Korean Peninsula. President Trump committed to provide security guarantees to the DPRK, and Chairman Kim Jong Un reaffirmed his firm and unwavering commitment to complete denuclearization of the Korean Peninsula.

Convinced that the establishment of new U.S.–DPRK relations will contribute to the peace and prosperity of the Korean Peninsula and of the world, and recognizing that mutual confidence building can promote the denuclearization of the Korean Peninsula, President Trump and Chairman Kim Jong Un state the following:

1.   The United States and the DPRK commit to establish new U.S.–DPRK relations in accordance with the desire of the peoples of the two countries for peace and prosperity.

2.   The United States and the DPRK will join their efforts to build a lasting and stable peace regime on the Korean Peninsula.

3.   Reaffirming the April 27, 2018 Panmunjom Declaration, the DPRK commits to work toward complete denuclearization of the Korean Peninsula.

4.   The United States and the DPRK commit to recovering POW/MIA remains, including the immediate repatriation of those already identified.

Having acknowledged that the U.S.–DPRK summit—the first in history—was an epochal event of great significance in overcoming decades of tensions and hostilities between the two countries and for the opening up of a new future, President Trump and Chairman Kim Jong Un commit to implement the stipulations in this joint statement fully and expeditiously. The United States and the DPRK commit to hold follow-on negotiations, led by the U.S. Secretary of State, Mike Pompeo, and a relevant high-level DPRK official, at the earliest possible date, to implement the outcomes of the U.S.–DPRK summit.

President Donald J. Trump of the United States of America and Chairman Kim Jong Un of the State Affairs Commission of the Democratic People's Republic of Korea have committed to cooperate for the development of new U.S.-DPRK relations and for the promotion of peace, prosperity, and security of the Korean Peninsula and of the world.

DONALD J. TRUMP
President of the United States of America

KIM JONG UN
Chairman of the State Affairs Commission
of the Democratic People's Republic of Korea

Sentosa Island
June 12, 2018
Singapore

SOURCE: Executive Office of the President. "Joint Statement by President Trump and Chairman of the State Affairs Commission Kim Jong Un of North Korea." June 12, 2018. *Compilation of Presidential Documents* 2018, no. 00422 (June 12, 2018). https://www.gpo.gov/fdsys/pkg/DCPD-201800422/pdf/DCPD-201800422.pdf.

## *Trump, Kim Hold Joint Press Conference following Historic Summit*

**June 12, 2018**

*President Trump.* So we're signing a very important document, a pretty comprehensive document. And we've had a really great term together, a great relationship. I'll be giving a news conference at 2:30, which is in a little bit less than 2 hours. And we'll discuss this at great length. In the meantime, I believe that they'll be handing it out on behalf of Chairman Kim or myself. And we're both very honored to sign the document. Thank you.

Would you like to say something to the press?

*Chairman Kim.* Today we had a historic meeting and decided to leave the past behind. And we are about to sign a historic document. The world will see a major change. I would like to express my gratitude to President Trump to make this meeting happen. Thank you.

*President Trump.* Thank you very much.

Okay. Okay.

*[At this point, President Trump and Chairman Kim signed the joint statement.]*

*North Korea's Nuclear Weapons Program*

Q. Mr. President, did he agree to denuclearize, sir?

*President Trump.* We're starting that process very quickly. Very, very quickly. Absolutely.

*North Korea–U.S. Relations*

Q. Mr. President, 100-percent denuclearization?

Q. Did you talk about Otto Warmbier, sir?

*Q.* Mr. Kim, did you agree to give up your nuclear arms?

*President Trump.* You'll be seeing everything in just a little while. The letter that we're signing is very comprehensive, and I think both sides are going to be very impressed with the result. A lot of good will went into this, a lot of work, a lot of preparation. I want to thank everybody on both sides. Secretary Pompeo and all of his counterparts, they were absolutely fantastic.

Thank you very much. That's fantastic. Thank you very much.

Thank you very much, everybody. We'll see you a little bit later. And we're very proud of what took place today. I think our whole relationship with North Korea and the Korean Peninsula is—it's going to be a very much different situation than it has in the past. We both want to do something. We both are going to do something. And we have developed a very special bond. So people are going to be very impressed. People are going to be very happy. And we're going to take care of a very big and very dangerous problem for the world.

And I want to thank Chairman Kim. We spent a lot of time together today, a very intensive time. And I would actually say that it worked out for both of us far better than anybody could have expected. I think far better—I watched the various news reports. I would say far better than anybody even predicted.

And this is going to lead to more and more and more. And it's an honor to be with you, a very great honor.

Thank you. Thank you to all of your representatives very much.

Thank you very much, everybody. Thank you.

*North Korea–U.S. Relations*

*Q.* Mr. Kim, will you invite Chairman Kim to the White House?

*President Trump.* Absolutely, I will.

*Q.* Mr. Kim, would you like to come to Washington?

*President Trump.* Thank you. Thank you, everybody.

SOURCE: Executive Office of the President. "Remarks on Signing a Joint Statement with Chairman of the State Affairs Commission Kim Jong Un of North Korea and an Exchange with Reporters on Sentosa Island, Singapore." June 12, 2018. https://www.gpo.gov/fdsys/pkg/DCPD-201800421/pdf/DCPD-201800421.pdf.

## OTHER HISTORIC DOCUMENTS OF INTEREST

### FROM THIS VOLUME

**FROM PREVIOUS *HISTORIC DOCUMENTS***

# IMF Issues Financial Support during Argentina Financial Crisis

JUNE 20, AUGUST 29, AND OCTOBER 26, 2018

Argentina, Latin America's third-largest economy, spiraled deeper into economic turmoil in 2018. By fall, the nation was facing inflation over 30 percent and interest rates as high as 60 percent, the monthly gross domestic product (GDP) had fallen sharply, and the president's approval rating plummeted. Despite promises that he would revive the economy, the president's economic plans only resulted in an increasing number of Argentinians falling into poverty. The crisis led to the request of a $50 billion standby loan from the International Monetary Fund (IMF), which the government initially intended to use only to shore up investor confidence. However, within months of asking for the arrangement, Argentina requested an emergency disbursement of the loan, and then an increase in the total loan amount.

## NATION DEVOLVES INTO CRISIS

Argentina is no stranger to difficult economic conditions. From 1998 to 2002, the nation experienced a severe economic depression that resulted in a 28 percent contraction in its economy. The government collapsed, unemployment was widespread, more than 50 percent of Argentinians were living below the poverty line, and 25 percent were considered indigent. Many Argentinians blamed the IMF for the crisis, and in 2004, the body admitted that its "surveillance failed to highlight the growing vulnerabilities in the authorities' choice of policies and the IMF erred by supporting inadequate policies too long." The nation fell deeper into the red as it tried to maintain its locked-in exchange rate against the U.S. dollar. Some of the funds pledged by the IMF to assist in the financial crisis were utilized to sustain that so-called peg, which was eventually eliminated toward the end of the crisis. "In retrospect, the resources used in an attempt to preserve the peg could have been better used to mitigate some of the inevitable costs of exit," the IMF said in 2004.

Argentina's economy would eventually begin growing again, albeit slowly, under President Nestor Kirchner, who led the country until his death in 2007, the same year Argentina paid off its previous loan to the IMF. Kirchner was succeeded by his wife, Cristina Fernandez, who took a different tack on the economy upon assuming office. Fernandez increased public spending and heavily subsidized consumer services including utilities. The government also restricted access to the dollar and tightly controlled its exchange rate, but that left the economy without access to global financial markets and rampant inflation. President Mauricio Macri was elected in 2015 with a promise to institute reforms that would restart economic stagnation. He began by removing Fernandez's protectionist policies to reopen Argentina to foreign trade, cut government spending, and reduce taxes. Initially, the reforms worked. Inflation fell, and the poverty rate was on the decline.

In December 2017, however, the nation experienced its worst drought in three decades, which hampered its corn and soybean harvests. At the same time, interest rate hikes in the United States strengthened the dollar worldwide, and foreign investors began putting their money into the U.S. dollar rather than smaller, emerging markets like Argentina. Argentina's debt became increasingly expensive for investors who had a growing lack of confidence in the government to shore up its financial woes. Lower-than-anticipated foreign investment and increasing commodity prices triggered a currency devaluation.

In turn, the government instituted emergency efforts like increasing export taxes, shrinking the size of the government, raising utility rates, and decreasing pension benefits. Macri aimed to cut Argentina's fiscal deficit to 1.3 percent of GDP by 2019, which would require increased foreign investment, something that proved difficult as the dollar continued to improve against the peso. The reforms didn't go far enough toward addressing runaway inflation, growing debt, an ever-expanding fiscal deficit, and flagging investor confidence. Argentinians took to the streets to protest the government and its seemingly ineffective economic strategies.

## IMF AGREES TO ASSIST

As the economy continued to contract, Macri's government turned to the IMF in May 2018 and requested a $50 billion standby loan. To gain approval for the loan, Argentina was required to submit a plan detailing its proposed efforts for economic improvement. The plan included four key provisions including expediting the reduction of the government's deficit to restore the primary balance by 2020, reducing inflation by establishing a more independent central bank and policies such as an exchange rate based on market forces, steady spending on social programs as a share of GDP, and rebuilding foreign exchange reserves held by the central bank. The goal was also to bring inflation down into the single digits by the end of 2021. The request was approved on June 20 and quickly made $15 billion available to Argentina's government. The remaining $35 billion would be provided at the nation's request over the three-year term of the agreement, but disbursement would be based on quarterly IMF reviews of Argentina's work to improve its fiscal situation. Macri said he did not intend to utilize the money but that it would instead be used to increase consumer and foreign investor confidence. According to the IMF Executive Board, Argentina's government intended to "treat the remainder of the arrangement as precautionary."

In a statement announcing the standby arrangement, the IMF said the government's plan "aims to strengthen the country's economy by restoring market confidence via a consistent macroeconomic program that lessens financing needs, puts Argentina's public debt on a firm downward trajectory, and strengthens the plan to reduce inflation by setting more realistic inflation targets and reinforcing the independence of the central bank." It added, "Importantly, the plan includes steps to protect society's most vulnerable by maintaining social spending and, if social conditions were to deteriorate, by providing room for greater spending on Argentina's social safety net."

On August 29, amid ongoing economic strain, Argentina requested an emergency release of the $50 billion loan fund. The peso lost 12 percent following the news, reaching a loss of half its value since the start of 2018, and the central bank raised interest rates from 45 percent to 60 percent. Macri said the move was intended to eliminate uncertainty because the nation had "seen new expressions of lack of confidence in the markets, specifically over our financing capacity in 2019." The IMF agreed to allow the Argentinian government access to the funds in return for a revision of its economic plan "with a focus on better insulating Argentina from the recent shifts in global financial markets, including through stronger monetary and fiscal policies and a deepening of efforts to support the most vulnerable in society," said IMF Managing Director Christine Lagarde. The revised economic plan included expanded austerity measures and new export taxes. Understanding that the IMF remains unpopular in Argentina, Lagarde sought to reassure the public that the government was driving the reforms, noting that "the Argentine authorities will be critical in steering Argentina through the current difficult circumstances and will ultimately strengthen the economy for the benefit of all Argentines."

One month later, Argentina requested that the IMF expand the total loan package to $57.1 billion, which the IMF agreed to in October. Lagarde called the $57.1 billion package "the biggest loan in the history of the IMF" but cautioned that it came with explicit provisions. Argentina would be required to reach zero deficit for 2019, and the central bank could only intervene to stabilize the peso in rare instances. The latter provision is considered among many in the Argentinian media to be the reason why the central bank's president, Luis Caputo, resigned. Caputo cited personal reasons for his resignation, but one person familiar with the situation told the *Financial Times* that Caputo "was asking for permission to intervene in the foreign exchange markets and that caused very great fear at the IMF." The resignation resulted in an immediate 5 percent dip in the peso.

## UNIONS STRIKE, MACRI FACES BACKLASH

The expanded IMF loan led to renewed protests against Macri and his government. In September, Argentina's unions called for a nationwide strike. The move resulted in a closure of bus and train lines and the grounding of flights. Banks, stores, and schools closed, and some hospitals were forced to provide only emergency services due to staffing shortages. Those striking demanded that the government help citizens who were dealing with cutbacks in subsidies and high prices for consumer goods. "These are humiliating times for our country. It's the people who are saying, 'enough,'" said Hugo Moyano, the secretary general of Argentina's largest union confederation, CGT.

Macri was a prime target of the protests. The president campaigned on a platform that promised to eliminate poverty and increase jobs. However, the worsening economic situation actually deepened the nation's poverty level, and work remained scarce. Added to that, the IMF's unpopularity with the Argentinian people, and the austerity measures instituted by his government, President Macri's popularity took a significant hit and his approval rating dipped below 27 percent by October. Spurred by what they saw as Macri's inability to control the crisis, opposition parties in Parliament began working together to pass measures popular with the public, including one that would lower utility tariffs. Macri was forced to veto the measure to maintain progress on his economic reform package. It is likely that Macri will face a difficult reelection battle in 2019. Argentinian newspapers reported that his predecessor, Fernandez, was a likely challenger, despite having been charged in a bribery scandal in September 2018.

—Heather Kerrigan

*Following is a June 20, 2018, press release from the International Monetary Fund (IMF) Executive Board regarding the approval of Argentina's $50 billion standby* *loan; a statement by the IMF Managing Director on August 29, 2018, upon Argentina's request for emergency disbursement of funds; and an October 26, 2018, press release from the IMF Executive Board announcing the agreement of an expanded loan amount for Argentina.*

# IMF Executive Board Approves $50 Billion Loan Plan for Argentina

June 20, 2018

The Executive Board of the International Monetary Fund (IMF) today approved a three-year Stand-By Arrangement (SBA) for Argentina amounting to US$50 billion (equivalent to SDR 35.379 billion, or about 1,110 percent of Argentina's quota in the IMF).

The Board's decision allows the authorities to make an immediate purchase of US$15 billion (equivalent to SDR 10,614 billion, or 333 percent of Argentina's quota). One half of this amount (US$7.5 billion) will be used for budget support. The remaining amount of IMF financial support (US$35 billion) will be made available over the duration of the arrangement, subject to quarterly reviews by the Executive Board. The authorities have indicated that they intend to draw on the first tranche of the arrangement but subsequently treat the remainder of the arrangement as precautionary.

The Argentine authorities' economic plan backed by the SBA aims to strengthen the country's economy by restoring market confidence via a consistent macroeconomic program that lessens financing needs, puts Argentina's public debt on a firm downward trajectory, and strengthens the plan to reduce inflation by setting more realistic inflation targets and reinforcing the independence of the central bank. Importantly, the plan includes steps to protect society's most vulnerable by maintaining social spending and, if social conditions were to deteriorate, by providing room for greater spending on Argentina's social safety net.

Following the Executive Board discussion of Argentina's economic plan, Ms. Christine Lagarde, Managing Director and Chair, summarized the Board's findings:

"For the past 2½ years, Argentina has been engaged in a systemic transformation of its economy, including deep changes to foreign exchange markets, subsidies, and taxation, as well as improvements to their official statistics. Nonetheless, a recent shift in market sentiment and an ill-fated confluence of factors have placed Argentina under significant balance of payments pressures. Amid these challenging circumstances, the Government has requested IMF support in implementing its own policy plans.

"The authorities' intended policies seek to address longstanding vulnerabilities, ensure that debt remains sustainable, reduce inflation, and foster growth and job creation, while reducing poverty.

"Given the large fiscal deficits over the past several years, the Government's economic program is anchored on the goal of achieving federal government primary balance by 2020. This will be key to restoring market confidence. Improving the budgetary process and providing this medium-term anchor for fiscal policy will help to entrench these gains.

"The authorities also aim to rebuild the credibility of the inflation targeting framework, including by strengthening central bank independence and ending direct and indirect central bank financing of the government. These efforts are expected to bring inflation to single digits by end-2021.

"The authorities are committed to a floating, market-determined exchange rate. They intend to limit foreign exchange intervention to periods of significant volatility and market dysfunction, and to rebuild reserve buffers.

"The program places considerable emphasis on maintaining social cohesion, encouraging gender equality, and protecting society's most vulnerable. The authorities, at the highest level, are strongly committed to these principles. The most vulnerable population will be assisted by well-designed government support programs that will be prioritized within the program targets. The Government has also prioritized gender equity to realize the potential and benefits from Argentine women fully participating, on equal footing, in the economy.

"The Argentine Government has demonstrated its strong ownership of the program, which is custom-tailored for the situation faced by the people of Argentina. There are evident risks to the program but steadfast implementation of the policy plans will allow the country to fully capitalize on its economic potential, and to ensure that all Argentines are included in the country's future prosperity."

## ANNEX

### Recent economic developments

Argentina's financial markets came under sudden pressure in April as the result of a confluence of factors. A severe drought led to a sharp decline in agricultural production and export revenue, world energy prices increased, and global financial conditions tightened through an appreciation of the U.S. dollar and an upward shift in U.S. interest rates. These changes interacted with vulnerabilities that Argentina's policy path had embedded, including significant fiscal and external financing requirements. These economic forces manifested themselves principally in the form of pressure on the Argentine peso, market anxiety about the roll-over of short-term central bank paper, and an increase in Argentina's sovereign risk premium.

### Program summary

The IMF-support economic plan aims to strengthen the Argentine economy by focusing on four key pillars:

- **Restore market confidence.** The government has committed to a clear macroeconomic program that lessens federal financing needs and puts public debt on a firm downward trajectory. This will help create a clear path to strong, sustained, and equitable growth and robust job creation. Anchoring this effort is a fiscal adjustment that ensures that the federal government reaches primary balance by 2020, with a significant up-front adjustment to secure a primary deficit of 1.3 percent of GDP in 2019.

- **Protect society's most vulnerable.** Steps will be taken to strengthen the social safety net, including through a redesign of assistance programs (which are often overlapping, yet still result in gaps in coverage) and through measures to increase female labor force participation (by eliminating the second-earner tax penalty and providing working families with assistance with childcare). The level of social spending will be protected under the program. Also, if needed, additional spending on pre-identified, high-quality, means-tested social assistance projects will be accommodated. The authorities' goal is to continue to reduce poverty rates throughout the course of the arrangement even if there were to be a slower-than-expected economic rebound.

- **Strengthen the credibility of the central bank's inflation targeting framework.** The government has pledged to provide the central bank with the institutional and operational independence and autonomy that is needed to achieve effectively inflation objectives. In addition, the central bank has adopted a new credible path of disinflation to bring inflation to single digits by the end of the three-year SBA period. Plans are also being developed to ensure the central bank has a healthy balance sheet and full financial autonomy. The plan also foresees steps to diminish the Central Bank's vulnerability from a short term peso denominated debt (LEBACs).

- **Progressively lessen the strains on the balance of payments.** This would involve rebuilding international reserves and reducing Argentina's vulnerability to pressures on the capital account.

*[Financial tables have been omitted.]*

SOURCE: International Monetary Fund. "IMF Executive Board Approves US$50 Billion Stand-By Arrangement for Argentina." June 20, 2018. https://www.imf.org/en/News/Articles/2018/06/20/pr18245-argentina-imf-executive-board-approves-us50-billion-stand-by-arrangement.

## IMF Responds to Argentina Request for Emergency Loan Disbursement

**August 29, 2018**

Ms. Christine Lagarde, the International Monetary Fund's Managing Director, made the following statement today regarding Argentina.

"President Macri and I had a productive conversation today. He indicated his desire to work toward strengthening the policies underpinning the Stand-By Arrangement with the IMF.

"In consideration of the more adverse international market conditions, which had not been fully anticipated in the original program with Argentina, the authorities will be working to revise the government's economic plan with a focus on better insulating Argentina from the recent shifts in global financial markets, including through stronger monetary and fiscal policies and a deepening of efforts to support the most vulnerable in society.

"I stressed my support for Argentina's policy efforts and our readiness to assist the government in developing its revised policy plans. I have instructed IMF staff to work with the Argentine authorities to strengthen the Fund-supported arrangement and to reexamine the phasing of the financial program. I have agreed that we would aim to reach a rapid conclusion of these discussions to present to our Executive Board for approval.

"I am confident that the strong commitment and determination of the Argentine authorities will be critical in steering Argentina through the current difficult circumstances and will ultimately strengthen the economy for the benefit of all Argentines."

SOURCE: International Monetary Fund. "Statement by the IMF's Managing Director on Argentina." August 29, 2018. https://www.imf.org/en/News/Articles/2018/08/29/pr18336-argentina-statement-by-the-imf-managing-director.

# IMF Extends Argentina Loan Amount

**October 26, 2018**

The Executive Board of the International Monetary Fund (IMF) completed today the first review of Argentina's economic performance under the 36-month Stand-By Arrangement (SBA) that was approved on June 20, 2018.

The completion of the review allows the authorities to draw the equivalent of about US$5.7 billion (SDR 4.10 billion), bringing total disbursements since June to about US$20.4 billion (SDR 14.71 billion). The Board also approved an augmentation of the Stand-By Arrangement to increase access to about US$56.3 billion (equivalent to SDR 40.71 billion or 1,277 percent of quota)[1]. The authorities have requested the use of this IMF financing as budget support.

Argentina's strengthened economic plan aims to bolster confidence and stabilize the economy through a reduction in the budget deficit, the adoption of a simpler monetary policy framework, and freely floating the exchange rate (with foreign currency intervention limited to cases of an extreme overshooting of the currency). Protecting the most vulnerable in Argentina continues to be a central component of the authorities' efforts including by prioritizing social assistance spending and planning for an increase in spending on social assistance programs in the event that social conditions deteriorate.

Following the Executive Board discussion of Argentina's economic plan, Ms. Christine Lagarde, the IMF's Managing Director, stated:

"Argentina has faced difficult market conditions but the authorities have remained steadfastly committed to the Stand-By Arrangement's main policy objectives to address long-standing vulnerabilities, protect the vulnerable, ensure that the public debt remains sustainable, reduce inflation, and foster growth and job creation.

"To achieve these goals, the authorities have redoubled their reform efforts by accelerating the reduction in the fiscal deficit to reach primary balance in 2019 and achieve a primary surplus starting in 2020. The 2019 budget, which is anchored by this target, has been approved by the Lower House. Its passage into law will be key to restoring confidence and ensuring policy continuity.

"The authorities have redesigned their monetary policy framework with strict limits on the growth in the monetary base. This framework is expected to provide a simpler and more effective anchor that will decisively lower inflation and inflation expectations.

"The authorities are allowing the currency to freely float. However, in the event that there is a significant overshooting of the exchange rate, the Central Bank is prepared to intervene in a limited, simple, and rules-based way.

"The program continues to emphasize improving gender equality, protecting society's most vulnerable, and laying the foundation for growth and job creation. The authorities have already taken measures to increase social assistance programs and have prioritized social assistance and childcare spending in the 2019 Budget.

"Despite the challenging environment the government has proactively strengthened its policy plans. Important challenges remain. However, full implementation of the policies that underpin the Stand-By Arrangement, together with strong support from the international community, should allow the country to return to macroeconomic stability and fulfill its full economic potential, for the benefit of all Argentines."

### Annex

The main elements of Argentina's revised economic plan are summarized below:

**Fiscal Policy:** The authorities are fully committed to reducing the federal government's financing needs and placing public debt on a firm downward path. They aim to strengthen the country's fiscal position by achieving a primary balance in 2019 and primary surpluses starting in 2020. To this end, the government is seeking support in the Argentine Congress for revenue-enhancing and cost-cutting measures that include: introducing taxes on exports, increasing the wealth tax, scaling back inefficient energy subsidies, reprioritizing capital spending, and improving the structure of federal transfers to provinces.

**Monetary Policy:** To decisively reduce inflation, the Central Bank will shift toward a stronger, simpler, and more verifiable monetary policy regime, temporarily replacing the inflation targeting regime with a monetary base target. At the center of the new framework is a commitment to cap the growth of money to zero percent per month (calculated as the change in the monthly average) until June 2019, with the aim of decisively bringing down inflation and inflation expectations. This framework is supplemented by a commitment not to allow short-term rates to fall below 60 percent until 12-month inflation expectations decisively fall for at least two consecutive months.

**Exchange Rate Policy:** The Central Bank of Argentina (BCRA) has adopted a floating exchange rate regime without intervention. However, in the event of extreme overshooting of the exchange rate, the BCRA may conduct limited intervention in foreign exchange markets to prevent disorderly market conditions. Such intervention would be unsterilized.

**Social Protection and Gender Equality.** The draft federal budget strengthens the social safety net. The floor on social assistance spending and the framework for adjusting social spending will be maintained. The draft budget increases social spending and preserves health spending (while better targeting health outlays to the most vulnerable). It also includes a 12 percent expansion of public childcare in an effort to raise female labor force participation (particularly for lower income households). With the support of the World Bank, the National Social Security Administration (ANSES) will continue to improve targeting and expand coverage of the universal child allowance (AUH). Finally, the government has also developed a system to improve the monitoring of social conditions to better respond to emerging needs of low income households.

**Augmentation and Re-phasing of Fund Resources.** Under the revised arrangement, Fund resources for Argentina in 2018-19 have increased by US$19 billion. A total of about US$56.3 billion would be made available to Argentina for the duration of the program through 2021. Fund disbursements for the remainder of 2018 would more than double compared to the original Fund-supported program, to a total of US$13.4 billion (on top of the US$15 billion already disbursed). Planned disbursements in 2019 are also nearly doubled, to US$22.8 billion, with US$5.9 billion planned for 2020-21. The resources available in the program are no longer expected to be treated as precautionary and the authorities have requested the use of the IMF financing for budget support.

---

[1]US dollar amounts have been calculated using today's exchange rate:   SDR ONE EQUALS U.S. DOLLARS - 1.38371/U.S. DOLLAR ONE EQUALS SDR - 0.722697

SOURCE: International Monetary Fund. "IMF Executive Board Completes First Review under Argentina's Stand-By Arrangement, Approves US$5.7 Billion Disbursement." October 26, 2018. https://www.imf.org/en/News/Articles/2018/10/26/pr18395-argentina-imf-executive-board-completes-first-review-under-argentina-stand-arrangement.

## OTHER HISTORIC DOCUMENTS OF INTEREST

### FROM PREVIOUS HISTORIC DOCUMENTS

# Supreme Court Rules on Trump Travel Ban

JUNE 26, 2018

On June 26, 2018, the Supreme Court rejected a challenge to President Donald Trump's so-called travel ban, which restricts travel to the United States by citizens from seven countries, a majority of which are predominantly Muslim. The Court's 5–4 decision in *Trump v. Hawaii* capped two years of tumultuous litigation over multiple iterations of the travel ban. Chief Justice John Roberts wrote the majority opinion, upholding the ban against both statutory and constitutional challenges, both of which were rooted in the argument that the president's own incendiary comments about the need for the ban, which he had repeatedly referred to on the campaign trail as the "Muslim Ban," undermined its legitimacy and proved that its real justification was religious animosity. Chief Justice Roberts rejected these arguments while nevertheless making it clear that the Court was expressing "no view on the soundness of the policy." The Court emphasized that, in the context of national security and foreign affairs, it would give broad deference to the president's judgments and not substitute its own assessment of the facts.

## MULTIPLE TRAVEL BAN ATTEMPTS

Almost immediately after taking office, in January 2017, President Trump, who had routinely made anti-Muslim statements during his campaign, hastily drafted and issued what would be the first of three travel bans. He did not seek input from the Departments of State, Defense, Homeland Security, or Justice or any of the multiple agencies responsible for its enforcement. This ban suspended for ninety days the entry of all foreign nationals from seven countries: Iran, Iraq, Libya, Somalia, Sudan, Syria, and Yemen. The ban took effect as soon as it was signed, without advance warning, leading to chaos at airports around the world. Almost immediately, multiple courts entered nationwide injunctions on the enforcement of the first version of the travel ban and then, again, on a second version that replaced the first two months later. The second travel ban suspended entry of nationals from six countries for ninety days to prevent dangerous individuals from entering while the government worked to establish "adequate standards . . . to prevent infiltration by foreign terrorists." According to the order, the countries—Iran, Libya, Somalia, Sudan, Syria, and Yemen—had been selected because each "is a state sponsor of terrorism, has been significantly compromised by terrorist organizations or contains active conflict zones."

On September 24, 2017, the day that the second travel ban expired, President Trump signed Presidential Proclamation 9545. This third version of the travel ban, more carefully drafted and reflecting input from multiple agencies, detailed the results of a worldwide review to identify the countries that it found to have deficient information-sharing practices and to present national security concerns. Based on these findings, the president ordered an indefinite ban on travel to the United States from five of the six countries listed in the previous ban (Iran, Libya, Somalia, Syria, and Yemen, dropping Sudan). It also imposed new restrictions on citizens of three more—North Korea, Chad, and certain government officials from Venezuela. It later dropped Chad from the list.

The State of Hawaii, as the administrator of the University of Hawaii, which recruits students and faculty from many of these countries, challenged the proclamation (except as it applied to North Korea and Venezuela), arguing that it contravenes provisions of the Immigration and Nationality Act (INA) and violates the Establishment Clause of the First Amendment because its motivation was animus to Islam and not concerns for national security. The federal district court issued a nationwide preliminary injunction barring enforcement of the entry restrictions. The Ninth Circuit Court of Appeals affirmed the injunction, ruling that the president had likely exceeded his powers under the INA, but not reaching the constitutional questions. The Supreme Court agreed to hear the case.

## SUPREME COURT RULES IN FAVOR OF THE TRAVEL BAN

Chief Justice Roberts wrote the 5–4 opinion in *Hawaii v. Trump*, joined by the more conservative block of the Court's justices: Anthony Kennedy, Clarence Thomas, Samuel Alito, and Neil Gorsuch. The first issue addressed by the opinion is whether the president had the authority to issue the third iteration of the travel ban. The Constitution, in Article I, specifically grants Congress the power to establish rules governing immigration. Congress exercised this power when it passed the INA, a law that determines the process for foreign nationals to seek entry into the United States and sets out numerous grounds that would make someone inadmissible or ineligible for a visa. Section 1182(f) of the INA specifically grants the president the broad discretion to suspend any foreigner's entry if he finds it is in the best interest of the country:

> *Whenever the President finds that the entry of any aliens or of any class of aliens into the United States would be detrimental to the interests of the United States, he may by proclamation, and for such period as he shall deem necessary, suspend the entry of all aliens or any class of aliens as immigrants or nonimmigrants, or impose on the entry of aliens any restrictions he may deem to be appropriate.*

The chief justice described the "plain language" of this law as conferring on the president "broad discretion" and "ample power" to decide whether and when to bar entry of any aliens whenever the president finds it to be in the national interest. According to the Court, "the President has undoubtedly fulfilled that requirement here." The only requirement in this law is that the president "find" that the entry of the covered aliens "would be detrimental to the interests of the United States." Here, the opinion outlines how the president ordered multiple agencies to conduct a comprehensive evaluation of every country in the world and determine how they comply with information and risk assessment requirements. The president then issued the proclamation that contained thorough descriptions of the process and resulting recommendations that support the restrictions.

The proclamation, he explained, sets forth the findings that certain entry restrictions were necessary to "prevent the entry of those foreign nationals about whom the United States Government lacks sufficient information." Chief Justice Roberts rejected the plaintiffs' arguments that the president's findings supporting the travel ban were insufficient and unpersuasive, first by entertaining the possibility that the deference inherent in the law was so great that it only requires the president to make a "finding" and not to "explain that finding with sufficient detail to enable judicial review." But the opinion does not pursue this possibility, because Justice Roberts instead finds that the stated reasons for the travel ban are squarely within the scope of presidential authority under the INA "even assuming that some form of review is appropriate." The findings contained in this twelve-page proclamation, the chief justice wrote, are more detailed than those issued by any past presidential proclamations. For example, President Bill Clinton, in 1996, barred entry of certain people from Sudan with only a single sentence of explanation.

Due to the broad deference inherent in the law, together with the deference tradition-ally accorded to a president in the national security sphere, the Court concluded that the president's travel ban falls well within the delegation of powers in the INA.

## Supreme Court Rejects First Amendment Argument

After resolving the statutory challenges to the president's travel ban, the Court turned to the constitutional challenge. The First Amendment contains the provision that "Congress shall make no law respecting the establishment of religion or prohibiting the free exer-cise thereof." Courts have interpreted the Establishment Clause to forbid the government from officially preferring one religion over another. The plaintiffs in this case argued that the true purpose of the travel ban was "religious animus" against Muslims and that the facially neutral stated purposes were merely pretextual, as evidenced by the presi-dent's own comments. The opinion catalogues some of President Trump's statements regarding the travel ban, stating that they cast "doubt on the official objective of the Proclamation." These include, among others, calling for a "total and complete shutdown of Muslims entering the United States," "Islam hates us," and the retweeting of anti-Mus-lim propaganda videos. Chief Justice Roberts contrasts these statements with expres-sions of religious tolerance by other presidents including George Washington, Dwight D. Eisenhower, and George W. Bush, noting that presidents have "performed unevenly in living up to those inspiring words." After making this possibly subtle reproach to the president, Chief Justice Roberts declined to address the plaintiffs' arguments that President Trump's words do violence to our constitutional traditions, instead clearly stat-ing that "the issue before us is not whether to denounce the statements." The only issue for the Court, he wrote, is to determine "the significance of those statements in reviewing a Presidential directive, neutral on its face, addressing a matter within the core of execu-tive responsibility."

Unlike most Establishment Clause claims, this case arose in the context of a national security directive regulating the entry of aliens to the country. Courts have recognized that such decisions fall to the political branches of government, generally free of judicial control. The Court cited a case from 1972, *Kleindienst v. Mandel*, for the principle that, in the immigration context, the Court will generally not look beyond the "facially legitimate and *bona fide*" reasons given for executive action. According to the Court, such judicial restraint in matters of national security is critical to allow the president the flexibility "to respond to changing world conditions." Nevertheless, the Court, for the purposes of this case, assumed it could consider extrinsic evidence to "look behind the face of the Proclamation to the extent of applying rational basis review." But, under this standard, Roberts explained, the ban will be upheld if it is "plausibly related to the Government's stated objective." Applying this lenient standard, the Court ruled that the travel ban pre-sented a sufficient national security justification. In particular, the Court pointed to the fact that the stated purpose of the order was clearly legitimate—protecting the country from entry of people who have not been adequately vetted. He also cited the fact that the text of the proclamation does not mention religion and that it covers a slim portion of the world's Muslim population as supporting the travel ban's legitimacy.

## JUSTICE SOTOMAYOR'S DISSENTING OPINION

The 5–4 decision drew four other opinions: two short concurrences, one by Justice Kennedy and one by Justice Thomas, and two dissenting opinions. In a passionate twenty-eight page, sharply worded dissent, Justice Sonia Sotomayor, joined by Justice Ruth Bader Ginsburg, argued that this opinion is inconsistent with the recently decided case of *Masterpiece Cakeshop v. Colorado Civil Rights Commission*. In that case, the Court relied on stray remarks from a state commissioner expressing hostility to religion and the failure to disavow those remarks to find a violation of the Establishment Clause, leading the Court to rule in favor of a Christian baker who refused to sell a wedding cake to a same-sex couple. "Those principles should apply equally here," she wrote, after having quoted multiple statements from the president as evidence of the proclamation's religious animus. Sotomayor added, "the words of the President and his advisers create the strong perception that the Proclamation is contaminated by impermissible discriminatory animus against Islam and its followers."

She also accused the majority of "unquestioning acceptance" of the president's national security claims, calling out "stark parallels" in reasoning with *Korematsu v. United States*, the 1944 case in which the Supreme Court upheld the forced relocation of Japanese Americans to internment camps. Chief Justice Roberts forcefully rejected the *Korematsu* comparison, writing "it is wholly inapt to liken that morally repugnant order to the facially neutral policy denying certain foreign nationals the privilege of admission." He took the opportunity to expressly declare that *Korematsu* "has no place in law under the Constitution." Justice Sotomayor responded that this ruling "merely replaces one 'gravely wrong' decision with another."

## IMPACT OF THE COURT'S DECISION

This decision, with its emphasis on the broad discretion and authority of the president to suspend entry to this country of foreign aliens for purposes of national security, signals a hands-off approach by the Court in matters of immigration. This is likely to have immediate implications. When the Court's decision came down in June, the administration was imposing a "zero tolerance" policy for illegal immigrants that resulted in the separation of children from parents crossing the U.S.–Mexico border illegally. A federal judge in California issued a halt to these separations and ordered the reunification of families. In the run-up to the midterm elections, President Trump ordered active-duty troops to the southern border to stop a slow-moving caravan of several thousand migrants traveling from Central America to the United States. Two days after the elections, he reversed long-standing federal and international asylum laws by issuing new rules giving the president vast powers to deny asylum to any migrant crossing the border into the United States. These new rules cite the same authority relied on by the Court in *Trump v. Hawaii* to uphold the travel ban. Similarly, the president has ordered an end to the Deferred Action for Childhood Arrivals (DACA), the rule giving temporary status to the immigrants brought to the United States as children. This order is currently on hold as it works its way through the courts, but it is likely to reach the Supreme Court.

—Melissa Feinberg

*Following are excerpts from the Supreme Court's ruling in* Trump v. Hawaii, *in which the Court ruled 5–4 on June 26, 2018, to uphold President Donald Trump's travel ban.*

# Supreme Court Issues Ruling on Trump Travel Ban

**June 26, 2018**

*[Footnotes have been omitted.]*

## SUPREME COURT OF THE UNITED STATES

No. 17–965

Donald J. Trump, President of the
United States, et al., Petitioners

*v.*

Hawaii, et al.

On Writ of Certiorari to The
United States Court of Appeals
for the Ninth Circuit

[June 26, 2018]

CHIEF JUSTICE ROBERTS delivered the opinion of the Court.

Under the Immigration and Nationality Act, foreign nationals seeking entry into the United States undergo a vetting process to ensure that they satisfy the numerous requirements for admission. The Act also vests the President with authority to restrict the entry of aliens whenever he finds that their entry "would be detrimental to the interests of the United States." 8 U. S. C. §1182(f). Relying on that delegation, the President concluded that it was necessary to impose entry restrictions on nationals of countries that do not share adequate information for an informed entry determination, or that otherwise present national security risks. Presidential Proclamation No. 9645, 82 Fed. Reg. 45161 (2017) (Proclamation). The plaintiffs in this litigation, respondents here, challenged the application of those entry restrictions to certain aliens abroad. We now decide whether the President had authority under the Act to issue the Proclamation, and whether the entry policy violates the Establishment Clause of the First Amendment.

*[Section I, which details the legal history of presidential travel bans and the parties to this case, and Section II, which briefly discusses whether the Court has the authority to review the ban—deciding, for purposes of this case, to assume that it does—have been omitted.]*

## III

The INA establishes numerous grounds on which an alien abroad may be inadmissible to the United States and ineligible for a visa. [*citation omitted*] Congress has also delegated to the President authority to suspend or restrict the entry of aliens in certain circumstances. The principal source of that authority, §1182(f), enables the President to "suspend the entry of all aliens or any class of aliens" whenever he "finds" that their entry "would be detrimental to the interests of the United States." . . .

. . . By its plain language, §1182(f) grants the President broad discretion to suspend the entry of aliens into the United States. The President lawfully exercised that discretion based on his findings—following a worldwide, multi-agency review—that entry of the covered aliens would be detrimental to the national interest. And plaintiffs' attempts to identify a conflict with other provisions in the INA, and their appeal to the statute's purposes and legislative history, fail to overcome the clear statutory language.

## A

The text of §1182(f) states:

> "Whenever the President finds that the entry of any aliens or of any class of aliens into the United States would be detrimental to the interests of the United States, he may by proclamation, and for such period as he shall deem necessary, suspend the entry of all aliens or any class of aliens as immigrants or nonimmigrants, or impose on the entry of aliens any restrictions he may deem to be appropriate."

> By its terms, §1182(f) exudes deference to the President in every clause. . . .

. . . The Proclamation falls well within this comprehensive delegation. The sole prerequisite set forth in §1182(f) is that the President "find[ ]" that the entry of the covered aliens "would be detrimental to the interests of the United States." The President has undoubtedly fulfilled that requirement here. He first ordered DHS and other agencies to conduct a comprehensive evaluation of every single country's compliance with the information and risk assessment baseline. The President then issued a Proclamation setting forth extensive findings describing how deficiencies in the practices of select foreign governments—several of which are state sponsors of terrorism—deprive the Government of "sufficient information to assess the risks [those countries' nationals] pose to the United States." Proclamation §1(h)(i). Based on that review, the President found that it was in the national interest to restrict entry of aliens who could not be vetted with adequate information—both to protect national security and public safety, and to induce improvement by their home countries. The Proclamation therefore "craft[ed] . . . country-specific restrictions that would be most likely to encourage cooperation given each country's distinct circumstances," while securing the Nation "until such time as improvements occur." *Ibid.*

Plaintiffs believe that these findings are insufficient. They argue, as an initial matter, that the Proclamation fails to provide a persuasive rationale for why nationality alone renders the covered foreign nationals a security risk. And they further discount the President's stated concern about deficient vetting because the Proclamation allows many aliens from the designated countries to enter on nonimmigrant visas. . . .

. . . But even assuming that some form of review is appropriate, plaintiffs' attacks on the sufficiency of the President's findings cannot be sustained. The 12-page

Proclamation—which thoroughly describes the process, agency evaluations, and recommendations underlying the President's chosen restrictions—is more detailed than any prior order a President has issued under §1182(f). Contrast Presidential Proclamation No. 6958, 3 CFR 133 (1996) (President Clinton) (explaining in one sentence why suspending entry of members of the Sudanese government and armed forces "is in the foreign policy interests of the United States"); Presidential Proclamation No. 4865, 3 CFR 50–51 (1981) (President Reagan) (explaining in five sentences why measures to curtail "the continuing illegal migration by sea of large numbers of undocumented aliens into the southeastern United States" are "necessary").

Moreover, plaintiffs' request for a searching inquiry into the persuasiveness of the President's justifications is inconsistent with the broad statutory text and the deference traditionally accorded the President in this sphere. "Whether the President's chosen method" of addressing perceived risks is justified from a policy perspective is "irrelevant to the scope of his [§1182(f)] authority." *Sale*, 509 U. S., at 187–188. . . .

. . . In short, the language of §1182(f) is clear, and the Proclamation does not exceed any textual limit on the President's authority.

## B

Confronted with this "facially broad grant of power," 878 F. 3d, at 688, plaintiffs focus their attention on statutory structure and legislative purpose. They seek support in, first, the immigration scheme reflected in the INA as a whole, and, second, the legislative history of §1182(f) and historical practice. Neither argument justifies departing from the clear text of the statute.

*[The Court's further examination of the plaintiffs' unsuccessful arguments regarding the INA and its legislative history has been omitted. Also omitted is Section III C, in which the Court rejects another argument based in statutory interpretation.]*

## IV

### A

We now turn to plaintiffs' claim that the Proclamation was issued for the unconstitutional purpose of excluding Muslims.

*[An initial discussion in which the Court concludes that the plaintiffs have standing to have their arguments heard has been omitted.]*

### B

The First Amendment provides, in part, that "Congress shall make no law respecting an establishment of religion, or prohibiting the free exercise thereof." Our cases recognize that "[t]he clearest command of the Establishment Clause is that one religious denomination cannot be officially preferred over another." *Larson* v. *Valente*, 456 U. S. 228, 244 (1982). Plaintiffs believe that the Proclamation violates this prohibition by singling out Muslims for disfavored treatment. The entry suspension, they contend, operates as a "religious gerrymander," in part because most of the countries covered by the Proclamation have Muslim-majority populations. And in their view, deviations from the information-sharing baseline criteria suggest that the results of the multi-agency review were "foreordained." Relying on Establishment Clause precedents concerning laws and policies applied domestically, plaintiffs allege that the primary purpose of the Proclamation was religious animus and that the President's stated concerns about vetting protocols and national security were but pretexts for discriminating against Muslims. Brief for Respondents 69-73.

At the heart of plaintiffs' case is a series of statements by the President and his advisers casting doubt on the official objective of the Proclamation. For example, while a candidate on the campaign trail, the President published a "Statement on Preventing Muslim Immigration" that called for a "total and complete shutdown of Muslims entering the United States until our country's representatives can figure out what is going on." App 158 That statement remained on his campaign website until May 2017. *Id.* at 130. Then-candidate Trump also stated that "Islam hates us" and asserted that the United States was "having problems with Muslims coming into the country." *Id.* at 120, 159. Shortly after being elected, when asked whether violence in Europe had affected his plans to "ban Muslim immigration," the President replied, "You know my plans. All along, I've been proven to be right." *Id.* at 123

One week after his inauguration, the President issued EO–1. In a television interview, one of the President's campaign advisers explained that when the President "first announced it, he said, 'Muslim ban.' He called me up. He said, 'Put a commission together. Show me the right way to do it legally.'" *Id.*, at 125. The adviser said he assembled a group of Members of Congress and lawyers that "focused on, instead of religion, danger. . . . [The order] is based on places where there [is] substantial evidence that people are sending terrorists into our country." *Id.*, at 229.

Plaintiffs also note that after issuing EO–2 to replace EO–1, the President expressed regret that his prior order had been "watered down" and called for a "much tougher version" of his "Travel Ban." Shortly before the release of the Proclamation, he stated that the "travel ban . . . should be far larger, tougher, and more specific," but "stupidly that would not be politically correct." *Id.*, at 132–133. More recently, on November 29, 2017, the President retweeted links to three anti-Muslim propaganda videos. In response to questions about those videos, the President's deputy press secretary denied that the President thinks Muslims are a threat to the United States, explaining that "the President has been talking about these security issues for years now, from the campaign trail to the White House" and "has addressed these issues with the travel order that he issued earlier this year and the companion proclamation." *IRAP* v. *Trump*, 883 F. 3d 233, 267 (CA4 2018).

The President of the United States possesses an extraordinary power to speak to his fellow citizens and on their behalf. Our Presidents have frequently used that power to espouse the principles of religious freedom and tolerance on which this Nation was founded. In 1790 George Washington reassured the Hebrew Congregation of Newport, Rhode Island that "happily the Government of the United States . . . gives to bigotry no sanction, to persecution no assistance [and] requires only that they who live under its protection should demean themselves as good citizens." 6 Papers of George Washington 285 (D. Twohig ed. 1996). President Eisenhower, at the opening of the Islamic Center of Washington, similarly pledged to a Muslim audience that "America would fight with her whole strength for your right to have here your own church," declaring that "[t]his concept is indeed a part of America." Public Papers of the Presidents, Dwight D. Eisenhower, June

28, 1957, p. 509 (1957). And just days after the attacks of September 11, 2001, President George W. Bush returned to the same Islamic Center to implore his fellow Americans— Muslims and non-Muslims alike—to remember during their time of grief that "[t]he face of terror is not the true faith of Islam," and that America is "a great country because we share the same values of respect and dignity and human worth." *Public Papers of the Presidents*, George W. Bush, Vol. 2, Sept. 17, 2001, p. 1121 (2001). Yet it cannot be denied that the Federal Government and the Presidents who have carried its laws into effect have— from the Nation's earliest days—performed unevenly in living up to those inspiring words.

Plaintiffs argue that this President's words strike at fundamental standards of respect and tolerance, in violation of our constitutional tradition. But the issue before us is not whether to denounce the statements. It is instead the significance of those statements in reviewing a Presidential directive, neutral on its face, addressing a matter within the core of executive responsibility. In doing so, we must consider not only the statements of a particular President, but also the authority of the Presidency itself.

The case before us differs in numerous respects from the conventional Establishment Clause claim. Unlike the typical suit involving religious displays or school prayer, plaintiffs seek to invalidate a national security directive regulating the entry of aliens abroad. Their claim accordingly raises a number of delicate issues regarding the scope of the constitutional right and the manner of proof. The Proclamation, moreover, is facially neutral toward religion. Plaintiffs therefore ask the Court to probe the sincerity of the stated justifications for the policy by reference to extrinsic statements—many of which were made before the President took the oath of office. These various aspects of plaintiffs' challenge inform our standard of review.

## C

For more than a century, this Court has recognized that the admission and exclusion of foreign nationals is a "fundamental sovereign attribute exercised by the Government's political departments largely immune from judicial control." *Fiallo* v. *Bell*, 430 U. S. 787, 792 (1977); see *Harisiades* v. *Shaughnessy*, 342 U. S. 580, 588–589 (1952) ("[A]ny policy toward aliens is vitally and intricately interwoven with contemporaneous policies in regard to the conduct of foreign relations [and] the war power."). Because decisions in these matters may implicate "relations with foreign powers," or involve "classifications defined in the light of changing political and economic circumstances," such judgments "are frequently of a character more appropriate to either the Legislature or the Executive." *Mathews* v. *Diaz*, 426 U. S. 67, 81 (1976). . . .

. . . The upshot of our cases in this context is clear: "Any rule of constitutional law that would inhibit the flexibility" of the President "to respond to changing world conditions should be adopted only with the greatest caution," and our inquiry into matters of entry and national security is highly constrained. *Mathews*, 426 U. S., at 81–82. We need not define the precise contours of that inquiry in this case. A conventional application of *Mandel*, asking only whether the policy is facially legitimate and bona fide, would put an end to our review. But the Government has suggested that it may be appropriate here for the inquiry to extend beyond the facial neutrality of the order. See Tr. of Oral Arg. 16–17, 25–27 (describing *Mandel* as "the starting point" of the analysis). For our purposes today, we assume that we may look behind the face of the Proclamation to the extent of applying rational basis review. That standard of review considers whether the entry policy is plausibly related to the Government's stated objective to protect the country and improve vetting processes. See *Railroad Retirement Bd.* v. *Fritz*, 449 U. S. 166, 179 (1980). As a result, we may consider plaintiffs' extrinsic evidence, but will uphold the policy so long as it can reasonably be understood to result from a justification independent of unconstitutional grounds.

## D

Given the standard of review, it should come as no surprise that the Court hardly ever strikes down a policy as illegitimate under rational basis scrutiny. On the few occasions where we have done so, a common thread has been that the laws at issue lack any purpose other than a "bare . . . desire to harm a politically unpopular group." *Department of Agriculture* v. *Moreno*, 413 U. S. 528, 534 (1973). . . .

. . . The Proclamation does not fit this pattern. It cannot be said that it is impossible to "discern a relationship to legitimate state interests" or that the policy is "inexplicable by anything but animus." Indeed, the dissent can only attempt to argue otherwise by refusing to apply anything resembling rational basis review. But because there is persuasive evidence that the entry suspension has a legitimate grounding in national security concerns, quite apart from any religious hostility, we must accept that independent justification.

The Proclamation is expressly premised on legitimate purposes: preventing entry of nationals who cannot be adequately vetted and inducing other nations to improve their practices. The text says nothing about religion. Plaintiffs and the dissent nonetheless emphasize that five of the seven nations currently included in the Proclamation have Muslim-majority populations. Yet that fact alone does not support an inference of religious hostility, given that the policy covers just 8% of the world's Muslim population and is limited to countries that were previously designated by Congress or prior administrations as posing national security risks. . . .

. . . The Proclamation, moreover, reflects the results of a worldwide review process undertaken by multiple Cabinet officials and their agencies. . . .

. . . More fundamentally, plaintiffs and the dissent challenge the entry suspension based on their perception of its effectiveness and wisdom. They suggest that the policy is overbroad and does little to serve national security interests. But we cannot substitute our own assessment for the Executive's predictive judgments on such matters, all of which "are delicate, complex, and involve large elements of prophecy." *Chicago & Southern Air Lines, Inc.* v. *Waterman S. S. Corp.*, 333 U. S. 103, 111 (1948); see also *Regan* v. *Wald*, 468 U. S. 222, 242–243 (1984) (declining invitation to conduct an "independent foreign policy analysis"). While we of course "do not defer to the Government's reading of the First Amendment," the Executive's evaluation of the underlying facts is entitled to appropriate weight, particularly in the context of litigation involving "sensitive and weighty interests of national security and foreign affairs." *Humanitarian Law Project*, 561 U. S., at 33–34.

*[Discussion of three additional features of the ban that support its legitimacy has been omitted. This included the fact that some countries have been removed from the ban, the existence of exceptions for some categories of foreign nationals, and the existence of a waiver program.]*

Finally, the dissent invokes *Korematsu* v. *United States*, 323 U. S. 214 (1944). Whatever rhetorical advantage the dissent may see in doing so, *Korematsu* has nothing to do with this case. The forcible relocation of U.S. citizens to concentration camps, solely and explicitly on the basis of race, is objectively unlawful and outside the scope of Presidential authority. But it is wholly inapt to liken that morally repugnant order to a facially neutral policy denying certain foreign nationals the privilege of admission. See *post,* at 26–28. The entry suspension is an act that is well within executive authority and could have been taken by any other President—the only question is evaluating the actions of this particular President in promulgating an otherwise valid Proclamation.

The dissent's reference to *Korematsu,* however, affords this Court the opportunity to make express what is already obvious: *Korematsu* was gravely wrong the day it was decided, has been overruled in the court of history, and—to be clear—"has no place in law under the Constitution." 323 U. S., at 248 (Jackson, J., dissenting).

\* \* \*

Under these circumstances, the Government has set forth a sufficient national security justification to survive rational basis review. We express no view on the soundness of the policy. We simply hold today that plaintiffs have not demonstrated a likelihood of success on the merits of their constitutional claim.

# V

. . . The judgment of the Court of Appeals is reversed, and the case is remanded for further proceedings consistent with this opinion.

*It is so ordered.*

*[The concurring opinions of Justices Kennedy and Thomas, and the dissenting opinion of Justice Breyer, have been omitted.]*

JUSTICE SOTOMAYOR, with whom JUSTICE GINSBURG joins, dissenting.

The United States of America is a Nation built upon the promise of religious liberty. Our Founders honored that core promise by embedding the principle of religious neutrality in the First Amendment. The Court's decision today fails to safeguard that fundamental principle. It leaves undisturbed a policy first advertised openly and unequivocally as a "total and complete shutdown of Muslims entering the United States" because the policy now masquerades behind a façade of national-security concerns. But this repackaging does little to cleanse Presidential Proclamation No. 9645 of the appearance of discrimination that the President's words have created. Based on the evidence in the record, a reasonable observer would conclude that the Proclamation was motivated by anti-Muslim animus. That alone suffices to show that plaintiffs are likely to succeed on the merits of their Establishment Clause claim. The majority holds otherwise by ignoring the facts, misconstruing our legal precedent, and turning a blind eye to the pain and suffering the Proclamation inflicts upon countless families and individuals, many of whom are United States citizens. Because that troubling result runs contrary to the Constitution and our precedent, I dissent.

# I

Plaintiffs challenge the Proclamation on various grounds, both statutory and constitutional. Ordinarily, when a case can be decided on purely statutory grounds, we strive to follow a "prudential rule of avoiding constitutional questions." *Zobrest v. Catalina Foothills School Dist.,* 509 U. S. 1, 8 (1993). But that rule of thumb is far from categorical, and it has limited application where, as here, the constitutional question proves far simpler than the statutory one. Whatever the merits of plaintiffs' complex statutory claims, the Proclamation must be enjoined for a more fundamental reason: It runs afoul of the Establishment Clause's guarantee of religious neutrality.

*[A review of the Establishment Clause of the Constitution has been omitted.]*

# B

## 1

Although the majority briefly recounts a few of the statements and background events that form the basis of plaintiffs' constitutional challenge, that highly abridged account does not tell even half of the story. The full record paints a far more harrowing picture, from which a reasonable observer would readily conclude that the Proclamation was motivated by hostility and animus toward the Muslim faith.

During his Presidential campaign, then-candidate Donald Trump pledged that, if elected, he would ban Muslims from entering the United States. Specifically, on December 7, 2015, he issued a formal statement "calling for a total and complete shutdown of Muslims entering the United States." . . .

On December 8, 2015, Trump justified his proposal during a television interview by noting that President Franklin D. Roosevelt "did the same thing" with respect to the internment of Japanese Americans during World War II. In January 2016, during a Republican primary debate, Trump was asked whether he wanted to "rethink [his] position" on "banning Muslims from entering the country." He answered, "No." . . .

*[Additional discussion of Trump's comments related to his travel ban during his candidacy, and the early Court rulings against the first two iterations of the ban, has been omitted.]*

While litigation over EO–2 was ongoing, President Trump repeatedly made statements alluding to a desire to keep Muslims out of the country. For instance, he said at a rally of his supporters that EO–2 was just a "watered down version of the first one" and had been "tailor[ed]" at the behest of "the lawyers." He further added that he would prefer "to go back to the first [executive order] and go all the way" and reiterated his belief that it was "very hard" for Muslims to assimilate into Western culture. During a rally in April 2017, President Trump recited the lyrics to a song called "The Snake," a song about a woman who nurses a sick snake back to health but then is attacked by the snake, as a warning about Syrian refugees entering the country. And in June 2017, the President stated on Twitter that the Justice Department had submitted a "watered down, politically correct version" of the "original Travel Ban" "to S[upreme] C[ourt]." The President went on to tweet: "People, the lawyers and the courts can call it whatever they want, but I am calling it what we need and what it is, a TRAVEL BAN!" Id., at 132–133. He added: "That's right, we need a TRAVEL BAN for certain DANGEROUS countries, not some politically correct term that won't help us protect our people!" Then, on August 17, 2017, President Trump issued yet another tweet about Islam, once more referencing the story about General Pershing's massacre of Muslims in the Philippines: "Study what General Pershing . . . did to terrorists when caught. There was no more Radical Islamic Terror for 35 years!"

In September 2017, President Trump tweeted that "[t]he travel ban into the United States should be far larger, tougher and more specific—but stupidly, that would not be politically correct!" Later that month, on September 24, 2017, President Trump issued Presidential Proclamation No. 9645, 82 Fed. Reg. 45161 (2017) (Proclamation), which restricts entry of certain nationals from six Muslim-majority countries. On November 29, 2017, President Trump "retweeted" three anti-Muslim videos, entitled "Muslim Destroys a Statue of Virgin Mary!", "Islamist mob pushes teenage boy off roof and beats him to death!", and "Muslim migrant beats up Dutch boy on crutches!" . . .

## 2

As the majority correctly notes, "the issue before us is not whether to denounce" these offensive statements. Rather, the dispositive and narrow question here is whether a reasonable observer, presented with all "openly available data," the text and "historical context" of the Proclamation, and the "specific sequence of events" leading to it, would conclude that the primary purpose of the Proclamation is to disfavor Islam and its adherents by excluding them from the country. The answer is unquestionably yes.

Taking all the relevant evidence together, a reasonable observer would conclude that the Proclamation was driven primarily by anti-Muslim animus, rather than by the Government's asserted national-security justifications. Even before being sworn into office, then-candidate Trump stated that "Islam hates us," warned that "[w]e're having problems with the Muslims, and we're having problems with Muslims coming into the country," id., at 121, promised to enact a "total and complete shut down of Muslims entering the United States," and instructed one of his advisers to find a "lega[l]" way to enact a Muslim ban. The President continued to make similar statements well after his inauguration, as detailed above.

Moreover, despite several opportunities to do so, President Trump has never disavowed any of his prior statements about Islam. . . .

Ultimately, what began as a policy explicitly "calling for a total and complete shutdown of Muslims entering the United States" has since morphed into a "Proclamation" putatively based on national-security concerns. But this new window dressing cannot conceal an unassailable fact: the words of the President and his advisers create the strong perception that the Proclamation is contaminated by impermissible discriminatory animus against Islam and its followers.

## II

Rather than defend the President's problematic statements, the Government urges this Court to set them aside and defer to the President on issues related to immigration and national security. The majority accepts that invitation and incorrectly applies a watered-down legal standard in an effort to short circuit plaintiffs' Establishment Clause claim. . . .

The President's statements, which the majority utterly fails to address in its legal analysis, strongly support the conclusion that the Proclamation was issued to express hostility toward Muslims and exclude them from the country. Given the overwhelming record evidence of anti-Muslim animus, it simply cannot be said that the Proclamation has a legitimate basis. . . .

The majority insists that the Proclamation furthers two interrelated national-security interests: "preventing entry of nationals who cannot be adequately vetted and inducing other nations to improve their practices." But the Court offers insufficient support for its view "that the entry suspension has a legitimate grounding in [those] national security concerns, quite apart from any religious hostility." Indeed, even a cursory review of the Government's asserted national-security rationale reveals that the Proclamation is nothing more than a "'religious gerrymander.'" . . .

. . . [T]he worldwide review does little to break the clear connection between the Proclamation and the President's anti-Muslim statements. For "[n]o matter how many officials affix their names to it, the Proclamation rests on a rotten foundation." The President campaigned on a promise to implement a "total and complete shutdown of Muslims" entering the country, translated that campaign promise into a concrete policy, and made several statements linking that policy (in its various forms) to anti-Muslim animus.

Ignoring all this, the majority empowers the President to hide behind an administrative review process that the Government refuses to disclose to the public. Furthermore, evidence of which we can take judicial notice indicates that the multiagency review process could not have been very thorough. Ongoing litigation under the Freedom of Information Act shows that the September 2017 report the Government produced after its review process was a mere 17 pages. That the Government's analysis of the vetting practices of hundreds of countries boiled down to such a short document raises serious questions about the legitimacy of the President's proclaimed national-security rationale.

Beyond that, Congress has already addressed the national-security concerns supposedly undergirding the Proclamation through an "extensive and complex" framework governing "immigration and alien status." The Immigration and Nationality Act sets forth, in painstaking detail, a reticulated scheme regulating the admission of individuals to the United States. . . .

Put simply, Congress has already erected a statutory scheme that fulfills the putative national-security interests the Government now puts forth to justify the Proclamation. Tellingly, the Government remains wholly unable to articulate any credible national-security interest that would go unaddressed by the current statutory scheme absent the Proclamation. The Government also offers no evidence that this current vetting scheme, which involves a highly searching consideration of individuals required to obtain visas for entry into the United States and a highly searching consideration of which countries are eligible for inclusion in the Visa Waiver Program, is inadequate to achieve the Proclamation's proclaimed objectives of "preventing entry of nationals who cannot be adequately vetted and inducing other nations to improve their [vetting and information-sharing] practices." . . .

Moreover, the Proclamation purports to mitigate national-security risks by excluding nationals of countries that provide insufficient information to vet their nationals. Yet, as plaintiffs explain, the Proclamation broadly denies immigrant visas to all nationals of those countries, including those whose admission would likely not implicate these information deficiencies (e.g., infants, or nationals of countries included in the Proclamation who are long-term residents of and traveling from a country not covered by the Proclamation). In addition, the Proclamation permits certain nationals from the countries named in the Proclamation to obtain nonimmigrant visas, which undermines the Government's assertion that it does not already have the capacity and sufficient information to vet these individuals adequately. . . .

In sum, none of the features of the Proclamation highlighted by the majority supports the Government's claim that the Proclamation is genuinely and primarily rooted in a legitimate national-security interest. What the unrebutted evidence actually shows is that a reasonable observer would conclude, quite easily, that the primary purpose and function of the Proclamation is to disfavor Islam by banning Muslims from entering our country. . . .

## IV

The First Amendment stands as a bulwark against official religious prejudice and embodies our Nation's deep commitment to religious plurality and tolerance. That constitutional promise is why, "[f]or centuries now, people have come to this country from every corner of the world to share in the blessing of religious freedom." Instead of vindicating those principles, today's decision tosses them aside. In holding that the First Amendment gives way to an executive policy that a reasonable observer would view as motivated by animus against Muslims, the majority opinion upends this Court's precedent, repeats tragic mistakes of the past, and denies countless individuals the fundamental right of religious liberty. . . .

In the intervening years since *Korematsu*, our Nation has done much to leave its sordid legacy behind. Today, the Court takes the important step of finally overruling *Korematsu*, denouncing it as "gravely wrong the day it was decided." This formal repudiation of a shameful precedent is laudable and long overdue. But it does not make the majority's decision here acceptable or right. By blindly accepting the Government's misguided invitation to sanction a discriminatory policy motivated by animosity toward a disfavored group, all in the name of a superficial claim of national security, the Court redeploys the same dangerous logic underlying *Korematsu* and merely replaces one "gravely wrong" decision with another.

Our Constitution demands, and our country deserves, a Judiciary willing to hold the coordinate branches to account when they defy our most sacred legal commitments. Because the Court's decision today has failed in that respect, with profound regret, I dissent.

Source: Supreme Court of the United States. *Trump v. Hawaii.* 585 U.S. ____ (2018). https://www.supreme court.gov/opinions/17pdf/17-965_h315.pdf.

## OTHER HISTORIC DOCUMENTS OF INTEREST

### FROM THIS VOLUME

### FROM PREVIOUS *HISTORIC DOCUMENTS*

# Justice Kennedy Announces Retirement from Supreme Court; Kavanaugh Nominated

JUNE 27, AND SEPTEMBER 26 AND 27, 2018

In a letter to President Donald Trump, dated June 27, 2018, Justice Anthony Kennedy announced his intent to retire from the Supreme Court by the end of July. This announcement marked the end of the thirty-year career of a conservative jurist originally nominated by President Ronald Reagan in 1987. Kennedy had earned a reputation as an occasionally unpredictable swing vote who, while voting most frequently with the conservatives, was also the pivotal vote for many key liberal decisions. His announcement gave President Trump a second Supreme Court seat to fill and the opportunity to put his stamp on the Supreme Court for decades to come. With the likelihood that the appointment would move the Court further to the right and cement a 5–4 conservative majority, everyone anticipated a contentious confirmation battle over Trump's pick, D.C. Circuit Court Judge Brett Kavanaugh. But the confirmation process erupted when accusations of sexual assault dating from the nominee's high school years became public, leading to historic and dramatic testimony before the Senate Judiciary Committee, watched live by more than twenty million people. In the end, the Senate voted to confirm Kavanaugh by one of the narrowest margins in history.

## KENNEDY'S LEGAL LEGACY

Justice Kennedy was the ninety-third justice to serve on the Supreme Court, where he spent much of his career in the Court's ideological middle. This made him the necessary fifth vote on virtually every important and closely fought case and, for this reason, the most important vote on the Court. Perhaps most notably, Kennedy left behind a legacy as a champion of LGBTQ rights, having authored a series of opinions that extended, for the first time, constitutional protections to gay and lesbian Americans. Most of these cases were decided 5–4, including a 2003 opinion striking down sodomy laws used to prosecute gay men, and culminating in 2015 with *Obergefell v. Hodges*, which legalized same-sex marriage. His opinions frequently spoke of "dignity," as when addressing marriage equality, he wrote, "They ask for equal dignity in the eyes of the law. The Constitution grants them that right." Earlier in his years on the bench, he and Justice Sandra Day O'Connor had been swing votes in *Planned Parenthood v. Casey*, the 1992 case that upheld abortion rights. He was the fifth vote in a series of cases making it unconstitutional to impose the death penalty on juveniles, the intellectually disabled, and in nonhomicide cases. Nevertheless, he voted against overturning the death penalty generally and rarely granted a stay of execution.

Kennedy also joined with the conservative justices to write many influential 5–4 decisions. He wrote the opinion in *Citizens United*, the controversial case that held that stopping corporations or unions from spending money in support of or against candidates violates the First Amendment, opening the floodgates of corporate money into American elections. He voted with the majority in a pair of decisions in 2008 and 2010, which, for the first time, held that the Second Amendment provided an individual the right to keep and bear arms. Hours before he announced his retirement, Kennedy voted with the majority of the Court to restrict public-sector unions from collecting dues from nonmembers.

## President Trump Nominates Brett Kavanaugh

On July 9, 2018, President Trump announced that Kavanaugh, fifty-three, was his pick for the open seat on the Supreme Court, and he called for a "swift" confirmation in the Senate. Kavanaugh, a judge on the U.S. Court of Appeals for the District of Columbia, had been a law clerk for Justice Kennedy and then a participant in the most contentious partisan battles of the subsequent decades. He worked for independent counsel Kenneth W. Starr to impeach President Bill Clinton and for George W. Bush in the Florida vote recount, including working on the appeals in the *Bush v. Gore* case that determined the winner of the 2000 presidential election. He then spent four years working on President Bush's staff before becoming a federal judge. An ideological conservative, Judge Kavanaugh was expected to push the Court to the right on many issues. Although Democrats prepared for a confirmation battle, Senate Majority Leader Mitch McConnell, R-Ky., had in 2017 changed Senate rules to allow the confirmation of a Supreme Court justice with only a simple majority of votes. Prior to that, it took sixty votes to confirm a Supreme Court judge. Now Judge Kavanaugh could be appointed to a lifetime tenure on the Court without a single Democratic vote. In his public statement, he said, "If confirmed by the Senate, I will keep an open mind on every case."

Four days of confirmation hearings began on September 4, 2018, during which Democrats pressed Kavanaugh on his views on abortion, precedent, and presidential power. Kavanaugh carefully avoided answering most questions, sticking to a well-rehearsed script, declining to answer any "hypothetical questions," and repeating that he is a strong believer in judicial precedent. Republicans hoped to have a vote of the full Senate before October 1, the first day of the Supreme Court's new term.

## Accusations of Sexual Assault and Misconduct

During the summer before these confirmation hearings, Sen. Dianne Feinstein, D-Calif., ranking member of the Judiciary Committee, received a letter from a constituent, Christine Blasey Ford, a psychology professor at Palo Alto University and research psychologist at Stanford University School of Medicine. In her letter dated July 30, 2018, Ford wrote that Kavanaugh had sexually assaulted her when the pair were high school students. Because Ford asked for privacy, Sen. Feinstein did not share the letter with other senators or with the press. She also did not bring up the matter when Kavanaugh met with her to discuss his nomination.

In the week after the conclusion of Kavanaugh's Senate testimony, however, reports of the existence of such a letter began to circulate in the media, although the letter's author was unknown. Sen. Feinstein released a brief statement acknowledging the existence of the letter and saying that she had turned it over to the Federal Bureau of Investigation (FBI). On September 16, Ford, stating that she feared her identity was about to be made public, gave an interview to the *Washington Post* detailing her allegations. She said that when she was fifteen, she attended a house party with other local-area high school students, where Kavanaugh and a friend trapped her in an upstairs bedroom. Ford says Kavanaugh held her on the bed, tried to forcibly remove her clothes, and covered her mouth to muffle her screams. In a statement from the White House, Kavanaugh denied the allegations. The next week, a second accuser came forward. Deborah Ramirez was a student at Yale University with Kavanaugh and gave an interview with the *New Yorker* detailing accusations of sexual misconduct from that time. Again, Kavanaugh denied all allegations, and Democratic senators demanded that the White House rescind the nomination. After a week of negotiations with both parties, the Senate Judiciary Committee moved to set a special session to hear publicly from both Ford and Kavanaugh about the allegations.

## Ford and Kavanaugh Testify

On September 27, an extraordinary and emotional spectacle played out in a special session of the Senate Judiciary Committee. The morning started with four hours of testimony from Dr. Ford, who, in her early comments, stated, "I am here today not because I want to be. I am terrified. I am here because I believe it is my civic duty to tell you what happened to me while Brett Kavanaugh and I were in high school." She went on to describe, in detail, how she felt, over thirty years ago, when an allegedly drunken Kavanaugh and his friend, Mark Judge, locked her in an empty bedroom, before Kavanaugh pinned her to the bed and attempted to rip off her clothes. "I believed he was going to rape me," she said and, describing how he held his hand over her mouth when she tried to scream, added, "It was hard for me to breathe, and I thought that Brett was accidentally going to kill me." In a powerful moment, Sen. Patrick Leahy, D-Vt., asked Ford to describe her most vivid memory from the night. "Indelible in the hippocampus is the laughter," Ford responded, using both emotional and scientific terms, "the uproarious laughter between the two and their having fun at my expense." When Sen. Dick Durbin, D-Ill., addressing a Republican staffer's suggestion that she was mistaken about the identity of her assailant, asked her, "Dr. Ford, with what degree of certainty do you believe Brett Kavanaugh assaulted you?" she leaned forward to the microphone and answered, "One hundred percent."

A few hours later, in stark contrast to the quiet and careful tone of the morning session, Kavanaugh went on the attack in his response. He appeared angry as he yelled his forty-five-minute-long opening statement. "This confirmation process has become a national disgrace," he said, describing it as a "circus," a "calculated and orchestrated political hit, fueled with apparent pent-up anger about President Trump and the 2016 election." He even called the allegations against him "revenge on behalf of the Clintons." He accused the senators of replacing their role of "advice and consent" with "search and destroy." This attack on the process reminded many commentators of the 1991 confirmation hearings for Justice Clarence Thomas, who had been accused of sexual harassment by Anita Hill. In his testimony, he accused the Senate of a "high-tech lynching."

Kavanaugh unequivocally denied all allegations of sexual assault and, characterizing his high school days, stated, "I liked beer. I still like beer. But I did not drink beer to the point of blacking out, and I never sexually assaulted anyone." When the question period began, Kavanaugh was combative with the Democratic senators. In an awkward exchange with Sen. Amy Klobuchar, D-Minn., about whether he had ever experienced drinking that impacted his memory, Kavanaugh attempted to turn the question back on her, answering, "I don't know. Have you?" and then, again, when she asked him whether his answer was that it had not happened, he responded, "Yeah, and I'm curious if you have." Republican Sen. Lindsey Graham, R-S.C., by contrast, used his allotted questioning time to accuse Democrats of using the allegations to help them win 2018 elections. Addressing his Republican colleagues, he shouted, "If you vote no, you're legitimizing the most despicable thing I have seen in my time in politics." A number of witnesses provided sworn statements to the Senate Judiciary Committee, none of which corroborated either Dr. Ford's or Judge Kavanaugh's testimony. Instead, as Kavanaugh said in his testimony, "All of the people identified by Dr. Ford as being present at the party have said they do not remember any such party ever happening."

The next day after the hearing, the Senate Judiciary Committee voted in favor of advancing Kavanaugh's nomination. But, in a surprising move, Sen. Jeff Flake, R-Ariz., asked for a weeklong delay on a full Senate vote in order to allow the FBI to investigate Ford's allegations. Knowing that Sen. Flake's vote would be needed to confirm Judge Kavanaugh, Senate Republicans and the White House agreed to this request. President Trump ordered an investigation that was restricted in both time and scope. The FBI could not interview either Ford or Kavanaugh and was not given the power to subpoena either witnesses or evidence. When the FBI report concluded, it did not result in any new information. This left Republicans feeling more comfortable voting for confirmation, while Democrats claimed that the report was "incomplete." In the end, on October 6, while protestors shouted "Shame," the Senate voted to confirm Kavanaugh to a lifetime position on the Supreme Court by a vote of 50–48, the narrowest margin in 137 years.

## KAVANAUGH CONFIRMATION CREATES CONSERVATIVE MAJORITY

The legal impact of Kavanaugh's confirmation will be the creation of a solid conservative majority on the Supreme Court, potentially for a generation to come. A *Washington Post–ABC News* poll showed that 43 percent of Americans believe Court rulings will be more politically motivated with Judge Kavanaugh on the Court, leading to fears the bruising confirmation battle will weaken the federal judiciary.

Politically, the impact of the bitter and divisive confirmation battle, occurring one month before the 2018 midterm elections, was to electrify the voters of both major political parties and fuel massive voter turnout across the board. Republicans were able to characterize the mostly female protesters who thronged the Capitol during the hearings as an "angry mob." Sen. Mitch McConnell, R-Ky., in an interview with the *Washington Post*, said, "I want to thank the mob, because they've done the one thing we were having trouble doing which was energizing the base." President Trump spoke at a rally the day of the Kavanaugh confirmation, urging his supporters to focus on Supreme Court seats when they vote. "It could be three, it could even be four, it could be a lot," he said. "And if you allow the wrong people to get into office, things could change. . . . You don't hand matches to an arsonist, and you don't give power to an angry left-wing mob." In the end, four red-state Democratic senators who voted against confirmation of Judge Kavanaugh lost their seats in the midterm elections. In particular, political commentators opined that the "Kavanaugh effect" was responsible for the defeat of Sen. Heidi Heitkamp, D-N.D., and Claire McCaskill, D-Mo.

While Judge Kavanaugh may have helped Republicans pick up seats in the Senate, his confirmation likely contributed to turning out female voters in record numbers to fuel historic Democratic victories and send record numbers of women to the House of Representatives. Much of the increase in Democratic strength over previous midterms came from college-educated, suburban women, a group that polls show believed Dr. Ford over Judge Kavanaugh by more than 60 percent. Discussing the gender gap on Fox News, Sen. Graham, Judge Kavanaugh's loudest supporter, said, "We've got to address the suburban women problem, because it's real."

—Melissa Feinberg

*Following is the full text of Justice Anthony Kennedy's resignation letter to the Supreme Court, dated June 27, 2018; the text of Dr. Christine Blasey Ford's testimony before the Senate Judiciary Committee as submitted on September 26, 2018; and the text of Judge Brett Kavanaugh's testimony, as delivered before the Senate Judiciary Committee on September 27, 2018.*

# Justice Kennedy Announces His Retirement

**June 27, 2018**

My dear Mr. President,

   This letter is a respectful and formal notification of my decision, effective July 31 of this year, to end my regular active status as an Associate Justice of the Supreme Court, while continuing to serve in a senior status, as provided in 28 U.S.C. § 371(b).

   For a member of the legal profession it is the highest of honors to serve on this Court. Please permit me by this letter to express my profound gratitude for having had the privilege to seek in each case how best to know, interpret, and defend the Constitution and the laws that must always conform to its mandates and promises.

Respectfully and sincerely,
Anthony M. Kennedy
The President
The White House
Washington, D.C. 20500

SOURCE: Supreme Court of the United States. Chambers of Justice Anthony M. Kennedy. June 27, 2018. https://www.supremecourt.gov/publicinfo/press/Letter_to_the_President_June27.pdf.

# Dr. Ford Delivers Testimony during Kavanaugh Nomination Hearings

**September 26, 2018**

### Written Testimony of Dr. Christine Blasey Ford
### United States Senate Judiciary Committee September 26, 2018

Chairman Grassley, Ranking Member Feinstein, Members of the Committee. My name is Christine Blasey Ford. I am a Professor of Psychology at Palo Alto University and a Research Psychologist at the Stanford University School of Medicine.

I was an undergraduate at the University of North Carolina and earned my degree in Experimental Psychology in 1988. I received a Master's degree in 1991 in Clinical Psychology from Pepperdine University. In 1996, I received a PhD in Educational Psychology from the University of Southern California. I earned a Master's degree in Epidemiology from the Stanford University School of Medicine in 2009.

I have been married to Russell Ford since 2002 and we have two children.

I am here today not because I want to be. I am terrified. I am here because I believe it is my civic duty to tell you what happened to me while Brett Kavanaugh and I were in high school. I have described the events publicly before. I summarized them in my letter to Ranking Member Feinstein, and again in my letter to Chairman Grassley. I understand and appreciate the importance of your hearing from me directly about what happened to me and the impact it has had on my life and on my family.

I grew up in the suburbs of Washington, D.C. I attended the Holton-Arms School in Bethesda, Maryland, from 1980 to 1984. Holton-Arms is an all-girls school that opened in 1901. During my time at the school, girls at Holton-Arms frequently met and became friendly with boys from all-boys schools in the area, including Landon School, Georgetown Prep, Gonzaga High School, country clubs, and other places where kids and their families socialized. This is how I met Brett Kavanaugh, the boy who sexually assaulted me.

In my freshman and sophomore school years, when I was 14 and 15 years old, my group of friends intersected with Brett and his friends for a short period of time. I had been friendly with a classmate of Brett's for a short time during my freshman year, and it was through that connection that I attended a number of parties that Brett also attended. We did not know each other well, but I knew him and he knew me. In the summer of 1982, like most summers, I spent almost every day at the Columbia Country Club in Chevy Chase, Maryland swimming and practicing diving.

One evening that summer, after a day of swimming at the club, I attended a small gathering at a house in the Chevy Chase/Bethesda area. There were four boys I remember being there: Brett Kavanaugh, Mark Judge, P.J. Smyth, and one other boy whose name I cannot recall. I remember my friend Leland Ingham attending. I do not remember all of the details of how that gathering came together, but like many that summer, it was almost surely a spur of the moment gathering. I truly wish I could provide detailed answers to all of the questions that have been and will be asked about how I got to the party, where it took place, and so forth. I don't have all the answers, and I don't remember as much as I would like to. But the details about that night that bring me here today are ones I will never forget. They have been seared into my memory and have haunted me episodically as an adult.

When I got to the small gathering, people were drinking beer in a small living room on the first floor of the house. I drank one beer that evening. Brett and Mark were visibly drunk. Early in the evening, I went up a narrow set of stairs leading from the living room to a second floor to use the bathroom. When I got to the top of the stairs, I was pushed from behind into a bedroom. I couldn't see who pushed me. Brett and Mark came into the bedroom and locked the door behind them. There was music already playing in the bedroom. It was turned up louder by either Brett or Mark once we were in the room. I was pushed onto the bed and Brett got on top of me. He began running his hands over my body and grinding his hips into me. I yelled, hoping someone downstairs might hear me, and tried to get away from him, but his weight was heavy. Brett groped me and tried to take off my clothes. He had a hard time because he was so drunk, and because I was wearing a one-piece bathing suit under my clothes. I believed he was going to rape me. I tried to yell for help. When I did, Brett put his hand over my mouth to stop me from screaming. This was what terrified me the most, and has had the most lasting impact on my life. It was hard for me to breathe, and I thought that Brett was accidentally going to kill me. Both Brett and Mark were drunkenly laughing during the attack. They both seemed to be having a good time. Mark was urging Brett on, although at times he told Brett to stop. A couple of times I made eye contact with Mark and thought he might try to help me, but he did not.

During this assault, Mark came over and jumped on the bed twice while Brett was on top of me. The last time he did this, we toppled over and Brett was no longer on top of me. I was able to get up and run out of the room. Directly across from the bedroom was a small bathroom. I ran inside the bathroom and locked the door. I heard Brett and Mark leave the bedroom laughing and loudly walk down the narrow stairs, pin-balling off the walls on the way down. I waited and when I did not hear them come back up the stairs, I left the bathroom, ran down the stairs, through the living room, and left the house. I remember being on the street and feeling an enormous sense of relief that I had escaped from the house and that Brett and Mark were not coming after me.

Brett's assault on me drastically altered my life. For a very long time, I was too afraid and ashamed to tell anyone the details. I did not want to tell my parents that I, at age 15, was in a house without any parents present, drinking beer with boys. I tried to convince myself that because Brett did not rape me, I should be able to move on and just pretend that it had never happened. Over the years, I told very few friends that I had this traumatic experience. I told my husband before we were married that I had experienced a sexual assault. I had never told the details to anyone until May 2012, during a couples counseling session. The reason this came up in counseling is that my husband and I had completed an extensive remodel of our home, and I insisted on a second front door, an idea that he and others disagreed with and could not understand. In explaining why I wanted to have a second front door, I described the assault in detail. I recall saying that the boy who assaulted me could someday be on the U.S. Supreme Court and spoke a bit about his background. My husband recalls that I named my attacker as Brett Kavanaugh.

After that May 2012 therapy session, I did my best to suppress memories of the assault because recounting the details caused me to relive the experience, and caused panic attacks and anxiety. Occasionally I would discuss the assault in individual therapy, but talking about it caused me to relive the trauma, so I tried not to think about it or discuss it. But over the years, I went through periods where I thought about Brett's attack. I confided in some close friends that I had an experience with sexual assault. Occasionally I stated that my assailant was a prominent lawyer or judge but I did not use his name. I do not recall each person I spoke to about Brett's assault, and some friends have reminded me of these conversations since the publication of The Washington Post story on September 16, 2018. But until July 2018, I had never named Mr. Kavanaugh as my attacker outside of therapy.

This all changed in early July 2018. I saw press reports stating that Brett Kavanaugh was on the "short list" of potential Supreme Court nominees. I thought it was my civic duty to relay the information I had about Mr. Kavanaugh's conduct so that those considering his potential nomination would know about the assault.

On July 6, 2018, I had a sense of urgency to relay the information to the Senate and the President as soon as possible before a nominee was selected. I called my congressional representative and let her receptionist know that someone on the President's shortlist had attacked me. I also sent a message to The Washington Post's confidential tip line. I did not use my name, but I provided the names of Brett Kavanaugh and Mark Judge. I stated that Mr. Kavanaugh had assaulted me in the 1980s in Maryland. This was an extremely hard thing for me to do, but I felt I couldn't NOT do it. Over the next two days, I told a couple of close friends on the beach in California that Mr. Kavanaugh had sexually assaulted me. I was conflicted about whether to speak out.

On July 9, 2018, I received a call from the office of Congresswoman Anna Eshoo after Mr. Kavanaugh had become the nominee. I met with her staff on July 18 and with her on July 20, describing the assault and discussing my fear about coming forward. Later, we discussed the possibility of sending a letter to Ranking Member Feinstein, who is one of my state's Senators, describing what occurred. My understanding is that Representative Eshoo's office delivered a copy of my letter to Senator Feinstein's office on July 30, 2018. The letter included my name, but requested that the letter be kept confidential.

My hope was that providing the information confidentially would be sufficient to allow the Senate to consider Mr. Kavanaugh's serious misconduct without having to make myself, my family, or anyone's family vulnerable to the personal attacks and invasions of privacy we have faced since my name became public. In a letter on August 31, 2018, Senator Feinstein wrote that she would not share the letter without my consent. I greatly appreciated this commitment. All sexual assault victims should be able to decide for themselves whether their private experience is made public.

As the hearing date got closer, I struggled with a terrible choice: Do I share the facts with the Senate and put myself and my family in the public spotlight? Or do I preserve our privacy and allow the Senate to make its decision on Mr. Kavanaugh's nomination without knowing the full truth about his past behavior?

I agonized daily with this decision throughout August and early September 2018. The sense of duty that motivated me to reach out confidentially to The Washington Post, Representative Eshoo's office, and Senator Feinstein's office was always there, but my fears of the consequences of speaking out started to increase.

During August 2018, the press reported that Mr. Kavanaugh's confirmation was virtually certain. His allies painted him as a champion of women's rights and empowerment. I believed that if I came forward, my voice would be drowned out by a chorus of powerful supporters. By the time of the confirmation hearings, I had resigned myself to remaining quiet and letting the Committee and the Senate make their decision without knowing what Mr. Kavanaugh had done to me.

Once the press started reporting on the existence of the letter I had sent to Senator Feinstein, I faced mounting pressure. Reporters appeared at my home and at my job demanding information about this letter, including in the presence of my graduate students. They called my boss and co-workers and left me many messages, making it clear that my name would inevitably be released to the media. I decided to speak out publicly to a journalist who had responded to the tip I had sent to The Washington Post and who had gained my trust. It was important to me to describe the details of the assault in my own words.

Since September 16, the date of The Washington Post story, I have experienced an outpouring of support from people in every state of this country. Thousands of people who have had their lives dramatically altered by sexual violence have reached out to share their own experiences with me and have thanked me for coming forward. We have received tremendous support from friends and our community.

At the same time, my greatest fears have been realized—and the reality has been far worse than what I expected. My family and I have been the target of constant harassment and death threats. I have been called the most vile and hateful names imaginable. These messages, while far fewer than the expressions of support, have been terrifying to receive and have rocked me to my core. People have posted my personal information on the internet. This has resulted in additional emails, calls, and threats. My family and I were forced to move out of our home. Since September 16, my family and I have been living in various secure locales, with guards. This past Tuesday evening, my work email account was hacked and messages were sent out supposedly recanting my description of the sexual assault.

Apart from the assault itself, these last couple of weeks have been the hardest of my life. I have had to relive my trauma in front of the entire world, and have seen my life picked apart by people on television, in the media, and in this body who have never met me or spoken with me. I have been accused of acting out of partisan political motives. Those who say that do not know me. I am a fiercely independent person and I am no one's pawn. My motivation in coming forward was to provide the facts about how Mr. Kavanaugh's actions have damaged my life, so that you can take that into serious consideration as you make your decision about how to proceed. It is not my responsibility to determine whether Mr. Kavanaugh deserves to sit on the Supreme Court. My responsibility is to tell the truth.

I understand that the Majority has hired a professional prosecutor to ask me some questions, and I am committed to doing my very best to answer them. At the same time, because the Committee Members will be judging my credibility, I hope to be able to engage directly with each of you.

At this point, I will do my best to answer your questions.

SOURCE: U.S. Senate Judiciary Committee. "Written Testimony of Dr. Christine Blasey Ford." Submitted September 26, 2018. Delivered September 27, 2018. https://www.judiciary.senate.gov/imo/media/doc/09-27-18%20Ford%20Testimony%20Updated.pdf.

# Kavanaugh Delivers Testimony to Senate Judiciary Committee

**September 27, 2018**

Mr. Chairman, Ranking Member Feinstein, members of the committee, thank you for allowing me to make my statement. I wrote it myself yesterday afternoon and evening. No one has seen a draft, or it, except for one of my former law clerks. This is my statement.

Less than two weeks ago, Dr. Ford publicly accused me of committing wrongdoing at an event more than 36 years ago when we were both in high school. I denied the allegation immediately, categorically and unequivocally. All four people allegedly at the event, including Dr. Ford's longtime friend, Ms. Keyser, have said they recall no such event. Her longtime friend, Ms. Keyser, said under penalty of felony that she does not know me, and does not believe she ever saw me at a party, ever.

Here is the quote from Ms. Keyser's attorney's letter: quote, "Simply put, Ms. Keyser does not know Mr. Kavanaugh, and she has no recollection of ever being at a party or gathering where he was present, with or without Dr. Ford," end quote. Think about that fact.

The day after the allegation appeared, I told this committee that I wanted a hearing as soon as possible to clear my name. I demanded a hearing for the very next day. Unfortunately, it took the committee 10 days to get to this hearing. In those 10 long days, as was predictable, and as I predicted, my family and my name have been totally and permanently destroyed by vicious and false additional accusations. The 10-day delay has been harmful to me and my family, to the Supreme Court and to the country.

When this allegation first arose, I welcomed any kind of investigation, Senate, FBI or otherwise. The committee now has conducted a thorough investigation, and I've cooperated fully. I know that any kind of investigation—Senate, FBI, Montgomery County Police—whatever, will clear me. Listen to the people I know. Listen to the people who've known me my whole life. Listen to the people I've grown up with, and worked with, and played with, and coached with, and dated, and taught, and gone to games with, and had beers with. And listen to the witnesses who allegedly were at this event 36 years ago. Listen to Ms. Keyser. She does not know me. I was not at the party described by Dr. Ford.

This confirmation process has become a national disgrace. The Constitution gives the Senate an important role in the confirmation process, but you have replaced advice and consent with search and destroy.

Since my nomination in July, there's been a frenzy on the left to come up with something, anything to block my confirmation. Shortly after I was nominated, the Democratic Senate leader said he would, quote, "oppose me with everything he's got." A Democratic senator on this committee publicly—publicly referred to me as evil—evil. Think about that word. It's said that those who supported me were, quote, "complicit in evil." Another Democratic senator on this committee said, quote, "Judge Kavanaugh is your worst nightmare." A former head of the Democratic National Committee said, quote, "Judge Kavanaugh will threaten the lives of millions of Americans for decades to come."

I understand the passions of the moment, but I would say to those senators, your words have meaning. Millions of Americans listen carefully to you. Given comments like those, is it any surprise that people have been willing to do anything to make any physical threat against my family, to send any violent e-mail to my wife, to make any kind of allegation against me and against my friends. To blow me up and take me down.

You sowed the wind for decades to come. I fear that the whole country will reap the whirlwind.

The behavior of several of the Democratic members of this committee at my hearing a few weeks ago was an embarrassment. But at least it was just a good old-fashioned attempt at Borking.

Those efforts didn't work. When I did at least OK enough at the hearings that it looked like I might actually get confirmed, a new tactic was needed.

Some of you were lying in wait and had it ready. This first allegation was held in secret for weeks by a Democratic member of this committee, and by staff. It would be needed only if you couldn't take me out on the merits.

When it was needed, this allegation was unleashed and publicly deployed over Dr. Ford's wishes. And then—and then as no doubt was expected—if not planned—came a long series of false last-minute smears designed to scare me and drive me out of the process before any hearing occurred.

Crazy stuff. Gangs, illegitimate children, fights on boats in Rhode Island. All nonsense, reported breathlessly and often uncritically by the media.

This has destroyed my family and my good name. A good name built up through decades of very hard work and public service at the highest levels of the American government.

This whole two-week effort has been a calculated and orchestrated political hit, fueled with apparent pent-up anger about President Trump and the 2016 election. Fear that has been unfairly stoked about my judicial record. Revenge on behalf of the Clintons, and millions of dollars in money from outside left-wing opposition groups.

This is a circus. The consequences will extend long past my nomination. The consequences will be with us for decades. This grotesque and coordinated character assassination will dissuade competent and good people of all political persuasions, from serving our country.

And as we all know, in the United States political system of the early 2000s, what goes around comes around. I am an optimistic guy. I always try to be on the sunrise side of the mountain, to be optimistic about the day that is coming.

But today, I have to say that I fear for the future. Last time I was here, I told this committee that a federal judge must be independent, not swayed by public or political pressure.

I said I was such a judge, and I am. I will not be intimidated into withdrawing from this process. You've tried hard. You've given it your all. No one can question your effort, but your coordinated and well-funded effort to destroy my good name and to destroy my family will not drive me out. The vile threats of violence against my family will not drive me out.

You may defeat me in the final vote, but you'll never get me to quit. Never.

I'm here today to tell the truth. I've never sexually assaulted anyone. Not in high school, not in college, not ever. Sexual assault is horrific. One of my closest friends to this day is a woman who was sexually abused and who, in the 1990s when we were in our 30s, confided in me about the abuse and sought my advice. I was one of the only people she consulted.

Allegations of sexual assault must always be taken seriously, always. Those who make allegations always deserve to be heard.

At the same time, the person who was the subject of the allegations also deserves to be heard. Due process is a foundation of the American rule of law. Due process means listening to both sides.

As I told you at my hearing three weeks ago, I'm the only child of Martha and Ed Kavanaugh. They're here today. When I was 10, my mom went to law school. And as a lawyer, she worked hard and overcame barriers, including the workplace sexual harassment that so many women faced (ph) at that time and still face today.

She became a trailblazer, one of Maryland's earliest women prosecutors and trial judges. She and my dad taught me the importance of equality and respect for all people, and she inspired me to be a lawyer and a judge.

Last time I was here, I told you that when my mom was a prosecutor and I was in high school, she used to practice her closing arguments at the dining room table, on my dad and me.

As I told you, her trademark line was, "Use your common sense. What rings true? What rings false?" Her trademark line is a good reminder, as we sit here today, some 36 years after the alleged event occurred when there is no corroboration and indeed it is refuted by the people allegedly there.

After I've been in the public arena for 26 years without even a hint—a whiff—of an allegation like this. And when my nomination to the Supreme Court was just about to be voted on, at a time when I'm called "evil" by a Democratic member of this committee, while Democratic opponents of my nomination say people will die if I am confirmed.

This onslaught of last-minute allegations does not ring true. I'm not questioning that Dr. Ford may have been sexually assaulted by some person in some place at some time. But I have never done this. To her or to anyone. That's not who I am. It is not who I was. I am innocent of this charge.

I intend no ill will to Dr. Ford and her family. The other night, Ashley and my daughter, Liza, said their prayers. And little Liza—all of 10 years old—said to Ashley, "We should pray for the woman." It's a lot of wisdom from a 10-year old. We mean—we mean no ill will.

First, let's start with my career. For the last 26 years, since 1992, I have served in many high profile and sensitive government positions for which the FBI has investigated my background six separate times. Six separate FBI background investigations over 26 years. All of them after the elent (ph)—event alleged here. I have been in the public arena and under extreme public scrutiny for decades.

In 1992, I worked for the Office of Solicitor General in the Department of Justice. In 1993, I clerked on the Supreme Court for Justice Anthony Kennedy. I spent 4 years at the Independent Counsel's office during the 1990s. That office was the subject of enormous scrutiny from the media and the public. During 1998, the year of the impeachment of President Clinton, our office generally and I personally were in the middle of an intense national media and political spotlight.

I and other leading members of Ken Starr's office were opposition researched from head to toe, from birth through the present day. Recall the people who were exposed that year of 1998 as having in engaged in some sexual wrongdoing or indiscretions in their pasts. One person on the left even paid a million dollars for people to report evidence of sexual wrongdoing, and it worked. Exposed some prominent people. Nothing about me.

From 2001 to 2006, I worked for President George W. Bush in the White House. As Staff Secretary, I was by President Bush's side for 3 years and was entrusted with the nation's most sensitive secrets. I traveled on Air Force One all over the country and the world with President Bush. I went everywhere with him, from Texas to Pakistan, from Alaska to Australia, from Buckingham Palace to the Vatican. Three years in the West Wing, 5 1/2 years in the White House.

I was then nominated to be a judge on the D.C. Circuit. I was thoroughly vetted by the White House, the FBI, the American Bar Association, and this committee. I sat before this committee for two thorough confirmation hearings in 2004 and 2006.

For the past 12 years leading up to my nomination for this job, I've served in a very public arena as a federal judge on what is often referred to as the second-most important court in the country. I've handled some of the most significant sensitive cases affecting the lives and liberties of the American people.

I have been a good judge. And for this nomination, another FBI background investigation, another American Bar Association investigation, 31 hours of hearings, 65 senator meetings, 1,200 written questions, more than all previous Supreme Court nominees combined.

Throughout that entire time, throughout my 53 years and 7 months on this Earth, until last week, no one ever accused me of any kind of sexual misconduct. No one, ever. A lifetime. A lifetime of public service and a lifetime of high-profile public service at the highest levels of American government and never a hint of anything of this kind, and that's because nothing of this kind ever happened.

Second, let's turn to specifics. I categorically and unequivocally deny the allegation against me by Dr. Ford. I never had any sexual or physical encounter of any kind with Dr. Ford. I never attended a gathering like the one Dr. Ford describes in her allegation. I've never sexually assaulted Dr. Ford or anyone.

Again, I am not questioning that Dr. Ford may have been sexually assaulted by some person in some place at some time. But I have never done that to her or to anyone.

Dr. Ford's allegation stems from a party that she alleges occurred during the summer of 1982, 36 years ago. I was 17 years old, between my junior and senior years of high school at Georgetown Prep, a rigorous all-boys Catholic Jesuit High School in Rockville, Maryland. When my friends and I spent time together at parties on weekends, it was usually the—with friends from nearby Catholic all-girls high schools, Stone Ridge, Holy Child, Visitation, Immaculata, Holy Cross.

Dr. Ford did not attend one of those schools. She attended an independent private school named Holton-Arms and she was a year behind me. She and I did not travel in the same social circles. It is possible that we met at some point at some events, although I do not recall that. To repeat, all of the people identified by Dr. Ford as being present at the party have said they do not remember any such party ever happening.

Importantly her friend, Ms. Keyser, has not only denied knowledge of the party, Ms. Keyser said under penalty of felony she does not know me, does not recall ever being at a party with me ever. And my two male friends who were allegedly there, who knew me well, have told this committee under penalty of felony that they do not recall any such party and that I never did or would do anything like this.

Dr. Ford's allegation is not merely uncorroborated, it is refuted by the very people she says were there, including by a long-time friend of hers. Refuted.

Third, Dr. Ford has said that this event occurred at a house near Columbia Country Club, which is at the corner of Connecticut Avenue in the East-West Highway in Chevy Chase, Maryland. In her letter to Senator Feinstein, she said that there were four other people at the house but none of those people, nor I, lived near Columbia Country Club.

As of the summer of 1982, Dr. Ford was 15 and could not drive yet and she did not live near Columbia Country Club. She says confidently that she had one beer at the party, but she does not say how she got to the house in question or how she got home or whose house it was.

Fourth, I have submitted to this committee detailed calendars recording my activities in the summer of 1982. Why did I keep calendars? My dad started keeping detailed calendars of his life in 1978. He did so as both a calendar and a diary. He was a very organized guy, to put it mildly. Christmas time, we'd sit around and he regales us with old stories, old milestones, old weddings, old events from his calendars.

In ninth grade—in ninth grade, in 1980, I started keeping calendars of my own. For me, also, it's both a calendar and a diary. I've kept such calendar as diaries for the last 38 years; mine are not as good as my dad's in some years. And when I was a kid, the calendars are about what you would expect from a kid; some goofy parts, some embarrassing parts.

But I did have the summer of 1982 documented pretty well. The event described by Dr. Ford, presumably happened on a weekend because I believed everyone worked and had jobs in the summers. And in any event, a drunken early evening event of the kind she describes, presumably happened on a weekend.

If it was a weekend, my calendars show that I was out of town almost every weekend night before football training camp started in late August. The only weekend nights that I was in D.C. were Friday, June 4, when I was with my dad at a pro golf tournament and had my high school achievement test at 8:30 the next morning.

I also was in D.C. on Saturday night, August 7th. But I was at a small gathering at Becky's house in Rockville with Matt, Denise, Laurie and Jenny. Their names are all listed on my calendar. I won't use their last names here.

And then on the weekend of August 20 to 22nd, I was staying at the Garrets' (ph) with Pat (ph) and Chris (ph) as we did final preparations for football training camp that began on Sunday, the 22nd. As the calendars confirm, the—that weekend before a brutal training camp schedule was no time for parities [sic].

So let me emphasize this point. If the party described by Dr. Ford happened in the summer of 1982 on a weekend night, my calendar shows all but definitively that I was not there.

During the weekdays in the summer of 1982, as you can see, I was out of town for two weeks of the summer for a trip to the beach with friends and at the legendary Five-Star Basketball Camp in Honesdale, Pennsylvania. When I was in town, I spent much of my time working, working out, lifting weights, playing basketball, or hanging out and having some beers with friends as we talked about life, and football, and school and girls.

Some have noticed that I didn't have church on Sundays on my calendars. I also didn't list brushing my teeth. And for me, going to church on Sundays was like brushing my teeth, automatic. It still is.

In the summer of 1981, I had worked construction. In the summer of 1982, my job was cutting lawns. I had my own business of sorts. You see some specifics about the lawn cutting listed on the August calendar page, when I had to time the last lawn cuttings of the summer of various lawns before football training camp.

I played in a lot of summer league basketball games for the Georgetown Prep team at night at Blair High School in Silver Spring. Many nights, I worked out with other guys at Tobin's house. He was the great quarterback on our football team and his dad ran work-outs—or lifted weights at Georgetown Prep in preparation for the football season. I attended and watched many sporting events, as is my habit to this day.

The calendars show a few weekday gatherings at friends' houses after a workout or just to meet up and have some beers. But none of those gatherings included the group of people that Dr. Ford has identified. And as my calendars show, I was very precise about listing who was there; very precise.

And keeping—keep in mind, my calendars also were diaries of sorts, forward-looking and backward-looking, just like my dad's. You can see, for example, that I crossed out missed workouts and the canceled doctor's appointments, and that I listed the precise people who had shown up for certain events. The calendars are obviously not dispositive on their own, but they are another piece of evidence for you to consider.

Fifth, Dr. Ford's allegation is radically inconsistent with my record and my character from my youth to the present day. As students at an all-boys catholic Jesuit school, many of us became friends and remain friends to this day with students at local catholic all-girls schools.

One feature of my life that has remained true to the present day is that I have always had a lot of close female friends. I'm not talking about girlfriends; I'm talking about friends who are women. That started in high school. Maybe it was because I'm an only child and had no sisters.

But anyway, we had no social media, or texts, or e-mail and we talked on the phone. I remember talking almost every night it seemed, to my friends Amy, or Julie, or Kristin, or Karen, or Suzanne, or Moira, or Megan, or Nikki (ph). The list goes on—friends for a lifetime, built on a foundation of talking through school and life, starting at age 14. Several of those great women are in the seats right behind me today.

My friends and I sometimes got together and had parties on weekends. The drinking age was 18 in Maryland for most of my time in high school, and was 18 in D.C. for all of my time in high school. I drank beer with my friends. Almost everyone did. Sometimes I had too many beers. Sometimes others did. I liked beer. I still like beer. But I did not drink beer to the point of blacking out, and I never sexually assaulted anyone.

There is a bright line between drinking beer, which I gladly do, and which I fully embrace, and sexually assaulting someone, which is a violent crime. If every American who drinks beer or every American who drank beer in high school is suddenly presumed guilty of sexual assault, will be an ugly, new place in this country. I never committed sexual assault.

As high school students, we sometimes did goofy or stupid things. I doubt we are alone in looking back in high school and cringing at some things.

For one thing, our yearbook was a disaster. I think some editors and students wanted the yearbook to be some combination of Animal House, Caddy Shack and Fast Times at Ridgemont High, which were all recent movies at that time. Many of us went along in the yearbook to the point of absurdity. This past week, my friends and I have cringed when we read about it and talked to each other.

One thing in particular we're sad about: one of our good—one of our good female friends who we would admire and went to dances with had her names used on the yearbook page with the term "alumnus." That yearbook reference was clumsily intended to show affection, and that she was one of us. But in this circus, the media's interpreted the term is related to sex. It was not related to sex. As the woman herself noted to the media on the record, she and I never had any six—sexual interaction of—at all. I'm so sorry to her for that yearbook reference. This may sound a bit trivial, given all that we are here for, but one thing I want to try to make sure—sure of in the future is my friendship with her. She was and is a great person.

As to sex, this is not a topic I ever imagined would come up at a judicial confirmation hearing, but I want to give you a full picture of who I was. I never had sexual intercourse, or anything close to it, during high school, or for many years after that. In some crowds, I was probably a little outwardly shy about my inexperience; tried to hide that. At the same time, I was also inwardly proud of it. For me and the girls who I was friends with, that lack of major rampant sexual activity in high school was a matter of faith and respect and caution.

The committee has a letter from 65 women who knew me in high school. They said that I always treated them with dignity and respect. That letter came together in one night, 35 years after graduation, while a sexual assault allegation was pending against me in a very fraught (ph) and public situation where they knew—they knew they'd be vilified if they defended me. Think about that. They put theirselves (sic) on the line for me. Those are some awesome women, and I love all of them.

You also have a letter from women who knew me in college. Most were varsity athletes, and they described that I treated them as friends and equals, and supported them in their sports at a time when women's sports was emerging in the wake of Title IX. I thank all of them for all of their texts, and their emails, and their support. One of those women friends from college, a self-described liberal and feminist, sent me a text last night that said, quote, "Deep breaths. You're a good man, a good man, a good man."

A text yesterday from another of those women friends from college said, quote, "Brett, be strong. Pulling for you to my core." A third text yesterday from yet another of those women I'm friends with from college said, "I'm holding you in the light of God."

As I said in my opening statement the last time I was with you, cherish your friends, look out for your friends, lift up your friends, love your friends. I've felt that love more over the last two weeks than I ever have in my life. I thank all my friends. I love all my friends.

Throughout my life, I've devoted huge efforts to encouraging and promoting the careers of women. I will put my record up against anyone's, male or female. I am proud of the letter from 84 women—84 women—who worked with me at the Bush White House from 2001 to 2006, and described me as, quote, "a man of the highest integrity."

Read the op-ed from Sarah Day (ph) from Yarmouth, Maine. She worked in Oval Office operations, outside of President Bush's office. Here's what she recently wrote in centralmaine.com, and today she stands by her comments.

Quote, "Brett was an advocate for young women like me. He encouraged me to take on more responsibility and to feel confident in my role. In fact, during the 2004 Republican National Convention, Brett gave me the opportunity to help with the preparation and review of the president's remarks, something I never (ph) . . .

. . . "something I never would have had the chance to do if he had not included me. And he didn't just include me in the work. He made sure I was at Madison Square Garden to watch the president's speech, instead of back at the hotel, watching it on TV." End quote.

As a judge since 2006, I've had the privilege of hiring four recent law school graduates to serve as my law clerks each year. The law clerks for federal judges are the best and brightest graduates of American law schools. They work for one-year terms for judges after law school, and then they move on in their careers.

For judges, training these young lawyers is an important responsibility. The clerks will become the next generation of American lawyers and leaders, judges and senators.

Just after I took the bench in 2006, there was a major New York Times story about the low numbers of women law clerks at the Supreme Court and federal appeals courts.

I took notice, and I took action. A majority of my 48 law clerks over the last 12 years have been women.

In a letter to this committee, my women law clerks said I was one of the strongest advocates in the federal judiciary for women lawyers. And they wrote that the legal profession is fairer and more equal because of me.

In my time on the bench, no federal judge—not a single one in the country—has sent more women law clerks to clerk on the Supreme Court than I have.

Before this allegation arose two weeks ago, I was required to start making certain administrative preparations for my possible transfer to the Supreme Court, just in case I was confirmed.

As part of that, I had to, in essence, contingently hire a first group of four law clerks who could be available to clerk at the Supreme Court for me on a moment's notice.

I did so, and contingently hired four law clerks. All four are women. If confirmed, I'll be the first justice in the history of the Supreme Court to have a group of all-women law clerks.

That is who I am. That is who I was. Over the past 12 years, I've taught constitutional law to hundreds of students, primarily at Harvard Law School, where (ph) I was hired by then-dean and now-Justice Elena Kagan.

One of my former women students, a Democrat, testified to this committee that I was an even-handed professor who treats people fairly and with respect.

In a letter to this committee, my former students—male and female alike—wrote that I displayed "a character that impressed us all." I loved teaching law. But thanks to what some of you on this side of the committee have unleashed, I may never be able to teach again.

For the past seven years, I've coached my two daughters' basketball teams. You saw many of those girls when they came to my hearing for a couple of hours. You have a letter from the parents of the girls I coach, that describe my dedication, commitment and character.

I coach because I know that a girl's confidence on the basketball court translates into confidence in other aspects of life. I love coaching more than anything I've ever done in my whole life. But thanks to what some of you on this side of the committee have unleashed, I may never be able to coach again.

I've been a judge for 12 years. I have a long record of service to America and to the Constitution. I revere the Constitution. I am deeply grateful to President Trump for nominating me. He was so gracious to my family and me on the July night he announced my nomination at the White House. I thank him for his steadfast support.

When I accepted the president's nomination, Ashley and I knew this process would be challenging. We never expected that it would devolve into this. Explaining this to our daughters has been about the worst experience of our lives.

Ashley has been a rock. I thank God every day for Ashley and my family. We live in a country devoted to due process and the rule of law. That means taking allegations seriously.

But if the mere allegation—the mere assertion of an allegation—a refuted allegation from 36 years ago is enough to destroy a person's life and career, we will have abandoned the basic principles of fairness and due process that define our legal system and our country.

I ask you to judge me by the standard that you would want applied to your father, your husband, your brother or your son. My family and I intend no ill will toward Dr. Ford or her family.

But I swear today—under oath, before the Senate and the nation; before my family and God—I am innocent of this charge.

SOURCE: Bloomberg Government. "Senate Judiciary Committee Hearing on the Nomination of Brett M. Kavanaugh to Be an Associate Justice of the Supreme Court, Day 5, Focusing on Allegations of Sexual Assault." September 27, 2018. https://www.bgov.com/core/news/#!/articles/PFQQJF8JMDC0. Transcript provided courtesy of Bloomberg Government (www.bgov.com) (877-498-3587).

## OTHER HISTORIC DOCUMENTS OF INTEREST

### FROM PREVIOUS HISTORIC DOCUMENTS

# Supreme Court Rules on Public-Sector Unions

JUNE 27, 2018

On June 27, 2018, the Supreme Court overturned a forty-year-old precedent to hold, in *Janus v. American Federation of State, County, and Municipal Employees*, that public-sector unions cannot charge any fees to nonunion employees without their explicit consent. According to the Court, these fees violate the free speech rights of the nonunion members by "compelling them to subsidize private speech on matters of substantial public concern." Although one of the most significant decisions to impact labor unions in decades, the ruling was not unexpected. In the 5–4 ruling, conservative justices found a First Amendment violation when nonunion members are "forced to subsidize a union." The fees that the Court held to be unconstitutional are generally a fraction of union member fees, and they cannot, by law, cover any political activity. Their purpose has been to prevent nonunion workers from gaining all the benefits of collective bargaining but without paying anything for them. By declaring these fees unconstitutional, twenty-two states will need to change their laws, and thousands of collective bargaining agreements that cover millions of public employees will need to be renegotiated. Unions decried the decision as a devastating blow and predict they will suffer a loss of resources, political strength, and the ability to advocate for workers.

## Illinois Law under Supreme Court Scrutiny

Under Illinois law, if a majority of state employees in a particular unit vote to be represented by a union, that union will be designated as the exclusive representative of all the employees. Employees are not obligated to join the union, but the union is obligated, by law, to represent the interests of all employees, whether members or not. Union members must pay full union dues, but those who decline to join the union have been assessed a fee, referred to as an "agency" fee or a "fair share" fee, that is calculated as a percentage of the union dues. Since 1947, it has been settled law that states can choose to allow this type of fee. When these fees were challenged in 1977, the Supreme Court, in *Abood v. Detroit Board of Education*, crafted a compromise: unions would still be allowed to charge the fees, with the added requirement that unions cannot use any fee paid by a nonmember for political purposes. Illinois law reflected these precedents when it allowed public-sector unions to charge nonmembers a fee to compensate the union for certain collective bargaining and contract administration expenses "affecting wages, hours, and conditions of employment." Illinois did not allow the union to charge for expenditures "related to the election or support of any candidate for public office."

Mark Janus worked as a child support specialist, employed by the Illinois Department of Healthcare and Family Services, where he was one of the 35,000 public employees in Illinois who were represented by American Federation of State, County, and Municipal

Employees (AFSCME). He refused to join the union because he objected to "many of the public policy positions that [it] advocates." Under his collective bargaining agreement, he was assessed an agency fee of $44.85 per month, which is 78.06 percent of full union dues. Claiming that "all nonmember fee deductions are coerced political speech," Janus challenged the Illinois statute authorizing the imposition of the agency fees. Both the District Court and the Court of Appeals for the Seventh Circuit rejected his claims, holding that they were foreclosed by settled Supreme Court precedent. The Supreme Court agreed to hear the case.

## Supreme Court Overturns Forty-Year Precedent

Because Janus's case involved settled precedent, when the Court agreed to hear the appeal, it was clear that the justices intended to consider overruling their previous judgment. Generally, the Supreme Court follows the principle of *stare decisis*, which is Latin for "to stand by things decided," and, in practice, means that the Court will not overturn past decisions absent strong grounds for doing so. The Supreme Court has explained the reasoning behind this preference for *stare decisis* in a past case, stating "it promotes the even-handed, predictable, and consistent development of legal principles, fosters reliance on judicial decisions, and contributes to the actual and perceived integrity of the judicial process." In *Janus v. American Federation of State, County, and Municipal Employees*, however, the Court found that it had erred in 1977 when it decided *Abood* and explicitly overturned it. In an opinion written by Justice Samuel Alito and joined by Chief Justice John Roberts and Justices Clarence Thomas, Anthony Kennedy, and Neil Gorsuch, the Court ruled that agency fees violate the First Amendment and cannot continue.

Justice Alito's opinion first considered whether the earlier *Abood* case was consistent with First Amendment principles and found it lacking. Among other rights, the First Amendment protects freedom of speech and includes, as Justice Alito writes, "both the right to speak freely and the right to refrain from speaking at all." This is violated when laws compel individuals to "mouth support for views they find objectionable." By way of example, he argued that everyone would agree that it would violate the First Amendment if the state required residents "to sign a document expressing support for a particular set of positions on controversial public issues." In fact, speech that is compelled could be considered worse than speech that is prevented, because, in that situation, "individuals are coerced into betraying their convictions." To support the argument that similar First Amendment concerns are raised by compelling a person to *subsidize* the speech of others, Justice Alito quoted Thomas Jefferson: "To compel a man to furnish contributions of money for the propagation of opinions which he disbelieves and abhors is sinful and tyrannical." Having shown that "the compelled subsidization of private speech seriously impinges on First Amendment rights," the opinion concluded that it cannot be casually allowed. Justice Alito then reviewed the stated reasons that the *Abood* decision relied upon to allow agency fees and was unimpressed.

First, in *Abood*, the Supreme Court pointed to the state's interest in "labor peace," that is the need to avoid "conflict and disruption," to support the need for agency fees. Such fears, Justice Alito asserted, have been shown to be unfounded in the decades since the case was decided. Here, the opinion points to the federal employment arena that does not allow such fees, and yet 27 percent of federal employees are in unions. Similarly, in the twenty-eight states that forbid such fees, "millions of public employees" are represented by unions, all without the "pandemonium" predicted by *Abood*. This led Alito to conclude:

"Whatever may have been the case 41 years ago when *Abood* was decided, it is thus now undeniable that 'labor peace' can readily be achieved 'through means significantly less restrictive of associational freedoms' than the assessment of agency fees."

Justice Alito also dismissed the second argument, that agency fees are necessary to prevent "free riders" from "enjoying the benefits of union representation without shouldering the costs." The opinion quotes the petitioner, Janus, who strenuously objects to the idea that he is "a free rider on a bus headed for a destination that he wishes to reach," describing himself instead as "more like a person shanghaied for an unwanted voyage." Justice Alito doubled down on this metaphor when he read his opinion from the bench, calling those who object to paying agency fees captives, not free riders, because they don't want to make the trip at all. The avoidance of free riders is not, the opinion concludes, a compelling interest to justify imposing fees. Finding otherwise would, Justice Alito wrote, lead to "startling consequences." By way of example, he asked whether the government could require seniors, veterans, or physicians to pay for the services of lobbying groups that claim to speak on their behalf, even if they object to the service. The answer, the opinion makes clear, is no. "In simple terms," Alito stated, rejecting the "free-rider" justification for the fees, "the First Amendment does not permit the government to compel a person to pay for another party's speech just because the government thinks that the speech furthers the interests of the person who does not want to pay."

## Dissent Objects to "Weaponizing the First Amendment"

In a sign of profound disagreement, Justice Elena Kagan read a summary of her strongly worded dissent from the bench. Her opinion was joined by Justices Ruth Bader Ginsburg, Stephen Breyer, and Sonia Sotomayor. "There is no sugarcoating today's opinion," she wrote. "The majority overthrows a decision entrenched in this nation's law—and in its economic life—for over 40 years." Her dissent began by praising the *Abood* decision for striking a workable balance between the First Amendment rights of employees and the interest of government employers to run their workforces as they see fit. A balance, she noted, built into the laws of twenty-two states, underpinning thousands of contracts involving millions of employees. Despite the vast impact of this decision, Justice Kagan described the majority opinion as acting "with no real clue of what will happen next—of how its action will alter public sector labor relations. It does so even though the government services affected—policing, firefighting, teaching, transportation, sanitation (and more)—affect the quality of life of tens of millions of Americans." She wrote, "Rarely if ever has the Court overruled a decision—let alone one of this import—with so little regard for the usual principles of *stare decisis*."

The dissent criticized the majority for casting aside precedent, for acting with disregard to the real-world impacts of its decision, and for taking a side in a policy dispute that almost evenly divided the states. But, more broadly, the dissent criticized the constitutional tool wielded by the majority to do this. In the most widely quoted part of her dissenting opinion, Justice Kagan berated the majority for "weaponizing the First Amendment, in a way that unleashes judges, now and in the future, to intervene in economic and regulatory policy." Speech is a part of every human interaction, so inevitably it is part of virtually all policy making, and this, together with the majority's aggressive reliance on the First Amendment to upend precedent, led Justice Kagan to fear that potentially every aspect of human interaction could become subject to intervention by the courts. She described this as a dangerous road, and, borrowing the language of "black-robed rulers" from the late justice Antonin Scalia, she concluded: "at every stop are black-robed rulers overriding citizens' choices. The First Amendment was meant for better things."

## PUBLIC-SECTOR UNIONS BRACE FOR LOSSES

The direct impact of the decision in *Janus* will be felt only by public-sector unions because the First Amendment only restricts government action and does not apply to private-sector unions. This is not much of a limitation, however, because most union activity in the United States is currently in the public sector. While enrollment in all unions has been on the decline, currently only 6.5 percent of private-sector employees are unionized, in contrast to more than a third of public workers. The decision will also only impact public-sector unions in the twenty-two states where agency fees had been mandatory. In these states, union representation has been high; some states have more than sixty percent of public workers in unions.

Public-sector unions began preparing for losses in membership and revenue that could weaken their ability to represent employees in labor disputes and to collectively bargain on their behalf. After the *Janus* decision, unions are still obligated to represent all employees when they negotiate for better wages, benefits, pensions, or working conditions. But now employees are no longer required to pay anything for these services. This undermines the economic incentives for workers to join unions and threatens to weaken their influence. Fred Redmond, international vice president of the United Steelworkers union, wrote in a letter to the *New York Times*, "We can safely assume that neither Mark Janus, the plaintiff in the case, nor any other objector to fair-share fees, is willing to renounce his union-won paychecks and other benefits. They just don't want to pay for them." Further supporting this fear of hemorrhaging membership is the experience of states that have recently outlawed agency fees. Michigan public-sector union membership dropped 20 percent within three years of making the fees illegal. Labor experts predict that teachers' unions could lose up to a third of their membership as a result of the decision, and the National Education Association, the nation's largest union, which that represents three million teachers, said that it is likely to lose 31,000 agency fee payers in the first year of its next budget cycle and is preparing for budget cuts totaling $50 million over two years.

In some states, those cuts materialized quickly, as unions began refunding nonmember fees. In Pennsylvania, this amounted to an estimated 15 percent loss of the $42.5 million collected by unions in 2017, according to the state's Office of Administration. In terms of membership losses, by the close of 2018, many public-sector unions were actually experiencing increases in their membership rather than the anticipated losses. Unions admitted, however, that they had conducted membership drives in anticipation of the Court's ruling, and it is possible that individuals are still unaware of the *Janus* decision and their rights under the ruling.

Since the ruling, roughly a third of the states affected by the *Janus* decision have passed laws designed to soften its impact on unions. Rhode Island, for example, is now letting police unions limit representation in grievance hearings to union members, and New York passed a law limiting access to employees' personal data in order to prevent it from passing to antiunion groups lobbying members to leave the union. In New Jersey, union employees were provided only a limited timeframe to withdraw their membership.

—Melissa Feinberg

*Following are excerpts from the Supreme Court's decision in* Janus v. American Federation of State, County, and Municipal Employees, *on June 27, 2018, in which the Court ruled that public-service unions cannot charge any fees to nonunion employees without their explicit consent.*

# Supreme Court Issues Ruling
# on Public-Sector Union Dues

**June 27, 2018**

*[Footnotes have been omitted.]*

### SUPREME COURT OF THE UNITED STATES

No. 16-1466

Mark Janus, Petitioner

*v.*

American Federation of
State, County, and Municipal
Employees, Council 31, et al.

On Writ of Certiorari to
the United States Court of
Appeals for the Seventh
Circuit

[June 27, 2018]

JUSTICE ALITO delivered the opinion of the Court.

Under Illinois law, public employees are forced to subsidize a union, even if they choose not to join and strongly object to the positions the union takes in collective bargaining and related activities. We conclude that this arrangement violates the free speech rights of nonmembers by compelling them to subsidize private speech on matters of substantial public concern.

We upheld a similar law in *Abood* v. *Detroit Bd. of Ed.*, 431 U. S. 209 (1977), and we recognize the importance of following precedent unless there are strong reasons for not doing so. But there are very strong reasons in this case. Fundamental free speech rights are at stake. *Abood* was poorly reasoned. It has led to practical problems and abuse. It is inconsistent with other First Amendment cases and has been undermined by more recent decisions. Developments since *Abood* was handed down have shed new light on the issue of agency fees, and no reliance interests on the part of public sector unions are sufficient to justify the perpetuation of the free speech violations that *Abood* has countenanced for the past 41 years. *Abood* is therefore overruled.

*[Section I, which describes the legal background of the case and the parties to the litigation, and Section II, which deals with a jurisdictional issue, have been omitted.]*

# III

In *Abood*, the Court upheld the constitutionality of an agency-shop arrangement like the one now before us, but in more recent cases we have recognized that this holding is "something of an anomaly," *Knox* v. *Service Employees*, 567 U. S. 298, 311 (2012), and that *Abood*'s "analysis is questionable on several grounds." We have therefore refused to extend *Abood* to situations where it does not squarely control, while leaving for another day the question whether *Abood* should be overruled. . . .

We now address that question. We first consider whether *Abood*'s holding is consistent with standard First Amendment principles.

# A

The First Amendment, made applicable to the States by the Fourteenth Amendment, forbids abridgment of the freedom of speech. We have held time and again that freedom of speech "includes both the right to speak freely and the right to refrain from speaking at all." *[citation omitted]* The right to eschew association for expressive purposes is likewise protected. *Roberts* v. *United States Jaycees*, 468 U. S. 609, 623 (1984) ("Freedom of association . . . plainly presupposes a freedom not to associate"); see *Pacific Gas & Elec.*, *supra*, at 12 ("[F]orced associations that burden protected speech are impermissible"). As Justice Jackson memorably put it: "If there is any fixed star in our constitutional constellation, it is that no official, high or petty, can prescribe what shall be orthodox in politics, nationalism, religion, or other matters of opinion or *force citizens to confess by word or act their faith therein*." *West Virginia Bd. of Ed.* v. *Barnette*, 319 U. S. 624, 642 (1943) (emphasis added).

Compelling individuals to mouth support for views they find objectionable violates that cardinal constitutional command, and in most contexts, any such effort would be universally condemned. Suppose, for example, that the State of Illinois required all residents to sign a document expressing support for a particular set of positions on controversial public issues—say, the platform of one of the major political parties. No one, we trust, would seriously argue that the First Amendment permits this.

Perhaps because such compulsion so plainly violates the Constitution, most of our free speech cases have involved restrictions on what can be said, rather than laws compelling speech. But measures compelling speech are at least as threatening.

Free speech serves many ends. It is essential to our democratic form of government, see, *e.g.*, *Garrison* v. *Louisiana*, 379 U. S. 64, 74–75 (1964), and it furthers the search for truth, see, *e.g.*, *Thornhill* v. *Alabama*, 310 U. S. 88, 95 (1940). Whenever the Federal Government or a State prevents individuals from saying what they think on important matters or compels them to voice ideas with which they disagree, it undermines these ends.

When speech is compelled, however, additional damage is done. In that situation, individuals are coerced into betraying their convictions. Forcing free and independent individuals to endorse ideas they find objectionable is always demeaning, and for this reason, one of our landmark free speech cases said that a law commanding "involuntary affirmation" of objected-to beliefs would require "even more immediate and urgent grounds" than a law demanding silence. *Barnette*, *supra*, at 633; see also *Riley*, *supra*, at 796–797 (rejecting "deferential test" for compelled speech claims).

Compelling a person to *subsidize* the speech of other private speakers raises similar First Amendment concerns. *Knox*, *supra*, at 309; *United States* v. *United Foods, Inc.*, 533

U. S. 405, 410 (2001); *Abood, supra*, at 222, 234–235. As Jefferson famously put it, "to compel a man to furnish contributions of money for the propagation of opinions which he disbelieves and abhor[s] is sinful and tyrannical." A Bill for Establishing Religious Freedom, in 2 Papers of Thomas Jefferson 545 (J. Boyd ed. 1950) (emphasis deleted and footnote omitted); see also *Hudson*, 475 U. S., at 305, n. 15. We have therefore recognized that a "'significant impingement on First Amendment rights'" occurs when public employees are required to provide financial support for a union that "takes many positions during collective bargaining that have powerful political and civic consequences." *Knox, supra*, at 310–311 (quoting *Ellis v. Railway Clerks*, 466 U. S. 435, 455 (1984)).

*[A discussion of case law has been omitted.]*

## B

In *Abood*, the main defense of the agency-fee arrangement was that it served the State's interest in "labor peace," 431 U. S., at 224. By "labor peace," the *Abood* Court meant avoidance of the conflict and disruption that it envisioned would occur if the employees in a unit were represented by more than one union. In such a situation, the Court predicted, "inter-union rivalries" would foster "dissension within the work force," and the employer could face "conflicting demands from different unions." *Id.*, at 220–221. Confusion would ensue if the employer entered into and attempted to "enforce two or more agreements specifying different terms and conditions of employment." *Id.*, at 220. And a settlement with one union would be "subject to attack from [a] rival labor organizatio[n]." *Id.*, at 221.

We assume that "labor peace," in this sense of the term, is a compelling state interest, but *Abood* cited no evidence that the pandemonium it imagined would result if agency fees were not allowed, and it is now clear that *Abood*'s fears were unfounded. The *Abood* Court assumed that designation of a union as the exclusive representative of all the employees in a unit and the exaction of agency fees are inextricably linked, but that is simply not true.

The federal employment experience is illustrative. Under federal law, a union chosen by majority vote is designated as the exclusive representative of all the employees, but federal law does not permit agency fees. See 5 U. S. C. §§7102, 7111(a), 7114(a). Nevertheless, nearly a million federal employees—about 27% of the federal work force—are union members. The situation in the Postal Service is similar. Although permitted to choose an exclusive representative, Postal Service employees are not required to pay an agency fee, 39 U. S. C. §§1203(a), 1209(c), and about 400,000 are union members. Likewise, millions of public employees in the 28 States that have laws generally prohibiting agency fees are represented by unions that serve as the exclusive representatives of all the employees. Whatever may have been the case 41 years ago when *Abood* was handed down, it is now undeniable that "labor peace" can readily be achieved "through means significantly less restrictive of associational freedoms" than the assessment of agency fees. *Harris, supra*, at ___ (slip op., at 30) (internal quotation marks omitted).

## C

In addition to the promotion of "labor peace," *Abood* cited "the risk of 'free riders'" as justification for agency fees, 431 U. S., at 224. Respondents and some of their *amici* endorse this reasoning, contending that agency fees are needed to prevent nonmembers from enjoying the benefits of union representation without shouldering the costs. Brief for Union Respondent 34–36; Brief for State Respondents 41–45; see, *e.g.*, Brief for International Brotherhood of Teamsters as *Amicus Curiae* 3–5.

Petitioner strenuously objects to this free-rider label. He argues that he is not a free rider on a bus headed for a destination that he wishes to reach but is more like a person shanghaied for an unwanted voyage.

Whichever description fits the majority of public employees who would not subsidize a union if given the option, avoiding free riders is not a compelling interest. As we have noted, "free-rider arguments . . . are generally insufficient to overcome First Amendment objections." *Knox*, 567 U. S., at 311. To hold otherwise across the board would have startling consequences. Many private groups speak out with the objective of obtaining government action that will have the effect of benefiting nonmembers. May all those who are thought to benefit from such efforts be compelled to subsidize this speech?

Suppose that a particular group lobbies or speaks out on behalf of what it thinks are the needs of senior citizens or veterans or physicians, to take just a few examples. Could the government require that all seniors, veterans, or doctors pay for that service even if they object? It has never been thought that this is permissible. "[P]rivate speech often furthers the interests of nonspeakers," but "that does not alone empower the state to compel the speech to be paid for." *Lehnert* v. *Ferris Faculty Assn.*, 500 U. S. 507, 556 (1991) (Scalia, J., concurring in judgment in part and dissenting in part). In simple terms, the First Amendment does not permit the government to compel a person to pay for another party's speech just because the government thinks that the speech furthers the interests of the person who does not want to pay.

Those supporting agency fees contend that the situation here is different because unions are statutorily required to "represen[t] the interests of all public employees in the unit," whether or not they are union members. §315/6(d); see, *e.g.*, Brief for State Respondents 40–41, 45; *post*, at 7 (KAGAN, J., dissenting). Why might this matter?

We can think of two possible arguments. It might be argued that a State has a compelling interest in requiring the payment of agency fees because (1) unions would otherwise be unwilling to represent nonmembers or (2) it would be fundamentally unfair to require unions to provide fair representation for nonmembers if nonmembers were not required to pay. Neither of these arguments is sound.

First, it is simply not true that unions will refuse to serve as the exclusive representative of all employees in the unit if they are not given agency fees. As noted, unions represent millions of public employees in jurisdictions that do not permit agency fees. No union is ever compelled to seek that designation. On the contrary, designation as exclusive representative is avidly sought. Why is this so?

Even without agency fees, designation as the exclusive representative confers many benefits. As noted, that status gives the union a privileged place in negotiations over wages, benefits, and working conditions. See §315/6(c). Not only is the union given the exclusive right to speak for all the employees in collective bargaining, but the employer is required by state law to listen to and to bargain in good faith with only that union. §315/7. Designation as exclusive representative thus "results in a tremendous increase in the power" of the union. *American Communications Assn.* v. *Douds*, 339 U. S. 382, 401 (1950).

In addition, a union designated as exclusive representative is often granted special privileges, such as obtaining information about employees, see §315/6(c), and having dues and fees deducted directly from employee wages, §§315/6(e)–(f). The collective-bargaining agreement in this case guarantees a long list of additional privileges.

See App. 138–143.

These benefits greatly outweigh any extra burden imposed by the duty of providing fair representation for nonmembers. . . .

. . . Nor can such fees be justified on the ground that it would otherwise be unfair to require a union to bear the duty of fair representation. That duty is a necessary concomitant of the authority that a union seeks when it chooses to serve as the exclusive representative of all the employees in a unit. As explained, designating a union as the exclusive representative of nonmembers substantially restricts the nonmembers' rights. *Supra*, at 2–3. Protection of their interests is placed in the hands of the union, and if the union were free to disregard or even work against those interests, these employees would be wholly unprotected. That is why we said many years ago that serious "constitutional questions [would] arise" if the union were *not* subject to the duty to represent all employees fairly. *Steele, supra*, at 198.

In sum, we do not see any reason to treat the free-rider interest any differently in the agency-fee context than in any other First Amendment context. See *Knox*, 567 U. S., at 311, 321. We therefore hold that agency fees cannot be upheld on free-rider grounds.

*[Sections IV and V have been omitted. In these sections, the Court addresses and rejects alternative arguments in support of agency fees.]*

# VI

*[A discussion of* stare decisis *has been omitted.]*

\* \* \*

We recognize that the loss of payments from nonmembers may cause unions to experience unpleasant transition costs in the short-term, and may require unions to make adjustments in order to attract and retain members. But we must weigh these disadvantages against the considerable windfall that unions have received under *Abood* for the past 41 years. It is hard to estimate how many billions of dollars have been taken from nonmembers and transferred to public sector unions in violation of the First Amendment. Those unconstitutional exactions cannot be allowed to continue indefinitely. . . .

# VII

For these reasons, States and public sector unions may no longer extract agency fees from nonconsenting employees. Under Illinois law, if a public sector collective bargaining agreement includes an agency-fee provision and the union certifies to the employer the amount of the fee, that amount is automatically deducted from the nonmember's wages. §315/6(e). No form of employee consent is required.

This procedure violates the First Amendment and cannot continue. Neither an agency fee nor any other payment to the union may be deducted from a nonmember's wages, nor may any other attempt be made to collect such a payment, unless the employee affirmatively consents to pay. By agreeing to pay, nonmembers are waiving their First Amendment rights, and such a waiver cannot be presumed. Rather, to be effective, the waiver must be freely given and shown by "clear and compelling" evidence. Unless employees clearly and affirmatively consent before any money is taken from them, this standard cannot be met.

\* \* \*

*Abood* was wrongly decided and is now overruled. The judgment of the United States Court of Appeals for the Seventh Circuit is reversed, and the case is remanded for further proceedings consistent with this opinion.

*It is so ordered.*

*[The dissenting opinion of Justice Sotomayor has been omitted.]*

JUSTICE KAGAN, with whom JUSTICE GINSBURG, JUSTICE BREYER, and JUSTICE SOTOMAYOR join, dissenting.

For over 40 years, *Abood* v. *Detroit Bd. of Ed.*, 431 U. S. 209 (1977), struck a stable balance between public employees' First Amendment rights and government entities' interests in running their workforces as they thought proper. Under that decision, a government entity could require public employees to pay a fair share of the cost that a union incurs when negotiating on their behalf over terms of employment. But no part of that fair-share payment could go to any of the union's political or ideological activities.

That holding fit comfortably with this Court's general framework for evaluating claims that a condition of public employment violates the First Amendment. The Court's decisions have long made plain that government entities have substantial latitude to regulate their employees' speech—especially about terms of employment—in the interest of operating their workplaces effectively.

Not any longer. Today, the Court succeeds in its 6-year campaign to reverse *Abood*. Its decision will have large-scale consequences. Public employee unions will lose a secure source of financial support. State and local governments that thought fair-share provisions furthered their interests will need to find new ways of managing their workforces. Across the country, the relationships of public employees and employers will alter in both predictable and wholly unexpected ways.

Rarely if ever has the Court overruled a decision—let alone one of this import—with so little regard for the usual principles of *stare decisis*. There are no special justifications for reversing *Abood*. It has proved workable. No recent developments have eroded its underpinnings. And it is deeply entrenched, in both the law and the real world. More than 20 States have statutory schemes built on the decision. Those laws underpin thousands of ongoing contracts involving millions of employees. Reliance interests do not come any stronger than those surrounding *Abood*. And likewise, judicial disruption does not get any greater than what the Court does today. I respectfully dissent.

*[Sections I, II, and III, detailing the facts in the case and the majority's findings, have been omitted.]*

## IV

There is no sugarcoating today's opinion. The majority overthrows a decision entrenched in this Nation's law—and in its economic life—for over 40 years. As a result, it prevents the

American people, acting through their state and local officials, from making important choices about workplace governance. And it does so by weaponizing the First Amendment, in a way that unleashes judges, now and in the future, to intervene in economic and regulatory policy. . . .

And maybe most alarming, the majority has chosen the winners by turning the First Amendment into a sword, and using it against workaday economic and regulatory policy. Today is not the first time the Court has wielded the First Amendment in such an aggressive way. *[citation omitted]* And it threatens not to be the last. Speech is everywhere—a part of every human activity (employment, health care, securities trading, you name it). For that reason, almost all economic and regulatory policy affects or touches speech. So the majority's road runs long. And at every stop are black-robed rulers overriding citizens' choices. The First Amendment was meant for better things. It was meant not to undermine but to protect democratic governance—including over the role of public sector unions.

SOURCE: Supreme Court of the United States. *Janus v. American Federation of State, County, and Municipal Employees*. 585 U.S. _____ (2018). https://www.supremecourt.gov/opinions/17pdf/16-1466_2b3j.pdf.

## OTHER HISTORIC DOCUMENTS OF INTEREST

### FROM PREVIOUS *HISTORIC DOCUMENTS*

- Supreme Court Rules on Union Contributions by Public Employees, *2014*, p. 296

# July

# Facebook, Twitter, and YouTube Executives Testify before Congress on Content Filtering

JULY 17, 2018

Facing mounting criticisms of censorship from conservative lawmakers, representatives from three of the largest technology companies, Twitter, Facebook, and Alphabet, Inc.—parent company of Google and YouTube—came before the House Judiciary Committee in the summer of 2018 to explain their policies on content moderation. The companies' platforms had increasingly become lightning rods for criticism as their roles as conveyers—and arbiters—of news and information had grown. Conservative lawmakers charged each company with employing politically motivated content removal practices, while their Democratic counterparts criticized the companies' role in the spread of misinformation. The companies, which rely on a mix of human reviewers and algorithms to review online content, vehemently denied any politically motivated censorship and sought to explain the steps they were taking to curb misinformation online. Top executives from Twitter and Facebook appeared again before Congress at the end of the summer to face additional questions on suspicious activity, Russian interference, online abuse, and perceived biases in content moderation. Each hearing signaled mounting pressure on social media platforms to curb abuses but also demonstrated that government regulators are struggling to keep pace with the platforms' growth and evolution.

## FILTERING: CENSORSHIP VERSUS FREE SPEECH

The top public policy officials from Twitter, Facebook, and Alphabet, Inc., appeared before the House Judiciary Committee on July 17, 2018, to provide testimony on their respective companies' increasingly central role to modern discourse, politics, and news. Committee members, especially Republican lawmakers, said they specifically wanted to hear about the companies' approach to content moderation and the steps they were taking to curb the spread of misinformation.

A founding principle of each platform is the free flow of ideas, that social media platforms should simply be a vessel for users and their views. As social media use has spread and the platforms have matured, this principle has bumped up against the reality that for many users, social media is their primary source of news and information. That changing dynamic has forced technology companies into the uncomfortable position of increasingly moderating content that is shared via their platforms. While these companies have typically maintained a red-line restriction on violent or hate-filled content, efforts by some parties to manipulate social platforms for their own benefit—including activists, politicians, and even foreign governments—have complicated decision-making processes about what content is permissible and what should be removed. This decision-making process, known as content filtering, has attracted increased attention from U.S. lawmakers and with it various calls for regulatory changes.

## TECHNOLOGY EXECUTIVES EXPLAIN EFFORTS TO ADDRESS "NEW AND CHALLENGING LEGAL AND POLICY QUESTIONS"

Facebook Vice President for Global Policy Management Monika Bickert opened her testimony by reaffirming Facebook's commitment to a free and open spread of information. "Freedom of expression is one of our core values, and we believe that the Facebook community is richer and stronger when a broad range of viewpoints is represented," she said. Bickert acknowledged, however, the "new and challenging legal and policy questions" facing the company. "Assessing whether a specific piece of content belongs on Facebook often requires making a nuanced determination, and while we won't get it right every time, we learn from our mistakes and are always working to improve," Bickert stated. Bickert cited steps the company has taken to better hone its content moderation and removal process, noting that Facebook had engaged a former Republican senator and a national civil liberties and civil rights leader to advise the company on potential bias, in addition to soliciting additional feedback from more than 100 external groups. Providing additional oversight to its content review team, establishing a more robust appeals process for people to contest content decisions, and ongoing tweaks to its algorithm rounded out Facebook's efforts to improve its content moderation. "We hope that these improvements and safeguards will help ensure that Facebook remains a platform for a wide range of ideas and enables the broadest spectrum of free expression possible," Bickert said.

Twitter Public Policy Senior Strategist Nick Pickles echoed many of the same sentiments as those of Bickert. Twitter's purpose, according to Pickles, "is to serve the public conversation." That purpose comes with certain responsibilities, he said, such as ensuring "that all voices can be heard," "that everyone feels safe participating in the conversation," and "people can trust in the credibility of the conversation and those taking part." Pickles cited more than thirty policy and product changes made by Twitter to improve users' experiences and discussed the company's efforts to engage outside experts around content moderation. Pickles largely leaned on Twitter's terms of service and rules as evidence of the company's efforts to police content and discussions on the platform. The rules, Pickles explained, are part of the company's effort to "keep Twitter safe for all viewpoints and opinions, even those viewpoints and opinions that some of our users may find objectionable or with which they vehemently disagree." Reports of abuse are addressed both through manual review by Twitter employees and "machine learning," he said, declaring that the company's approach had "proven effective." Pickles concluded his opening statement by directly addressing censorship concerns. "Let me make clear to the Committee today that these claims are unfounded and false," he said. "In fact, we have deliberately taken this approach as a robust defense against bias, as it requires us to define and act upon bad conduct, not a specific type of speech. Our purpose is to serve the conversation, not to make value judgments on personal beliefs."

YouTube Global Policy Lead Juniper Downs represented YouTube parent company Alphabet, Inc., and sought to reassure policymakers that there was no bias in YouTube and Google's search results. "Supporting the free flow of ideas is core to our mission to organize and make the world's information universally accessible and useful," Downs stated. While "not all speech is protected," Downs said, Google follows the law in every country it operates in, including blocking content when necessary. Downs focused her testimony on explaining how Google Search and YouTube evaluate, return, and improve search results for users. Google, Downs said, makes "thousands of improvements" every year to Search, undergoes rigorous user testing and evaluation, and employs External Search Quality Evaluators to measure the quality of search results following public guidelines posted by the company. YouTube also uses public guidelines to help police appropriate content and advertisements while giving users tools to filter out additional content. Downs joined her fellow witnesses by stating directly that Google stays above the political fray. "Our policies do not target particular political beliefs," Downs stated, adding that any content policies developed at Google are done in a "politically neutral way." "Giving preference to content of one political ideology over another would fundamentally conflict with our goal of providing services that work for everyone," Downs said.

### Republicans See Bias; Democrats, an "Imaginary Narrative"

House Judiciary Committee Chairman Bob Goodlatte, R-Va., invited the representatives to discuss content moderation and to "answer questions on their content moderation practices and how they can be better stewards of free speech in the United States and abroad." But Goodlatte, together with other conservative lawmakers on the panel, overwhelmingly focused on perceived bias against conservatives.

Goodlatte conceded that since an earlier hearing in April 2018, Congress has "seen numerous efforts by these companies to improve transparency" but repeatedly pressed, often from different angles, the technology representatives on their filtering practices. For example, Goodlatte questioned whether the companies were "using their market power to push the envelope on filtering decisions to favor the content the companies prefer." Other conservative lawmakers followed suit. Rep. Lamar Smith, R-Tex., accused Google of censoring the word *Jesus* in some search results. Rep. Steve King, R-Iowa, asked Facebook why traffic to conspiracy theory site Gateway Pundit had dropped recently. The companies vehemently denied the charges; declined to discuss individual websites; or, in some cases, said they were not allowed to respond.

House Democrats sharply criticized the hearing and their Republican counterparts. Rep. David Cicilline, D-R.I., said Facebook has "bent over backwards to placate and mollify conservatives," pointing to Facebook's refusal to remove unsubstantiated conspiracy theories. "There is no evidence that the algorithms of social networks or search results are biased against conservatives. It is a made-up narrative pushed by the conservative propaganda machine to convince voters of a conspiracy that does not exist," he said. Other Democrats were equally blunt. Rep. Ted Lieu, D-Calif., called it a "dumb hearing," while Rep. Jamie B. Raskin, D-Md., rebuked Republicans for pushing an "imaginary narrative." Others asked the committee to focus on threats from Russia: the top Democrat on the committee, Rep. Jerrold Nadler, D-N.Y., unsuccessfully asked the panel to adjourn to a private session to discuss the matter. The various witnesses stressed that their companies strive to treat all groups fairly, regardless of political viewpoint.

### A Continued Effort to Restore Trust

The hearing demonstrated lawmakers' increased scrutiny of technology companies, particularly in the wake of the 2016 election, but also underscored the companies' desire to restore public trust and be responsive to lawmakers' concerns. Days after the Judiciary Committee hearing, Twitter announced that it had removed 70 million suspicious accounts from its platform. The purge focused on "bots" and other suspicious accounts, which many users purchased to inflate their following on the influential platform. Months earlier, a report by the *New York Times* had thrust the practice of buying followers and retweets into the national spotlight and prompted investigations in at least two states and calls in Congress for intervention by the Federal Trade Commission. For Twitter, the suspicious accounts presented a deeper threat than increased regulatory oversight: potential alienation of its user base. Executives acknowledged the practice devalued the influence accumulated by legitimate users.

Facebook and Twitter reappeared before Congress in early September, this time sending COO Sheryl Sandberg and CEO Jack Dorsey, respectively. (Google declined the invitation.) The Senate Intelligence Committee and the House Energy and Commerce Committee grilled Sandberg and Dorsey on their companies' efforts to prevent foreign governments from spreading misinformation and potential political bias in their content monitoring efforts, as well as asking about bullying, hate speech, and efforts to incite violence using their platforms. The hearings involved a significant amount of partisan finger pointing, with Republicans charging both companies with bias while Democrats lamented wasting a hearing on a fake controversy. Sandberg and Dorsey offered few new insights, focusing on what their companies had done to counter foreign interference, address the proliferation of fake accounts, and increase transparency in the last year. Both executives and lawmakers agreed that more must be done to inform Americans about the content they consume online and the other users with whom they interact.

—Robert Howard

*Following are the prepared testimonies of Facebook Head of Global Policy Management Monika Bickert, Twitter Public Policy Senior Strategist Nick Pickles, and YouTube Global Head of Public Policy and Government Relations Juniper Downs, for a July 17, 2018, hearing before the House Judiciary Committee.*

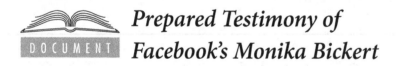

# Prepared Testimony of
# Facebook's Monika Bickert

**July 17, 2018**

## I. Introduction

Chairman Goodlatte, Ranking Member Nadler, and distinguished members of the Committee, thank you for the opportunity to appear before you today to discuss social media content filtering practices. My name is Monika Bickert, and I am the Vice President for Global Policy Management at Facebook, heading our efforts related to Product Policy and Counterterrorism.

Facebook's mission is to give people the power to build community and bring the world closer together. More than two billion people come to our platform each month to stay connected with friends and family, to discover what's going on in the world, to build their businesses, and to share and express what matters most to them.

Freedom of expression is one of our core values, and we believe that the Facebook community is richer and stronger when a broad range of viewpoints is represented. We are committed to encouraging dialogue and the free flow of ideas by designing our products to give people a voice and by implementing standards to ensure fair and transparent processes for removing content that doesn't belong on Facebook.

People share billions of pictures, stories, and videos on Facebook daily. Being at the forefront of such a high volume of content sharing means that we are also at the forefront of new and challenging legal and policy questions, including questions around how to keep our community safe and the dialogue on our platform healthy. Assessing whether a specific piece of content belongs on Facebook often requires making a nuanced determination, and while we won't get it right every time, we learn from our mistakes and are always working to improve. Conversations like the one we're having here today are part of that process.

We know that there have been a number of high-profile content removal incidents affecting individuals across the political spectrum, and we are taking a variety of steps to respond to the concerns raised by this Committee and others. Among other things, we have engaged an outside advisor, former Senator Jon Kyl, to advise the company on potential bias against conservative voices. Laura Murphy, a national civil liberties and civil rights leader also is getting feedback directly from civil rights groups to help advise Facebook on the best path forward. We already partner with over 100 groups across the political spectrum, and we believe this external feedback will help us improve over time and ensure we can most effectively serve our diverse community. And we are continuing to expand our list of outside partner organizations to ensure we receive feedback on our content policies from a diverse set of viewpoints.

We also are instituting additional controls and oversight around our content review team, including robust escalation procedures and updated reviewer training materials, and have launched an appeals process to enable people to contest content decisions with which they disagree. In addition, we constantly work to refine and enhance the quality of our machine learning, which is a first line of defense for content assessment on our platform. We hope that these improvements and safeguards will help ensure that Facebook remains a platform for a wide range of ideas and enables the broadest spectrum of free expression possible.

These recent efforts dovetail with our broader long-term efforts to foster conversations among diverse voices and create a safe community, which I'd like to turn to next.

*[Section II, discussing Facebook's news feed and community standards, has been omitted.]*

### III. False News and News Feed Quality

As part of Facebook's broader efforts to ensure that time spent on our platform is time well-spent, we are taking steps to reduce the spread of false news. False news is an issue that negatively impacts the quality of discourse on both the right and the left, and we are committed to reducing it. One of the best ways to do this is to require people to use the names they are known by, and we've gotten increasingly better at finding and disabling fake accounts. We have disabled thousands of accounts tied to organized, financially motivated fake news spammers. These investigations have been used to improve our automated systems that find fake accounts. We now block millions of fake accounts each day as people try to create them—and before they've done any harm. We are investing heavily in new technology and hiring thousands more people to tackle the problem of inauthenticity on the platform.

This year, we announced major changes to News Feed that are designed to help bring people closer together by encouraging more meaningful connections on Facebook. Because space in News Feed is limited, showing more posts from friends and family and updates that spark conversation means we'll show less public content, including videos and other posts from publishers or businesses. We've also taken steps to make sure the news people see, while less overall, is high quality. People tell us they don't like stories that are misleading, sensational or spammy. That includes clickbait headlines that withhold key information in order to get attention and lure visitors into clicking on a link.

In 2017, we worked hard to reduce fake news and clickbait, and to destroy the economic incentives for spammers to generate these articles in the first place. In 2018, we are working to prioritize news from publications that the community rates as trustworthy, news that people find informative, and news that is relevant to people's local community.

We have partnered with third-party fact checking organizations to limit the reach of false news and to let people know when they are sharing news stories (excluding opinion and satire) that have been disputed or debunked. Third-party fact-checkers on Facebook are signatories to the non-partisan International Fact-Checking Network Code of Principles. In the United States, Facebook's third-party fact-checking is conducted by the Associated Press, Factcheck.org, PolitiFact, Snopes, and the Weekly Standard Fact Check.

We recognize that some people may ask whether, in today's world, is it possible to have a set of fact-checkers that are widely recognized as objective. While we work with the International Fact-Checking Network to make sure all our partners have high standards of accuracy, fairness, and transparency, we know that this is still not a perfect process.

If questions are raised around a fact-checker's rating of a specific story, publishers may reach out directly to the third-party fact-checking organizations and indicate that (1) they believe the fact-checker's rating is inaccurate, or (2) they have corrected the rated content. To dispute a rating, the publisher must indicate why the original rating was inaccurate. To issue a correction, the publisher must correct the false content and clearly state that a correction was made directly on the story. If a rating is successfully corrected or disputed, the demotion on the content will be lifted and the strike against the domain or Page will be removed. Fact-checkers are asked to respond to requests in a reasonable time period—ideally one business day for a simple correction, and up to a few business days for more complex disputes.

We've also made some changes to how we let people know that a story is disputed so that they can learn more and come to their own conclusions. And we are continually working with publishers, fact-checking organizations, and other members of our community to refine these processes and to ensure that people can have confidence in the news that they read and share on Facebook.

## IV. Advertising on Facebook

Similar to our Community Standards, we have Advertising Policies that outline which ads are and are not allowed on Facebook. Unlike posts from friends or Pages, ads receive paid distribution, which means we have an even higher standard for what is allowed. Our publicly-available Advertising Policies outline our standards; among other things, we do not permit ads that violate our Community Standards, ads for illegal products and services, ads with adult content, or ads that are misleading or false.

We are continually working to improve our efforts to enforce our advertising policies. We review many ads proactively using automated and manual tools, and reactively when people hide, block, or mark ads as offensive. We are taking concrete steps to strengthen both our automated and our manual review, and we are expanding our global ads review teams. We also are investing more in machine learning to better understand when to flag and take down ads. Enforcement is never perfect, but we are working on getting better at finding and removing improper ads.

We recently announced changes designed to bring more transparency and accountability to ads and Pages on Facebook. These changes are designed to prevent future abuse in elections and to help ensure that people on Facebook have the information that they need to assess political and issue ads, as well as content on Pages. Our goal is transparency, and we will continue to strive to find the right balance that is not over- or underinclusive.

As part of these changes, now all election-related and issue ads on Facebook and Instagram in the U.S. must be clearly labeled—including a "paid for by" disclosure from the advertiser at the top of the ad. This will help ensure that people can see who is paying for the ad. When people click on the label, they'll be taken to an archive with more information, such as the campaign budget associated with an individual ad and how many people saw it. That same archive can be reached at https://www.facebook.com/political-contentads. People on Facebook visiting the archive can see and search ads with political or issue content that an advertiser has run in the U.S. for up to seven years. Advertisers wanting to run ads with political content in the U.S. will need to verify their identity and location. This creates greater transparency around ads across the political spectrum, and allows people to easily understand why they are seeing ads, who paid for them, and what other ads those advertisers are running. . . .

*[Section V, discussing Facebook's learning from past mistakes, has been omitted.]*

## VI. Conclusion

In closing, I want to reiterate our deep commitment to building a community that encourages and fosters free expression. We want Facebook to be a place where individuals with diverse viewpoints can connect and exchange ideas. We recognize that people have questions about our efforts to achieve these goals, and we are committed to working with the members of this Committee, our regulators, and others in the tech industry and civil society to continue the dialogue around these issues. I appreciate the opportunity to be here today, and I look forward to your questions.

SOURCE: House of Representatives Committee on the Judiciary. "Testimony of Monika Bickert, Vice President for Global Policy Management, Facebook." July 17, 2018. https://docs.house.gov/meetings/JU/JU00/20180717/108546/HHRG-115-JU00-Wstate-BickertM-20180717.pdf.

# Prepared Testimony of
# Twitter's Nick Pickles

DOCUMENT

July 17, 2018

Chairman Goodlatte, Ranking Member Nadler, and Members of the Committee:

Thank you for the opportunity to appear here today. We appreciate the Committee's inquiries about Twitter's content moderation policies, and we are pleased to be here to share our story.

We are delighted that in the United States, all 100 senators, 50 governors and almost every member of the House of Representatives have official Twitter accounts, which are used to engage in local, national, and global conversations on a wide range of issues of civic importance. We also partner with news organizations on a regular basis to live-stream congressional hearings and political events, giving users a front-row seat to history from their smartphones or computer screens.

Our purpose is to serve the public conversation.

As part of that, there are certain responsibilities we consider core to our company. We must ensure that all voices can be heard. We must make it so that everyone feels safe participating in the conversation—whether they are speaking or simply listening. And we must ensure people can trust in the credibility of the conversation and those taking part.

Our commitment to this work is at the very heart of why people come to Twitter.

We are also committed to improving the health of the public conversation and the health of the conversation on Twitter. Consistent with that effort, we have made more than 30 policy and product changes since the beginning of last year aimed at improving health on our platform. Our data show we are making progress in advancing this goal.

We are also seeking to collaborate with outside experts to better define and measure the health of the public conversation. We have requested proposals and will be announcing the outcome of that process soon. And we are committed to sharing the results of our collaboration so that other organizations can benefit from that work.

Threats of violence, abusive conduct, and harassment can have the effect of bullying voices into silence, thereby robbing other Twitter users of valuable perspectives and threatening the freedom of expression that Twitter seeks to foster. We want to ensure that Twitter continues to be a safe space for our users to share their viewpoints with the broader Twitter community.

To do that, we must keep Twitter safe for all viewpoints and opinions, even those viewpoints and opinions that some of our users may find objectionable or with which they vehemently disagree—so long as the content is not in violation of the Twitter Rules. We do not believe that censorship will solve political or societal challenges or that removing certain content could resolve disagreements or address prejudices. We are committed to protecting speech and promoting the health of the public conversation on our platform.

Accordingly, the Twitter Rules prohibit certain types of behavior on our platform. Because abusive activity—and the challenge of detecting and curtailing it—is not static and has evolved over time, those rules continue to be developed and refined over the years as well.

Our rules are laid out in detailed and plain language in our Help Center, which can be found at help.twitter.com. They are not based on ideology or a particular set of beliefs.

Instead, the Twitter Rules are based on behavioral contexts. For example, our rules prohibit making specific threats of violence or wishing for the serious physical harm, death, or disease of an individual or group of people.

Our rules also govern other abusive activity on the platform. For example, we prohibit malicious automation, spam, impersonation accounts, and the use of multiple accounts for overlapping purposes. Again, all of these rules are based on problematic behaviors, not the content of the Tweets or any ideology.

We also have stringent rules and policies that govern advertising on the platform. Advertising on Twitter generally takes the form of promoted Tweets, which advertisers can use to reach new users. Because promoted Tweets are presented to users from accounts they have not yet chosen to follow, Twitter applies a robust set of policies that prohibit, among other things, ads for illegal goods and services, ads making misleading or deceptive claims, ads for drugs or drug paraphernalia, ads containing hate content, sensitive topics, and violence, and ads containing offensive or inflammatory content. These policies are laid out at twitter.com/adspolicy.

We see a range of groups across the political spectrum use our advertising products to promote content about a variety of issues ranging from immigration to tax reform. Like any account that uses our advertising products, those groups are all bound by the same Twitter ads policies and Twitter Rules.

Both organic and promoted content can be reported by our users. We address such reports with a combination of technology and human review approaches. Machine learning improvements are enabling us to be more proactive in finding those who are being disruptive, but user reports are still a highly valuable part of our work. When evaluating these reports, we take into account a variety of factors and context, including whether the behavior is directed at an individual, a group, or a protected category of people. We also take into account whether the user has a history of violating our policies as well as the severity of the violation.

Accounts that violate our policies and the Twitter Rules can be subject to a range of enforcement actions, including temporary and, in some cases, permanent suspension. We recognize that a lack of transparency in enforcement actions can lead to a lack of public understanding about what an individual may have done to warrant action, and we have taken meaningful steps to address this where possible. For example, where appropriate, users are now notified of the specific Tweet that we determined to be in violation of our rules; we also alert those users to the specific rule they violated.

Our Safety Center houses information about our rules, tools, philosophy, and partnerships to further explain our work in this area. We explain our approach to enforcement in greater detail here: help.twitter.com/en/rules-and-policies/enforcement-philosophy.

Because our enforcement process typically relies on both automated and manual human review, we often have to make tough calls, and we do not always get things right—especially given the scope and scale of a platform such as Twitter, where users collectively post hundreds of millions of Tweets each day. When we make a mistake, we acknowledge it and strive to learn from it. We are committed to being direct and engaged with our users and the public—including elected officials—when we get things wrong.

Where we identify suspicious account activity (e.g., exceptionally high-volume Tweeting with the same hashtag, or mentioning the same @handle without a reply from the account being addressed), we automatically send the account owner a test to confirm he or she is still in control of the account. These automated tests vary depending on the type of suspicious activity we detect, and may involve the account owner completing a simple reCAPTCHA challenge or a password reset request. We do not immediately remove content as part of these automated tests, but limit its visibility until the test is passed.

This approach has proven effective in helping us address malicious automation and spam on our platform. In May 2018, for example, our systems identified and challenged more than 9.9 million potentially spammy or automated accounts per week. That is an increase from 6.4 million in December 2017, and 3.2 million in September.

Due to technology and process improvements during the past year, we are now removing 214 percent more accounts for violating our spam policies on a year-on-year basis.

At the same time, the average number of spam reports we received through our reporting flow continued to drop—from an average of approximately 25,000 per day in March, to approximately 17,000 per day in May. We've also seen a 10 percent drop in spam reports from search as a result of our recent changes.

These metrics demonstrate our progress, but our work will never be complete. Bad actors change their behavior and we are constantly evaluating new threats and behavior. Among other things, we rely on our detection tools to identify people who have been suspended from the platform and who have created a new Twitter account or those who use multiple accounts for the same purpose.

We have also taken additional proactive steps recently to make follower counts more meaningful and accurate by removing locked accounts from follower counts globally. This step is a reflection of our ongoing commitment to the health of Twitter and a desire to ensure indicators that users rely on to make judgements about an account are as accurate as possible. Our process applies to all accounts active on the platform, regardless of the content they post.

Another critical part of our commitment to health is changing how we think about the areas on Twitter where our systems curate how information is presented. In places like search and conversations where we try to present content we believe you are most likely to find interesting, we are increasingly relying on behavior to help us make those determinations.

To help us do that, we recently took steps to more effectively address behaviors and activity on the platform that do not necessarily violate our policies, but that distort and detract from the public conversation. Most significantly, this approach enables us to improve the overall health of the conversation without needing to remove content from Twitter. Ultimately, everyone's comments and perspectives are available, but those who are simply looking to disrupt the conversation will not be rewarded by having their Tweets placed at the top of the conversation or search results.

Early results demonstrated that this approach has a positive impact, resulting in a four percent decrease in abuse reports from search and eight percent fewer abuse reports from conversations.

Some critics have described the sum of all of this work as a banning of conservative voices. Let me make clear to the Committee today that these claims are unfounded and false. In fact, we have deliberately taken this approach as a robust defense against bias, as it requires us to define and act upon bad conduct, not a specific type of speech. Our purpose is to serve the conversation, not to make value judgments on personal beliefs.

Our success as a company depends on making Twitter a safe place for free expression and a place that serves healthy public conversation. We know that Twitter plays an increasingly vital role in the world, and we know there is much work for us to do to make it even better. And we are committed to continue to improve transparency and visibility to the people using our service.

Thank you again, and I look forward to your questions.

SOURCE: House of Representatives Committee on the Judiciary. "Statement of Nick Pickles, Senior Strategist, Public Policy, Twitter, Inc. before the Committee on the Judiciary United States House of Representatives." July 17, 2018. https://docs.house.gov/meetings/JU/JU00/20180717/108546/HHRG-115-JU00-Wstate-PicklesN-20180717.pdf.

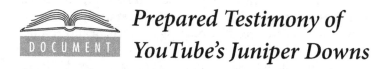

# Prepared Testimony of YouTube's Juniper Downs

July 17, 2018

## I. Introduction

Chairman Goodlatte, Ranking Member Nadler, and members of the Committee: Thank you for the opportunity to appear before you today. My name is Juniper Downs, and I serve as the global policy lead for YouTube.

The Internet has been a force for creativity, learning, and access to information. Products like Google Search and YouTube have expanded economic opportunity for small businesses to market and sell their goods; have given artists, creators, and journalists a platform to share their work, connect with an audience, and enrich civic discourse; and have enabled billions to benefit from a bigger, broader understanding of the world.

Supporting the free flow of ideas is core to our mission to organize and make the world's information universally accessible and useful. We build tools that empower users to access, create, and share information like never before—giving them more choice, opportunity, and exposure to a diversity of opinions. We build those products for everyone, in the US and around the world. People will value these services only so long as they continue to trust them to work well and provide them with the most relevant and useful information. We have a natural and long-term incentive to make sure that our products work for users of all viewpoints.

We strive to make information from the web available to all our users, but not all speech is protected. We respect the laws of the nearly 200 countries in which we offer services. Once we are on notice of content that may violate local law, we evaluate it and block it for the relevant jurisdiction. For many issues, such as privacy, defamation, or hate speech, our legal obligations may vary country by country as different jurisdictions have come to different conclusions about how to deal with these complex issues. In the case of all legal removals, we share information about government requests for removal in our Transparency Report.

Where we have developed our own content policies, we enforce them in a politically neutral way. Giving preference to content of one political ideology over another would fundamentally conflict with our goal of providing services that work for everyone.

## II. Search

Google Search has come a long way since we started in 1998, but our goal remains the same: to provide users with the most relevant information for their searches from the most authoritative sources. Search reflects the content available on the web—hundreds of billions of web pages—and the web is dynamic with many thousands of pieces of new content posted every minute. For a typical query, there are thousands, even millions, of webpages with potentially relevant information. Search handles trillions of queries each year, and every day 15% of the queries we process are ones we've never seen before. For example, we could not have anticipated queries about the soccer team trapped in caves in Thailand, but our systems quickly adapted to return results about the rescue mission. Building a search engine that can serve the most useful results for all these queries is a complex challenge that requires ongoing research, quality testing, and investment.

To give users results that are useful and relevant in a fraction of a second, Google ranking systems sort through the webpages in our Search index. These ranking systems analyze what users are looking for and what information web pages contain. We analyze search queries, rank useful pages, and consider context (such as location and language), to return relevant and useful information.

Sometimes, the correct treatment for a given page is that it shouldn't be ranked at all. When deciding whether to block a page outright from our results, we're strongly guided by the law, relying whenever possible on the decisions of courts. There are some other narrow circumstances in which we may remove links from Search results, including when we identify violations of our webmaster guidelines, which guard against deceptive or manipulative behavior designed to deceive users or game our systems.

Every year we make thousands of improvements to Search to improve the quality of results for the wide range of queries Google sees every day. In 2017, we ran over 270,000 experiments, with trained external Search Quality Evaluators and live user tests, resulting in more than 2400 improvements to Search. Our ranking and algorithmic improvements have one purpose only: improving our Search results for our users.

We put all possible changes through rigorous user testing and evaluation. We work with external Search Quality Evaluators from a range of backgrounds and geographies to measure the quality of search results on an ongoing basis. These Evaluators assess how well a website gives searchers what they're looking for and rate the quality of results based on the expertise, authoritativeness, and trustworthiness of the content. These ratings help us benchmark the quality of our results and make sure these meet a high bar for users of Google Search all around the world. To ensure a consistent approach, we publish Search Quality Evaluator Guidelines to give these Evaluators guidance and examples for appropriate ratings. We make these guidelines publicly available on our How Search Works website.

## III. YouTube

YouTube's mission is to give everyone a voice and show them the world. It has democratized how stories—and whose stories—get told. We work to provide a place where people can listen, share, build community, and be successful. To put our work in context, it's important to recognize the scale of our services. More than one and a half billion people come to YouTube every month. We see well over 450 hours of video uploaded every minute. Most of this content is positive—ranging from how-to videos, family vloggers, and funny pet videos, to educational and cultural content and more. In fact, learning and educational content drives over a billion views on YouTube every single day. Many creators are able to make a living using the platform. YouTube channels making over six figures in revenue are up 40 percent over the last year. And digital platforms like YouTube have long been a place for breaking news, exposing injustices, and sharing content from previously inaccessible places.

We are dedicated to access to information and freedom of expression, but it's not anything goes on YouTube. We've developed robust Community Guidelines to provide clear guidance about what is not allowed on YouTube. For example, we do not allow pornography, incitement to violence, or harassment. We work hard to maintain an environment that benefits creators, advertisers, and viewers alike. Keeping YouTube free from dangerous, illegal, or illicit content not only protects our users, it's a business imperative.

In addition, we may impose certain restrictions on content, including disabling advertising on videos that don't comply with our Advertiser Friendly Guidelines, and age-restricting content that may not be appropriate for all audiences. We also provide user controls, like Restricted Mode, an optional setting for users who want to filter out more mature content. Of course videos that are unavailable in Restricted Mode or are not monetized through advertising remain available on the site.

Our policies do not target particular political beliefs. To determine when videos should be removed, demonetized, or age restricted, we look at the context, including whether content is clearly documentary, educational, or satirical. As an example, videos that discuss or depict mature subjects including death and tragedy, highly sexualized content, violence, or excessive profanity, are likely to be unavailable in Restricted Mode.

We don't always get it right, and sometimes our system de-monetizes content when it should not. We hear these concerns from creators of all stripes—from gamers, to various underrepresented communities, to both liberals and conservatives. Accordingly, we have a robust process for appeal of both demonetization and removal decisions. We encourage our users to take advantage of this process if they feel we have treated content in a way that is inconsistent with our policies. We also work hard to keep creators informed around changes to the platform, particularly around monetization and our advertiser-friendly guidelines. We engage in open and frequent communication with our creators through partner managers, blog posts, product forums, social accounts, and email notifications.

As I mentioned at the start, we build our products for all of our users from all political stripes around the globe. The long term success of our business is directly related to our ability to earn and maintain the trust of our users. We will continue to pursue that trust by encouraging and acting on feedback about ways we can improve.

Thank you for the opportunity to outline our efforts in this space. I'm happy to answer any questions you might have.

SOURCE: House of Representatives Committee on the Judiciary. "Written Testimony of Juniper Downs, Director, Public Policy and Government Relations, Google House Judiciary Committee." July 17, 2018. https://docs.house.gov/meetings/JU/JU00/20180717/108546/HHRG-115-JU00-Wstate-DownsJ-20180717.pdf.

## Other Historic Documents of Interest

# State Officials Investigate Sexual Abuse by Catholic Clergy

JULY 28, AUGUST 14, AND SEPTEMBER 6, 2018

For decades, the Catholic Church has been beset with scandal over allegations of child sexual abuse by priests worldwide. In the United States, such allegations have drawn increased attention since 2002, when the *Boston Globe* published a series of reports detailing clerical sexual abuse in Massachusetts and church officials' efforts to hide it and keep victims quiet. Sixteen years later, an investigation by a Pennsylvania grand jury brought fresh attention to the controversy. The panel's findings of widespread clerical sexual abuse and church cover-ups spurred officials in at least a dozen other states and the U.S. Department of Justice to launch similar investigations.

## Pennsylvania Grand Jury Finds Widespread Abuse

On August 14, 2018, the office of Pennsylvania Attorney General Josh Shapiro released a report detailing the findings of a grand jury investigation into allegations of clerical sexual abuse in six of the commonwealth's eight Catholic dioceses. (Similar investigations of the Philadelphia and Altoona-Johnstown dioceses were previously conducted.) The investigation was conducted over a two-year period and involved the examination of 500,000 subpoenaed internal diocese documents dating back to 1947, as well as testimony from dozens of victims.

The panel's findings revealed widespread abuse across Pennsylvania, citing evidence that 301 "predator priests" had sexually abused more than 1,000 children while serving in active ministry. Jurors wrote that there were likely thousands more victims who were too afraid to come forward or whose records had been lost by the church. The report described in vivid detail numerous incidents of groping, molestation, and rape in all six dioceses, as well as a systematic effort by senior church officials to cover-up abuse allegations and avoid scandal. "They protected their institution at all costs," said Shapiro. "As the grand jury found, the church showed a complete disdain for victims."

Special agents from the Federal Bureau of Investigation's National Center for the Analysis of Violent Crime collaborated with the grand jury to review "a significant portion" of the evidence the panel received, with a focus on the church's strategies for concealing abuse. According to the grand jury's report, the agents identified a series of church practices that provided "a playbook for concealing the truth." For example, officials would use terms such as *inappropriate contact* or *boundary issues* instead of rape to describe alleged abuse. The dioceses also assigned priests who had not been trained to handle sexual abuse cases to investigate their colleagues and declined to report allegations to law enforcement. If officials determined a priest needed to be removed from his parish, they often reassigned him to another parish—possibly one in another state—while concealing from the community the reason for the change. The report listed the accused priests' names and detailed how they were transferred from parish to parish, noting that many of the officials who protected those priests and allowed them to remain in ministry either kept their office or advanced within the church. "Priests were raping little boys and girls, and the men of God who were responsible for them not only did nothing; they hid it all. For decades," wrote the jury. "Monsignors, auxiliary bishops, bishops, archbishops, cardinals have mostly been protected; many, including some named in this report, have been promoted."

Due to the church's cover-up, the grand jury said, nearly every instance of abuse they had identified was too old to be prosecuted. However, Shapiro did file charges against a priest in the Greensburg diocese who was found to be sexually abusing a seven-year-old boy. The priest pled guilty prior to the report's release and was awaiting sentencing at the time of its publication. Another priest, in the Erie diocese, also faced charges for assaulting a boy since the latter was eight years old.

The grand jury proposed several changes to Pennsylvania laws related to child sex abuse, including eliminating the criminal statute of limitations, which currently allows victims to come forward with allegations until they are fifty years old. They also recommended creating a two-year "civil window" to allow older victims to sue the church for damages and called for passage of a new statute stating that confidentiality agreements signed by victims do not prevent them from contacting police about abuse. In releasing the report, Shapiro declared his support for each of the grand jury's recommendations and called on the commonwealth's bishops to support the "common-sense reforms." The church has historically resisted such proposals.

The report's publication was delayed by at least a month following a legal challenge by more than two dozen current and retired clergy members who were named in the document. Some claimed the grand jury's findings were false or misleading and that the report's publication would violate their constitutional rights to due process. Pennsylvania's Supreme Court ruled on July 27 that the report could be released but that some of the priests' names had to be redacted first. Most dioceses sought to preempt the report by releasing information about the accused priests and abuse allegations prior to its publication. On August 1, for example, Bishop Ronald Gainer of the Harrisburg diocese released a list of seventy-one priests, deacons, and seminarians accused of "substantiated" sexual misconduct and issued a public apology.

In response to the report, Cardinal Daniel DiNardo, president of the U.S. Conference of Catholic Bishops, and Bishop Timothy L. Doherty, chair of the bishops' Committee for the Protection of Children and Young People, said they were "shamed by and sorry for the sins and omissions by Catholic priests and Catholic bishops." Other church officials were unapologetic. "There was no cover-up going on," claimed Bishop David Zubik of Pittsburgh. "We have over the course of the last 30 years, for sure, been transparent about everything that has in fact been transpiring." The Vatican declined to comment on the grand jury's findings.

## HIGH-PROFILE SCANDALS PLAGUE THE CHURCH

The Pennsylvania grand jury's report dealt another blow to the Catholic Church in a year already marked by several high-profile scandals. At the beginning of the year, Pope Francis dispatched Vatican investigators to Chile to interview victims of clerical abuse and explore allegations that senior church officials engaged in a cover-up. The resulting 2,300-page report accused church officials of failing to investigate credible allegations, finding that in some cases they destroyed documents to conceal abuse. As of July 2018, Chilean special prosecutors were investigating nearly seventy clergy and laypeople for their involvement in the sexual abuse of more than 100 potential victims. Earlier, in May 2018, Australian Archbishop of Adelaide Philip Wilson was sentenced to twelve months in prison for covering up sexual abuse of minors committed by a priest in the 1970s. The sentence was later overturned but made Wilson one of the highest-ranking Catholic officials to be convicted of such a crime.

One of the most recognized Catholic Church officials in the United States, Cardinal Theodore McCarrick, was also caught up in the abuse scandal. After becoming ordained in 1958, McCarrick rose quickly through the church's ranks, holding such prominent offices as archbishop of Newark, New Jersey, and archbishop of Washington, D.C., before becoming a cardinal. In June 2018, the Archdiocese of New York determined that an accusation McCarrick had molested a sixteen-year-old altar boy in the 1970s was credible. The eighty-eight-year-old cardinal was subsequently removed from active ministry. "While I have absolutely no recollection of this reported abuse, and believe in my innocence, I am sorry for the pain the person who brought the charges has gone through, as well as for the scandal such charges cause our people," he said. Shortly thereafter, reports surfaced that McCarrick had sexually abused young priests and men who were studying to become priests for years. According to an investigation by the *New York Times*, church officials knew about McCarrick's activities since at least 1994, when the first documented complaint against him was made. On July 28, the Vatican announced that Pope Francis had accepted McCarrick's resignation from the College of Cardinals and barred him from exercising in any public ministry. The pope also directed McCarrick to observe "a life of prayer and penance until the accusations made against him are examined in a regular canonical trial." McCarrick was the highest-ranking U.S. church official to be removed from office as a result of sexual abuse allegations.

## More States Open Investigations

The grand jury's findings spurred attorneys general in at least a dozen other states and Washington, D.C., to launch their own investigations of clerical sexual abuse. Missouri Attorney General Josh Hawley was the first to announce state action following the Pennsylvania report, opening an investigation into clergy in the St. Louis area. The Archdiocese of St. Louis had reportedly requested the investigation and was cooperating with Hawley, who also requested records from the state's four other archdioceses.

In early September, New York Attorney General Barbara Underwood subpoenaed the state's eight dioceses for records related to child sex abuse, to be examined as part of a civil investigation led by her office's Charities Bureau. Underwood also announced a new hotline and online complaint center for victims and witnesses of clerical child sex abuse to report incidents directly to her office. In a prior announcement, Underwood revealed that her office's Criminal Division was seeking partnerships with district attorneys to investigate and prosecute criminal offenses. (New York's district attorneys are the only officials with the authority to convene grand juries.) "The Pennsylvania grand jury report shined a light on incredibly disturbing and depraved acts by Catholic clergy, assisted by a culture of secrecy and cover-ups in the dioceses," Underwood said. "Victims in New York deserve to be heard as well—and we are going to do everything in our power to bring them the justice they deserve."

In neighboring New Jersey, Attorney General Gurbir Grewal formed a new task force to investigate sexual abuse allegations and possible cover-ups by church officials. The task force was given the authority to subpoena internal documents and testimony from the state's six dioceses and present evidence to a grand jury. As in New York, Grewal announced a new hotline for victims. "I was deeply troubled to read the allegations contained in last month's Pennsylvania grand jury report," said Grewal. "We owe it to the people of New Jersey to find out whether the same thing happened here. If it did, we will take action against those responsible."

Illinois Attorney General Lisa Madigan sought meetings with church officials in September to discuss the Pennsylvania report, which named several priests with Illinois connections. Officials from all six of the state's dioceses met with Madigan, who went on to publicize the preliminary findings of her office's investigation in December. Madigan concluded that the church withheld the names of at least 500 priests who had been accused of sexual abuse. The church said the allegations against these men were not credible, but Madigan's investigation found that many accusations were not investigated at all, while others were discounted because they only involved one victim or because the accused priest had since died. She also found evidence that the church sought to discredit victims' allegations by "focusing on the survivors' personal lives." Madigan declared that the dioceses were incapable of investigating themselves and called on the bishops to report all abuse allegations to law enforcement. Madigan's successor, Kwame Raoul, has promised to continue the investigation.

In addition to the state-level investigations, various media reports indicated that the U.S. Department of Justice subpoenaed documents from at least seven of Pennsylvania's Catholic dioceses in October. The agency's investigation is reportedly the first national probe of its size and scope into sexual abuse by Catholic clergy.

—Linda Grimm

*Following is Vatican News' announcement on July 28, 2018, that Pope Francis accepted the resignation of Cardinal Theodore McCarrick; the introduction to the Pennsylvania grand jury's report on clerical sexual abuse, published on August 14, 2018; and press releases issued by New York Attorney General Barbara Underwood and New Jersey Attorney General Gurbir Grewal on September 6, 2018, announcing investigations into clerical sexual abuse in their states and related hotlines.*

# *Vatican Announces Pope Francis Accepted Cardinal McCarrick's Resignation*

DOCUMENT

---

**July 28, 2018**

Pope Francis on Saturday accepted the resignation of Cardinal Theodore McCarrick, Archbishop emeritus of Washington (USA), from the cardinalate.

At the same time, the Holy Father barred him from the exercise of any public ministry, according to a statement from the Holy See Press Office on Saturday.

Pope Francis directed Cardinal McCarrick to observe "a life of prayer and penance until the accusations made against him are examined in a regular canonical trial."

The Pope also imposed on Cardinal McCarrick "the obligation to remain in a house yet to be indicated to him".

Cardinal McCarrick sent his letter of resignation as a member of the College of Cardinals to Pope Francis on Friday evening.

SOURCE: Vatican News. "Pope Francis Accepts Resignation of Cardinal McCarrick." July 28, 2018. https://www.vaticannews.va/en/pope/news/2018-07/pope-francis-cardinal-mccarrick-resignation.html.

# Pennsylvania Grand Jury Investigation Report

**August 14, 2018**

*[The Introduction summarizing the report is included. All other sections from the report have been omitted.]*

## I. Introduction

We, the members of this grand jury, need you to hear this. We know some of you have heard some of it before. There have been other reports about child sex abuse within the Catholic Church. But never on this scale. For many of us, those earlier stories happened someplace else, someplace away. Now we know the truth: it happened everywhere.

We were given the job of investigating child sex abuse in *six* dioceses—every diocese in the state except Philadelphia and Altoona-Johnstown, which were the subject of previous grand juries. These six dioceses account for 54 of Pennsylvania's 67 counties. We heard the testimony of dozens of witnesses concerning clergy sex abuse. We subpoenaed, and reviewed, half a million pages of internal diocesan documents. They contained credible allegations against over *three hundred* predator priests. Over *one thousand* child victims were identifiable, from the church's own records. We believe that the real number—of children whose records were lost, or who were afraid ever to come forward—is in the thousands.

Most of the victims were boys; but there were girls too. Some were teens; many were pre pubescent. Some were manipulated with alcohol or pornography. Some were made to masturbate their assailants, or were groped by them. Some were raped orally, some vaginally, some anally. But all of them were brushed aside, in every part of the state, by church leaders who preferred to protect the abusers and their institution above all.

As a consequence of the coverup, almost every instance of abuse we found is too old to be prosecuted. But that is not to say there are no more predators. This grand jury has issued presentments against a priest in the Greensburg [D]iocese and a priest in the Erie Diocese, who has been sexually assaulting children within the last decade. We learned of these abusers directly from their dioceses—which we hope is a sign that the church is finally changing its ways. And there may be more indictments in the future; investigation continues.

But we are not satisfied by the few charges we can bring, which represent only a tiny percentage of all the child abusers we saw. We are sick over all the crimes that will go unpunished and uncompensated. This report is our only recourse. We are going to name their names, and describe what they did—both the sex offenders and those who concealed them. We are going to shine a light on their conduct, because that is what the victims deserve. And we are going to make our recommendations for how the laws should change so that maybe no one will have to conduct another inquiry like this one. We hereby exercise our historical and statutory right as grand jurors to inform the public of our findings.

This introduction will briefly describe the sections of the report that follow. We know it is very long. But the only way to fix these problems is to appreciate their scope.

## The dioceses

This section of the report addresses each diocese individually, through two or more case studies that provide examples of the abuse that occurred and the manner in which diocesan leaders "managed" it. While each church district had its idiosyncrasies, the pattern was pretty much the same. The main thing was not to help children, but to avoid "scandal." That is not our word, but theirs; it appears over and over again in the documents we recovered. Abuse complaints were kept locked up in a "secret archive." That is not our word, but theirs; the church's Code of Canon Law specifically requires the diocese to maintain such an archive. Only the bishop can have the key.

The strategies were so common that they were susceptible to behavioral analysis by the Federal Bureau of Investigation. For our benefit, the FBI agreed to assign members of its National Center for the Analysis of Violent Crime to review a significant portion of the evidence received by the grand jury. Special agents testified before us that they had identified a series of practices that regularly appeared, in various configurations, in the diocesan files they had analyzed. It's like a playbook for concealing the truth:

First, make sure to use euphemisms rather than real words to describe the sexual assaults in diocese documents. Never say "rape"; say "inappropriate contact" or "boundary issues."

Second, don't conduct genuine investigations with properly trained personnel. Instead, assign fellow clergy members to ask inadequate questions and then make credibility determinations about the colleagues with whom they live and work.

Third, for an appearance of integrity, send priests for "evaluation" at church-run psychiatric treatment centers. Allow these experts to "diagnose" whether the priest was a pedophile, based largely on the priest's "self-reports," and regardless of whether the priest had actually engaged in sexual contact with a child.

Fourth, when a priest does have to be removed, don't say why. Tell his parishioners that he is on "sick leave," or suffering from "nervous exhaustion." Or say nothing at all.

Fifth, even if a priest is raping children, keep providing him housing and living expenses, although he may be using these resources to facilitate more sexual assaults.

Sixth, if a predator's conduct becomes known to the community, don't remove him from the priesthood to ensure that no more children will be victimized. Instead, transfer him to a new location where no one will know he is a child abuser.

Finally and above all, don't tell the police. Child sexual abuse, even short of actual penetration, is and has for all relevant times been a crime. But don't treat it that way; handle it like a personnel matter, "in house."

To be sure, we did come across some cases in which members of law enforcement, despite what may have been the dioceses' best efforts, learned of clergy sex abuse allegations. Some of these were many decades ago, and police or prosecutors at the time simply deferred to church officials. Other reports arose more recently, but involved old conduct, and so were quickly rejected on statute of limitations grounds without looking into larger patterns and potential continuing risks. We recognize that victims in these circumstances were understandably disappointed there was no place they could go to be heard.

But we have heard them, and will tell their stories, using the church's own records, which we reproduce in the body of the report where appropriate. In the Diocese of Allentown, for example, documents show that a priest was confronted about an abuse complaint. He admitted, "Please help me. I sexually molested a boy." The diocese concluded that "the experience will not necessarily be a horrendous trauma" for the victim, and that the family should just be given "an opportunity to ventilate." The priest was left in unrestricted ministry for several more years, despite his own confession.

Similarly in the Diocese of Erie, despite a priest's admission to assaulting at least a dozen young boys, the bishop wrote to thank him for "all that you have done for God's people. . . The Lord, who sees in private, will reward." Another priest confessed to anal and oral rape of at least 15 boys, as young as seven years old. The bishop later met with the abuser to commend him as "a person of candor and sincerity," and to compliment him "for the progress he has made" in controlling his "addiction." When the abuser was finally removed from the priesthood years later, the bishop ordered the parish not to say why; "nothing else need be noted."

In the Diocese of Greensburg, a priest impregnated a 17-year-old, forged the head pastor's signature on a marriage certificate, then divorced the girl months later. Despite having sex with a minor, despite fathering a child, despite being married and being divorced, the priest was permitted to stay in ministry thanks to the diocese's efforts to find a "benevolent bishop" in another state willing to take him on. Another priest, grooming his middle school students for oral sex, taught them how Mary had to "bite off the cord" and "lick" Jesus clean after he was born. It took another 15 years, and numerous additional reports of abuse, before the diocese finally removed the priest from ministry.

A priest in the Diocese of Harrisburg abused five sisters in a single family, despite prior reports that were never acted on. In addition to sex acts, the priest collected samples of the girls' urine, pubic hair, and menstrual blood. Eventually, his house was searched and his collection was found. Without that kind of incontrovertible evidence, apparently, the diocese remained unwilling to err on the side of children even in the face of multiple reports of abuse. As a high-ranking official said about one suspect priest: "At this point we are at impasse—allegations and no admission." Years later, the abuser did admit what he had done, but by then it was too late.

Elsewhere we saw the same sort of disturbing disdain for victims. In the Diocese of Pittsburgh, church officials dismissed an incident of abuse on the ground that the 15-year-old had "pursued" the priest and "literally seduced" him into a relationship. After the priest was arrested, the church submitted an evaluation on his behalf to the court. The evaluation acknowledged that the priest had admitted to "sado-masochistic" activities with several boys—but the sadomasochism was only "mild," and at least the priest was not "psychotic."

The Diocese of Scranton also chose to defend its clergy abusers over its children. A diocese priest was arrested and convicted after decades of abuse reports that had been ignored by the church. The bishop finally took action only as the sentencing date approached. He wrote a letter to the judge, with a copy to a state senator, urging the court to release the defendant to a Catholic treatment center. He emphasized the high cost of incarceration. In another case, a priest raped a girl, got her pregnant, and arranged an abortion. The bishop expressed his feelings in a letter: "This is a very difficult time in your life, and I realize how upset you are. I too share your grief." But the letter was not for the girl. It was addressed to the rapist.

### The church and child abuse, past and present

We know that the bulk of the discussion in this report concerns events that occurred before the early 2000's. That is simply because the bulk of the material we received from the dioceses concerned those events. The information in these documents was previously kept hidden from those whom it most affected. It is exposed now only because of the existence of this grand jury.

That historical record is highly important, for present and future purposes. The thousands of victims of clergy child sex abuse in Pennsylvania deserve an accounting, to use as best they can to try to move on with their lives. And the citizens of Pennsylvania deserve an accounting as well, to help determine how best to make appropriate improvements in the law.

At the same time, we recognize that much has changed over the last fifteen years. We agreed to hear from each of the six dioceses we investigated, so that they could inform us about recent developments in their jurisdictions. In response, five of the bishops submitted statements to us, and the sixth, the bishop of Erie, appeared before us in person. His testimony impressed us as forthright and heartfelt. It appears that the church is now advising law enforcement of abuse reports more promptly. Internal review processes have been established. Victims are no longer quite so invisible.

But the full picture is not yet clear. We know that child abuse in the church has not yet disappeared, because we are charging two priests, in two different dioceses, with crimes that fall within the statute of limitations. One of these priests ejaculated in the mouth of a seven-year-old. The other assaulted two different boys, on a monthly basis, for a period of years that ended only in 2010.

And we know there might be many additional recent victims, who have not yet developed the resources to come forward either to police or to the church. As we have learned from the experiences of the victims who we saw, it takes time. We hope this report will encourage others to speak.

What we can say, though, is that despite some institutional reform, individual leaders of the church have largely escaped public accountability. Priests were raping little boys and girls, and the men of God who were responsible for them not only did nothing; they hid it all. For decades. Monsignors, auxiliary bishops, bishops, archbishops, cardinals have mostly been protected; many, including some named in this report, have been promoted. Until that changes, we think it is too early to close the book on the Catholic Church sex scandal.

### Recommendations

Grand jurors are just regular people who are randomly selected for service. We don't get paid much, the hours are bad, and the work can be heartbreaking. What makes it worthwhile is knowing we can do some kind of justice. We spent 24 months dredging up the most depraved behavior, only to find that the laws protect most of its perpetrators, and leave its victims with nothing. We say laws that do that need to change.

First, we ask the Pennsylvania legislature to stop shielding child sexual predators behind the criminal statute of limitations. Thanks to a recent amendment, the current law permits victims to come forward until age 50. That's better than it was before, but still not good enough; we should just get rid of it. We heard from plenty of victims who are now in their 50's, 60's, 70's, and even one who was 83 years old. We want future victims to know they will always have the force of the criminal law behind them, no matter how long they live. And we want future child predators to know they should always be looking over their shoulder—no matter how long they live.

Second, we call for a "civil window" law, which would let older victims sue the diocese for the damage inflicted on their lives when they were kids. We saw these victims; they are marked for life. Many of them wind up addicted, or impaired, or dead before their time. The law in force right now gives child sex abuse victims twelve years to sue, once they turn 18. But victims who are already in their 30's and older fell under a different law; they only got two years. For victims in this age range, the short two-year period would have expired back in the 1990's or even earlier—long before revelations about the institutional nature of clergy sex abuse. We think that's unacceptable. These victims ran out of time to sue before they even knew they had a case; the church was still successfully hiding its complicity. Our proposal would open a limited "window" offering them a chance, finally, to be heard in court. All we're asking is to give those two years back.

Third, we want improvement to the law for mandated reporting of abuse. We saw from diocesan records that church officials, going back decades, were insisting they had no duty to report to the government when they learned of child abuse in their parishes. New laws make it harder to take that position; but we want them tighter. The law penalizes a "continuing" failure to report, but only if the abuse of "the child" is "active." We're not sure what that means and we don't want any wiggle room. Make it clear that the duty to report a child abuser continues as long as there's reason to believe he will do it again—whether or not he's "active" on any particular day, and whether or not he may pick a different kid next time.

Fourth, we need a law concerning confidentiality agreements. They've become a hot topic in recent months in sexual harassment cases—but it turns out the church has been using them for a long time. The subpoenaed records contained quite a few confidentiality agreements, going back decades: payouts sealed by silence. There are arguments on both sides about whether it's proper to use these agreements in securing lawsuit settlements. But there should be no room for debate on one point: no non-disclosure agreement can or should apply to criminal investigations. If the subject of a civil lawsuit happens also to concern criminal activity, then a confidentiality agreement gives neither party either the right or the obligation to decline cooperation with law enforcement. All future agreements should have to say that in big bold letters. And all this should be enacted into a law.

We believe these proposals will assist in the exposure and prosecution of child sexual abuse, and so it is within the scope of our duty to make them. But to be honest it's not enough. We don't just want this abuse punished by criminal and civil penalties. We want it not to happen at all. We think it's reasonable to expect one of the world's great religions, dedicated to the spiritual well-being of over a billion people, to find ways to organize itself so that the shepherds stop preying upon the flock. If it does nothing else, this report removes any remaining doubt that the failure to prevent abuse was a systemic failure, an institutional failure. There are things that the government can do to help. But we hope there will also be self-reflection within the church, and a deep commitment to creating a safer environment for its children.

## Profiles

This final section of the report is possibly the most important. It contains profiles of more than 300 clergy members, from all six dioceses we investigated. By comparison, estimates of the number of abusive priests identified since 2002 in the Boston, Massachusetts archdiocese range from about 150 to 250. The 2005 Philadelphia archdiocese grand jury report identified over 60 priests. The 2016 Altoona-Johnstown report named about 50 abusers. We believe ours is the largest grand jury report of its kind to date.

Each of the profiles is a summary of the abuse allegations against individual priests and of the church's response over time to those allegations. The profiles are based largely on the wealth of internal documents surrendered by the dioceses. In many cases, we also received testimony from the victims. And, on over a dozen occasions, the priests themselves appeared before us. Most of them admitted what they had done.

Even out of these hundreds of odious stories, some stood out. There was the priest, for example, who raped a seven-year-old girl—while he was visiting her in the hospital after she'd had her tonsils out. Or the priest who made a nine-year-old give him oral sex, then rinsed out the boy's mouth with holy water to purify him. Or the boy who drank some juice at his priest's house, and woke up the next morning bleeding from his rectum, unable to remember anything from the night before. Or the priest, a registered psychologist, who "treated" a young parishioner with depression by attempting to hypnotize her and directing her to take off her clothes, piece by piece.

One priest was willing to admit to molesting boys, but denied reports from two girls who had been abused; "they don't have a penis," he explained. Another priest, asked about abusing his parishioners, refused to commit: "with my history," he said, "anything is possible." Yet another priest finally decided to quit after years of child abuse complaints, but asked for, and received, a letter of reference for his next job—at Walt Disney World.

We came across a file in which the diocese candidly conceded that "this is one of our worst ones"—but of course told no one about him. Actually we came across the same statement in the files of several other priests. Then there was the file with a simple celebratory notation: "bad abuse case. [Victim] sued us . . . we won." And this happy note, in a case in which a seven-year-old girl was molested by a priest from outside the diocese: *[Redacted—Ongoing Appellate Litigation]*

In addition to describing the abuse and its handling, each of the profiles also includes a list, as complete as we could make it, of the subject priest's places of assignment over the course of his career. That doesn't mean we received abuse reports associated with each of those assignments. But the assignment list should provide parishioners with a way to determine whether priests who were credibly accused of abuse ever served in their area.

We should emphasize that, while the list of priests is long, we don't think we got them all. We feel certain that many victims never came forward, and that the dioceses did not create written records every single time they heard something about abuse. We also couldn't fully account for out-of-state travel. Many priests who served in Pennsylvania also spent some of their careers in other parts of the country. If they abused children elsewhere, reports might have made their way back to diocesan files here. But we suspect that a lot did not.

Although this section of our report is as comprehensive as we could make it, we did not automatically name every priest who was mentioned in the documents. We actually received files on over 400 priests from the dioceses. Some of these are not presented here because the information contained in the file was too scanty to make a reasonable determination about what had happened. On other occasions, we present a profile anonymously, because the case reveals a lot about the diocese's behavior, but nothing significant about the priest's. And in numerous other cases, the evidence contained in the file was clear, but the misconduct was outside the purpose of this investigation, which focused on criminal child sex abuse. As a result, we do not include files involving sex between priests and adults, substance abuse, or financial wrongdoing, unless these relate directly to abuse of children.

Many of the priests who we profile here are dead. We decided it was crucial to include them anyway, because we suspect that many of their victims may still be alive—including unreported victims who may have thought they were the only one. Those victims deserve to know they were not alone. It was not their fault.

We need to end with this note. During our deliberations, one of the victims who had appeared before us tried to kill herself. From her hospital bed, she asked for one thing: that we finish our work and tell the world what really happened. We feel a debt to this woman, and to the many other victims who so exposed themselves by giving us their stories. We hope this report will make good on what we owe.

SOURCE: Office of the Attorney General of the Commonwealth of Pennsylvania. "Report I of the 40th Statewide Investigating Grand Jury." Released August 14, 2018. https://www.attorneygeneral.gov/wp-content/uploads/2018/08/A-Report-of-the-Fortieth-Statewide-Investigating-Grand-Jury_Cleland-Redactions-8-12-08_Redacted.pdf.

# *New Jersey Attorney General Announces Sexual Abuse Task Force*

**September 6, 2018**

Attorney General Gurbir S. Grewal today announced that he is forming a task force to investigate allegations of sexual abuse by members of the clergy within the Catholic dioceses of New Jersey, as well as any efforts to cover up such abuse.

Attorney General Grewal has appointed former Acting Essex County Prosecutor Robert D. Laurino to head the task force. An experienced sex crimes prosecutor, Laurino will oversee a team of detectives and prosecutors from across the state's County Prosecutor's Offices and the Division of Criminal Justice (DCJ), and will report directly to DCJ Director Veronica Allende. Attorney General Grewal has authorized the task force to present evidence to a state grand jury, including through the use of subpoenas to compel testimony and the production of documents, in addition to other investigative tools.

To help identify potential victims, Attorney General Grewal also has established a new dedicated hotline to report allegations of sexual abuse by members of the clergy. The hotline will be staffed by trained professionals and operate on a 24/7 basis. The toll-free number is 855-363-6548.

Today's announcement follows the recent publication of a report by a Pennsylvania grand jury alleging more than 1,000 victims of sexual abuse by Roman Catholic priests in that state over a 70-year period. The report, which was the result of a multi-year investigation led by Pennsylvania Attorney General Josh Shapiro, also detailed allegations of a cover-up by church leaders and accusations of sexual abuse against at least four priests who spent part of their ministries in New Jersey.

"I was deeply troubled to read the allegations contained in last month's Pennsylvania grand jury report," said Attorney General Grewal. "The report revealed that sexual assaults on children—and efforts to cover up such assaults—were far more widespread in Pennsylvania than we ever thought possible. We owe it to the people of New Jersey to find out whether the same thing happened here. If it did, we will take action against those responsible."

"No person is above the law and no institution is immune from accountability," continued Attorney General Grewal. "We will devote whatever resources are necessary to uncover the truth and bring justice to victims. I commend Attorney General Josh Shapiro for his investigation in Pennsylvania, and we will work to ensure that our investigation in New Jersey is done professionally and thoroughly."

"I am extremely honored that the Attorney General would ask me to take on such an extraordinarily important investigation," said Laurino. "Having been a special victims prosecutor for most of my professional career, I am prepared to do everything possible to give a voice to those who were abused. I hope that we will finally be able to give these individuals some degree of closure in their lives."

In addition to investigating allegations of sexual abuse by clergy, the task force will conduct a comprehensive review of existing agreements between the Catholic dioceses of New Jersey and state law enforcement. In 2002, each of the state's dioceses entered into a Memorandum of Understanding (MOU) with the Attorney General's Office and various County Prosecutors' Offices. These MOUs mandated that the dioceses establish policies and procedures to ensure that their leaders and employees report information to prosecutors about potential cases of sexual abuse within their churches and cooperate in any resulting law enforcement investigations. As part of the efforts announced today, the task force will determine whether the dioceses complied with the MOUs' mandatory reporting requirements and whether any additional action is necessary.

"We want victims to know that we stand ready to investigate their cases and will do everything in our power to bring those responsible for these crimes to justice," said DCJ Director Veronica Allende. "The key is obtaining adequate evidence, and we urge anyone with information about sexual abuse by members of the clergy to contact us confidentially through our new hotline."

Laurino has been a member of the Essex County Prosecutors Office since 1980. He served as Acting Prosecutor from June 2017 until this month, and previously served as Acting Prosecutor from January 2010 to February 2011. Laurino has completed over 100 jury trials and has handled thousands of cases involving sexual violence.

Laurino has served as a faculty member for the National District Attorneys Association, the New Jersey Attorney General's Advocacy Institute, the New York Prosecutors Training Institute, and AEquitas: The Prosecutors' Resource on Violence Against Women, where he has taught trial advocacy courses on matters concerning sexual assault, ethics, and DNA evidence. Laurino has published and continues to lecture nationally on issues involving sexual violence, forensic evidence, attorney ethics, and the abuse of individuals with disabilities. A cum laude graduate of Villanova University, Laurino received a master's degree from Rutgers University. Laurino graduated from Seton Hall University School of Law, where he was an editor of the law review.

"Bob Laurino has spent much of his career investigating and prosecuting sexual violence, and he is a highly respected expert and advocate in this area," said Attorney General Grewal. "His passion and expertise make him the right person to lead this task force."

Information about the task force is available at www.nj.gov/oag/clergy-abuse.

SOURCE: Office of the Attorney General of the State of New Jersey. "AG Grewal Establishes Task Force to Investigate Allegations of Sexual Abuse by Clergy in Catholic Dioceses of New Jersey." September 6, 2018. https://nj.gov/oag/newsreleases18/pr20180906a.html.

# New York Attorney General Announces Civil Investigation, Sexual Abuse Hotline

**September 6, 2018**

Today, New York Attorney General Barbara D. Underwood announced a clergy abuse hotline and online complaint form through which victims and anyone with information can provide information—part of the Attorney General's ongoing investigation into sexual abuse of children within the New York dioceses of the Catholic Church.

Victims and anyone with information about abuse can call the hotline at 1-800-771-7755 or file a complaint online at ag.ny.gov/ClergyAbuse. An investigator will review all allegations; the Attorney General and our law enforcement partners will seek to protect victims' and witnesses' identities.

The Attorney General's Charities Bureau has launched a civil investigation into how the dioceses and other church entities—which are non-profit institutions—reviewed and potentially covered up allegations of extensive sexual abuse of minors.

As announced last month, the Attorney General's Criminal Division is also seeking to partner with District Attorneys—who are the only entities that currently have the power to convene grand juries to investigate these matters—to investigate and, if warranted, prosecute any individuals who have committed criminal offenses that fall within the applicable statutes of limitations.

"The Pennsylvania grand jury report shined a light on incredibly disturbing and depraved acts by Catholic clergy, assisted by a culture of secrecy and cover ups in the dioceses. Victims in New York deserve to be heard as well—and we are going to do everything in our power to bring them the justice they deserve," said Attorney General Underwood. "I urge all victims and anyone else with information to contact our hotline. And make no mistake: the only way that justice can fully and truly be served is for the legislature to finally pass the Child Victims Act."

It is important to note that many cases of abuse may not be prosecutable given New York's statutes of limitations. The Attorney General has repeatedly urged the legislature to pass the Child Victims Act, which would allow all victims to file civil suits until age 50 and seek criminal charges until age 28. Under current law, victims only have until age 23 to file civil cases or seek criminal charges for most types of child sexual abuse; some of the most serious child sex crimes have no time limit on the bringing of criminal charges, but only for conduct that occurred in 2001 or later.

However, the Attorney General encourages any victim of sexual abuse by Catholic clergy to participate in this investigation, even if they believe that their information may be outside the statute of limitations for a court case. All victim information will be helpful to understanding and reforming the institutional approach of the Church, regardless of whether an individual case can be prosecuted.

"I continue to encourage District Attorneys in all counties to work with the Attorney General's Office to investigate allegations of sexual abuse in the Catholic Diocese. Past victims and current victims deserve to have their complaints aggressively investigated and those who have committed these horrific crimes must be held accountable," said District Attorneys Association of New York President, Albany County District Attorney David Soares. "DAASNY is ready to collaborate with the Attorney General's office to investigate complaints from victims and witnesses."

SOURCE: Office of the Attorney General of New York State. "A.G. Underwood Announces Clergy Abuse Hotline—Part of Investigation into Sexual Abuse of Children within NY Dioceses of Catholic Church." September 6, 2018. https://ag.ny.gov/press-release/ag-underwood-announces-clergy-abuse-hotline-part-investigation-sexual-abuse-children.

## OTHER HISTORIC DOCUMENTS OF INTEREST

### FROM PREVIOUS HISTORIC DOCUMENTS

- Catholic Bishops on Sexual Abuse by Priests, *2002*, p. 868

# Turkish Central Bank on Adjustments to Alleviate Financial Crisis

JULY 31, AUGUST 13, AND SEPTEMBER 13, 2018

In 2018, the Turkish Central Bank undertook a number of measures to alleviate a financial downturn. The economic situation was brought on by a culmination of factors including poor financial management exacerbated by sanctions and tariffs levied by the United States as well as decreasing investor confidence in emerging markets including Turkey. Despite urgings by Turkish President Recep Tayyip Erdoğan against doing so, the Central Bank was forced to raise its key interest rate to prevent further inflation and devaluation of the lira. By the end of the year, Turkey was still teetering on the brink of a full-blown economic crisis.

## TURKEY VEERS INTO FINANCIAL CRISIS

Erdoğan was prime minister before becoming Turkey's first-ever popularly elected president in 2014, a role he leveraged as a mandate for expansion of executive authority. His growing stranglehold on power survived a coup attempt in July 2016, which led to the declaration of multiple states of emergency. In April 2017, Turkish voters handed Erdoğan another victory when they declared in a referendum their preference for a presidential system of government over the existing parliamentary one. This provided sweeping new powers to Erdoğan, who in turn called for early presidential and parliamentary elections to be held, moving the date from November 2019 to June 2018. The president was easily reelected to a second five-year term, and his party, the Justice and Development Party (*Adalet ve Kalkınma Partisi* [AKP]), was able to retain its hold on parliament by partnering with the Nationalist Action Party (*Milliyetçi Hareket Partisi* [MHP]). Erdoğan's grip on power and concerns over the seeming violation of democratic norms in Turkey and potential human rights abuses soured Turkey's relationship with the West. Still, Erdoğan remained popular among a large segment of the Turkish population, who were reaping the benefits of the economic growth experienced under his watch. Since Erdoğan became prime minister following an economic downturn in the early 2000s, Turkey's economy grew substantially, bolstered by a construction boom, expanding international investment, and cheap credit.

That rapid growth began to slow in 2018, as investors started moving toward more financially stable markets in the West. Instead of adjusting his economic strategies, Erdoğan doubled down on his policies, which value short-term growth driven by consumer spending and massive government-funded projects over incremental economic gains amounting to long-term stability. Ahead of the June election, Erdoğan questioned the independence of the Turkish Central Bank and its decision to raise the top interest rate seventy-five basis points to 13.5 percent. In an interview with Bloomberg, Erdoğan said he would "have to give off the image of a president who's influential on monetary policies" and promised to tighten his control over the bank if reelected. Durmus Yilmaz, who led Turkey's Central Bank from 2006 to 2011, cautioned that such tactics had been tried in the past and resulted in interest rates reaching 400 percent.

After he was reelected, Erdoğan followed through on his promise to better control economic decisions and fired the finance and treasury minister, a former Merrill Lynch chief economist. In his place, Erdoğan appointed his son-in-law and then announced that the president had the exclusive power to appoint those at the Central Bank who set interest rates. Instead of taking the advice of economists and allowing the Central Bank to act independently of politics and increase interest rates to keep inflation in check, Erdoğan instead encouraged the bank to keep borrowing costs low, and possibly decrease them, as a means to fuel economic expansion. Erdoğan has long touted an opinion that high interest rates lead to high inflation, but there are few economists who support that view. By August, the value of the lira against the U.S. dollar had depreciated 40 percent since the beginning of the year, and inflation hit nearly 18 percent.

## FACTORS CONTRIBUTING TO TURKEY'S FINANCIAL CRISIS

Poor financial management was not the only factor contributing to Turkey's financial crisis in 2018. Turkey was suffering from a significant trade deficit that reached 5.5 percent of gross domestic product in 2017. While not an unusually high level for an emerging economy, that deficit has to be made up either by foreign investment or other borrowing to pay the debt holders. In 2018 alone, a portion of this debt was coming due, and Turkey would need to pay or refinance tens of billions of dollars.

Another factor, one that caused a similar economic downturn in Argentina in 2018, was a decreasing interest among investors to put their money in emerging foreign markets. During the global economic collapse from 2008 to 2009, advanced economies kept their interest rates low as a means to jumpstart economic activity. Without expectation of a strong return, investors turned to emerging markets, and Turkey was particularly attractive given its economic growth that averaged 6.8 percent between 2010 and 2017. By 2018, these investors were growing concerned because many of the projects supporting economic expansion had been financed not in lira but in dollars, and as the dollar grew in strength, the debt owed became more expensive. Investors worried that Turkish companies would be unable to pay back the debt, which could result in widespread bankruptcy. With the U.S. Federal Reserve deciding to raise interest rates, a signal that the markets were growing again, investors left Turkey and instead turned to the dollar to get a better, and likely safer, return on their investment.

Turkey's relationship with the United States also pushed the economy deeper into crisis. The U.S. Treasury Department in August issued sanctions against Turkey's justice and interior ministers in an attempt to force the country's hand to release detained U.S. pastor Andrew Brunson. Brunson was arrested in Turkey in 2016, a country he had lived in for more than two decades, and was accused of conspiring with those who were attempting to overthrow Erdoğan's government. According to a 2017 letter from members of Congress to Erdoğan, there was "no evidence to substantiate the charges against [Brunson]" or any indication that he was a member of the organization leading the 2016 coup attempt. The U.S. ambassador to Turkey, John Bass, said Brunson's detention appeared to be "simply because he's an American citizen who as a man of faith was in contact with a range of people in this country who he was trying to help . . . and for some reason, some specific set of his interactions suddenly are being classified as support for terrorism." When sanctions were ineffective at securing Brunson's release, President Donald Trump announced that the United States would double tariffs on Turkish steel and aluminum, a move Erdoğan referred to as "economic war." Brunson was not released until October, and the Turkish government hoped that would result in a lifting of tariffs to jump-start confidence and reinvestment in its economy. Although Trump said the pastor's release would "lead to good, perhaps great, relations" between the United States and Turkey, the president did not lift the aluminum and steel sanctions by the end of 2018.

## PATHWAYS OUT OF CRISIS

Many economists, including those close to Erdoğan, agreed that preventing a financial crisis required raising interest rates. Doing so would likely weaken demand and encourage renewed investment in the lira, which would in turn reduce the costs of imports, give Turkish citizens more buying power, and ultimately strengthen the economy. But Erdoğan's reluctance to do so fed the cycle of weakened consumer and foreign investor confidence because investors did not believe the president would do what was necessary to shore up the economy. The Turkish Central Bank promised to "use all available instruments in pursuit of the price stability objective" and vowed to maintain a "tight stance" on monetary policy until the outlook improved. But it failed to act in a substantial way to increase investor confidence and shore up flagging growth, instead insinuating that the market fluctuations occurring in Turkey were a normal, short-term impact of the rapid growth seen over the previous two decades. Mustafa Sentop, the deputy speaker of parliament from Erdoğan's AKP, expressed the government's confidence in the economy: "We don't believe Turkey will have a problem in funding this debt."

In September, the Central Bank did increase the policy rate, the bank's benchmark interest rate, slightly from 17.75 percent to 24 percent despite Erdoğan urging otherwise. And late that month, Turkey's finance minister, Berat Albayrak, announced a new economic plan, the Medium Term Programme, aimed at ending the current financial downturn and putting Turkey back on the path to growth. The plan would "rein in inflation, spur growth and cut the current account deficit," Albayrak said. He explained that in the short term, economic growth would slow, but that it would pick up again in 2021. The plan aimed for a budget deficit–to–GDP ratio of 1.9 percent in 2018 that would shrink to 1.7 percent by 2021. "Our major intention is to support stabilization process with discipline in public finance," the finance minister said.

As a last resort, Turkey could appeal to the International Monetary Fund (IMF) for financial assistance. Argentina, which faced many of the same economic challenges as Turkey in 2018, ended up requesting a $57.1 billion IMF standby loan to dig out of its financial crisis. That same option would be available to Turkey; however, Erdoğan's government was unlikely to request IMF aid because the president was credited with helping Turkey pay back the loan it took from the IMF in the early 2000s in the face of another financial crisis. According to Erdoğan's son-in-law and finance minister, Turkey had "no need of the IMF."

—Heather Kerrigan

*Following are three press releases from the Turkish Central Bank on July 31, August 13, and September 13, 2018, on the nation's economy and the actions taken by the bank to address concerns.*

## Turkey's Central Bank Addresses Financial Concerns

DOCUMENT

**July 31, 2018**

### Inflation Developments

1. In June, consumer prices rose by 2.61 percent and annual inflation increased by 3.24 points to 15.39 percent. The rise in annual inflation was widespread across subcategories, with the most significant contribution coming from unprocessed food. Cost pressures from recent exchange rate developments drove prices higher in many related items. Producer prices exerted even stronger upward pressure on consumer prices compared to a month earlier. Thus, core indicators saw a notable increase in both their annual inflation rates and underlying trends.

2. Annual inflation in food and non-alcoholic beverages rose by 7.89 points to 18.89 percent in June. This increase was driven by the unprocessed food inflation that soared due to vegetables prices. In this period, there was significant divergence between the producer prices for PPI for agriculture and the consumer prices for food. The widening gap between producer and consumer price levels for some vegetables signaled market problems associated with the distribution channel. Meanwhile, processed food prices recorded increases across all subcategories, pushing annual processed food inflation up to 14.47 percent. In the upcoming period, bread and raw milk reference purchase prices might put upward pressure on processed food prices.

3. Energy prices increased by 1.01 percent in June and annual energy inflation rose by 1.82 points to 16.99 percent. Solid fuel, bottled gas and administered municipal water prices were up, whereas fuel prices remained flat due to the new sliding-scale tariff system. In the period ahead, administered energy prices will likely reflect the cumulative cost pressures from exchange rates and oil prices.

4. In June, annual services inflation increased by 1.44 points to 10.96 percent. The rise in services inflation was widespread across subcategories. Communication services inflation went up on the back of internet tariffs, while transport services inflation was driven higher by cumulative cost pressures and the buoyant domestic and international tourism industry. The tourism upsurge was the main driver of price hikes in related subcategories, such as catering, accommodation and package tours. In summary, prices of services reflected not only cost pressures from exchange rates, oil prices and food prices but also demand-side effects of the favorable tourism outlook.

5. Annual core goods inflation rose by 2.57 points to 18.55 percent in June, largely due to recent exchange rate developments. Thus, prices of durable goods and other core goods posted sharp widespread increases. Clothing inflation, however, remained flat in this period. The exchange rate-driven rise in costs is likely to put further inflationary pressure on prices of core goods in coming months.

## Factors Affecting Inflation

6. Economic activity proved a little stronger than projected in the first quarter of 2018. Gross Domestic Product (GDP) increased by 2.0 percent on a quarterly basis and 7.4 percent on an annual basis. Main driver of quarterly growth was domestic demand, particularly private consumption in the first quarter. Investment offered rather limited support to growth due to the muted course of machinery-equipment investments. Net exports contributed positively to quarterly growth owing both to the contraction in imports coupled with the rebound in tourism.

7. Recently released data indicate a more significant rebalancing trend in economic activity. Data for the second quarter reveal that external demand maintains its strength. Amid favorable global growth outlook, rising external demand and flexibility in diversifying export markets continue to stimulate exports. The Committee noted that the rebound in revenues from tourism and other services is rather brisk, and under these circumstances, net exports will provide positive contribution to quarterly growth in the second quarter as well. In the upcoming period, exports of goods and services are expected to boost growth further and the slowdown in import demand resulting from the subdued domestic demand is likely to have further positive repercussions on the current account balance.

8. In the second quarter, signs of deceleration in domestic demand became more visible. In this period, the depreciation in the Turkish lira accompanied by the increased financial volatility, perceptions of uncertainty and financing costs decelerated domestic demand both through the consumption and investment expenditures channels. The slowdown in domestically-oriented sectors, particularly sectors affiliated to construction, confirms this outlook. Meanwhile, accommodative stance of the public sector conducted through expenditures and fiscal measures are projected to moderate the slowdown in domestic demand to some extent. Survey indicators point that the rebalancing process in economic activity may continue in the third quarter.

9. The ongoing improvement in the labor market came to [a] halt in the second quarter, as the economic activity started to lose pace and converge to its underlying trend. Employment in the services and industrial sectors posted mild increases in April, while the evident fall in construction employment led to a quarterly decline in non-farm employment.

10. In sum, data for the second quarter indicate that economic activity has assumed a rebalancing process both in terms of growth rate and composition. However, the downside risks to the magnitude and duration of the slowdown in economic activity are kept alive by the high level of financial volatility and perceptions of uncertainty.

## Monetary Policy and Risks

11. The Committee evaluated the medium-term inflation forecasts for the July Inflation Report as well. Accordingly, year-end consumer inflation forecasts for 2018 and 2019 were revised upwards by 5 points and 2.8 points, respectively compared to the April forecast. With a tight policy stance that focuses on bringing inflation down with enhanced policy coordination, inflation is projected to converge gradually to the target. Accordingly, inflation is projected to be 13.4 percent at the end of 2018 and then fall to 9.3 percent at the end of 2019,

6.7 percent at the end of 2020, stabilizing around 5 percent over the medium term. Forecasts are based on a monetary policy framework that envisaged that the tight monetary policy stance will be maintained for an extended period.

12. Cost factors and volatility in food prices have been the main drivers of the recent upsurge in inflation. On the other hand, price increases have shown a generalized pattern across subsectors. Despite the milder impact of demand conditions on inflation, elevated levels of inflation and inflation expectations continue to pose risks on the pricing behavior. Accordingly, the Committee assessed that it might be necessary to maintain a tight monetary stance for an extended period.

13. The Central Bank will continue to use all available instruments in pursuit of the price stability objective. Tight stance in monetary policy will be maintained decisively until inflation outlook displays a significant improvement. Inflation expectations, pricing behavior, lagged impact of recent monetary policy decisions, contribution of fiscal policy to rebalancing process, and other factors affecting inflation will be closely monitored and, if needed, further monetary tightening will be delivered.

14. The outlook that the medium-term projections presented in the Inflation Report is based on the Monetary Policy Committee's judgments and assumptions. Nevertheless, various risks to these factors may affect the inflation outlook and necessitate changes in the monetary policy stance envisaged in the baseline scenario. The Committee evaluated that risks to the medium-term inflation outlook are mostly on the upside.

15. The pricing behavior, developments in global risk appetite, the contribution of fiscal policy to the rebalancing, and the lagged effects of the monetary policy will be monitored closely in the coming period. Should these factors deviate from the baseline scenario, the monetary policy stance will be reviewed depending on the change in the inflation outlook.

SOURCE: Central Bank of the Republic of Turkey. "Press Release on Summary of the Monetary Policy Committee Meeting (No. 2018-29)." July 31, 2018. http://www.tcmb.gov.tr/wps/wcm/connect/e64d08d2-746c-499d-b164-1e4e43a96383/ANO2018-29.pdf?MOD=AJPERES&CACHEID=ROOTWORKSPACE-e64d08d2-746c-499d-b164-1e4e43a96383-mjL.GY9.

# Turkish Central Bank
# Announces Financial Controls

**August 13, 2018**

To support financial stability and sustain the effective functioning of markets, the following measures have been introduced:

I. Turkish lira liquidity management:

   1) In the framework of intraday and overnight standing facilities, the Central Bank will provide all the liquidity the banks need.

   2) Discount rates for collaterals against Turkish lira transactions will be revised based on type and maturity, thus providing banks with flexibility in their collateral management. Through this regulation, the discounted value of banks' current unencumbered collaterals is projected to increase by approximately 3,8 billion Turkish liras.

3) Collateral FX deposit limits for Turkish lira transactions of banks have been raised to 20 billion euros from 7,2 billion euros.

4) As cited in the Monetary and Exchange Rate Policy Text for 2018, when deemed necessary, in addition to one-week repo auctions, which are the main funding instrument of the Central Bank, traditional repo auctions or deposit selling auctions may be held with maturities no longer than 91 days.

5) For the days with relatively higher funding need, more than one repo auction may be conducted with maturities between 6 and 10 days.

6) To provide flexibility in banks' collateral management, upon the request of banks, a portion of or the entire amount of the winning bids in one-week repo auctions will be allowed to be used in deposit transactions instead of repo transactions at the Central Bank Interbank Money Market with the same interest rate and maturity.

II. FX liquidity management:

1) Banks will be able to borrow FX deposits in one-month maturity in addition to one-week maturity.

2) The Central Bank will resume its intermediary function at the FX deposit market. Accordingly, through the intermediation of the Central Bank, banks will be able to borrow from and lend to each other at the FX deposit market as per the rules set by the Implementation Instructions on the Foreign Exchange and Banknotes Markets.

3) Banks' current foreign exchange deposit limits of around 50 billion US dollars may be increased and utilization conditions may be improved if deemed necessary.

4) Banks will continue to purchase foreign banknotes from the Central Bank via foreign exchange transactions within their pre-determined limits at the Foreign Exchange and Banknotes Markets.

The Central Bank will closely monitor the market depth and price formations, and take all necessary measures to maintain financial stability, if deemed necessary.

SOURCE: Central Bank of the Republic of Turkey. "Press Release on Financial Markets." August 13, 2018. http://www.tcmb.gov.tr/wps/wcm/connect/836da9dd-1b87-41ef-8bbd-9ba8c9b2591f/ANO2018-31 .pdf?MOD=AJPERES&CACHEID=ROOTWORKSPACE-836da9dd-1b87-41ef-8bbd-9ba8c9b2591f-mkNFYFB.

DOCUMENT

# Central Bank Increases Interest Rate

**September 13, 2018**

## Participating Committee Members

Murat Çetinkaya (Governor), Ömer Duman, Uğur Namık Küçük, Emrah Şener, Murat Uysal, Abdullah Yavaş.

The Monetary Policy Committee (the Committee) has decided to increase the policy rate (one week repo auction rate) from 17.75 percent to 24 percent.

Recently released data indicate a more significant rebalancing trend in the economic activity. External demand maintains its strength, while slowdown in domestic demand accelerates.

Recent developments regarding the inflation outlook point to significant risks to price stability. Price increases have shown a generalized pattern across subsectors, reflecting the movements in exchange rates. Deterioration in the pricing behavior continues to pose upside risks on the inflation outlook, despite weaker domestic demand conditions. Accordingly, the Committee has decided to implement a strong monetary tightening to support price stability.

The Central Bank will continue to use all available instruments in pursuit of the price stability objective. Tight stance in monetary policy will be maintained decisively until inflation outlook displays a significant improvement. Inflation expectations, pricing behavior, lagged impact of recent monetary policy decisions, contribution of fiscal policy to rebalancing process, and other factors affecting inflation will be closely monitored and, if needed, further monetary tightening will be delivered.

It should be emphasized that any new data or information may lead the Committee to revise its stance.

The summary of the Monetary Policy Committee Meeting will be released within five working days.

SOURCE: Central Bank of the Republic of Turkey. "Decision of the Monetary Policy Committee." September 13, 2018. http://www.tcmb.gov.tr/wps/wcm/connect/f492fc92-9166-4d4f-a385-03ec 6cb663a6/ANO2018-38.pdf?MOD=AJPERES&CACHEID=ROOTWORKSPACE-f492fc92-9166-4d4f-a385-03ec6cb663a6-mniBDT2.

## OTHER HISTORIC DOCUMENTS OF INTEREST

### FROM THIS VOLUME

- IMF Issues Financial Support during Argentina Financial Crisis, p. 354

### FROM PREVIOUS *HISTORIC DOCUMENTS*

- Turkish President Responds to Referendum and State of Emergency, *2017*, p. 213

# August

# Pope Declares Death Penalty Unacceptable

AUGUST 2, 2018

For hundreds of years, the Catholic Church permitted executions as a form of criminal punishment, until Pope John Paul II revised Catholic doctrine to significantly narrow the circumstances in which the church viewed the death penalty as an appropriate sentence. In 2018, at Pope Francis's direction, the doctrine was further revised to declare the death penalty "unacceptable" in all cases. While senior Catholic officials characterized the change as consistent with recent church teachings, some conservatives argued the pope was rewriting doctrine to suit his personal views. Some also questioned the revision's significance since most countries no longer use the death penalty.

## POPE FRANCIS CHALLENGES DEATH PENALTY

Since his election in 2013, Pope Francis has repeatedly spoken against the death penalty and asserted that its use is never justified. "Today capital punishment is unacceptable, however serious the condemned's crime may have been," he wrote in a 2015 letter to the president of the International Commission Against the Death Penalty. The pope argued that the death penalty "entails cruel, inhumane, and degrading treatment" regardless of the method used by authorities and noted that some executions have been badly botched. He further observed that some convictions carrying the death sentence have been wrong and overturned; therefore capital punishment should not be used because of the "defective selectivity of the criminal justice system and in the face of the possibility of judicial error." The death penalty, he stated, "does not render justice to the victims, but rather fosters vengeance." Pope Francis reiterated his arguments during an address to Congress in 2015 and urged lawmakers to put a stop to executions. "I am convinced that this way is the best, since every life is sacred, every human person is endowed with an inalienable dignity, and society can only benefit from the rehabilitation of those convicted of crimes," he said.

Upon marking the twenty-fifth anniversary of the Catechism of the Catholic Church in October 2017, the pope requested that the church doctrine's discussion of the death penalty be revised to more explicitly oppose capital punishment. "It is, in itself, contrary to the Gospel, because a decision is voluntarily made to suppress a human life, which is always sacred in the eyes of the Creator and of whom, in the last analysis, only God can be the true judge and guarantor," he said. The pope added that the death penalty also eliminates any possibility that the accused might seek forgiveness and start a new life.

## REVISION TO CHURCH DOCTRINE APPROVED

On August 2, 2018, the Vatican released a revision to section 2267 of the Catechism of the Catholic Church, which deals specifically with capital punishment. "The death penalty is inadmissible because it is an attack on the inviolability and dignity of the person," the revised text read, adding that the church "works with determination for its abolition worldwide." The new text had been approved by Pope Francis in May during an audience with the prefect for the Congregation for the Doctrine of the Faith, Spanish Cardinal Luis Ladaria.

That same day, the Office of the Congregation for the Doctrine of Faith published a letter from Ladaria to the bishops explaining the change to church doctrine. (The bishops have primary responsibility for teaching and promoting the catechism.) The letter stated that Pope Francis had requested a reformulation of church teachings on the death penalty so that they would "better reflect the development of the doctrine on this point that has taken place in recent times," citing previous statements by Pope John Paul II and Pope Benedict XVI that supported the death penalty's abolition. Pope John Paul II had said "the dignity of human life must never be taken away, even in the case of someone who has done great evil," while Pope Benedict XVI called on world leaders to make "every effort to elim-inate the death penalty" and told Catholics that ending capital punishment was an essen-tial part of "conforming penal law both to the human dignity of prisoners and the effective maintenance of public order."

The letter further noted that the catechism had been revised by Pope John Paul II in 1997 to say that the death penalty could be used if it is "the only practicable way to defend the lives of human beings effectively against the aggressor," though the updated doctrine stated that the instances in which capital punishment is necessary "are very rare, if not practically nonexistent." Additionally, the revised text stated that if nonlethal forms of punishment were determined to be sufficient, the authorities should limit themselves to such measures because they are "more in keeping with the concrete conditions of the com-mon good and more in conformity to the dignity of the human person." At the time, the change in doctrine was meant to increase its alignment with the "culture of life" promoted by Pope John Paul II that emphasized the value of each person and the need to protect every human life.

Ladaria wrote that the changes approved by Pope Francis centered on the "clearer awareness of the Church for the respect due to every human life" and the church's under-standing that penal actions applied by states "should be oriented above all to the rehabili-tation and social reintegration" of criminals. "Today the increasing understanding that the dignity of a person is not lost even after committing the most serious crimes, the deep-ened understanding of the significance of penal sanctions applied by the State, and the development of more efficacious detention systems that guarantee the due protection of citizens have given rise to a new awareness that recognizes the inadmissibility of the death penalty," he explained.

Catholics opposed to the death penalty praised the change in doctrine, including Sister Helen Prejean, a globally recognized advocate for death row inmates and author of the book *Dead Man Walking: An Eyewitness Account of the Death Penalty in the United States*. "It's a happy day. I'm clicking my heels," she said. "What I'm particularly delighted about is there's no loopholes. It's unconditional." Some conservatives and traditionalists took issue with the revision. "I think a lot of the pro-life people will feel that [Pope Francis] has undercut us," said Bill Donohue, president of the Catholic League. "Why the need for the change? I see nothing in the comments coming from the Vatican that explains why something broke. This will only add to the confusion in the laity."

## DEATH PENALTY ON THE DECLINE

Some observers questioned how impactful the change in doctrine would be, since, according to Amnesty International, a majority of countries have already banned the death penalty, including those in Europe and Latin America with large Catholic populations. Many of these same observers speculated that the change could be most impactful in the United States, where thirty states have statutes allowing for the use of the death penalty. By not completely rejecting the death penalty, Pope John Paul II's revision to catechism gave Catholic public officials in the United States leeway to support for capital punishment without contradicting their religious beliefs. Similarly, a Pew Research Center poll conducted in the spring of 2018 found that 53 percent of U.S. Catholics support the death penalty.

Pope Francis's change to church doctrine was expected to create some uncomfortable situations for Catholic politicians such as Nebraska Gov. Pete Ricketts, whose state was scheduled to execute a convicted murderer on August 14. State lawmakers had repealed the death penalty in 2015, but Ricketts pushed for—and personally helped to finance—a referendum that restored the punishment. Ricketts stated that the execution would continue as scheduled and affirmed that "capital punishment remains the will of the people and the law of the state of Nebraska," despite the change to church teachings.

Notably, while the catechism is considered binding for Catholics, there are no penalties for the faithful who disagree with or do not completely follow church doctrine. "We're not at the point where the church will deny communion to somebody who votes to uphold the death penalty," said Robert Dunham, executive director of the Death Penalty Information Center. "But I think it is getting harder and harder for the pro–death penalty Catholic legislators to reconcile their religious beliefs with their political beliefs." Chester Gillis, professor of theology at Georgetown University, observed that there are "lots of other teachings in the Catholic Church that not everybody abides by," noting, for example, that the church considers birth control a mortal sin. "If true there would be a lot of couples in mortal sin," he said.

Even without a ban on capital punishment, executions have become less common in the United States. According to Dunham's group, of the states that have death penalty statutes, only ten have conducted executions since 2014. Similarly, twenty-three people were executed in 2017, compared to ninety-eight people in 1999.

John Carr, director of the Initiative on Catholic Social Thought and Public Life at Georgetown University, suggested the change in church teachings could have a somewhat indirect effect. "I think what this does is get people to reexamine their own attitudes and convictions," he said. "The death penalty in the United States probably will not come to an end through an act of Congress or a Supreme Court decision. It will essentially fade away as prosecutors don't ask for it, juries don't recommend it, and the rest of us don't support it."

—Linda Grimm

*Following is the text of the revised Catechism of the Catholic Church, published by the Vatican on August 2, 2018; and a letter to Catholic bishops from the prefect of the Office of the Congregation for the Doctrine of the Faith on August 2, 2018, explaining the change in doctrine.*

# Revision to Catholic Church
# Catechism on the Death Penalty

**August 2, 2018**

The death penalty

2267. Recourse to the death penalty on the part of legitimate authority, following a fair trial, was long considered an appropriate response to the gravity of certain crimes and an acceptable, albeit extreme, means of safeguarding the common good.

Today, however, there is an increasing awareness that the dignity of the person is not lost even after the commission of very serious crimes. In addition, a new understanding has emerged of the significance of penal sanctions imposed by the state. Lastly, more effective systems of detention have been developed, which ensure the due protection of citizens but, at the same time, do not definitively deprive the guilty of the possibility of redemption.

Consequently, the Church teaches, in the light of the Gospel, that "the death penalty is inadmissible because it is an attack on the inviolability and dignity of the person", and she works with determination for its abolition worldwide.

SOURCE: Holy See Press Office. "New Revision of Number 2267 of the Catechism of the Catholic Church on the Death Penalty – Rescriptum 'ex Audentia SS.mi,' 02.08.2018." August 2, 2018. https://press.vatican .va/content/salastampa/en/bollettino/pubblico/2018/08/02/180802a.html.

# Letter to Bishops Explaining Revision
# to Catholic Church Catechism

**August 2, 2018**

*[All footnotes have been omitted.]*

1. The Holy Father Pope Francis, in his Discourse on the occasion of the twenty-fifth anniversary of the publication of the Apostolic Constitution *Fidei depositum*, by which John Paul II promulgated the *Catechism of the Catholic Church*, asked that the teaching on the death penalty be reformulated so as to better reflect the development of the doctrine on this point that has taken place in recent times. This development centers principally on the clearer awareness of the Church for the respect due to every human life. Along this line, John Paul II affirmed: "Not even a murderer loses his personal dignity, and God himself pledges to guarantee this."

2. It is in the same light that one should understand the attitude towards the death penalty that is expressed ever more widely in the teaching of pastors and in the sensibility of the people of God. If, in fact, the political and social situation of the past made the death

penalty an acceptable means for the protection of the common good, today the increasing understanding that the dignity of a person is not lost even after committing the most serious crimes, the deepened understanding of the significance of penal sanctions applied by the State, and the development of more efficacious detention systems that guarantee the due protection of citizens have given rise to a new awareness that recognizes the inadmissibility of the death penalty and, therefore, calling for its abolition.

3. In this development, the teaching of the Encyclical Letter *Evangelium vitæ* of John Paul II is of great importance. The Holy Father enumerated among the signs of hope for a new culture of life "a growing public opposition to the death penalty, even when such a penalty is seen as a kind of 'legitimate defense' on the part of society. Modern society in fact has the means of effectively suppressing crime by rendering criminals harmless without definitively denying them the chance to reform." The teaching of *Evangelium vitæ* was then included in the *editio typica* of the *Catechism of the Catholic Church*. In it, the death penalty is not presented as a proportionate penalty for the gravity of the crime, but it can be justified if it is "the only practicable way to defend the lives of human beings effectively against the aggressor," even if in reality "cases of absolute necessity for suppression of the offender today are very rare, if not practically non-existent" (n. 2267).

4. John Paul II also intervened on other occasions against the death penalty, appealing both to respect for the dignity of the person as well as to the means that today's society possesses to defend itself from criminals. Thus, in the *Christmas Message* of 1998, he wished "the world the consensus concerning the need for urgent and adequate measures . . . to end the death penalty." The following month in the United States, he repeated, "A sign of hope is the increasing recognition that the dignity of human life must never be taken away, even in the case of someone who has done great evil. Modern society has the means of protecting itself, without definitively denying criminals the chance to reform. I renew the appeal I made most recently at Christmas for a consensus to end the death penalty, which is both cruel and unnecessary."

5. The motivation to be committed to the abolition of the death penalty was continued with the subsequent Pontiffs. Benedict XVI recalled "the attention of society's leaders to the need to make every effort to eliminate the death penalty." He later wished a group of the faithful that "your deliberations will encourage the political and legislative initiatives being promoted in a growing number of countries to eliminate the death penalty and to continue the substantive progress made in conforming penal law both to the human dignity of prisoners and the effective maintenance of public order."

6. In this same prospective, Pope Francis has reaffirmed that "today capital punishment is unacceptable, however serious the condemned's crime may have been." The death penalty, regardless of the means of execution, "entails cruel, inhumane, and degrading treatment." Furthermore, it is to be rejected "due to the defective selectivity of the criminal justice system and in the face of the possibility of judicial error." It is in this light that Pope Francis has asked for a revision of the formulation of the *Catechism of the Catholic Church* on the death penalty in a manner that affirms that "no matter how serious the crime that has been committed, the death penalty is inadmissible because it is an attack on the inviolability and the dignity of the person."

7. The new revision of number 2267 of the *Catechism of the Catholic Church*, approved by Pope Francis, situates itself in continuity with the preceding Magisterium while bringing

forth a coherent development of Catholic doctrine. The new text, following the footsteps of the teaching of John Paul II in *Evangelium vitæ*, affirms that ending the life of a criminal as punishment for a crime is inadmissible because it attacks the dignity of the person, a dignity that is not lost even after having committed the most serious crimes. This conclusion is reached taking into account the new understanding of penal sanctions applied by the modern State, which should be oriented above all to the rehabilitation and social reintegration of the criminal. Finally, given that modern society possesses more efficient detention systems, the death penalty becomes unnecessary as protection for the life of innocent people. Certainly, it remains the duty of public authorities to defend the life of citizens, as has always been taught by the Magisterium and is confirmed by the *Catechism of the Catholic Church* in numbers 2265 and 2266.

8. All of this shows that the new formulation of number 2267 of the *Catechism* expresses an authentic development of doctrine that is not in contradiction with the prior teachings of the Magisterium. These teachings, in fact, can be explained in the light of the primary responsibility of the public authority to protect the common good in a social context in which the penal sanctions were understood differently, and had developed in an environment in which it was more difficult to guarantee that the criminal could not repeat his crime.

9. The new revision affirms that the understanding of the inadmissibility of the death penalty grew "in the light of the Gospel." The Gospel, in fact, helps to understand better the order of creation that the Son of God assumed, purified, and brought to fulfillment. It also invites us to the mercy and patience of the Lord that gives to each person the time to convert oneself.

10. The new formulation of number 2267 of the *Catechism of the Catholic Church* desires to give energy to a movement towards a decisive commitment to favor a mentality that recognizes the dignity of every human life and, in respectful dialogue with civil authorities, to encourage the creation of conditions that allow for the elimination of the death penalty where it is still in effect.

*The Sovereign Pontiff Francis, in the Audience granted to the undersigned Secretary of the Congregation for the Doctrine of the Faith on 28 June 2018, has approved the present Letter, adopted in the Ordinary Session of this Congregation on 13 June 2018, and ordered its publication.*

*Rome, from the Office of the Congregation for the Doctrine of the Faith, 1 August 2018, Memorial of Saint Alphonsus Liguori.*

Luis F. Card. Ladaria, S.I.
*Prefect*

X Giacomo Morandi
*Titular Archbishop of Cerveteri*
*Secretary*

SOURCE: Holy See Press Office. "Letter to the Bishops regarding the New Revision of Number 2267 of the Catechism of the Catholic Church on the Death Penalty, from the Congregation for the Doctrine of the Faith, 02.08.2018." August 2, 2018. https://press.vatican.va/content/salastampa/en/bollettino/pubblico/2018/08/02/180802b.html.

## OTHER HISTORIC DOCUMENTS OF INTEREST

# Zimbabwe's President Remarks on Historic Election

AUGUST 2, 3, AND 27, 2018

In November 2017, Robert Mugabe, the longtime leader of Zimbabwe, stepped down from his position after a bloodless takeover by the country's military. Mugabe was replaced by his former vice president, Emmerson Mnangagwa, who served as interim president until elections could be held in the summer of 2018. Mnangagwa went on to narrowly defeat his opponents in that election, the first held since Zimbabwe declared independence in which Mugabe was not a candidate. According to international election observers, the 2018 vote was marred by irregularities and voter intimidation. Mnangagwa's primary opponent challenged the results, but the country's Constitutional Court refused to reverse the outcome.

## Mugabe Fires Mnangagwa

Mugabe was Zimbabwe's first president after the country declared independence from Great Britain in 1980. Although he was at first revered for replacing the foreign, white minority government and promising to bring power back to the citizens, his government quickly became dictatorial. Mugabe's nearly forty-year reign was characterized by corruption, a violent crackdown on any opposition, and vote rigging to ensure the president retained his hold on power. Mugabe's mismanagement resulted in Zimbabwe's economic collapse, which led to staggering inflation and widespread unemployment.

In November 2017, amid speculation about who might replace the ninety-three-year-old president, Mugabe fired his vice president, Mnangagwa. Many in the nation viewed this as a power grab by Mugabe's wife, Grace, to pave the way for her to become the next president. Mugabe's office refuted those arguments, instead saying the vice president had been disloyal to Mugabe. In response to the firing, a segment of the Zimbabwe Defence Forces (ZDF) surrounded the presidential palace and seized control of the nation's state-run broadcast network. The military denied that it had conducted a coup but said the president would not be released until those responsible for "committing crimes that are causing social and economic suffering in the country" were brought "to justice." Zimbabweans protested in the capital, demanding Mugabe's resignation. On November 19, Mugabe's Zimbabwe African National Union–Patriotic Front (ZANU-PF) ousted him as leader, replacing him with Mnangagwa. On November 21, Mugabe announced his intent to resign in a letter to parliament. Mnangagwa was sworn in as interim president on November 24, 2017, promising to serve only until the next democratic election could be held.

## Mnangagwa Victorious in Presidential Race

In January 2018, Mnangagwa's government announced that parliamentary and presidential elections would be held within five months. It was not until May that a July 30 date was set for the election. Twenty-three candidates submitted their names to take part in the presidential race. Joining Mnangagwa on the ballot were Nelson Chamisa, the leader of Movement for Democratic Change (MDC) Alliance, ZANU-PF's main opposition comprised of seven political parties. Early polling showed Mnangagwa with a wide lead, but as the election drew near, Chamisa began gaining ground.

The July 30 vote was largely peaceful, with upward of 70 percent of the more than five million registered voters in Zimbabwe casting a ballot. The Zimbabwe Electoral Commission (ZEC) on August 1 announced the results of the parliamentary election, in which ZANU-PF claimed more than two-thirds of the seats. At the same time, the commission stated that it would delay the presidential results to provide more time for verification. By law, the ZEC had until August 4 to release the results, and if no candidate had more than 50 percent of the vote, a runoff would be held on September 8. Mnangagwa's opponents, including the MDC Alliance, accused the commission of postponing the results in an effort to rig the outcome in the president's favor. Chamisa declared himself the winner.

Opposition supporters took to the streets in the capital of Harare, and after police were unable to quell the unrest, Zimbabwe's military was sent in. They responded with tear gas, water cannons, and in some instances by firing live rounds into the crowd, injuring many and killing six. Mnangagwa pleaded for calm in the interim, writing on Twitter, "We must all demonstrate patience and maturity, and act in a way that puts our people and their safety first." He also blamed the MDC Alliance for the protests, saying that "we hold the party and its leadership responsible for any loss of life, injury or damage of property that arise from these acts of political violence which they have aided and abetted." On August 2, police arrested twenty-seven MDC Alliance leaders, all of whom were later released on bail, for their part in the violence. They also issued an arrest warrant for Chamisa, but he was never taken into custody.

On August 3, the ZEC released the results of the presidential election. Mnangagwa narrowly defeated Chamisa, 50.7 percent to 44.3 percent. In response, Mnangagwa tweeted, "This is a new beginning. Let us join hands, in peace, unity & love, & together build a new Zimbabwe for all!" The MDC Alliance rejected the results and alleged widespread irregularities in the vote tally, as well as voter suppression. According to the MDC, 21 percent of official result forms were not posted at the corresponding polling station as required by law. Chamisa again claimed victory. "We won but they declared the opposite. You voted but they cheated. Over 2.5 ml votes can't be ignored. We're doing all to secure your vote & defend your WILL. Change is coming!" he wrote on Twitter.

## ELECTION OUTCOME CHALLENGED

The European Union and United States sent representatives to monitor the vote, marking the first time in sixteen years that outside observers were allowed into the country during an election. In a statement, the European Union noted that it found concerns related to "intimidation of voters, [the electoral commission's] lack of transparency in preparations, media bias, and some problems around polling stations on election day." The International Republican Institute and the National Democratic Institute, two U.S. election observer groups, also found "numerous incidents of food and agricultural assistance and extreme media bias" that favored Mnangagwa.

On August 10, the MDC Alliance filed a challenge with the Constitutional Court, alleging that the election was marred by "mammoth theft and fraud" and that Mnangagwa was incorrectly declared the victor. The MDC Alliance stated that 40,000 more presidential ballots were cast than parliamentary ones, which they found highly suspicious considering Mnangagwa avoided a runoff by only 30,000 votes. The court was given fourteen days to reach a decision. The court issued its unanimous verdict on August 24, upholding the ZEC results. Chief Justice Luke Malaba called the MDC Alliance claims "bold and unsubstantiated." He added that the most accurate evidence in the case would be the votes themselves but that the MDC had not requested a recount. While stating that they would respect the court's decision, the MDC Alliance vowed to "doggedly pursue all constitutionally permissible avenues to ensure that the sovereign will of the people is protected and guaranteed."

Mnangagwa's inauguration was delayed until August 27 to allow the Constitutional Court to review the challenge to the ZEC results. At his inauguration, Mnangagwa promised his government would serve the will of the people, and he vowed to root out corruption wherever it existed. He also asked that the nation, including those who opposed his candidacy, come together for the good of Zimbabwe. "I exhort us to commit ourselves to collectively develop our motherland. We are all Zimbabweans; what unites us is greater than what could ever divide us."

—Heather Kerrigan

*Following is a tweet from Emmerson Mnangagwa on August 2, 2018, announcing his victory as president of Zimbabwe; an August 3, 2018, tweet from Nelson Chamisa alleging the vote outcome was incorrect; and a press release from the Office of the President of Zimbabwe, released on August 27, 2018, upon Mnangagwa's inauguration.*

DOCUMENT  *Mnangagwa Declares Victory*

**August 2, 2018**

Thank you Zimbabwe!
I am humbled to be elected President of the Second Republic of Zimbabwe.
Though we may have been divided at the polls, we are united in our dreams.
This is a new beginning. Let us join hands, in peace, unity & love, & together build a new Zimbabwe for all!

SOURCE: President of Zimbabwe (@edmnangagwa). Twitter post. August 2, 2018. https://twitter .com/edmnangagwa/status/1025155847691952129?ref_src=twsrc%5Etfw%7Ctwcamp%5Etweetembe d%7Ctwterm%5E1025155847691952129&ref_url=https%3A%2F%2Fwww.theguardian.com%2Fwor ld%2F2018%2Faug%2F02%2Fmnangagwas-zanu-pf-on-track-to-pull-off-narrow-win-in-zimbabwe-election.

## *Chamisa Alleges Vote Rigging*

**August 3, 2018**

I'm aware of your anxieties, concerns and worries. Your hopes & aspirations I so dearly carry. We won but they declared the opposite. You voted but they cheated. Over 2.5 ml votes can't be ignored. We're doing all to secure your vote & defend your WILL. Change is coming! #Godisinit

SOURCE: Nelson Chamisa (@nelsonchamisa). Twitter post. August 3, 2018. https://twitter.com/nelson chamisa/status/1025614028444459008.

## *Mnangagwa Inaugurated President of Zimbabwe*

**August 27, 2018**

President Mnangagwa was yesterday sworn in as the third President of the Republic of Zimbabwe and Second Executive President since the Constitutional amendments of 1987. Mr Canaan Banana was the first ceremonial President from 1980 until 1987 when former President, Mr Robert Mugabe took over as the first Executive President after the Constitution was amended.

Taking oath of office, President Mnangagwa promised a new Zimbabwe in the Second Republic underpinned by servant leadership where corruption and unnecessary bureaucracy in service delivery will not be tolerated.

The Second Republic was born yesterday following President Mnangagwa's inauguration as the Second Executive President of Zimbabwe at the National Sports Stadium in Harare.

In the new Zimbabwe, he said, all citizens will be equal before the law and prosecution of corrupt cases will be done without fear or favour.

Addressing a bumper crowd at the giant National Sports Stadium, President Mnangagwa said those appointed to serve in public offices should also adopt his servant leadership approach to transform the country.

"I am your listening President, a servant leader," President Mnangagwa said.

"In this vein, those who will occupy public office at any level, under my Government will be required to exercise servant leadership in the execution of their duties and to be humble and responsive in their interactions and dealings with the citizenry.

"Equally, the bureaucracy in the Second Republic will be expected to be development oriented, responsive to the people's needs as well as exhibit high principles of professional ethics and integrity.

"My administration will therefore expect public sector officials to deliver quality and timely services to the people as well as facilitate business, trade and investment. Bureaucratic bottlenecks, unnecessary delays, lethargic and corrupt activities will not be tolerated.

"We must as a society encourage and inculcate the culture of hard honest work. The prosecution of perpetrators of corruption will be carried out without fear or favour. In the Second Republic, no person or entity will be allowed to steal, loot or pocket that which belongs to the people of Zimbabwe. No one is above the law. This is a New Zimbabwe, the Zimbabwe we all want."

President Mnangagwa continued: "As per our pledge during the campaign trail, my Government will be implementing the Constitutional provisions with regards the devolution of Government powers and responsibilities. Provinces will now be expected to plan and grow their provincial economies.

"Economic development at every level is the ultimate goal. I therefore challenge local authorities in the Second Republic, to be the engines of local economic development and growth. My Government will not stand by and watch people suffer due to dereliction of duty, corruption or incompetence within our local authorities.

"It will not be easy, but as the Holy Bible teaches us: 'For you have need of endurance, so that when you have done the will of God, you may receive what was promised.'

"We have indeed endured; we have toiled; and now as we walk in unity the path that lies ahead, we will reap a better and more prosperous future.

"As I have repeatedly said in the past months, real change does not happen overnight. However, inspired by our national anthem, we must work together, nothing is beyond our reach. With love and unity, we will reach the Promised Land, we will build the Zimbabwe we all want, brick upon brick, stone upon stone."

President Mnangagwa said he was humbled by the confidence reposed in him by the people of Zimbabwe and would do everything in his capacity to bring positive change in the country.

"I am emboldened and inspired by your collective hopes, dreams and desires; and the trust reposed in me. I will work tirelessly, as a servant leader, to improve the quality of life for all of us," he said.

"To all my colleagues and other political parties who contested in the just ended harmonised elections, especially those represented in Parliament, I exhort us to commit ourselves to collectively develop our motherland. We are all Zimbabweans; what unites us is greater than what could ever divide us.

"Let me assure you that tomorrow is brighter! Let us look forward to the journey ahead, a journey we will walk together as one people, a united people. A journey of development, progress and prosperity in our New Zimbabwe. Together, let us explore new frontiers in every facet and sphere of our economy and society. Let us endeavour to climb new heights. Let us arise and shine, for indeed our light has surely come."

SOURCE: President and Cabinet of Zimbabwe. "ED Promises a New Zimbabwe." August 27, 2018. http://www.theopc.gov.zw/index.php/326-ed-promises-a-new-zimbabwe.

## OTHER HISTORIC DOCUMENTS OF INTEREST

**FROM PREVIOUS *HISTORIC DOCUMENTS***

# Cohen, Manafort Reach Plea Agreements in Special Counsel Probe

AUGUST 21, SEPTEMBER 14, AND
NOVEMBER 26 AND 29, 2018

In May 2017, the Department of Justice announced that it would appoint a special counsel to investigate possible links between the campaign of President Donald Trump and members of the Russian government. Despite various attempts to undermine the investigation, by the close of 2018, the probe led by Special Counsel Robert Mueller had resulted in charges against at least thirty-two individuals and three companies. Five of those individuals were either Trump campaign officials or close confidantes of the president. This included Trump's personal lawyer, Michael Cohen, who pled guilty to nine counts, including campaign finance fraud, tax evasion, and lying to Congress, and Trump's former campaign manager, Paul Manafort, who was convicted by a jury for crimes the Mueller team uncovered in 2017.

## Cohen Pleads Guilty to Eight Charges

Cohen, Trump's longtime personal lawyer, was caught up in the Mueller probe in April 2018 when the Federal Bureau of Investigation (FBI) raided Cohen's hotel room and office, seizing business records and emails. Cohen first joined the Trump organization in 2006, after formerly serving as a personal injury lawyer and taxi fleet manager. Cohen also served as co-president of Trump Entertainment, served on the board of the Eric Trump Foundation, and for a short time was deputy finance chair of the Republican National Committee. Cohen was frequently referred to in the media as Trump's "fixer" and was known as one of the president's closest advisers.

According to Cohen's lawyer, Stephen Ryan, the FBI raid and seizure of communications between Cohen and his clients was related to a referral made by Special Counsel Mueller's office to the U.S. Attorney's Office for the Southern District of New York. The raid was carried out as part of an investigation into possible bank and tax fraud. The raid also sought information on alleged campaign finance violations related to a possible $130,000 hush-money payment made to adult film actress Stephanie Clifford, commonly referred to by her stage name, Stormy Daniels, and a $150,000 payment to *Playboy* model Karen McDougal. Those two payments were reportedly made on behalf of then-candidate Donald Trump, with whom the women said they had past affairs. Ryan called the raid, which was conducted without prior warning, "completely inappropriate and unnecessary," and noted that Cohen had already provided thousands of documents to members of Congress who were conducting their own investigation into possible links between the Trump campaign and the Russian government. President Trump called the raid "a disgraceful situation" and "a total witch hunt."

Following the raid on Cohen's home and office, the judge presiding over the case, Kimba Wood, appointed Barbara S. Jones as special master to determine which of the nearly four million files contained content protected by attorney–client privilege. Jones was not directed to individually review every document but rather only those that lawyers representing Cohen and Trump had deemed privileged. On June 4, Jones submitted a report indicating that most of the material seized was not protected and could be used by federal prosecutors.

On August 21, Cohen surrendered to the FBI and was charged in federal court with eight counts: five counts related to tax evasion, one count of making false statements to a bank, one count of causing an unlawful corporate contribution, and one count of an excessive campaign contribution. While the tax evasion and bank fraud charges were related to Cohen's taxi medallion and real estate entities, the other two were tied to Cohen's work with then-candidate Trump. The campaign finance violation and unlawful corporate contribution stemmed from the payments made to Clifford and McDougal. By law, campaign expenditures coordinated with a candidate or the candidate's committee are limited to $2,700 per election cycle. Further, federal law indicates that money spent to protect a candidate's political changes could be considered a campaign contribution and therefore subject to federal reporting requirements and spending caps. According to the charges, Cohen had "in coordination and at the direction of a candidate for federal office" made the $150,000 payment "for the principal purpose of influencing an election," while the $130,000 payment was deemed an excessive campaign contribution done at the direction of that candidate for office. In court, Cohen said that $130,000 "was later repaid to me by the candidate."

President Trump was not named in the court filing, but it does reference "Individual-1" who had become president of the United States by January 2017. Cohen also did not refer to Trump by name in court, although after the guilty plea was made, Cohen's lawyer, Lanny Davis, said, "Donald Trump directed [Cohen] to commit a crime by making payments to two women for the principal purpose of influencing an election." Trump's lawyer, Rudy Giuliani, said the charges against Cohen did not make any "allegation of wrongdoing against the President," adding, "It is clear that, as the prosecutor noted, Mr. Cohen's actions reflect a pattern of lies and dishonesty over a significant period of time."

Cohen pled guilty to all charges levied against him and was released on a $500,000 bond and scheduled for sentencing on December 12. The charges to which Cohen pled guilty had a maximum penalty of sixty-five years in prison; however, because of the plea deal Cohen reached with investigators, the maximum was lowered to five.

## MANAFORT CONVICTED ON EIGHT COUNTS

On the same day Cohen pled guilty, Trump's former campaign chair, Paul Manafort, was convicted in Virginia on bank and tax fraud charges. On October 30, 2017, Manafort and his business partner, Rick Gates, became the first individuals charged under the Mueller investigation. Charges against the pair included money laundering, false statements to the Justice Department, failure to register as a foreign agent under the Foreign Agent Registration Act, failure to file reports regarding foreign bank and financial accounts, and acts of conspiracy against the United States. The charges alleged, in part, that from 2006 through at least 2015, Manafort and Gates conducted lobbying for a pro-Russian political party in Ukraine headed by an individual with ties to Russian President Vladimir Putin. The millions earned from these efforts were hidden from U.S. authorities through money laundering. The pair is also said to have knowingly lied to the Justice Department about their lobbying activities. At the time of the indictment, White House Press Secretary Sarah

Huckabee Sanders said the charges supported what the president had said "from day one. There's been no evidence of Trump–Russia collusion, and nothing in the indictment today changes that at all." Indeed, the charges did not amount to collusion and were largely tangential to the primary purpose of Mueller's investigation, but the media speculated that they were intended to put pressure on other members of Trump's orbit.

While Gates agreed to a plea bargain in February 2018, Manafort chose to go to trial. His trial on the eighteen criminal counts Mueller filed against him began on July 31, 2018. Prosecutors used the time to paint a picture of Manafort as a dishonest and ruthless political operative. Manafort, prosecutors said, offered those connected to the Russian government access to the Trump campaign in exchange for funds to help pay off the massive debts Manafort had incurred through his opulent lifestyle. According to prosecutors, before he was asked to leave the campaign in August 2016, Manafort organized a meeting at Trump Tower in New York with Russian nationals who promised they had damaging information on Democratic presidential candidate Hillary Clinton. Although there was no direct discussion in court about Russian attempts to influence the election, the prosecution sought to make clear that Manafort was a man desperate to shore up his financial situation and that he would do it through any means possible. During the trial, Gates testified against Manafort, providing information on how he helped the accused hide his foreign earnings from the United States. Gates also admitted that he stole money from Manafort. According to the *New York Times*, Gates told friends he found it unfair that he was paid $240,000 per year when Manafort was earning tens of millions of dollars. This led the defense, which called no witnesses of its own, to focus its time on casting Gates as a habitual liar who was the mastermind behind Manafort's alleged crimes.

After just over a week of trial, the jury went into deliberations. Prosecutors considered the case an easy win, but the jury made two significant requests of Judge T. S. Ellis III that called into question whether the highly technical testimony presented in the case overshadowed some of what the prosecution saw as straightforward allegations. The jury asked Judge Ellis to define the phrase "beyond a reasonable doubt" and also asked what to do if they could not "come to a consensus on a single count." After four days of deliberation, the jury reached a conclusion, announcing that they had deadlocked on ten charges and were only able to convict Manafort on eight felony counts. Five of the guilty counts were tax fraud charges from 2010 through 2014 for filing false returns, one count was for failure to file a foreign banking and financial record in 2012, and the remaining two were for bank fraud charges related to loans Manafort took out in 2015 and 2016. The other ten counts, including three counts of not filing a disclosure of a foreign bank account and seven counts of committing or conspiring to commit bank fraud, were declared a mistrial. The judge set a deadline of August 29 for the prosecution to decide whether to retry Manafort on those ten counts.

After the verdict, President Trump expressed sympathy for his former campaign chair. "I feel very badly for Paul Manafort and his wonderful family. 'Justice' took a 12 year old tax case, among other things, applied tremendous pressure on him and, unlike Michael Cohen, he refused to "break"—make up stories in order to get a 'deal.' Such respect for a brave man!" the president tweeted. He went on to add that Manafort was a "good man" who had been subject to Mueller's "witch hunt" despite having spent years doing excellent work for people like Ronald Reagan. Manafort's lawyer said his client was "disappointed at not getting acquittals all the way through, or a complete hung jury on all counts. However, he would like to thank Judge Ellis for granting him a fair trial, thank the jury for their very long and hard-fought deliberations. He is evaluating all of his options at this point." The judge set a date for a sentencing hearing for February 8, 2019; that date was later canceled pending the outcome of a separate dispute with the Mueller team. Manafort faced up to eighty years in prison for the counts on which he was found guilty.

## MANAFORT VIOLATES PLEA AGREEMENT

Manafort faced a second trial in neighboring Washington, D.C., in September on charges of money laundering, witness tampering, and failure to register as a foreign agent. Notably, neither the Washington nor the Virginia cases was a direct link between Mueller's primary focus to determine whether there was a link between the Trump campaign and the Russian government, although Mueller's mandate did allow him to refer for prosecution other crimes discovered in the course of his investigation. Ahead of the start of the September trial, Manafort reached a deal with the government and agreed to plead guilty to conspiracy to defraud the United States and witness tampering. Manafort also pled guilty to the remaining counts against him, including the ten declared a mistrial in the Virginia case. According to the agreement, as long as Manafort sufficiently cooperated with investigators, those charges would be dropped and no further charges would be filed related to Manafort's alleged participation in criminal activity related to the case.

On November 26, Mueller submitted a status report related to the plea agreement, in which he noted, "After signing the plea agreement, Manafort committed federal crimes by lying to the Federal Bureau of Investigation and the Special Counsel's Office on a variety of subject matters, which constitute breaches of the agreement." The court documents added, "As the defendant has breached the plea agreement, there is no reason to delay his sentencing." Mueller's office did not indicate what Manafort had lied about, and Manafort's lawyers said he had "provided truthful information." The Mueller team went on to submit 800 heavily redacted pages of evidence to support their claims. In some instances, media outlets that obtained the redacted documents were able to easily remove the redaction and learned that the Mueller team believed Manafort lied about sharing Trump campaign polling data with someone linked to Russian intelligence services, as well as lied about a payment he received from someone accused of being a Russian intelligence operative.

In late November, U.S. District Judge Amy Berman Jackson stated that she needed to rule on whether Manafort was in violation of the plea deal he struck with Mueller's team before he could be sentenced in the Washington case. In January 2019, Judge Jackson set a date of February 4 to decide whether Manafort violated the plea agreement. That hearing would be sealed. Mueller's team said that while they did not intend to pursue additional charges against Manafort for lying to investigators, they did believe that Manafort should not receive credit during his sentencing for agreeing to cooperate with the Mueller team. Judge Jackson ultimately ruled on February 13 that Manafort had intentionally violated the terms of his plea agreement.

## COHEN PLEADS GUILTY TO LYING TO CONGRESS

Cohen, who had been cooperating for months with federal investigators in New York as well as with the Mueller team, in November found himself subject to additional charges, this time for lying to Congress about negotiations to build a Trump hotel in Russia. The charges stemmed from a letter sent by Cohen to the House and Senate Intelligence Committees on August 28, 2017, indicating that negotiations for a possible hotel in Moscow ended in January 2016. However, according to federal prosecutors, planning for the hotel continued much longer and extended into Trump's campaign for president. Prosecutors said Cohen lied to "minimize links between the Moscow Project and Individual 1 and give the false impression that the Moscow Project ended before the Iowa caucus and the very first primary in hopes of limiting the ongoing Russia investigations." The court filing stated, "As late as approximately June 2016, Cohen . . . discussed the status and progress of the Moscow Project with Individual 1 on more than three occasions."

Cohen's lawyer tweeted that the plea deal "reaffirmed what he said last July 2 and told me many times since—that he decided to put his wife, daughter, son and country first. Today he again told the truth and nothing but the truth. @realDonaldTrump called him a liar. Who do you believe?" Trump again asserted that he had "nothing to do with Russia." He added, "I don't have any jobs in Russia. I'm all over the world, but we're not involved in Russia." The president called Cohen "a weak person and not a very smart person" and said that it was inconsequential whether the dates of the ongoing conversations were right or wrong "because I was allowed to do whatever I wanted during the campaign. I was running my business."

Cohen accepted another plea agreement with Mueller's team and pled guilty to the charge of lying to Congress. At his sentencing hearing for the nine total charges against him (those filed in August along with lying to Congress), Cohen said he took "full responsibility for each act that I pled guilty to: The personal ones to me and those involving the president of the United States of America." He added, "Recently, the president tweeted a statement calling me weak and it was correct but for a much different reason than he was implying. It was because time and time again I felt it was my duty to cover up his dirty deeds." Cohen was sentenced to three years in prison for the first eight charges and three months for lying to Congress, along with a fine, restitution, and forfeiture amounting to nearly $2 million. Cohen was given until March 6, 2019, to report to prison.

On January 18, 2019, *BuzzFeed News* released a report claiming that Trump directed Cohen to lie to Congress and that the Mueller investigation had knowledge of the situation. In a rare response to the press, Mueller's office rejected the allegations in the article. The statement from the special counsel's office said only, "BuzzFeed's description of specific statements to the special counsel's office, and characterization of documents and testimony obtained by this office, regarding Michael Cohen's congressional testimony are not accurate." *BuzzFeed News*, however, stood by its story.

That same month, Cohen agreed to testify at a public hearing before the House Oversight and Reform Committee on February 7 to give a full account of his work with Trump. Cohen quickly rescinded his agreement to appear, citing threats by President Trump and his associates against Cohen's family. On January 24, the Senate Intelligence Committee subpoenaed Cohen to appear at a private hearing on February 12, 2019.

—Heather Kerrigan

*Following is an August 21, 2018, release from the Department of Justice, announcing Michael Cohen's intent to enter a guilty plea on charges including tax evasion and campaign finance violations; a plea deal filed on September 14, 2018, by Paul Manafort related to charges brought by Special Counsel Robert Mueller; a report filed by Mueller's office on November 26, 2018, indicating that Manafort failed to comply with the terms of his plea agreement; and a November 29, 2018, plea agreement offered to Cohen for lying to Congress.*

# Cohen Pleads Guilty to Tax Evasion and Campaign Finance Violations

**August 21, 2018**

## Plea Follows Filing of Eight Count Criminal Information Alleging Concealment of More Than $4 Million in Unreported Income, $280,000 in Unlawful Campaign Contributions

Robert Khuzami, Attorney for the United States, Acting Under Authority Conferred by 28 U.S.C. § 515, William F. Sweeney Jr., the Assistant Director-in-Charge of the New York Field Office of the Federal Bureau of Investigation ("FBI"), and James D. Robnett, the Special Agent-in-Charge of the New York Field Office of the Internal Revenue Service, Criminal Investigation ("IRS-CI"), announced today the guilty plea of MICHAEL COHEN to charges of tax evasion, making false statements to a federally-insured bank, and campaign finance violations. The plea was entered followed the filing of an eight-count criminal information, which alleged that COHEN concealed more than $4 million in personal income from the IRS, made false statements to a federally-insured financial institution in connection with a $500,000 home equity loan, and, in 2016, caused $280,000 in payments to be made to silence two women who otherwise planned to speak publicly about their alleged affairs with a presidential candidate, thereby intending to influence the 2016 presidential election. COHEN pled guilty today before U.S. District Judge William H. Pauley III.

Attorney for the United States Robert Khuzami said: "Michael Cohen is a lawyer who, rather than setting an example of respect for the law, instead chose to break the law, repeatedly over many years and in a variety of ways. His day of reckoning serves as a reminder that we are a nation of laws, with one set of rules that applies equally to everyone."

FBI Assistant Director-in-Charge William F. Sweeney Jr. said: "This investigation uncovered crimes of fraud, deception and evasion, conducted through a string of financial transactions that were carefully constructed and concealed to protect a variety of interests. But as we all know, the truth can only remain hidden for so long before the FBI brings it to light. We are all expected to follow the rule of law, and the public expects us—the FBI— to enforce the law equally. Today, Mr. Cohen has been reminded of this important lesson, as he acknowledged with his guilty plea."

IRS-CI Special Agent-in-Charge James D. Robnett said: "Today's guilty plea exemplifies IRS Special Agents' rigorous pursuit of tax evasion and sends the clear message that the tax laws apply to everybody. Mr. Cohen's greed to hide his income from the IRS cheats all the honest taxpayers, and we should not expect law abiding citizens to foot the bill for those who circumvent the system to evade paying their fair share."

According to the allegations in the Information unsealed today as well as statements made in Manhattan federal court:

From 2007 through January 2017, COHEN was an attorney and employee of a Manhattan-based real estate company (the "Company"). COHEN held the title of "Executive Vice President" and "Special Counsel" to the owner of the Company ("Individual-1"). In January 2017, COHEN left the Company and began holding himself out as the "personal attorney" to Individual-1, who by that time had become the President of the United States.

In addition to working for and earning income from the Organization, at all times relevant to this Information, COHEN owned taxi medallions in New York City and Chicago worth millions of dollars. COHEN owned these taxi medallions as investments and leased the medallions to operators who paid COHEN a portion of the operating income.

### The Tax Evasion Scheme

In late 2013, COHEN retained an accountant ("Accountant-1") for the purpose of handling COHEN's personal and entity tax returns. After being retained, Accountant-1 filed amended 2011 and 2012 Form 1040 tax returns with the Internal Revenue Service ("IRS"). For tax years 2013 through 2016, Accountant-1 prepared individual returns for COHEN and returns for COHEN's medallion and real estate entities. To confirm he had reviewed and approved these returns, both COHEN and his wife signed a Form 8879 for tax years 2013 through 2016, and filed manually for tax year 2012. Between 2012 and the end of 2016, COHEN earned more than $2.4 million in income from a series of personal loans made by COHEN to a taxi operator to whom COHEN leased certain of his Chicago taxi medallions ("Taxi Operator-1"), none of which he disclosed to the IRS.

As a further part of the scheme to evade paying income taxes, COHEN also concealed more than $1.3 million in income he received from another taxi operator to whom COHEN leased certain of his New York medallions ("Taxi Operator-2"). This income took two forms. First, COHEN did not report the substantial majority of a bonus payment of at least $870,000, which was made by Taxi Operator-2 in 2012 to induce COHEN to allow Taxi Operator-2 to operate certain of COHEN's medallions. Second, between 2012 and 2016, COHEN concealed nearly $1 million in taxable income he received from Taxi Operator-2's operation of certain of COHEN's taxi medallions.

To ensure the concealment of this additional operator income, COHEN arranged to receive a portion of the medallion income personally, as opposed to having the income paid to COHEN's medallion entities. Paying the medallion entities would have alerted Accountant-1, who prepared the returns for those entities, to the existence of the income such that it would have been included on COHEN's tax returns.

As a further part of his scheme to evade taxes, COHEN also hid the following additional sources of income from Accountant-1 and the IRS:

- A $100,000 payment received, in 2014, for brokering the sale of a piece of property in a private aviation community in Ocala, Florida.

- Approximately $30,000 in profit made, in 2014, for brokering the sale of a Birkin Bag, a highly coveted French handbag that retails for between $11,900 to $300,000, depending on the type of leather or animal skin used.

- More than $200,000 in consulting income earned in 2016 from an assisted living company purportedly for COHEN's "consulting" on real estate and other projects.

In total, COHEN failed to report more than $4 million in income, resulting in the avoidance of taxes of more than $1.4 million due to the IRS.

### False Statements to a Bank

In 2010, COHEN, through companies he controlled, executed a $6.4 million promissory note with a bank ("Bank-1"), collateralized by COHEN's taxi medallions and personally guaranteed by COHEN. A year later, in 2011, COHEN personally obtained a $6 million line of credit from Bank-1 (the "Line of Credit"), also collateralized by his taxi medallions. By February 2013, COHEN had increased the Line of Credit from $6 million to $14 million, thereby increasing COHEN's personal medallion liabilities at Bank-1 to more than $20 million.

In November 2014, COHEN refinanced his medallion debt at Bank-1 with another bank ("Bank-2"), who shared the debt with a New York-based credit union (the "Credit Union"). The transaction was structured as a package of individual loans to the entities that owned COHEN's New York medallions. Following the loans' closing, COHEN's medallion debt at Bank-1 was paid off with funds from Bank-2 and the Credit Union, and the Line of Credit with Bank-1 was closed.

In 2013, in connection with a successful application for a mortgage from another Bank ("Bank-3") for his Park Avenue condominium (the "2013 Application"), COHEN disclosed only the $6.4 million medallion loan he had with Bank-1 at the time. As noted above, COHEN also had a larger, $14 million Line of Credit with Bank-1 secured by his medallions, which COHEN did not disclose in the 2013 Application.

In February 2015, COHEN, in an attempt to secure financing from Bank-3 to purchase a summer home for approximately $8.5 million, again concealed the $14 million Line of Credit. Specifically, in connection with this proposed transaction, Bank-3 obtained a 2014 personal financial statement COHEN had provided to Bank-2 while refinancing his medallion debt. Bank-3 questioned COHEN about the $14 million Line of Credit reflected on that personal financial statement, because COHEN had omitted that debt from the 2013 Application to Bank-3. COHEN misled Bank-3, stating, in writing, that the $14 million Line of Credit was undrawn and that he would close it. In truth and in fact, COHEN had effectively overdrawn the Line of Credit, having swapped it out for a fully drawn, larger loan shared by Bank-2 and the Credit Union upon refinancing his medallion debt. When Bank-3 informed COHEN that it would only provide financing if COHEN closed the Line of Credit, COHEN lied again, misleadingly stating in an email: "The medallion line was closed in the middle of November 2014."

In December 2015, COHEN contacted Bank-3 to apply for a home equity line of credit ("HELOC"). In so doing, COHEN again significantly understated his medallion debt. Specifically, in the HELOC application, COHEN, together with his wife, represented a positive net worth of more than $40 million, again omitting the $14 million in medallion debt with Bank-2 and the Credit Union. Because COHEN had previously confirmed in writing to Bank-3 that the $14 million Line of Credit had been closed, Bank-3 had no reason to question COHEN about the omission of this liability on the HELOC application. In addition, in seeking the HELOC, COHEN substantially and materially understated his monthly expenses to Bank-3 by omitting at least $70,000 in monthly interest payments due to Bank-2 on the true amount of his medallion debt.

In April 2016, Bank-3 approved COHEN for a $500,000 HELOC. By fraudulently concealing truthful information about his financial condition, COHEN obtained a HELOC that Bank-3 would otherwise not have approved.

## Campaign Finance Violations

The Federal Election Campaign Act of 1971, as amended, Title 52, United States Code, Section 30101, et seq., (the "Election Act"), regulates the influence of money on politics. At all relevant times, the Election Act set certain limitations and prohibitions, among them: (a) individual contributions to any presidential candidate, including expenditures coordinated with a candidate or his political committee, were limited to $2,700 per election, and presidential candidates and their committees were prohibited from accepting contributions from individuals in excess of this limit; and (b) Corporations were prohibited from making contributions directly to presidential candidates, including expenditures coordinated with candidates or their committees, and candidates were prohibited from accepting corporate contributions.

On June 16, 2015, Individual-1 began his presidential campaign. While COHEN continued to work at the Company and did not have a formal title with the campaign, he had a campaign email address and, at various times, advised the campaign, including on matters of interest to the press, and made televised and media appearances on behalf of the campaign.

In August 2015, the Chairman and Chief Executive of Corporation-1, a media company that owns, among other things, a popular tabloid magazine ("Chairman-1" and "Magazine-1," respectively"), in coordination with COHEN and one or more members of the campaign, offered to help deal with negative stories about Individual-1's relationships with women by, among other things, assisting the campaign in identifying such stories so they could be purchased and their publication avoided. Chairman-1 agreed to keep COHEN apprised of any such negative stories.

Consistent with the agreement described above, Corporation-1 advised COHEN of negative stories during the course of the campaign, and COHEN, with the assistance of Corporation-1, was able to arrange for the purchase of two stories so as to suppress them and prevent them from influencing the election.

First, in June 2016, a model and actress ("Woman-1") began attempting to sell her story of her alleged extramarital affair with Individual-1 that had taken place in 2006 and 2007, knowing the story would be of considerable value because of the election. Woman-1 retained an attorney ("Attorney-1"), who in turn contacted the editor-in-chief of Magazine-1 ("Editor-1"), and offered to sell Woman-1's story to Magazine-1. Chairman-1 and Editor-1 informed COHEN of the story. At COHEN's urging and subject to COHEN's promise that Corporation-1 would be reimbursed, Editor-1 ultimately began negotiating for the purchase of the story.

On August 5, 2016, Corporation-1 entered into an agreement with Woman-1 to acquire her "limited life rights" to the story of her relationship with "any then-married man," in exchange for $150,000 and a commitment to feature her on two magazine covers and publish more than 100 magazine articles authored by her. Despite the cover and article features to the agreement, its principal purpose, as understood by those involved, including COHEN, was to suppress Woman-1's story so as to prevent it from influencing the election.

Between late August 2016 and September 2016, COHEN agreed with Chairman-1 to assign the rights to the non-disclosure portion of Corporation-1's agreement with Woman-1 to COHEN for $125,000. COHEN incorporated a shell entity called "Resolution Consultants LLC" for use in the transaction. Both Chairman-1 and COHEN ultimately signed the agreement, and a consultant for Corporation-1, using his own shell entity, provided COHEN with an invoice for the payment of $125,000. However, in early October 2016, after the assignment agreement was signed but before COHEN had paid the $125,000, Chairman-1 contacted COHEN and told him, in substance, that the deal was off and that COHEN should tear up the assignment agreement.

Second, on October 8, 2016, an agent for an adult film actress ("Woman-2") informed Editor-1 that Woman-2 was willing to make public statements and confirm on the record her alleged past affair with Individual-1. Chairman-1 and Editor-1 then contacted COHEN and put him in touch with Attorney-1, who was also representing Woman-2. Over the course of the next few days, COHEN negotiated a $130,000 agreement with Attorney-1 to himself purchase Woman-2's silence, and received a signed confidential settlement agreement and a separate side letter agreement from Attorney-1.

COHEN did not immediately execute the agreement, nor did he pay Woman-2. On the evening of October 25, 2016, with no deal with Woman-2 finalized, Attorney-1 told Editor-1 that Woman-2 was close to completing a deal with another outlet to make her story public. Editor-1, in turn, texted COHEN that "[w]e have to coordinate something on the matter [Attorney-1 is] calling you about or it could look awfully bad for everyone." Chairman-1 and Editor-1 then called COHEN through an encrypted telephone application. COHEN agreed to make the payment, and then called Attorney-1 to finalize the deal.

The next day, on October 26, 2016, COHEN emailed an incorporating service to obtain the corporate formation documents for another shell corporation, Essential Consultants LLC, which COHEN had incorporated a few days prior. Later that afternoon, COHEN drew down $131,000 from the fraudulently obtained HELOC and requested that it be deposited into a bank account COHEN had just opened in the name of Essential Consultants. The next morning, on October 27, 2016, COHEN went to Bank-3 and wired approximately $130,000 from Essential Consultants to Attorney-1. On the bank form to complete the wire, COHEN falsely indicated that the "purpose of wire being sent" was "retainer." On November 1, 2016, COHEN received from Attorney-1 copies of the final, signed confidential settlement agreement and side letter agreement.

COHEN caused and made the payments described herein in order to influence the 2016 presidential election. In so doing, he coordinated with one or more members of the campaign, including through meetings and phone calls, about the fact, nature, and timing of the payments. As a result of the payments solicited and made by COHEN, neither Woman-1 nor Woman-2 spoke to the press prior to the election.

In January 2017, COHEN in seeking reimbursement for election-related expenses, presented executives of the Company with a copy of a bank statement from the Essential Consultants bank account, which reflected the $130,000 payment COHEN had made to the bank account of Attorney-1 in order to keep Woman-2 silent in advance of the election, plus a $35 wire fee, adding, in handwriting, an additional "$50,000." The $50,000 represented a claimed payment for "tech services," which in fact related to work COHEN had solicited from a technology company during and in connection with the campaign. COHEN added these amounts to a sum of $180,035. After receiving this document, executives of the Company "grossed up" for tax purposes COHEN's requested reimbursement of $180,000 to $360,000, and then added a bonus of $60,000 so that COHEN would be paid $420,000 in total. Executives of the Company also determined that the $420,000 would be paid to COHEN in monthly amounts of $35,000 over the course of 12 months, and that COHEN should send invoices for these payments.

On February 14, 2017, COHEN sent an executive of the Company ("Executive-1") the first of his monthly invoices, requesting "[p]ursuant to [a] retainer agreement, . . . payment for services rendered for the months of January and February, 2017." The invoice listed $35,000 for each of those two months. Executive-1 forwarded the invoice to another executive of the Company ("Executive-2") the same day by email, and it was approved.

Executive-1 forwarded that email to another employee at the Company, stating: "Please pay from the Trust. Post to legal expenses. Put 'retainer for the months of January and February 2017' in the description."

Throughout 2017, COHEN sent to one or more representatives of the Company monthly invoices, which stated, "Pursuant to the retainer agreement, kindly remit payment for services rendered for" the relevant month in 2017, and sought $35,000 per month. The Company accounted for these payments as legal expenses. In truth and in fact, there was no such retainer agreement, and the monthly invoices COHEN submitted were not in connection with any legal services he had provided in 2017.

During 2017, pursuant to the invoices described above, COHEN received monthly $35,000 reimbursement checks, totaling $420,000.

* * *

COHEN, 51, of NEW YORK, NEW YORK, pleaded guilty to five counts of willful tax evasion; one count of making false statements to a bank; one count of causing an unlawful campaign contribution; and one count of making an excessive campaign contribution.

COHEN'S sentencing is scheduled for December 12 at 11 a.m.

*[A chart identifying the charges and the maximum penalties has been omitted.]*

The maximum potential sentences in this case are prescribed by Congress and are provided here for informational purposes only, as any sentencings of the defendant will be determined by the judge.

Mr. Khuzami praised the work of the FBI, the IRS, and the Special Agents of the U.S. Attorney's Office.

This case is being handled by the Office's Public Corruption Unit. Assistant U.S. Attorneys Andrea M. Griswold, Rachel Maimin, Thomas McKay, and Nicolas Roos are in charge of the prosecution.

SOURCE: U.S. Department of Justice. "Michael Cohen Pleads Guilty in Manhattan Federal Court to Eight Counts, Including Criminal Tax Evasion and Campaign Finance Violations." August 21, 2018. https://www.justice.gov/usao-sdny/pr/michael-cohen-pleads-guilty-manhattan-federal-court-eight-counts-including-criminal-tax.

# Manafort Offered Plea Agreement

**September 14, 2018**

Re: United States v. Paul J. Manafort, Jr., Crim. No. 17-201-1 (ABJ)

Dear Counsel:

This letter sets forth the full and complete plea offer to your client Paul J. Manafort, Jr. (herein after referred to as "your client" or "defendant") from the Special Counsel's Office (hereinafter also referred to as "the Government" or "this Office"). If your client accepts the terms and conditions of this offer, please have your client execute this document in the space provided below. Upon receipt of the executed document, this letter will become the Plea Agreement (hereinafter referred to as the "Agreement"). The terms of the offer are as follows.

### 1.  Charges and Statutory Penalties

Your client agrees to plead guilty in the above-captioned case to all elements of all objects of all the charges in a Superseding Criminal Information, which will encompass the charges in Counts One and Two of a Superseding Criminal Information, charging your client with:

A.  conspiracy against the United States, in violation of 18 U.S.C. § 371 (which includes a conspiracy to: (a) money launder (in violation of 18 U.S.C. § 1956); (b) commit tax fraud (in violation of 26 U.S.C. § 7206(1)); (c) fail to file Foreign Bank Account Reports (in violation of 31 U.S.C. §§ 5314 and 5322(b)); (d) violate the Foreign Agents Registration Act (in violation of 22 U.S.C. §§ 612, 618(a)(1), and 618(a)(2)); and (e) to lie to the Department of Justice (in violation of 18 U.S.C. § 1001(a) and 22 U.S.C. §§ 612 and 618(a)(2)); and

B.  conspiracy against the United States, in violation of 18 U.S.C. § 371, to wit: conspiracy to obstruct justice by tampering with witnesses while on pre-trial release (in violation of 18 U.S.C. § 1512).

The defendant also agrees not to appeal any trial or pre-trial issue in the Eastern District of Virginia, or to challenge in the district court any such issue, and admits in the attacked "Statement of Offense" his guilt of the remaining counts against him in United States v. Paul J. Manafort, Jr., Crim. No. 1:18-cr-83 (TSE) (hereafter "Eastern District of Virginia.") A copy of the Superseding Criminal Information and Statement of Offense are attached.

Your client understands that each violation of 18 U.S.C. § 371 carries a maximum sentence of 5 years' imprisonment; a fine of not more than $250,000, pursuant to 18 U.S.C. § 3571(b)(3); a term of supervised release of not more than 3 years, pursuant to 18 U.S.C. § 3583(b)(2); and an obligation to pay any applicable interest or penalties on fines and restitution not timely made, and forfeiture. . . .

### 2.  Factual Stipulations

Your client agrees that the attached Statement of the Offense fairly and accurately describes and summarizes your client's actions and involvement in the offenses to which your client is pleading guilty, as well as crimes charged in the Eastern District of Virginia that remain outstanding, as well as additional acts taken by him. Please have your client sign and return the Statement of the Offense, along with this Agreement.

### 3.  Additional Charges

In consideration of your client's guilty plea to the above offenses, and upon the completion of full completion of full cooperation as described herein and fulfillment of all the other obligations herein, no additional criminal charges will be brought against the defendant for his heretofore disclosed participation in criminal activity, including money laundering, false statements, personal and corporate tax, and FBAR offenses, bank fraud, Foreign Agents Registration Act violations for his work in Ukraine, and obstruction of justice. In addition, subject to the terms of this Agreement, at the time of sentence or at the completion of his successful cooperation, whichever is later, the Government will move to dismiss the remaining counts of the Indictment in this matter and in the Eastern District of Virginia and your client waives venue as to such charges in the event he breaches this agreement. Your client also waives all rights under the Speedy Trial act as to any outstanding charges.

*[Sections detailing sentencing guidelines have been omitted.]*

### 7.   Court Not Bound by this Agreement or the Sentencing Guidelines

Your client understands that the sentence in this case will be imposed in accordance with 18 U.S.C. § 3553(a), upon consideration of the Sentencing Guidelines. Your client further understands that the sentence to be imposed is a matter solely within the discretion of the Courts. Your client acknowledges that the Courts are not obligated to follow any recommendation of the Government at the time of sentencing or to grant a downward departure based on your client's substantial assistance to the Government, even if the Government files a motion pursuant to Section 5K1.1 of the Sentencing Guidelines. Your client understands that neither the Government's recommendation nor the Sentencing Guidelines are binding on the Courts.

Your client acknowledges that your client's entry of a guilty plea to the charged offenses authorizes the Court to impose any sentence, up to and including the statutory maximum sentence, which may be greater than the applicable Guidelines range determined by the Court. Although the parties agree that the sentences there and in the Eastern District of Virginia should run concurrently to the extent there is factual overlap (i.e. the tax and foreign bank account charges), that recommendation is not binding on either Court. The Government cannot, and does not, make any promise or representation as to what sentences your client will receive. Moreover, your client acknowledges that your client will have no right to withdraw your client's plea of guilty should the Courts impose sentences that are outside the Guidelines range or if the Courts do not follow the Government's sentencing recommendation. The Government and your client will be bound by this Agreement, regardless of the sentence imposed by the Courts. Any effort by your client to withdraw the guilty plea because of the length of the sentence shall constitute a breach of this Agreement.

### 8.   Cooperation

Your client shall cooperate fully, truthfully, completely, and forthrightly with the Government and other law enforcement authorities identified by the Government in any and all matters as to which the Government deems the cooperation relevant. This cooperation will include, but is not limited to, the following:

(a)   The defendant agrees to be fully debriefed and to attend all meetings at which his presence is requested, concerning his participation in and knowledge of all criminal activities.

(b)   The defendant agrees to furnish to the Government all documents and other material that may be relevant to the investigation and that are in the defendant's possession or control and to participate in undercover activities pursuant to the specific instructions of law enforcement agents to the Government.

(c)   The defendant agrees to testify at any proceeding in the District of Colombia *[sic]* or elsewhere as requested by the Government.

(d) The defendant consents to adjournments of his sentences as requested by the Government.

(e) The defendant agrees that all of the defendant's obligations under this agreement continue after the defendant is sentenced here and in the Eastern District of Virginia; and

(f) The defendant must at all times give complete, truthful, and accurate information and testimony, and must not commit, or attempt to commit, any further crimes.

Your client acknowledges and understands that, during the course of the cooperation outlines in this Agreement, your client will be interviewed by law enforcement agents and/or Government attorneys. Your client waives any right to have counsel present during these interviews and agrees to meet with law enforcement agents and Government attorneys outside of the presence of counsel. If, at some future point, you or your client desire to have counsel present during interviews by law enforcement agents and/or Government attorneys, and you communicate this decision in writing to this Office, this Office will honor this request, and this change will have no effect on any other terms and conditions of this Agreement.

Your client shall testify fully, completely and truthfully before any and all Grand Juries in the District of Columbia and elsewhere, and at any and all trials of cases or other court proceedings in the District of Columbia and elsewhere, at which your client's testimony may be deemed relevant by the Government.

Your client understands and acknowledges that nothing in this Agreement allows your client to commit any criminal violation of local, state or federal law during the period of your client's cooperation with law enforcement authorities or at any time prior to the sentencing in this case. The commission of a criminal offense during the period of your client's cooperation or at any time prior to sentencing will constitute a breach of this Agreement and will relieve the Government of all of its obligations under this Agreement, including, but not limited to, its obligation to inform this Court of any assistance your client has provided. However, your client acknowledges and agrees that such a breach of this Agreement will not entitle your client to withdraw your client's plea of guilty or relieve your client of the obligations under this Agreement.

Your client agrees that the sentencing in this case and in the Eastern District of Virginia may be delayed until your client's efforts to cooperate have been completed, as determined by the Government, so that the Courts will have the benefit of all relevant information before a sentence is imposed.

## 9. Government's Obligations

The Government will bring to the Courts' attention at the time of sentencing the nature and extent of your client's cooperation or lack of cooperation. The Government will evaluate the full nature and extent of your client's cooperation to determine whether your client has provided substantial assistance in the investigation or prosecution of another person who has committed an offense. If this Office determines that the defendant has provided substantial assistance in the investigation or prosecution of another person who has committed an offense. If this Office determines the defendant has provided substantial assistance in the form of truthful information and, where applicable, testimony, the Office will file motions pursuant to Section 5K1.1 of the United States Sentencing

Guidelines. Defendant will then be free to argue for any sentence below the advisory Sentencing Guidelines range calculated by the Probation Office, including probation. . . .

*[Sections detailing Manafort's waiver of certain rights, restitution, and forfeiture have been omitted.]*

### 13. Breach of Agreement

Your client understands and agrees that, if after entering this Agreement, your client fails specifically to perform or to fulfill completely each and every one of your client's obligations under this Agreement, or engages in any criminal activity prior to sentencing or during his cooperation (whichever is later), your client will have breached this Agreement. Should it be judged by the Government in its sole discretion that the defendant has failed to cooperate fully, has intentionally given false, misleading or incomplete information or testimony, has committed or attempted to commit any further crimes, or has otherwise violated any provision of this agreement, the defendant will not be released from his pleas of guilty but the Government will be released from its obligations under this agreement, including (a) not to oppose a downward adjustment of two levels for acceptance of responsibility described above, and to make the motion for an additional one-level reduction described above and (b) to file the motion for a downward departure for cooperation described above. Moreover, the Government may withdraw the motion described above, if such motion has been filed prior to sentencing. In the event that it is judged by the Government that there has been a breach: (a) your client will be fully subject to criminal prosecution, in addition to the charges contained in the Superseding Criminal Information, for any crimes to which he has not pled guilty, including perjury and obstruction of justice; and (b) the Government and any other party will be free to use against your client, directly and indirectly, in any criminal or civil proceeding, all statements made by your client, including the Statement of Offense, and any of the information or materials provided by your client, including such statements, information, and materials provided pursuant to this Agreement or during the course of any debriefings conducted in anticipation of, or after entry of, this Agreement, whether or not the debriefings were previously a part of proffer-protected debriefings, and your client's statements made during proceedings before the Court pursuant to Rule 11 of the Federal Rules of Criminal Procedure.

Your client understands and agrees that the Government shall be required to prove a breach of this Agreement only by good faith.

Nothing in this Agreement shall be construed to protect your client from prosecution for any crimes not included within this Agreement or committed by your client after the execution of this Agreement. Your client understands and agrees that the Government reserves the right to prosecute your client for any such offenses. Your client further understands that any perjury, false statements or declarations, or obstruction of justice relating to your client's obligations under this Agreement shall constitute a breach of this Agreement. In the event of such a breach, your client will not be allowed to withdraw your client's guilty plea. . . .

*[Manafort's signed acceptance of the agreement has been omitted.]*

SOURCE: U.S. Department of Justice. *United States v. Paul J. Manafort, Jr., Criminal no. 17-201-1 (ABJ).* Document 422. Filed September 14, 2018. https://www.justice.gov/file/1094151/download.

# Mueller's Office Indicates Manafort Violated Terms of Plea Agreement

**November 26, 2018**

UNITED STATES DISTRICT COURT
FOR THE DISTRICT OF COLUMBIA

UNITED STATES OF AMERICA

v.

PAUL J. MANAFORT, JR.,                    Crim. No. 17-201-1 (ABJ)

Defendant.

## JOINT STATUS REPORT

The United States of America, by and through Special Counsel Robert S. Mueller, III, and Paul J. Manafort, Jr., by and through counsel, respectfully submit this joint status report to request, in light of recent developments, that the Court direct the preparation of a Presentence Investigation Report and schedule sentencing in this matter, as well as set a schedule for any pre-sentencing submissions and motions.

The government reports that:

1. On September 14, 2018, one business day before jury selection was scheduled in this matter, defendant Paul J. Manafort, Jr., pleaded guilty to a superseding information, charging him with two criminal conspiracy counts that encompassed all the criminal conduct alleged in the Superseding Indictment in this district. As the Court is aware, that criminal conduct occurred over a decade, up through April 2018.

2. Manafort pleaded pursuant to a plea agreement that required his "fully, truthfully, completely, and forthrightly" cooperating with the government. Plea Agreement, Doc. 422 ¶ 8; Plea Hr'g Tr. 39:10-17, 48:11-16, Sept. 14, 2018. The plea agreement provides that if the defendant fails to fulfill completely "each and every one" of his obligations under this agreement, or "engages in any criminal activity prior to sentencing," the defendant will be in breach of the agreement. A breach relieves the government of any obligations it has under the agreement, including its agreement to a reduction in the Sentencing Guidelines for acceptance of responsibility, but leaves intact all the obligations of the defendant as well as his guilty pleas. Plea Agreement, Doc. 422 ¶¶ 4B, 8, & 13. Plea Agreement, Doc. 422 ¶¶ 7 & 9.

3. After signing the plea agreement, Manafort committed federal crimes by lying to the Federal Bureau of Investigation and the Special Counsel's Office on a variety of subject matters, which constitute breaches of the agreement. The government will file a detailed sentencing submission to the Probation Department and the Court in advance of sentencing that sets forth the nature of the defendant's crimes and lies, including those after signing the plea agreement herein.

4. As the defendant has breached the plea agreement, there is no reason to delay his sentencing herein.

The defendant reports that:

5. After signing the plea agreement, Manafort met with the government on numerous occasions and answered the government's questions. Manafort has provided information to the government in an effort to live up to his cooperation obligations. He believes he has provided truthful information and does not agree with the government's characterization or that he has breached the agreement. Given the conflict in the parties' positions, there is no reason to delay the sentencing herein, and he asks the Court to set a sentencing date in this matter.

*[Signatures have been omitted.]*

SOURCE: U.S. Department of Justice. *United States v. Paul J. Manafort, Jr., Criminal no. 17-201-1 (ABJ).* Document 455. Filed November 26, 2018.

# *Cohen Accepts Plea Agreement for Lying to Congress*

**November 29, 2018**

Dear Mr. Petrillo and Ms. Lester:

This letter sets forth the full and complete plea offer to your client, Michael Cohen (hereinafter referred to as "your client" or "defendant"), from the Special Counsel's Office (hereinafter also referred to as "the Government" or "this Office"). If your client accepts the terms and conditions of this offer, please have your client execute this document in the space provided below. Upon receipt of the executed document, this letter will become the Plea Agreement (hereinafter referred to as "this Agreement"). The terms of the offer are as follows:

### 1.   Charges and Statutory Penalties

Your client agrees to waive indictment and plead guilty to a Criminal Information, a copy of which is attached, charging your client with making false statements of the U.S. Congress, in violation of 18 U.S.C. § 1001(a)(2).

Your client understands that a violation of 18 U.S.C. § 1001 carries a maximum sentence of 5 years' imprisonment; a fine of not more than $250,000, pursuant to 18 U.S.C. § 3571(b)(3); a term of supervised release of not more than 3 years, pursuant to 18 U.S.C. § 3583(b)(2); and an obligation to pay any applicable interest or penalties on fines and restitution not timely made. . . .

## 2.  Plea

Your client understands and acknowledges that this Agreement is contingent upon the entry of a guilty plea by the defendant in this case. If your client fails to enter a guilty plea, this Agreement and any proceedings pursuant to this Agreement may be withdrawn or voided in whole or in part at the option of this Office.

## 3.  Factual Stipulations

Your client agrees that the factual allegations found within the Criminal Information fairly and accurately describe your client's actions and involvement in the offense to which your client is pleading guilty.

## 4.  Additional Charges

In consideration of your client's guilty plea to the above offense, your client will not be further prosecuted criminally by this Office for the conduct set forth in the attached Criminal Information; for any other false statements made by him to the U.S. Congress or to this Office in connection with the conduct described in the Criminal Information; and for obstructing, aiding or abetting in the obstruction of, or conspiring to obstruct or commit perjury before congressional or grand jury investigations in connection with the conduct described in the Criminal Information.

*[Sections detailing sentencing guidelines have been omitted.]*

## 7.  Reservation of Allocution and Cooperation

The Government and your client reserve the right to describe fully, both orally and in writing, to the sentencing judge, the nature and seriousness of your client's misconduct, including any misconduct not described in the charges to which your client is pleading guilty.

The Government agrees to bring the Court's attention at sentencing in this matter and in *United States v. Cohen*, No. 1:18-cr-602 (WHP) (S.D.N.Y.) the nature and extent of the defendant's cooperation with this Office, on the condition that your client continues to respond and provide truthful information regarding any and all matters as to which this Office deems relevant. The defendant must at all times give complete, truthful, and accurate information and testimony, and must not commit, or attempt to commit, any further crimes.

The Government agrees not to oppose the transfer of this case in its entirety or for the purposes of sentencing to the Judge in *United States v. Cohen*, No. 1:18-cr-602 (WHP) (S.D.N.Y.).

The parties also reserve the right to inform the presentence report writer and the Court of any relevant facts, to dispute any factual inaccuracies in the presentence report, and to contest any matters not provided for in this Agreement. In the event that the Court considers any Sentencing Guidelines adjustments, departures, or calculations different from any agreements contained in this Agreement, or contemplates a sentence outside the Guidelines range based upon the general sentencing factors listed in 18 U.S.C. § 3553(a), the parties reserve the right to answer any related inquiries from the Court. In addition, if in this Agreement the parties have agreed to recommend or refrain from recommending to the Court a particular resolution of any sentencing issue, the parties reserve the right to full allocution in any post-sentence litigation. The parties retain the full right of allocution in connection with any post-sentence motion which may be filed in this matter and/or any proceeding(s) before the Bureau of Prisons. In addition, your client acknowledges that the Government is not obligated and does not intend to file any post-sentence downward departure motion in this case pursuant to Rule 35(b) of the Federal Rules of Criminal Procedure.

## 8.   Court Not Bound by this Agreement or the Sentencing Guidelines

Your client understands that the sentence in this case will be imposed in accordance with 18 U.S.C. § 3553(a), upon consideration of the Sentencing Guidelines. Your client further understands that the sentence to be imposed is a matter solely within the discretion of the Court. Your client acknowledges that the Court is not obligated to follow any recommendation of the Government at the time of sentencing. Your client understands that neither the Government's recommendation nor the Sentencing Guidelines are binding on the Court.

Your client acknowledges that your client's entry of a guilty plea to the charged offense authorizes the Court to impose any sentence, up to and including the statutory maximum sentence, which may be greater than the applicable Guidelines range. The Government cannot, and does not, make any promise or representation as to what sentence your client will receive. Moreover, it is understood that your client will have no right to withdraw your client's plea of guilty should the Court impose a sentence that is outside the Guidelines range or if the Court does not follow the Government's sentencing recommendation. The Government and your client will be bound by this Agreement, regardless of the sentence imposed by the Court. Any effort by your client to withdraw the guilty plea because of the length of the sentence shall constitute a breach of this Agreement.

*[Sections detailing Cohen's waiver of certain rights, restitution, and forfeiture have been omitted.]*

## 11.   Breach of Agreement

Your client understands and agrees that, if after entering this Agreement, your client fails specifically to perform or to fulfill completely each and every one of your client's obligations under this Agreement, or engages in any criminal activity prior to sentencing, your client will have breached this Agreement. In the event of such a breach: (a) the Government will be free from its obligations under this Agreement; (b) your client will not have the right to withdraw the guilty plea; (c) your client will be fully subject to criminal prosecution for any other crimes, including perjury and obstruction of justice; and (d) the Government will be free to use against your client, directly and indirectly, in any criminal or civil proceeding, all statements made by your client and any of the information or materials provided by your client, including such statements, information and materials provided pursuant to this Agreement or during the course of any debriefings conducted in anticipation of, or after entry of, this Agreement, whether or not the debriefings were previously characterized as "off-the-record" debriefings, and including your client's statements made during proceedings before the Court pursuant to Rule 11 of the Federal Rules of Criminal Procedure.

Your client understands and agrees that the Government shall be required to prove a breach of this Agreement only by a preponderance of the evidence, except where such breach is based on a violation of federal, state, or local criminal law, which the Government need prove only by probable cause in order to establish a breach of this Agreement.

Nothing in this Agreement shall be construed to permit your client to commit perjury, to make false statements or declarations, to obstruct justice, or to protect your client from prosecution for any crimes not included within this Agreement or committed by your client after the execution of this Agreement. Your client understands and agrees that the Government reserves the right to prosecute your client for any such offenses. Your client further understands that any perjury, false statements or declarations, or obstruction of justice relating to your client's obligations under this Agreement that takes place after execution of this Agreement shall constitute a breach of this Agreement. In the event of such a breach, your client will not be allowed to withdraw your client's guilty plea. . . .

*[Cohen's acceptance of the plea agreement has been omitted.]*

SOURCE: U.S. Department of Justice. *United States v. Michael Cohen.* Plea Agreement. November 29, 2018. https://www.justice.gov/file/1115566/download.

## OTHER HISTORIC DOCUMENTS OF INTEREST

### FROM THIS VOLUME

- Department of Justice Issues Indictments against Russians; Trump and Putin Meet for Summit, p. 125

### FROM PREVIOUS *HISTORIC DOCUMENTS*

- Former FBI Director Robert Mueller Appointed Special Counsel on U.S. Election–Russia Investigation, Issues Indictments, *2017*, p. 270
- CIA and FBI Release Findings on Russian Involvement in U.S. Election, *2016*, p. 511

# Australian Prime Minister Resigns following Leadership Challenge

AUGUST 24, 2018

On August 24, 2018, Scott Morrison was sworn in as Australia's fifth prime minister in as many years. The preceding decade of Australian politics had been marked by a series of abrupt intraparty leadership upheavals that were set off by competing members of the majority party, often stemmed from professional rivalries, and played out through escalating policy disputes. In 2018, Prime Minister Malcolm Turnbull became the latest casualty of the country's fractured political process after a series of disagreements and growing demands related to national energy policy led to a turbulent and bitter challenge from conservative factions of Turnbull's own center-right party. The challenge and Turnbull's subsequent resignation ultimately caused the Coalition-led government to lose its narrow majority in parliament.

## A CONSERVATIVE INSURGENCY

In August 2018, emboldened by an increasingly vocal far-right conservative faction, Home Affairs Minister Peter Dutton initiated a leadership "spill"—a vote in parliament by members of the prime minister's party to replace him or her. The center-right Coalition, made up of Turnbull and Dutton's Liberal Party and the National Party, held a single-seat majority over the opposition center-left Labor Party. Turnbull pledged to resign from parliament entirely if he lost the vote, but hoping to gain an advantage of surprise, he headed off the process by declaring his own position open to nomination without leaving time for rivals to secure votes. Dutton was the only candidate nominated. On August 21, in a party room ballot, Turnbull held on to power by a 48–35 vote. Following the vote, numerous cabinet ministers who had supported Dutton offered their resignation, most of which Turnbull declined in an effort to restore a semblance of unity to the fractured party. (Turnbull did accept Dutton's resignation.)

Dutton refused to abandon his insurrection, and Turnbull's unconvincing victory left him vulnerable as dissenting party members pressed for a second challenge. Dutton was perceived as a hardline conservative; his aggressive campaign, combined with his low popularity among moderate voters, created opportunities for more centrist candidates to emerge. Turnbull said he would resign after a majority of party members called for a second spill, which became a three-way challenge between Dutton, Foreign Minister Julie Bishop, and Treasurer Scott Morrison. Bishop was eliminated in the first round of voting and resigned from the cabinet, ending her tenure as deputy party leader. Morrison went on to secure a narrow victory in a subsequent run-off against Dutton by a 45–40 vote, suggesting that deep fault lines remain within the Liberal Party.

A former Turnbull ally, Morrison initially distanced himself from the internal conflict, but as a more moderate alternative to Dutton, and more broadly palatable to Liberal

Party voters, he seized control without having to claim ownership of the spill. Like Dutton, Morrison rose to prominence over his nationalist rhetoric and hardline stance on immigration. As minister of immigration and border patrol, he enforced aggressive policies to stop asylum seekers from reaching Australia by boat, including by creating offshore detention centers—a practice widely condemned by human rights groups and the United Nations. Analysts observed that the perception of Morrison as a moderate is an indication of how far to the right Australia's conservative politics have shifted in recent years. At his swearing in, Morrison called for unity within his party. "Our job . . . is to ensure that we not only bring our party back together, which has been bruised and battered this week, but that will enable us to ensure we bring the parliament back together," he said.

Following the vote, Turnbull reaffirmed his intention to leave parliament, officially resigning on August 31. A by-election was held to fill Turnbull's vacated seat, which had generally been considered safely within Liberal Party control. However, his Wentworth electorate rejected the Liberal Party in the largest-ever swing against a sitting government, giving the seat to independent candidate Kerryn Phelps and costing the Coalition their majority in the lower house of parliament. Despite being the principle agitator of a conflict that served only to cause further damage to his party, Dutton maintained that he did not regret his actions, claiming the spill was necessary to resolve lingering animosity from the Turnbull–Tony Abbot split of 2015.

## A Decade of Dysfunction and Eroding Discourse

Dysfunctional politics are not new to Australia: since 2007, no prime minister has served a full term before being deposed by rivals, and Turnbull himself supported a similar coup against Abbott in 2015. As opposed to the protracted and weighty American impeachment process, Australian leaders are much more easily removed and replaced, requiring only a simple majority of ministers of their own party to wrest control and select a new leader. The practice is driven by the logic that replacing an unpopular leader will boost a party's favorability in opinion polls before an election; however, the turbulence caused by frequent leadership replacements has fueled uncertainty among voters and foreign allies alike, in addition to disrupting domestic and foreign policy. Foreign governments are often left wondering whether any Australian leader will be in office long enough to follow through on bilateral agreements, while the public feels left out of the process, fueling a sentiment that elected officials are more focused on internal power plays and political machinations than actual governance. In this context, the electoral loss of Turnbull's seat was unsurprising. As Phelps observed in her October 20 election-night address, "we have . . . tapped into a sentiment in the Australian people, to talk about the issues that are important to them, not the issues about survival for a particular political party."

## Party Ruptures Fueled by Contentious Energy and Emissions Debate

Compared to previous leadership spills, the 2018 contest was particularly chaotic for the Liberal Party and largely a problem of its own making. As a *Sydney Morning Herald* analyst put it, "factional foot stamping . . . caused an earthquake" as festering internal rivalries escalated over a proposed energy policy. Energy historically has been, and will continue to be, a thorny issue as Australia (a leading exporter of coal and natural gas) attempts to shore up domestic energy infrastructure while recognizing the growing need to identify climate-resilient policies. (This debate played out against the backdrop of a record-breaking drought and abnormally early and strong bushfires in New South Wales.) Previous Australian governments have struggled with the issue, and earlier attempts to legislate emission reductions had been politically damaging to Liberal Party leaders.

In late 2017, Turnbull had proposed the National Energy Guarantee, which was a broad bill meant to align Australian policy with the country's commitments under the Paris Agreement. Turnbull had gathered the necessary support of a majority, but a small group of conservative members led by former prime minister Abbott remained staunchly opposed to the bill and threatened to vote against the legislation—a move that would have publicly demonstrated a loss of confidence in Turnbull's leadership. Abbott, who had set Australia's emissions reductions targets under the Paris Agreement when he was prime minister, was the most vocal opponent of the bill, arguing that Australia should not pursue emission reductions as long as other major polluters were not meeting their own commitments.

To assuage these concerns, Turnbull removed emission targets from the legislation and instead signaled a plan to pursue a similar goal through regulation. Turnbull's capitulation only emboldened his critics, who convinced him to accede to escalating demands while his progressive supporters were dismayed to watch policies shifting further to the right. In his effort to stave off rebellion, Turnbull effectively abandoned all efforts toward climate policy and removed the regulatory provisions related to emissions reductions from the bill as well. While the Coalition held an emergency session on energy policy, conservative members began to sound out a leadership challenge, and Dutton was approached and urged to run. The opposition Labor Party characterized Turnbull as a "white flag prime minister" as he continued to give ground to conservatives. This hastened the erosion of Turnbull's public support, which in turn strengthened conservatives' case for his removal.

## TURNBULL STEPS DOWN

Speaking to reporters on August 24, Turnbull remarked, "This week has been so dispiriting, because it just appears to be . . . vengeance, personal ambition, and factional feuding." He said, "Australians will be just dumbstruck and so appalled . . . by this sort of disloyalty" and "insurgency" when it was possible that differences in policy could have been resolved "with a little bit of goodwill." Yet he also said he remained "very optimistic and positive about our nation's future." Turnbull declared that the Coalition government had implemented "enormous reforms and very, very substantial achievements," adding that his party had delivered on its promises of job creation and economic growth. He thanked his government and his cabinet ministers as well as the Australian people "for everything they have done for me. It has been such a privilege to be the leader of this great nation."

New measures to encourage leadership stability within the Liberal Party were announced on December 2. It was resolved that a two-thirds vote, rather than a simple majority, would be required to remove an elected Liberal Party prime minister. Speaking with reporters, Morrison acknowledged that both lawmakers and the public were tired of the "coup culture" in the capital. The move mirrored a similar step taken by former prime minister Kevin Rudd, whose Labor Party had placed restrictions on spills five years earlier.

Australia's next federal election must be held by May 18, 2019. The Coalition government faced persistently poor polling since 2016, and with the opposition leveraging the chaotic and divisive Turnbull ouster as a campaign talking point, the Liberal Party is expected to perform poorly. Morrison was tasked with reconciling divisions within the party and promised to "provide the stability and the unity and the direction and the purpose that the Australian people expect." Pledging to ensure that his cabinet reflects conservative and liberal traditions in the party, he extended an invitation to Bishop and Dutton to join his cabinet and presented the start of his tenure as a "new generation" of Liberal leadership.

—Megan Howes

*Following is a statement and exchange with reporters by former prime minister Malcolm Turnbull on August 24, 2018, about the Liberal Party leadership challenges and his resignation from parliament.*

# Turnbull Makes Statement, Answers Reporter Questions on Leadership Change

DOCUMENT

---

It may surprise you on a day like this, but I remain very optimistic and positive about our nation's future.

I want to thank the Australian people for the support they've given me and my Government over the last nearly three years. We've been able to achieve as a progressive Government, as a progressive Liberal Coalition Government, enormous reforms and very, very substantial achievements.

You know, the foundation of everything you do in Government is a strong economy and we have delivered—as we promised—jobs and growth. You may have heard that before. We've got record jobs growth in Australia last year. We have strong economic growth, 3.1%, as you know, higher than any of the G7 economies.

That has enabled us to do so much more. Despite the minority position in the Senate and the one-seat majority in the House of Representatives, we've been able to deliver substantial taxation reforms. Much more than many of you, probably any of you, thought possible.

Substantial personal income tax reforms, the biggest in more than 20 years.

Tax reductions for small and medium businesses, overwhelmingly Australian, family-owned businesses.

We have also been able to get on with the job of important historic infrastructure. I'm very proud that we are underway with Snowy Hydro 2.0, I know sometimes my opponents in the Labor Party say that I'm not committed to renewables. Well I tell you, we're building and we're going to build the biggest single renewable project in Australia since Snowy Hydro 1.0. So that is a substantial commitment. Plus we're getting on and building the Western Sydney Airport, the Inland Rail and we'll build a railway from Melbourne out to Tullamarine. So many other big infrastructure projects and we've been able to do it, because of strong economic growth.

We've also taken a different approach, I have been a reforming Liberal Prime Minister. Of course one of the many difficult political challenges that we face, particularly in the

Coalition, has been the issue of marriage equality. Now, we have delivered that. Same-sex marriage is legal. We went through a postal vote, as you know, which was hugely successful. Again, much more successful than many thought and we have delivered that historic reform, a very substantial one.

We have also established a National Redress Scheme for the Victims of Child Sexual Abuse. We have provided record support for mental health services and indeed for health services right across the board, whether it is hospitals, Medicare, the Pharmaceutical Benefits Scheme. None of those things could have been done without the strong economy that we've delivered.

Childcare reforms also have been once-in-a-generation reforms.

But I have taken a different approach as a Federal leader, as a federal Government, to the way we engage with cities. As you know, historically, federal governments played a limited role, a sort of an ad hoc role, with cities. Very often you had federal governments, state government and local government, often moving in roughly the same direction, but being like ships in the night. The City Deals program has been a real innovation. A very, very welcome reform and working very well, enabling for the first time to see federal government money systematically going into work in partnership with communities, so that you agree on what your vision is and then get on and do it.

I want to say also that keeping Australians safe is obviously the single most importantly priority of Government. I have had outstanding Ministers in that area, particularly Marise Payne the Defence Minister and the Defence Industry Minister Christopher Pyne. We have embarked on the largest investment in our defence capabilities ever, in peacetime. Of course it's not simply a matter of ensuring that our men and women in the ADF have the capabilities, both to give them the force they need and to ensure that they are safe in all the circumstances they're engaging in. But it also is part of an agenda to ensure that defence industry, these advanced industries, provide the lead, the opportunities, to build the Australian economy. It is all part of our economic plan.

Clearly as Prime Minister I've had a great deal to do in terms of our international agenda. We've been able to secure, again, a reform or an achievement that many people thought was impossible, which was the Trans-Pacific Partnership. When Donald Trump pulled out of that everyone thought it was dead. I was mocked, as you know, by some for keeping at it. But we managed to secure the TPP-11, the Trans-Pacific Partnership continued. The fact that it has continued, not only creates export opportunities for Australians, but it also provides a foundation for a trade deal for the US to re-enter at some point in the future and for others to do as well.

We have also of course, I was able to secure and then maintain the resettlement deal with the United States for refugees on Manus and Nauru. That was a challenging exercise, to maintain that, but of course hundreds of refugees are now being resettled without providing the incentive for the people smugglers to get back into business again and maintaining that strong border protection has been critically important.

I was also able to ensure that when the US put tariffs on steel and aluminium on countries right around the world, Australia was exempted from that. Again, a great example of the way in which I have sought always to stand up for Australian jobs, Australian workers and our industries.

We've been able to ensure that we could bring back the rule of law in the building sector with the Australian Building and Construction Commission. That was obviously one of the double dissolution triggers, but again many thought that was impossible. But we were able to achieve it.

So I think it has been a challenging time to be Prime Minister, but I'm very proud of our record.

I'm very proud of my Government and my Ministers' record in achievement. I want to thank them. I want to thing all my colleagues. I want to thank my staff, but above all I want to thank my wife Lucy for her love and support. I want to thank our children, Alex and his wife Yvonne and our daughter Daisy and her husband James.

It isn't easy being either married to or the child of a politician, let alone a Prime Minister. Often children get attention from the media and others that they frankly, don't deserve, in terms of people wanting to sort of have a crack at their father, by going after them. So it's been tough on them at times, but I want to thank them for their solidarity and loyalty and love. Our grandchildren of course are a great joy. I look forward to spending some more time with them and with Lucy.

But finally, I want to thank the Australian people for everything they have done for me. It has been such a privilege to be the leader of this great nation.

I love Australia. I love Australians. We are the most successful multicultural society in the world, and I have always defended that and advanced that as one of our greatest assets. We must never allow the politics of race or division or of setting Australians against each other, to become part of our political culture.

We have so much going for us in this country. We have to be proud of it and cherish it.

Now, I suppose I should say something about the events of the last week or so. Look, I think you all know what's happened. There was a determined insurgency from a number of people both in the Party Room and backed by voices, powerful voices in the media really to if not bring down the Government, certainly bring down my Prime Ministership. It was extraordinary. It was described as madness by many and I think it's difficult to describe it in any other way.

In the Party Room meeting today I was impressed by how many of my colleagues spoke or voted for loyalty above disloyalty. How the insurgents were not rewarded by electing Mr Dutton, for example, but instead my successor—who I wish the very best, of course—Scott Morrison, a very loyal and effective Treasurer. I want to thank him of course for his great work, but above all I want to thank Julie Bishop. She is a very dear friend. We've been friends for over 30 years. We sometimes wonder whether we should remind people of that, but nonetheless, she's a very dear friend. She's been an extraordinary Foreign Minister, I would say our finest Foreign Minister. She has been a loyal deputy and just a great colleague and friend. So I thank Julie very much. As you know, she's stood down as the deputy and she's succeeded by Josh Frydenberg. Again, I wish Josh all the best, he's been a very loyal and capable minister.

So, that is what I have to say to you today, I'm happy to take some questions. Hang on, hang on you can't all talk at once. I'm going to, given that I'm about to no longer be the Prime Minister, I'm going to ask Laura Tingle to ask me a question.

**Journalist:** You talk[ed] about bullying yesterday and you talked about the insurgency today. One of the frustrations that voters have had with your Prime Ministership is the sense that you conceded too regularly to the conservatives and to the right. Do you regret doing that given that they came for you anyway? And what is your view of what is going to happen to climate policy and energy policy now?

**Turnbull:** Okay, well Laura, what I have done always is to try to keep the Party together. That has meant that from time to time I have had to compromise and make concessions.

Really it's something I learned from my first time as leader, that you have to work so hard to keep the show together. That's the bottom line. But, you look at what we've achieved, it's a very long list.

In terms of energy policy and climate policy, I think the truth is that the Coalition finds it very hard to get agreement on anything to do with emissions. That's the truth. I mean the National Energy Guarantee was or is, a vitally piece of economic reform. It remains the Government's policy, of course. But with a one-seat majority in the House, unless you can command all or almost all your votes, you can't get it passed. I want to thank Josh for the work that he's done on that.

But if I can say this; the emissions policy, emissions issues and climate policy issues have the same problem within the Coalition of bitterly entrenched views that are actually sort of more ideological views, than views based as I say, in engineering and economics. It's a bit like same-sex marriage used to be. Almost an insoluble problem. Now, we were able to sort that out, that was a very significant achievement in my time as Prime Minister. I'm actually I think the first Prime Minister to support legalising same-sex marriage, but most importantly, was able to get it done.

As for what the future holds in terms of energy policy, again you'll have to talk to Scott about that. But clearly there's a great foundation in the announcements we have already made, arising out of the ACCCC report. The next person I'm going to invite to ask me a question is Mr Coorey.

**Journalist:** The Party is very split over this, it's exposed quite a division down the middle. What's your message on unity, do you think the party can unify?

**Turnbull:** Well Phil it's obvious. Australians will be just dumbstruck and so appalled by the conduct of the last week. You know, to imagine that a Government would be rocked by this sort of disloyalty and deliberate, you know, insurgency is the best way to describe it, deliberate, destructive action, at a time when there are differences on policy, but frankly, all of them were resolvable, able to be resolved with a little bit of goodwill. Of course, a month ago, as I said yesterday, we were a little behind in the national polls and a little bit ahead in our own polls. So I think many Australians will just be shaking their heads in disbelief at what's been done.

**Journalist:** And unity, Prime Minister?

**Turnbull:** Well unity Phil, disunity is death in Australian politics, as everyone says. It's perfectly obvious. But the people who chose—Peter Dutton and Tony Abbott and others—who chose to deliberately attack the Government from within, they did so because they wanted to bring the Government down. They wanted to bring my Prime Ministership down. While the consequence is that I'm no longer PM, of course, instead of Mr Dutton being Prime Minister, we'll no doubt in due course we'll have Mr Morrison. Murpharoo?

**Journalist:** Prime Minister, I have so many questions . . . But I have to ask this one for news purposes, this is what we need to know. You did tell us yesterday that you intended to exit the Parliament?

**Turnbull:** Yes.

**Journalist:** When do you intend to exit the Parliament, is it now or at the next election?

**Turnbull:** Oh no, I'll be leaving the Parliament in, not before too long. As I have always said, I've been very clear about that. It's not a secret. Now I'm just going to go to Chris Uhlmann, is he here? No, alright what about you, KG?

**Journalist:** Mr. Turnbull, do you have any regrets as you look back at the three years of being PM?

**Turnbull:** Oh I'm sure if I have time to reflect on them, I'm sure I'll think of a few. But at the moment I'm really just focused on taking a very positive approach to all of these issues. I think again, I've got great optimism for Australia. I'm proud of the achievements of the Government.

You know, I talk about my team and my office, you know Clive and Sally and Boldy and the whole team. I have never worked with a better team of people than I have in my office. They are outstanding and we have run a very good Government. In the sense that the Cabinet hasn't leaked very much, despite your best efforts to cause it to do so. We've been united, we've had a thoroughly traditional approach, so that's been good.

Okay now, I have a thoroughly traditional grandson. Here he is, here's Jack and here's Daisy, and here's Alice and Lucy. Okay now I'm going to take a couple more. No, you're right, perhaps just one more. David?

**Journalist:** Mr. Turnbull, the discussion about the ballot this week has been dominated by talk about the petition. You've been blamed in some quarters for the "chaos", in inverted commas. What do you say to those who say it was wrong for you to insist on the 43 names and to insist on those names?

**Turnbull:** Well look, I mean this is a matter of political history and we might wrap up with that. The fact is there was a leadership ballot on Tuesday which I won convincingly.

The proposition that there should be almost immediately another ballot, is really unprecedented. So it was reasonable for me to say: "Well, if you want to call another party meeting, you better tell me why, show me evidence that a majority want to do that."

So insofar as there has been chaos this week, it has been created by the wreckers. I have done everything I can to maintain the stability of government and the stability of the Party. But, of course if people are determined to wreck, then we know they will continue to do so. . . .

Look, I came into politics at the very mature age of 50. I've had a very good time here in the Parliament. I've always been focused on what I can deliver for the Australian people.

Again, the critical thing is with politics, it's not about the politicians. That's why this week has been so dispiriting, because it just appears to be, you know, vengeance, personal ambition, factional feuding, or however you'd describe it. It hasn't had anything to do with 25 million Australians and the Australian[s] we should be focused on above all else, are these little ones, you know, it is the next generation that we are working for here in this place. And we have achieved a great deal.

There are some things that I would have liked to have completed or done more on. But to be really honest with you, we have got so much more done in this Government and particularly in this Parliament, than I expected and certainly a lot more than any of you expected, sceptics that you all are.

So look, thank you all very much and I wish you all the best.

Above all I wish the new prime minister-elect the very best and his team.

Thank you. . . .

Source: Office of Malcolm Turnbull. "Press Statement - Parliament House - 24 August 2018." August 24, 2018. https://www.malcolmturnbull.com.au/media/press-statement-palriament-house-24-august-2018.

## OTHER HISTORIC DOCUMENTS OF INTEREST

### FROM PREVIOUS *HISTORIC DOCUMENTS*

# President Trump on New Trade Pact with Mexico and Canada

AUGUST 31, OCTOBER 2, AND DECEMBER 1, 2018

Year-long negotiations between the United States, Canada, and Mexico on a trade pact to replace the existing North American Free Trade Agreement (NAFTA) reached a conclusion in late 2018, when the leaders of all three nations signed a trilateral deal. To go into effect, the agreement would need to be ratified by the legislature of each country, something likely to prove most difficult in the United States, where Democrats had just won control of the House of Representatives.

## BREAKDOWN IN NAFTA

NAFTA was signed into law by President Bill Clinton in December 1993. At the time, the deal was widely supported by both Democrats and Republicans, and it aimed to increase jobs and encourage economic development for all three nations by lowering trade restrictions. Since its inception, politicians and economists have debated whether NAFTA helps or hurts the United States. The conclusion, at least among economists, is that the impact is likely a wash. The terms of the agreement allowed many U.S. companies to save money by moving their operations to Mexico, which can be a job killer in the United States. However, it is possible that those jobs would have disappeared from the United States anyway because Mexican companies were opening their own factories and could promise cheaper goods and labor to U.S. companies. And, because trade between the United States, Canada, and Mexico was easier under the agreement, the United States was selling more goods to its neighbors, thus creating jobs. Since NAFTA, the United States has had a trade surplus with Canada but a trade deficit with Mexico. Even so, U.S. consumers benefitted from lower prices of goods purchased from Mexico, a factor for keeping inflation in check.

As a candidate, Donald Trump promised to focus on trade and, more specifically, to eliminate NAFTA, which he called "the worst deal maybe ever signed." Trump said the trade pact had resulted in millions of American factory jobs lost because its provisions encourage U.S. companies to move abroad. In his first 100 days as president, Trump threatened to unilaterally withdraw the United States from NAFTA if Canada and Mexico did not want to negotiate a new deal. This drew mixed responses from the president's own party, where support for free trade is generally more robust than it is among Democrats. It also raised questions among members of Congress about whether the president had the power to remove the United States from the deal because the Constitution provides Congress the power to "regulate commerce with foreign nations."

Both Canada and Mexico expressed a desire to come to the negotiating table to establish a new, more modern trade agreement. In August 2017, U.S. Trade Representative Robert Lighthizer began the trilateral negotiations with an ambitious goal of drafting a new agreement by the close of the year. Additional meetings were held in September,

October, and November, but the original deadline passed without an agreement, as did two more set for March and May 2018. Negotiations were stalled in mid-2018 when the Trump administration imposed tariffs on all steel and aluminum imports, and Canada and Mexico responded in kind. Canada completely pulled out of negotiations in July, shortly after President Trump announced that he would not approve any trade agreement until after the November 2018 midterm elections. Negotiations continued with Mexico, and Lighthizer expressed his hope that an agreement could be reached with Mexico "and that as a result of that Canada will come in and begin to compromise."

## TRADE DEAL WITH MEXICO

Mexico's leaders remained at the bargaining table after Canada's departure, driven primarily by a desire to establish an agreement that could be wrapped up before Mexican President Enrique Peña Nieto left office. The incoming president, Andrés Manuel López Obrador, who would take office on December 1, was highly critical of NAFTA and Peña Nieto's work with President Trump, signaling that he may request changes if negotiations on the agreement were not completed before Peña Nieto's departure. Despite NAFTA's popularity with the Mexican public, it had checkered support among influential politicians in the country.

On August 26, President Trump and U.S. Trade Representative Lighthizer announced that an agreement with Mexico had been reached to replace NAFTA. "It's a big day for trade. It's a big day for our country," Trump said. The new trade deal was largely a continuation of NAFTA with some adjustments. The agreement would run for sixteen years and would be reviewed every six years with the option for extension. Included within the trade deal were provisions that increased from 62.5 percent to 75 percent how many of the components of each car must be manufactured in either the United States or Mexico for the vehicle to qualify as duty-free. It also required that 40 percent to 45 percent of the parts used in cars receiving duty-free treatment be manufactured by individuals earning at least $16 per hour, substantially higher than the normal rate in Mexico. Administration officials admitted that because the cost of labor and parts would increase, it was possible that could be passed on to consumers, who would pay more to buy a car. However, the administration noted that the terms would make it less attractive for companies to move their operations to Mexico in search of cheaper labor or parts, a win for American workers in the automotive sector.

On August 31, President Trump sent a message to Congress notifying them, as required by law, of his "intention to enter into a trade agreement with Mexico—and with Canada if it is willing, in a timely manner, to meet the high standards for free, fair, and reciprocal trade contained therein." According to the president's letter to Congress, the agreement is "a great deal for the American people. It sets a new tone for all trade agreements, proof of the high standard that my Administration will require of any country entering a new trade agreement with the United States." The agreement, which the president said he wanted to enter into at the end of November, would require the consent of Congress within ninety days.

## CANADA KEPT OUT OF INITIAL AGREEMENT

Absent from the U.S.–Mexico deal was an agreement over how to address the steel and aluminum import tariffs Trump imposed in the summer, which Lighthizer said was an issue the two governments were working through. A bigger factor, however, was that Canada had been shut out of what Trump was referring to as the U.S.–Mexico trade agreement. "There is no political necessity to keep Canada in the new NAFTA deal. If we don't make a fair deal for the U.S. after decades of abuse, Canada will be out," Trump said on Twitter. Lighthizer cautioned that negotiators would continue to work with their Canadian counterparts with the intent of including them in the final agreement. Marcelo Ebrard, the incoming Mexican foreign minister, said Canadian participation was "indispensable for being able to renew the treaty."

The involvement of the Canadians was not just of interest to some U.S. officials and the Mexican government; it was also necessary for Canada to sign off if the trade agreement were to represent a complete overhaul or replacement of NAFTA. Trump said he welcomed the participation of the Canadians if they were willing "to negotiate fairly" but cautioned that if they failed to do so, he would not hesitate to levy additional duties on the country. "The easiest thing we can do is tariff their cars coming in" as a means of retaliation. A spokesperson for Canadian Foreign Minister Chrystia Freeland said, "We will only sign a new NAFTA that is good for Canada and good for the middle class." Congressional Republicans, who had been tepid in their support for Trump's NAFTA overhaul plans, stressed the importance of ensuring that Canada was part of the final agreement. Sen. Orrin Hatch, R-Utah, chair of the Senate Finance Committee, said "a final agreement should include Canada" to ensure that the trade deal reaped all possible benefits for American workers and the American economy.

Canadian representatives quickly returned to Washington to rejoin the talks in late August, with Freeland noting that there was "a lot of goodwill" in the negotiations and that they would be working "very intensely" to secure a final agreement as soon as possible. "We continue to be encouraged by the constructive atmosphere that I think both countries are bringing to the table," Freeland said. President Trump set a new deadline of September 30 for the three countries to come to an agreement, which would allow Congress time to approve the deal before the end of the year and before the new Congress was seated.

## NEW TRADE PACT SIGNED AT G-20

Negotiators from the three nations met the president's September 30 deadline. The United States–Mexico–Canada Agreement (USMCA) made a number of changes to existing NAFTA language, primarily meant to expand access for Mexican and Canadian producers to American markets, allow U.S. dairy producers more access to Canada, and incentivize the purchase of vehicles produced by workers making a fair wage. It kept in place some of the components of the U.S.–Mexico agreement, including the requirement that 75 percent of the parts of a vehicle be manufactured in the United States, Mexico, or Canada to qualify for duty-free treatment. Thirty percent of the car would need to be made by workers earning at least $16 per hour, a threshold that would increase to 40 percent in 2023. Canada secured a victory for itself by maintaining the Chapter 19 provision that allows the three countries to challenge antidumping and countervailing duties to a special panel rather than challenging a specific trade practice in U.S. court, which is more difficult. Other provisions included expanding market protections for U.S. drug manufacturers in Canada, one requiring Mexican trucks to meet U.S. safety standards if they crossed the border into the United States, and one allowing Mexican workers more opportunity to organize into labor unions. The agreement also provided additional protection for intellectual property rights and banned the use of Chapter 11 bankruptcy for resolving disputes with governments (with the exception of U.S. oil companies). Two side letters were included with the trade deal, which promised that Canada and Mexico could continue to send auto parts and vehicles into the United States duty-free. Notably, the two countries did not reach an agreement on the existing steel and aluminum tariffs.

On November 30, President Trump, President Peña Nieto, and Canadian Prime Minister Justin Trudeau signed the USMCA at the Group of 20 meeting in Argentina. Once signed, the agreement required ratification by the legislature of each signatory. This was expected to be relatively easy in Canada, where the prime minister's party held control of parliament. In Mexico, newly inaugurated president Obrador said he did not intend to request changes to the agreement before it was sent to the General Congress for approval.

In the United States, passage would be led by Democrats in the House once the new Congress was seated in January 2019. Some Democrats have long been objectors to NAFTA and had worked with the White House to negotiate the USMCA. Others, however, including incoming Speaker of the House Nancy Pelosi, complained that the labor and environmental standards in the new agreement were not tough enough. To put pressure on Congress to pass the USMCA, on December 1, Trump told the press corps traveling with him from Argentina that he would formally terminate NAFTA in "a relatively short period of time," which he said would give Congress a choice between either USMCA or no trilateral trade deal. There is a provision under the existing NAFTA deal that the president can withdraw the United States from participation in the deal. However, many in Congress believe the body would need to pass legislation to fully repeal NAFTA. If the president were to withdraw from NAFTA without congressional backing, it is likely the issue would end up in court.

—Heather Kerrigan

*Following are two documents dated August 31, 2018, announcing President Donald Trump's intent to enter into a trade agreement; the text of an October 2, 2018, exchange with reporters on the U.S.–Mexico–Canada (USMCA) trade agreement; and a Q&A with reporters on December 1, 2018, regarding the signing of the USMCA.*

 *President Trump Files Notice of Intent to Enter into a Trade Agreement*

**August 31, 2018**

Consistent with section 106(a)(1)(A) of the Bipartisan Congressional Trade Priorities and Accountability Act of 2015 (Public Law 114-26, Title I) (the "Act"), I have notified the Congress of my intention to enter into a trade agreement with Mexico—and with Canada if it is willing, in a timely manner, to meet the high standards for free, fair, and reciprocal trade contained therein.

Consistent with section 106(a)(1)(A) of the Act, this notice shall be published in the *Federal Register*.

DONALD J. TRUMP
The White House, August 31, 2018.

Source: Executive Office of the President. "Notice—Notice of Intention to Enter into a Trade Agreement." August 31, 2018. *Compilation of Presidential Documents* 2018, no. 00570 (August 31, 2018). https://www .govinfo.gov/content/pkg/DCPD-201800570/pdf/DCPD-201800570.pdf.

## President Trump Announces Trade Deal to Congress

**August 31, 2018**

*Dear Mr. Speaker: (Dear Mr. President:)*

On May 18, 2017, my Administration notified the Congress that I intended to initiate trade negotiations with Canada and Mexico. Negotiations began on August 16, 2017. Since that time, my Administration has worked hard with Mexico and Canada to reach a modern trade agreement that sets high standards for free, fair, and reciprocal trade.

I am pleased to report that in only 1 year, we have made dramatic progress toward such an agreement:

- It will help American farmers by ensuring fairer market conditions and improved market access for United States agricultural products.

- It will create a more level playing field for American workers—due in part to improved rules of origin for automobiles, trucks, and other products.

- It will include the toughest and most comprehensive labor and environmental rules of any United States trade deal. For the first time in North America, those rules will be enforceable—and they will be strictly enforced.

- It will encourage innovation by providing new and improved protections for United States intellectual property.

- It will contain the strongest disciplines on digital trade of any international agreement, and will provide a firm foundation for the expansion of trade in innovative products and services.

- It will create a more level playing field for American service industries, including the critical sector of financial services.

- It will provide the most robust protections against currency manipulation of any United States trade deal.

- It will give United States policymakers new weapons against the harmful, market-distorting effect of state-owned enterprises on private companies.

In short, this agreement is a great deal for the American people. It sets a new tone for all trade agreements, proof of the high standard that my Administration will require of any country entering a new trade agreement with the United States.

I intend to enter into the agreement by the end of November 2018. Accordingly, pursuant to section 106(a)(1)(A) of the Bipartisan Congressional Trade Priorities and Accountability Act of 2015 (Public Law 114–26, Title I), I hereby notify the House of

Representatives and the Senate that I intend to enter into a trade agreement with Mexico—and with Canada if it is willing, in a timely manner, to meet the high standards for free, fair, and reciprocal trade contained therein.

My Administration looks forward to continued collaboration with the Congress to develop legislation to approve and implement this agreement.

Sincerely,

DONALD J. TRUMP

NOTE: Identical letters were sent to Paul D. Ryan, Speaker of the House of Representatives, and Michael R. Pence, President of the Senate.

SOURCE: Executive Office of the President. "Letter to Congressional Leaders on Intention to Enter into a Trade Agreement." August 31, 2018. *Compilation of Presidential Documents* 2018, no. 00571 (August 31, 2018). https://www.govinfo.gov/content/pkg/DCPD-201800571/pdf/DCPD-201800571.pdf.

# President Trump Addresses USMCA Questions

**October 2, 2018**

*[Only portions of the exchange with reporters related to the trade agreement have been included.]*

*The President.* The deal we made with Canada and Mexico has gotten tremendous reviews, as you see. It's been very well received by farmers and ranchers and industrialists and workers, generally. And it's been really something. And I think it's also going to be a very good deal for Mexico. And I believe it's going to be a very good deal for Canada.

But it's gotten tremendous reviews, and it's going through the process. And even many of the Democrats, including Chuck Schumer, came out and said nice things. So that's very nice to hear that. So it's nice to see a little bit of a bipartisan approach.

But the trade deal—the big trade deal—the largest deal ever made, so far, in trade—I expect to top it with China or EU or something. But this is the largest ever made. And as you know, now we're working on China. We're working on Japan. We're working on EU. But these are great deals for our Nation and great deals for our workers. So——

*Democratic Support for the United States–Mexico–Canada Agreement*

Q. What do you have to do to get Democrats to support your trade deals?

*The President.* Oh, I think the Democrats are going to like the trade deal. They already do. A lot of them have come out and said very positive things about it.

We seem to have great support for the trade bill. It covers just about everybody.

Source: Executive Office of the President. "Remarks on the United States–Mexico–Canada Agreement and an Exchange with Reporters prior to Departure for Philadelphia, Pennsylvania." October 2, 2018. *Compilation of Presidential Documents* 2018, no. 00660 (October 2, 2018). https://www.govinfo.gov/content/pkg/DCPD-201800660/pdf/DCPD-201800660.pdf.

# President Trump Answers Questions on USMCA

**December 1, 2018**

*[Only portions of the exchange with reporters related to the trade agreement have been included.]*

## North American Free Trade Agreement/United States–Mexico–Canada Agreement

Q. Is there any chance we can get the NAFTA termination stuff on the record?

*The President.* Ready? I will be formally terminating NAFTA shortly. Just so you understand, when I do that, if for any reason we're unable to make the deal, that's—*[inaudible]*—because Congress, then Congress will have a choice of approving the USMCA, which is a phenomenal deal. Much, much better than NAFTA. A great deal.

*[At this point, the President spoke off the record, and no transcript was provided. He then continued his on-the-record remarks as follows]*

So we'll be terminating NAFTA in the not-too-distant future. We are delaying it.

*[The President spoke off the record, and no transcript was provided. His on-the-record exchange with reporters then continued as follows.]*

## North American Free Trade Agreement/United States–Mexico–Canada Agreement/ Federal Government Funding Extension

Q. Can we say this is a 6-month termination?

*The President.* Say that it's a 6-month term, and I'll be terminating it within a relatively short period of time. We get rid of NAFTA. It's been a disaster for the United States. It's caused us tremendous amounts of unemployment and loss and company loss and everything else. That'll be terminated.

And so Congress will have a choice of the USMCA or pre-NAFTA, which worked very well. You got out; you negotiate your deals. It worked very well. Okay?

Thank you. . . .

Source: Executive Office of the President. "Remarks on China-United States Trade Relations and an Exchange with Reporters aboard Air Force One while En Route to Joint Base Andrews, Maryland." December 1, 2018. *Compilation of Documents* 2018, no. 00829 (December 1, 2018). https://www.govinfo.gov/content/pkg/DCPD-201800829/pdf/DCPD-201800829.pdf.

## OTHER HISTORIC DOCUMENTS OF INTEREST

### FROM THIS VOLUME

U.S. and Chinese Officials Respond to Trade Dispute, p. 163

### FROM PREVIOUS *HISTORIC DOCUMENTS*

RNC and DNC Leaders Remark on Super Tuesday; Trump and Clinton Accept Nominations, *2016*, p. 127

Clinton Remarks on House Passage of NAFTA, *1993*, p. 953

# September

# India Supreme Court Decriminalizes Homosexuality and Adultery

SEPTEMBER 6 AND SEPTEMBER 27, 2018

In 2018, the India Supreme Court issued a series of landmark rulings, including those striking down colonial-era laws that criminalized homosexuality and adultery. The Court also ordered that one of Hinduism's holiest sites, the Sabarimala temple, must lift its ban preventing women of certain ages from entering. While celebrated by lesbian, gay, bisexual, and transgender (LGBT) advocates and women's rights groups, India's political, social, and religious conservatives balked at the Court's decisions, expressing concerns that changes to the law would threaten India's traditions and ethos.

## COURT LIFTS BAN ON HOMOSEXUAL RELATIONS

Since 1861, the Indian Penal Code included a law (Section 377) prohibiting "carnal intercourse against the order of nature with any man, woman or animal." While the law technically bans a variety of sexual actions—including those between heterosexual men and women—it has largely been understood as a ban on homosexual sex. The rule was imposed when India was still a colony under British rule and was part of a package of anti-vice and immorality laws instituted across the British Empire. It carried a ten-year prison sentence as punishment for anyone found guilty of homosexuality.

Prosecutions under the law were reportedly rare; however, LGBT groups and other Section 377 critics said it was often used to blackmail homosexuals and it inhibited the fight against HIV/AIDS. Between 2016 and 2018, Mumbai-based LGBT rights group Humsafar Trust said it handled eighteen cases of gay men who were being blackmailed by police or others who threatened to report them to authorities. The group also received more than fifty complaints of harassment or discrimination in the workplace that homosexuals did not report because of the law.

Legal challenges to Section 377 were filed in 1994 and 2001 but were shuffled back and forth among courts that did not want to issue a ruling on the matter. In 2009, the Delhi High Court ruled in favor of decriminalizing homosexuality, but the decision was overturned by the Supreme Court in December 2013 following a campaign by conservative political, social, and religious groups. At the time, the Supreme Court said the issue should be dealt with by parliament. However, just over two years later, in February 2016, the Supreme Court agreed to revisit its ruling after LGBT activists filed a curative petition (a formal request to review an earlier Court ruling perceived to be a "miscarriage of justice") with the Court. More than two dozen LGBT Indians were listed as co-petitioners. The lawyers leading the challenge to Section 377 observed that these individuals were willing to risk arrest by coming out publicly in order to end the suffering caused by the law. The legal team also estimated that roughly 6 to 8 percent of the Indian population—or as many as 104 million people—might be LGBT.

A five-justice panel heard oral arguments in the case over a four-day period in July 2018. On September 6, the justices issued a unanimous decision decriminalizing homosexuality. The ruling comprised four separate written judgments, one of which was authored by Chief Justice Dipak Misra. "Criminalising carnal intercourse . . . is irrational, arbitrary, and manifestly unconstitutional," he wrote. "Social exclusion, identity seclusion and isolation from the social mainstream are still the stark realities faced by individuals today, and it is only when each and every individual is liberated from the shackles of such bondage . . . that we can call ourselves a truly free society." Justice Indu Malhotra wrote that "history owes an apology" to LGBT people, while Justice DY Chandrachud said the government had no right to control Indians' private lives. The Court noted that some provisions of Section 377, such as those pertaining to sexual relations with children, would remain in place under its ruling. The decision is also specifically focused on sexual relations; the Court did not provide an opinion on same-sex marriage or other LGBT rights.

Legal experts and Court observers said a 2017 decision by the Supreme Court that affirmed Indians' fundamental right to privacy provided the legal foundation for the homosexuality ruling. As part of the Court's written opinion in the privacy case, the justices said that sexual orientation was "an essential attribute of privacy" and therefore the Court's 2013 ruling on Section 377 was wrong. Observers also said it was significant that Prime Minister Narendra Modi's government declined to file an argument in the 2018 homosexuality case, despite previously expressing support for the law. India's government is largely controlled by the Bharatiya Janata Party, a conservative Hindu group that has generally espoused traditionalist views. "[Homosexuality] is not a normal thing," said Subramanian Swamy, a Bharatiya Janata Party MP. "We cannot celebrate it. We should invest in medical research to see if it can be cured."

LGBT rights advocates celebrated the Supreme Court's decision. "I was turning into a cynical human being with very little belief in the system, but honestly this has really shown once again that we are a functional democracy where freedom of choice, speech and rights still exist," said Ritu Dalmia, one of the advocates listed on the petition to the Court. "It's like a second freedom struggle where finally we have thrown a British law out of this country," said LGBT activist Harish Iyer. "I think the next step would be to get anti-discrimination laws in place, or anti-bullying laws." The Indian National Congress, the country's main opposition party, welcomed the Court's ruling on Twitter, writing, "We join the people of India and the LGBTQ community in their victory over prejudice. We welcome the progressive and decisive verdict from SC and hope this is the beginning of a more equal and inclusive society."

## ADULTERY LAW STRUCK DOWN

Just a few weeks later, the Supreme Court struck down a separate colonial-era law: Section 497 of the Indian Penal Code, which criminalized consensual sexual relations between a man and a married woman without the consent of the woman's husband. Men found guilty of violating the law could be sentenced up to five years in prison, ordered to pay a fine, or both. The law did not allow women to file complaints against adulterous husbands, nor could they be held liable for their participation in adulterous acts.

In August 2017, Indian businessman Joseph Shine filed a petition to the Supreme Court challenging the law's constitutionality. Shine argued that the law was not only arbitrary, it discriminated against both men and women. "Married women are not a special case for the purpose of prosecution for adultery. They are not in any way situated

differently than men," Shine wrote. He added that the law "indirectly discriminates against women by holding an erroneous presumption that women are the property of men." Shine's arguments echoed those made by women's rights groups, which claimed that Section 497 treated women like men's property and deprived them of both dignity and individual choice.

The Supreme Court's decision was once again unanimous. The panel of justices held that the law "perpetuates the subordinate status of women, denies dignity and sexual autonomy, and is based on gender stereotypes." Chief Justice Misra wrote, "A husband is not the master. Equality is the governing parameter." Announcing the ruling from the bench, Misra added, "Adultery can be grounds for civil issues including dissolution of marriage, but it cannot be a criminal offence . . . adultery might not be the cause of an unhappy marriage, it could be the result of an unhappy marriage." Unlike the Court's decision on Section 377, its ruling on Section 497 struck down the law entirely.

Women's groups celebrated the ruling. "Scrapping it was long overdue and is very welcome," said Kavita Krishnan, secretary of the All India Progressive Women's Association. "Our political class should have decriminalised adultery and homosexuality a long time ago, instead of leaving it to the courts." These groups also expressed hope that the ruling would spur a conversation about other women's issues and support their call for the criminalization of marital rape.

The government had opposed Shine's position, arguing, "Diluting adultery laws will impact the sanctity of marriages. Making adultery legal will hurt marriage bonds." Modi himself had expressed an interest in revising the law to make it gender neutral rather than have adultery decriminalized. Conservative groups were also disappointed by the Court's ruling. "Our society is not ready for this, we do not have to blindly follow western norms," said Ajay Gautam, founder of the far-right group Hum Hindu. "Public morality and the social fabric will collapse if extra-marital relations are allowed," he added. "We will help the government in drafting a counter to this that can be issued as an executive order to criminalise these immoral acts again."

## COURT ORDERS SACRED TEMPLE TO PERMIT ALL WOMEN ENTRY

Continuing its rapid-fire issuance of September rulings, the Supreme Court on September 28 ordered the operators of the Sabarimala temple to allow women of all ages to enter. The temple is one of Hinduism's holiest sites and draws tens of millions of pilgrims each year. However, most of these pilgrims are men because women of "menstruating age"—or those between the ages of ten and fifty—are prohibited from visiting. Temple officials claimed the ban was fundamental to their religious beliefs because Hindus believe that the deity to whom the temple is dedicated, Lord Ayyappa, is celibate and cannot have contact with women of menstruating age. Some further believe that menstruating women are impure, or that they would be a temptation to Lord Ayyappa and thus should be denied entry.

In its 4–1 decision, the Supreme Court said that religious freedom could not be used to justify sexist policies and that restrictions like those in place at the Sabarimala temple "can't be held as essential religious practice." Chief Justice Misra added, "Religion cannot be the cover to deny women the right to worship. To treat women as children of a lesser God is to blink at constitutional morality." Justice Malhotra dissented, writing, "Religious practices cannot solely be tested on the basis of the right to equality. It is up to the worshippers, not the court, to decide what is the religion's essential practice."

The ruling followed a multiyear effort initiated by women's rights groups in 2015 to ensure women could enter temples and mosques across India. A Mumbai court had ruled in 2016 that women had the right to enter any place of worship that men were permitted to enter and that the government should protect that right. Also in 2016, the Bombay High Court ruled that the Shani Shingnapur temple had to lift a ban that prevented any women from entering.

Sabarimala temple officials said they would appeal the Supreme Court's ruling. In defiance of the decision, conservative Hindu groups, devotees, and right-wing politicians have prevented women from entering the temple, at times clashing with police. Thousands have been arrested for their involvement in violent demonstrations. Some Hindu women have participated in the protests, saying they do not want the right to visit the temple. On November 13, the Supreme Court agreed to review its ruling and said all forty-nine petitions it had received would be heard on January 22, 2019.

—Linda Grimm

*Following is the conclusion of the India Supreme Court's ruling on Section 377 of the Indian Penal Code, issued on September 6, 2018; and excerpts of the judgment written by Chief Justice Dipak Misra to explain the Court's September 27, 2018, ruling on Section 497.*

# India Supreme Court Ruling on Homosexuality Ban

**September 6, 2018**

*[All footnotes have been omitted.]*

## Q. Conclusions

253. In view of the aforesaid analysis, we record our conclusions in seriatim:-

i.   The eminence of identity which has been luculently stated in the **NALSA** case very aptly connects human rights and the constitutional guarantee of right to life and liberty with dignity. With the same spirit, we must recognize that the concept of identity which has a constitutional tenability cannot be pigeonholed singularly to one's orientation as it may keep the individual choice at bay. At the core of the concept of identity lies self-determination, realization of one's own abilities visualizing the opportunities and rejection of external views with a clear conscience that is in accord with constitutional norms and values or principles that are, to put in a capsule, "constitutionally permissible."

ii.  In **Suresh Koushal** (supra), this Court overturned the decision of the Delhi High Court in **Naz Foundation** (supra) thereby upholding the constitutionality of Section 377 IPC and stating a ground that the LGBT community comprised only a minuscule fraction of the total population and that the mere fact

that the said Section was being misused is not a reflection of the *vires* of the Section. Such a view is constitutionally impermissible.

iii.   Our Constitution is a living and organic document capable of expansion with the changing needs and demands of the society. The Courts must commemorate that it is the Constitution and its golden principles to which they bear their foremost allegiance and they must robe themselves with the armoury of progressive and pragmatic interpretation to combat the evils of inequality and injustice that try to creep into the society. The role of the Courts gains more importance when the rights which are affected belong to a class of persons or a minority group who have been deprived of even their basic rights since time immemorial.

iv.   The primary objective of having a constitutional democracy is to transform the society progressively and inclusively. Our Constitution has been perceived to be transformative in the sense that the interpretation of its provisions should not be limited to the mere literal meaning of its words; instead they ought to be given a meaningful construction which is reflective of their intent and purpose in consonance with the changing times. Transformative constitutionalism not only includes within its wide periphery the recognition of the rights and dignity of individuals but also propagates the fostering and development of an atmosphere wherein every individual is bestowed with adequate opportunities to develop socially, economically and politically. Discrimination of any kind strikes at the very core of any democratic society. When guided by transformative constitutionalism, the society is dissuaded from indulging in any form of discrimination so that the nation is guided towards a resplendent future.

v.   Constitutional morality embraces within its sphere several virtues, foremost of them being the espousal of a pluralistic and inclusive society. The concept of constitutional morality urges the organs of the State, including the Judiciary, to preserve the heterogeneous nature of the society and to curb any attempt by the majority to usurp the rights and freedoms of a smaller or minuscule section of the populace. Constitutional morality cannot be martyred at the altar of social morality and it is only constitutional morality that can be allowed to permeate into the Rule of Law. The veil of social morality cannot be used to violate fundamental rights of even a single individual, for the foundation of constitutional morality rests upon the recognition of diversity that pervades the society.

vi.   The right to live with dignity has been recognized as a human right on the international front and by number of precedents of this Court and, therefore, the constitutional courts must strive to protect the dignity of every individual, for without the right to dignity, every other right would be rendered meaningless. Dignity is an inseparable facet of every individual that invites reciprocative respect from others to every aspect of an individual which he/she perceives as an essential attribute of his/her individuality, be it an orientation or an optional expression of choice. The Constitution has ladened the judiciary with the very important duty to protect and ensure the right of every individual including the right to express and choose without any impediments so as to enable an individual to fully realize his/her fundamental right to live with dignity.

vii.    Sexual orientation is one of the many biological phenomena which is natural and inherent in an individual and is controlled by neurological and biological factors. The science of sexuality has theorized that an individual exerts little or no control over who he/she gets attracted to. Any discrimination on the basis of one's sexual orientation would entail a violation of the fundamental right of freedom of expression.

viii.    After the privacy judgment in **Puttaswamy** (supra), the right to privacy has been raised to the pedestal of a fundamental right. The reasoning in **Suresh Koushal** (supra), that only a minuscule fraction of the total population comprises of LGBT community and that the existence of Section 377 IPC abridges the fundamental rights of a very minuscule percentage of the total populace, is found to be a discordant note. The said reasoning in *Suresh Koushal* (supra), in our opinion, is fallacious, for the framers of our Constitution could have never intended that the fundamental rights shall be extended for the benefit of the majority only and that the Courts ought to interfere only when the fundamental rights of a large percentage of the total populace is affected. In fact, the said view would be completely against the constitutional ethos, for the language employed in Part III of the Constitution as well as the intention of the framers of our Constitution mandates that the Courts must step in whenever there is a violation of the fundamental rights, even if the right/s of a single individual is/are in peril.

ix.    There is a manifest ascendance of rights under the Constitution which paves the way for the doctrine of progressive realization of rights as such rights evolve with the evolution of the society. This doctrine, as a natural corollary, gives birth to the doctrine of non-retrogression, as per which there must not be atavism of constitutional rights. In the light of the same, if we were to accept the view in *Suresh Koushal* (supra), it would tantamount to a retrograde step in the direction of the progressive interpretation of the Constitution and denial of progressive realization of rights.

x.    Autonomy is individualistic. Under the autonomy principle, the individual has sovereignty over his/her body. He/she can surrender his/her autonomy wilfully to another individual and their intimacy in privacy is a matter of their choice. Such concept of identity is not only sacred but is also in recognition of the quintessential facet of humanity in a person's nature. The autonomy establishes identity and the said identity, in the ultimate eventuate, becomes a part of dignity in an individual.

xi.    A cursory reading of both Sections 375 IPC and 377 IPC reveals that although the former Section gives due recognition to the absence of 'wilful and informed consent' for an act to be termed as rape, per contra, Section 377 does not contain any such qualification embodying in itself the absence of 'wilful and informed consent' to criminalize carnal intercourse which consequently results in criminalizing even voluntary carnal intercourse between homosexuals, heterosexuals, bisexuals and transgenders. Section 375 IPC, after the coming into force of the Criminal Law (Amendment) Act, 2013, has not used the words 'subject to any other provision of the IPC.' This indicates that Section 375 IPC is not subject to Section 377 IPC.

xii.   The expression 'against the order of nature' has neither been defined in Section 377 IPC nor in any other provision of the IPC. The connotation given to the expression by various judicial pronouncements includes all sexual acts which are not intended for the purpose of procreation. Therefore, if coitus is not performed for procreation only, it does not per se make it 'against the order of nature.'

xiii.   Section 377 IPC, in its present form, being violative of the right to dignity and the right to privacy, has to be tested, both, on the pedestal of Articles 14 and 19 of the Constitution as per the law laid down in *Maneka Gandhi* (supra) and other later authorities.

xiv.   An examination of Section 377 IPC on the anvil of Article 14 of the Constitution reveals that the classification adopted under the said Section has no reasonable nexus with its object as other penal provisions such as Section 375 IPC and the POCSO Act already penalize non-consensual carnal intercourse. Per contra, Section 377 IPC in its present form has resulted in an unwanted collateral effect whereby even 'consensual sexual acts,' which are neither harmful to children nor women, by the LGBTs have been woefully targeted thereby resulting in discrimination and unequal treatment to the LGBT community and is, thus, violative of Article 14 of the Constitution.

xv.   Section 377 IPC, so far as it criminalises even consensual sexual acts between competent adults, fails to make a distinction between non-consensual and consensual sexual acts of competent adults in private space which are neither harmful nor contagious to the society. Section 377 IPC subjects the LGBT community to societal pariah and dereliction and is, therefore, manifestly arbitrary, for it has become an odious weapon for the harassment of the LGBT community by subjecting them to discrimination and unequal treatment. Therefore, in view of the law laid down in *Shayara Bano* (supra), Section 377 IPC is liable to be partially struck down for being violative of Article 14 of the Constitution.

xvi.   An examination of Section 377 IPC on the anvil of Article 19(1)(a) reveals that it amounts to an unreasonable restriction, for public decency and morality cannot be amplified beyond a rational or logical limit and cannot be accepted as reasonable grounds for curbing the fundamental rights of freedom of expression and choice of the LGBT community. Consensual carnal intercourse among adults, be it homosexual or heterosexual, in private space, does not in any way harm the public decency or morality. Therefore, Section 377 IPC in its present form violates Article 19(1)(a) of the Constitution.

xvii.   Ergo, Section 377 IPC, so far as it penalizes any consensual sexual relationship between two adults, be it homosexuals (man and a man), heterosexuals (man and a woman) or lesbians (woman and a woman), cannot be regarded as constitutional. However, if anyone, by which we mean both a man and a woman, engages in any kind of sexual activity with an animal, the said aspect of Section 377 is constitutional and it shall remain a penal offence under Section 377 IPC. Any act of the description covered under Section 377 IPC done between two individuals without the consent of any one of them would invite penal liability under Section 377 IPC.

xviii. The decision in *Suresh Koushal* (supra), not being in consonance with what we have stated hereinabove, is overruled.

254. The Writ Petitions are, accordingly, disposed of. There shall be no order as to costs.

SOURCE: Supreme Court of India. "In the Supreme Court of India, Criminal Original Jurisdiction, Writ Petition (Criminal) No. 76 of 2016." September 6, 2018. https://www.sci.gov.in/supreme court/2016/14961/14961_2016_Judgement_06-Sep-2018.pdf.

# Excerpts from Court Ruling on Adultery Law

**September 27, 2018**

*[All footnotes have been omitted.]*

Joseph Shine                                                    . . . Petitioner(s)

VERSUS

Union of India                                                 . . . Respondent(s)

## JUDGMENT

### Dipak Misra, CJI (For himself and A.M. Khanwilkar, J.)

The beauty of the Indian Constitution is that it includes 'I,' 'you' and 'we.' Such a magnificent, compassionate and monumental document embodies emphatic inclusiveness which has been further nurtured by judicial sensitivity when it has developed the concept of golden triangle of fundamental rights. If we have to apply the parameters of a fundamental right, it is an expression of judicial sensibility which further enhances the beauty of the Constitution as conceived of. In such a situation, the essentiality of the rights of women gets the real requisite space in the living room of individual dignity rather than the space in an annexe to the main building. That is the manifestation of concerned sensitivity. Individual dignity has a sanctified realm in a civilized society. The civility of a civilization earns warmth and respect when it respects more the individuality of a woman. The said concept gets a further accent when a woman is treated with the real spirit of equality with a man. Any system treating a woman with indignity, inequity and inequality or discrimination invites the wrath of the Constitution. Any provision that might have, few decades back, got the stamp of serene approval may have to meet its epitaph with the efflux of time and growing constitutional precepts and progressive perception. A woman cannot be asked to think as a man or as how the society desires. Such a thought is abominable, for it slaughters her core identity. And, it is time to say that a husband is not the master. Equality is the governing parameter. All historical perceptions should evaporate and their obituaries be written. . . .

2. At this juncture, it is necessary to state that though there is necessity of certainty of law, yet with the societal changes and more so, when the rights are expanded by the Court in respect of certain aspects having regard to the reflective perception of the organic and living Constitution, it is not apposite to have an inflexible stand on the foundation that the concept of certainty of law should be allowed to prevail and govern. The progression in law and the perceptual shift compels the present to have a penetrating look to the past.

3. When we say so, we may not be understood that precedents are not to be treated as such and that in the excuse of perceptual shift, the binding nature of precedent should not be allowed to retain its status or allowed to be diluted. When a constitutional court faces such a challenge, namely, to be detained by a precedent or to grow out of the same because of the normative changes that have occurred in the other arenas of law and the obtaining precedent does not cohesively fit into the same, the concept of cohesive adjustment has to be in accord with the growing legal interpretation and the analysis has to be different, more so, where the emerging concept recognises a particular right to be planted in the compartment of a fundamental right, such as Articles 14 and 21 of the Constitution. In such a backdrop, when the constitutionality of a provision is assailed, the Court is compelled to have a keen scrutiny of the provision in the context of developed and progressive interpretation. A constitutional court cannot remain entrenched in a precedent, for the controversy relates to the lives of human beings who transcendentally grow. It can be announced with certitude that transformative constitutionalism asserts itself every moment and asserts itself to have its space. It is abhorrent to any kind of regressive approach. The whole thing can be viewed from another perspective. What might be acceptable at one point of time may melt into total insignificance at another point of time. However, it is worthy to note that the change perceived should not be in a sphere of fancy or individual fascination, but should be founded on the solid bedrock of change that the society has perceived, the spheres in which the legislature has responded and the rights that have been accentuated by the constitutional courts. To explicate, despite conferring many a right on women within the parameters of progressive jurisprudence and expansive constitutional vision, the Court cannot conceive of women still being treated as a property of men, and secondly, where the delicate relationship between a husband and wife does not remain so, it is seemingly implausible to allow a criminal offence to enter and make a third party culpable.

*[Sections 4–17 have been omitted and contain discussion of legal precedent and relevant portions of the Indian Penal Code.]*

18. At this juncture, we think it seemly to state that we are only going to deal with the constitutional validity of Section 497 IPC and Section 198 CrPC. The learned counsel for the petitioner submits that the provision by its very nature is arbitrary and invites the frown of Article 14 of the Constitution. . . .

*[Sections 19–21 have been omitted and contain discussion of legal precedent.]*

22. We may now proceed to test the provision on the touchstone of the aforesaid principles. On a reading of the provision, it is demonstrable that women are treated as subordinate to men inasmuch as it lays down that when there is connivance or consent of the man, there is no offence. This treats the woman as a chattel. It treats her as the property of man and totally subservient to the will of the master. It is a reflection of the social dominance that was prevalent when the penal provision was drafted.

23. As we notice, the provision treats a married woman as a property of the husband. It is interesting to note that Section 497 IPC does not bring within its purview an extra marital relationship with an unmarried woman or a widow. The dictionary meaning of 'adultery' is that a married person commits adultery if he has sex with a woman with whom he has not entered into wedlock. . . . However, the provision has made it a restricted one as a consequence of which a man, in certain situations, becomes criminally liable for having committed adultery while, in other situations, he cannot be branded as a person who has committed adultery so as to invite the culpability of Section 497 IPC. Section 198 CrPC deals with a 'person aggrieved.' Sub-section (2) of Section 198 treats the husband of the woman as deemed to be aggrieved by an offence committed under Section 497 IPC and in the absence of husband, some person who had care of the woman on his behalf at the time when such offence was committed with the leave of the court. It does not consider the wife of the adulterer as an aggrieved person. The offence and the deeming definition of an aggrieved person, as we find, is absolutely and manifestly arbitrary as it does not even appear to be rational and it can be stated with emphasis that it confers a licence on the husband to deal with the wife as he likes which is extremely excessive and disproportionate. We are constrained to think so, as it does not treat a woman as an abettor but protects a woman and simultaneously, it does not enable the wife to file any criminal prosecution against the husband. Indubitably, she can take civil action but the husband is also entitled to take civil action. However, that does not save the provision as being manifestly arbitrary. That is one aspect of the matter. If the entire provision is scanned being Argus-eyed, we notice that on the one hand, it protects a woman and on the other, it does not protect the other woman. The rationale of the provision suffers from the absence of logicality of approach and, therefore, we have no hesitation in saying that it suffers from the vice of Article 14 of the Constitution being manifestly arbitrary.

24. Presently, we shall address the issue against the backdrop of Article 21 of the Constitution. For the said purpose, it is necessary to devote some space with regard to the dignity of women and the concept of gender equality.

*[Sections 25–40 have been omitted and contain discussion of legal precedent.]*

41. From the aforesaid analysis, it is discernible that the Court, with the passage of time, has recognized the conceptual equality of woman and the essential dignity which a woman is entitled to have. There can be no curtailment of the same. But, Section 497 IPC effectively does the same by creating invidious distinctions based on gender stereotypes which creates a dent in the individual dignity of women. Besides, the emphasis on the element of connivance or consent of the husband tantamounts to subordination of women. Therefore, we have no hesitation in holding that the same offends Article 21 of the Constitution.

42. Another aspect needs to be addressed. The question we intend to pose is whether adultery should be treated as a criminal offence. Even assuming that the new definition of adultery encapsules within its scope sexual intercourse with an unmarried woman or a widow, adultery is basically associated with the institution of marriage. There is no denial of the fact that marriage is treated as a social institution and regard being had to various aspects that social history has witnessed in this country, the Parliament has always made efforts to maintain the rights of women. For instance, Section 498-A IPC deals with husband or relative of husband of a woman subjecting her to cruelty. The Parliament has also brought in the Protection of Women from Domestic Violence Act, 2005. This enactment protects women. It also enters into the matrimonial sphere. The offences under the provisions of the said enactment are different from the provision that has been conceived of under Section 497 IPC or, for that matter, concerning bringing of adultery within the net of a criminal offence. There can be no shadow of doubt that adultery can be a ground for any kind of civil wrong including dissolution of marriage. But the pivotal question is whether it should be treated as a criminal offence. When we say so, it is not to be understood that there can be any kind of social licence that destroys the matrimonial home. It is an ideal condition when the wife and husband maintain their loyalty. We are not commenting on any kind of ideal situation but, in fact, focusing on whether the act of adultery should be treated as a criminal offence. . . .

*[Sections 43–48 have been omitted and discuss various definitions of crime.]*

49. We have referred to the aforesaid theories and authorities to understand whether adultery that enters into the matrimonial realm should be treated as a criminal offence. There can be many a situation and we do not intend to get into the same. Suffice it to say, it is different from an offence committed under Section 498-A or any violation of the Protection of Women from Domestic Violence Act, 2005 or, for that matter, the protection conceived of under Section 125 of the Code of Criminal Procedure or Sections 306 or 304B or 494 IPC. These offences are meant to sub-serve various other purposes relating to a matrimonial relationship and extinction of life of a married woman during subsistence of marriage. Treating adultery an offence, we are disposed to think, would tantamount to the State entering into a real private realm. Under the existing provision, the husband is treated as an aggrieved person and the wife is ignored as a victim. Presently, the provision is reflective of a tripartite labyrinth. A situation may be conceived of where equality of status and the right to file a case may be conferred on the wife. In either situation, the whole scenario is extremely private. It stands in contradistinction to the demand for dowry, domestic violence, sending someone to jail for non-grant of maintenance or filing a complaint for second marriage. Adultery stands on a different footing from the aforesaid offences. We are absolutely conscious that the Parliament has the law making power. We make it very clear that we are not making law or legislating but only stating that a particular act, i.e., adultery does not fit into the concept of a crime. We may repeat at the cost of repetition that if it is treated as a crime, there would be immense intrusion into the extreme privacy of the matrimonial sphere. It is better to be left as a ground for divorce. For any other purpose as the Parliament has perceived or may, at any time, perceive, to treat it as a criminal offence will offend the two facets of Article 21 of the Constitution, namely, dignity of husband and wife, as the case may be, and the privacy attached to a relationship between the two. Let it be clearly stated, by no stretch of imagination, one can say, that Section 498-A or any other provision, as mentioned hereinbefore, also enters into

the private realm of matrimonial relationship. In case of the said offences, there is no third party involved. It is the husband and his relatives. There has been correct imposition by law not to demand dowry or to treat women with cruelty so as to compel her to commit suicide. The said activities deserve to be punished and the law has rightly provided so. . . .

53. In case of adultery, the law expects the parties to remain loyal and maintain fidelity throughout and also makes the adulterer the culprit. This expectation by law is a command which gets into the core of privacy. That apart, it is a discriminatory command and also a socio-moral one. Two individuals may part on the said ground but to attach criminality to the same is inapposite.

54. We may also usefully note here that adultery as a crime is no more prevalent in People's Republic of China, Japan, Australia, Brazil and many western European countries. The diversity of culture in those countries can be judicially taken note of. Non-criminalisation of adultery, apart from what we have stated hereinabove, can be proved from certain other facets. When the parties to a marriage lose their moral commitment of the relationship, it creates a dent in the marriage and it will depend upon the parties how they deal with the situation. Some may exonerate and live together and some may seek divorce. It is absolutely a matter of privacy at its pinnacle. The theories of punishment, whether deterrent or reformative, would not save the situation. A punishment is unlikely to establish commitment, if punishment is meted out to either of them or a third party. Adultery, in certain situations, may not be the cause of an unhappy marriage. It can be the result. It is difficult to conceive of such situations in absolute terms. The issue that requires to be determined is whether the said 'act' should be made a criminal offence especially when on certain occasions, it can be the cause and in certain situations, it can be the result. If the act is treated as an offence and punishment is provided, it would tantamount to punishing people who are unhappy in marital relationships and any law that would make adultery a crime would have to punish indiscriminately both the persons whose marriages have been broken down as well as those persons whose marriages are not. A law punishing adultery as a crime cannot make distinction between these two types of marriages. It is bound to become a law which would fall within the sphere of manifest arbitrariness.

55. In this regard, another aspect deserves to be noted. The jurisprudence in England, which to a large extent, is adopted by this country has never regarded adultery as a crime except for a period of ten years in the reign of Puritanical Oliver Cromwell. As we see the international perspective, most of the countries have abolished adultery as a crime. We have already ascribed when such an act is treated as a crime and how it faces the frown of Articles 14 and 21 of the Constitution. Thinking of adultery from the point of view of criminality would be a retrograde step. This Court has travelled on the path of transformative constitutionalism and, therefore, it is absolutely inappropriate to sit in a time machine to a different era where the machine moves on the path of regression. Hence, to treat adultery as a crime would be unwarranted in law.

56. As we have held that Section 497 IPC is unconstitutional and adultery should not be treated as an offence, it is appropriate to declare Section 198 CrPC which deals with the procedure for filing a complaint in relation to the offence of adultery as unconstitutional. When the substantive provision goes, the procedural provision has to pave the same path.

57. In view of the foregoing analysis, the decisions in *Sowmithri Vishnu* (supra) and *V. Revathi* (supra) stand overruled and any other judgment following precedents also stands overruled.

58. Consequently, the writ petition is allowed to the extent indicated hereinbefore.

Source: Supreme Court of India. "In the Supreme Court of India, Criminal Original Jurisdiction, Writ Petition (Criminal) No. 194 of 2017." September 27, 2018. https://www.sci.gov.in/supreme court/2017/32550/32550_2017_Judgement_27-Sep-2018.pdf.

## OTHER HISTORIC DOCUMENTS OF INTEREST

### FROM PREVIOUS *HISTORIC DOCUMENTS*

# Census Bureau Releases Annual Report on Poverty in the United States

SEPTEMBER 12, 2018

On September 12, 2018, the U.S. Census Bureau released its annual report on the number of Americans living in poverty, along with a supplemental measure of these statistics that is designed to account for factors such as government safety-net programs including the Supplemental Nutrition Assistance Program (SNAP), commonly referred to as food stamps. The supplemental report noted no statistically significant decrease in either the rate or number of people in poverty, but the traditional report did note a small decrease in the poverty rate, the third consecutive annual decline. This was coupled with an increase in real median household income.

## POVERTY RATE DECLINES FOR THIRD CONSECUTIVE YEAR

The 2018 release of the annual Census Bureau report, *Income and Poverty in the United States*, indicated a decrease of 0.4 percentage points in the official poverty rate from 12.7 percent 2016 to 12.3 percent in 2017; the number of individuals in poverty—39.7 million—was not statistically different from the prior year. As defined by the Department of Health and Human Services, the 2017 poverty threshold was $24,600 for a family of four or $12,060 for an individual.

When the poverty rate was first established in 1959, 22.4 percent of Americans were considered to be living in poverty, and that metric fell quickly over the next decade. Since then, however, progress has been uneven. The 2017 poverty rate was in line with the rate in 1970. Over that forty-seven-year period, the rate has increased fourteen times and decreased seventeen, according to the Census Bureau. "Year-to-year increases in poverty in the 14 years when the rate went up tended to be higher, an average of 0.8 percentage points. In contrast, the average annual drop in the 17 years when poverty declined was 0.6 percentage points," wrote Ashley Edwards, the Census Bureau's Poverty Statistics Branch chief.

The 12.3 percent poverty rate was the lowest since 2006, the year before the most recent recession, indicating that the economic situation in the United States was reaching its pre-recession level. Further indicative of the ongoing economic improvement, the Census Bureau reported that "[f]rom 2016 to 2017 the number of people in poverty decreased for people in families; people living in the West; people living outside metropolitan statistical areas; all workers; workers who worked less than full-time, year-round; people with a disability; people with a high school diploma but no college degree; and people with some college but no degree." Individuals with at least a bachelor's degree were the only group to experience an increase in the poverty rate or number of people in poverty, but among all educational attainment groups, those with at least a bachelor's degree still had the lowest poverty rate.

For those aged eighteen to sixty-four, the poverty rate decreased from 11.6 percent in 2016 to 11.2 percent, or 22.2 million, in 2017. For those over age sixty-five, 9.2 percent, or 4.7 million individuals, were living in poverty. Neither the rate nor the number was statistically different from that measured in 2016. Similarly, those under age eighteen had a poverty rate of 17.5 percent, or 12.8 million individuals, and neither measurement was statistically different from 2016. Children represented 32.3 percent of people in poverty in 2017, despite representing only 22.7 percent of the total U.S. population. The Census Bureau did find one significant decrease in the child poverty rate, specifically for those classified as children living in unrelated subfamilies. These children, who make up less than 1 percent of all U.S. children, have a parent or parents who are not related to the head of the household by birth, marriage, or adoption. The poverty rate for these children declined 10.5 percentage points to 37.5 percent.

The poverty rate was statistically different for only one of the four Census regions, the West. The 2017 poverty rate was 11.8 percent, or 9.1 million individuals, down from 12.8 percent and 9.8 million the year before. In the Northeast and Midwest, the poverty rate was 11.4 percent, while the South had the highest poverty rate among the four regions at 13.6 percent. West Virginia and Delaware were the only two states to see their poverty rates increase from 2016 to 2017. Twenty states experienced a decrease in the rate, while the other thirty-eight states remained unchanged. In Delaware, the rate increased significantly, from 11.7 percent to 13.6 percent, knocking out any postrecession gains. Researchers in Delaware believe this may be driven by the state's changing demographics.

Among racial groups, the poverty rate for non-Hispanic whites was 8.7 percent, or 17 million individuals, which was not statistically different from 2016. This group accounted for 42.8 percent of all people in poverty in the United States in 2017. Blacks and Asians did not experience statistically different poverty rates from 2016 to 2017, which were at 21.2 percent and 10 percent, respectively, in 2017. For Hispanics, the poverty rate fell from 19.4 percent in 2016 to 18.3 percent, or 10.8 million, in 2017. The number of Hispanics in poverty was not statistically different from the prior year.

The number of shared households, those with one or more additional nonhousehold member, spouse, or partner aged eighteen or older—not counting those enrolled in school up to age twenty-four—was 19.5 percent, or 24.9 million households in 2018. The number and percentage were not statistically different from 2017 and were still higher than the 2007 prerecession level of 19.7 million households. According to the report, it can be difficult to fully determine the impact shared households have on the overall poverty rate. For example, young adults aged twenty-five to thirty-four living with their parents in 2018 had an official 2017 poverty rate of 6.2 percent, but if poverty status was determined based solely upon the income of that individual, the rate would have been 35.4 percent. Further, "although 6.1 percent of families including at least one adult child (aged 25 to 34) of the householder were in poverty in 2017, the poverty rate for these families would have increased to 12.5 percent if the young adult were not living in—and contributing to—the household."

Median household income was $61,372 in 2017, up 1.8 percent over 2016 when adjusted for inflation, marking the third consecutive annual increase in this metric. Median household income was the highest on record since 1967 without adjusting for the change in how Census asks and measures this metric. (If adjusted, median household income in 2017 was similar to that in prior years.) However, this metric fell short of the 3.2 percent increase from 2015 to 2016 and was lower than overall economic growth, which has averaged more than 2 percent. This means that the average American household is not keeping pace with economic expansion.

The numbers in the report also indicated that inequality was continuing to grow. In 2017, median household income rose 2.6 percent for non-Hispanic white households, rose 3.7 percent for Hispanic households, but fell 0.2 percent for black households. Depth of poverty, a measure of how close families in poverty come to the poverty line, showed further growth in inequality. From 1975 to 2017, the percent of families living at half of the poverty threshold nearly doubled. "While any reduction in poverty or increase in income is a step in the right direction, most families have just barely made up the ground lost over the past decade," said Elise Gould, senior economist at the Washington-based Economic Policy Institute." In 2017 . . . well-worn patterns of inequality reemerged, with stronger growth at the top than for typical households," she added.

## SUPPLEMENTAL REPORT

The official Census estimate of poverty takes account of money earned before taxes and includes various sources of private and government income, including Social Security and cash assistance. It does not, however, account for programs intended to lift low-income Americans out of poverty, such as refundable tax credits, or the value of in-kind benefits like SNAP or housing subsidies. The official estimate also does not account for children under the age of fifteen who are unrelated to anyone in their household or expenses related to health insurance, child care, housing, and transportation and the regional variance in those costs. To provide a more accurate measure of poverty that takes into account these factors, in 2011, the Census Bureau released its first supplemental poverty report.

Released at the same time as the official report, the 2018 supplemental report recorded a poverty rate of 13.9 percent, higher than the official rate of 12.3 percent. The poverty rate for most groups was higher than the official definition, with the exception of two key demographics, children, who recorded a poverty rate of 15.6 percent in the supplemental report and 17.5 percent in the official measure, and cohabiting partner units who had a 13.3 percent supplemental poverty rate but a 25.1 percent official rate.

The supplemental poverty report shows the impact of social programs on the number and rate of those in poverty. For example, Social Security benefits kept 27 million Americans out of poverty, while refundable tax credits lifted 8.3 million out of poverty. Refundable tax credits, which include the Earned Income Tax Credit and the child tax credit, kept 4.5 million children from falling into poverty. The supplemental report also notes that by subtracting medical expenses from income, the poverty rate increases by 3.4 percentage points, which would classify 10.9 million more Americans as living in poverty. "Medical expenses were the largest contributor to increasing the number of individuals in poverty," the report states.

## UNEMPLOYMENT REACHES LOWEST LEVEL IN FOUR DECADES; INEQUALITY CONTINUES

After being stuck at 4.1 percent since October 2017, the U.S. unemployment rate dipped to 3.9 percent in April 2018 and continued its downward trend throughout the year, reaching 3.7 percent in September, the lowest since 1969. The White House celebrated the report and the ongoing expansion of the U.S. economy. "The American economy continues to fire on all cylinders," said Department of Labor Secretary Alexander Acosta. "During the past few months, we have seen GDP growth exceed 4 percent, consumer confidence rise to an 18-year high, and the stock market set new records."

While the unemployment rate was the focal point of the jobs report, it contained somewhat disappointing statistics elsewhere. In September, for example, the economy gained only 134,000 jobs, its lowest for the year, down significantly from the 270,000 added in August. Economists speculated that this was likely caused by the impact of Hurricane Florence, which may have hampered hiring in the southeastern United States. Additionally, while unemployment claims were continuing to fall and the labor force participation rate was holding steady at 62.7 percent, in September, the number of involuntarily part-time workers—those seeking full-time work but forced to accept a part-time position—increased to 4.6 million. In 2000, that number was 3.2 million.

Wage growth also fell slightly, from 2.9 percent in August to 2.8 percent in September. Analysts puzzled over why wage growth was so slow, given that a low unemployment rate means that employers face a smaller labor pool, which generally results in higher salaries. In the 1990s and early 2000s, the most recent period reflecting 2018's economic growth, wages rose at an annual rate of 4 percent. According to the Bureau of Labor Statistics, gains in full-time median weekly earnings were lower than inflation through the last quarter of 2017 and the first half of 2018. Any minor increases experienced by workers were largely wiped out by higher costs for necessities such as gas and rent. A Brookings Institution report by Ryan Nunn and Jay Shambaugh found that "workers simply aren't getting ahead" because "real wage growth has been consistently hovering around zero."

—Heather Kerrigan

*Following are excerpts from the U.S. Census Bureau report on poverty in the United States, released on September 12, 2018; and excerpts from the U.S. Census Bureau supplemental poverty report, also released on September 12, 2018.*

# Census Bureau Report on Poverty in the United States

DOCUMENT

September 12, 2018

*[All portions of the report not corresponding to poverty have been omitted. Tables, graphs, and footnotes, and references to them, have been omitted.]*

## INTRODUCTION

The U.S. Census Bureau collects data and publishes estimates on income and poverty in order to evaluate national economic trends as well as to understand their impact on the well-being of households, families, and individuals. This report presents data on income and poverty in the United States based on information collected in the 2018 and earlier Current Population Survey (CPS) Annual Social and Economic Supplements (ASEC) conducted by the Census Bureau.

This report contains two main sections, one focuses on income and the other on poverty. Each section presents estimates by characteristics such as race, Hispanic origin, nativity, and region. Other topics, such as earnings and family poverty rates are included only in the relevant section.

## Summary of Findings

- Real median household income increased 1.8 percent between 2016 and 2017. This is the third consecutive annual increase in median household income.

- The 2017 real median earnings of all male workers increased 3.0 percent from 2016, while real median earnings for their female counterparts saw no statistically significant change between 2016 and 2017.

- In 2017, the real median earnings of men and women working full-time, year-round each decreased from their respective 2016 medians by 1.1 percent.

- The number of men and women with earnings working full-time, year-round increased by 1.4 million and 1.0 million, respectively, between 2016 and 2017.

- The official poverty rate decreased by 0.4 percentage points between 2016 and 2017. This is the third consecutive annual decrease in the poverty rate.

- The number of people in poverty in 2017 was not statistically different from 2016.

For most demographic groups . . . , the 2017 median household income estimates were higher or were not statistically different from the 2016 estimates. Householders aged 15 to 24 were the only group to experience a decline in median household income between 2016 and 2017. For most demographic groups . . . , poverty rates in 2017 were either lower than in 2016 or not statistically different. The only group to experience a statistically significant increase in poverty rates from 2016 to 2017 were people with at least a bachelor's degree.

*[The section on income in the United States has been omitted.]*

## POVERTY IN THE UNITED STATES

### Highlights

- The official poverty rate in 2017 was 12.3 percent, down 0.4 percentage points from 12.7 percent in 2016. This is the third consecutive annual decline in poverty. Since 2014, the poverty rate has fallen 2.5 percentage points from 14.8 percent to 12.3 percent.

- In 2017 there were 39.7 million people in poverty, not statistically different from the number in poverty in 2016.

- Between 2016 and 2017, the poverty rate for adults aged 18 to 64 declined 0.4 percentage points, from 11.6 percent to 11.2 percent, while poverty rates for individuals under the age of 18 and for people aged 65 and older were not statistically different from 2016.

- Between 2016 and 2017, people with at least a bachelor's degree were the only group to have an increase in the poverty rate or the number of people in poverty.

Among this group, the poverty rate increased 0.3 percentage points and the number in poverty increased by 363,000 individuals between 2016 and 2017. Even with this increase, among educational attainment groups, people with at least a bachelor's degree had the lowest poverty rates in 2017.

- From 2016 to 2017 the number of people in poverty decreased for people in families; people living in the West; people living outside metropolitan statistical areas; all workers; workers who worked less than full-time, year-round; people with a disability; people with a high school diploma but no college degree; and people with some college but no degree.

## Race and Hispanic Origin

The poverty rate for non-Hispanic Whites was 8.7 percent in 2017 with 17.0 million individuals in poverty. Neither the poverty rate nor the number in poverty was statistically different from 2016. The poverty rate for non-Hispanic Whites was lower than the poverty rates for other racial groups. Non-Hispanic Whites accounted for 60.5 percent of the total population and 42.8 percent of the people in poverty in 2017.

The poverty rate for Blacks was 21.2 percent in 2017, representing 9.0 million people in poverty. For Asians, the 2017 poverty rate and the number in poverty were 10.0 percent and 2.0 million, respectively. Among Blacks and Asians, neither the poverty rate nor the number in poverty was statistically different from 2016. The poverty rate for Hispanics was 18.3 percent in 2017, down from 19.4 percent in 2016. In 2017, the number of Hispanics in poverty was 10.8 million, not significantly different from the number in 2016.

## Sex

In 2017, the poverty rate for males was 11.0 percent, not statistically different from 2016. The 2017 poverty rate for females was 13.6 percent, down from 14.0 percent in 2016.

The poverty rate in 2017 for women aged 18 to 64 was 13.0 percent while the poverty rate for men aged 18 to 64 was 9.4 percent. The poverty rate for women aged 65 and older was 10.5 percent while the poverty rate for men aged 65 and older was 7.5 percent. For people under the age of 18, the poverty rate for girls (17.7 percent) and the poverty rate for boys (17.3 percent) were not statistically different.

## Age

Between 2016 and 2017, the poverty rate for people aged 18 to 64 decreased to 11.2 percent, down from 11.6 percent. The number of people in poverty within this age group was 22.2 million in 2017, not statistically different from 2016. For people aged 65 and older, the 2017 poverty rate was 9.2 percent, representing 4.7 million individuals in poverty. Neither the poverty rate nor the number in poverty was statistically different from 2016 for this age group.

For people under the age of 18, 17.5 percent (12.8 million) were in poverty in 2017, neither estimate statistically different from 2016. This group represented 22.7 percent of the total population in 2017 and 32.3 percent of the people in poverty.

Related children are people under the age of 18 related to the householder by birth, marriage, or adoption who are not themselves householders or spouses of householders.

In 2017, 17.1 percent (12.4 million) of related children under the age of 18 were in poverty, not statistically different from 2016.

The number and percent of related children in poverty were not statistically different from 2016 to 2017 across all household types—those living with married, female, or male householders. In 2017, the proportion and number of related children in poverty were 8.4 percent and 4.2 million among married-couple families, 40.8 percent and 7.2 million among female-householder families, and 19.1 percent and 1.0 million among male-householder families.

One group of children did experience a statistically-significant decline in their poverty rate: children living in unrelated sub-families. These are children whose parents (or parent) are not related by birth, marriage, or adoption to the householder. The poverty rate for these children fell by 10.5 percentage points: from 48.0 percent in 2016 to 37.5 percent in 2017. Note, however, that these children represent less than 1.0 percent of all children.

The poverty rate and the number in poverty for related children under the age of 6 were 19.2 percent and 4.5 million in 2017, not statistically different from 2016. About half (48.4 percent) of related children under the age of 6 in families with a female householder were in poverty. This was more than four times the rate of their counterparts in married-couple families (9.5 percent).

## Nativity

The poverty rate for the native-born population decreased to 11.9 percent in 2017, down from 12.3 percent in 2016. The number of native-born individuals in poverty was 33.1 million in 2017, not significantly different from 2016. Among the foreign-born population, 14.5 percent and 6.6 million were in poverty in 2017. Neither the poverty rate nor the number of foreign-born individuals in poverty were statistically different from the 2016 estimate.

The poverty rate in 2017 for foreign-born naturalized citizens (10.1 percent) was lower than the poverty rates for noncitizens and native-born citizens (18.6 percent and 11.9 percent, respectively). Neither the poverty rate nor the number of foreign-born naturalized citizens in poverty in 2017 (2.2 million) were statistically different from the 2016 estimate. The poverty rate for those who were not U.S. citizens in 2017 was 18.6 percent, representing 4.4 million individuals in poverty. Neither the 2017 poverty rate for noncitizens nor the number in poverty were significantly different from the 2016 estimate. Within the foreign-born population in 2017, 48.1 percent were naturalized U.S. citizens, while the remaining were not citizens of the United States.

## Region

Between 2016 and 2017, the West was the only region to experience a statistically-significant change in the poverty rate or the number of people in poverty. The 2017 poverty rate and number in poverty for the West was 11.8 percent and 9.1 million, down from 12.8 percent and 9.8 million in 2016. In 2017, the poverty rate and the number in poverty was 11.4 percent and 6.4 million for the Northeast, 11.4 percent and 7.6 million for the Midwest, and 13.6 percent and 16.6 million for the South. The South had the highest poverty rate in 2017 relative to the other three regions.

## Residence

Inside metropolitan statistical areas, the poverty rate and the number of people in poverty in 2017 were 11.9 percent and 33.3 million, neither statistically different from 2016. Among those living outside metropolitan statistical areas, the poverty rate decreased to 14.8 percent in 2017, down from 15.8 percent in 2016. The number in poverty decreased to 6.4 million, down from 6.9 million.

The 2017 poverty rate for those living inside metropolitan areas but not in principal cities was 9.7 percent, and the number in poverty was 17.1 million. Among those who lived in principal cities, the poverty rate in 2017 was 15.6 percent and the number in poverty was 16.2 million. Neither group experienced a statistically-significant change in the poverty rate nor in the number in poverty between 2016 and 2017.

## Work Experience

In 2017, 5.3 percent of workers aged 18 to 64 were in poverty, a decline from 5.8 percent in 2016. For those who worked full-time, year-round, 2.2 percent were in poverty in 2017, not statistically different from 2016. Those working less than full-time, year-round had a poverty rate in 2017 of 13.4 percent, down from 14.7 percent in 2016.

Among those aged 18 to 64 who did not work at least 1 week during the calendar year, 30.7 percent were in poverty in 2017, not statistically different from 2016. Those who did not work at least 1 week in 2017 represented 23.2 percent of all people aged 18 to 64, while they made up 63.4 percent of people aged 18 to 64 in poverty.

## Disability Status

For people aged 18 to 64 with a disability, the poverty rate in 2017 was 24.9 percent, down from 26.8 percent in 2016. The number in poverty with a disability was 3.8 million, a decline from 4.1 million in 2016. In 2017, 10.1 percent of people aged 18 to 64 without a disability were in poverty, representing 18.4 million people. Neither the poverty rate nor the number in poverty without a disability showed any statistical change between 2016 and 2017.

Among people aged 18 to 64, those with a disability represented 7.6 percent of all people, compared with 16.9 percent of people aged 18 to 64 in poverty.

## Educational Attainment

In 2017, 24.5 percent of people aged 25 and older without a high school diploma were in poverty, not significantly different from 2016. The 2017 poverty rate for those with a high school diploma but with no college was 12.7 percent, down from 13.3 percent in 2016. For those with some college but no degree, 8.8 percent were in poverty in 2017, a decline from 9.4 percent in 2016.

Among people with at least a bachelor's degree, the poverty rate and the number in poverty were 4.8 percent and 3.7 million in 2017, up from 4.5 percent and 3.3 million in 2016. This was the only group to have an increase in the poverty rate or the number of people in poverty between 2016 and 2017. Even with this increase, among educational attainment groups, people with at least a bachelor's degree had the lowest poverty rates in

2017. People with at least a bachelor's degree in 2017 represented 35.0 percent of all people aged 25 and older, compared with 16.5 percent of people aged 25 and older in poverty.

## Families

The poverty rate for primary families in 2017 was 9.3 percent, representing 7.8 million families, a decline from 9.8 percent and 8.1 million families in 2016. The poverty rate for unrelated subfamilies was 30.8 percent, representing 137,000 families, a decline from 40.6 percent and 202,000 families in 2016.

The poverty rate and the number in poverty in 2017 were 4.9 percent and 3.0 million for married-couple primary families, 25.7 percent and 4.0 million for primary families with a female householder, and 12.4 percent and 793,000 for primary families with a male householder. None of these family types experienced a statistically-significant change in the rate or number of families in poverty between 2016 and 2017.

## Depth of Poverty

Categorizing a person as "in poverty" or "not in poverty" is one way to describe his or her economic situation. The income-to-poverty ratio and the income deficit or surplus describe additional aspects of economic well-being. While the poverty rate shows the proportion of people with income below the relevant poverty threshold, the income-to-poverty ratio gauges the depth of poverty and shows how close a family's income is to its poverty threshold. The income-to-poverty ratio is reported as a percentage that compares a family's or an unrelated person's income with the applicable threshold. For example, a family with an income-to-poverty ratio of 125 percent has income that is 25 percent above its poverty threshold.

The income deficit or surplus shows how many dollars a family's or an individual's income is below (or above) their poverty threshold. For those with an income deficit, the measure is an estimate of the dollar amount necessary to reach their poverty threshold.

## Ratio of Income to Poverty

. . . In 2017, 18.5 million people reported family income below one-half of their poverty threshold. They represented 5.7 percent of all people and 46.7 percent of those in poverty. Approximately 16.7 percent of individuals had family income below 125 percent of their threshold, 21.0 percent had family income below 150 percent of their poverty threshold, and 29.7 percent had family income below 200 percent of their threshold.

Of the 18.5 million people in 2017 with family income below one-half of their poverty threshold, 5.9 million were individuals under the age of 18, 11.0 million were aged 18 to 64, and 1.7 million were aged 65 and older. The demographic makeup of the population differs at varying degrees of poverty.

In 2017, people under the age of 18 represented:

- 22.7 percent of the overall population.

- 19.8 percent of people in families with income above 200 percent of their poverty threshold.

- 27.9 percent of people in families with income between 100 percent and 200 percent of their poverty threshold.

- 31.6 percent of people in families below 50 percent of their poverty threshold.

By comparison, people aged 65 and older represented:

- 15.8 percent of the overall population.

- 15.7 percent of people in families with income above 200 percent of their poverty threshold.

- 19.1 percent of people in families between 100 percent and 200 percent of their poverty threshold.

- 8.9 percent of people in families below 50 percent of their poverty threshold.

## Income Deficit

The income deficit for families in poverty (the difference in dollars between a family's income and its poverty threshold) averaged $10,819 in 2017, not statistically different than the inflation-adjusted income deficit for families in poverty in 2016. The average income deficit was larger for families with a female householder ($11,460) than for married-couple families ($10,309).

The average per capita income deficit was also larger for families with a female householder ($3,391) than for married-couple families ($2,817). For unrelated individuals, the average income deficit for those in poverty was $7,327 in 2017. The $7,013 deficit for unrelated women was lower than the $7,744 deficit for unrelated men.

## Shared Households

Shared households are defined as households that include at least one "additional" adult, a person aged 18 or older, who is not the householder, spouse, or cohabiting partner of the householder. Adults aged 18 to 24 who are enrolled in school are not counted as additional adults.

In 2018, the number and percentage of shared households remained higher than in 2007, the year before the most recent recession. In 2007, 17.0 percent of all households were shared households, totaling 19.7 million shared households. In 2018, 19.5 percent of all households were shared households, totaling 24.9 million shared households. The number and percentage of shared households in 2018 were not statistically different from 2017.

In 2018, an estimated 28.1 percent (12.6 million) of adults aged 25 to 34 were additional adults in someone else's household, neither of which was statistically different from 2017. Of young adults aged 25 to 34, 16.8 percent lived with their parents in 2018, not statistically different from 2017. However, the number of these young adults residing with their parents increased by 430,000 individuals between 2017 and 2018, to 7.5 million.

It is difficult to assess the precise impact of household sharing on overall poverty rates. Adults aged 25 to 34 living with their parents in 2018 had an official 2017 poverty rate of 6.2 percent (when the entire family's income is compared with the threshold that includes the young adult as a member of the family). However, if poverty status had been determined using only the young adult's own income, 35.4 percent of those aged 25 to 34 would have been below the poverty threshold for a single person under the age of 65. However, although 6.1 percent of families including at least one adult child (aged 25 to 34) of the householder were in poverty in 2017, the poverty rate for these families would have increased to 12.5 percent if the young adult were not living in—and contributing to—the household.

*[The sections discussing additional information on income and poverty and sources and estimates have been omitted.]*

SOURCE: U.S. Census Bureau. "Income and Poverty in the United States: 2017." September 12, 2018. https://www.census.gov/content/dam/Census/library/publications/2018/demo/p60-263.pdf.

# Census Bureau Report on Supplemental Poverty Measures

**September 12, 2018**

*[All footnotes, figures, tables (except Table A.2), graphics, and references to them have been omitted.]*

## INTRODUCTION

Since the publication of the first official U.S. poverty estimates, researchers and policy-makers have continued to discuss the best approach to measure income and poverty in the United States. Beginning in 2011, the U.S. Census Bureau began publishing the Supplemental Poverty Measure (SPM), which extends the official poverty measure by taking account of many of the government programs designed to assist low-income families and individuals that are not included in the official poverty measure. This is the eighth report describing the SPM, released by the Census Bureau, with support from the Bureau of Labor Statistics (BLS). This report presents updated estimates of the prevalence of poverty in the United States using the official measure and the SPM based on information collected in 2018 and earlier Current Population Survey Annual Social and Economic Supplements (CPS ASEC).

*[The background discussion has been omitted.]*

## POVERTY ESTIMATES FOR 2017: OFFICIAL AND SPM

. . . 13.9 percent of people were poor using the SPM definition of poverty, higher than the 12.3 percent using the official definition of poverty with the comparable universe. While for most groups, SPM rates were higher than official poverty rates, the SPM shows lower poverty rates for children and individuals living in cohabiting partner units. Official and SPM poverty rates for individuals living in female reference person units and individuals who did not work were not statistically different. Note that poverty rates for those aged 65 and older were higher under the SPM compared with the official measure. This partially reflects that the official thresholds are set lower for units with householders in this age group, while the SPM thresholds do not vary by age.

Estimates for the SPM are available back to 2009. Since the SPM's initial production, the SPM rate has been higher than the official poverty rate. . . . The SPM has ranged from 0.6 to 1.6 percentage points higher than the official measure since 2009. In 2017, the gap between the SPM and the official measure was the largest since 2009.

. . . In 2017, the gap between the official poverty measure and the SPM for children narrowed to 1.9 percentage points, lower than all previous years.

## Poverty Rates by State: Official and SPM

To create state-level estimates using the CPS ASEC, the Census Bureau recommends using 3-year averages for additional statistical reliability. . . . The 3-year average poverty rate for the United States in 2015–2017 was 12.9 percent with the official measure and 14.1 percent using the SPM.

While the SPM national poverty rate was higher than the official, that difference varies by geographic area. . . . States where the SPM rates were higher than official are shaded orange; states where SPM was lower than official are shaded blue; and states where the differences in the rates were not statistically significant are grey.

The 16 states for which the SPM rates were higher than the official poverty rates were California, Colorado, Connecticut, Delaware, Florida, Hawaii, Illinois, Maryland, Massachusetts, Nevada, New Hampshire, New Jersey, New York, Oregon, Texas, and Virginia. The SPM rate for the District of Columbia was also higher. Higher SPM rates by state may occur for many reasons. Geographic adjustments for housing costs and/or different mixes of housing tenure may result in higher SPM thresholds. Higher nondiscretionary expenses, such as taxes or medical expenses, may also drive higher SPM rates.

The 18 states where SPM rates were lower than the official poverty rates were Alabama, Arkansas, Idaho, Kansas, Kentucky, Louisiana, Maine, Michigan, Mississippi, Montana, New Mexico, Ohio, Oklahoma, Rhode Island, South Carolina, South Dakota, West Virginia, and Wisconsin. Lower SPM rates could occur due to lower thresholds reflecting lower housing costs, a different mix of housing tenure, or more generous noncash benefits.

The 16 states that were not statistically different under the two measures include Alaska, Arizona, Georgia, Indiana, Iowa, Minnesota, Missouri, Nebraska, North Carolina, North Dakota, Pennsylvania, Tennessee, Utah, Vermont, Washington, and Wyoming.

## The SPM and the Effect of Cash and Noncash Transfers, Taxes, and Other Nondiscretionary Expenses

This section moves away from comparing the SPM with the official measure and looks only at the SPM. This analysis allows one to gauge the effects of taxes and transfers and other necessary expenses using the SPM as a measure of economic well-being. Income used for estimating the official poverty measure includes cash benefits from the government (e.g., Social Security, unemployment insurance benefits, public assistance benefits, and workers' compensation benefits), but does not take account of taxes or noncash benefits aimed at improving the economic situation of the poor. The SPM incorporates all of these elements, adding in cash benefits, and noncash transfers, while subtracting necessary expenses, such as taxes, medical expenses, and expenses related to work. An important contribution of the SPM is that it allows us to gauge the potential magnitude of the effect of tax credits and transfers in alleviating poverty. We can also examine the effects of nondiscretionary expenses, such as work and medical expenses. . . .

Removing one item from the calculation of SPM resources and recalculating poverty rates shows, for example, that Social Security benefits decrease the SPM rate by 8.4 percentage points, from 22.3 percent to 13.9 percent. This means that with Social Security benefits, 27.0 million fewer people are living below the poverty line. When including refundable tax credits (the Earned Income Tax Credit [EITC] and the refundable portion of the child tax credit) in resources, 8.3 million fewer people are considered poor, all else constant. On the other hand, when the SPM subtracts amounts paid for child support, income and payroll taxes, work-related expenses, and medical expenses, the number and percentage in poverty are higher. When subtracting medical expenses from income, the SPM rate is 3.4 percentage points higher. In numbers, 10.9 million more people are classified as poor.

In comparison to 2016, the 2017 anti-poverty impacts of Social Security and child support received increased, with Social Security lifting 0.9 million more individuals out of poverty and child support received lifting 0.2 million additional individuals out of poverty. Conversely, child support paid pushed 0.1 million fewer individuals into poverty in 2017 than in 2016.

. . . In 2017, accounting for refundable tax credits resulted in a 6.1 percentage point decrease in the child poverty rate, representing 4.5 million children prevented from falling into poverty by the inclusion of these credits. Subtracting medical expenses, such as contributions toward the cost of medical care and health insurance premiums, from the income of families with children resulted in a child poverty rate 3.1 percentage points higher. For the 65 and older group, SPM rates increased by about 5.4 percentage points with the subtraction of medical expenses from income, while Social Security benefits lowered poverty rates by 34.6 percentage points for the 65 and older group, lifting 17.7 million individuals above the poverty line.

## Summary

This report provides estimates of the SPM for the United States. The results shown illustrate differences between the official measure of poverty and a poverty measure that takes account of noncash benefits received by families and nondiscretionary expenses that they must pay. The SPM also employs a poverty threshold that is updated by the BLS with information on expenditures for food, clothing, shelter, and utilities. Results showed higher poverty rates using the SPM than the official measure for most groups, with children being an exception with lower poverty rates using the SPM.

The SPM allows us to examine the effect of taxes, noncash transfers, and necessary expenses on the poor and on important groups within the population in poverty. As such, there are lower percentages of the SPM poverty populations in the very high and very low resource categories than we find using the official measure. Since noncash benefits help those in extreme poverty, there were lower percentages of individuals with resources below half the SPM threshold for most groups. In addition, the effect of benefits received from each program and taxes and other nondiscretionary expenses on SPM rates were examined.

**Table A.2** Number and Percentage of People in Poverty by Different Poverty Measures: 2017

(Numbers in thousands, margin of error in thousands or percentage points as appropriate. For information on confidentiality protection, sampling error, nonsampling error, and definitions, see www2.census.gov/programs-surveys/cps/techdocs /cpsmar18.pdf)

| Characteristic | Number** (in thousands) | Official** | | | | SPM | | | | Difference | |
| | | Number | | Percent | | Number | | Percent | | | |
| | | Estimate | Margin of error† (±) | Estimate | Margin of error† (±) | Estimate | Margin of error† (±) | Estimate | Margin of error† (±) | Number | Percent |
| **All people** | **323,156** | **39,804** | **924** | **12.3** | **0.3** | **44,972** | **993** | **13.9** | **0.3** | **\*5,168** | **\*1.6** |
| **Sex** | | | | | | | | | | | |
| Male | 158,426 | 17,427 | 486 | 11.0 | 0.3 | 20,717 | 501 | 13.1 | 0.3 | \*3,289 | \*2.1 |
| Female | 164,730 | 22,377 | 530 | 13.6 | 0.3 | 24,255 | 570 | 14.7 | 0.3 | \*1,878 | \*1.1 |
| **Age** | | | | | | | | | | | |
| Under 18 years | 73,963 | 12,914 | 434 | 17.5 | 0.6 | 11,521 | 399 | 15.6 | 0.5 | \*–1,393 | \*–1.9 |
| 18 to 64 years | 198,113 | 22,209 | 564 | 11.2 | 0.3 | 26,244 | 628 | 13.2 | 0.3 | \*4,035 | \*2.0 |
| 65 years and older | 51,080 | 4,681 | 190 | 9.2 | 0.4 | 7,207 | 274 | 14.1 | 0.5 | \*2,526 | \*4.9 |
| **Type of Unit** | | | | | | | | | | | |
| Married couple | 193,567 | 11,020 | 491 | 5.7 | 0.3 | 16,879 | 663 | 8.7 | 0.3 | \*5,859 | \*3.0 |
| Cohabiting partners | 26,833 | 6,729 | 332 | 25.1 | 1.0 | 3,558 | 298 | 13.3 | 1.1 | \*–3,171 | \*–11.8 |
| Female reference person | 42,454 | 11,111 | 458 | 26.2 | 0.9 | 11,408 | 448 | 26.9 | 0.9 | 297 | 0.7 |
| Male reference person | 14,626 | 1,641 | 193 | 11.2 | 1.2 | 2,382 | 208 | 16.3 | 1.3 | \*741 | \*5.1 |
| Unrelated individuals | 45,676 | 9,303 | 340 | 20.4 | 0.6 | 10,745 | 375 | 23.5 | 0.7 | \*1,441 | \*3.2 |

*(Continued)*

(Continued)

| Characteristic | Number** (in thousands) Estimate | Official** | | | | SPM | | | | Difference | |
|---|---|---|---|---|---|---|---|---|---|---|---|
| | | Number | | Percent | | Number | | Percent | | | |
| | | Estimate | Margin of error† (±) | Estimate | Margin of error† (±) | Estimate | Margin of error† (±) | Estimate | Margin of error† (±) | Number | Percent |
| **Race[1] and Hispanic Origin** | | | | | | | | | | | |
| White | 247,695 | 26,522 | 719 | 10.7 | 0.3 | 30,433 | 780 | 12.3 | 0.3 | *3,911 | *1.6 |
| White, not Hispanic | 195,530 | 17,037 | 574 | 8.7 | 0.3 | 19,249 | 594 | 9.8 | 0.3 | *2,212 | *1.1 |
| Black | 42,564 | 9,007 | 372 | 21.2 | 0.9 | 9,394 | 410 | 22.1 | 1.0 | *387 | *0.9 |
| Asian | 19,484 | 1,953 | 190 | 10.0 | 1.0 | 2,948 | 204 | 15.1 | 1.0 | *995 | *5.1 |
| Hispanic (any race) | 59,227 | 10,835 | 425 | 18.3 | 0.7 | 12,654 | 488 | 21.4 | 0.8 | *1,819 | *3.1 |
| **Nativity** | | | | | | | | | | | |
| Native born | 277,748 | 33,198 | 858 | 12.0 | 0.3 | 35,538 | 864 | 12.8 | 0.3 | *2,340 | *0.8 |
| Foreign born | 45,408 | 6,607 | 295 | 14.5 | 0.6 | 9,435 | 367 | 20.8 | 0.7 | *2,828 | *6.2 |
| Naturalized citizen | 21,854 | 2,213 | 146 | 10.1 | 0.6 | 3,513 | 195 | 16.1 | 0.8 | *1,300 | *6.0 |
| Not a citizen | 23,554 | 4,394 | 238 | 18.7 | 0.9 | 5,921 | 297 | 25.1 | 1.1 | *1,527 | *6.5 |
| **Educational Attainment** | | | | | | | | | | | |
| Total aged 25 and older | 219,830 | 22,163 | 516 | 10.1 | 0.2 | 27,801 | 635 | 12.6 | 0.3 | *5,638 | *2.6 |
| No high school diploma | 22,411 | 5,485 | 217 | 24.5 | 0.9 | 6,429 | 259 | 28.7 | 1.0 | *943 | *4.2 |

| Characteristic | Number** (in thousands) | Official** Number Estimate | Official** Number Margin of error† (±) | Official** Percent Estimate | Official** Percent Margin of error† (±) | SPM Number Estimate | SPM Number Margin of error† (±) | SPM Percent Estimate | SPM Percent Margin of error† (±) | Difference Number | Difference Percent |
|---|---|---|---|---|---|---|---|---|---|---|---|
| High school, no college | 62,685 | 7,942 | 285 | 12.7 | 0.4 | 10,038 | 350 | 16.0 | 0.5 | *2,095 | *3.3 |
| Some college | 57,810 | 5,075 | 206 | 8.8 | 0.4 | 6,263 | 247 | 10.8 | 0.4 | *1,189 | *2.1 |
| Bachelor's degree or higher | 76,924 | 3,661 | 181 | 4.8 | 0.2 | 5,072 | 207 | 6.6 | 0.3 | *1,411 | *1.8 |
| **Tenure** | | | | | | | | | | | |
| Owner | 214,924 | 15,185 | 534 | 7.1 | 0.2 | 19,764 | 612 | 9.2 | 0.3 | *4,579 | *2.1 |
| Owner/mortgage | 138,946 | 7,152 | 365 | 5.1 | 0.3 | 10,492 | 478 | 7.6 | 0.3 | *3,340 | *2.4 |
| Owner/no mortgage/rent free | 79,339 | 8,718 | 435 | 11.0 | 0.5 | 9,886 | 444 | 12.5 | 0.5 | *1,168 | *1.5 |
| Renter | 104,871 | 23,934 | 691 | 22.8 | 0.6 | 24,594 | 706 | 23.5 | 0.6 | *660 | *0.6 |
| **Residence[2]** | | | | | | | | | | | |
| Inside metropolitan statistical areas | 280,048 | 33,408 | 866 | 11.9 | 0.3 | 39,472 | 955 | 14.1 | 0.3 | *6,064 | *2.2 |
| Inside principal cities | 104,068 | 16,241 | 635 | 15.6 | 0.5 | 18,216 | 687 | 17.5 | 0.5 | *1,974 | *1.9 |
| Outside principal cities | 175,980 | 17,167 | 584 | 9.8 | 0.3 | 21,257 | 666 | 12.1 | 0.4 | *4,090 | *2.3 |
| Outside metropolitan statistical areas | 43,108 | 6,396 | 526 | 14.8 | 0.7 | 5,500 | 463 | 12.8 | 0.6 | *–897 | *–2.1 |

(Continued)

(Continued)

| Characteristic | Number** (in thousands) | Official** | | | | SPM | | | | Difference | |
|---|---|---|---|---|---|---|---|---|---|---|---|
| | | Number | | Percent | | Number | | Percent | | | |
| | | Estimate | Margin of error† (±) | Estimate | Margin of error† (±) | Estimate | Margin of error† (±) | Estimate | Margin of error† (±) | Number | Percent |
| **Region** | | | | | | | | | | | |
| Northeast | 56,065 | 6,381 | 340 | 11.4 | 0.6 | 7,976 | 396 | 14.2 | 0.7 | *1,594 | *2.8 |
| Midwest | 67,481 | 7,661 | 397 | 11.4 | 0.6 | 7,198 | 372 | 10.7 | 0.6 | *−463 | *−0.7 |
| South | 122,480 | 16,662 | 593 | 13.6 | 0.5 | 18,147 | 651 | 14.8 | 0.5 | *1,485 | *1.2 |
| West | 77,130 | 9,100 | 400 | 11.8 | 0.5 | 11,652 | 404 | 15.1 | 0.5 | *2,552 | *3.3 |
| **Health Insurance Coverage** | | | | | | | | | | | |
| With private insurance | 217,007 | 11,219 | 493 | 5.2 | 0.2 | 17,872 | 602 | 8.2 | 0.3 | *6,653 | *3.1 |
| With public, no private insurance | 77,606 | 21,838 | 584 | 28.1 | 0.7 | 19,851 | 579 | 25.6 | 0.7 | *−1,987 | *−2.6 |
| Not insured | 28,543 | 6,748 | 311 | 23.6 | 0.9 | 7,249 | 343 | 25.4 | 1.0 | *502 | *1.8 |
| **Work Experience** | | | | | | | | | | | |
| Total 18 to 64 years | 198,113 | 22,209 | 564 | 11.2 | 0.3 | 26,244 | 628 | 13.2 | 0.3 | *4,035 | *2.0 |
| All workers | 152,199 | 8,135 | 259 | 5.3 | 0.2 | 12,172 | 362 | 8.0 | 0.2 | *4,037 | *2.7 |
| Worked full-time, year-round | 109,700 | 2,422 | 128 | 2.2 | 0.1 | 5,368 | 205 | 4.9 | 0.2 | *2,946 | *2.7 |
| Less than full-time, year-round | 42,499 | 5,714 | 224 | 13.4 | 0.5 | 6,804 | 270 | 16.0 | 0.6 | *1,090 | *2.6 |
| Did not work at least 1 week | 45,914 | 14,073 | 440 | 30.7 | 0.7 | 14,072 | 434 | 30.6 | 0.7 | −1 | Z |

| Characteristic | Number** (in thousands) Estimate | Official** Number Estimate | Margin of error[†] (±) | Percent Estimate | Margin of error[†] (±) | SPM Number Estimate | Margin of error[†] (±) | Percent Estimate | Margin of error[†] (±) | Difference Number | Percent |
|---|---|---|---|---|---|---|---|---|---|---|---|
| **Disability Status[3]** | | | | | | | | | | | |
| Total 18 to 64 years | 198,113 | 22,209 | 564 | 11.2 | 0.3 | 26,244 | 628 | 13.2 | 0.3 | *4,035 | *2.0 |
| With a disability | 15,116 | 3,764 | 170 | 24.9 | 1.0 | 3,550 | 163 | 23.5 | 1.0 | *–213 | *–1.4 |
| With no disability | 182,042 | 18,412 | 504 | 10.1 | 0.3 | 22,656 | 576 | 12.4 | 0.3 | *4,244 | *2.3 |

*An asterisk preceding an estimate indicates change is statistically different from zero at the 90 percent confidence level.

**Includes unrelated individuals under the age of 15.

[†]The margin of error (MOE) is a measure of an estimate's variability. The larger the MOE in relation to the size of the estimate, the less reliable the estimate. This number, when added to and subtracted from the estimate, forms the 90 percent confidence interval. The MOEs shown in this table are based on standard errors calculated using replicate weights. For more information, see "Standard Errors and Their Use" at < www2.census.gov/library/publications/2018/demo/p60-263sa.pdf>.

Z Represents or rounds to zero.

[1]Federal surveys give respondents the option of reporting more than one race. Therefore, two basic ways of defining a race group are possible. A group such as Asian may be defined as those who reported Asian and no other race (the race-alone or single-race concept) or as those who reported Asian regardless of whether they also reported another race (the race-alone-or-in-combination concept). This table shows data using the first approach (race alone). The use of the single-race population does not imply that it is the preferred method of presenting or analyzing data. The Census Bureau uses a variety of approaches. Information on people who reported more than one race, such as White and American Indian and Alaska Native or Asian and Black or African American, is available from the 2010 Census through American FactFinder. About 2.9 percent of people reported more than one race in the 2010 Census. Data for American Indians and Alaska Natives, Native Hawaiians and Other Pacific Islanders, and those reporting two or more races are not shown separately.

[2]For information on metropolitan statistical areas and principal cities, see <www.census.gov/programs-surveys/metro-micro/about/glossary.html>.

[3]The sum of those with and without a disability does not equal the total because disability status is not defined for individuals in the U.S. Armed Forces.

NOTE: Details may not sum due to rounding.

SOURCE: U.S. Census Bureau. "The Supplemental Poverty Measure: 2017." September 12, 2018. https://www.census.gov/content/dam/Census/library/publications/2018/demo/p60-265.pdf.

# OTHER HISTORIC DOCUMENTS OF INTEREST

## FROM THIS VOLUME

## FROM PREVIOUS *HISTORIC DOCUMENTS*

# Prime Minister May, EU Remark on Brexit Negotiations

SEPTEMBER 21, OCTOBER 22, NOVEMBER 25 AND 26, DECEMBER 10 AND 17, 2018

After more than a year of protracted negotiations, the European Union and the United Kingdom edged toward an agreement on the terms of the United Kingdom's departure from the European Union—a process known popularly as Brexit. In early 2018, negotiators settled preliminary issues, including a "divorce" lump-sum payment by the United Kingdom, the rights of each other's expatriate citizens to continue living and working in their adoptive countries, and the transition period for the United Kingdom to stop being bound by EU single-market rules. Negotiations in the latter half of 2018 focused on the nature of the UK's relationship with the European Union post-Brexit. The UK government's goal was to exit both the EU's political institutions (its representation in the EU's decision-making bodies) and the economic ones, namely the EU's single market and customs union. The final sticking point was how to avoid Brexit causing the imposition of border controls between Northern Ireland, which is part of the United Kingdom, and the Republic of Ireland, which intended to remain in the European Union. An arrangement called a backstop was agreed to by negotiators to ensure continued free movement of goods and people in Ireland, both north and south of the border. But Brexit's most fervent supporters quickly turned against the backstop, fearful it would keep the United Kingdom too closely aligned with the European Union.

## CONSERVATIVES FORCE BREXIT CONSIDERATION

The genesis of the UK's departure from the European Union was a speech then–Prime Minister David Cameron gave in January 2013 when he pledged, if reelected, to hold a referendum giving UK citizens an in-or-out option on EU membership. The United Kingdom first joined the European Union in 1973. Over the next four decades, as the EU became more closely integrated politically and economically, hostility toward the European Union inside the United Kingdom mounted, especially from Cameron's party, the Conservatives. Cameron's referendum pledge was an attempt to assuage the anti-EU bloc and prevent a split in the party.

Having won reelection in 2015, Cameron renegotiated the UK's terms of EU membership. While remaining a full member, the EU agreed to increase the number of areas where the UK had a way to opt out of EU policies. This deal in tow, Cameron scheduled his promised in-or-out referendum for June 23, 2016. Like most Conservatives, he campaigned on the Remain side. Nearly all the parliamentarians from the other parties, including Labour, the Liberal Democrats, and the Scottish National Party, also urged Remain. Exceptionally, Northern Ireland's Democratic Unionist Party (DUP), however, sided with the Leave campaign. The DUP is the main party representing Northern Ireland's

Protestant UK-supporting community. Its overarching mission is to keep Northern Ireland permanently part of the UK and prevent reunification with the Republic of Ireland.

The referendum campaign grew heated, with immigration a flashpoint. The Leave side blamed the EU for what it said was excessive immigration into the UK. When the results were announced in the early hours of June 24, it caused a political earthquake. The Leave side had won by 52 percent to 48 percent, albeit with significant regional differences, with Scotland, Northern Ireland, and the capital of London voting Remain. Cameron resigned immediately as prime minister, to be replaced in July by Theresa May, a longtime Conservative parliamentarian and government minister. May was a low-profile Remain supporter during the campaign, but following the result, she pledged to deliver Brexit. EU leaders reacted by expressing regret and sadness while urging the UK government to proceed promptly with the necessary procedural steps. Under Article 50 of the EU Treaty—a provision only added as recently as 2009—that process would begin with the UK notifying the EU in writing of its intent to leave. May moved slowly in pulling the trigger on Article 50, knowing that once activated, it put the UK on course to exit precisely two years later, regardless of whether a withdrawal agreement was in place by then.

May consulted her Conservative colleagues on approach but largely ignored those from across the political aisle—an oversight she would pay dearly for later. In January 2017, she announced her negotiating goals. Deferring to the wishes of the anti-EU Conservatives, she immediately excluded two "soft Brexit" options. First, the UK would not stay in the EU customs union, the arrangement under which goods are traded tariff free between EU member states with a common tariff on goods imported into the EU. May argued that leaving the customs union was necessary to give the UK free rein when negotiating trade agreements with non-EU countries post-Brexit. She also ruled out remaining part of the EU single market, a zone of 500 million consumers in twenty-eight countries with common standards in areas including consumer protection, workers' rights, and environmental protection. Such a path is the one that Iceland, Liechtenstein, and Norway have taken since 1994, eschewing full EU membership but being part of the single market. May's rationale for excluding this solution was that it would bind the UK to follow EU standards it had no say in setting and give citizens of all single-market member countries—thirty-one in total, with a combined population of 515 million—the right to live in the United Kingdom. After 2004, when ten Central and Eastern European countries had joined the EU, the UK experienced an influx of about one million of these countries' nationals, who came in search of higher-paying jobs. The influx had fueled anti-immigrant sentiment, helping the Leave side to win the Brexit referendum.

## EU Steers Brexit Talks

On March 29, 2017, with its negotiating red lines agreed, the UK government triggered Article 50. The next step was for the EU to adopt its negotiating mandate, which it did in May 2017. The European Commission, the EU's executive arm, led the negotiations that began in June. When May was elected prime minister in July 2016, she notably appointed three vocal Brexit backers to the top three Brexit-related ministerial posts: Boris Johnson as foreign secretary, David Davis as Brexit secretary, and Liam Fox as trade secretary. Her reasoning for this was that it was better to place the so-called Three Brexiteers inside the cabinet than to have them on the fringes constantly expressing dissatisfaction with her activities. However, as the months progressed, the situation created frustration on all sides, especially from Davis and Johnson, who could not steer the negotiations in the direction they wanted. The chief EU negotiator, Commissioner Michel Barnier, proved an implacable interlocutor. The UK government had thought that they could, when necessary, go over Barnier's head and negotiate more favorable terms directly from EU member state leaders. They soon learned that this would not work. EU leaders were largely content to delegate the negotiating to Barnier, and they remained unified in supporting him.

By the end of 2017, Brexit was completely dominating the political agenda in the UK. In the EU, by contrast, while the top-tier leadership regularly took stock of the progress the talks were making (or not making), they were focusing on other priorities, too. It was generally agreed that Barnier, a seasoned EU diplomat with decades of negotiating experience, had a better command of the issues than did Davis, his UK counterpart. The EU side consistently set the negotiating calendar, agenda, and overall structure. When the talks were stalling, Barnier would point out that the clock was ticking and that deal or no deal, the UK was on course to exit the EU on March 29, 2019.

Prime Minister May's hand had meanwhile been weakened by a strategic gamble she made that went badly awry. With opinion polls putting the Conservatives ahead of the main opposition Labour Party, May called a snap general election for June 2017. She hoped to increase her slim parliamentary majority and gain a bigger buffer that she might well need when seeking parliamentary approval of a future Brexit deal. However, the lead evaporated during the campaign, and Labour kept gaining ground. On election day, the Conservatives lost their overall parliamentary majority but remained the largest party. May's government became reliant on the votes of the ten DUP parliamentarians. They were all hardline backers of Brexit and also demanded that she rule out any deal that would put distance between Northern Ireland and the rest of the UK. May's margin for maneuver in the negotiations became further reduced by her reliance on DUP support.

As 2018 proceeded, EU and UK negotiators reached agreement on the key withdrawal issues. First, the so-called divorce bill, a monetary lump sum that the UK agreed to pay to the EU in return for continued access to the single market for a transition period that would end on December 31, 2020, was set at approximately £50 billion ($59 billion). The two sides also resolved the complicated issue of their expatriate citizens' employment, pension, and residence rights. Some three million EU citizens were living in the UK, while more than a million UK citizens were living in the EU. Many of the EU citizens in the UK were from Central and Eastern Europe. They comprised a sizable share of the UK workforce in some sectors, notably agriculture and health care. Mindful of how reliant economically the UK was on their labor, the government agreed to grant them "settled status" whereby they could continue to live there post-Brexit. The EU granted reciprocal rights to UK expatriates living in the remaining twenty-seven EU member states. Most of these UK citizens live in France, Ireland, and Spain.

## Northern Ireland "Backstop" Slows Negotiations

The final issue that needed to be resolved was Northern Ireland. Because Great Britain—England, Scotland, and Wales—is an island, the UK's only land border with the EU post-Brexit would be Northern Ireland. May had already said no to the options of the UK staying part of the EU customs union or single market. In addition, to ensure the UK's continued unity and to meet DUP demands, she had ruled out Northern Ireland having a different arrangement with the EU than the rest of the UK. Ordinarily, the consequence of taking this path would be a need to introduce border controls, in particular goods inspections, at the Northern Ireland land border. This posed a huge problem, however, because both goods and people have moved freely across the Northern Ireland border ever since the 1998 Good Friday Agreement that ended the violent thirty-year conflict between Irish nationalists and UK unionists. The Good Friday Agreement, which the UK was legally bound to fully implement, guaranteed continued free flow of people and goods in Ireland—in other words, to prevent a new hard border from emerging in Northern Ireland. Marrying all of her negotiating goals and pre-existing obligations proved a difficult task, and throughout the summer of 2018, the status of Northern Ireland dominated the Brexit negotiations.

Following a meeting with her cabinet ministers in July, Prime Minister May clarified her government's position. The goal would be to "create a UK–EU free trade agreement which establishes a common rule book for industrial goods and agricultural products." May added, "This maintains high standards in these areas, but we will also ensure that no new changes in the future take place without the approval of our parliament." After meeting with EU leaders in Salzburg in September 2018, she further refined her goals. She opposed any agreement with the EU that left Northern Ireland in the EU customs union but the rest of the UK out of it. She pledged to pursue a "third option" that would "avoid a hard border between Ireland and Northern Ireland, while respecting the referendum results and the integrity of the United Kingdom." But that left open the primary question of how that could be accomplished.

The solution that EU and UK negotiators developed in October was an arrangement referred to as the backstop. According to the backstop agreement, during the transition period from March 29, 2019, until December 31, 2020, the UK and EU would work to conclude a free-trade agreement that was deep and comprehensive enough to avoid the need for border checks in Northern Ireland. If they failed to finalize this deal by December 31, 2020, the entire United Kingdom would temporarily remain inside the EU customs union until the deal was concluded, and Northern Ireland would, in addition, temporarily align with some EU single-market rules.

In a statement to the UK parliament on October 15, May stressed that the backstop would be temporary and that "we are not going to be trapped permanently in a single customs territory unable to do meaningful trade deals." In a separate statement a week later, however, May admitted that she was unable to extract from the EU a legally binding commitment to the temporary nature of the backstop. In essence, as the terms of the EU–UK relationship were still to be negotiated, the EU was unwilling to be bound up front to concluding that agreement within a prescribed timeframe or with a predetermined outcome. The backstop was the final piece of the Withdrawal Agreement, and the EU side made clear it was done with negotiating. EU leaders gave their stamp of approval to the Withdrawal Agreement in November. European leaders including German Chancellor Angela Merkel and European Commission President Jean-Claude Juncker voiced sadness over the UK's imminent departure but pledged to proceed with ratifying the Agreement.

Meanwhile, in London, the Agreement's future was looking increasingly in peril. As the UK parliament digested its terms and conditions, those on the anti-EU side became fixated on the backstop. They argued that the backstop could leave the UK permanently stuck in the EU customs union, because there was no way to exit as long as the EU did not conclude a new free trade agreement with the UK. A growing number of Conservative parliamentarians announced they would vote against the Agreement. So too did the DUP. Because she had made little effort to involve other political parties in the Brexit negotiations, May was unable to muster support from across the political aisle for her deal. As she could only afford a handful of defections from her Conservative colleagues and DUP allies, given how slim the government's majority was, it appeared that the Agreement would fail to pass parliament.

## BREXIT VOTE POSTPONED, FAILS

The UK parliament vote was originally scheduled for December 2018. However, seeing that she was on course to lose the vote, May postponed it until January in the hopes she could win firmer commitments from EU leaders about the temporary nature of the backstop. The EU gave some oral reassurances but would not give a legally binding commitment, nor would it agree to substantively alter the Agreement itself. When debate in parliament resumed in early 2019, it was clear May faced an uphill battle. The Brexiteers, including Johnson and Davis, had long since deserted May, both resigning their ministerial posts in 2018. May had replaced Davis with another Brexit advocate, Dominic Raab, but he had resigned a few months later, unhappy with the direction the negotiations had taken.

On January 15, 2019, May suffered the heaviest parliamentary defeat of any UK prime minister in the country's history. Only 202 out of 650 parliamentarians voted for the Agreement, with 432 voting against. About one hundred of her Conservative colleagues had rejected the deal, as did the DUP and all other parties. The scale of the defeat was devastating. And yet, when a no-confidence vote in May's government was held the following day, she narrowly survived. May's pro-Brexit Conservative colleagues and the DUP backed her, despite having inflicted a humiliating defeat on her the day before. They did this out of fear that a new election would usher in a new government led by Labour leader Jeremy Corbyn, who politically was significantly left leaning and was unpredictable on the EU withdrawal.

By late January, there was uncertainty over the direction the UK was headed, with an array of scenarios plausible. These included the UK revoking its Article 50 notice and staying in the EU, May getting the Agreement changed and passed by parliament, a substantive renegotiation of the Agreement, a general election and new government, a second referendum, a delayed departure date, and a "hard Brexit." The latter was the term used to describe the UK leaving the EU without any formal agreement in place. This was a source of anxiety in many quarters, given the legal uncertainty and economic turmoil it would likely create.

Because the UK has no written constitution and a long tradition of a strong legislature, parliament became emboldened and seemed determined to steer the UK toward a softer Brexit and quite possibly a delayed one, too. Opinion polls showed that the British public continued to be evenly split on whether to leave or remain inside the EU. As another referendum would take many months to organize, the UK would need to seek permission from the EU to delay its departure date if it wished to avoid a hard Brexit. The EU leadership indicated they would only grant this delay if the UK made its long-term intentions clear. It was also possible for the UK simply to remain inside the EU. This had been made easier by an EU Court of Justice judgment from December 2018, which ruled that the UK government could unilaterally revoke its Article 50 notification at any time prior to the Withdrawal Agreement entering into force. As the clock ticked toward the scheduled March 29 exit day, uncertainty and anxiety over the UK's future was as great as it had ever been.

—Brian Beary

*Following are five statements delivered by British prime minister Theresa May on September 21, October 22, November 26, December 10, and December 17, 2018, regarding negotiations for a British exit from the European Union; and the text of a November 25, 2018, European Council conclusion regarding Britain's decision to invoke Article 50 and withdraw from the European Union.*

## *Prime Minister May Remarks on Meeting with EU Leaders*

**September 21, 2018**

Yesterday, I was in Salzburg for talks with European leaders.

I have always said that these negotiations would be tough—and they were always bound to be toughest in the final straight.

While both sides want a deal, we have to face up to the fact that—despite the progress we have made—there are two big issues where we remain a long way apart.

The first is our economic relationship after we have left.

Here, the EU is still only offering us two options.

The first option would involve the UK staying in the European Economic Area and a customs union with the EU.

In plain English, this would mean we'd still have to abide by all the EU rules, uncontrolled immigration from the EU would continue and we couldn't do the trade deals we want with other countries.

That would make a mockery of the referendum we had two years ago.

The second option would be a basic free trade agreement for Great Britain that would introduce checks at the Great Britain/EU border. But even worse, Northern Ireland would effectively remain in the Customs Union and parts of the Single Market, permanently separated economically from the rest of the UK by a border down the Irish Sea.

Parliament has already—unanimously—rejected this idea.

Creating any form of customs border between Northern Ireland and the rest of the UK would not respect that Northern Ireland is an integral part of the United Kingdom, in line with the principle of consent, as set out clearly in the Belfast/Good Friday Agreement.

It is something I will never agree to—indeed, in my judgement it is something no British Prime Minister would ever agree to. If the EU believe I will, they are making a fundamental mistake. Anything which fails to respect the referendum or which effectively divides our country in two would be a bad deal and I have always said no deal is better than a bad deal.

But I have also been clear that the best outcome is for the UK to leave with a deal. That is why, following months of intensive work and detailed discussions, we proposed a third option for our future economic relationship, based on the frictionless trade in goods. That is the best way to protect jobs here and in the EU and to avoid a hard border between Ireland and Northern Ireland, while respecting the referendum result and the integrity of the United Kingdom.

Yesterday Donald Tusk said our proposals would undermine the single market. He didn't explain how in any detail or make any counter-proposal. So we are at an impasse.

The second issue is connected to the first. We both agree that the Withdrawal Agreement needs to include a backstop to ensure that if there's a delay in implementing our new relationship, there still won't be a hard border between Ireland and Northern Ireland.

But the EU is proposing to achieve this by effectively keeping Northern Ireland in the Customs Union.

As I have already said, that is unacceptable. We will never agree to it. It would mean breaking up our country.

We will set out our alternative that preserves the integrity of the UK. And it will be in line with the commitments we made back in December—including the commitment that no new regulatory barriers should be created between Northern Ireland and the rest of the UK unless the Northern Ireland Executive and Assembly agree.

As I told EU leaders, neither side should demand the unacceptable of the other.

We cannot accept anything that threatens the integrity of our union, just as they cannot accept anything that threatens the integrity of theirs.

We cannot accept anything that does not respect the result of the referendum, just as they cannot accept anything that is not in the interest of their citizens.

Throughout this process, I have treated the EU with nothing but respect. The UK expects the same. A good relationship at the end of this process depends on it.

At this late stage in the negotiations, it is not acceptable to simply reject the other side's proposals without a detailed explanation and counter proposals.

So we now need to hear from the EU what the real issues are and what their alternative is so that we can discuss them. Until we do, we cannot make progress.

In the meantime, we must and will continue the work of preparing ourselves for no deal.

In particular, I want to clarify our approach to two issues.

First, there are over 3 million EU citizens living in the UK who will be understandably worried about what the outcome of yesterday's summit means for their future.

I want to be clear with you that even in the event of no deal your rights will be protected. You are our friends, our neighbours, our colleagues. We want you to stay.

Second, I want to reassure the people of Northern Ireland that in the event of no deal we will do everything in our power to prevent a return to a hard border.

Let me also say this.

The referendum was the largest democratic exercise this country has ever undergone. To deny its legitimacy or frustrate its result threatens public trust in our democracy.

That is why for over two years I have worked day and night to deliver a deal that sees the UK leave the EU.

I have worked to bring people with me even when that has not always seemed possible.

No one wants a good deal more than me.

But the EU should be clear: I will not overturn the result of the referendum. Nor will I break up my country.

We need serious engagement on resolving the two big problems in the negotiations. We stand ready.

SOURCE: Office of the Prime Minister of the United Kingdom. "PM Brexit Negotiations Statement: 21 September 2018." September 21, 2018. https://www.gov.uk/government/news/pm-brexit-negotiations-statement-21-september-2018.

# May on Issues related to Brexit Agreement

October 22, 2018

*[Portions of the prime minister's speech unrelated to Brexit have been omitted.]*

Turning to Brexit, Mr Speaker, let me begin with the progress we have made on both the Withdrawal Agreement and the political declaration on our future relationship.

As I reported to the House last Monday, the shape of the deal across the vast majority of the Withdrawal Agreement is now clear.

Since Salzburg we have agreed the broad scope of provisions that set out the governance and dispute resolution arrangements for our Withdrawal Agreement.

We have developed a Protocol relating to the UK Sovereign Base Areas in Cyprus.

Following discussions with Spain—and in close co-operation with the Government of Gibraltar—we have also developed a Protocol and a set of underlying memoranda relating to Gibraltar, heralding a new era in our relations.

And we have broad agreement on the structure and scope of the future relationship, with important progress made on issues like security, transport and services.

And this progress in the last three weeks builds on the areas where we have already reached agreement—on citizens' rights, on the financial settlement, on the Implementation Period, and in Northern Ireland, agreement on the preservation of the particular rights for UK and Irish citizens—and on the special arrangements between us such as the Common Travel Area, which has existed since before either the UK or Ireland ever became members of the European Economic Community.

Mr Speaker, taking all of this together, 95 per cent of the Withdrawal Agreement and its protocols are now settled.

There is one real sticking point left, but a considerable one, which is how we guarantee that—in the unlikely event our future relationship is not in place by the end of the Implementation Period—there is no return to a hard border between Northern Ireland and Ireland.

The commitment to avoiding a hard border is one this House emphatically endorsed and enshrined in law in the Withdrawal Act earlier this year.

As I set out last week, the original backstop proposal from the EU was one we could not accept, as it would mean creating a customs border down the Irish Sea and breaking up the integrity of our United Kingdom.

I do not believe that any UK Prime Minister could ever accept this.

And I certainly will not.

But as I said in my Mansion House speech: We chose to leave; we have a responsibility to help find a solution. So earlier this year, we put forward a counter-proposal for a temporary UK–EU joint customs territory for the backstop.

And in a substantial shift in their position since Salzburg, the EU are now actively working with us on this proposal.

But a number of issues remain.

The EU argue that they cannot give a legally binding commitment to a UK-wide customs arrangement in the Withdrawal Agreement, so their original proposal must remain a possibility.

Furthermore, Mr Speaker, people are understandably worried that we could get stuck in a backstop that is designed only to be temporary.

And there are also concerns that Northern Ireland could be cut off from accessing its most important market—Great Britain.

During last week's Council, I had good discussions with Presidents Juncker, Tusk and Macron, Chancellor Merkel and Taoiseach Varadkar and others about how to break this impasse.

I believe there are four steps we need to take.

First, we must make the commitment to a temporary UK–EU joint customs territory legally binding, so the Northern Ireland only proposal is no longer needed.

This would not only protect relations North–South, but also, vitally, East–West.

This is critical: the relationship between Northern Ireland and the rest of the UK is an integral strand of the Belfast Good Friday Agreement. So to protect that Agreement we need to preserve the totality of relationships it sets out.

Nothing we agree with the EU under Article 50 should risk a return to a hard border, or threaten the delicate constitutional and political arrangements underpinned by the Belfast Good Friday Agreement.

The second step, is to create an option to extend the Implementation Period as an alternative to the backstop.

Mr Speaker, I have not committed to extending the Implementation Period.

I do not want to extend the Implementation Period—and I do not believe that extending it will be necessary.

I see any extension—or being in any form of backstop—as undesirable. By far the best outcome for the UK, for Ireland and for the EU—is that our future relationship is agreed and in place by 1st January 2021.

I have every confidence that it will be. And the European Union have said they will show equal commitment to this timetable.

But the impasse we are trying to resolve is about the insurance policy if this does not happen.

So what I am saying is that—if at the end of 2020 our future relationship was not quite ready—the proposal is that the UK would be able to make a sovereign choice between the UK-wide customs backstop or a short extension of the Implementation Period.

And Mr Speaker, there are some limited circumstances in which it could be argued that an extension to the Implementation Period might be preferable, if we were certain it was only for a short time

For example, a short extension to the Implementation Period would mean only one set of changes for businesses—at the point we move to the future relationship.

But in any such scenario we would have to be out of this Implementation Period well before the end of this Parliament.

The third step, Mr Speaker, is to ensure that were we to need either of these insurance policies—whether the backstop or a short extension to the Implementation Period—we could not be kept in either arrangement indefinitely.

We would not accept a position in which the UK, having negotiated in good faith an agreement which prevents a hard border in Northern Ireland, nonetheless finds itself locked into an alternative, inferior arrangement against our will.

The fourth step, Mr Speaker, is for the Government to deliver the commitment we have made to ensure full continued access for Northern Ireland's businesses to the whole of the UK internal market.

Northern Ireland's businesses rely heavily on trade with their largest market—Great Britain—and we must protect this in any scenario.

Mr Speaker, let us remember that all of these steps are about insurance policies that no-one in the UK or the EU wants or expects to use.

So we cannot let this become the barrier to reaching the future partnership we all want to see.

We have to explore every possible option to break the impasse and that is what I am doing.

When I stood in Downing Street and addressed the nation for the first time, I pledged that the government I lead will not be driven by the interests of the privileged few but of ordinary working families.

And that is what guides me every day in these negotiations.

Before any decision, I ask: how do I best deliver the Brexit that the British people voted for.

How do I best take back control of our money, borders and laws.

How do I best protect jobs and make sure nothing gets in the way of our brilliant entrepreneurs and small businesses.

And how do I best protect the integrity of our precious United Kingdom, and protect the historic progress we have made in Northern Ireland.

And, if doing those things means I get difficult days in Brussels, then so be it. The Brexit talks are not about my interests. They are about the national interest—and the interests of the whole of our United Kingdom.

Serving our national interest will demand that we hold our nerve through these last stages of the negotiations, the hardest part of all.

It will mean not giving in to those who want to stop Brexit with a politicians vote—politicians telling the people they got it wrong the first time and should try again.

And it will mean focusing on the prize that lies before us: the great opportunities that we can open up for our country when we clear these final hurdles in the negotiations.

That is what I am working to achieve. And I commend this Statement to the House.

SOURCE: Office of the Prime Minister of the United Kingdom. "PM's Statement on European Council: 22 October 2018." October 22, 2018. https://www.gov.uk/government/speeches/pms-statement-on-euro pean-council-22-october-2018.

# *European Council Agrees to Brexit Plan*

**November 25, 2018**

### *Conclusions – 25 November 2018*

1. The European Council endorses the Agreement on the withdrawal of the United Kingdom of Great Britain and Northern Ireland from the European Union and the European Atomic Energy Community. On this basis, the European Council invites the Commission, the European Parliament and the Council to take the necessary steps to

ensure that the agreement can enter into force on 30 March 2019, so as to provide for an orderly withdrawal.

2. The European Council approves the Political Declaration setting out the framework for the future relationship between the European Union and the United Kingdom of Great Britain and Northern Ireland. The European Council restates the Union's determination to have as close as possible a partnership with the United Kingdom in the future in line with the Political Declaration. The Union's approach will continue to be defined by the overall positions and principles set out in the previously agreed European Council's guidelines. The European Council will remain permanently seized of the matter.

3. The European Council thanks Michel Barnier for his tireless efforts as the Union's chief negotiator and for his contribution to maintaining the unity among EU27 Member States throughout the negotiations on the withdrawal of the United Kingdom from the European Union.

SOURCE: Council of the European Union. "Special Meeting of the European Council (Art. 50), 25 November 2018." November 25, 2018. https://www.consilium.europa.eu/media/37103/25-special-euco-final-conclusions-en.pdf.

# *Prime Minister May Addresses Brexit Agreement*

**November 26, 2018**

With permission, Mr Speaker, I would like to make a Statement on the conclusion of our negotiations to leave the European Union.

At yesterday's Special European Council in Brussels, I reached a deal with the leaders of the other 27 EU Member States on a Withdrawal Agreement that will ensure our smooth and orderly departure on 29th March next year; and, tied to this Agreement, a Political Declaration on an ambitious future partnership that is in our national interest.

Mr Speaker, this is the right deal for Britain because it delivers on the democratic decision of the British people.

It takes back control of our borders. It ends the free movement of people in full once and for all, allowing the government to introduce a new skills-based immigration system.

It takes back control of our laws. It ends the jurisdiction of the European Court of Justice in the UK and means instead our laws being made in our Parliaments, enforced by our courts.

And it takes back control of our money. It ends the vast annual payments we send to Brussels. So instead we can spend taxpayers' money on our own priorities, including the £394 million a week of extra investment into our long-term plan for the NHS.

By creating a new Free Trade Area with no tariffs, fees, charges, quantitative restrictions or rules of origin checks, this deal protects jobs, including those that rely on integrated supply chains.

It protects our security with a close relationship on defence and on tackling crime and terrorism, which will help to keep all our people safe.

And it protects the integrity of our United Kingdom, meeting our commitments in Northern Ireland and delivering for the whole UK family, including our Overseas Territories and the Crown Dependencies.

Mr Speaker, on Gibraltar, we have worked constructively with the governments of Spain and Gibraltar—and I want to pay tribute in particular to Gibraltar's Chief Minister Fabian Picardo for his statesmanship in these negotiations.

We have ensured that Gibraltar is covered by the whole Withdrawal Agreement and by the Implementation Period.

And for the future partnership, the UK government will be negotiating for the whole UK family, including Gibraltar.

As Fabian Picardo said this weekend:

Every aspect of the response of the United Kingdom was agreed with the Government of Gibraltar. We have worked seamlessly together in this as we have in all other aspects of this two year period of negotiation. Most importantly, the legal text of the draft Withdrawal Agreement has not been changed. That is what the Spanish Government repeatedly sought. But they have not achieved that. The United Kingdom has not let us down.

Mr Speaker, our message to the people of Gibraltar is clear: we will always stand by you. We are proud that Gibraltar is British and our position on sovereignty has not and will not change.

Mr Speaker, the Withdrawal Agreement will ensure that we leave the European Union on 29th March next year in a smooth and orderly way.

It protects the rights of EU citizens living in the UK and UK citizens living in the EU, so they can carry on living their lives as before.

It delivers a time-limited Implementation Period to give business time to prepare for the new arrangements. During the Implementation Period trade will continue on current terms so businesses only have to face one set of changes. It ensures a fair settlement of our financial obligations—less than half of what some originally expected and demanded.

And it meets our commitment to ensure there is no hard border between Northern Ireland and Ireland—and also no customs border in the Irish Sea—in the event that the future relationship is not ready by the end of the implementation period.

Mr Speaker, I know some Members remain concerned that we could find ourselves stuck in this backstop.

So let me address this directly.

First, this is an insurance policy that no-one wants to use.

Both the UK and the EU are fully committed to having our future relationship in place by 1st January 2021.

And the Withdrawal Agreement has a legal duty on both sides to use best endeavours to avoid the backstop ever coming into force.

If, despite this, the future relationship is not ready by the end of 2020, we would not be forced to use the backstop. We would have a clear choice between the backstop or a short extension to the Implementation Period.

If we did choose the backstop, the legal text is clear that it should be temporary and that the Article 50 legal base cannot provide for a permanent relationship.

And there is now more flexibility that it can be superseded either by the future relationship, or by alternative arrangements which include the potential for facilitative arrangements and technologies to avoid a hard border on the island of Ireland. There is also a termination clause, which allows the backstop to be turned off when we have fulfilled our commitments on the Northern Ireland border. And there is a unilateral right to trigger a review through the Joint Committee and the ability to seek independent arbitration if the EU does not use good faith in this process.

Furthermore, as a result of the changes we have negotiated, the legal text is now also clear that once the backstop has been superseded, it shall "cease to apply".

So if a future Parliament decided to then move from an initially deep trade relationship to a looser one, the backstop could not return.

Mr Speaker, I do not pretend that either we or the EU are entirely happy with these arrangements. And that's how it must be—were either party entirely happy, that party would have no incentive to move on to the future relationship.

But there is no alternative deal that honours our commitments to Northern Ireland which does not involve this insurance policy. And the EU would not have agreed any future partnership without it.

Put simply, there is no deal that comes without a backstop, and without a backstop there is no deal.

Mr Speaker, the Withdrawal Agreement is accompanied by a Political Declaration, which sets out the scope and terms of an ambitious future relationship between the UK and the EU.

It is a detailed set of instructions to negotiators that will be used to deliver a legal agreement on our future relationship after we have left.

The linkage clause between the Withdrawal Agreement and this declaration requires both sides to use best endeavours to get this legal text agreed and implemented by the end of 2020.

And both sides are committed to making preparations for an immediate start to the formal negotiations after our withdrawal.

The declaration contains specific detail on our future economic relationship.

This includes a new Free Trade Area with no tariffs, fees, quantitative restrictions or rules of origin checks—an unprecedented economic relationship that no other major economy has.

It includes liberalisation in trade in services well beyond WTO commitments and building on recent EU Free Trade Agreements.

It includes new arrangements for our financial services sector—ensuring market access cannot be withdrawn on a whim and providing stability and certainty for our world-leading industry.

And it ensures we will leave EU programmes that do not work in our interests: so we will be out of the Common Agricultural Policy that has failed our farmers and out of the Common Fisheries Policy that has failed our coastal communities.

Instead as the Political Declaration sets out, we will be "an independent coastal state" once again. We will take back full sovereign control over our waters. So we will be able to decide for ourselves who we allow to fish in our waters.

The EU have maintained throughout this process that they wanted to link overall access to markets to access to fisheries. They failed in the Withdrawal Agreement, and they failed again in the Political Declaration.

It is no surprise some are already trying to lay down markers again for the future relationship, but they should be getting used to the answer by now: it is not going to happen.

Finally, the declaration is clear that whatever is agreed in the future partnership must recognise the development of an independent UK trade policy beyond this economic partnership.

So for the first time in forty years, the UK will be able to strike new trade deals and open up new markets for our goods and services in the fastest growing economies around the world.

Mr Speaker, as I set out for the House last week, the future relationship also includes a comprehensive new security partnership with close reciprocal law enforcement and judicial co-operation to keep all our people safe.

At the outset we were told that being outside of free movement and outside of the Schengen area, we would be treated like any other non-EU state on security.

But this deal delivers the broadest security partnership in the EU's history, including arrangements for effective data exchange on Passenger Name Records, DNA, fingerprints, and vehicle registration data, as well as extradition arrangements like those in the European Arrest Warrant.

And it opens the way to sharing the types of information included in the ECRIS and SIS II databases on wanted or missing persons and criminal records.

Mr Speaker, this has been a long and complex negotiation.

It has required give and take on both sides. That is the nature of a negotiation.

But this deal honours the result of the referendum while providing a close economic and security relationship with our nearest neighbours and in so doing offers a brighter future for the British people outside of the EU.

And I can say to the House with absolute certainty that there is not a better deal available. My fellow leaders were very clear on that themselves yesterday.

Mr Speaker, our duty—as a Parliament over these coming weeks—is to examine this deal in detail, to debate it respectfully, to listen to our constituents and decide what is in our national interest.

There is a choice which this House will have to make.

We can back this deal, deliver on the vote of the referendum and move on to building a brighter future of opportunity and prosperity for all our people.

Or this House can choose to reject this deal and go back to square one. Because no-one knows what would happen if this deal doesn't pass. It would open the door to more division and more uncertainty, with all the risks that will entail.

Mr Speaker, I believe our national interest is clear.

The British people want us to get on with a deal that honours the referendum and allows us to come together again as a country, whichever way we voted.

This is that deal. A deal that delivers for the British people.

And I commend this Statement to the House.

Source: Office of the Prime Minister of the United Kingdom. "PM's Statement on the Special European Council: 26 November 2018." November 26, 2018. https://www.gov.uk/government/speeches/pms-statement-on-the-special-european-council-26-november-2018.

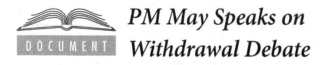

## PM May Speaks on Withdrawal Debate

**December 10, 2018**

Mr Speaker, with permission I would like to make a statement on Exiting the European Union.

We have now had three days of debate on the Withdrawal Agreement setting out the terms of our departure from the EU and the Political Declaration setting out our future relationship after we have left.

I have listened very carefully to what has been said, in this chamber and out of it, by members from all sides.

From listening to those views it is clear that while there is broad support for many of the key aspects of the deal, on one issue—the Northern Ireland backstop—there remains widespread and deep concern.

As a result, if we went ahead and held the vote tomorrow the deal would be rejected by a significant margin.

We will therefore defer the vote scheduled for tomorrow and not proceed to divide the House at this time.

I set out in my speech opening the debate last week the reasons why the backstop is a necessary guarantee to the people of Northern Ireland and why—whatever future relationship you want—there is no deal available that does not include the backstop.

Behind all those arguments are some inescapable facts.

The fact that Northern Ireland shares a land border with another sovereign state.

The fact that the hard-won peace that has been built in Northern Ireland over the last two decades has been built around a seamless border.

And the fact that Brexit will create a wholly new situation: on 30 March the Northern Ireland/Ireland border will for the first time become the external frontier of the European Union's single market and customs union.

The challenge this poses must be met not with rhetoric but with real and workable solutions.

Businesses operate across that border. People live their lives crossing and re-crossing it every day.

I have been there and spoken to some of those people. They do not want their everyday lives to change as a result of the decision we have taken. They do not want a return to a hard border.

And if this House cares about preserving our Union, it must listen to those people, because our Union will only endure with their consent.

We had hoped that the changes we have secured to the backstop would reassure Members that we could never be trapped in it indefinitely.

I hope the House will forgive me if I take a moment to remind it of those changes.

The customs element of the backstop is now UK-wide. It no longer splits our country into two customs territories. This also means that the backstop is now an uncomfortable arrangement for the EU, so they won't want it to come into use, or persist for long if it does.

Both sides are now legally committed to using best endeavours to have our new relationship in place before the end of the implementation period, ensuring the backstop is never used.

If our new relationship isn't ready, we can now choose to extend the implementation period, further reducing the likelihood of the backstop coming into use.

If the backstop ever does come into use, we now don't have to get the new relationship in place to get out of it. Alternative arrangements that make use of technology could be put in place instead.

The treaty is now clear that the backstop can only ever be temporary.

And there is now a termination clause.

But I am clear from what I have heard in this place and from my own conversations that these elements do not offer a sufficient number of colleagues the reassurance that they need.

I spoke to a number of EU leaders over the weekend, and in advance of the European Council I will go to see my counterparts in other member states and the leadership of the Council and the Commission.

I will discuss with them the clear concerns that this House has expressed.

We are also looking closely at new ways of empowering the House of Commons to ensure that any provision for a backstop has democratic legitimacy and to enable the House to place its own obligations on the government to ensure that the backstop cannot be in place indefinitely.

Mr Speaker, having spent the best part of two years poring over the detail of Brexit, listening to the public's ambitions, and yes, their fears too, and testing the limits of what the other side is prepared to accept, I am in absolutely no doubt that this deal is the right one.

It honours the result of the referendum. It protects jobs, security and our Union. But it also represents the very best deal that is actually negotiable with the EU.

I believe in it—as do many Members of this House. And I still believe there is a majority to be won in this House in support of it, if I can secure additional reassurance on the question of the backstop.

And that is what my focus will be in the days ahead.

But Mr Speaker, if you take a step back, it is clear that this House faces a much more fundamental question.

Does this House want to deliver Brexit? And if it does, does it want to do so through reaching an agreement with the EU?

If the answer is yes, and I believe that is the answer of the majority of this House, then we all have to ask ourselves whether we are prepared to make a compromise.

Because there will be no enduring and successful Brexit without some compromise on both sides of the debate.

Many of the most controversial aspects of this deal—including the backstop—are simply inescapable facts of having a negotiated Brexit.

Those members who continue to disagree need to shoulder the responsibility of advocating an alternative solution that can be delivered.

And do so without ducking its implications.

So if you want a second referendum to overturn the result of the first, be honest that this risks dividing the country again, when as a House we should be striving to bring it back together.

If you want to remain part of the Single Market and the Customs Union, be open that this would require free movement, rule-taking across the economy, and ongoing financial contributions—none of which are in my view compatible with the result of the referendum.

If you want to leave without a deal, be upfront that in the short term, this would cause significant economic damage to parts of our country who can least afford to bear the burden.

I do not believe that any of those courses of action command a majority in this House.

But notwithstanding that fact, for as long as we fail to agree a deal, the risk of an accidental no deal increases.

So the government will step up its work in preparation for that potential outcome and the Cabinet will hold further discussions on it this week.

The vast majority of us, Mr Speaker, accept the result of the referendum, and want to leave with a deal. We have a responsibility to discharge.

If we will the ends, we must also will the means.

I know that members across the House appreciate how important that responsibility is.

And I am very grateful to all members—on this side of the House and a few on the other side too—who have backed this deal and spoken up for it.

Many others, I know, have been wrestling with their consciences, particularly over the question of the backstop: seized of the need to face-up to the challenge posed by the Irish border, but genuinely concerned about the consequences.

I have listened. I have heard those concerns and I will now do everything I possibly can to secure further assurances.

If I may conclude on a personal note, Mr Speaker.

On the morning after the referendum two and a half years ago, I knew that we had witnessed a defining moment for our democracy.

Places that didn't get a lot of attention at elections and which did not get much coverage on the news were making their voices heard and saying that they wanted things to change.

I knew in that moment that Parliament had to deliver for them.

But of course that does not just mean delivering Brexit. It means working across all areas—building a stronger economy, improving public services, tackling social injustices—to make this a country that truly works for everyone, a country where nowhere and nobody is left behind.

And these matters are too important to be afterthoughts in our politics—they deserve to be at the centre of our thinking.

But that can only happen if we get Brexit done and get it done right.

And even though I voted Remain, from the moment I took up the responsibility of being Prime Minister of this great country I have known that my duty is to honour the result of that vote.

And I have been just as determined to protect the jobs that put food on the tables of working families and the security partnerships that keep each one of us safe.

And that is what this deal does. It gives us control of our borders, our money and our laws. It protects jobs, security and our Union. It is the right deal for Britain.

I am determined to do all I can to secure the reassurances this House requires, to get this deal over the line and deliver for the British people.

And I commend this statement to the House.

SOURCE: Office of the Prime Minister of the United Kingdom. "PM's Statement on Exiting the European Union: 10 December 2018." December 10, 2018. https://www.gov.uk/government/speeches/pms-statement-on-exiting-the-european-union-10-december-2018.

## PM May Discusses
## Brexit Backstop

**December 17, 2018**

*[Portions of the speech not related to Brexit have been omitted.]*

Mr Speaker, at this Council I faithfully and firmly reflected the concerns of this House over the Northern Ireland backstop.

I explained the assurances we had already agreed with the EU were insufficient for this House—and that we had to go further in showing that we never want to use this backstop and, if it is used, it must be a temporary arrangement.

Some of the resulting exchanges at this Council were robust.

But I make no apology for standing up for the interests of this House and the interests of our whole United Kingdom.

In response, the EU 27 published a series of conclusions.

They made clear that it is their—and I quote—"firm determination to work speedily on a subsequent agreement that establishes by 31st December 2020 alternative arrangements, so that the backstop will not need to be triggered."

The House will forgive me, but I think this bears repeating: "the backstop will not need to be triggered."

They underlined that "if the backstop were nevertheless to be triggered, it would apply temporarily."

They said that in this event the EU "would use its best endeavours to negotiate and conclude expeditiously a subsequent agreement that would replace the backstop."

And they gave a new assurance in relation to the Future Partnership with the UK, to make it even less likely that the backstop would ever be needed by stating that the EU "stands ready to embark on preparations immediately after signature of the Withdrawal Agreement to ensure that negotiations can start as soon as possible after the UK's withdrawal."

Mr Speaker, in these conclusions, in their statements at the Council and in their private meetings with me, my fellow EU leaders could not have been clearer—they do not want to use this backstop. They want to agree the best possible future relationship with us. There is no plot to keep us in the backstop.

Indeed, President Macron said on Friday—"we can clarify and reassure . . . the backstop is not our objective, it is not a durable solution and nobody is trying to lock the UK into the backstop."

As formal conclusions from a European Council, these commitments have legal status and should be welcomed. They go further than the EU has ever done previously in trying to address the concerns of this House.

And of course they sit on top of the commitments that we have already negotiated in relation to the backstop: including . . .

. . . ensuring the customs element is UK-wide;

. . . that both sides are legally committed to using best endeavours to have our new relationship in place before the end of the Implementation Period;

. . . that if the new relationship isn't ready we can choose to extend the Implementation Period instead of the backstop coming into force;

. . . that if the backstop does come in, we can use alternative arrangements, not just the future relationship, to get out of it;

. . . that the treaty is clear the backstop can only ever be temporary;

. . . and that there is an explicit termination clause.

But Mr Speaker, I know this House is still deeply uncomfortable about the backstop.

And I understand that. And I want us to go further still in the reassurances we secure.

Discussions with my EU partners—including Presidents Tusk, Juncker and others—have shown that further clarification following the Council's conclusions is in fact possible.

So discussions are continuing to explore further political and legal assurances.

We are also looking closely at new ways of empowering the House of Commons to ensure that any provision for a backstop has democratic legitimacy and to enable the House to place its own obligations on the government to ensure that the backstop cannot be in place indefinitely.

But it is now only just over 14 weeks until the UK leaves the EU. And I know many Members of this House are concerned that we need to take a decision soon.

My Rt Hon Friend, the Leader of the House, will set out business on Thursday in the usual way.

But I can confirm today that we intend to return to the Meaningful Vote debate in the week commencing 7th January and hold the vote the following week.

Mr Speaker, when we have the vote, Members will need to reflect carefully on what is in the best interests of our country.

I know that there are a range of very strongly held personal views on this issue across the House. And I respect all of them.

But expressing our personal views is not what we are here to do.

We asked the British people to take this decision.

472 current Members of this House voted for the Referendum in June 2015, with just 32 voting against.

And the British people responded by instructing us to leave the European Union.

Similarly 438 current Members of this House voted to trigger Article 50, to set the process of our departure in motion, with only 85 of today's Members voting against.

Now we must honour our duty to finish the job.

I know this is not everyone's perfect deal. It is a compromise.

But if we let the perfect be the enemy of the good then we risk leaving the EU with no deal.

Of course we have prepared for no deal, and tomorrow the Cabinet will be discussing the next phase in ensuring we are ready for that scenario.

But let us not risk the jobs, services and security of the people we serve by turning our backs on an agreement with our neighbours that honours the referendum and provides for a smooth and orderly exit.

Avoiding no deal is only possible if we can reach an agreement or if we abandon Brexit entirely.

And as I said in the debate earlier this month—"do not imagine that if we vote this down, a different deal is going to miraculously appear."

If you want proof, look at the Conclusions of this Council.

As President Juncker said: "it is the best deal possible and the only deal possible."

And any proposal for the future relationship—whether Norway, Canada, or any other variety that has been mentioned—would require agreeing this Withdrawal Agreement.

The Leader of the Opposition—as well as some others—are trying to pretend they could do otherwise.

This is a fiction.

Finally let us not break faith with the British people by trying to stage another referendum.

Another vote which would do irreparable damage to the integrity of our politics, because it would say to millions who trusted in democracy, that our democracy does not deliver.

Another vote which would likely leave us no further forward than the last.

And another vote which would further divide our country at the very moment we should be working to unite it.

And let us not follow the Leader of the Opposition in thinking about what gives him the best chance of forcing a General Election.

For at this critical moment in our history, we should be thinking not about our party's interests, but about the national interest.

Let us a find a way to come together and work together in the national interest to see this Brexit through.

Mr Speaker, I will work tirelessly over these new few weeks to fulfil my responsibility as Prime Minister to find a way forwards.

Over the last two weeks, I have met quite a number of colleagues and I am happy to continue to do so on this important issue so that we can fulfil our responsibilities to the British people.

So together, we can take back control of our borders, laws and money; while protecting the jobs, the security and the integrity of our precious United Kingdom.

So together we can move on to finalising the future relationship with the European Union and the trade deals with the rest of the world that can fuel our prosperity for years to come.

And so together we can get this Brexit done and shift the national focus to our domestic priorities—investing in our NHS, our schools and housing; tackling the injustices that so many still face; and building a country that truly works for everyone.

For these are the ways in which, together, this House will best serve the interests of the British people.

And I commend this Statement to the House.

SOURCE: Office of the Prime Minister of the United Kingdom. "PM Statement on European Council: 17 December 2018." December 17, 2018. https://www.gov.uk/government/speeches/pm-statement-on-european-council-17-december-2018.

## OTHER HISTORIC DOCUMENTS OF INTEREST

### FROM PREVIOUS *HISTORIC DOCUMENTS*

# Trump Addresses the UN
# General Assembly

Held at United Nations (UN) headquarters in New York City in September 2018, the 73rd session of the General Assembly featured remarks by representatives of nearly all 193 UN member states. While many global issues were discussed, the session's official theme was "making the United Nations relevant to all people" and "shared responsibilities for peaceful, equitable and sustainable societies." U.S. President Donald Trump's remarks stood in stark contrast to other leaders' focus on the importance of multilateralism; Trump offered a staunch defense of national sovereignty and continued to criticize UN entities.

## TRUMP CALLS FOR PROTECTION OF NATIONAL SOVEREIGNTY

Throughout his speech, Trump repeatedly expressed nationalist views consistent with the "America First" theme of his campaign and early presidency. "America is governed by Americans," he said. "We reject the ideology of globalism, and we embrace the doctrine of patriotism. Around the world, responsible nations must defend against threats to sovereignty not just from global governance, but also from other, new forms of coercion and domination." Trump argued that the United States and other nations must act to protect their sovereignty because "sovereign and independent nations are the only vehicle where freedom has ever survived, democracy has ever endured, or peace has ever prospered." New opportunities for cooperation and peacemaking will present themselves, Trump claimed, when "nations respect the rights of their neighbors and defend the interests of their people." The United States "will always choose independence and cooperation over global governance, control, and domination," he said.

Trump declared that his administration's approach to international relations had yielded significant successes to date. His assertion that his administration "has accomplished more than almost any administration in the history of our country" in less than two years drew uncharacteristic laughter from other leaders in the chamber. "Didn't expect that reaction, but that's okay," Trump responded. The president went on to cite "highly productive conversations and meetings" with North Korean Supreme Leader Kim Jong Un as a major achievement, noting that their discussions led to a halt in nuclear testing and dismantling of some of that country's military facilities. Trump also said that his trip to Saudi Arabia prompted Persian Gulf states to open a new center targeting terrorist financing, enforce new sanctions, and collaborate with the United States on counterterrorism efforts, in addition to providing aid in Yemen and Syria. The president further observed that the United States was working with nations in the region to develop a strategic alliance that would help the Middle East achieve "prosperity, stability, and security across their home region." Additionally, Trump said the Islamic State of Iraq and the Levant's (ISIL) "bloodthirsty killers" had been driven from territory in Iraq and Syria that the group previously occupied, thanks to U.S. military action and partnerships with allies.

While Trump used his speech to lob criticisms at a number of targets—from the Venezuelan government to unfair trade practices—he reserved his harshest judgments for Iran. The president continued to accuse Iran's "brutal regime" and "corrupt dictatorship" of fueling and financing the long-running Syrian civil war. Iran's leaders "sow chaos, death, and destruction" and "plunder the nation's resources to enrich themselves and to spread mayhem across the Middle East" and beyond, he claimed. The Iranian people were outraged by their government's actions and neighboring countries have "paid a heavy toll," he said, which is why there was strong support in the region for the United States' decision to withdraw from the "horrible" Iran nuclear deal and reimpose sanctions. Trump argued that the nuclear deal and subsequent lifting of sanctions had created a "windfall" for Iran, which was in turn used to increase military spending and financial support for terrorism. He promised to impose another round of sanctions against Iran in November and said the United States was trying to persuade other countries to cut their imports of Iranian crude oil. "We cannot allow the world's leading sponsor of terrorism to possess the planet's most dangerous weapons," he said. "We ask all nations to isolate Iran's regime as long as its aggression continues. And we ask all nations to support Iran's people as they struggle to reclaim their religious and righteous destiny."

Trump also persisted in criticizing UN institutions, though he affirmed the United States' commitment to making the UN "more effective and accountable." The president reminded world leaders that he warned them in 2017 that the UN Human Rights Council had become "a grave embarrassment" due to its protection of some of the most egregious human rights abusers. The United States had presented a path to reform, Trump said, but since no action was taken, it had no choice but to withdraw from the council. "We will not return until real reform is enacted," he pledged. The United States would no longer recognize the International Criminal Court (ICC) for similar reasons, he said, claiming that the organization had "no jurisdiction, no legitimacy, and no authority." (The ICC is an independent entity, but the UN Security Council may refer cases to the court or temporarily suspend its investigations.) Echoing the nationalist sentiments expressed elsewhere in his speech, Trump said the United States would never surrender its sovereignty to "an unelected, unaccountable, global bureaucracy."

The United States' rejection of multilateral agreements and institutions continued in early October when administration officials announced a withdrawal from two accords: the 1955 Treaty of Amity with Iran, which sought to normalize relations between the two countries, and an optional protocol under the 1961 Vienna Convention of Diplomatic Relations that requires certain disputes between nations to be settled by the International Court of Justice (ICJ)—the UN's primary judicial body. The move came the same day the ICJ ordered the United States to ensure that new sanctions against Iran do not impact humanitarian aid or civil aviation safety. Speaking to reporters about the announcement, U.S. National Security Advisor John Bolton called the ICJ "politicized and ineffective" and said the United States would review all international agreements that required it to participate in cases before the court. "The United States will not sit idly by as baseless politicized claims are brought against us," he said.

## World Leaders Defend Multilateralism

Trump's remarks were discordant to those offered by other leaders during the General Assembly, many of whom stressed the importance of multilateralism. On the session's opening day, UN Secretary General António Guterres said that the world was suffering from a "trust deficit disorder" and called on governments to work together to counter unilateralism and encourage international cooperation. "Today, world order is increasingly chaotic," he said. "Power relations are less clear. Universal values are being eroded. Democratic principles are under siege." Guterres warned that people were losing faith in political establishments amid rising populism and polarization in many nations. "The world is more connected, yet societies are becoming more fragmented," he said. "Challenges are growing outward, while many people are turning inward."

Heads of state and government or ministers from nearly every continent offered their own defense of multilateralism, with some also advocating support for specific UN agreements. French President Emmanuel Macron provided a key voice in the debate, declaring that "nationalism always leads to defeat" and that "we should only triumph through bolstered multilateralism." Macron blamed the "crisis of the very foundations of today's world" on unilateralism and argued that protectionism and isolationism were only creating more problems, citing the ongoing Israeli–Palestinian conflict as one example. In an apparent reference to Trump's remarks, Macron said that even those who criticized globalization "have all benefitted from the way global order is structured." He called for new policies to combat inequality, which he said had given rise to increased nationalism, and said that universal values should guide international cooperation.

Swiss President Alain Berset lamented the tendency of some leaders to respond to global problems such as extremism, migration, and climate change with "nationalist isolation" and "a growing mistrust with regard to cooperation between states." Berset spoke of "a real crisis in multilateralism—paradoxically at the very moment when we are trying to forge the main pillars of the global governance of the future" and said the UN was best-suited to tackle modern-day global challenges. His remarks also emphasized Switzerland's support for the ICC and criticized protectionist trade policies.

Other voices included Chinese Foreign Minister Wang Yi, who described the UN as a "symbol of multilateralism" and called on the international community to "stand united under the umbrella of multilateralism, uphold the central role of the UN in international affairs, and provide more predictability and stability in this turbulent world." Brazilian President Michel Temer added that "protectionism may even sound seductive, but it is through openness and integration that harmony, growth, and progress can be achieved." Rwandan President Paul Kagame also expressed support for multilateralism, though he observed that the current "two-track system of global governance," in which a few countries determine the standards for everyone else, is "unsustainable." Kagame said that "addressing this imbalance in the very foundation of our system is what will give shape to a revival of multilateral cooperation, and renew the legitimacy of the international institutions, that are so crucial to our planet's future."

## Iran Responds to Trump

In what was widely characterized as a direct response to Trump, Iranian President Hassan Rouhani used his General Assembly remarks to highlight the global suffering caused by the "recklessness and disregard of some states for international values and institutions." Rouhani also challenged the idea that it is possible to achieve security and peace by denying those things to others. "Confronting multilateralism is not a sign of strength, rather it is a symptom of a weakness of intellect."

Addressing the Trump-maligned nuclear deal, Rouhani said Iran was pleased that the international community "did not acquiesce to the U.S.'s illegal and unilateral withdrawal," an acknowledgement that China, Russia, and European parties to the agreement continued to abide by its terms. Rouhani declared that sanctions are a form of "economic terrorism" and warned that no country can be forced to the negotiating table. "If so, what follows is the accumulation of the grapes of wrath . . . to be reaped later by the oppressors," he said. He also invited Trump to return to the negotiating table if he was displeased with the terms of the deal.

Rouhani continued to challenge Trump's statements after returning to Iran, claiming that the United States "had no achievements in this public assembly" and noting that "everyone laughed" at Trump's claims to have accomplished so much in the first year of his presidency. Rouhani further stated that only "one or two countries" continued to support the United States. "It's a historic political isolation that is rare for America," he said.

—Linda Grimm

*Following is the text of President Donald Trump's remarks to the UN General Assembly, as delivered on September 25, 2018.*

# President Trump Remarks to the United Nations General Assembly

**September 25, 2018**

Madam President, Mr. Secretary-General, world leaders, Ambassadors, and distinguished delegates: One year ago, I stood before you for the first time in this grand hall. I addressed the threats facing our world, and I presented a vision to achieve a brighter future for all of humanity.

Today I stand before the United Nations General Assembly to share the extraordinary progress we've made. In less than 2 years, my administration has accomplished more than almost any administration in the history of our country. *[Laughter]* America's—so true. *[Laughter]* Didn't expect that reaction, but that's okay. *[Laughter]*

America's economy is booming like never before. Since my election, we've added $10 trillion in wealth. The stock market is at an all-time high in history, and jobless claims are at a 50-year low. African American, Hispanic American, and Asian American unemployment have all achieved their lowest levels ever recorded. We've added more than 4 million new jobs, including half a million manufacturing jobs.

We have passed the biggest tax cuts and reforms in American history. We've started the construction of a major border wall, and we have greatly strengthened border security. We have secured record funding for our military: $700 billion this year and $716 billion next year. Our military will soon be more powerful than it has ever been before. In other words, the United States is stronger, safer, and a richer country than it was when I assumed office less than 2 years ago.

We are standing up for America and for the American people. And we are also standing up for the world. This is great news for our citizens and for peace-loving people everywhere. We believe that when nations respect the rights of their neighbors and defend the interests of their people, they can better work together to secure the blessings of safety, prosperity, and peace.

Each of us here today is the emissary of a distinct culture, a rich history, and a people bound together by ties of memory, tradition, and the values that make our homelands like nowhere else on Earth.

That is why America will always choose independence and cooperation over global governance, control, and domination. I honor the right of every nation in this room to pursue its own customs, beliefs, and traditions. The United States will not tell you how to live or work or worship. We only ask that you honor our sovereignty in return.

From Warsaw to Brussels to Tokyo to Singapore, it has been my highest honor to represent the United States abroad. I have forged close relationships and friendships and strong partnerships with the leaders of many nations in this room, and our approach has always yielded incredible change.

With support from many countries here today, we have engaged with North Korea to replace the specter of conflict with a bold and new push for peace. In June, I traveled to Singapore to meet face to face with North Korea's leader, Chairman Kim Jong Un. We had highly productive conversations and meetings, and we agreed that it was in both countries' interest to pursue the denuclearization of the Korean Peninsula. Since that meeting, we have already seen a number of encouraging measures that few could have imagined only a short time ago.

The missiles and rockets are no longer flying in every direction. Nuclear testing has stopped. Some military facilities are already being dismantled. Our hostages have been released. And as promised, the remains of our fallen heroes are being returned home to lay at rest in American soil.

I would like to thank Chairman Kim for his courage and for the steps he has taken, though much work remains to be done. The sanctions will stay in place until denuclearization occurs. I also want to thank the many member states who helped us reach this moment, a moment that is actually far greater than people would understand—far greater—but for also their support and the critical support that we will all need going forward. A special thanks to President Moon of South Korea, Prime Minister Abe of Japan, and President Xi of China.

In the Middle East, our new approach is also yielding great strides and very historic change. Following my trip to Saudi Arabia last year, the Gulf countries opened a new center to target terrorist financing. They are enforcing new sanctions, working with us to identify and track terrorist networks, and taking more responsibility for fighting terrorism and extremism in their own region. The U.A.E., Saudi Arabia, and Qatar have pledged billions of dollars to aid the people of Syria and Yemen. And they are pursuing multiple avenues to ending Yemen's horrible, horrific civil war.

Ultimately, it is up to the nations of the region to decide what kind of future they want for themselves and their children. For that reason, the United States is working with the Gulf Cooperation Council, Jordan, and Egypt to establish a regional strategic alliance so that Middle Eastern nations can advance prosperity, stability, and security across their home region.

Thanks to the United States military and our partnership with many of your nations, I am pleased to report that the bloodthirsty killers known as ISIS have been driven out from the territory they once held in Iraq and Syria. We will continue to work with friends and allies to deny radical Islamic terrorists any funding, territory, or support, or any means of infiltrating our borders.

The ongoing tragedy in Syria is heartbreaking. Our shared goals must be the de-escalation of military conflict, along with a political solution that honors the will of the

Syrian people. In this vein, we urge the United Nations–led peace process be reinvigo-rated. But, rest assured, the United States will respond if chemical weapons are deployed by the Assad regime. I commend the people of Jordan and other neighboring countries for hosting refugees from this very brutal civil war. As we see in Jordan, the most compassion-ate policy is to place refugees as close to their homes as possible to ease their eventual return to be part of the rebuilding process. This approach also stretches finite resources to help far more people, increasing the impact of every dollar spent.

Every solution to the humanitarian crisis in Syria must also include a strategy to address the brutal regime that has fueled and financed it: the corrupt dictatorship in Iran. Iran's leaders sow chaos, death, and destruction. They do not respect their neighbors or borders, or the sovereign rights of nations. Instead, Iran's leaders plunder the nation's resources to enrich themselves and to spread mayhem across the Middle East and far beyond.

The Iranian people are rightly outraged that their leaders have embezzled billions of dollars from Iran's treasury, seized valuable portions of the economy, and looted the peo-ple's religious endowments, all to line their own pockets and send their proxies to wage war. Not good. Iran's neighbors have paid a heavy toll for the regime's agenda of aggression and expansion. That is why so many countries in the Middle East strongly supported my decision to withdraw the United States from the horrible 2015 Iran nuclear deal and reim-pose nuclear sanctions.

The Iran deal was a windfall for Iran's leaders. In the years since the deal was reached, Iran's military budget grew nearly 40 percent. The dictatorship used the funds to build nuclear-capable missiles, increase internal repression, finance terrorism, and fund havoc and slaughter in Syria and Yemen.

The United States has launched a campaign of economic pressure to deny the regime the funds it needs to advance its bloody agenda. Last month, we began re-imposing hard-hitting nuclear sanctions that had been lifted under the Iran deal. Additional sanctions will resume November 5, and more will follow. And we're working with countries that import Iranian crude oil to cut their purchases substantially.

We cannot allow the world's leading sponsor of terrorism to possess the planet's most dangerous weapons. We cannot allow a regime that chants "Death to America" and that threatens Israel with annihilation to possess the means to deliver a nuclear warhead to any city on Earth. Just can't do it. We ask all nations to isolate Iran's regime as long as its aggres-sion continues. And we ask all nations to support Iran's people as they struggle to reclaim their religious and righteous destiny.

This year, we also took another significant step forward in the Middle East. In recog-nition of every sovereign state to determine its own capital, I moved the U.S. Embassy in Israel to Jerusalem. The United States is committed to a future of peace and stability in the region, including peace between the Israelis and the Palestinians. That aim is advanced, not harmed, by acknowledging the obvious facts.

America's policy of principled realism means we will not be held hostage to old dog-mas, discredited ideologies, and so-called experts who have been proven wrong over the years, time and time again. This is true not only in matters of peace, but in matters of prosperity. We believe that trade must be fair and reciprocal. The United States will not be taken advantage of any longer.

For decades, the United States opened its economy—the largest, by far, on Earth—with few conditions. We allowed foreign goods from all over the world to flow freely across our borders. Yet other countries did not grant us fair and reciprocal access to their markets in return. Even worse, some countries abused their openness to dump their products, subsidize their goods, target our industries, and manipulate their currencies to gain unfair advantage over our country. As a result, our trade deficit ballooned to nearly $800 billion a year.

For this reason, we are systematically renegotiating broken and bad trade deals. Last month, we announced a groundbreaking U.S.-Mexico trade agreement. And just yesterday I stood with President Moon to announce the successful completion of the brand new U.S.-Korea trade deal. And this is just the beginning.

Many nations in this hall will agree that the world trading system is in dire need of change. For example, countries were admitted to the World Trade Organization that violate every single principle on which the organization is based. While the United States and many other nations play by the rules, these countries use government-run industrial planning and state-owned enterprises to rig the system in their favor. They engage in relentless product dumping, forced technology transfer, and the theft of intellectual property.

The United States lost over 3 million manufacturing jobs, nearly a quarter of all steel jobs, and 60,000 factories after China joined the WTO. And we have racked up $13 trillion in trade deficits over the last two decades. But those days are over. We will no longer tolerate such abuse. We will not allow our workers to be victimized, our companies to be cheated, and our wealth to be plundered and transferred. America will never apologize for protecting its citizens.

The United States has just announced tariffs on another $200 billion in Chinese-made goods for a total, so far, of $250 billion. I have great respect and affection for my friend, President Xi, but I have made clear our trade imbalance is just not acceptable. China's market distortions and the way they deal cannot be tolerated. As my administration has demonstrated, America will always act in our national interest.

I spoke before this body last year and warned that the U.N. Human Rights Council had become a grave embarrassment to this institution, shielding egregious human rights abusers while bashing America and its many friends. Our Ambassador to the United Nations, Nikki Haley, laid out a clear agenda for reform, but despite reported and repeated warnings, no action at all was taken. So the United States took the only responsible course: We withdrew from the Human Rights Council, and we will not return until real reform is enacted.

For similar reasons, the United States will provide no support in recognition to the International Criminal Court. As far as America is concerned, the ICC has no jurisdiction, no legitimacy, and no authority. The ICC claims near-universal jurisdiction over the citizens of every country, violating all principles of justice, fairness, and due process. We will never surrender America's sovereignty to an unelected, unaccountable, global bureaucracy.

America is governed by Americans. We reject the ideology of globalism, and we embrace the doctrine of patriotism. Around the world, responsible nations must defend against threats to sovereignty not just from global governance, but also from other, new forms of coercion and domination.

In America, we believe strongly in energy security for ourselves and for our allies. We have become the largest energy producer anywhere on the face of the Earth. The United States stands ready to export our abundant, affordable supply of oil, clean coal, and natural gas.

OPEC and OPEC nations are, as usual, ripping off the rest of the world, and I don't like it. Nobody should like it. *[Laughter]* We defend many of these nations for nothing, and then they take advantage of us by giving us high oil prices. Not good.

We want them to stop raising prices, we want them to start lowering prices, and they must contribute substantially to military protection from now on. We are not going to put up with it—these horrible prices—much longer.

Reliance on a single foreign supplier can leave a nation vulnerable to extortion and intimidation. That is why we congratulate European states, such as Poland, for leading the construction of a Baltic pipeline so that nations are not dependent on Russia to meet their energy needs. Germany will become totally dependent on Russian energy if it does not immediately change course.

Here in the Western Hemisphere, we are committed to maintaining our independence from the encroachment of expansionist foreign powers. It has been the formal policy of our country since President Monroe that we reject the interference of foreign nations in this hemisphere and in our own affairs. The United States has recently strengthened our laws to better screen foreign investments in our country for national security threats and we welcome cooperation with countries in this region and around the world that wish to do the same. You need to do it for your own protection.

The United States is also working with partners in Latin America to confront threats to sovereignty from uncontrolled migration. Tolerance for human struggling and human smuggling and trafficking is not humane. It's a horrible thing that's going on, at levels that nobody has ever seen before. It's very, very cruel.

Illegal immigration funds criminal networks, ruthless gangs, and the flow of deadly drugs. Illegal immigration exploits vulnerable populations, hurts hard-working citizens, and has produced a vicious cycle of crime, violence, and poverty. Only by upholding national borders, destroying criminal gangs, can we break this cycle and establish a real foundation for prosperity.

We recognize the right of every nation in this room to set its own immigration policy in accordance with its national interests, just as we ask other countries to respect our own right to do the same, which we are doing. That is one reason the United States will not participate in the new Global Compact on Migration. Migration should not be governed by an international body unaccountable to our own citizens. Ultimately, the only long-term solution to the migration crisis is to help people build more hopeful futures in their home countries. Make their countries great again. *[Laughter]*

Currently, we are witnessing a human tragedy, as an example, in Venezuela. More than 2 million people have fled the anguish inflicted by the socialist Maduro regime and its Cuban sponsors. Not long ago, Venezuela was one of the richest countries on Earth. Today, socialism has bankrupted the oil-rich nation and driven its people into abject poverty.

Virtually everywhere socialism or communism has been tried, it has produced suffering, corruption, and decay. Socialism's thirst for power leads to expansion, incursion, and oppression. All nations of the world should resist socialism and the misery that it brings to everyone.

In that spirit, we ask the nations gathered here to join us in calling for the restoration of democracy in Venezuela. Today we are announcing additional sanctions against the repressive regime, targeting Maduro's inner circle and close advisers.

We are grateful for all the work the United Nations does around the world to help people build better lives for themselves and their families.

The United States is the world's largest giver in the world, by far, of foreign aid. But few give anything to us. That is why we are taking a hard look at U.S. foreign assistance. That will be headed up by Secretary of State Mike Pompeo. We will examine what is working, what is not working, and whether the countries who receive our dollars and our protection also have our interests at heart. Moving forward, we are only going to give foreign aid to those who respect us and, frankly, are our friends. And we expect other countries to pay their fair share for the cost of their defense.

The United States is committed to making the United Nations more effective and accountable. I have said many times that the United Nations has unlimited potential. As part of our reform effort, I have told our negotiators that the United States will not pay more than 25 percent of the U.N. peacekeeping budget. This will encourage other countries to step up, get involved, and also share in this very large burden.

And we are working to shift more of our funding from assessed contributions to voluntary so that we can target American resources to the programs with the best record of success. Only when each of us does our part and contributes our share can we realize the U.N.'s highest aspirations. We must pursue peace without fear, hope without despair, and security without apology.

Looking around this hall where so much history has transpired, we think of the many before us who have come here to address the challenges of their nations and of their times. And our thoughts turn to the same question that ran through all their speeches and resolutions, through every word and every hope. It is the question of what kind of world will we leave for our children and what kind of nations they will inherit.

The dreams that fill this hall today are as diverse as the people who have stood at this podium and as varied as the countries represented right here in this body are. It really is something. It really is great, great history.

There is India, a free society over a billion people, successfully lifting countless millions out of poverty and into the middle class. There is Saudi Arabia, where King Salman and the Crown Prince are pursuing bold new reforms. There is Israel, proudly celebrating its 70th anniversary as a thriving democracy in the Holy Land. In Poland, a great people are standing up for their independence, their security, and their sovereignty.

Many countries are pursuing their own unique visions, building their own hopeful futures, and chasing their own wonderful dreams of destiny, of legacy, and of a home. The whole world is richer, humanity is better, because of this beautiful constellation of nations, each very special, each very unique, and each shining brightly in its part of the world. In each one, we see awesome promise of a people bound together by a shared past and working toward a common future.

As for Americans, we know what kind of future we want for ourselves. We know what kind of a nation America must always be. In America, we believe in the majesty of freedom and the dignity of the individual. We believe in self-government and the rule of law. And we prize the culture that sustains our liberty: a culture built on strong families, deep faith, and fierce independence. We celebrate our heroes, we treasure our traditions, and above all, we love our country.

Inside everyone in this great chamber today, and everyone listening all around the globe, there is the heart of a patriot that feels the same powerful love for your nation, the same intense loyalty to your homeland. The passion that burns in the hearts of patriots and the souls of nations has inspired reform and revolution, sacrifice and selflessness, scientific breakthroughs and magnificent works of art. Our task is not to erase it, but to embrace it. To build with it. To draw on its ancient wisdom. And to find within it the will to make our nations greater, our regions safer, and the world better.

To unleash this incredible potential in our people, we must defend the foundations that make it all possible. Sovereign and independent nations are the only vehicle where freedom has ever survived, democracy has ever endured, or peace has ever prospered. And so we must protect our sovereignty and our cherished independence above all.

When we do, we will find new avenues for cooperation unfolding before us. We will find new passion for peacemaking rising within us. We will find new purpose, new resolve, and new spirit flourishing all around us, and making this a more beautiful world in which to live.

So together, let us choose a future of patriotism, prosperity, and pride. Let us choose peace and freedom over domination and defeat. And let us come here to this place to stand for our people and their nations, forever strong, forever sovereign, forever just, and forever thankful for the grace and the goodness and the glory of God.

Thank you, God bless you, and God bless the nations of the world. Thank you very much.

Thank you.

SOURCE: Executive Office of the President. "Remarks to the United Nations General Assembly in New York City." September 25, 2018. *Compilation of Presidential Documents* 2018, no. 00631 (September 25, 2018). https://www.govinfo.gov/content/pkg/DCPD-201800631/pdf/DCPD-201800631.pdf.

## OTHER HISTORIC DOCUMENTS OF INTEREST

### FROM THIS VOLUME

### FROM PREVIOUS *HISTORIC DOCUMENTS*

# Swedish Parliament Vote of No Confidence in Prime Minister

SEPTEMBER 25 AND OCTOBER 22, 2018

Sweden's government was in limbo for more than three months following its September 2018 general election. None of the country's political parties secured a majority of seats in parliament, and the vote left the traditional center-left and center-right political blocs deadlocked. Prime Minister Stefan Löfven lost a no-confidence vote in parliament following the election, leaving Speaker Andreas Norlén in charge of talks with the various party leaders to agree on a new government. Most were staunchly opposed to collaborating with the Sweden Democrats, a far-right, anti-immigrant party that won the third-largest number of seats in the election, which complicated negotiations. Disagreements among the parties and an unwillingness of some center-right parties to work with the center-left led to an impasse, and a new government was not formed until January 2019.

## GENERAL ELECTION LEADS TO HUNG PARLIAMENT

Swedish voters went to the polls on September 9 to elect 349 lawmakers to the country's Riksdag. Any of Sweden's political parties would need to win 175 seats to secure a majority in parliament. At the time, Löfven's Social Democratic Party and the Green Party comprised a minority government that was able to pass legislation with the support of the Left Party.

When the results were tallied, the Social Democratic Party had won 28.4 percent of the vote, preserving its nearly 100-year record of winning the most votes in general elections. However, it was the worst showing for the party in a century. Sweden's other major party, the Moderate Party, also lost support, although it received the second-highest number of votes (19.8 percent). The votes lost by these major parties were cast instead for smaller political organizations, including the center-right Centre Party, the conservative Christian Democrats, and the formerly communist Left Party. Most notably, the far-right, anti-immigrant Sweden Democrats won 17.6 percent of the vote, which was less than the 25 percent some pre-election polls projected the party would win but more than the 12.9 percent the party won in the 2014 general election. As a result, the Sweden Democrats would take 62 seats in parliament, making them the third-largest party in parliament behind the Social Democratic Party with 101 seats and the Moderate Party with 70 seats.

Electoral gains by the Sweden Democrats reflected similar outcomes for far-right groups participating in recent elections across Western Europe, fueled by the continent's ongoing migrant crisis. In 2017, elections in France and Germany saw populist and anti-immigrant parties drawing a larger percentage of the vote, with the far-right Alternative for Germany Party winning seats in parliament for the first time. Far-right parties are also now part of the governments of Italy, Austria, Norway, and Finland.

Immigration, migrant integration, and welfare programs had been the central themes of Sweden's 2018 campaign. The September poll was the first general election to be held since the government had allowed more than 160,000 migrants to enter the country in 2015—the most per capita of any European nation. The migrants' arrival prompted concerns that Sweden's already strained welfare system—which was facing doctor and teacher shortages, limited police capacity, and long waits for some medical procedures—would not be able to handle the influx. The Sweden Democrats said the government had prioritized asylum seekers and called for "tight responsible immigration policies," including a freeze on migrant entry. Löfven had described the vote as "a referendum about our welfare" but said it was also about "decency" and "not letting the Sweden Democrats, an extremist party, a racist party, get any influence in the government."

Not only did no party win a majority of seats in parliament, but Sweden's two traditional political blocs—the center-left and the center-right—were deadlocked, with each having received about 40 percent of the vote. (The center-left bloc comprises of the Social Democratic, Left, and Green Parties, while the center-right bloc comprises of the Moderate, Liberal, and Christian Democrat Parties.) In order to form a new government, center-right and center-left parties would need to forge cross-bloc alliances, or one bloc would have to collaborate with the Sweden Democrats. Most of the parties staunchly opposed any kind of agreement with the Sweden Democrats given its far-right policies and its roots as an organization formed by white supremacists. Political observers said it was unlikely that the Social Democratic and Moderate Party would partner to form a government. Most speculated that Moderate Party leader Ulf Kristersson would try to form a minority center-right government.

Kristersson called on Löfven to resign and help the center-right bloc form a new government after election. Löfven responded that he would not step down and said it would be "illogical" for the larger center-left bloc to facilitate an Alliance government. (*Alliance* is a term often used to refer to Sweden's center-right parties.) Löfven said he wanted to form a coalition or come to some agreement with the Centre and Liberal Parties, but leaders of both organizations said they preferred to remain part of the center-right bloc. Löfven also cautioned against any collaboration with the Sweden Democrats, saying the party "can never, and will never, offer anything that will help society. They will only increase division and hate."

The Sweden Democrats celebrated the election outcome, with leader Jimmie Åkesson positioning himself as a "kingmaker" at a postelection event. "We will have an immense influence over what happens in Sweden in the coming weeks, months, years," he told supporters. Åkesson expressed interest in working with other parties to form a new government, but especially the Moderate Party.

## Löfven Dismissed following No-Confidence Vote

Swedish law dictates that the sitting prime minister face a no-confidence vote in parliament after a general election. Sweden also has a system of negative parliamentarism, which means that only no votes are counted. In the case of no-confidence votes, a prime minister and his or her government may remain in place if fewer than 175 members of parliament vote against them.

The vote on Löfven was held on September 25. More than half the Riksdag, or 204 members of parliament, voted against the prime minister, declaring their lack of confidence in him. The Sweden Democrats joined the Alliance to vote against him. Speaker Andreas Norlén subsequently dismissed Löfven as prime minister but asked him to lead a caretaker government while a new government was formed. The vote outcome also meant that Norlén would be responsible for leading talks to form a new government. The speaker would be able to call up to four votes for the Riksdag to approve a new government; if none of the four votes resulted in a government's approval, a snap election would have to be called within three months.

Shortly before the no-confidence vote, Kristersson said that Sweden needed a new government with "broad political support to undertake reforms" and continued to claim that he had enough support to become the next prime minister. Löfven countered that the Moderate Party would not be able to form a new government without the support of the Social Democratic Party, adding that "unless the combined center-right parties are willing to break their promise never to give the Sweden Democrats power over the government, a so-called Alliance government is unrealistic with this distribution of seats."

## SWEDEN STRUGGLES TO FORM A NEW GOVERNMENT

Uncertainty hung over Sweden for the next three and a half months as party leaders struggled to overcome their differences to form a new government. Norlén began meeting with party representatives and his deputy speakers on September 27 to try to develop an agreeable proposal for a new government and prime minister. On October 2, Norlén asked Kristersson to put together a plan for a new government, with a deadline of October 13. Once Kristersson's plan was presented to Norlén, the speaker would decide whether to put it to a vote in parliament. "The parties have to rethink their positions in order for a government to be formed," Norlén said. "I am the speaker, not a magician." Kristersson told reporters that he would "do all I can to build an Alliance government" and that he would focus his efforts on Alliance members and the Social Democratic Party. Löfven said he would not support an Alliance government, while the Sweden Democrats said they would block any government that did not give their party a say in policy development.

Ultimately, Kristersson was unable to come up with a plan before his deadline, so Norlén turned to Löfven, asking him to form a government by October 29. Löfven said he would speak to all mainstream parties, stating that a solution would "require humility and compromise from all parties." The former prime minister, however, was also unsuccessful. "In light of the responses I have had so far, in the current situation, the possibility does not exist for me to build a government that can be accepted by parliament," Löfven said, though he noted that his talks with other party leaders had "been sincere" and led to "greater understanding of each other's positions."

Norlén's next step was to put Kristersson forward as prime minister. Norlén announced his decision on November 5 and said he would formally nominate the Moderate Party leader on November 12, giving him one week to find coalition partners before facing a vote in parliament. On November 14, 195 members of the Riksdag voted against Kristersson's proposal to form a minority coalition government with the Christian Democrats. Members of the Social Democratic, Liberal, and Centre Parties said they voted against Kristersson's proposal because they were concerned the minority coalition would be too fragile and reliant on the Sweden Democrats to pass laws.

The next day, Norlén asked Centre Party leader Annie Lööf to try to determine what kind of government may be able to win parliament's approval, giving her a week to complete the task. Lööf's assignment was notably different than that of Kristersson or Löfven because she was not asked to form a coalition. This meant Lööf was not being considered as a candidate for prime minister. "I am going to try to put the question of prime minister to the side in order to find broad agreements and broad backing for the reforms that Sweden needs," Lööf said.

On November 22, Lööf said she had tried to build consensus with all groups except the Left Party and the Sweden Democrats while keeping the Alliance together, but that "all these solutions have been blocked by one party or several parties saying no." It was once again up to Norlén, she said, to determine the next step in the process. Media reports indicated that thus far the Moderate and Christian Democrat Parties had refused to work with the center-left bloc, particularly the Social Democratic Party, while the Centre and Liberal Parties were adamantly opposed to working with the Sweden Democrats.

On November 23, Norlén said he would formally nominate Löfven as prime minister on December 3. "It is still a difficult political situation and there is, of course, no guarantee that his candidature will be successful," Norlén said of his decision. One week after Löfven's nomination, Lööf said her party would vote against him because he was unwilling to meet their policy demands, including lower income taxes and labor law reforms. "We would have needed to see considerably more liberal political reforms in order for the Centre Party to be able to come to an agreement and allow Stefan Löfven four more years," she said. When the vote on Löfven was held on December 14, 200 votes were cast against him and his proposed Social Democratic–Green Party government.

No further progress was made before the end of the year, and speculation mounted that a snap election would be necessary. Then on January 11, 2019, Lööf announced that the Centre, Green, and Liberal Parties had reached an agreement with the Social Democratic Party. Under the deal, a new government would be formed by the Social Democratic and Green Parties, with Löfven as prime minister. The Centre and Liberal Parties would back the new government's legislative proposals in the Riksdag. Löfven reportedly made several concessions to the two groups during negotiations, including a promise to implement new labor laws and housing regulations to appease the Centre Party. Parliament voted on the proposal on January 19. While 153 members voted against the new government, it was not enough to defeat Löfven and his coalition, meaning he would once again serve as prime minister.

—Linda Grimm

*Following is information provided by Speaker Andreas Norlén about the Riksdag's no-confidence vote on Prime Minister Stefan Löfven on September 25, 2018; and a statement by Norlén on October 22, 2018, about Löfven's efforts to form a new government.*

# Information about the
# Vote on Prime Minister

**September 25, 2018**

On 25 September, a vote was held on the Prime Minister in order to determine the support for Prime Minister Stefan Löfven (Social Democratic Party) in the newly elected Riksdag. The results of the vote show that the Prime Minister does not have the confidence of the new Riksdag, as more than half of the members of the Riksdag voted against him.

These are the results of the vote in the Chamber:

- No: 204 votes

- Yes: 142 votes

- Absent: 3 members

The count was 204 votes against and 142 votes in favour of the Prime Minister. The Speaker Andreas Norlén has now dismissed Stefan Löfven from office as Prime Minister, but has at the same time assigned Stefan Löfven to lead a caretaker government.

"I will now start my work of presenting a proposal for Prime Minister to the Riksdag. The first thing on my agenda will be to call the representatives of all the parties for talks", says the Speaker Andreas Norlén.

On Thursday, the Speaker Andreas Norlén will initiate talks with the representatives of the party groups in the Riksdag, a process known as the Speaker's interview rounds. Further information about these talks will be available shortly.

SOURCE: Sveriges Riksdag. "Information about the Vote on the Prime Minister and the Continued Process." September 25, 2018. http://www.riksdagen.se/en/the-election-2018/information-about-the-vote-on-the-prime-minister-and-the-continued-process.

# Statement by the Speaker on Stefan Löfven's Progress Report

**October 22, 2018**

At a meeting with the Speaker of the Riksdag Andreas Norlén on 22 October, Stefan Löfven (Social Democratic Party) provided a status report on his task of exploring the possibilities of forming a government.

"I have had a meeting with Stefan Löfven today, during which he presented his work with the task of exploring the possibilities of forming a government. He will continue this work during the assigned period," says the Speaker Andreas Norlén after the meeting.

"We have a complicated political situation, where the parties actively need to hold discussions with each other in order to progress. In such situations, internal work is also necessary. The time aspect is important, but at the same time, it is important to respect the fact that the work of the parties can take time. The process now being used to explore the possibilities of forming a government has been used by Speakers of the Riksdag since 1976. I, too, have chosen to follow established practice and provide this framework for the parties' discussions," continues the Speaker.

Stefan Löfven's (Social Democratic Party) task of exploring the possibilities of forming a government that is tolerated by the Riksdag is based on the same criteria as that previously given to Ulf Kristersson (Moderate Party). The final report is due on Monday 29 October at the latest. Further information about the forms for the final report will be issued at the end of the week.

## Background

On Thursday 27 September, the Speaker started the assignment of preparing a proposal for a new Prime Minister for the Riksdag to take a stand on. The assignment includes interview rounds with representatives of all the parties in the Riksdag and deliberations with the Deputy Speakers.

The Speaker has spoken to the party representatives, conferred with the Deputy Speakers and informed the Head of State of the current situation. On 2 October, Ulf Kristersson (Moderate Party) was given the task of exploring the possibilities of forming a government that is tolerated by the Riksdag, and a final report on the task was presented on 13 October. On 15 October, the task of exploring the possibilities of forming a government was given to Stefan Löfven (Social Democratic Party). . . .

SOURCE: Sveriges Riksdag. "Statement by the Speaker on Stefan Löfven's (Social Democratic Party) Progress Report." October 22, 2018. http://www.riksdagen.se/en/news/2018/okt/22/statement-by-the-speaker-on-stefan-lofvens-social-democratic-party-progress-report.

## OTHER HISTORIC DOCUMENTS OF INTEREST

### FROM PREVIOUS *HISTORIC DOCUMENTS*

# October

# United Nations Remarks on Election in Democratic Republic of the Congo

OCTOBER 6, NOVEMBER 22, AND DECEMBER 22, 2018

After two years of delays, the Democratic Republic of the Congo (DRC) held an election to determine outgoing president Joseph Kabila's successor on December 30, 2018. The run-up to the vote was marked by protests demanding Kabila leave office, claims by opposition leaders that government loyalists were collaborating to extend the president's term, and numerous challenges to electoral preparations. United Nations (UN) officials closely monitored the situation and continually urged calm and collaboration to ensure the election's credibility. While the vote proceeded peacefully, the official results were met with shock and suspicion when announced in January 2019 after more delays.

## ELECTIONS POSTPONED IN 2016 AND 2017

The DRC was originally scheduled to hold a presidential election in November 2016, shortly before the end of Kabila's second term. However, in October 2016, the country's Constitutional Court approved a request from the Independent National Electoral Commission (CENI) to postpone the election to give the commission more time to update voter registration lists. The move was widely viewed as an effort by Kabila's allies to extend his time in office and prompted widespread public protests calling for the president to step down. The government acted quickly to try to suppress the demonstrations. International organizations including the United Nations and Human Rights Watch reported that hundreds of Congolese were killed or wounded in violent clashes between government security forces and protestors, with hundreds more unlawfully arrested and detained. The United States and the European Union imposed sanctions on several government officials in response to the crackdown.

Amid growing internal and international pressure, Kabila's government and the opposition came together for talks mediated by the National Episcopal Conference of Congo (CENCO), which resulted in an agreement to hold the presidential election in 2017. Per the agreement's terms, Kabila would remain in power until that time, but a transitional government would be installed by March 2017. Kabila was also prevented from pursuing a constitutional amendment that would allow him to run for a third consecutive term.

The deal was not fully implemented. CENI officials said in July 2017 that it would not be possible to hold elections before the end of the year because it needed more time to prepare. The commission announced in November that the election would instead take place on December 23, 2018. Additionally, Kabila appointed all members of the transitional government in April and May 2017, despite previously agreeing that the opposition could select the interim officials. While some opposition members were given cabinet posts, most of the appointed officials had served in the previous government, and Kabila loyalists were named to many key ministries, including justice and foreign affairs.

## Vote Preparations Lag

Twenty-one candidates were approved to run in the 2018 presidential election, but three emerged as the primary contenders: Emmanuel Ramazani Shadary, a former interior minister from Kabila's Governing People's Party for Reconstruction and Democracy; Felix Tshisekedi, leader of the main opposition group Union for Democracy and Social Progress; and Martin Fayulu, leader of the Engagement for Citizenship and Development opposition party. The opposition coalition had been working on an agreement through which Fayulu would represent all parties as a common candidate, but Tshisekedi pulled out of the agreement to stand on his own. Fayulu was still generally viewed as the common opposition candidate since he was backed by seven opposition leaders.

In the run-up to election day, significant concerns remained about the country's ability to prepare for the vote and ensure its credibility. Opposition parties were particularly uneasy about CENI's insistence that new touch-screen voting machines be used, claiming that these "cheating machines" could be used to manipulate the election results. CENI officials argued the machines were critical to conducting the poll because it was too difficult to print, distribute, and count paper ballots. UN Security Council members visited the DRC in early October to meet with Kabila and CENCO and to conduct a working session with CENI to discuss election-related challenges and progress. The Security Council's "priority objective" was for the DRC to have on-time elections that were "credible, transparent, and held in a calm climate," said François Delattre, permanent representative of France to the UN and leader of the council's mission to the DRC. "We have signaled the Council's willingness to accompany the DRC on the road to peace, stability and prosperity," he added.

Despite the numerous challenges of holding a national election with approximately 40 million voters across a large, impoverished country with poor infrastructure, officials repeatedly rejected offers of assistance from outside parties. MONUSCO, the UN's stabilization mission in the DRC, had offered the use of helicopters and planes to help transport voting machines to polling stations, for example, but CENI declined. Election preparations remained a focus for the UN Security Council, which issued a statement in November urging all parties "to work together to address issues of common concern without further delay in the interest of building trust and reaching the largest possible consensus on the technical organization of elections."

On December 20, CENI announced that the election would be postponed for one week due to delays caused by a warehouse fire, which destroyed roughly 80 percent of the voting machines for the capital, Kinshasa, and the Ebola outbreak in the eastern part of the country. UN Security Council members "expressed their hope that this delay will permit the creation of favourable conditions for the Congolese people to express themselves freely" on election day.

## Election Results Delayed, Challenged

The election finally took place on December 30. Issues ranging from power outages to late openings and a lack of voting materials were reported at polling places across the country. Officials also made a late decision to suspend voting in three cities due to the Ebola outbreak and ethnic violence. Roughly 40,000 election observers were dispatched by CENCO to help monitor the polls.

Fayulu was expected to win, given his significant lead in pre-election opinion polls. Election results were supposed to be announced on January 6, 2019, but were delayed for several days, fueling rumors that officials were trying to influence the outcome. When CENI reported the vote tallies on January 10, Congolese reacted with shock: Tshisekedi was "provisionally declared the elected president" with 38.5 percent of the vote, compared to Fayulu with 34.8 percent, and Shadary with 23.8 percent. Fayulu claimed there had been an "electoral coup" and insisted Tshisekedi won only because he made a power-sharing deal with the government—a claim that seemed more credible following the government's quick acceptance of the vote count. CENCO also questioned CENI's tallies, stating that the results did not match the data collected by its monitors. While CENCO did not name its expected winner, it was reported that the group's data showed Fayulu with a comfortable margin of victory.

Fayulu appealed to the Constitutional Court for a recount, but his appeal was rejected on January 20. Tshisekedi was sworn in four days later. His inauguration marked the first time that an opposition leader assumed the presidency since the DRC gained independence from Belgium, as well as the first peaceful transfer of power.

—Linda Grimm

*Following is a press release issued by the UN Security Council on October 6, 2018, during members' visit to the Democratic Republic of the Congo; a statement by the UN Security Council on November 22, 2018, about the country's electoral preparations; and a statement by the UN Security Council on December 22, 2018, in response to the election's postponement.*

# UN Security Council Calls December Election an Historic Opportunity

**October 6, 2018**

The United Nations Security Council is on a visit to the Democratic Republic of the Congo (DRC), where on Saturday the body's 15 members pledged to support the process in the run-up to long-delayed elections, set for late December, and called for the polls to be credible and peaceful.

"The Security Council must put all its weight [behind] our priority objective: elections by 23 December, which are credible, transparent, and held in a calm climate," François Delattre, the Permanent Representative of France to the UN and leader of the Council mission, said on Friday evening during a press briefing in Kinshasa, the Congolese capital.

The DRC is scheduled to hold long-delayed elections on December 23, 2018. President Joseph Kabila has declared he will not stand for the polls, in line with the country's Constitution.

On Saturday, the Security Council delegation had a "significant and in-depth" meeting with President Kabila, which Ambassador Delattre described as the "high point of the Council's mission in Kinshasa."

"We have signaled the Council's willingness to accompany the DRC on the road to peace, stability and prosperity," Mr. Delatter [sic] stated, adding: "The 23 December elections mark a historic opportunity on this path. They are paving the way for the country's first democratic and peaceful transition."

Arriving in Kinshasa Friday afternoon, the Security Council delegation held a two-hour "working session" discussing the progress and challenges of the electoral process with the office of the Independent National Electoral Commission (CENI).

The President of the CENI, Corneille Nangaa, thanked the Council for the considerable support of the UN to the elections process. "Today we have more than 130 international MONUSCO experts who are our advisers," Nangaa told reporters, referring to acronym for the UN stabilization mission in the country.

He also made clear that the DRC Government had decided "not to solicit other financial and logistical support from partners".

Mr. Nangaa went on to stress the need to reconcile a critical double imperative: the credibility of polls and their holding on 23 December.

The Security Council also met on Saturday with the National Episcopal Conference of the Congo (CENCO), which facilitated the signing by the Government and the opposition of the so-called 'New Year's Eve agreement' on December 31, 2016, by which elections were to be held before the end of 2017. After a postponement, marked by violent protests, the polls were finally announced for late December 2018.

For CENCO, the meeting with the Council delegation was an opportunity to express "the fears, difficulties and worries" related to the electoral process, but also to emphasize that "the process is moving forward".

"CENCO has been inviting political and social actors to seek consensus around the problems that divide them," Fr André Masinganda, the First Deputy Secretary-General of CENCO, told Radio Okapi, citing, among others, problems related to the electoral register and the voting machine.

SOURCE: United Nations. "In DR Congo, UN Security Council Says December Polls Are 'Historic Opportunity' for Country." October 6, 2018. https://news.un.org/en/story/2018/10/1022452.

# UN Security Council Statement on DRC Election Preparation

DOCUMENT

**November 22, 2018**

The following Security Council press statement was issued today by Council President Ma Zhaoxu (China):

The members of the Security Council expressed their conviction that the elections of 23 December 2018, as an expression of the sovereignty of the people and government of the Democratic Republic of the Congo, constitute a historic opportunity for the first democratic and peaceful transfer of power in the DRC, the consolidation of stability in the country and the creation of the conditions for its development.

The members of the Security Council welcomed the progress made in the technical preparations for the elections and the efforts of the Congolese government in financing the elections. They welcomed the decision of the government of the Democratic Republic of the Congo to invite international observer missions, including from the African Union and the Southern African Development Community (SADC), and encouraged the extension of further invitations to other observers. They expressed concern regarding the deficit in trust and remaining differences among Congolese political actors and encouraged them, as well as the Independent National Electoral Commission (CENI), to work together to address issues of common concern without further delay in the interest of building trust and reaching the largest possible consensus on the technical organization of elections, including regarding the voting machines and the voter registry.

In the run-up to the start of the official electoral campaign on 22 November, the members of the Security Council urged all parties—government and opposition—to engage peacefully and constructively in the electoral process, in order to ensure transparent, peaceful and credible elections and to preserve peace and stability in the Democratic Republic of the Congo and the region. They further recalled the importance of ensuring the safety and security of candidates and voters during the campaign period.

The members of the Security Council underlined the importance of the entire Congolese political class and the institutions responsible for organizing elections remaining committed to ensuring the success of the electoral process, leading to a peaceful transfer of power, in accordance with the Congolese Constitution and the 31 December 2016 Agreement (the Agreement).

The members of the Security Council called upon all political parties, their supporters, and other political actors to remain fully committed to the Congolese Constitution, the Agreement and the electoral timeline, which together represent the only viable path out of the current political situation. They reiterated that the effective, swift and sincere implementation of the Agreement, including the Agreement's confidence-building measures in full, such as liberalizing further political space in the Democratic Republic of the Congo, releasing detained members of the political opposition and of civil society, respecting human rights and fundamental freedoms such as freedom of opinion and expression, freedom of the press, and the right of peaceful assembly, are essential for peaceful and credible elections on 23 December, a democratic transition of power, and the peace and stability of the Democratic Republic of the Congo.

The members of the Security Council encouraged all Congolese stakeholders to create all necessary conditions to ensure a violence-free environment conducive to the peaceful conduct of political activities, to ensure that the elections take place with the requisite conditions of transparency and credibility, including the full and effective participation of women at all stages, and are conducted in accordance with the Democratic Republic of the Congo's international obligations.

The members of the Security Council urged all parties to continue to reject violence of any kind, exercise maximum restraint in their actions and statements by refraining from provocations such as violence and violent speeches and to address their differences peacefully.

The members of the Security Council called on the international community and neighbouring governments to actively support the electoral process in the DRC and to take active steps to prevent any external actions, which would interfere negatively on the election process, its outcome or its legitimacy.

The members of the Security Council reiterated their condemnation of all armed groups active in the Democratic Republic of the Congo. They further reiterated their demand that all armed groups cease immediately all forms of violence, and immediately and permanently disband and lay down their arms.

The members of the Security Council also stressed that international and United Nations staff, including election observers, peacekeepers and experts working in the Democratic Republic of the Congo, must be able to safely carry out their tasks. They recalled that the government bears the primary responsibility to protect international staff within its territory and to hold perpetrators accountable. They further recalled that involvement in planning, directing, sponsoring or conducting attacks against Peacekeepers from the United Nations Organization Stabilization Mission in the Democratic Republic of the Congo (MONUSCO) or United Nations and associated personnel, including members of the Group of Experts, constitutes a basis for sanctions designations pursuant to Security Council resolutions.

Finally, the members of the Security Council encouraged the Congolese Government and the CENI to make appropriate and timely use of the cooperation offered and the resources deployed by MONUSCO and make any request for logistical support without further delay to enable MONUSCO to provide such assistance.

SOURCE: United Nations. "Security Council Press Statement on Electoral Preparations in Democratic Republic of Congo." November 22, 2018. https://www.un.org/press/en/2018/sc13599.doc.htm.

# UN Security Council Remarks on Election Postponement

**December 22, 2018**

The following Security Council press statement was issued today by Council President Kacou Houadja Léon Adom (Côte d'Ivoire):

The members of the Security Council took note of the decision by the National Independent Electoral Commission of the Democratic Republic of the Congo (CENI) to delay until 30 December the presidential, parliamentary and provincial elections previously scheduled for 23 December.

The members of the Security Council reaffirmed its strong commitment to the sovereignty, independence, unity and territorial integrity of the Democratic Republic of the Congo.

The members of the Security Council expressed their hope that this delay will permit the creation of favourable conditions for the Congolese people to express themselves freely on the 30 December. They called for continuous dialogue and transparency with all political stakeholders during this period in order to ensure trust is maintained until the elections are held.

The members of the Security Council called on all parties to engage peacefully and constructively in the electoral process to ensure transparent, peaceful and credible

elections that will result in a transfer of power in accordance with the Congolese Constitution and the 31 December 2016 Agreement.

The members of the Security Council expressed their condolences to the families of the victims, including the Russian pilots, following the crash of a CENI-chartered airplane during electoral preparation operations. They further expressed their support to CENI's efforts to ensure all logistical preparations are made on time for the election date and reiterated MONUSCO's [United Nations Organization Stabilization Mission in the Democratic Republic of the Congo] readiness to provide support if requested.

SOURCE: United Nations. "Security Council Press Statement on Decision to Postpone Elections in Democratic Republic of Congo." December 22, 2018. https://www.un.org/press/en/2018/sc13648.doc.htm.

## OTHER HISTORIC DOCUMENTS OF INTEREST

### FROM PREVIOUS *HISTORIC DOCUMENTS*

# IPCC and U.S. Reports Warn
# of Climate Change Impacts

OCTOBER 8, NOVEMBER 10, NOVEMBER 12, NOVEMBER 17,
AND NOVEMBER 23, 2018

Fall 2018 saw the release of two prominent scientific reports that outlined how industrial emissions are destabilizing the global climate system and warned of detrimental impacts to all ecosystems, human communities, and major economies. Against a backdrop of rising seas and extreme weather events around the world, both reports articulated what a best-case scenario for climate change looks like in the decades to come and outlined pathways to avoid the worst possible consequences.

## IPCC Says Time and Carbon Budgets Running Out

On October 8, 2018, the Intergovernmental Panel on Climate Change (IPCC), a consortium of the world's leading climate scientists, issued a momentous report throwing into stark relief the anticipated global ecological and humanitarian tolls of climate change. "Special Report on Global Warming of 1.5°C" was commissioned by the United Nations to assess the feasibility of limiting average global temperature rise to 1.5°C (34.7°F) above pre-industrial levels, and to better understand the dangers of exceeding this threshold. Drawing on more than 6,000 peer-reviewed studies, the report was intended to serve as the primary scientific guide informing implementation of the Paris Agreement, under which most countries resolved to limit global average temperature rise to "well below 2 degrees Celsius," while striving for a safer 1.5°C.

The IPCC report concluded that the 1.5°C threshold could be crossed as early as 2030, and that limiting warming to this level will require an economic and technological transformation of unprecedented speed and scale. Concerted and far-reaching changes would be needed across energy and transportation, as well as industrial, urban, and agricultural systems, the authors wrote. According to the report, limiting global temperature rise to 1.5°C by 2100 will require annual carbon emissions to be halved in the next twelve years and to reach net-zero by mid-century. Reaching these targets would require a virtual abandonment of coal and other fossil fuels in the next two decades, concurrent with substantial investments to scale renewable energy up to 70 percent to 85 percent of global energy generation (from 25 percent now). The IPCC outlined four possible pathways to reach this target with different combinations of land and energy use policies and technological shifts. Most of the report's proposed scenarios would cause global temperatures to exceed the 1.5°C threshold for a few decades before dropping back down. While all scenarios rely to some extent on carbon removal to compensate for rising temperatures, the technology necessary to accomplish this is unproven at scale. The sooner the world takes meaningful action to reduce emissions before 2030, the less daunting and destabilizing emission management and climate-related crises will be, the report declared.

The IPCC report also compared the projected impacts of global warming at the 1.5°C and 2°C (35.6°F) levels on food security, public health, ecological functions, and the global economy, finding that the half-degree difference was significant. Half of a degree more warming would expose tens of millions more people worldwide to dangerous heat waves, water shortages, coastal flooding, and food insecurity, the report stated. Global crop yields would suffer, particularly in sub-Saharan Africa, Southeast Asia, and Central and South America. At 1.5°C, the Arctic would likely have one sea ice–free summer per century, but at 2°C it would have one per decade, committing the world to several additional feet of sea level rise. Similar trends would be seen across a range of variables: corn crop failure in the tropics would become twice as likely, global fisheries would lose 50 percent productivity, and 99 percent of the world's coral reefs would die off. Compared to a 1.5°C increase, a 2°C warming would reduce freshwater availability by half in the Mediterranean and Middle East, a region already water scarce and politically volatile.

The report was largely met with alarm from global leaders and a broad acknowledgement of the need for action across public and private sectors. Only a handful of countries are on track to meet their first commitments under the Paris Agreement, which would have put the world on an initial path toward 2.6°C (36.68°F) warming by 2100. If these commitments are not met and current environmental policies are maintained, the world is expected to see warming greater than 3°C (37.4°F) by 2100.

Attempts to officially incorporate the report into global climate negotiations failed at the annual United Nations climate talks in December 2018. The United States joined delegates from Saudi Arabia, Russia, and Kuwait in opposing a strong acknowledgement of the findings and rejecting language to "welcome" the new information into climate negotiations, instead suggesting a more muted offer to "take note." Speaking to *The Guardian*, Norwegian Minister of Environment Ola Elvestuen said, "We have to find solutions even though the U.S. isn't there. . . . The next four to 12 years are crucial ones, where we will set the path to how the world will develop in the decades ahead." While battles play out in the arena of international diplomacy, many cities in the U.S. and around the world independently resolved to align their policies and infrastructure with climate change science. To aid these efforts, eighteen of the IPCC report authors produced a separate guide that translates findings into specific recommendations for city-level action.

## NATIONAL CLIMATE ASSESSMENT CONCLUDES
## CLIMATE CHANGE A PROFOUND THREAT

On November 23, the second volume of the Fourth National Climate Assessment was published, presenting a similarly unambiguous warning of the consequences of climate change for the United States. Per congressional mandate, the report is produced every four years by the U.S. Global Change Research Program, a consortium of thirteen federal agencies including the U.S. Department of Defense, Environmental Protection Agency, and National Aeronautics and Space Administration. The assessment laid out the threats that a changing climate would pose to the American economy, infrastructure, and public health and emphasized the importance of defining mitigation and adaptation strategies to avoid the worst ecological, economic, and social costs.

The 2018 report echoed many of the findings cited in previous editions, but since 2014, economic research has lent greater precision to estimated costs of projected impacts. According to the report, the current climate trajectory could cut up to 10 percent of American gross domestic product by 2100—more than double the losses caused by the

Great Recession of 2008. Costs to the U.S. economy of approximately $500 billion a year will be most significantly felt across agriculture, fisheries, infrastructure, and international trade. The report concluded that while every part of the United States would be affected, the nation's farm belt would be expected to be one of the hardest-hit regions, as extreme heat and droughts, wildfires on rangelands, and heavy downpours disrupt agricultural productivity. Severe flooding was also a concern identified by the report because it "could affect the economic stability of local governments, businesses and the broader economy." The report noted that warming oceans are already impacting fisheries. For example, in 2012, record ocean temperatures caused lobster catches in Maine to peak a month earlier than normal, affecting an unprepared distribution chain. The country's position in international trade would be compromised as well. The report found that extreme weather events were "virtually certain to increasingly affect U.S. trade and economy, including import and export prices and businesses with overseas operations and supply chains." Additionally, the report explored climate change's threat to public health. Rising temperatures would increase the frequency, intensity and duration of dangerous heat waves, the report said, while harmful ozone levels and air pollution would exacerbate respiratory and cardiovascular problems, putting vulnerable communities at greater risk. A wetter and warmer world also would expand the range of disease-carrying insects, exposing more people to viruses such as West Nile and Lyme. "The impacts and costs of climate change were already being felt in the United States, and changes in the likelihood or severity of some recent extreme weather events can now be attributed with increasingly higher confidence to human-caused warming," the report stated, with authors noting that future disruptions have the potential to create financial and legal challenges that have not yet been addressed.

The report's findings directly contradicted President Donald Trump's opposition to environmental regulations, which he argued hinder economic growth. Downplaying the report's significance, the White House issued a statement criticizing the report as largely based on "the most extreme scenario." Some degree of uncertainty is inherent in climate projections, but many of the 2014 National Climate Assessment's predictions had been realized, such as a forecast that coastal cities would see more flooding as sea levels rise. High-tide flooding now posed regular risks to communities and infrastructure in low-lying southeastern cities such as Miami, Florida, and Charleston, South Carolina.

## CLIMATE CHANGE IN PARADISE

While climate change itself cannot be singled out as a direct cause of any given event, it is generally believed to exacerbate conditions that make such events possible. Scientists found, for example, that rising temperatures and decreased humidity dry out vegetation, making wildfires worse. Climate change also led to an increase in extreme Santa Ana winds, which can speed the spread of wildfires.

In November 2018, one of the most destructive wildfires on record blazed through Paradise, California, and beyond into the mountains of Butte County, killing at least eighty-five people. Known as the Camp Fire, the disaster was declared a public health emergency, as smoky air enveloped millions of people and toxic ash blew into cities downwind. Smoldering debris from 19,000 properties presented a monumental clean-up task for the Federal Emergency Management Agency, on a scale some likened to the disaster response after the attacks of September 11, 2001. The fire caused an estimated $7 billion in property damage before it was finally contained on November 25.

President Trump repeatedly denied a link between the Camp Fire and global warming and said the disaster would not change his opinion on climate change. He initially blamed California's poor forest management for the fire and threatened to withhold federal relief funds for fire victims, even though most forestland in California is maintained by the federal government. Following a concerted push for aid by state officials and California's U.S. senators, the president walked back his comments and signed a major disaster declaration on November 12, which made more federal funds available to supplement local recovery efforts. Speaking to reporters in Chico, California, several days later, Trump skirted questions about whether he thought state officials should have done anything differently, saying only, "A lot of lessons have been learned."

Victims of the Camp Fire later sued Pacific Gas & Electric (PG&E), the state's largest utility, claiming it misled Californians about safety-related maintenance efforts. PG&E equipment was suspected of causing the Camp Fire after the company reported employees found a damaged transmission tower and power pole near the location where the wildfire started. Facing billions of dollars in liability for fire damage, PG&E filed for bankruptcy in January 2019.

—Megan Howes

*Following are excerpts from the Summary for Policymakers of the IPCC Special Report on Global Warming of 1.5°C published on October 8, 2018; select tweets from President Donald Trump on November 10 and November 12, 2018, remarking on issues related to the Camp Fire; remarks made by President Donald Trump on a November 17, 2018, visit to the Camp Fire incident command post; and the summary findings of the Fourth National Climate Assessment, published on November 23, 2018.*

# IPCC Special Report on Global Warming of 1.5°C

**October 8, 2018**

*[The following sections have been excerpted from a report summary developed by the IPCC for policymakers. All footnotes, tables, and figures have been omitted.]*

### Projected Climate Change, Potential Impacts and Associated Risks

B.1   Climate models project robust differences in regional climate characteristics between present-day and global warming of 1.5°C, and between 1.5°C and 2°C. These differences include increases in: mean temperature in most land and ocean regions (*high confidence*), hot extremes in most inhabited regions (*high confidence*), heavy precipitation in several regions (*medium confidence*), and the probability of drought and precipitation deficits in some regions (*medium confidence*). . . .

B.2   By 2100, global mean sea level rise is projected to be around 0.1 metre lower with global warming of 1.5°C compared to 2°C (*medium confidence*). Sea level will continue to rise well beyond 2100 (*high confidence*), and the magnitude and rate of this rise depend on future emission pathways. A slower rate of sea level rise enables greater opportunities for adaptation in the human and ecological systems of small islands, low-lying coastal areas and deltas (*medium confidence*)....

B.3    On land, impacts on biodiversity and ecosystems, including species loss and extinction, are projected to be lower at 1.5°C of global warming compared to 2°C. Limiting global warming to 1.5°C compared to 2°C is projected to lower the impacts on terrestrial, freshwater and coastal ecosystems and to retain more of their services to humans (*high confidence*)....

B.4    Limiting global warming to 1.5°C compared to 2°C is projected to reduce increases in ocean temperature as well as associated increases in ocean acidity and decreases in ocean oxygen levels (*high confidence*). Consequently, limiting global warming to 1.5°C is projected to reduce risks to marine biodiversity, fisheries, and ecosystems, and their functions and services to humans, as illustrated by recent changes to Arctic sea ice and warm-water coral reef ecosystems (*high confidence*)....

B.5    Climate-related risks to health, livelihoods, food security, water supply, human security, and economic growth are projected to increase with global warming of 1.5°C and increase further with 2°C....

B.6    Most adaptation needs will be lower for global warming of 1.5°C compared to 2°C (*high confidence*). There are a wide range of adaptation options that can reduce the risks of climate change (*high confidence*). There are limits to adaptation and adaptive capacity for some human and natural systems at global warming of 1.5°C, with associated losses (*medium confidence*). The number and availability of adaptation options vary by sector (*medium confidence*)....

## Emission Pathways and System Transitions
## Consistent with 1.5°C Global Warming

C.1    In model pathways with no or limited overshoot of 1.5°C, global net anthropogenic $CO_2$ emissions decline by about 45% from 2010 levels by 2030 (40–60% interquartile range), reaching net zero around 2050 (2045–2055 interquartile range). For limiting global warming to below 2°C $CO_2$ emissions are projected to decline by about 25% by 2030 in most pathways (10–30% interquartile range) and reach net zero around 2070 (2065–2080 interquartile range). Non-$CO_2$ emissions in pathways that limit global warming to 1.5°C show deep reductions that are similar to those in pathways limiting warming to 2°C. (*high confidence*)

C.1.1    $CO_2$ emissions reductions that limit global warming to 1.5°C with no or limited overshoot can involve different portfolios of mitigation measures, striking different balances between lowering energy and resource intensity, rate of decarbonization, and the reliance on carbon dioxide removal. Different portfolios face different implementation challenges and potential synergies and trade-offs with sustainable development. (*high confidence*)

C.1.2    Modelled pathways that limit global warming to 1.5°C with no or limited overshoot involve deep reductions in emissions of methane and black carbon (35% or more of both by 2050 relative to 2010). These pathways also reduce most of the cooling aerosols, which partially offsets mitigation effects for two to three decades. Non-$CO_2$ emissions can be reduced as a result of broad mitigation measures in the energy sector. In addition, targeted non-$CO_2$ mitigation measures can reduce nitrous oxide and methane from agriculture, methane from the waste sector, some sources of black carbon, and hydrofluorocarbons. High bioenergy demand can increase emissions of nitrous oxide in some 1.5°C pathways, highlighting the importance of appropriate management approaches. Improved air quality resulting from projected reductions in many non-$CO_2$ emissions provide direct and immediate population health benefits in all 1.5°C model pathways. (*high confidence*)

C.1.3    Limiting global warming requires limiting the total cumulative global anthropogenic emissions of $CO_2$ since the pre-industrial period, that is, staying within a total carbon budget (*high confidence*). By the end of 2017, anthropogenic $CO_2$ emissions since the pre-industrial period are estimated to have reduced the total carbon budget for 1.5°C by approximately 2200 ± 320 $GtCO_2$ (*medium confidence*). The associated remaining budget is being depleted by current emissions of 42 ± 3 $GtCO_2$ per year (*high confidence*). . . . .

C.1.4    Solar radiation modification (SRM) measures are not included in any of the available assessed pathways. Although some SRM measures may be theoretically effective in reducing an overshoot, they face large uncertainties and knowledge gaps as well as substantial risks and institutional and social constraints to deployment related to governance, ethics, and impacts on sustainable development. They also do not mitigate ocean acidification. (*medium confidence*)

C.2     Pathways limiting global warming to 1.5°C with no or limited overshoot would require rapid and far-reaching transitions in energy, land, urban and infrastructure (including transport and buildings), and industrial systems (*high confidence*). These systems transitions are unprecedented in terms of scale, but not necessarily in terms of speed, and imply deep emissions reductions in all sectors, a wide portfolio of mitigation options and a significant upscaling of investments in those options (*medium confidence*).

C.2.1    Pathways that limit global warming to 1.5°C with no or limited overshoot show system changes that are more rapid and pronounced over the next two decades than in 2°C pathways (*high confidence*). The rates of system changes associated with limiting global warming to 1.5°C with no or limited overshoot have occurred in the past within specific sectors, technologies and spatial contexts, but there is no documented historic precedent for their scale (*medium confidence*).

C.2.2    In energy systems, modelled global pathways (considered in the literature) limiting global warming to 1.5°C with no or limited overshoot generally meet energy service demand with lower energy use, including through enhanced energy efficiency, and show faster electrification of energy end use compared to 2°C (*high confidence*). In 1.5°C pathways with no or limited overshoot, low-emission energy sources are projected to have a higher share, compared with 2°C pathways, particularly before 2050 (*high confidence*). In 1.5°C pathways with no or limited overshoot, renewables are projected to supply 70–85% (interquartile range) of electricity in 2050 (*high confidence*). In electricity generation, shares of nuclear and fossil fuels with carbon dioxide capture and storage (CCS) are modelled to increase in most 1.5°C pathways with no or limited overshoot. In modelled 1.5°C pathways with limited or no overshoot, the use of CCS would allow the electricity generation share of gas to be approximately 8% (3–11% interquartile range) of global electricity in 2050, while the use of coal shows a steep reduction in all pathways and would be reduced to close to 0% (0–2% interquartile range) of electricity (*high confidence*). While acknowledging the challenges, and differences between the options and national circumstances, political, economic, social and technical feasibility of solar energy, wind energy and electricity storage technologies have substantially improved over the past few years (*high confidence*). These improvements signal a potential system transition in electricity generation.

C.2.3    $CO_2$ emissions from industry in pathways limiting global warming to 1.5°C with no or limited overshoot are projected to be about 65–90% (interquartile range) lower in 2050 relative to 2010, as compared to 50–80% for global warming of 2°C (*medium confidence*). Such reductions can be achieved through combinations of new and existing technologies and practices, including electrification, hydrogen, sustainable bio-based feedstocks, product substitution, and carbon capture, utilization and storage (CCUS). These options are technically proven at various scales but their large-scale deployment may be limited by economic, financial, human capacity and institutional constraints in specific contexts, and specific characteristics of large-scale industrial installations. In industry, emissions reductions by energy and process efficiency by themselves are insufficient for limiting warming to 1.5°C with no or limited overshoot (*high confidence*).

C.2.4    The urban and infrastructure system transition consistent with limiting global warming to 1.5°C with no or limited overshoot would imply, for example, changes in land and urban planning practices, as well as deeper emissions reductions in transport and buildings compared to pathways that limit global warming below 2°C (*medium confidence*). Technical measures and practices enabling deep emissions reductions include various energy efficiency options. In pathways limiting global warming to 1.5°C with no or limited overshoot, the electricity share of energy demand in buildings would be about 55–75% in 2050 compared to 50–70% in 2050 for 2°C global warming (*medium confidence*). In the transport sector, the share of low-emission final energy would rise from less than 5% in 2020 to about 35–65% in 2050 compared to 25–45% for 2°C of global warming (*medium confidence*). Economic, institutional and socio-cultural barriers may inhibit these urban and infrastructure system transitions, depending on national, regional and local circumstances, capabilities and the availability of capital (*high confidence*).

C.2.5    Transitions in global and regional land use are found in all pathways limiting global warming to 1.5°C with no or limited overshoot, but their scale depends on the pursued mitigation portfolio. Model pathways that limit global warming to 1.5°C with no or limited overshoot project a 4 million $km^2$ reduction to a 2.5 million $km^2$ increase of non-pasture agricultural land for food and feed crops and a 0.5–11 million $km^2$ reduction of pasture land, to be converted into a 0–6 million $km^2$ increase of agricultural land for energy crops and a 2 million $km^2$ reduction to 9.5 million $km^2$ increase in forests by 2050 relative to 2010 (*medium confidence*). Land-use transitions of similar magnitude can be observed in modelled 2°C pathways (*medium confidence*). Such large transitions pose profound challenges for sustainable management of the various demands on land for human settlements, food, livestock feed, fibre, bioenergy, carbon storage, biodiversity and other ecosystem services (*high confidence*). Mitigation options limiting the demand for land include sustainable intensification of land-use practices, ecosystem restoration and changes towards less resource-intensive diets (*high confidence*). The implementation of land-based mitigation options would require overcoming socio-economic, institutional, technological, financing and environmental barriers that differ across regions (*high confidence*).

C.2.6   Additional annual average energy-related investments for the period 2016 to 2050 in pathways limiting warming to 1.5°C compared to pathways without new climate policies beyond those in place today are estimated to be around 830 billion USD2010 (range of 150 billion to 1700 billion USD2010 across six models). This compares to total annual average energy supply investments in 1.5°C pathways of 1460 to 3510 billion USD2010 and total annual average energy demand investments of 640 to 910 billion USD2010 for the period 2016 to 2050. Total energy-related investments increase by about 12% (range of 3% to 24%) in 1.5°C pathways relative to 2°C pathways. Annual investments in low-carbon energy technologies and energy efficiency are upscaled by roughly a factor of six (range of factor of 4 to 10) by 2050 compared to 2015 (*medium confidence*).

C.2.7   Modelled pathways limiting global warming to 1.5°C with no or limited overshoot project a wide range of global average discounted marginal abatement costs over the 21st century. They are roughly 3–4 times higher than in pathways limiting global warming to below 2°C (*high confidence*). The economic literature distinguishes marginal abatement costs from total mitigation costs in the economy. The literature on total mitigation costs of 1.5°C mitigation pathways is limited and was not assessed in this Report. Knowledge gaps remain in the integrated assessment of the economy-wide costs and benefits of mitigation in line with pathways limiting warming to 1.5°C.

C.3     All pathways that limit global warming to 1.5°C with limited or no overshoot project the use of carbon dioxide removal (CDR) on the order of 100–1000 GtCO$_2$ over the 21st century. CDR would be used to compensate for residual emissions and, in most cases, achieve net negative emissions to return global warming to 1.5°C following a peak (*high confidence*). CDR deployment of several hundreds of GtCO$_2$ is subject to multiple feasibility and sustainability constraints (*high confidence*). Significant near-term emissions reductions and measures to lower energy and land demand can limit CDR deployment to a few hundred GtCO$_2$ without reliance on bioenergy with carbon capture and storage (BECCS) (*high confidence*).

C.3.1   Existing and potential CDR measures include afforestation and reforestation, land restoration and soil carbon sequestration, BECCS, direct air carbon capture and storage (DACCS), enhanced weathering and ocean alkalinization. These differ widely in terms of maturity, potentials, costs, risks, co-benefits and trade-offs (*high confidence*). To date, only a few published pathways include CDR measures other than afforestation and BECCS.

C.3.2   In pathways limiting global warming to 1.5°C with limited or no overshoot, BECCS deployment is projected to range from 0–1, 0–8, and 0–16 GtCO$_2$ yr$^{-1}$ in 2030, 2050, and 2100, respectively, while agriculture, forestry and land-use (AFOLU) related CDR measures are projected to remove 0–5, 1–11, and 1–5 GtCO$_2$ yr$^{-1}$ in these years (*medium confidence*). The upper end of these deployment ranges by mid-century exceeds the BECCS potential of up to 5 GtCO$_2$ yr$^{-1}$ and afforestation potential of up to 3.6 GtCO$_2$ yr$^{-1}$ assessed based on recent literature (*medium confidence*). Some pathways avoid BECCS deployment completely through demand-side measures and greater reliance on AFOLU-related CDR measures (*medium confidence*). The use of bioenergy can be as high or even higher when BECCS is excluded compared to when it is included due to its potential for replacing fossil fuels across sectors (*high confidence*).

C.3.3   Pathways that overshoot 1.5°C of global warming rely on CDR exceeding residual CO$_2$ emissions later in the century to return to below 1.5°C by 2100, with larger overshoots requiring greater amounts of CDR (*high confidence*). Limitations on the speed, scale, and societal acceptability of CDR deployment hence determine the ability to return global warming to below 1.5°C following an overshoot. Carbon cycle and climate system understanding is still limited about the effectiveness of net negative emissions to reduce temperatures after they peak (*high confidence*).

C.3.4   Most current and potential CDR measures could have significant impacts on land, energy, water or nutrients if deployed at large scale (*high confidence*). Afforestation and bioenergy may compete with other land uses and may have significant impacts on agricultural and food systems, biodiversity, and other ecosystem functions and services (*high confidence*). Effective governance is needed to limit such trade-offs and ensure permanence of carbon removal in terrestrial, geological and ocean reservoirs (*high confidence*). Feasibility and sustainability of CDR use could be enhanced by a portfolio of options deployed at substantial, but lesser scales, rather than a single option at very large scale (*high confidence*).

C.3.5   Some AFOLU-related CDR measures such as restoration of natural ecosystems and soil carbon sequestration could provide co-benefits such as improved biodiversity, soil quality, and local food security. If deployed at large scale, they would require governance systems enabling sustainable land management to conserve and protect land carbon stocks and other ecosystem functions and services (*medium confidence*).

## Strengthening the Global Response in the Context of Sustainable Development and Efforts to Eradicate Poverty

D.1   Estimates of the global emissions outcome of current nationally stated mitigation ambitions as submitted under the Paris Agreement would lead to global greenhouse gas emissions in 2030 of 52–58 GtCO$_2$eq yr$^{-1}$ (*medium confidence*). Pathways reflecting these ambitions would not limit global warming to 1.5°C, even if supplemented by very challenging increases in the scale and ambition of emissions reductions after 2030 (*high confidence*). Avoiding overshoot and reliance on future large-scale deployment of carbon dioxide removal (CDR) can only be achieved if global CO$_2$ emissions start to decline well before 2030 (*high confidence*).

D.1.1   Pathways that limit global warming to 1.5°C with no or limited overshoot show clear emission reductions by 2030 (*high confidence*). All but one show a decline in global greenhouse gas emissions to below 35 GtCO$_2$eq yr$^{-1}$ in 2030, and half of available pathways fall within the 25–30 GtCO$_2$eq yr$^{-1}$ range (interquartile range), a 40–50% reduction from 2010 levels (*high confidence*). Pathways reflecting current nationally stated mitigation ambition until 2030 are broadly consistent with cost-effective pathways that result in a global warming of about 3°C by 2100, with warming continuing afterwards (*medium confidence*).

D.1.2   Overshoot trajectories result in higher impacts and associated challenges compared to pathways that limit global warming to 1.5°C with no or limited overshoot (*high confidence*). Reversing warming after an overshoot of 0.2°C or larger during this century would require upscaling and deployment of CDR at rates and volumes that might not be achievable given considerable implementation challenges (*medium confidence*).

D.1.3   The lower the emissions in 2030, the lower the challenge in limiting global warming to 1.5°C after 2030 with no or limited overshoot (*high confidence*). The challenges from delayed actions to reduce greenhouse gas emissions include the risk of cost escalation, lock-in in carbon-emitting infrastructure, stranded assets, and reduced flexibility in future response options in the medium to long term (*high confidence*). These may increase uneven distributional impacts between countries at different stages of development (*medium confid*ence).

D.2   The avoided climate change impacts on sustainable development, eradication of poverty and reducing inequalities would be greater if global warming were limited to 1.5°C rather than 2°C, if mitigation and adaptation synergies are maximized while trade-offs are minimized (*high confidence*).

D.2.1   Climate change impacts and responses are closely linked to sustainable development which balances social well-being, economic prosperity and environmental protection. The United Nations Sustainable Development Goals (SDGs), adopted in 2015, provide an established framework for assessing the links between global warming of 1.5°C or 2°C and development goals that include poverty eradication, reducing inequalities, and climate action. (*high confidence*)

D.2.2   The consideration of ethics and equity can help address the uneven distribution of adverse impacts associated with 1.5°C and higher levels of global warming, as well as those from mitigation and adaptation, particularly for poor and disadvantaged populations, in all societies (*high confidence*).

D.2.3   Mitigation and adaptation consistent with limiting global warming to 1.5°C are underpinned by enabling conditions, assessed in this Report across the geophysical, environmental-ecological, technological, economic, socio-cultural and institutional dimensions of feasibility. Strengthened multilevel governance, institutional capacity, policy instruments, technological innovation and transfer and mobilization of finance, and changes in human behaviour and lifestyles are enabling conditions that enhance the feasibility of mitigation and adaptation options for 1.5°C-consistent systems transitions. (*high confidence*)

D.3   Adaptation options specific to national contexts, if carefully selected together with enabling conditions, will have benefits for sustainable development and poverty reduction with global warming of 1.5°C, although trade-offs are possible (*high confidence*).

D.3.1 Adaptation options that reduce the vulnerability of human and natural systems have many synergies with sustainable development, if well managed, such as ensuring food and water security, reducing disaster risks, improving health conditions, maintaining ecosystem services and reducing poverty and inequality (*high confidence*). Increasing investment in physical and social infrastructure is a key enabling condition to enhance the resilience and the adaptive capacities of societies. These benefits can occur in most regions with adaptation to 1.5°C of global warming (*high confidence*).

D.3.2 Adaptation to 1.5°C global warming can also result in trade-offs or maladaptations with adverse impacts for sustainable development. For example, if poorly designed or implemented, adaptation projects in a range of sectors can increase greenhouse gas emissions and water use, increase gender and social inequality, undermine health conditions, and encroach on natural ecosystems (*high confidence*). These trade-offs can be reduced by adaptations that include attention to poverty and sustainable development (*high confidence*).

D.3.3 A mix of adaptation and mitigation options to limit global warming to 1.5°C, implemented in a participatory and integrated manner, can enable rapid, systemic transitions in urban and rural areas (*high confidence*). These are most effective when aligned with economic and sustainable development, and when local and regional governments and decision makers are supported by national governments (*medium confidence*).

D.3.4 Adaptation options that also mitigate emissions can provide synergies and cost savings in most sectors and system transitions, such as when land management reduces emissions and disaster risk, or when low-carbon buildings are also designed for efficient cooling. Trade-offs between mitigation and adaptation, when limiting global warming to 1.5°C, such as when bioenergy crops, reforestation or afforestation encroach on land needed for agricultural adaptation, can undermine food security, livelihoods, ecosystem functions and services and other aspects of sustainable development. (*high confidence*)

D.4 Mitigation options consistent with 1.5°C pathways are associated with multiple synergies and trade-offs across the Sustainable Development Goals (SDGs). While the total number of possible synergies exceeds the number of trade-offs, their net effect will depend on the pace and magnitude of changes, the composition of the mitigation portfolio and the management of the transition. (*high confidence*)

D.4.1 1.5°C pathways have robust synergies particularly for the SDGs 3 (health), 7 (clean energy), 11 (cities and communities), 12 (responsible consumption and production) and 14 (oceans) (*very high confidence*). Some 1.5°C pathways show potential trade-offs with mitigation for SDGs 1 (poverty), 2 (hunger), 6 (water) and 7 (energy access), if not managed carefully (*high confidence*).

D.4.2 1.5°C pathways that include low energy demand, low material consumption, and low GHG-intensive food consumption have the most pronounced synergies and the lowest number of trade-offs with respect to sustainable development and the SDGs (*high confidence*). Such pathways would reduce dependence on CDR. In modelled pathways, sustainable development, eradicating poverty and reducing inequality can support limiting warming to 1.5°C (*high confidence*).

D.4.3   1.5°C and 2°C modelled pathways often rely on the deployment of large-scale land-related measures like afforestation and bioenergy supply, which, if poorly managed, can compete with food production and hence raise food security concerns (*high confidence*). The impacts of carbon dioxide removal (CDR) options on SDGs depend on the type of options and the scale of deployment (*high confidence*). If poorly implemented, CDR options such as BECCS and AFOLU options would lead to trade-offs. Context-relevant design and implementation requires considering people's needs, biodiversity, and other sustainable development dimensions (*very high confidence*).

D.4.4   Mitigation consistent with 1.5°C pathways creates risks for sustainable development in regions with high dependency on fossil fuels for revenue and employment generation (*high confidence*). Policies that promote diversification of the economy and the energy sector can address the associated challenges (*high confidence*).

D.4.5   Redistributive policies across sectors and populations that shield the poor and vulnerable can resolve trade-offs for a range of SDGs, particularly hunger, poverty and energy access. Investment needs for such complementary policies are only a small fraction of the overall mitigation investments in 1.5°C pathways. (*high confidence*)

D.5   Limiting the risks from global warming of 1.5°C in the context of sustainable development and poverty eradication implies system transitions that can be enabled by an increase of adaptation and mitigation investments, policy instruments, the acceleration of technological innovation and behaviour changes (*high confidence*).

D.5.1   Directing finance towards investment in infrastructure for mitigation and adaptation could provide additional resources. This could involve the mobilization of private funds by institutional investors, asset managers and development or investment banks, as well as the provision of public funds. Government policies that lower the risk of low-emission and adaptation investments can facilitate the mobilization of private funds and enhance the effectiveness of other public policies. Studies indicate a number of challenges, including access to finance and mobilization of funds. (*high confidence*)

D.5.2   Adaptation finance consistent with global warming of 1.5°C is difficult to quantify and compare with 2°C. Knowledge gaps include insufficient data to calculate specific climate resilience-enhancing investments from the provision of currently underinvested basic infrastructure. Estimates of the costs of adaptation might be lower at global warming of 1.5°C than for 2°C. Adaptation needs have typically been supported by public sector sources such as national and subnational government budgets, and in developing countries together with support from development assistance, multilateral development banks, and United Nations Framework Convention on Climate Change channels (*medium confidence*). More recently there is a growing understanding of the scale and increase in non-governmental organizations and private funding in some regions (*medium confidence*). Barriers include the scale of adaptation financing, limited capacity and access to adaptation finance (*medium confidence*).

D.5.3 Global model pathways limiting global warming to 1.5°C are projected to involve the annual average investment needs in the energy system of around 2.4 trillion USD2010 between 2016 and 2035, representing about 2.5% of the world GDP (*medium confidence*).

D.5.4 Policy tools can help mobilize incremental resources, including through shifting global investments and savings and through market and non-market based instruments as well as accompanying measures to secure the equity of the transition, acknowledging the challenges related with implementation, including those of energy costs, depreciation of assets and impacts on international competition, and utilizing the opportunities to maximize co-benefits (*high confidence*).

D.5.5 The systems transitions consistent with adapting to and limiting global warming to 1.5°C include the widespread adoption of new and possibly disruptive technologies and practices and enhanced climate-driven innovation. These imply enhanced technological innovation capabilities, including in industry and finance. Both national innovation policies and international cooperation can contribute to the development, commercialization and widespread adoption of mitigation and adaptation technologies. Innovation policies may be more effective when they combine public support for research and development with policy mixes that provide incentives for technology diffusion. (*high confidence*)

D.5.6 Education, information, and community approaches, including those that are informed by indigenous knowledge and local knowledge, can accelerate the wide-scale behaviour changes consistent with adapting to and limiting global warming to 1.5°C. These approaches are more effective when combined with other policies and tailored to the motivations, capabilities and resources of specific actors and contexts (*high confidence*). Public acceptability can enable or inhibit the implementation of policies and measures to limit global warming to 1.5°C and to adapt to the consequences. Public acceptability depends on the individual's evaluation of expected policy consequences, the perceived fairness of the distribution of these consequences, and perceived fairness of decision procedures (*high confidence*).

D.6 Sustainable development supports, and often enables, the fundamental societal and systems transitions and transformations that help limit global warming to 1.5°C. Such changes facilitate the pursuit of climate-resilient development pathways that achieve ambitious mitigation and adaptation in conjunction with poverty eradication and efforts to reduce inequalities (*high confidence*).

D.6.1 Social justice and equity are core aspects of climate-resilient development pathways that aim to limit global warming to 1.5°C as they address challenges and inevitable trade-offs, widen opportunities, and ensure that options, visions, and values are deliberated, between and within countries and communities, without making the poor and disadvantaged worse off (*high confidence*).

D.6.2   The potential for climate-resilient development pathways differs between and within regions and nations, due to different development contexts and systemic vulnerabilities (*very high confidence*). Efforts along such pathways to date have been limited (*medium confidence*) and enhanced efforts would involve strengthened and timely action from all countries and non-state actors (*high confidence*).

D.6.3   Pathways that are consistent with sustainable development show fewer mitigation and adaptation challenges and are associated with lower mitigation costs. The large majority of modelling studies could not construct pathways characterized by lack of international cooperation, inequality and poverty that were able to limit global warming to 1.5°C. (*high confidence*)

D.7   Strengthening the capacities for climate action of national and sub-national authorities, civil society, the private sector, indigenous peoples and local communities can support the implementation of ambitious actions implied by limiting global warming to 1.5°C (*high confidence*). International cooperation can provide an enabling environment for this to be achieved in all countries and for all people, in the context of sustainable development. International cooperation is a critical enabler for developing countries and vulnerable regions (*high confidence*).

D.7.1   Partnerships involving non-state public and private actors, institutional investors, the banking system, civil society and scientific institutions would facilitate actions and responses consistent with limiting global warming to 1.5°C (*very high confidence*).

D.7.2   Cooperation on strengthened accountable multilevel governance that includes non-state actors such as industry, civil society and scientific institutions, coordinated sectoral and cross-sectoral policies at various governance levels, gender-sensitive policies, finance including innovative financing, and cooperation on technology development and transfer can ensure participation, transparency, capacity building and learning among different players (*high confidence*).

D.7.3   International cooperation is a critical enabler for developing countries and vulnerable regions to strengthen their action for the implementation of 1.5°C-consistent climate responses, including through enhancing access to finance and technology and enhancing domestic capacities, taking into account national and local circumstances and needs (*high confidence*).

D.7.4   Collective efforts at all levels, in ways that reflect different circumstances and capabilities, in the pursuit of limiting global warming to 1.5°C, taking into account equity as well as effectiveness, can facilitate strengthening the global response to climate change, achieving sustainable development and eradicating poverty (*high confidence*).

SOURCE: Intergovernmental Panel on Climate Change. "Special Report on Global Warming of 1.5°C: Summary for Policymakers." October 8, 2018. https://archive.ipcc.ch/pdf/special-reports/sr15/sr15_spm_final.pdf.

## President Trump Comments on Camp Fire in California

**November 10, 2018**

There is no reason for these massive, deadly and costly forest fires in California except that forest management is so poor. Billions of dollars are given each year, with so many lives lost, all because of gross mismanagement of the forests. Remedy now, or no more Fed payments!

SOURCE: Donald Trump (@realDonaldTrump). Twitter post. November 10, 2018. https://twitter.com/realDonaldTrump/status/1061168803218948096.

## President Trump Announces Disaster Declaration for California

**November 12, 2018**

I just approved an expedited request for a Major Disaster Declaration for the State of California. Wanted to respond quickly in order to alleviate some of the incredible suffering going on. I am with you all the way. God Bless all of the victims and families affected.

SOURCE: Donald Trump (@realDonaldTrump). Twitter post. November 12, 2018. https://twitter.com/realDonaldTrump/status/1062153051459469312.

## President Trump Remarks and Exchange with Reporters on the Camp Fire Incident

**November 17, 2018**

Well, thank you, Jerry. And I just want to also thank FEMA; law enforcement—you folks have been incredible; first responders; the firefighters. They're out there now. They want to be fighting—you know, they've got a lot of territory to cover.

Still going very heavily. There's a big area of very intense flame right now that's next to a very explosive area, wouldn't you say? I mean, that's a very big problem out there going. And they're fighting, and they're fighting like hell.

We've never seen anything like this. In California, we've never seen anything like this, Jerry. It's like total devastation. . . .

But again, the men and women that are fighting this fire are incredible. You know that more than 70 people are lost, are gone. And we're looking for hundreds of people right now. There are literally hundreds that they're looking for.

And hopefully, that's going to be a good conclusion instead of a bad conclusion. Maybe they left, and maybe they're with their loved ones somewhere else, and we just don't know about it. But they're looking for hundreds of people. And we'll know the answer to that over the next 48 hours, I think, for the most part. . . .

Q. Mr. President, do you see any role of climate change in the—in these fires that we've seen in California recently? . . .

*The President.* Well, I think you have a lot of factors. We have the management factor that I know Jerry has really been up on and very well. And Gavin is going to—we're going to be looking at it together. And right now that seems to be a very big problem. And we're going to get that problem solved.

In the farm bill, we're putting quite a bit of money—about $500 million—in the farm bill for management and maintenance of the forests beyond this area. But really, management—$500 million. That will be in the farm bill. We just put it in. The farm bill is moving along pretty rapidly for our great farmers. But we have a new category and that's management and maintenance of the forests. It's very important. . . .

Q. Does seeing this devastation, though, change your opinion at all on climate change, Mr. President?

*The President.* No. No. I have a strong opinion. I want great climate. We're going to have that. And we're going to have forests that are very safe, because we can't go through this every year. We go through this—and we're going to have safe forests. And that's happening as we speak—as we speak. . . .

Q. You said there needs to be changes with fire management. Should the State and local officials have done anything differently at this point?

*The President.* No, we're going to work together with the Federal Government. No, State, local, and Federal Government. Federal Government is going to work with the State and local, and we're going to help them with funding. And we're going to take—it's going to take a lot of funding, I will tell you that.

Q. Should they have done things differently before this point?

*The President.* A lot of things have been learned. A lot of things have been learned. And they've been working very hard, and I think you're going to see something very spectacular over the next number of years. . . .

SOURCE: Executive Office of the President. "Remarks at the Camp Fire Incident Command Post and an Exchange with Reporters in Chico, California." November 17, 2018. *Compilation of Presidential Documents* 2018, no. 000797 (November 17, 2018). https://www.govinfo.gov/content/pkg/DCPD-201800797/pdf/DCPD-201800797.pdf.

# Fourth National Climate Assessment Summary Findings

November 23, 2018

*[The following key findings have been excerpted from the Summary Findings of the Fourth National Climate Assessment.]*

## Communities

Climate change creates new risks and exacerbates existing vulnerabilities in communities across the United States, presenting growing challenges to human health and safety, quality of life, and the rate of economic growth. . . .

## Economy

Without substantial and sustained global mitigation and regional adaptation efforts, climate change is expected to cause growing losses to American infrastructure and property and impede the rate of economic growth over this century. . . .

## Interconnected Impacts

Climate change affects the natural, built, and social systems we rely on individually and through their connections to one another. These interconnected systems are increasingly vulnerable to cascading impacts that are often difficult to predict, threatening essential services within and beyond the Nation's borders. . . .

## Actions to Reduce Risks

Communities, governments, and businesses are working to reduce risks from and costs associated with climate change by taking action to lower greenhouse gas emissions and implement adaptation strategies. While mitigation and adaptation efforts have expanded substantially in the last four years, they do not yet approach the scale considered necessary to avoid substantial damages to the economy, environment, and human health over the coming decades. . . .

## Water

The quality and quantity of water available for use by people and ecosystems across the country are being affected by climate change, increasing risks and costs to agriculture, energy production, industry, recreation, and the environment. . . .

## Health

Impacts from climate change on extreme weather and climate-related events, air quality, and the transmission of disease through insects and pests, food, and water increasingly threaten the health and well-being of the American people, particularly populations that are already vulnerable. . . .

*Indigenous Peoples*

Climate change increasingly threatens Indigenous communities' livelihoods, economies, health, and cultural identities by disrupting interconnected social, physical, and ecological systems. . . .

*Ecosystems and Ecosystem Services*

Ecosystems and the benefits they provide to society are being altered by climate change, and these impacts are projected to continue. Without substantial and sustained reductions in global greenhouse gas emissions, transformative impacts on some ecosystems will occur; some coral reef and sea ice ecosystems are already experiencing such transformational changes. . . .

*Agriculture and Food*

Rising temperatures, extreme heat, drought, wildfire on rangelands, and heavy downpours are expected to increasingly disrupt agricultural productivity in the United States. Expected increases in challenges to livestock health, declines in crop yields and quality, and changes in extreme events in the United States and abroad threaten rural livelihoods, sustainable food security, and price stability. . . .

*Infrastructure*

Our Nation's aging and deteriorating infrastructure is further stressed by increases in heavy precipitation events, coastal flooding, heat, wildfires, and other extreme events, as well as changes to average precipitation and temperature. Without adaptation, climate change will continue to degrade infrastructure performance over the rest of the century, with the potential for cascading impacts that threaten our economy, national security, essential services, and health and well-being. . . .

*Oceans and Coasts*

Coastal communities and the ecosystems that support them are increasingly threatened by the impacts of climate change. Without significant reductions in global greenhouse gas emissions and regional adaptation measures, many coastal regions will be transformed by the latter part of this century, with impacts affecting other regions and sectors. Even in a future with lower greenhouse gas emissions, many communities are expected to suffer financial impacts as chronic high-tide flooding leads to higher costs and lower property values. . . .

*Tourism and Recreation*

Outdoor recreation, tourist economies, and quality of life are reliant on benefits provided by our natural environment that will be degraded by the impacts of climate change in many ways. . . .

SOURCE: U.S. Global Change Research Program. "Summary Findings of the Fourth National Climate Assessment." November 23, 2018. https://nca2018.globalchange.gov/downloads/NCA4_Ch01_Summary-Findings.pdf.

## OTHER HISTORIC DOCUMENTS OF INTEREST

### FROM THIS VOLUME

- United Nations Climate Change Releases First Annual Report, p. 270

### FROM PREVIOUS *HISTORIC DOCUMENTS*

- United States Withdraws from the Paris Climate Accord, *2016*, p. 323
- U.S. and Chinese Presidents Remark on Ratification of Paris Climate Agreement, *2016*, p. 407
- United Nations Climate Change Conference Reaches Historic Agreement, *2015*, p. 656

# Armenian Prime Minister Resigns

OCTOBER 16, 2018

In 2018, Armenia experienced a peaceful public revolution that ushered in a new government, putting an end to more than twenty-five years of Republican Party leadership. Revolution leader Nikol Pashinyan, a member of parliament and vocal critic of the government, was installed as the country's new prime minister in May. Just five months later, Pashinyan resigned to force snap parliamentary elections that he said were needed to realign the distribution of seats in the National Assembly with Armenia's new political reality. The December election resulted in a major victory for Pashinyan's political alliance while dealing a huge blow to the Republican Party.

## A CHANGE OF POWER

Armenia's Republican Party dominated the country's political and economic spheres since it declared independence from the Soviet Union in 1991. In recent years, the Armenian opposition grew stronger as the public became increasingly frustrated with government corruption and cronyism. Public anger boiled over in 2008 following a presidential election that opposition leaders and supporters claimed was rife with election fraud. That disputed vote brought Serzh Sargsyan into office amid mass public protests in the capital city of Yerevan that prompted outgoing president Robert Kocharyan to declare a state of emergency. Sargsyan was reelected in 2013.

Armenian presidents are limited to serving two terms, meaning that Sargsyan was due to step down in April 2018. In 2015, however, a Republican Party–backed constitutional referendum resulted in the transfer of most of the Armenian president's powers to the office of prime minister, creating an opportunity for Sargsyan to extend his leadership of the government. Sargsyan promised in 2017 that he would not seek the prime minister's office, but the National Assembly voted him into the post on April 17, 2018, without considering any other candidates. The move angered Armenians who viewed it as Sargsyan's attempt to cling to power.

Anticipating the assembly's decision, Pashinyan, a member of parliament and a former newspaper editor, began to walk across central Armenia in protest on March 31. Pashinyan had been a vocal critic of the Armenian government for years and helped to organize the street protests after the 2008 election. Pashinyan was arrested in 2009 on charges of fomenting unrest and spent two years in prison. He was elected to parliament in 2012, joining a small group of only nine opposition lawmakers.

Pashinyan's protest soon gave rise to a national, peaceful revolution that saw tens of thousands of Armenians take to the streets to demand Sargsyan's resignation. Pashinyan described the movement as a "velvet revolution," a reference to the peaceful transition of power that occurred in Czechoslovakia in 1989. Demonstrations began on April 13 in Yerevan but soon spread to other major cities. Soldiers from Armenia's peacekeeping force joined marches in the capital wearing their uniforms, putting additional pressure on the prime minister to step down. Pashinyan and two opposition allies were briefly detained on April 22 after a short meeting with Sargsyan (the prime minister walked out after just a few minutes, claiming the opposition was trying to blackmail him). On April 23, Sargsyan bowed to the mounting public pressure and announced his resignation. "I was wrong," he said in a statement. "The street movement is against my tenure. I am fulfilling your demand." Karen Karapetyan, who had just stepped down as prime minister before Sargsyan took the post, became acting prime minister.

The protests continued while members of parliament debated the path forward. Armenian law requires parliament to elect a new prime minister within two weeks of the former officeholder's resignation, and up to two votes may be held. If lawmakers do not agree on a candidate, snap elections must be called within thirty to forty days. Lawmakers generally agreed that snap elections would become necessary after Sargsyan's resignation, but opposition leaders did not want the Republican Party to oversee the poll. On May 1, the National Assembly voted down Pashinyan's first bid to become prime minister by a vote of 56–45 after nine hours of debate. He was the only candidate. Pashinyan subsequently called for nationwide strike. His supporters brought the country to a halt on May 2 as they blocked major roads and public transportation and forced the closure of schools, universities, and government institutions. The next day, Republican Party leadership announced it would support whichever candidate for prime minister was nominated by one-third of lawmakers. The party would not nominate its own candidate, it added. The news meant Pashinyan was all but certain to become prime minister, and he soon called for an end to the protests. "The issue has practically been solved," he said.

The National Assembly voted on Pashinyan's candidacy for the second time on May 8. This time he was elected by a vote of 59–42. "Your victory is not that I was elected as prime minister of Armenia; your victory is that you decided who should be prime minister of Armenia," he told a supportive crowd in the capital after the vote. Pashinyan said his first priority as prime minister would be to organize a new, fair parliamentary election because the makeup of the National Assembly no longer reflected Armenia's political reality. He also pledged to end the oligarchy and nepotism in government. Pashinyan promised to maintain the country's close relationship with Russia while focusing on addressing domestic issues, a message he had often shared during the protests. Analysts suggested such rhetoric helped dissuade Russia from meddling in the Armenian revolution. Russian President Vladimir Putin had previously intervened in former Soviet states, such as Georgia and Ukraine, where popular uprisings were seen as a threat to Russian interests. Russian officials indicated no intent to become involved in Armenia and called for a peaceful transition of power. The new prime minister also said he would "step up cooperation" with the United States and the European Union.

## Pashinyan Resigns

Armenian municipal elections held in September 2018 resulted in a landslide victory for the My Step Alliance—the political bloc that includes Pashinyan's Civil Contract Party. The alliance won more than 80 percent of the vote in the capital, which is home to almost 40 percent of Armenia's population. Pashinyan viewed the strong win as a mandate to push for snap parliamentary elections before the end of the year. However, on October 2, the National Assembly passed a Republican Party–backed bill seeking changes to parliamentary regulations that would have made it much more difficult for Pashinyan to dissolve parliament and schedule new elections. The measure received support from members of the Prosperous Armenia Party and the Armenian Revolutionary Federation; six cabinet members affiliated with those parties were subsequently dismissed by Pashinyan. The prime minister urged President Armen Sarkissian not to sign the "counterrevolutionary" bill into law, claiming that the Republican Party had "waged a war against their people." Tens of thousands of Armenians—summoned by Pashinyan—gathered outside the National Assembly building to protest the vote. The demonstration ended after Pashinyan met with various party leaders in parliament and received assurances that snap elections would not be impeded. Pashinyan soon stated his intention to resign to force an election.

Pashinyan officially resigned on October 16. Explaining to the Armenian people that he did not want to leave office, Pashinyan said his resignation was intended to "bring to completion our non-violent velvet revolution by holding snap elections and reinstating the people's power," adding that it would "usher in a completely new era." He reassured the public that the government would continue to fulfill its duties and he would continue to serve as prime minister until the election was held. "If you vote for our political team in December," he stated, "I shall be reelected as Prime Minister." Pashinyan sought to reassure "the parliamentary majority" that he and his supporters "are not seeking and will never look for enemies in Armenia" and said he wished all parties success in the election.

## SNAP ELECTIONS HELD

The day of Pashinyan's resignation, his government proposed electoral system changes that they hoped to implement before snap elections. The changes included lowering the vote thresholds for political parties and alliances to win seats in parliament from 5 percent and 7 percent, respectively, to 4 percent and 6 percent. At least four political entities would need to have representation in parliament, as opposed to the current three. Another change would have adjusted the way seats are distributed in the National Assembly. Many believed the existing system helped the Republican Party secure a major victory in the 2017 parliamentary elections and maintain its long-held grip on Armenian politics.

The National Assembly voted on these proposals on October 22, but the Republican Party boycotted the vote, meaning there were not enough lawmakers present to pass the bill. (The Armenian Constitution requires any change to the Electoral Code to be approved by at least sixty-three members of parliament.) Republican Party Vice President Armen Ashotyan said the electoral system should not be changed so close to an election, declaring "it is simply absurd to build democracy in the country with undemocratic methods." Pashinyan accused the Republican Party of "sabotaging" his government's efforts, claiming it hoped to "turn the fresh parliamentary elections into an instrument for revenge." However, he said, even if the existing Electoral Code remained in place, "the victory of the people is inevitable and cannot be stolen by anyone." The government reintroduced the bill, but it failed to gain approval again in a second vote.

On November 1, the National Assembly was dissolved, and Pashinyan signed a decree setting the snap election for December 9. The poll took place as scheduled, with election monitors from the Organization for Security and Co-operation in Europe reporting the vote had been free and fair. Approximately 49 percent of registered voters participated. Results released by the Central Election Commission showed the My Step Alliance won approximately 70 percent of the votes, returning Pashinyan to the prime minister's office and securing 88 seats in the new 132-seat parliament. The Prosperous Armenia Party won 8 percent of the votes, making it the second most vote-getting party or alliance. The Republican Party received only 4.7 percent of the vote. "Armenian citizens created a revolutionary majority at the parliament," said Pashinyan. "If this trend continues, the majority won't face any problems in implementing legislative changes."

—Linda Grimm

*Following is a speech by Armenian Prime Minister Nikol Pashinyan on October 16, 2018, announcing his resignation.*

## Prime Minister Nikol Pashinyan Announces Resignation

**October 16, 2018**

Dear compatriots,

My dear people,

Proud citizens of the Republic of Armenia,

As I said before, I am resigning today from the office of Prime Minister of Armenia. The purpose of this resignation is not to leave the post of prime minister, which means getting rid of the responsibility assumed before you, but to bring to completion our non-violent velvet revolution by holding snap elections and reinstating the people's power.

The roadmap to early parliamentary elections is as follows: after my resignation, the President of the Republic of Armenia immediately accepts the government's resignation. The Parliament fails to elect a prime minister twice over the next 14 days, due to which the National Assembly is dissolved, and the President calls preterm parliamentary elections.

During this time, the members of government will continue to fulfill their duties, I will continue to fulfill the constitutional powers of Prime Minister of the Republic of Armenia, that is, I will continue to be the guarantor of the people's victory, and if you vote for our political team in December, I shall be reelected as Prime Minister.

Many are afraid and wonder if we are prepared for the scenario where Parliament nominates another candidate for the post of prime minister. I do not even want to say that the events of October 2 demonstrated that we are more than prepared for any scenario because not a single force can stand before the people's will and wishes.

But now I do not want to think of any such scenario, because as much contradictions and heated debates we were to have with a number of parliamentary forces, I do not think that they may have an intent or purpose to act against the people and the national security of the Republic of Armenia.

Parliamentary forces have shown that regardless of all contradictions and misinterpretations, our statehood, its stability and security represent a red line for them, and I believe that they will never cross that line. Especially as the RPA, the Tsarukyan bloc and the ARF faction have publicly stated that they are not going to nominate or elect a prime minister.

I also want to tell the representatives of the parliamentary majority that while we have been criticizing them so far, we are not seeking and will never look for enemies in Armenia.

All the way through my political career, I have said and I want to reiterate now that I never had and will never have enemies in Armenia. Wishing all political forces every success in the proposed snap parliamentary elections, I would like to reaffirm that our government shall guarantee the free expression of people's will during the elections.

Dear compatriots,

Although this resignation is of formal nature, the moment is truly exciting because we thereby recap yet another stage in our revolution and usher in a completely new era.

And now, looking back at the past five months of my premiership, I want to thank you for your endless support and trust.

I also want to apologize to all those whom I have disappointed by failing to meet their legitimate hopes. Nevertheless, my dear compatriots, you may rest assured that I am not indifferent and keep in mind all your grievances; all your dreams are in my heart: they give me wings and strength to stand in front of you, and state with confidence that everything will be OK; everything is going to be fine.

Be prepared for ever new victories, for building a powerful, free and happy Armenia.

I love you all. I am proud of all of you. I bow before you and kiss you all. And therefore,

Long live Freedom!

Long live the Republic of Armenia!

Long live our children who are living and will live in a free and happy Armenia!

SOURCE: Office of the Prime Minister of the Republic of Armenia. "Address to the Nation by Prime Minister Nikol Pashinyan." October 16, 2018. http://www.primeminister.am/en/statements-and-messages/item/2018/10/16/Nikol-Pashinyan-message-16-10.

## OTHER HISTORIC DOCUMENTS OF INTEREST

### FROM PREVIOUS *HISTORIC DOCUMENTS*

- Treaty on Eurasian Economic Union Takes Effect, *2015*, p. 3

# Turkish President, U.S. Leaders Remark on Journalist Killed in Saudi Arabia

OCTOBER 17, OCTOBER 23, AND NOVEMBER 20, 2018

The October 2018 disappearance of *Washington Post* columnist Jamal Khashoggi from the Saudi Arabian consulate in Istanbul, Turkey, caused an international scandal that challenged U.S.–Saudi Arabia relations and drew increased attention to the Saudi-backed war in Yemen. The Saudi journalist—who previously served as a spokesman and adviser to several senior Saudi officials—had been living in the United States in self-imposed exile since June 2017, after his advocacy for democratic reforms and vocal criticism of Crown Prince Mohammed bin Salman made him a target of government-sanctioned harassment. The crown prince's crackdown on dissent inside and outside of the country prompted immediate speculation that Khashoggi had been kidnapped or worse, and that Mohammed bin Salman was directly involved. While Saudi officials initially claimed that Khashoggi left the consulate unharmed, in the face of mounting evidence compiled by Turkish investigators, they eventually acknowledged he had been killed by "rogue" Saudi agents, maintaining the crown prince's distance from the incident. President Donald Trump's response to the admission, which emphasized the importance of maintaining a relationship with Saudi Arabia over Khashoggi's death, was roundly criticized by many U.S. lawmakers, who in turn decided to pursue their own punitive actions.

## KHASHOGGI DISAPPEARS

Khashoggi first visited the Saudi consulate in Istanbul on September 28, seeking paperwork that would allow him to marry his Turkish fiancée, Hatice Cengiz. He was told to come back for an appointment on October 2. Khashoggi returned to the consulate with his fiancée at the scheduled time. Cengiz waited for hours outside the building before asking consulate staff about Khashoggi's whereabouts. After being told the journalist had left the consulate via a back entrance, Cengiz reported Khashoggi as missing to the Turkish authorities, who soon began an investigation. The next day, Saudi officials confirmed Khashoggi's disappearance while reiterating that he left the consulate on his own, unharmed. Turkish officials contested that claim, saying that video captured by cameras outside the consulate indicated he was still inside the building.

On October 6, a Saudi security team arrived in Istanbul to assist the police and other security forces with their investigation. A few days later Turkish officials released photos of fifteen Saudis who arrived in Istanbul on October 1 and October 2 and allegedly comprised a "hit squad" charged with killing Khashoggi. Officials described the men as security, intelligence, and forensic experts, several of whom were close to Mohammed bin Salman or had served on the crown prince's security team. The team reportedly killed

Khashoggi within two hours of entering the consulate, then dismembered him with a bone saw that one team member—reportedly an autopsy specialist—flew into Turkey specifically for that purpose. Several news reports indicated that the Turkish government had obtained audio recordings from inside the consulate that confirmed Khashoggi's death. Turkish officials did not receive permission from Saudi Arabia to search the consulate until mid-October, following the arrival of a second Saudi delegation in Istanbul. The two countries also formed a joint working group to help continue the investigation.

## SAUDI OFFICIALS CHANGE THEIR STORY

Saudi officials did not acknowledge that Khashoggi had been killed until October 19. In a statement read on state television, officials claimed Khashoggi had been accidentally strangled during a fistfight in the consulate and that his body had been given to a "local collaborator" for disposal. Eighteen people had been arrested for their involvement in the incident—fifteen of whom matched the men identified by Turkish officials earlier in the month. The other three were consulate staff. Five high-ranking Saudi officials had also been dismissed, according to the statement, including deputy director of Saudi intelligence Major General Ahmed al Assiri, who reportedly organized the operation, and Saud al-Qahtani, a close aide to Mohammed bin Salman and leader of the Center for Studies and Media Affairs at the Royal Court. Additionally, King Salman appointed the crown prince to oversee a restructuring of the country's intelligence services.

Turkish officials continued to counter the Saudi version of events. On October 23, Turkish president Recep Tayyip Erdoğan declared before a meeting of the Justice and Development Party Parliamentary Group that "the findings and evidence so far show Khashoggi was the victim of a vicious murder" that was "a planned operation, not a spontaneous development." Erdoğan said the evidence continued to raise questions such as from whom the team of Saudis received orders, why it took so long for Saudi officials to open the consulate to investigators, and why "so many inconsistent statements [have] been made while the murder was so clear." While suggesting that Khashoggi's killing was coordinated by officials at the highest levels of the Saudi government, Erdoğan did not mention the crown prince by name. He also called for the eighteen people detained by the Saudis to be tried in Turkey.

Two days later, Saudi officials acknowledged evidence from Turkish investigators that Khashoggi's death had been a premeditated assassination. Blame for the incident was still placed squarely on the fifteen-man team, which Saudi officials claimed had gone "rogue." On November 15, the Saudi public prosecutor announced charges against eleven men involved in Khashoggi's murder, saying the death penalty would be sought in five cases. The prosecutor also provided an updated explanation of what happened in the consulate: the team was supposed to bring Khashoggi back to Saudi Arabia for questioning, but the tranquilizer they injected into the journalist triggered an overdose that caused his death. The prosecutor also acknowledged that the team dismembered Khashoggi's body but insisted it was a last-minute decision to do so, despite Turkish officials' repeated assertion that the bone saw had been brought into the country.

## THE UNITED STATES RESPONDS

President Trump and administration officials initially declined to issue a definitive statement on Khashoggi's disappearance or potential U.S. action against those involved in the incident. Secretary of State Mike Pompeo traveled to Saudi Arabia and Turkey in mid-October to meet with leadership and discuss the investigation. Speaking briefly to reporters on October 17, Pompeo said he "stressed the importance of them conducting a complete investigation into the disappearance of Jamal Khashoggi" during his meetings and that Saudi officials had committed to "a thorough, complete, and transparent investigation." The Saudi government had "promised accountability for each of those persons whom they determine . . . deserves accountability," he added. Pompeo skirted reporters' questions about whether Khashoggi was dead and whether he believed Saudi officials' insistence that their government was not involved, saying he was "waiting for the investigation to be completed." The president made similar comments the next day, though he speculated that Khashoggi was dead and promised "severe" consequences if it was determined that Saudi Arabia was involved.

The consequences began to take shape in late October, when the State Department revoked visas for or put on a visa blacklist twenty-one Saudis identified as being involved in Khashoggi's killing. This was followed on November 15 by the U.S. Treasury Department's imposition of sanctions against seventeen Saudis, many of whom also faced charges by the Saudi public prosecutor. Notably, the seventeen individuals included Qahtani, who was not charged by the prosecutor but was targeted for sanctions for helping to plan and execute the operation. The sanctions froze any assets under U.S. jurisdiction, prohibited transactions with the individuals, and prevented them from traveling to the United States.

Soon after, various news outlets began reporting that a classified Central Intelligence Agency (CIA) assessment of Khashoggi's assassination concluded that Mohammed bin Salman ordered the killing. This conclusion was based on various communications that had been intercepted by the CIA, including a call that Khalid bin Salman, the Saudi ambassador to the United States and the crown prince's brother, had placed with Khashoggi, during which he instructed the journalist to go to the consulate in Istanbul to get his marriage documents and reassured him it would be safe to do so. This call was reportedly placed at the crown prince's direction. The assessment also used Turkish officials' audio recordings from inside the consulate to confirm that Khashoggi had been killed shortly after entering the building, and in the consul general's office. A spokeswoman for the Saudi Embassy in Washington, D.C., issued a statement asserting, "The claims in this purported assessment are false."

President Trump maintained there was no conclusive evidence connecting the crown prince to the murder. A statement by Trump on November 20 emphasized the strength and importance of the United States' relationship with Saudi Arabia. Trump highlighted an agreement through which Saudi Arabia was expected to spend or invest $450 billion in the United States—$110 billion of which was earmarked for military equipment purchases. "If we foolishly cancel these contracts, Russia and China would be the enormous beneficiaries," he said. The president also favorably compared Saudi Arabia to other actors in the region, namely Iran, which he blamed for the "bloody proxy war" in Yemen while claiming Saudi Arabia would "gladly withdraw" from the conflict if Iran agreed to leave. Only after these comments did Trump state that "the crime against Jamal Khashoggi was a terrible one, and one that our country does not condone," noting that the United States had already imposed sanctions on numerous Saudis. He restated denials from Mohammed bin Salman and King Salman that they were involved in the operation and seemed to question the CIA's conclusion that the crown prince knew about it, saying, "Maybe he did and maybe he didn't." Regardless of Khashoggi's death, Trump went on, the United States "intends to remain a steadfast partner of Saudi Arabia to ensure the interests of our country, Israel, and all other partners in the region."

The president's statement drew sharp criticisms from Khashoggi's colleagues and members of Congress. *Washington Post* publisher and CEO Fred Ryan declared Trump's statement to be "a betrayal of long-established American values of respect for human rights and the expectation of trust and honesty in our strategic relationships." He called on Congress to "stand up for America's true values and lasting interests." Sen. Lindsey Graham, R-S.C., said the crown prince's behavior had shown disrespect for the United States' relationship with Saudi Arabia and made him "beyond toxic" and suggested there would be bipartisan support for tough sanctions against members of the royal family. On the other side of the aisle, Sen. Dianne Feinstein, D-Calif., said she would vote against any future arms deals with Saudi Arabia, urged consideration of sanctions against Mohammed bin Salman, and called for the Saudi ambassador to the United States to be dismissed.

The Senate actively pursued additional actions against the Saudi Arabian government, including through legislation seeking to block weapons sales to the country and impose sanctions on officials involved in Khashoggi's killing and the war in Yemen. In December, the Senate passed a bill to end U.S. military assistance to Saudi Arabia for the Yemen war and approved a separate resolution declaring Mohammed bin Salman responsible for Khashoggi's death. The measures signaled a remarkable break with the White House, though neither was taken up by the House before the end of the year. "The fact that we haven't forced [the crown prince] to come clean is creating a problem," said Senate Foreign Relations Committee Chair Bob Corker, R-Tenn. The Yemen bill "allows us to somehow or other address this since the administration appears unwilling to do so," he added. "We cannot sweep under the rug the callous disregard for human life and flagrant violations of international norms the Saudis are showing," said Sen. Robert Menendez, D-N.J., the ranking member on the Senate Foreign Relations Committee. In an unusual move, the Saudi Foreign Ministry issued a statement criticizing the Senate's action, saying the resolution blaming the crown prince was based on "unsubstantiated claims and allegations and contained blatant interference in the kingdom's internal affairs, undermining the kingdom's regional and international role."

—Linda Grimm

*Following is U.S. Secretary of State Mike Pompeo's remarks on October 17, 2018, regarding the investigation into Khashoggi's death; Turkish President Recep Tayyip Erdoğan's speech to the Justice and Development Party Parliamentary Group on October 23, 2018, about Turkey's investigation and initial findings; and a statement by President Donald Trump on November 20, 2018, about Khashoggi and the United States' relationship with Saudi Arabia.*

# U.S. Secretary of State Remarks on Khashoggi Investigation

**October 17, 2018**

SECRETARY POMPEO: We're on our way to Turkey, where I'll meet with President Erdogan this morning, if all goes as planned. Yesterday I had the chance to have a number of meetings, extended meetings, with King Salman and the crown prince, Adel al-Jubeir, the foreign minister. In each of those meetings I stressed the importance of them conducting a complete investigation into the disappearance of Jamal Khashoggi, and they made a commitment; they said they would do that and they said it would be a thorough, complete, and transparent investigation. We'll all see the results of that. They made a commitment that they would show the entire world the results of their investigation. They also indicated they would get this done quickly. I don't know the precise timeline, but they indicated that they understood the importance of getting that done in a timely, rapid fashion so that they could begin to answer important questions.

We also had the chance to talk about lots of other elements of the relationship between our two countries. We have many overlapping interests, places we work together, places where Saudi Arabia and the United States are trying to achieve important things around the world, and we spent time discussing those as well.

QUESTION: Sir, did they tell you what happened to Jamal Khashoggi?

SECRETARY POMPEO: They told me they were going to conduct a thorough, complete, transparent investigation. They made a commitment, too, to hold anyone connected to any wrongdoing that may be found accountable for that, whether they are a senior officer or official. They promised accountability for each of those persons whom they determine as a result of their investigation has—deserves accountability.

QUESTION: Including a member of the royal family?

SECRETARY POMPEO: They made no exceptions to who they would hold accountable. They were just—they were very clear. They understand the importance of this issue. They are determined to get to the bottom of it, and that they will conduct the report, and we'll all get a chance to see it. They each promised that they would achieve that for us.

QUESTION: And did they say that Mr. Khashoggi is alive or dead?

SECRETARY POMPEO: I don't want to talk about any of the facts. They didn't want to either, in that they want to have the opportunity to complete this investigation in a thorough way.

QUESTION: Do you believe the denials?

SECRETARY POMPEO: And I think that's—I think that's—I think that's a reasonable thing to do to give them that opportunity, and then we'll all get to judge, we'll all get to evaluate the work that they do.

QUESTION: With the reports coming from Turkey, what gives you the benefit of the doubt of believing them so far right now?

SECRETARY POMPEO: I'm waiting for the investigation to be completed. They promised that they would achieve that, and I'm counting on it, and they gave me their word. And we'll all get to see if they deliver against that commitment.

QUESTION: Did you talk about repercussions in case the Saudis are found to be involved?

SECRETARY POMPEO: We talked about the importance of completing the investigation.

QUESTION: And what happens if the Saudis are found to be involved, for the U.S.?

SECRETARY POMPEO: We talked about the importance of the investigation, completing it in a timely fashion, and making sure that it was sufficiently transparent that we could evaluate the work that had been done to get to the bottom of it. So that was the purpose of the visit. In that sense it was incredibly successful. We received commitments that they would complete this, and I am counting on them to do that. So thanks, everybody.

QUESTION: Did they tell you something different, though, in private about this?

SECRETARY POMPEO: Have a good morning and we'll see you all on the other side.

SOURCE: U.S. Department of State. "Remarks to Traveling Press." October 17, 2018. https://www.state.gov/secretary/remarks/2018/10/286696.htm.

DOCUMENT

# President Erdoğan Comments on Khashoggi's Death

**October 23, 2018**

*[The following remarks have been excerpted from the full text of a speech Erdoğan delivered before his political party's parliamentary group meeting.]*

My dear friends;

In this part of our parliamentary party group discussion, I would like to make a comprehensive evaluation as regards the murder of the journalist Jamal Khashoggi that was proven definitely to take place in Consulate General of Saudi Arabia in Istanbul. First and foremost, I wish God's Peace on the soul of the late Jamal Khashoggi, and my condolences to his family, fiancée, friends, compatriots in Saudi Arabia and the media world.

Before all else, let's have a small refresher. Jamal Khashoggi first entered Saudi Arabia's Istanbul consulate on Friday, September 28, at 11:50, for marriage transactions. It can be understood that team that planned and carried out the murder was informed about Khashoggi's visit, in other words, this was the first step of the plan or the process of building the road map. Furthermore, the fact that some consular officials went to their home country in a hurry indicates that the preparation work and planning were done there.

On October 1, at 16:30, the day before the operation, a team of three people arrived in Istanbul on a chartered flight, checked into a hotel first and then went to the Consulate General of Saudi Arabia in Istanbul. In the meantime, another team from the consulate went on a reconnaissance mission in Belgrad Forest in Istanbul and Yalova. On October 2, at 01:45, the second group of three people arrived in Istanbul on another chartered flight and checked into a hotel. The third group of nine people, including generals, arrived in Istanbul on a private flight and went to another hotel.

This team, consisting of fifteen people in total, arrived in the Consulate General of Saudi Arabia in Istanbul separately between 09:50 and 11:00 and regrouped there. First, the hard drive of the consulate's CCTV system was removed. And Jamal Khashoggi at 11:50 was called to confirm his appointment that day. Khashoggi, who arrived in Istanbul from London in the early hours of the same day, walks into the consulate at 13:08. Of course, his fiancée is with him. And after that time, nothing is heard of him.

Khashoggi's fiancée contacted Turkish authorities at 17:50 saying that he might have been detained by force, or something might have happened to him. As a result, the Istanbul Police Department immediately launched an investigation. Upon inspection of CCTV footage, it became clear that Khashoggi had not left the consulate building. Of course, no action was taken regarding the consulate building and its staff, as they were under the protective cover of diplomatic immunity in accordance with the Vienna Convention [on Consular Relations]. Now, the Vienna Convention is also discussed and there have been statements recently made by [European Commission Vice President and High Representative for Foreign Affairs and Security Policy Federica] Mogherini in order to talk over this Vienna Convention once more. An actual operation could not be conducted at the first stage about the Consulate General and its staff.

As our police and intelligence forces dug deeper into the issue, our Istanbul Chief Public Prosecutor's Office launched an official investigation. As the investigation advanced, interesting facts emerged. Starting from the day before the murder, it became known that fifteen Saudi security, intelligence personnel, and forensic specialists arrived in our country. Six of those people left the country on the evening of October 2nd at 18:20, and the remaining seven left at 22:50 on private planes. The person who attempted to disguise himself to look like Jamal Khashoggi with his clothes, glasses and beard—along with another individual accompanying him—also left after midnight for Riyadh on a commercial flight. The staff at work at the consulate on that day were confined to a room on the grounds that there was an inspection taking place. The staff who were not present were given permission to not come to work, on the same grounds.

The Saudi Arabian administration denied the allegations regarding Khashoggi's killing in a statement made on October 4. Moreover—this is important—the Consul General of Saudi Arabia on October 6 invited a Reuters reporter into the consulate showing them closets, doors, and electricity panels in a reckless attempt to defend himself. Meanwhile, our police and intelligence units as well as our prosecutors kept digging deep and uncovered new information and documents. Our foreign ministry was in constant discussion and shared information with their counterparts.

A delegation of representatives from Saudi Arabia came to our country on October 11 and established contact points. The Saudi authorities announced that they would allow the search of the consulate building, as a result of the issue's consistent presence on Turkey's and the global media agenda.

My dear friends;

Of course, first, some things must be asked, and the answers must be sought, because this incident takes place in Istanbul and we have a responsibility. So as those in a position of responsibility it is our right to question this. As the fog around the issue began to dissipate, other countries also began to act. We have stated that under no circumstance will we remain silent about this murder, and that we will take any steps required by conscience and law. In addition, we waited for the results of the investigations so as to not misjudge anyone.

In the first phone call we made with Salman bin Abdulaziz, the King of Saudi Arabia and the Custodian of the Two Mosques, on October 14, we explained the matter to him in the light of our findings and everything we have discovered. In this meeting, I explained to him the meeting I had with a delegation he had previously sent to investigate the event and expressed our decision for establishing a joint working group, and informed him by saying that 'our joint investigation group started to work' and we agreed on this issue.

Upon the king's order, teams containing prosecutors and members of the police department entered the Saudi consulate and searched the premises. Of course, as the consul general had not allowed this, I spoke to the delegation who had come in about the insufficiency of this consul general, which I reiterated to the king. And the day after we spoke the consul general was removed from his post. During this time, the Saudi consul general in Istanbul returned to his country.

On October 18, another search of the consulate took place. Seventeen days after the murder, on October 19, the Saudi Arabian administration officially admitted that Jamal Khashoggi was killed inside the consulate building. In a statement made by the Saudi administration, it was said that Khashoggi had perished during a brawl that took place inside the consulate. On the night of that very same day we had another phone call with King Salman bin Abdulaziz. After the admission of the murder, it was expressed that the eighteen people involved in the incident were arrested. The list of people given to us was determined to be the same names that our security and intelligence personnel had identified as being involved in the incident. The list of people included fifteen people who came to Turkey plus three people. These three people were working at the consulate. These developments are of course important in reaching an official admission of murder.

On October 21, we had a comprehensive telephone conversation with the U.S. President Donald Trump, agreeing to bring these events into the light by all means. As a country, Turkey managed this process with the utmost due diligence, in line with international law and our legislative system. Despite this fact, various media organizations carried out smear campaigns targeting Turkey to implicate our country and to distract people from focusing on the actual targets. We know who are behind these smear campaigns and what their motivations are. These plots to destroy the reputation of our country could not and will not stop us from uncovering the truth of this matter.

Before anything else, this murder took place in Saudi Arabia's consulate building which is considered Saudi soil. However, it should be remembered that it is still within Turkey's borders. Moreover, the Vienna Convention, as well as other forms of international law, cannot allow the investigation of such a brutal murder to be concealed under diplomatic immunity. We will surely investigate this murder committed within our borders with all its dimensions and do what has to be done to this end. Furthermore, Jamal Khashoggi is not just a Saudi citizen but also an internationally renowned journalist, which gives us an additional responsibility on an international level. Turkey is following up on this matter not just as a matter of its right to sovereignty, but also on behalf of the international community and the collective conscience of humanity.

All the information and evidence that has been uncovered thus far lead to the conclusion that Jamal Khashoggi was the victim of a gruesome murder. Concealing such an atrocity would hurt the collective conscience of humanity. We expect the same sensitivity from all parties in the matter, especially the Saudi Arabian administration.

My dear friends;

The Saudi administration has taken a significant step by admitting to the murder. From now on, we expect them to openly identify all of those responsible in the event, from the highest to the lowest level, and punish them before the law. We have strong indications that the murder was not the result of a spontaneous event but that of a planned operation.

In light of the existing information, these questions continue to be on people's minds: Why did the fifteen people, all connected to the event, meet in Istanbul on the day of the murder? On whose orders did these people come? Why was the consulate building opened for investigation days after [the event] and not immediately? Why were there so many inconsistent statements made despite it being so obvious that it was a murder? Why is the body of a person who was admittedly murdered still absent? If the statement that the body was given to a local accomplice is true, then who is this local accomplice? The one talking about the presence of a local accomplice is not an ordinary person but an authorized official of Saudi Arabia. Then you have to reveal this local accomplice.

No one should think that this matter will be closed before all of these questions are answered. Some of the information that our police and intelligence units are still evaluating already points towards the event being a planned operation. As the assessment of the information is completed, it will be added into the prosecutor's case. Blaming this on some security and intelligence officers will satisfy neither us nor the international community. The conscience of humanity will only be satisfied when all those from the person who gave the order to anybody who carried it out are brought to account.

Personally, I do not doubt the sincerity of the Custodian of the Two Mosques, King Salman bin Abdulaziz. With that said, it is of utmost importance that such a critical investigation be led by a truly impartial and just committee—nobody connected to the murder should be a part of the investigation team. Considering that this was a political killing, accomplices in various different countries—if they do exist—have to be investigated. This is required by international law, Islamic law and, I believe, also by Saudi law.

As Turkey, we will follow this matter until the very end, making sure that whatever international law and our legislation require will get done. In fact, I am making a call from here today. This call is to the high-level officials, primarily King Salman bin Abdul Aziz, the Custodian of the Two Mosques. The incident took place in Istanbul. Therefore the adjudication of these fifteen plus three, these eighteen people, should be carried out in Istanbul. That is my proposal. The decision is at his discretion. But this is my proposal, my request, because this is where the incident occurred. That is why it's important.

SOURCE: Presidency of the Republic of Turkey. "Speech at AK Parti Group Meeting." October 23, 2018. Translated by SAGE Publishing. https://www.tccb.gov.tr/konusmalar/353/99308/ak-parti-grup-toplan tisinda-yaptiklari-konusma.

# President Trump Statement on U.S.–Saudi Arabia Relationship

**November 20, 2018**

The world is a very dangerous place!

The country of Iran, as an example, is responsible for a bloody proxy war against Saudi Arabia in Yemen, trying to destabilize Iraq's fragile attempt at democracy, supporting the terror group Hezbollah in Lebanon, propping up dictator Bashar Assad in Syria (who has killed millions of his own citizens), and much more. Likewise, the Iranians have killed many Americans and other innocent people throughout the Middle East. Iran states openly, and with great force, "Death to America!" and "Death to Israel!" Iran is considered "the world's leading sponsor of terror."

On the other hand, Saudi Arabia would gladly withdraw from Yemen if the Iranians would agree to leave. They would immediately provide desperately needed humanitarian assistance. Additionally, Saudi Arabia has agreed to spend billions of dollars in leading the fight against Radical Islamic Terrorism.

After my heavily negotiated trip to Saudi Arabia last year, the Kingdom agreed to spend and invest $450 billion in the United States. This is a record amount of money. It will create hundreds of thousands of jobs, tremendous economic development, and much additional wealth for the United States. Of the $450 billion, $110 billion will be spent on the purchase of military equipment from Boeing, Lockheed Martin, Raytheon and many other great U.S. defense contractors. If we foolishly cancel these contracts, Russia and China would be the enormous beneficiaries—and very happy to acquire all of this newfound business. It would be a wonderful gift to them directly from the United States!

The crime against Jamal Khashoggi was a terrible one, and one that our country does not condone. Indeed, we have taken strong action against those already known to have participated in the murder. After great independent research, we now know many details of this horrible crime. We have already sanctioned 17 Saudis known to have been involved in the murder of Mr. Khashoggi, and the disposal of his body.

Representatives of Saudi Arabia say that Jamal Khashoggi was an "enemy of the state" and a member of the Muslim Brotherhood, but my decision is in no way based on that—this is an unacceptable and horrible crime. King Salman and Crown Prince Mohammad bin Salman vigorously deny any knowledge of the planning or execution of the murder of Mr. Khashoggi. Our intelligence agencies continue to assess all information, but it could very well be that the Crown Prince had knowledge of this tragic event—maybe he did and maybe he didn't!

That being said, we may never know all of the facts surrounding the murder of Mr. Jamal Khashoggi. In any case, our relationship is with the Kingdom of Saudi Arabia. They have been a great ally in our very important fight against Iran. The United States intends to remain a steadfast partner of Saudi Arabia to ensure the interests of our country, Israel and all other partners in the region. It is our paramount goal to fully eliminate the threat of terrorism throughout the world!

I understand there are members of Congress who, for political or other reasons, would like to go in a different direction—and they are free to do so. I will consider whatever ideas are presented to me, but only if they are consistent with the absolute security and safety of America. After the United States, Saudi Arabia is the largest oil producing nation in the world. They have worked closely with us and have been very responsive to my requests to keeping oil prices at reasonable levels—so important for the world. As President of the United States I intend to ensure that, in a very dangerous world, America is pursuing its national interests and vigorously contesting countries that wish to do us harm. Very simply it is called America First!

SOURCE: Executive Office of the President. "Statement on Standing with Saudi Arabia." November 20, 2018. *Compilation of Presidential Documents* 2018, no. 00802 (November 20, 2018). https://www.govinfo.gov/content/pkg/DCPD-201800802/pdf/DCPD-201800802.pdf..

## OTHER HISTORIC DOCUMENTS OF INTEREST

# United Nations Briefing on the Humanitarian Crisis in Yemen

OCTOBER 23, 2018

In 2018, the United Nations declared Yemen the site of the world's worst humanitarian crisis. Three-quarters of the country's population was in need of some form of aid, and children under the age of five were dying at a rate of one every ten minutes from a preventable cause. A majority of Yemenis lacked access to basic human needs like clean water, food, and health care. Factors driving the crisis included an unstable government, a failing economy, soaring food and fuel prices, air strikes that destroyed infrastructure, limited access for aid workers, and disrupted shipments of vital supplies. The United Nations repeatedly appealed to its member states for the billions of dollars it needed to provide aid to the eight million citizens it was serving in any given month, a twofold increase from 2017. UN member states also continued to push for a political solution to the crisis, one that respected the country's sovereignty and considered the demands of all parties in the conflict.

## YEMEN CONFLICT DRIVES HUMANITARIAN CRISIS

The humanitarian crisis in Yemen had been slowly building since 2011, when the Arab Spring uprisings deposed Ali Abdullah Saleh, who had served as president for more than three decades. His successor, Abdu Rabbu Mansour Hadi, struggled to address a growing insurgency led by the Houthis, a minority Shia group. In early 2015, Saleh aligned with the Houthis, sparking a civil war that forced Hadi and his government into exile. The Houthis gained control of large swaths of Yemen, including the capital city of Sana'a, along with weapons and military vehicles that were used against the Hadi government and its supporters.

The internal conflict quickly became a proxy war between Iran, which backed the Houthi rebels, and Saudi Arabia, which led a coalition of primarily Sunni Arab Middle Eastern states in support of the Hadi government. While Iran provided training, arms, and strategic military support to the Houthis, the Saudi coalition aided the Hadi government's military response and carried out thousands of air strikes that were initially intended to root out Houthi rebels. Given Yemen's strategic importance in the region and a desire among primarily Western governments to stop Iran from widening its influence, the Saudi coalition quickly drew logistical and intelligence support from countries like the United States, United Kingdom, and France.

More than a year after the fighting began, in October 2016, the United Nations special envoy to Yemen submitted for consideration a road map for peace between the Houthis and Hadi's government. The road map required that Hadi step down after a transitional government was installed and that the Houthis withdraw from territory they had seized. Hadi and his supporters quickly rejected the proposal. The Houthis, however, accepted the road map at the same time they announced that they had formed a new Yemeni government, the Government of National Salvation (GNS). Despite receiving a vote of confidence in Yemen's parliament, the GNS failed to garner international recognition of its legitimacy.

## COMPOUNDING HEALTH AND SECURITY CRISIS

The conflict wore on without any progress toward peace or the installation of a new government. That instability contributed to the deepening humanitarian crisis, which by April 2018 had been labeled the world's worst by the United Nations. According to UN Secretary General António Guterres, almost half of all children aged six months to five years were chronically malnourished and a majority of the population lacked access to food, clean drinking water, and medical treatment. The poor sanitary conditions and scarce clean water resulted in the worst documented cholera outbreak in history, with more than one million suspected cases reported between fall 2016 and spring 2018. The World Health Organization reported 2,200 cholera-related deaths by December 2017. According to Guterres, cholera and other preventable diseases had become a "death sentence" for Yemenis.

The unrelenting air strikes carried out by the Saudi coalition were a key contributor to the cholera outbreak and the larger humanitarian crisis in the country. According to the United Nations, of the 18,000 air strikes attributed to the coalition, nearly one-third hit nonmilitary targets, killing civilians and destroying infrastructure including schools, hospitals, roads, bridges, and wastewater treatment plants. These bombings made it difficult for aid workers to reach those in need of assistance, especially in the most remote parts of the country. Concern over whether Saudi Arabia was contributing to the crisis more than it was assisting led the U.S. House and Senate in late 2018 to consider resolutions to withdraw U.S. support from the coalition. "Our involvement in this war," said Rep. Barbara Lee, D-Calif., "quite frankly, is shameful."

## YEMENIS ON THE BRINK OF FAMINE

Actions by the warring Houthis and Hadi government and its supporters also created an economic crisis. The government had not paid more than one million public workers on a consistent basis since August 2016, and farmland was frequently destroyed by air strikes, robbing Yemenis of any opportunity to support themselves and their families. Those who remained employed were often earning less than $2 per day. The United Nations reported that this forced families to decide between purchasing food and transporting a sick relative to a health clinic for life-saving care.

Before the civil war, Yemen was heavily reliant on imports of both food and fuel. When the fighting started, the Houthis began charging fees to allow these goods to travel into their territory. Additionally, a Saudi blockade at the nation's ports that was intended to stop Iranian weapons from entering the country actually resulted in making food and fuel more difficult and expensive to obtain. When added to the hyperinflation brought on by mismanagement of the economy by the Hadi government and its Saudi supporters, food and fuel became unattainable for most Yemenis. The World Food Programme reported that food prices rose an average of 137 percent since the civil war began. That lack of access to affordable food resulted in an estimated 85,000 children under the age of five dying from malnutrition since the civil war began, according to a report by Save the Children.

In October 2018, the United Nations warned that half of the country was on the brink of famine. While the Saudis called the food crisis exaggerated, Mark Lowcock, UN Under Secretary General for Humanitarian Affairs and Emergency Relief Coordinator, told the Security Council that the famine was "much bigger than anything any professional in this field has encounter[ed] during their working lives." UN member states remained committed to providing the aid necessary but admitted that a larger political solution was required to lift the country out of famine and end the humanitarian crisis. "There is simply no alternative to a political solution. The dire situation the Under-Secretary-General described is yet another reminder that this war and the suffering of the Yemeni people can only end at the negotiating table, not on the battlefield," said Ambassador Jonathan Cohen, U.S. Deputy Permanent Representative to the United Nations.

—Heather Kerrigan

*Following are remarks delivered on October 23, 2018, at a UN Security Briefing by U.S. Deputy Permanent Representative to the United Nations Ambassador Jonathan Cohen, regarding the humanitarian crisis in Yemen; and an October 23, 2018, press release documenting a United Nations Security Council briefing on the situation in Yemen.*

# U.S. Ambassador on Crisis in Yemen

**October 23, 2018**

AS DELIVERED

Thank you, Mr. President. And let me add our voice to those thanking you, Under-Secretary-General Lowcock, for your deeply concerning, sobering, and important briefing today. We are very grateful for the hard work that you do and that your team does on the ground in Yemen every day.

The stories behind the huge numbers of people affected by the crisis have become all too familiar. Babies ravaged by hunger, too weak to cry. Parents choosing between critical medical care for a child or food for their family.

And now, as the Under-Secretary-General argued, continued deterioration and newly acute risk are apparent in every grim update—most recently, in reports of over 20,000 newly displaced in northern Yemen due to fighting there. There are alternatives to this. The suffering of the Yemeni people is not inevitable. But unless the fighting stops and there are immediate efforts to stabilize the Yemeni rial, the suffering of those who are already severely food insecure in Yemen will continue to worsen.

In this regard, no one has worked harder or more tirelessly to bring about a political solution than UN Special Envoy Martin Griffiths. He has our full support, and we need him to succeed.

Mr. President, until we achieve a political solution, we implore all parties to take necessary measures to protect civilians and critical civilian infrastructure and to ensure unfettered access for humanitarian goods and personnel and the movement of essential commercial goods.

The parties must adhere to their obligations under international law and recognize that damage to ports and other civilian infrastructure will further drive food insecurity. In this regard, we urge parties to consider all possible measures to further mitigate and reduce unnecessary suffering from this conflict. We thank the United Nations for its efforts to maintain a deconfliction mechanism in this context to allow aid and commercial goods to flow despite the fighting.

Mr. President, we share the Under-Secretary-General's assessment that humanitarian assistance, especially in the past year, has been critical in staving off the worst outcomes and mitigating Yemeni suffering. The United States is one of the largest donors of humanitarian assistance in Yemen, providing more than $1.2 billion in humanitarian aid since fiscal year 2017, including food, medical care, safe drinking water, shelter, psychosocial support, and supplies to fight the spread of disease. U.S. contributions to UN World Food Program operations have also been vital.

But as the Under-Secretary-General said, we can and must do more. And so we are. In addition to continued humanitarian relief, we are expanding non-humanitarian assistance to address the consequences of conflict, including supporting efforts to enhance the Central Bank of Yemen's ability to function so that it can begin to address Yemen's deteriorating economic situation and the currency depreciation that has made it even harder for Yemenis to afford to survive.

We'll continue those efforts and hope that all parties will also recognize and help respond to the suffering. At the same time, there is simply no alternative to a political solution. The dire situation the Under-Secretary-General described is yet another reminder that this war and the suffering of the Yemeni people can only end at the negotiating table, not on the battlefield.

Thank you.

SOURCE: U.S. Mission to the United Nations. "Remarks at a UN Security Council Briefing on the Situation in Yemen." October 23, 2018. https://usun.state.gov/remarks/8677.

# UN Briefing on Humanitarian Crisis in Yemen

DOCUMENT

**October 23, 2018**

To stem the growing threat of famine in Yemen, the international community must act urgently to unblock imports, ensure distribution of aid and counteract a lack of foreign exchange in the war-torn gulf nation, the United Nations top humanitarian affairs official told the Security Council this afternoon.

"There is now a clear and present danger of an imminent famine engulfing Yemen: much bigger than anything any professional in this field has encounter[ed] during their working lives," Mark Lowcock, Under-Secretary-General for Humanitarian Affairs and Emergency Relief Coordinator said in a briefing on the Yemen crisis that focused on food security.

Half the country—some 14 million people—are threatened by famine in a worst-case scenario, Mr. Lowcock said. Fighting around the key port of Hodeidah continues to choke off life-sustaining supplies, Government regulations have hampered commercial imports and the collapse of the economy means that there is no foreign exchange to pay for essential goods.

To avert catastrophe, he called on all stakeholders to urgently support a humanitarian ceasefire in and around all importation infrastructure and to do everything possible to facilitate the delivery of humanitarian assistance as required under international law. The United Nations, as he already has indicated, is ready to play an enhanced role in ensuring the appropriate use of key facilities especially around Hodeidah.

Restrictions must be lifted and main transport routes kept open and safe so that essential aid and imports are allowed to reach their destinations, he stressed. A larger and faster injection of foreign exchange through the Central Bank is also urgently needed, along with expedited credit for trade and payment of pensioners and civil servants. Increased funding is needed to match the scale of the crisis, he added. Finally, and most importantly, he called upon belligerents to seize this moment to engage fully and openly with the Special Envoy to end the conflict.

Council members took the floor to affirm the urgency to avert famine in Yemen, with many also sounding the alarm on the other aspects of the humanitarian crisis. They also called on all parties to the conflict to respect international humanitarian law by allowing unhindered access for aid and other essential goods. While stressing that the Russian Federation will continue its unpoliticized aid to Yemen, that country's representative also underscored that the solution lies in the political dimension.

Most speakers echoed that, asserting that only an inclusive United Nations-led and Yemeni-owned political process can end the suffering. They called on all parties in the country to pursue that process through the United Nations Special Envoy, with Kuwait's representative affirming the continued relevance of the Gulf Initiative in that context. Some called for greater Council pressure on the parties to bring the parties back to the negotiating table.

Yemen's representative, emphasizing his Government's commitment to international humanitarian and human rights law, called on the Security Council to act with strength to bring the Houthis to the negotiating table and to abide by Security Council resolutions so that his people's suffering can end.

Describing Government strategies to decentralize humanitarian assistance so it can be distributed to those in need, he said that it has also taken measures to restore the economy through the banking system, including meeting the needs of small traders and the oil company. Actions, he added, have also been taken to neutralize the Houthi black market.

He announced that measures to control credit lines will be postponed awaiting dialogue with traders on the situation. Calling for assistance in building up foreign currency supplies, similar to what Saudi Arabia has done, he thanked that country, the United Arab Emirates and other donors, as well as the United Nations, for their assistance. He also called on all donors to meet the needs set out in the 2018 humanitarian appeal for his country.

Also speaking were representatives of the United Kingdom, China, France, Netherlands, Poland, Ethiopia, Peru, Sweden, Equatorial Guinea, Kazakhstan, Cote d'Ivoire, United States and Bolivia.

The meeting began at 3 p.m. and ended at 4:47 p.m.

## Briefing

MARK LOWCOCK, Under-Secretary-General for Humanitarian Affairs and Emergency Relief Coordinator, while noting assessments were ongoing, underscored that "there is now a clear and present danger of an imminent famine engulfing Yemen: much bigger than anything any professional in this field has encounter[ed] during their working lives". Although he had warned of famine twice in the past, he stressed that the situation is now much graver than on either of those occasions because of the sheer number of people at risk—possibly reaching 14 million, half the total population of the country—and the fact that the immune systems of millions of people are collapsing from being on mere survival rations for years on end.

Recalling that last month he told the Council about the intensification of fighting around Hodeidah, choking the lifeline of aid operations and commercial imports, he reported that the situation around that city has worsened over the past several days. Due to ongoing hostilities, the eastern road from Hodeidah to Sana'a remains blocked and clashes continue to prevent access to a major milling facility, with several humanitarian warehouses occupied for over two months. The parties to the conflict continue to violate international humanitarian law through mass civilian casualties and damage to critical infrastructure. Delays in issuing visas, restrictions on importation of equipment and cargo, retraction of permits, interference in humanitarian assessment exercises and moni-toring, all further limit the ability to provide life-saving assistance. The relief effort will ultimately simply be overwhelmed, he warned.

Yemen is still almost entirely reliant on imports for food, fuel and medicines, and available foreign exchange has been inadequate to finance the imports needed, given the collapse in the economy, he continued. That has been partially mitigated by aid generously funded by donors, with aid agencies implementing the world's largest humanitarian oper-ation. Some 200 organizations are working through the United Nations Humanitarian Response Plan and have delivered assistance in all 33 districts this year. As many as 8 million people are receiving life-saving assistance every month, but the aid operation cannot conceivably meet the needs of all Yemenis.

For that purpose, he said that his call last month for an urgent and substantial injec-tion of foreign exchange and the resumption of payments to pensioners and key public sector workers has resulted in a pledge from Saudi Arabia and the United Arab Emirates for $70 million to cover allowances for 135,000 teachers. However, action in that area looks to be too small and too slow to reverse the trajectory towards famine. Those involved must address the matter with great urgency.

Meanwhile, the Government of Yemen appears to be planning further restriction on trade in essential commodities, with only a handful of necessary lines of credit being issued since June, mostly in just the last few days, he continued. The alarming effect of those regulations is that two vessels carrying substantial amounts of fuel have been refused entry at the Government's request in the past few days increasing the possibility of famine.

To avert catastrophe, he called on all stakeholders to urgently support a humanitarian ceasefire in and around all importation infrastructure and to do everything possible to facilitate the delivery of humanitarian assistance required under international law. The United Nations, as he has already indicated, is ready to play an enhanced role in ensuring the appropriate use of key facilities especially around Hodeidah.

To ensure essential aid and imports reached their destinations, restrictions must be lifted and main transport routes kept open and safe, he emphasized. A larger and faster injection of foreign exchange through the Central Bank is also urgently needed, along with expedited credit for trade and payment of pensioners and civil servants. Increased funding is needed to match the scale of the crisis. Finally, and most importantly, he called upon belligerents to seize this moment to engage fully and openly with the Special Envoy to end the conflict.

## Statements

KAREN PIERCE (<u>United Kingdom</u>) said the numbers cited by the Under-Secretary-General are horrifying. The fact that the crisis does not seem to be getting better is something the Council should take a deep interest in. Noting the number of children facing severe malnutrition, as well as the rising number of cholera cases, she welcomed the support extended by the United Arab Emirates and Saudi Arabia and highlighted the $125 million assistance package announced by the United Kingdom on World Food Day. Voicing concerns about the falling value of the Yemeni rial, rising consumer prices and the Central Bank of Yemen's struggle to pay salaries, she urged the Government to take action to stabilize the rial, and in the meantime, to pause implementation of its decree that would prevent staple goods from entering the country. Emphasizing that unhindered humanitarian access is essential to avert famine, she said the Houthis should stop interfering with the humanitarian response so that food, fuel and medicine can reach those in need in Yemen's north. Military operations must be carried out in accordance with international humanitarian law, including the protection of civilians and civilian infrastructure. Stressing that only a political settlement will allow the humanitarian situation to be properly addressed, she called on all parties to engage with the Special Envoy in good faith.

BADER ABDULLAH N. M. ALMUNAYEKH (<u>Kuwait</u>) said the deterioration of the humanitarian situation is the unavoidable result of the armed conflict which affects, first and foremost, the economy. Given the non-payment of salaries and the rial's depreciation, the international community has a responsibility to support the Yemeni Government's economic response, as well as the Special Envoy's efforts. He commended Saudi Arabia's support to the Central Bank, including a recent cash injection of $200 million, bringing the total Saudi contribution to $3.2 billion, in addition to $70 million for teachers' salaries. Pointing to the Houthis' coup against the legitimate Government in Yemen and their seizing control of all State institutions by force, he said they are refusing to cooperate with political efforts to end the crisis, as seen most recently in Geneva. That group is also seizing and looting humanitarian assistance. His country stands ready to support international efforts to prioritize a political solution based on international resolutions, despite security challenges, including the targeting of Saudi territory with ballistic missiles and other weapons. Efforts to end the crisis must stem from a political solution based on the Gulf initiative, the outcome of the national dialogue and relevant Security Council resolutions.

MA SHAOXU (<u>China</u>) said the international community should take action to alleviate the grave humanitarian situation. Parties to the conflict should create conditions for easing the humanitarian situation by abiding by international law, ceasing hostilities and ensuring humanitarian access and the transport of relief supplies. The international community should sustain humanitarian efforts and continue to provide medicine, food and other supplies in a target manner to ease the suffering of the Yemeni people. Emphasizing that the political process is fundamental for ending the conflict, he said the international community should step up support for the Special Envoy's efforts, including a sustainable negotiating process. He went on to recall the President of China's recent announcement of a fresh assistance initiative for Yemen.

ANNE GUEGUEN (France), expressing deep concern at the humanitarian situation, said that, now, more than ever, it is essential to guarantee respect for international humanitarian law, protection of civilians and humanitarian access, as well as efforts to restore the Yemeni economy. That involves nothing more than implementation of the Security Council's recent presidential statement. Protection of civilians from artillery fire, especially in densely populated cities like Hodeidah, must be guaranteed, and humanitarian workers, operating in a very dangerous environment, must be protected. Humanitarian and commercial access must also be guaranteed, with the ports of Hodeidah and Saleef staying open to receive at least food and fuel. Galloping inflation and the rial's depreciation must be contained. She appealed to the parties to engage fully with the Special Envoy to relaunch dialogue and advance the political process. Only a political solution will bring a sustainable end to the Yemeni people's suffering, she said.

KAREL JAN GUSTAAF VAN OOSTEROM (Netherlands) stated that, with 172,000 severely malnourished children and 11 million Yemenis on the brink of an entirely man-made famine, he stressed that Yemen is a clear example of the relationship between conflict and hunger. Noting that Security Council resolution 2417 (2018) commits the Council to address man-made crises with man-made solutions, he said it was unconscionable that no discernible action has been taken. He called for Houthi-affiliated militia to immediately abandon all humanitarian warehouses they have occupied for two months in Hodeidah and for the Yemeni Government to address with utmost urgency the import delays. The road connecting Hodeidah and Sana'a must also be opened. Turning to international humanitarian law, he said hostilities continue to be a major factor in the current tipping point, with shelling and air strikes killing scores of civilians and hitting hospitals and water sanitation facilities, which increases the risk of cholera. All parties are called to take urgent steps, as humanitarian actors on the ground warn that anything short of a halt to hostilities may be insufficient to avert a famine.

JOANNA WRONECKA (Poland) said that the briefing clearly shows that there is a desperate urgency to respond to the humanitarian crisis in Yemen, with the tragic plight of children of particular concern. She urged all parties to the conflict and those with influence over them to help save those children from the horrors of war and starvation. The full functioning of the port in Hodeidah must be ensured, and the effects of severe inflation reversed. Recalling the urgent steps called for in the Council statements of the past year, she said that they were still very much relevant. It is time for concrete actions to put the conflict to an end through an inclusive United Nations-led political process.

VASSILY A. NEBENZIA (Russian Federation), affirming the urgency of the humanitarian situation in Yemen, said that providing humanitarian assistance in Yemen on a non-discriminatory basis must be ensured immediately, with all ports opened and made operational and all transport unimpeded. His country will continue its unpoliticized aid, but the solution lies in the political dimension. The Council must get the parties to come to the table for that purpose. He called on all parties to show restraint and refrain from using force. The building of trust and the winding down of offensives are ways to assist the Special Envoy work. Unfortunately, the region's multiple crises have been dealt with on an ad-hoc basis, he observed, noting that his country has long proposed a new security architecture in the Middle East that would allow replacement of force and threats with peaceful resolution of conflicts.

TAYE ATSKE SELASSIE AMDE (Ethiopia), affirmed that the humanitarian situation in Yemen remained of deep concern. The port of Hodeidah must remain open and functional and the continued economic decline mitigated. Welcoming announcements of donor contributions to pay teachers' salaries, he stressed that safe and unhindered humanitarian access remains vital. He strongly appealed to all parties to exercise maximum restraint. Most urgently, a comprehensive political solution must be brought about through diplomacy that respects the sovereignty and territorial integrity of the country. The Council must strengthen its strong support for the work of the Special Envoy in that regard.

GUSTAVO MEZA-CUADRA (Peru) said the situation in Yemen, scene of the worst humanitarian crisis in the world today, reflects the Council's failure to meet its responsibilities for international peace and security and for the protection of millions of vulnerable Yemenis. Abandoning the Yemeni people will lead to extremism, and in turn, terrorism. The Houthis should be held accountable for the crimes they have committed, he said, adding that Peru is waiting for a credible investigation into the bombing of a bus in August in which tens of children died. Impunity is unacceptable, he emphasized. Noting that only one container-bearing vessel has entered the port of Hodeidah since November 2017, he said military objectives must not be a condition for humanitarian assistance and access. He reiterated Peru's support for the Special Envoy's efforts to re-establish dialogue between the parties to the conflict. Further, Council members, including those with influence, must do more to alleviate the situation. "The time to act is now and we cannot remain passive witnesses to this tragedy," he said.

OLOF SKOOG (Sweden) said it is "just staggering" that an additional 5.6 million people may face food insecurity in coming months, bringing the total number in pre-famine conditions to 14 million. To help reverse it, he called for urgent economic measures including expanding liquidity to stabilize the currency, expediting lines of credit for importers, and ensuring payment of civil servants. The food crisis is aggravated by military escalation, with conflict in Hodeidah causing casualties and also hampering aid and imports, and continued fighting on the road to Sana'a impacting the lifeline to northern Yemen. He called for a durable ceasefire, safe and unhindered humanitarian access and respect for international humanitarian law, stressing that only a negotiated political solution can end "this futile war".

NARCISO SIPACO RIBALA (Equatorial Guinea) said three years of conflict and the resulting collapse of the economy have exhausted the Yemeni people's ability to cope. The international community must urgently find a strategy to halt the fall of the rial, which has lost more than half its value since the conflict started. Parties to the conflict must refrain from actions that would block the delivery and distribution of humanitarian supplies. Noting the large number of cholera cases and fatalities, he hailed efforts led by the World Health Organization (WHO) and the United Nations Children's Fund (UNICEF), including the just-completed vaccination campaign that will hopefully halt the spread of the pandemic. He called on all parties to respect international humanitarian law, ensure the protection of civilians and civilian infrastructure, and make sure that Yemenis find a way out of the crisis. He also called on all parties to participate in the Special Envoy's efforts.

DIDAR TEMENOV (Kazakhstan) said that he strongly supports the United Nations call on all parties to safeguard civilian lives, prevent deaths and injuries, allow freedom of movement, and protect hospitals, clinics and schools, in accordance with international humanitarian and human rights law. He welcomed the coordinated efforts of stakeholders to provide aid to the people of Hodeidah and endorsed the United Nations call on all parties to refrain from the use of explosive weapons in populated areas. He underscored that all parties to the conflict should facilitate the continuation and expansion of commercial imports into all ports, including by addressing the delays linked to Government's Decree 75 and other restrictions. Presently, commercial imports through the Hodeidah and Saleef ports continue to be below the needs of the population served. He acknowledged the importance of concerted action to address distortions in the Yemeni economy, including by supporting the currency and expanding lines of credit for importers. He also urged parties to engage in good faith and without preconditions in the political process, to demonstrate flexibility and to resolve complex issues.

GBOLIÉ DESIRÉ WULFRAN IPO (Côte d'Ivoire) called on all parties to immediately cease hostilities and to resume negotiations within the framework of the Special Envoy's peace plan. Restrictions on the delivery of humanitarian assistance must also be lifted. Parties to the conflict must take ownership of the Special Envoy's peace plan, he said, inviting the Special Envoy to pursue his efforts.

JONATHAN R. COHEN (United States) said the suffering of the Yemeni people is not inevitable, but unless the fighting stops and efforts are made to stabilize the rial, that suffering will continue. The Special Envoy's efforts must succeed, but in the meantime, all parties must protect civilians and civilian infrastructure and guarantee unfettered humanitarian access. Damage to ports and other infrastructure will further drive food insecurity, he said, sharing the Under-Secretary-General's assessment that humanitarian assistance is critical for staving off the worst outcome. The United States is one of the biggest providers of humanitarian assistance to Yemen, but as the Under-Secretary-General said, "we can and must do more". He said his country is expanding non-humanitarian assistance, including by enhancing the Yemeni central bank's ability to function. He emphasized, however, that there is simply no alternative to a political solution. The suffering can only end at the negotiating table, not on the battlefield.

SACHA SERGIO LLORENTTY SOLÍZ (Bolivia), Council President for October, spoke in his national capacity, stressing that the Council cannot plead ignorance about the severity of the crisis in Yemen after repeated dire warnings, noted that it went beyond the food security crisis to encompass 16,000 civilian deaths in the fighting and many succumbing to cholera and other diseases. Military action in Yemen will not solve the problem, he said, calling on all parties to cease hostilities immediately, allow unhindered humanitarian aid and begin negotiations on a peaceful solution to the conflict under the leadership of the United Nations Special Envoy.

AHMED AWAD AHMED BINMUBARAK (Yemen) said that no reality should be imposed on the Yemeni people by the Security Council, which should implement its resolutions. His country had gone to great lengths to adhere to Council resolutions despite the Houthi assault and their subsequent refusal to participate in peace talks. The suffering of the Yemeni people is the result of a coup by an extremist militia, an agent of Iran and Hizbullah, following efforts of his Government to build a democratic State where the rights of all are protected. The militia's attacks have not spared any segment of society from killing, torture and victimization by land mines. They continue to recruit children to fight in their ranks, to assault humanitarian and aid workers, target aid vessels, to use food aid to engage fighters and to hijack fuel supplies. In addition, kidnapping and torture is being used to make money from innocent civilians.

His Government has affirmed its commitment to international human rights and humanitarian law, he said, describing Government strategies to decentralize humanitarian assistance so it can be distributed to those in need. The President has also taken measures to restore the economy through the banking system, including meeting the needs of small traders and the oil company. Actions have also been taken to neutralize the Houthi black market. In addition, he announced that measures to control credit lines will be postponed awaiting dialogue with traders to alleviate the credit situation. Calling for assistance in building up foreign currency supplies, similar to what Saudi Arabia has done, he thanked that country, the United Arab Emirates and other donors, as well as the United Nations. He called on all donors to meet the needs set out in the 2018 humanitarian appeal. He also stressed that the suffering in Yemen cannot end until the crisis caused by the Houthi coup is ended through the framework adopted by the Security Council, which must send a clear message that it will not stay silen[t] as outrages continue.

SOURCE: United Nations. "International Community Must Take Action to Stop Catastrophic Famine in Yemen, Top Humanitarian Affairs Official Tells Security Council." October 23, 2018. https://www .un.org/press/en/2018/sc13550.doc.htm.

## OTHER HISTORIC DOCUMENTS OF INTEREST

### FROM PREVIOUS *HISTORIC DOCUMENTS*

- Yemeni Rebels Fire on U.S. Ship; New Rebel Government Established, *2016*, p. 559

# Brazilian President Comments on General Election

OCTOBER 28 AND NOVEMBER 7, 2018

October 2018 saw Brazilians head to the polls for the first general election since a widespread corruption scandal ensnared dozens of politicians and led to the impeachment of former president Dilma Rousseff. The election was widely viewed as a referendum on the Workers' Party, to which Rousseff and her predecessor Luiz Inácio Lula da Silva belonged, and the political left. Voters had grown disillusioned by the many corruption scandals plaguing the Workers' Party, with just 17 percent of Brazilians expressing confidence in the national government according to a Gallup poll. Longtime legislator and far-right politician Jair Bolsonaro effectively mobilized this discontent, blaming liberals for the country's problems and taking tough stances on crime and corruption. He quickly amassed support despite his record of controversial remarks and mounted a major challenge to little-known Workers' Party candidate Fernando Haddad, ultimately securing a comfortable victory following a divisive campaign.

## Haddad and Bolsonaro Lead Crowded Field

Thirteen presidential candidates registered to participate in the first round of Brazil's general election, scheduled for October 7. However, two men soon emerged as the leading candidates.

Representing the Workers' Party was Fernando Haddad, a former education minister and São Paolo mayor. Haddad was the party's second choice for presidential candidate. Party leaders had previously selected the highly popular former president Luiz Inácio Lula da Silva, affectionately known by Brazilians as "Lula," as their candidate. Lula was arrested in April 2018 on charges of corruption and money laundering stemming from the Operation Car Wash corruption scandal involving dozens of politicians, many of whom belonged to the Workers' Party. Lula was later convicted of those crimes and is currently serving a twelve-year prison sentence. On August 31, Brazil's Superior Electoral Court rejected Lula's candidacy, prompting the party to turn to Haddad. "From now on, Haddad will be Lula for millions of Brazilians," the former president wrote in an endorsement letter from his prison cell. Since Haddad was not well known outside of São Paolo, much of his campaign focused on linking his name with Lula's. At the same time, Haddad tried to distance himself from Operation Car Wash and party members charged with corruption. He also sought to position himself as a more moderate candidate than Lula, one who was seeking gradual reforms while expanding social programs and increasing state-provided benefits, to appeal to a wider audience among Brazil's polarized electorate.

The other leading candidate was Jair Bolsonaro of the Social Liberal Party, a rightwing conservative group. Although Bolsonaro's party was relatively small and had only one seat in the Chamber of Deputies (Brazil's lower chamber of Congress), he quickly gained broad support during the campaign for strong law-and-order rhetoric and promises to crack down on crime and corruption. Bolsonaro had served in the Chamber of Deputies as a federal deputy for Rio de Janeiro since 1991 and was a former army captain. Despite his legislative and military experience, Bolsonaro's supporters generally viewed him as an outsider who could bring change to a corruption-ridden political system. His outspoken, antiestablishment style—and his avid use of social media to communicate— gave rise to the nickname "Trump of the Tropics," though some observers said a comparison to Philippine President Rodrigo Duterte would be more apt.

Even before running for president, Bolsonaro was perhaps best known for his dislike of "political correctness" and controversial remarks that disparaged women, homosexuals, and black Brazilians. He once told a female lawmaker that she was not worth sexually assaulting because she was "very ugly," for example, and claimed that having a female child was a "weakness." At other times, Bolsonaro praised Brazil's former military dictatorship, during which hundreds of people were killed or disappeared, as a "glorious period" and suggested the country should return to similar hardline tactics. He had also declared himself "in favor of torture" and said a "policeman who doesn't kill isn't a policeman." Such remarks earned him particularly strong support from the police and armed forces.

## Bitter Divisions, Violence Mark Campaign

Brazil's stagnant economy, widespread corruption, and rising crime rates created a frustrated and highly polarized electorate and led to a bitter campaign between Haddad and Bolsonaro. As tensions mounted, a wave of political violence broke out across the country. Widely reported incidents included a Bolsonaro voter killing a Haddad supporter in a bar and Bolsonaro supporters carving a swastika into the skin of a woman who was carrying an LGBT flag and wearing an anti-Bolsonaro sticker. News reports suggested that targets of political violence were primarily Haddad supporters, but Bolsonaro claimed his supporters were being hurt as well. In fact, Bolsonaro himself was stabbed during a campaign rally on September 6. According to Agência Pública, an independent journalism group, Bolsonaro supporters were the alleged attackers in fifty violent incidents between September 30 and October 10; by comparison, six incidents had Bolsonaro supporters as victims. Bolsonaro's critics blamed him for inciting the violence with his divisive and discriminatory language. They pointed to examples such as Bolsonaro's statement that he would rather have a dead son than a homosexual son, contrasted against videos of soccer fans shouting, "Bolsonaro will kill all queers" at games. Bolsonaro initially dismissed the claims, telling reporters, "A guy with my T-shirt goes too far. What has that got to do with me? I am not in control of the millions and millions of people who support me." However, Bolsonaro later tweeted that he did not want votes from those who commit violence against Brazilians who did not support him.

Another major issue during the election cycle was the spread of fake news via Facebook and WhatsApp, a messaging service offered by the social media giant. Some of the fake stories claimed that Haddad and his vice-presidential running mate, Manuela D'Ávila, wanted to "sexualize" children based on an initiative Haddad oversaw as minister of education that produced educational material intended to combat homophobia. Other common themes included that Bolsonaro planned to increase taxes on the poorest Brazilians rather than abolishing them as he had promised and that the knife attack against him was faked to drum up support. Another false report that gained significant traction in early October was that electronic voting machines had been tampered with to autocomplete votes for Haddad. Two dozen media organizations collaborated to establish a news monitoring project called Comprova, which investigated allegations of more than 100 fake news stories on WhatsApp and Facebook during the campaign and election. Those involved in the effort said it was likely misinformation was much more widespread on WhatsApp, where message encryption prevented fact checkers and electoral authorities from evaluating content. WhatsApp tried to limit the spread of fake news by restricting the number of recipients a message could be forwarded to, running public advertisements instructing Brazilians on identifying fake news, and blocking "bot" accounts. The Superior Electoral Court also took some action to address the issue, including through an October 8 order that Facebook remove links to more than thirty fake news stories about Haddad and D'Ávila. In late October, the court opened an investigation into allegations that pro-Bolsonaro companies and businessmen had been funding fake news dissemination, which would be a violation of electoral law if found to be true.

Social media platforms also provided a vehicle for the women-led anti-Bolsonaro campaign #elenao, or #nothim, in response to Bolsonaro's misogynistic comments. Women also led nationwide protests against Bolsonaro on September 29, with tens of thousands of people participating in marches in cities including São Paolo, Rio de Janeiro, and Brasilia.

## VICTORY FOR BOLSONARO

Brazil's president and vice president are chosen through a two-round electoral system. A presidential candidate must receive more than 50 percent of the overall vote to be declared the winner in the first round. If no candidate receives more than 50 percent, there is a run-off vote between the two candidates who received the most votes. The first round of voting in the 2018 general election took place on October 7. Bolsonaro received 46 percent of the first-round vote, just shy of the 50 percent threshold. Haddad came in second, with 29 percent of the vote.

The second round of voting was conducted on October 28. The Superior Electoral Court announced Bolsonaro as the winner later that evening. He received roughly 55 percent of the vote compared to Haddad's 45 percent. "We couldn't keep on flirting with communism, populism and left-wing extremism," Bolsonaro said after the results were announced. "We all knew where Brazil was heading." Calling himself a "defender of freedom," Bolsonaro said his government would protect Brazilians who "follow their duties and respect the laws." Outgoing president Michel Temer said, "The people today have exercised their power," and this was done with "all tranquility, with all harmony, with all sovereignty that the people knew how to exercise today." He also noted Bolsonaro's enthusiasm and desire for unity and harmony. Temer said the presidential transition would begin the next day, stressing the importance of working together "to maintain, to continue what we have already done."

After a meeting with the president-elect on November 7, Temer spoke of the two men's willingness "to collaborate intensely," noting that he had invited Bolsonaro to travel with him on his remaining trips abroad and pledged to work with him to identify and pass legislative priorities before the end of the year. "I think that what this political-administrative moment means, is [that it is] no longer a political-electoral moment, in which there were controversies, but a political-administrative moment, in which all Brazilians must unite, fraternally, and walk hand in hand for the prosperity of Brazil," Temer said.

Bolsonaro was sworn into office on January 1, 2019. The new president promised to build a "society without discrimination or division" and called for a "national pact" to eliminate corruption, crime, and economic mismanagement. "The national motto is order and progress. No society can develop without respecting these," he said. In a swipe at liberals, Bolsonaro said Brazil would free itself from socialism and political correctness and would "return to being a country free of ideological constrictions."

Brazilians remain sharply divided over Bolsonaro and the country's future. While his supporters celebrated his victory, others have expressed concerns about the intolerance his presidency may sow or a potential return to hardline policies. Bolsonaro will also need to negotiate an interesting legislative environment. While the Social Liberal Party now holds fifty-two seats in the Chamber of Deputies, the Workers' Party maintains the largest representation with fifty-six seats. Additionally, a record thirty political parties have seats in Congress.

—Linda Grimm

*Following are statements by former Brazilian president Michel Temer on October 28 and November 7, 2018, in response to the second-round general election results and his meeting with President-elect Jair Bolsonaro, respectively.*

# Statement by President Temer on the Second Round Election Results

**October 28, 2018**

Good evening. I want to make a brief statement regarding the election of the new President of the Federative Republic of Brazil. And the first message I want to send is exactly and precisely that the people today have exercised their power. By the way, when the elections take place, it is the right time for the people to exercise a power that is theirs. The power to say who is going to run the country. And this was done with all tranquility, with all harmony, with all sovereignty that the people knew how to exercise today.

I just greeted President-elect Jair Bolsonaro. I could see his enthusiasm, not only when he talked to me, but also when he made a statement that seeks precisely the country's unity, that seek the pacification of the country, that seek harmony in the country. It is what everyone wishes and surely I can say again, witnessing the words of the president-elect, that he will seek precisely this.

I would also like to say, at this moment, I am once again communicating to all of you that, starting tomorrow, we will begin the transition. And in the transition, regarding physical infrastructure, of course we organised the Centro Cultural Banco do Brasil and I will offer to him also, to his team, the Granja do Torto. If he wants to occupy it, he can. The transition is already practically formatted, organised. This will lead to a transition book to reveal what has been done and what still needs to be done or will continue to be done.

Especially on the economic level, we must work together to maintain, to continue what we have already done, that everyone has done. The economic policy that has prevailed in the country, in addition to other environmental, educational and health policies.

I have absolute conviction, as the president-elect has declared, that he will have, as I have already said, a government of great peace, a very harmonious government, which is what our country needs the most.

Thank you very much. . . .

*[A brief Q&A with reporters has been omitted.]*

Source: Presidency of the Republic of Brazil. "Press Statement by the President of the Republic, Michel Temer, after the Results of the Second Round Elections." October 28, 2018. http://www.brazil.gov.br/government/speeches/2018/10/press-statement-by-the-president-of-the-republic-michel-temer-after-the-results-of-the-second-round-elections.

# Statement by President Temer on Meeting with President-elect Jair Bolsonaro

**November 7, 2018**

Well, I want to address everyone to, repeating the words of president-elect Jair Bolsonaro, to say that I had the pleasure of receiving him. And, while meeting with him, we were able, naturally, to deliver to him what our government has done over these two-and-a-half years and what still remains to be done . . . and, of course, what remains to be done, for the sovereign appreciation of the President-elect.

I also added that we are here, naturally, willing to collaborate intensely. It is not only a formal collaboration, but it is a true collaboration. And I even asked his excellency, the president-elect, to send us any bills that are still pending in the Chamber of Deputies and Senate which it is in their interest to see approved. If so, we will make every effort to obtain approval. First point.

Secondly, I invited President Bolsonaro, if he can, to travel with me abroad. There are some scheduled trips. I even mentioned the G20, which will be at the end of the month. I don't know if the president can, but I told him that when he wants to, we can go abroad together.

And of course, we will also deliver, let us say, symbolically, the keys to where the cabinet will be. And on day one, on January 1st, I will be pleased to hand over to President Bolsonaro, who has conducted a wonderful election campaign . . . I shall have the pleasure, let us say, symbolically, of handing over the keys to the Planalto Palace.

President Bolsonaro was kind enough to say, as he just mentioned, that he relies on our collaboration now and eventually, if necessary, with us, with our collaboration, in directing any talks that we may have after President Bolsonaro, already elected, has taken office.

But it is with great pleasure that I received him here. And I think that what this political-administrative moment means, is [that it is] no longer a political-electoral moment, in which there were controversies, but a political-administrative moment, in which all Brazilians must unite, fraternally, and walk hand in hand for the prosperity of Brazil.

I have already seen that this is exactly and precisely the position of President-elect Bolsonaro. So let us all go forward together, for the good of the country.

Thank you for your visit.

SOURCE: Presidency of the Republic of Brazil. "Press Statement by the President of the Republic, Michel Temer, after Meeting with President-elect Jair Bolsonaro - Planalto Palace." November 7, 2018. http://www.brazil.gov.br/government/speeches/2018/11/press-statement-by-the-president-of-the-republic-michel-temer-after-meeting-with-president-elect-jair-bolsonaro-planalto-palace.

## OTHER HISTORIC DOCUMENTS OF INTEREST

### FROM PREVIOUS *HISTORIC DOCUMENTS*

# November

# Federal Officials Remark on Immigration Procedures; Supreme Court Denies Asylum Policy Stay

NOVEMBER 1 AND 9, AND DECEMBER 20 AND 21, 2018

Since he took office in January 2017, the administration of President Donald Trump has enacted multiple policies aimed at curbing illegal immigration, specifically at the U.S.–Mexico border. In November 2018, the president signed a proclamation that would deny asylum to any migrant entering the United States from Mexico illegally. Civil rights groups sued the administration in federal court, and a judge barred the proclamation from taking effect. The Trump administration sought relief from the Ninth Circuit, and while that case was pending asked the U.S. Supreme Court for a stay of the initial ruling. The Court in December denied that request. Also in December 2018, the Department of Homeland Security (DHS) announced a policy of returning illegal immigrants crossing the southern U.S. border to Mexico while they await an immigration decision. The administration said the program removed the incentive to attempt illegally immigrating to the United States, because immigrants would no longer be able to wait in the country for a court date. Immigration groups promised to challenge that policy as well.

## TRUMP ADDRESSES THE NATION ON ILLEGAL IMMIGRATION

Stemming the flow of illegal immigration into the United States was a lynchpin of Trump's campaign for president. Almost immediately after he took office, his administration began drafting policies aimed at slowing immigration and curbing potential criminals and terrorists from entering the United States. Many, including three separate iterations of a ban blocking travel from seven predominantly Muslim countries, were challenged in court. In mid-2018, public outcry grew over an administration policy known as "zero tolerance" that resulted in the separation of parents from their children at the U.S.–Mexico border. These children were subsequently housed in detention facilities, pictures of which were carried by media outlets showing some children held in cages. The president signed an executive order in June ending the separation of migrant families, and a court ordered all separated children to be reunified with their parents or another adult who could take custody of the child.

Despite public criticism and frequent legal challenges, the president's position on stopping illegal immigration into the United States was unwavering, especially as it pertained to crossings made along the U.S.–Mexico border. "Illegal immigration affects the lives of all Americans. Illegal immigration hurts American workers; burdens American taxpayers; and undermines public safety; and places enormous strain on local schools, hospitals, and communities in general, taking precious resources away from the poorest Americans who need them most," President Trump said in a November address to the nation. The president explained that his administration continued to support legal migration and that he intended only to target the illegal border crossers, who he said numbered 1,500 to 2,000 per day.

In his November address, the president expressed concern about existing U.S. immigration law and the number of immigrants arriving from Mexico who are able to claim asylum and who must have their cases heard by an immigration judge. Due to the backlog of cases, hearing these claims can take more than three years. Under previous administrations, immigrants who are not considered dangerous to national security are sometimes released into the United States to await an immigration court date at which they must appear or risk deportation. "The overwhelming majority of claims are rejected by the courts, but by that time, the alien has usually long since disappeared into our country. So they never get to see the judge. They never get to have a ruling. They don't care because they're in the country and nobody knows where they are," the president claimed. According to the Justice Department, an estimated 60 to 75 percent of nondetained immigrants do appear for their court hearings, while the remainder are decided without the migrant present. Even so, Trump said his administration would no longer allow for release into the United States while an immigration case is pending.

## Asylum Proclamation Challenged in Court

During his address to the nation, President Trump remarked on a migrant caravan that was making its way from Central America through Mexico, with the intent of crossing into the United States. According to the president, members of this caravan were offered asylum by the Mexican government but rejected it. This, the president said, "demonstrate[s] that these migrants are not legitimate asylum seekers. They're not looking for protection. Because if they were, they'd be able to get it from Mexico." But, Trump said, "they don't want to stay; they want to come into the United States. So this is no longer safety, and asylum is about safety."

In response to this caravan, on November 9, the president signed a proclamation that would temporarily suspend "the entry of certain aliens in order to address the problem of large numbers of aliens traveling through Mexico to enter our country unlawfully or without proper documentation." The intent of the proclamation was to encourage migrants seeking lawful entry into the United States to access designated ports of entry so they could be appropriately processed. Under the proclamation, those "entering through the southern border, even those without proper documentation, may, consistent with this proclamation, avail themselves of our asylum system, provided that they properly present themselves for inspection at a port of entry." But those "who enter the United States unlawfully through the southern border in contravention of this proclamation will be ineligible to be granted asylum under the regulation promulgated by the Attorney General and the Secretary of Homeland Security that became effective earlier today."

Trump's proclamation was almost immediately challenged in court by immigration groups, who said it ran contrary to immigration laws. Under previous immigration rules, a migrant was allowed to seek asylum in the United States based on a "well-founded fear of persecution" regardless of how or where he or she entered, whether illegally or legally. According to the court filing, the ports through which the Trump administration was trying to funnel migrants are limited, and those arriving could expect to wait months to file an asylum claim.

On November 19, U.S. District Judge Jon Tigar agreed that the proclamation was not in line with federal law and issued a temporary restraining order against it. The Justice Department requested a stay, saying that Tigar's ruling "jeopardizes important national interests" and would prohibit the Trump administration from addressing "a major crisis" at the U.S.–Mexico border. Tigar rejected the government's request for a stay, noting that it had "not shown that the rule is a lawful exercise of executive branch authority," nor had it addressed the harm likely to "be suffered by asylum-seekers with legitimate claims." In mid-December, with the temporary restraining order about to expire, Tigar issued a preliminary injunction preventing the Trump administration from enacting the proclamation.

The Trump administration turned to the Supreme Court, asking for a stay on Tigar's order while it appealed the ruling to the U.S. Court of Appeals for the Ninth Circuit. According to the government's petition, Tigar's order would negatively impact "a coordinated effort by the President, the Attorney General, and the Secretary to re-establish sovereign control over the southern border, reduce illegal and dangerous border crossings, and conduct sensitive and ongoing diplomatic negotiations." In a two-sentence statement on December 21, the Supreme Court rejected the government's request for a stay but noted that Justices Clarence Thomas, Samuel Alito, Neil Gorsuch, and Brett Kavanaugh all supported the government's request. By the end of 2018, the case remained pending before the Ninth Circuit and is likely to be appealed to the Supreme Court if the Trump administration does not receive a favorable ruling.

## Migrants to Await Immigration Decisions in Mexico

On December 20, Homeland Security Secretary Kirstjen Nielsen announced that her department had reached an agreement that would require asylum seekers arriving at the U.S.–Mexico border to wait in Mexico while their cases are heard. "Aliens trying to game the system to get into our country illegally will no longer be able to disappear into the United States, where many skip their court dates. Instead, they will wait for an immigration court decision while they are in Mexico. 'Catch and release' will be replaced with 'catch and return,'" Nielsen said. The administration argued that invoking the authority in Section 235(b)(2)(C) of the Immigration and Nationality Act would reduce illegal immigration because one of the incentives for migrants to come to the United States—being released into the United States while awaiting a court date—was eliminated. The decision would allow DHS to focus more on those with legitimate asylum claims and help the immigration courts better handle the 750,000 immigration cases currently before it. DHS officials expected the policy would also save money on detention and legal costs.

In what appeared to be a significant diplomatic win for the Trump administration, Nielsen said the United States had made the Mexican government aware of their decision and that Mexico had in turn agreed to "implement essential measures on their side of the border. We expect affected migrants will receive humanitarian visas to stay on Mexican soil, the ability to apply for work, and other protections while they await a U.S. legal determination." However, Roberto Velasco, a spokesperson for the Mexican Foreign Ministry, said the announcement by the Trump administration was not an agreement but rather "a unilateral move by the United States that we have to respond to." In a statement, the Foreign Ministry said it was temporarily authorizing "the entry of certain foreign persons from the United States who have entered the country through a port of entry or who have been apprehended between ports of entry, have been interviewed by the authorities of migratory control of that country, and have received a summons to appear before an immigration judge." The Mexican government did not intend to establish detention centers for the migrants awaiting an asylum decision but said those individuals would be allowed to travel freely throughout the country and provided work permits.

The announcements from Mexico and the United States contained few details about how the policy would work in practice and sowed confusion at ports of entry and in immigration courts. It is likely the DHS decision will be challenged by immigration rights groups in court.

—Heather Kerrigan

*Following is the text of an address delivered by President Donald Trump on illegal immigration and border security on November 1, 2018; the text of a November 9, 2018, proclamation on the administration's asylum policy; a press release from the Department of Homeland Security on December 20, 2018, detailing immigration procedures at the U.S.–Mexico border; and the text of a U.S. Supreme Court decision on December 21, 2018, denying the government's request for a stay in the case of* Trump v. East Bay Sanctuary Covenant.

DOCUMENT

# President Speaks with Reporters on Illegal Immigration

**November 1, 2018**

*[Footnotes have been omitted.]*

*The President.* Well, thank you very much, everyone. Appreciate it. And good afternoon. I would like to provide an update to the American people regarding the crisis on our southern border, and crisis it is.

Illegal immigration affects the lives of all Americans. Illegal immigration hurts American workers; burdens American taxpayers; and undermines public safety; and places enormous strain on local schools, hospitals, and communities in general, taking precious resources away from the poorest Americans who need them most. Illegal immigration costs our country billions and billions of dollars each year.

America is a welcoming country. And under my leadership, it's a welcoming country. We lead the world in humanitarian protection and assistance, by far. It's nobody even close. We have the largest and most expansive immigration programs anywhere on the planet.

We've issued 40 million green cards since 1970, which means the permanent residency and a path to citizenship for many, many people. But we will not allow our generosity to be abused by those who would break our laws, defy our rules, violate our borders, break into our country illegally. We won't allow it.

Mass, uncontrolled immigration is especially unfair to the many wonderful, law-abiding immigrants already living here who followed the rules and waited their turn.

Some have been waiting for many years. Some have been waiting for a long time. They've done everything perfectly. And they're going to come in. At some point, they're going to come in. In many cases, very soon. We need them to come in, because we have companies coming into our country; they need workers. But they have to come in on a merit basis, and they will come in on a merit basis.

The communities are often left to bear the cost and the influx of people that come in illegally. We can't allow that. There's a limit to how many people a nation can responsibly absorb into their societies. Every day, above and beyond our existing lawful admission programs, roughly 1,500 to 2,000 people try crossing our borders illegally.

We do a very good job considering the laws are so bad. They're not archaic, they're incompetent. It's not that they're old, they're just bad. And we can't get any Democrat votes to change them. It's only the Republicans that are in unison; they want to change them. They want to make strong borders, want to get rid of any crime because of the borders, of which there's a lot.

And we've done a great job with the laws that we have. We're moving in tremendous numbers of people to get out the MS-13 gangs and others [sic] gangs that illegally come into our country. And we're getting them out by the thousands.

But this is a perilous situation, and it threatens to become even more hazardous as our economy gets better and better. A lot of the cause of this problem is the fact that we right now have the hottest economy anywhere in the world. It's doing better than any economy in the world. Jobs, unemployment—you look at any number.

Right now we have more workers than any time in the history of our country. We have more people working, which is a tremendous statement. More people working than at any time in the history of our country. And people want to come in, and in some cases, they want to take advantage of that, and that's okay. And we want them to come in, but they have to come in through merit. They have to come in legally.

At this very moment, large, well-organized caravans of migrants are marching towards our southern border. Some people call it an "invasion." It's like an invasion. They have violently overrun the Mexican border. You saw that 2 days ago. These are tough people, in many cases. A lot of young men, strong men, and a lot of men that maybe we don't want in our country. But again, we'll find that out through the legal process.

But they've overrun the Mexican police, and they've overrun and hurt badly Mexican soldiers. So this isn't an innocent group of people. This is a large number of people that are tough. They've injured, they've attacked, and the Mexican police and military has actually suffered. And I appreciate what Mexico is trying to do.

So let me begin by stating that these illegal caravans will not be allowed into the United States, and they should turn back now, because they're wasting their time. They should apply to come into our country. We want them to come into our country very much. We need people to help us. We have all of these companies that are coming in. We've never had anything like this. We have car companies coming in. We have Foxconn— so involved with the manufacturing of Apple products—coming in in Wisconsin. We have a lot of companies coming in, but they have to apply, and they have to be wonderful people that are going to love our country and work hard.

And we've already dispatched, for the border, the United States military. And they will do the job. They are setting up right now, and they're preparing. We hope nothing happens. But if it does, we are totally prepared. Greatest military anywhere in the world, and it's going to be, and is now, in great shape. No longer depleted like it was when I took over as the President of the United States.

The Government of Mexico has generously offered asylum, jobs, education, and medical care for people within the caravan, but many members of the caravan have refused these offers, which demonstrate that these migrants are not legitimate asylum seekers. They're not looking for protection. Because if they were, they'd be able to get it from Mexico. Mexico has agreed to take them in and encouraged to stay. But they don't want to stay; they want to come into the United States. So this is no longer safety, and asylum is about safety.

Asylum is not a program for those living in poverty. There are billions of people in the world living at the poverty level. The United States cannot possibly absorb them all. Asylum is a very special protection intended only for those fleeing government persecution based on race, religion, and other protected status.

These caravans and illegal migrants are drawn to our country by Democrat-backed laws and left-wing judicial rulings. We're getting rulings that are so ridiculous, so bad. They're writing the laws. Can't do that. Collectively known as—as an example, catch-and-release. It's a disgrace that we have to put up with it.

These policies lead to the release of illegal aliens into our communities after they've been apprehended. But we're not releasing anymore. Big change, as of a couple of days ago. We're going to no longer release. We're going to catch; we're not going to release. They're going to stay with us until the deportation hearing or the asylum hearing takes place. So we're not releasing them into the community.

We have millions of people that, over the years, have been released into the community. They never show up for the trials. They never come back. They're never seen again. And those people, they know who they are. And we know a lot of where they are and who they are. And those people will be deported, directly deported.

The biggest loophole drawing illegal aliens to our borders is the use of fraudulent or meritless asylum claims to gain entry into our great country. An alien simply crosses the border illegally, finds a Border Patrol agent, and using well-coached language—by lawyers and others that stand there and—trying to get fees or whatever they can get—they're given a phrase to read. They never heard of the phrase before. They don't believe in the phrase. But they're given a little legal statement to read, and they read it. And now, all of a sudden, they're supposed to qualify. But that's not the reason they're here.

This merely asserts the need for asylum, and then often released into the United States, and they await a lengthy court process. The court process will takes [sic] years sometimes for them to attend. Well, we're not releasing them into our country any longer. They'll wait for long periods of time. We're putting up massive cities of tents. The military is helping us incredibly well.

I want to thank the Army Corps of Engineers. They've been so efficient, so good, so talented. And we have thousands of tents. We have a lot of tents; we have a lot of everything. And we're going to hold them right there. We're not letting them into our country. And then, they never show up—almost. It's, like, a level of 3 percent. They never show up for the trial. So by the time their trial comes, they're gone. Nobody knows where they are. But we know where a lot of them are, and they're going to be deported.

There are now nearly 700,000 aliens inside the United States awaiting adjudication of their claims. Most of these people we have no idea how they got there, why they got there. And the number is actually going to be a much larger number as we look at all of the data. So if you look at just at a minimal number, it's the size of Vermont, or bigger. And the overall number could be 10 million people; it could be 12 million people; it could be 20 million people. The recordkeeping from past administrations has not exactly been very good.

As human smugglers and traffickers have learned how the game is played and how to game the system, we have witnessed a staggering 1,700 [percent] increase in asylum claims since the year 2010. They understand the law better than the lawyers understand the law. You have a lot of professionalism there. You have a lot of professionalism involved with setting up the caravans. You take a look at the way that's happening. Even the countries, you look at Honduras and El Salvador, and you look at what's happening at the different levels and different countries or what's happening on the streets. There's a lot of professionalism taking place, and there seems to be a lot of money passing. And then, all of a sudden, out of the blue, these big caravans are formed, and they start marching up. They've got a long way to go.

On average, once released, an asylum case takes 3½ years to complete. Think of it. Somebody walks into our country, reads a statement given by a lawyer, and we have a 3½-year court case for one person, whereas other people tell them: "Out. Get out. Just get out." Other countries: "Get out. We have a border. Get out."

We go through years and years of litigation, because of the Democrats and the incompetent, very, very stupid laws that we have. They're the laughingstock all over the world, including the people that are marching up. They understand. But the difference is, we're not allowing them in, and we're not releasing, and we're not doing any of the things that were done for so many years that really are terrible for our country.

The overwhelming majority of claims are rejected by the courts, but by that time, the alien has usually long since disappeared into our country. So they never get to see the judge. They never get to have a ruling. They don't care because they're in the country and nobody knows where they are.

All told, there are approximately 1 million aliens who have received final orders of removal. They've actually got final orders of removal. You don't have to go to court anymore. The courts have already issued the orders of removal, and we've gotten a lot of them. But who remain at large in our country. So we're moving them out.

This endemic abuse of the asylum system makes a mockery of our immigration system, displacing legitimate asylum seekers—and there are legitimate asylum seekers—while rewarding those who abuse or defraud our system, which is almost everybody. Everybody is abusing it and just doing things to our system which were unthinkable, I'm sure even by the Democrats who were largely responsible for getting it done.

These individuals disrespect the foundations of American government by voluntarily choosing to break the law as their first act on American soil.

Furthermore, contained within this giant flow of illegal migration to our southwest border is the movement of illicit and deadly narcotics. It's in the southwest, most of it comes in. Nearly 100 percent of heroin in the United States enters through the southern border. Think of that: One-hundred percent, almost, of heroin comes in through the southern border, along with roughly 90 percent of cocaine and the majority of meth and a substantial portion of the ultralethal fentanyl killing our youth. The fentanyl is killing our youth.

These drugs destroy the lives and kill much more than 70,000 Americans every single year. And the number goes up. It goes up and up and up, because we are so foolish with our laws that we allow this to happen. A death toll equivalent of the size of an entire American city every year.

The current influx, if not halted, threatens to overwhelm our immigration system and our communities and poses unacceptable dangers to the entire Nation. We have to have our borders. Can't let drugs come in. Not just—it's not just people. It's people; it's drugs. It's human traffickers.

Human trafficking is now at the highest level in the world that it's ever been. That's because of the internet. Think of it: human trafficking. You think back 200 years, 500 years. Human trafficking, where they steal children; in many cases, women, unfortunately. They steal women. The human traffickers, the lowest scum on Earth. The lowest scum on Earth. And it's at a level that it's never been. Worldwide, never been at a level like this.

If these caravans are allowed into our country, only bigger and more emboldened caravans will follow. And you see that's what's happening now. We have one that's coming up, and it's being somewhat dissipated, as they march. But then, other people are joining it. And then, it gets bigger. And now, if you look back at Honduras, and if you look at El Salvador, other ones are solving, and they're forming. They're forming. You have new ones that are forming. And we call it "caravan number two"—is unbelievably rough people. Very, very hard for the military to stop it. Our military will have no problem. But very, very hard. Mexico is having a very, very hard time with it.

Once they arrive, the Democrat Party's vision is to offer them free health care, free welfare, free education, and even the right to vote. You and the hard-working taxpayers of our country will be asked to pick up the entire tab. And that's what's happening—medical and, in many cases, they've got some big medical problems before they get here.

No nation can allow itself to be overwhelmed by uncontrolled masses of people rushing their border. That's what's happening. They are rushing our border. They are coming up. And even before you get to the caravan, just on a daily basis, people coming in. And it's a very bad thing for our country. It's sad in many ways, but it's a very bad thing for our country and, again, costs us billions and billions and billions of dollars a year.

And I will therefore take every lawful action at my disposal to address this crisis. And that's what we're doing. The United States military, great people.

My administration is finalizing a plan to end the rampant abuse of our asylum system—it's abused—to halt the dangerous influx, and to establish control over America's sovereign borders. We've got borders. And once that control is set and standardized and made very strong—including the building of the wall, which we've already started; $1.6 billion spent last year; $1.6 billion this year. We have another $1.6 [billion] that will be coming, but we want to build it at one time. All it does is turn people in a different direction if you don't. We want to build it at one time.

Under this plan, the illegal aliens will no longer get a free pass into our country by lodging meritless claims in seeking asylum. Instead, migrants seeking asylum will have to present themselves lawfully at a port of entry. So they are going to have to lawfully present themselves at a port of entry. Those who choose to break our laws and enter illegally will no longer be able to use meritless claims to gain automatic admission into our country. We will hold them—for a long time, if necessary.

The only long-term solution to the crisis, and the only way to ensure the endurance of our Nation as a sovereign country, is for Congress to overcome "open borders" obstruction. That's exactly what it is: It's "open borders" obstruction. No votes. You can come up with the greatest border plan, the greatest immigration plan; you won't get one vote from a Democrat. They have terrible policy. In many cases, they're terrible politicians. But the one thing I give them great credit for: They vote as a bloc. They stick together.

And we will end catch-and-release. We're not releasing any longer. We also must finish the job that we started by being strong at the border. When we're strong at the border, people will turn away, and they won't bother. You will see, in a year from now, or in certainly a period of time from now, despite our very good economy, which some of them come for that—I can't blame them for that; you have to do it legally—but you will see that the numbers of people trying to get in will be greatly reduced.

But that can only happen if we're strong at the border. And the southern border is a big problem, and it's a tremendous problem for drugs pouring in and destroying our youth and, really, destroying the fabric of our country. There's never been a drug problem like we have today. And as I said, much of it comes from the southern border.

So, in the meantime, I will fulfill my sacred obligation to protect our country and defend the United States of America. And this is a defense of our country. We have no choice. We have no choice. We will defend our borders; we will defend our country.

Thank you very much.

*[A Q&A with reporters has been omitted.]*

SOURCE: Executive Office of the President. "Remarks on Illegal Immigration and Border Security and an Exchange with Reporters." November 1, 2018. *Compilation of Presidential Documents* 2018, no. 00758 (November 1, 2018). https://www.govinfo.gov/content/pkg/DCPD-201800758/pdf/DCPD-201800758.pdf.

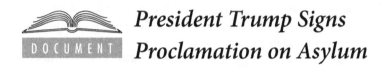

# *President Trump Signs Proclamation on Asylum*

**November 9, 2018**

*By the President of the United States of America*

*A Proclamation*

The United States expects the arrival at the border between the United States and Mexico (southern border) of a substantial number of aliens primarily from Central America who appear to have no lawful basis for admission into our country. They are traveling in large, organized groups through Mexico and reportedly intend to enter the United States unlawfully or without proper documentation and to seek asylum, despite the fact that, based on past experience, a significant majority will not be eligible for or be granted that benefit. Many entered Mexico unlawfully—some with violence—and have rejected opportunities to apply for asylum and benefits in Mexico. The arrival of large numbers of aliens will contribute to the overloading of our immigration and asylum system and to the release of thousands of aliens into the interior of the United States. The continuing and threatened mass migration of aliens with no basis for admission into the United States through our southern border has precipitated a crisis and undermines the integrity of our borders. I therefore must take immediate action to protect the national interest, and to maintain the effectiveness of the asylum system for legitimate asylum seekers who demonstrate that they have fled persecution and warrant the many special benefits associated with asylum.

In recent weeks, an average of approximately 2,000 inadmissible aliens have entered each day at our southern border. In Fiscal Year 2018 overall, 124,511 aliens were found inadmissible at ports of entry on the southern border, while 396,579 aliens were apprehended entering the United States unlawfully between such ports of entry. The great number of aliens who cross unlawfully into the United States through the southern border consumes tremendous resources as the Government seeks to surveil, apprehend, screen, process, and detain them.

Aliens who enter the United States unlawfully or without proper documentation and are subject to expedited removal may avoid being promptly removed by demonstrating, during an initial screening process, a credible fear of persecution or torture. Approximately 2 decades ago, most aliens deemed inadmissible at a port of entry or apprehended after unlawfully entering the United States through the southern border were single adults who were promptly returned to Mexico, and very few asserted a fear of return. Since then, however, there has been a massive increase in fear-of-persecution or torture claims by aliens who enter the United States through the southern border. The vast majority of such aliens are found to satisfy the credible-fear threshold, although only a fraction of the claimants whose claims are adjudicated ultimately qualify for asylum or other protection. Aliens found to have a credible fear are often released into the interior of the United States, as a result of a lack of detention space and a variety of other legal and practical difficulties, pending adjudication of their claims in a full removal proceeding in immigration court. The immigration adjudication process often takes years to complete because of the growing volume of claims and because of the need to expedite proceedings for detained aliens. During that time, many released aliens fail to appear for hearings, do not comply with subsequent orders of removal, or are difficult to locate and remove.

Members of family units pose particular challenges. The Federal Government lacks sufficient facilities to house families together. Virtually all members of family units who enter the United States through the southern border, unlawfully or without proper documentation, and that are found to have a credible fear of persecution, are thus released into the United States. Against this backdrop of near-assurance of release, the number of such aliens traveling as family units who enter through the southern border and claim a credible fear of persecution has greatly increased. And large numbers of family units decide to make the dangerous and unlawful border crossing with their children.

The United States has a long and proud history of offering protection to aliens who are fleeing persecution and torture and who qualify under the standards articulated in our immigration laws, including through our asylum system and the Refugee Admissions Program. But our system is being overwhelmed by migration through our southern border. Crossing the border to avoid detection and then, if apprehended, claiming a fear of persecution is in too many instances an avenue to near-automatic release into the interior of the United States. Once released, such aliens are very difficult to remove. An additional influx of large groups of aliens arriving at once through the southern border would add tremendous strain to an already taxed system, especially if they avoid orderly processing by unlawfully crossing the southern border.

The entry of large numbers of aliens into the United States unlawfully between ports of entry on the southern border is contrary to the national interest, and our law has long recognized that aliens who seek to lawfully enter the United States must do so at ports of entry. Unlawful entry puts lives of both law enforcement and aliens at risk. By contrast, entry at ports of entry at the southern border allows for orderly processing, which enables the efficient deployment of law enforcement resources across our vast southern border.

Failing to take immediate action to stem the mass migration the United States is currently experiencing and anticipating would only encourage additional mass unlawful migration and further overwhelming of the system.

Other presidents have taken strong action to prevent mass migration. In Proclamation 4865 of September 29, 1981 (High Seas Interdiction of Illegal Aliens), in response to an influx of Haitian nationals traveling to the United States by sea, President Reagan suspended the entry of undocumented aliens from the high seas and ordered the Coast Guard to intercept such aliens before they reached United States shores and to return them to their point of origin. In Executive Order 12807 of May 24, 1992 (Interdiction of Illegal Aliens), in response to a dramatic increase in the unlawful mass migration of Haitian nationals to the United States, President Bush ordered additional measures to interdict such Haitian nationals and return them to their home country. The Supreme Court upheld the legality of those measures in *Sale v. Haitian Centers Council, Inc.*, 509 U.S. 155 (1993).

I am similarly acting to suspend, for a limited period, the entry of certain aliens in order to address the problem of large numbers of aliens traveling through Mexico to enter our country unlawfully or without proper documentation. I am tailoring the suspension to channel these aliens to ports of entry, so that, if they enter the United States, they do so in an orderly and controlled manner instead of unlawfully. Under this suspension, aliens entering through the southern border, even those without proper documentation, may, consistent with this proclamation, avail themselves of our asylum system, provided that they properly present themselves for inspection at a port of entry. In anticipation of a large group of aliens arriving in the coming weeks, I am directing the Secretary of Homeland Security to commit additional resources to support our ports of entry at the southern border to assist in processing those aliens—and all others arriving at our ports of entry—as efficiently as possible.

But aliens who enter the United States unlawfully through the southern border in contravention of this proclamation will be ineligible to be granted asylum under the regulation promulgated by the Attorney General and the Secretary of Homeland Security that became effective earlier today. Those aliens may, however, still seek other forms of protection from persecution or torture. In addition, this limited suspension will facilitate ongoing negotiations with Mexico and other countries regarding appropriate cooperative arrangements to prevent unlawful mass migration to the United States through the southern border. Thus, this proclamation is also necessary to manage and conduct the foreign affairs of the United States effectively.

*Now, Therefore, I, Donald J. Trump,* by the authority vested in me by the Constitution and the laws of the United States of America, including sections 212(f) and 215(a) of the Immigration and Nationality Act (INA) (8 U.S.C. 1182(f) and 1185(a), respectively) hereby find that, absent the measures set forth in this proclamation, the entry into the United States of persons described in section 1 of this proclamation would be detrimental to the interests of the United States, and that their entry should be subject to certain restrictions, limitations, and exceptions. I therefore hereby proclaim the following:

*Section 1. Suspension and Limitation on Entry.* The entry of any alien into the United States across the international boundary between the United States and Mexico is hereby suspended and limited, subject to section 2 of this proclamation. That suspension and limitation shall expire 90 days after the date of this proclamation or the date on which an agreement permits the United States to remove aliens to Mexico in compliance with the terms of section 208(a)(2)(A) of the INA (8 U.S.C. 1158(a)(2)(A)), whichever is earlier.

*Sec. 2. Scope and Implementation of Suspension and Limitation on Entry.* (a) The suspension and limitation on entry pursuant to section 1 of this proclamation shall apply only to aliens who enter the United States after the date of this proclamation.

(b) The suspension and limitation on entry pursuant to section 1 of this proclamation shall not apply to any alien who enters the United States at a port of entry and properly presents for inspection, or to any lawful permanent resident of the United States.

(c) Nothing in this proclamation shall limit an alien entering the United States from being considered for withholding of removal under section 241(b)(3) of the INA (8 U.S.C. 1231(b)(3)) or protection pursuant to the regulations promulgated under the authority of the implementing legislation regarding the Convention Against Torture and Other Cruel, Inhuman or Degrading Treatment or Punishment, or limit the statutory processes afforded to unaccompanied alien children upon entering the United States under section 279 of title 6, United States Code, and section 1232 of title 8, United States Code.

(d) No later than 90 days after the date of this proclamation, the Secretary of State, the Attorney General, and the Secretary of Homeland Security shall jointly submit to the President, through the Assistant to the President for National Security Affairs, a recommendation on whether an extension or renewal of the suspension or limitation on entry in section 1 of this proclamation is in the interests of the United States.

*Sec. 3. Interdiction.* The Secretary of State and the Secretary of Homeland Security shall consult with the Government of Mexico regarding appropriate steps—consistent with applicable law and the foreign policy, national security, and public-safety interests of the United States—to address the approach of large groups of aliens traveling through Mexico with the intent of entering the United States unlawfully, including efforts to deter, dissuade, and return such aliens before they physically enter United States territory through the southern border.

*Sec. 4. Severability.* It is the policy of the United States to enforce this proclamation to the maximum extent possible to advance the interests of the United States. Accordingly:

(a) if any provision of this proclamation, or the application of any provision to any person or circumstance, is held to be invalid, the remainder of this proclamation and the application of its other provisions to any other persons or circumstances shall not be affected thereby; and

(b) if any provision of this proclamation, or the application of any provision to any person or circumstance, is held to be invalid because of the failure to follow certain procedures, the relevant executive branch officials shall implement those procedural requirements to conform with existing law and with any applicable court orders.

*Sec. 5. General Provisions.* (a) Nothing in this proclamation shall be construed to impair or otherwise affect:

(i) the authority granted by law to an executive department or agency, or the head thereof; or

(ii) the functions of the Director of the Office of Management and Budget relating to budgetary, administrative, or legislative proposals.

(b) This proclamation shall be implemented consistent with applicable law and subject to the availability of appropriations.

(c) This proclamation is not intended to, and does not, create any right or benefit, substantive or procedural, enforceable at law or in equity by any party against the United States, its departments, agencies, or entities, its officers, employees, or agents, or any other person.

*In Witness Whereof,* I have hereunto set my hand this ninth day of November, in the year of our Lord two thousand eighteen, and of the Independence of the United States of America the two hundred and forty-third.

DONALD J. TRUMP

SOURCE: Executive Office of the President. "Proclamation 9822—Addressing Mass Migration through the Southern Border of the United States." November 9, 2018. *Compilation of Presidential Documents 2018*, no. 00780 (November 9, 2018). https://www.govinfo.gov/content/pkg/DCPD-201800780/pdf/DCPD-201800780.pdf.

# DHS Announces Policy for
# U.S.–Mexico Border

**December 20, 2018**

Today, Secretary of Homeland Security Kirstjen M. Nielsen announced historic action to confront the illegal immigration crisis facing the United States. Effective immediately, the United States will begin the process of invoking Section 235(b)(2)(C) of the Immigration and Nationality Act. Under the Migration Protection Protocols (MPP), individuals arriving in or entering the United States from Mexico—illegally or without proper documentation—may be returned to Mexico for the duration of their immigration proceedings.

"Today we are announcing historic measures to bring the illegal immigration crisis under control," said Secretary Nielsen. "We will confront this crisis head on, uphold the rule of law, and strengthen our humanitarian commitments. Aliens trying to game the system to get into our country illegally will no longer be able to disappear into the United States, where many skip their court dates. Instead, they will wait for an immigration court decision while they are in Mexico. 'Catch and release' will be replaced with 'catch and return.' In doing so, we will reduce illegal migration by removing one of the key incentives that encourages people from taking the dangerous journey to the United States in the first place. This will also allow us to focus more attention on those who are actually fleeing persecution.

"Let me be clear: we will undertake these steps consistent with all domestic and international legal obligations, including our humanitarian commitments. We have notified the Mexican government of our intended actions. In response, Mexico has made an independent determination that they will commit to implement essential measures on their side of the border. We expect affected migrants will receive humanitarian visas to stay on Mexican soil, the ability to apply for work, and other protections while they await a U.S. legal determination."

## Background

Illegal aliens have exploited asylum loopholes at an alarming rate. Over the last five years, DHS has seen a 2000 percent increase in aliens claiming credible fear (the first step to asylum), as many know it will give them an opportunity to stay in our country, even if they do not actually have a valid claim to asylum. As a result, the United States has an overwhelming asylum backlog of more than 786,000 pending cases. Last year alone the number of asylum claims soared 67 percent compared to the previous year. Most of these claims are not meritorious—in fact nine out of ten asylum claims are not granted by a federal immigration judge. However, by the time a judge has ordered them removed from the United States, many have vanished.

## Process

- Aliens trying to enter the U.S. to claim asylum will no longer be released into our country, where they often disappear before a court can determine their claim's merits.

- Instead, those aliens will be processed by DHS and given a "Notice to Appear" for their immigration court hearing.

- While they wait in Mexico, the Mexican government has made its own determination to provide such individuals humanitarian visas, work authorization, and other protections. Aliens will have access to immigration attorneys and to the U.S. for their court hearings.

- Aliens whose claims are upheld by U.S. judges will be allowed in. Those without valid claims will be deported to their home countries.

**Anticipated Benefits**

- As we implement, illegal immigration and false asylum claims are expected to decline.

- Aliens will not be able to disappear into U.S. before court decision.

- More attention can be focused on more quickly assisting legitimate asylum-seekers, as fraudsters are disincentivized from making the journey.

- Precious border security personnel and resources will be freed up to focus on protecting our territory and clearing the massive asylum backlog.

- Vulnerable populations will get the protection they need while they await a determination in Mexico.

SOURCE: U.S. Department of Homeland Security. "Secretary Kirstjen M. Nielsen Announces Historic Action to Confront Illegal Immigration." December 20, 2018. https://www.dhs.gov/news/2018/12/20/secretary-nielsen-announces-historic-action-confront-illegal-immigration.

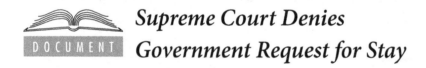

# Supreme Court Denies Government Request for Stay

**December 21, 2018**

(ORDER LIST: 586 U.S.)

FRIDAY, DECEMBER 21, 2018

ORDER IN PENDING CASE

18A615    TRUMP, PRESIDENT OF U.S., ET AL. V. E. BAY SANCTUARY COV., ET AL.

The application for stay presented to Justice Kagan and by her referred to the Court is denied.

Justice Thomas, Justice Alito, Justice Gorsuch, and Justice Kavanaugh would grant the application for stay.

SOURCE: Supreme Court of the United States. *Trump v. East Bay Sanctuary Covenant.* 586 U.S. ___ (2018). https://www.supremecourt.gov/orders/courtorders/122118zr_986b.pdf.

## OTHER HISTORIC DOCUMENTS OF INTEREST

### FROM THIS VOLUME

### FROM PREVIOUS *HISTORIC DOCUMENTS*

# Donald Trump and Nancy Pelosi Respond to Midterm Elections

NOVEMBER 7, 2018

On November 6, 2018, voters across the country went to the polls to elect all 435 members of the House of Representatives, thirty-five senators, thirty-six governors, and thousands of other state and local leaders. Nationally, Democrats won back control of the House, but in the Senate, Republicans were able to expand their majority by two seats. A divided Congress all but ensured that the gridlock plaguing Washington would continue. In the states, voters became increasingly entrenched in their partisan preferences, with Republicans maintaining their hold on a majority of governorships and state legislative chambers.

## DEMOCRATS WIN CONTROL OF HOUSE, REPUBLICANS MAINTAIN SENATE

Democrats were the heavy favorite to win back control of the House of Representatives in the 2018 midterm elections, with political news website FiveThirtyEight.com giving the party an 85 percent chance of gaining control in the days heading into the election. Those predictions proved correct, with Democrats taking 235 seats and the Republicans 199. Nearly 60 million Americans voted for House Democrats during the midterm, according to FiveThirtyEight's founder Nate Silver, which was high even for a wave election year. The Democratic vote was driven by a number of factors, including discontent with the current administration of President Donald Trump, an anti-incumbent sentiment even within the party, and enthusiasm for the record number of women seeking a House seat.

One of the most talked-about House races was in New York's 14th Congressional District, where Alexandria Ocasio-Cortez defeated ten-term incumbent and Democratic Caucus Chair Joe Crowley during the state's Democratic primary on June 26. She went on to easily defeat her Republican challenger in November. At twenty-nine years old, Ocasio-Cortez was the youngest woman ever elected to Congress. North Carolina's 9th District also drew nationwide attention, albeit after the election took place. The district's Republican incumbent lost in the primary to Mark Harris, a pastor. Democrats selected businessman Dan McCready in their primary. Although the district leans Republican, the Democratic Congressional Campaign Committee considered it a possible pickup for Democrats. When the votes were tallied on November 6, it appeared that Harris was ahead by fewer than 1,000 votes. But because of a number of allegations of voter fraud, the state's Board of Elections refused to certify the results. An investigation accused a Harris operative of directing the illegal collection of absentee ballots from voters. (State law only allows for the voter or a close relative to mail an absentee ballot.) Harris denied any knowledge of the wrongdoing and called for a new election, which the Board of Elections agreed to in February 2019.

In the Senate, Democrats did not have a clear path to victory. They were defending twenty-six of the thirty-five seats up for election, and many were in states that voted for Trump in 2016. Among the most closely watched Senate races were those in North Dakota and Texas. In North Dakota, the Democratic incumbent, Sen. Heidi Heitkamp, was up against Republican Kevin Cramer. Heitkamp won her seat in 2012, by less than a percentage point. Cramer was a popular member of the House, where he had served since 2013. FiveThirtyEight.com considered the state the fourth most Republican in the country, and it voted for Trump 63 percent to Democratic challenger Hillary Clinton's 27 percent in the 2016 presidential election. Few polls showed Heitkamp in the lead ahead of election day, and her vote against Supreme Court nominee Judge Brett Kavanaugh all but sealed her fate. Heitkamp was defeated 55.5 percent to 44.5 percent. In Texas, Sen. Ted Cruz faced off against Rep. Beto O'Rourke, a rising Democratic star who was frequently compared to former president Barack Obama. Texas had not elected a Democrat in a statewide race since 1994, so the fact that Cruz was facing a legitimate challenge was itself surprising. O'Rourke was drawing record crowds around the state, particularly in college towns, and raised an unprecedented amount of money as a Democrat in Texas, especially one who rejected money from political action committees. Texas has the lowest midterm turnout rate in the nation, and O'Rourke sought to drive the state's young voting population to the polls. Cruz, who drew on support from the president, called O'Rourke out of touch and touted his own record in Congress supporting Texans. Ultimately, Cruz defeated O'Rourke 50.9 percent to 48.3 percent. Republicans would go on to hold onto the Senate, with fifty-three seats to the Democrats' forty-five. (There are two Independent members of the Senate, both of whom caucus with the Democrats.)

The 116th Congress would be the most diverse in history. A record 131 women—116 in the House and 15 in the Senate—would serve in the new Congress. A total of 34 percent of incoming House Democrats are people of color, and the average age of the body is forty-seven, a full decade younger than the 115th Congress. Two members—Deb Haaland of New Mexico and Sharice Davids of Kansas—would be the first Native American women to serve in Congress. Ilhan Omar of Minnesota and Rashida Tlaib of Michigan would be the first Muslim women in Congress; the pair were also the first Somali American and Palestinian American in Congress, respectively. A number of states also had historic firsts, with Iowa sending its first women to the House, Texas its first Hispanic women, and Massachusetts its first black congresswoman. Both the Hispanic and Black caucuses would have their largest delegations ever in the 116th Congress, at thirty-nine and fifty-five members, respectively.

## Trump, Pelosi Celebrate Victories, Call for Bipartisanship

President Trump held a press conference on November 7 to address the election outcomes. He spent the bulk of his remarks focused on gains in the Senate, noting, "It was a big day yesterday, an incredible day. And last night the Republican Party defied history to expand our Senate majority while significantly beating expectations in the House." Trump said that the two-seat pickup in the Senate was the biggest gain for the president's party in a midterm election during the president's first term in office since 1962. Trump called the pickup in the Senate a repudiation of how Democrats handled the hearings and confirmation of Supreme Court Justice Kavanaugh. He added that those Republican candidates who embraced the Trump administration's "message of low taxes, low regulations, low crime, strong borders, and great judges excelled last night," while those who chose to shy away from the president "did very poorly."

House Minority Leader Nancy Pelosi, who was widely expected to reprise her role as Speaker of the House in the new Congress, spoke to the press about the Democratic victories on November 7. "It's a great day for the American people," she said, explaining that "Americans elected an extraordinary class of dynamic and diverse Democratic candidates, Members-Elect who reflect their districts and who embody the bountiful diversity of our nation." According to Pelosi, the focus of Democratic candidates on health care was key to their victory. Pelosi said Democrats embraced that as a central component of their campaign "because we knew how important health care is, not only to the good health of families, but to the financial well-being of their families." The result, Pelosi said, was "a resounding verdict against congressional Republicans' attacks on Medicare, Medicaid, and the Affordable Care Act, and people with pre-existing conditions in districts everywhere in America." Pelosi noted that the ability of Democrats to retake the House was also driven by a desire among voters "to restore the health of our democracy." She added, "The American people . . . want to put an end to unchecked GOP control of Washington, restoring again the checks and balances envisioned by our Founders."

Both Trump and Pelosi called for greater unity between the two parties heading into 2019. "Hopefully, we can all work together next year to continue delivering for the American people, including on economic growth, infrastructure, trade, lowering the cost of prescription drugs," Trump said, adding, "Now is the time for members of both parties to join together, put partisanship aside, and keep the American economic miracle going strong." Pelosi noted that when Democrats controlled the House during the presidency of George W. Bush, they were able to work with the White House to pass major legislation on issues including taxes and the environment. "Over the years, we've been able to work together regionally, bipartisan across the aisle, across the Capitol and down Pennsylvania Avenue. I hope that we can do that because we want to create jobs from sea to shining sea," Pelosi said.

## REPUBLICANS REIGN SUPREME IN STATE-LEVEL RACES

Voters were not just selecting members of Congress in the 2018 midterm elections; they also chose their own state legislators, governors, secretaries of state, and other state- and local-level positions. In the states, the 2018 election outcomes were an affirmation of entrenched partisan preference, with Democrats doing well where they were already the dominant party and Republicans performing similarly with their base. When the votes were counted, Democrats gained seven governorships and six legislative chambers, but Republicans maintained their dominance, holding a majority of governorships and almost two-thirds of all state legislative chambers. According to the National Conference of State Legislatures, for the first time since 1914, all but one partisan state legislature was controlled by a single party. Only Minnesota had a split legislature, with Democrats in control of the state House and Republicans controlling the Senate. (Nebraska has a unicameral, nonpartisan legislature.) President Trump celebrated the Republican victories. "We have four Governors' races crucial to 2020 and the Presidential race: Florida, Iowa, Ohio, and Georgia. The big ones. . . . Can't get much more important than that. They were incredible. They were actually incredible campaigns too." He added, "Republicans will control the majority of Governorships across the country, including three great women who worked very hard: the Governors of Alabama, South Dakota, and Iowa. They worked very, very hard. And they're very talented."

The most-watched races in the states were in the south in Georgia and Florida. In Georgia, Republican Secretary of State Brian Kemp ran against Democrat Stacey Abrams, a former minority leader of the state House. If elected, Abrams would have become the first black female governor in the country. Kemp drew criticism throughout the race for retaining his position as secretary of state, overseeing an election in which he was also a candidate. The race drew a spate of lawsuits alleging voter suppression because more than 3,000 voters were incorrectly flagged by the state's voter registration system as noncitizens, while tens of thousands of registrations were improperly put on hold. Both instances disproportionally impacted the state's African American population. Ultimately, Abrams fell nearly 55,000 votes short of Kemp, too large a margin for an automatic recount. In a speech, Abrams said hers was not a true concession "because concession means to acknowledge an action is right, true, or proper." Criticizing Kemp for using his position to suppress voters, Abrams said, "More than 200 years into Georgia's democratic experiment, the state failed its voters." She added, "eight years of systemic disenfranchisement, disinvestment and incompetence had its desired effect on the electoral process in Georgia."

In neighboring Florida, former Republican member of Congress Ron DeSantis faced off against Andrew Gillum, the Democratic mayor of Tallahassee. On election night, Gillum conceded defeat, although by a narrow margin, but a week later, he withdrew his concession after the secretary of state announced that the race was close enough to trigger an automatic recount. Gillum, who would have become the first black governor of Florida if elected, was ultimately defeated by around 34,000 votes when the results were certified in mid-November.

Wisconsin stood out as a bright spot for Democrats on election night. The state's Republican incumbent governor, Scott Walker, was defeated by Tony Evers, the state superintendent of public education, by just more than one percentage point. In the lame-duck session between November 6 and the end of the year, the Republican-led Wisconsin legislature passed a series of bills that were signed by Walker limiting the power of the incoming governor and attorney general. The new laws, similar to those considered by both Democratic and Republican majorities in other states, weakened the governor's rulemaking authority and temporarily gave the Republican-controlled legislature the ability to make most appointments on an economic development board. The laws also gave the legislature the power to decide whether to withdraw Wisconsin from lawsuits, a move aimed at preventing the new Democratic attorney general from removing Wisconsin from a nationwide lawsuit challenging the Affordable Care Act. Democratic groups filed a lawsuit against the series of lame-duck laws in January 2019.

—Heather Kerrigan

*Following is the text of a press conference given by President Donald Trump on November 7, 2018, regarding the outcome of the midterm elections; and remarks delivered by House Minority Leader Nancy Pelosi, also on November 7, 2018, on the Democrats regaining control of the House.*

# President Trump Responds to Midterm Elections

November 7, 2018

*The President.* Thank you. Thank you very much. Please, thank you.

It was a big day yesterday, an incredible day. And last night the Republican Party defied history to expand our Senate majority while significantly beating expectations in the House for the midtown—and midterm year. We did this in spite of a very dramatic fundraising disadvantage driven by Democrats' wealthy donors and special interests and very hostile media coverage, to put it mildly. The media coverage set a new record and a new standard.

We also had a staggering number of House retirements. So it's a little tough. These are seats that could've been held pretty easily, and we had newcomers going in, and a lot of them worked very hard. But it's very difficult when you have that many retirements.

We held a large number of campaign rallies with large, large numbers of people going to every one—to the best of my knowledge, we didn't have a vacant or an empty seat; I'm sure you would have reported it if you spotted one—including 30 rallies in the last 60 days. And we saw the candidates that I supported achieve tremendous success last night.

As an example, of the 11 candidates we campaigned with during the last week, 9 won last night. This vigorous campaigning stopped the blue wave that they talked about. I don't know if there ever was such a thing, but could've been. If we didn't do the campaigning, probably, there could've been. And the history really will see what a good job we did in the final couple of weeks in terms of getting some tremendous people over the finish line. They really are tremendous people, but many of them were not known. But they will be known.

This election marks the largest Senate gains for a President's party in a first midterm election since at least President Kennedy's in 1962. There have been only four midterm elections since 1934 in which a President's party has gained even a single Senate seat. As of now, we picked up, it looks like, three. Could be four. Perhaps it could be two. But we picked up a lot. And most likely, the number will be three. You people probably know that better than I do at this point, because you've looked at the more recent numbers.

Fifty-five is the largest number of Republican Senators in the last 100 years. In the last 80 years, a sitting President's party has only gained a cumulative total of eight Senate seats, averaging one per decade. So if we picked up two, three, or four, that's a big percentage of that number. So in the last 80 years—you think of that—only eight seats.

In President Obama's first midterm election, he lost six Senate seats, including in the deep-blue State of Massachusetts. Republicans captured at least four Senate seats held by Democrat incumbents. And these are tremendously talented, hard-working people that did this: Indiana, North Dakota, Florida, Missouri. We also won two open Senate seats in Tennessee—I want to congratulate our great champion who did such a great job in Tennessee, Marsha—and in Utah. And Arizona is looking very good. Really, very good. She's done a terrific job. That was a tough race, and she's done a fantastic job.

In each of these open seats, Democrats recruited very strong candidates with substantial fundraising and media support. We were getting bombarded with money on the other side.

In the House, Republicans dramatically outperformed historical precedence and overcame a historic number of retirements, the most House Republican retirements in 88 years; 43 House Republicans retired.

Now, I will say this—that, in many cases, they were chairmen of committees, and they left because they weren't chairmen, because the Republicans have a rule—for 6 years. And what that does is wonderful in one way; it lets people come through the system and become chairman. And in another way, it drives people out. Because when they're a chairman, they don't want to go and not be a chairman. You're the chairman of a committee, and you're a big deal, and all of a sudden, you're not doing that anymore. So they leave. We had a lot of them leave. It's—I guess you can flip a coin as to which system is better. The Democrats do the other. Some of their folks have been on these committees for a long time as chairman.

In 2010, President Obama's first midterm, he lost 63 seats. By contrast, as of the most current count, it looks like around 27 House seats or something. And we'll figure that out pretty soon.

We also had a slew of historic wins in the Governors' races—the Governors' races were incredible—against very well-funded, talented, and skilled Democrat candidates and people that worked very, very hard, respectfully, for those candidates, like Oprah Winfrey, who I like. *[Laughter]* I don't know if she likes me anymore, but that's okay. She used to. But she worked very hard in Georgia. Very, very hard.

And if you look at them, we have four Governors' races crucial to 2020 and the Presidential race: Florida, Iowa, Ohio, and Georgia. The big ones: Florida, Iowa, Ohio, and Georgia. Can't get much more important than that. They were incredible. They were actually incredible campaigns too. Incredible.

As of right now, Republicans will control the majority of Governorships across the country, including three great women who worked very hard: the Governors of Alabama, South Dakota, and Iowa. They worked very, very hard. And they're very talented.

By expanding our Senate majority, the voters have also clearly rebuked the Senate Democrats for their handling of the Kavanaugh hearings. That was a factor, I think maybe a very big factor. The way that was handled, I think, was—tremendous energy was given to the Republican Party by the way they treated then-Judge Kavanaugh, now Justice Kavanaugh. And expressed their support for confirming more great pro-Constitution judges.

Candidates who embraced our message of low taxes, low regulations, low crime, strong borders, and great judges excelled last night. They excelled. They really—I mean, we have a list of people that were fantastic, and I'm just going to point them out: Mike Bost; Rodney Davis; Andy Barr was fantastic. I went to Kentucky—for the most part, I didn't campaign for the House, but I did actually make a special trip for Andy Barr because he was in a very tough race in Kentucky, and he won. That was a very tough race. The polls were all showing that he was down and down substantially. And he won. And that one I did do. Pete Stauber of Minnesota, great guy; he's new and ran a fantastic race.

On the other hand, you had some that decided to "let's stay away." "Let's stay away." They did very poorly. I'm not sure that I should be happy or sad, but I feel just fine about it. Carlos Curbelo; Mike Coffman—too bad, Mike. *[Laughter]* Mia Love. I saw Mia Love. She'd call me all the time to help her with a hostage situation, being held hostage in Venezuela. But Mia Love gave me no love—*[laughter]*—and she lost. Too bad. Sorry about that, Mia. *[Laughter]*

And Barbara Comstock was another one. I mean, I think she could have won that race, but she didn't want to have any embrace. For that, I don't blame her. But she lost, substantially lost. Peter Roskam didn't want the embrace. Erik Paulsen didn't want the embrace. And in New Jersey, I think he could have done well, but didn't work out too good. Bob Hugin, I feel badly because I think that's something that could have been won. That's a race that could have been won. John Faso.

Those are some of the people that, you know, decided for their own reason not to embrace, whether it's me or what we stand for. But what we stand for meant a lot to most people. And we've had tremendous support and tremendous support in the Republican Party. Among the biggest support in the history of the party. I've actually heard, at 93 percent, it's a record. But I won't say that, because who knows. But we've had tremendous support.

America is booming like never before, doing fantastic. We have Larry Kudlow here, and he said the numbers are as good as he's ever seen—numbers—at any time for our country. But he's a young man, so he hasn't seen that many numbers. *[Laughter]* Where's Larry? You're a young man, right, Larry? And you haven't been doing this too long, but they're as good as you've ever seen. And we may have—if you have a question for Larry, we'll do that.

But I want to send my warmest appreciation in regards to Majority Leader Mitch McConnell. We really worked very well together. We have been working very well together. We actually have a great relationship. People just don't understand that, which is fine.

And also to, perhaps—it looks like, I would think—Speaker Nancy Pelosi. And I give her a lot of credit. She works very hard, and she's worked long and hard. I give her a great deal of credit for what she's done and what she's accomplished.

Hopefully, we can all work together next year to continue delivering for the American people, including on economic growth, infrastructure, trade, lowering the cost of prescription drugs. These are some of things that the Democrats do want to work on, and I really believe we'll be able to do that. I think we're going to have a lot of reason to do it.

And I will say, just as a matter of business, I was with some very successful people last night. We were watching the returns. So if the Republicans won—and let's say we held on by two or one or three—it would've been very hard out of that many Republicans to ever even get support among Republicans, because there will always be one or two or three people that, for a good reason or for a bad reason or for grandstanding—we have that too; you've seen that. You've seen that. Plenty of grandstanding. But for certain reasons, that many people, you're always going to have a couple that won't do it. So that puts us in a very bad position.

In other words, had we kept it, and this is no—I'm saying this for a very basic reason; it's common sense—it puts us in a very tough position. We win by one or two or three, and you'll have one or two or three or four or five, even, come over and say, you know: "Look, we're not going to along with this. We want this, this, this." And all of a sudden, we can't even—we wouldn't even be able to get it, in many cases, out of the Republicans' hands before we sent it on to the Senate.

And now we have a much easier path, because the Democrats will come to us with a plan for infrastructure, a plan for health care, a plan for whatever they are looking at, and we'll negotiate. And as you know, it's been very hard in the Senate, because we need, essentially, 10 votes from Democrats, and we don't get those votes. Because the Democrats do really stick together well. I don't agree with them on a lot of policy, but I agree with them on sticking together. They stick together great.

So now we go into the Senate. We don't have the 10 votes. And what happens? It doesn't get passed. Even if it gets out of the House, it doesn't get passed. So under the new concept of what we're doing, I say: "Come on. Let me see what you have." They want to do things. You know, I keep hearing about investigations fatigue. Like from the time—almost from the time I announced I was going to run, they've been giving us this investigation fatigue. It's been a long time. They've got nothing. Zero. You know why? Because there is nothing.

But they can play that game, but we can play it better. Because we have a thing called the United States Senate. And a lot of very questionable things were done between leaks of classified information and many other elements that should not have taken place. And all you're going to do is end up in back and forth and back and forth. And 2 years is going to go up, and we won't have done a thing.

I really think, and I really respected what Nancy said last night about bipartisanship and getting together and uniting. She used the word "uniting" and she used the bipartisanship statement, which is so important, because that's what we should be doing. So we can look at us, they can look at us, and then we can look at them, and it'll go back and forth. And it'll probably be very good for me politically. I could see it being extremely good politically, because I think I'm better at that game than they are, actually. *[Laughter]*

But we'll find out. I mean, you know, we'll find out. Or we can work together. You can't do them simultaneously, by the way. Just think if somebody said, "Oh, you can do them both." No, you can't. Because if they're doing that, we're not doing the other, just so you understand. So we won't be doing that.

But now what happens is, we send it to the Senate, and we'll get a hundred-percent Democrat support, and we'll get some Republican support. And if it's good, I really believe we have Republicans that will help with the approval process, and they will really help with the approval process.

So it really could be a beautiful bipartisan type of situation. If we won by one or two or three or four or five, that wouldn't happen. And the closer it is, the worse it is. This way, they'll come to me, we'll negotiate. Maybe we'll make a deal, maybe we won't. That's possible. But we have a lot of things in common on infrastructure.

We want to do something on health care; they want to do something on health care. There are a lot of great things that we can do together. And now we'll send it up, and we will really get—we'll get the Democrats, and we'll get the Republicans, or some of the Republicans. And I'll make sure that we send something up that the Republicans can support, and they're going to want to make sure they send something up that the Democrats can support.

So our great country is booming like never before, and we're thriving on every single level, both in terms of economic and military strength; in terms of development. In terms of GDP, we're doing unbelievably.

I will tell you, our trade deals are coming along fantastically. The USMCA and South Korea is finished. USMCA has gotten rave reviews. Not going to lose companies anymore to other countries. They're not going to do that, because they have a tremendous economic incentive; it's—meaning, it's prohibitive for them to do that. So it's not going to be like NAFTA, which is one of the worst deals I've ever seen—although we've made some other pretty bad ones too.

Now is the time for members of both parties to join together, put partisanship aside, and keep the American economic miracle going strong. It is a miracle. We're doing so well. And I've said it at a lot of rallies. Some of you have probably heard it so much you don't want to hear it again. But when people come to my office—Presidents, Prime Ministers—they all congratulate me, almost the first thing, on what we've done economically. Because it is really amazing.

And our steel industry is back. Our aluminum industry is starting to do really well. These are industries that were dead. Our miners are working again.

We must all work together to protect our military—we have to do that—to support our law enforcement, secure our borders, and advance really great policy, including environmental policy. We want crystal-clean water. We want beautiful, perfect air. Air and water, it has to be perfect.

At the same time, we don't want to put ourselves at a disadvantage to other countries who are very competitive with us and who don't abide by the rules at all. We don't want to hurt our jobs. We don't want to hurt our factories. We don't want companies leaving. We want to be totally competitive, and we are.

And right now we have just about the cleanest air, the cleanest water we've ever had, and it's always going to be that way. We insist on it. So environmental is very important to me.

*[A Q&A with reporters present at the event has been omitted.]*

SOURCE: Executive Office of the President. "The President's News Conference." November 7, 2018. *Compilation of Presidential Documents 2018*, no. 00771 (November 7, 2018). https://www.govinfo.gov/content/pkg/DCPD-201800771/pdf/DCPD-201800771.pdf.

# *Minority Leader Pelosi on Midterm Victories*

**November 7, 2018**

<u>Leader Pelosi.</u> Good afternoon, everyone. And a good afternoon it is. It's a great day for the American people.

The biggest winner yesterday was the health care for American people, for our seniors, and hard-working American families. Health care was on the ballot, and health care won.

Yesterday, Americans elected an extraordinary class of dynamic and diverse Democratic candidates, Members-Elect who reflect their districts and who embody the bountiful diversity of our nation.

Women led the way to victory with at least 30 new women coming to the Congress. Is that not exciting? And there are still some races that are not finalized yet, so there could be more.

Democrats also secured big wins in the governorships across the country. And while it is my responsibility to win the House for the Democrats, the winning of governorships is essential, essential to good policy in our country and open elections and the rest.

So victories in Wisconsin, Illinois, Kansas, Maine, Michigan, New Mexico and Nevada. We are very proud in New Mexico that our colleague, Michelle Lujan Grisham, is now the Governor. In Colorado, Jared Polis is now the Governor, our current colleague, even though that's replacing a Democratic Governor, great Governor, Governor Hickenlooper, so that wasn't a pickup, but it is a Democratic Member there. Tim Walz in Minnesota, our colleague, again, winning in Minnesota.

So, for us, seeing the extraordinary leadership of eight Members going into Governors' offices, seeing an increased number of Democratic governorships, it was a great night for the American people.

We won because from the beginning we focused on health care. Two years ago today, the day after the election, not the same date, but the same day after the election, everyone came together and said we see the urgency, we want to take responsibility, and that gave us opportunity to protect the Affordable Care Act. That was so essential to the health and financial security of America's working families, and we knew it would be a target of the Trump Administration.

So just so you know, that by that Sunday, we had mobilized many of the groups outside. They were self-mobilized as well, but we all came together, depending on where we might be on the spectrum in other issues, to say this was our focus.

We made a plan to launch our campaign on the weekend of Martin Luther King Day. You know when that is, in January. And we did. After the President's inauguration, as you know, something historic happened in our country, the Women's March. And much of that was about health care, women's reproductive health. Health care, the beat goes on.

Over the course of that next year and a half, working with the outside groups—and they deserve a great deal of credit—and I'm proud of our Democratic unity in the Congress of the United States and our inside maneuvering. That unity was essential to the clarity of our message and our differentiation from the Republicans on that subject. But working together, voting together, we were able to make our case.

The outside groups, and we participated in some of this, but the outside groups had 10,000 events across the country speaking out about the risks that were involved in the Republican policy in terms of health care in our country, their assaults on Medicare, Medicaid, their assaults on the benefit of a pre-existing medical condition being taken away, all of that, so much more. The issue about the cost of prescription drugs, all of those issues by groups, coalitions, Protect Our Care, Little Lobbyists, patient advocacy groups across the country, labor unions, veterans, the list goes on and on, so many people who were involved in that leading up to this being on the ballot.

And some of you have said to me, how did this emerge as the issue in the campaign? My answer is, we made our own environment because we knew how important health care is, not only to the good health of families, but to the financial well-being of their families, health care costs being such a major assault on their economic security.

It was, and when we put together our For the People agenda, our first priority was to lower health care costs by lowering the cost of prescription drugs. Leader Mitch McConnell went forth and really admitted that Medicare and Medicaid and some aspects of Social Security disability benefits were on the chopping block. The President pulled his punch when it came time to lowering the cost of prescription drugs by enabling the Secretary [of HHS] to negotiate for that.

So this is very important. That was For the People, lower health care costs, bigger paychecks by building the infrastructure of America, integrity in government by reducing the role of big dark money in the political spectrum. That was our agenda. Our candidates ran with it. But health care, health care, health care in every household in America is an important issue.

The man whose office I occupy now, Speaker Tip O'Neill, he said all politics is local. When it comes to health care, all politics is personal.

And so, again, we made our own environment. While the GOP tried relentlessly to distract and divide, our candidates kept their focus on that subject. When I say 'our candidates,' our candidates for reelection as well.

Voters delivered a resounding verdict against congressional Republicans' attacks on Medicare, Medicaid, and the Affordable Care Act, and people with pre-existing conditions in districts everywhere in America. They want new direction, a House that will—now they want a new direction, a House that will work to make progress in the lives of America's families and seniors.

Democrats pledge, again, a new majority, our For the People agenda, lower health care costs, lower prescription drugs, bigger paychecks, building infrastructure, clean up corruption to make America work for the American people's interest, not the special interests.

Yesterday's election was not only a vote to protect America's health care. It was a vote to restore the health of our democracy. The health of our democracy. Under the Constitution, I'm proud that the legislative branch is Article I, the first branch of government, the legislative branch, right after that beautiful preamble stating our purpose, Article I, the legislative branch. It is there as a co-equal branch of the other branches of government and a check and balance on other branches of government.

The American people had put want to put an end to unchecked GOP control of Washington, restoring again the checks and balances envisioned by our Founders. That's a responsibility we have when we take that oath to protect and defend the Constitution, and we, as Democrats, are here to strengthen the institution in which we serve and not to have it be a rubber stamp for President Trump.

House Democrats will honor our responsibility to the Constitution, as I said, have a conscience. How we will open, how we will do things, we will open the Congress with a rule that will insist upon openness and transparency so that the American people can see the impact of public policy on their lives, putting an end to what the Republicans did with their tax scam in the dark of night, the speed of light, no hearings on a bill that would have trillions of dollars of impact on our economy. That's over.

We will strive in that openness with the American people as our partners because they will see the impact of legislation on their lives. We will strive for bipartisanship. We believe that we have a responsibility to seek common ground where we can. Where we cannot, we must stand our ground, but we must try. And so openness and transparency, accountability, bipartisanship, a very important part of how we will go forward.

We believe that's the responsibility we have to honor the vision of our Founders. They gave us in their Declaration a call for life, liberty, and the pursuit of happiness. How beautiful. They also gave us guidance on how to achieve that: E Pluribus Unum, from many, one. They couldn't imagine how many there would be or how different we would be from each other, but they knew that we had to strive for oneness.

Recognizing that this is a marketplace of ideas, we have different views on the role of government, and that's a healthy debate for the American people to witness and for us to have. We do so with confidence in our values and our proposals, but also with humility to listen and hear what others may have to say. And so that will be the kind of Congress that we have, one again that honors the guidance of E Pluribus Unum.

Last night, I had a conversation with President Trump about how we could work together. One of the issues that came up was part of our For the People agenda, building the infrastructure of America, and I hope that we can achieve that. He talked about it during his campaign, and, really, didn't come through with it in his first two years in office, but that issue has not been a partisan issue in the Congress of the United States.

Over the years, we've been able to work together regionally, bipartisan across the aisle, across the Capitol and down Pennsylvania Avenue. I hope that we can do that because we want to create jobs from sea to shining sea. We want good paying jobs, whether it's about surface transportation, water systems, my colleague Congressman Eshoo is here, a champion on broadband, always on high-speed broadband across America to end the digital divide, especially into rural areas as well as urban areas, and then in schools, housing, and the rest.

Those jobs, those initiatives will create good paying jobs but will also generate other economic growth in their regions. So we hope that we can work in a bipartisan way in that way.

The other issue that we could hopefully work on is lowering the cost of prescription drugs, and that is something the President has talked about. We had it in our '6 for '06' 12 years ago when we won the House. Five of those six became law. The one we couldn't get 60 votes in the Senate for was enabling the Secretary [of HHS] to negotiate for lower prescription drug prices. We hope to get that done now because that is a big impact on America's families' budget.

And then the third really caffeinating issue for us is integrity in government, to reduce the role of special interest money, and I commend all of our candidates for their commitment to the health care agenda, to a bigger paycheck agenda, and also to the good government agenda.

They have written letters saying that they want H.R. 1, which is our Better Deal for America's Democracy, to be something they vote on. But I say to them, when you come here, you will have an impact on what that legislation is. You may want to make some additions or some tweaking, but nonetheless, our newcomers will be part of putting together how the agenda goes forward, and we look forward to that invigoration of the Congress.

I also spoke to Mitch McConnell, Leader McConnell this morning on how we can work together, especially on infrastructure. I did receive a call of congratulations from Speaker Ryan, and I welcomed that, and we discussed how it is to win and how it is not to win.

In any event, the concern that he was expressing was about some of his colleagues who will no longer be serving. On that point, I want to make a couple of I want to say something because in winning this election, not only are we on the right side of history, we're on the right side of the future. This is where we have to go. But once we talk about the challenges that we face, we had to jump over gerrymandered lines all over the country.

So when we talk about our success, it's about the grassroots operation owning the ground. All of these groups that care about health care, many of them out there helped elect people who share their values about lowering health care costs, removing lifetime caps, even annual caps on insurance coverage, and certainly restoring the benefit of pre-existing conditions not being a barrier to coverage.

Most importantly, though, the quality of our candidates, they are spectacular from every walk of life, and some of them from a couple of different walks of life. And when they come here, they'll bring their experience, their knowledge, and especially their values to the Congress. We look forward to that. This is no easy feat to win this election. I hear the President attributed it to this, that, and the other thing, but when we think of how gerrymandered the country is, how we hope to change that, but nonetheless, how we were able to succeed in this election is a tribute again to the quality of our candidates, the determination of our grassroots folks across the country, and the values that we share with the American people.

In terms of working with the President, I will I just would say that I worked very productively with President Bush when we had the majority and he had the Presidency. We passed one of the biggest energy bills in the history of our country. We passed one of the biggest tax bills in terms of stimulus for low income people as well as middle income people in his Presidency, and the list goes on. PEPFAR, he wanted PEPFAR. We wanted and there was so many issues that we worked together although we vehemently opposed the war in Iraq.

But the point is, is that we worked together. The President said: I'll wait for them to send me something. Well, we have ideas, and we can send him something, but the fact is that we'd like to work together so our legislation will be bipartisan. We're not going for the lowest common denominator. We're going for the boldest common denominator. Our position will be a consensus within our own party for what we can support but also welcoming other ideas.

So we look forward to a new kind of a new era in terms of what is happening. This past two years, it seemed like a very, very long time in terms of the path that it's taken us down. And I think of our Founders and their courage, their vision, what they had in mind for us, E Pluribus Unum, from many, one, when I think of the American people and how beautifully diverse we are and how newcomers to our country have constantly reinvigorated America, when I think of our beautiful planet, and, of course, our own country, God's gift to us and how it has been neglected and degraded in this past couple of years, I think that there is plenty of opportunity for us to match our legislation with the rhetoric that we are hearing.

It might surprise you to note that the President I quoted the most on the campaign trail—what would you think? Ronald Reagan. And I'll just—I won't read you the whole quote, but I'll read you just one paragraph. Ronald Reagan said: 'This is the last speech that I will make as President of the United States, and I want to—it's fitting to be leave final thought, an observation about a country which I love.'

His last speech. That's quite a headliner, right, in your business, Ronald Reagan's last speech.

He said: 'Thanks to each new wave of new arrivals to this land of opportunity, we are a nation forever young, forever bursting with energy and new ideas, and always on the cutting edge, always leading the world to the next frontier. This quality is vital to our future as a nation.'

He goes on to say: 'If we ever close the door to new Americans, our leadership in the world would soon be lost. If we ever close the door, our leadership will soon be lost.'

So in that respect for the vision of our Founders, the diversity of our country, the beauty of our land, the values in our Constitution, first and foremost, we think there is an opportunity to work together. One sign of good faith on the part of the President to work together [would be] for them to withdraw their assault on the pre-existing condition benefit, which the Republican attorneys general across the country have put forth, and which this administration has said they will not defend the law of the land, they will join in that lawsuit. That's just wrong. That's just wrong. So we think, again, as a sign of good faith and in keeping with what they are saying on the campaign trail, prove it. Withdraw the lawsuit. So that would be one place that we could start.

In any event, next week we look forward to welcoming our new class of freshmen. We will celebrate their diversity, the freshness of their thinking and the rest, and they will immediately be incorporated into our building a consensus of how we go forward in a very open, transparent, bipartisan, unifying Congress.

*[A Q&A with reporters has been omitted.]*

SOURCE: Office of Rep. Nancy Pelosi. "Pelosi Remarks at Press Conference at the U.S. Capitol." November 7, 2018. https://www.speaker.gov/newsroom/press-releases/11718-4.

## OTHER HISTORIC DOCUMENTS OF INTEREST

### FROM THIS VOLUME

### FROM PREVIOUS *HISTORIC DOCUMENTS*

# Martial Law Declared in Ukraine

NOVEMBER 26, NOVEMBER 27, AND DECEMBER 20, 2018

Tensions between Russia and Ukraine flared in November 2018 when Russian security forces seized three Ukrainian ships attempting to sail through the Kerch Strait. Russian officials claimed the ships had illegally crossed the country's borders, but the Ukrainian government argued the Kerch Strait was shared territorial water. Russia's actions were roundly condemned by the international community as a continued violation of Ukraine's sovereignty. The Ukrainian government quickly moved to impose martial law to enable the country to bolster its defenses against what officials described as a serious threat of Russian aggression.

## RUSSIA SEIZES UKRAINIAN SHIPS, BLOCKS KERCH STRAIT

On November 25, Russian security forces opened fire on two Ukrainian armored artillery ships and a tugboat seeking to enter the Sea of Azov via the Kerch Strait, which separates the Crimean peninsula from mainland Russia. (The Kerch Strait is the only entry point to the sea.) The three ships were subsequently seized and their twenty-four crew members detained. Russia also closed the Kerch Strait, claiming the ships were executing dangerous maneuvers and might have been attempting to sabotage Russia's newly constructed bridge to the peninsula.

The two countries have been locked in conflict since 2014, when Russia annexed the Ukrainian peninsula of Crimea. The annexation followed a public referendum and vote by the regional Crimean parliament in favor of secession. The central Ukrainian government and Western nations called the vote a sham that was held under the duress of a Russian military incursion. (Russian forces had begun entering and occupying territory on the peninsula in February 2014.) Ukraine does not recognize the annexation and maintains that the border between the two countries goes through the Kerch Strait. Unrest flared in eastern Ukraine following the annexation, with pro-Russian separatists and Russian forces taking up arms against the Ukrainian government. More than 10,000 people have been killed in the ongoing conflict.

For months prior to the Kerch Strait incident, tensions between Russia and Ukraine had been building. In March, Ukrainian border guards impounded a Russian fishing boat and detained its crew, keeping them in custody until October. Russia's Kerch Bridge opened in May, at which point Russian border guards began conducting inspections of foreign ships sailing in the Sea of Azov. Nearly 300 Ukrainian and other foreign vessels had since been stopped. Ukrainian officials claimed these inspections hurt the country's trade because roughly 7 percent of Ukrainian exports travel from ports along the Sea of Azov.

The Ukrainian government decried the November seizure of its ships and personnel, claiming that Russia had violated a fifteen-year-old treaty in which the Sea of Azov was declared shared territorial waters and the international law of the sea, which allows "innocent" passage through any strait. However, Russia's Federal Security Service (FSB) claimed the ships had illegally entered the country's territory and had been asked to leave before they were fired upon. Officials argued that new rules implemented in 2015 require any vessel sailing through the strait to obtain permission at least forty-eight hours in advance. The Ukrainian ships, they said, had only provided last-minute notification of their intention to traverse the strait. To reinforce this argument, officials repeatedly asserted that two Ukrainian military ships had followed these rules and passed through the strait on September 23 without incident. Ukrainian officials denied this, saying the ships did not seek permission from Russia because they already had the right to sail through the shared waters. Russia later broadcast what officials claimed were confessions from several of the detained sailors that the incident was a deliberate provocation by the Ukrainian government. Ukrainian officials countered that the statements were coerced and suggested the sailors had been abused.

Russian President Vladimir Putin initially characterized the conflict as "a border incident, nothing more," but later claimed Ukrainian President Petro Poroshenko was exploiting the situation to drum up support ahead of a planned 2019 election. "Clearly, they are in the middle of an election campaign right now, and they want to aggravate the situation in order to raise the ratings of one of the contenders, I mean the incumbent president and the current government," Putin said during his annual news conference. "It is ultimately bad for the interests of the Ukrainian people and state." Members of Putin's administration made similar claims. "There is no doubt that it was done by blessing or, perhaps, even a direct order from the top," said Russian Foreign Minister Sergey Lavrov. "Ukraine had undoubtedly hoped to get additional benefits from the situation, expecting the U.S. and Europe to blindly take the provocateurs' side." Russian officials also said the Ukrainian sailors would not be released until they faced criminal trial.

## INTERNATIONAL RESPONSE

At both countries' request, an emergency meeting of the United Nations (UN) Security Council was held on November 26 to discuss the incident. The council heard from both the Russian and Ukrainian representatives after rejecting a provisional agenda item proposed by Russia that characterized the altercation as a violation of its borders. Briefing council members, UN Under Secretary General for Political Affairs Rosemary DiCarlo urged both countries to "refrain from any ratcheting up of actions or rhetoric" and reminded them of "the need to contain this incident so as to prevent a serious escalation that may have unforeseen consequences."

Leaders of many Western nations denounced Russia's actions. In a statement, North Atlantic Treaty Organization (NATO) members said, "There is no justification for Russia's use of military force against Ukrainian ships and naval personnel. We call on Russia to release the Ukrainian sailors and ships it seized, without delay." NATO members also reiterated their "full support to Ukraine's sovereignty and territorial integrity within its internationally recognised borders and territorial waters." U.S. Ambassador to the UN Nikki Haley called Russia's actions "outrageous" and "reckless," while British Foreign Secretary Jeremy Hunt said Russia had shown "contempt for international norms and Ukrainian sovereignty." European Union spokesperson Maja Kocijančič said the incident demonstrated "how instability and tensions are bound to rise when the basic rules of international cooperation are disregarded." She added, "The construction of the Kerch Bridge took place without Ukraine's consent and constitutes another violation of Ukraine's sovereignty and territorial integrity."

On December 17, the UN General Assembly adopted a resolution urging Russia to withdraw from Crimea and "end its temporary occupation of Ukraine's territory without delay." The resolution condemned Russia's construction of the Kerch Strait Bridge and called for the release of Ukraine's ships and sailors. However, the assembly rejected a proposed amendment calling for both countries to conduct full independent investigations of the incident. Russia's First Deputy U.N. Ambassador Dmitry Polyansky said his government regretted the vote, he said of the resolution. "The Kiev regime thus receives new signals that it's allowed everything and all will be forgiven, while Russia will be unconditionally blamed in advance for all its sins and crimes," he said.

## UKRAINIAN GOVERNMENT IMPOSES MARTIAL LAW

On November 26, the day after the Kerch Strait incident, Poroshenko announced that he would seek parliament's approval to impose martial law in the ten Ukrainian regions that border Russia, the Transnistria region, the Sea of Azov, and the Black Sea. "Russia has been waging a hybrid war against our country for five years," said Poroshenko during a televised address about his proposal. "But with an attack on Ukrainian military boats it moved to a new stage of aggression." The president said intelligence reports suggested an "extremely serious threat of a land-based operation against Ukraine," noting that Russia had amassed planes, helicopters, tanks, and other military equipment "several dozens of kilometers from our border." Poroshenko said the imposition of martial law did not signify a declaration of war. Rather, its purpose was to strengthen Ukrainian defenses against potential Russian aggression so that the military could be mobilized quickly if necessary. The president reassured Ukrainians that he did not intend to implement any measures restricting individual freedoms or censoring speech, though such limitations would be permitted under Ukrainian law. Some of the measures included in the proposed martial law decree involved calling military reservists to duty, planning air defenses for critical government facilities, and enhancing cybersecurity mechanisms. It would also ban Russian men between the ages of sixteen and sixty from entering Ukraine except for humanitarian purposes.

Parliament took up the president's proposal that same day in an emergency session. During five hours of heated debate, several lawmakers expressed concerns about provisions they claimed could severely limit civil liberties. "We do not support the destruction of human rights under the guise of martial law!" yelled Yulia Tymoshenko, a former prime minister and a presidential candidate. Others accused Poroshenko of using the crisis for his own political benefit and questioned whether the proposed sixty-day duration of martial law would allow him to delay the presidential election. Lawmakers agreed to several revisions that addressed some concerns, including a change that limited the period of martial law to thirty days. Despite the highly charged debate, the revised decree was approved overwhelmingly. Immediately after its approval, parliament voted to schedule the presidential election for March 31, 2019, to further assuage concerns about the timing of martial law.

Lawmakers were not the only ones who had concerns about martial law. According to a poll by Rating Group Ukraine, 58 percent of Ukrainians believed Russia had committed "an act of military aggression" in the Kerch Strait, but 60 percent opposed martial law. Some analysts also questioned the timing and motivations of the martial law decree, asking why, for example, similar action had not been pursued when Russia invaded Crimea, or at any other time when violence escalated during the ongoing conflict.

Martial law began on November 28 and ended on December 27. Announcing its expiration, Poroshenko said martial law had been "timely and necessary" and had increased the military's "ability to respond to the threat of a full-fledged Russian invasion." Specifically, he noted Ukraine had relocated troops to areas most vulnerable to Russian attack and had strengthened its air defenses in the south and east. Poroshenko added that if not for the upcoming presidential election, he would have requested an extension of martial law because the "Russian threat does not go away."

Russia has since impounded the seized Ukrainian ships and repeatedly dismissed demands by Ukrainian officials and the international community to release the sailors. At the time of writing, no trial date had been set for the detained men.

—Linda Grimm

*Following are remarks by Ukrainian President Petro Poroshenko on November 26, 2018, announcing his proposal to declare martial law; a statement by NATO members on November 27, 2018, responding to the incident in the Kerch Strait; and comments made by Russian President Vladimir Putin about the situation with Ukraine during a December 20, 2018, news conference.*

# Ukrainian President Remarks on Introduction of Martial Law

**November 26, 2018**

Fellow Ukrainians!

Today, the Parliament will consider the issue of extreme importance, which directly concerns your protection, your security, the security of Ukraine, its sovereignty and territorial integrity.

According to the decision of the National Security and Defense Council of Ukraine adopted tonight, as President and as Supreme Commander-in-Chief of the Armed Forces of Ukraine, I have fulfilled my constitutional duty and a few hours ago, by my decree, I introduced martial law all over Ukraine starting from 9 am, November 28.

Russia has been waging a hybrid war against our country for five years. But with an attack on Ukrainian military boats it moved to a new stage of aggression. No one will say now: "They are not there". No one camouflages into green humanoids or militiamen. This is a bold and frank participation of the regular units of the Russian Federation, their demonstrative attack on the detachment of the Ukrainian Armed Forces. This is a qualitatively different situation, a qualitatively different threat.

And this attack, of course, is not accidental. This is clearly an element planned by Russians in the escalation of the situation in the waters of the Sea of Azov, which has been lasting for several months. And I'm sure this is still not a culmination.

Security officials and diplomats have informed you today at a press conference about all the circumstances of yesterday's incident.

Reconnaissance data suggest an extremely serious threat of a land-based operation against Ukraine. I have a document of intelligence in my hands, a summary of our intelligence data. Here on several pages is a detailed description of all the forces of the enemy located at a distance of literally several dozens of kilometers from our border. Ready at any moment for an immediate invasion of Ukraine. A rifle hanging on the wall will go off sooner or later. And these are planes, helicopters, tanks, missile complexes, armored personnel carriers, salvo fire systems.

Of all the options provided by the Law "On the Legal Status of Martial Law", the Decree, my Decree "On the Imposition of Martial Law" includes only those that deal mainly with various military activities—we must strengthen the security right now. (Measures—ed.) that in case of the invasion will allow us to react as quickly as possible, mobilize all resources as soon as possible. Especially since the boys and girls from the first wave of the reserve, which already have military experience, are ready to pack rucksacks right now and resources will be mobilized—both human, arms and financial.

I emphasize that I do not envisage any measures in the Decree related to the restriction of the rights and freedoms of citizens, introduction of censorship, etc. I hope that both politicians and mass media will act responsibly and adequately in the current situation and will not attack Ukraine with the theses borrowed from Russian propagandists.

Nor do I plan to resort to full or partial mobilization so far—this opportunity remains open only if Russia resorts to further escalation.

Martial law does not mean the declaration of war. It is introduced solely for the purpose of strengthening Ukraine's defense against the background of growing aggressiveness from Russia. Martial law does not mean our retreat from the political-diplomatic settlement in the east. Today, I informed our western partners about this in detail. From the very morning, I have had detailed talks with NATO Secretary General Jens Stoltenberg, with Polish President Andrzej Duda, since Poland represents Ukraine's position and is the initiator of the consideration of the situation at the UN Security Council, with German Chancellor Angela Merkel and with many others. Consultations will be continued this evening. And I can tell you that their attention to the situation in the east and directly in the waters of the Sea of Azov has increased substantially. Today, we are heard much better than yesterday or the day before yesterday.

Dear friends, fellow Ukrainians.

Our joint responsibility, first of all mine, as of Supreme Commander-in-Chief, is to protect Ukraine. And Ukraine's defense is not only the defense of territory or military equipment. This is primarily the protection of people. We must be as prepared as possible for any action by our aggressive, volatile and, unfortunately, pretty unpredictable neighbor.

Of course, it is related to the protection of the right to free choice as well. Only a reliable defense, only doubling and tripling our defensive efforts guarantees peace that is needed, inter alia, for the conduct of the elections.

The NSDC recommended me today to introduce martial law for 60 days. I want to announce to you my decision—I will propose to the Parliament to introduce martial law for 30 days. For what? For martial law not to overlap with the beginning of the election campaign by a single day. So that no one of those who care for their party, their political interest more than for the nation and Ukrainian interest have a reason for dirty political speculations or insinuations.

Martial law will last 30 days and will end in mid-December. It is in December, in early December, that I will submit a draft resolution to the Parliament on the date of the presidential elections to be held in accordance with the Constitution on March 31, 2019. Period. As Supreme Commander-in-Chief, I will make every effort to stay within this short term and squeeze out the maximum opportunities from this month to increase our readiness to repel a possible full-scale offensive of the aggressor country—Russia.

Glory to Ukraine!

SOURCE: President of Ukraine. "Statement by the President of Ukraine on the Approval of the Decree on the Introduction of Martial Law in Ukraine." November 26, 2018. https://www.president.gov.ua/en/news/zayava-prezidenta-ukrayini-shodo-zatverdzhennya-ukazu-pro-vv-51362.

# NATO Statement on Developments near the Sea of Azov

**November 27, 2018**

In view of Russia's use of military force against Ukraine near the Sea of Azov and the Kerch Strait, NATO Allies call on Russia to ensure unhindered access to Ukrainian ports and allow freedom of navigation.

There is no justification for Russia's use of military force against Ukrainian ships and naval personnel. We call on Russia to release the Ukrainian sailors and ships it seized, without delay.

We call for calm and restraint.

We reiterate our full support to Ukraine's sovereignty and territorial integrity within its internationally recognised borders and territorial waters. We strongly condemn Russia's illegal and illegitimate annexation of Crimea, which we do not and will not recognise. Russia's construction and partial opening of the Kerch Strait bridge represents another violation of Ukraine's sovereignty and territorial integrity.

NATO stands with Ukraine, and will continue to provide political and practical support to the country within the framework of our established cooperation. NATO will continue to monitor the situation.

SOURCE: North Atlantic Treaty Organization. "North Atlantic Council Statement on Developments near the Sea of Azov." November 27, 2018. https://www.nato.int/cps/en/natohq/news_160859.htm.

# Russian President Remarks on Ukrainian Relations

**December 20, 2018**

*[The following questions and answers have been excerpted from the transcript of President Vladimir Putin's annual press conference.]*

**Yegor Sozayev-Guryev [Reporter]:** I have a question about the precedent in the Kerch Strait, I wonder about the future of the captured Ukrainian military. What will happen to them? Do you think this provocation was a success? . . .

**Vladimir Putin:** With regard to your first question, you said: "Do you think this provocation was a success?" First, let us state that it was a provocation, and you agree with that. This is already a good start.

Now, whether it was a success or not, I believe provocations are a bad thing whatever way you look at them. Provocations seek to aggravate things. Why do our Ukrainian partners need things to go that way? Clearly, they are in the middle of an election campaign right now, and they want to aggravate the situation in order to raise the ratings of one of the contenders, I mean the incumbent president and the current government. Well, this is bad, it is ultimately bad for the interests of the Ukrainian people and state. However, it is possible to move forward without any provocations and do so calmly, as before.

Whether it was a success or not, I mean in terms of improving popularity ratings, maybe it was, as Mr. Poroshenko's ratings seem to have increased a little and he has moved from the fifth position to the second or third, where the figure fluctuates around 12 percent. Ms. Tymoshenko, I believe, has 20 percent or even more, whereas Zelinsky, Boyko and Poroshenko have around 12 percent each. In this sense, yes, he probably achieved the goal. At the expense of the country's interests, I believe. This is a bad way to boost ratings.

With regard to the future of the Ukrainian servicemen, they were sent on this mission and some of them were expected to die in the process. I can see that the leadership is very upset by the fact that no one died. They expected some of them to die. Thank God, this did not happen. An investigation is underway. Once it is over, we will know what to do with them. . . .

**Roman Tsymbalyuk [Reporter]:** Mr. President, I would like to ask you how much money you are spending on the occupied Donbass? Under your leadership, people there are living in poverty. . . . My question is what are the terms . . . of exchange of Ukrainian political prisoners and Ukrainian servicemen. You do need your Russian citizens back, don't you? . . . Doesn't it seem to you that a direct dialogue between the presidents of Ukraine and Russia will never take place until you change your job? Thank you.

**Vladimir Putin:** Regarding the suffering of the people who live in Donbass. You are a Ukrainian citizen, aren't you? And you consider the people who live on this territory to be the citizens of your country. Can you tell me who established the blockade between Donbass and the rest of Ukraine? Did Russia do it? The Ukrainian authorities did it: they imposed a total economic blockade of the territory they consider to be their own. They shoot at the people they consider to be their own citizens. People are killed there almost every day, peaceful civilians, by the way.

We do render humanitarian and other assistance and support to the people who live on that territory. But we do it only to prevent them from being finally crushed, devoured and torn to pieces, and we will continue doing it. Because attempts to solve these political issues by force—and we have seen this being done by the current Kiev authorities for several years—are doomed to failure. This has to be kept in mind.

Now concerning how to settle these relations and who will and will not remain in power. It is not about personalities, it is about the attitude towards people. We want to see peace and prosperity on the entire territory of Ukraine, including Donbass. We are interested in it because Ukraine remains one of our biggest trade and economic partners.

Trade between Ukraine and Russia, in spite of all the efforts of the current Kiev authorities, is growing, it has grown in the outgoing year, it has grown during the current year. Is it strange? No, it is not strange because these are natural ties. These natural ties will sooner or later make themselves felt. But as long as the Kiev corridors of power are peopled by Russophobes who do not understand the interests of their own people this abnormal situation will persist. Regardless of who is in power at the Kremlin.

We have attended to the issue of exchange all along. Mr. Medvedchuk, on instructions from Poroshenko, by the way, has been constantly engaged in this. He came to Moscow just recently and raised the issue of the release of Ukrainian servicemen detained in the Kerch Strait, in the Black Sea to be more precise. Yes, Medvedchuk raised this issue. However, as I have said, these issues could only be tackled after the criminal case is closed. . . .

**Ilya Petrenko [Reporter]:** . . . I would like to inquire about a recent decision to simplify procedures for the people of Ukraine to obtain Russian citizenship. . . . If this is so essential, and if this is needed to help people in eastern Ukraine, why didn't we do it earlier? Are you not afraid that bureaucracy will persist, and that papers will, from now on, be placed to the left, rather than the right? . . .

**Vladimir Putin:** Regarding naturalisation, this does not have to do only with what is taking place in southeastern Ukraine. Our initiatives do not target exclusively people living in these territories. The Government is currently working on amendments to the relevant law on citizenship and naturalisation. What for? These efforts are designed to show that we do not seek and will not support policies of division or the ones designed to alienate the peoples of Russia and Ukraine. What are the current [Ukrainian] authorities doing? What is their mission? What are they trying to achieve on the back of Russophobia they are promoting? They are practically admitting that they are pursuing a historic task of separating the peoples of Russia and Ukraine. This is what they are up to. And for that, they can get away with anything.

Your colleague from the Ukrainian media talked about the challenges faced by people living in Donbass and the Lugansk Region, and their poor living standards. But is it any better in Ukraine? The situation is quite similar compared to Donbass, and it is getting worse all the time. Anything can be forgiven within the country, and even more so outside it against the backdrop of war, hostilities and tensions. And they are getting paid for this. They are about to receive another IMF tranche. We do understand what this is all about: just enough to pay out pensions and salaries to social sector employees, and the future generations will have to foot the bill. For this reason the overall situation is quite unfavourable. I believe this to be the case for the economy, society and domestic political processes. But our nations are very close and share the same history, so we will do everything to move in this direction.

The law on citizenship is currently being amended, and it will be adopted in early 2019. . . .

**Galina Polonskaya [Reporter]:** . . . The UN adopted a resolution about Russia's militarisation of the Sea of Azov, Crimea, and part of the Black Sea. After what happened with the Ukrainian ships in the Kerch Strait, there were reports that Russia was sending military equipment to Crimea. Why should Russia reinforce its military presence in Crimea? Is Russia ready to declare the entire water area of the Sea of Azov its territory? Thank you.

**Vladimir Putin:** Look, in 2014, people living in Crimea came out for the referendum and ultimately voted for reunification with the Russian Federation. From that moment, after the relevant domestic procedures, Crimea became part of the Russian Federation, part of Russia. Therefore, we are entitled to and will continue to pursue our military policy on any part of our territory, as we see fit to ensure national security. Crimea is no exception. If the General Staff, if the border guards believe that we need to do something extra in some area, we will do it. Russia's security in this area will certainly be ensured. We are not going to overdo it there, but what needs to be done, will be done. This is the first point.

Now about the Sea of Azov and the Kerch Strait. We almost immediately announced that we intended to build a bridge to link up with Crimea, which we did. First we built an energy bridge, then a gas pipe, and now we are building two power plants there, in Sevastopol and in Simferopol, with a total capacity of 940 megawatts. We are building the Tavrida road, to be completed by the end of 2020. Next year, I think, the two-lane road will open, and by the end of 2020, a four-lane road.

We will develop the local infrastructure. That is, it is not only about reinforcing the military component, but above all, the civilian, infrastructure component. All this will certainly be implemented. We have a federal targeted programme for the development of Crimea. For the next two years, we have allocated 300 billion rubles for the development of the peninsula. All this will progress. Along with that, the military component will be strengthened, as far as we need it.

As for the Kerch straits, the situation is difficult, in terms of nature. These straits are very narrow and rather shallow. Their depth is about 13 metres. Let me emphasise that pilotage has always been conducted there. The construction of the bridge does not interfere with anything. Pilots escort ships as they used to.

Freight turnover is growing, in particular, in the ports of the Sea of Azov, this is true. But work there is organised and all participants in these economic activities know how this is being done. There is a queue there. Sometimes it is bigger and sometimes it is smaller. Just look at the number of vessels in front of the entrance to the port of Novorossiysk. There are quite a few of them.

I will have to repeat this once again: On September 11 of the past year Ukrainian vessels, including warships, fulfilled all requirements of passage through these straits and under the bridge and were calmly led by our pilots into the Sea of Azov and further on to their destination in the Sea. Nobody interfered with them—just helped.

This time everything was different. This is a deliberate provocation in the course of Mr. Poroshenko's election campaign. We have already shown in the media the logbook that contains the order to "enter secretly." What does "secretly" mean? Nobody can say what might happen there without pilotage, all the more so when some politicians say in public that they are ready to blow up the bridge. Naturally, we cannot allow this to happen. This would be simply absurd for us, period. As for routine activities, nobody restricts them.

Now a few words about the regime in the Sea of Azov. We have a treaty dating back to 2003, I think. What does it say? It reads that there is a coastal area of five kilometres, not the usual 12 sea miles in accordance with the international Law of the Sea, but five kilometres off the coast. These are the territorial waters of a state, in this case of Russia or Ukraine, and the rest is common sea. Incidentally, our fishermen were once captured although they did not enter the five km zone. Nonetheless, they were seized and their captain is still detained. And your Euronews channel does not even mention this as if this is how it should be. The same is true of other Russian seamen: there is a dry-cargo vessel with its crew out there somewhere, but nobody recalls anything. Therefore, we should observe these agreements and abstain from announcing any unilateral actions.

As for warships, they should be in constant contact with our border guards. The border guards conduct their border mission. In conditions of martial law, I can hardly imagine warships going to and fro, but in general we would like to normalise the situation. We do not create any obstacles to vessels, including warships. Let me repeat that last September vessels were led by our pilot and nobody interfered with them, on the contrary we only helped.

This is a complicated problem, which we will certainly keep working on. . . .

SOURCE: President of Russia. "Vladimir Putin's Annual News Conference." December 20, 2018. http://en.kremlin.ru/events/president/news/59455.

## OTHER HISTORIC DOCUMENTS OF INTEREST

### FROM PREVIOUS *HISTORIC DOCUMENTS*

# December

# Former President George H. W. Bush Dies

DECEMBER 1 AND DECEMBER 5, 2018

Former U.S. president George H. W. Bush died on November 30, 2018, at his home in Houston, Texas, at the age of ninety-four. Bush was widely memorialized as a pragmatic and temperate leader who presided over a transitional era of American influence in the world with integrity and optimism. Americans of both parties and leaders abroad mourned the passing of the forty-first president and contemplated what some described as a bygone era of public service and civility in American politics.

## POLITICS AND PUBLIC SERVICE

Six months after Japan's 1941 attack on Pearl Harbor propelled the United States into conflict, Bush celebrated his eighteenth birthday and enlisted as a naval aviator. Bush went on to fly fifty-eight combat missions in the Pacific theater and was rescued at sea after his plane was shot down by enemy fire. After the war, he started a successful oil business in Midland, Texas, before pursuing a political career. He was twice elected to represent the 7th Congressional District of Texas in the U.S. House of Representatives before an unsuccessful 1970 run for Senate. In 1971, Bush became President Richard Nixon's ambassador to the United Nations. One year later, he was tapped to chair the Republican National Committee in the midst of the Watergate scandal, then was appointed by President Gerald Ford to lead the Central Intelligence Agency. Bush was President Ronald Reagan's running mate on the Republican ticket in 1980 and served as vice president throughout the Reagan administration until his own 1988 bid for the White House.

Bush often framed his public service as a civic duty. He underscored this theme in accepting his party's nomination for the presidency at the Republican National Convention in New Orleans: "I am a man who sees life in terms of missions—missions defined and missions completed," he told delegates. Bush assumed office on January 20, 1989, following a landslide victory over Massachusetts governor Michael Dukakis. Bush said he hoped to usher in a more moderate era of politics after the tumultuous Reagan years. With measured and restrained leadership and an enduring commitment to diplomacy, he steered the nation through a transitional period that he described in his diary as "a fascinating time of change in the world itself."

## INTERNATIONAL DIPLOMACY AND A TAXING DOMESTIC RECORD

Bush's administration balanced two competing forces in American politics that emerged over the twentieth century: the global responsibilities of a central power in foreign affairs and the rise of the cultural right wing in domestic politics. Bush was a skilled diplomat, adept at building coalitions and dealing with adversaries in uncommonly good faith. His single term had a monumental impact on global politics: his administration oversaw a peaceful conclusion to the Cold War and dissolution of the Soviet Union, facilitated reunification of Germany and the liberation of Eastern Europe, and led a multinational coalition to expel Iraqi invaders from Kuwait. The swift conclusion to conflict in the Persian Gulf earned him a standing ovation when he addressed a joint session of Congress that spring, and his approval ratings briefly soared to nearly 85 percent, according to a *New York Times*/CBS poll.

On the home front, Bush struggled to translate his foreign-policy prowess to his domestic record. He inherited the party of Reagan, which for a quarter of a century had drifted further to the right, and throughout his presidency, Bush struggled to work with a solidly Democratic legislative branch while satisfying conservative voices in his party. He saw success in negotiating the North American Free Trade Agreement, passed the landmark Americans with Disabilities Act, and signed into law sweeping amendments to the 1970 Clean Air Act. However, it was his decision to enact spending cuts and tax revenue increases to manage the growing national deficit that loomed largest over his domestic legacy.

Early in Bush's presidency, the U.S. economy slipped into a modest recession, and unemployment rose to almost 8 percent in June of 1992. Bush had campaigned vehemently against tax increases, making an explicit, now infamous campaign promise: "Read my lips: no new taxes." Yet he compromised to reach a budget deal with Congress that stabilized government finances through tax increases on the wealthy and new rules to limit spending. Bush's about-face on tax increases came a few months before the 1990 midterm elections and set the stage for later presidential primary challenges. Although the deal ultimately created the conditions for his successor to eliminate the federal budget deficit and laid the groundwork for a decade of economic prosperity, these long-term benefits were not realized before Bush's first term ended and the president's compromise split conservatives along a deepening fault line. Led by Republican whip Newt Gingrich, young and more conservative House members openly opposed the deal, while older, more moderate Republicans, many of whom had served alongside Bush for decades, stood by the president.

In the 1992 presidential election, an unexpectedly strong third-party challenge by fellow Texan and billionaire Ross Perot left Bush with just 38 percent of the vote—the lowest of any incumbent president in eighty years, consigning him to a short list of one-term presidents. For all his success in the international arena, his presidency faltered as voters perceived him as detached from their everyday concerns, and his loss marked a generational shift in American leadership. Yet Bush remained graceful in defeat, writing in a note to incoming president and former Arkansas governor Bill Clinton: "Don't let the critics discourage you or push you off course. You will be our President when you read this note. I wish you well."

## A KINDER AND GENTLER LEGACY

Bush was lionized in death as he was not always in life. While his bipartisan civility may have been genuine, his legacy is marred by times when principles did not win out over political expediency. The tension between these competing influences manifested most memorably in an anti-Dukakis attack ad overtly steeped in racial overtones, which has become an archetypal reference point for dog-whistle racism in modern politics. Additionally, Bush opposed President Lyndon B. Johnson's landmark Civil Rights Act as a Senate candidate in Texas. He later reflected on this decision, saying, "I generally favor the goals as outlined in [Johnson's] Great Society. . . . I took some of the far-right positions to get elected. I hope I never do it again." In a late-2010s era of #MeToo, Bush faced renewed criticism for defending Justice Clarence Thomas, his Supreme Court nominee, amid allegations of sexual harassment.

Despite these criticisms, friends, colleagues, and formal rivals said Bush's defining traits were an essential dignity and willingness to compromise in the interest of effective governance. He openly expressed distaste for the rancor that increasingly characterizes Republican leadership and pointedly refused to endorse Donald Trump's candidacy in 2016. He enjoyed greater popularity after leaving office and was awarded the Presidential Medal of Freedom by President Barack Obama in 2011. The contrasts between Bush and his son, President George W. Bush, led many Americans to appreciate his optimistic but measured leadership. He was hardly the towering figure of Reagan, whose two terms cast a long shadow, but neither was he as remote, and his humanity was central to his influence. In a 2013 interview, former secretary of state James Baker said, "Whether they agreed with him on certain policy positions or not, people respected him, and liked him."

Bush largely represented a "kinder" and "gentler" strain of Republican politics—the oft-quoted words from his 1989 inaugural address that described his vision for the nation. Bush talked about "a thousand points of light" in reference to community and charitable groups "spread like stars throughout the nation." Always one to eschew self-promotion, when granddaughter Jenna Bush Hager (then a correspondent for the *Today Show*) asked him in a 2012 interview about his legacy, he replied, "I want somebody else to define the legacy. I've kind of banned use of the *L* word. History will point out some of the things I did wrong and some of the things I did right."

## AMERICA'S LAST GREAT SOLDIER-STATESMAN

On December 5, a state funeral was held for Bush at the National Cathedral in Washington, D.C. In attendance were all four living former presidents, as well as thousands of foreign leaders, lawmakers, Supreme Court justices, and former officials in Bush's administration, including Baker and Vice President Dan Quayle. President Trump attended but had no speaking role given his history of animosity with the Bush family. In an earlier statement, the president and First Lady Melania Trump said Bush's "essential authenticity, disarming wit, and unwavering commitment to faith, family, and country" had "inspired generations of his fellow Americans to public service."

President George W. Bush eulogized his father as "a diplomat of unmatched skill, a commander in chief of formidable accomplishment, and a gentleman who executed the duties of his office with dignity and honor." Stories shared in the days following his death highlighted the elder Bush's civility, his commitment to the institutions of government, and his uncommonly strong faith in alliances. Jon Meacham, Pulitzer Prize–winning historian and Bush's biographer, called him "America's last great soldier-statesman, a 20th-century founding father." Former Canadian prime minister Brian Mulroney remarked that during the first Bush administration, "every single head of government in the world knew that they were dealing with a gentleman and genuine leader, one that was distinguished, resolute and brave." A common thread across his obituaries was nostalgia for a time when American politics operated in good faith and a shared value of the greater good. He was described as having believed in the essential goodness of the American public and in the nobility of the American experiment, with an unaffected vision of politics as a means for public service.

In his death, Bush has been venerated as one of the last moderate members of the Grand Old Party. There was less of an overt sense of rebuke to the Trump administration at Bush's funeral than there had been during the September memorial service for Sen. John McCain, R-Ariz., but the tacit contrasts in values and temperaments between the former and current president were unmistakable. Following the state funeral, a service was held in Houston before Bush was interred at his presidential library in College Station, Texas, alongside former first lady Barbara Bush, who passed in April 2018, and daughter Robin, who died of leukemia at age three. At his request, "Hail to the Chief" was not performed at the burial, but fighter jets executed a "missing man" formation flyover. Echoing the sense of duty through which he dedicated his career, Rev. Dr. Russell Jones Levenson concluded the homily with "Mr. President, mission complete."

—Megan Howes

*Following is a statement by President Donald Trump and First Lady Melania Trump on December 1, 2018, in response to former president George H.W. Bush's passing; and a transcript of the eulogy delivered by former president George W. Bush at his father's state funeral on December 5, 2018.*

# *President and First Lady Remark on the Passing of Former President George H. W. Bush*

DOCUMENT

**December 1, 2018**

Melania and I join with a grieving Nation to mourn the loss of former President George H.W. Bush, who passed away last night.

Through his essential authenticity, disarming wit, and unwavering commitment to faith, family, and country, President Bush inspired generations of his fellow Americans to public service—to be, in his words, "a thousand points of light" illuminating the greatness, hope, and opportunity of America to the world.

President Bush always found a way to set the bar higher. As a young man, he captained the Yale baseball team and served as the youngest aviator in the United States Navy during the Second World War. Later in life, he rose to the pinnacle of American politics as a Congressman from Texas, envoy to China, Director of Central Intelligence, Vice President of eight years to President Ronald Reagan, and finally President of the United States.

With sound judgement, common sense, and unflappable leadership, President Bush guided our Nation, and the world, to a peaceful and victorious conclusion of the Cold War. As President, he set the stage for the decades of prosperity that have followed. And through all that he accomplished, he remained humble, following the quiet call to service that gave him a clear sense of direction.

Along with his full life of service to country, we will remember President Bush for his devotion to family—especially the love of his life, Barbara. His example lives on, and will continue to stir future Americans to pursue a greater cause. Our hearts ache with his loss, and we, with the American people, send our prayers to the entire Bush family, as we honor the life and legacy of 41.

SOURCE: Executive Office of the President. "Statement on the Death of Former President George H.W. Bush." December 1, 2018. *Compilation of Presidential Documents* 2018, no. 00826 (December 1, 2018). https://www.govinfo.gov/content/pkg/DCPD-201800826/pdf/DCPD-201800826.pdf.

# Eulogy Delivered by Former President George W. Bush

**December 5, 2018**

Distinguished guests, including our presidents and first ladies, government officials, foreign dignitaries, and friends: Jeb, Neil, Marvin, Doro, and I, and our families, thank you all for being here.

I once heard it said of man that "the idea is to die young as late as possible."

At age 85, a favorite pastime of George H.W. Bush was firing up his boat, the Fidelity, and opening up the three-300 horsepower engines to fly—joyfully fly—across the Atlantic, with Secret Service boats straining to keep up.

At 90, George H.W. Bush parachuted out of an aircraft and landed on the grounds of St. Ann's by the Sea in Kennebunkport, Maine—the church where his mom was married and where he'd worshiped often. Mother liked to say he chose the location just in case the chute didn't open.

In his 90's, he took great delight when his closest pal, James A. Baker, smuggled a bottle of Grey Goose vodka into his hospital room. Apparently, it paired well with the steak Baker had delivered from Morton's.

To his very last days, Dad's life was instructive. As he aged, he taught us how to grow old with dignity, humor, and kindness—and, when the good Lord finally called, how to meet him with courage and with joy in the promise of what lies ahead.

One reason Dad knew how to die young is that he almost did it—twice. When he was a teenager, a staph infection nearly took his life. A few years later he was alone in the Pacific on a life raft, praying that his rescuers would find him before the enemy did.

God answered those prayers. It turned out he had other plans for George H.W. Bush. For Dad's part, I think those brushes with death made him cherish the gift of life. And he vowed to live every day to the fullest.

Dad was always busy—a man in constant motion—but never too busy to share his love of life with those around him. He taught us to love the outdoors. He loved watching dogs flush a covey. He loved landing the elusive striper. And once confined to a wheelchair, he seemed happiest sitting in his favorite perch on the back porch at Walker's Point contemplating the majesty of the Atlantic. The horizons he saw were bright and hopeful. He was a genuinely optimistic man. And that optimism guided his children and made each of us believe that anything was possible.

He continually broadened his horizons with daring decisions. He was a patriot. After high school, he put college on hold and became a Navy fighter pilot as World War II broke out. Like many of his generation, he never talked about his service until his time as a public figure forced his hand. We learned of the attack on Chichi Jima, the mission completed, the shoot-down. We learned of the death of his crewmates, whom he thought about throughout his entire life. And we learned of his rescue.

And then, another audacious decision; he moved his young family from the comforts of the East Coast to Odessa, Texas. He and Mom adjusted to their arid surroundings quickly. He was a tolerant man. After all, he was kind and neighborly to the women with whom he, Mom and I shared a bathroom in our small duplex—even after he learned their profession—ladies of the night.

Dad could relate to people from all walks of life. He was an empathetic man. He valued character over pedigree. And he was no cynic. He looked for the good in each person—and usually found it.

Dad taught us that public service is noble and necessary; that one can serve with integrity and hold true to the important values, like faith and family. He strongly believed that it was important to give back to the community and country in which one lived. He recognized that serving others enriched the giver's soul. To us, his was the brightest of a thousand points of light.

In victory, he shared credit. When he lost, he shouldered the blame. He accepted that failure is part of living a full life, but taught us never to be defined by failure. He showed us how setbacks can strengthen.

None of his disappointments could compare with one of life's greatest tragedies, the loss of a young child. Jeb and I were too young to remember the pain and agony he and Mom felt when our 3-year-old sister died. We only learned later that Dad, a man of quiet faith, prayed for her daily. He was sustained by the love of the almighty and the real and enduring love of our mom. Dad always believed that one day he would hug his precious Robin again.

He loved to laugh, especially at himself. He could tease and needle, but never out of malice. He placed great value on a good joke. That's why he chose Simpson to speak. On email, he had a circle of friends with whom he shared or received the latest jokes. His grading system for the quality of the joke was classic George Bush. The rare 7s and 8s were considered huge winners—most of them off-color.

George Bush knew how to be a true and loyal friend. He honored and nurtured his many friendships with his generous and giving soul. There exist thousands of handwritten notes encouraging, or sympathizing, or thanking his friends and acquaintances.

He had an enormous capacity to give of himself. Many a person would tell you that Dad became a mentor and a father figure in their life. He listened and he consoled. He was their friend. I think of Don Rhodes, Taylor Blanton, Jim Nantz, Arnold Schwarzenegger, and perhaps the unlikeliest of all, the man who defeated him, Bill Clinton. My siblings and I refer to the guys in this group as "brothers from other mothers."

He taught us that a day was not meant to be wasted. He played golf at a legendary pace. I always wondered why he insisted on speed golf. He was a good golfer.

Well, here's my conclusion: He played fast so that he could move on to the next event, to enjoy the rest of the day, to expend his enormous energy, to live it all. He was born with just two settings: full throttle, then sleep.

He taught us what it means to be a wonderful father, grandfather, and great-grandfather. He was firm in his principles and supportive as we began to seek our own ways. He encouraged and comforted, but never steered. We tested his patience—I know I did—but he always responded with the great gift of unconditional love.

Last Friday, when I was told he had minutes to live, I called him. The guy who answered the phone said, "I think he can hear you, but hasn't said anything most of the day. I said, "Dad, I love you, and you've been a wonderful father." And the last words he would ever say on earth were, "I love you, too."

To us, he was close to perfect. But, not totally perfect. His short game was lousy. He wasn't exactly Fred Astaire on the dance floor. The man couldn't stomach vegetables, especially broccoli. And by the way, he passed these genetic defects along to us.

Finally, every day of his 73 years of marriage, Dad taught us all what it means to be a great husband. He married his sweetheart. He adored her. He laughed and cried with her. He was dedicated to her totally.

In his old age, Dad enjoyed watching police show reruns, volume on high, all the while holding Mom's hand. After Mom died, Dad was strong, but all he really wanted to do was to hold Mom's hand, again.

Of course, Dad taught me another special lesson. He showed me what it means to be a president who serves with integrity, leads with courage, and acts with love in his heart for the citizens of our country. When the history books are written, they will say that George H.W. Bush was a great president of the United States—a diplomat of unmatched skill, a commander in chief of formidable accomplishment, and a gentleman who executed the duties of his office with dignity and honor.

In his Inaugural Address, the 41st president of the United States said this: "We cannot hope only to leave our children a bigger car, a bigger bank account. We must hope to give them a sense of what it means to be a loyal friend, a loving parent, a citizen who leaves his home, his neighborhood and town better than he found it. What do we want the men and women who work with us to say when we are no longer there? That we were more driven to succeed than anyone around us? Or that we stopped to ask if a sick child had gotten better, and stayed a moment there to trade a word of friendship?"

Well, Dad—we're going remember you for exactly that and so much more.

And we're going to miss you. Your decency, sincerity, and kind soul will stay with us forever. So, through our tears, let us see the blessings of knowing and loving you—a great and noble man, and the best father a son or daughter could have.

And in our grief, let us smile knowing that Dad is hugging Robin and holding Mom's hand again.

SOURCE: George W. Bush Presidential Center. "Remarks by President George W. Bush at the State Funeral of President George H.W. Bush." December 5, 2018. https://www.bushcenter.org/about-the-center/news room/press-releases/2018/12/gwb-eulogy-of-george-hw-bush.html.

## OTHER HISTORIC DOCUMENTS OF INTEREST

### FROM PREVIOUS *HISTORIC DOCUMENTS*

# French President Comments on Yellow Vest Protests

DECEMBER 1 AND DECEMBER 10, 2018

Angered by a new fuel tax, hundreds of thousands of French drivers took to the streets in November 2018 to protest rising gas prices. The protests soon evolved into a national movement of working- and middle-class French who felt neglected by the economic policies of President Emmanuel Macron and demanded higher wages and a reduced cost of living. After weeks of protests and increasing pressure, the government abandoned the fuel tax and announced a minimum wage hike, among other economic policy changes. These concessions failed to appease protestors, who continued their weekly demonstrations as Macron traveled the country meeting with voters and local officials in town hall–style sessions to address their concerns.

## LES GILETS JAUNES

The yellow vest protests began as a response to the French government's proposal to increase taxes on diesel fuel and gasoline. The government had already raised its hydrocarbon tax at the beginning of 2018, adding nearly eight cents and four cents to the per-liter cost of diesel and gasoline, respectively. The new tax would increase these prices by another six cents and three cents, beginning January 1, 2019. Macron and his government said the tax was necessary to help fight climate change and protect the environment, with revenue generated by the tax to fund renewable energy investments.

The fuel tax increase angered many French who live in rural areas of the country and must drive long distances to work. Combined with rising fuel prices, the higher tax would make gas too expensive, they argued. (Diesel fuel prices had risen by about 23 percent in France since the start of the year.) An online petition against rising fuel costs eventually spurred the organization of protests across France on November 17. Protestors became known as *les gilets jaunes*, or "the yellow vests," because they donned the bright-yellow roadside safety vests that French law requires all drivers to carry in their vehicles.

The protests began in rural areas of France's thirteen provinces, but they quickly spread to metropolitan areas and cities, including Paris, with hundreds of thousands of people participating in demonstrations. As the movement grew, so did the protestors' complaints and demands. The yellow vests soon comprised not only French motorists but also a broad swath of people from the working and middle classes who were dissatisfied by their increased cost of living and quality of life. Protestors variously called for a higher minimum wage, increased pensions and social security benefits, and more opportunities for the public to have a say in policymaking. Others called for the dissolution of the National Assembly, new elections, and Macron's resignation.

While the movement lacked national leadership and its demands were diverse, the yellow vests generally coalesced around a shared perception that Macron had become a president for the rich who was disconnected from and neglecting ordinary people. Macron's controversial reduction of France's "wealth tax"—which taxed all assets over €1.3 million (approximately $1.5 million) before Macron narrowed it to tax only real estate assets—and continued loosening of labor laws were among the policies that created this perception. Unemployment also remained high at about 9 percent and was particularly problematic for young people, approximately 20 percent of whom did not have a job.

## RIOTS IN PARIS

The protests peaked during the first weekend in December, when demonstrations in Paris turned into riots and violence broke out on the famous Avenue des Champs Élysées. Until that time, the yellow vest demonstrations had mostly been peaceful and in many areas consisted primarily of roadblocks at big intersections, toll plazas, and other high-traffic locations. Rioters defaced Paris's famed Arc de Triomphe and Tomb of the Unknown Soldier, looted shops, vandalized buildings, and set cars on fire, with some reports indicating that police were attacked. More than 100 people were injured and over 400 were arrested in the worst unrest seen by the City of Lights since the student protests of 1968. Officials estimated the riots caused about $3.4 million worth of damage. Officials also attributed much of the violence to *casseurs*, or ultra-left and ultra-right anarchists.

Speaking to reporters at the G-20 summit in Argentina on December 1, Macron condemned the violence in Paris and promised that those responsible would be held accountable. "I will never condone violence," he said. "No cause can justify an attack on law enforcement officers, the looting of shops, the burning of public and private buildings, the threatening of passer-by and journalists and the desecration of the l'Arc de Triomphe." Macron toured the damage and reportedly held an emergency meeting with top ministers upon returning to Paris. Some speculated that the government would declare a state of emergency, but no such announcement was made. Macron said that he sympathized with his "fellow citizens" but that he would not give in to violence. He said that the government would not repeal the fuel tax increase but that he was open to discussion about how the tax would be applied, signaling, for example, that the tax could be adjusted when gas prices spike to ease the financial burden on drivers. Macron further acknowledged that past policies had encouraged people to move out of France's cities and travel by road, saying "we pushed them into this situation." Macron's political rivals were quick to criticize his remarks: National Rally political party leader Marine Le Pen said the president was "devoid of any solutions," while Socialist Olivier Faure wrote that the president "says that he hears [the complaints], but does not understand."

Anticipating another wave of violent protest, many Parisian landmarks, shops, and restaurants were closed the following weekend. Prime Minister Édouard Philippe said that 89,000 police officers would be on duty across France and armored tanks would be deployed in Paris to help limit the violence. More riots shook the capital and other major cities across France, but the protests were less violent than those of the prior weekend.

## GOVERNMENT ABANDONS FUEL TAX, ANNOUNCES ADDITIONAL ACTIONS

The ongoing yellow vest protests posed the greatest challenge Macron had faced since taking office in May 2017. A late-November poll by Ifop-Fiducial found that Macron's approval rating had fallen to 23 percent from 29 percent in October, while Philippe's approval rating had fallen ten points to 26 percent. A separate poll conducted by Harris Interactive on December 2 found that 72 percent of French people supported the yellow vest movement, though 85 percent disapproved of the recent violence. Macron also faced pressure from France's provincial governments. On December 4, French newspaper *L'Opinion* published a letter from twelve of the country's thirteen regional leaders calling for a moratorium on the fuel tax and urging the government to take the time to consider how its proposal could be improved.

That day, Philippe announced a six-month suspension of the proposed fuel tax, saying that "no tax deserves to endanger the unity of the nation." He expressed the government's hope that the suspension would "bring calm and serenity back" to France and "enable real dialogue" with protestors. (The government reportedly invited yellow vest representatives to participate in talks before the Paris riots and after, but protestors left the first meeting after realizing it was not being recorded and cancelled the second meeting due to safety concerns.) Philippe also announced that planned increases in gas and electricity prices would be suspended for three months. The suspension marked the government's first significant policy concession to the protestors, but many said it was not enough. Benjamin Cauchy, an unofficial leader of the yellow vest movement, described the announcement as a "first step," adding, "we will not settle for a crumb." The government abandoned the fuel tax altogether on December 5, but this failed to quell the protests due to the movement's expanded demands.

On December 10, Macron met with representatives from five major trade unions and three employers' organizations, as well as local government officials, to discuss protestors' grievances and potential responses. Macron delivered a televised address to the nation later that evening, during which he declared an "economic and social state of emergency" and announced additional reforms. Macron pledged to increase the minimum wage by 7 percent, with increased costs to be covered by the government, not employers. He also promised to end taxes on overtime pay and cancel a planned tax increase for low-income pensioners. Additionally, Macron said employers would be encouraged to give employees tax-free year-end bonuses. However, the president reiterated his position against reinstating the wealth tax, which he claimed would weaken France and hinder job creation. "We have come to the crossroad of our country and our future," Macron declared. He acknowledged the deep anger felt by many struggling French and that his government had not responded to their concerns quickly enough, but he also urged calm and peace. "Calm and republican order must reign," the president said. "No lasting project can be achieved when there is no social peace."

Despite winning additional concessions from Macron, French discontent with the government continued to expand. Around the time of the president's announcement, students began protesting his proposed changes to the baccalaureate exam they must take to attend college, claiming the changes would foster inequality by limiting opportunities for some students. Two road transportation unions called for worker strikes to protest changes to overtime payments. Yellow vest protests continued through February, though demonstrations have generally become smaller over time. At the same time Macron sought to improve his image and ease tensions through the Grand National Debate, a series of town hall–style meetings and debates with local leaders and constituents across France that was intended to collect input on topics including taxes, democracy, and environmental policies.

—Linda Grimm

*Following is a statement by French President Emmanuel Macron on December 1, 2018, in response to the riots in Paris; and a national address by Macron on December 10, 2018, during which he announced a minimum wage increase and other economic actions.*

## Macron Responds to Riots in Paris

**December 1, 2018**

During his statement at the end of the G20 in Argentina, the President commented on the violence:

"What happened today in Paris has nothing to do with a peaceful expression of a legitimate anger. No cause can justify an attack on law enforcement officers, the looting of shops, the burning of public and private buildings, the threatening of passer-by and journalists and the desecration of the l'Arc de Triomphe. The perpetrators of these violent acts do not want any change nor improvement, their sole desire is chaos: they are betraying the cause they claimed they are fighting for and are manipulating others. They will be identified and brought to justice to answer for their actions. Upon my return tomorrow, I will summon an interministerial meeting with the competent services. I will always respect protests, I will always listen to oppositions but I will never condone violence."

SOURCE: President of the Republic of France. "What Happened Today in Paris Has Nothing to Do with a Peaceful Expression of a Legitimate Anger." December 1, 2018. Translated by SAGE Publishing. https://www.elysee.fr/emmanuel-macron/2018/12/01/ce-quil-sest-passe-aujourdhui-a-paris-na-rien-a-voir-avec-lexpression-pacifique-dune-colere-legitime.

## Macron Delivers National Address on Yellow Vest Protests

**December 10, 2018**

My dear French compatriots, we have come to the crossroad of our country and our future. The events witnessed in the past few weeks on the French and Oversea Territories have deeply troubled the Nation. They brought together legitimate claims and a series of unacceptable acts of violence and let me be very clear: these acts of violence will not benefit from any indulgence.

We all saw the ugly games of opportunists who are struggling to leverage on sincere angers to lead them astray. We all saw reckless politicians whose only aim was to trouble the Republic, seek for disorder and anarchy. No anger is grounded when it leads to an attack on a police or gendarme officer or to the destruction of shops and public buildings.

The very existence of our freedom is based on the fact that everyone can express his opinions that others don't share without fear of these differences.

When violence takes the upper hand, freedom ceases to exist. Henceforth, calm and republican order must reign. No lasting project can be achieved when there is no social peace, we shall deploy all resources to restore peace. It is within this context that I instructed the government to take stringent measures.

However, first and foremost, I will like to acknowledge the fact that people are angry and annoyed, and this annoyance is shared by many among us, so many French people share this indignation, which I will not confine to the unacceptable behaviors that are been condemned here.

It all began with anger against a tax and the Prime Minister provided a solution by cancelling it and by removing all increases provided to take effect from the beginning of next year, however, the root of this anger is deeper and I feel it in so many respects. This situation could be an opportunity for us.

This is the case of a couple of employees who cannot end up a month but who gets up early every day and return late and who work very far from their home.

It is the case of a single mother, a widow or a divorcee, who no longer lives, who does have the means to pay for the child care of his/her children, nor is she/he able to improve his/her monthly income and has no hope. For the first time, I met them, these courageous women who are shouting their distress at so many roundabouts!

It is the case of low-income pensioners who contributed all through their lives and often helped both parents and children and are unable to make it.

It is the case of underprivileged persons, people living with disabilities who place is not well defined in the society. Their distress is not new but we cowardly end up getting used to it and basically, everything was happening as if they were forgotten or discarded.

The result of the social malaise of the past forty years is resurfacing: the discomfort of workers who are completely loss; the unrest on the territories, villages as well as neighborhoods where publics services are shrinking and living conditions are deteriorating, the democratic unrest that gives room to the feeling of not being heard; discomfort with respect to the evolutions of our society, a hustled secularism before some life styles that create barriers and distance.

Their roots are traced far back into history, but it is here now.

There is no doubt that we were unable to provide a sufficiently quick and fast response for the past one and the half year. I take my share of this responsibility. I may have made you feel that I do not care that I had other priorities. I am also aware that I may have hurt some of you with my statements. Tonight, let me be very clear with you. If I fought to hustle the political system, habits and hypocrisies in place, it is specifically because I believe more than everything in our country and that I love this country because my legitimacy comes from nothing else than you, not even a title, a party or any coterie.

Several other countries are experiencing this malaise that we are witnessing today, but I deeply believe that together we can find a solution. That is my desire for France because it is our vocation over the years to path the unexplored way for ourselves and for the world.

That is my burning wish for France because people who are so divided, who no longer respect their laws and the friendship that binds them together are heading to their ruin.

This is my desire because it is by sensing this crisis that I solicited your vote to reconcile and bring together. Let me reassure you that I have not forgotten this commitment and this pressing need.

Today, I will start by declaring an economic and social state of emergency. We want to build a country of value, of work, a France where our children will live better than us. This can only be done through better schools, universities, learning and trainings that will provide the younger and youngest generations what is needed to live freely and work properly.

I confirm that investment in the Nation, in schools and in training is an unprecedented concept.

We all want to build a France where everyone should live with dignity from his work? On this point, our progress has been very slow. I want to take rapid and concrete decisions on this matter. I therefore ask the government and the Parliament to take the necessary measures to ensure that people live better from their jobs as from the beginning of next year. The minimum wage (SMIC) of an employee will increase by 100 euro per month as from 2019 without costing a single euro for the employer.

I want to reconnect with a good grasp, which stated that the increased of accepted work is also an increase of income; from 2019, extra hours will be paid without taxes or charges. And I want to see a genuine improvement right away; for this reason I will ask all employers who can, to pay a bonus at the end of the year to their employees and this bonus will be exempted from any tax or charges.

Pensioners constitute a valuable part of our Nation. For those who earn less than 2,000 Euro per month, in 2019, we will cancel the increase of supplementary social security contribution (CSG) borne this year; the effort requested from them was too much and was unjust. As from tomorrow, the Prime Minister will present all these decisions to parliamentarians.

However, we will not stop there. I am pleading with our large companies, and our wealthier fellow citizens, to help the Nation succeed; I will meet them this week and will take decisions in this respect. I know that some of you may desire a review of the wealth tax reform, but for close to 40 years, this reform has been operational, do we live better now? The wealthy people were leaving and our country was growing weaker. In compliance with the commitments taken before you, this tax was cancelled for those who are investing in our economy and hence help to create jobs; and in the contrary, it was maintained for those who have real estate properties.

Going back will weaken us meanwhile we are in a course of recreating jobs in all sectors of activities. That notwithstanding, the Government and the Parliament will have to go further to put an end to undue advantages as well as tax evasions. The manager of a French Company must pay his taxes in France and large companies that make profits in France must also pay taxes there, that is justice.

As you can see, we are responding to the socio-economic emergency by strong measures, by more rapid tax reductions, by a better control of expenditures rather than setbacks.

I intend to urge the Government continue with the ambition of transforming our country, an option that the people chose some 18 months ago; we have a great task ahead of us that of conducting a deep reform of the State, compensating unemployment and pensioners. These reforms are indispensable: We all need fairer, simpler and clearer rules, and especially those that compensate workers.

But today, what we need the more is to reconnect with our collective project. For the Nation of France and for Europe. Reason why the national debate earlier declared must be inclusive. Is based on this ground that we shall all take our responsibilities. The responsibility of producing in order to redistribute, the responsibility to learn in a bid to become a free citizen, the responsibility to change in order to take into account the urgency of our climate and budget liabilities.

To succeed, we must come together and tackle all key issues relating to our Nation. I will not dodge away from issues affecting representation; the possibility to listen to the various currents of opinion better apprehended in their diversity, a fairer electoral law, the inclusion of white ballots and even citizens not belonging to political parties should be allowed to take part in the debate. I also wish that issues on our tax system be raised so that it could lead to justice and efficiency in our country. Let us tackle the questions of our daily life in order to address the issue of climate change: accommodation, transportation and heating system. And good solutions will also emerge from the field.

Don't hesitate to ask question related to the organization of the State, the manner in which it is run and governed from Paris, of course highly centralized for decades now. Don't forget the issue of public service in all our territories.

I also want the Nation to come to a mutual agreement on the meaning of our deep identity, that we should address the issue of migration. We must face all these questions.

These substantive changes require a thorough and shared reflection, which must be conducted within an unprecedented debate. This debate must take place at the national level in our institutions, each will have its share that is: the Government, assemblies, social partners and associations, you will also take part. I intend to personally ensure the coordination, receive the various opinions, measure the heartbeat of our country.

However, the magnitude of such a debate cannot be restricted only to institutional representatives; it should also take place everywhere on the field and there are natural partners and some citizens that must receive the request and serve as relays: these are the mayors who are the administrators of the Republic on the field. It is for this reason that I will personally meet the Mayors of France, region after region to lay down a solid bedrock for a new social contract for our Nation.

We will not resume the normal course of our lives, as it has always been the case in the past with similar crisis, without really understanding the situation and without attempting to change it. We are at a turning point for our country: through dialogue, respect and commitment, we shall overcome.

We have got down to task and I will be back to give you an account of what has been done.

My sole preoccupation, is you, my only struggle is for you.

Our only battle is for France.

Long live the Republic, long live France.

SOURCE: President of the Republic of France. "Address of the President of the Republic Emmanuel Macron to the Nation." December 10, 2018. Translated by SAGE Publishing. https://www.elysee.fr/emmanuel-macron/2018/12/10/adresse-du-president-de-la-republique-du-lundi-10-decembre-2018.

## OTHER HISTORIC DOCUMENTS OF INTEREST

### FROM PREVIOUS HISTORIC DOCUMENTS

# Nobel Peace Prize Awarded to Antirape Activists

DECEMBER 10, 2018

Since 1901, the Nobel Peace Prize has been awarded ninety-nine times to 133 laureates, both individuals and organizations. In his will establishing the prize, Alfred Nobel outlined three types of peace work that could qualify for the award: contributions to fraternity between nations, to the abolition or reduction of standing armies, or to the holding and promotion of peace congresses. After years of speculation that he would win the annual award, on December 10, 2018, the Nobel Committee presented the peace prize to Denis Mukwege, a gynecological surgeon from the Democratic Republic of the Congo (DRC). Mukwege shared the prize with Nadia Murad, an Iraqi woman forced into sexual slavery by the Islamic State of Iraq and the Levant (ISIL). The pair were honored for their work to end mass rape and other forms of sexual abuse used as a weapon of war.

## African, Middle Eastern Activists Share Nobel Peace Prize

The Norwegian Nobel Committee does not immediately publicize the names of all those nominated for the annual award, waiting until fifty years after the award is presented to make the names public. At times, organizations will share information on who they nominated, and bookmakers around the world frequently publicize the odds of potential victors. In 2018, there were thought to be more than 330 candidates under consideration by the five-member committee. According to *Time* Magazine, favorites among odds makers were the leaders of North and South Korea, Kim Jong Un and Moon Jae-in, U.S. President Donald Trump, Pope Francis, the United Nations High Commissioner for Refugees, and the American Civil Liberties Union.

On October 5, 2018, Berit Reiss-Andersen, chair of the committee, ended speculation when she announced that the award would be shared by Mukwege and Murad. She explained the committee's decision was rooted in a desire "to send out a message of awareness that women, who constitute half of the population in most communities, actually are used as a weapon of war, and that they need protection and that the perpetrators have to be prosecuted and held responsible for their actions." Andersen said, "A more peaceful world can only be achieved if women and their fundamental rights and security are recognized and protected in war." She added that the pair "put their personal security at risk by courageously combatting war crime and seeking justice for victims." When asked whether the award was inspired by the global #MeToo movement against sexual assault and harassment, Andersen explained that "#MeToo and war crimes [are] not quite the same thing," but "it is important to see the suffering of women, to see the abuses . . . it is also important that women leave the concept of shame and speak up."

Mukwege is known in the DRC as "the man who mends women." He and his colleagues have treated an estimated 30,000 women, most of whom are survivors of sexual violence. Many of his patients receive surgery for vaginal fistula, a tear in the muscle caused by violent rape, and he also provides counseling to address the psychological challenges posed by the sexual violence perpetrated by government security forces and armed militias. Mukwege said in past interviews that he sees some women for the same problem multiple times and has treated children as young as two as well as the elderly. Mukwege learned of the award while he was in the operating room and said the prize "reflects the recognition of suffering and the lack of a just reparation for women victims of rape and sexual violence in all countries of the world and on all continents." He dedicated the award to women around the world "bruised by conflict and facing everyday violence."

Murad, a member of the Yazidi minority in Iraq, was abducted and sold into sexual slavery by ISIL in 2014. Her six brothers and mother were all murdered by the terrorist group. After three months of captivity, Murad escaped to Mosul with the help of a Sunni family. Unlike many other women who have escaped ISIL and who prefer to remain anonymous, Murad wanted her name and picture to be used as she advocated before international bodies, calling on them to recognize and address the genocide of the Yazidi people and use of sexual assault as a weapon of war. Murad said she was "incredibly honored and humbled" to receive the Nobel Peace Prize, which she said she shared "with Yazidis, Iraqis, Kurds, other persecuted minorities, and all of the countless victims of sexual violence around the world."

## Awardees Urge Global Action against Sexual Violence

At the December award ceremony in Oslo, both Mukwege and Murad used their lectures to call on the international community to do more to combat sexual violence against women. "Thank you very much for this honour," said Murad, the second-youngest Nobel Peace Prize awardee in history, "but the fact remains that the only prize in the world that can restore our dignity is justice and the prosecution of criminals. There is no award that can compensate for our people and our loved ones who were killed solely because they were Yazidis." Murad described her childhood growing up in Kojo, a village in Northern Iraq and one of the first in the country captured by ISIL. Murad explained that both the Iraqi government and Kurdish leaders failed to protect the Yazidi minority in her community, but she reserved her sharpest criticism for countries around the world, who she said stood idly by as the Yazidis were rounded up and sold into slavery. "In the 21st century, in the age of globalization and human rights, more than 6,500 Yazidi children and women became captive and were sold, bought, and sexually and psychologically abused. Despite our daily appeals since 2014, the fate of more than 3,000 children and women in the grip of ISIS is still unknown," Murad said. "It is inconceivable that the conscience of the leaders of 195 countries around the world is not mobilised to liberate these girls. What if they were a commercial deal, an oil field or a shipment of weapons? Most certainly, no efforts would be spared to liberate them."

Mukwege similarly used his lecture to call for international action and justice for the victims of sexual violence. "This human tragedy will continue if those responsible are not prosecuted. Only the fight against impunity can break the spiral of violence," he said. Mukwege spoke of his years treating the victims of sexual violence and explained that they had taught him "that the problem could not be solved in the operating room, but that we had to combat the root causes of these atrocities." The violence in the DRC, according to Mukwege, resulted in "hundreds of thousands of women raped, over 4 million people displaced within the country and the loss of 6 million human lives." Mukwege said it was not only those perpetrating the violence who were responsible for the chaos and destruction in the DRC but also those in the international community who turned a blind eye to the crisis. "The Congolese people have been humiliated, abused and massacred for more than two decades in plain sight of the international community," Mukwege said. "I call upon you . . . to stand up and together say loudly: 'The violence in the DRC, it's enough! Enough is enough! Peace, now!'"

## ADDITIONAL NOBEL AWARDEES

The Nobel Prize is also given out in the categories of Physiology or Medicine, Physics, Chemistry, Literature, and Economic Sciences. The Swedish Academy, a panel of writers and scholars responsible for awarding the Nobel Prize in Literature, announced in May that it would not select a winner for 2018 but would instead choose two in 2019. That decision was driven by a scandal surrounding Jean-Claude Arnault, a photographer whose wife is a member of the academy, and who jointly own a cultural center in Stockholm that receives academy funding. In November 2017, *Dagens Nyheter*, a Swedish newspaper, reported that Arnault had sexually assaulted or harassed at least eighteen women. According to his accusers, Arnault used his connections to the Swedish Academy to coerce women into sex. The allegations resulted in high-profile resignations from the academy, which the body said contributed to its decision to postpone the award. "We find it necessary to commit time to recovering public confidence . . . before the next laureate can be announced," said interim permanent secretary Anders Olsson. "This is out of respect for previous and future literature laureates, the Nobel Foundation, and the general public."

The Swedish Academy only awards the Nobel Prize in Literature, so its decision did not affect the prizes in the four other categories. The prize for Physics was awarded to Arthur Ashkin, Gérard Monurou, and Donna Strickland—who was only the third woman to win the Physics prize—for their work in the field of laser physics. The Nobel Prize in Chemistry was similarly split, with half going to Frances H. Arnold and the other half shared by George P. Smith and Sir Gregory P. Winter, all of whom focused on the principles of evolution in their enzyme research meant to address chemical issues in the human body. The Physiology or Medicine prize was awarded to James P. Allison and Tasuku Honjo, who made a landmark discovery in the fight against cancer. The Economic Sciences prize was given to William D. Nordhaus and Paul M. Romer for their work in macroeconomic analysis.

—Heather Kerrigan

*Following is the text of the Nobel Peace Prize lectures delivered on December 10, 2018, by awardees Nadia Murad and Denis Mukwege.*

# *Nadia Murad Delivers Nobel Lecture*

**December 10, 2018**

Your Majesties, Your Royal Highnesses, Excellencies, Distinguished Members of the Committee, Ladies and Gentlemen, my warm greetings to you.

I would like to thank The Nobel Committee for bestowing this honour on me. It is a great honour to have been awarded this valuable prize with my friend Dr Denis Mukwege, who has been working tirelessly to help victims of sexual violence and to be a voice for those women who have been subjected to violence.

I want to talk to you from the bottom of my heart and to share with you how the course of my life and the life of the entire Yazidi community have changed because of this genocide, and how ISIS tried to eradicate one of the components of Iraq by taking women into captivity, killing men and destroying our pilgrimage sites and houses of worship.

Today is a special day for me. It is the day when good has triumphed over evil, the day when humanity defeated terrorism, the day that the children and women who have suffered persecution have triumphed over the perpetrators of these crimes.

I hope that today marks the beginning of a new era—when peace is the priority, and the world can collectively begin to define a new roadmap to protect women, children and minorities from persecution, in particular victims of sexual violence.

I lived my childhood as a village girl in Kojo, south of Sinjar region. I did not know anything about the Nobel Peace Prize. I knew nothing about the conflicts and killings that took place in our world every day. I did not know that human beings could perpetrate such hideous crimes against each other.

As a young girl, I dreamed of finishing high school. It was my dream to have a beauty parlour in our village and to live near my family in Sinjar. But this dream became a nightmare. Unexpected things happened. Genocide took place. As a consequence, I lost my mother, six of my brothers and my brothers' children. Every Yazidi family has a similar story, one more horrible than the other because of this genocide.

Yes, our lives have changed overnight, in a way we can hardly understand. Every Yazidi family counts members that are separated from each other. The social fabric of a peaceful community has been torn apart, a whole society that was carrying high the banner of peace and the culture of tolerance has become fuel for a useless war.

In our history, we have been subjected to many campaigns of genocide because of our beliefs and religion. As a result of these genocides, there are only a few Yazidis left in Turkey. In Syria, there were about 80,000 Yazidis, today there are only 5000. In Iraq, the Yazidis face the same fate, their number is decreasing significantly. The goal of ISIS to eradicate this religion will be achieved unless the Yazidis are provided the appropriate protection. This is also the case for other minorities in Iraq and Syria.

After the failure of the Government of Iraq and the Government of Kurdistan to protect us, the international community also failed to save us from ISIS and to prevent the occurrence of the genocide against us, and stood idly by watching the annihilation of a complete community. Our homes, our families, our traditions, our people, our dreams were all destroyed.

After the genocide, we received international and local sympathy, and many countries recognized this genocide, but the genocide did not stop. The threat of annihilation still exists.

The predicament of the Yazidis in the prisons of ISIS has not changed. They have not been able to leave the camps, nothing of what ISIS destroyed has been rebuilt. So far, the perpetrators of the crimes which led to this genocide have not been brought to justice. I do not seek more sympathy; I want to translate those feelings into actions on the ground.

If the international community is serious about providing assistance to the victims of this genocide, and if we want the Yazidis to leave displacement camps and return to their areas, and give them confidence again, the international community should provide them with international protection under United Nations supervision. Without this international protection, there is no guarantee that we will not be subjected to other genocides from other terrorist groups. The international community must be committed to providing asylum and immigration opportunities to those who have become victims of this genocide.

Today is a special day for all Iraqis, not only because I am the first Iraqi to win the Nobel Peace Prize. It is also the day when we celebrate the victory of liberating Iraqi territory from the terrorist organization of ISIS. The Iraqis from the North to the South united their forces and fought a long battle on behalf of the world against this extremist terrorist organization.

This unity gave us strength. We also need to unite our efforts to investigate the crimes of ISIS and prosecute those who welcomed, helped and joined them to control vast areas in Iraq. There should be no place for terrorism and extremist ideas in post-ISIS Iraq; we must join forces in building our country; we must contribute together to achieve security, stability and prosperity for the benefit of all Iraqis.

We have to remember every day how the terrorist organization of ISIS and those who carry its ideas attacked the Yazidis with unprecedented brutality in 2014 with the aim of ending the existence of one of the original components of the Iraqi society. They committed this genocide for the sole reason that we are Yazidis who have different beliefs and customs and who are against killing each other or holding people in captivity or enslaving them.

In the 21st century, in the age of globalization and human rights, more than 6,500 Yazidi children and women became captive and were sold, bought, and sexually and psychologically abused. Despite our daily appeals since 2014, the fate of more than 3,000 children and women in the grip of ISIS is still unknown. Young girls at the prime of life are sold, bought, held captive and raped every day. It is inconceivable that the conscience of the leaders of 195 countries around the world is not mobilised to liberate these girls. What if they were a commercial deal, an oil field or a shipment of weapons? Most certainly, no efforts would be spared to liberate them.

Every day I hear tragic stories. Hundreds of thousands and even millions of children and women around the world are suffering from persecution and violence. Every day I hear the screams of children in Syria, Iraq and Yemen. Every day we see hundreds of women and children in Africa and other countries becoming murder projects fuel for wars, without anyone moving in to help them or hold to account those who commit these crimes.

For almost four years, I have been travelling around the world to tell my story and that of my community and other vulnerable communities, without having achieved any justice. The perpetrators of sexual violence against Yazidi and other women and girls are yet to be prosecuted for these crimes. If justice is not done, this genocide will be repeated against us and against other vulnerable communities. Justice is the only way to achieve peace and co-existence among the various components of Iraq. If we do not want to repeat cases of rape and captivity against women, we must hold to account those who have used sexual violence as a weapon to commit crimes against women and girls.

Thank you very much for this honour, but the fact remains that the only prize in the world that can restore our dignity is justice and the prosecution of criminals. There is no award that can compensate for our people and our loved ones who were killed solely because they were Yazidis. The only prize that will restore a normal life between our people and our friends is justice and protection for the rest of this community.

We celebrate these days the 70th anniversary of the Universal Declaration of Human Rights, which aims at preventing genocides and calls for the prosecution of their perpetrators. My community has been subjected to genocide for more than four years. The international community did nothing to deter it nor to stop it. It did not bring the perpetrators to justice. Other vulnerable communities have been subjected to ethnic cleansing, racism and identity change in plain sight of the international community.

The protection of the Yazidis and all vulnerable communities around the world is the responsibility of the international community and international institutions in charge of defending human rights, the protection of minorities, the protection of the rights of women and children, especially in areas where conflicts and internal wars take place.

I had the privilege of participating in the Paris Peace Conference. This conference celebrated the 100th anniversary of the end of World War I. But how many genocides and wars have taken place since World War I ended? The victims of wars, in particular internal wars, are countless. The world condemned these wars and recognised these genocides. It however failed to put an end to acts of war and to prevent their recurrence.

It is true that there are numerous conflicts and problems in the world, but there are also many initiatives to support the victims and huge efforts are exerted to bring about justice.

For without the initiative taken by the government of Baden-Württemberg and Mr Kretschmann and their assistance, I would not have been able to enjoy my freedom today, to denounce the crimes of ISIS and tell the truth about the sufferings of the Yazidis. It is my view that all victims deserve a safe haven until justice is done for them.

Education plays an essential role in nurturing civilized societies that believe in tolerance and peace. Therefore, we must invest in our children because children, like a blank slate, can be taught tolerance and co-existence instead of hatred and sectarianism. Women must also be the key to solving many problems and must be involved in building lasting peace among communities. With the voice and participation of women, we can make fundamental changes in our communities.

I am proud of the Yazidis, for their strength and patience. Our community has been targeted many times and threatened in its existence, yet we continue to struggle for our right to exist. The Yazidi community embodies peace and tolerance and must be considered an example for the world.

I would like to take this opportunity to address my thanks to the persons who defended and carried my message since the first day, in particular my team who stood by my side day in day out.

I thank all the governments that recognized the Yazidi genocide and the governments that provided support to vulnerable communities. Thank you Canada and Australia for hosting victims of the Yazidi genocide. I thank France and President Macron for their humanitarian support to our cause. My thanks go to the people of Iraqi Kurdistan for their support all along the last four years to the internally displaced people. I thank the Emir of Kuwait and the government of Norway for organising the Conference for the Reconstruction of Iraq. I thank my friend Amal Clooney and her team for their huge efforts to hold ISIS to account. I thank Greece for the unlimited support to refugees.

Let us all unite to fight injustice and oppression; Let us raise our voices together and say: No to violence, yes to peace, no to slavery, yes to freedom, no to racial discrimination, yes to equality and to human rights for all.

No to exploiting women and children, yes to providing a decent and independent life to them, no to impunity for criminals, yes to holding criminals accountable and to achieving justice.

Thank you for your hospitality and kind attention. May you all live in lasting Peace.

SOURCE: The Nobel Foundation. "Nadia Murad—Nobel Lecture." December 10, 2018. ©The Nobel Foundation. https://www.nobelprize.org/prizes/peace/2018/murad/55705-nadia-murad-nobel-lecture-2.

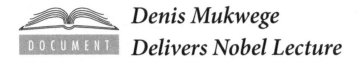

DOCUMENT

## *Denis Mukwege Delivers Nobel Lecture*

**December 10, 2018**

In the tragic night of 6 October 1996, rebels attacked our hospital in Lemera, in the Democratic Republic of Congo (RDC). More than thirty people were killed. Patients were slaughtered in their beds point blank. Unable to flee, the staff were killed in cold blood.

I could not have imagined that it was only the beginning.

Forced to leave Lemera in 1999, we set up the Panzi hospital in Bukavu where I still work as an obstetrician-gynaecologist today.

The first patient admitted was a rape victim who had been shot in her genitals.

The macabre violence knew no limit.

Sadly, this violence has never stopped.

One day like any other, the hospital received a phone call.

At the other end of the line, a colleague in tears implored: "Please send us an ambulance fast. Please hurry."

So we sent an ambulance, as we normally do.

Two hours later, the ambulance returned.

Inside was a little girl about eighteen months old. She was bleeding profusely and was immediately taken to the operating room.

When I arrived, all the nurses were sobbing. The baby's bladder, genitals and rectum were severely injured.

By the penetration of an adult.

We prayed in silence: my God, tell us what we are seeing isn't true.

Tell us it's a bad dream.

Tell us when we wake up, everything will be alright.

But it was not a bad dream.

It was the reality.

It has become our new reality in the DRC.

When another baby arrived, I realized that the problem could not be solved in the operating room, but that we had to combat the root causes of these atrocities.

I decided to travel to the village of Kavumu to talk to the men: why don't you protect your babies, your daughters, your wives? And where are the authorities?

To my surprise, the villagers knew the suspect. Everyone was afraid of him, since he was a member of the provincial Parliament and enjoyed absolute power over the population.

For several months, his militia has been terrorising the whole village. It had instilled fear by killing a human rights defender who had had the courage to report the facts. The deputy got away with no consequences. His parliamentary immunity enabled him to abuse with impunity.

The two babies were followed by several dozens of other raped children.

When the forty-eighth victim arrived, we were desperate.

With other human rights defenders, we went to a military court. At last, the rapes were prosecuted and judged as crimes against humanity.

The rapes of babies in Kavumu stopped.

And so did the calls to Panzi hospital.

But these babies' psychological, sexual and reproductive health is severely impaired.

What happened in Kavumu and what is still going on in many other places in Congo, such as the rapes and massacres in Béni and Kasaï, was made possible by the absence of the rule of law, the collapse of traditional values and the reign of impunity, particularly for those in power.

Rape, massacres, torture, widespread insecurity and a flagrant lack of education create a spiral of unprecedented violence.

The human cost of this perverted, organized chaos has been hundreds of thousands of women raped, over 4 million people displaced within the country and the loss of 6 million human lives. Imagine, the equivalent of the entire population of Denmark decimated.

United Nations peacekeepers and experts have not been spared, either. Several of them have been killed on duty. Today, the United Nations Mission is still in the DRC to prevent the situation from degenerating further.

We are grateful to them.

However, despite their efforts, this human tragedy will continue if those responsible are not prosecuted. Only the fight against impunity can break the spiral of violence.

We all have the power to change the course of history when the beliefs we are fighting for are right.

—

Your Majesties, Your Royal Highnesses, Your Excellencies, Distinguished members of the Nobel Committee, dear Madam Nadia Murad, Ladies and Gentlemen, Friends of peace,

It is in the name of the Congolese people that I accept the Nobel Peace Prize. It is to all victims of sexual violence across the world that I dedicate this prize.

It is with humility that I come before you to raise the voice of the victims of sexual violence in armed conflicts and the hopes of my compatriots.

I take this opportunity to thank everyone who, over the years, has supported our battle. I am thinking, in particular, of the organizations and institutions of friendly countries, my colleagues, my family and my dear wife Madeleine.

—

My name is Denis Mukwege. I come from one of the richest countries on the planet. Yet the people of my country are among the poorest of the world.

The troubling reality is that the abundance of our natural resources—gold, coltan, cobalt and other strategic minerals—is the root cause of war, extreme violence and abject poverty.

We love nice cars, jewellery and gadgets. I have a smartphone myself. These items contain minerals found in our country. Often mined in inhuman conditions by young children, victims of intimidation and sexual violence.

When you drive your electric car; when you use your smart phone or admire your jewellery, take a minute to reflect on the human cost of manufacturing these objects.

As consumers, let us at least insist that these products are manufactured with respect for human dignity.

Turning a blind eye to this tragedy is being complicit.

It's not just perpetrators of violence who are responsible for their crimes, it is also those who choose to look the other way.

My country is being systematically looted with the complicity of people claiming to be our leaders. Looted for their power, their wealth and their glory. Looted at the expense of millions of innocent men, women and children abandoned in extreme poverty. While the profits from our minerals end up in the pockets of a predatory oligarchy.

For twenty years now, day after day, at Panzi hospital, I have seen the harrowing consequences of the country's gross mismanagement.

Babies, girls, young women, mothers, grandmothers, and also men and boys, cruelly raped, often publicly and collectively, by inserting burning plastic or sharp objects in their genitals.

I'll spare you the details.

The Congolese people have been humiliated, abused and massacred for more than two decades in plain sight of the international community.

Today, with access to the most powerful communication technology ever, no one can say: "I didn't know".

—

With this Nobel Peace Prize, I call on the world to be a witness and I urge you to join us in order to put an end to this suffering that shames our common humanity.

The people of my country desperately need peace.

But:

How to build peace on mass graves?

How to build peace without truth nor reconciliation?

How to build peace without justice nor reparation?

As I speak to you, a report is gathering mold in an office drawer in New York. It was drafted following a professional investigation into war crimes and human rights violations perpetrated in Congo. This investigation explicitly names the victims, the places and the dates, but leaves the perpetrators nameless.

This Mapping Report by the office of the United Nations High Commissioner for Human Rights describes no fewer than 617 war crimes and crimes against humanity and perhaps even crimes of genocide.

What is the world waiting for before taking this into account? There is no lasting peace without justice. Yet, justice in not negotiable.

Let us have the courage to take a critical and impartial look at what has been going on for too long in the Great Lakes Region.

Let us have the courage to reveal the names of the perpetrators of the crimes against humanity to prevent them from continuing to plague the region.

Let us have the courage to recognize our past mistakes.

Let us have the courage to tell the truth, to remember and commemorate.

Dear Congolese compatriots, let us have the courage to take our destiny in our own hands. Let us build peace, build our country's future, and together build a better future for Africa. No one else will do it for us.

—

Ladies and Gentlemen, Friends of peace,

The picture I have painted for you depicts a dark reality.

But let me tell you Sarah's story.

Sarah was referred to the hospital in critical condition. An armed group had attacked her village, massacred her whole family, and had left her alone.

Sarah was taken to the forest as a hostage, and tied to a tree. Naked. Sarah was gang-raped every day until she lost consciousness.

The aim of these rapes used as a weapon of war is to destroy the victim, her family and her community. In short, to destroy the social fabric.

When she arrived at the hospital, Sarah could not walk or even stand on her feet. She could not control her bladder nor her bowels.

Because of the seriousness of her genital, urinary and digestive injuries coupled with an infection, no one could imagine her one day being able to get back on her feet.

Yet, with each passing day, the desire to continue to live sparkled in Sarah's eyes. Every passing day, it was she who encouraged the medical staff not to lose hope.

Today, Sarah is a beautiful, smiling, strong and charming woman.

Sarah has committed herself to helping people who have survived a history like hers.

Sarah received fifty US dollars, a grant our Dorcas transit house gives to women who are ready to rebuild their lives socio-economically.

Today, Sarah runs her small business. She has bought a plot of land. The Panzi Foundation has helped her with sheeting to make a roof. She has built a little house. She is independent and proud.

Her experience shows that, no matter how difficult and hopeless the situation, with determination there is always hope at the end of the tunnel.

If a woman like Sarah does not give up, who are we to do so?

This is Sarah's story. Sarah is Congolese. But there are Sarahs in the Central African Republic, Colombia, Bosnia, Myanmar, Iraq and many other conflict-riven countries in the world.

—

At Panzi, our holistic care programme—which includes medical, psychological, socio-economic and legal support—shows that even if the road to recovery is long and difficult, victims have the potential to turn their suffering into power.

They can become agents of positive change in society. This is the case already at City of Joy, our rehabilitation centre in Bukavu where women receive support to regain control of their destiny.

However, they cannot succeed on their own and our role is to listen to them, as today we listen to Madam Nadia Murad.

Dear Nadia, your courage, your audacity, your ability to give us hope, are a source of inspiration for the entire world and for me personally.

—

The Nobel Peace Prize awarded to us today will be of value only if it leads to concrete change in the lives of victims of sexual violence all over the world and the restoration of peace in our countries.

So, what can we do?

What can you do?

First, it is incumbent upon all of us to act in this direction.

Taking action is a choice.

It is a choice:

- whether or not we stop violence against women,

- whether or not we create a positive masculinity which promotes gender equality, in times of peace and in times of war.

It is a choice:

- – whether or not to support a woman,
- – whether or not to protect her,
- – whether or not to defend her rights,
- – whether or not to fight on her side in countries ravaged by conflict.

It is a choice: whether or not to build peace in the countries in conflict.

Taking action means saying 'no' to indifference.

If there is a war to be waged, it is the war against the indifference which is eating away at our societies.

Second, we are all indebted to these women and their loved-ones and we must all take ownership of this fight; including states by ceasing to welcome leaders who have tolerated, or worse, used sexual violence to take power.

States must stop welcoming them by rolling out the red carpet, and instead draw a red line against the use of rape as a weapon of war.

This red line would consist of imposing economic and political sanctions on these leaders and taking them to court.

Doing the right thing is not hard. It is a matter of political will.

Third, we must acknowledge the suffering of the survivors of all acts of violence against women in armed conflicts and support their holistic recovery process.

I insist on reparations: the measures that give survivors compensation and satisfaction and enable them to start a new life. It is a human right.

I call on States to support the initiative to create a Global Fund for reparations for victims of sexual violence in armed conflicts.

Fourth, on behalf of all widows, all widowers and orphans of the massacres committed in the DRC and all Congolese in love with peace, I call on the international community to finally consider the "Mapping Project report" and its recommendations.

May justice prevail.

This would allow the Congolese people to weep for their loved-ones, to mourn their dead, to forgive their torturers, to overcome their suffering and finally to project themselves into a serene future.

Finally, after twenty years of bloodshed, rape and massive population displacements, the Congolese people are desperately awaiting implementation of the responsibility to protect the civilian population when their government cannot or does not want to do so. The people are waiting to explore the path to a lasting peace.

To achieve peace, there has to be adherence to the principle of free, transparent, credible and peaceful elections.

"People of the Congo, let us get to work!" Let's build a State at the heart of Africa where the government serves its people. A State under the rule of law, capable of bringing lasting and harmonious development not just of the DRC but of the whole of Africa, where all political, economic and social actions will be based on a people-centred approach to restore human dignity of all citizens.

Your Majesties, Distinguished Members of the Nobel Committee, Ladies and Gentlemen, Friends of peace,

The challenge is clear. It is within our reach.

For all Sarahs, for all women, for all men and children of Congo, I call upon you not only to award this Nobel Peace Prize to my country's people, but to stand up and together say loudly: "The violence in the DRC, it's enough! Enough is enough! Peace, now!"
Thank you.

Denis Mukwege

SOURCE: The Nobel Foundation. "Denis Mukwege—Nobel Lecture." December 10, 2018. ©The Nobel Foundation. https://www.nobelprize.org/prizes/peace/2018/mukwege/55721-denis-mukwege-nobel-lecture-2.

## OTHER HISTORIC DOCUMENTS OF INTEREST

### FROM THIS VOLUME

### FROM PREVIOUS *HISTORIC DOCUMENTS*

# President Trump and Democrats Remark on Federal Government Shutdown

DECEMBER 11 AND 22, 2018, AND JANUARY 25, 2019

For thirty-five days, from midnight on December 22, 2018, until January 25, 2019, the federal government experienced its longest shutdown in history. The fiscal 2019 lapse in funding stemmed from disagreement between Democrats and Republicans over whether to provide $5.7 billion to President Donald Trump for a wall along the U.S.–Mexico border, one of the president's key campaign promises. The January 2019 stopgap bill that allowed the government to temporarily reopen for three weeks included no funding for the border wall, and the final fiscal 2019 spending legislation passed in February provided only $1.375 billion for steel border fencing. In response, after signing the funding measure into law, President Trump declared a national emergency in an attempt to gain access to money for the border wall. Sixteen states filed a challenge against the declaration in court, and House Democrats promised to bring to the floor a bill blocking the president's action.

## BORDER WALL LEADS TO FUNDING LAPSE

As a candidate, Trump promised to build a wall along the U.S.–Mexico border to stop illegal immigration that he said brought a steady flow of drugs and criminals into the United States. On the campaign trail, Trump promised that he would force Mexico to pay for the wall, something the country refused to do. In his first week as president, on January 25, 2017, Trump signed an executive order calling on the Department of Homeland Security (DHS) to "plan, design, and construct a physical wall along the southern border." The president wanted this barrier to be a solid wall, different from the collection of vertical steel slats, metal mesh fences, and metal posts already in place along nearly one-third of the 2,000-mile border. To provide the initial funds needed for construction, the president asked Congress for $1.6 billion. The House approved the funds as part of a larger national security spending bill, but the Senate never took it up because it was opposed by nearly all Democrats and some Republicans.

The president reprised his request for wall funding during the fiscal 2018 budget negotiations that took place in the summer and fall of 2017. Democrats and Republicans were unable to reach a consensus on whether or how to provide funding. At the same time, they were struggling to determine how to deal with other immigration concerns, namely whether those covered under the Deferred Action for Childhood Arrivals (DACA) policy should be offered further protections in exchange for wall funding or deported. These disagreements prevented Congress from passing a full-year budget and required that the federal government be funded through a series of continuing resolutions, two of which caused brief lapses in government funding and resulted in a total three days of shutdown. Ultimately, the omnibus spending bill signed in March 2018 did not address the fate of DACA recipients, nor did it provide Trump the funds he requested for his border wall. Instead, it allowed $1.6 billion for repair of existing sections of border barrier and thirty-three new miles of fencing but not the concrete-style wall the president sought.

Throughout 2018, the president continued to call on Congress to provide funding for a border wall. While awaiting the funds, the administration enacted several new policies to address illegal immigration along the U.S.–Mexico border, most of which were challenged in court. By the time fiscal 2019 began, on October 1, 2018, Democrats and Republicans were still at an impasse on the border wall and were also facing the impending midterm election. The compounding challenges forced Congress to again punt the issue of full-year spending in favor of minibus appropriations bills and a short-term continuing resolution. But after Democrats won back control of the House, Republicans hastened their attempts to get a budget complete before the new Congress was seated in January 2019. Their efforts proved unsuccessful.

## Negotiations Stall, Leading to Government Shutdown

On December 11, with the threat of a partial federal government shutdown just over a week away, President Trump met with House Minority Leader Nancy Pelosi, D-Calif., who was widely expected to reprise her role as Speaker in the new Congress, and Senate Minority Leader Chuck Schumer, D-N.Y. The meeting began on a high note with a brief discussion about the need for bipartisanship. The trio addressed two bills making their way through Congress that had broad support on both sides of the aisle, a criminal justice system overhaul and a farm bill, that the president hoped would come up for a vote. But the conversation quickly pivoted to the border wall. "One way or the other, it's going to get built. I'd like not to see a government closing, a shutdown. We will see what happens over the next short period of time. But the wall is a very important thing to us," Trump said.

Almost immediately, Trump and Pelosi went toe to toe on the wall, with Pelosi asking why Republicans had not attempted to pass a funding measure in the House, where they had control. The president asserted doing so would be meaningless because he did not have sixty votes in the Senate for final passage of a border-wall funding bill. Trump and Pelosi also argued over the semantics of whether to refer to the impending shutdown as the "Trump shutdown" or the "Pelosi shutdown." Schumer interrupted a heated exchange to explain that the Senate, House, and White House all agree that secure borders are a necessity. But, Schumer said, the most likely way to get funding for border security would be to revive legislation passed in 2017 that provided more than $1 billion to DHS, with the caveat that it could not be used for wall construction. "We want to do the same thing we did last year, this year. That's our proposal. If it's good then, it's good now, and it won't shut down the government," Schumer said. Trump responded, "Chuck, we can build a much bigger section with more money," adding that he would not sign any bill that is "not good border security." Pelosi and Schumer insisted what was currently being offered in Congress—a variation of the 2017 legislation—was what DHS had asked for.

Despite noting during the meeting with Pelosi and Schumer that he would be "proud" to shut down the government over the border security issue, just a few days later, media reports indicated that the president was considering backing a two-week stopgap spending measure that included no wall funding but that would allow the government to remain open while further budget negotiations took place. After meetings with the White House, on December 18, Senate Majority Leader Mitch McConnell, R-Ky., said that the president was "flexible" on border wall funding. Shortly after, White House Press Secretary Sarah Huckabee Sanders said the president would be willing to accept less than the $5.7 billion he initially requested for the wall.

One day later, on December 19, the Senate passed a short-term spending bill to keep the government open through February 8, 2019, but without any funding for the border wall. In a reversal, Trump refused to support the bill and said he would not sign any legislation that did not include money for the border wall. When the Senate bill arrived in the House, Republicans added $5.7 billion for the border wall before passing the legislation and sending it back to the Senate. That bill failed in the Senate, and both chambers adjourned without a spending bill in place, thus setting in motion a partial government shutdown beginning at midnight on December 22. The two chambers would only briefly gavel in for pro forma sessions before the 116th Congress was seated on January 3, 2019.

## PRESIDENT SIGNS FUNDING BILL, DECLARES NATIONAL EMERGENCY

The partial government shutdown affected an estimated 800,000 federal workers, with 420,000 expected to work without pay and the remainder furloughed. Those expected to report for work were primarily in positions deemed vital to national health and safety, including Transportation Security Administration (TSA) staff, border patrol agents, and federal prison guards. Although Congress passed a bill before it adjourned guaranteeing back pay for federal workers once the government reopened, over the course of the five-week shutdown the news was flooded with stories about federal workers forced to seek food assistance, skip mortgage payments, and forgo buying medication. As the shutdown stretched on, Americans who did not work in the public sector began to wonder whether they would receive their tax refunds, if welfare benefits would be paid on time, and when they might be able to again visit the national parks.

When the new Congress was seated on January 3, 2019, a series of bills was placed on the House floor. The first funded DHS through February 8, and the second was a package of five appropriations bills that funded the rest of the government for the remainder of the fiscal year. Both bills passed, primarily along party lines. In total, the bills contained $1.3 billion for border security, but no funds were appropriated for a border wall. Those bills—and a number of other funding measures that followed—were nonstarters in the Senate, where McConnell refused to bring to the floor any legislation that did not have support from the president. It was not until January 24 that McConnell brought two proposals to a full Senate vote. One, supported by Republicans, would reopen the federal government, provide money for the border wall, extend protections for current DACA recipients for three years but limit any new applicants who could qualify, and make it more difficult for migrants to seek asylum. That proposal failed 50–47, falling ten votes short of the sixty-vote threshold required for passage of a spending bill. The second bill, supported by Democrats, was similar to what the Senate had passed in December and reopened the government without additional funding for the border wall. That bill also failed, by a vote of 52–44.

On January 25, facing a public relations nightmare that was souring voter sentiment for both parties, the House and Senate passed a three-week continuing resolution that included no money for the border wall. The president, denying that it was a concession, agreed to sign it. To secure Trump's signature, the two parties agreed that they would spend the next three weeks negotiating on DHS funding and the border wall. In a speech in the Rose Garden announcing the end of the shutdown, Trump encouraged Democrats and Republicans to "operate in good faith . . . for the benefit of our whole beautiful, wonderful nation." He expressed optimism that the House and Senate could reach an agreement and discussed why he felt a wall was vital to national safety. The president wrote in a separate tweet that if those negotiations produced nothing, "it's off to the races." Speculation was rampant about what that might mean and if the president intended to shut down the government again or if he would declare a national emergency. When the final funding bill for fiscal 2019 did not include the $5.7 billion in wall funding, on February 15, 2019, President Trump declared a national emergency with regard to the crisis on the border, hoping doing so would secure the funds for the wall. Immediately, a group of sixteen states—most of which were led by Democratic governors—filed suit in federal court, and House Democratic leadership vowed to put a bill on the floor to overturn the declaration.

—Heather Kerrigan

*Following is the text of a meeting between President Donald Trump, Rep. Nancy Pelosi, D-Calif., and Sen. Chuck Schumer, D-N.Y., on December 11, 2018; a statement by Pelosi and Schumer on December 22, 2018, at the start of the government shutdown; and the text of a Rose Garden statement delivered by President Trump on January 25, 2019, announcing the end of the shutdown.*

# Trump Hosts House and Senate Democratic Leaders

**December 11, 2018**

*The President.* Okay, thank you very much. It's a great honor to have Nancy Pelosi with us and Chuck Schumer with us. And we've actually worked very hard on a couple of things that are happening. Criminal justice reform—as you know, we've just heard word—got word that Mitch McConnell and the group, we're going to be putting it up for a vote. We have great Democrat support, great Republican support. So, criminal justice reform, something that people have been trying to get—how long, Nancy? Many years.

*Speaker-Designate Pelosi.* A long time.

*The President.* Many, many years. Looks like it's going to be passing, hopefully—famous last words—on a very bipartisan way. And it's really something we're all very proud of. And again, tremendous support from Republicans and tremendous support from Democrats. And I think it's going to get a very good vote. And we'll see soon enough. But it will be up for a vote very shortly. A lot of years they've been waiting for it.

The other thing, the farm bill is moving along nicely. And I guess they'll be voting on Friday or so. But pretty close.

*Leader Schumer.* Soon. Soon.

*Speaker-Designate Pelosi.* Possibly.

*The President.* And we think the farm bill is in very good shape. A lot of good things are happening with it, and our farmers are well taken care of. And again, that will be quite bipartisan and it will happen pretty soon.

And then we have the easy one, the wall. That will be the one that will be the easiest of all. What do you think, Chuck? Maybe not?

*Leader Schumer.* It's called "funding the government," Mr. President.

*The President.* [*Laughter*] So we're going to see. But I will tell you, the wall will get built. We'll see what happens.

It is not an easy situation because the Democrats have a different view, I think, than— I can say—the Republicans. We have great Republican support. We don't have Democrat support. But we're going to talk about that now. We're going to see.

One thing that I do have to say is: Tremendous amounts of wall have already been built, and a lot of—a lot of wall. When you include the renovation of existing fences and walls, we've renovated a tremendous amount and we've done a lot of work. In San Diego, we're building new walls right now. And we've—right next to San Diego, we've completed a major section of wall and it's really worked well.

So, a lot of wall has been built. We don't talk about that, but we might as well start, because it's building—it's being built right now, big sections of wall. And we will continue that.

And one way or the other, it's going to get built. I'd like not to see a government closing, a shutdown. We will see what happens over the next short period of time. But the wall is a very important thing to us.

I might put it a different way. Border security is extremely important, and we have to take care of border security. When you look at what happened with the caravans, with the people, with a lot of—we shut it down; we had no choice. We shut it down. But it could be a lot easier if we had real border security.

I just want to pay my respects to the Border Patrol agents and officers. They've been incredible. The ICE agents and officers, they've been incredible. And very importantly, our military. Our military went in and they did an incredible job. They have been really, really spectacular.

A lot of the people that wanted to come into the country, and really, they were to come in no matter how they wanted to come in—they were going to come in even in a rough way—many of these people are leaving now and they're going back to their countries: Honduras, Guatemala, El Salvador, and other countries. They're leaving. If you noticed, it's getting a lot less crowded in Mexico. And a lot of them are going to stay in Mexico, and the Mexican government has been working with us very well. So we appreciate that. But they haven't been coming into our country. We can't let people come in that way.

So that's pretty much it. We're going to talk about the wall. I wanted to talk about criminal justice reform, just to let you know how positive that is. I want to talk about the farm bill, how positive that is. And I want to talk about the wall. And I will tell you, it's a tough issue because we are in very opposite sides of—I really think I can say "border security," but certainly the wall.

But the wall will get built. A lot of the wall is built. It's been very effective. I asked for a couple of notes on that. If you look at San Diego, illegal traffic dropped 92 percent once the wall was up. El Paso, illegal traffic dropped 72 percent, then ultimately 95 percent, once the wall was up.

In Tucson, Arizona, illegal traffic dropped 92 percent. Yuma, it dropped illegal traffic 95 to 96 percent.

I mean—and when I say "dropped," the only reason we even have any percentage where people got through is because they walk and go around areas that aren't built. It dropped virtually 100 percent in the areas where the wall is. So, I mean, it's very effective.

If you really want to find out how effective a wall is, just ask Israel—99.9 percent effective. And our wall will be every bit as good as that, if not better.

So we've done a lot of work on the wall; a lot of wall is built. A lot of people don't know that. A lot of wall is renovated. We have walls that were in very bad condition that are now in A1 tip-top shape. And, frankly, some wall has been reinforced by our military. Our military has done a fantastic job. So the wall will get built, but we may not—we may not have an agreement today. We probably won't. But we have an agreement on other things that are really good.

Nancy, would you like to say something?

*Speaker-Designate Pelosi.* Well, thank you, Mr. President, for the opportunity to meet with you so that we can work together in a bipartisan way to meet the needs of the American people.

I think the American people recognize that we must keep government open, that a shutdown is not worth anything, and that you should not have a Trump shutdown. You have the White House—

*The President.* Did you say "Trump"? Oh, oh.

*Speaker-Designate Pelosi.* A "Trump Shutdown." You Have The White House—

*The President.* I was going to call it a "Pelosi shutdown."

*Speaker-Designate Pelosi.* You have the Senate. You have the House of Representatives. You have the votes. You should pass it right now.

*The President.* No, we don't have the votes, Nancy, because in the Senate, we need 60 votes and we don't have it.

*Speaker-Designate Pelosi.* No, no, but in the House, you could bring it up right now, today.

*The President.* Yeah, but I can't—excuse me. But I can't get it passed in the House if it's not going to pass in the Senate. I don't want to waste time.

*Speaker-Designate Pelosi.* Well, the fact is you can get it started that way.

*The President.* The House we can get passed very easily, and we do.

*Speaker-Designate Pelosi.* Okay, then do it. Then do it.

*The President.* But the problem is the Senate, because we need 10 Democrats to vote, and they won't vote.

*Speaker-Designate Pelosi.* No, no, that's not the point, Mr. President. The point is—

*The President.* It's sort of the point.

*Speaker-Designate Pelosi.* —that there are equities to be weighed. And we are here to have a conversation—

*The President.* Correct.

*Speaker-Designate Pelosi.* —in a careful way. So I don't think we should have a debate in front of the press on this. But the fact is, the House Republicans could bring up this bill, if they had the votes, immediately, and set the tone for what you want.

*The President.* If we thought we were going to get it passed in the Senate, Nancy, we would do it immediately. We would get it passed very easily in the House.

*Speaker-Designate Pelosi.* No, that's not the point. That's not the point.

*The President.* Nancy, I'd have it passed in two seconds. It doesn't matter, though, because we can't get it passed in the Senate because we need 10 Democrat votes. That's the problem.

*Speaker-Designate Pelosi.* Well, again, let us have our conversation—

*The President.* That's right.

*Speaker-Designate Pelosi.* —and then we can meet with the press again. But the fact is, is that legislating—which is what we do—

*The President.* Right.

*Speaker-Designate Pelosi.* —you begin, you make your point, you state your case. That's what the House Republicans could do, if they had the votes. But there are no votes in the House, a majority of votes, for a wall—no matter where you start.

*Leader Schumer.* That is exactly right. You don't have the votes in the House.

*The President.* If I needed the votes for the wall in the House, I would have them—in one session, it would be done.

*Speaker-Designate Pelosi.* Well, then go do it. Go do it.

*The President.* It doesn't help because we need 10 Democrats in the Senate.

*Speaker-Designate Pelosi.* No, don't put it on the Senate. Put it on the negotiation.

*The President.* Okay, let me ask you this. Just—and we're doing this in a very friendly manner. It doesn't help for me to take a vote in the House, where I will win easily with the Republicans—

*Speaker-Designate Pelosi.* You will not win.

*The President.* It doesn't help to take that vote because I'm not going to get the vote of the Senate.

*Speaker-Designate Pelosi.* Well, don't blame it on the Senate, Mr. President.

*The President.* I need 10 senators. That's the problem.

*Speaker-Designate Pelosi.* Mr. President, you have the White House, you have the Senate.

*The President.* I have the White House.

*Speaker-Designate Pelosi.* You have the House of Representatives.

*The President.* The White House is done. And the House would give me the vote if I wanted it. But I can't because I need—

*Speaker-Designate Pelosi.* But you can't—you can't—

*The President.* Nancy, I need 10 votes from Chuck.

*Leader Schumer.* All right, let me say something here.

*Speaker-Designate Pelosi.* Mr. President, let me—let me just say one thing. The fact is you do not have the votes in the House.

*The President.* Nancy, I do. And we need border security.

*Speaker-Designate Pelosi.* Well, let's take the vote and we'll find out.

*The President.* Nancy. Nancy. We need border security. It's very simple.

*Speaker-Designate Pelosi.* Of course we do.

*The President.* We need border security.

*Speaker-Designate Pelosi.* We do.

*The President.* People are pouring into our country, including terrorists. We have terrorists. We caught 10 terrorists over the last very short period of time. Ten. These are very serious people. Our border agents, all of our law enforcement has been incredible what they've done. But we caught 10 terrorists. These are people that were looking to do harm.

We need the wall. We need—more important than anything, we need border security, of which the wall is just a piece. But it's important.

Chuck, did you want to say something?

*Leader Schumer.* Yeah. Here's what I want to say: We have a lot of disagreements here. The Washington Post today gave you a whole lot of Pinocchios because they say you constantly misstate how much the wall is—how much of the wall is built and how much is there.

But that's not the point here. We have a disagreement about the wall—

*The President.* Well, the Washington Post—[*laughter*].

*Leader Schumer.* —whether it's effective or it isn't. Not on border security, but on the wall.

We do not want to shut down the government. You have called 20 times to shut down the government. You say, "I want to shut down the government." We don't. We want to come to an agreement. If we can't come to an agreement, we have solutions that will pass the House and Senate right now, and will not shut down the government. And that's what we're urging you to do. Not threaten to shut down the government—

*The President.* Chuck—

*Leader Schumer.* —because you—

*The President.* You don't want to shut down the government, Chuck.

*Leader Schumer.* Let me just finish. Because you can't get your way.

*The President.* Because the last time you shut it down you got killed.

*Leader Schumer.* Yeah. Let me say something, Mr. President. You just say, "My way, or we'll shut down the government." We have a proposal that Democrats and Republicans will support to do a CR that will not shut down the government. We urge you to take it.

*The President.* And if it's not good border security, I won't take it.

*Speaker-Designate Pelosi.* It is good border security.

*Leader Schumer.* It is very good border security.

*The President.* And if it's not good border security, I won't take it.

*Speaker-Designate Pelosi.* It's actually what the border security asked for.

*Leader Schumer.* It's what the border—

*The President.* Because when you look at these numbers of the effectiveness of our border security, and when you look at the job that we're doing with our military—

*Leader Schumer.* You just said it is effective.

*The President.* Can I be—can I tell you something?

*Leader Schumer.* Yeah, you just said it's effective.

*The President.* Without a wall—these are only areas where you have the walls.

*Leader Schumer.* We want to do this—

*The President.* Where you have walls, Chuck, it's effective. Where you don't have walls, it is not effective.

*Speaker-Designate Pelosi.*  Wait a second. Let's call a halt to this.

*Leader Schumer.* Yeah.

*Speaker-Designate Pelosi.* Let's call a halt to this. We've come in here as the first branch of government: Article I, the legislative branch. We're coming in, in good faith, to negotiate with you about how we can keep the government open.

*Leader Schumer.* Open.

*The President.* We're going to keep it open—

*Speaker-Designate Pelosi.* The American—

*The President.* —if we have border security.

*Speaker-Designate Pelosi.* The American—

*The President.* If we don't have border security, Chuck—

*Speaker-Designate Pelosi.* I'm with you.

*The President.* —we're not going to keep it open.

*Speaker-Designate Pelosi.* I'm with you. We are going to have border security.

*Leader Schumer.* And it's the same border—

*Speaker-Designate Pelosi.* Effective border security.

*Leader Schumer.* You're bragging about what has been done.

*The President.* By us.

*Leader Schumer.* We want to do the same thing we did last year, this year. That's our proposal. If it's good then, it's good now, and it won't shut down the government.

*The President.* Chuck, we can build a much bigger section with more money.

*Leader Schumer.* Let's debate—

*Speaker-Designate Pelosi.* We have taken—

*Leader Schumer.* Let's debate in private.

*Speaker-Designate Pelosi.* We have taken this conversation—

*Leader Schumer.* Okay?

*The President.* Okay.

*Leader Schumer.* Yeah.

*Speaker-Designate Pelosi.* —to a place that is devoid, frankly, of fact. And we can dispel that.

*The President.* We need border security. And I think we all agree that we need border security.

*Leader Schumer.* Yes, we do.

*The President.* Is that right?

*Leader Schumer.* We do.

*The President.* See? We get along. [*Laughter*]
    Thank you, everybody.

*[A Q&A with reporters has been omitted.]*

Source: Executive Office of the President. "Remarks and an Exchange with Reporters during a Meeting with Senate Minority Leader Charles E. Schumer and Speaker-Designate of the House of Representatives Nancy Pelosi." December 11, 2018. *Compilation of Presidential Documents* 2018, no. 00842 (December 11, 2018). https://www.govinfo.gov/content/pkg/DCPD-201800842/pdf/DCPD-201800842.pdf.

# Pelosi and Schumer Remark on Government Shutdown

**December 22, 2018**

"Regrettably, America has now entered a Trump Shutdown. Republicans control the House, the Senate, and the White House. But instead of honoring his responsibility to the American people, President Trump threw a temper tantrum and convinced House Republicans to push our nation into a destructive Trump Shutdown in the middle of the holiday season. President Trump has said more than 25 times that he wanted a shutdown and now he has gotten what he wanted.

"Democrats have offered Republicans multiple proposals to keep the government open, including one that already passed the Senate unanimously, and all of which include funding for strong, sensible, and effective border security—not the president's ineffective and expensive wall. If President Trump and Republicans choose to continue this Trump Shutdown, the new House Democratic majority will swiftly pass legislation to re-open government in January."

SOURCE: Office of Rep. Nancy Pelosi. "Joint Statement from Leaders Pelosi and Schumer Statement on Trump Government Shutdown." December 22, 2018. https://www.speaker.gov/newsroom/122118-2.

# President Trump Announces End of Government Shutdown

**January 25, 2019**

Thank you very much. My fellow Americans, I am very proud to announce today that we have reached a deal to end the shutdown and reopen the Federal Government. As everyone knows, I have a very powerful alternative, but I didn't want to use it at this time. Hopefully, it will be unnecessary.

I want to thank all of the incredible Federal workers, and their amazing families, who have shown such extraordinary devotion in the face of this recent hardship. You are fantastic people. You are incredible patriots. Many of you have suffered far greater than anyone, but your families would know or understand. And not only did you not complain, but in many cases you encouraged me to keep going because you care so much about our country and about its border security.

Again, I thank you. All Americans, I thank you. You are very, very special people. I am so proud that you are citizens of our country. When I say "Make America Great Again," it could never be done without you. Great people.

In a short while, I will sign a bill to open our government for three weeks until February 15. I will make sure that all employees receive their back pay very quickly, or as soon as possible. It'll happen fast. I am asking Senate Majority Leader Mitch McConnell to put this proposal on the floor immediately.

After 36 days of spirited debate and dialogue, I have seen and heard from enough Democrats and Republicans that they are willing to put partisanship aside—I think—and put the security of the American people first. I do believe they're going to do that. They have said they are for complete border security, and they have finally and fully acknowledged that having barriers, fencing, or walls—or whatever you want to call it—will be an important part of the solution.

A bipartisan Conference Committee of House and Senate lawmakers and leaders will immediately begin reviewing the requests of our Homeland Security experts—and experts they are—and also law enforcement professionals, who have worked with us so closely. We want to thank Border Patrol, ICE, and all law enforcement. Been incredible.

Based on operational guidance from the experts in the field, they will put together a Homeland Security package for me to shortly sign into law.

Over the next 21 days, I expect that both Democrats and Republicans will operate in good faith. This is an opportunity for all parties to work together for the benefit of our whole beautiful, wonderful nation.

If we make a fair deal, the American people will be proud of their government for proving that we can put country before party. We can show all Americans, and people all around the world, that both political parties are united when it comes to protecting our country and protecting our people.

Many disagree, but I really feel that, working with Democrats and Republicans, we can make a truly great and secure deal happen for everyone.

Walls should not be controversial. Our country has built 654 miles of barrier over the last 15 years, and every career Border Patrol agent I have spoken with has told me that walls work. They do work. No matter where you go, they work. Israel built a wall—99.9 percent successful. Won't be any different for us.

They keep criminals out. They save good people from attempting a very dangerous journey from other countries—thousands of miles—because they think they have a glimmer of hope of coming through. With a wall, they don't have that hope. They keep drugs out, and they dramatically increase efficiency by allowing us to patrol far larger areas with far fewer people. It's just common sense. Walls work.

That's why most of the Democrats in Congress have voted in the past for bills that include walls and physical barriers and very powerful fences. The walls we are building are not medieval walls. They are smart walls designed to meet the needs of frontline border agents, and are operationally effective. These barriers are made of steel, have see-through visibility, which is very important, and are equipped with sensors, monitors, and cutting-edge technology, including state-of-the-art drones.

We do not need 2,000 miles of concrete wall from sea to shining sea—we never did; we never proposed that; we never wanted that—because we have barriers at the border where natural structures are as good as anything that we can build. They're already there. They've been there for millions of years.

Our proposed structures will be in pre-determined high-risk locations that have been specifically identified by the Border Patrol to stop illicit flows of people and drugs. No border security plan can ever work without a physical barrier. Just doesn't happen.

At the same time, we need to increase drug detection technology and manpower to modernize our ports of entry, which are obsolete. The equipment is obsolete. They're old. They're tired. This is something we have all come to agree on, and will allow for quicker and safer commerce. These critical investments will improve and facilitate legal trade and travel through our lawful ports of entry.

Our plan also includes desperately needed humanitarian assistance for those being exploited and abused by coyotes, smugglers, and the dangerous journey north.

The requests we have put before Congress are vital to ending the humanitarian and security crisis on our southern border. Absolutely vital. Will not work without it.

This crisis threatens the safety of our country and thousands of American lives. Criminal cartels, narco-terrorists, transnational gangs like MS-13, and human traffickers are brazenly violating U.S. laws and terrorizing innocent communities.

Human traffickers—the victims are women and children. Maybe to a lesser extent, believe or not, children. Women are tied up. They're bound. Duct tape put around their faces, around their mouths. In many cases, they can't even breathe. They're put in the backs of cars or vans or trucks. They don't go through your port of entry. They make a right turn going very quickly. They go into the desert areas, or whatever areas you can look at. And as soon as there's no protection, they make a left or a right into the United States of America. There's nobody to catch them. There's nobody to find them.

They can't come through the port, because if they come through the port, people will see four women sitting in a van with tape around their face and around their mouth. Can't have that.

And that problem, because of the Internet, is the biggest problem—it's never been like this before—that you can imagine. It's at the worst level—human trafficking—in the history of the world. This is not a United States problem; this is a world problem. But they come through areas where they have no protection, where they have no steel barriers, where they have no walls. And we can stop almost 100 percent of that.

The profits reaped by these murderous organizations are used to fund their malign and destabilizing conduct throughout this hemisphere.

Last year alone, ICE officers removed 10,000 known or suspected gang members, like MS-13 and members as bad as them. Horrible people. Tough. Mean. Sadistic. In the last two years, ICE officers arrested a total of 266,000 criminal aliens inside of the United States, including those charged or convicted of nearly 100,000 assaults, 30,000 sex crimes, and 4,000 homicides or, as you would call them, violent, vicious killings. It can be stopped.

Vast quantities of lethal drugs—including meth, fentanyl, heroin, and cocaine—are smuggled across our southern border and into U.S. schools and communities. Drugs kill much more than 70,000 Americans a year and cost our society in excess of $700 billion.

The sheer volume of illegal immigration has overwhelmed federal authorities and stretched our immigration system beyond the breaking point. Nearly 50 migrants a day are being referred for medical assistance—they are very, very sick—making this a health crisis as well. It's a very big health crisis. People have no idea how big it is, unless you're there.

Our backlog in the immigration courts is now far greater than the 800,000 cases that you've been hearing about over the last couple of years. Think of that, though: 800,000 cases because our laws are obsolete. So obsolete. They're the laughing stock all over the world. Our immigration laws, all over the world—they've been there for a long time—are the laughing stock, all over the world.

We do not have the necessary space or resources to detain, house, vet, screen, and safely process this tremendous influx of people. In short, we do not have control over who is entering our country, where they come from, who they are, or why they are coming.

The result, for many years, is a colossal danger to public safety. We're going to straighten it out. It's not hard. It's easy, if given the resources.

Last month was the third straight month in a row with 60,000 apprehensions on our southern border. Think of that. We apprehended 60,000 people. That's like a stadium full of people. A big stadium.

There are many criminals being apprehended, but vast numbers are coming because our economy is so strong. We have the strongest economy now in the entire world. You see what's happening. We have nowhere left to house them and no way to promptly remove them. We can't get them out because our laws are so obsolete, so antiquated, and so bad.

Without new resources from Congress, we will be forced to release these people into communities—something we don't want to do—called catch-and-release. You catch them. Even if they are criminals, you then release them. And you can't release them from where they came, so they go into our country and end up in places you would least suspect. And we do as little releasing as possible, by they're coming by the hundreds of thousands.

I have had zero Democrat lawmakers volunteer to have them released into their districts or states. And I think they know that, and that's what we're going to be discussing over the next three weeks.

The painful reality is that the tremendous economic and financial burdens of illegal immigration fall on the shoulders of low-income Americans, including millions of wonderful, patriotic, law-abiding immigrants who enrich our nation.

As Commander in Chief, my highest priority is the defense of our great country. We cannot surrender operational control over the nation's borders to foreign cartels, traffickers, and smugglers. We want future Americans to come to our country legally and through a system based on merit. We need people to come to our country. We have great companies moving back into the United States. And we have the lowest employment and the best employment numbers that we've ever had. There are more people working today in the United States than have ever worked in our country. We need people to come in to help us—the farms, and with all of these great companies that are moving back. Finally, they're moving back. People said it couldn't happen. It's happening.

And we want them to enjoy the blessings of safety and liberty, and the rule of law. We cannot protect and deliver these blessings without a strong and secure border.

I believe that crime in this country can go down by a massive percentage if we have great security on our southern border. I believe drugs, large percentages of which come through the southern border, will be cut by a number that nobody will believe.

So let me be very clear: We really have no choice but to build a powerful wall or steel barrier. If we don't get a fair deal from Congress, the Government will either shut down on February 15, again, or I will use the powers afforded to me under the laws and the Constitution of the United States to address this emergency. We will have great security.

And I want to thank you all very much. Thank you very much.

SOURCE: Executive Office of the President. "Remarks on the Federal Government Shutdown." January 25, 2019. *Compilation of Presidential Documents* 2019, no. 00049 (January 25, 2019). https://www.govinfo.gov/content/pkg/DCPD-201900049/pdf/DCPD-201900049.pdf.

## OTHER HISTORIC DOCUMENTS OF INTEREST

### FROM THIS VOLUME

# Fed Hikes Interest Rate; Treasury Secretary Remarks on Economy

DECEMBER 19 AND 23, 2018

After strong growth for much of the year, the U.S. economy ended 2018 on a downswing, with the Dow Jones Industrial Average, NASDAQ, and S&P 500 tumbling to near ten-year lows. The decline was driven by a number of factors, including a decision by the Federal Reserve to raise its benchmark interest rate for the fourth time in a year, an ongoing trade war between the world's two biggest economies—the United States and China—and slowing growth both domestically and globally. Seeking to calm the markets, Treasury Secretary Steven Mnuchin took the unusual step of contacting the six largest banks in the country to determine whether they had appropriate liquidity for continuing to lend to consumers and businesses. His unexpected remarks, intended to promote investor confidence, had the opposite effect and instead sparked confusion about whether greater concern over the state of the U.S. economy was warranted.

## FEDERAL RESERVE RAISES KEY INTEREST RATE

In the depth of the 2007 to 2009 recession, the Federal Reserve Board of Governors announced that it was cutting a key economic indicator, the short-term interest rate, to near zero. That target interest rate dictates the rate banks pay when lending to each other or borrowing money from the federal government. Establishing a baseline near zero was unprecedented and was intended to slowly encourage the economy to pick up by giving banks the ability to increase lending at higher interest rates. It was not until 2015 that the Federal Reserve decided to begin raising the interest rate again, an indicator that the economy was on steady footing and that both banks and consumers could withstand higher interest rates.

Gradual increases continued, and on December 19, 2018, the Federal Reserve announced that it would raise its key interest rate to a range of 2.25 percent to 2.5 percent, the highest level since 2008. According to the Federal Open Market Committee (FOMC), the Federal Reserve body responsible for policymaking, the rate was raised because of indications "that the labor market has continued to strengthen and that economic activity has been rising at a strong rate. Job gains have been strong, on average, in recent months, and the unemployment rate has remained low. Household spending has continued to grow strongly, while growth of business fixed investment has moderated from its rapid pace earlier in the year." According to some economists, the justification for raising rates a fourth time in 2018 may have also been driven by fear among central bank members surrounding rapid, and likely unsustainable, economic growth caused by an increase in government spending and tax cuts.

The announcement of the increase was coupled with a lowered expectation for future rate increases. In September 2018, the FOMC predicted three rate hikes in 2019, but that was adjusted downward in its December 2018 statement to indicate it would focus on "gradual" increases moving forward. "The Committee judges that some further gradual increases in the target range for the federal funds rate will be consistent with sustained expansion of economic activity, strong labor market conditions, and inflation near the Committee's symmetric 2 percent objective over the medium term," the FOMC said. After 2019, the FOMC was likely to vote to hike the interest rate only once in 2020, followed by decreases in the benchmark rate beginning in 2021 to promote economic growth. The official statement, and corresponding remarks made by Powell, indicated that the FOMC would be more data dependent in determining when future rate increases were warranted, noting that the body would continue to monitor domestic and global economic developments, labor market conditions, inflation expectations, and other financial indicators.

The announcement from the Federal Reserve in December also adjusted downward its expectations for gross domestic product (GDP) growth. In September, the Federal Reserve estimated GDP would rise 3.1 percent for 2018 and 2.5 percent in 2019. Those rates were adjusted to 3.0 for 2018, 2.3 for 2019, and 2.0 for 2020 but were accompanied by a note that economic growth was still "rising at a strong rate." These growth predictions were in stark contrast to those developed by the Trump administration, which believed the tax cut package signed into law at the close of 2017 would help drive an annualized GDP growth rate of 3 percent in the years after it went into effect.

The Federal Reserve and Chair Powell had endured weeks of attacks from President Donald Trump leading up to the decision to raise the rate. Trump accused the Fed of being the "greatest threat" to economic growth and tweeted on December 17, "It is incredible that with a very strong dollar and virtually no inflation, the outside world blowing up around us, Paris is burning and China way down, the Fed is even considering yet another interest rate hike. Take the Victory!" But in a speech announcing the decision, Powell said the Fed was undeterred by the president's statements and that they had no impact to stop "us from doing what we think is the right thing to do." Powell called the increase "appropriate for what is a very healthy economy."

## Stocks Suffer Worst Week in a Decade

Stocks tumbled at the news of the rate hike, with the Dow Jones closing down 352 points, a 733-point drop from the high it had reached earlier in the day, and the S&P 500 dipped to a fifteen-month low. Ultimately, the week of December 17–21, 2018, marked one of the biggest weekly declines for U.S. stocks in nearly a decade. The S&P 500 fell 7 percent, the NASDAQ fell 8.36 percent, and the Dow Jones fell 6.8 percent by the end of the week. According to economic experts, the decline put the United States in bear market territory—which occurs once an index loses 20 percent of its value—after years of significant gains. Reasons for the sudden and sharp decline included slowing economic growth in both the United States and globally, falling oil prices, and the ongoing U.S.–China trade war. Investors were also concerned about volatility in D.C. politics, with a partial government shutdown that began at midnight on December 22 and fears that the president wanted to fire the Federal Reserve chair. "The market volatility is being driven by computer algorithm trading programs that instantly buy or sell everything, depending on the news they are getting fed. There's too much news," said Ed Yardeni, president of Yardeni Research, an analytical and investment strategy company.

The stock market went on to end 2018 down. The Dow Jones had a 5.6 percent loss for 2018, the S&P 500 a 6.2 percent drop, and the NASDAQ was down 3.9 percent. Although a bear market was possible for 2019, most economists appeared confident that a recession was unlikely. "A cyclical bear market historically produces a decline of 25 percent from top to bottom on average," Bruce Bittles, chief investment strategist at Baird, wrote to clients. "A recession would likely cause significantly more damage."

## MNUCHIN ATTEMPTS TO SHORE UP CONFIDENCE

On December 23, Treasury Secretary Mnuchin unexpectedly tweeted a statement noting that he had contacted the CEOs of the six largest banks in the nation—Bank of America, Citi, Goldman Sachs, JPMorgan Chase, Morgan Stanley, and Wells Fargo—and that each individual bank affirmed "that they have ample liquidity available for lending to consumer, business markets, and all other market operations." Mnuchin added that he intended to convene a call on December 24 with the President's Working Group on Financial Markets, a body comprised of representatives from the Federal Reserve, Securities and Exchange Commission, and Commodity Futures Trading Commission. This group, which tends only to meet to address a financial crisis, would "discuss coordination efforts to assure normal market operations."

Mnuchin's actions appeared to be an attempt to instill greater confidence among investors in the tumbling market, but economic analysts worried it could have the opposite effect, especially in light of the ongoing tumult caused by the partial federal government shutdown. "More than anything else right now, Washington and politics are absolutely driving investor sentiment and market direction and that can turn on a dime," said Oliver Pursche, board member at Bruderman Asset Management, a financial services company. "Panic feeds panic and this looks like panic in the administration," said Diane Swonk, chief economist at Grant Thornton, adding, "Suggesting you might know something that no one else is worried about creates more unease." Economist Paul Krugman tweeted, "This is amazing. It's as if Mnuchin was trying to create a panic over something nobody was worried about until this release."

When U.S. markets reopened on December 24, stocks slid again over the fear Mnuchin sparked but recovered by late morning. Trump took to Twitter and blamed the initial drop on the Federal Reserve, writing, "They don't have a feel for the Market, they don't understand necessary Trade Wars or Strong Dollars or even Democrat Shutdowns over Borders. The Fed is like a powerful golfer who can't score because he has no touch—he can't putt!" That morning's tweet sent stocks tumbling again. The Dow Jones ended a shortened trading day, due to the Christmas Eve holiday, 650 points lower than its open. The S&P 500 was down 2.7 percent and the NASDAQ down 2.2 percent. Those declines for the Dow Jones and S&P 500 marked the biggest Christmas Eve decline ever.

—Heather Kerrigan

*Following is the text of a December 19, 2018, press release from the Federal Reserve announcing its intent to raise the benchmark interest rate to 2.5 percent; and the text of a December 23, 2018, tweet from Treasury Secretary Steven Mnuchin regarding his conversations with the country's largest banks.*

# Fed Raises Interest Rates for Fourth Time in 2018

**December 19, 2018**

Information received since the Federal Open Market Committee met in November indicates that the labor market has continued to strengthen and that economic activity has been rising at a strong rate. Job gains have been strong, on average, in recent months, and the unemployment rate has remained low. Household spending has continued to grow strongly, while growth of business fixed investment has moderated from its rapid pace earlier in the year. On a 12-month basis, both overall inflation and inflation for items other than food and energy remain near 2 percent. Indicators of longer-term inflation expectations are little changed, on balance.

Consistent with its statutory mandate, the Committee seeks to foster maximum employment and price stability. The Committee judges that some further gradual increases in the target range for the federal funds rate will be consistent with sustained expansion of economic activity, strong labor market conditions, and inflation near the Committee's symmetric 2 percent objective over the medium term. The Committee judges that risks to the economic outlook are roughly balanced, but will continue to monitor global economic and financial developments and assess their implications for the economic outlook.

In view of realized and expected labor market conditions and inflation, the Committee decided to raise the target range for the federal funds rate to 2-1/4 to 2-1/2 percent.

In determining the timing and size of future adjustments to the target range for the federal funds rate, the Committee will assess realized and expected economic conditions relative to its maximum employment objective and its symmetric 2 percent inflation objective. This assessment will take into account a wide range of information, including measures of labor market conditions, indicators of inflation pressures and inflation expectations, and readings on financial and international developments.

Voting for the FOMC monetary policy action were: Jerome H. Powell, Chairman; John C. Williams, Vice Chairman; Thomas I. Barkin; Raphael W. Bostic; Michelle W. Bowman; Lael Brainard; Richard H. Clarida; Mary C. Daly; Loretta J. Mester; and Randal K. Quarles.

SOURCE: U.S. Federal Reserve. "Federal Reserve Issues FOMC Statement." December 19, 2018. https://www.federalreserve.gov/newsevents/pressreleases/monetary20181219a.htm.

# Treasury Secretary Addresses Bank Liquidity

**December 23, 2018**

Today I convened individual calls with the CEOs of the nation's six largest banks. See attached statement.

\*\*\*

**U.S. Treasury Department**
**Office of Public Affairs**

**Secretary Mnuchin convened individual calls with the CEOs**
**of the nation's six largest banks**

*The banks all confirmed ample liquidity is available for lending to*
*consumer and business markets.*

Washington—Secretary Mnuchin conducted a series of calls today with the CEOs of the nations six largest banks: Brian Moynihan, Bank of America; Michael Corbat, Citi; David Solomon, Goldman Sachs; Jamie Dimon, JP Morgan Chase, James Gorman, Morgan Stanley; Tim Sloan, Wells Fargo. The CEOs confirmed that they have ample liquidity available for lending to consumer, business markets, and all other market operations. He also confirmed that they have not experienced any clearance or margin issues and that the markets continue to function properly.

Tomorrow, the Secretary will convene a call with the President's Working Group on financial markets, which he chairs. This includes the Board of Governors of the Federal Reserve System, the Securities and Exchange Commission, and the Commodities Futures Trading Commission. He has also invited the office of the Comptroller of the Currency, and the Federal Deposit Insurance Corporation to participate as well. These key regulators will discuss coordination efforts to assure normal market operations.

"We continue to see strong economic growth in the U.S. economy with robust activity from consumers and businesses," stated Secretary Mnuchin and added "With the government shutdown, Treasury will have critical employees to maintain its core operations at Fiscal Services, IRS, and other critical functions within the department."

SOURCE: Secretary Steven Mnuchin (@stevenmnuchin1). Twitter post. December 23, 2018. https://twitter.com/stevenmnuchin1/status/1076958380361543681.

## OTHER HISTORIC DOCUMENTS OF INTEREST

### FROM THIS VOLUME

### FROM PREVIOUS *HISTORIC DOCUMENTS*

# President Trump Announces U.S. Troops to Withdraw from Syria; Defense Leaders Resign

DECEMBER 19 AND DECEMBER 20, 2018

In December 2018, President Donald Trump surprised administration officials and U.S. lawmakers by announcing he would withdraw more than 2,000 American troops from Syria. Trump explained the dramatic shift in foreign policy by declaring the United States had defeated the Islamic State in the Levant (ISIL) in Syria. U.S. coalition partners expressed confusion over the announcement, which also created chaos within the Trump administration. U.S. Defense Secretary Jim Mattis resigned shortly after the announcement, followed by Brett McGurk, the special presidential envoy to the coalition fighting ISIL. The resignation of two top officials whose experience was widely viewed as counterbalance to a sometimes unpredictable president sent U.S. foreign policy deeper into a period of instability.

## AMERICAN INVOLVEMENT IN SYRIA

Syria plunged into an intractable civil war in 2011, as the government of President Bashar al-Assad struggled to maintain control amid the democratization efforts sweeping the Middle East during the Arab Spring. At the conflict's onset, the United States offered minimal support for opposition forces, supplying the Free Syrian Army with nonlethal aid such as food rations, medicine, and vehicles. As the fighting intensified, the American government began providing training, money, and intelligence to select Syrian rebel commanders. Terrorist organizations, including ISIL and al-Nusra Front, quickly found new footing and strength within the vacuum created by the multisided conflict. Behind the scenes, the conflict increasingly evolved into a proxy war for powers seeking to shape the region. Western democracies, including the United States, United Kingdom, and France, backed opposition forces while Russia and Iran backed the Assad government. Three years into the conflict, the United States increased its involvement. Together with the United Kingdom, France, Jordan, Turkey, Canada, Australia, and other allies, the United States sent first military advisers and later soldiers into the country in 2014. Coalition forces primarily focused on fighting and destabilizing ISIL and other terrorist organizations, but their active military involvement also projected Western power to check Russia and Iran.

Following the 2016 U.S. presidential election, the Trump administration signaled little change regarding America's involvement in Syria. One year after his inauguration, President Trump indicated he would maintain a similar open-ended military presence in Syria to further erode ISIL's base of power, counter Iran's influence, and oust Assad. In September 2018, reports indicated the president had agreed to keep U.S. forces in Syria beyond the end of the year while launching a new diplomatic push aimed at establishing a stable government that may or may not include Assad. However, President Trump reportedly told advisers in private that he wanted to withdraw American troops from the country.

## "We Have Won"

On the morning of December 19, 2018, President Trump acted on his private conversations with advisers and announced the withdrawal of U.S. troops from Syria. In an abrupt statement via Twitter, President Trump proclaimed, "We have defeated ISIS in Syria, my only reason for being there during the Trump Presidency." In a video posted to Twitter later that day, President Trump reaffirmed that the United States had "won against ISIS," adding, "Our boys, our young women, our men—they're all coming back, and they're coming back now."

The announcement took the world by surprise and brought swift and immediate condemnation from lawmakers from both parties. Sen. Lindsey Graham, R-S.C., one of the president's top allies in the Senate, said he had been "blindsided" and demanded to know why Congress was not informed of the decision. In a letter signed by five other senators, Graham asked President Trump to reconsider his decision, stressing the importance of retaining a U.S. presence in the region. "We believe that such action at this time is a premature and costly mistake that not only threatens the safety and security of the United States, but also emboldens ISIS, Bashar al Assad, Iran, and Russia," the senators wrote.

Democrats were even more incredulous, suggesting that the move was an effort to distract from the administration's various controversies and legal challenges, including those posed by the Mueller probe. House Minority Leader Nancy Pelosi, D-Calif., called it a "hasty announcement" that was motivated by the president's "personal or political objectives," noting that the president went public with his decision one day after former national security adviser Michael Flynn—who had admitted "he was a registered foreign agent for a country with clear interests in the Syrian conflict"—had appeared in court for sentencing.

U.S. allies offered more muted reactions, though some expressed concern about the long-term consequences of an American withdrawal. The British government remarked that while coalition forces had eroded ISIL's standing, "we must not lose sight of the threat they pose." ISIL "will remain a threat," the government's statement read, "even without territory." Israel's Prime Minister Benjamin Netanyahu said it was "an American decision" and later affirmed it would not change his country's policies, despite speculation among some analysts and media outlets that U.S. withdrawal would hamper Israeli efforts to counter Iranian influence in the region. "We are standing steadfast on our red lines in Syria and everywhere else," Netanyahu said. Conversely, the Russian Foreign Ministry welcomed the decision, saying it could open the door to "a political solution" to the ongoing conflict and the formation of a Syrian constitutional committee.

Trump administration officials expressed public concern that a withdrawal would hurt Western efforts within the entire region and cede U.S. influence in Syria to Russia and Iran. Officials, including personnel directing coalition forces on the ground, were also concerned that the decision would abandon key American allies in the region. Specifically, they noted that U.S. withdrawal could leave Kurdish allies vulnerable to attack from Turkey. Pulling support would also make it more difficult for America to gain the trust of local fighters for counterterrorism operations in Afghanistan, Yemen, Somalia, and other regions where U.S. forces are operating.

## Top Administration Officials Rebuke Trump

The loudest and most stinging rebuke came from Secretary Mattis, who resigned his cabinet-level position the day after Trump's announcement. In a letter delivered to the White House and later circulated throughout the Defense Department, Secretary Mattis reaffirmed the progress the American military had made over his tenure and condemned the president's approach to foreign affairs as destructive to American influence and power. In subtle jabs to the president's decision to withdraw from Syria, Secretary Mattis wrote that "our strength as a nation is inextricably linked to the strength of our unique and comprehensive system of alliances and partnerships." He specifically cited the importance of the North Atlantic Treaty Organization, a defense alliance President Trump frequently derides, as well as coalition forces fighting in Syria.

Secretary Mattis's core complaint was that President Trump was surrendering U.S. influence to adversaries. "I believe we must be resolute and unambiguous in our approach to those countries whose strategic interests are increasingly in tension with ours," he wrote. "My views on treating allies with respect and also being clear-eyed about both malign actors and strategic competitors are strongly held." Secretary Mattis continued, "Because you have the right to have a Secretary of Defense whose views are better aligned with yours on these and other subjects, I believe it is right for me to step down from my position."

Congressional officials from both sides of the aisle applauded Secretary Mattis and expressed concern about the future. "This is scary," tweeted Sen. Mark Warner, D-Va., later adding that Secretary Mattis is "an island of stability amidst the chaos of the Trump administration." Sen. Ben Sasse, R-Neb., called it "a sad day for America because Secretary Mattis was giving advice the President needs to hear."

Other top American officials followed suit. Brett McGurk, special presidential envoy to the coalition fighting ISIL, announced his resignation two days after Mattis. In an e-mail to colleagues, McGurk wrote that the president's decision "came as a shock and was a complete reversal of policy that was articulated to us," adding that it "left our coalition partners confused and our fighting partners bewildered." McGurk said he "ultimately concluded that I could not carry out these new instructions and maintain my integrity."

The United States began withdrawing military equipment from Syria in January 2019. As of this writing, troops have yet to leave the country. News reports have cited Defense Department officials as saying it may take four to six months to complete withdrawal, although National Security Adviser John Bolton has said troop withdrawal was dependent on several factors that could keep U.S. soldiers on the ground even longer.

—Robert Howard

*Following is a tweet posted by President Donald Trump on December 19, 2018, announcing a withdrawal of U.S. troops from Syria; and the resignation letter of U.S. Secretary of Defense James Mattis, delivered on December 20, 2018.*

# President Trump Announces Troop Withdrawal from Syria

**December 19, 2018**

We have defeated ISIS in Syria, my only reason for being there during the Trump Presidency.

SOURCE: Donald Trump (@realDonaldTrump). Twitter post. December 19, 2018. https://twitter.com/realDonaldTrump/status/1075397797929775105.

# *Defense Secretary Mattis Resignation Letter*

DOCUMENT

December 20, 2018

Dear Mr. President:

I have been privileged to serve as our country's 26th Secretary of Defense which has allowed me to serve alongside our men and women of the Department in defense of our citizens and our ideals.

I am proud of the progress that has been made over the past two years on some of the key goals articulated in our National Defense Strategy: putting the Department on a more sound budgetary footing, improving readiness and lethality in our forces, and reforming the Department's business practices for greater performance. Our troops continue to provide the capabilities needed to prevail in conflict and sustain strong U.S. global influence.

One core belief I have always held is that our strength as a nation is inextricably linked to the strength of our unique and comprehensive system of alliances and partnerships. While the US remains the indispensable nation in the free world, we cannot protect our interests or serve that role effectively without maintaining strong alliances and showing respect to those allies. Like you, I have said from the beginning that the armed forces of the United States should not be the policeman of the world. Instead, we must use all tools of American power to provide for the common defense, including providing effective leadership to our alliances. NATO's 29 democracies demonstrated that strength in their commitment to fighting alongside us following the 9-11 attack on America. The Defeat-ISIS coalition of 74 nations is further proof.

Similarly, I believe we must be resolute and unambiguous in our approach to those countries whose strategic interests are increasingly in tension with ours. It is clear that China and Russia, for example, want to shape a world consistent with their authoritarian model—gaining veto authority over other nations' economic, diplomatic, and security decisions—to promote their own interests at the expense of their neighbors, America and our allies. That is why we must use all the tools of American power to provide for the common defense.

My views on treating allies with respect and also being clear-eyed about both malign actors and strategic competitors are strongly held and informed by over four decades of immersion in these issues. We must do everything possible to advance an international order that is most conducive to our security, prosperity and values, and we are strengthened in this effort by the solidarity of our alliances.

Because you have the right to have a Secretary of Defense whose views are better aligned with yours on these and other subjects, I believe it is right for me to step down from my position. The end date for my tenure is February 28, 2019, a date that should allow sufficient time for a successor to be nominated and confirmed as well as to make sure the Department's interests are properly articulated and protected at upcoming events to include Congressional posture hearings and the NATO Defense Ministerial meeting in February. Further, that a full transition to a new Secretary of Defense occurs well in advance of the transition of Chairman of the Joint Chiefs of Staff in September in order to ensure stability within the Department.

I pledge my full effort to a smooth transition that ensures the needs and interests of the 2.15 million Service Members and 732,079 DoD civilians receive undistracted attention of the Department at all times so that they can fulfill their critical, round-the-clock mission to protect the American people.

I very much appreciate this opportunity to serve the nation and our men and women in uniform.

Jim N. Mattis

SOURCE: U.S. Department of Defense. "Letter from Secretary James N. Mattis." December 20, 2018. https://media.defense.gov/2018/Dec/20/2002075156/-1/-1/1/LETTER-FROM-SECRETARY-JAMES-N-MATTIS.PDF.

## OTHER HISTORIC DOCUMENTS OF INTEREST

### FROM THIS VOLUME

### FROM PREVIOUS *HISTORIC DOCUMENTS*

# President Trump Remarks on Criminal Justice Overhaul

DECEMBER 21, 2018

In one of its final acts, the 115th Congress passed a landmark bill reforming the U.S. criminal justice system in December 2018. The First Step Act represented the most substantial change in a generation to the prison and sentencing laws that caused the federal prison population to balloon and created a criminal justice system that lawmakers on both sides of the aisle viewed as costly and unfair. Republican and Democratic leaders supported the bill, which passed the House and Senate with overwhelming bipartisan support before being signed into law by President Donald Trump. The bill's passage marked a rare instance of cross-party collaboration in a bitterly divided Washington, and observers expected it would have a pronounced effect on the U.S. criminal justice system.

## A Rare Bipartisan Opportunity

President Trump signed the First Step Act—also known by its longer title, "Formerly Incarcerated Reenter Society Transformed Safely Transitioning Every Person Act"—into law on December 21, 2018. Trump highlighted the bill's "incredible bipartisan support," calling the Republican and Democratic lawmakers surrounding him at the signing ceremony in the Oval Office a "cross-section of everybody in our country." The president also spoke about the historic difficulty of pursuing criminal justice reform. "Everybody said it couldn't be done," he noted. "They said the conservatives won't approve it. They said the liberals won't approve it. . . . It's been many, many years, numerous decades, and nobody came close."

The bill was the first major overhaul of the American criminal justice system since 1994. At that time, in the face of rising crime rates, President Bill Clinton championed and signed into law the Violent Crime Control and Law Enforcement Act, the largest crime-control bill in U.S. history. While proponents applauded the bill for cracking down on violent offenders, critics claimed it accelerated mass incarceration and created a much more punitive criminal justice system, especially for communities of color and low-level, nonviolent offenders.

It was against this backdrop that advocates sought reforms, working through multiple presidencies and Congresses to overhaul criminal justice and sentencing in the United States. A coalition of religious leaders, scholars, and activists pressured U.S. leaders to prioritize reforms that would reduce punitive prison sentences and put fewer people behind bars. Many saw the election of Trump, who ran on a "tough on crime" platform in 2016, as closing the window for serious reforms. But in the fall of 2018, Trump publicly threw his support behind reform measures working their way through the Republican-controlled Congress, signaling renewed hope that an overhaul of the criminal justice system was possible.

## Reforms Aimed at Reducing Recidivism, Easing Sentences

At the heart of the First Step Act are measures aimed at easing mass sentencing laws and keeping people convicted of crimes from returning to prison. The law invests in incentives and programs that improve prison conditions and better prepare low-risk prisoners for reentry into their communities. Enhanced job training, expanded early-release programs, and modified sentencing laws—including those adjusting mandatory minimum sentences for nonviolent drug offenders—seek to reduce mass incarceration.

Federal sentencing laws were a major focus of the reform package, and according to supporters, each change was likely to lead to shorter prison sentences, especially for nonviolent offenders and those with minimal criminal histories. The law made retroactive the changes enacted by the Fair Sentencing Act of 2010, which reduced the disparity between crack and powder cocaine sentences at the federal level for nearly 2,600 federal inmates. Specifically, this measure sought to address the fact that African Americans disproportionately receive harsher sentences for selling crack than the white drug dealers who sell powdered cocaine.

Other provisions of the First Step Act included expanding the use of the "safety valve." This exception allows judges to skirt federal mandatory minimum sentences and was previously only available to nonviolent offenders with no criminal history. The First Step Act would allow judges the opportunity to apply the exception to those with a limited criminal history. The law also eased what is known as the federal "three strikes" rule that automatically imposed life sentences on individuals convicted three or more times of a certain set of crimes, including drug offenses. The new law would instead allow for a twenty-five-year sentence to be imposed. The First Step Act also addressed what is known as the "stacking mechanism," which makes possession of a firearm a federal crime if the individual has that weapon in the course of committing another crime. According to the new law, the stacking mechanism could only be used against individuals with previous convictions.

To further address recidivism and prison overcrowding, the law expanded programs that reward prisoners for good behavior while behind bars. Under existing law, inmates without a disciplinary record were eligible to reduce their sentences by forty-seven days per year; the First Step Act increased this to fifty-four days per year. Notably, the change would be applied retroactively, allowing thousands of prisoners to qualify for early release. Prisoners electing to participate in vocational and rehabilitative programs could earn credit under the new law toward early release to a halfway house or home confinement.

Altogether, the First Step Act promised major changes for federal prisoners while also establishing policies for states, which house much of the U.S. prison population, to emulate. The law fell short of a more expansive overhaul proposed in Congress during the Obama administration and reforms sought by some liberal and conservative activists, but officials from both sides of the political spectrum applauded its passage.

## Strange Political Bedfellows Help Push the Bill to Passage

Politically, the bill marked a strong shift for the Republican Party. The conservative movement long championed a tough stance on crime, and in 2016, Trump made that a key tenet of his platform with a promise to support more stringent prison sentences and a zero-tolerance policy. Yet diverse forces, from the president to his top advisers to liberal advocacy groups and reformers, were able to overcome a polarized and often gridlocked Washington.

Advocates from the far left, including the American Civil Liberties Union, together with more establishment Democrats, such as the Center for American Progress, linked arms with staunch conservatives such as the American Conservative Union and antigovernment libertarians including the Koch brothers to push lawmakers to reconsider the way the federal government administers justice three decades after the war on crime peaked. "We have the clearest path forward that we have had in years," said Holly Harris, the executive director of the Justice Action Network, a bipartisan coalition supporting criminal justice reform. "This would be the first time that these members have voted on a piece of legislation that turns away from the lock-'em-up-and-throw-away-the-keys policies of the 1990s. That is groundbreaking."

Jared Kushner, Trump's son-in-law and one of his key advisers, was widely viewed as the primary driver behind the president's shift in position. Kushner's desire for a change in federal sentencing guidelines stemmed from his own personal experience with them: his father was incarcerated for fourteen months at a federal prison in Alabama after being convicted on tax evasion, witness tampering, and illegal campaign contributions. Kushner spent time on Capitol Hill, working with both Democratic and Republican lawmakers, and is considered the driving force behind the decision of Senate Majority Leader Mitch McConnell, R-Ky., to bring the criminal justice overhaul bill to a floor vote. During the First Step Act signing ceremony, Trump recognized Kushner's efforts and said that the First Step Act would "keep our communities safer, and provide hope and a second chance, to those who earn it. In addition to everything else, billions of dollars will be saved."

Lawmakers from both parties extoled the bill's virtues. "This bill in its entirety has been endorsed by the political spectrum of America," said Sen. Richard Durbin, D-Ill. "I can't remember any bill that has this kind of support, left and right, liberal and conservative, Democrat and Republican." Sen. John Cornyn, R-Tex., the majority whip, remarked, "We're not just talking about money. We're talking about human potential." He continued, "We're investing in the men and women who want to turn their lives around once they're released from prison, and we're investing in so doing in stronger and more viable communities." Others spoke about what the bill meant to them personally. "This is literally one of the reasons I came to the United States Senate, to get something like this done," said Sen. Cory Booker, D-N.J., one of three African American senators.

While widely viewing it as a groundbreaking achievement, advocates were quick to point out that the law is named "First Step" for a reason. State-level reforms passed in recent years, including laws legalizing marijuana and defelonizing drug offenses, have gone further to reform the criminal justice system.

—Robert Howard

*Following are remarks by President Donald Trump on December 21, 2018, prior to signing the First Step Act of 2018 and the Juvenile Justice Reform Act of 2018 into law.*

# *President Trump Remarks on Signing Criminal Justice Reform Legislation*

**December 21, 2018**

*The President.* Thank you very much. I appreciate everybody being here. We've had a very busy two or three days. It's been very positive. Things are happening that haven't happened in our government for a long time. . . .

*[A section of the president's statement pertaining to border security has been omitted.]*

Now to a very positive note: criminal justice reform. Everybody said it couldn't be done. *[Laughter]* They said the conservatives won't approve it. They said the liberals won't approve it. They said nobody is going to approve it; everybody is going to be against it. It's been many, many years, numerous decades, and nobody came close.

And I just want to thank all of the people standing behind me. I want to thank my daughter Ivanka, my son-in-law Jared Kushner. I want to thank—*[applause]*—and I have to say, I want to thank Paul and Kevin. I want to thank Mitch. I want to thank Nancy and Chuck, as I say, affectionately, actually. *[Laughter]* But I do. I want to thank everybody. This was incredible bipartisan support. Mike, you were great—Mike Pence. Everybody. Everybody worked so hard on this.

And I look at, you know, behind me—I said, this is a cross-section of everybody in our country. We have everybody here. I won't go into details, because I'll get myself into trouble if I go into too many of those details. *[Laughter]* We have everybody wanting this. We had a few people that didn't, and that's okay. It's impossible to get a hundred percent. But we passed this in the Senate, 87 to 12. That's unheard of. And the one person that missed the vote was actually in Afghanistan doing a very good job: Lindsey Graham. And I think I can honestly say that he would have voted in favor. *[Laughter]* Lindsey was for it. And so it's 88 to 12.

And then, in the House, we passed it 358 to 36. And you look at this vote—358 to 36—it's impossible; you don't have votes like that. Hopefully, we can do so well for border security, but it won't happen. *[Laughter]* Hard to believe. Because border security, to me, is simpler.

Criminal justice reform—and I must tell you, I've been a little bit of a student over the last 4 or 5 weeks too, because I started off a little bit on the negative side and said, what does it all mean? And then, I'd speak to people that are really involved. I'd look at States. The State of Texas—Texas is a tough State for criminal justice. Very tough. They passed it a long time ago. It's had a huge impact. Kentucky—we have Matt here, and we have Mitch here. Matt. Kentucky passed it. Georgia passed it. And they've had tremendous, tremendous results, results that are incredible. And other States also. And other States that are known for being tough on crime, tough on whatever you want to say.

So I started looking at it very closely. And when you have somebody put in jail for 54 years because he did something that has no chance of him coming out and totally nonviolent, but there was a violation of a rule, that's tough stuff.

Alice Johnson, I let her out. She was in jail for 22 years. She had another 28 years. And the crime was, let's say—I think most of you would agree—was not worthy of a 50-year term in prison. And she came out, and I'll never forget the look on her face. She walked out of jail after 22 years, and she was with her family. She was with her family. And they greeted her at the door, and everyone—she had grandsons; big, strong, beautiful guys. They grabbed their grandmother, and they were all crying. Everybody was crying. I said, what a beautiful thing that is. Everybody—big family. Everybody, they were gathered around—there was this large circle—hugging and kissing each other. She was in for 22 years. She had another 28 years to go.

There was another case where a judge came to me—a good man—and he was mandated to put a young man in jail for 28, approximately, years. And he wanted him to go to jail for 2 years. He said he did commit a problem, but he was mandated to put him in jail for 28 years. And he actually left the bench; he quit. He was a highly respected judge and is a respected person. He left the bench. He was so saddened that there was nothing he could do, because this young man was mandated to spend almost a good portion of the rest of his life, about 28 years, in jail. And the judge had no power to do anything about it, yet he was a judge.

And he's actually taken up a crusade for this, and he left the bench. He quit, as a judge. He said, "When I can't give this man 2 or 5 years, when he has to be in jail for the best part of his life, then I don't want to be a judge anymore." I never forgot it. This was 2 months ago that I met this gentleman, the judge.

So criminal justice reform is an incredible, beyond bipartisan, signing. We'll be doing that in just a moment. But what I wanted to do was maybe go around and ask some of these incredible leaders; these are political leaders—Senators, Congressmen—but they're also leaders from around the country, a couple from around the world, and some stars. We have some big stars in this room too. And we've had tremendous support. Shocking. To me it was shocking.

And I will say this: Nobody thought 3, 4 months ago this was something that we couldn't even think about. I had a man come up to me yesterday. You know, we passed the biggest tax cuts in the history of our country. We've done regulation cuts that has never been done before, more than any other President. And a man came up to me, who's a top lawyer in the—in this country, very, very knowledgeable in this subject. He said: "Sir, this is the single biggest thing you've done. Far bigger than tax cuts. Far bigger than regulation cuts. Far bigger than anything you've done." And I started to argue with him. And then, after a while, I said, "Why am I arguing?" *[Laughter]* I said: "Let's take it. What difference is it?" I said, "We'll take it."

*[Remarks by other officials in the room, and a Q&A with reporters, has been omitted.]*

SOURCE: Executive Office of the President. "Remarks on Signing Criminal Justice Reform Legislation and an Exchange with Reporters." December 21, 2018. *Compilation of Presidential Documents* 2018, no. 00859 (December 21, 2018). https://www.govinfo.gov/content/pkg/DCPD-201800859/pdf/DCPD-201800859.pdf.

NOTE: The language of the First Step Act is available from Congress.gov, https://www.congress.gov/115/bills/s756/BILLS-115s756enr.pdf.

## OTHER HISTORIC DOCUMENTS OF INTEREST

### FROM PREVIOUS *HISTORIC DOCUMENTS*

# Index